FYI
RE: MEDAL OF HONOR TOTALS

As of July 1, 1985, there are 3,412 awards of the Medal of
Honor (Navy, Army and Air Force) on record. (This does not
include, of course, the 911 names struck by an Army board
of review in 1917.)

The total number of recipients of the Medal of Honor is 3,394.
This tally includes Mary Walker but not Billy Mitchell. The
criterion for inclusion is the awarding of the actual medal;
whaterver the intent of the authorizing legislation, General
Mitchell's medal was not the Medal of Honor.

The reason for the discrepancy in totals is simple: there are
several men who have been awarded two medals. First, there
are thirteen who have received two medals for two separate
actions:

Thomas Custer	Both Civil War
John Cooper	Civil War & 1865
Patrick Mullen	Civil War & 1865
Frank Baldwin	Civil War & Indian Campaigns
Henry Hogan	Both Indian Campaigns
William Wilson	Both Indian Campaigns
Albert Weisbogel	1874 & 1876
Robert Sweeney	1881 & 1883
Louis Williams	1883 & 1884
John King	1901 & 1909
Daniel Daly	Boxer Bebellion & Haiti
John McCloy	Boxer Rebellion & Veracruz
Smedley Butler	Veracruz & Haiti

The five remaining double recipients are five Marines who
received both the Navy and Army Medals of Honor for the same
actions in World War I. This was due to the unique command
structure of the time, whereby Marine and Army units served
together. Because each of the Marines' actions was performed
with an Army unit involved, they were considered eligible
for the Army's award as well. The five Marines are:

Louis Cukela
Ernest Janson*
John Kelly
Matej Kocak
John Pruitt

*Ernest Janson received his Army medal under the name
of Charles Hoffman, for reasons unknown.

Denis Kennedy
Boston Publishing Co.
July 1985

18

The Congressional Medal of Honor

"The President may award, and present in the name of Congress, a medal of honor of appropriate design, with ribbons and appurtnances, to a person who, while a member of the [armed forces], distinguished himself conspicuously by gallantry and intrepidity at the risk of his life above and beyond the call of duty —

"(1) while engaged in an action against an enemy of the United States;

"(2) while engaged in military operations involving conflict with an opposing foreign force; or

"(3) while serving with friendly foreign forces engaged in an armed conflict against an opposing armed force in which the United States is not a belligerent party."

THE CONGRESSIONAL MEDAL OF HONOR

THE NAMES, THE DEEDS

Sharp & Dunnigan

PUBLICATIONS

BOX 660 FOREST RANCH,
CALIF

October 15, 1984
First Printing

Library of Congress Cataloging in Publication Data
Main entry under title:

The Congressional Medal of Honor.

    Includes index.
    1. Medal of Honor.   2. United States – Armed Forces –
Biography.   I. Sharp & Dunnigan Publications.
UB433.C65   1984   355.1'342'0922 [B]   84-51095
Library of Congress Catalog Number 84-51095

Sharp & Dunnigan Publications
Forest Ranch, California
95942 U.S.A.

ISBN 0-918495-01-6

DEDICATION

This book is dedicated to those who's deeds are recorded by name herein; to those who's deeds of valor were recognized by one of the honors listed below; and to those who's deeds have neither record nor recognition, but who met the call of duty when duty itself was above and beyond.

ORDER OF PRECEDENCE OF MILITARY DECORATIONS

The following is the order of precedence for military decorations of the United States, based on degrees of valor and meritorious achievement, and the date each medal was established:

U.S. ARMY AND U.S. AIR FORCE

1. Medal of Honor (1862)
2. Distinguished Service Cross (1918)/Air Force Cross (1960)
3. Defense Distinguished Service Medal (1970)
4. Distinguished Service Medal (1918)
5. Silver Star (1918)
6. Defense Superior Service Medal (1976)
7. Legion of Merit (1942)
8. Distinguished Flying Cross
9. Soldier's Medal (1926)/Airman's Medal (1960)
10. Bronze Star (1942)
11. Meritorious Service Medal (1969)
12. Air Medal (1942)
13. Joint Service Commendation Medal (1963)
14. Army Commendation Medal (formerly Commendation Ribbon) (1945)/Air Force Commendation Medal (1958)
15. Purple Heart (1782)

U.S. NAVY AND MARINE CORPS

1. Medal of Honor (1862)
2. Navy Cross (1919)
3. Defense Distinguished Service Medal (1970)
4. Distinguished Service Medal (1918)
5. Silver Star (1918)
6. Defense Superior Service Medal (1976)
7. Legion of Merit (1942)
8. Navy and Marine Corps Medal (1942)
9. Bronze Star (1942)
10. Meritorious Service Medal (1969)
11. Air Medal (1942)
12. Joint Service Commendation Medal (1967)
13. Navy Commendation Medal (formerly Navy Commendation Ribbon) (1944)
14. Purple Heart (1782)

ACKNOWLEDGEMENTS

The publishers would like to thank the members of the Senate Committee on Veterans' Affairs, 96th Congress, for having the foresight and imagination to have commissioned, *MEDAL OF HONOR RECIPIENTS 1863-1978 "In the name of the Congress of the United States."*

And so it follows, our deep appreciation to those who carried out that directive, Specifically: "Sister Maria Veronica, IHM, Medal of Honor archivist, Freedoms Foundation at Valley Forge, Pennsylvania; the members of the Medal of Honor Roundtable and, in particular, Gerald F. White, national director, and Rudolph J. Frederick, editor-in-chief, both of the Medal of Honor History Roundtable; and GySgt. James McGinn and GySgt. David Kennedy, both of the ODASD(A)OSD(C), White House Correspondents."

The publishers would also like to express our gratitude to Edward A. Michalski, A.V. Division DDI, OASD(PA), Department of Defense and the Medals and Decorations sections of the United States Army and the United States Marine Corps.

Our thanks also to Congressional staff member Stephen Hardesty (former S/Sgt. USMC). and S/Sgt. Stuart Kelly USMC, for their effort on final update.

CONTENTS

PREFACE

It is said that an American fights for three things:
His brothers in arms, who share his darkest hours,
His home,
and his country, regardless of the politics of the moment. He
always fights as a free man,
and he will lay his life on the line.

98th CONGRESS
2d Session **H.R. 5515**

IN THE SENATE OF THE UNITED STATES

May 9 (legislative day, April 30), 1984
Received

May 10 (legislative day, April 30), 1984
Ordered held at the desk

AN ACT

To authorize the President to award the Medal of Honor to the unknown American who lost his life while serving in the Armed Forces of the United States in Southeast Asia during the Vietnam era and who has been selected to be buried in the Memorial Amphitheater at Arlington National Cemetery.

Be it enacted by the Senate and House of Representatives of the United States of America in Congress assembled, That the President may award, and present in the name of Congress, the Medal of Honor to the unknown American who lost his life while serving in Southeast Asia during the Vietnam era as a member of the Armed Forces of the United States and who has been selected to lie buried in the Memorial Amphitheater of the National Cemetery at Arlington, Virginia, as authorized by section 9 of the National Cemeteries Act of 1973 (Public Law 93-43).

May 3, 1984
Passed House by voice vote

May 16, 1984
Passed Senate without amendment by voice vote

May 25, 1984
Signed by the President. Became Public Law 98-301.

May 28, 1984
Memorial Day Services, Arlington National Cemetery, Arlingon, Virginia
    "An American hero has returned home . . . Today, we simply say with pride, thank you dear son. May God cradle you in his arms.
    "We present to you the Congressional Medal of Honor, for services above and beyond the call of duty – in action with the enemy during the Vietnam Era." — Ronald Reagan, President of the United States.

PART I
HISTORICAL BACKGROUND

THE MEDAL OF HONOR

The Medal of Honor is the highest military award for bravery that can be given to any individual in the United States of America. Conceived in the early 1860's and first presented in 1863, the medal has a colorful and inspiring history which has culminated in the standards applied today for awarding this respected honor.

In their provisions for judging whether a man is entitled to the Medal of Honor, each of the armed services has set up regulations which permit no margin of doubt or error. The deed of the person must be proved by incontestable evidence of at least two eyewitnesses; it must be so outstanding that it clearly distinguishes his gallantry beyond the call of duty from lesser forms of bravery; it must involve the risk of his life; and it must be the type of deed which, if he had not done it, would not subject him to any justified criticism.

A recommendation for the Army or Air Force Medal must be made within 2 years from the date of the deed upon which it depends. Award of the medal must be made within 3 years after the date of the deed. The recommendation for a Navy Medal of Honor must be made within 3 years and awarded within 5 years.

Apart from the great honor which it conveys, there are certain small privileges which accompany the Medal of Honor. Its recipients can, under certain conditions, obtain free air transportation on military aircraft within the continental United States on a "space available" basis. A veteran who has been awarded the medal for combat in any war is eligible for a special pension of $200 per month, starting from the date he applies for the pension.

The Medal of Honor is presented to its recipients by a high official "in the name of the Congress of the United States." For this reason it is sometimes called the Congressional Medal of Honor.

As a general rule, the Medal of Honor may be awarded for a deed of personal bravery or self-sacrifice above and beyond the call of duty only while the person is a member of the Armed Forces of the United States in action against an enemy of the United States, or while engaged in military operations involving conflict with an opposing foreign force, or while serving with friendly foreign forces engaged in armed conflict against an opposing armed force in which the United States is not a belligerent party. However, until passage of Public Law 88–77, the Navy could and did award Medals of Honor for bravery in the line of the naval profession. Such awards recognized bravery in saving life, and deeds of valor performed in submarine rescues, boiler explosions, turret fires, and other types of disaster unique to the naval profession.

2

Congress has often voted special medals for important victories and other contributions to the Nation, the first having been awarded to General Washington for his success at Boston in 1776. These are truly Congressional medals to honor individuals and events. By Congressional action, and signed by the President, the Medal of Honor was awarded to the following Unknown Soldiers: Britain and France, on March 4, 1921; United States—World War I, on August 24, 1921; Italy, on October 12, 1921; Belgium, on December 1, 1922; and Rumania, on June 6, 1923. On two occasions the Army Medal of Honor has been awarded by separate acts of Congress—the first being the act of December 1927 honoring Captain Charles A. Lindbergh; the second being the act of 21 March 1935 honoring Major General Adolphus W. Greely. In each case, the medal presented was the Army Medal of Honor in use at the time, not a special medal struck for the purpose expressed in each act of Congress. In addition, five members of the Navy—Machinist Floyd Bennett, Commander Richard E. Byrd, Jr., Boatswain's Mate George R. Cholister, Ensign Henry C. Drexler, and Lieutenant Richmond P. Hobson, each received the Navy Medal of Honor by acts of Congress. By Congressional approval the Medal of Honor was also awarded to the American Unknown Soldier of World War II, on March 9, 1948; and to the American Unknown Soldier of the Korean conflict on August 31, 1957. On May 28, 1984 the medal was awarded to the Unknown American of the Vietnam era.

"IN THE NAME OF THE CONGRESS OF THE UNITED STATES"

The Medal of Honor was not the idea of any one American. Like most of the ideas which have flowered into institutions and practices in our Nation, it was the result of group thought and action and evolved in response to a need of the times.

In the winter of 1861-62, following the beginning of hostilities in the Civil War, there was much thought in Washington concerning the necessity for recognizing the deeds of the American soldiers, sailors, and marines who were distinguishing themselves in the fighting.

The American Nation, which had given little thought to its Armed Forces during times of peace, now found them to be the focal point of attention. The serviceman, unpublicized and isolated during the preceding years, many of which were spent guarding the national frontiers against Indian raids and the coastline against smugglers, now became a great looming figure in the fight to preserve the Union. Overnight, he ceased to be a man plying some remote and mysterious trade out on the plains of Kansas or North Dakota, or on some ship at sea. He was the boy next door, or indeed the son of the household, sent out to fight for a cause that, in a very real sense, lay close to home.

His contribution was not just in fighting, but in fighting gallantly, sometimes displaying a sheer heroism which, when looked upon by the Nation in whose name it was called forth, quite naturally caused that Nation to seek some means of rewarding him.

But the thought did not stop there. For the first time since the Revolution, Americans realized not only what important citizens its soldiers, sailors, and marines were, but how important they had always been. They realized that the far-off lonely trooper, walking his post on the frontier, or the equally lonely sailor or marine standing watch from the bridge of his ship at sea along the coast, during the years of "peace," had been doing the same essential work as that of the soldier, sailor, or marine of the Civil War—protecting the Nation. And they realized that in doing this work they had very often displayed a little-known and unrecognized heroism which, by its nature, rendered them capable of being killed in action in their posts of duty, just as they could have been during the winter of 1861–62.

In looking back for a precedent for honoring our servicemen, Americans could note the "Certificate of Merit," which had been authorized for soldiers in 1847. Originally this award did not provide a medal, but rather a certificate signed by the President. Later, in 1905, a medal and ribbon bar for wear on the uniform were authorized. Congress also passed a provision that holders of the certificate who were still in the service should have extra pay of $2 per month. But money alone could not honor the servicemen for his deed.

There also had been a method of honoring officers by means of the "brevet" system of promotions, whereby an officer mentioned for gallantry in dispatches could be granted a "brevet rank" higher than that of his actual rank, and be entitled to wear the insignia which went with the brevet. But this system had fallen victim to a series of political abuses, and by 1861 much of its honor had grown meaningless.

The best precedent for honoring servicemen—and the only precedent in our Nation's history which had involved the award of decorations—went back to 1782. On August 7 of that year, in Newburg, N.Y., George Washington had created the Purple Heart as a decoration for "singular meritorious action." Three men had received the award in 1783. The records show no others.

The philosophy behind the Purple Heart had been that since his honor is something which no true soldier, sailor or marine likes to talk about, those who sought to honor him should give him a token of that honor which he could wear without words.

A similar philosophy and purpose characterized the American people and the Congress of the United States in 1861. Senator James W. Grimes, of Iowa, took the lead as chairman of the Senate Naval Committee. He introduced a bill to create a Navy medal. It was passed by both Houses of Congress and approved by President Abraham Lincoln on December 21, 1861. It established a Medal of Honor for enlisted men of the Navy and Marine Corps—the first decoration formally authorized by the American Government to be worn as a badge of honor.

Action on the Army medal was started 2 months later, when, on February 17, 1862, Senator Henry Wilson, of Massachusetts, introduced a Senate resolution providing for presentation of "medals of honor" to enlisted men of the Army and Voluntary Forces who "shall most distinguish themselves by their gallantry in action, and other soldierlike qualities."

President Lincoln's approval made the resolution law on July 12, 1862. It was amended by an act approved on March 3, 1863, which extended its provision to include officers as well as enlisted men, and made the provisions retroactive to the beginning of the Civil War.

This legislation was to stand as the basis upon which the Army Medal of Honor could be awarded until July 9, 1918, when it was superseded by a completely revised statute.

As soon as the Navy Medal of Honor had been authorized, Secretary of the Navy Gideon Welles wrote to James Pollock, Director of the U.S. Mint at Philadelphia, asking for his assistance in obtaining a design for the medal. Pollock had submitted five designs to the Navy by the time the Army bill had been introduced in the Senate. When he heard that a similar medal was being considered for the Army, Pollock wrote to Secretary of War Edwin M. Stanton, enclosing one of the designs prepared for the Navy, and pointing out that it would be appropriate for use by the Army as well. Two more designs were submitted to the Navy on May 6, 1862, and on May 9, the Navy approved one of them.

In bas-relief, on the star, the Union held a shield in her right hand against an attacker, who crouched to the left, holding forked-tongued serpents which struck at the shield. In the left hand of the Union was held the fasces, the ancient Roman symbol of unified authority, an ax bound in staves of wood—still a common symbol on many of our 10-cent pieces. The 34 stars which encircle these figures represent the number of States at the time the medal was designed. The reverse of the medal bore a blank for the name of the awardee and the date and place of his deed.

On November 17, 1862, the War Department contracted with the firm of William Wilson & Son, Philadelphia, where the Navy medals were being made, for 2,000 of the same type of medals for the Army. The only difference between the Army medal and that of the Navy was that the Army medal, instead of being attached to its ribbon by an anchor, was attached by means of the American Eagle symbol, standing on crossed cannon and cannon balls.

And now the Navy and the Army had a Medal of Honor. Heroic deeds would entitle their authors to the decoration. On March 25, 1863, the first Army medals were awarded "in the name of the Congress of the United States." A few days later, on April 3, 1863, the first Navy medals were awarded sailors and marines.

PROTECTING THE MEDAL

There were some sincere men who believed that the idea of a Medal of Honor would not prove popular with Americans. By the end of the Civil War, and in succeeding years, this view was definitely proved to be incorrect. If anything, the medal was too popular, and the glory which it conferred upon its recipients had the effect of inspiring the human emotion of envy in many breasts. A flood of imitations sprang up following the Civil War, and had the effect of causing Congress, eventually, to take steps to protect the dignity of the original medal.

The abuses and confusion as to who earned and who did not earn the Medal of Honor were stated as early as 1869, when M. H. Beaumont, publisher of a magazine named The Soldier's Friend, wrote from New York to the War Department, indicating that he had been repeatedly requested to publish the names of all Medal of Honor recipients.

"There are some who are using medals for the purpose of soliciting charity," he wrote, "who obtained them surreptitiously."

Adjutant General Townsend agreed that the publication of a list would be a good idea. He pointed out that some of the awardees had never applied for their medals, and that publication might help lead to their delivery. A list was sent to Beaumont on September 29, 1869, and published in The Soldier's Friend shortly afterward.

The number of abuses rose—with increased applications by ex-soldiers, who, following the Civil War, began to present claims for the Medal of Honor without any sound documentation, and after passage of an inordinate amount of time from the dates upon which they alleged to have been earned. These events led to the creation of boards of review, not only of individual acts, but of the whole policy involved in the award to the Medal of Honor.

Public interest in the history of the medal was quickened. Four editions of a book edited by Brig. Gen. Theophilus F. Rodenbaugh, himself a medal recipient, were published in rapid succession. These were entitled "Uncle Sam's Medal of Honor Men" (1886), "The Bravest Five Hundred of '61" (1891), "Fighting for Honor" (1893), and "Sabre and Bayonet" (1897).

President Harry S. Truman, in 1946, ordered the Navy and the Army to publish information on the Medal of Honor recipients in their respective services. In July 1948, the United States Army published the information in a book entitled "The Medal of Honor of the United States Army." In 1949, the Navy published a book entitled "Medal of Honor, the Navy." In compiling this report, the committee is indebted to both of these publications and has used a great deal of material from each.

Interest in perpetuating the ideals of the medal was mounting on the part of medal recipients themselves. On April 23, 1890, the Medal of Honor Legion was organized at Washington as a local society. It was made a national organization during the grand encampment of the Grand Army of the Republic in Boston, on August 14, 1890, and was incorporated by Act of Congress on August 4, 1955. Today it is known as the Legion of Valor of the United States of America. The objectives of the Legion of Valor are—

> To promote true fellowship among our members;
> To advance the best interests of members of the Armed Forces of the United States and to enhance their prestige and understanding by example and personal activity;
> To extend all possible relief to needy members, their widows, and children; and
> To stimulate patriotism in the minds of our youth and to engender a national pride and interest in the Armed Forces of the United States.

The Congressional Medal of Honor Society of the United States, was chartered by the 85th Congress under a legislative act signed into law by President Eisenhower on August 14, 1958. The purposes of the society are—

"To form a bond of friendship and comradeship among all holders of the Medal of Honor.

"To protect, uphold, and preserve the dignity and honor of the medal at all times and on all occasions.

"To protect the name of the medal, and individual holders of the medal from exploitation.

"To provide appropriate aid to all persons to whom the medal has been awarded, their widows or their children.

"To serve our country in peace as we did in war.

"To inspire and stimulate our youth to become worthy citizens of our country.

"To foster and perpetuate Americanism.

"The Society will *not* participate in local or national politics, nor will the Society lend its support for the purpose of obtaining special legislative considerations."

On June 26, 1897, the Secretary of War, R. A. Alger, announced that paragraph 177 of the Army regulations was revised, at the direction of President William McKinley, and that new regulations would henceforth define the award of the Medal of Honor.

The resulting regulations gave the War Department an authoritative and comprehensive system for dealing with award of the medal. Later, an act of Congress, approved on April 24, 1904, made it mandatory that all claims for the medal should be accompanied by official documents describing the deed involved.

At about the same time, the design of the Army Medal of Honor was changed. Initially, the Army and Navy Medal of Honor were the same design, except that the Navy medal was attached to its ribbon by an anchor while the Army medal was attached to its ribbon by means of the American Eagle, standing on crossed cannon and cannon balls.

Late in 1903, Brig. Gen. Horace Porter had several designs prepared by Messrs. Arthur, Bertrand & Berenger, of Paris, and sent them to the Adjutant General, recommending that one of them should be approved by the Medal of Honor Legion, which, at that time, was headed by Maj. Gen. Daniel E. Sickles. Following approval of this organization, the Secretary of War approved the new design and a rosette, fixing his signature to the plan on January 28, 1904.

Just 2 weeks earlier, Representative Cordell Hull, of Tennessee, had introduced the act of 1904, providing for the changes in issuance of the medal. It was approved on April 23, 1904, and it authorized "three thousand medals of honor prepared * * * upon a new design."

It remained only to protect the new design from abuse. Early in 1904, a patent was applied for, and on November 22, 1904, Gen. G. L. Gillespie was awarded Patent Serial No. 197,369, covering the new Medal of Honor, specified as U.S. Patent Office Design No. 37,236. The final step for protection of the new design was taken on December 19, 1904, when General Gillespie transferred the Medal of Honor patent "to W. H. Taft and his successor or successors as Secretary of War of the United States of America."

The medal as officially described is made of silver, heavily electroplated in gold. The chief feature of the old medal, the five-pointed star, has been retained, and in its center appears the head of the heroic Minerva, the highest symbol of wisdom and righteous war. Surrounding this central feature in circular form are the words "United States of America" representing nationality. An open laurel wreath, enameled in green, encircles the star, and the oak leaves at the bases of the prongs of the star are likewise enameled in green to give them prominence.

The medal is suspended by a blue silk ribbon, spangled with 13 white stars representing the original States, and this ribbon is attached to an eagle supported upon a horizontal bar. Upon the bar, which is attached to two points of the star, appears the word "Valor," indicative of the distinguished service represented by the medal.

The reverse of the medal is plain so that the name of the recipient may be engraved thereon. On the reverse of the bar are stamped the words "The Congress To."

The patent which had been taken out for protection of the design of the medal expired on November 21, 1918. When this situation was referred to the Judge Advocate General of the Army for an opinion, he stated that this method of protecting the design should be replaced by legislative action forbidding imitations on the part of Congress. A bill for this purpose was recommended by the War Department, passed Congress, and was approved by the President on February 24, 1923. Imitation of the design of the medal was now forbidden by law.

THE "PYRAMID OF HONOR"

The Medal of Honor, which had begun as an idea in the minds of a few people back in 1861, had become a reality occupying the attention and energies of many Americans by 1904. Not all of the extraordinary examples of courage or of service were of the type which would deserve the Medal of Honor. At the same time, all of them deserved recognition, and each degree of valor or service could be looked upon as a step in the direction of that extraordinary service of heroism above and beyond the call of duty which is rewarded, once it has been proved, by the award of the Medal of Honor.

The problem of recognition of these lesser deeds was solved by the creation of a system of decorations arranged in an ascending order, with the lowest awards being the most widely distributed—and the Medal of Honor as the final, supreme award, its distribution limited strictly to the handful of those meeting the most severe tests of heroism. Thus, between the medals most widely distributed—and the Medal of Honor, held by only a few, there came all the other awards of Americans in uniform—arranged as a "pyramid of honor," with the Medal of Honor being the highest point, at the very top.

The legislation of 1904 gave the medal the maximum protection it had yet achieved. Now thought began to turn to the matter of presentation of the medal as a means through which it could be further dignified.

There had been a few scattered instances in which the medal was presented by the President or other high official. The six survivors of the Mitchell Raid through Georgia were awarded the first Army Medals of Honor on March 25, 1863, by Secretary of War Stanton. After presentation of the medals in his office, Secretary Stanton then took the six to the White House for a visit with President Lincoln. A few days later, on April 3, 1863, the first Navy Medals of Honor were awarded to a number of sailors taking part in the attacks on Forts Jackson, Fisher, and St. Philip, on April 24, 1862.

When Ulysses S. Grant became President, he presented the medal in the White House on two separate occasions. While in some cases soldiers and sailors of the Civil War had been given their medals at military formations and mentioned in the orders of the day, there is only one occasion recorded in which this custom was continued after the Civil War.

In some cases, the medals had been sent to awardees by registered mail. And, unfortunately, in some cases these medals had been returned to the War and Navy Departments because the recipients who had earned them had been discharged and their whereabouts were unknown.

On December 9, 1904, Maj. William E. Birkhimer, who had been a brigadier general of volunteers during the Spanish-American War and who was himself a medal recipient, suggested to the Military Secretary in Washington that "every possible attention should be paid to formality and solemnity of circumstance" whenever the medal was given to its recipients. His suggestion was passed up through channels to the Chief of Staff, and after extensive exchanges of correspondence, President Theodore Roosevelt, on September 20, 1905, signed an Executive order directing that ceremonies of award "will always be made with formal and impressive ceremonial," and that the recipient "will, when practicable, be ordered to Washington, D. C., and the presentation will be made by the President, as Commander in Chief, or by such representative as the President may designate." If it should be impracticable for the awardee to come to Washington, the order provided, the Chief of Staff would prescribe the time and place of the ceremony in each case.

The first White House presentation of the medal under the terms of this order was made by President Roosevelt on January 10, 1906.

On April 27, 1916, Congress approved an act which provided for the creation of a "Medal of Honor Roll," upon which honorably discharged medal recipients who earned the medal in combat and who had attained the age of 65 years were to be recorded, with each enrolled person to receive a special pension of $10 per month for life. The primary purpose of this act was to give medal recipients the same special recognition shown to holders of similar British and French decorations for valor. Limiting the award to the nominal sum of $10 monthly emphasized that it was not given as a pension, but to provide a small amount for personal comforts in the advanced years of life, at a time when needs are generally not very acute, especially in cases in which the veteran is in receipt of pension benefits. The amount was not made larger both because it was contrary to the policy of Congress to recognize distinguished service by pensions, and because to combine an award for conspicuous gallantry with a pension would diminish the honor attached to the award of the medal.

The passage of this act marked the successful culmination of a 26-year effort by the Medal of Honor Legion—the organization of medal recipients which was formed back in 1890—to obtain, in the words of one of its first documents, "such legislation from Congress as will tend to give the Medal of Honor the same position among the military orders of the world which similar medals occupy." Bills aimed at this type of legislation had been introduced into Congress recurrently following the organization of the Medal of Honor Legion—none of them meeting with success.

The successful bill was introduced by Representative Isaac R. Sherwood, of New York, who was a Civil War veteran, breveted brigadier general by Lincoln. He had fought in 43 battles, being under fire 123 days, and had been complimented in special orders for gallantry in action six times. He had led a full-dress congressional discussion of the Medal of Honor question on the floor of the House on July 6, 1914.

The Medal of Honor Roll, established by an Act of Congress, 27 April 1916, provided that upon attaining age 65 each recipient of the Medal of Honor who was honorably discharged from the service by muster-out, resignation, or otherwise, would have his name entered on the Roll and be eligible for a special pension of $10 per month for life. The Act was amended 14 August 1961 to increase the amount of pension to $100 per month, decrease the age to 50 and remove the requirement of separation from the service. It was further amended 13 October 1964 to decrease the age to 40, and on 31 October 1965 to delete the age of the awardee as a requirement and, most recently, on 18 October 1978, to raise the amount of the special pension to $200 per month. In addition the act provided for enrollment "upon written application being made to the Secretary of the proper department"—War or Navy—"and subject to the conditions and requirements hereinafter contained," of "the name of each surviving person who has served in the military or naval service of the United States in any war, who has attained or shall attain the age of 65 years * * *." It then laid down the condition that the applicant's Medal of Honor should have been earned by action involving actual conflict with an enemy, distinguished by conspicuous gallantry or intrepidity, at the risk of life, above and beyond the call of duty.

The act specified that the Secretary of War or of the Navy would be responsible to decide whether each applicant would be entitled to the benefits of the act.

If the official award as originally made appeared to the War Department to conform to the criteria established by the statute, this automatically entitled the applicant to the pension without further investigation. If, on the other hand, a doubt arose as to whether or not the applicant was entitled to entry on the roll, then, to quote the act further, "all official correspondence, orders, reports, recommendations, requests, and other evidence now on file in any public office or department shall be considered."

What was to be done if, after the consideration of these documents, the War Department felt that the applicant was ineligible was defined on June 3, 1916, in section 122 of the Army reorganization bill. This act provided for appointment by the Secretary of War of a board of five retired general officers for the purpose of "investigating and reporting upon past awards or issue of the so-called congressional medal of honor by or through the War Department; this with a view to ascertain what medals of honor, if any, have been awarded or issued for any cause other than distinguished conduct * * * involving actual conflict with an enemy * * *."

"And in any case," this act continued, "in which said board shall find and report that said medal was issued for any cause other than that hereinbefore specified, the name of the recipient of the medal so issued shall be stricken permanently from the official Medal of Honor list. It shall be a misdemeanor for him to wear or publicly display such medal, and, if he shall still be in the Army, he shall be required to return said medal to the War Department for cancellation."

By October 16, 1916, the Board created by this act had met, gathered all Medal of Honor records, prepared statistics, classified cases and organized evidence which might be needed in its deliberations. Between October 16, 1916, and January 17, 1917, all of the 2,625 Medals of Honor which had been awarded up to that time were considered by the Board, and on February 15, 1917, 910 names were stricken from the list.

Of these 910 names, 864 were involved in one group—a case in which the medal had been given to members of a single regiment. The regiment's (27th Maine Volunteer Infantry) enlistment was to have expired in June of 1863. As an inducement to keep the regiment on active duty during a critical period, President Lincoln authorized Medals of Honor for any of its members who volunteered for another tour of duty. The 309 men who volunteered for extended duty, in the face of more action and possible death, certainly were demonstrating "soldierlike" qualities, and as such were entitled to the Medal under one proviso of the original law. But their act in no way measured up to the 1916 standards. A clerical error compounded the abuse. Not only did the 309 volunteers receive the medal, but the balance of the regiment, which had gone home in spite of the President's offer, was awarded it also. In this group case as well as in the remaining 46 scattered cases, the Board felt that the medal had not been properly awarded for distinguished services, by the definition of the act of June 3, 1916. Among the 46 others who lost their medal was William F. Cody, better known as Buffalo Bill.

In its final report, the Board indicated that in the large majority of cases "the medals have been awarded for distinguished conduct in action, measuring that term by the highest standard, and there can be no question as to the propriety of the award."

In some cases, the Board reported, the rewards the men received were "greater than would now be given for the same acts," but in the absence of evidence to the contrary, "and because there has been no high judicial interpretation of the Medal of Honor laws" the Board found that there were "but few instances where the medal has not been awarded for distinguished services."

The 910 cases which did not pass the Board's investigation were turned over to the War Department, and against each of the names involved was stamped the inscription, "Stricken from the list February 15, 1917, Adverse Action Medal of Honor Board—A. G. 2411162."

There have been no instances of cancellation of Medal of Honor awards within the naval service.

This Board had few legal definitions to guide it in its work. It had to work with a quantity of regulations and precedents in making its decisions, and this mass of information was uncoordinated and even, in some cases, conflicting. For example, the act of April 27, 1916, provided for a "Medal of Honor Roll" for those who met the definition of valor above and beyond the call of duty; whereas the original act creating the Medal on July 12, 1862, specified only gallantry in action and "other soldierlike qualities" as the basis for award.

In 1918, Congress decided to clear away any inconsistencies of the legislation which had grown around the Army medal and make a set of perfectly clear rules for its award. On July 9, 1918, an act was approved which stated as follows:

"* * * the provisions of existing law relating to the award of Medals of Honor * * * are amended so that the President is authorized to present, in the name of the Congress, a Medal of Honor only to each person who, while an officer or enlisted man of the Army, shall hereafter, in action involving actual conflict with an enemy, distinguish himself conspicuously by gallantry and intrepidity at risk of his life above and beyond the call of duty."

At one stroke, by use of the word "hereafter," this legislation wiped out of existence the War Department's problem of acting on numerous ancient and complicated claims for medals originating as far back as the Civil War. At the same time, it clearly defined the type of deed which could earn a medal.

But these were not the only provisions of this 1918 act. It directed that enlisted men who were medal recipients should receive $2 per month extra in their military pay. This matter of an extra $2 per month was intertwined with the Certificate of Merit. The 1918 legislation abolished the Certificate of Merit and replaced it by a new medal—the Distinguished Service Medal—still retaining the extra pay feature.

The Distinguished Service Cross was brought into existence to more fully single out and honor combat gallantry. The committee on Military Affairs, which had prepared the bill, stated that, "It is believed that if a secondary medal * * * had been authorized in the past, the award of the * * * Medal of Honor would have been much more jealously guarded than it was for many years. And it is certain that the establishment of such a secondary medal now will go far toward removing the temptation to laxity with regard to future awards of the greater medal."

However, it would have been illogical to have a "secondary" medal which carried the old Certificate of Merit provision of $2 extra pay per month, while the "greater medal"—the Medal of Honor—had no such provision attached to it. Therefore, the extra pay feature was added to the award of the Medal of Honor.

But possibly the most important and far-reaching effect of this 1918 legislation was the fact that for the first time in American history it was established by law that there were degrees of service to the country, each worthy of recognition, but only *one* of which could be accorded supreme recognition. In addition to the Distinguished Service

Cross, the 1918 act also created the Army Distinguished Service Medal and the Army Silver Star Citation, each of them lower in precedence. The Silver Star became a formal decoration, with its own distinctive ribbon, in 1932.

This legislation also made it clear that recommendations for such Army awards had to be made within 2 years after the act involved, and laid down the time limit of 3 years as that in which the medals involved could be issued, following the date of the act meriting their award. It provided that not more than one medal should be issued to any one person, but that for each succeeding act justifying the award a suitable bar or other device could be awarded by the President. The President was authorized to delegate award of all four medals with which this 1918 act was concerned—the Medal of Honor, Distinguished Service Cross, Distinguished Service Medal, and Silver Star—to commanding generals of armies or higher units in the field.

The act of July 9, 1918, was the genesis of what has been called the "Pyramid of Honor," a hierarchy of military decorations awarded for combat valor and meritorious service at the top of which is placed the Medal of Honor. The Medal of Honor is restricted to the few who qualify by the most rigid definition of courage and valor in combat. Next in order of precedence is the Distinguished Service Cross, with less rigid restrictions, allowing more to qualify for this award for combat valor. Beneath the Distinguished Service Cross is the Distinguished Service Medal, which can be awarded for exceptionally meritorious service. The complete hierarchy consists at present of 12 awards for valor and/or service, ranging from the Medal of Honor at the top to the Purple Heart at the base of the "Pyramid of Honor."

A second Medal of Honor, commonly referred to as the (new) Medal of Honor, was approved by act of Congress of February 4, 1919, for award to any person in the naval service of the United States who while in action involving "actual conflict" with the enemy distinguished himself conspicuously by gallantry and intrepidity at the risk of his life above and beyond the call of duty and without detriment to the mission. The old Medal of Honor was retained for noncombat service.

The new Navy Medal of Honor was designed by Tiffany & Company of New York—hence the reference to it as the "Tiffany Cross"—and is a gold cross pattee, 35 millimeters across, on a wreath of oak and laurel leaves. The center of the cross bears the eagle design from the United States seal within an octagon bearing the inscription, "United States Navy, 1917–1918." A plain anchor appears on each arm of the cross. Except for the embossed words, "Awarded to," the reverse is plain. The medal is suspended from a ribbon consisting of a triple chevron of 13 white stars on a light blue field, the star at the point of the chevron being uppermost. At the crest of the ribbon is a bar which bears the single word "Valour." It is worn at the neck as a pendant, suspended from the band by means of its ribbon. The ribbon bar worn in lieu of either the original Medal of Honor or the second Medal of Honor is light blue and is embroidered with 5 white stars.

The act of Congress, approved February 4, 1919, which established the new Navy Medal of Honor, also provided for the adoption of a Navy Distinguished Service Medal, a Navy Cross and a gold star to be awarded in lieu of a second or additional award of any Navy decoration.

The new Navy Medal of Honor was made obsolete by an act of Congress approved August 7, 1942. This act restored the dual status of the old Navy Medal of Honor, thereby authorizing its award for combat or noncombat service above and beyond the call of duty. It also reversed the relative position of the Distinguished Service Medal and Navy Cross and established the Silver Star, the Legion of Merit, and the Navy and Marine Corps Medal as Navy decorations. In addition, it also abolished duplication of awards.

In order to insure fairness to all, Gen. John J. Pershing issued instructions to various commanding officers of the American Expeditionary Forces to submit recommendations for award of the Medal of Honor, Distinguished Service Cross, and Distinguished Service Medal. Recommendations were to come from regimental commanders, or, in the cases of men not in regiments, from the commanders corresponding as nearly as possible to the grade of regimental commander. General Pershing also appointed a board of officers at his headquarters to consider recommendations for the decorations. The recommendations so screened were then passed on to the Commander in Chief.

From these procedures there evolved the methods of examining possible awards which were used throughout World War II. Among the major requirements established at Headquarters, AEF, was one which specified that each recommendation for a Medal of Honor must cite a specific action on a particular day or in a particular engagement, giving the place and details of the action and the numbers of troops involved. It was also specified that each recommendation must be accompanied by sworn statements of two or more persons who were eyewitnesses of the action for which the medal was recommended.

Five days after the Armistice, General Pershing not only directed that a careful review be made of each case which had been submitted for award of the Distinguished Service Cross, but he also sent to headquarters of each division an officer thoroughly familiar with the forms necessary to substantiate awards of the Medal of Honor. He ordered that these officers were to be given every possible assistance in obtaining necessary evidence for Medal of Honor award in these cases, so that the Distinguished Service Cross would not be given when a case merited the Medal of Honor.

Up to November 23, 1918, 24 Medal of Honor recommendations had been received in the Personnel Bureau, AEF, and 4 approved, as mentioned above. As of that date, the Personnel Bureau became the Personnel Division of The Adjutant General's Office, U.S. Army, and Lt. Col. J. A. Ulio continued as chief of the Decorations Section within this new Division.

Medal of Honor recommendations and those pertaining to other decorations were handled at General Pershing's headquarters at Chaumont, France, between November 1918 and July 1919. They were submitted to the War Department, and during this period 78 Medal of Honor awards were made.

General Pershing personally reviewed each recommendation and the supporting documents.

Until June 30, 1921, the Badge and Medal Section in The Adjutant General's Office functioned within very limited areas of administration. On that date, the Secretary of War directed The Adjutant General to take over all operating functions connected with the award of Army medals and decorations.

The last Medal of Honor which could be awarded under the legislations of 1918—which specified that the award could be made not more than 3 years from the date of the act which won it—was presented to the American Unknown Soldier on Armistice Day of 1921. The bill which allowed it to be awarded to an unidentified soldier was signed by the President on August 24, 1921.

The medal was pinned on the flag draping the coffin of the Unknown Soldier at Arlington National Cemetery by President Warren G. Harding, at services in the amphitheater of the cemetery. At the same time, the President pinned to the flag high awards of Great Britain, France, Belgium, Italy, Rumania, Czechoslovakia, and Poland. All of these nations had authorized award of their highest decorations to the American Unknown Soldier, and the ceremony was attended by dignitaries of each of these countries.

During the post-World War I period special congressional action and Executive orders allowed the award of the Medal of Honor to Unknown Soldiers of nations which had been our allies in the conflict. On March 4, 1921, an act was approved awarding the medal to the Unknown British and French Soldiers, and on October 12, 1921, a similar act awarded it to the Italian Unknown Soldier.

Authorization to award the medal to the Belgian Unknown Soldier was given by Executive order of the President on December 1, 1922, and a similar authorization was given in the case of the Unknown Rumanian Soldier on June 6, 1923.

The Medal of Honor was also awarded to the Unknown American of World War II by act of Congress approved March 9, 1948, and to the Unknown American of the Korean conflict by act of Congress approved August 31, 1957, and of the Vietnam era on May 28, 1984.

In the winter of 1919–20, there was some discussion of changing the design of the Army medal once again, in order to beautify it, but the prevailing opinion was in favor of leaving it unchanged, and the design remained the same as it is today.

During the period of 1927–30, the Army War College, which has the mission of training selected officers for duty with the General Staff of the War Department and for high command, made studies of the principles and technical aspects of administration of Medal of Honor awards. Ten student officers had been assigned to make a study of the system of rewards in the Army as early as 1924. Three years later, in 1927, using the earlier study as a guide and source of material, a study of greater scope was finished at the War College.

A third study of the subject was made later.

When the time limitation on awards of the medal—contained in the 1918 legislation—expired for the second time, on April 7, 1923, many applications for War Department decorations which already had been filed with the Department during the first 4 postwar years still remained pending in the archives of The Adjutant General and the General Staff. On May 26, 1928, an extension was made part of an act of Congress in order to allow clearing up of these cases. It provided for consideration of recommendations pending at that date in the War and Navy Departments and the Marine Corps, with awards to be made in such cases as could be shown worthy.

On October 14, 1927, The Permanent Board of Awards was established by the Secretary of the Navy Curtis D. Wilbur to consider recommendations for awards of naval decorations to members of the military forces and to those attached to or serving with the Navy in any capacity. The Board was composed of two rear admirals of the line of the Navy and a brigadier general of the Marine Corps, with a lieutenant commander of the line of the Navy who served as recorder. The ranks and the number of members composing the Board have varied through the years, depending on conditions of world affairs, and the name of the Board was changed to Navy Department Board of Decorations and Medals.

During World War II and the Korean conflict, the Secretary of the Navy delegated authority to certain designated commands in the theaters of operations to award decorations without reference to the Secretary of the Navy (Navy Department Board of Decorations and Medals). Such authority excluded the Medal of Honor, the Distinguished Service Medal, all awards to flag officers, the Navy and Marine Corps Medal, and unit awards.

All of these procedures and policies, based upon congressional legislation, may seem dry and uninteresting. Legal terminology does not make for glamour. Records of proceedings of a board of review do not lend themselves to heroics. And the precise wording of regulations and bulletins, spelling out the law with care and repetition hardly constitutes the material of an adventure story. But it is precisely *because* of these legalistic safeguards that the Medal of Honor is a symbol of such glorious tradition today. The hours which were spent—thousands of them—from 1861 to the present day in the work of legislation, definition, administration, review of applications and recommendations, were unglamorous hours which painfully built the firm base for the pinnacle which bears the Medal of Honor. As a result of this painstaking work, the Nation was prepared, when World War II struck, to administer a swift and accurate reward for many provable cases of valor in action. Since World War II, through both the Korean conflict and the Vietnam era, these procedures have stood intact to continue to provide the Nation with an efficient manner of rewarding such conspicuous valor.

The Air Force Medal of Honor was established by Congress on July 6, 1960. Designed by the Institute of Heraldry, U.S. Army, the medal is a gold finished five pointed bronze star (one point down) 2″ in diameter. It's points are tipped with trefoils and joined by a green enamel laurel wreath edged in gold. In the center of the star is a likeness of the head of the Statue of Liberty surrounded by an amulet of 34 stars (the number of states in 1862). The star is suspended from a gold design of thunderbolts taken from the Air Force coat of arms. This in turn is attached to a horizontal bar bearing the word "Valor". The bar is suspended from a light blue silk-moiré neck ribbon behind an octagonal shaped pad of the ribbon bearing 13 white stars.

MASTER SERGEANT
GARY I. GORDON
UNITED STATES ARMY

Master Sergeant Gary I. Gordon, United States Army, distinguished himself by actions above and beyond the call of duty on 3 October 1993, while serving as Sniper Team Leader, United States Army Special Operations Command with Task Force Ranger in Mogadishu, Somalia. Master Sergeant Gordon's sniper team provided precision fires from the lead helicopter during an assault, and at two helicopter crash sites, while subjected to intense automatic weapons and rocket propelled grenade fires. When Master Sergeant Gordon learned that ground forces were to immediately available to secure the second crash site, he and another sniper unhesitatingly volunteered to be inserted to protect the four critically wounded personnel, despite being well aware of the growing number of enemy personnel closing in on the site. After his third request to be inserted, Master Sergeant Gordon received permission to perform his volunteer mission. When debris and enemy ground fires at the site caused him to abort the first attempt, Master Sergeant Gordon was inserted one hundred meters south of the crash site. Equipped with only his sniper rifle and a pistol, Master Sergeant Gordon and his fellow sniper, while under intense small arms fire from the enemy, fought their way through a dense maze of shanties and shacks to reach the critically injured crew members. Master Sergeant Gordon immediately pulled the pilot and the other crew members from the aircraft, establishing a perimeter which placed him and his fellow sniper in the most vulnerable position. Master Sergeant Gordon used his long range rifle and side arm to kill an undetermined number of attackers until he depleted his ammunition. Master Sergeant Gordon then went back to the wreckage, recovering some of the crew's weapons and ammunition. Despite the fact that he was critically low on ammunition he provided some of it to the dazed pilot and then radioed for help. master Sergeant Gordon _____ the _____ _____ing the downed crew. After his team member

SERGEANT FIRST CLASS
RANDALL D. SHUGHART
UNITED STATES ARMY

Sergeant First Class Randall D. Shughart, United States Army, distinguished himself by actions above and beyond the call of duty on 3 October 1993, while serving as a Sniper Team Member, United States Army Special Operations Command with Task Force Ranger in Mogadishu, Somalia. Sergeant First Class Shughart provided precision sniper fires from the lead helicopter during an assault on a building and at two helicopter crash sites, while subjected to intense automatic weapons and rocket propelled grenade fires. While providing critical suppressive fires at the second crash site, Sergeant First Class Shughart and his team leader learned that ground forces were not immediately available to secure the site. Sergeant First Class Shughart and this team leader unhesitatingly volunteered to be inserted to protect the four critically wounded personnel, despite being well aware of the growing number of enemy personnel closing in on the site. After their third request to be inserted, Sergeant First Class Shughart and his team leader received permission to perform this volunteer mission. When debris and enemy ground fires at the site caused them to abort the first attempt, Sergeant First Class Shughart and his team leader were inserted one hundred meters south of the crash site. Equipped with only his sniper rifle and a pistol, Sergeant First Class Shughart and his team leader, while under intense small arms fire from the enemy, fought their way through a dense maze of shanties and shacks to reach the critically injured crew members. Sergeant First Class Shughart pulled the pilot and the other crew members from the aircraft, establishing a perimeter which placed him and his fellow sniper in the most vulnerable position. Sergeant First Class Shughart used his long range rifle and side arm to kill an undetermined number of attackers while traveling the perimeter, protecting the downed crew. Sergeant First Class Shughart continued his protective fire until he depleted his ammunition and was fatally wounded. His actions saved the pilot's life. Sergeant First Class Shughart's extraordinary heroism and devotion to duty were in keeping with the highest standards of military service and reflect great credit on him, his unit, and the United States Army.

PART II
CITATIONS OF AWARDS OF THE MEDAL OF HONOR
BY WAR, CAMPAIGN, CONFLICT OR ERA

[Asterisk (*) Indicates Posthumous Award]

VIETNAM

(VIETNAM ERA)

*ADAMS, WILLIAM E. ✓

Rank and organization: Major, U.S. Army, A/227th Assault Helicopter Company, 52d Aviation Battalion, 1st Aviation Brigade. *Place and Date:* Kontum Province, Republic of Vietnam, 25 May 1971. *Entered Service at:* Kansas City, Mo. *Born:* 16 June 1939, Casper, Wyo. *Citation:* Maj. Adams distinguished himself on 25 May 1971 while serving as a helicopter pilot in Kontum Province in the Republic of Vietnam. On that date, Maj. Adams volunteered to fly a lightly armed helicopter in an attempt to evacuate 3 seriously wounded soldiers from a small fire base which was under attack by a large enemy force. He made the decision with full knowledge that numerous anti-aircraft weapons were positioned around the base and that the clear weather would afford the enemy gunners unobstructed view of all routes into the base. As he approached the base, the enemy gunners opened fire with heavy machineguns, rocket-propelled grenades and small arms. Undaunted by the fusillade, he continued his approach determined to accomplish the mission. Displaying tremendous courage under fire, he calmly directed the attacks of supporting gunships while maintaining absolute control of the helicopter he was flying. He landed the aircraft at the fire base despite the ever-increasing enemy fire and calmly waited until the wounded soldiers were placed on board. As his aircraft departed from the fire base, it was struck and seriously damaged by enemy anti-aircraft fire and began descending. Flying with exceptional skill, he immediately regained control of the crippled aircraft and attempted a controlled landing. Despite his valiant efforts, the helicopter exploded, overturned, and plummeted to earth amid the hail of enemy fire. Maj. Adams' conspicuous gallantry, intrepidity, and humanitarian regard for his fellow man were in keeping with the most cherished traditions of the military service and reflected utmost credit on him and the U.S. Army.

*ALBANESE, LEWIS

Rank and organization: Private First Class, U.S. Army, Company B, 5th Battalion (Airmobile), 7th Cavalry, 1st Cavalry Division. *Place and date:* Republic of Vietnam, 1 December 1966. *Entered service at:* Seattle, Wash. *Born:* 27 April 1946, Venice, Italy. *G.O. No.:* 12, 3 April 1968. *Citation:* For conspicuous gallantry and intrepidity in action at the risk of his life and beyond the call of duty. Pfc. Albanese's platoon, while advancing through densely covered terrain to establish a blocking position, received intense automatic weapons fire from close range. As other members maneuvered to assault the enemy position, Pfc. Albanese was ordered to provide security for the left flank of the platoon. Suddenly, the left flank received fire from enemy located in a well-concealed ditch. Realizing the imminent danger to his comrades from this fire, Pfc. Albanese fixed his bayonet and moved aggressively into the ditch. His action silenced the sniper fire, enabling the platoon to resume movement toward the main enemy position. As the platoon continued to advance, the sound of heavy firing emanated from the left flank from a pitched battle that ensued in the ditch which Pfc. Albanese had entered. The ditch was actually a well-organized complex of enemy defenses designed to bring devastating flanking fire on the forces attacking the main position. Pfc. Albanese, disregarding the danger to himself, advanced 100 meters along the trench and killed 6 of the snipers, who were armed with automatic weapons. Having exhausted his ammunition, Pfc. Albanese was mortally wounded when he engaged and killed 2 more enemy soldiers in fierce hand-to-hand combat. His unparalled actions saved the lives of many members of his platoon who otherwise would have fallen to the sniper fire from the ditch, and enabled his platoon to successfully advance against an enemy force of overwhelming numerical superiority. Pfc. Albanese's extraordinary heroism and supreme dedication to his comrades were commensurate with the finest traditions of the military service and remain a tribute to himself, his unit, and the U.S. Army.

*ANDERSON, JAMES, JR.

Rank and organization: Private First Class, U.S. Marine Corps, 2d Platoon, Company F, 2d Battalion, 3d Marines, 3d Marine Division. *Place and date:* Republic of Vietnam, 28 February 1967. *Entered service at:* Los Angeles, Calif. *Born:* 22 January 1947, Los Angeles, Calif. *Citation:* For conspicuous gallantry and intrepidity at the risk of his life above and beyond the call of duty. Company F was advancing in dense jungle northwest of Cam Lo in an effort to extract a heavily besieged reconnaissance patrol. Pfc. Anderson's platoon was the lead element and had advanced only about 200 meters when they were brought under extremely intense enemy small-arms and automatic weapons fire. The platoon reacted swiftly, getting on line as best they could in the thick terrain, and began returning fire. Pfc. Anderson found himself tightly bunched together with the other members of the platoon only 20 meters from the enemy positions. As the fire fight continued several of the men were wounded by the deadly enemy assault. Suddenly, an enemy grenade landed in the midst of the marines and rolled alongside Pfc. Anderson's head. Unhesitatingly and with complete disregard for his personal safety, he reached out, grasped the grenade, pulled it to his chest and curled around it as it went off. Although several marines received shrapnel from the grenade, his body absorbed the major force of the explosion. In this singularly heroic act, Pfc. Anderson saved his comrades from serious injury and possible death. His personal heroism, extraordinary valor, and inspirational supreme self-sacrifice reflected great credit upon himself and the Marine Corps and upheld the highest traditions of the U.S. Naval Service. He gallantly gave his life for his country.

*ANDERSON, RICHARD A.

Rank and organization: Lance Corporal, U.S. Marine Corps, Company E, 3d Reconnaissance Battalion, 3d Marine Division. *Place and date:* Quang Tri Province, Republic of Vietnam, 24 August 1969. *Entered service at:* Houston, Tex. *Born:* 16 April 1948, Washington, D.C. *Citation:* For conspicuous gallantry and intrepidity at the risk of his life above and beyond the call of duty while serving as an assistant team leader with Company E, in connection with combat operations against an armed enemy. While conducting a patrol during the early morning hours L/Cpl. Anderson's reconnaissance team came under a heavy volume of automatic weapons and machinegun fire from a numerically's superior and well concealed enemy force. Although painfully wounded in both legs and knocked to the ground during the initial moments of the fierce fire fight, L/Cpl. Anderson assumed a prone position and continued to deliver intense suppressive fire in an attempt to repulse the attackers. Moments later he was wounded a second time by an enemy soldier who had approached to within 8 feet of the team's position. Undaunted, he continued to pour a relentless stream of fire at the assaulting unit, even while a companion was treating his leg wounds. Observing an enemy grenade land between himself and the other marine, L/Cpl. Anderson immediately rolled over and covered the lethal weapon with his body, absorbing the full effects of the detonation. By his indomitable courage, inspiring initiative, and selfless devotion to duty, L/Cpl. Anderson was instrumental in saving several marines from serious injury or possible death. His actions were in keeping with the highest traditions of the Marine Corps and of the U.S. Naval Service. He gallantly gave his life in the service of his country.

ANDERSON, WEBSTER

Rank and organization: Sergeant First Class, U.S. Army, Battery A, 2d Battalion, 320th Artillery 101st Airborne Infantry Division (Airmobile). *Place and date:* Tam Ky, Republic of Vietnam, 15 October 1967. *Entered service at:* Winnsboro, S.C. *Born:* 15 July 1933, Winnsboro, S.C. *Citation:* Sfc. Anderson (then S/Sgt.), distinguished himself by conspicuous gallantry and intrepidity in action while serving as chief of section in Battery A, against a hostile force. During the early morning hours Battery A's defensive position was attacked by a determined North Vietnamese Army infantry unit supported by heavy mortar, recoilless rifle, rocket propelled grenade and automatic weapon fire. The initial enemy onslaught breached the battery defensive perimeter. Sfc. Anderson, with complete disregard for his personal safety, mounted the exposed parapet of his howitzer position and became the mainstay of the defense of the battery position. Sfc. Anderson directed devastating direct howitzer fire on the assaulting enemy while providing rifle and grenade defensive fire against enemy soldiers attempting to overrun his gun section position. While protecting his crew and directing their fire against the enemy from his exposed position, 2 enemy grenades exploded at his feet knocking him down and severely wounding him in the legs. Despite the excruciating pain and though not able to stand, Sfc. Anderson valorously propped himself on the parapet and continued to direct howitzer fire upon the closing enemy and to encourage his men to fight on. Seeing an enemy grenade land within the gunpit near a wounded member of his gun-crew, Sfc. Anderson heedless of his own safety, seized the grenade and attempted to throw it over the parapet to save his men. As the grenade was thrown from the position it exploded and Sfc. Anderson was again greviously wounded. Although only partially conscious and severely wounded, Sfc. Anderson refused medical evacuation and continued to encourage his men in the defense of the position. Sfc. Anderson by his inspirational leadership, professionalism, devotion to duty and complete disregard for his welfare was able to maintain the defense of his section position and to defeat a determined attack. Sfc. Anderson's gallantry and extraordinary heroism at the risk of his life above and beyond the call of duty are in the highest traditions of the military service and reflect great credit upon himself, his unit, and the U.S. Army.

*ASHLEY, EUGENE, JR.

Rank and organization: Sergeant First Class, U.S. Army, Company C, 5th Special Forces Group (Airborne), 1st Special Forces. *Place and date:* Near Lang Vei, Republic of Vietnam, 6th and 7th February 1968. *Entered service at:* New York, N.Y. *Born:* 12 October 1931, Wilmington, N.C. *Citation:* Sfc. Ashley, distinguished himself by conspicuous gallantry and intrepidity while serving with Detachment

A–101, Company C. Sfc. Ashley was the senior special forces Advisor of a hastily organized assault force whose mission was to rescue entrapped U.S. special forces advisors at Camp Lang Vei. During the initial attack on the special forces camp by North Vietnamese army forces, Sfc. Ashley supported the camp with high explosive and illumination mortar rounds. When communications were lost with the main camp, he assumed the additional responsibility of directing air strikes and artillery support. Sfc. Ashley organized and equipped a small assault force composed of local friendly personnel. During the ensuing battle, Sfc. Ashley led a total of 5 vigorous assaults against the enemy, continuously exposing himself to a voluminous hail of enemy grenades, machinegun and automatic weapons fire. Throughout these assaults, he was plagued by numerous boobytrapped satchel charges in all bunkers on his avenue of approach. During his fifth and final assault, he adjusted air strikes nearly on top of his assault element, forcing the enemy to withdraw and resulting in friendly control of the summit of the hill. While exposing himself to intense enemy fire, he was seriously wounded by machinegun fire but continued his mission without regard for his personal safety. After the fifth assault he lost consciousness and was carried from the summit by his comrades only to suffer a fatal wound when an enemy artillery round landed in the area. Sfc. Ashley displayed extraordinary heroism in risking his life in an attempt to save the lives of his entrapped comrades and commanding officer. His total disregard for his personal safety while exposed to enemy observation and automatic weapons fire was an inspiration to all men committed to the assault. The resolute valor with which he led 5 gallant charges placed critical diversionary pressure on the attacking enemy and his valiant efforts carved a channel in the overpowering enemy forces and weapons positions through which the survivors of Camp Lang Vei eventually escaped to freedom. Sfc. Ashley's bravery at the cost of his life was in the highest traditions of the military service, and reflects great credit upon himself, his unit, and the U.S. Army.

*AUSTIN, OSCAR P.

Rank and organization: Private First Class, U.S. Marine Corps, Company E, 2d Battalion, 7th Marines, 1st Marine Division, (Rein), FMF. *Place and date:* West of Da Nang, Republic of Vietnam, 23 February 1969. *Entered service at:* Phoenix, Ariz. *Born:* 15 January 1948, Nacogdoches, Tex. *Citation:* For conspicuous gallantry and intrepidity at the risk of his life above and beyond the call of duty while serving as an assistant machine gunner with Company E, in connection with operations against enemy forces. During the early morning hours Pfc. Austin's observation post was subjected to a fierce ground attack by a large North Vietnamese Army force supported by a heavy volume of handgrenades, satchel charges, and small arms fire. Observing that 1 of his wounded companions had fallen unconscious in a position dangerously exposed to the hostile fire, Pfc. Austin unhesitatingly left the relative security of his fighting hole and, with complete disregard for his safety, raced across the fire-swept terrain to assist the marine to a covered location. As he neared the casualty, he observed an enemy grenade land nearby and, reacting instantly, leaped between the injured marine and the lethal object, absorbing the effects of its detonation. As he ignored his painful injuries and turned to examine the wounded man, he saw a North Vietnamese Army soldier aiming a weapon at his unconscious companion. With full knowledge of the probable consequences and thinking only to protect the marine, Pfc. Austin resolutely threw himself between the casualty and the hostile soldier, and, in doing, was mortally wounded. Pfc. Austin's indomitable courage, inspiring initiative and selfless devotion to duty upheld the highest traditions of the Marine Corps and the U.S. Naval Service. He gallantly gave his life for his country.

BACA, JOHN P.

Rank and organization: Specialist Fourth Class, U.S. Army, Company D, 1st Battalion, 12th Calvary, 1st Calvary Division. *Place and date:* Phuoc Long Province, Republic of Vietnam, 10 February 1970. *Entered service at:* Fort Ord, Calif. *Born:* 10 January 1949, Providence, R.I. *Citation:* For conspicuous gallantry and intrepidity in action at the risk of his life above and beyond the call of duty. Sp4c. Baca, Company D, distinguished himself while serving on a recoilless rifle team during a night ambush mission. A platoon from his company was sent to investigate the detonation of an automatic ambush device forward of his unit's main position and soon came under intense enemy fire from concealed positions along the trail. Hearing the heavy firing from the platoon position and realizing that his recoilless rifle team could assist the members of the beseiged patrol, Sp4c. Baca led his team through the hail of enemy fire to a firing position within the patrol's defensive perimeter. As they prepared to engage the enemy, a fragmentation grenade was thrown into the midst of the patrol. Fully aware of the danger to his comrades, Sp4c. Baca unhesitatingly, and with complete disregard for his own safety, covered the grenade with his steel helmet and fell on it as the grenade exploded, thereby absorbing the lethal fragments and concussion with his body. His gallant action and total disregard for his personal well-being directly saved 8 men from certain serious injury or death. The extraordinary courage and selflessness displayed by Sp4c. Baca, at the risk of his life, are in the highest traditions of the military service and reflect great credit on him, his unit, and the U.S. Army.

BACON, NICKY DANIEL

Rank and organization: Staff Sergeant, U.S. Army, Company B, 4th Battalion, 21st Infantry, 11th Infantry Brigade, Americal Division. *Place and date:* West of Tam Ky, Republic of Vietnam, 26 August 1968. *Entered service at:* Phoenix, Ariz. *Born:* 25 November 1945, Caraway, Ark. *Citation:* For conspicuous gallantry and intrepidity in action at the risk of his life above and beyond the call of duty. S/Sgt. Bacon distinguished himself while serving as a squad leader with the 1st Platoon, Company B, during an operation west of Tam Ky. When Company B came under fire from an enemy bunker line to the front, S/Sgt. Bacon quickly organized his men and led them forward in an assault. He advanced on a hostile bunker and destroyed it with grenades. As he did so, several fellow soldiers including the 1st Platoon leader, were struck by machinegun fire and fell wounded in an exposed position forward of the rest of the platoon. S/Sgt. Bacon immediately assumed command of the platoon and assaulted the hostile gun position, finally killing the enemy guncrew in a singlehanded effort. When the 3d Platoon moved to S/Sgt. Bacon's location, its leader was also wounded. Without hesitation S/Sgt. Bacon took charge of the additional platoon and continued the fight. In the ensuing action he personally killed 4 more enemy soldiers and silenced an antitank weapon. Under his leadership and example, the members of both platoons accepted his authority without question. Continuing to ignore the intense hostile fire, he climbed up on the exposed deck of a tank and directed fire into the enemy position while several wounded men were evacuated. As a result of S/Sgt. Bacon's extraordinary efforts, his company was able to move forward, eliminate the enemy positions, and rescue the men trapped to the front. S/Sgt. Bacon's bravery at the risk of his life was in the highest traditions of the military service and reflects great credit upon himself, his unit, and the U.S. Army.

BAKER, JOHN F., JR.

Rank and organization: Sergeant (then Pfc.), U.S. Army, Company A, 2d Battalion, 27th Infantry, 25th Infantry Division. *Place and date:* Republic of Vietnam, 5 November 1966. *Entered service at:* Moline, Ill. *Born:* 30 October 1945, Davenport, Iowa. *Citation:* For conspicuous gallantry and intrepidity in action at the risk of his life above and beyond the call of duty. En route to assist another unit that was engaged with the enemy, Company A came under intense enemy fire and the lead man was killed instantly. Sgt. Baker immediately moved to the head of the column and together with another soldier knocked out 2 enemy bunkers. When his comrade was mortally wounded, Sgt. Baker, spotting 4 Viet Cong snipers, killed all of them, evacuated the fallen soldier and returned to lead repeated assaults against the enemy positions, killing several more Viet Cong. Moving to attack 2 additional enemy bunkers, he and another soldier drew intense enemy fire and Sgt. Baker was blown from his feet by an enemy grenade. He quickly recovered and singlehandedly destroyed 1 bunker before the other soldier was wounded. Seizing his fallen comrade's machinegun, Sgt. Baker charged through the deadly fusillade to silence the other bunker. He evacuated his comrade, replenished his ammunition and returned to the forefront to brave the enemy fire and continue the fight. When the forward element was ordered to withdraw, he carried 1 wounded man to the rear. As he returned to evacuate another soldier, he was taken under fire by snipers, but raced beyond the friendly troops to attack and kill the snipers. After evacuating the wounded man, he returned to cover the deployment of the unit. His ammunition now exhausted, he dragged 2 more of his fallen comrades to the rear. Sgt. Baker's selfless heroism, indomitable fighting spirit, and extraordinary gallantry were directly responsible for saving the lives of several of his comrades, and inflicting serious damage on the enemy. His acts were in keeping with the highest traditions of the U.S. Army and reflect great credit upon himself and the Armed Forces of his country.

BALLARD, DONALD E.

Rank and organization: Hospital Corpsman Second Class, U.S. Navy, Company M, 3d Battalion, 4th Marines, 3d Marine Division. *Place and date:* Quang Tri Province, Republic of Vietnam, 16 May 1968. *Entered service at:* Kansas City, Mo. *Born:* 5 December 1945, Kansas City, Mo. *Citation:* For conspicuous gallantry and intrepidity at the risk of his life and beyond the call of duty while serving as a HC2c. with Company M, in connection with operations against enemy aggressor forces. During the afternoon hours, Company M was moving to join the remainder of the 3d Battalion in Quang Tri Province. After treating and evacuating 2 heat casualties, HC2c. Ballard was returning to his platoon from the evacuation landing zone when the company was ambushed by a North Vietnamese Army unit employing automatic weapons and mortars, and sustained numerous casualties. Observing a wounded marine, HC2c. Ballard unhesitatingly moved across the fire-swept terrain to the injured man and swiftly rendered medical assistance to his comrade. HC2c. Ballard then directed 4 marines to carry the casualty to a position of relative safety. As the 4 men prepared to move the wounded marine, an enemy soldier suddenly left his concealed position and, after hurling a handgrenade which landed near the casualty, commenced firing upon the small group of men. Instantly shouting a warning to the marines, HC2c. Ballard fearlessly threw himself upon the lethal explosive device to protect his comrades from the deadly blast. When the grenaded failed to detonate, he calmly arose from his dangerous position and resolutely continued his determined efforts in treating other marine casualties. HC2c. Ballard's heroic actions and selfless concern for the welfare of his companions served to inspire all who observed him and prevented possible injury or death to his fellow marines. His courage, daring initiative, and unwavering devotion to duty in the face of extreme personal danger, sustain and enhance the finest traditions of the U.S. Naval Service.

*BARKER, JEDH COLBY

Rank and organization: Lance Corporal, U.S. Marine Corps, Company F, 2d Battalion, 4th Marines, 3d Marine Division (Rein), FMF. *Place and date:* Near Con Thein, Republic of Vietnam, 21 September 1967. *Entered service at:* Park Ridge, N.J. *Born:* 20 June 1945, Franklin, N.H. *Citation:* For conspicuous gallantry and intrepidity at the risk of his life above and beyond the call of duty while serving as a machine gunner with Company F. During a reconnaissance operation L/Cpl. Barker's squad was suddenly hit by enemy sniper fire. The squad immediately deployed to a combat formation and advanced to a strongly fortified enemy position, when it was again struck by small arms and automatic weapons fire, sustaining numerous casualties. Although wounded by the initial burst of fire, L/Cpl. Barker boldly remained in the open, delivering a devastating volume of accurate fire on the numerically superior force. The enemy was intent upon annihilating the small marine force and, realizing that L/Cpl. Barker was a threat to their position, directed the preponderance of their fire on his position. He was again wounded, this time in the right hand, which prevented him from operating his vitally needed machinegun. Suddenly and without warning, an enemy grenade landed in the midst of the few surviving marines. Unhesitatingly and with complete disregard for his personal safety, L/Cpl. Barker threw himself upon the deadly grenade, absorbing with his body the full and tremendous force of the explosion. In a final act of bravery, he crawled to the side of a wounded comrade and administered first aid before succumbing to his grevious wounds. His bold initiative, intrepid fighting spirit and unwavering devotion to duty in the face of almost certain death undoubtedly saved his comrades from further injury or possible death and reflected great credit upon himself, the Marine Corps, and the U.S. Naval Service. He gallantly gave his life for his country.

*BARNES, JOHN ANDREW III

Rank and organization: Private First Class, U.S. Army, Company C, 1st Battalion, 503d Infantry 173d Airborne Brigade. *Place and date:* Dak To, Republic of Vietnam, 12 November 1967. *Entered service at:* Boston, Mass. *Born:* 16 April 1945, Boston, Mass. *Citation:* For conspicuous gallantry and intrepidity in action at the risk of his life above and beyond the call of duty. Pfc. Barnes distinguished himself by exceptional heroism while engaged in combat against hostile forces. Pfc. Barnes was serving as a grenadier when his unit was attacked by a North Vietnamese force, estimated to be a battalion. Upon seeing the crew of a machinegun team killed, Pfc. Barnes, without hesitation, dashed through the bullet swept area, manned the machinegun, and killed 9 enemy soldiers as they assaulted his position. While pausing just long enough to retrieve more ammunition, Pfc. Barnes observed an enemy grenade thrown into the midst of some severely wounded personnel close to his position. Realizing that the grenade could further injure or kill the majority of the wounded personnel, he sacrificed his life by throwing himself directly onto the handgrenade as it exploded. Through is indomitable courage, complete disregard for his own safety, and profound concern for his fellow soldiers, he averted a probable loss of life and injury to the wounded members of his unit. Pfc. Barnes' extraordinary heroism, and intrepidity at the cost of his life, above and beyond the call of duty, are in the highest traditions of military service and reflect great credit upon himself, his unit, and the U.S. Army.

BARNUM, HARVEY C., JR.

Rank and organization: Captain (then Lt.), U.S. Marine Corps, Company H, 2d Battalion, 9th Marines, 3d Marine Division (Rein). *Place and date:* Ky Phu in Quang Tin Province, Republic of Vietnam, 18 December 1965. *Entered service at:* Cheshire, Conn. *Born:* 21 July 1940, Cheshire, Conn. *Citation:* For conspicuous gallantry and intrepidity at the risk of his life above and beyond the call of duty. When the company was suddenly pinned down by a hail of extremely accurate enemy fire and was quickly separated from the remainder of the battalion by over 500 meters of open and fire-swept ground, and casualties mounted rapidly. Lt. Barnum quickly made a hazardous reconnaissance of the area, seeking targets for his artillery. Finding the rifle company commander mortally wounded and the radio operator killed, he, with complete disregard for his safety, gave aid to the dying commander, then removed the radio from the dead operator and strapped it to himself. He immediately assumed command of the rifle company, and moving at once into the midst of the heavy fire, rallying and giving encouragement to all units, reorganized them to replace the loss of key personnel and led their attack on enemy positions from which deadly fire continued to come. His sound and swift decisions and his obvious calm served to stabilize the badly decimated units and his gallant example as he stood exposed repeatedly to point out targets served as an inspiration to all. Provided with 2 armed helicopters, he moved fearlessly through enemy fire to control the air attack against the firmly entrenched enemy while skillfully directing 1 platoon in a successful counterattack on the key enemy positions. Having thus cleared a small area, he requested and directed the landing of 2 transport helicopters for the evacuation of the dead and wounded. He then assisted in the mopping up and final seizure of the battalion's objective. His gallant initiative and heroic conduct reflected great credit upon himself and were in keeping with the highest traditions of the Marine Corps and the U.S. Naval Service.

BEIKIRCH, GARY B.

Rank and organization: Sergeant, U.S. Army, Company B, 5th Special Forces Group, 1st Special Forces. *Place and date:* Kontum Province, Republic of Vietnam, 1 April 1970. *Entered service at:* Buffalo, N.Y. *Born:* 29 August 1947, Rochester, N.Y. *Citation:* For conspicuous gallantry and intrepidity in action at the risk of his life above and beyond the call of duty. Sgt. Beikirch, medical aidman, Detachment B–24, Company B, distinguished himself during the defense of Camp Dak Seang. The allied defenders suffered a number of casualties as a result of an intense, devastating attack launched by the enemy from well-concealed positions surrounding the camp. Sgt. Beikirch, with complete disregard for his personal safety, moved unhesitatingly through the withering enemy fire to his fallen comrades, applied first aid to their wounds and assisted them to the medical aid station. When informed that a seriously injured American officer was lying in an exposed position, Sgt. Beikirch ran immediately through the hail of fire. Although he was wounded seriously by fragments from an exploding enemy mortar shell, Sgt. Beikirch carried the officer to a medical aid station. Ignoring his own serious injuries, Sgt. Beikirch left the relative safety of the medical bunker to search for and evacuate other men who had been injured. He was again wounded as he dragged a critically injured Vietnamese soldier to the medical bunker while simultaneously applying mouth-to-mouth resuscitation to sustain his life. Sgt. Beikirch again refused treatment and continued his search for other casualties until he collapsed. Only then did he permit himself to be treated. Sgt. Beikirch's complete devotion to the welfare of his comrades, at the risk of his life are in keeping with the highest traditions of the military service and reflect great credit on him, his unit, and the U.S. Army.

*BELCHER, TED

Rank and organization: Sergeant, U.S. Army, Company C, 1st Battalion, 14th Infantry, 25th Infantry Division. *Place and date:* Plei Djerang, Republic of Vietnam, 19 November 1966. *Entered service at:* Huntington, W. Va. *Born:* 21 July 1924, Accoville, W. Va. *Citation:* Distinguishing himself by conspicuous gallantry and intrepidity at the risk of his life. Sgt. Belcher's unit was engaged in a search and destroy mission with Company B, 1st Battalion, 14th Infantry, the Battalion Reconnaissance Platoon and a special forces company of civilian irregular defense group personnel. As a squad leader of the 2d Platoon of Company C, Sgt. Belcher was leading his men when they encountered a bunker complex. The reconnaissance platoon, located a few hundred meters northwest of Company C, received a heavy volume of fire from well camouflaged snipers. As the 2d Platoon moved forward to assist the unit under attack, Sgt. Belcher and his squad, advancing only a short distance through the dense jungle terrain, met heavy and accurate automatic weapons and sniper fire. Sgt. Belcher and his squad were momentarily stopped by the deadly volume of enemy fire. He quickly gave the order to return fire and resume the advance toward the enemy. As he moved up with his men, a handgrenade landed in the midst of the sergeant's squad. Instantly realizing the immediate danger to his men, Sgt. Belcher, unhesitatingly and with complete disregard for his safety, lunged forward, covering the grenade with his body. Absorbing the grenade blast at the cost of his life, he saved his comrades from becoming casualties. Sgt. Belcher's profound concern for his fellow soldiers, at the risk of his life above and beyond the call of duty are in keeping with the highest traditions of the U.S. Army and reflect credit upon himself and the Armed Forces of his country.

*BELLRICHARD, LESLIE ALLEN

Rank and organization: Private First Class, U.S. Army, Company C, 1st Battalion, 8th Infantry. *Place and date:* Kontum Province, Republic of Vietnam, 20 May 1967. *Entered service at:* Oakland, Calif. *Born:* 4 December 1941, Janesville, Wis. *Citation:* For conspicuous gallantry and intrepidity in action at the risk of his life above and beyond the call of duty. Acting as a fire team leader with Company C, during combat operations Pfc. Bellrichard was with 4 fellow soldiers in a foxhole on their unit's perimeter when the position came under a massive enemy attack. Following a 30-minute mortar barrage, the enemy launched a strong ground assault. Pfc. Bellrichard rose in face of a group of charging enemy soldiers and threw handgrenades into their midst, eliminating several of the foe and forcing the remainder to withdraw. Failing in their initial attack, the enemy repeated the mortar and rocket bombardment of the friendly perimeter, then once again charged against the defenders in a concerted effort to overrun the position. Pfc. Bellrichard resumed throwing handgrenades at the onrushing attackers. As he was about to hurl a grenade, a mortar round exploded just in front of his position, knocking him into the foxhole and causing him to lose his grip on the already armed grenade. Recovering instantly, Pfc. Bellrichard recognized the threat to the lives of his 4 comrades and threw himself upon the grenade, shielding his companions from the blast that followed. Although severely wounded, Pfc. Bellrichard struggled into an upright position in the foxhole and fired his rifle at the enemy until he succumbed to his wounds. His selfless heroism contributed greatly to the successful defense of the position, and he was directly responsible for saving the lives of several of his comrades. His acts are in keeping with the highest traditions of the military service and reflect great credit upon himself and the U.S. Army.

BENAVIDEZ, ROY P.

Rank and Organization: Master Sergeant, Detachment B-56, 5th Special Forces Group, Republic of Vietnam. *Place and Date:* West of Loc Ninh on 2 May 1968. *Entered Service at:* Houston, Texas June 1955. *Date and Place of Birth:* 5 August 1935, DeWitt County, Cuero, Texas. Master Sergeant (then Staff Sergeant) Roy P. Benavidez, 455-02-5039, United States Army, who distinguished himself by a series of daring and extremely valorous actions on 2 May 1968 while assigned to Detachment B-56, 5th Special Forces Group (Airborne), 1st Special Forces, Republic of Vietnam. On the morning of 2 May 1968, a 12-man Special Forces Reconnaissance Team was inserted by helicopters in a dense jungle area west of Loc Ninh, Vietnam to gather intelligence information about confirmed large-scale enemy activity. This area was controlled and routinely patrolled by the North Vietnamese Army. After a short period of time on the ground, the team met heavy enemy resistance, and requested emergency extraction. Three helicopters attempted extraction, but were unable to land due to intense enemy small arms and anti-aircraft fire. Sergeant Benavidez was at the Forward Operating Base in Loc Ninh monitoring the operation by radio when these helicopters returned to off-load wounded crewmembers and to assess aircraft damage. Sergeant Benavidez voluntarily boarded a returning aircraft to assist in another extraction attempt. Realizing that all the team members were either dead or wounded and unable to move to the pickup zone, he directed the aircraft to a nearby clearing where he jumped from the hovering helicopter, and ran approximately 75 meters under withering small arms fire to the crippled team. Prior to reaching the team's position he was wounded in his right leg, face, and head. Despite these painful injuries, he took charge, repositioning the team members and directing their fire to facilitate the landing of an extractrion aircraft, and the loading of wounded and dead team members. He then threw smoke cannisters to direct the aircraft to the team's position. Despite his severe wounds and under intense enemy fire, he carried and dragged half of the wounded team members to the awaiting aircraft. He then provided protective fire by running alongside the aircraft as it moved to pick up the remaining team members. As the enemy's fire intensified, he hurried to recover the body and classified documents on the dead team leader. When he reached the leader's body, Sergeant Benavidez was severely wounded by small arms fire in the abdomen and grenade fragments in his back. At nearly the same moment, the aircraft pilot was mortally wounded, and his helicopter crashed. Athough in extremely critical condition due to his multiple wounds, Sergeant Benavidez secured the classified documents and made his way back to the wreckage, where he aided the wounded out of the overturned aircraft, and gathered the stunned survivors into a defenseive perimeter. Under increasing enemy automatic weapons and grenade fire, he moved around the perimeter distributing water and ammunition to his weary men, reinstilling in them a will to live and fight. Facing a buildup of enemy opposition with a beleaguered team, Sergeant Benavidez mustered his strength, began calling in tactical air strikes and directed the fire from supporting gunships to suppress the enemy's fire and so permit another extraction attempt. He was wounded again in hs thigh by small arms fire while administering first aid to a wounded team member just before another extraction helicopter was able to land. His indomitable spirit kept him going as he began to ferry his comrades to the craft. On his second trip with the wounded, he was clubbed from additional wounds to his head and arms before killing his adversary. He then continued under devastating fire to carry the wounded to the helicopter. Upon reaching the aircraft, he spotted and killed two enemy soldiers who were rushing the craft from an angle that prevented the aircraft door gunner from firing upon them. With little strength remaining, he made one last trip to the perimeter to ensure that all classified material had been collected or destroyed, and to bring in the remaining wounded. Only then, in extremely serious condition from numerous wounds and loss of blood, did he allow himself to be pulled into the extraction aircraft. Sergeant Benavidez' gallant choice to join voluntarily his comrades who were in critical straits, to expose himself constantly to withering enemy fire, and his refusal to be stopped despite numerous severe wounds, saved the lives of at least eight men. His fearless personal leadership, tenacious devotion to duty, and extremely valorous actions in the face of overwhelming odds were in keeping with the highest traditions of the military service, and reflect the utmost credit on him and the United States Army. (This awards supersedes the Distinguished Service Cross awarded to Master Sergeant Roy P. Benavidez for extraordinary heroism on 2 May 1968, as announced in United States Army, Vietnam, General Orders 3752, 1968.)

*BENNETT, STEVEN L.

Rank and organization: Captain, U.S. Air Force. 20th Tactical Air Support Squadron, Pacific Air Forces. *Place and date:* Quang Tri, Republic of Vietnam, 29 June 1972. *Entered service at:* Lafayette, La. *Born:* 22 April 1946, Palestine, Tex. *Citation:* Capt. Bennett was the pilot of a light aircraft flying an artillery adjustment mission along a heavily defended segment of route structure. A large concentration of enemy troops was massing for an attack on a friendly unit. Capt. Bennett requested tactical air support but was advised that none was available. He also requested artillery support but this too was denied due to the close proximity of friendly troops to the target. Capt. Bennett was determined to aid the endangered unit and elected to strafe the hostile positions. After 4 such passes, the enemy force began to retreat. Capt. Bennett continued the attack, but, as he completed his fifth strafing pass, his aircraft was struck by a surface-to-air missile, which severely damaged the left engine and the left main landing gear. As fire spread in the left engine, Capt. Bennett realized that recovery at a friendly airfield was impossible. He instructed his observer to prepare for an ejection, but was informed by the observer that his parachute had been shredded by the force of the impacting missile. Although Capt. Bennett had a good parachute, he knew that if he ejected, the observer would have no chance of survival. With complete disregard for his own life, Capt. Bennett elected to ditch the aircraft into the Gulf of Tonkin, even though he realized that a pilot of this type aircraft had never survived a ditching. The ensuing impact upon the water caused the aircraft to cartwheel and severely damaged the front cockpit, making escape for Capt. Bennett impossible. The observer successfully made his way out of the aircraft and was rescued. Capt. Bennett's unparalleled concern for his companion, extraordinary heroism and intrepidity above and beyond the call of duty, at the cost of his life, were in keeping with the highest traditions of the military service and reflect great credit upon himself and the U.S. Air Force.

*BENNETT, THOMAS W.

Rank and organization: Corporal, U.S. Army, 2d Platoon, Company B, 1st Battalion, 14th Infantry. *Place and date:* Chu Pa Region, Pleiku Province, Republic of Vietnam, 9–11 February 1969. *Entered service at:* Fairmont, W. Va. *Born:* 7 April 1947, Morgantown, W. Va. *Citation:* For conspicuous gallantry and intrepidity in action at the risk of his life above and beyond the call of duty. Cpl. Bennett distinguished himself while serving as a platoon medical aidman with the 2d Platoon, Company B, during a reconnaissance-in-force mission. On 9 February the platoon was moving to assist the 1st Platoon of Company D which had run into a North Vietnamese ambush when it became heavily engaged by the intense small arms, automatic weapons, mortar and rocket fire from a well fortified and numerically superior enemy unit. In the initial barrage of fire, 3 of the point members of the platoon fell wounded. Cpl. Bennett, with complete disregard for his safety, ran through the heavy fire to his fallen comrades, administered life-saving first aid under fire and then made repeated trips carrying the wounded men to positions of relative safety from which they would be medically evacuated from the battle position. Cpl. Bennett repeatedly braved the intense enemy fire moving across open areas to give aid and comfort to his wounded comrades. He valiantly exposed himself to the heavy fire in order to retrieve the bodies of several fallen personnel. Throughout the night and following day, Cpl. Bennett moved from position to position treating and comforting the several personnel who had suffered shrapnel and gunshot wounds. On 11 February, Company B again moved in an assault on the well fortified enemy positions and became heavily engaged with the numerically superior enemy force. Five members of the company fell wounded in the initial assault. Cpl. Bennett ran to their aid without regard to the heavy fire. He treated 1 wounded comrade and began running toward another seriously wounded man. Although the wounded man was located forward of the company position covered by heavy enemy grazing fire and Cpl. Bennett was warned that it was impossible to reach the position, he leaped forward with complete disregard for his safety to save his comrade's life. In attempting to save his fellow soldier, he was mortally wounded. Cpl. Bennett's undaunted concern for his comrades at the cost of his life above and beyond the call of duty are in keeping with the highest traditions of the military service and reflect great credit upon himself, his unit, and the U.S. Army.

*BLANCHFIELD, MICHAEL R.

Rank and organization: Specialist Fourth Class, U.S. Army, Company A, 4th Battalion, 503d Infantry, 173d Airborne Brigade. *Place and date:* Binh Dinh Province, Republic of Vietnam, 3 July 1969. *Entered service at:* Chicago, Ill. *Born:* 4 January 1950, Minneapolis, Minn. *Citation:* For conspicuous gallantry and intrepidity in action at the risk of his life above and beyond the call of duty. Sp4c. Blanchfield distinguished himself while serving as a rifleman in Company A on a combat patrol. The patrol surrounded a group of houses to search for suspects. During the search of 1 of the huts, a man suddenly ran out toward a nearby tree line. Sp4c. Blanchfield, who was on guard outside the hut, saw the man, shouted for him to halt, and began firing at him as the man ignored the warning and continued to run. The suspect suddenly threw a grenade toward the hut and its occupants. Although the exploding grenade severely wounded Sp4c. Blanchfield and several others, he regained his feet to continue the pursuit of the enemy. The fleeing enemy threw a second grenade which landed near Sp4c. Blanchfield and several members of his patrol. Instantly realizing the danger, he shouted a warning to his comrades. Sp4c. Blanchfield unhesitatingly and with complete disregard for his safety, threw himself on the grenade, absorbing the full and fatal impact of the explosion. By his gallant action and self-sacrifice, he was able to save the lives and prevent injury to 4 members of the patrol and several Vietnamese civilians in the immediate area. Sp4c. Blanchfield's extraordinary courage and gallantry at the cost of his life above and beyond the call of duty are in keeping with the highest traditions of the military service and reflect great credit upon himself, his unit, and the U.S. Army.

*BOBO, JOHN P.

Rank and organization: Second Lieutenant, U.S. Marine Corps Reserve, 3d Battalion, 9th Marines, 3d Marine Division (Rein), FMF. *Place and date:* Quang Tri Province, Republic of Vietnam, 30 March 1967. *Entered service at:* Buffalo, N.Y. *Born:* 14 February 1943, Niagara Falls, N.Y. *Citation:* For conspicuous gallantry and intrepidity at the risk of his life above and beyond the call of duty. Company I was establishing night ambush sites when the command group was attacked by a reinforced North Vietnamese company supported by heavy automatic weapons and mortar fire. 2d Lt. Bobo immediately organized a hasty defense and moved from position to position encouraging the outnumbered marines despite the murderous enemy fire. Recovering a rocket launcher from among the friendly casualties, he organized a new launcher team and directed its fire into the enemy machinegun positions. When an exploding enemy mortar round severed 2d Lt. Bobo's right leg below the knee, he refused to be evacuated and insisted upon being placed in a firing position to cover the movement of the command group to a better location. With a web belt around his leg serving as a tourniquet and with his leg jammed into the dirt to curtain the bleeding, he remained in this position and delivered devastating fire into the ranks of the enemy attempting to overrun the marines. 2d Lt. Bobo was mortally wounded while firing his weapon into the mainpoint of the enemy attack but his valiant spirit inspired his men to heroic efforts, and his tenacious stand enabled the command group to gain a protective position where it repulsed the enemy onslaught. 2d Lt. Bobo's superb leadership, dauntless courage, and bold initiative reflected great credit upon himself and upheld the highest traditions of the Marine Corps and the U.S. Naval Service. He gallantly gave his life for his country.

BONDSTEEL, JAMES LEROY

Rank and organization: Staff Sergeant, U.S. Army, Company A, 2d Battalion, 2d Infantry, 1st Infantry Division. *Place and date:* An Loc Province, Republic of Vietnam, 24 May 1969. *Entered service at:* Detroit, Mich. *Born:* 18 July 1947, Jackson, Mich. *Citation:* For conspicuous gallantry and intrepidity in action at the risk of his life above and beyond the call of duty. S/Sgt. Bondsteel distinguished himself while serving as a platoon sergeant with Company A, near the village of Lang Sau. Company A was directed to assist a friendly unit which was endangered by intense fire from a North Vietnamese Battalion located in a heavily fortified base camp. S/Sgt. Bondsteel quickly organized the men of his platoon into effective combat teams and spearheaded the attack by destroying 4 enemy occupied bunkers. He then raced some 200 meters under heavy enemy fire to reach an adjoining platoon which had begun to falter. After rallying this unit and assisting their wounded, S/Sgt. Bondsteel returned to his own sector with critically needed munitions. Without pausing he moved to the forefront and destroyed 4 enemy occupied bunkers and a machinegun which had threatened his advancing platoon. Although painfully wounded by an enemy grenade, S/Sgt. Bondsteel refused medical attention and continued his assault by neutralizing 2 more enemy bunkers nearby. While searching one of these emplacements S/Sgt. Bondsteel narrowly escaped death when an enemy soldier detonated a grenade at close range. Shortly thereafter, he ran to the aid of a severely wounded officer and struck down an enemy soldier who was threatening the officer's life. S/Sgt. Bondsteel then continued to rally his men and led them through the entrenched enemy until his company was relieved. His exemplary leadership and great personal courage throughout the 4-hour battle ensured the success of his own and nearby units, and resulted in the saving of numerous lives of his fellow soldiers. By individual acts of bravery he destroyed 10 enemy bunkers and accounted for a large toll of the enemy, including 2 key enemy commanders. His extraordinary heroism at the risk of his life was in the highest traditions of the military service and reflect great credit on him, his unit, and the U.S. Army.

*BOWEN, HAMMETT L., Jr.

Rank and organization: Staff Sergeant, U.S. Army, Company C, 2d Battalion, 14th Infantry, 25th Infantry Division. *Place and date:* Binh Duong Province, Republic of Vietnam, 27 June 1969. *Entered service at:* Jacksonville, Fla. *Born:* 30 November 1947, Lagrange, Ga. *Citation:* S/Sgt. Bowen distinguished himself while serving as a platoon sergeant during combat operations in Binh Duong Province, Republic of Vietnam. S/Sgt. Bowen's platoon was advancing on a reconnaissance mission into enemy controlled terrain when it came under the withering crossfire of small arms and grenades from an enemy ambush force. S/Sgt. Bowen placed heavy suppressive fire on the enemy positions and ordered his men to fall back. As the platoon was moving back, an enemy grenade was thrown amid S/Sgt. Bowen and 3 of his men. Sensing the danger to his comrades, S/Sgt. Bowen shouted a warning to his men and hurled himself on the grenade, absorbing the explosion with his body while saving the lives of his fellow soldiers. S/Sgt. Bowen's extraordinary courage and concern for his men at the cost of his life served as an inspiration to his comrades and are in the highest traditions of the military service and the U.S. Army.

BRADY, PATRICK HENRY

Rank and organization: Major, U.S. Army, Medical Service Corps, 54th Medical Detachment, 67th Medical Group, 44th Medical Brigade. *Place and date:* Near Chu Lai, Republic of Vietnam, 6 January 1968. *Entered service at:* Seattle, Wash. *Born:* 1 October 1936, Philip, S. Dak. *Citation:* For conspicuous gallantry and intrepidity in action at the risk of his life above and beyond the call of duty, Maj. Brady distinguished himself while serving in the Republic of Vietnam commanding a UH-1H ambulance helicopter, volunteered to rescue wounded men from a site in enemy held territory which was reported to be heavily defended and to be blanketed by fog. To reach the site he descended through heavy fog and smoke and hovered slowly along a valley trail, turning his ship sideward to blow away the fog with the backwash from his rotor blades. Despite the unchallenged, close-range enemy fire, he found the dangerously small site, where he successfully landed and evacuated 2 badly wounded South Vietnamese soldiers. He was then called to another area completely covered by dense fog where American casualties lay only 50 meters from the enemy. Two aircraft had previously been shot down and others had made unsuccessful attempts to reach this site earlier in the day. With unmatched skill and extraordinary courage, Maj. Brady made 4 flights to this embattled landing zone and successfully rescued all the wounded. On his third mission of the day Maj. Brady once again landed at a site surrounded by the enemy. The friendly ground force, pinned down by enemy fire, had been unable to reach and secure the landing zone. Although his aircraft had been badly damaged and his controls partially shot away during his initial entry into this area, he returned minutes later and rescued the remaining injured. Shortly thereafter, obtaining a replacement aircraft, Maj. Brady was requested to land in an enemy minefield where a platoon of American soldiers was trapped. A mine detonated near his helicopter, wounding 2 crewmembers and damaging his ship. In spite of this, he managed to fly 6 severely injured patients to medical aid. Throughout that day Maj. Brady utilized 3 helicopters to evacuate a total of 51 seriously wounded men, many of whom would have perished without prompt medical treatment. Maj. Brady's bravery was in the highest traditions of the military service and reflects great credit upon himself and the U.S. Army.

*BRUCE, DANIEL D.

Rank and organization: Private First Class, U.S. Marine Corps, Headquarters and Service Company, 3d Battalion, 5th Marines, 1st Marine Division. *Place and date:* Fire Support Base Tomahawk, Quang Nam Province, Republic of Vietnam, 1 March 1969. *Entered service at:* Chicago, Ill. *Born:* 18 May 1950, Michigan City, Ind. *Citation:* For conspicuous gallantry and intrepidity at the risk of his life above and beyond the call of duty while serving as a mortar man with Headquarters and Service Company 3d Battalion, against the enemy. Early in the morning Pfc. Bruce was on watch in his night defensive position at fire support base tomahawk when he heard movements ahead of him. An enemy explosive charge was thrown toward his position and he reacted instantly, catching the device and shouting to alert his companions. Realizing the danger to the adjacent position with its 2 occupants, Pfc. Bruce held the device to his body and attempted to carry it from the vicinity of the entrenched marines. As he moved away, the charge detonated and he absorbed the full force of the explosion. Pfc. Bruce's indomitable courage, inspiring valor and selfless devotion to duty saved the lives of 3 of his fellow marines and upheld the highest traditions of the Marine Corps and the U.S. Naval Service. He gallantly gave his life for his country.

*BRYANT, WILLIAM MAUD

Rank and organization: Sergeant First Class, U.S. Army, Company A, 5th Special Forces Group, 1st Special Forces. *Place and date:* Long Khanh Province, Republic of Vietnam, 24 March 1969. *Entered service at:* Detroit, Mich. *Born:* 16 February 1933, Cochran, Ga. *Citation:* For conspicuous gallantry and intrepidity in action at the risk of his life above and beyond the call of duty. Sfc. Bryant, assigned to Company A, distinguished himself while serving as commanding officer of Civilian Irregular Defense Group Company 321, 2d Battalion, 3d Mobile Strike Force Command, during combat operations. The battalion came under heavy fire and became surrounded by the elements of 3 enemy regiments. Sfc. Bryant displayed extraordinary heroism throughout the succeeding 34 hours of incessant attack as he moved throughout the company position heedless of the intense hostile fire while establishing and improving the defensive perimeter, directing fire during critical phases of the battle, distributing ammunition, assisting the wounded, and providing the leadership and inspirational example of courage to his men. When a helicopter drop of ammunition was made to resupply the beleaguered force, Sfc. Bryant with complete disregard for his safety ran through the heavy enemy fire to retrieve the scattered ammunition boxes and distributed needed ammunition to his men. During a lull in the intense fighting, Sfc. Bryant led a patrol outside the perimeter to obtain information of the enemy. The patrol came under intense automatic weapons fire and was pinned down. Sfc. Bryant singlehandedly repulsed 1 enemy attack on his small force and by his heroic action inspired his men to fight off other assaults. Seeing a wounded enemy soldier some distance from the patrol location, Sfc. Bryant crawled forward alone under heavy fire to retrieve the soldier for intelligence purposes. Finding that the enemy soldier had expired, Sfc. Bryant crawled back to his patrol and led his men back to the company position where he again took command of the defense. As the siege continued, Sfc. Bryant organized and led a patrol in a daring attempt to break through the enemy encirclement. The patrol had advanced some 200 meters by heavy fighting when it was pinned down by the intense automatic weapons fire from heavily fortified bunkers and Sfc. Bryant was severely wounded. Despite his wounds he rallied his men, called for helicopter gunship support, and directed heavy suppressive fire upon the enemy positions. Following the last gunship attack, Sfc. Bryant fearlessly charged an enemy automatic weapons position, overrunning it, and singlehandedly destroying its 3 defenders. Inspired by his heroic example, his men renewed their attack on the entrenched enemy. While regrouping his small force for the final assault against the enemy, Sfc. Bryant fell mortally wounded by an enemy rocket. Sfc. Bryant's selfless concern for his comrades, at the cost of his life above and beyond the call of duty are in keeping with the highest traditions of the military service and reflect great credit upon himself, his unit, and the U.S. Army.

BUCHA, PAUL WILLIAM

Rank and organization: Captain, U.S. Army, Company D, 3d Battalion. 187th Infantry, 3d Brigade, 101st Airborne Division. Place and date: Near Phuoc Vinh, Binh Duong Province, Republic of Vietnam, 16-19 March 1968. Entered service at: U.S. Military Academy, West Point, N.Y. Born: 1 August 1943, Washington, D.C. Citation: For conspicuous gallantry and intrepidity in action at the risk of his life above and beyond the call of duty. Capt. Bucha distinguished himself while serving as commanding officer, Company D, on a reconnaissance-in-force mission against enemy forces near Phuoc Vinh, The company was inserted by helicopter into the suspected enemy stronghold to locate and destroy the enemy. During this period Capt. Bucha aggressively and courageously led his men in the destruction of enemy fortifications and base areas and eliminated scattered resistance impeding the advance of the company. On 18 March while advancing to contact, the lead elements of the company became engaged by the heavy automatic weapon, heavy machinegun, rocket propelled grenade, claymore mine and small-arms fire of an estimated battalion-size force. Capt. Bucha, with complete disregard for his safety, moved to the threatened area to direct the defense and ordered reinforcements to the aid of the lead element. Seeing that his men were pinned down by heavy machinegun fire from a concealed bunker located some 40 meters to the front of the positions, Capt. Bucha crawled through the hail of fire to singlehandedly destroy the bunker with grenades. During this heroic action Capt. Bucha received a painful shrapnel wound. Returning to the perimeter, he observed that his unit could not hold its positions and repel the human wave assaults launched by the determined enemy. Capt. Bucha ordered the withdrawal of the unit elements and covered the withdrawal to positions of a company perimeter from which he could direct fire upon the charging enemy. When 1 friendly element retrieving casualties was ambushed and cut off from the perimeter, Capt. Bucha ordered them to feign death and he directed artillery fire around them. During the night Capt. Bucha moved throughout the position, distributing ammunition, providing encouragement and insuring the integrity of the defense. He directed artillery, helicopter gunship and Air Force gunship fire on the enemy strong points and attacking forces, marking the positions with smoke grenades. Using flashlights in complete view of enemy snipers, he directed the medical evacuation of 3 air-ambulance loads of seriously wounded personnel and the helicopter supply of his company. At daybreak Capt. Bucha led a rescue party to recover the dead and wounded members of the ambushed element. During the period of intensive combat, Capt. Bucha, by his extraordinary heroism, inspirational example, outstanding leadership and professional competence, led his company in the decimation of a superior enemy force which left 156 dead on the battlefield. His bravery and gallantry at the risk of his life are in the highest traditions of the military service, Capt. Bucha has reflected great credit on himself, his unit, and the U.S. Army.

*BUKER, BRIAN L.

Rank and organization: Sergeant, U.S. Army, Detachment B–55, 5th Special Forces Group, 1st Special Forces. *Place and date:* Chau Doc Province, Republic of Vietnam, 5 April 1970. *Entered service at:* Bangor, Maine. *Born:* 3 November 1949, Benton, Maine. *Citation:* For conspicuous gallantry and intrepidity in action at the risk of life above and beyond the call of duty. Sgt. Buker, Detachment B–55, distinguished himself while serving as a platoon adviser of a Vietnamese mobile strike force company during an offensive mission. Sgt. Buker personally led the platoon, cleared a strategically located well-guarded pass, and established the first foothold at the top of what had been an impenetrable mountain fortress. When the platoon came under the intense fire from a determined enemy located in 2 heavily fortified bunkers, and realizing that withdrawal would result in heavy casualties, Sgt. Buker unhesitatingly, and with complete disregard for his personal safety, charged through the hail of enemy fire and destroyed the first bunker with handgrenades. While reorganizing his men for the attack on the second bunker, Sgt. Buker was seriously wounded. Despite his wounds and the deadly enemy fire, he crawled forward and destroyed the second bunker. Sgt. Buker refused medical attention and was reorganizing his men to continue the attack when he was mortally wounded. As a direct result of his heroic actions, many casualties were averted, and the assault of the enemy position was successful. Sgt. Buker's extraordinary heroism at the cost of his life are in the highest traditions of the military service and reflect great credit on him, his unit, and the U.S. Army.

*BURKE, ROBERT C.

Rank and organization: Private First Class, U.S. Marine Corps, Company I, 3d Battalion, 27th Marines, 1st Marine Division (Rein), FMF. *Place and date:* Southern Quang Nam Province Republic of Vietnam, 17 May 1968. *Entered service at:* Chicago, Ill. *Born:* 7 November 1949, Monticello, Ill. *Citation:* For conspicuous gallantry and intrepidity at the risk of his life above and beyond the call of duty for service as a machine gunner with Company I. While on Operation ALLEN BROOK, Company I was approaching a dry river bed with a heavily wooded treeline that borders the hamlet of Le Nam (1), when they suddenly came under intense mortar, rocket propelled grenades, automatic weapons and small-arms fire from a large, well concealed enemy force which halted the company's advance and wounded several marines. Realizing that key points of resistance had to be eliminated to allow the units to advance and casualties to be evacuated, Pfc. Burke, without hesitation, seized his machinegun and launched a series of 1-man assaults against the fortified emplacements. As he aggressively maneuvered to the edge of the steep river bank, he delivered accurate suppressive fire upon several enemy bunkers, which enabled his comrades to advance and move the wounded marines to positions of relative safety. As he continued his combative actions, he located an opposing automatic weapons emplacement and poured intense fire into the position, killing 3 North Vietnamese soldiers as they attempted to flee. Pfc. Burke then fearlessly moved from one position to another, quelling the hostile fire until his weapon malfunctioned. Obtaining a casualty's rifle and handgrenades, he advanced further into the midst of the enemy fire in an assault against another pocket of resistance, killing 2 more of the enemy. Observing that a fellow marine had cleared his malfunctioning machinegun he grasped his weapon and moved into a dangerously exposed area and saturated the hostile treeline until he fell mortally wounded. Pfc. Burke's gallant actions upheld the highest traditions of the Marine Corps and the U.S. Naval Service. He gallantly gave his life for his country.

*CAPODANNO, VINCENT R.

Rank and organization: Lieutenant, U.S. Navy, Chaplain Corps, 3d Battalion, 5th Marines, 1st Marine Division (Rein), FMF. *Place and date:* Quang Tin Province, Republic of Vietnam, 4 September 1967. *Entered service at:* Staten Island, N.Y. *Born:* 13 February 1929, Staten Island, N.Y. *Citation:* For conspicuous gallantry and intrepidity at the risk of his life above and beyond the call of duty as Chaplain of the 3d

Battalion, in connection with operations against enemy forces. In response to reports that the 2d Platoon of M Company was in danger of being overrun by a massed enemy assaulting force, Lt. Capodanno left the relative safety of the company command post and ran through an open area raked with fire, directly to the beleaguered platoon. Disregarding the intense enemy small-arms, automatic-weapons, and mortar fire, he moved about the battlefield administering last rites to the dying and giving medical aid to the wounded. When an exploding mortar round inflicted painful multiple wounds to his arms and legs, and severed a portion of his right hand, he steadfastly refused all medical aid. Instead, he directed the corpsmen to help their wounded comrades and, with calm vigor, continued to move about the battlefield as he provided encouragement by voice and example to the valiant marines. Upon encountering a wounded corpsman in the direct line of fire of an enemy machine gunner positioned approximately 15 yards away, Lt. Capodanno rushed a daring attempt to aid and assist the mortally wounded corpsman. At that instant, only inches from his goal, he was struck down by a burst of machinegun fire. By his heroic conduct on the battlefield, and his inspiring example, Lt. Capodanno upheld the finest traditions of the U.S. Naval Service. He gallantly gave his life in the cause of freedom.

*CARON, WAYNE MAURICE

Rank and organization: Hospital Corpsman Third Class, U.S. Navy, Headquarters and Service Company, 3d Battalion, 7th Marines, 1st Marine Division (Rein), FMF. *Place and date:* Quang Nam Province, Republic of Vietnam, 28 July 1968. *Entered service at:* Boston, Mass. *Born:* 2 November 1946, Middleboro, Mass. *Citation:* For conspicuous gallantry and intrepidity at the risk of his life above and beyond the call of duty while serving as platoon corpsman with Company K, during combat operations against enemy forces. While on a sweep through an open rice field HC3c. Caron's unit started receiving enemy small-arms fire. Upon seeing 2 marine casualties fall, he immediately ran forward to render first aid, but found that they were dead. At this time, the platoon was taken under intense small-arms and automatic-weapons fire, sustaining additional casualties. As he moved to the aid of his wounded comrades, HC3c. Caron was hit in the arm by enemy fire. Although knocked to the ground, he regained his feet and continued to the injured marines. He rendered medical assistance to the first marine he reached, who was grievously wounded, and undoubtedly was instrumental in saving the man's life. HC3c. Caron then ran toward the second wounded marine, but was again hit by enemy fire, this time in the leg. Nonetheless, he crawled the remaining distance and provided medical aid for this severely wounded man. HC3c. Caron started to make his way to yet another injured comrade, when he was again struck by enemy small-arms fire. Courageously and with unbelievable determination, HC3c. Caron continued his attempt to reach the third marine until he was killed by an enemy rocket round. His inspiring valor, steadfast determination and selfless dedication in the face of extreme danger, sustain and enhance the finest traditions of the U.S. Naval Service.

*CARTER, BRUCE W.

Rank and organization: Private First Class, U.S. Marine Corps, Company H, 2d Battalion, 3d Marines, 3d Marine Division (Rein), FMF. *Place and date:* Quang Tri Province, Republic of Vietnam, 7 August 1969. *Entered service at:* Jacksonville, Fla. *Born:* 7 May 1950, Schenectady, N.Y. *Citation:* For conspicuous gallantry and intrepidity at the risk of his life above and beyond the call of duty while serving as grenadier with Company H in connection with combat operations against the enemy. Pfc. Carter's unit was maneuvering against the enemy during Operation Idaho Canyon and came under a heavy volume of fire from a numerically superior hostile force. The lead element soon became separated from the main body of the squad by a brush fire. Pfc. Carter and his fellow marines were pinned down by vicious crossfire when, with complete disregard for his safety, he stood in full view of the North Vietnamese Army soldiers to deliver a devastating volume of fire at their positions. The accuracy and aggressiveness of his attack caused several enemy casualties and forced the remainder of the soldiers to retreat from the immediate area. Shouting directions to the marines around him, Pfc. Carter then commenced leading them from the path of the rapidly approaching brush fire when he observed a hostile grenade land between him and his companions. Fully aware of the probable consequences of his action but determined to protect the men following him, he unhesitatingly threw himself over the grenade, absorbing the full effects of its detonation with his body. Pfc. Carter's indomitable courage, inspiring initiative, and selfless devotion to duty upheld the highest traditions of the Marine Corps and the U.S. Naval Service. He gallantly gave his life in the service of his country.

CAVAIANI, JON R.

Rank and organization: Staff Sergeant, U.S. Army, Vietnam Training Advisory Group, Republic of Vietnam. *Place and date:* Republic of Vietnam, 4 and 5 June 1971. *Entered service at:* Fresno, Calif. *Born:* 2 August 1943, Royston, England. *Citation:* S/Sgt. Cavaiani distinguished himself by conspicuous gallantry and intrepidity at the risk of life above and beyond the call of duty in action in the Republic of Vietnam on 4 and 5 June 1971 while serving as a platoon leader to a security platoon providing security for an isolated radio relay site located within enemy-held territory. On the morning of 4 June 1971, the entire camp came under an intense barrage of enemy small arms, automatic weapons, rocket-propelled grenade and mortar fire from a superior size enemy force. S/Sgt. Cavaiani acted with complete disregard for his personal safety as he repeatedly exposed himself to heavy enemy fire in order to move about the camp's perimeter directing the platoon's fire and rallying the platoon in a desperate fight for survival. S/Sgt. Cavaiani also returned heavy suppressive fire upon the assaulting enemy force during this period with a variety of weapons. When the entire platoon was to be evacuated, S/Sgt. Cavaiani unhesitatingly volunteered to remain on the ground and direct the helicopters into the landing zone. S/Sgt. Cavaiani was able to direct the first 3 helicopters in evacuating a major portion of the platoon. Due to intense increase in enemy fire, S/Sgt. Cavaiani was forced to remain at the camp overnight where he calmly directed the remaining platoon members in strengthening their defenses. On the morning of 5 June, a heavy ground fog restricted visibility. The superior size enemy force launched a major ground attack in an attempt to completely annihilate the remaining small force. The enemy force advanced in 2 ranks, first firing a heavy volume of small arms automatic weapons and rocket-propelled grenade fire while the second rank continuously threw a steady barrage of handgrenades at the beleaguered force. S/Sgt. Cavaiani returned a heavy barrage of small arms and handgrenade fire on the assaulting enemy force but was unable to slow them down. He ordered the remaining platoon members to attempt to escape while he provided them with cover fire. With 1 last courageous exertion, S/Sgt. Cavaiani recovered a machinegun, stood up, completely exposing himself to the heavy enemy fire directed at him, and began firing the machinegun in a sweeping motion along the 2 ranks of advancing enemy soldiers. Through S/Sgt. Cavaiani's valiant efforts with complete disregard for his safety, the majority of the remaining platoon members were able to escape. While inflicting severe losses on the advancing enemy force, S/Sgt. Cavaiani was wounded numerous times. S/Sgt. Cavaiani's conspicuous gallantry, extraordinary heroism and intrepidity at the risk of his life, above and beyond the call of duty, were in keeping with the highest traditions of the military service and reflect great credit upon himself and the U.S. Army.

CLAUSEN, RAYMOND M.

Rank and organization: Private First Class, U.S. Marine Corps, Marine Medium Helicopter Squadron 263, Marine Aircraft Group 16, 1st Marine Aircraft Wing. *Place and date:* Republic of Vietnam, 31 January 1970. *Entered service at:* New Orleans, La. *Born:* 14 October 1947, New Orleans, La. *Citation:* For conspicuous gallantry and intrepidity at the risk of his life above and beyond the call of duty while serving with Marine Medium Helicopter Squadron 263 during operations against enemy forces. Participating in a helicopter rescue mission to extract elements of a platoon which had inadvertently entered a minefield while attacking enemy positions, Pfc. Clausen skillfully guided the helicopter pilot to a landing in an area cleared by 1 of several mine explosions. With 11 marines wounded, 1 dead, and the remaining 8 marines holding their positions for fear of detonating other mines, Pfc. Clausen quickly leaped from the helicopter and, in the face of enemy fire, moved across the extremely hazardous mine-laden area to assist in carrying casualties to the waiting helicopter and in placing them aboard. Despite the ever-present threat of further mine explosions, he continued his valiant efforts, leaving the comparatively safe area of the helicopter on 6 separate occasions to carry out his rescue efforts. On 1 occasion while he was carrying 1 of the wounded, another mine detonated, killing a corpsman and wounding 3 other men. Only when he was certain that all marines were safely aboard did he signal the pilot to lift the helicopter. By the courageous, determined and inspiring efforts in the face of the utmost danger, Pfc. Clausen upheld the highest traditions of the Marine Corps and of the U.S. Naval Service.

*COKER, RONALD L.

Rank and organization: Private First Class, U.S. Marine Corps, Company M, 3d Battalion, 3d Marine Division (Rein), FMF. *Place and date:* Quang Tri Province, Republic of Vietnam, 24 March 1969. *Entered service at:* Denver, Colo. *Born:* 9 August 1947, Alliance, Colo. *Citation:* For conspicuous gallantry and intrepidity at the risk of his life above and beyond the call of duty while serving as a rifleman with Company M in action against enemy forces. While serving as point man for the 2d Platoon, Pfc. Coker was leading his patrol when he encountered 5 enemy soldiers on a narrow jungle trail. Pfc. Coker's squad aggressively pursued them to a cave. As the squad neared the cave, it came under intense hostile fire, seriously wounding 1 marine and forcing the others to take cover. Observing the wounded man lying exposed to continuous enemy fire, Pfc. Coker disregarded his safety and moved across the fire-swept terrain toward his companion. Although wounded by enemy small-arms fire, he continued to crawl across the hazardous area and skillfully threw a handgrenade into the enemy positions, suppressing the hostile fire sufficiently to enable him to reach the wounded man. As he began to drag his injured comrade toward safety, a grenade landed on the wounded marine. Unhesitatingly, Pfc. Coker grasped it with both hands and turned away from his wounded companion, but before he could dispose of the grenade it exploded. Severely wounded, but undaunted, he refused to abandon his comrade. As he moved toward friendly lines, 2 more enemy grenades exploded near him, inflicting still further injuries. Concerned only for the safety of his comrade, Pfc. Coker, with supreme effort continued to crawl and pull the wounded marine with him. His heroic deeds inspired his fellow marines to such aggressive action that the enemy fire was suppressed sufficiently to enable others to reach him and carry him to a relatively safe area where he succumbed to his extensive wounds. Pfc. Coker's indomitable courage, inspiring initiative and selfless devotion to duty upheld the highest traditions of the Marine Corps and of the U.S. Naval Service. He gallantly gave his life for his country.

*CONNOR, PETER S.

Rank and organization: Staff Sergeant, U.S. Marine Corps, Company F, 2d Battalion, 3d Marines, 1st Marine Division (Rein), FMF. *Place and date:* Quang Ngai Province, Republic of Vietnam, 25 February 1966. *Entered service at:* South Orange, N.J. *Born:* 4 September 1932, Orange, N.J. *Citation:* For conspicuous gallantry and intrepidity in action against enemy Viet Cong forces at the risk of his life above and beyond the call of duty. Leading his platoon on a search and destroy operation in an area made particularly hazardous by extensive cave and tunnel complexes, S/Sgt. Connor maneuvered his unit aggressively forward under intermittent enemy small-arms fire. Exhibiting particular alertness and keen observation, he spotted an enemy spider hole emplacement approximately 15 meters to his front. He pulled the pin from a fragmentation grenade intending to charge the hole boldly and drop the missile into its depths. Upon pulling the pin he realized that the firing mechanism was faulty, and that even as he held the safety device firmly in place, the fuse charge was already activated. With only precious seconds to decide, he further realized that he could not cover the distance to the small opening of the spider hole in sufficient time, and that to hurl the deadly bomb in any direction would result in death or injury to some of his comrades tactically deployed near him. Manifesting extraordinary gallantry and with utter disregard for his personal safety, he chose to hold the grenade against his body in order to absorb the terrific explosion and spare his comrades. His act of extreme valor and selflessness in the face of virtually certain death, although leaving him mortally wounded, spared many of his fellow marines from death or injury. His gallant action in giving his life in the cause of freedom reflects the highest credit upon the Marine Corps and the Armed Forces of the United States.

*COOK, DONALD GILBERT

Rank and organization: Colonel, United States Marine Corps, Prisoner of War by the Viet Cong in the Republic of Vietnam. *Place and date:* Vietnam, 31 December, 1964 to 8 December, 1967. *Entered service at: Brooklyn, New York. Date and place of birth:* 9 August 1934, Brooklyn New York. For conspicuous gallantry and intrepidity at the risk of his life above and beyond the call of duty while interned as a Prisoner of War by the Viet Cong in the Republic of Vietnam during the period 31 December 1964 to 8 December 1967. Despite the fact that by so doing he would bring about harsher treatment for himself, Colonel (then Captain) Cook established himself as the senior prisoner, even though in actuality he was not. Repeatedly assuming more than his share of their health, Colonel Cook willingly and unselfishly put the interests of his comrades before that of his own well-being and, eventually, his life. Giving more needy men his medicine and drug allowance while constantly nursing them, he risked infection from contagious diseases while in a rapidly deteriorating state of health. This unselfish and exemplary conduct, coupled with his refusal to stray even the slightest from the Code of Conduct, earned him the deepest respect from not only his fellow prisoners, but his captors as well. Rather than negotiate for his own release or better treatment, he steadfastly frustrated attempts by the Viet Cong to break his indomitable spirit, and passed this same resolve on to the men whose well-being he so closely associated himself. Knowing his refusals would prevent his release prior to the end of the war, and also knowing his chances for prolonged survival would be small in the event of continued refusal, he chose nevertheless to adhere to a Code of Conduct far above that which could be expected. His personal valor and exceptional spirit of loyalty in the face of almost certain death reflected the highest credit upon Colonel Cook, the Marine Corps, and the United States Naval Service.

*CREEK, THOMAS E.

Rank and Organization: Lance Corporal, U.S. Marine Corps, Company I 3d Battalion, 9th Marines, 3d Marine Division (Rein), FMF. *Place and Date:* Near Cam Lo, Republic of Vietnam, 13 February, 1969. *Entered Service at: Amarillo, Texas. Born:* 7 April 1950, Joplin, Mo. *Citation:* For conspicuous gallantry and intrepidity at the risk of his life above and beyond the call of duty while serving as a rifleman with Company I in action against enemy forces. L/Cpl. Creek's squad was providing security for a convoy moving to resupply the Vandegrift Command Base when an enemy command detonated mine destroyed 1 of the vehicles and halted the convoy near the Cam Lo Resettlement Village. Almost immediately, the marines came under a heavy volume of hostile mortar fire followed by intense small-arms fire from a well-concealed enemy force. As his squad deployed to engage the enemy, L/Cpl. Creek quickly moved to a fighting position and aggressively engaged in the fire fight. Observing a position from which he could more effectively deliver fire against the hostile forces, he completely disregarded his own safety as he fearlessly dashed across the fire-swept terrain and was seriously wounded by enemy fire. At the same time, an enemy grenade was thrown into the gully where he had fallen, landing between him and several companions. Fully realizing the inevitable results of his action, L/Cpl. Creek rolled on the grenade and absorbed the full force of the explosion with his body, thereby saving the lives of 5 of his fellow marines. As a result of his heroic action, his men were inspired to such aggressive action that the enemy was defeated and the convoy was able to continue its vital mission. L/Cpl. Creek's indomitable courage, inspired the Marine Corps and the U.S. Naval Service. He gallantly gave his life for his country.

*CRESCENZ, MICHAEL J.

Rank and organization: Corporal, U.S. Army, Company A, 4th Battalion, 31st Infantry, 196th Infantry Brigade, American Division. *Place and date:* Hiep Duc Valley area, Republic of Vietnam, 20 November 1968. Entered service at: Philadelphia, PA. *Born:* 14 January 1949, Philadelphia, PA. *Citation:* Cpl. Crescenz distinguished himself by conspicious gallantry and intrepidity in action while serving as a rifleman with Company A. In the morning his unit engaged a large, well-entrenched force of the North Vietnamese Army whose initial burst of fire pinned down the lead squad and killed the 2 point men, halting the advance of Company A. Immediately, Cpl. Crescenz left the relative safety of his own position, seized a nearby machinegun and, with complete disregard for his safety, charged 100 meters up a slope toward the enemy's bunkers which he effectively silenced, killing the 2 occupants of each. Undaunted by the withering machinegun fire around him, Cpl. Crescenz courageously moved forward toward a third bunker which he also succeeded in silencing, killing 2 more of the enemy and momentarily clearing the route of advance for his comrades. Suddenly, intense machinegun fire erupted from an unseen, camouflaged bunker. Realizing the danger to his fellow soldiers, Cpl. Crescenz disregarded the barrage of hostile fire directed at him and daringly advanced toward the position. Assaulting with his machinegun, Cpl. Crescenz was within 5 meters of the bunker when he was mortally wounded by the fire from the enemy machinegun. As a direct result of his heroic actions, his company was able to maneuver freely with minimal danger and to complete its mission, defeating the enemy. Cpl. Crescenz's bravery and extraordinary heroism at the cost of his life are in the highest traditions of the military service and reflect great credit on himself, his unit, and the U.S. Army.

*CUTINHA, NICHOLAS J.

Rank and organization: Specialist Fourth Class, U.S. Army, Company C, 4th Battalion, 9th Infantry Regiment, 25th Infantry Division. *Place and date:* Near Gia Dinh, Republic of Vietnam, 2 March 1968. *Entered service at:* Coral Gables, Fla. *Born:* 13 January 1945, Fernandina Beach, Fla. *Citation:* For conspicuous gallantry and intrepidity in action at the risk of his life above and beyond the call of duty. While serving as a machine gunner with Company C, Sp4c. Cutinha accompanied his unit on a combat mission near Gia Dinh. Suddenly his company came under small arms, automatic weapons, mortar and rocket propelled grenade fire, from a battalion size enemy unit. During the initial hostile attack, communication with the battalion was lost and the company commander and numerous members of the company became casualties. When Sp4c. Cutinha observed that his company was pinned down and disorganized, he moved to the front with complete disregard for his safety, firing his machinegun at the charging enemy. As he moved forward he drew fire on his own position and was seriously wounded in the leg. As the hostile fire intensified and half of the company was killed or wounded, Sp4c. Cutinha assumed command of all the survivors in his area and initiated a withdrawal while providing covering fire for the evacuation of the wounded. He killed several enemy soldiers but sustained another leg wound when his machinegun was destroyed by incoming rounds. Undaunted, he crawled through a hail of enemy fire to an operable machinegun in order to continue the defense of his injured comrades who were being administered medical treatment. Sp4c. Cutinha maintained this position, refused assistance, and provided defensive fire for his comrades until he fell mortally wounded. He was solely responsible for killing 15 enemy soldiers while saving the lives of at least 9 members of his own unit. Sp4c. Cutinha's gallantry and extraordinary heroism were in keeping with the highest traditions of the military service and reflect great credit upon himself, his unit, and the U.S. Army.

*DAHL, LARRY G.

Rank and organization: Specialist Fourth Class, U.S. Army, 359th Transportation Company, 27th Transportation Battalion, U.S. Army Support Command. *Place and date:* An Khe, Binh Dinh Province, Republic of Vietnam, 23 February 1971. *Entered service at:* Portland, Oreg. *Born:* 6 October 1949, Oregon City, Oreg. *Citation:* Sp4c. Dahl distinguished himself by conspicuous gallantry and intrepidity while serving as a machine gunner on a gun truck near An Khe, Binh Dinh Province. The gun truck in which Sp4c. Dahl was riding was sent with 2 other gun trucks to assist in the defense of a convoy that had been ambushed by an enemy force. The gun trucks entered the battle zone and engaged the attacking enemy troops with a heavy volume of machinegun fire, causing a large number of casualties. After a brief period of intense fighting the attack subsided. As the gun trucks were preparing to return to their normal escort duties, an enemy handgrenade was thrown into the truck in which Sp4c. Dahl was riding. Instantly realizing the great danger, Sp4c. Dahl called a warning to his companions and threw himself directly onto the grenade. Through his indomitable courage, complete disregard for his safety, and profound concern for his fellow soldiers, Sp4c. Dahl saved the lives of the other members of the truck crew while sacrificing his own. Sp4c. Dahl's conspicuous gallantry, extraordinary heroism, and intrepidity at the cost of his life, above and beyond the call of duty, are in keeping with the highest traditions of the military service and reflect great credit on himself, his unit and the U.S. Army.

*DAVIS, RODNEY MAXWELL

Rank and organization: Sergeant, U.S. Marine Corps, Company B, 1st Battalion, 5th Marines, 1st Marine Division. *Place and date:* Quang Nam Province, Republic of Vietnam, 6 September 1967. *Entered service at:* Macon, Ga. *Born:* 7 April 1942, Macon, Ga. *Citation:* For conspicuous gallantry and intrepidity at the risk of his life above and beyond the call of duty while serving as the right guide of the 2d Platoon, Company B, in action against enemy forces. Elements of the 2d Platoon were pinned down by a numerically superior force of attacking North Vietnamese Army Regulars. Remnants of the platoon were located in a trench line where Sgt. Davis was directing the fire of his men in an attempt to repel the enemy attack. Disregarding the enemy handgrenades and high volume of small arms and mortar fire, Sgt. Davis moved from man to man shouting words of encouragement to each of them while firing and throwing grenades at the onrushing enemy. When an enemy grenade landed in the trench in the midst of his men, Sgt. Davis, realizing the gravity of the situation, and in a final valiant act of complete self-sacrifice, instantly threw himself upon the grenade, absorbing with his body the full and terrific force of the explosion. Through his extraordinary initiative and inspiring valor in the face of almost certain death, Sgt. Davis saved his comrades from injury and possible loss of life, enabled his platoon to hold its vital position, and upheld the highest traditions of the Marine Corps and the U.S. Naval Service. He gallantly gave his life for his country.

DAVIS, SAMMY L.

Rank and organization: Sergeant, U.S. Army, Battery C, 2d Battalion, 4th Artillery, 9th Infantry Division. *Place and date:* West of Cai Lay, Republic of Vietnam, 18 November 1967. *Entered service at:* Indianapolis, Ind. *Born:* 1 November 1946, Dayton, Ohio. *Citation:* For conspicuous gallantry and intrepidity in action at the risk of his life and beyond the call of duty. Sgt. Davis (then Pfc.) distinguished himself during the early morning hours while serving as a cannoneer with Battery C, at a remote fire support base. At approximately 0200 hours, the fire support base was under heavy enemy mortar attack. Simultaneously, an estimated reinforced Viet Cong battalion launched a fierce ground assault upon the fire support base. The attacking enemy drove to within 25 meters of the friendly positions. Only a river separated the Viet Cong from the fire support base. Detecting a nearby enemy position, Sgt. Davis seized a machinegun and provided covering fire for his guncrew, as they attempted to bring direct artillery fire on the enemy. Despite his efforts, an enemy recoilless rifle round scored a direct hit upon the artillery piece. The resultant blast hurled the guncrew from their weapon and blew Sgt. Davis into a foxhole. He struggled to his feet and returned to the howitzer, which was burning furiously. Ignoring repeated warnings to seek cover, Sgt. Davis rammed a shell into the gun. Disregarding a withering hail of enemy fire directed against his position, he aimed and fired the howitzer which rolled backward, knocking Sgt. Davis violently to the ground. Undaunted, he returned to the weapon to fire again when an enemy mortar round exploded within 20 meters of his position, injuring him painfully. Nevertheless, Sgt. Davis loaded the artillery piece, aimed and fired. Again he was knocked down by the recoil. In complete disregard for his safety, Sgt. Davis loaded and fired 3 more shells into the enemy. Disregarding his extensive injuries and his inability to swim, Sgt. Davis picked up an air mattress and struck out across the deep river to rescue 3 wounded comrades on the far side. Upon reaching the 3 wounded men, he stood upright and fired into the dense vegetation to prevent the Viet Cong from advancing. While the most seriously wounded soldier was helped across the river, Sgt. Davis protected the 2 remaining casualties until he could pull them across the river to the fire support base. Though suffering from painful wounds, he refused medical attention, joining another howitzer crew which fired at the large Viet Cong force until it broke contact and fled. Sgt. Davis' extraordinary heroism, at the risk of his life, are in keeping with the highest traditions of the military service and reflect great credit upon himself and the U.S. Army.

DAY, GEORGE E.

Rank and organization: Colonel (then Major), U.S. Air Force, Forward Air Controller Pilot of an F–100 aircraft. *Place and date:* North Vietnam, 26 August 1967. *Entered service at:* Sioux City, Iowa. *Born:* 24 February 1925, Sioux City, Iowa. *Citation:* On 26 August 1967, Col. Day was forced to eject from his aircraft over North Vietnam when it was hit by ground fire. His right arm was broken in 3 places, and his left knee was badly sprained. He was immediately captured by hostile forces and taken to a prison camp where he was interrogated and severely tortured. After causing the guards to relax their vigilance, Col. Day escaped into the jungle and began the trek toward South Vietnam. Despite injuries inflicted by fragments of a bomb or rocket, he continued southward surviving only on a few berries and uncooked frogs. He successfully evaded enemy patrols and reached the Ben Hai River, where he encountered U.S. artillery barrages. With the aid of a bamboo log float, Col. Day swam across the river and entered the demilitarized zone. Due to delirium, he lost his sense of direction and wandered aimlessly for several days. After several unsuccessful attempts to signal U.S. aircraft, he was ambushed and recaptured by the Viet Cong, sustaining gunshot wounds to his left hand and thigh. He was returned to the prison from which he had escaped and later was moved to Hanoi after giving his captors false information to questions put before him. Physically, Col. Day was totally debilitated and unable to perform even the simplest task for himself. Despite his many injuries, he continued to offer maximum resistance. His personal bravery in the face of deadly enemy pressure was significant in saving the lives of fellow aviators who were still flying against the enemy. Col. Day's conspicuous gallantry and intrepidity at the risk of his life above and beyond the call of duty are in keeping with the highest traditions of the U.S. Air Force and reflect great credit upon himself and the U.S. Armed Forces.

*DE LA GARZA, EMILIO A., JR.

Rank and organization: Lance Corporal, U.S. Marine Corps, Company E, 2d Battalion, 1st Marines, 1st Marine Division. *Place and date:* Near Da Nang, Republic of Vietnam, 11 April 1970. *Entered service at:* Chicago, Ill. *Born:* 23 June 1949, East Chicago, Ind. *Citation:* For conspicuous gallantry and intrepidity at the risk of his life above and beyond the call of duty while serving as a machine gunner with Company E. Returning with his squad from a night ambush operation, L/Cpl. De La Garza joined his platoon commander and another marine in searching for 2 enemy soldiers who had been observed fleeing for cover toward a small pond. Moments later, he located 1 of the enemy soldiers hiding among the reeds and brush. As the 3 marines attempted to remove the resisting soldier from the pond, L/Cpl. De La Garza observed him pull the pin on a grenade. Shouting a warning, L/Cpl. De La Garza placed himself between the other 2 marines and the ensuing blast from the grenade, thereby saving the lives of his comrades at the sacrifice of his life. By his prompt and decisive action, and his great personal valor in the face of almost certain death, L/Cpl. De La Garza upheld and further enhanced the finest traditions of the Marine Corps and the U.S. Naval Service.

DETHLEFSEN, MERLYN HANS

Rank and organization: Major (then Capt.), U.S. Air Force. *Place and date:* In the air over North Vietnam, 10 March 1967. *Entered service at:* Royal, Iowa. *Born:* 29 June 1934, Greenville, Iowa. *Citation:* Maj. Dethlefsen was 1 of a flight of F–105 aircraft engaged in a fire suppression mission designed to destroy a key antiaircraft defensive complex containing surface-to-air missiles (SAM), an exceptionally heavy concentration of antiaircraft artillery, and other automatic weapons. The defensive network was situated to dominate the approach and provide protection to an important North Vietnam industrial center that was scheduled to be attacked by fighter bombers immediately after the strike by Maj. Dethlefsen's flight. In the initial attack on the defensive complex the lead aircraft was crippled, and Maj. Dethlefsen's aircraft was extensively damaged by the intense enemy fire. Realizing that the success of the impending fighter bomber attack on the center now depended on his ability to effectively suppress the defensive fire, Maj. Dethlefsen ignored the enemy's overwhelming firepower and the damage to his aircraft and pressed his attack. Despite a continuing hail of antiaircraft fire, deadly surface-to-air missiles, and counterattacks by MIG interceptors, Maj. Dethlefsen flew repeated close range strikes to silence the enemy defensive positions with bombs and cannon fire. His action in rendering ineffective the defensive SAM and antiaircraft artillery sites enabled the ensuing fighter bombers to strike successfully the important industrial target without loss or damage to their aircraft, thereby appreciably reducing the enemy's ability to provide essential war material. Maj. Dethlefsen's consummate skill and selfless dedication to this significant mission were in keeping with the highest traditions of the U.S. Air Force and reflect great credit upon himself and the Armed Forces of his country.

*DEVORE, EDWARD A., Jr.

Rank and organization: Specialist Fourth Class, U.S. Army, Company B, 4th Battalion, 39th Infantry, 9th Infantry Division. *Place and date:* Near Saigon, Republic of Vietnam, 17 March 1968. *Entered service at:* Harbor City, Calif. *Born:* 15 June 1947, Torrance, Calif. *Citation:* For conspicuous gallantry and intrepidity in action at the risk of his life above and beyond the call of duty. Sp4c. DeVore, distinguished himself by exceptionally valorous actions on the afternoon of 17 March 1968, while serving as a machine gunner with Company B, on a reconnaissance-in-force mission approximately 5 kilometers south of Saigon. Sp4c. DeVore's platoon, the company's lead element, abruptly came under intense fire from automatic weapons, claymore mines, rockets and grenades from well-concealed bunkers in a nipa palm swamp. One man was killed and 3 wounded about 20 meters from the bunker complex. Sp4c. DeVore raced through a hail of fire to provide a base of fire with his machinegun, enabling the point element to move the wounded back to friendly lines. After supporting artillery, gunships and airstrikes had been employed on the enemy positions, a squad was sent forward to retrieve their fallen comrades. Intense enemy frontal and enfilading automatic weapons fire pinned down this element in the kill zone. With complete disregard for his personal safety, Sp4c. DeVore assaulted the enemy positions. Hit in the shoulder and knocked down about 35 meters short of his objectives, Sp4c. DeVore, ignoring his pain and the warnings of his fellow soldiers, jumped to his feet and continued his assault under intense hostile fire. Although mortally wounded during this advance, he continued to place highly accurate suppressive fire upon the entrenched insurgents. By drawing the enemy fire upon himself, Sp4c. DeVore enabled the trapped squad to rejoin the platoon in safety. Sp4c. DeVore's extraordinary heroism and devotion to duty in close combat were in keeping with the highest traditions of the military service and reflect great credit upon himself, the 39th Infantry, and the U.S. Army.

*DIAS, RALPH E.

Rank and organization: Private First Class, U.S. Marine Corps, 3d Platoon, Company D, 1st Battalion, 7th Marines, 1st Marine Division (Rein) FMF. *Place and date:* Que Son Mountains, Republic of Vietnam, 12 November 1969. *Entered service at:* Pittsburgh, Pa. *Born:* 15 July 1950, Shelocta, Indiana County, Pa. *Citation:* As a member of a reaction force which was pinned down by enemy fire while assisting a platoon in the same circumstance, Pfc. Dias, observing that both units were sustaining casualties, initiated an aggressive assault against an enemy machinegun bunker which was the principal source of hostile fire. Severely wounded by enemy snipers while charging across the open area, he pulled himself to the shelter of a nearby rock. Braving enemy fire for a second time, Pfc. Dias was again wounded. Unable to walk, he crawled 15 meters to the protection of a rock located near his objective and, repeatedly exposing himself to intense hostile fire, unsuccessfully threw several handgrenades at the machinegun emplacement. Still determined to destroy the emplacement, Pfc. Dias again moved into the open and was wounded a third time by sniper fire. As he threw a last grenade which destroyed the enemy position, he was mortally wounded by another enemy round. Pfc. Dias' indomitable courage, dynamic initiative, and selfless devotion to duty upheld the highest traditions of the Marine Corps and the U.S. Naval Service. He gallantly gave his life in the service to his country.

*DICKEY, DOUGLAS E.

Rank and organization: Private First Class, U.S. Marine Corps, Company C, 1st Battalion, 4th Marines, 9th Marine Amphibious Brigade, 3d Marine Division (Rein). *Place and date:* Republic of Vietnam, 26 March 1967. *Entered service at:* Cincinnati, Ohio. *Born:* 24 December 1946, Greenville, Darke, Ohio. *Citation:* For conspicuous gallantry and intrepidity at the risk of his life above and beyond the call of duty. While participating in Operation Beacon Hill 1, the 2d Platoon was engaged in a fierce battle with the Viet Cong at close range in dense jungle foliage. Pfc. Dickey had come forward to replace a radio operator who had been wounded in this intense action and was being treated by a medical corpsman. Suddenly an enemy grenade landed in the midst of a group of marines, which included the wounded radio operator who was immobilized. Fully realizing the inevitable result of his actions, Pfc. Dickey, in a final valiant act, quickly and unhesitatingly threw himself upon the deadly grenade, absorbing with his body the full and complete force of the explosion. Pfc. Dickey's personal heroism, extraordinary valor and selfless courage saved a number of his comrades from certain injury and possible death at the cost of his life. His actions reflected great credit upon himself, the Marine Corps and the U.S. Naval Service. He gallantly gave his life for his country.

DIX, DREW DENNIS

Rank and organization: Staff Sergeant, U.S. Army, U.S. Senior Advisor Group, IV Corps, Military Assistance Command. *Place and date:* Chau Doc Province, Republic of Vietnam, 31 January and 1 February 1968. *Entered service at:* Denver, Colo. *Born:* 14 December 1944, West Point, N.Y. *Citation:* For conspicuous gallantry and intrepidity in action at the risk of his life above and beyond the call of duty. S/Sgt. Dix distinguished himself by exceptional heroism while serving as a unit adviser. Two heavily armed Viet Cong battalions attacked the Province capital city of Chau Phu resulting in the complete breakdown and fragmentation of the defenses of the city. S/Sgt. Dix, with a patrol of Vietnamese soldiers, was recalled to assist in the defense of Chau Phu. Learning that a nurse was trapped in a house near the center of the city, S/Sgt. Dix organized a relief force, successfully rescued the nurse, and returned her to the safety of the Tactical Operations Center. Being informed of other trapped civilians within the city, S/Sgt. Dix voluntarily led another force to rescue 8 civilian employees located in a building which was under heavy mortar and small-arms fire. S/Sgt. Dix then returned to the center of the city. Upon approaching a building, he was subjected to intense automatic rifle and machinegun fire from an unknown number of Viet Cong. He personally assaulted the building, killing 6 Viet Cong, and rescuing 2 Filipinos. The following day S/Sgt. Dix, still on his own volition, assembled a 20-man force and though under intense enemy fire cleared the Viet Cong out of the hotel, theater, and other adjacent buildings within the city. During this portion of the attack, Army Republic of Vietnam soldiers inspired by the heroism and success of S/Sgt. Dix, rallied and commenced firing upon the Viet Cong. S/Sgt. Dix captured 20 prisoners, including a high ranking Viet Cong official. He then attacked enemy troops who had entered the residence of the Deputy Province Chief and was successful in rescuing the official's wife and children. S/Sgt. Dix's personal heroic actions resulted in 14 confirmed Viet Cong killed in action and possibly 25 more, the capture of 20 prisoners, 15 weapons, and the rescue of the 14 United States and free world civilians. The heroism of S/Sgt. Dix was in the highest tradition and reflects great credit upon the U.S. Army.

*DOANE, STEPHEN HOLDEN

Rank and organization: First Lieutenant, U.S. Army, Company B, 1st Battalion, 5th Infantry, 25th Infantry Division. *Place and date:* Hau Nghia Province, Republic of Vietnam, 25 March 1969. *Entered service at:* Albany, N.Y. *Born:* 13 October 1947, Beverely, Mass. *Citation:* For conspicuous gallantry and intrepidity in action at the risk of his life above and beyond the call of duty. First Lt. Doane was serving as a platoon leader when his company, engaged in a tactical operation, abruptly contacted an enemy force concealed in protected bunkers and trenches. Three of the leading soldiers were pinned down by enemy crossfire. One was seriously wounded. After efforts of 1 platoon to rescue these men had failed, it became obvious that only a small group could successfully move close enough to destroy the enemy position and rescue or relieve the trapped soldiers. 1st Lt. Doane, although fully aware of the danger of such an action, crawled to the nearest enemy bunker and silenced it. He was wounded but continued to advance to a second enemy bunker. As he prepared to throw a grenade, he was again wounded. Undaunted, he deliberately pulled the pin on the grenade and lunged with it into the enemy bunker, destroying this final obstacle. 1st Lt. Doane's supreme act enabled his company to rescue the trapped men without further casualties. The extraordinary courage and selflessness displayed by this officer were an inspiration to his men and are in the highest traditions of the U.S. Army.

DOLBY, DAVID CHARLES

Rank and organization: Sergeant (then SP4c.), U.S. Army, Company B, 1st Battalion (Airborne), 8th Cavalry, 1st Cavalry Division (Airmobile). *Place and date:* Republic of Vietnam, 21 May 1966. *Entered service at:* Philadelphia, Pa. *Born:* 14 May 1946, Norristown, Pa. *G.O. No.:* 45, 20 October 1967. *Citation:* For conspicuous gallantry and intrepidity at the risk of life above and beyond the call of duty, when his platoon, while advancing tactically, suddenly came under intense fire from the enemy located on a ridge immediately to the front. Six members of the platoon were killed instantly and a number were wounded, including the platoon leader. Sgt. Dolby's every move brought fire from the enemy. However, aware that the platoon leader was critically wounded, and that the platoon was in a precarious situation, Sgt. Dolby moved the wounded men to safety and deployed the remainder of the platoon to engage the enemy. Subsequently, his dying platoon leader ordered Sgt. Dolby to withdraw the forward elements to rejoin the platoon. Despite the continuing intense enemy fire and with utter disregard for his own safety, Sgt. Dolby positioned abled-bodied men to cover the withdrawal of the forward elements, assisted the wounded to the new position, and he, alone, attacked enemy positions until his ammunition was expended. Replenishing his ammunition, he returned to the area of most intense action, singlehandedly killed 3 enemy machine gunners and neutralized the enemy fire, thus enabling friendly elements on the flank to advance on the enemy redoubt. He defied the enemy fire to personally carry a seriously wounded soldier to safety where he could be treated and, returning to the forward area, he crawled through withering fire to within 50 meters of the enemy bunkers and threw smokegrenades to mark them for air strikes. Although repeatedly under fire at close range from enemy snipers and automatic weapons, Sgt. Dolby directed artillery fire on the enemy and succeeded in silencing several enemy weapons. He remained in his exposed location until his comrades had displaced to more secure positions. His actions of unsurpassed valor during 4 hours of intense combat were a source of inspiration to his entire company, contributed significantly to the success of the overall assault on the enemy position, and were directly responsible for saving the lives of a number of his fellow soldiers. Sgt. Dolby's heroism was in the highest tradition of the U.S. Army.

DONLON, ROGER HUGH C.

Rank and organization: Captain, U.S. Army. *Place and date:* Near
Nam Dong, Republic of Vietnam, 6 July 1964. *Entered service at:* Fort
Chaffee, Ark. *Born:* 30 January 1934, Saugerties, N.Y. *G.O. No.:* 41,
17 December 1964. *Citation:* For conspicuous gallantry and intrepidity
at the risk of his life above and beyond the call of duty while defending a U.S. military installation against a fierce attack by hostile forces.
Capt. Donlon was serving as the commanding officer of the U.S. Army
Special Forces Detachment A-726 at Camp Nam Dong when a reinforced Viet Cong battalion suddenly launched a full-scale, predawn attack on the camp. During the violent battle that ensued, lasting 5
hours and resulting in heavy casualties on both sides, Capt. Donlon
directed the defense operations in the midst of an enemy barrage of
mortar shells, falling grenades, and extremely heavy gunfire. Upon the
initial onslaught, he swiftly marshaled his forces and ordered the
removal of the needed ammunition from a blazing building. He then
dashed through a hail of small arms and exploding handgrenades to
abort a breach of the main gate. En route to this position he detected
an enemy demolition team of 3 in the proximity of the main gate and
quickly annihilated them. Although exposed to the intense grenade attack, he then succeeded in reaching a 60mm mortar position despite
sustaining a severe stomach wound as he was within 5 yards of the
gunpit. When he discovered that most of the men in this gunpit were
also wounded, he completely disregarded his own injury, directed their
withdrawal to a location 30 meters away, and again risked his life by
remaining behind and covering the movement with the upmost effectiveness. Noticing that his team sergeant was unable to evacuate the
gunpit he crawled toward him and, while dragging the fallen soldier
out of the gunpit, an enemy mortar exploded and inflicted a wound in
Capt. Donlon's left shoulder. Although suffering from multiple wounds,
he carried the abandoned 60mm mortar weapon to a new location 30
meters away where he found 3 wounded defenders. After administering first aid and encouragement to these men, he left the weapon with
them, headed toward another position, and retrieved a 57mm recoilless
rifle. Then with great courage and coolness under fire, he returned to
the abandoned gunpit, evacuated ammunition for the 2 weapons, and
while crawling and dragging the urgently needed ammunition, received
a third wound on his leg by an enemy handgrenade. Despite his critical
physical condition, he again crawled 175 meters to an 81mm mortar
position and directed firing operations which protected the seriously
threatened east sector of the camp. He then moved to an eastern
60mm mortar position and upon determining that the vicious enemy
assault had weakened, crawled back to the gunpit with the 60mm mortar, set it up for defensive operations, and turned it over to 2 defenders with minor wounds. Without hesitation, he left this sheltered position, and moved from position to position around the beleaguered
perimeter while hurling handgrenades at the enemy and inspiring his
men to superhuman effort. As he bravely continued to move around
the perimeter, a mortar shell exploded, wounding him in the face and
body. As the long awaited daylight brought defeat to the enemy forces
and their retreat back to the jungle leaving behind 54 of their dead,

many weapons, and grenades, Capt. Donlon immediately reorganized his defenses and administered first aid to the wounded. His dynamic leadership, fortitude, and valiant efforts inspired not only the American personnel but the friendly Vietnamese defenders as well and resulted in the successful defense of the camp. Capt. Donlon's extraordinary heroism, at the risk of his life above and beyond the call of duty are in the highest traditions of the U.S. Army and reflect great credit upon himself and the Armed Forces of his country.

DUNAGAN, KERN W.

Rank and organization: Major, U.S. Army, Company A, 1st Battalion, 46 Infantry, Americal Division. *Place and date:* Quang Tin Province, Republic of Vietnam, 13 May 1969. *Entered service at:* Los Angeles, Calif. *Born:* 20 February 1934, Superior, Ariz. *Citation:* For conspicuous gallantry and intrepidity in action at the risk of his life above and beyond the call of duty. Maj. (then Capt.) Dunagan distinguished himself during the period May 13 and 14, 1969, while serving as commanding officer, Company A. On May 13, 1969, Maj. Dunagan was leading an attack to relieve pressure on the battalion's forward support base when his company came under intense fire from a well-entrenched enemy battalion. Despite continuous hostile fire from a numerically superior force, Maj. Dunagan repeatedly and fearlessly exposed himself in order to locate enemy positions, direct friendly supporting artillery, and position the men of his company. In the early evening, while directing an element of his unit into perimeter guard, he was seriously wounded during an enemy mortar attack, but he refused to leave the battlefield and continued to supervise the evacuation of dead and wounded and to lead his command in the difficult task of disengaging from an aggressive enemy. In spite of painful wounds and extreme fatigue, Maj. Dunagan risked heavy fire on 2 occasions to rescue critically wounded men. He was again seriously wounded. Undaunted, he continued to display outstanding courage, professional competence, and leadership and successfully extricated his command from its untenable position on the evening of May 14. Having maneuvered his command into contact with an adjacent friendly unit, he learned that a 6-man party from his company was under fire and had not reached the new perimeter. Maj. Dunagan unhesitatingly went back and searched for his men. Finding 1 soldier critically wounded, Maj. Dunagan, ignoring his wounds, lifted the man to his shoulders and carried him to the comparative safety of the friendly perimeter. Before permitting himself to be evacuated, he insured all of his wounded received emergency treatment and were removed from the area. Throughout the engagement, Maj. Dunagan's actions gave great inspiration to his men and were directly responsible for saving the lives of many of his fellow soldiers. Maj. Dunagan's extraordinary heroism above and beyond the call of duty, are in the highest traditions of the U.S. Army and reflect great credit on him, his unit, and the U.S. Army.

*DURHAM, HAROLD BASCOM, Jr.

Rank and organization: Second Lieutenant, U.S. Army, Battery C, 6th Battalion, 15th Artillery, 1st Infantry Division. *Place and date:*

Republic of Vietnam, 17 October 1967. *Entered service at:* Atlanta, Ga. *Born:* 12 October 1942, Rocky Mount, N.C. *Citation:* 2d Lt. Durham, Artillery, distinguished himself by conspicuous gallantry and intrepidity at the cost of his life above and beyond the call of duty while assigned to Battery C. 2d Lt. Durham was serving as a forward observer with Company D, 2d Battalion, 28th Infantry during a battalion reconnaissance-in-force mission. At approximately 1015 hours contact was made with an enemy force concealed in well-camouflaged positions and fortified bunkers. 2d Lt. Durham immediately moved into an exposed position to adjust the supporting artillery fire onto the insurgents. During a brief lull in the battle he administered emergency first aid to the wounded in spite of heavy enemy sniper fire directed toward him. Moments later, as enemy units assaulted friendly positions, he learned that Company A, bearing the brunt of the attack, had lost its forward observer. While he was moving to replace the wounded observer, the enemy detonated a claymore mine, severely wounding him in the head and impairing his vision. In spite of the intense pain, he continued to direct the supporting artillery fire and to employ his individual weapon in support of the hard pressed infantrymen. As the enemy pressed their attack, 2d Lt. Durham called for supporting fire to be placed almost directly on his position. Twice the insurgents were driven back, leaving many dead and wounded behind. 2d Lt. Durham was then taken to a secondary defensive position. Even in his extremely weakened condition, he continued to call artillery fire onto the enemy. He refused to seek cover and instead positioned himself in a small clearing which offered a better vantage point from which to adjust the fire. Suddenly, he was severely wounded a second time by enemy machinegun fire. As he lay on the ground near death, he saw two Viet Cong approaching, shooting the defenseless wounded men. With his last effort, 2d Lt. Durham shouted a warning to a nearby soldier who immediately killed the insurgents. 2d Lt. Durham died moments later, still grasping the radio handset. 2d Lt. Durham's gallant actions in close combat with an enemy force are in keeping with the highest traditions of the military service and reflect great credit upon himself, his unit, and the U.S. Army.

*ENGLISH, GLENN H., JR.

Rank and organization: Staff Sergeant, U.S. Army, Company E, 3d Battalion, 503 Infantry, 173d Airborne Brigade. *Place and date:* Phu My District, Republic of Vietnam, 7 September 1970. *Entered service at:* Philadelphia, Pa. *Born:* 23 April 1940, Altoona, Pa. *Citation:* S/Sgt. English was riding in the lead armored personnel carrier in a 4-vehicle column when an enemy mine exploded in front of his vehicle. As the vehicle swerved from the road, a concealed enemy force waiting in ambush opened fire with automatic weapons and anti-tank grenades, striking the vehicle several times and setting it on fire. S/Sgt. English escaped from the disabled vehicle and, without pausing to extinguish the flames on his clothing, rallied his stunned unit. He then led it in a vigorous assault, in the face of heavy enemy automatic weapons fire, on the entrenched enemy position. This prompt and courageous action routed the enemy and saved his unit from destruction. Following the assault, S/Sgt. English heard the cries of 3 men still trapped inside the vehicle. Paying no heed to warnings that the ammunition and fuel in the burning personnel carrier might explode at any moment, S/Sgt. English raced to the vehicle and climbed inside to rescue his wounded comrades. As he was lifting 1 of the men to safety, the vehicle exploded, mortally wounding him and the man he was attempting to save. By his extraordinary devotion to duty, indomitable courage, and utter disregard for his own safety, S/Sgt. English saved his unit from destruction and selflessly sacrificed his life in a brave attempt to save 3 comrades. S/Sgt. English's conspicuous gallantry and intrepidity in action at the cost of his life were an inspiration to his comrades and are in the highest traditions of the U.S. Army.

*ESTOCIN, MICHAEL J.

Rank and organization: Captain (then Lt. Cmdr.), U.S. Navy, Attack Squadron 192, USS *Ticonderoga* (CVA-14). *Place and date:* Haiphong, North Vietnam, 20 and 26 April 1967. *Entered service at:* Akron, Ohio, 20 July 1954. *Born:* 27 April 1931, Turtle Creek, Pa. *Citation:* For conspicuous gallantry and intrepidity at the risk of his life above and beyond the call of duty on 20 and 26 April 1967 as a pilot in Attack Squadron 192, embarked in USS *Ticonderoga* (CVA-14). Leading a 3-plane group of aircraft in support of a coordinated strike against two thermal powerplants in Haiphong, North Vietnam, on 20 April 1967, Capt. Estocin provided continuous warnings to the strike group leaders of the surface-to-air missile (SAM) threats, and personally neutralized 3 SAM sites. Although his aircraft was severely damaged by an exploding missile, he reentered the target area and relentlessly prosecuted a SHRIKE attack in the face of intense antiaircraft fire. With less than 5 minutes of fuel remaining he departed the target area and commenced inflight refueling which continued for over 100 miles. Three miles aft of *Ticonderoga*, and without enough fuel for a second approach, he disengaged from the tanker and executed a precise approach to a fiery arrested landing. On 26 April 1967, in support of a coordinated strike against the vital fuel facilities in Haiphong, he led an attack on a threatening SAM site, during which his aircraft was seriously damaged by an exploding SAM; nevertheless, he regained control of his burning aircraft and courageously launched his SHRIKE missiles before departing the area. By his inspiring courage and unswerving devotion to duty in the face of grave personal danger, Captain Estocin upheld the highest traditions of the U.S. Naval Service.

*EVANS, DONALD W., JR.

Rank and organization: Specialist Fourth Class, U.S. Army, Company A, 2d Battalion, 12 Infantry, 4th Infantry Division. *Place and date:* Tri Tam, Republic of Vietnam, 27 January 1967. *Entered service at:* Covina, Calif. *Born:* 23 July 1943, Covina, Calif. *Citation:* For conspicuous gallantry and intrepidity in action at the risk of his life above and beyond the call of duty. He left his position of relative safety with his platoon which had not yet been committed to the battle to answer the calls for medical aid from the wounded men of another platoon which was heavily engaged with the enemy force. Dashing across 100 meters of open area through a withering hail of enemy fire and exploding grenades, he administered lifesaving treatment to 1 individual and continued to expose himself to the deadly enemy fire as he moved to treat each of the other wounded men and to offer them encouragement. Realizing that the wounds of 1 man required immediate attention, Sp4c. Evans dragged the injured soldier back across the dangerous fire-swept area, to a secure position from which he could be further evacuated. Miraculously escaping the enemy fusillade, Sp4c. Evans returned to the forward location. As he continued the treatment of the wounded, he was struck by fragments from an enemy grenade. Despite his serious and painful injury he succeeded in evacuating another wounded comrade, rejoined his platoon as it was committed to battle and was soon treating other wounded soldiers. As he evacuated another wounded man across the fire covered field, he was severely wounded. Continuing to refuse medical attention and ignoring advice to remain behind, he managed with his waning strength to move yet another wounded comrade across the dangerous open area to safety. Disregarding his painful wounds and seriously weakened from profuse bleeding, he continued his lifesaving medical aid and was killed while treating another wounded comrade. Sp4c. Evan's extraordinary valor, dedication and indomitable spirit saved the lives of several of his fellow soldiers, served as an inspiration to the men of his company, were instrumental in the success of their mission, and reflect great credit upon himself and the Armed Forces of his country.

*EVANS, RODNEY J.

Rank and organization: Sergeant, U.S. Army, Company D, 1st Battalion, 12th Cavalry, 1st Cavalry Divison. *Place and date:* Tay Ninh Province, Republic of Vietnam, 18 July 1969. *Entered service at:* Montgomery, Ala. *Born:* 17 July 1948, Chelsea, Mass. *Citation:* For conspicuous gallantry and intrepidity in action at the risk of his life above and beyond the call of duty. Sgt. Evans distinguished himself by extraordinary heroism while serving as a squad leader in a reconnaissance sweep through heavy vegetation to reconnoiter a strong enemy position. As the force approached a well-defined trail, the platoon scout warned that the trail was boobytrapped. Sgt. Evans led his squad on a route parallel to the trail. The force had started to move forward when a nearby squad was hit by the blast of a concealed mine. Looking to his right Sgt. Evans saw a second enemy device. With complete disregard for his safety he shouted a warning to his men, dived to the ground and crawled toward the mine. Just as he reached it an enemy soldier detonated the explosive and Sgt. Evans absorbed the full impact with his body. His gallant and selfless action saved his comrades from probable death or injury and served as an inspiration to his entire unit. Sgt. Evans' gallantry in action at the cost of his life were in keeping with the highest traditions of the military service and reflect great credit upon himself, his unit, and the U.S. Army.

FERGUSON, FREDERICK EDGAR

Rank and organization: Chief Warrant Officer, U.S. Army, Company C, 227th Aviation Battalion, 1st Cavalry Division (Airmobile). *Place and date:* Hue, Republic of Vietnam, 31 January 1968. *Entered service at:* Phoenix, Ariz. *Born:* 18 August 1939, Pilot Point, Tex. *Citation:* For conspicuous gallantry and intrepidity in action at the risk of his life above and beyond the call of duty. CWO Ferguson, U.S. Army, distinguished himself while serving with Company C. CWO Ferguson, commander of a resupply helicopter monitoring an emergency call from wounded passengers and crewmen of a downed helicopter under heavy attack within the enemy controlled city of Hue, unhesitatingly volunteered to attempt evacuation. Despite warnings from all aircraft to stay clear of the area due to heavy antiaircraft fire, CWO Ferguson began a low-level flight at maximum airspeed along the Perfume River toward the tiny, isolated South Vietnamese Army compound in which the crash survivors had taken refuge. Coolly and skillfully maintaining his course in the face of intense, short range fire from enemy occupied buildings and boats, he displayed superior flying skill and tenacity of purpose by landing his aircraft in an extremely confined area in a blinding dust cloud under heavy mortar and small-arms fire. Although the helicopter was severely damaged by mortar fragments during the loading of the wounded, CWO Ferguson disregarded the damage and, taking off through the continuing hail of mortar fire, he flew his crippled aircraft on the return route through the rain of fire that he had experienced earlier and safely returned his wounded passengers to friendly control. CWO Ferguson's extraordinary determination saved the lives of 5 of his comrades. His actions are in the highest traditions of the military service and reflect great credit on himself and the U.S. Army.

*FERNANDEZ, DANIEL

Rank and organization: Specialist Fourth Class, U.S. Army, Company C, 1st Battalion, 5th Infantry (Mechanized) 25th Infantry Division. *Place and date:* Cu Chi, Hau Nghia Province, Republic of Vietnam, 18 February 1966. *Entered service at:* Albuquerque, N. Mex. *Born:* 30 June 1944, Albuquerque, N. Mex. *G.O. No.:* 21, 26 April 1967. *Citation:* For conspicuous gallantry and intrepidity at the risk of his life above and beyond the call of duty. Sp4c. Fernandez demonstrated indomitable courage when the patrol was ambushed by a Viet Cong rifle company and driven back by the intense enemy automatic weapons fire before it could evacuate an American soldier who had been wounded in the Viet Cong attack. Sp4c. Fernandez, a sergeant and 2 other volunteers immediately fought their way through devastating fire and exploding grenades to reach the fallen soldier. Upon reaching their fallen comrade the sergeant was struck in the knee by machinegun fire and immobilized. Sp4c. Fernandez took charge, rallied the left flank of his patrol and began to assist in the recovery of the wounded sergeant. While first aid was being administered to the wounded man, a sudden increase in the accuracy and intensity of enemy fire forced the volunteer group to take cover. As they did, an enemy grenade landed in the midst of the group, although some men did not see it. Realizing there was no time for the wounded sergeant or the other men to protect themselves from the grenade blast, Sp4c. Fernandez vaulted over the wounded sergeant and threw himself on the grenade as it exploded, saving the lives of his 4 comrades at the sacrifice of his life. Sp4c. Fernandez' profound concern for his fellow soldiers, at the risk of his life above and beyond the call of duty are in the highest traditions of the U.S. Army and reflect great credit upon himself and the Armed Forces of his country.

FISHER, BERNARD FRANCIS

Rank and organization: Major, U.S. Air Force, 1st Air Commandos. *Place and date:* Bien Hoa and Pleiku, Vietnam, 10 March 1966. *Entered service at:* Kuna, Idaho. *Born:* 11 January 1927, San Bernardino, Calif. *Citation:* For conspicuous gallantry and intrepidity at the risk of his life above and beyond the call of duty. On that date, the special forces camp at A Shau was under attack by 2,000 North Vietnamese Army regulars. Hostile troops had positioned themselves between the airstrip and the camp. Other hostile troops had surrounded the camp and were continuously raking it with automatic weapons fire from the surrounding hills. The tops of the 1,500-foot hills were obscured by an 800 foot ceiling, limiting aircraft maneuverability and forcing pilots to operate within range of hostile gun positions, which often were able to fire down on the attacking aircraft. During the battle, Maj. Fisher observed a fellow airman crash land on the battle-torn airstrip. In the belief that the downed pilot was seriously injured and in imminent danger of capture, Maj. Fisher announced his intention to land on the airstrip to effect a rescue. Although aware of the extreme danger and likely failure of such an attempt, he elected to continue. Directing his own air cover, he landed his aircraft and taxied almost the full length of the runway, which was littered with battle debris and parts of an exploded aircraft. While effecting a successful rescue of the downed pilot, heavy ground fire was observed, with 19 bullets striking his aircraft. In the face of the withering ground fire, he applied power and gained enough speed to lift-off at the overrun of the airstrip. Maj. Fisher's profound concern for his fellow airman, and at the risk of his life above and beyond the call of duty are in the highest traditions of the U.S. Air Force and reflect great credit upon himself and the Armed Forces of his country.

FITZMAURICE, MICHAEL JOHN

Rank and organization: Specialist Fourth Class, U.S. Army, Troop D, 2d Squadron, 17th Cavalry, 101st Airborne Division. *Place and date:* Khesanh, Republic of Vietnam, 23 March 1971. *Entered service at:* Jamestown, N. Dak. *Born:* 9 March 1950, Jamestown, N. Dak. *Citation:* For conspicuous gallantry and intrepidity in action at the risk of his life above and beyond the call of duty. Sp4c. Fitzmaurice, 3d Platoon, Troop D, distinguished himself at Khesanh. Sp4c. Fitzmaurice and 3 fellow soldiers were occupying a bunker when a company of North Vietnamese sappers infiltrated the area. At the onset of the attack Sp4c. Fitzmaurice observed 3 explosive charges which had been thrown into the bunker by the enemy. Realizing the imminent danger to his comrades, and with complete disregard for his personal safety, he hurled 2 of the charges out of the bunker. He then threw his flak vest and himself over the remaining charge. By this courageous act he absorbed the blast and shielded his fellow-soldiers. Although suffering from serious multiple wounds and partial loss of sight, he charged out of the bunker, and engaged the enemy until his rifle was damaged by the blast of an enemy handgrenade. While in search of another weapon, Sp4c. Fitzmaurice encountered and overcame an enemy sapper in hand-to-hand combat. Having obtained another weapon, he returned to his original fighting position and inflicted additional casualties on the attacking enemy. Although seriously wounded, Sp4c. Fitzmaurice refused to be medically evacuated, preferring to remain at his post. Sp4c. Fitzmaurice's extraordinary heroism in action at the risk of his life contributed significantly to the successful defense of the position and resulted in saving the lives of a number of his fellow soldiers. These acts of heroism go above and beyond the call of duty, are in keeping with the highest traditions of the military service, and reflect great credit on Sp4c. Fitzmaurice and the U.S. Army.

*FLEEK, CHARLES CLINTON

Rank and organization: Sergeant, U.S. Army, Company C, 1st Battalion, 27th Infantry, 25th Infantry Division. *Place and date:* Binh Duong Province, Republic of Vietnam, 27 May 1967. *Entered service at:* Cincinnati, Ohio. *Born:* 28 August 1947, Petersburg, Ky. *Citation:* For conspicuous gallantry and intrepidity in action at the risk of his life above and beyond the call of duty. Sgt. Fleek distinguished himself while serving as a squad leader in Company C, during an ambush operation. Sgt. Fleek's unit was deployed in ambush locations when a large enemy force approached the position. Suddenly, the leading enemy element, sensing the ambush, halted and started to withdraw. Reacting instantly, Sgt. Fleek opened fire and directed the effective fire of his men upon the numerically superior enemy force. During the fierce battle that followed, an enemy soldier threw a grenade into the squad position. Realizing that his men had not seen the grenade, Sgt. Fleek, although in a position to seek cover, shouted a warning to his comrades and threw himself onto the grenade, absorbing its blast. His gallant action undoubtedly saved the lives or prevented the injury of at least 8 of his fellow soldiers. Sgt. Fleek's gallantry and willing self-sacrifice were in keeping with the highest traditions of the military service and reflect great credit on himself, his unit, and the U.S. Army.

FLEMING, JAMES P.

Rank and organization: Captain, U.S. Air Force, 20th Special Operations Squadron. *Place and date:* Near Duc Co, Republic of Vietnam, 26 November 1968. *Entered service at:* Pullman, Wash. *Born:* 12 March 1943, Sedalia, Mo. *Citation:* For conspicuous gallantry and intrepidity in action at the risk of his life above and beyond the call of duty. Capt. Fleming (then 1st Lt.) distinguished himself as the Aircraft Commander of a UH-IF transport Helicopter. Capt. Fleming went to the aid of a 6-man special forces long range reconnaissance patrol that was in danger of being overrun by a large, heavily armed hostile force. Despite the knowledge that 1 helicopter had been downed by intense hostile fire, Capt. Fleming descended, and balanced his helicopter on a river bank with the tail boom hanging over open water. The patrol could not penetrate to the landing site and he was forced to withdraw. Dangerously low on fuel, Capt. Fleming repeated his original landing maneuver. Disregarding his own safety, he remained in this exposed position. Hostile fire crashed through his windscreen as the patrol boarded his helicopter. Capt. Fleming made a successful takeoff through a barrage of hostile fire and recovered safely at a forward base. Capt. Fleming's profound concern for his fellowmen, and at the risk of his life above and beyond the call of duty are in keeping with the highest traditions of the U.S. Air Force and reflect great credit upon himself and the Armed Forces of his country.

FOLEY, ROBERT F.

Rank and organization: Captain, U.S. Army, Company A, 2d Battalion, 27th Infantry, 25th Infantry Division. *Place and date:* Near Quan Dau Tieng, Republic of Vietnam, 5 November 1966. *Entered service at:* Newton, Mass. *Born:* 30 May 1941, Newton, Mass. *Citation:* For conspicuous gallantry and intrepidity in action at the risk of his life above and beyond the call of duty. Capt. Foley's company was ordered to extricate another company of the battalion. Moving through the dense jungle to aid the besieged unit, Company A encountered a strong enemy force occupying well concealed, defensive positions, and the company's leading element quickly sustained several casualties. Capt. Foley immediately ran forward to the scene of the most intense action to direct the company's efforts. Deploying 1 platoon on the flank, he led the other 2 platoons in an attack on the enemy in the face of intense fire. During this action both radio operators accompanying him were wounded. At grave risk to himself he defied the enemy's murderous fire, and helped the wounded operators to a position where they could receive medical care. As he moved forward again 1 of his machinegun crews was wounded. Seizing the weapon, he charged forward firing the machinegun, shouting orders and rallying his men, thus maintaining the momentum of the attack. Under increasingly heavy enemy fire he ordered his assistant to take cover and, alone, Capt. Foley continued to advance firing the machinegun until the wounded had been evacuated and the attack in this area could be resumed. When movement on the other flank was halted by the enemy's fanatical defense, Capt. Foley moved to personally direct this critical phase of the battle. Leading the renewed effort he was blown off his feet and wounded by an enemy grenade. Despite his painful wounds he refused medical aid and perservered in the forefront of the attack on the enemy redoubt. He led the assault on several enemy gun emplacements and, singlehandedly, destroyed 3 such positions. His outstanding personal leadership under intense enemy fire during the fierce battle which lasted for several hours, inspired his men to heroic efforts and was instrumental in the ultimate success of the operation. Capt. Foley's magnificent courage, selfless concern for his men and professional skill reflect the utmost credit upon himself and the U.S. Army.

*FOLLAND, MICHAEL FLEMING

Rank and organization: Corporal, U.S. Army, Company D, 2d Battalion, 3d Infantry, 199th Infantry Brigade. *Place and date:* Long Khanh, Providence, Republic of Vietnam, 3 July 1969. *Entered service at:* Richmond, Va. *Born:* 15 April 1949, Richmond, Va. *Citation:* For conspicuous gallantry and intrepidity in action at the risk of his life above and beyond the call of duty. Cpl. Folland distinguished himself while serving as an ammunition bearer with the weapons platoon of Company D, during a reconnaissance patrol mission. As the patrol was moving through a dense jungle area, it was caught in an intense cross-fire from heavily fortified and concealed enemy ambush positions. As the patrol reacted to neutralize the ambush, it became evident that the heavy weapons could not be used in the cramped fighting area. Cpl. Folland dropped his recoilless rifle ammunition, and ran forward to join his commander in an assault on the enemy bunkers. The assaulting force moved forward until it was pinned down directly in front of the heavily fortified bunkers by machinegun fire. Cpl. Folland stood up to draw enemy fire on himself and to place suppressive fire on the enemy positions while his commander attempted to destroy the machinegun positions with grenades. Before the officer could throw a grenade, an enemy grenade landed in the position. Cpl. Folland alerted his comrades and his commander hurled the grenade from the position. When a second enemy grenade landed in the position, Cpl. Folland again shouted a warning to his fellow soldiers. Seeing that no one could reach the grenade and realizing that it was about to explode, Cpl. Folland, with complete disregard for his safety, threw himself on the grenade. By his dauntless courage, Cpl. Folland saved the lives of his comrades although he was mortally wounded by the explosion. Cpl. Folland's extraordinary heroism, at the cost of his life, was in keeping with the highest traditions of the military service and reflects great credit upon himself, his unit, and the U.S. Army.

*FOSTER, PAUL HELLSTROM

Rank and organization: Sergeant, U.S. Marine Corps Reserve, 2d Battalion, 4th Marines, 3d Marine Division. *Place and date:* Near Con Thien, Republic of Vietnam, 14 October 1967. *Entered service at:* San Francisco, Calif. *Born:* 17 April 1939, San Mateo, Calif. *Citation:* For conspicuous gallantry and intrepidity at the risk of his life above and beyond the call of duty while serving as an artillery liaison operations chief with the 2d Battalion. In the early morning hours the 2d Battalion was occupying a defensive position which protected a bridge on the road leading from Con Thien to Cam Lo. Suddenly, the marines' position came under a heavy volume of mortar and artillery fire, followed by an aggressive enemy ground assault. In the ensuing engagement, the hostile force penetrated the perimeter and brought a heavy concentration of small arms, automatic weapons, and rocket fire to bear on the battalion command post. Although his position in the fire support coordination center was dangerously exposed to enemy fire and he was wounded when an enemy handgrenade exploded near his position, Sgt. Foster resolutely continued to direct accurate mortar and artillery fire on the advancing North Vietnamese troops. As the attack continued, a handgrenade landed in the midst of Sgt. Foster and his 5 companions. Realizing the danger, he shouted a warning, threw his armored vest over the grenade, and unhesitatingly placed his body over the armored vest. When the grenade exploded, Sgt. Foster absorbed the entire blast with his body and was mortally wounded. His heroic actions undoubtedly saved his comrades from further injury or possible death. Sgt. Foster's courage, extraordinary heroism, and unfaltering devotion to duty reflected great credit upon himself and the Marine Corps and upheld the highest traditions of the U.S. Naval Service. He gallantly gave his life for his country.

FOX, WESLEY L.

Rank and organization: Captain, U.S. Marine Corps, Company A, 1st Battalion, 9th Marines, 3d Marine Division. *Place and date:* Quang Tri Province, Republic of Vietnam, 22 February 1969. *Entered service at:* Leesburg, Va. *Born:* 30 September 1931, Herndon, Va. *Citation:* For conspicuous gallantry and intrepidity at the risk of his life above and beyond the call of duty while serving as commanding officer of Company A, in action against the enemy in the northern A Shau Valley. Capt. (then 1st Lt.) Fox's company came under intense fire from a large well concealed enemy force. Capt. Fox maneuvered to a position from which he could assess the situation and confer with his platoon leaders. As they departed to execute the plan he had devised, the enemy attacked and Capt. Fox was wounded along with all of the other members of the command group, except the executive officer. Capt. Fox continued to direct the activity of his company. Advancing through heavy enemy fire, he personally neutralized 1 enemy position and calmly ordered an assault against the hostile emplacements. He then moved through the hazardous area coordinating aircraft support with the activities of his men. When his executive officer was mortally wounded, Capt. Fox reorganized the company and directed the fire of his men as they hurled grenades against the enemy and drove the hostile forces into retreat. Wounded again in the final assault, Capt. Fox refused medical attention, established a defensive posture, and supervised the preparation of casualties for medical evacuation. His indomitable courage, inspiring initiative, and unwavering devotion to duty in the face of grave personal danger inspired his marines to such aggressive action that they overcame all enemy resistance and destroyed a large bunker complex. Capt. Fox's heroic actions reflect great credit upon himself and the Marine Corps, and uphold the highest traditions of the U.S. Naval Service.

*FRATELLENICO, FRANK R.

Rank and organization: Corporal, U.S. Army, Company B, 2d Battalion, 502d Infantry, 1st Brigade, 101st Airborne Division. *Place and date:* Quang Tri Province, Republic of Vietnam, 19 August 1970. *Entered service at:* Albany, N.Y. *Born:* 14 July 1951, Sharon, Conn. *Citation:* Cpl. Fratellenico distinguished himself while serving as a rifleman with Company B. Cpl. Fratellenico's squad was pinned down by intensive fire from 2 well-fortified enemy bunkers. At great personal risk Cpl. Fratellenico maneuvered forward and, using handgrenades, neutralized the first bunker which was occupied by a number of enemy soldiers. While attacking the second bunker, enemy fire struck Cpl. Fratellenico, causing him to fall to the ground and drop a grenade which he was preparing to throw. Alert to the imminent danger to his comrades, Cpl. Fratellenico retrieved the grenade and fell upon it an instant before it exploded. His heroic actions prevented death or serious injury to 4 of his comrades nearby and inspired his unit which subsequently overran the enemy position. Cpl. Fratellenico's conspicuous gallantry, extraordinary heroism, and intrepidity at the cost of his life, above and beyond the call of duty, are in keeping with the highest traditions of the military service and reflect great credit on him, his unit, and the U.S. Army.

*FOURNET, DOUGLAS B.

Rank and organization: First Lieutenant, U.S. Army, Company B, 1st Battalion, 7th Cavalry, 1st Cavalry Division (Airmobile). *Place and date:* A Shau Valley, Republic of Vietnam, 4 May 1968. *Entered service at:* New Orleans, La. *Born:* 7 May 1943, Lake Charles, La. *Citation:* For conspicuous gallantry and intrepidity in action at the risk of his life above and beyond the call of duty. 1st Lt. Fournet, Infantry, distinguished himself in action while serving as rifle platoon leader of the 2d Platoon, Company B. While advancing uphill against fortified enemy positions in the A Shau Valley, the platoon encountered intense sniper fire, making movement very difficult. The right flank man suddenly discovered an enemy claymore mine covering the route of advance and shouted a warning to his comrades. Realizing that the enemy would also be alerted, 1st Lt. Fournet ordered his men to take cover and ran uphill toward the mine, drawing a sheath knife as he approached it. With complete disregard for his safety and realizing the imminent danger to members of his command, he used his body as a shield in front of the mine as he attempted to slash the control wires leading from the enemy positions to the mine. As he reached for the wire the mine was detonated, killing him instantly. Five men nearest the mine were slightly wounded, but 1st Lt. Fournet's heroic and unselfish act spared his men of serious injury or death. His gallantry and willing self-sacrifice are in keeping with the highest traditions of the military service and reflect great credit upon himself, his unit, and the U.S. Army.

*FOUS, JAMES W.

Rank and organization: Private First Class, U.S. Army, Company E, 4th Battalion, 47th Infantry, 9th Infantry Division. *Place and date:* Kien Hoa Province, Republic of Vietnam, 14 May 1968. *Entered service at:* Omaha, Nebr. *Born:* 14 October 1946, Omaha, Nebr. *Citation:* For conspicuous gallantry and intrepidity in action at the risk of his life above and beyond the call of duty. Pfc. Fous distinguished himself at the risk of his life while serving as a rifleman with Company E. Pfc. Fous was participating in a reconnaissance-in-force mission when his unit formed its perimeter defense for the night. Pfc. Fous, together with 3 other American soldiers, occupied a position in a thickly vegetated area facing a woodline. Pfc. Fous detected 3 Viet Cong maneuvering toward his position and, after alerting the other men, directed accurate fire upon the enemy soldiers, silencing 2 of them. The third Viet Cong soldier managed to escape in the thick vegetation after throwing a handgrenade into Pfc. Fous' position. Without hesitation, Pfc. Fous shouted a warning to his comrades and leaped upon the lethal explosive, absorbing the blast with his body to save the lives of the 3 men in the area at the sacrifice of his life. Pfc. Fous' extraordinary heroism at the cost of his life were in keeping with the highest traditions of the military service and reflect great credit upon himself, his unit, and the U.S. Army.

FRITZ, HAROLD A.

Rank and organization: Captain, U.S. Army, Troop A, 1st Squadron, 11th Armored Cavalry Regiment. *Place and date:* Binh Long Province, Republic of Vietnam, 11 January 1969. *Entered service at:* Milwaukee, Wis. *Born:* 21 February 1944, Chicago, Ill. *Citation:* For conspicuous gallantry and intrepidity in action at the risk of his life above and beyond the call of duty. Capt. (then 1st Lt.) Fritz, Armor, U.S. Army, distinguished himself while serving as a platoon leader with Troop A, near Quan Loi. Capt. Fritz was leading his 7-vehicle armored column along Highway 13 to meet and escort a truck convoy when the column suddenly came under intense crossfire from a reinforced enemy company deployed in ambush positions. In the initial attack, Capt. Fritz' vehicle was hit and he was seriously wounded. Realizing that his platoon was completely surrounded, vastly outnumbered, and in danger of being overrun, Capt. Fritz leaped to the top of his burning vehicle and directed the positioning of his remaining vehicles and men. With complete disregard for his wounds and safety, he ran from vehicle to vehicle in complete view of the enemy gunners in order to reposition his men, to improve the defenses, to assist the wounded, to distribute ammunition, to direct fire, and to provide encouragement to his men. When a strong enemy force assaulted the position and attempted to overrun the platoon, Capt. Fritz manned a machinegun and through his exemplary action inspired his men to deliver intense and deadly fire which broke the assault and routed the attackers. Moments later a second enemy force advanced to within 2 meters of the position and threatened to overwhelm the defenders. Capt. Fritz, armed only with a pistol and bayonet, led a small group of his men in a fierce and daring charge which routed the attackers and inflicted heavy casualties. When a relief force arrived, Capt. Fritz saw that it was not deploying effectively against the enemy positions, and he moved through the heavy enemy fire to direct its deployment against the hostile positions. This deployment forced the enemy to abandon the ambush site and withdraw. Despite his wounds, Capt. Fritz returned to his position, assisted his men, and refused medical attention until all of his wounded comrades had been treated and evacuated. The extraordinary courage and selflessness displayed by Capt. Fritz, at the repeated risk of his own life above and beyond the call of duty, were in keeping with the highest traditions of the U.S. Army and reflect the greatest credit upon himself, his unit, and the Armed Forces.

*GARDNER, JAMES A.

Rank and organization: First Lieutenant, U.S. Army, Headquarters and Headquarters Company, 1st Battalion (Airborne), 327th Infantry, 1st Brigade, 101st Airborne Division. *Place and date:* My Canh, Vietnam, 7 February 1966. *Entered service at:* Memphis, Tenn. *Born:* 7 February 1943, Dyersburg, Tenn. *Citation:* For conspicuous gallantry and intrepidity in action at the risk of his life above and beyond the call of duty. 1st Lt. Gardner's platoon was advancing to relieve a company of the 1st Battalion that had been pinned down for several hours by a numerically superior enemy force in the village of My Canh, Vietnam. The enemy occupied a series of strongly fortified bunker positions which were mutually supporting and expertly concealed. Approaches to the position were well covered by an integrated pattern of fire including automatic weapons, machineguns and mortars. Air strikes and artillery placed on the fortifications had little effect. 1st Lt. Gardner's platoon was to relieve the friendly company by encircling and destroying the enemy force. Even as it moved to begin the attack, the platoon was under heavy enemy fire. During the attack, the enemy fire intensified. Leading the assault and disregarding his own safety, 1st Lt. Gardner charged through a withering hail of fire across an open rice paddy. On reaching the first bunker he destroyed it with a grenade and without hesitation dashed to the second bunker and eliminated it by tossing a grenade inside. Then, crawling swiftly along the dike of a rice paddy, he reached the third bunker. Before he could arm a grenade, the enemy gunner leaped forth, firing at him. 1st Lt. Gardner instantly returned the fire and killed the enemy gunner at a distance of 6 feet. Following the seizure of the main enemy position, he reorganized the platoon to continue the attack. Advancing to the new assault position, the platoon was pinned down by an enemy machinegun emplaced in a fortified bunker. 1st Lt. Gardner immediately collected several grenades and charged the enemy position, firing his rifle as he advanced to neutralize the defenders. He dropped a grenade into the bunker and vaulted beyond. As the bunker blew up, he came under fire again. Rolling into a ditch to gain cover, he moved toward the new source of fire. Nearing the position, he leaped from the ditch and advanced with a grenade in one hand and firing his rifle with the other. He was gravely wounded just before he reached the bunker, but with a last valiant effort he staggered forward and destroyed the bunker, and its defenders with a grenade. Although he fell dead on the rim of the bunker, his extraordinary actions so inspired the men of his platoon that they resumed the attack and completely routed the enemy. 1st Lt. Gardner's conspicuous gallantry were in the highest traditions of the U.S. Army.

*GERTSCH, JOHN G.

Rank and organization: Staff Sergeant, U.S. Army, Company E, 1st Battalion, 327th Infantry, 101st Airborne Division. *Place and date:* A Shau Valley, Republic of Vietnam, 15 to 19 July 1969. *Entered service at:* Buffalo, N.Y. *Born:* 29 September 1944, Jersey City, N.J.: *Citation:* S/Sgt. Gertsch distinguished himself while serving as a platoon sergeant and platoon leader during combat operations in the A Shau Valley. During the initial phase of an operation to seize a strongly defended enemy position, S/Sgt. Gertsch's platoon leader was seriously wounded and lay exposed to intense enemy fire. Forsaking his own safety, without hesitation S/Sgt. Gertsch rushed to aid his fallen leader and dragged him to a sheltered position. He then assumed command of the heavily engaged platoon and led his men in a fierce counterattack that forced the enemy to withdraw. Later, a small element of S/Sgt. Gertsch's unit was reconnoitering when attacked again by the enemy. S/Sgt. Gertsch moved forward to his besieged element and immediately charged, firing as he advanced. His determined assault forced the enemy troops to withdraw in confusion and made possible the recovery of 2 wounded men who had been exposed to heavy enemy fire. Sometime later his platoon came under attack by an enemy force employing automatic weapons, grenade, and rocket fire. S/Sgt. Gertsch was severely wounded during the onslaught but continued to command his platoon despite his painful wound. While moving under fire and encouraging his men he sighted an aidman treating a wounded officer from an adjacent unit. Realizing that both men were in imminent danger of being killed, he rushed forward and positioned himself between them and the enemy nearby. While the wounded officer was being moved to safety S/Sgt. Gertsch was mortally wounded by enemy fire. Without S/Sgt. Gertch's courage, ability to inspire others, and profound concern for the welfare of his men, the loss of life among his fellow soldiers would have been significantly greater. His conspicuous gallantry, extraordinary heroism, and intrepidity at the cost of his life, above and beyond the call of duty, are in the highest traditions of the U.S. Army and reflect great credit on him and the Armed Forces of his country.

*GONZALEZ, ALFREDO

Rank and organization: Sergeant, U.S. Marine Corps, Company A, 1st Battalion, 1st Marines, 1st Marine Division (Rein), FMF. *Place and date:* Near Thua Thien, Republic of Vietnam, 4 February 1968. *Entered service at:* San Antonio, Tex. *Born:* 23 May 1946, Edinburg Tex. *Citation:* For conspicuous gallantry and intrepidity at the risk of his life above and beyond the call of duty while serving as platoon commander, 3d Platoon, Company A. On 31 January 1968, during the initial phase of Operation Hue City, Sgt. Gonzalez' unit was formed as a reaction force and deployed to Hue to relieve the pressure on the beleaguered city. While moving by truck convoy along Route No. 1, near the village of Lang Van Lrong, the marines received a heavy volume of enemy fire. Sgt. Gonzalez aggressively maneuvered the marines in his platoon, and directed their fire until the area was cleared of snipers. Immediately after crossing a river south of Hue, the column was again hit by intense enemy fire. One of the marines on top of a tank was wounded and fell to the ground in an exposed position. With complete disregard for his safety, Sgt. Gonzalez ran through the fire-swept area to the assistance of his injured comrade. He lifted him up and though receiving fragmentation wounds during the rescue, he carried the wounded marine to a covered position for treatment. Due to the increased volume and accuracy of enemy fire from a fortified machinegun bunker on the side of the road, the company was temporarily halted. Realizing the gravity of the situation, Sgt. Gonzalez exposed himself to the enemy fire and moved his platoon along the east side of a bordering rice paddy to a dike directly across from the bunker. Though fully aware of the danger involved, he moved to the fire-swept road and destroyed the hostile position with handgrenades. Although seriously wounded again on 3 February, he steadfastly refused medical treatment and continued to supervise his men and lead the attack. On 4 February, the enemy had again pinned the company down, inflicting heavy casualties with automatic weapons and rocket fire. Sgt. Gonzalez, utilizing a number of light antitank assault weapons, fearlessly moved from position to position firing numerous rounds at the heavily fortified enemy emplacements. He successfully knocked out a rocket position and suppressed much of the enemy fire before falling mortally wounded. The heroism, courage, and dynamic leadership displayed by Sgt. Gonzalez reflected great credit upon himself and the Marine Corps, and were in keeping with the highest traditions of the U.S. Naval Service. He gallantly gave his life for his country.

*GRAHAM, JAMES A.

Rank and organization: Captain, U.S. Marine Corps, Company F, 2d Battalion, 5th Marines, 1st Marine Division. *Place and date:* Republic of Vietnam, 2 June 1967. *Entered service at:* Prince Georges, Md. *Born:* 25 August 1940, Wilkinsburg, Allegheny County, Pa. *Citation:* For conspicuous gallantry and intrepidity at the risk of his life above and beyond the call of duty. During Operation Union II, the 1st Battalion, 5th Marines, consisting of Companies A and D, with Capt. Graham's company attached launched an attack against an enemy occupied position with 2 companies assaulting and 1 in reserve. Company F, a leading company, was proceeding across a clear paddy area 1,000 meters wide, attacking toward the assigned objective, when it came under fire from mortars and small arms which immediately inflicted a large number of casualties. Hardest hit by the enemy fire was the 2d platoon of Company F, which was pinned down in the open paddy area by intense fire from 2 concealed machineguns. Forming an assault unit from members of his small company headquarters, Capt. Graham boldly led a fierce assault through the second platoon's position, forcing the enemy to abandon the first machinegun position, thereby relieving some of the pressure on his second platoon, and enabling evacuation of the wounded to a more secure area. Resolute to silence the second machinegun, which continued its devastating fire, Capt. Graham's small force stood steadfast in its hard won enclave. Subsequently, during the afternoon's fierce fighting, he suffered 2 minor wounds while personally accounting for an estimated 15 enemy killed. With the enemy position remaining invincible upon each attempt to withdraw to friendly lines, and although knowing that he had no chance of survival, he chose to remain with 1 man who could not be moved due to the seriousness of his wounds. The last radio transmission from Capt. Graham reported that he was being assaulted by a force of 25 enemy soldiers; he died while protecting himself and the wounded man he chose not to abandon. Capt. Graham's actions throughout the day were a series of heroic achievements. His outstanding courage, superb leadership and indomitable fighting spirit undoubtedly saved the second platoon from annihilation and reflected great credit upon himself, the Marine Corps, and the U.S. Naval Service. He gallantly gave his life for his country.

*GRANDSTAFF, BRUCE ALAN

Rank and organization: Platoon Sergeant, U.S. Army, Company B, 1st Battalion, 8th Infantry. *Place and date:* Pleiku Province, Republic of Vietnam, 18 May 1967. *Entered service at:* Spokane, Wash. *Born:* 2 June 1934, Spokane, Wash. *Citation:* For conspicuous gallantry and intrepidity in action at the risk of his life above and beyond the call of duty. P/Sgt. Grandstaff distinguished himself while leading the

Weapons Platoon, Company B, on a reconnaissance mission near the Cambodian border. His platoon was advancing through intermittent enemy contact when it was struck by heavy small arms and automatic weapons fire from 3 sides. As he established a defensive perimeter, P/Sgt. Grandstaff noted that several of his men had been struck down. He raced 30 meters through the intense fire to aid them but could only save 1. Denied freedom to maneuver his unit by the intensity of the enemy onslaught, he adjusted artillery to within 45 meters of his position. When helicopter gunships arrived, he crawled outside the defensive position to mark the location with smoke grenades. Realizing his first marker was probably ineffective, he crawled to another location and threw his last smoke grenade but the smoke did not penetrate the jungle foilage. Seriously wounded in the leg during this effort he returned to his radio and, refusing medical aid, adjusted the artillery even closer as the enemy advanced on his position. Recognizing the need for additional firepower, he again braved the enemy fusillade, crawled to the edge of his position and fired several magazines of tracer ammunition through the jungle canopy. He succeeded in designating the location to the gunships but this action again drew the enemy fire and he was wounded in the other leg. Now enduring intense pain and bleeding profusely, he crawled to within 10 meters of an enemy machinegun which had caused many casualties among his men. He destroyed the position with handgrenades but received additional wounds. Rallying his remaining men to withstand the enemy assaults, he realized his position was being overrun and asked for artillery directly on his location. He fought until mortally wounded by an enemy rocket. Although every man in the platoon was a casualty, survivors attest to the indomitable spirit and exceptional courage of this outstanding combat leader who inspired his men to fight courageously against overwhelming odds and cost the enemy heavy casualties. P/Sgt. Grandstaff's selfless gallantry, above and beyond the call of duty, are in the highest traditions of the U.S. Army and reflect great credit upon himself and the Armed Forces of his country.

*GRANT, JOSEPH XAVIER

Rank and organization: Captain (then 1st Lt.), U.S. Army, Company A, 1st Battalion, 14th Infantry, 25th Infantry Division. *Place and date:* Republic of Vietnam, 13 November 1966. *Entered service at:* Boston, Mass. *Born:* 28 March 1940, Cambridge, Mass. *G.O. No.:* 4, 29 January 1968. *Citation:* For conspicuous gallantry and intrepidity in action at the risk of his life above and beyond the call of duty. Company A was participating in a search and destroy operation when the leading platoon made contact with the enemy and a fierce fire-fight ensued. Capt. Grant was ordered to disengage the 2 remaining platoons and to maneuver them to envelop and destroy the enemy. After beginning their movement, the platoons encountered intense enemy automatic weapons and mortar fire from the front and flank. Capt. Grant was ordered to deploy the platoons in a defensive position. As this action was underway, the enemy attacked, using "human wave" assaults, in an attempt to literally overwhelm Capt. Grant's force. In a magnificent display of courage and leadership, Capt. Grant moved under intense fire along the hastily formed defensive line repositioning soldiers to fill gaps created by the mounting casualties and inspiring and directing the efforts of his men to successfully repel the determined enemy onslaught. Seeing a platoon leader wounded, Capt. Grant hastened to his aid, in the face of the mass of fire of the entire enemy force, and moved him to a more secure position. During this action, Capt. Grant was wounded in the shoulder. Refusing medical treatment, he returned to the forward part of the perimeter, where he continued to lead and to inspire his men by his own indomitable example. While attempting to evacuate a wounded soldier, he was pinned down by fire from an enemy machinegun. With a supply of handgrenades, he crawled forward under a withering hail of fire and knocked out the machinegun, killing the crew, after which he moved the wounded man to safety. Learning that several other wounded men were pinned down by enemy fire forward of his position, Capt. Grant disregarded his painful wound and led 5 men across the fireswept open ground to effect a rescue. Following return of the wounded men to the perimeter, a concentration of mortar fire landed in their midst and Capt. Grant was killed instantly. His heroic actions saved the lives of a number of his comrades and enabled the task force to repulse the vicious assaults and defeat the enemy. Capt. Grant's actions reflect great credit upon himself and were in keeping with the finest traditions of the U.S. Army.

*GRAVES, TERRENCE COLLINSON

Rank and organization: Second Lieutenant, U.S. Marine Corps, 3d Force Reconnaissance Company, 3d Reconnaissance Battalion, 3d Marine Division (Rein), FMF. *Place and date:* Quang Tri Province, Republic of Vietnam, 16 February 1968. *Entered service at:* New York *Born:* 6 July 1945, Corpus Christi, Tex. *Citation:* For conspicuous gallantry and intrepidity at the risk of his life above and beyond the call of duty as a platoon commander with the 3d Force Reconnaissance Company. While on a long-range reconnaissance mission, 2d Lt. Graves' 8-man patrol observed 7 enemy soldiers approaching their position. Reacting instantly, he deployed his men and directed their fire on the approaching enemy. After the fire had ceased, he and 2 patrol members commenced a search of the area, and suddenly came under a heavy volume of hostile small arms and automatic weapons fire from a numerically superior enemy force. When 1 of his men was hit by the enemy fire, 2d Lt. Graves moved through the fire-swept area to his radio and, while directing suppressive fire from his men, requested air support and adjusted a heavy volume of artillery and helicopter gunship fire upon the enemy. After attending the wounded, 2d Lt. Graves, accompanied by another marine, moved from his relatively safe position to confirm the results of the earlier engagement. Observing that several of the enemy were still alive, he launched a determined assault, eliminating the remaining enemy troops. He then began moving the patrol to a landing zone for extraction, when the unit again came under intense fire which wounded 2 more marines and 2d Lt. Graves. Refusing medical attention, he once more adjusted air strikes and artillery fire upon the enemy while directing the fire of his men. He led his men to a new landing site into which he skillfully guided the incoming aircraft and boarded his men while remaining exposed to the hostile fire. Realizing that 1 of the wounded had not embarked, he directed the aircraft to depart and, along with another marine, moved to the side of the casualty. Confronted with a shortage of ammunition, 2d Lt. Graves utilized supporting arms and directed fire until a second helicopter arrived. At this point, the volume of enemy fire intensified, hitting the helicopter and causing it to crash shortly after liftoff. All aboard were killed. 2d Lt. Graves' outstanding courage, superb leadership and indomitable fighting spirit throughout the day were in keeping with the highest traditions of the Marine Corps and the U.S. Naval Service. He gallantly gave his life for his country.

*GUENETTE, PETER M.

Rank and organization: Specialist Fourth Class, U.S. Army, Company D, 2d Battalion (Airborne), 506th Infantry, 101st Airborne Division (Airmobile). *Place and date:* Quan Tan Uyen Province, Republic of Vietnam, 18 May 1968. *Entered service at:* Albany, N.Y. *Born:* 4 January 1948, Troy, N.Y. *Citation:* For conspicuous gallantry and intrepidity in action at the risk of his life above and beyond the call of duty. Sp4c. Guenette distinguished himself while serving as a machine gunner with Company D, during combat operations. While Sp4c. Guenette's platoon was sweeping a suspected enemy base camp, it came under light harassing fire from a well equipped and firmly entrenched squad of North Vietnamese Army regulars which was serving as a delaying force at the entrance to their base camp. As the platoon moved within 10 meters of the fortified positions, the enemy fire became intense. Sp4c. Guenette and his assistant gunner immediately began to provide a base of suppressive fire, ceasing momentarily to allow the assistant gunner time to throw a grenade into a bunker. Seconds later, an enemy grenade was thrown to Sp4c. Guenette's right flank. Realizing that the grenade would kill or wound at least 4 men and destroy the machinegun, he shouted a warning and smothered the grenade with his body, absorbing its blast. Through his actions, he prevented loss of life or injury to at least 3 men and enabled his comrades to maintain their fire superiority. By his gallantry at the cost of his life in keeping with the highest traditions of the military service, Sp4c. Guenette has reflected great credit on himself, his unit, and the U.S. Army.

HAGEMEISTER, CHARLES CRIS

Rank and organization: Specialist Fifth Class (then Sp4c.) U.S. Army, Headquarters and Headquarters Company, 1st Battalion, 5th Cavalry, 1st Cavalry Division (Airmobile). *Place and date:* Binh Dinh Province, Republic of Vietnam, 20 March 1967. *Entered service at:* Lincoln, Nebr. *Born:* 21 August 1946, Lincoln, Nebr. *Citation:* For conspicuous gallantry and intrepidity in action at the risk of his life above and beyond the call of duty. While conducting combat operations against a hostile force, Sp5c. Hagemeister's platoon suddenly came under heavy attack from 3 sides by an enemy force occupying well concealed, fortified positions and supported by machineguns and mortars. Seeing 2 of his comrades seriously wounded in the initial action, Sp5c. Hagemeister unhesitatingly and with total disregard for his safety, raced through the deadly hail of enemy fire to provide them medical aid. Upon learning that the platoon leader and several other soldiers also had been wounded, Sp5c. Hagemeister continued to brave the withering enemy fire and crawled forward to render lifesaving treatment and to offer words of encouragement. Attempting to evacuate the seriously wounded soldiers, Sp5c. Hagemeister was taken under fire at close range by an enemy sniper. Realizing that the lives of his fellow soldiers depended on his actions, Sp5c. Hagemeister seized a rifle from a fallen comrade, killed the sniper, 3 other enemy soldiers who were attempting to encircle his position and silenced an enemy machinegun that covered the area with deadly fire. Unable to remove the wounded to a less exposed location and aware of the enemy's efforts to isolate his unit, he dashed through the fusillade of fire to secure help from a nearby platoon. Returning with help, he placed men in positions to cover his advance as he moved to evacuate the wounded forward of his location. These efforts successfully completed, he then moved to the other flank and evacuated additional wounded men despite the fact that his every move drew fire from the enemy. Sp5c. Hagemeister's repeated heroic and selfless actions at the risk of his life saved the lives of many of his comrades and inspired their actions in repelling the enemy assault. Sp5c. Hagemeister's indomitable courage was in the highest traditions of the U.S. Armed Forces and reflect great credit upon himself.

*HAGEN, LOREN D.

Rank and organization: First Lieutenant, U.S. Army, Infantry, U.S. Army Training Advisory Group. *Place and date:* Republic of Vietnam, 7 August 1971. *Entered service at:* Fargo, N. Dak. *Born:* 25 February 1946, Fargo, N. Dak. *Citation:* 1st Lt. Hagen distinguished himself in action while serving as the team leader of a small reconnaissance team operating deep within enemy-held territory. At approximately 0630 hours on the morning of 7 August 1971 the small team came under a fierce assault by a superior-sized enemy force using heavy small arms, automatic weapons, mortar, and rocket fire. 1st Lt. Hagen immediately began returning small-arms fire upon the attackers and successfully led this team in repelling the first enemy onslaught. He then quickly deployed his men into more strategic defense locations before the enemy struck again in an attempt to overrun and annihilate the beleaguered team's members. 1st Lt. Hagen repeatedly exposed himself to the enemy fire directed at him as he constantly moved about the team's perimeter, directing fire, rallying the members, and resupplying the team with ammunition, while courageously returning small arms and handgrenade fire in a valorous attempt to repel the advancing enemy force. The courageous actions and expert leadership abilities of 1st Lt. Hagen were a great source of inspiration and instilled confidence in the team members. After observing an enemy rocket make a direct hit on and destroy 1 of the team's bunkers, 1st Lt. Hagen moved toward the wrecked bunker in search for team members despite the fact that the enemy force now controlled the bunker area. With total disregard for his own personal safety, he crawled through the enemy fire while returning small-arms fire upon the enemy force. Undaunted by the enemy rockets and grenades impacting all around him, 1st Lt. Hagen desperately advanced upon the destroyed bunker until he was fatally wounded by enemy small arms and automatic weapons fire. With complete disregard for his personal safety, 1st Lt. Hagen's courageous gallantry, extraordinary heroism, and intrepidity above and beyond the call of duty, at the cost of his own life, were in keeping with the highest traditions of the military service and reflect great credit upon him and the U.S. Army.

*HARTSOCK, ROBERT W.

Rank and organization: Staff Sergeant, U.S. Army, 44th Infantry Platoon, 3d Brigade, 25th Infantry Division. *Place and date:* Hau Nghia, Province, Republic of Vietnam, 23 February 1969. *Entered service at:* Fairmont, W. Va. *Born:* 24 January 1945, Cumberland, Md. *Citation:* For conspicuous gallantry and intrepidity in action at the risk of his life above and beyond the call of duty. S/Sgt. Hartsock, distinguished himself in action while serving as section leader with the 44th Infantry Platoon. When the Dau Tieng Base Camp came under a heavy enemy rocket and mortar attack, S/Sgt. Hartsock and his platoon commander spotted an enemy sapper squad which had infiltrated the camp undetected. Realizing the enemy squad was heading for the brigade tactical operations center and nearby prisoner compound, they concealed themselves and, although heavily outnumbered, awaited the approach of the hostile soldiers. When the enemy was almost upon them, S/Sgt. Hartsock and his platoon commander opened fire on the squad. As a wounded enemy soldier fell, he managed to detonate a satchel charge he was carrying. S/Sgt. Hartsock, with complete disregard for his life, threw himself on the charge and was gravely wounded. In spite of his wounds, S/Sgt. Hartsock crawled about 5 meters to a ditch and provided heavy suppressive fire, completely pinning down the enemy and allowing his commander to seek shelter. S/Sgt. Hartsock continued his deadly stream of fire until he succumbed to his wounds. S/Sgt. Hartsock's extraordinary heroism and profound concern for the lives of his fellow soldiers were in keeping with the highest traditions of the military service and reflect great credit on him, his unit, and the U.S. Army.

*HARVEY, CARMEL BERNON, JR.

Rank and organization: Specialist Fourth Class, U.S. Army, Company B, 1st Battalion, 5th Cavalry, 1st Cavalry Division (Airmobile). *Place and date:* Binh Dinh Province, Republic of Vietnam, 21 June 1967. *Entered service at:* Chicago, Ill. *Born:* 6 October 1946, Montgomery, W. Va. *Citation:* For conspicuous gallantry and intrepidity in action at the risk of his life above and beyond the call of duty. Sp4c. Harvey distinguished himself as a fire team leader with Company B, during combat operations. Ordered to secure a downed helicopter, his platoon established a defensive perimeter around the aircraft, but shortly thereafter a large enemy force attacked the position from 3 sides. Sp4c. Harvey and 2 members of his squad were in a position directly in the path of the enemy onslaught, and their location received the brunt of the fire from an enemy machinegun. In short order, both of his companions were wounded, but Sp4c. Harvey covered this loss by increasing his deliberate rifle fire at the foe. The enemy machinegun seemed to concentrate on him and the bullets struck the ground all around his position. One round hit and armed a grenade attached to his belt. Quickly, he tried to remove the grenade but was unsuccessful. Realizing the danger to his comrades if he remained and despite the hail of enemy fire, he jumped to his feet, shouted a challenge at the enemy, and raced toward the deadly machinegun. He nearly reached the enemy position when the grenade on his belt exploded, mortally wounding Sp4c. Harvey, and stunning the enemy machinegun crew. His final act caused a pause in the enemy fire, and the wounded men were moved from the danger area. Sp4c. Harvey's dedication to duty, high sense of responsibility, and heroic actions inspired the others in his platoon to decisively beat back the enemy attack. His acts are in keeping with the highest traditions of the military service and reflect great credit upon himself and the U.S. Army.

HERDA, FRANK A.

Rank and organization: Specialist Fourth Class, U.S. Army, Company A, 1st Battalion (Airborne), 506th Infantry, 101st Airborne Division (Airmobile). *Place and date:* Near Dak To, Quang Trang Province, Republic of Vietnam, 29 June 1968. *Entered service at:* Cleveland, Ohio. *Born:* 13 September 1947, Cleveland, Ohio. *Citation:* For conspicuous gallantry and intrepidity in action at the risk of his life above and beyond the call of duty. Sp4c. Herda (then Pfc.) distinguished himself while serving as a grenadier with Company A. Company A was part of a battalion-size night defensive perimeter when a large enemy force initiated an attack on the friendly units. While other enemy elements provided diversionary fire and indirect weapons fire to the west, a sapper force of approximately 30 men armed with handgrenades and small charges attacked Company A's perimeter from the east. As the sappers were making a last, violent assault, 5 of them charged the position defended by Sp4c. Herda and 2 comrades, 1 of whom was wounded and lay helpless in the bottom of the foxhole. Sp4c. Herda fired at the aggressors until they were within 10 feet of his position and 1 of their grenades landed in the foxhole. He fired 1 last round from his grenade launcher, hitting 1 of the enemy soldiers in the head, and then, with no concern for his safety, Sp4c. Herda immediately covered the blast of the grenade with his body. The explosion wounded him grievously, but his selfless action prevented his 2 comrades from being seriously injured or killed and enabled the remaining defender to kill the other sappers. By his gallantry at the risk of his life in the highest traditions of the military service, Sp4c. Herda has reflected great credit on himself, his unit, and the U.S. Army.

*HIBBS, ROBERT JOHN

Rank and organization: Second Lieutenant, U.S. Army, Company B, 2d Battalion, 28th Infantry, 1st Infantry Division. *Place and date:* Don Dien Lo Ke, Republic of Vietnam, 5 March 1966. *Entered service at:* Des Moines, Iowa. *Born:* 21 April 1943, Omaha, Nebr. *G.O. No.:* 8, 24 February 1967. *Citations:* For conspicuous gallantry and intrepidity at the risk of life above and beyond the call of duty. 2d Lt. Hibbs was in command of a 15-man ambush patrol of the 2d Battalion, when his unit observed a company of Viet Cong advancing along the road toward the 2d Battalion's position. Informing his command post by radio of the impending attack, he prepared his men for the oncoming Viet Cong, emplaced 2 mines in their path and, when the insurgents were within 20 feet of the patrol's position, he fired the 2 antipersonnel mines, wounding or killing half of the enemy company. Then, to cover the withdrawal of his patrol, he threw handgrenades, stepped onto the open road, and opened fire on the remainder of the Viet Cong force of approximately 50 men. Having rejoined his men, he was leading them toward the battalion perimeter when the patrol encountered the rear elements of another Viet Cong company deployed to attack the battalion. With the advantage of surprise, he directed a charge against the Viet Cong, which carried the patrol through the insurgent force, completely disrupting its attack. Learning that a wounded patrol member was wandering in the area between the 2 opposing forces and although moments from safety and wounded in the leg himself, he and a sergeant went back to the battlefield to recover the stricken man. After they maneuvered through the withering fire of 2 Viet Cong machineguns, the sergeant grabbed the dazed soldier and dragged him back toward the friendly lines while 2d Lt. Hibbs remained behind to provide covering fire. Armed with only an M–16 rifle and a pistol, but determined to destroy the enemy positions, he then charged the 2 machinegun emplacements and was struck down. Before succumbing to his mortal wounds, he destroyed the starlight telescopic sight attached to his rifle to prevent its capture and use by the Viet Cong. 2d Lt. Hibb's profound concern for his fellow soldiers, and his intrepidity at the risk of his life above and beyond the call of duty are in the highest traditions of the U.S. Army and reflect great credit upon himself and the Armed Forces of his country.

*HOLCOMB, JOHN NOBLE

Rank and organization: Sergeant, U.S. Army, Company D, 2d Battalion, 7th Cavalry, 1st Cavalry Division. *Place and date:* Near Quan Loi, Republic of Vietnam, 3 December 1968. *Entered service at:* Corvallis, Oreg. *Born:* 11 June 1946, Baker, Oreg. *Citation:* For conspicuous gallantry and intrepidity in action at the risk of his life above and beyond the call of duty. Sgt. Holcomb distinguished himself while serving as a squad leader in Company D during a combat assault mission. Sgt. Holcomb's company assault had landed by helicopter and deployed into a hasty defensive position to organize for a reconnaissance-in-force mission when it was attacked from 3 sides by an estimated battalion-size enemy force. Sgt. Holcomb's squad was directly in the path of the main enemy attack. With complete disregard for the heavy fire, Sgt. Holcomb moved among his men giving encouragement and directing fire on the assaulting enemy. When his machine gunner was knocked out, Sgt. Holcomb seized the weapon, ran to a forward edge of the position, and placed withering fire on the enemy. His gallant actions caused the enemy to withdraw. Sgt. Holcomb treated and carried his wounded to a position of safety and reorganized his defensive sector despite a raging grass fire ignited by the incoming enemy mortar and rocket rounds. When the enemy assaulted the position a second time, Sgt. Holcomb again manned the forward machinegun, devastating the enemy attack and forcing the enemy to again break contact and withdraw. During the enemy withdrawal an enemy rocket hit Sgt. Holcomb's position, destroying his machinegun and severely wounding him. Despite his painful wounds, Sgt. Holcomb crawled through the grass fire and exploding mortar and rocket rounds to move the members of his squad, everyone of whom had been wounded, to more secure positions. Although grievously wounded and sustained solely by his indomitable will and courage, Sgt. Holcomb as the last surviving leader of his platoon organized his men to repel the enemy, crawled to the platoon radio and reported the third enemy assault on his position. His report brought friendly supporting fires on the charging enemy and broke the enemy attack. Sgt. Holcomb's inspiring leadership, fighting spirit, in action at the cost of his life were in keeping with the highest traditions of the military service and reflect great credit on himself, his unit, and the U.S. Army.

HOOPER, JOE R.

Rank and organization: Staff Sergeant, U.S. Army, Company D, 2d Battalion (Airborne), 501st Infantry, 101st Airborne Division. *Place and date:* Near Hue, Republic of Vietnam, 21 February 1968. *Entered service at:* Los Angeles, Calif. *Born:* 8 August 1938, Piedmont, S.C. *Citation:* For conspicuous gallantry and intrepidity in action at the risk of his life above and beyond the call of duty. Staff Sergeant (then Sgt.) Hooper, U.S. Army, distinguished himself while serving as squad leader with Company D. Company D was assaulting a heavily defended enemy position along a river bank when it encountered a withering hail of fire from rockets, machineguns and automatic weapons. S/Sgt. Hooper rallied several men and stormed across the river, overrunning several bunkers on the opposite shore. Thus inspired, the rest of the company moved to the attack. With utter disregard for his own safety, he moved out under the intense fire again and pulled back the wounded, moving them to safety. During this act S/Sgt. Hooper was seriously wounded, but he refused medical aid and returned to his men. With the relentless enemy fire disrupting the attack, he singlehandedly stormed 3 enemy bunkers, destroying them with handgrenade and rifle fire, and shot 2 enemy soldiers who had attacked and wounded the Chaplain. Leading his men forward in a sweep of the area, S/Sgt. Hooper destroyed 3 buildings housing enemy riflemen. At this point he was attacked by a North Vietnamese officer whom he fatally wounded with his bayonet. Finding his men under heavy fire from a house to the front, he proceeded alone to the building, killing its occupants with rifle fire and grenades. By now his initial body wound had been compounded by grenade fragments, yet despite the multiple wounds and loss of blood, he continued to lead his men against the intense enemy fire. As his squad reached the final line of enemy resistance, it received devastating fire from 4 bunkers in line on its left flank. S/Sgt. Hooper gathered several handgrenades and raced down a small trench which ran the length of the bunker line, tossing grenades into each bunker as he passed by, killing all but 2 of the occupants. With these positions destroyed, he concentrated on the last bunkers facing his men, destroying the first with an incendiary grenade and neutralizing 2 more by rifle fire. He then raced across an open field, still under enemy fire, to rescue a wounded man who was trapped in a trench. Upon reaching the man, he was faced by an armed enemy soldier whom he killed with a pistol. Moving his comrade to safety and returning to his men, he neutralized the final pocket of enemy resistance by fatally wounding 3 North Vietnamese officers with rifle fire. S/Sgt. Hooper then established a final line and reorganized his men, not accepting treatment until this was accomplished and not consenting to evacuation until the following morning. His supreme valor, inspiring leadership and heroic self-sacrifice were directly responsible for the company's success and provided a lasting example in personal courage for every man on the field. S/Sgt. Hooper's actions were in keeping with the highest traditions of the military service and reflect great credit upon himself and the U.S. Army.

*HOSKING, CHARLES ERNEST, JR.

Rank and organization: Master Sergeant, U.S. Army, Company A, 5th Special Forces Group (Airborne), 1st Special Forces. *Place and date:* Phuoc Long Province, Republic of Vietnam, 21 March 1967. *Entered service at:* Fort Dix, N.J. *Born:* 12 May 1924, Ramsey, N.J. *Citation:* For conspicuous gallantry and intrepidity in action at the risk of his life above and beyond the call of duty. M/Sgt. Hosking (then Sfc.), Detachment A–302, Company A, greatly distinguished himself while serving as company advisor in the III Corps Civilian Irregular Defense Group Reaction Battalion during combat operations in Don Luan District. A Viet Cong suspect was apprehended and subsequently identified as a Viet Cong sniper. While M/Sgt. Hosking was preparing the enemy for movement back to the base camp, the prisoner suddenly grabbed a handgrenade from M/Sgt. Hosking's belt, armed the grenade, and started running towards the company command group which consisted of 2 Americans and 2 Vietnamese who were standing a few feet away. Instantly realizing that the enemy intended to kill the other men, M/Sgt. Hosking immediately leaped upon the Viet Cong's back. With utter disregard for his personal safety, he grasped the Viet Cong in a "Bear Hug" forcing the grenade against the enemy soldier's chest. He then wrestled the Viet Cong to the ground and covered the enemy's body with his body until the grenade detonated. The blast instantly killed both M/Sgt. Hosking and the Viet Cong. By absorbing the full force of the exploding grenade with his body and that of the enemy, he saved the other members of his command group from death or serious injury. M/Sgt. Hosking's risk of his life above and beyond the call of duty are in the highest tradition of the U.S. Army and reflect great credit upon himself and the Armed Forces of his country.

HOWARD, JIMMIE E.

Rank and organization: Gunnery Sergeant (then S/Sgt.) U.S. Marine Corps, Company C, 1st Reconnaissance Battalion, 1st Marine Division. *Place and date:* Republic of Vietnam, 16 June 1966. *Entered service at:* Burlington, Iowa. *Born:* 27 July 1929, Burlington, Iowa. *Citation:* For conspicuous gallantry and intrepidity at the risk of his own life above and beyond the call of duty. G/Sgt. Howard and his 18-man platoon were occupying an observation post deep within enemy-controlled territory. Shortly after midnight a Viet Cong force of estimated battalion size approached the marines' position and launched a vicious attack with small arms, automatic weapons, and mortar fire. Reacting swiftly and fearlessly in the face of the overwhelming odds, G/Sgt. Howard skillfully organized his small but determined force into a tight perimeter defense and calmly moved from position to position to direct his men's fire. Throughout the night, during assault after assault, his courageous example and firm leadership inspired and motivated his men to withstand the unrelenting fury of the hostile fire in the seemingly hopeless situation. He constantly shouted encouragement to his men and exhibited imagination and resourcefulness in directing their return fire. When fragments of an exploding enemy grenade wounded him severely and prevented him from moving his legs, he distributed his ammunition to the remaining members of his platoon and proceeded to maintain radio communications and direct air strikes on the enemy with uncanny accuracy. At dawn, despite the fact that 5 men were killed and all but 1 wounded, his beleaguered platoon was still in command of its position. When evacuation helicopters approached his position, G/Sgt. Howard warned them away and called for additional air strikes and directed devastating small-arms fire and air strikes against enemy automatic weapons positions in order to make the landing zone as secure as possible. Through his extraordinary courage and resolute fighting spirit, G/Sgt. Howard was largely responsible for preventing the loss of his entire platoon. His valiant leadership and courageous fighting spirit served to inspire the men of his platoon to heroic endeavor in the face of overwhelming odds, and reflect the highest credit upon G/Sgt. Howard, the Marine Corps, and the U.S. Naval Service.

HOWARD, ROBERT L.

Rank and organization: First Lieutenant, U.S. Army, 5th Special Forces Group (Airborne), 1st Special Forces. *Place and date:* Republic of Vietnam, 30 December 1968. *Entered service at:* Montgomery, Ala. *Born:* 11 July 1939, Opelika, Ala. *Citation:* For conspicuous gallantry and intrepidity in action at the risk of his life above and beyond the call of duty. 1st Lt. Howard (then Sfc.), distinguished himself while serving as platoon sergeant of an American-Vietnamese platoon which was on a mission to rescue a missing American soldier in enemy controlled territory in the Republic of Vietnam. The platoon had left its helicopter landing zone and was moving out on its mission when it was attacked by an estimated 2-company force. During the initial engagement, 1st Lt. Howard was wounded and his weapon destroyed by a grenade explosion. 1st Lt. Howard saw his platoon leader had been wounded seriously and was exposed to fire. Although unable to walk, and weaponless, 1st Lt. Howard unhesitatingly crawled through a hail of fire to retrieve his wounded leader. As 1st Lt. Howard was administering first aid and removing the officer's equipment, an enemy bullet struck 1 of the ammunition pouches on the lieutenant's belt, detonating several magazines of ammunition. 1st Lt. Howard momentarily sought cover and then realizing that he must rejoin the platoon, which had been disorganized by the enemy attack, he again began dragging the seriously wounded officer toward the platoon area. Through his outstanding example of indomitable courage and bravery,

1st Lt. Howard was able to rally the platoon into an organized defense force. With complete disregard for his safety, 1st Lt. Howard crawled from position to position, administering first aid to the wounded, giving encouragement to the defenders and directing their fire on the encircling enemy. For 3½ hours 1st Lt. Howard's small force and supporting aircraft successfully repulsed enemy attacks and finally were in sufficient control to permit the landing of rescue helicopters. 1st Lt. Howard personally supervised the loading of his men and did not leave the bullet-swept landing zone until all were aboard safely. 1st Lt. Howard's gallantry in action, his complete devotion to the welfare of his men at the risk of his life were in keeping with the highest traditions of the military service and reflect great credit on himself, his unit, and the U.S. Army.

*HOWE, JAMES D.

Rank and organization: Lance Corporal, U.S. Marine Corps, Company I, 3d Battalion, 7th Marines, 1st Marine Division. *Place and date:* Republic of Vietnam, 6 May 1970. *Entered service at:* Fort Jackson, S.C. *Born:* 17 December 1948, Six Mile, Pickens, S.C. *Citation:* For conspicuous gallantry and intrepidity at the risk of his life above and beyond the call of duty while serving as a rifleman with Company I, during operations against enemy forces. In the early morning hours L/Cpl. Howe and 2 other marines were occupying a defensive position in a sandy beach area fronted by bamboo thickets. Enemy sappers suddenly launched a grenade attack against the position, utilizing the cover of darkness to carry out their assault. Following the initial explosions of the grenades, L/Cpl. Howe and his 2 comrades moved to a more advantageous position in order to return suppressive fire. When an enemy grenade landed in their midst, L/Cpl. Howe immediately shouted a warning and then threw himself upon the deadly missile, thereby protecting the lives of the fellow marines. His heroic and selfless action was in keeping with the finest traditions of the Marine Corps and of the U.S. Naval Service. He valiantly gave his life in the service of his country.

*INGALLS, GEORGE ALAN

Rank and organization: Specialist Fourth Class, U.S. Army, Company A, 2d Battalion, 5th Cavalry, 1st Cavalry Division (Airmobile). *Place and date:* Near Duc Pho, Republic of Vietnam, 16 April 1967. *Entered service at:* Los Angeles, Calif. *Born:* 9 March 1946, Hanford, Calif. *Citation:* For conspicuous gallantry and intrepidity in action at the risk of his life above and beyond the call of duty. Sp4c. Ingalls, a member of Company A, accompanied his squad on a night ambush mission. Shortly after the ambush was established, an enemy soldier entered the killing zone and was shot when he tried to evade capture. Other enemy soldiers were expected to enter the area, and the ambush was maintained in the same location. Two quiet hours passed without incident, then suddenly a handgrenade was thrown from the nearby dense undergrowth into the center of the squad's position. The grenade did not explode, but shortly thereafter a second grenade landed directly between Sp4c. Ingalls and a nearby comrade. Although he could have jumped to a safe position, Sp4c. Ingalls, in a spontaneous act of great courage, threw himself on the grenade and absorbed its full blast. The explosion mortally wounded Sp4c. Ingalls, but his heroic action saved the lives of the remaining members of his squad. His gallantry and selfless devotion to his comrades are in keeping with the highest traditions of the military service and reflects great credit upon Sp4c. Ingalls, his unit, and the U.S. Army.

JACKSON, JOE M.

Rank and organization: Lieutenant Colonel, U.S. Air Force, 311th Air Commando Squadron, Da Nang, Republic of Vietnam. *Place and date:* Kham Duc, Republic of Vietnam, 12 May 1968. *Entered service at:* Newman, Ga. *Born:* 14 March 1923, Newman, Ga. *Citation:* For conspicuous gallantry and intrepidity in action at the risk of his life above and beyond the call of duty. Lt. Col. Jackson distinguished himself as pilot of a C–123 aircraft. Lt. Col. Jackson volunteered to attempt the rescue of a 3-man USAF Combat Control Team from the special forces camp at Kham Duc. Hostile forces had overrun the forward outpost and established gun positions on the airstrip. They were raking the camp with small arms, mortars, light and heavy automatic weapons, and recoilless rifle fire. The camp was engulfed in flames and ammunition dumps were continuously exploding and littering the runway with debris. In addition, 8 aircraft had been destroyed by the intense enemy fire and 1 aircraft remained on the runway reducing its usable length to only 2,200 feet. To further complicate the landing, the weather was deteriorating rapidly, thereby permitting only 1 airstrike prior to his landing. Although fully aware of the extreme danger and likely failure of such an attempt. Lt. Col. Jackson elected to land his aircraft and attempt to rescue. Displaying superb airmanship and extraordinary heroism, he landed his aircraft near the point where the combat control team was reported to be hiding. While on the ground, his aircraft was the target of intense hostile fire. A rocket landed in front of the nose of the aircraft but failed to explode. Once the combat control team was aboard, Lt. Col. Jackson succeeded in getting airborne despite the hostile fire directed across the runway in front of his aircraft. Lt. Col. Jackson's profound concern for his fellowmen, at the risk of his life above and beyond the call of duty are in keeping with the highest traditions of the U.S. Air Force and reflect great credit upon himself, and the Armed Forces of his country.

JACOBS, JACK H.

Rank and organization: Captain, U.S. Army, U.S. Army Element, U.S. Military Assistance Command, Republic of Vietnam. *Place and date:* Kien Phong Province, Republic of Vietnam, 9 March 1968. *Entered service at:* Trenton, N.J. *Born:* 2 August 1945, Brooklyn, N.Y. *Citation:* For conspicuous gallantry and intrepidity in action at the risk of his life above and beyond the call of duty. Capt. Jacobs (then 1st Lt.), Infantry, distinguished himself while serving as assistant battalion advisor, 2d Battalion, 16th Infantry, 9th Infantry Division, Army of the Republic of Vietnam. The 2d Battalion was advancing to contact when it came under intense heavy machinegun and mortar fire from a Viet Cong battalion positioned in well fortified bunkers. As the 2d Battalion deployed into attack formation its advance was halted by devastating fire. Capt. Jacobs, with the command element of the lead company, called for and directed air strikes on the enemy positions to facilitate a renewed attack. Due to the intensity of the enemy fire and heavy casualties to the command group, including the company commander, the attack stopped and the friendly troops became disorganized. Although wounded by mortar fragments, Capt. Jacobs assumed command of the allied company, ordered a withdrawal from the exposed position and established a defensive perimeter. Despite profuse bleeding from head wounds which impaired his vision, Capt. Jacobs, with complete disregard for his safety, returned under intense fire to evacuate a seriously wounded advisor to the safety of a wooded area where he administered lifesaving first aid. He then returned through heavy automatic weapons fire to evacuate the wounded company commander. Capt. Jacobs made repeated trips across the fire-swept open rice paddies evacuating wounded and their weapons. On 3 separate occasions, Capt. Jacobs contacted and drove off Viet Cong squads who were searching for allied wounded and weapons, singlehandedly killing 3 and wounding several others. His gallant actions and extraordinary heroism saved the lives of 1 U.S. advisor and 13 allied soldiers. Through his effort the allied company was restored to an effective fighting unit and prevented defeat of the friendly forces by a strong and determined enemy. Capt. Jacobs, by his gallantry and bravery in action in the highest traditions of the military service, has reflected great credit upon himself, his unit, and the U.S. Army.

JENKINS, DON J.

Rank and organization: Staff Sergeant, U.S. Army, Company A, 2d Battalion, 39th Infantry, 9th Infantry Division. *Place and date:* Kien Phong Province, Republic of Vietnam, 6 January 1969. *Entered service at:* Nashville, Tenn. *Born:* 18 April 1948, Quality, Ky. *Citation:* For conspicuous gallantry and intrepidity in action at the risk of his life above and beyond the call of duty. S/Sgt. Jenkins (then Pfc.), Company A, distinguished himself while serving as a machine gunner on a reconnaissance mission. When his company came under heavy cross-fire from an enemy complex, S/Sgt. Jenkins unhesitatingly maneuvered forward to a perilously exposed position and began placing suppressive fire on the enemy. When his own machinegun jammed, he immediately obtained a rifle and continued to fire into the enemy bunkers until his machinegun was made operative by his assistant. He exposed himself to extremely heavy fire when he repeatedly both ran and crawled across open terrain to obtain resupplies of ammunition until he had exhausted all that was available for his machinegun. Displaying tremendous presence of mind, he then armed himself with 2 antitank weapons and, by himself, maneuvered through the hostile fusillade to within 20 meters of an enemy bunker to destroy that position. After moving back to the friendly defensive perimeter long enough to secure yet another weapon, a grenade launcher, S/Sgt. Jenkins moved forward to a position providing no protection and resumed placing accurate fire on the enemy until his ammunition was again exhausted. During this time he was seriously wounded by shrapnel. Undaunted and displaying great courage, he moved forward 100 meters to aid a friendly element that was pinned down only a few meters from the enemy. This he did with complete disregard for his own wound and despite having been advised that several previous rescue attempts had failed at the cost of the life of 1 and the wounding of others. Ignoring the continuing intense fire and his painful wounds, and hindered by darkness, he made 3 trips to the beleaguered unit, each time pulling a wounded comrade back to safety. S/Sgt. Jenkins' extraordinary valor, dedication, and indomitable spirit inspired his fellow soldiers to repulse the determined enemy attack and ultimately to defeat the larger force. S/Sgt. Jenkins risk of his life reflect great credit upon himself, his unit, and the U.S. Army.

*JENKINS, ROBERT H., JR.

Rank and organization: Private First Class, U.S. Marine Corps, 3d Reconnaissance Battalion, 3d Marine Division (Rein), FMF. *Place and date:* Fire Support Base Argonne, Republic of Vietnam, 5 March 1969. *Entered service at:* Jacksonville, Fla. *Born:* 1 June 1948, Interlachen, Fla. *Citation:* For conspicuous gallantry and intrepidity at the risk of his life above and beyond the call of duty while serving as a machine gunner with Company C, 3d Reconnaissance Battalion, in connection with operations against enemy forces. Early in the morning Pfc. Jenkins' 12-man reconnaissance team was occupying a defensive position at Fire Support Base Argonne south of the Demilitarized Zone. Suddenly, the marines were assaulted by a North Vietnamese Army platoon employing mortars, automatic weapons, and handgrenades. Reacting instantly, Pfc. Jenkins and another marine quickly moved into a 2-man fighting emplacement, and as they boldly delivered accurate machinegun fire against the enemy, a North Vietnamese soldier threw a handgrenade into the friendly emplacement. Fully realizing the inevitable results of his actions, Pfc. Jenkins quickly seized his comrade, and pushing the man to the ground, he leaped on top of the marine to shield him from the explosion. Absorbing the full impact of the detonation, Pfc. Jenkins was seriously injured and subsequently succumbed to his wounds. His courage, inspiring valor and selfless devotion to duty saved a fellow marine from serious injury or possible death and upheld the highest traditions of the Marine Corps and the U.S. Naval Service. He gallantly gave his life for his country.

JENNINGS, DELBERT O.

Rank and organization: Staff Sergeant, U.S. Army, Company C, 1st Battalion (Airborne), 12th Cavalry, 1st Air Cavalry Division. *Place and date:* Kim Song Valley, Republic of Vietnam, 27 December 1966. *Entered service at:* San Francisco, Calif. *Born:* 23 July 1936, Silver City, N. Mex. *Citation:* For conspicuous gallantry and intrepidity at the risk of life above and beyond the call of duty. Part of Company C was defending an artillery position when attacked by a North Vietnamese Army regiment supported by mortar, recoilless-rifle, and machinegun fire. At the outset, S/Sgt. Jennings sprang to his bunker, astride the main attack route, and slowed the on-coming enemy wave with highly effective machinegun fire. Despite a tenacious defense in which he killed at least 12 of the enemy, his squad was forced to the rear. After covering the withdrawal of the squad, he rejoined his men, destroyed an enemy demolition crew about to blow up a nearby howitzer, and killed 3 enemy soldiers at his initial bunker position. Ordering his men back into a secondary position, he again covered their withdrawal, killing 1 enemy with the butt of his weapon. Observing that some of the defenders were unaware of an enemy force in their rear, he raced through a fire-swept area to warn the men, turn their fire on the enemy, and lead them into the secondary perimeter. Assisting in the defense of the new position, he aided the air-landing of reinforcements by throwing white phosphorous grenades on the landing zone despite dangerously silhouetting himself with the light. After helping to repulse the final enemy assaults, he led a group of volunteers well beyond friendly lines to an area where 8 seriously wounded men lay. Braving enemy sniper fire and ignoring the presence of boobytraps in the area, they recovered the 8 men who would have probably perished without early medical treatment. S/Sgt. Jenning's extraordinary heroism and inspirational leadership saved the lives of many of his comrades and contributed greatly to the defeat of a superior enemy force. His actions stand with the highest traditions of the military profession and reflect great credit upon himself, his unit, and the U.S. Army.

*JIMENEZ, JOSE FRANCISCO

Rank and organization: Lance Corporal, U.S. Marine Corps, Company K, 3d Battalion, 7th Marines, 1st Marine Division. *Place and date:* Quang Nam Province, Republic of Vietnam, 28 August 1969. *Entered service at:* Phoenix, Ariz. *Born:* 20 March 1946, Mexico City, Mex. *Citation:* For conspicuous gallantry and intrepidity at the risk of his life above and beyond the call of duty while serving as a fire team leader with Company K, in operations against the enemy. L/Cpl. Jimenez' unit came under heavy attack by North Vietnamese soldiers concealed in well camouflaged emplacements. L/Cpl. Jimenez reacted by seizing the initiative and plunging forward toward the enemy positions. He personally destroyed several enemy personnel and silenced an antiaircraft weapon. Shouting encouragement to his companions, L/Cpl. Jimenez continued his aggressive forward movement. He slowly maneuvered to within 10 feet of hostile soldiers who were firing automatic weapons from a trench and, in the face of vicious enemy fire, destroyed the position. Although he was by now the target of concentrated fire from hostile gunners intent upon halting his assault, L/Cpl. Jimenez continued to press forward. As he moved to attack another enemy soldier, he was mortally wounded. L/Cpl. Jimenez' indomitable courage, aggressive fighting spirit and unfaltering devotion to duty upheld the highest traditions of the Marine Corps and of the U.S. Naval Service.

JOEL, LAWRENCE

Rank and organization: Specialist Sixth Class (then Sp5c), U.S. Army, Headquarters and Headquarters Company, 1st Battalion (Airborne), 503d Infantry, 173d Airborne Brigade. *Place and date:* Republic of Vietnam, 8 November 1965, *Entered service at:* New York City, N.Y. *G.O. No.:* 15, 5 April 1967. *Born:* 22 February 1928, Winston-Salem, N.C. *Citation:* For conspicuous gallantry and intrepidity at the risk of life above and beyond the call of duty. Sp6c. Joel demonstrated indomitable courage, determination, and professional skill when a numerically superior and well-concealed Viet Cong element launched a vicious attack which wounded or killed nearly every man in the lead squad of the company. After treating the men wounded by the initial burst of gunfire, he bravely moved forward to assist others who were wounded while proceeding to their objective. While moving from man to man, he was struck in the right leg by machinegun fire. Although painfully wounded his desire to aid his fellow soldiers transcended all personal feeling. He bandaged his own wound and self-administered morphine to deaden the pain enabling him to continue his dangerous undertaking. Through this period of time, he constantly shouted words of encouragement to all around him. Then, completely ignoring the warnings of others, and his pain, he continued his search for wounded, exposing himself to hostile fire; and, as bullets dug up the dirt around him, he held plasma bottles high while kneeling completely engrossed in his life saving mission. Then, after being struck a second time and with a bullet lodged in his thigh, he dragged himself over the battlefield and succeeded in treating 13 more men before his medical supplies ran out. Displaying resourcefulness, he saved the life of 1 man by placing a plastic bag over a severe chest wound to congeal the blood. As 1 of the platoons pursued the Viet Cong, an insurgent force in concealed positions opened fire on the platoon and wounded many more soldiers. With a new stock of medical supplies, Sp6c. Joel again shouted words of encouragement as he crawled through an intense hail of gunfire to the wounded men. After the 24 hour battle subsided and the Viet Cong dead numbered 410, snipers continued to harass the company. Throughout the long battle, Sp6c. Joel never lost sight of his mission as a medical aidman and continued to comfort and treat the wounded until his own evacuation was ordered. His meticulous attention to duty saved a large number of lives and his unselfish, daring example under most adverse conditions was an inspiration to all. Sp6c. Joel's profound concern for his fellow soldiers, at the risk of his life above and beyond the call of duty are in the highest traditions of the U.S. Army and reflect great credit upon himself and the Armed Forces of his country.

JOHNSON, DWIGHT H.

Rank and organization: Specialist Fifth Class, U.S. Army, Company B, 1st Battalion, 69th Armor, 4th Infantry Division. *Place and date:* Near Dak To, Kontum Province, Republic of Vietnam, 15 January 1968. *Entered service at:* Detriot, Mich. *Born:* 7 May 1947, Detroit, Mich. *Citation:* For conspicuous gallantry and intrepidity at the risk of his life above and beyond the call of duty. Sp5c. Johnson, a tank driver with Company B, was a member of a reaction force moving to aid other elements of his platoon, which was in heavy contact with a battalion size North Vietnamese force. Sp5c. Johnson's tank, upon reaching the point of contact, threw a track and became immobilized. Realizing that he could do no more as a driver, he climbed out of the vehicle, armed only with a .45 caliber pistol. Despite intense hostile fire, Sp5c. Johnson killed several enemy soldiers before he had expended his ammunition. Returning to his tank through a heavy volume of antitank rocket, small arms and automatic weapons fire, he obtained a submachinegun with which to continue his fight against the advancing enemy. Armed with this weapon, Sp5c. Johnson again braved deadly enemy fire to return to the center of the ambush site where he courageously eliminated more of the determined foe. Engaged in extremely close combat when the last of his ammunition was expended, he killed an enemy soldier with the stock end of his submachinegun. Now weaponless, Sp5c. Johnson ignored the enemy fire around him, climbed into his platoon sergeant's tank, extricated a wounded crewmember and carried him to an armored personnel carrier. He then returned to the same tank and assisted in firing the main gun until it jammed. In a magnificent display of courage, Sp5c. Johnson exited the tank and again armed only with a .45 caliber pistol, engaged several North Vietnamese troops in close proximity to the vehicle. Fighting his way through devastating fire and remounting his own immobilized tank, he remained fully exposed to the enemy as he bravely and skillfully engaged them with the tank's externally-mounted .50 caliber machinegun; where he remained until the situation was brought under control. Sp5c. Johnson's profound concern for his fellow soldiers, at the risk of his life above and beyond the call of duty are in keeping with the highest traditions of the military service and reflect great credit upon himself and the U.S. Army.

*JOHNSON, RALPH H.

Rank and organization: Private First Class, U.S. Marine Corps, Company A, 1st Reconnaissance Battalion, 1st Marine Division (Rein), FMF. *Place and date:* Near the Quan Duc Valley, Republic of Vietnam, 5 March 1968. *Entered service at:* Oakland, Calif. *Born:* 11 January 1949, Charleston, S.C. *Citation:* For conspicuous gallantry and intrepidity at the risk of his life above and beyond the call of duty while serving as a reconnaissance scout with Company A, in action against the North Vietnamese Army and Viet Cong forces. In the early morning hours during Operation ROCK, Pfc. Johnson was a member of a 15-man reconnaissance patrol manning an observation post on Hill 146 overlooking the Quan Duc Valley deep in enemy controlled territory. They were attacked by a platoon-size hostile force employing automatic weapons, satchel charges and handgrenades. Suddenly, a handgrenade landed in the 3-man fighting hole occupied by Pfc. Johnson and 2 fellow marines. Realizing the inherent danger to his 2 comrades, he shouted a warning and unhesitatingly hurled himself upon the explosive device. When the grenade exploded, Pfc. Johnson absorbed the tremendous impact of the blast and was killed instantly. His prompt and heroic act saved the life of 1 marine at the cost of his life and undoubtedly prevented the enemy from penetrating his sector of the patrol's perimeter. Pfc. Johnson's courage, inspiring valor and selfless devotion to duty were in keeping with the highest traditions of the Marine Corps and the U.S. Naval Service. He gallantly gave his life for his country.

*JOHNSTON, DONALD R.

Rank and organization: Specialist Fourth Class, U.S. Army, Company D, 1st Battalion, 8th Cavalry, 1st Cavalry Division. *Place and date:* Tay Ninh Province, Republic of Vietnam, 21 March 1969. *Entered service at:* Columbus, Ga. *Born:* 19 November 1947, Columbus, Ga. *Citation:*

For conspicuous gallantry and intrepidity in action at the risk of his life above and beyond the call of duty. Sp4c. Johnston distinguished himself while serving as a mortarman with Company D, at a fire support base in Tay Ninh Province. Sp4c. Johnston's company was in defensive positions when it came under a devastating rocket and mortar attack. Under cover of the bombardment, enemy sappers broke through the defensive perimeter and began hurling explosive charges into the main defensive bunkers. Sp4c. Johnston and 6 of his comrades had moved from their exposed positions to 1 of the bunkers to continue their fight against the enemy attackers. As they were firing from the bunker, an enemy soldier threw 3 explosive charges into their position. Sensing the danger to his comrades, Sp4c. Johnston, with complete disregard for his safety, hurled himself onto the explosive charges, smothering the detonations with his body and shielding his fellow soldiers from the blast. His heroic action saved the lives of 6 of his comrades. Sp4c. Johnston's concern for his fellow men at the cost of his life were in the highest traditions of the military service and reflect great credit upon himself, his unit, and the U.S. Army.

*JONES, WILLIAM A., III

Rank and organization: Colonel, U.S. Air Force, 602d Special Operations Squadron, Nakon Phanom Royal Thai Air Force Base, Thailand. *Place and date:* Near Dong Hoi, North Vietnam, 1 September 1968. *Entered service at:* Charlottesville, Va. *Born:* 31 May 1922, Norfolk, Va. *Citation:* For conspicuous gallantry and intrepidity in action at the risk of his life above and beyond the call of duty. Col. Jones distinguished himself as the pilot of an A–1H Skyraider aircraft near Dong Hoi, North Vietnam. On that day, as the on-scene commander in the attempted rescue of a downed U.S. pilot, Col. Jones' aircraft was repeatedly hit by heavy and accurate antiaircraft fire. On one of his low passes, Col. Jones felt an explosion beneath his aircraft and his cockpit rapidly filled with smoke. With complete disregard of the possibility that his aircraft might still be burning, he unhesitatingly continued his search for the downed pilot. On this pass, he sighted the survivor and a multiple-barrel gun position firing at him from near the top of a karst formation. He could not attack the gun position on that pass for fear he would endanger the downed pilot. Leaving himself exposed to the gun position, Col. Jones attacked the position with cannon and rocket fire on 2 successive passes. On his second pass, the aircraft was hit with multiple rounds of automatic weapons fire. One round impacted the Yankee Extraction System rocket mounted directly behind the headrest, igniting the rocket. His aircraft was observed to burst into flames in the center fuselage section, with flames engulfing the cockpit area. He pulled the extraction handle, jettisoning the canopy. The influx of fresh air made the fire burn with greater intensity for a few moments, but since the rocket motor had already burned, the extraction system did not pull Col. Jones from the aircraft. Despite searing pains from severe burns sustained on his arms, hands, neck, shoulders, and face, Col. Jones pulled his aircraft into a climb and attempted to transmit the location of the downed pilot and the enemy gun position to the other aircraft in the area. His calls were blocked by other aircraft transmissions repeatedly directing him to bail out and within seconds his transmitters were disabled and he could receive only on 1 channel. Completely disregarding his injuries, he elected to fly his crippled aircraft back to his base and pass on essential information for the rescue rather than bail out. Col. Jones successfully landed his heavily damaged aircraft and passed the information to a debriefing officer while on the operating table. As a result of his heroic actions and complete disregard for his personal safety, the downed pilot was rescued later in the day. Col. Jones' profound concern for his fellow man at the risk of his life, above and beyond the call of duty, are in keeping with the highest traditions of the U.S. Air Force and reflect great credit upon himself and the Armed Forces of his country.

*KAROPCZYC, STEPHEN EDWARD

Rank and organization: First Lieutenant, U.S. Army, Company A, 2d Battalion, 35th Infantry, 25th Infantry Division. *Place and date:* Kontum Province, Republic of Vietnam, 12 March 1967. *Entered service at:* Bethpage, N.Y. *Born:* 5 March 1944, New York, N.Y. *Citation:* For conspicuous gallantry and intrepidity in action at the risk of his life above and beyond the call of duty. While leading the 3d Platoon, Company A, on a flanking maneuver against a superior enemy force, 1st Lt. Karopczyc observed that his lead element was engaged with a small enemy unit along his route. Aware of the importance of quickly pushing through to the main enemy force in order to provide relief for a hard-pressed friendly platoon, he dashed through the intense enemy fire into the open and hurled colored smoke grenades to designate the foe for attack by helicopter gunships. He moved among his men to embolden their advance, and he guided their attack by marking enemy locations with bursts of fire from his own weapon. His forceful leadership quickened the advance, forced the enemy to retreat, and allowed his unit to close with the main hostile force. Continuing the deployment of his platoon, he constantly exposed himself as he ran from man to man to give encouragement and to direct their efforts. A shot from an enemy sniper struck him above the heart but he refused aid for this serious injury, plugging the bleeding wound with his finger until it could be properly dressed. As the enemy strength mounted, he ordered his men to organize a defensive position in and around some abandoned bunkers where he conducted a defense against the increasingly strong enemy attacks. After several hours, a North Vietnamese soldier hurled a handgrenade to within a few feet of 1st Lt. Karopczyc and 2 other wounded men. Although his position protected him, he leaped up to cover the deadly grenade with a steel helmet. It exploded to drive fragments into 1st Lt. Karopczyc's legs, but his action prevented further injury to the 2 wounded men. Severely weakened by his multiple wounds, he continued to direct the actions of his men until he succumbed 2 hours later. 1st Lt. Karopczyc's heroic leadership, unyielding perseverance, and selfless devotion to his men were directly responsible for the successful and spirited action of his platoon throughout the battle and are in keeping with the highest traditions of the U.S. Army.

*KAWAMURA, TERRY TERUO

Rank and organization: Corporal, U.S. Army, 173d Engineer Company, 173d Airborne Brigade, Republic of Vietnam. *Place and date:* Camp Radcliff, Republic of Vietnam, 20 March 1969. *Entered service at:* Oahu, Hawaii. *Born:* 10 December 1949, Wahiawa, Oahu, Hawaii. *Citation:* For conspicuous gallantry and intrepidity in action at the risk of his life above and beyond the call of duty. Cpl. Kawamura distinguished himself by heroic action while serving as a member of the 173d Engineer Company. An enemy demolition team infiltrated the unit quarters area and opened fire with automatic weapons. Disregarding the intense fire, Cpl. Kawamura ran for his weapon. At that moment, a violent explosion tore a hole in the roof and stunned the occupants of the room. Cpl. Kawamura jumped to his feet, secured his weapon and, as he ran toward the door to return the enemy fire, he observed that another explosive charge had been thrown through the hole in the roof to the floor. He immediately realized that 2 stunned fellow soldiers were in great peril and shouted a warning. Although in a position to escape, Cpl. Kawamura unhesitatingly wheeled around and threw himself on the charge. In completely disregarding his safety, Cpl. Kawamura prevented serious injury or death to several members of his unit. The extraordinary courage and selflessness displayed by Cpl. Kawamura are in the highest traditions of the military service and reflect great credit upon himself, his unit, and the U.S. Army.

KAYS, KENNETH MICHAEL

Rank and organization: Private First Class, U.S. Army, Headquarters and Headquarters Company, 1st Battalion, 506th Infantry, 101st Airborne Division. *Place and date:* Thua Thien Province, Republic of Vietnam, 7 May 1970. *Entered service at:* Fairfield, Ill. *Born:* 22 September 1949, Mount Vernon, Ill. *Citation:* For conspicuous gallantry intrepidity in action at the risk of his life above and beyond the call of duty. Pfc. (then Pvt.) Kays distinguished himself while serving as a medical aidman with Company D, 1st Battalion, 101st Airborne Division near Fire Support Base Maureen. A heavily armed force of enemy sappers and infantrymen assaulted Company D's night defensive position, wounding and killing a number of its members. Disregarding the intense enemy fire and ground assault, Pfc. Kays began moving toward the perimeter to assist his fallen comrades. In doing so he became the target of concentrated enemy fire and explosive charges, 1 of which severed the lower portion of his left leg. After applying a tourniquet to his leg, Pfc. Kays moved to the fire-swept perimeter, administered medical aid to 1 of the wounded, and helped move him to an area of relative safety. Despite his severe wound and excruciating pain, Pfc. Kays returned to the perimeter in search of other wounded men. He treated another wounded comrade, and, using his own body as a shield against enemy bullets and fragments, moved him to safety. Although weakened from a great loss of blood, Pfc. Kays resumed his heroic lifesaving efforts by moving beyond the company's perimeter into enemy held territory to treat a wounded American lying there. Only after his fellow wounded soldiers had been treated and evacuated did Pfc. Kays allow his own wounds to be treated. These courageous acts by Pfc. Kays resulted in the saving of numerous lives and inspired others in his company to repel the enemy. Pfc. Kays' heroism at the risk of his life are in keeping with the highest traditions of the service and reflect great credit on him, his unit, and the U.S. Army.

*KEDENBURG, JOHN J.

Rank and organization: Specialist Fifth Class, U.S. Army, 5th Special Forces Group (Airborne), 1st Special Forces. *Place and date:* Republic of Vietnam, 13 June 1968. *Entered service at:* Brooklyn, N.Y. *Born:* 31 July 1946, Brooklyn, N.Y. *Citation:* For conspicuous gallantry and intrepidity in action at the risk of his life above and beyond the call of duty. Sp5c. Kedenburg, U.S. Army, Command and Control Detachment North, Forward Operating Base 2, 5th Special Forces Group (Airborne), distinguished himself while serving as advisor to a long-range reconnaissance team of South Vietnamese irregular troops. The team's mission was to conduct counterguerrilla operations deep within enemy-held territory. Prior to reaching the day's objective, the team was attacked and encircled by a battalion-size North Vietnamese Army force. Sp5c. Kedenburg assumed immediate command of the team which succeeded, after a fierce fight, in breaking out of the encirclement. As the team moved through thick jungle to a position from which it could be extracted by helicopter, Sp5c. Kedenburg conducted a gallant rear guard fight against the pursuing enemy and called for tactical air support and rescue helicopters. His withering fire against the enemy permitted the team to reach a preselected landing zone with the loss of only 1 man, who was unaccounted for. Once in the landing zone, Sp5c. Kedenburg deployed the team into a perimeter defense against the numerically superior enemy force. When tactical air support arrived, he skillfully directed air strikes against the enemy, suppressing their fire so that helicopters could hover over the area and drop slings to be used in the extraction of the team. After half of the team was extracted by helicopter, Sp5c. Kedenburg and the remaining 3 members of the team harnessed themselves to the sling on a second hovering helicopter. Just as the helicopter was to lift them out of the area, the South Vietnamese team member who had been unaccounted for after the initial encounter with the enemy appeared in the landing zone. Sp5c. Kedenburg unhesitatingly gave up his place in the sling to the man and directed the helicopter pilot to leave the area. He then continued to engage the enemy who were swarming into the landing zone, killing 6 enemy soldiers before he was overpowered. Sp5c. Kedenburg's inspiring leadership, consummate courage and willing self-sacrifice permitted his small team to inflict heavy casualties on the enemy and escape almost certain annihilation. His actions reflect great credit upon himself and the U.S. Army.

*KEITH, MIGUEL

Rank and organization: Lance Corporal, U.S. Marine Corps, Combined Action Platoon 1-3-2, III Marine Amphibious Force. *Place and date:* Quang Ngai Province, Republic of Vietnam, 8 May 1970. *Entered service at:* Omaha, Nebr. *Born:* 2 June 1951, San Antonio, Tex. *Citation:* For conspicuous gallantry and intrepidity at the risk of his life above and beyond the call of duty while serving as a machine gunner with Combined Action Platoon 1–3–2. During the early morning L/Cpl. Keith was seriously wounded when his platoon was subjected to a heavy ground attack by a greatly outnumbering enemy force. Despite his painful wounds, he ran across the fire-swept terrain to check the security of vital defensive positions and then, while completely exposed to view, proceeded to deliver a hail of devastating machinegun fire against the enemy. Determined to stop 5 of the enemy soldiers approaching the command post, he rushed forward, firing as he advanced. He succeeded in disposing of 3 of the attackers and in dispersing the remaining 2. At this point, a grenade detonated near L/Cpl. Keith, knocking him to the ground and inflicting further severe wounds. Fighting pain and weakness from loss of blood, he again braved the concentrated hostile fire to charge an estimated 25 enemy soldiers who were massing to attack. The vigor of his assault and his well placed fire eliminated 4 of the enemy soldiers while the remainder fled for cover. During this valiant effort, he was mortally wounded by an enemy soldier. By his courageous and inspiring performance in the face of almost overwhelming odds, L/Cpl. Keith contributed in large measure to the success of his platoon in routing a numerically superior enemy force, and upheld the finest traditions of the Marine Corps and of the U.S. Naval Service.

KELLER, LEONARD B.

Rank and organization: Sergeant, U.S. Army, Company A, 3d Battalion, 60th Infantry, 9th Infantry Division. *Place and date:* Ap Bac Zone, Republic of Vietnam, 2 May 1967. *Entered service at:* Chicago, Ill. *Born:* 25 February 1947, Rockford, Ill. *Citation:* For conspicuous gallantry and intrepidity in action at the risk of his life above and beyond the call of duty. Sweeping through an area where an enemy ambush had occurred earlier, Sgt. Keller's unit suddenly came under intense automatic weapons and small-arms fire from a number of enemy bunkers and numerous snipers in nearby trees. Sgt. Keller quickly moved to a position where he could fire at a bunker from which automatic fire was received, killing 1 Viet Cong who attempted to escape. Leaping to the top of a dike, he and a comrade charged the enemy bunkers, dangerously exposing themselves to the enemy fire. Armed with a light machinegun, Sgt. Keller and his comrade began a systematic assault on the enemy bunkers. While Sgt. Keller neutralized the fire from the first bunker with his machinegun, the other soldier threw in a handgrenade killing its occupant. Then he and the other soldier charged a second bunker, killing its occupant. A third bunker contained an automatic rifleman who had pinned down much of the friendly platoon. Again, with utter disregard for the fire directed to them, the 2 men charged, killing the enemy within. Continuing their attack, Sgt. Keller and his comrade assaulted 4 more bunkers, killing the enemy within. During their furious assault, Sgt. Keller and his comrade had been almost continuously exposed to intense sniper fire as the enemy desperately sought to stop their attack. The ferocity of their assault had carried the soldiers beyond the line of bunkers into the treeline, forcing snipers to flee. The 2 men gave immediate chase, driving the enemy away from the friendly unit. When his ammunition was exhausted, Sgt. Keller returned to the platoon to assist in the evacuation of the wounded. The 2-man assault had driven an enemy platoon from a well prepared position, accounted for numerous enemy dead, and prevented further friendly casualties. Sgt. Keller's selfless heroism and indomitable fighting spirit saved the lives of many of his comrades and inflicted serious damage on the enemy. His acts were in keeping with the highest traditions of the military service and reflect great credit upon himself and the U.S. Army.

KELLEY, THOMAS G.

Rank and organization: Lieutenant Commander, U.S. Navy, River Assault Division 152. *Place and date:* Ong Muong Canal, Kien Hoa Province, Republic of Vietnam, 15 June 1969. *Entered service at:* Boston, Mass. *Born:* 13 May 1939, Boston, Mass. *Citation:* For conspicuous gallantry and intrepidity at the risk of his life above and beyond the call of duty in the afternoon while serving as commander of River Assault Division 152 during combat operations against enemy aggressor forces. Lt. Comdr. (then Lt.) Kelley was in charge of a column of 8 river assault craft which were extracting 1 company of U.S. Army infantry troops on the east bank of the Ong Muong Canal in Kien Hoa Province, when 1 of the armored troop carriers reported a mechanical failure of a loading ramp. At approximately the same time, Viet Cong forces opened fire from the opposite bank of the canal. After issuing orders for the crippled troop carrier to raise its ramp manually, and for the remaining boats to form a protective cordon around the disabled craft, Lt. Comdr. Kelley realizing the extreme danger to his column and its inability to clear the ambush site until the crippled unit was repaired, boldly maneuvered the monitor in which he was embarked to the exposed side of the protective cordon in direct line with the enemy's fire, and ordered the monitor to commence firing. Suddenly, an enemy rocket scored a direct hit on the coxswain's flat, the shell penetrating the thick armor plate, and the explosion spraying shrapnel in all directions. Sustaining serious head wounds from the blast, which hurled him to the deck of the monitor, Lt. Comdr. Kelley disregarded his severe injuries and attempted to continue directing the other boats. Although unable to move from the deck or to speak clearly into the radio, he succeeded in relaying his commands through 1 of his men until the enemy attack was silenced and the boats were able to move to an area of safety. Lt. Comdr. Kelley's brilliant leadership, bold initiative, and resolute determination served to inspire his men and provide the impetus needed to carry out the mission after he was medically evacuated by helicopter. His extraordinary courage under fire, and his selfless devotion to duty sustain and enhance the finest traditions of the U.S. Naval Service.

KELLOGG, ALLAN JAY, Jr.

Rank and organization: Gunnery Sergeant, U.S. Marine Corps (then S/Sgt.), Company G, 2d Battalion, 5th Marines, 1st Marine Division. *Place and date:* Quang Nam Province, Republic of Vietnam, 11 March 1970. *Entered service at:* Bridgeport, Conn. *Born:* 1 October 1943, Bethel, Conn. *Citation:* For conspicuous gallantry and intrepidity at the risk of his life above and beyond the call of duty while serving as a platoon sergeant with Company G, in connection with combat operations against the enemy on the night of 11 March 1970. Under the leadership of G/Sgt. Kellogg, a small unit from Company G was evacuating a fallen comrade when the unit came under a heavy volume of small arms and automatic weapons fire from a numerically superior enemy force occupying well-concealed emplacements in the surrounding jungle. During the ensuing fierce engagement, an enemy soldier managed to maneuver through the dense foliage to a position near the marines, and hurled a handgrenade into their midst which glanced off the chest of G/Sgt. Kellogg. Quick to act, he forced the grenade into the mud in which he was standing, threw himself over the lethal weapon and absorbed the full effects of its detonation with his body, thereby preventing serious injury or possible death to several of his fellow marines. Although suffering multiple injuries to his chest and his right shoulder and arm, G/Sgt. Kellogg resolutely continued to direct the efforts of his men until all were able to maneuver to the relative safety of the company perimeter. By his heroic and decisive action in risking his life to save the lives of his comrades, G/Sgt. Kellogg reflected the highest credit upon himself and upheld the finest traditions of the Marine Corps and the U.S. Naval Service.

KERREY, JOSEPH R.

Rank and organization: Lieutenant, Junior Grade, U.S. Naval Reserve, Sea, Air, and Land Team (SEAL). *Place and date:* Near Nha Trang Bay, Republic of Vietnam, 14 March 1969. *Entered service at:* Omaha, Nebr. *Born:* 27 August 1943, Lincoln, Nebr. *Citation:* For conspicuous gallantry and intrepidity at the risk of his life above and beyond the call of duty while serving as a SEAL team leader during action against enemy aggressor (Viet Cong) forces. Acting in response to reliable intelligence, Lt. (jg.) Kerrey led his SEAL team on a mission to capture important members of the enemy's area political cadre known to be located on an island in the bay of Nha Trang. In order to surprise the enemy, he and his team scaled a 350-foot sheer cliff to place themselves above the ledge on which the enemy was located. Splitting his team in 2 elements and coordinating both, Lt. (jg.) Kerrey led his men in the treacherous downward descent to the enemy's camp. Just as they neared the end of their descent, intense enemy fire was directed at them, and Lt. (jg.) Kerrey received massive injuries from a grenade which exploded at his feet and threw him backward onto the jagged rocks. Although bleeding profusely and suffering great pain, he displayed outstanding courage and presence of mind in immediately directing his element's fire into the heart of the enemy camp. Utilizing his radioman, Lt. (jg.) Kerrey called in the second element's fire support which caught the confused Viet Cong in a devastating crossfire. After successfully suppressing the enemy's fire, and although immobilized by his multiple wounds, he continued to maintain calm, superlative control as he ordered his team to secure and defend an extraction site. Lt. (jg.) Kerrey resolutely directed his men, despite his near-unconscious state, until he was eventually evacuated by helicopter. The havoc brought to the enemy by this very successful mission cannot be over-estimated. The enemy soldiers who were captured provided critical intelligence to the allied effort. Lt. (jg.) Kerrey's courageous and inspiring leadership, valiant fighting spirit, and tenacious devotion to duty in the face of almost overwhelming opposition sustain and enhance the finest traditions of the U.S. Naval Service.

KINSMAN, THOMAS JAMES

Rank and organization: Specialist Fourth Class, U.S. Army, Company B, 3d Battalion, 60th Infantry, 9th Infantry Division. *Place and date:* Near Vinh Long, Republic of Vietnam, 6 February 1968. *Entered service at:* Seattle, Wash. *Born:* 4 March 1945, Renton, Wash. *Citation:* For conspicuous gallantry and intrepidity in action at the risk of his life above and beyond the call of duty Sp4c. Kinsman (then Pfc.) distinguished himself in action in the afternoon while serving as a rifleman with Company B, on a reconnaissance-in-force mission. As his company was proceeding up a narrow canal in armored troops carriers, it came under sudden and intense rocket, automatic weapons and small-arms fire from a well entrenched Viet Cong force. The company immediately beached and began assaulting the enemy bunker complex. Hampered by exceedingly dense undergrowth which limited visibility to 10 meters, a group of 8 men became cut off from the main body of the company. As they were moving through heavy enemy fire to effect a link-up, an enemy soldier in a concealed position hurled a grenade into their midst. Sp4c. Kinsman immediately alerted his comrades of the danger, then unhesitatingly threw himself on the grenade and blocked the explosion with his body. As a result of his courageous action, he received severe head and chest wounds. Through his indomitable courage, complete disregard for his personal safety and profound concern for his fellow soldiers, Sp4c. Kinsman averted loss of life and injury to the other 7 men of his element. Sp4c. Kinsman's extraordinary heroism at the risk of his life, above and beyond the call of duty, are in keeping with the highest traditions of the military service and reflect great credit upon himself, his unit, and the U.S. Army.

LAMBERS, PAUL RONALD

Rank and organization: Staff Sergeant, U.S. Army, Company A, 2d Battalion, 27th Infantry, 25th Infantry Division. *Place and date:* Tay Ninh Province, Republic of Vietnam, 20 August 1968. *Entered service at:* Holland, Mich. *Born:* 25 June 1942, Holland, Mich. *Citation:* For conspicuous gallantry and intrepidity in action at the risk of his life above and beyond the call of duty. S/Sgt. (then Sgt.) Lambers distinguished himself in action while serving with the 3d Platoon, Company A. The unit had established a night defensive position astride a suspected enemy infiltration route, when it was attacked by an estimated Viet Cong battalion. During the initial enemy onslaught, the platoon leader fell seriously wounded and S/Sgt. Lambers assumed command of the platoon. Disregarding the intense enemy fire, S/Sgt. Lambers left his covered position, secured the platoon radio and moved to the command post to direct the defense. When his radio became inoperative due to enemy action, S/Sgt. Lambers crossed the fire swept position to secure the 90mm recoilless rifle crew's radio in order to re-establish communications. Upon discovering that the 90mm recoilless rifle was not functioning, S/Sgt. Lambers assisted in the repair of the weapon and directed cannister fire at point blank range against the attacking enemy who had breached the defensive wire of the position. When the weapon was knocked out by enemy fire, he singlehandedly repulsed a penetration of the position by detonating claymore mines and throwing grenades into the midst of the attackers, killing 4 more of the Viet Cong with well aimed handgrenades. S/Sgt. Lambers maintained command of the platoon elements by moving from position to position under the hail of enemy fire, providing assistance where the assault was the heaviest and by his outstanding example inspiring his men to the utmost efforts of courage. He displayed great skill and valor throughout the 5-hour battle by personally directing artillery and helicopter fire, placing them at times within 5 meters of the defensive position. He repeatedly exposed himself to hostile fire at great risk to his own life in order to redistribute ammunition and to care for seriously wounded comrades and to move them to sheltered positions. S/Sgt. Lambers' superb leadership, professional skill and magnificent courage saved the lives of his comrades, resulted in the virtual annihilation of a vastly superior enemy force and were largely instrumental in thwarting an enemy offensive against Tay Ninh City. His gallantry at the risk of his life is in keeping with the highest traditions of the military service and reflects great credit upon himself, his unit, and the U.S. Army.

LANG, GEORGE C.

Rank and organization: Specialist Fourth Class, U.S. Army, Company A, 4th Battalion, 47th Infantry, 9th Infantry Division. *Place and date:* Kien Hoa Province, Republic of Vietnam, 22 February 1969. *Entered service at:* Brooklyn, N.Y. *Born:* 20 April 1947, Flushing, N.Y. *Citation:* For conspicuous gallantry and intrepidity in action at the risk of his life above and beyond the call of duty. Sp4c. Lang, Company A, was serving as a squad leader when his unit, on a reconnaissance-in-force mission, encountered intense fire from a well fortified enemy bunker complex. Sp4c. Lang observed an emplacement from which heavy fire was coming. Unhesitatingly, he assaulted the position and destroyed it with handgrenades and rifle fire. Observing another emplacement approximately 15 meters to his front, Sp4c. Lang jumped across a canal, moved through heavy enemy fire to within a few feet of the position, and eliminated it, again using handgrenades and rifle fire. Nearby, he discovered a large cache of enemy ammunition. As he maneuvered his squad forward to secure the cache, they came under fire from yet a third bunker. Sp4c. Lang immediately reacted, assaulted his position, and destroyed it with the remainder of his grenades. After returning to the area of the arms cache, his squad again came under heavy enemy rocket and automatic weapons fire from 3 sides and suffered 6 casualties. Sp4c. Lang was 1 of those seriously wounded. Although immobilized and in great pain, he continued to direct his men until his evacuation was ordered over his protests. The sustained extraordinary courage and selflessness exhibited by this soldier over an extended period of time were an inspiration to his comrades and are in keeping with the highest traditions of the U.S. Army.

*LANGHORN, GARFIELD M.

Rank and organization: Private First class, U.S. Army, Troop C, 7th Squadron (Airmobile), 17th Cavalry, 1st Aviation Brigade. *Place and date:* Pleiku Province, Republic of Vietnam, 15 January 1969. *Entered service at:* Brooklyn, N.Y. *Born:* 10 September 1948, Cumberland, Va. *Citation:* For conspicuous gallantry and intrepidity in action at the risk of his life above and beyond the call of duty. Pfc. Langhorn distinguished himself while serving as a radio operator with Troop C, near Plei Djereng in Pleiku Province. Pfc. Langhorn's platoon was inserted into a landing zone to rescue 2 pilots of a Cobra helicopter shot down by enemy fire on a heavily timbered slope. He provided radio coordination with the command-and-control aircraft overhead while the troops hacked their way through dense undergrowth to the wreckage, where both aviators were found dead. As the men were taking the bodies to a pickup site, they suddenly came under intense fire from North Vietnamese soldiers in camouflaged bunkers to the front and right flank, and within minutes they were surrounded. Pfc. Langhorn immediately radioed for help from the orbiting gunships, which began to place minigun and rocket fire on the aggressors. He then lay between the platoon leader and another man, operating the radio and providing covering fire for the wounded who had been moved to the center of the small perimeter. Darkness soon fell, making it impossible for the gunships to give accurate support, and the aggressors began to probe the perimeter. An enemy handgrenade landed in front of Pfc. Langhorn and a few feet from personnel who had become casualties. Choosing to protect these wounded, he unhesitatingly threw himself on the grenade, scooped it beneath his body and absorbed the blast. By sacrificing himself, he saved the lives of his comrades. Pfc. Langhorn's extraordinary heroism at the cost of his life was in keeping with the highest traditions of the military service and reflect great credit on himself, his unit, and the U.S. Army.

*LaPOINTE, JOSEPH G., Jr.

Rank and organization: Specialist Fourth Class, U.S. Army, 2d Squadron, 17th Cavalry, 101st Airborne Division. *Place and date:* Quang Tin Province, Republic of Vietnam, 2 June 1969. *Entered service at:* Cincinnati, Ohio. *Born:* 2 July 1948, Dayton, Ohio. *Citation:* For conspicuous gallantry and intrepidity in action at the risk of his life above and beyond the call of duty. Sp4c. LaPointe, Headquarters and Headquarters Troop, 2d Squadron, distinguished himself while serving as a medical aidman during a combat helicopter assault mission. Sp4c. LaPointe's patrol was advancing from the landing zone through an adjoining valley when it suddenly encountered heavy automatic weapons fire from a large enemy force entrenched in well fortified bunker positions. In the initial hail of fire, 2 soldiers in the formation vanguard were seriously wounded. Hearing a call for aid from 1 of the wounded, Sp4c. LaPointe ran forward through heavy fire to assist his fallen comrades. To reach the wounded men, he was forced to crawl directly in view of an enemy bunker. As members of his unit attempted to provide covering fire, he administered first aid to 1 man, shielding the other with his body. He was hit by a burst of fire from the bunker while attending the wounded soldier. In spite of his painful wounds, Sp4c. LaPointe continued his lifesaving duties until he was again wounded and knocked to the ground. Making strenuous efforts, he moved back again into a shielding position to continue administering first aid. An exploding enemy grenade mortally wounded all 3 men. Sp4c. LaPointe's courageous actions at the cost of his life were an inspiration to his comrades. His gallantry and selflessness are in the highest traditions of the military service and reflect great credit on him, his unit, and the U.S. Army.

LASSEN, CLYDE EVERETT

Rank and organization: Lieutenant, U.S. Navy, Helicopter Support Squadron 7, Detachment 104, embarked in U.S.S. *Preble* (DLG-15). *Place and date:* Republic of Vietnam, 19 June 1968. *Entered service at:* Jacksonville, Fla. *Born:* 14 March 1942, Fort Myers, Fla. *Citation:* For conspicuous gallantry and intrepidity at the risk of his life above and beyond the call of duty as pilot and aircraft commander of a search and rescue helicopter, attached to Helicopter Support Squadron 7, during operations against enemy forces in North Vietnam. Launched shortly after midnight to attempt the rescue of 2 downed aviators, Lt. (then Lt. (jg.)) Lassen skillfully piloted his aircraft over unknown and hostile terrain to a steep, tree-covered hill on which the survivors had been located. Although enemy fire was being directed at the helicopter, he initially landed in a clear area near the base of the hill, but, due to the dense undergrowth, the survivors could not reach the helicopter. With the aid of flare illumination, Lt. Lassen successfully accomplished a hover between 2 trees at the survivors' position. Illumination was abruptly lost as the last of the flares were expended, and the helicopter collided with a tree, commencing a sharp descent. Expertly righting his aircraft and maneuvering clear, Lt. Lassen remained in the area, determined to make another rescue attempt, and encouraged the downed aviators while awaiting resumption of flare illumination. After another unsuccessful, illuminated rescue attempt, and with his fuel dangerously low and his aircraft significantly damaged, he launched again and commenced another approach in the face of the continuing enemy opposition. When flare illumination was again lost, Lt. Lassen, fully aware of the dangers in clearly revealing his position to the enemy, turned on his landing lights and completed the landing. On this attempt, the survivors were able to make their way to the helicopter. En route to the coast he encountered and successfully evaded additional hostile antiaircraft fire and, with fuel for only 5 minutes of flight remaining, landed safely aboard U.S.S. *Jouett* (DLG-29).

*LAUFFER, BILLY LANE

Rank and organization: Private First Class, U.S. Army, Company C, 2d Battalion, 5th Cavalry, 1st Air Cavalry Division. *Place and date:* Near Bon Son in Binh Dinh Province, Republic of Vietnam, 21 September 1966. *Entered service at:* Phoenix, Ariz. *Born:* 20 October 1945, Murray, Ky. *Citation:* For conspicuous gallantry and intrepidity in action at the risk of his life above and beyond the call of duty. Pfc. Lauffer's squad, a part of Company C, was suddenly struck at close range by an intense machinegun crossfire from 2 concealed bunkers astride the squad's route. Pfc. Lauffer, the second man in the column, saw the leadman fall and noted that the remainder of the squad was unable to move. Two comrades, previously wounded and being carried on litters, were lying helpless in the beaten zone of the enemy fire. Reacting instinctively, Pfc. Lauffer quickly engaged both bunkers with fire from his rifle, but when the other squad members attempted to maneuver under his covering fire, the enemy fusillade increased in volume and thwarted every attempt to move. Seeing this and his wounded comrades helpless in the open, Pfc. Lauffer rose to his feet and charged the enemy machinegun positions, firing his weapon and drawing the enemy's attention. Keeping the enemy confused and off balance, his 1-man assault provided the crucial moments for the wounded point man to crawl to a covered position, the squad to move the exposed litter patients to safety, and his comrades to gain more advantageous positions. Pfc. Lauffer was fatally wounded during his selfless act of courage and devotion to his fellow soldiers. His gallantry at the cost of his life served as an inspiration to his comrades and saved the lives of an untold number of his companions. His actions are in keeping with the highest traditions of military service and reflect great credit upon himself, his unit, and the U.S. Army.

*LAW, ROBERT D.

Rank and organization: Specialist Fourth Class, U.S. Army, Company I (Ranger), 75th Infantry, 1st Infantry Division. *Place and date:* Tinh Phuoc Thanh Province, Republic of Vietnam, 22 February 1969. *Entered service at:* Dallas, Tex. *Born:* 15 September 1944, Fort Worth, Tex. *Citation:* For conspicuous gallantry and intrepidity in action at the risk of his life above and beyond the call of duty. Sp4c. Law distinguished himself while serving with Company I. While on a long-range reconnaissance patrol in Tinh Phuoc Thanh Province, Sp4c. Law and 5 comrades made contact with a small enemy patrol. As the opposing elements exchanged intense fire, he maneuvered to a perilously exposed position flanking his comrades and began placing suppressive fire on the hostile troops. Although his team was hindered by a low supply of ammunition and suffered from an unidentified irritating gas in the air, Sp4c. Law's spirited defense and challenging counterassault rallied his fellow soldiers against the well-equipped hostile troops. When an enemy grenade landed in his team's position, Sp4c. Law, instead of diving into the safety of a stream behind him, threw himself on the grenade to save the lives of his comrades. Sp4c. Law's extraordinary courage and profound concern for his fellow soldiers were in keeping with the highest traditions of the military service and reflect great credit on himself, his unit, and the U.S. Army.

LEE, HOWARD V.

Rank and organization: Major, U.S. Marine Corps, Company E, 2d Battalion, 4th Marines, 3d Marine Division (Rein). *Place and date:* Near Cam Lo, Republic of Vietnam, 8 and 9 August 1966. *Entered service at:* Dumfries, Va. *Born:* 1 August 1933, New York, N.Y. *Citation:* For conspicuous gallantry and intrepidity at the risk of his life above and beyond the call of duty. A platoon of Maj. (then Capt.)

Lee's company, while on an operation deep in enemy territory, was attacked and surrounded by a large Vietnamese force. Realizing that the unit had suffered numerous casualties, depriving it of effective leadership, and fully aware that the platoon was even then under heavy attack by the enemy, Maj. Lee took 7 men and proceeded by helicopter to reinforce the beleaguered platoon. Maj. Lee disembarked from the helicopter with 2 of his men and, braving withering enemy fire, led them into the perimeter, where he fearlessly moved from position to position, directing and encouraging the overtaxed troops. The enemy then launched a massive attack with the full might of their forces. Although painfully wounded by fragments from an enemy grenade in several areas of his body, including his eye, Maj. Lee continued undauntedly throughout the night to direct the valiant defense, coordinate supporting fire, and apprise higher headquarters of the plight of the platoon. The next morning he collapsed from his wounds and was forced to relinquish command. However the small band of marines had held their position and repeatedly fought off many vicious enemy attacks for a grueling 6 hours until their evacuation was effected the following morning. Maj. Lee's actions saved his men from capture, minimized the loss of lives, and dealt the enemy a severe defeat. His indomitable fighting spirit, superb leadership, and great personal valor in the face of tremendous odds, reflect great credit upon himself and are in keeping with the highest traditions of the Marine Corps and the U.S. Naval Service.

*LEE, MILTON A.

Rank and organization: Private First Class, U.S. Army, Company B, 2d Battalion, 502d Infantry, 1st Brigade, 101st Airborne Division (Airmobile). *Place and date:* Near Phu Bai, Thua Thien Province, Republic of Vietnam, 26 April 1968. *Entered service at:* San Antonio, Tex. *Born:* 28 February 1949, Shreveport, La. *Citation:* For conspicuous gallantry and intrepidity in action at the risk of his life above and beyond the call of duty. Pfc. Lee distinguished himself near the city of Phu Bai in the Province of Thua Thien. Pfc. Lee was serving as the radio telephone operator with the 3d Platoon, Company B. As lead element for the company, the 3d Platoon received intense surprise hostile fire from a force of North Vietnamese Army regulars in well-concealed bunkers. With 50 percent casualties, the platoon maneuvered to a position of cover to treat their wounded and reorganize, while Pfc. Lee moved through the heavy enemy fire giving lifesaving first aid to his wounded comrades. During the subsequent assault on the enemy defensive positions, Pfc. Lee continuously kept close radio contact with the company commander, relaying precise and understandable orders to his platoon leader. While advancing with the front rank toward the objective, Pfc. Lee observed 4 North Vietnamese soldiers with automatic weapons and a rocket launcher lying in wait for the lead element of the platoon. As the element moved forward, unaware of the concealed danger, Pfc. Lee immediately and with utter disregard for his own personal safety, passed his radio to another soldier and charged through the murderous fire. Without hesitation he continued his assault, overrunning the enemy position, killing all occupants and capturing 4 automatic weapons and a rocket launcher. Pfc.

Lee continued his 1-man assault on the second position through a heavy barrage of enemy automatic weapons fire. Grievously wounded, he continued to press the attack, crawling forward into a firing position and delivering accurate covering fire to enable his platoon to maneuver and destroy the position. Not until the position was overrun did Pfc. Lee falter in his steady volume of fire and succumb to his wounds. Pfc. Lee's heroic actions saved the lives of the lead element and were instrumental in the destruction of the key position of the enemy defense. Pfc. Lee's gallantry at the risk of life above and beyond the call of duty are in keeping with the highest traditions of the military service and reflect great credit on himself, the 502d Infantry, and the U.S. Army.

*LEISY, ROBERT RONALD

Rank and organization: Second Lieutenant, U.S. Army, Infantry, Company B, 1st Battalion, 8th Cavalry, 1st Cavalry Division. *Place and date:* Phuoc Long Province, Republic of Vietnam, 2 December 1969. *Entered service at:* Seattle, Wash. *Born:* 1 March 1945, Stockton, Calif. *Citation:* For conspicuous gallantry and intrepidity in action at the risk of his life above and beyond the call of duty. 2d Lt. Leisy, Infantry, Company B, distinguished himself while serving as platoon leader during a reconnaissance mission. One of his patrols became heavily engaged by fire from a numerically superior enemy force located in a well-entrenched bunker complex. As 2d Lt. Leisy deployed the remainder of his platoon to rescue the beleaguered patrol, the platoon also came under intense enemy fire from the front and both flanks. In complete disregard for his safety, 2d Lt. Leisy moved from position to position deploying his men to effectively engage the enemy. Accompanied by his radio operator he moved to the front and spotted an enemy sniper in a tree in the act of firing a rocket-propelled grenade at them. Realizing there was neither time to escape the grenade nor shout a warning, 2d Lt. Leisy unhesitatingly, and with full knowledge of the consequences, shielded the radio operator with his body and absorbed the full impact of the explosion. This valorous act saved the life of the radio operator and protected other men of his platoon who were nearby from serious injury. Despite his mortal wounds, 2d Lt. Leisy calmly and confidently continued to direct the platoon's fire. When medical aid arrived, 2d Lt. Leisy valiantly refused attention until the other seriously wounded were treated. His display of extraordinary courage and exemplary devotion to duty provided the inspiration and leadership that enabled his platoon to successfully withdraw without further casualties. 2d Lt. Leisy's gallantry at the cost of his life are in keeping with the highest traditions of the military service and reflect great credit on him, his unit, and the U.S. Army.

LEMON, PETER C.

Rank and organization: Sergeant, U.S. Army, Company E, 2d Battalion, 8th Cavalry, 1st Cavalry Division. *Place and date:* Tay Ninh Province, Republic of Vietnam, 1 April 1970. *Entered service at:* Tawas City, Mich. *Born:* 5 June 1950, Toronto, Canada. *Citation:* For conspicuous gallantry and intrepidity in action at the risk of his life above and beyond the call of duty. Sgt. Lemon (then Sp4c.), Company

E, distinguished himself while serving as an assistant machine gunner during the defense of Fire Support Base Illingworth. When the base came under heavy enemy attack, Sgt. Lemon engaged a numerically superior enemy with machinegun and rifle fire from his defensive position until both weapons malfunctioned. He then used handgrenades to fend off the intensified enemy attack launched in his direction. After eliminating all but 1 of the enemy soldiers in the immediate vicinity, he pursued and disposed of the remaining soldier in hand-to-hand combat. Despite fragment wounds from an exploding grenade, Sgt. Lemon regained his position, carried a more seriously wounded comrade to an aid station, and, as he returned, was wounded a second time by enemy fire. Disregarding his personal injuries, he moved to his position through a hail of small arms and grenade fire. Sgt. Lemon immediately realized that the defensive sector was in danger of being overrun by the enemy and unhesitatingly assaulted the enemy soldiers by throwing handgrenades and engaging in hand-to-hand combat. He was wounded yet a third time, but his determined efforts successfully drove the enemy from the position. Securing an operable machinegun, Sgt. Lemon stood atop an embankment fully exposed to enemy fire, and placed effective fire upon the enemy until he collapsed from his multiple wounds and exhaustion. After regaining consciousness at the aid station, he refused medical evacuation until his more seriously wounded comrades had been evacuated. Sgt. Lemon's gallantry and extraordinary heroism, are in keeping with the highest traditions of the military service and reflect great credit on him, his unit, and the U.S. Army.

*LEONARD, MATTHEW

Rank and organization: Platoon Sergeant, U.S. Army, Company B, 1st Battalion, 16th Infantry, 1st Infantry Division. *Place and date:* Near Suoi Da, Republic of Vietnam, 28 February 1967. *Entered service at:* Birmingham, Ala. *Born:* 26 November 1929, Eutaw, Ala. *Citation:* For conspicuous gallantry and intrepidity in action at the risk of his life above and beyond the call of duty. His platoon was suddenly attacked by a large enemy force employing small arms, automatic weapons, and handgrenades. Although the platoon leader and several other key leaders were among the first wounded, P/Sgt. Leonard quickly rallied his men to throw back the initial enemy assaults. During the short pause that followed, he organized a defensive perimeter, redistributed ammunition, and inspired his comrades through his forceful leadership and words of encouragement. Noticing a wounded companion outside the perimeter, he dragged the man to safety but was struck by a sniper's bullet which shattered his left hand. Refusing medical attention and continuously exposing himself to the increasing fire as the enemy again assaulted the perimeter, P/Sgt. Leonard moved from position to position to direct the fire of his men against the well camouflaged foe. Under the cover of the main attack, the enemy moved a machinegun into a location where it could sweep the entire perimeter. This threat was magnified when the platoon machinegun in this area malfunctioned. P/Sgt. Leonard quickly crawled to the gun position and was helping to clear the malfunction when the gunner and other men in the vicinity were wounded by fire from the enemy machinegun. P/Sgt. Leonard rose to his feet, charged the enemy gun, and destroyed the hostile crew despite being hit several times by enemy fire. He moved to a tree, propped himself against it, and continued to engage the enemy until he succumbed to his many wounds. His fighting spirit, heroic leadership, and valiant acts inspired the remaining members of his platoon to hold back the enemy until assistance arrived. P/Sgt. Leonard's profound courage and devotion to his men are in keeping with the highest traditions of the military service, and his gallant actions reflect great credit upon himself and the U.S. Army.

LEVITOW, JOHN L.

Rank and organization: Sergeant, U.S. Air Force, 3d Special Operations Squadron. *Place and date:* Long Binh Army Post, Republic of Vietnam, 24 February 1969. *Entered service at:* New Haven, Conn. *Born:* 1 November 1945, Hartford, Conn. *Citation:* For conspicuous gallantry and intrepidity in action at the risk of his life above and beyond the call of duty. Sgt. Levitow (then A1c.), U.S. Air Force, distinguished himself by exceptional heroism while assigned as a loadmaster aboard an AC–47 aircraft flying a night mission in support of Long Binh Army Post. Sgt. Levitow's aircraft was struck by a hostile mortar round. The resulting explosion ripped a hole 2 feet in diameter through the wing and fragments made over 3,500 holes in the fuselage. All occupants of the cargo compartment were wounded and helplessly slammed against the floor and fuselage. The explosion tore an activated flare from the grasp of a crewmember who had been launching flares to provide illumination for Army ground troops engaged in combat. Sgt. Levitow, though stunned by the concussion of the blast and suffering from over 40 fragment wounds in the back and legs, staggered to his feet and turned to assist the man nearest to him who had been knocked down and was bleeding heavily. As he was moving his wounded comrade forward and away from the opened cargo compartment door, he saw the smoking flare ahead of him in the aisle. Realizing the danger involved and completely disregarding his own wounds, Sgt. Levitow started toward the burning flare. The aircraft was partially out of control and the flare was rolling wildly from side to side. Sgt. Levitow struggled forward despite the loss of blood from his many wounds and the partial loss of feeling in his right leg. Unable to grasp the rolling flare with his hands, he threw himself bodily upon the burning flare. Hugging the deadly device to his body, he dragged himself back to the rear of the aircraft and hurled the flare through the open cargo door. At that instant the flare separated and ignited in the air, but clear of the aircraft. Sgt. Levitow, by his selfless and heroic actions, saved the aircraft and its entire crew from certain death and destruction. Sgt. Levitow's gallantry, his profound concern for his fellowmen, at the risk of his life above and beyond the call of duty are in keeping with the highest traditions of the U.S. Air Force and reflect great credit upon himself and the Armed Forces of his country.

LITEKY, ANGELO J.

Rank and organization: Chaplain (Capt.), U.S. Army, Headquarters and Headquarters Company, 199th Infantry Brigade. *Place and date:*

Near Phuoc-Lac, Bien Hoa Province, Republic of Vietnam, 6 December 1967. *Entered service at:* Fort Hamilton, N.Y. *Born:* 14 February 1931, Washington, D.C. *Citation:* Chaplain Liteky distinguished himself by exceptional heroism while serving with Company A, 4th Battalion, 12th Infantry, 199th Light Infantry Brigade. He was participating in a search and destroy operation when Company A came under intense fire from a battalion size enemy force. Momentarily stunned from the immediate encounter that ensued, the men hugged the ground for cover. Observing 2 wounded men, Chaplain Liteky moved to within 15 meters of an enemy machinegun position to reach them, placing himself between the enemy and the wounded men. When there was a brief respite in the fighting, he managed to drag them to the relative safety of the landing zone. Inspired by his courageous actions, the company rallied and began placing a heavy volume of fire upon the enemy's positions. In a magnificent display of courage and leadership, Chaplain Liteky began moving upright through the enemy fire, administering last rites to the dying and evacuating the wounded. Noticing another trapped and seriously wounded man, Chaplain Liteky crawled to his aid. Realizing that the wounded man was too heavy to carry, he rolled on his back, placed the man on his chest and through sheer determination and fortitude crawled back to the landing zone using his elbows and heels to push himself along. Pausing for breath momentarily, he returned to the action and came upon a man entangled in the dense, thorny underbrush. Once more intense enemy fire was directed at him, but Chaplain Liteky stood his ground and calmly broke the vines and carried the man to the landing zone for evacuation. On several occasions when the landing zone was under small arms and rocket fire, Chaplain Liteky stood up in the face of hostile fire and personally directed the medivac helicopters into and out of the area. With the wounded safely evacuated, Chaplain Liteky returned to the perimeter, constantly encouraging and inspiring the men. Upon the unit's relief on the morning of 7 December 1967, it was discovered that despite painful wounds in the neck and foot, Chaplain Liteky had personally carried over 20 men to the landing zone for evacuation during the savage fighting. Through his indomitable inspiration and heroic actions, Chaplain Liteky saved the lives of a number of his comrades and enabled the company to repulse the enemy. Chaplain Liteky's actions reflect great credit upon himself and were in keeping with the highest traditions of the U.S. Army.

LITTRELL, GARY LEE

Rank and organization: Sergeant First Class, U.S. Army, Advisory Team 21, II Corps Advisory Group. *Place and date:* Kontum Province, Republic of Vietnam, 4–8 April 1970. *Entered service at:* Los Angeles, Calif. *Born:* 26 October 1944, Henderson, Ky. *Citation:* For conspicuous gallantry and intrepidity in action at the risk of his life above and beyond the call of duty. Sfc. Littrell, U.S. Military Assistance Command, Vietnam, Advisory Team 21, distinguished himself while serving as a Light Weapons Infantry Advisor with the 23d Battalion, 2d Ranger Group, Republic of Vietnam Army, near Dak Seang. After establishing a defensive perimeter on a hill on April 4, the battalion was subjected to an intense enemy mortar attack which killed the Vietnamese commander, 1 advisor, and seriously wounded all the advisors except Sfc. Littrell. During the ensuing 4 days, Sfc. Littrell exhibited near superhuman endurance as he singlehandedly bolstered the besieged battalion. Repeatedly abandoning positions of relative safety, he directed artillery and air support by day and marked the unit's location by night, despite the heavy, concentrated enemy fire. His dauntless will instilled in the men of the 23d Battalion a deep desire to resist. Assault after assault was repulsed as the battalion responded to the extraordinary leadership and personal example exhibited by Sfc. Littrell as he continuously moved to those points most seriously threatened by the enemy, redistributed ammunition, strengthened faltering defenses, cared for the wounded and shouted encouragement to the Vietnamese in their own language. When the beleaguered battalion was finally ordered to withdraw, numerous ambushes were encountered. Sfc. Littrell repeatedly prevented widespread disorder by directing air strikes to within 50 meters of their position. Through his indomitable courage and complete disregard for his safety, he averted excessive loss of life and injury to the members of the battalion. The sustained extraordinary courage and selflessness displayed by Sfc. Littrell over an extended period of time were in keeping with the highest traditions of the military service and reflect great credit on him and the U.S. Army.

LIVINGSTON, JAMES E.

Rank and organization: Captain, U.S. Marine Corps, Company E, 2d Battalion, 4th Marines, 9th Marine Amphibious Brigade. *Place and date:* Dai Do, Republic of Vietnam, 2 May 1968. *Entered service at:* McRae, Ga. *Born:* 12 January 1940, Towns, Telfair County, Ga. *Citation:* For conspicuous gallantry and intrepidity at the risk of his life above and beyond the call of duty while serving as Commanding Officer, Company E, in action against enemy forces. Company E launched a determined assault on the heavily fortified village of Dai Do, which had been seized by the enemy on the preceding evening isolating a marine company from the remainder of the battalion. Skillfully employing screening agents, Capt. Livingston maneuvered his men to assault positions across 500 meters of dangerous open rice paddy while under intense enemy fire. Ignoring hostile rounds impacting near him, he fearlessly led his men in a savage assault against enemy emplacements within the village. While adjusting supporting arms fire, Capt. Livingston moved to the points of heaviest resistance, shouting words of encouragement to his marines, directing their fire, and spurring the dwindling momentum of the attack on repeated occasions. Although twice painfully wounded by grenade fragments, he refused medical treatment and courageously led his men in the destruction of over 100 mutually supporting bunkers, driving the remaining enemy from their positions, and relieving the pressure on the stranded marine company. As the 2 companies consolidated positions and evacuated casualties, a third company passed through the friendly lines launching an assault on the adjacent village of Dinh To, only to be halted by a furious counterattack of an enemy battalion. Swiftly assessing the situation and disregarding the heavy volume of enemy fire, Capt. Livingston boldly maneuvered the remaining effective men of his company forward, joined forces with the heavily engaged marines, and halted the enemy's counterattack. Wounded a third time and unable to walk, he steadfastly remained in the dangerously exposed area, deploying his men to more tenable positions and supervising the evacuation of casualties. Only when assured of the safety of his men did he allow himself to be evacuated. Capt. Livingston's gallant actions uphold the highest traditions of the Marine Corps and the U.S. Naval Service.

*LONG, DONALD RUSSELL

Rank and organization: Sergeant, U.S. Army, Troop C, 1st Squadron, 4th Cavalry, 1st Infantry Division. *Place and date:* Republic of Vietnam, 30 June 1966. *Entered service at:* Ashland, Ky. *Born:* 27 August 1939, Blackfork, Ohio. *G.O. No.:* 13, 4 April 1968. *Citation:* For conspicuous gallantry and intrepidity in action at the risk of his life above and beyond the call of duty. Troops B and C, while conducting a reconnaissance mission along a road were suddenly attacked by a Viet Cong regiment, supported by mortars, recoilless rifles and machineguns, from concealed positions astride the road. Sgt. Long abandoned the relative safety of his armored personnel carrier and braved a withering hail of enemy fire to carry wounded men to evacuation helicopters. As the platoon fought its way forward to resupply advanced elements, Sgt. Long repeatedly exposed himself to enemy fire at point blank range to provide the needed supplies. While assaulting the Viet Cong position, Sgt. Long inspired his comrades by fearlessly standing unprotected to repel the enemy with rifle fire and grenades as they attempted to mount his carrier. When the enemy threatened to overrun a disabled carrier nearby, Sgt. Long again disregarded his own safety to help the severely wounded crew to safety. As he was handing arms to the less seriously wounded and reorganizing them to press the attack, an enemy grenade was hurled onto the carrier deck. Immediately recognizing the imminent danger, he instinctively shouted a warning to the crew and pushed to safety one man who had not heard his warning over the roar of battle. Realizing that these actions would not fully protect the exposed crewmen from the deadly explosion, he threw himself over the grenade to absorb the blast and thereby saved the lives of 8 of his comrades at the expense of his life. Throughout the battle, Sgt. Long's extraordinary heroism, courage and supreme devotion to his men were in the finest tradition of the military service, and reflect great credit upon himself and the U.S. Army.

*LOZADA, CARLOS JAMES

Rank and organization: Private First Class, U.S. Army, Company A, 2d Battalion, 503d Infantry, 173d Airborne Brigade. *Place and date:* Dak To, Republic of Vietnam, 20 November 1967. *Entered service at:* New York, N.Y. *Born:* 6 September 1946, Caguas, Puerto Rico. *Citation:* For conspicuous gallantry and intrepidity in action at the risk of his life above and beyond the call of duty. Pfc. Lozada, U.S. Army, distinguished himself at the risk of his life above and beyond the call of duty in the battle of Dak To. While serving as a machine gunner with 1st Platoon, Company A, Pfc. Lozada was part of a 4-man early warning outpost, located 35 meters from his company's lines. At 1400 hours a North Vietnamese Army company rapidly approached the outpost along a well defined trail. Pfc. Lozada alerted his comrades and commenced firing at the enemy who were within 10 meters of the outpost. His heavy and accurate machinegun fire killed at least 20 North Vietnamese soldiers and completely disrupted their initial attack. Pfc. Lozada remained in an exposed position and continued to pour deadly fire upon the enemy despite the urgent pleas of his comrades to withdraw. The enemy continued their assault, attempting to envelop the outpost. At the same time enemy forces launched a heavy attack on the forward west flank of Company A with the intent to cut them off from their battalion. Company A was given the order to withdraw. Pfc. Lozada apparently realized that if he abandoned his position there would be nothing to hold back the surging North Vietnamese soldiers and that the entire company withdrawal would be jeopardized. He called for his comrades to move back and that he would stay and provide cover for them. He made this decision realizing that the enemy was converging on 3 sides of his position and only meters away, and a delay in withdrawal meant almost certain death. Pfc. Lozada continued to deliver a heavy, accurate volume of suppressive fire against the enemy until he was mortally wounded and had to be carried during the withdrawal. His heroic deed served as an example and an inspiration to his comrades throughout the ensuing 4-day battle. Pfc. Lozada's actions are in the highest traditions of the U.S. Army and reflect great credit upon himself, his unit, and the U.S. Army.

*LUCAS, ANDRE C.

Rank and organization: Lieutenant Colonel, U.S. Army, 2d Battalion, 506th Infantry, 101st Airborne Division. *Place and date:* Fire Support Base Ripcord, Republic of Vietnam, 1 to 23 July 1970. *Entered service at:* West Point, N.Y. *Born:* 2 October 1930, Washington D.C. *Citation:* Lt. Col. Lucas distinguished himself by extraordinary heroism while serving as the commanding officer of the 2d Battalion. Although the fire base was constantly subjected to heavy attacks by a numerically superior enemy force throughout this period, Lt. Col. Lucas, forsaking his own safety, performed numerous acts of extraordinary valor in directing the defense of the allied position. On 1 occasion, he flew in a helicopter at treetop level above an entrenched enemy directing the fire of 1 of his companies for over 3 hours. Even though his helicopter was heavily damaged by enemy fire, he remained in an exposed position until the company expended its supply of grenades. He then transferred to another helicopter, dropped critically needed grenades to the troops, and resumed his perilous mission of directing fire on the enemy. These courageous actions by Lt. Col. Lucas prevented the company from being encircled and destroyed by a larger enemy force. On another occasion, Lt. Col. Lucas attempted to rescue a crewman trapped in a burning helicopter. As the flames in the aircraft spread, and enemy fire became intense, Lt. Col. Lucas ordered all members of the rescue party to safety. Then, at great personal risk, he continued the rescue effort amid concentrated enemy mortar fire, intense heat, and exploding ammunition until the aircraft was completely engulfed in flames. Lt. Col. Lucas was mortally wounded while directing the successful withdrawal of his battalion from the fire base. His actions throughout this extended period inspired his men to heroic efforts, and were instrumental in saving the lives of many of his fellow soldiers while inflicting heavy casualties on the enemy. Lt. Col. Lucas' conspicuous gallantry and intrepidity in action, at the cost of his own life, were in keeping with the highest traditions of the military service and reflect great credit on him, his unit and the U.S. Army.

LYNCH, ALLEN JAMES

Rank and organization: Sergeant, U.S. Army, Company D, 1st Battalion (Airmobile), 12th Cavalry, 1st Cavalry Division (Airmobile). *Place and date:* Near My An (2), Binh Dinh Province, Republic of Vietnam, 15 December 1967. *Entered service at:* Chicago, Ill. *Born:* 28 October 1945, Chicago, Ill. *Citation:* For conspicuous gallantry and intrepidity in action at the risk of his life above and beyond the call of duty. Sgt. Lynch (then Sp4c.) distinguished himself while serving as a radio telephone operator with Company D. While serving in the forward element on an operation near the village of My An, his unit became heavily engaged with a numerically superior enemy force. Quickly and accurately assessing the situation, Sgt. Lynch provided his commander with information which subsequently proved essential to the unit's successful actions. Observing 3 wounded comrades lying exposed to enemy fire, Sgt. Lynch dashed across 50 meters of open ground through a withering hail of enemy fire to administer aid. Reconnoitering a nearby trench for a covered position to protect the wounded from intense hostile fire, he killed 2 enemy soldiers at point blank range. With the trench cleared, he unhesitatingly returned to the fire-swept area 3 times to carry the wounded men to safety. When his company was forced to withdraw by the superior firepower of the enemy, Sgt. Lynch remained to aid his comrades at the risk of his life rather than abandon them. Alone, he defended his isolated position for 2 hours against the advancing enemy. Using only his rifle and a grenade, he stopped them just short of his trench, killing 5. Again, disregarding his safety in the face of withering hostile fire, he crossed 70 meters of exposed terrain 5 times to carry his wounded comrades to a more secure area. Once he had assured their comfort and safety, Sgt. Lynch located the counterattacking friendly company to assist in directing the attack and evacuating the 3 casualties. His gallantry at the risk of his life is in the highest traditions of the military service, Sgt. Lynch has reflected great credit on himself, the 12th Cavalry, and the U.S. Army.

MARM, WALTER JOSEPH, Jr.

Rank and organization: First Lieutenant (then 2d Lt.), U.S. Army, Company A, 1st Battalion, 7th Cavalry, 1st Cavalry Division (Airmobile). *Place and date:* Vicinity of Ia Drang Valley, Republic of Vietnam, 14 November 1965. *Entered service at:* Pittsburgh, Pa. *Born:* 20 November 1941, Washington, Pa. *G.O. No.:* 7, 15 February 1967. *Citation:* For conspicuous gallantry and intrepidity at the risk of life above and beyond the call of duty. As a platoon leader in the 1st Cavalry Division (Airmobile), 1st Lt. Marm demonstrated indomitable courage during a combat operation. His company was moving through the valley to relieve a friendly unit surrounded by an enemy force of estimated regimental size. 1st Lt. Marm led his platoon through withering fire until they were finally forced to take cover. Realizing that his platoon could not hold very long, and seeing four enemy soldiers moving into his position, he moved quickly under heavy fire and annihilated all 4. Then, seeing that his platoon was receiving intense fire from a concealed machinegun, he deliberately exposed himself to draw its fire. Thus locating its position, he attempted to destroy it with an antitank weapon. Although he inflicted casualties, the weapon did not silence the enemy fire. Quickly, disregarding the intense fire directed on him and his platoon, he charged 30 meters across open ground, and hurled grenades into the enemy position, killing some of the 8 insurgents manning it. Although severely wounded, when his grenades were expended, armed with only a rifle, he continued the momentum of his assault on the position and killed the remainder of the enemy. 1st Lt. Marm's selfless actions reduced the fire on his platoon, broke the enemy assault, and rallied his unit to continue toward the accomplishment of this mission. 1st Lt. Marm's gallantry on the battlefield and his extraordinary intrepidity at the risk of his life are in the highest traditions of the U.S. Army and reflect great credit upon himself and the Armed Forces of his country.

*MARTINI, GARY W.

Rank and organization: Private First Class, U.S. Marine Corps, Company F, 2d Battalion, 1st Marines, 1st Marine Division. *Place and date:* Binh Son, Republic of Vietnam, 21 April 1967. *Entered service at:* Portland, Oreg. *Born:* 21 September 1948, Lexington, Va. *Citation:* For conspicuous gallantry and intrepidity at the risk of his life above and beyond the call of duty. On 21 April 1967, during Operation UNION, elements of Company F, conducting offensive operations at Binh Son, encountered a firmly entrenched enemy force and immediately deployed to engage them. The marines in Pfc. Martini's platoon assaulted across an open rice paddy to within 20 meters of the enemy trench line where they were suddenly struck by handgrenades, intense small arms, automatic weapons, and mortar fire. The enemy onslaught killed 14 and wounded 18 marines, pinning the remainder of the platoon down behind a low paddy dike. In the face of imminent danger, Pfc. Martini immediately crawled over the dike to a forward open area within 15 meters of the enemy position where, continuously exposed to the hostile fire, he hurled handgrenades, killing several of the enemy. Crawling back through the intense fire, he rejoined his platoon which had moved to the relative safety of a trench line. From this position he observed several of his wounded comrades lying helpless in the fire-swept paddy. Although he knew that 1 man had been killed attempting to assist the wounded, Pfc. Martini raced through the open area and dragged a comrade back to a friendly position. In spite of a serious wound received during this first daring rescue, he again braved the unrelenting fury of the enemy fire to aid another companion lying wounded only 20 meters in front of the enemy trench line. As he reached the fallen marine, he received a mortal wound, but disregarding his own condition, he began to drag the marine toward his platoon's position. Observing men from his unit attempting to leave the security of their position to aid him, concerned only for their safety, he called to them to remain under cover, and through a final supreme effort, moved his injured comrade to where he could be pulled to safety, before he fell, succumbing to his wounds. Stouthearted and indomitable, Pfc. Martini unhesitatingly yielded his life to save 2 of his comrades and insure the safety of the remainder of his platoon. His outstanding courage, valiant fighting spirit and selfless devotion to duty reflected the highest credit upon himself, the Marine Corps, and the U.S. Naval Service. He gallantly gave his life for his country.

*MAXAM, LARRY LEONARD

Rank and organization: Corporal, U.S. Marine Corps, Company D, 1st Battalion, 4th Marines, 3d Marine Division (Rein), FMF. *Place and date:* Cam Lo District, Quang Tri Province, Republic of Vietnam, 2 February 1968. *Entered service at:* Los Angeles, Calif. *Born:* 9 January 1948, Glendale, Calif. *Citation:* For conspicuous gallantry and intrepidity at the risk of his life above and beyond the call of duty while serving as a fire team leader with Company D. The Cam Lo District Headquarters came under extremely heavy rocket, artillery, mortar, and recoilless rifle fire from a numerically superior enemy force, destroying a portion of the defensive perimeter. Cpl. Maxam, observing the enemy massing for an assault into the compound across the remaining defensive wire, instructed his assistant fire team leader to take charge of the fire team, and unhesitatingly proceeded to the weakened section of the perimeter. Completely exposed to the concentrated enemy fire, he sustained multiple fragmentation wounds from exploding grenades as he ran to an abandoned machinegun position. Reaching the emplacement, he grasped the machinegun and commenced to deliver effective fire on the advancing enemy. As the enemy directed maximum firepower against the determined marine, Cpl. Maxam's position received a direct hit from a rocket propelled grenade, knocking him backwards and inflicting severe fragmentation wounds to his face and right eye. Although momentarily stunned and in intense pain, Cpl. Maxam courageously resumed his firing position and subsequently was struck again by small-arms fire. With resolute determination, he gallantly continued to deliver intense machinegun fire, causing the enemy to retreat through the defensive wire to positions of cover. In a desperate attempt to silence his weapon, the North Vietnamese threw handgrenades and directed recoilless rifle fire against him inflicting 2 additional wounds. Too weak to reload his machinegun, Cpl. Maxam fell to a prone position and valiantly continued to deliver effective fire with his rifle. After 1½ hours, during which he was hit repeatedly by fragments from exploding grenades and concentrated small-arms fire, he succumbed to his wounds, having successfully defended nearly half of the perimeter singlehandedly. Cpl. Maxam's aggressive fighting spirit, inspiring valor and selfless devotion to duty reflected great credit upon himself and the Marine Corps and upheld the highest traditions of the U.S. Naval Service. He gallantly gave his life for his country.

McCLEERY, FINNIS D.

Rank and organization: Platoon Sergeant, U.S. Army, Company A, 1st Battalion, 6th U.S. Infantry. *Place and date:* Quang Tin Province, Republic of Vietnam, 14 May 1968. *Entered service at:* San Angelo, Tex. *Born:* 25 December 1927, Stephenville, Tex. *Citation:* For conspicuous gallantry and intrepidity in action at the risk of his life above and beyond the call of duty. P/Sgt. McCleery, U.S. Army, distinguished himself while serving as platoon leader of the 1st Platoon of Company A. A combined force was assigned the mission of assaulting a reinforced company of North Vietnamese Army regulars, well entrenched on Hill 352, 17 miles west of Tam Ky. As P/Sgt. McCleery led his men up the hill and across an open area to close with the enemy, his platoon and other friendly elements were pinned down by tremendously heavy fire coming from the fortified enemy positions. Realizing the severe damage that the enemy could inflict on the combined force in the event that their attack was completely halted, P/Sgt. McCleery rose from his sheltered position and began a 1-man assault on the bunker complex. With extraordinary courage, he moved across 60 meters of open ground as bullets struck all around him and rockets and grenades literally exploded at his feet. As he came within 30 meters of the key enemy bunker, P/Sgt. McCleery began firing furiously from the hip and throwing handgrenades. At this point in his assault, he was painfully wounded by shrapnel, but, with complete disregard for his wound, he continued his advance on the key bunker and killed all of its occupants. Having successfully and singlehandedly breached the enemy perimeter, he climbed to the top of the bunker he had just captured and, in full view of the enemy, shouted encouragement to his men to follow his assault. As the friendly forces moved forward, P/Sgt. McCleery began a lateral assault on the enemy bunker line. He continued to expose himself to the intense enemy fire as he moved from bunker to bunker, destroying each in turn. He was wounded a second time by shrapnel as he destroyed and routed the enemy from the hill. P/Sgt. McCleery is personally credited with eliminating several key enemy positions and inspiring the assault that resulted in gaining control of Hill 352. His extraordinary heroism at the risk of his life, above and beyond the call of duty, was in keeping with the highest standards of the military service, and reflects great credit on him, the Americal Division, and the U.S. Army.

*McDONALD, PHILL G.

Rank and organization: Private First Class, U.S. Army, Company A, 1st Battalion, 14th Infantry, 4th Infantry Division. *Place and date:* Near Kontum City, Republic of Vietnam, 7 June 1968. *Entered service at:* Beckley, W. Va. *Born:* 13 September 1941. Avondale, W. Va. *Citation:* For conspicuous gallantry and intrepidity in action at the risk of his life above and beyond the call of duty. Pfc. McDonald distinguished himself while serving as a team leader with the 1st Platoon of Company A. While on a combat mission his platoon came under heavy barrage of automatic weapons fire from a well concealed company-size enemy force. Volunteering to escort 2 wounded comrades to an evacuation point, Pfc. McDonald crawled through intense fire to destroy with a grenade an enemy automatic weapon threatening the safety of the evacuation. Returning to his platoon, he again volunteered to provide covering fire for the maneuver of the platoon from its exposed position. Realizing the threat he posed, enemy gunners concentrated their fire on Pfc. McDonald's position, seriously wounding him. Despite his painful wounds, Pfc. McDonald recovered the weapon of a wounded machine gunner to provide accurate covering fire for the gunner's evacuation. When other soldiers were pinned down by a heavy volume of fire from a hostile machinegun to his front, Pfc. McDonald crawled toward the enemy position to destroy it with grenades. He was mortally wounded in this intrepid action. Pfc. McDonald's gallantry at the risk of his life which resulted in the saving of the lives of his comrades, is in keeping with the highest traditions of the military service and reflects great credit upon himself, his unit, and the U.S. Army.

McGINTY, JOHN J. III

Rank and organization: Second Lieutenant (then S/Sgt.), U.S. Marine Corps, Company K, 3d Battalion, 4th Marines, 3d Marine Division, Fleet Marine Force. *Place and date:* Republic of Vietnam, 18 July 1966. *Entered service at:* Laurel Bay, S.C. *Born:* 21 January 1940, Boston, Mass. *Citation:* For conspicuous gallantry and intrepidity at the risk of his life above and beyond the call of duty. 2d Lt. McGinty's platoon, which was providing rear security to protect the withdrawal of the battalion from a position which had been under attack for 3 days, came under heavy small arms, automatic weapons and mortar fire from an estimated enemy regiment. With each successive human wave which assaulted his 32-man platoon during the 4-hour battle, 2d Lt. McGinty rallied his men to beat off the enemy. In 1 bitter assault, 2 of the squads became separated from the remainder of the platoon. With complete disregard for his safety, 2d Lt. McGinty charged through intense automatic weapons and mortar fire to their position. Finding 20 men wounded and the medical corpsman killed, he quickly reloaded ammunition magazines and weapons for the wounded men and directed their fire upon the enemy. Although he was painfully wounded as he moved to care for the disabled men, he continued to shout encouragement to his troops and to direct their fire so effectively that the attacking hordes were beaten off. When the enemy tried to out-flank his position, he killed 5 of them at point-blank range with his pistol. When they again seemed on the verge of overrunning the small force, he skillfully adjusted artillery and air strikes within 50 yards of his position. This destructive firepower routed the enemy, who left an estimated 500 bodies on the battlefield. 2d Lt. McGinty's personal heroism, indomitable leadership, selfless devotion to duty, and bold fighting spirit inspired his men to resist the repeated attacks by a fanatical enemy, reflected great credit upon himself, and upheld the highest traditions of the Marine Corps and the U.S. Naval Service.

McGONAGLE, WILLIAM L.[1]

Rank and organization: Captain (then Comdr.) U.S. Navy, U.S.S. *Liberty* (AGTR-5). *Place and date:* International waters, Eastern Mediterranean, 8–9 June 1967. *Entered service at:* Thermal, Calif. *Born:* 19 November 1925, Wichita, Kans. *Citation:* For conspicuous gallantry and intrepidity at the risk of his life above and beyond the call of duty. Sailing in international waters, the *Liberty* was attacked without warning by jet fighter aircraft and motor torpedo boats which inflicted many casualties among the crew and caused extreme damage to the ship. Although severely wounded during the first air attack, Capt. McGonagle remained at his battle station on the badly damaged bridge and, with full knowledge of the seriousness of his wounds, subordinated his own welfare to the safety and survival of his command. Steadfastly refusing any treatment which would take him away from his post, he calmly continued to exercise firm command of his ship. Despite continuous exposure to fire, he maneuvered his ship, directed its defense, supervised the control of flooding and fire, and saw to the care of the casualties. Capt. McGonagle's extraordinary valor under these conditions inspired the surviving members of the *Liberty*'s crew, many of them seriously wounded, to heroic efforts to overcome the battle damage and keep the ship afloat. Subsequent to the attack, although in great pain and weak from the loss of blood, Captain McGonagle remained at his battle station and continued to command his ship for more than 17 hours. It was only after rendezvous with a U.S. destroyer that he relinquished personal control of the *Liberty* and permitted himself to be removed from the bridge. Even then, he refused much needed medical attention until convinced that the seriously wounded among his crew had been treated. Capt. McGonagle's superb professionalism, courageous fighting spirit, and valiant leadership saved his ship and many lives. His actions sustain and enhance the finest traditions of the U.S. Naval Service.

*McKIBBEN, RAY

Rank and organization: Sergeant, U.S. Army, Troop B, 7th Squadron (Airmobile), 17th Cavalry. *Place and date:* Near Song Mao, Republic of Vietnam, 8 December 1968. *Entered service at:* Atlanta, Ga. *Born:* 27 October 1945. Felton, Ga. *Citation:* For conspicuous gallantry and intrepidity in action at the risk of his life above and beyond the call of duty, Sgt. McKibben distinguished himself in action while serving as team leader of the point element of a reconnaissance patrol of Troop B, operating in enemy territory. Sgt. McKibben was leading his point element in a movement to contact along a well-traveled trail when the lead element came under heavy automatic weapons fire from a fortified bunker position, forcing the patrol to take cover. Sgt. McKibben, appraising the situation and without regard for his own safety, charged through bamboo and heavy brush to the fortified position, killed the enemy gunner, secured the weapon and directed his patrol element forward. As the patrol moved out, Sgt. McKibben observed enemy movement to the flank of the patrol. Fire support from helicopter gunships was requested and the area was effectively neutralized. The patrol again continued its mission and as the lead element rounded the

---

[1] Captain McGonagle was granted the Medal of Honor for actions which took place in international waters in the Eastern Mediterranean rather than in Vietnam.

bend of a river it came under heavy automatic weapons fire from camouflaged bunkers. As Sgt. McKibben was deploying his men to covered positions, he observed one of his men fall wounded. Although bullets were hitting all around the wounded man, Sgt. McKibben, with complete disregard for his safety, sprang to his comrade's side and under heavy enemy fire pulled him to safety behind the cover of a rock emplacement where he administered hasty first aid. Sgt. McKibben, seeing that his comrades were pinned down and were unable to deliver effective fire against the enemy bunkers, again undertook a singlehanded assault of the enemy defenses. He charged through the brush and hail of automatic weapons fire closing on the first bunker, killing the enemy with accurate rifle fire and securing the enemy's weapon. He continued his assault against the next bunker, firing his rifle as he charged. As he approached the second bunker his rifle ran out of ammunition; however, he used the captured enemy weapon until it too was empty, at that time he silenced the bunker with well placed handgrenades. He reloaded his weapon and covered the advance of his men as they moved forward. Observing the fire of another bunker impeding the patrol's advance, Sgt. McKibben again singlehandedly assaulted the new position. As he neared the bunker he was mortally wounded but was able to fire a final burst from his weapon killing the enemy and enabling the patrol to continue the assault. Sgt. McKibben's indomitable courage, extraordinary heroism, profound concern for the welfare of his fellow soldiers and disregard for his personal safety saved the lives of his comrades and enabled the patrol to accomplish its mission. Sgt. McKibben's gallantry in action at the cost of his life above and beyond the call of duty are in the highest traditions of the military service and reflect great credit upon himself, his unit, and the U.S. Army.

*McMAHON, THOMAS J.

Rank and organization: Specialist Fourth Class, U.S. Army, Company A, 2d Battalion, 1st Infantry, 196th Infantry Brigade, Americal Division. *Place and date:* Quang Tin Province, Republic of Vietnam, 19 March 1969. *Entered service at:* Portland, Maine. *Born:* 24 June 1948, Washington, D.C. *Citation:* For conspicuous gallantry and intrepidity in action at the risk of his life above and beyond the call of duty. Sp4c. McMahon distinguished himself while serving as medical aid man with Company A. When the lead elements of his company came under heavy fire from well-fortified enemy positions, 3 soldiers fell seriously wounded. Sp4c. McMahon, with complete disregard for his safety, left his covered position and ran through intense enemy fire to the side of 1 of the wounded, administered first aid and then carried him to safety. He returned through the hail of fire to the side of a second wounded man. Although painfully wounded by an exploding mortar round while returning the wounded man to a secure position, Sp4c. McMahon refused medical attention and heroically ran back through the heavy enemy fire toward his remaining wounded comrade. He fell mortally wounded before he could rescue the last man. Sp4c. McMahon's undaunted concern for the welfare of his comrades at the cost of his life are in keeping with the highest traditions of the military service and reflect great credit on himself, his unit, and the U.S. Army.

McNERNEY, DAVID H.

Rank and organization: First Sergeant, U.S. Army, Company A, 1st Battalion, 8th Infantry, 4th Infantry Division. *Place and date:* Polei Doc, Republic of Vietnam, 22 March 1967. *Entered service at:* Fort Bliss, Tex. *Born:* 2 June 1931, Lowell, Mass. *Citation:* 1st Sgt. McNerney distinguished himself when his unit was attacked by a North Vietnamese battalion near Polei Doc. Running through the hail of enemy fire to the area of heaviest contact, he was assisting in the development of a defensive perimeter when he encountered several enemy at close range. He killed the enemy but was painfully injured when blown from his feet by a grenade. In spite of this injury, he assaulted and destroyed an enemy machinegun position that had pinned down 5 of his comrades beyond the defensive line. Upon learning his commander and artillery forward observer had been killed, he assumed command of the company. He adjusted artillery fire to within 20 meters of the position in a daring measure to repulse enemy assaults. When the smoke grenades used to mark the position were gone, he moved into a nearby clearing to designate the location to friendly aircraft. In spite of enemy fire he remained exposed until he was certain the position was spotted and then climbed into a tree and tied the identification panel to its highest branches. Then he moved among his men readjusting their position, encouraging the defenders and checking the wounded. As the hostile assaults slackened, he began clearing a helicopter landing site to evacuate the wounded. When explosives were needed to remove large trees, he crawled outside the relative safety of his perimeter to collect demolition material from abandoned rucksacks. Moving through a fusillade of fire he returned with the explosives that were vital to the clearing of the landing zone. Disregarding the pain of his injury and refusing medical evacuation 1st Sgt. McNerney remained with his unit until the next day when the new commander arrived. First Sgt. McNerney's outstanding heroism and leadership were inspirational to his comrades. His actions were in keeping with the highest traditions of the U.S. Army and reflect great credit upon himself and the Armed Forces of his country.

*McWETHY, EDGAR LEE, JR.

Rank and organization: Specialist Fifth Class, U.S. Army, Company B, 1st Battalion, 5th Cavalry, 1st Cavalry Division (Airmobile). *Place and date:* Binh Dinh Province, Republic of Vietnam, 21 June 1967. *Entered service at:* Denver, Colo. *Born:* 22 November 1944, Leadville, Colo. *Citation:* For conspicuous gallantry and intrepidity in action at the risk of his life above and beyond the call of duty. Serving as a medical aidman with Company B, Sp5c. McWethy accompanied his platoon to the site of a downed helicopter. Shortly after the platoon established a defensive perimeter around the aircraft, a large enemy force attacked the position from 3 sides with a heavy volume of automatic weapons fire and grenades. The platoon leader and his radio operator were wounded almost immediately, and Sp5c. McWethy rushed across the fire-swept area to their assistance. Although he could not help the mortally wounded radio operator, Sp5c. McWethy's timely first aid enabled the platoon leader to retain command during this critical period. Hearing a call for aid, Sp5c. McWethy started across the open toward the injured men, but was wounded in the head and knocked to the ground. He regained his feet and continued on but was hit again, this time in the leg. Struggling onward despite his wounds, he gained the side of his comrades and treated their injuries. Observing another fallen rifleman lying in an exposed position raked by enemy fire, Sp5c. McWethy moved toward him without hesitation. Although the enemy fire wounded him a third time, Sp5c. McWethy reached his fallen companion. Though weakened and in extreme pain, Sp5c. Mc-wethy gave the wounded man artificial respiration but suffered a fourth and fatal wound. Through his indomitable courage, complete disregard for his safety, and demonstrated concern for his fellow soldiers, Sp5c. McWethy inspired the members of his platoon and contributed in great measure to their successful defense of the position and the ultimate rout of the enemy force. Sp5c. McWethy's profound sense of duty, bravery, and his willingness to accept extraordinary risks in order to help the men of his unit are characteristic of the highest traditions of the military service and reflect great credit upon himself and the U.S. Army.

*MICHAEL, DON LESLIE

Rank and organization: Specialist Fourth Class, U.S. Army, Company C, 4th Battalion, 503d Infantry, 173d Airborne Brigade. *Place and date:* Republic of Vietnam, 8 April 1967. *Entered service at:* Montgomery, Ala. *Born:* 31 July 1947, Florence, Ala. *Citation:* For conspicuous gallantry and intrepidity at the risk of his life above and beyond the call of duty. Sp4c. Michael, U.S. Army, distinguished himself while serving with Company C. Sp4c. Michael was part of a platoon which was moving through an area of suspected enemy activity. While the rest of the platoon stopped to provide security, the squad to which Sp4c. Michael was assigned moved forward to investigate signs of recent enemy activity. After moving approximately 125 meters, the squad encountered a single Viet Cong soldier. When he was fired upon by the squad's machine gunner, other Viet Cong opened fire with automatic weapons from a well-concealed bunker to the squad's right front. The volume of enemy fire was so withering as to pin down the entire squad and halt all forward movement. Realizing the gravity of the situation, Sp4c. Michael exposed himself to throw 2 grenades, but failed to eliminate the enemy position. From his position on the left flank, Sp4c. Michael maneuvered forward with 2 more grenades until he was within 20 meters of the enemy bunkers, when he again exposed himself to throw 2 grenades, which failed to detonate. Undaunted, Sp4c. Michael made his way back to the friendly positions to obtain more grenades. With 2 grenades in hand, he again started his perilous move towards the enemy bunker, which by this time was under intense artillery fire from friendly positions. As he neared the bunker, an enemy soldier attacked him from a concealed position. Sp4c. Michael killed him with his rifle and, in spite of the enemy fire and the exploding artillery rounds, was successful in destroying the enemy positions. Sp4c. Michael took up pursuit of the remnants of the retreating enemy. When his comrades reached Sp4c. Michael, he had been mortally wounded. His inspiring display of determination and courage saved the lives of many of his comrades and successfully eliminated a destructive enemy force. Sp4c. Michael's actions were in keeping with the highest traditions of the military service and reflect the utmost credit upon himself and the U.S. Army.

MILLER, FRANKLIN D.

Rank and organization: Staff Sergeant, U.S. Army, 5th Special Forces Group, 1st Special Forces. *Place and date:* Kontum Province, Republic of Vietnam, 5 January 1970. *Entered service at:* Albuquerque, N. Mex. *Born:* 27 January 1945, Elizabeth City, N.C. *Citation:* For conspicuous gallantry and intrepidity in action at the risk of his life above and beyond the call of duty. S/Sgt. Miller, 5th Special Forces Group, distinguished himself while serving as team leader of an American-Vietnamese long-range reconnaissance patrol operating deep within enemy controlled territory. Leaving the helicopter insertion point, the patrol moved forward on its mission. Suddenly, 1 of the team members tripped a hostile boobytrap which wounded 4 soldiers. S/Sgt. Miller, knowing that the explosion would alert the enemy, quickly administered first aid to the wounded and directed the team into positions across a small stream bed at the base of a steep hill. Within a few minutes, S/Sgt. Miller saw the lead element of what he estimated to be a platoon-size enemy force moving toward his location. Concerned for the safety of his men, he directed the small team to move up the hill to a more secure position. He remained alone, separated from the patrol, to meet the attack. S/Sgt. Miller singlehandedly repulsed 2 determined attacks by the numerically superior enemy force and caused them to withdraw in disorder. He rejoined his team, established contact with a forward air controller and arranged the evacuation of his patrol. However, the only suitable extraction location in the heavy jungle was a bomb crater some 150 meters from the team location. S/Sgt. Miller reconnoitered the route to the crater and led his men through the enemy controlled jungle to the extraction site. As the evacuation helicopter hovered over the crater to pick up the patrol, the enemy launched a savage automatic weapon and rocket-propelled grenade attack against the beleaguered team, driving off the rescue helicopter. S/Sgt. Miller led the team in a valiant defense which drove back the enemy in its attempt to overrun the small patrol. Although seriously wounded and with every man in his patrol a casualty, S/Sgt. Miller moved forward to again singlehandedly meet the hostile attackers. From his forward exposed position, S/Sgt. Miller gallantly repelled 2 attacks by the enemy before a friendly relief force reached the patrol location. S/Sgt. Miller's gallantry, intrepidity in action, and selfless devotion to the welfare of his comrades are in keeping with the highest traditions of the military service and reflect great credit on him, his unit, and the U.S. Army.

*MILLER, GARY L.

Rank and organization: First Lieutenant, U.S. Army, Company A, 1st Battalion, 28th Infantry, 1st Infantry Division. *Place and date:* Binh Duong Province, Republic of Vietnam, 16 February 1969. *Entered service at:* Roanoke, Va. *Born:* 19 March 1947, Covington, Va. *Citation:* For conspicuous intrepidity and gallantry in action at the risk of his life above and beyond the call of duty. First Lt. Miller, Infantry, Company A, was serving as a platoon leader at night when his company ambushed a hostile force infiltrating from Cambodian sanctuaries. After contact with the enemy was broken, 1st Lt. Miller led a reconnaissance patrol from their prepared positions through the early evening darkness and dense tropical growth to search the area for enemy casualties. As the group advanced they were suddenly attacked. First Lt. Miller was seriously wounded. However, the group fought back with telling effect on the hostile force. An enemy grenade was thrown into the midst of the friendly patrol group and all took cover except 1st Lt. Miller, who in the dim light located the grenade and threw himself on it, absorbing the force of the explosion with his body. His action saved nearby members of his patrol from almost certain serious injury. The extraordinary courage and selflessness displayed by this officer were an inspiration to his comrades and are in the highest traditions of the U.S. Army.

MODRZEJEWSKI, ROBERT J.

Rank and organization: Major (then Capt.), U.S. Marine Corps, Company K, 3d Battalion, 4th Marines, 3d Marine Division, FMF. *Place and date:* Republic of Vietnam, 15 to 18 July 1966. *Entered service at:* Milwaukee, Wis. *Born:* 3 July 1934, Milwaukee, Wis. *Citation:* For conspicuous gallantry and intrepidity at the risk of his life above and beyond the call of duty. On 15 July, during Operation HASTINGS, Company K was landed in an enemy-infested jungle area to establish a blocking position at a major enemy trail network. Shortly after landing, the company encountered a reinforced enemy platoon in a well-organized, defensive position. Maj. Modrzejewski led his men in the successful seizure of the enemy redoubt, which contained large quantities of ammunition and supplies. That evening, a numerically superior enemy force counterattacked in an effort to retake the vital supply area, thus setting the pattern of activity for the next 2½ days. In the first series of attacks, the enemy assaulted repeatedly in overwhelming numbers but each time was repulsed by the gallant marines. The second night, the enemy struck in battalion strength, and Maj. Modrzejewski was wounded in this intensive action which was fought at close quarters. Although exposed to enemy fire, and despite his painful wounds, he crawled 200 meters to provide critically needed ammunition to an exposed element of his command and was constantly present wherever the fighting was heaviest, despite numerous casualties, a dwindling supply of ammunition and the knowledge that they were surrounded, he skillfully directed artillery fire to within a few meters of his position and courageously inspired the efforts of his company in repelling the aggressive enemy attack. On 18 July, Company K was attacked by a regimental-size enemy force. Although his unit was vastly outnumbered and weakened by the previous fighting, Maj. Modrzejewski reorganized his men and calmly moved among them to encourage and direct their efforts to heroic limits as they fought to overcome the vicious enemy onslaught. Again he called in air and artillery strikes at close range with devastating effect on the enemy, which together with the bold and determined fighting of the men of Company K, repulsed the fanatical attack of the larger North Vietnamese force. His unparalleled personal heroism and indomitable leadership inspired his men to a significant victory over the enemy force and reflected great credit upon himself, the Marine Corps, and the U.S. Naval Service.

*MOLNAR, FRANKIE ZOLY

Rank and organization: Staff Sergeant, U.S. Army, Company B, 1st Battalion, 8th Infantry, 4th Infantry Division. *Place and date:* Kontum Province, Republic of Vietnam, 20 May 1967. *Entered service at:* Fresno, Calif. *Born:* 14 February 1943, Logan, W. Va. *Citation:* For conspicuous gallantry and intrepidity in action at the risk of his life above and beyond the call of duty. S/Sgt. Molnar distinguished himself while serving as a squad leader with Company B, during combat operations. Shortly after the battalion's defensive perimeter was established, it was hit by intense mortar fire as the prelude to a massive enemy night attack. S/Sgt. Molnar immediately left his sheltered location to insure the readiness of his squad to meet the attack. As he crawled through the position, he discovered a group of enemy soldiers closing in on his squad area. His accurate rifle fire killed 5 of the enemy and forced the remainder to flee. When the mortar fire stopped, the enemy attacked in a human wave supported by grenades, rockets, automatic weapons, and small-arms fire. After assisting to repel the first enemy assault, S/Sgt. Molnar found that his squad's ammunition and grenade supply was nearly expended. Again leaving the relative safety of his position, he crawled through intense enemy fire to secure additional ammunition and distribute it to his squad. He rejoined his men to beat back the renewed enemy onslaught, and he moved about his area providing medical aid and assisting in the evacuation of the wounded. With the help of several men, he was preparing to move a severely wounded soldier when an enemy handgrenade was thrown into the group. The first to see the grenade, S/Sgt. Molnar threw himself on it and absorbed the deadly blast to save his comrades. His demonstrated selflessness and inspirational leadership on the battlefield were a major factor in the successful defense of the American position and are in keeping with the finest traditions of the U.S. Army. S/Sgt. Molnar's actions reflect great credit upon himself, his unit, and the U.S. Army.

*MONROE, JAMES H.

Rank and organization: Private First Class, U.S. Army, Headquarters and Headquarters Company, 1st Battalion, 8th Cavalry, 1st Cavalry Division (Airmobile). *Place and date:* Bong Son, Hoai Nhon Province, Republic of Vietnam, 16 February 1967. *Entered service at:* Chicago, Ill. *Born:* 17 October 1944, Aurora, Ill. *Citation:* For conspicuous gallantry and intrepidity in action at the risk of his life above and beyond the call of duty. His platoon was deployed in a night ambush when the position was suddenly subjected to an intense and accurate grenade attack, and 1 foxhole was hit immediately. Responding without hesitation to the calls for help from the wounded men Pfc. Monroe moved forward through heavy small-arms fire to the foxhole but found that all of the men had expired. He turned immediately and crawled back through the deadly hail of fire toward other calls for aid. He moved to the platoon sergeant's position where he found the radio operator bleeding profusely from fragmentation and bullet wounds. Ignoring the continuing enemy attack, Pfc. Monroe began treating the wounded man when he saw a live grenade fall directly in front of the position. He shouted a warning to all those nearby, pushed the wounded radio operator and the platoon sergeant to one side, and lunged forward to smother the grenade's blast with his body. Through his valorous actions, performed in a flash of inspired selflessness, Pfc. Monroe saved the lives of 2 of his comrades and prevented the probable injury of several others. His gallantry and intrepidity were in the highest traditions of the U.S. Army, and reflect great credit upon himself and the Armed Forces of his country.

*MORGAN, WILLIAM D.

Rank and organization: Corporal, U.S. Marine Corps, Company H, 2d Battalion, 9th Marines, 3d Marine Division. *Place and date:* Quang Tri Province, Republic of Vietnam, 25 February 1969. *Entered service at:* Pittsburgh, Pa. *Born:* 17 September 1947, Pittsburgh, Pa. *Citation:* For conspicuous gallantry and intrepidity at the risk of his life above and beyond the call of duty while serving as a squad leader with Company H, in operations against the enemy. While participating in Operation DEWEY CANYON southeast of Vandergrift Combat Base, 1 of the squads of Cpl. Morgan's platoon was temporarily pinned down and sustained several casualties while attacking a North Vietnamese Army force occupying a heavily fortified bunker complex. Observing that 2 of the wounded marines had fallen in a position dangerously exposed to the enemy fire and that all attempts to evacuate them were halted by a heavy volume of automatic weapons fire and rocket-propelled grenades. Cpl. Morgan unhesitatingly maneuvered through the dense jungle undergrowth to a road that passed in front of a hostile emplacement which was the principal source of enemy fire. Fully aware of the possible consequences of his valiant action, but thinking only of the welfare of his injured companions, Cpl. Morgan shouted words of encouragement to them as he initiated an aggressive assault against the hostile bunker. While charging across the open road, he was clearly visible to the hostile soldiers who turned their fire in his direction and mortally wounded him, but his diversionary tactic enabled the remainder of his squad to retrieve their casualties and overrun the North Vietnamese Army position. His heroic and determined actions saved the lives of 2 fellow marines and were instrumental in the subsequent defeat of the enemy. Cpl. Morgan's indomitable courage, inspiring initiative and selfless devotion to duty upheld the highest traditions of the Marine Corps and of the U.S. Naval Services. He gallantly gave his life for his country.

MORRIS, CHARLES B.

Rank and organization: Staff Sergeant (then Sgt.), U.S. Army, Company A, 2d Battalion (Airborne), 503d Infantry, 173d Airborne Brigade (Separate). *Place and date:* Republic of Vietnam, 29 June 1966. *Entered service at:* Roanoke, Va. *Born:* 29 December 1931, Carroll County, Va. *G.O. No.:* 51, 14 December 1967. *Citation:* For conspicuous gallantry and intrepidity at the risk of his life above and beyond the call of duty. Seeing indications of the enemy's presence in the area, S/Sgt. Morris deployed his squad and continued forward alone to make a reconnaissance. He unknowingly crawled within 20 meters of an enemy machinegun, whereupon the gunner fired, wounding him in the chest. S/Sgt. Morris instantly returned the fire and killed the gunner. Continuing to crawl within a few feet of the gun, he hurled a grenade and killed the remainder of the enemy crew. Although in pain and bleeding profusely, S/Sgt. Morris continued his reconnaissance. Returning to the platoon area, he reported the results of his reconnaissance to the platoon leader. As he spoke, the platoon came under heavy fire. Refusing medical attention for himself, he deployed his men in better firing positions confronting the entrenched enemy to his front. Then for 8 hours the platoon engaged the numerically superior enemy force. Withdrawal was impossible without abandoning many wounded and dead. Finding the platoon medic dead, S/Sgt. Morris administered first aid to himself and was returning to treat the wounded members of his squad with the medic's first aid kit when he was again wounded. Knocked down and stunned, he regained consciousness and continued to treat the wounded, reposition his men, and inspire and encourage their efforts. Wounded again when an enemy grenade shattered his left hand, nonetheless he personally took up the fight and armed and threw several grenades which killed a number of enemy soldiers. Seeing that an enemy machinegun had maneuvered behind his platoon and was delivering the fire upon his men, S/Sgt. Morris and another man crawled toward the gun to knock it out. His comrade was killed and S/Sgt. Morris sustained another wound, but, firing his rifle with 1 hand, he silenced the enemy machinegun. Returning to the platoon, he courageously exposed himself to the devastating enemy fire to drag the wounded to a protected area, and with utter disregard for his personal safety and the pain he suffered, he continued to lead and direct the efforts of his men until relief arrived. Upon termination of the battle, important documents were found among the enemy dead revealing a planned ambush of a Republic of Vietnam battalion. Use of this information prevented the ambush and saved many lives. S/Sgt. Morris' gallantry was instrumental in the successful defeat of the enemy, saved many lives, and was in the highest traditions of the U.S. Army.

*MURRAY, ROBERT C.

Rank and organization: Staff Sergeant, U.S. Army, Company B, 4th Battalion, 31st Infantry, 196th Infantry Brigade, 23d Infantry Division. *Place and date:* Near the village of Hiep Duc, Republic of Vietnam, 7 June 1970. *Entered service at:* New York, N.Y. *Born:* 10 December 1946, Bronx, N.Y. *Citation:* S/Sgt. Murray distinguished himself while serving as a squad leader with Company B. S/Sgt. Murray's squad was searching for an enemy mortar that had been threatening friendly positions when a member of the squad tripped an enemy grenade rigged as a booby trap. Realizing that he had activated the enemy booby trap, the soldier shouted for everybody to take cover. Instantly assessing the danger to the men of his squad, S/Sgt. Murray unhesitatingly and with complete disregard for his own safety, threw himself on the grenade absorbing the full and fatal impact of the explosion. By his gallant action and self sacrifice, he prevented the death or injury of the other members of his squad. S/Sgt. Murray's extraordinary courage and gallantry, at the cost of his life above and beyond the call of duty, are in keeping with the highest traditions of the military service and reflect great credit on him, his unit, and the U.S. Army.

*NASH, DAVID P.

Rank and organization: Private First Class, U.S. Army, Company B, 2d Battalion, 39th Infantry, 9th Infantry Division. *Place and date:* Giao Duc District, Dinh Tuong Province, Republic of Vietnam, 29 December 1968. *Entered service at:* Louisville, Ky. *Born:* 3 November 1947, Whitesville, Ky. *Citation:* For conspicuous gallantry and intrepidity in action at the risk of his life above and beyond the call of duty. Pfc. Nash distinguished himself while serving as a grenadier with Company B, in Giao Duc District. When an ambush patrol of which he was a member suddenly came under intense attack before reaching its destination, he was the first to return the enemy fire. Taking an exposed location, Pfc. Nash suppressed the hostile fusillade with a rapid series of rounds from his grenade launcher, enabling artillery fire to be adjusted on the enemy. After the foe had been routed, his small element continued to the ambush site where he established a position with 3 fellow soldiers on a narrow dike. Shortly past midnight, while Pfc. Nash and a comrade kept watch and the 2 other men took their turn sleeping, an enemy grenade wounded 2 soldiers in the adjacent position. Seconds later, Pfc. Nash saw another grenade land only a few feet from his own position. Although he could have escaped harm by rolling down the other side of the dike, he shouted a warning to his comrades and leaped upon the lethal explosive. Absorbing the blast with his body, he saved the lives of the 3 men in the area at the sacrifice of his life. By his gallantry at the cost of his life are in the highest traditions of the military service, Pfc. Nash has reflected great credit on himself, his unit, and the U.S. Army.

*NEWLIN, MELVIN EARL

Rank and organization: Private First Class, U.S. Marine Corps, 2d Battalion, 5th Marines, 1st Marine Division (Rein), FMF. *Place and date:* Quang Nam Province, Republic of Vietnam, 4 July 1967. *Entered service at:* Cleveland, Ohio. *Born:* 27 September 1948, Wellsville, Ohio. *Citation:* For conspicuous gallantry and intrepidity at the risk of his life above and beyond the call of duty while serving as a machine gunner attached to the 1st Platoon, Company F, 2d Battalion, on 3 and 4 July 1967. Pfc. Newlin, with 4 other marines, was manning a key position on the perimeter of the Nong Son outpost when the enemy launched a savage and well coordinated mortar and infantry assault, seriously wounding him and killing his 4 comrades. Propping himself against his machinegun, he poured a deadly accurate stream of fire into the charging ranks of the Viet Cong. Though repeatedly hit by small-arms fire, he twice repelled enemy attempts to overrun his position. During the third attempt, a grenade explosion wounded him again and knocked him to the ground unconscious. The Viet Cong guerrillas, believing him dead, bypassed him and continued their assault on the main force. Meanwhile, Pfc. Newlin regained consciousness, crawled back to his weapon, and brought it to bear on the rear of the enemy causing havoc and confusion among them. Spotting the enemy attempting to bring a captured 106 recoilless weapon to bear on other marine positions, he shifted his fire, inflicting heavy casualties on the enemy and preventing them from firing the captured weapon. He then shifted his fire back to the primary enemy force, causing the enemy to stop their assault on the marine bunkers and to once again attack his machinegun position. Valiantly fighting off 2 more enemy assaults, he firmly held his ground until mortally wounded. Pfc. Newlin had singlehandedly broken up and disorganized the entire enemy assault force, causing them to lose momentum and delaying them long enough for his fellow marines to organize a defense and beat off their secondary attack. His indomitable courage, fortitude, and unwavering devotion to duty in the face of almost certain death reflect great credit upon himself and the Marine Corps and upheld the highest traditions of the U.S. Naval Service.

*NOONAN, THOMAS P., JR.

Rank and organization: Lance Corporal, U.S. Marine Corps, Company G, 2d Battalion, 9th Marines, 3d Marine Division. *Place and date:* Near Vandergrift Combat Base, A Shau Valley, Republic of Vietnam, 5 February 1969. *Entered service at:* Brooklyn, N.Y. *Born:* 18 November 1943, Brooklyn, N.Y. *Citation:* For conspicuous gallantry and intrepidity at the risk of his life above and beyond the call of duty while serving as a fire team leader with Company G, in operations against the enemy in Quang Tri Province. Company G was directed to move from a position which they had been holding southeast of the Vandergrift Combat Base to an alternate location. As the marines commenced a slow and difficult descent down the side of the hill made extremely slippery by the heavy rains, the leading element came under a heavy fire from a North Vietnamese Army unit occupying well concealed positions in the rocky terrain. Four men were wounded, and repeated attempts to recover them failed because of the intense hostile fire. L/Cpl. Noonan moved from his position of relative security and, maneuvering down the treacherous slope to a location near the injured men, took cover behind some rocks. Shouting words of encouragement to the wounded men to restore their confidence, he dashed across the hazardous terrain and commenced dragging the most seriously wounded man away from the fire-swept area. Although wounded and knocked to the ground by an enemy round, L/Cpl. Noonan recovered rapidly and resumed dragging the man toward the marginal security of a rock. He was, however, mortally wounded before he could reach his destination. His heroic actions inspired his fellow marines to such aggressiveness that they initiated a spirited assault which forced the enemy soldiers to withdraw. L/Cpl. Noonan's indomitable courage, inspiring initiative, and selfless devotion to duty upheld the highest traditions of the Marine Corps and the U.S. Naval Service. He gallantly gave his life for his country.

NORRIS, THOMAS R.

Rank and organization: Lieutenant, U.S. Navy, SEAL Advisor, Strategic Technical Directorate Assistance Team, Headquarters, U.S. Military Assistance Command. *Place and date:* Quang Tri Province,

Republic of Vietnam, 10 to 13 April 1972. *Entered service at:* Silver Spring, Md. *Born:* 14 January 1944, Jacksonville, Fla. *Citation:* Lt. Norris completed an unprecedented ground rescue of 2 downed pilots deep within heavily controlled enemy territory in Quang Tri Province. Lt. Norris, on the night of 10 April, led a 5-man patrol through 2,000 meters of heavily controlled enemy territory, located 1 of the downed pilots at daybreak, and returned to the Forward Operating Base (FOB). On 11 April, after a devastating mortar and rocket attack on the small FOB, Lt. Norris led a 3-man team on 2 unsuccessful rescue attempts for the second pilot. On the afternoon of the 12th, a forward air controller located the pilot and notified Lt. Norris. Dressed in fishermen disguises and using a sampan, Lt. Norris and 1 Vietnamese traveled throughout that night and found the injured pilot at dawn. Covering the pilot with bamboo and vegetation, they began the return journey, successfully evading a North Vietnamese patrol. Approaching the FOB, they came under heavy machinegun fire. Lt. Norris called in an air strike which provided suppression fire and a smokescreen, allowing the rescue party to reach the FOB. By his outstanding display of decisive leadership, undaunted courage, and selfless dedication in the face of extreme danger, Lt. Norris enhanced the finest traditions of the U.S. Naval Service.

NOVOSEL, MICHAEL J.

Rank and organization: Chief Warrant Officer, U.S. Army, 82d Medical Detachment, 45th Medical Company, 68th Medical Group. *Place and date:* Kien Tuong Province, Republic of Vietnam, 2 October 1969. *Entered service at:* Kenner, La. *Born:* 3 September 1922, Etna, Pa. *Citation:* For conspicuous gallantry and intrepidity in action at the risk of his life above and beyond the call of duty. CWO Novosel, 82d Medical Detachment, distinguished himself while serving as commander of a medical evacuation helicopter. He unhesitatingly maneuvered his helicopter into a heavily fortified and defended enemy training area where a group of wounded Vietnamese soldiers were pinned down by a large enemy force. Flying without gunship or other cover and exposed to intense machinegun fire, CWO Novosel was able to locate and rescue a wounded soldier. Since all communications with the beleaguered troops had been lost, he repeatedly circled the battle area, flying at low level under continuous heavy fire, to attract the attention of the scattered friendly troops. This display of courage visibly raised their morale, as they recognized this as a signal to assemble for evacuation. On 6 occasions he and his crew were forced out of the battle area by the intense enemy fire, only to circle and return from another direction to land and extract additional troops. Near the end of the mission, a wounded soldier was spotted close to an enemy bunker. Fully realizing that he would attract a hail of enemy fire, CWO Novosel nevertheless attempted the extraction by hovering the helicopter backward. As the man was pulled on aboard, enemy automatic weapons opened fire at close range, damaged the aircraft and wounded CWO Novosel. He momentarily lost control of the aircraft, but quickly recovered and departed under the withering enemy fire. In all, 15 extremely hazardous extractions were performed in order to remove wounded personnel. As a direct result of his selfless conduct, the lives of 29 soldiers were saved. The extraordinary heroism displayed by CWO Novosel was an inspiration to his comrades in arms and reflect great credit on him, his unit, and the U.S. Army.

*OLIVE, MILTON L. III

Rank and organization: Private First Class, U.S. Army, Company B, 2d Battalion (Airborne), 503d Infantry, 173d Airborne Brigade. *Place and date:* Phu Cuong, Republic of Vietnam, 22 October 1965. *Entered service at:* Chicago, Ill. *Born:* 7 November 1946, Chicago, Ill. *G.O. No.:* 18, 26 April 1966. *Citation:* For conspicuous gallantry and intrepidity at the risk of his life above and beyond the call of duty. Pfc. Olive was a member of the 3d Platoon of Company B, as it moved through the jungle to find the Viet Cong operating in the area. Although the platoon was subjected to a heavy volume of enemy gunfire and pinned down temporarily, it retaliated by assaulting the Viet Cong positions, causing the enemy to flee. As the platoon pursued the insurgents, Pfc. Olive and 4 other soldiers were moving through the jungle together with a gernade was thrown into their midst. Pfc. Olive saw the grenade, and then saved the lives of his fellow soldiers at the sacrifice of his by grabbing the grenade in his hand and falling on it to absorb the blast with his body. Through his bravery, unhesitating actions, and complete disregard for his safety, he prevented additional loss of life or injury to the members of his platoon. Pfc. Olive's extraordinary heroism, at the risk of his life above and beyond the call of duty are in the highest traditions of the U.S. Army and reflect great credit upon himself and the Armed Forces of his country.

*OLSON, KENNETH L.

Rank and organization: Specialist Fourth Class, U.S. Army, Company A, 5th Battalion, 12th Infantry, 199th Infantry Brigade (Separate) (Light). *Place and date:* Republic of Vietnam, 13 May 1968. *Entered service at:* Minneapolis, Minn. *Born:* 26 May 1945, Willmar, Minn. *Citation:* For conspicuous gallantry and intrepidity in action at the risk of his life above and beyond the call of duty. Sp4c. Olson distinguished himself at the cost of his life while serving as a team leader with Company A. Sp4c. Olson was participating in a mission to reinforce a reconnaissance platoon which was heavily engaged with a well-entrenched Viet Cong force. When his platoon moved into the area of contact and had overrun the first line of enemy bunkers, Sp4c. Olson and a fellow soldier moved forward of the platoon to investigate another suspected line of bunkers. As the 2 men advanced they were pinned down by intense automatic weapons fire from an enemy position 10 meters to their front. With complete disregard for his safety, Sp4c. Olson exposed himself and hurled a handgrenade into the Viet Cong position. Failing to silence the hostile fire, he again exposed himself to the intense fire in preparation to assault the enemy position. As he prepared to hurl the grenade, he was wounded, causing him to drop the activated device within his own position. Realizing that it would explode immediately, Sp4c. Olson threw himself upon the grenade and pulled it in to his body to take the full force of the explosion. By this unselfish action Sp4c. Olson sacrificed his own life to save the lives of his fellow comrades-in-arms. His extraordinary heroism inspired his fellow soldiers to renew their efforts and totally defeat the enemy force. Sp4c. Olson's profound courage and intrepidity were in keeping with the highest traditions of the military service and reflect great credit upon himself, his unit, and the U.S. Army.

O'MALLEY, ROBERT E.

Rank and organization: Sergeant (then Cpl.), U.S. Marine Corps, Company I, 3d Battalion, 3d Marine Regiment, 3d Marine Division (Rein). *Place and date:* Near An Cu'ong 2, South Vietnam, 18 August 1965. *Entered service at:* New York, N.Y. *Born:* 3 June 1943, New York, N.Y. *Citation:* For conspicuous gallantry and intrepidity in action against the communist (Viet Cong) forces at the risk of his life above and beyond the call of duty. While leading his squad in the assault against a strongly entrenched enemy force, his unit came under intense small-arms fire. With complete disregard for his personal safety, Sgt. O'Malley raced across an open rice paddy to a trench line where the enemy forces were located. Jumping into the trench, he attacked the Viet Cong with his rifle and grenades, and singly killed 8 of the enemy. He then led his squad to the assistance of an adjacent marine unit which was suffering heavy casualties. Continuing to press forward, he reloaded his weapon and fired with telling effect into the enemy emplacement. He personally assisted in the evacuation of several wounded marines, and again regrouping the remnants of his squad, he returned to the point of the heaviest fighting. Ordered to an evacuation point by an officer, Sgt. O'Malley gathered his besieged and badly wounded squad, and boldly led them under fire to a helicopter for withdrawal. Although 3 times wounded in this encounter, and facing imminent death from a fanatic and determined enemy, he steadfastly refused evacuation and continued to cover his squad's boarding of the helicopters while, from an exposed position, he delivered fire against the enemy until his wounded men were evacuated. Only then, with his last mission accomplished, did he permit himself to be removed from the battlefield. By his valor, leadership, and courageous efforts in behalf of his comrades, he served as an inspiration to all who observed him, and reflected the highest credit upon the Marine Corps and the U.S. Naval Service.

*OUELLET, DAVID G.

Rank and organization: Seaman, U.S. Navy, River Squadron 5, My Tho Detachment 532. *Place and date:* Mekong River, Republic of Vietnam, 6 March 1967. *Entered service at:* Boston, Mass. *Born:* 13 June, 1944, Newton, Mass. *Citation:* For conspicuous gallantry and intrepidity at the risk of his life above and beyond the call of duty. As the forward machine gunner on River Patrol Boat (PBR) 124, which was on patrol during the early evening hours, Seaman Ouellet observed suspicious activity near the river bank, alerted his boat captain, and recommended movement of the boat to the area to investigate. While the PBR was making a high-speed run along the river bank, Seaman Ouellet spotted an incoming enemy grenade falling toward the boat. He immediately left the protected position of his gun mount and ran aft for the full length of the speeding boat, shouting to his fellow crewmembers to take cover. Observing the boat captain standing unprotected on the boat, Seaman Ouellet bounded on to the engine compartment cover, and pushed the boat captain down to safety. In the split second that followed the grenade's landing, and in the face of certain death, Seaman Ouellet fearlessly placed himself between the deadly missile and his shipmates, courageously absorbing most of the blast fragments with his body in order to protect his shipmates from injury and death. His extraordinary heroism and his selfless and courageous actions on behalf of his comrades at the expense of his life were in the finest traditions of the U.S. Naval Service.

PATTERSON, ROBERT MARTIN

Rank and organization: Sergeant, U.S. Army, Troop B, 2d Squadron, 17th Cavalry. *Place and date:* Near La Chu, Republic of Vietnam, 6 May 1968. *Entered service at:* Raleigh, N.C. *Born:* 16 April 1948, Durham, N.C. *Citation:* For conspicuous gallantry and intrepidity in action at the risk of his life above and beyond the call of duty. Sgt. Patterson (then Sp4c.) distinguished himself while serving as a fire team leader of the 3d Platoon, Troop B, during an assault against a North Vietnamese Army battalion which was entrenched in a heavily fortified position. When the leading squad of the 3d Platoon was pinned down by heavy interlocking automatic weapon and rocket propelled grenade fire from 2 enemy bunkers, Sgt. Patterson and the 2 other members of his assault team moved forward under a hail of enemy fire to destroy the bunkers with grenade and machinegun fire. Observing that his comrades were being fired on from a third enemy bunker covered by enemy gunners in 1-man spider holes, Sgt. Patterson, with complete disregard for his safety and ignoring the warning of his comrades that he was moving into a bunker complex, assaulted and destroyed the position. Although exposed to intensive small arm and grenade fire from the bunkers and their mutually supporting emplacements, Sgt. Patterson continued his assault upon the bunkers which were impeding the advance of his unit. Sgt. Patterson singlehandedly destroyed by rifle and grenade fire 5 enemy bunkers, killed 8 enemy soldiers and captured 7 weapons. His dauntless courage and heroism inspired his platoon to resume the attack and to penetrate the enemy defensive position. Sgt. Patterson's action at the risk of his life has reflected great credit upon himself, his unit, and the U.S. Army.

*PAUL, JOE C.

Rank and organization: Lance Corporal, U.S. Marine Corps, Company H, 2d Battalion, 4th Marines (Rein), 3d Marine Division (Rein). *Place and date:* near Chu Lai, Republic of Vietnam, 18 August 1965. *Entered service at:* Dayton, Ohio. *Born:* 23 April 1946, Williamsburg, Ky. *Citation:* For conspicuous gallantry and intrepidity at the risk of his life above and beyond the call of duty. In violent battle, L/Cpl. Paul's platoon sustained 5 casualties as it was temporarily pinned down, by devastating mortar, recoilless rifle, automatic weapons, and rifle fire delivered by insurgent communist (Viet Cong) forces in well entrenched positions. The wounded marines were unable to move from their perilously exposed positions forward of the remainder of their platoon, and were suddenly subjected to a barrage of white phosphorous rifle grenades. L/Cpl. Paul, fully aware that his tactics would almost certainly result in serious injury or death to himself, chose to disregard his safety and boldly dashed across the fire-swept rice paddies, placed himself between his wounded comrades and the enemy, and delivered effective suppressive fire with his automatic weapon in order to divert the attack long enough to allow the casualties to be evacuated. Although critically wounded during the course of the battle, he resolutely remained in his exposed position and continued to fire his rifle until he collapsed and was evacuated. By his fortitude and gallant spirit of self-sacrifice in the face of almost certain death, he saved the lives of several of his fellow marines. His heroic action served to inspire all who observed him and reflect the highest credit upon himself, the Marine Corps and the U.S. Naval Service. He gallantly gave his life in the cause of freedom.

PENRY, RICHARD A.

Rank and organization: Sergeant, U.S. Army, Company C, 4th Battalion, 12th Infantry, 199th Infantry Brigade. *Place and date:* Binh Tuy Province, Republic of Vietnam, 31 January 1970. *Entered service at:* Oakland, Calif. *Born:* 18 November 1948, Petaluma, Calif. *Citation:* For conspicuous gallantry and intrepidity in action at the risk of his life above and beyond the call of duty. Sgt. Penry, Company C, distinguished himself while serving as a rifleman during a night ambush mission. As the platoon was preparing the ambush position, it suddenly came under an intense enemy attack from mortar, rocket, and automatic weapons fire which seriously wounded the company commander and most of the platoon members, leaving small isolated groups of wounded men throughout the area. Sgt. Penry, seeing the extreme seriousness of the situation, worked his way through the deadly enemy fire to the company command post where he administered first aid to the wounded company commander and other personnel. He then moved the command post to a position which provided greater protection and visual communication and control of other platoon elements. Realizing the company radio was damaged and recognizing the urgent necessity to reestablish communications with the battalion headquarters, he ran outside the defensive perimeter through a fusilladc of hostile fire to retrieve a radio. Finding it inoperable, Sgt. Penry returned through heavy fire to retrieve 2 more radios. Turning his attention to the defense of the area, he crawled to the edge of the perimeter, retrieved needed ammunition and weapons and resupplied the wounded men. During a determined assault by over 30 enemy soldiers, Sgt. Penry occupied the most vulnerable forward position placing heavy, accurate fire on the attacking enemy and exposing himself several times to throw handgrenades into the advancing enemy troops. He succeeded virtually singlehandedly in stopping the attack. Learning that none of the radios were operable, Sgt. Penry again crawled outside the defensive perimeter, retrieved a fourth radio and established communications with higher headquarters. Sgt. Penry then continued to administer first aid to the wounded and repositioned them to better repel further enemy attacks. Despite continuous and deadly sniper fire, he again left the defensive perimeter, moved to within a few feet of enemy positions, located 5 isolated wounded soldiers, and led them to safety. When evacuation helicopters approached, Sgt. Penry voluntarily left the perimeter, set up a guiding beacon, established the priorities for evacuation and successively carried 18 wounded men to the extraction site. After all wounded personnel had been evacuated, Sgt. Penry joined another platoon and assisted in the pursuit of the enemy. Sgt. Penry's extraordinary heroism at the risk of his own life are in keeping with the highest traditions of the military service and reflect great credit on him, his unit, and the U.S. Army.

*PERKINS, WILLIAM THOMAS, Jr.

Rank and organization: Corporal, U.S. Marine Corps, Company C, 1st Battalion, 1st Marines, 1st Marine Division. *Place and date:* Quang Tri Province, Republic of Vietnam, 12 October 1967. *Entered service at:* San Francisco, Calif. *Born:* 10 August 1947, Rochester, N.Y. *Citation:* For conspicuous gallantry and intrepidity at the risk of his life above and beyond the call of duty while serving as a combat photographer attached to Company C. During Operation MEDINA, a major reconnaissance in force southwest of Quang Tri, Company C made heavy combat contact with a numerically superior North Vietnamese Army force estimated at from 2 to 3 companies. The focal point of the intense fighting was a helicopter landing zone which was also serving as the Command Post of Company C. In the course of a strong hostile attack, an enemy grenade landed in the immediate area occupied by Cpl. Perkins and 3 other marines. Realizing the inherent danger, he shouted the warning, "Incoming Grenade" to his fellow marines, and in a valiant act of heroism, hurled himself upon the grenade absorbing the impact of the explosion with his body, thereby saving the lives of his comrades at the cost of his life. Through his exceptional courage and inspiring valor in the face of certain death, Cpl. Perkins reflected great credit upon himself and the Marine Corps and upheld the highest traditions of the U.S. Naval Service. He gallantly gave his life for his country.

*PETERS, LAWRENCE DAVID

Rank and organization: Sergeant, U.S. Marine Corps, Company M, 3d Battalion, 5th Marines, 1st Marine Division. *Place and date:* Quang Tin Province, Republic of Vietnam, 4 September 1967. *Entered service at:* Binghamton, N.Y. *Born:* 16 September 1946, Johnson City, N.Y. *Citation:* For conspicuous gallantry and intrepidity at the risk of his life above and beyond the call of duty while serving as a squad leader with Company M. During Operation SWIFT, the marines of the 2d Platoon of Company M were struck by intense mortar, machinegun, and small-arms fire from an entrenched enemy force. As the company rallied its forces, Sgt. Peters maneuvered his squad in an assault on any enemy defended knoll. Disregarding his safety, as enemy rounds hit all about him, he stood in the open, pointing out enemy positions until he was painfully wounded in the leg. Disregarding his wound, he moved forward and continued to lead his men. As the enemy fire increased in accuracy and volume, his squad lost its momentum and was temporarily pinned down. Exposing himself to devastating enemy fire, he consolidated his position to render more effective fire. While directing the base of fire, he was wounded a second time in the face and neck from an exploding mortar round. As the enemy attempted to infiltrate the position of an adjacent platoon, Sgt. Peters stood erect in the full view of the enemy firing burst after burst forcing them to disclose their camouflaged positions. Sgt. Peters steadfastly continued to direct his squad in spite of 2 additional wounds, persisted in his efforts to encourage and supervise his men until he lost consciousness and succumbed. Inspired by his selfless actions, the squad regained fire superiority and once again carried the assault to the enemy. By his outstanding valor, indomitable fighting spirit and tenacious determination in the face of overwhelming odds, Sgt. Peters upheld the highest traditions of the Marine Corps and the U.S. Naval Service. He gallantly gave his life for his country.

*PETERSEN, DANNY J.

Rank and organization: Specialist Fourth Class, U.S. Army, Company B, 4th Battalion, 23d Infantry, 25th Infantry Division. *Place and date:* Tay Ninh Province, Republic of Vietnam, 9 January 1970. *Entered service at:* Kansas City, Mo. *Born:* 11 March 1949, Horton, Kans. *Citation:* Sp4c. Petersen distinguished himself while serving as an armored personnel carrier commander with Company B during a combat operation against a North Vietnamese Army Force estimated to be of battalion size. During the initial contact with the enemy, an armored personnel carrier was disabled and the crewmen were pinned down by the heavy onslaught of enemy small arms, automatic weapons and rocket-propelled grenade fire. Sp4c. Petersen immediately maneuvered his armored personnel carrier to a position between the disabled vehicle and the enemy. He placed suppressive fire on the enemy's well-fortified position, thereby enabling the crewmembers of the disabled personnel carrier to repair their vehicle. He then maneuvered his vehicle, while still under heavy hostile fire to within 10 feet of the enemy's defensive emplacement. After a period of intense fighting, his vehicle received a direct hit and the driver was wounded. With extraordinary courage and selfless disregard for his own safety, Sp4c. Petersen carried his wounded comrade 45 meters across the bullet-swept field to a secure area. He then voluntarily returned to his disabled armored personnel carrier to provide covering fire for both the other vehicles and the dismounted personnel of his platoon as they withdrew. Despite heavy fire from 3 sides, he remained with his disabled vehicle, alone and completely exposed. Sp4c. Petersen was standing on top of his vehicle, firing his weapon, when he was mortally wounded. His heroic and selfless actions prevented further loss of life in his platoon. Sp4c. Petersen's conspicuous gallantry and extraordinary heroism are in the highest traditions of the service and reflect great credit on him, his unit, and the U.S. Army.

*PHIPPS, JIMMY W.

Rank and organization: Private First Class, U.S. Marine Corps, Company B, 1st Engineer Battalion, 1st Marine Division (Rein), FMF. *Place and date:* Near An Hoa, Republic of Vietnam, 27 May 1969. *Entered service at:* Culver City, Calif. *Born:* 1 November 1950, Santa Monica, Calif. *Citation:* For conspicuous gallantry and intrepidity at the risk of his life above and beyond the call of duty while serving as a combat engineer with Company B in connection with combat operations against the enemy. Pfc. Phipps was a member of a 2-man combat engineer demolition team assigned to locate and destroy enemy artillery ordnance and concealed firing devices. After he had expended all of his explosives and blasting caps, Pfc. Phipps discovered a 175mm high explosive artillery round in a rice paddy. Suspecting that the enemy had attached the artillery round to a secondary explosive device, he warned other marines in the area to move to covered positions and prepared to destroy the round with a handgrenade. As he was attaching the handgrenade to a stake beside the artillery round, the fuse of the enemy's secondary explosive device ignited. Realizing that his assistant and the platoon commander were both within a few meters of him and that the imminent explosion could kill all 3 men, Pfc. Phipps grasped the handgrenade to his chest and dived forward to cover the enemy's explosive and the artillery round with his body, thereby shielding his companions from the detonation while absorbing the full and tremendous impact with his body. Pfc. Phipps' indomitable courage, inspiring initiative, and selfless devotion to duty saved the lives of 2 marines and upheld the highest traditions of the Marine Corps and the U.S. Naval Service. He gallantly gave his life for his country.

*PIERCE, LARRY S.

Rank and organization: Sergeant, U.S. Army, Headquarters and Headquarters Company, 1st Battalion (Airborne), 503d Infantry, 173d Airborne Brigade. *Place and date:* Near Ben Cat, Republic of Vietnam, 20 September 1965. *Entered service at:* Fresno, Calif. *Born:* 6 July 1941, Wewoka, Okla. *G.O. No.:* 7, 24 February 1966. *Citation:* For conspicuous gallantry and intrepidity at the risk of life above and beyond the call of duty. Sgt. Pierce was serving as squad leader in a reconnaissance platoon when his patrol was ambushed by hostile forces. Through his inspiring leadership and personal courage, the squad succeeded in eliminating an enemy machinegun and routing the opposing force. While pursuing the fleeing enemy, the squad came upon a dirt road and, as the main body of his men entered the road, Sgt. Pierce discovered an antipersonnel mine emplaced in the road bed. Realizing that the mine could destroy the majority of his squad, Sgt. Pierce saved the lives of his men at the sacrifice of his life by throwing himself directly onto the mine as it exploded. Through his indomitable courage, complete disregard for his safety, and profound concern for his fellow soldiers, he averted loss of life and injury to the members of his squad. Sgt. Pierce's extraordinary heroism, at the cost of his life, are in the highest traditions of the U.S. Army and reflect great credit upon himself and the Armed Forces of his country.

PITTMAN, RICHARD A.

Rank and organization: Sergeant (then L/Cpl.), U.S. Marine Corps, Company I, 3d Battalion, 5th Marines, 1st Marine Division (Rein) FMF. *Place and date:* near the Demilitarized Zone, Republic of Vietnam, 24 July 1966. *Entered service at:* Stockton, Calif. *Born:* 26 May 1945, French Camp, San Joaquin, Calif. *Citation:* For conspicuous gallantry and intrepidity at the risk of his life above and beyond the call of duty. While Company I was conducting an operation along the axis of a narrow jungle trail, the leading company elements suffered numerous casualties when they suddenly came under heavy fire from a well concealed and numerically superior enemy force. Hearing the engaged marines' calls for more firepower, Sgt. Pittman quickly exchanged his rifle for a machinegun and several belts of ammunition, left the relative safety of his platoon, and unhesitatingly rushed forward to aid his comrades. Taken under intense enemy small-arms fire at point blank range during his advance, he returned the fire, silencing the enemy position. As Sgt. Pittman continued to forge forward to aid members of the leading platoon, he again came under heavy fire from 2 automatic weapons which he promptly destroyed. Learning that there were additional wounded marines 50 yards further along the trail, he braved a withering hail of enemy mortar and small-arms fire to continue onward. As he reached the position where the leading marines had fallen, he was suddenly confronted with a bold frontal attack by 30 to 40 enemy. Totally disregarding his safety, he calmly established a position in the middle of the trail and raked the advancing enemy with devastating machinegun fire. His weapon rendered ineffective, he picked up an enemy submachinegun and, together with a pistol seized from a fallen comrade, continued his lethal fire until the enemy force had withdrawn. Having exhausted his ammunition except for a grenade which he hurled at the enemy, he then rejoined his platoon. Sgt. Pittman's daring initiative, bold fighting spirit and selfless devotion to duty inflicted many enemy casualties, disrupted the enemy attack and saved the lives of many of his wounded comrades. His personal valor at grave risk to himself reflects the highest credit upon himself, the Marine Corps, and the U.S. Naval Service.

*PITTS, RILEY L.

Rank and organization: Captain, U.S. Army, Company C, 2d Battalion, 27th Infantry, 25th Infantry Division. *Place and date:* Ap Dong, Republic of Vietnam, 31 October 1967. *Entered service at:* Wichita, Kans. *Born:* 15 October 1937, Fallis, Okla. *Citation:* Distinguishing himself by exceptional heroism while serving as company commander during an airmobile assault. Immediately after his company landed in the area, several Viet Cong opened fire with automatic weapons. Despite the enemy fire, Capt. Pitts forcefully led an assault which overran the enemy positions. Shortly thereafter, Capt. Pitts was ordered to move his unit to the north to reinforce another company heavily engaged against a strong enemy force. As Capt. Pitts' company moved forward to engage the enemy, intense fire was received from 3 directions, including fire from 4 enemy bunkers, 2 of which were within 15 meters of Capt. Pitts' position. The severity of the incoming fire prevented Capt. Pitts from maneuvering his company. His rifle fire proving ineffective against the enemy due to the dense jungle foliage, he picked up an M-79 grenade launcher and began pinpointing the targets. Seizing a Chinese Communist grenade which had been taken from a captured Viet Cong's web gear, Capt. Pitts lobbed the grenade at a bunker to his front, but it hit the dense jungle foliage and rebounded. Without hesitation, Capt. Pitts threw himself on top of the grenade which, fortunately, failed to explode. Capt. Pitts then directed the repositioning of the company to permit friendly artillery to be fired. Upon completion of the artillery fire mission, Capt. Pitts again led his men toward the enemy positions, personally killing at least 1 more Viet Cong. The jungle growth still prevented effective fire to be placed on the enemy. Capt. Pitts, displaying complete disregard for his life and personal safety, quickly moved to a position which permitted him to place effective fire on the enemy. He maintained a continuous fire, pinpointing the enemy's fortified positions, while at the same time directing and urging his men forward, until he was mortally wounded. Capt. Pitts' conspicuous gallantry, extraordinary heroism, and intrepidity at the cost of his life, above and beyond the call of duty, are in the highest traditions of the U.S. Army and reflect great credit upon himself, his unit, and the Armed Forces of his country.

PLESS, STEPHEN W.

Rank and organization: Major (then Capt.), U.S. Marine Corps, VMD-6, Mag-36, 1st Marine Aircraft Wing. *Place and date:* Near Quang Nai, Republic of Vietnam, 19 August 1967. *Entered service at:* Atlanta, Ga. *Born:* 6 September 1939, Newman, Ga. *Citation:* For conspicuous gallantry and intrepidity at the risk of his life above and beyond the call of duty while serving as a helicopter gunship pilot attached to Marine Observation Squadron 6 in action against enemy forces. During an escort mission Maj. Pless monitored an emergency call that 4 American soldiers stranded on a nearby beach were being overwhelmed by a large Viet Cong force. Maj. Pless flew to the scene and found 30 to 50 enemy soldiers in the open. Some of the enemy were bayonetting and beating the downed Americans. Maj. Pless displayed exceptional airmanship as he launched a devastating attack against the enemy force, killing or wounding many of the enemy and driving the remainder back into a treeline. His rocket and machinegun attacks were made at such low levels that the aircraft flew through debris created by explosions from its rockets. Seeing 1 of the wounded soldiers gesture for assistance, he maneuvered his helicopter into a position between the wounded men and the enemy, providing a shield which permitted his crew to retrieve the wounded. During the rescue the enemy directed intense fire at the helicopter and rushed the aircraft again and again, closing to within a few feet before being beaten back. When the wounded men were aboard, Maj. Pless maneuvered the helicopter out to sea. Before it became safely airborne, the overloaded aircraft settled 4 times into the water. Displaying superb airmanship, he finally got the helicopter aloft. Major Pless' extraordinary heroism coupled with his outstanding flying skill prevented the annihilation of the tiny force. His courageous actions reflect great credit upon himself and uphold the highest traditions of the Marine Corps and the U.S. Naval Service.

*PORT, WILLIAM D.

Rank and organization: Sergeant (then Pfc.), U.S. Army, Company C, 5th Battalion, 7th Cavalry, 1st Air Cavalry Division. *Place and date:* Que Son Valley, Heip Duc Province, Republic of Vietnam, 12 January 1968. *Entered service at:* Harrisburg, Pa. *Born:* 13 October 1941, Petersburg, Pa. *Citation:* For conspicuous gallantry and intrepidity at the risk of his life above and beyond the call of duty. Sgt. Port distinguished himself while serving as a rifleman with Company C, which was conducting combat operations against an enemy force in the Que Son Valley. As Sgt. Port's platoon was moving to cut off a reported movement of enemy soldiers, the platoon came under heavy fire from an entrenched enemy force. The platoon was forced to withdraw due to the intensity and ferocity of the fire. Although wounded in the hand as the withdrawal began, Sgt. Port, with complete disregard for his safety, ran through the heavy fire to assist a wounded comrade back to the safety of the platoon perimeter. As the enemy forces assaulted in the perimeter, Sgt. Port and 3 comrades were in position behind an embankment when an enemy grenade landed in their midst. Sgt. Port, realizing the danger to his fellow soldiers, shouted the warning, "Grenade," and unhesitatingly hurled himself towards the grenade to shield his comrades from the explosion. Through his exemplary courage and devotion he saved the lives of his fellow soldiers and gave the members of his platoon the inspiration needed to hold their position. Sgt. Port's selfless concern for his comrades, at the risk of his life above and beyond the call of duty are in keeping with the highest tradition of the military service and reflect great credit on himself, his unit, and the U.S. Army.

*POXON, ROBERT LESLIE

Rank and organization: First Lieutenant, U.S. Army, Troop B, 1st Squadron, 9th Cavalry, 1st Cavalry Division. *Place and date:* Tay Ninh Province, Republic of Vietnam, 2 June 1969. *Entered service at:* Detroit, Mich. *Born:* 3 January 1947, Detroit, Mich. *Citation:* For conspicuous gallantry and intrepidity in action at the risk of his life above and beyond the call of duty. 1st Lt. Poxon, Armor, Troop B, distinguished himself while serving as a platoon leader on a reconnaissance mission. Landing by helicopter in an area suspected of being occupied by the enemy, the platoon came under intense fire from enemy soldiers in concealed positions and fortifications around the landing zone. A soldier fell, hit by the first burst of fire. 1st Lt. Poxon dashed to his aid, drawing the majority of the enemy fire as he crossed 20 meters of open ground. The fallen soldier was beyond help and 1st Lt. Poxon was seriously and painfully wounded. 1st Lt. Poxon, with indomitable courage, refused medical aid and evacuation and turned his attention to seizing the initiative from the enemy. With sure instinct he marked a central enemy bunker as the key to success. Quickly instructing his men to concentrate their fire on the bunker, and in spite of his wound, 1st Lt. Poxon crawled toward the bunker, readied a handgrenade and charged. He was hit again but continued his assault. After succeeding in silencing the enemy guns in the bunker he was struck once again by enemy fire and fell, mortally wounded. 1st Lt. Poxon's comrades followed their leader, pressed the attack and drove the enemy from their positions. 1st Lt. Poxon's gallantry, indomitable will, and courage are in keeping with the highest traditions of the military service and reflect great credit upon himself, his unit, and the U.S. Army.

*PROM, WILLIAM R.

Rank and organization: Lance Corporal, U.S. Marine Corps, Company I, 3d Battalion, 3d Marines, 3d Marine Division (Rein), FMF.

Place and date: Near An Hoa, Republic of Vietnam. 9 February 1969. *Entered service at:* Pittsburgh, Pa. *Born:* 17 November 1948, Pittsburgh, Pa. *Citation:* For conspicuous gallantry and intrepidity at the risk of his life above and beyond the call of duty while serving as a machinegun squad leader with Company I, in action against the enemy. While returning from a reconnaissance operation during Operation TAYLOR COMMON, 2 platoons of Company I came under an intense automatic weapons fire and grenade attack from a well concealed North Vietnamese Army force in fortified positions. The leading, element of the platoon was isolated and several marines were wounded. L/Cpl. Prom immediately assumed control of 1 of his machineguns and began to deliver return fire. Disregarding his safety he advanced to a position from which he could more effectively deliver covering fire while first aid was administered to the wounded men. Realizing that the enemy would have to be destroyed before the injured marines could be evacuated, L/Cpl. Prom again moved forward and delivered a heavy volume of fire with such accuracy that he was instrumental in routing the enemy, thus permitting his men to regroup and resume their march. Shortly thereafter, the platoon again came under heavy fire in which 1 man was critically wounded. Reacting instantly, L/Cpl. Prom moved forward to protect his injured comrade. Unable to continue his fire because of his severe wounds, he continued to advance to within a few yards to the enemy positions. There, standing in full view of the enemy, he accurately directed the fire of his support elements until he was mortally wounded. Inspired by his heroic actions, the marines launched an assault that destroyed the enemy. L/Cpl. Prom's indomitable courage, inspiring initiative and selfless devotion to duty upheld the highest traditions of the Marine Corps and the U.S. Naval Service. He gallantly gave his life for his country.

*PRUDEN, ROBERT J.

Rank and organization: Staff Sergeant, U.S. Army, 75th Infantry, Americal Division. *Place and date:* Quang Ngai Province, Republic of Vietnam, 29 November 1969. *Entered service at:* Minneapolis, Minn. *Born:* 9 September 1949, St. Paul, Minn. *Citation:* For conspicuous gallantry and intrepidity in action at the risk of his life above and beyond the call of duty. S/Sgt. Pruden, Company G, distinguished himself while serving as a reconnaissance team leader during an ambush mission. The 6-man team was inserted by helicopter into enemy controlled territory to establish an ambush position and to obtain information concerning enemy movements. As the team moved into the preplanned area, S/Sgt. Pruden deployed his men into 2 groups on the opposite sides of a well used trail. As the groups were establishing their defensive positions, 1 member of the team was trapped in the open by the heavy fire from an enemy squad. Realizing that the ambush position had been compromised, S/Sgt. Pruden directed his team to open fire on the enemy force. Immediately, the team came under heavy fire from a second enemy element. S/Sgt. Pruden, with full knowledge of the extreme danger involved, left his concealed position and, firing as he ran, advanced toward the enemy to draw the hostile fire. He was seriously wounded twice but continued his attack until he fell for a third time, in front of the enemy positions. S/Sgt. Pruden's actions resulted in several enemy casualties and withdrawal of the remaining enemy force. Although grievously wounded, he directed his men into defensive positions and called for evacuation helicopters, which safely withdrew the members of the team. S/Sgt. Pruden's outstanding courage, selfless concern for the welfare of his men, and intrepidity in action at the cost of his life were in keeping with the highest traditions of the military service and reflect great credit upon himself, his unit, and the U.S. Army.

*RABEL, LASZLO

Rank and organization: Staff Sergeant, U.S. Army, 74th Infantry Detachment (Long Range Patrol), 173d Airborne Brigade. *Place and date:* Binh Dinh Province, Republic of Vietnam, 13 November 1968. *Entered service at:* Minneapolis, Minn. *Born:* 21 September 1939, Budapest, Hungary. *Citation:* For conspicuous gallantry and intrepidity in action at the risk of his life above and beyond the call of duty. S/Sgt. Rabel distinguished himself while serving as leader of Team Delta, 74th Infantry Detachment. At 1000 hours on this date, Team Delta was in a defensive perimeter conducting reconnaissance of enemy trail networks when a member of the team detected enemy movement to the front. As S/Sgt. Rabel and a comrade prepared to clear the area, he heard an incoming grenade as it landed in the midst of the team's perimeter. With complete disregard for his life, S/Sgt. Rabel threw himself on the grenade and, covering it with his body, received the complete impact of the immediate explosion. Through his indomitable courage, complete disregard for his safety and profound concern for his fellow soldiers, S/Sgt. Rabel averted the loss of life and injury to the other members of Team Delta. By his gallantry at the cost of his life in the highest traditions of the military service, S/Sgt. Rabel has reflected great credit upon himself, his unit, and the U.S. Army.

*RAY, DAVID ROBERT

Rank and organization: Hospital Corpsman Second Class, U.S. Navy, 2d Battalion, 11th Marines, 1st Marine Division (Rein), FMF. *Place and date:* Quang Nam Province, Republic of Vietnam, 19 March 1969. *Entered service at:* Nashville, Tenn. *Born:* 14 February 1945, McMinnville, Tenn. *Citation:* For conspicuous gallantry and intrepidity at the risk of his life above and beyond the call of duty while serving as a HC2c. with Battery D, 2d Battalion, at Phu Loc 6, near An Hoa. During the early morning hours, an estimated battalion-sized enemy force launched a determined assault against the battery's position, and succeeded in effecting a penetration of the barbed-wire perimeter. The initial burst of enemy fire caused numerous casualties among the marines who had immediately manned their howitzers during the rocket and mortar attack. Undaunted by the intense hostile fire, HC2c. Ray moved from parapet to parapet, rendering emergency medical treatment to the wounded. Although seriously wounded himself while administering first aid to a marine casualty, he refused medical aid and continued his lifesaving efforts. While he was bandaging and attempting to comfort another wounded marine, HC2c. Ray was forced to battle 2 enemy soldiers who attacked his position, personally killing 1 and wounding the other. Rapidly losing his strength as a result of his severe wounds, he nonetheless managed to move through the hail of enemy fire to other casualties. Once again, he was faced with the intense fire of oncoming enemy troops and, despite the grave personal danger and insurmountable odds, succeeded in treating the wounded and holding off the enemy until he ran out of ammunition, at which time he sustained fatal wounds. HC2c. Ray's final act of heroism was to protect the patient he was treating. He threw himself upon the wounded marine, thus saving the man's life when an enemy grenade exploded nearby. By his determined and persevering actions, courageous spirit, and selfless devotion to the welfare of his marine comrades, HC2c. Ray served to inspire the men of Battery D to heroic efforts in defeating the enemy. His conduct throughout was in keeping with the finest traditions of the U.S. Naval Service.

RAY, RONALD ERIC

Rank and organization: Captain (then 1st Lt.), U.S. Army, Company A, 2d Battalion, 35th Infantry, 25th Infantry Division. *Place and date:* Ia Drang Valley, Republic of Vietnam, 19 June 1966. *Entered service at:* Atlanta, Ga. *Born:* 7 December 1941, Cordelle, Ga. *Citation:* For conspicuous gallantry and intrepidity in action at the risk of his life above and beyond the call of duty. Capt. Ray distinguished himself while serving as a platoon leader with Company A. When 1 of his ambush patrols was attacked by an estimated reinforced Viet Cong company, Capt. Ray organized a reaction force and quickly moved through 2 kilometers of mountainous jungle terrain to the contact area. After breaking through the hostile lines to reach the beleaguered patrol, Capt. Ray began directing the reinforcement of the site. When an enemy position pinned down 3 of his men with a heavy volume of automatic weapons fire, he silenced the emplacement with a grenade and killed 4 Viet Cong with his rifle fire. As medics were moving a casualty toward a sheltered position, they began receiving intense hostile fire. While directing suppressive fire on the enemy position, Capt. Ray moved close enough to silence the enemy with a grenade. A few moments later Capt. Ray saw an enemy grenade land, unnoticed, near 2 of his men. Without hesitation or regard for his safety he dove between the grenade and the men, thus shielding them from the explosion while receiving wounds in his exposed feet and legs. He immediately sustained additional wounds in his legs from an enemy machinegun, but nevertheless he silenced the emplacement with another grenade. Although suffering great pain from his wounds, Capt. Ray continued to direct his men, providing the outstanding courage and leadership they vitally needed, and prevented their annihilation by successfully leading them from their surrounded position. Only after assuring that his platoon was no longer in immediate danger did he allow himself to be evacuated for medical treatment. By his gallantry at the risk of his life in the highest traditions of the military service, Capt. Ray has reflected great credit on himself, his unit, and the U.S. Army.

*REASONER, FRANK S.

Rank and organization: First Lieutenant, U.S. Marine Corps, Company A, 3d Reconnaissance Battalion, 3d Marine Division. *Place and date:* near Da Nang, Republic of Vietnam, 12 July 1965. *Entered service at:* Kellogg, Idaho. *Born:* 16 September 1937, Spokane, Wash. *Citation:* For conspicuous gallantry and intrepidity at the risk of his life above and beyond the call of duty. The reconnaissance patrol led by 1st Lt. Reasoner had deeply penetrated heavily controlled enemy territory when it came under extremely heavy fire from an estimated 50 to 100 Viet Cong insurgents. Accompanying the advance party and the point that consisted of 5 men, he immediately deployed his men for an assault after the Viet Cong had opened fire from numerous concealed positions. Boldly shouting encouragement, and virtually isolated from the main body, he organized a base of fire for an assault on the enemy positions. The slashing fury of the Viet Cong machinegun and automatic weapons fire made it impossible for the main body to move forward. Repeatedly exposing himself to the devastating attack he skillfully provided covering fire, killing at least 2 Viet Cong and effectively silencing an automatic weapons position in a valiant attempt to effect evacuation of a wounded man. As casualties began to mount his radio operator was wounded and 1st Lt. Reasoner immediately moved to his side and tended his wounds. When the radio operator was hit a second time while attempting to reach a covered position, 1st Lt. Reasoner courageously running to his aid through the grazing machinegun fire fell mortally wounded. His indomitable fighting spirit, valiant leadership and unflinching devotion to duty provided the inspiration that was to enable the patrol to complete its mission without further casualties. In the face of almost certain death he gallantly gave his life in the service of his country. His actions upheld the highest traditions of the Marine Corps and the U.S. Naval Service.

*ROARK, ANUND C.

Rank and organization: Sergeant, U.S. Army, Company C, 1st Battalion, 12th Infantry, 4th Infantry Division. *Place and date:* Kontum Province, Republic of Vietnam, 16 May 1968. *Entered service at:* Los Angeles, Calif. *Born:* 17 February 1948, Vallejo, Calif. *Citation:* For conspicuous gallantry and intrepidity in action at the risk of his life above and beyond the call of duty. Sgt. Roark distinguished himself by extraordinary gallantry while serving with Company C. Sgt. Roark was the point squad leader of a small force which had the mission of rescuing 11 men in a hilltop observation post under heavy attack by a company-size force, approximately 1,000 meters from the battalion perimeter. As lead elements of the relief force reached the besieged observation post, intense automatic weapons fire from enemy occupied bunkers halted their movement. Without hesitation, Sgt. Roark maneuvered his squad, repeatedly exposing himself to withering enemy fire to hurl grenades and direct the fire of his squad to gain fire superiority and cover the withdrawal of the outpost and evacuation of its casualties. Frustrated in their effort to overrun the position, the enemy swept the hilltop with small arms and volleys of grenades. Seeing a grenade land in the midst of his men, Sgt. Roark, with complete disregard for his safety, hurled himself upon the grenade, absorbing its blast with his body. Sgt. Roark's magnificent leadership and dauntless courage saved the lives of many of his comrades and were the inspiration for the successful relief of the outpost. His actions which culminated in the

136

supreme sacrifice of his life were in keeping with the highest traditions of the military service, and reflect great credit on himself and the U.S. Army.

ROBERTS, GORDON R.

Rank and organization: Sergeant (then Sp4c.), U.S. Army, Company B, 1st Battalion, 506th Infantry, 101st Airborne Division. *Place and date:* Thua Thien Province, Republic of Vietnam, 11 July 1969. *Entered service at:* Cincinnati, Ohio. *Born:* 14 June 1950, Middletown, Ohio. *Citation:* For conspicuous gallantry and intrepidity in action at the risk of his life above and beyond the call of duty. Sgt. Roberts distinguished himself while serving as a rifleman in Company B, during combat operations. Sgt. Roberts' platoon was maneuvering along a ridge to attack heavily fortified enemy bunker positions which had pinned down an adjoining friendly company. As the platoon approached the enemy positions, it was suddenly pinned down by heavy automatic weapons and grenade fire from camouflaged enemy fortifications atop the overlooking hill. Seeing his platoon immobilized and in danger of failing in its mission, Sgt. Roberts crawled rapidly toward the closest enemy bunker. With complete disregard for his safety, he leaped to his feet and charged the bunker, firing as he ran. Despite the intense enemy fire directed at him, Sgt. Roberts silenced the 2-man bunker. Without hesitation, Sgt. Roberts continued his 1-man assault on a second bunker. As he neared the second bunker, a burst of enemy fire knocked his rifle from his hands. Sgt. Roberts picked up a rifle dropped by a comrade and continued his assault, silencing the bunker. He continued his charge against a third bunker and destroyed it with well-thrown handgrenades. Although Sgt. Roberts was now cut off from his platoon, he continued his assault against a fourth enemy emplacement. He fought through a heavy hail of fire to join elements of the adjoining company which had been pinned down by the enemy fire. Although continually exposed to hostile fire, he assisted in moving wounded personnel from exposed positions on the hilltop to an evacuation area before returning to his unit. By his gallant and selfless actions, Sgt. Roberts contributed directly to saving the lives of his comrades and served as an inspiration to his fellow soldiers in the defeat of the enemy force. Sgt. Roberts' extraordinary heroism in action at the risk of his life were in keeping with the highest traditions of the military service and reflect great credit upon himself, his unit, and the U.S. Army.

*ROBINSON, JAMES W., JR.

Rank and organization: Sergeant, U.S. Army, Company D, 2d Battalion, 16th Infantry, 1st Infantry Division. *Place and date:* Republic of Vietnam, 11 April 1966. *Entered service at:* Chicago, Ill. *Born:* 30 August 1940, Hinsdale, Ill. *Citation:* For conspicuous gallantry and intrepidity in action at the risk of his life above and beyond the call of duty. Company C was engaged in fierce combat with a Viet Cong battalion. Despite the heavy fire, Sgt. Robinson moved among the men of his fire team, instructing and inspiring them, and placing them in advantageous positions. Enemy snipers located in nearby trees were inflicting heavy casualties on forward elements of Sgt. Robinson's unit.

Upon locating the enemy sniper whose fire was taking the heaviest toll, he took a grenade launcher and eliminated the sniper. Seeing a medic hit while administering aid to a wounded sergeant in front of his position and aware that now the 2 wounded men were at the mercy of the enemy, he charged through a withering hail of fire and dragged his comrades to safety, where he rendered first aid and saved their lives. As the battle continued and casualties mounted, Sgt. Robinson moved about under intense fire to collect from the wounded their weapons and ammunition and redistribute them to able-bodied soldiers. Adding his fire to that of his men, he assisted in eliminating a major enemy threat. Seeing another wounded comrade in front of his position, Sgt. Robinson again defied the enemy's fire to effect a rescue. In so doing he was himself wounded in the shoulder and leg. Despite his painful wounds, he dragged the soldier to shelter and saved his life by administering first aid. While patching his own wounds, he spotted an enemy machinegun which had inflicted a number of casualties on the American force. His rifle ammunition expended, he seized 2 grenades and, in an act of unsurpassed heroism, charged toward the entrenched enemy weapon. Hit again in the leg, this time with a tracer round which set fire to his clothing, Sgt. Robinson ripped the burning clothing from his body and staggered indomitably through the enemy fire, now concentrated solely on him, to within grenade range of the enemy machinegun position. Sustaining 2 additional chest wounds, he marshalled his fleeting physical strength and hurled the 2 grenades, thus destroying the enemy gun position, as he fell dead upon the battlefield. His magnificent display of leadership and bravery saved several lives and inspired his soldiers to defeat the numerically superior enemy force. Sgt. Robinson's conspicuous gallantry and intrepidity, at the cost of his life, are in keeping with the finest traditions of the U.S. Army and reflect great credit upon the 1st Infantry Division and the U.S. Armed Forces.

ROCCO, LOUIS R.

Rank and organization: Warrant Officer (then Sergeant First Class), U.S. Army, Advisory Team 162, U.S. Military Assistance Command. *Place and date:* Northeast of Katum, Republic of Vietnam, 24 May 1970. *Entered service at:* Los Angeles, Calif. *Born:* 19 November 1938, Albuquerque, N. Mex. *Citation:* WO Rocco distinguished himself when he volunteered to accompany a medical evacuation team on an urgent mission to evacuate 8 critically wounded Army of the Republic of Vietnam personnel. As the helicopter approached the landing zone, it became the target for intense enemy automatic weapons fire. Disregarding his own safety, WO Rocco identified and placed accurate suppressive fire on the enemy positions as the aircraft descended toward the landing zone. Sustaining major damage from the enemy fire, the aircraft was forced to crash land, causing WO Rocco to sustain a fractured wrist and hip and a severely bruised back. Ignoring his injuries, he extracted the survivors from the burning wreckage, sustaining burns to his own body. Despite intense enemy fire, WO Rocco carried each unconscious man across approximately 20 meters of exposed terrain to the Army of the Republic of Vietnam perimeter. On each trip, his severely burned hands and broken wrist caused excruciating pain, but the lives of the unconscious crash survivors were more important than his personal discomfort, and he continued his rescue efforts. Once inside the friendly position, WO Rocco helped administer first aid to his wounded comrades until his wounds and burns caused him to collapse and lose consciousness. His bravery under fire and intense devotion to duty were directly responsible for saving 3 of his fellow soldiers from certain death. His unparalleled bravery in the face of enemy fire, his complete disregard for his own pain and injuries, and his performance were far above and beyond the call of duty and were in keeping with the highest traditions of self-sacrifice and courage of the military service.

ROGERS, CHARLES CALVIN

Rank and organization: Lieutenant Colonel, U.S. Army, 1st Battalion, 5th Artillery, 1st Infantry Division. *Place and date:* Fishhook, near Cambodian border, Republic of Vietnam, 1 November 1968. *Entered service at:* Institute, W. Va. *Born:* 6 September 1929, Claremont, W. Va. *Citation:* For conspicuous gallantry and intrepidity in action at the risk of his life above and beyond the call of duty. Lt. Col. Rogers, Field Artillery, distinguished himself in action while serving as commanding officer, 1st Battalion, during the defense of a forward fire support base. In the early morning hours, the fire support base was subjected to a concentrated bombardment of heavy mortar, rocket and rocket propelled grenade fire. Simultaneously the position was struck by a human wave ground assault, led by sappers who breached the defensive barriers with bangalore torpedoes and penetrated the defensive perimeter. Lt. Col. Rogers with complete disregard for his safety moved through the hail of fragments from bursting enemy rounds to the embattled area. He aggressively rallied the dazed artillery crewmen to man their howitzers and he directed their fire on the assaulting enemy. Although knocked to the ground and wounded by an exploding round, Lt. Col. Rogers sprang to his feet and led a small counterattack force against an enemy element that had penetrated the howitzer positions. Although painfully wounded a second time during the assault, Lt. Col. Rogers pressed the attack killing several of the enemy and driving the remainder from the positions. Refusing medical treatment, Lt. Col. Rogers reestablished and reinforced the defensive positions. As a second human wave attack was launched against another sector of the perimeter, Lt. Col. Rogers directed artillery fire on the assaulting enemy and led a second counterattack against the charging forces. His valorous example rallied the beleaguered defenders to repulse and defeat the enemy onslaught. Lt. Col. Rogers moved from position to position through the heavy enemy fire, giving encouragement and direction to his men. At dawn the determined enemy launched a third assault against the fire base in an attempt to overrun the position. Lt. Col. Rogers moved to the threatened area and directed lethal fire on the enemy forces. Seeing a howitzer inoperative due to casualties, Lt. Col. Rogers joined the surviving members of the crew to return the howitzer to action. While directing the position defense, Lt. Col. Rogers was seriously wounded by fragments from a heavy mortar round which exploded on the parapet of the gun position. Although too severely wounded to physically lead the defenders, Lt. Col. Rogers continued to give encouragement and direction to his men in the defeating and repelling of the enemy attack. Lt. Col. Rogers' dauntless courage and heroism inspired the defenders of the fire support base to the heights of valor to defeat a determined and numerically superior enemy force. His relentless spirit of aggressiveness in action are in the highest traditions of the military service and reflects great credit upon himself, his unit, and the U.S. Army.

*RUBIO, EURIPIDES

Rank and organization: Captain, U.S. Army, Headquarters and Headquarters Company, 1st Battalion, 28th Infantry, 1st Infantry Division, RVN. *Place and date:* Tay Ninh Province, Republic of Vietnam, 8 November 1966. *Entered service at:* Fort Buchanan, Puerto Rico. *Born:* 1 March 1938, Ponce, Puerto Rico. *Citation:* For conspicuous gallantry and intrepidity in action at the risk of his life above and beyond the call of duty. Capt. Rubio, Infantry, was serving as communications officer, 1st Battalion, when a numerically superior enemy force launched a massive attack against the battalion defense position. Intense enemy machinegun fire raked the area while mortar rounds and rifle grenades exploded within the perimeter. Leaving the relative safety of his post, Capt. Rubio received 2 serious wounds as he braved the withering fire to go to the area of most intense action where he distributed ammunition, re-established positions and rendered aid to the wounded. Disregarding the painful wounds, he unhesitatingly assumed command when a rifle company commander was medically evacuated. Capt. Rubio was wounded a third time as he selflessly exposed himself to the devastating enemy fire to move among his men to encourage them to fight with renewed effort. While aiding the evacuation of wounded personnel, he noted that a smoke grenade which was intended to mark the Viet Cong position for air strikes had fallen dangerously close to the friendly lines. Capt. Rubio ran to reposition the grenade but was immediately struck to his knees by enemy fire. Despite his several wounds, Capt. Rubio scooped up the grenade, ran through the deadly hail of fire to within 20 meters of the enemy position and hurled the already smoking grenade into the midst of the enemy before he fell for the final time. Using the repositioned grenade as a marker, friendly air strikes were directed to destroy the hostile positions. Capt. Rubio's singularly heroic act turned the tide of battle, and his extraordinary leadership and valor were a magnificent inspiration to his men. His remarkable bravery and selfless concern for his men are in keeping with the highest traditions of the military service and reflect great credit on Capt. Rubio and the U.S. Army.

*SANTIAGO-COLON, HECTOR

Rank and organization: Specialist Fourth Class, U.S. Army, Company B, 5th Battalion, 7th Cavalry, 1st Cavalry Division (Airmobile). *Place and date:* Quang Tri Province, Republic of Vietnam, 28 June 1968. *Entered service at:* New York, N.Y. *Born:* 20 December 1942, Salinas, Puerto Rico. *Citation:* For conspicuous gallantry and intrepidity in action at the risk of his life above and beyond the call of duty. Sp4c. Santiago-Colon distinguished himself at the cost of his life while serving as a gunner in the mortar platoon of Company B. While serving as a perimeter sentry, Sp4c. Santiago-Colon heard distinct movement in the heavily wooded area to his front and flanks. Immediately he alerted his fellow sentries in the area to move to their foxholes and remain alert for any enemy probing forces. From the wooded area around his position heavy enemy automatic weapons and small-arms fire suddenly broke out, but extreme darkness rendered difficult the precise location and identification of the hostile force. Only the muzzle flashes from enemy weapons indicated their position. Sp4c. Santiago-Colon and the other members of his position immediately began to repel the attackers, utilizing handgrenades, antipersonnel mines and small-arms fire. Due to the heavy volume of enemy fire and exploding grenades around them, a North Vietnamese soldier was able to crawl, undetected, to their position. Suddenly, the enemy soldier lobbed a handgrenade into Sp4c. Santiago-Colon's foxhole. Realizing that there was no time to throw the grenade out of his position, Sp4c. Santiago-Colon retrieved the grenade, tucked it in to his stomach and, turning away from his comrades, absorbed the full impact of the blast. His heroic self-sacrifice saved the lives of those who occupied the foxhole with him, and provided them with the inspiration to continue fighting until they had forced the enemy to retreat from the perimeter. By his gallantry at the cost of his life and in the highest traditions of the military service, Sp4c. Santiago-Colon has reflected great credit upon himself, his unit, and the U.S. Army.

*SARGENT, RUPPERT L.

Rank and organization: First Lieutenant, U.S. Army, Company B, 4th Battalion, 9th Infantry, 25th Infantry Division. *Place and date:* Hau Nghia Province, Republic of Vietnam, 15 March 1967. *Entered service at:* Richmond, Va. *Born:* 6 January 1938, Hampton, Va. *Citation:* For conspicuous gallantry and intrepidity in action at the risk of his life above and beyond the call of duty. While leading a platoon of Company B, 1st Lt. Sargent was investigating a reported Viet Cong meetinghouse and weapons cache. A tunnel entrance which 1st Lt. Sargent observed was boobytrapped. He tried to destroy the boobytrap and blow the cover from the tunnel using handgrenades, but this attempt was not successful. He and his demolition man moved in to destroy the boobytrap and cover which flushed a Viet Cong soldier from the tunnel, who was immediately killed by the nearby platoon sergeant. 1st Lt. Sargent, the platoon sergeant, and a forward observer moved toward the tunnel entrance. As they approached, another Viet Cong emerged and threw 2 handgrenades that landed in the midst of the group. 1st Lt. Sargent fired 3 shots at the enemy then turned and unhesitatingly threw himself over the 2 grenades. He was mortally wounded, and his 2 companions were lightly wounded when the grenades exploded. By his courageous and selfless act of exceptional heroism, he saved the lives of the platoon sergeant and forward observer and prevented the injury or death of several other nearby comrades. 1st Lt. Sargent's actions were in keeping with the highest traditions of the military services and reflect great credit upon himself and the U.S. Army.

SASSER, CLARENCE EUGENE

Rank and organization: Specialist Fifth Class (then Pfc.), U.S. Army, Headquarters Company, 3d Battalion, 60th Infantry, 9th Infantry Division. *Place and date:* Ding Tuong Province, Republic of Vietnam, 10 January 1968. *Entered service at:* Houston, Tex. *Born:* 12 September 1947, Chenango, Tex. *Citation:* For conspicuous gallantry and intrepidity in action at the risk of his life above and beyond the call of duty. Sp5c. Sasser distinguished himself while assigned to Headquarters and Headquarters Company, 3d Battalion. He was serving as a medical aidman with Company A, 3d Battalion, on a reconnaissance in force operation. His company was making an air assault when suddenly it was taken under heavy small arms, recoilless rifle, machinegun and rocket fire from well fortified enemy positions on 3 sides of the landing zone. During the first few minutes, over 30 casualties were sustained. Without hesitation, Sp5c. Sasser ran across an open rice paddy through a hail of fire to assist the wounded. After helping 1 man to safety, was painfully wounded in the left shoulder by fragments of an exploding rocket. Refusing medical attention, he ran through a barrage of rocket and automatic weapons fire to aid casualties of the initial attack and, after giving them urgently needed treatment, continued to search for other wounded. Despite 2 additional wounds immobilizing his legs, he dragged himself through the mud toward another soldier 100 meters away. Although in agonizing pain and faint from loss of blood, Sp5c. Sasser reached the man, treated him, and proceeded on to encourage another group of soldiers to crawl 200 meters to relative safety. There he attended their wounds for 5 hours until they were evacuated. Sp5c. Sasser's extraordinary heroism is in keeping with the highest traditions of the military service and reflects great credit upon himself, his unit, and the U.S. Army.

*SEAY, WILLIAM W.

Rank and organization: Sergeant, U.S. Army, 62d Transportation Company (Medium Truck), 7th Transportation Battalion, 48th Transportation Group. *Place and date:* Near Ap Nhi, Republic of Vietnam, 25 August 1968. *Entered service at:* Montgomery, Ala. *Born:* 24 October 1948, Brewton, Ala. *Citation:* For conspicuous gallantry and intrepidity in action at the risk of his life above and beyond the call of duty. Sgt. Seay distinguished himself while serving as a driver with the 62d Transportation Company, on a resupply mission. The convoy with which he was traveling, carrying critically needed ammunition and supplies from Long Binh to Tay Ninh, was ambushed by a reinforced battalion of the North Vietnamese Army. As the main elements of the convoy entered the ambush killing zone, they were struck by intense rocket, machinegun and automatic weapon fire from the well concealed and entrenched enemy force. When his convoy was forced to stop, Sgt. Seay immediately dismounted and took a defensive position behind the wheels of a vehicle loaded with high-explosive ammunition. As the violent North Vietnamese assault approached to within 10 meters of the road, Sgt. Seay opened fire, killing 2 of the enemy. He then spotted a sniper in a tree approximately 75 meters to his front and killed him. When an enemy grenade was thrown under an ammunition trailer near his position, without regard for his own safety he left his protective cover, exposing himself to intense enemy fire, picked up the grenade, and threw it back to the North Vietnamese position, killing 4 more of the enemy and saving the lives of the men around him. Another enemy grenade landed approximately 3 meters from Sgt. Seay's position. Again Sgt. Seay left his covered position and threw the armed grenade back upon the assaulting enemy. After returning to his position he was painfully wounded in the right wrist; however, Sgt. Seay continued to give encouragement and direction to his fellow soldiers. After moving to the relative cover of a shallow ditch, he detected 3 enemy soldiers who had penetrated the position and were preparing to fire on his comrades. Although weak from loss of blood and with his right hand immobilized, Sgt. Seay stood up and fired his rifle with his left hand, killing all 3 and saving the lives of the other men in his location. As a result of his heroic action, Sgt. Seay was mortally wounded by a sniper's bullet. Sgt. Seay, by his gallantry in action at the cost of his life, has reflected great credit upon himself, his unit, and the U.S. Army.

*SHEA, DANIEL JOHN

Rank and organization: Private First Class, U.S. Army, Headquarters Company, 3d Battalion, 21st Infantry, 196th Infantry Brigade, Americal Division. *Place and date:* Quang Tri Province, Republic of Vietnam, 14 May 1969. *Entered service at:* New Haven, Conn. *Born:* 29 January 1947, Norwalk, Conn. *Citation:* For conspicuous gallantry and intrepidity in action at the risk of his life above and beyond the call of duty. Pfc. Shea, Headquarters and Headquarters Company, 3d Battalion, distinguished himself while serving as a medical aidman with Company C, 3d Battalion, during a combat patrol mission. As the lead platoon of the company was crossing a rice paddy, a large enemy force in ambush positions opened fire with mortars, grenades and automatic weapons. Under heavy crossfire from 3 sides, the platoon withdrew to a small island in the paddy to establish a defensive perimeter. Pfc. Shea, seeing that a number of his comrades had fallen in the initial hail of fire, dashed from the defensive position to assist the wounded. With complete disregard for his safety and braving the intense hostile fire sweeping the open rice paddy, Pfc. Shea made 4 trips to tend wounded soldiers and to carry them to the safety of the platoon position. Seeing a fifth wounded comrade directly in front of one of the enemy strongpoints, Pfc. Shea ran to his assistance. As he reached the wounded man, Pfc. Shea was grievously wounded. Disregarding his welfare, Pfc. Shea tended his wounded comrade and began to move him back to the safety of the defensive perimeter. As he neared the platoon position, Pfc. Shea was mortally wounded by a burst of enemy fire. By his heroic actions Pfc. Shea saved the lives of several of his fellow soldiers. Pfc. Shea's gallantry in action at the cost of his life were in keeping with the highest traditions of the military service and reflect great credit upon himself, his unit, and the U.S. Army.

*SHIELDS, MARVIN G.

Rank and organization: Construction Mechanic Third Class, U.S. Navy, Seabee Team 1104. *Place and date:* Dong Xoai, Republic of

Vietnam, 10 June 1965. *Entered service at:* Seattle, Wash. *Born:* 30 December 1939, Port Townsend, Wash. *Citation:* For conspicuous gallantry and intrepidity at the risk of his life above and beyond the call of duty. Although wounded when the compound of Detachment A-342, 5th Special Forces Group (Airborne), 1st Special Forces, came under intense fire from an estimated reinforced Viet Cong regiment employing machineguns, heavy weapons and small arms, Shields continued to resupply his fellow Americans who needed ammunition and to return the enemy fire for a period of approximately 3 hours, at which time the Viet Cong launched a massive attack at close range with flamethrowers, handgrenades and small-arms fire. Wounded a second time during this attack, Shields nevertheless assisted in carrying a more critically wounded man to safety, and then resumed firing at the enemy for 4 more hours. When the commander asked for a volunteer to accompany him in an attempt to knock out an enemy machinegun emplacement which was endangering the lives of all personnel in the compound because of the accuracy of its fire, Shields unhesitatingly volunteered for this extremely hazardous mission. Proceeding toward their objective with a 3.5-inch rocket launcher, they succeeded in destroying the enemy machinegun emplacement, thus undoubtedly saving the lives of many of their fellow servicemen in the compound. Shields was mortally wounded by hostile fire while returning to his defensive position. His heroic initiative and great personal valor in the face of intense enemy fire sustain and enhance the finest traditions of the U.S. Naval Service.

*SIJAN, LANCE P.

Rank and organization: Captain, U.S. Air Force, 4th Allied POW Wing, Pilot of an F-4C aircraft. *Place and date:* North Vietnam, 9 November 1967. *Entered service at:* Milwaukee, Wis. *Born:* 13 April 1942, Milwaukee, Wis. *Citation:* While on a flight over North Vietnam, Capt. Sijan ejected from his disabled aircraft and successfully evaded capture for more than 6 weeks. During this time, he was seriously injured and suffered from shock and extreme weight loss due to lack of food. After being captured by North Vietnamese soldiers, Capt. Sijan was taken to a holding point for subsequent transfer to a prisoner of war camp. In his emaciated and crippled condition, he overpowered 1 of his guards and crawled into the jungle, only to be recaptured after several hours. He was then transferred to another prison camp where he was kept in solitary confinement and interrogated at length. During interrogation, he was severely tortured; however, he did not divulge any information to his captors. Capt. Sijan lapsed into delirium and was placed in the care of another prisoner. During his intermittent periods of consciousness until his death, he never complained of his physical condition and, on several occasions, spoke of future escape attempts. Capt. Sijan's extraordinary heroism and intrepidity above and beyond the call of duty at the cost of his life are in keeping with the highest traditions of the U.S. Air Force and reflect great credit upon himself and the U.S. Armed Forces.

*SIMS, CLIFFORD CHESTER

Rank and organization: Staff Sergeant, U.S. Army, Company D, 2d Battalion (Airborne), 501st Infantry, 101st Airborne Division. *Place and date:* Near Hue, Republic of Vietnam, 21 February 1968. *Entered service at:* Jacksonville, Fla. *Born:* 18 June 1942, Port St. Joe, Fla. *Citation:* For conspicuous gallantry and intrepidity in action at the risk of his life above and beyond the call of duty. S/Sgt. Sims distinguished himself while serving as a squad leader with Company D. Company D was assaulting a heavily fortified enemy position concealed within a dense wooded area when it encountered strong enemy defensive fire. Once within the woodline, S/Sgt. Sims led his squad in a furious attack against an enemy force which had pinned down the 1st Platoon and threatened to overrun it. His skillful leadership provided the platoon with freedom of movement and enabled it to regain the initiative. S/Sgt. Sims was then ordered to move his squad to a position where he could provide covering fire for the company command group and to link up with the 3d Platoon, which was under heavy enemy pressure. After moving no more than 30 meters S/Sgt. Sims noticed that a brick structure in which ammunition was stocked was on fire. Realizing the danger, S/Sgt. Sims took immediate action to move his squad from this position. Though in the process of leaving the area 2 members of his squad were injured by the subsequent explosion of the ammunition, S/Sgt. Sims' prompt actions undoubtedly prevented more serious casualties from occurring. While continuing through the dense woods amidst heavy enemy fire, S/Sgt. Sims and his squad were approaching a bunker when they heard the unmistakable noise of a concealed boobytrap being triggered immediately to their front. S/Sgt. Sims warned his comrades of the danger and unhesitatingly hurled himself upon the device as it exploded, taking the full impact of the blast. In so protecting his fellow soldiers, he willingly sacrificed his life. S/Sgt. Sims' extraordinary heroism at the cost of his life is in keeping with the highest traditions of the military service and reflects great credit upon himself and the U.S. Army.

*SINGLETON, WALTER K.

Rank and organization: Sergeant, U.S. Marine Corps, Company A, 1st Battalion, 9th Marines, 3d Marine Division. *Place and date:* Gio Linh District, Quang Tri Province, Republic of Vietnam, 24 March 1967. *Entered service at:* Memphis, Tenn. *Born:* 7 December 1944, Memphis, Tenn. *Citation:* For conspicuous gallantry and intrepidity at the risk of his life above and beyond the call of duty. Sgt. Singleton's company was conducting combat operations when the lead platoon received intense small arms, automatic weapons, rocket, and mortar fire from a well entrenched enemy force. As the company fought its way forward, the extremely heavy enemy fire caused numerous friendly casualties. Sensing the need for early treatment of the wounded, Sgt. Singleton quickly moved from his relatively safe position in the rear of the foremost point of the advance and made numerous trips through the enemy killing zone to move the injured men out of the danger area. Noting that a large part of the enemy fire was coming from a hedgerow, he seized a machinegun and assaulted the key enemy location, delivering devastating fire as he advanced. He forced his way through the hedgerow directly into the enemy strong point. Although he was mortally wounded, his fearless attack killed 8 of the enemy and drove the remainder from the hedgerow. Sgt. Singleton's bold actions completely disorganized the enemy defense and saved the lives of many of his comrades. His daring initiative, selfless devotion to duty and indomitable fighting spirit reflected great credit upon himself and the Marine Corps, and his performance upheld the highest traditions of the U.S. Naval Service.

*SISLER, GEORGE K.

Rank and organization: First Lieutenant, U.S. Army, Headquarters and Headquarters Company, 5th Special Forces Group (Airborne), 1st Special Forces. *Place and date:* Republic of Vietnam. 7 February 1967. *Entered service at:* Dexter, Mo. *Born:* 19 September 1937, Dexter, Mo. *Citation:* For conspicuous gallantry and intrepidity at the risk of his life and above and beyond the call of duty. 1st Lt. Sisler was the platoon leader/adviser to a Special United States/Vietnam exploitation force. While on patrol deep within enemy dominated territory, 1st Lt. Sisler's platoon was attacked from 3 sides by a company sized enemy force. 1st Lt. Sisler quickly rallied his men, deployed them to a better defensive position, called for air strikes, and moved among his men to encourage and direct their efforts. Learning that 2 men had been wounded and were unable to pull back to the perimeter, 1st Lt. Sisler charged from the position through intense enemy fire to assist them. He reached the men and began carrying 1 of them back to the perimeter, when he was taken under more intensive weapons fire by the enemy. Laying down his wounded comrade, he killed 3 onrushing enemy soldiers by firing his rifle and silenced the enemy machinegun with a grenade. As he returned the wounded man to the perimeter, the left flank of the position came under extremely heavy attack by the superior enemy force and several additional men of his platoon were quickly wounded. Realizing the need for instant action to prevent his position from being overrun, 1st Lt. Sisler picked up some grenades and charged singlehandedly into the enemy onslaught, firing his weapon and throwing grenades. This singularly heroic action broke up the vicious assault and forced the enemy to begin withdrawing. Despite the continuing enemy fire, 1st Lt. Sisler was moving about the battlefield directing force and several additional men of his platoon were quickly wounded. His extraordinary leadership, infinite courage, and selfless concern for his men saved the lives of a number of his comrades. His actions reflect great credit upon himself and uphold the highest traditions of the military service.

*SKIDGEL, DONALD SIDNEY

Rank and organization: Sergeant, U.S. Army, Troop D, 1st Squadron, 9th Cavalry, 1st Cavalry Division. *Place and date:* Near Song Be, Republic of Vietnam, 14 September 1969. *Entered service at:* Bangor, Maine. *Born:* 13 October 1948, Caribou, Maine. *Citation:* For conspicuous gallantry and intrepidity in action at the risk of his life above and beyond the call of duty. Sgt. Skidgel distinguished himself while serving as a reconnaissance section leader in Troop D. On a road near Song Be in Binh Long Province, Sgt. Skidgel and his section with other elements of his troop were acting as a convoy security and screening force when contact occurred with an estimated enemy battalion concealed in tall grass and in bunkers bordering the road. Sgt. Skidgel maneuvered off the road and began placing effective machinegun fire on the enemy automatic weapons and rocket-propelled grenade positions. After silencing at least 1 position, he ran with his machinegun across 60 meters of bullet-swept ground to another location from which he continued to rake the enemy positions. Running low on ammunition, he returned to his vehicle over the same terrain. Moments later he was alerted that the command element was receiving intense automatic weapons, rocket-propelled grenade and mortar fire. Although he knew the road was saturated with enemy fire, Sgt. Skidgel calmly mounted his vehicle and with his driver advanced toward the command group in an effort to draw the enemy fire onto himself. Despite the hostile fire concentrated on him, he succeeded in silencing several enemy positions with his machinegun. Moments later Sgt. Skidgel was knocked down onto the rear fender by the explosion of an enemy rocket-propelled grenade. Ignoring his extremely painful wounds, he staggered back to his feet and placed effective fire on several other enemy positions until he was mortally wounded by hostile small arms fire. His selfless actions enabled the command group to withdraw to a better position without casualties and inspired the rest of his fellow soldiers to gain fire superiority and defeat the enemy. Sgt. Skidgel's gallantry at the cost of his life were in keeping with the highest traditions of the military service and reflect great credit upon himself, his unit, and the U.S. Army.

*SMEDLEY, LARRY E.

Rank and organization: Corporal, U.S. Marine Corps, Company D, 1st Battalion, 7th Marines, 1st Marine Division. *Place and date:* Quang Nam Province, Republic of Vietnam, 21 December 1967. *Entered service at:* Orlando, Fla. *Born:* 4 March 1949, Front Royal, Va. *Citation:* For conspicuous gallantry and intrepidity at the risk of his life above and beyond the call of duty while serving as a squad leader with company D, in connection with operations against the enemy. On the evenings of 20–21 December 1967, Cpl. Smedley led his 6-man squad to an ambush site at the mouth of Happy Valley, near Phouc Ninh (2) in Quang Nam Province. Later that night an estimated 100 Viet Cong and North Vietnamese Army regulars, carrying 122mm rocket launchers and mortars, were observed moving toward Hill 41. Realizing this was a significant enemy move to launch an attack on the vital Danang complex, Cpl. Smedley immediately took sound and courageous action to stop the enemy threat. After he radioed for a reaction force, he skillfully maneuvered his men to a more advantageous position and led an attack on the numerically superior enemy force. A heavy volume of fire from an enemy machinegun positioned on the left flank of the squad inflicted several casualties on Cpl. Smedley's unit. Simultaneously, an enemy rifle grenade exploded nearby, wounding him in the right foot and knocking him to the ground. Cpl. Smedley disregarded this serious injury and valiantly struggled to his feet, shouting words of encouragement to his men. He fearlessly led a charge against the enemy machinegun emplacement, firing his rifle and throwing grenades, until he was again struck by enemy fire and knocked to the ground. Gravely wounded and weak from loss of blood, he rose and commenced a 1-man assault against the enemy position. Although his aggressive and singlehanded attack resulted in the destruction of the machinegun, he was struck in the chest by enemy fire and fell mortally wounded. Cpl. Smedley's inspiring and courageous actions, bold initiative, and selfless devotion to duty in the face of certain death were in keeping with the highest traditions of the Marine Corps and the U.S. Naval Service. He gallantly gave his life for his country.

*SMITH, ELMELINDO R.

Rank and organization: Platoon Sergeant (then S/Sgt.), U.S. Army, 1st Platoon, Company C, 2d Battalion, 8th Infantry, 4th Infantry Division. *Place and date:* Republic of Vietnam, 16 February 1967. *Entered service at:* Honolulu, Hawaii. *Born:* 27 July 1935, Honolulu, Hawaii. *Citation:* For conspicuous gallantry and intrepidity at the risk of his life above and beyond the call of duty. During a reconnaissance patrol, his platoon was suddenly engaged by intense machinegun fire hemming in the platoon on 3 sides. A defensive perimeter was hastily established, but the enemy added mortar and rocket fire to the deadly fusillade and assaulted the position from several directions. With complete disregard for his safety, P/Sgt. Smith moved through the deadly fire along the defensive line, positioning soldiers, distributing ammunition and encouraging his men to repeal the enemy attack. Struck to the ground by enemy fire which caused a severe shoulder wound, he regained his feet, killed the enemy soldier and continued to move about the perimeter. He was again wounded in the shoulder and stomach but continued moving on his knees to assist in the defense. Noting the enemy massing at a weakened point on the perimeter, he crawled into the open and poured deadly fire into the enemy ranks. As he crawled on, he was struck by a rocket. Moments later, he regained consciousness, and drawing on his fast dwingling strength, continued to crawl from man to man. When he could move no farther, he chose to remain in the open where he could alert the perimeter to the approaching enemy. P/Sgt. Smith perished, never relenting in his determined effort against the enemy. The valorous acts and heroic leadership of this outstanding soldier inspired those remaining members of his platoon to beat back the enemy assaults. P/Sgt. Smith's gallant actions were in keeping with the highest traditions of the U.S. Army and they reflect great credit upon him and the Armed Forces of his country.

SPRAYBERRY, JAMES M.

Rank and organization: Captain (then 1st Lt.), U.S. Army, Company D, 5th Battalion, 7th Cavalry, 1st Cavalry Division (Airmobile). *Place and date:* Republic of Vietnam, 25 April 1968. *Entered service at:* Montgomery, Ala. *Born:* 24 April 1947, LaGrange, Ga. *Citation:* For conspicuous gallantry and intrepidity in action at the risk of his life above and beyond the call of duty. Capt. Sprayberry, Armour, U.S. Army, distinguished himself by exceptional bravery while serving as executive officer of Company D. His company commander and a great number of the men were wounded and separated from the main body of the company. A daylight attempt to rescue them was driven back by the well entrenched enemy's heavy fire. Capt. Sprayberry then organized and led a volunteer night patrol to eliminate the intervening enemy bunkers and to relieve the surrounded element. The patrol soon began receiving enemy machinegun fire. Capt. Sprayberry quickly moved the men to protective cover and without regard for his own safety, crawled within close range of the bunker from which the fire was coming. He silenced the machinegun with a handgrenade. Identifying several 1-man enemy positions nearby, Capt. Sprayberry immediately attacked them with the rest of his grenades. He crawled back for more grenades and when 2 grenades were thrown at his men from a position to the front, Capt. Sprayberry, without hesitation, again exposed himself and charged the enemy-held bunker killing its occupants with a grenade. Placing 2 men to cover his advance, he crawled forward and neutralized 3 more bunkers with grenades. Immediately thereafter, Capt. Sprayberry was surprised by an enemy soldier who charged from a concealed position. He killed the soldier with his pistol and with continuing disregard for the danger neutralized another enemy emplacement. Capt. Sprayberry then established radio contact with the isolated men, directing them toward his position. When the 2 elements made contact he organized his men into litter parties to evacuate the wounded. As the evacuation was nearing completion, he observed an enemy machinegun position which he silenced with a grenade. Capt. Sprayberry returned to the rescue party, established security, and moved to friendly lines with the wounded. This rescue operation, which lasted approximately 7½ hours, saved the lives of many of his fellow soldiers. Capt. Sprayberry personally killed 12 enemy soldiers, eliminated 2 machineguns, and destroyed numerous enemy bunkers. Capt. Sprayberry's indomitable spirit and gallant action at great personal risk to his life are in keeping with the highest traditions of the military service and reflect great credit upon himself, his unit, and the U.S. Army.

*STEINDAM, RUSSELL A.

Rank and organization: First Lieutenant, U.S. Army, Troop B, 3d Squadron, 4th Cavalry, 25th Infantry, Division. *Place and date:* Tay Ninh Province, Republic of Vietnam, 1 February 1970. *Entered service at:* Austin, Tex. *Born:* 27 August 1946, Austin, Tex. *Citation:* for conspicuous gallantry and intrepidity in action at the risk of his life above and beyond the call of duty. 1st Lt. Steindam, Troop B, while serving as a platoon leader, led members of his platoon on a night ambush operation. On the way to the ambush site, suspected enemy movement was detected on 1 flank and the platoon's temporary position was subjected to intense small arms and automatic weapons fire as well as a fusillade of hand and rocket-propelled grenades. After the initial barrage, 1st Lt. Steindam ordered fire placed on the enemy position and the wounded men to be moved to a shallow bomb crater. As he directed the return fire against the enemy from his exposed position, a fragmentation grenade was thrown into the site occupied by his command group. Instantly realizing the extreme gravity of the situation, 1st Lt. Steindam shouted a warning to alert his fellow soldiers in the immediate vicinity. Then, unhesitatingly and with complete disregard for his safety,1st Lt. Steindam deliberately threw himself on the grenade, absorbing the full and fatal force of the explosion as it detonated. By his gallant action and self-sacrifice, he was able to save the lives of the nearby members of his command group. The extraordinary courage and selflessness displayed by 1st Lt. Steindam were an inspiration to his comrades and are in the highest traditions of the U.S. Army.

*STEWART, JIMMY G.

Rank and organization: Staff Sergeant, U.S. Army, Company B, 2d Battalion, 12th Cavalry, 1st Cavalry Division (Airmobile). *Place and date:* Republic of Vietnam, 18 May 1966. *Entered service at:* Ashland, Ky. *Born:* 25 December 1942, West Columbia, W. Va. *Citation:* For conspicuous gallantry and intrepidity in action at the risk of his life above and beyond the call of duty. Early in the morning a reinforced North Vietnamese company attacked Company B, which was manning a defensive perimeter in Vietnam. The surprise onslaught wounded 5 members of a 6-man squad caught in the direct path of the enemy's thrust. S/Sgt. Stewart became a lone defender of vital terrain—virtually 1 man against a hostile platoon. Refusing to take advantage of a lull in the firing which would have permitted him to withdraw, S/Sgt. Stewart elected to hold his ground to protect his fallen comrades and prevent an enemy penetration of the company perimeter. As the full force of the platoon-sized man attack struck his lone position, he fought like a man possessed; emptying magazine after magazine at the determined, on-charging enemy. The enemy drove almost to his position and hurled grenades, but S/Sgt. Stewart decimated them by retrieving and throwing the grenades back. Exhausting his ammunition, he crawled under intense fire to his wounded team members and collected ammunition that they were unable to use. Far past the normal point of exhaustion, he held his position for 4 harrowing hours and through 3 assaults, annihilating the enemy as they approached and before they could get a foothold. As a result of his defense, the company position held until the arrival of a reinforcing platoon which counterattacked the enemy, now occupying foxholes to the left of S/Sgt. Stewart's position. After the counterattack, his body was found in a shallow enemy hole where he had advanced in order to add his fire to that of the counterattacking platoon. Eight enemy dead were found around his immediate position, with evidence that 15 others had been dragged away. The wounded whom he gave his life to protect, were recovered and evacuated. S/Sgt. Stewart's indomitable courage, in the face of overwhelming odds, stands as a tribute to himself and an inspiration to all men of his unit. His actions were in the highest traditions of the U.S. Army and the Armed Forces of his country.

STOCKDALE, JAMES B.

Rank and organization: Rear Admiral (then Captain), U.S. Navy. *Place and date:* Hoa Lo prison, Hanoi, North Vietnam, 4 September 1969. *Entered service at:* Abingdon, Ill. *Born:* 23 December 1923, Abingdon, Ill. *Citation:* For conspicuous gallantry and intrepidity at the risk of his life above and beyond the call of duty while senior naval officer in the Prisoner of War camps of North Vietnam. Recognized by his captors as the leader in the Prisoners' of War resistance to interrogation and in their refusal to participate in propaganda exploitation, Rear Adm. Stockdale was singled out for interrogation and attendant torture after he was detected in a covert communications attempt. Sensing the start of another purge, and aware that his earlier efforts at self-disfiguration to dissuade his captors from exploiting him for propaganda purposes had resulted in cruel and agonizing punishment, Rear Adm. Stockdale resolved to make himself a symbol of resistance regardless of personal sacrifice. He deliberately inflicted a near-mortal wound to his person in order to convince his captors of his willingness to give up his life rather than capitulate. He was subsequently discovered and revived by the North Vietnamese who, convinced of his indomitable spirit, abated in their employment of excessive harassment and torture toward all of the Prisoners of War. By his heroic action, at great peril to himself, he earned the everlasting gratitude of his fellow prisoners and of his country. Rear Adm. Stockdale's valiant leadership and extraordinary courage in a hostile environment sustain and enhance the finest traditions of the U.S. Naval Service.

*STONE, LESTER R., JR.

Rank and organization: Sergeant, U.S. Army, 1st Platoon, Company B, 1st Battalion, 20th Infantry, 11th Infantry Brigade, 23d Infantry Division (Americal). *Place and date:* West of Landing Zone Liz, Republic of Vietnam, 3 March 1969. *Entered service at:* Syracuse, N.Y. *Born:* 4 June 1947, Binghamton, N.Y. *Citation:* For conspicuous gallantry and intrepidity in action at the risk of his life above and beyond the call of duty. Sgt. Stone, distinguished himself while serving as squad leader of the 1st Platoon. The 1st Platoon was on a combat patrol mission just west of Landing Zone Liz when it came under intense automatic weapons and grenade fire from a well concealed company-size force of North Vietnamese regulars. Observing the platoon machinegunner fall critically wounded, Sgt. Stone remained in the exposed area to provide cover fire for the wounded soldier who was being pulled to safety by another member of the platoon. With enemy fire impacting all around him, Sgt. Stone had a malfunction in the machinegun, preventing him from firing the weapon automatically. Displaying extraordinary courage under the most adverse conditions, Sgt. Stone repaired the weapon and continued to place on the enemy positions effective suppressive fire which enabled the rescue to be completed. In a desparate attempt to overrun his position, an enemy force left its cover and charged Sgt. Stone. Disregarding the danger involved, Sgt. Stone rose to his knees and began placing intense fire on the enemy at pointblank range, killing 6 of the enemy before falling mortally wounded. His actions of unsurpassed valor were a source of inspiration to his entire unit, and he was responsible for saving the lives of a number of his fellow soldiers. His actions were in keeping with the highest traditions of the military profession and reflect great credit on him, his unit, and the U.S. Army.

*STOUT, MITCHELL W.

Rank and organization: Sergeant, U.S. Army, Battery C, 1st Battalion, 44th Artillery. *Place and date:* Khe Gio Bridge, Republic of

Vietnam, 12 March 1970. *Entered service at:* Raleigh, N.C. *Born:* 24 February 1950, Knoxville, Tenn. *Citation:* Sgt. Stout distinguished himself during an attack by a North Vietnamese Army Sapper company on his unit's firing position at Khe Gio Bridge. Sgt. Stout was in a bunker with members of a searchlight crew when the position came under heavy enemy mortar fire and ground attack. When the intensity of the mortar attack subsided, an enemy grenade was thrown into the bunker. Displaying great courage, Sgt. Stout ran to the grenade, picked it up, and started out of the bunker. As he reached the door, the grenade exploded. By holding the grenade close to his body and shielding its blast, he protected his fellow soldiers in the bunker from further injury or death. Sgt. Stout's conspicuous gallantry and intrepidity in action, at the cost of his own life, are in keeping with the highest traditions of the military service and reflect great credit upon him, his unit and the U.S. Army.

*STRYKER, ROBERT F.

Rank and organization: Specialist Fourth Class, U.S. Army, Company C, 1st Battalion, 26th Infantry, 1st Infantry Division. *Place and date:* Near Loc Ninh, Republic of Vietnam, 7 November 1967. *Entered service at:* Throop, N.Y. *Born:* 9 November 1944, Auburn, N.Y. *Citation:* For conspicuous gallantry and intrepidity at the risk of his life above and beyond the call of duty. Sp4c. Stryker, U.S. Army, distinguished himself while serving with Company C. Sp4c. Stryker was serving as a grenadier in a multicompany reconnaissance in force near Loc Ninh. As his unit moved through the dense underbrush, it was suddenly met with a hail of rocket, automatic weapons and small arms fire from enemy forces concealed in fortified bunkers and in the surrounding trees. Reacting quickly, Sp4c. Stryker fired into the enemy positions with his grenade launcher. During the devastating exchange of fire, Sp4c. Stryker detected enemy elements attempting to encircle his company and isolate it from the main body of the friendly force. Undaunted by the enemy machinegun and small-arms fire, Sp4c. Stryker repeatedly fired grenades into the trees, killing enemy snipers and enabling his comrades to sever the attempted encirclement. As the battle continued, Sp4c. Stryker observed several wounded members of his squad in the killing zone of an enemy claymore mine. With complete disregard for his safety, he threw himself upon the mine as it was detonated. He was mortally wounded as his body absorbed the blast and shielded his comrades from the explosion. His unselfish actions were responsible for saving the lives of at least 6 of his fellow soldiers. Sp4c. Stryker's great personal bravery was in keeping with the highest traditions of the military service and reflects great credit upon himself, his unit, and the U.S. Army.

STUMPF, KENNETH E.

Rank and organization: Staff Sergeant (then Sp4c.), U.S. Army, Company C, 1st Battalion, 35th Infantry, 25th Infantry Division. *Place and date:* Near Duc Pho, Republic of Vietnam, 25 April 1967. *Entered service at:* Milwaukee, Wis. *Born:* 28 September 1944, Neenah, Wis. *Citation:* For conspicuous gallantry and intrepidity in action at the risk of his life above and beyond the call of duty. S/Sgt. Stumpf distinguished himself while serving as a squad leader of the 3d Platoon, Company C, on a search and destroy mission. As S/Sgt. Stumpf's company approached a village, it encountered a North Vietnamese rifle company occupying a well fortified bunker complex. During the initial contact, 3 men from his squad fell wounded in front of a hostile machinegun emplacement. The enemy's heavy volume of fire prevented the unit from moving to the aid of the injured men, but S/Sgt. Stumpf left his secure position in a deep trench and ran through the barrage of incoming rounds to reach his wounded comrades. He picked up 1 of the men and carried him back to the safety of the trench. Twice more S/Sgt. Stumpf dashed forward while the enemy turned automatic weapons and machineguns upon him, yet he managed to rescue the remaining 2 wounded squad members. He then organized his squad and led an assault against several enemy bunkers from which continuously heavy fire was being received. He and his squad successfully eliminated 2 of the bunker positions, but one to the front of the advancing platoon remained a serious threat. Arming himself with extra handgrenades, S/Sgt. Stumpf ran over open ground, through a volley of fire directed at him by a determined enemy, toward the machinegun position. As he reached the bunker, he threw a handgrenade through the aperture. It was immediately returned by the occupants, forcing S/Sgt. Stumpf to take cover. Undaunted, he pulled the pins on 2 more grenades, held them for a few seconds after activation, then hurled them into the position, this time successfully destroying the emplacement. With the elimination of this key position, his unit was able to assault and overrun the enemy. S/Sgt. Stumpf's relentless spirit of aggressiveness, intrepidity, and ultimate concern for the lives of his men, are in the highest traditions of the military service and reflect great credit upon himself and the U.S. Army.

TAYLOR, JAMES ALLEN

Rank and organization: Captain (then 1st Lt.), U.S. Army, Troop B, 1st Cavalry, Americal Division. *Place and date:* West of Que Son, Republic of Vietnam, 9 November 1967. *Entered service at:* San Francisco, Calif. *Born:* 31 December 1937, Arcata, Calif. *Citation:* Capt. Taylor, Armor, was serving as executive officer of Troop B, 1st Squadron. His troop was engaged in an attack on a fortified position west of Que Son when it came under intense enemy recoilless rifle, mortar, and automatic weapons fire from an enemy strong point located immediately to its front. One armored cavalry assault vehicle was hit immediately by recoilless rifle fire and all 5 crewmembers were wounded. Aware that the stricken vehicle was in grave danger of exploding, Capt. Taylor rushed forward and personally extracted the wounded to safety despite the hail of enemy fire and exploding ammunition. Within minutes a second armored cavalry assault vehicle was hit by multiple recoilless rifle rounds. Despite the continuing intense enemy fire, Capt. Taylor moved forward on foot to rescue the wounded men from the burning vehicle and personally removed all the crewmen to the safety of a nearby dike. Moments later the vehicle exploded. As he was returning to his vehicle, a bursting mortar round painfully wounded Capt. Taylor, yet he valiantly returned to his vehicle to relocate the medical evacuation landing zone to an area closer to the front lines. As he was moving his vehicle, it came under machinegun fire from an enemy position not 50 yards away. Capt. Taylor engaged the position with his machinegun, killing the 3-man crew. Upon arrival at the new evacuation site, still another vehicle was struck. Once again Capt. Taylor rushed forward and pulled the wounded from the vehicle, loaded them aboard his vehicle, and returned them safely to the evacuation site. His actions of unsurpassed valor were a source of inspiration to his entire troop, contributed significantly to the success of the overall assault on the enemy position, and were directly responsible for saving the lives of a number of his fellow soldiers. His actions were in keeping with the highest traditions of the military profession and reflect great credit upon himself, his unit, and the U.S. Army.

*TAYLOR, KARL G., Sr.

Rank and organization: Staff Sergeant, U.S. Marine Corps, Company I, 3d Battalion, 26th Marine Regiment, 3d Marine Division (Rein), FMF. *Place and date:* Republic of Vietnam, 8 December 1968. *Entered service at:* Baltimore, Md. *Born:* 14 July 1939, Laurel, Md. *Citation:* For conspicuous gallantry and intrepidity at the risk of his life above and beyond the call of duty while serving at night as a company gunnery sergeant during Operation MEADE RIVER. Informed that the commander of the lead platoon had been mortally wounded when his unit was pinned down by a heavy volume of enemy fire, S/Sgt. Taylor along with another marine, crawled forward to the beleaguered unit through a hail of hostile fire, shouted encouragement and instructions to the men, and deployed them to covered positions. With his companion, he then repeatedly maneuvered across an open area to rescue those marines who were too seriously wounded to move by themselves. Upon learning that there were still other seriously wounded men lying in another open area, in proximity to an enemy machinegun position, S/Sgt. Taylor, accompanied by 4 comrades, led his men forward across the fire-swept terrain in an attempt to rescue the marines. When his group was halted by devastating fire, he directed his companions to return to the company command post; whereupon he took his grenade launcher and in full view of the enemy, charged across the open rice paddy toward the machinegun position, firing his weapon as he ran. Although wounded several times, he succeeded in reaching the machinegun bunker and silencing the fire from that sector, moments before he was mortally wounded. Directly instrumental in saving the lives of several of his fellow marines, S/Sgt. Taylor, by his indomitable courage, inspiring leadership, and selfless dedication, upheld the highest traditions of the Marine Corps and of the U.S. Naval Service.

THACKER, BRIAN MILES

Rank and organization: First Lieutenant, U.S. Army, Battery A, 1st Battalion, 92d Artillery. *Place and date:* Kontum Province, Republic of Vietnam, 31 March 1971. *Entered service at:* Salt Lake City, Utah. *Born:* 25 April 1945, Columbus, Ohio. *Citation:* For conspicuous gallantry and intrepidity in action at the risk of his life above and beyond the call of duty. 1st Lt. Thacker, Field Artillery, Battery A, distinguished himself while serving as the team leader of an Integrated Observation System collocated with elements of 2 Army of the Republic of Vietnam units at Fire Base 6. A numerically superior North Vietnamese Army force launched a well-planned, dawn attack on the small, isolated, hilltop fire base. Employing rockets, grenades, flamethrowers, and automatic weapons, the enemy forces penetrated the perimeter defenses and engaged the defenders in hand-to-hand combat. Throughout the morning and early afternoon, 1st Lt. Thacker rallied and encouraged the U.S. and Republic of Vietnam soldiers in heroic efforts to repulse the enemy. He occupied a dangerously exposed observation position for a period of 4 hours while directing friendly air strikes and artillery fire against the assaulting enemy forces. His personal bravery and inspired leadership enabled the outnumbered friendly forces to inflict a maximum of casualties on the attacking enemy forces and prevented the base from being overrun. By late afternoon, the situation had become untenable. 1st Lt. Thacker organized and directed the withdrawal of the remaining friendly forces. With complete disregard for his personal safety, he remained inside the perimeter alone to provide covering fire with his M–16 rifle until all other friendly forces had escaped from the besieged fire base. Then, in an act of supreme courage, he called for friendly artillery fire on his own position to allow his comrades more time to withdraw safely from the area and, at the same time, inflict even greater casualties on the enemy forces. Although wounded and unable to escape from the area himself, he successfully eluded the enemy forces for 8 days until friendly forces regained control of the fire base. The extraordinary courage and selflessness displayed by 1st Lt. Thacker were an inspiration to his comrades and are in the highest traditions of the military service.

THORNTON, MICHAEL EDWIN

Rank and organization: Petty Officer, U.S. Navy, Navy Advisory Group. *Place and date:* Republic of Vietnam, 31 October 1972. *Entered service at:* Spartanburg, S.C. *Born:* 23 March 1949, Greenville, S.C. *Citation:* For conspicuous gallantry and intrepidity at the risk of his life above and beyond the call of duty while participating in a daring operation against enemy forces. PO Thornton, as Assistant U.S. Navy Advisor, along with a U.S. Navy lieutenant serving as Senior Advisor, accompanied a 3-man Vietnamese Navy SEAL patrol on an intelligence gathering and prisoner capture operation against an enemy-occupied naval river base. Launched from a Vietnamese Navy junk in a rubber boat, the patrol reached land and was continuing on foot toward its objective when it suddenly came under heavy fire from a numerically superior force. The patrol called in naval gunfire support and then engaged the enemy in a fierce firefight, accounting for many enemy casualties before moving back to the waterline to prevent encirclement. Upon learning that the Senior Advisor had been hit by enemy fire and was believed to be dead, PO Thornton returned through a hail of fire to the lieutenant's last position; quickly disposed of 2 enemy soldiers about to overrun the position, and succeeded in removing the seriously wounded and unconscious Senior Naval Advisor to the water's edge. He then inflated the lieutenant's lifejacket and towed him seaward for approximately 2 hours until picked up by support craft. By his extraordinary courage and perseverance, PO Thornton was directly responsible for saving the life of his superior officer and enabling the safe extraction of all patrol members, thereby upholding the highest traditions of the U.S. Naval Service.

THORSNESS, LEO K.

Rank and organization: Lieutenant Colonel (then Maj.), U.S. Air Force, 357th Tactical Fighter Squadron. *Place and date:* Over North Vietnam, 19 April 1967. *Entered service at:* Walnut Grove, Minn. *Born:* 14 February 1932, Walnut Grove, Minn. *Citation:* For conspicuous gallantry and intrepidity in action at the risk of his life above and beyond the call of duty. As pilot of an F–105 aircraft, Lt. Col. Thorsness was on a surface-to-air missile suppression mission over North Vietnam. Lt. Col. Thorsness and his wingman attacked and silenced a surface-to-air missile site with air-to-ground missiles, and then destroyed a second surface-to-air missile site with bombs. In the attack on the second missile site, Lt. Col. Thorsness' wingman was shot down by intensive antiaircraft fire, and the 2 crewmembers abandoned their aircraft. Lt. Col. Thorsness circled the descending parachutes to keep the crewmembers in sight and relay their position to the Search and Rescue Center. During this maneuver, a MIG–17 was sighted in the area. Lt. Col. Thorsness immediately initiated an attack and destroyed the MIG. Because his aircraft was low on fuel, he was forced to depart the area in search of a tanker. Upon being advised that 2 helicopters were orbiting over the downed crew's position and that there were hostile MIGs in the area posing a serious threat to the helicopters, Lt. Col. Thorsness, despite his low fuel condition, decided to return alone through a hostile environment of surface-to-air missile and antiaircraft defenses to the downed crew's position. As he approached the area, he spotted 4 MIG–17 aircraft and immediately initiated an attack on the MIGs, damaging 1 and driving the others away from the rescue scene. When it became apparent that an aircraft in the area was critically low on fuel and the crew would have to abandon the aircraft unless they could reach a tanker, Lt. Col. Thorsness, although critically short on fuel himself, helped to avert further possible loss of life and a friendly aircraft by recovering at a forward operating base, thus allowing the aircraft in emergency fuel condition to refuel safely. Lt. Col. Thorsness' extraordinary heroism, self-sacrifice, and personal bravery involving conspicuous risk of life were in the highest traditions of the military service, and have reflected great credit upon himself and the U.S. Air Force.

VARGAS, M. SANDO, JR. JAY R.

Rank and organization: Major (then Capt.), U.S. Marine Corps, Company G, 2d Battalion, 4th Marines, 9th Marine Amphibious Brigade. *Place and date:* Dai Do, Republic of Vietnam, 30 April to 2 May 1968. *Entered service at:* Winslow, Ariz. *Born:* 29 July 1940, Winslow, Ariz. *Citation:* For conspicuous gallantry and intrepidity at the risk of his life above and beyond the call of duty while serving as commanding officer, Company G, in action against enemy forces from 30 April to 2 May 1968. On 1 May 1968, though suffering from wounds he had incurred while relocating his unit under heavy enemy fire the preceding day, Maj. Vargas combined Company G with two other companies and led his men in an attack on the fortified village of Dai Do. Exercising expert leadership, he maneuvered his marines across 700 meters of open rice paddy while under intense enemy mortar, rocket and artillery fire and obtained a foothold in 2 hedgerows on the enemy perimeter, only to have elements of his company become pinned down by the intense enemy fire. Leading his reserve platoon to the aid of his beleaguered men, Maj. Vargas inspired his men to renew their relentless advance, while destroying a number of enemy bunkers. Again wounded by grenade fragments, he refused aid as he moved about the hazardous area reorganizing his unit into a strong defense perimeter at the edge of the village. Shortly after the objective was secured the enemy commenced a series of counterattacks and probes which lasted throughout the night but were unsuccessful as the gallant defenders of Company G stood firm in their hard-won enclave. Reinforced the following morning, the marines launched a renewed assault through Dai Do on the village of Dinh To, to which the enemy retaliated with a massive counterattack resulting in hand-to-hand combat. Maj. Vargas remained in the open, encouraging and rendering assistance to his marines when he was hit for the third time in the 3-day battle. Observing his battalion commander sustain a serious wound, he disregarded his excruciating pain, crossed the fire-swept area and carried his commander to a covered position, then resumed supervising and encouraging his men while simultaneously assisting in organizing the battalion's perimeter defense. His gallant actions uphold the highest traditions of the Marine Corps and the U.S. Naval Service.

*WARREN, JOHN E., JR.

Rank and organization: First Lieutenant, U.S. Army, Company C, 2d Battalion, (Mechanized), 22d Infantry, 25th Infantry Division. *Place and date:* Tay Ninh Province, Republic of Vietnam, 14 January 1969. *Entered service at:* New York, N.Y. *Born:* 16 November 1946, Brooklyn, N.Y. *Citation:* For conspicuous gallantry and intrepidity in action at the risk of his life above and beyond the call of duty. 1st Lt. Warren, distinguished himself at the cost of his life while serving as a platoon leader with Company C. While moving through a rubber plantation to reinforce another friendly unit, Company C came under intense fire from a well-fortified enemy force. Disregarding his safety, 1st Lt. Warren with several of his men began maneuvering through the hail of enemy fire toward the hostile positions. When he had come to within 6 feet of one of the enemy bunkers and was preparing to toss a handgrenade into it, an enemy grenade was suddenly thrown into the middle of his small group. Thinking only of his men, 1st Lt. Warren fell in the direction of the grenade, thus shielding those around him from the blast. His action, performed at the cost of his life, saved 3 men from serious or mortal injury. First Lt. Warren's ultimate action of sacrifice to save the lives of his men was in keeping with the highest traditions of the military service and reflects great credit on him, his unit, and the U.S. Army.

*WATTERS, CHARLES JOSEPH

Rank and organization: Chaplain (Maj.), U.S. Army, Company A, 173d Support Battalion, 173d Airborne Brigade. *Place and date:* Near Dak To Province, Republic of Vietnam, 19 November 1967. *Entered service at:* Fort Dix, N.J. *Born:* 17 January 1927, Jersey City, N.J. *Citation:* For conspicuous gallantry and intrepidity in action at the risk of his life above and beyond the call of duty. Chaplain Watters distinguished himself during an assault in the vicinity of Dak To. Chaplain Watters was moving with one of the companies when it engaged a heavily armed enemy battalion. As the battle raged and the casualties mounted, Chaplain Watters, with complete disregard for his safety, rushed forward to the line of contact. Unarmed and completely exposed, he moved among, as well as in front of the advancing troops, giving aid to the wounded, assisting in their evacuation, giving words of encouragement, and administering the last rites to the dying. When a wounded paratrooper was standing in shock in front of the assaulting forces, Chaplain Watters ran forward, picked the man up on his shoulders and carried him to safety. As the troopers battled to the first enemy entrenchment, Chaplain Watters ran through the intense enemy fire to the front of the entrenchment to aid a fallen comrade. A short time later, the paratroopers pulled back in preparation for a second assault. Chaplain Watters exposed himself to both friendly and enemy fire between the 2 forces in order to recover 2 wounded soldiers. Later, when the battalion was forced to pull back into a perimeter, Chaplain Watters noticed that several wounded soldiers were lying outside the newly formed perimeter. Without hesitation and ignoring attempts to restrain him, Chaplain Watters left the perimeter three times in the face of small arms, automatic weapons, and mortar fire to carry and to assist the injured troopers to safety. Satisfied that all of the wounded were inside the perimeter, he began aiding the medics—applying field bandages to open wounds, obtaining and serving food and water, giving spiritual and mental strength and comfort. During his ministering, he moved out to the perimeter from position to position redistributing food and water, and tending to the needs of his men. Chaplain Watters was giving aid to the wounded when he himself was mortally wounded. Chaplain Watters' unyielding perseverance and selfless devotion to his comrades was in keeping with the highest traditions of the U.S. Army.

*WAYRYNEN, DALE EUGENE

Rank and organization: Specialist Fourth Class, U.S. Army, Company B, 2d Battalion, 502d Infantry, 1st Brigade, 101st Airborne Division. *Place and date:* Quang Ngai, Province, Republic of Vietnam, 18 May 1967. *Entered service at:* Minneapolis, Minn. *Born:* 18 January 1947, Moose Lake, Minn. *Citation:* For conspicuous gallantry and intrepidity in action at the risk of his life above and beyond the call of duty. Sp4c. Wayrynen distinguished himself with Company B, during combat operations near Duc Pho. His platoon was assisting in the night evacuation of the wounded from an earlier enemy contact when the leadman of the unit met face to face with a Viet Cong soldier. The American's shouted warning also alerted the enemy who immediately swept the area with automatic weapons fire from a strongly built bunker close to the trail and threw handgrenades from another nearby fortified position. Almost immediately, the leadman was wounded and knocked from his feet. Sp4c. Wayrynen, the second man in the formation, leaped beyond his fallen comrade to kill another enemy soldier who appeared on the trail, and he dragged his injured companion back to where the point squad had taken cover. Suddenly, a live enemy grenade landed in the center of the tightly grouped men. Sp4c. Wayrynen, quickly assessing the danger to the entire squad as well as to his platoon leader who was nearby, shouted a warning, pushed one soldier out of the way, and threw himself on the grenade at the moment it exploded. He was mortally wounded. His deep and abiding concern for his fellow soldiers was significantly reflected in his supreme and courageous act that preserved the lives of his comrades. Sp4c. Wayrynen's heroic actions are in keeping with the highest traditions of the service, and they reflect great credit upon himself and the U.S. Army.

*WEBER, LESTER W.

Rank and organization: Lance Corporal, U.S. Marine Corps, Company M, 3d Battalion, 7th Marines, 1st Marine Division. *Place and date:* Quang Nam Province, Republic of Vietnam, 23 February 1969. *Entered service at:* Chicago, Ill. *Born:* 30 July 1948, Aurora, Ill. *Citation:* For conspicuous gallantry and intrepidity at the risk of his life above and beyond the call of duty while serving as a machinegun squad leader with Company M, in action against the enemy. The 2d Platoon of Company M was dispatched to the Bo Ban area of Hieu Duc District to assist a squad from another platoon which had become heavily engaged with a well entrenched enemy battalion. While moving through a rice paddy covered with tall grass L/Cpl. Weber's platoon came under heavy attack from concealed hostile soldiers. He reacted by plunging into the tall grass, successfully attacking 1 enemy and forcing 11 others to break contact. Upon encountering a second North Vietnamese Army soldier he overwhelmed him in fierce hand-to-hand combat. Observing 2 other soldiers firing upon his comrades from behind a dike, L/Cpl. Weber ignored the frenzied firing of the enemy and racing across the hazardous area, dived into their position. He neutralized the position by wrestling weapons from the hands of the 2 soldiers and overcoming them. Although by now the target for concentrated fire from hostile riflemen, L/Cpl. Weber remained in a dangerously exposed position to shout words of encouragement to his emboldened companions. As he moved forward to attack a fifth enemy soldier, he was mortally wounded. L/Cpl. Weber's indomitable courage, aggressive fighting spirit and unwavering devotion to duty upheld the highest traditions of the Marine Corps and of the U.S. Naval Service. He gallantly gave his life for his country.

WETZEL, GARY GEORGE

Rank and organization: Specialist Fourth Class (then Pfc.), U.S. Army, 173d Assault Helicopter Company. *Place and date:* Near Ap Dong An, Republic of Vietnam, 8 January 1968. *Entered service at:* Milwaukee, Wis. *Born:* 29 September 1947, South Milwaukee, Wis.

Citation: Sp4c. Wetzel, 173d Assault Helicopter Company, distinguished himself by conspicuous gallantry and intrepidity at the risk of his life, above and beyond the call of duty. Sp4c. Wetzel was serving as door gunner aboard a helicopter which was part of an insertion force trapped in a landing zone by intense and deadly hostile fire. Sp4c. Wetzel was going to the aid of his aircraft commander when he was blown into a rice paddy and critically wounded by 2 enemy rockets that exploded just inches from his location. Although bleeding profusely due to the loss of his left arm and severe wounds in his right arm, chest, and left leg, Sp4c. Wetzel staggered back to his original position in his gun-well and took the enemy forces under fire. His machinegun was the only weapon placing effective fire on the enemy at that time. Through a resolve that overcame the shock and intolerable pain of his injuries, Sp4c. Wetzel remained at his position until he had eliminated the automatic weapons emplacement that had been inflicting heavy casualties on the American troops and preventing them from moving against this strong enemy force. Refusing to attend his own extensive wounds, he attempted to return to the aid of his aircraft commander but passed out from loss of blood. Regaining consciousness, he persisted in his efforts to drag himself to the aid of his fellow crewman. After an agonizing effort, he came to the side of the crew chief who was attempting to drag the wounded aircraft commander to the safety of a nearby dike. Unswerving in his devotion to his fellow man, Sp4c. Wetzel assisted his crew chief even though the lost consciousness once again during this action. Sp4c. Wetzel displayed extraordinary heroism in his efforts to aid his fellow crewmen. His gallant actions were in keeping with the highest traditions of the U.S. Army and reflect great credit upon himself and the Armed Forces of his country.

*WHEAT, ROY M.

Rank and organization: Lance Corporal, U.S. Marine Corps, Company K, 3d Battalion, 7th Marine, 1st Marine Division. *Place and date:* Republic of Vietnam, 11 August 1967. *Entered service at:* Jackson, Miss. *Born:* 24 July 1947, Moselle, Miss. *Citation:* For conspicuous gallantry and intrepidity at the risk of his life above and beyond the call of duty. L/Cpl. Wheat and 2 other marines were assigned the mission of providing security for a Navy construction battalion crane and crew operating along Liberty Road in the vicinity of the Dien Ban District, Quang Nam Province. After the marines had set up security positions in a tree line adjacent to the work site, L/Cpl. Wheat reconnoitered the area to the rear of their location for the possible presence of guerrillas. He then returned to within 10 feet of the friendly position, and here unintentionally triggered a well concealed, bounding type, antipersonnel mine. Immediately, a hissing sound was heard which was identified by the 3 marines as that of a burning time fuse. Shouting a warning to his comrades, L/Cpl. Wheat in a valiant act of heroism hurled himself upon the mine, absorbing the tremendous impact of the explosion with his body. The inspirational personal heroism and extraordinary valor of his unselfish action saved his fellow marines from certain injury and possible death, reflected great credit upon himself, and upheld the highest traditions of the Marine Corps and the U.S. Naval Service. He gallantly gave his life for his country.

*WICKAM, JERRY WAYNE

Rank and organization: Corporal, U.S. Army, Troop F, 2d Squadron, 11th Armored Cavalry Regiment. *Place and date:* Near Loc Ninh, Republic of Vietnam, 6 January 1968. *Entered service at:* Chicago, Ill. *Born:* 19 January 1942, Rockford, Ill. *Citation:* For conspicuous gallantry and intrepidity in action at the risk of his life above and beyond the call of duty. Cpl. Wickam, distinguished himself while serving with Troop F. Troop F was conducting a reconnaissance in force mission southwest of Loc Ninh when the lead element of the friendly force was subjected to a heavy barrage of rocket, automatic weapons, and small-arms fire from a well concealed enemy bunker complex. Disregarding the intense fire, Cpl. Wickam leaped from his armored vehicle and assaulted one of the enemy bunkers and threw a grenade into it, killing 2 enemy soldiers. He moved into the bunker, and with the aid of another soldier, began to remove the body of one Viet Cong when he detected the sound of an enemy grenade being charged. Cpl. Wickam warned his comrade and physically pushed him away from the grenade thus protecting him from the force of the blast. When a second Viet Cong bunker was discovered, he ran through a hail of enemy fire to deliver deadly fire into the bunker, killing one enemy soldier. He also captured 1 Viet Cong who later provided valuable information on enemy activity in the Loc Ninh area. After the patrol withdrew and an airstrike was conducted, Cpl. Wickam led his men back to evaluate the success of the strike. They were immediately attacked again by enemy fire. Without hesitation, he charged the bunker from which the fire was being directed, enabling the remainder of his men to seek cover. He threw a grenade inside of the enemy's position killing 2 Viet Cong and destroying the bunker. Moments later he was mortally wounded by enemy fire. Cpl. Wickam's extraordinary heroism at the cost of his life were in keeping with the highest traditions of the military service and reflect great credit upon himself and the U.S. Army.

*WILBANKS, HILLIARD A.

Rank and organization: Captain, U.S. Air Force, 21st Tactical Air Support Squadron, Nha Trang AFB, RVN. *Place and date:* Near Dalat, Republic of Vietnam, 24 February 1967. *Entered service at:* Atlanta, Ga. *Born:* 26 July 1933, Cornelia, Ga. *Citation:* For conspicuous gallantry and intrepidity in action at the risk of his life above and beyond the call of duty. As a forward air controller Capt. Wilbanks was pilot of an unarmed, light aircraft flying visual reconnaissance ahead of a South Vietnam Army Ranger Battalion. His intensive search revealed a well-concealed and numerically superior hostile force poised to ambush the advancing rangers. The Viet Cong, realizing that Capt. Wilbanks's discovery had compromised their position and ability to launch a surprise attack, immediately fired on the small aircraft with all available firepower. The enemy then began advancing against the exposed forward elements of the ranger force which were pinned down by devastating fire. Capt. Wilbanks recognized that close support aircraft could not arrive in time to enable the rangers to withstand the advancing enemy, onslaught. With full knowledge of the limitations of his unarmed, unarmored, light reconnaissance aircraft, and the great danger imposed by the enemy's vast firepower, he unhesitatingly assumed a covering, close support role. Flying through a hail of withering fire at treetop level, Capt. Wilbanks passed directly over the advancing enemy and inflicted many casualties by firing his rifle out of the side window of his aircraft. Despite increasingly intense antiaircraft fire, Capt. Wilbanks continued to completely disregard his own safety and made repeated low passes over the enemy to divert their fire away from the rangers. His daring tactics successfully interrupted the enemy advance, allowing the rangers to withdraw to safety from their perilous position. During his final courageous attack to protect the withdrawing forces, Capt. Wilbanks was mortally wounded and his bullet-riddled aircraft crashed between the opposing forces. Capt. Wilbanks' magnificent action saved numerous friendly personnel from certain injury or death. His unparalleled concern for his fellow man and his extraordinary heroism were in the highest traditions of the military service, and have reflected great credit upon himself and the U.S. Air Force.

*WILLETT, LOUIS E.

Rank and organization: Private First Class, U.S. Army, Company C, 1st Battalion, 12th Infantry, 4th Infantry Division. *Place and date:* Kontum Province, Republic of Vietnam, 15 February 1967. *Entered service at:* Brooklyn, N.Y. *Born:* 19 June 1945, Brooklyn, N.Y. *Citation:* For conspicuous gallantry and intrepidity at the risk of his life above and beyond the call of duty. Pfc. Willett distinguished himself while serving as a rifleman in Company C, during combat operations. His squad was conducting a security sweep when it made contact with a large enemy force. The squad was immediately engaged with a heavy volume of automatic weapons fire and pinned to the ground. Despite the deadly fusillade, Pfc. Willett rose to his feet firing rapid bursts from his weapon and moved to a position from which he placed highly effective fire on the enemy. His action allowed the remainder of his squad to begin to withdraw from the superior enemy force toward the company perimeter. Pfc. Willett covered the squad's withdrawal, but his position drew heavy enemy machinegun fire, and he received multiple wounds enabling the enemy again to pin down the remainder of the squad. Pfc. Willett struggled to an upright position, and, disregarding his painful wounds, he again engaged the enemy with his rifle to allow his squad to continue its movement and to evacuate several of his comrades who were by now wounded. Moving from position to position, he engaged the enemy at close range until he was mortally wounded. By his unselfish acts of bravery, Pfc. Willett insured the withdrawal of his comrades to the company position, saving their lives at the cost of his life. Pfc. Willett's valorous actions were in keeping with the highest traditions of the U.S. Army and reflect great credit upon himself and the Armed Forces of his country.

WILLIAMS, CHARLES Q.

Rank and organization: First Lieutenant (then 2d Lt.), U.S. Army, 5th Special Forces Group. *Place and date:* Dong Xoai, Republic of Vietnam, 9 to 10 June 1965. *Entered service at:* Fort Jackson, S.C. *Born:* 17 September 1933, Charleston, S.C. *G.O. No.:* 30, 5 July 1966. *Citation:* 1st Lt. Williams distinguished himself by conspicuous gallantry and intrepidity at the risk of his life above and beyond the call of duty while defending the Special Forces Camp against a violent attack by hostile forces that lasted for 14 hours. 1st Lt. Williams was serving as executive officer of a Special Forces Detachment when an estimated Vietcong reinforced regiment struck the camp and threatened to overrun it and the adjacent district headquarters. He awoke personnel, organized them, determined the source of the insurgents' main effort and led the troops to their defensive positions on the south and west walls. Then, after running to the District Headquarters to establish communications, he found that there was no radio operational with which to communicate with his commanding officer in another compound. To reach the other compound, he traveled through darkness but was halted in this effort by a combination of shrapnel in his right leg and the increase of the Vietcong gunfire. Ignoring his wound, he returned to the district headquarters and directed the defense against the first assault. As the insurgents attempted to scale the walls and as some of the Vietnamese defenders began to retreat, he dashed through a barrage of gunfire, succeeded in rallying these defenders, and led them back to their positions. Although wounded in the thigh and left leg during this gallant action, he returned to his position and, upon being told that communications were reestablished and that his commanding officer was seriously wounded, 1st Lt. Williams took charge of actions in both compounds. Then, in an attempt to reach the communications bunker, he sustained wounds in the stomach and right arm from grenade fragments. As the defensive positions on the walls had been held for hours and casualties were mounting, he ordered the consolidation of the American personnel from both compounds to establish a defense in the district building. After radio contact was made with a friendly air controller, he disregarded his wounds and directed the defense from the District building, using descending flares as reference points to adjust air strikes. By his courage, he inspired his team to hold out against the insurgent force that was closing in on them and throwing grenades into the windows of the building. As daylight arrived and the Vietcong continued to besiege the stronghold, firing a machinegun directly south of the district building, he was determined to eliminate this menace that threatened the lives of his men. Taking a 3.5 rocket launcher and a volunteer to load it, he worked his way across open terrain, reached the berm south of the district headquarters, and took aim at the Vietcong machinegun 150 meters away. Although the sight was faulty, he succeeded in hitting the machinegun. While he and the loader were trying to return to the district headquarters, they were both wounded. With a fourth wound, this time in the right arm and leg, and realizing he was unable to carry his wounded comrade back to the district building, 1st Lt. Williams pulled him to a covered position and then made his way back to the district building where he sought the help of others who went out and evacuated the injured soldier. Although seriously wounded and tired, he continued to direct the air strikes closer to the defensive position. As morning turned to afternoon and the Vietcong pressed their effort with direct recoilless rifle fire into the building, he ordered the evacuation of the seriously wounded to the safety of the communications bunker. When informed that helicopters would attempt to land as the hostile gunfire had abated, he led his team from the building to the artillery position, making certain of the timely evacuation of the wounded from the communications area, and then on to the pickup point. Despite resurgent Vietcong gunfire, he directed the rapid evacuation of all personnel. Throughout the long battle, he was undaunted by the vicious Vietcong assault and inspired the defenders in decimating the determined insurgents. 1st Lt. Williams' extraordinary heroism, are in the highest traditions of the U.S. Army and reflect great credit upon himself and the Armed Forces of his country.

*WILLIAMS, DEWAYNE T.

Rank and organization: Private First Class, U.S. Marine Corps, Company H, 2d Battalion, 1st Marines, 1st Marine Division. *Place and date:* Quang Nam Province, Republic of Vietnam, 18 September 1968. *Entered service at:* Saint Clair, Mich. *Born:* 18 September 1949, Brown City, Mich. *Citation:* For conspicuous gallantry and intrepidity at the risk of his life above and beyond the call of duty while serving as a rifleman with the 1st Platoon, Company H, in action against communist insurgent forces. Pfc. Williams was a member of a combat patrol sent out from the platoon with the mission of establishing positions in the company's area of operations, from which it could intercept and destroy enemy sniper teams operating in the area. In the night as the patrol was preparing to move from its daylight position to a preselected night position, it was attacked from ambush by a squad of enemy using small arms and handgrenades. Although severely wounded in the back by the close intense fire, Pfc. Williams, recognizing the danger to the patrol, immediately began to crawl forward toward a good firing position. While he was moving under the continuing intense fire, he heard one of the members of the patrol sound the alert that an enemy grenade had landed in their position. Reacting instantly to the alert, he saw that the grenade had landed close to where he was lying and without hesitation, in a valiant act of heroism, rolled on top of the grenade as it exploded, absorbing the full and tremendous impact of the explosion with his body. Through his extraordinary initiative and inspiring valor in the face of certain death, he saved the other members of his patrol from serious injury and possible loss of life, and enabled them to successfully defeat the attackers and hold their position until assistance arrived. His personal heroism and devotion to duty upheld the highest traditions of the Marine Corps and the U.S. Naval Service. He gallantly gave his life for his country.

WILLIAMS, JAMES E.

Rank and organization: Boatswain's Mate First Class (PO1c.), U.S. Navy, River Section 531, My Tho, RVN, *Place and date:* Mekong River, Republic of Vietnam, 31 October 1966. *Entered service at:* Columbia, S.C. *Born:* 13 June 1930, Rock Hill, S.C. *Citation:* For conspicuous gallantry and intrepidity at the risk of his life above and beyond the call of duty. PO1c. Williams was serving as Boat Captain and Patrol Officer aboard River Patrol Boat (PBR) 105 accompanied by another patrol boat when the patrol was suddenly taken under fire by 2 enemy sampans. PO1c. Williams immediately ordered the fire returned, killing the crew of 1 enemy boat and causing the other sampan to take refuge in a nearby river inlet. Pursuing the fleeing sampan, the U.S. patrol encountered a heavy volume of small-arms fire from enemy forces, at close range, occupying well-concealed positions along the river bank. Maneuvering through this fire, the patrol confronted a numerically superior enemy force aboard 2 enemy junks and 8 sampans augmented by heavy automatic weapons fire from ashore. In the savage battle that ensued, PO1c. Williams, with utter disregard for his safety exposed himself to the withering hail of enemy fire to direct counter-fire and inspire the actions of his patrol. Recognizing the overwhelming strength of the enemy force, PO1c. Williams deployed his patrol to await the arrival of armed helicopters. In the course of his movement his discovered an even larger concentration of enemy boats. Not waiting for the arrival of the armed helicopters, he displayed great initiative and boldly led the patrol through the intense enemy fire and damaged or destroyed 50 enemy sampans and 7 junks. This phase of the action completed, and with the arrival of the armed helicopters, PO1c. Williams directed the attack on the remaining enemy force. Now virtually dark, and although PO1c. Williams was aware that his boats would become even better targets, he ordered the patrol boats' search lights turned on to better illuminate the area and moved the patrol perilously close to shore to press the attack. Despite a waning supply of ammunition the patrol successfully engaged the enemy ashore and completed the rout of the enemy force. Under the leadership of PO1c. Williams, who demonstrated unusual professional skill and indomitable courage throughout the 3 hour battle, the patrol accounted for the destruction or loss of 65 enemy boats and inflicted numerous casualties on the enemy personnel. His extraordinary heroism and exemplary fighting spirit in the face of grave risks inspired the efforts of his men to defeat a larger enemy force, and are in keeping with the finest traditions of the U.S. Naval Service.

*WILSON, ALFRED M.

Rank and organization: Private First Class, U.S. Marine Corps, Company M, 3d Battalion, 9th Marines, 3d Marine Division. *Place and date:* Quang Tri Province, Republic of Vietnam, 3 March 1969. *Entered service at:* Abilene, Tex. *Born:* 13 January 1948, Olney, Ill. *Citation:* For conspicuous gallantry and intrepidity at the risk of his life above and beyond the call of duty while serving as a rifleman with Company M in action against hostile forces. While returning from a reconnaissance-in-force mission in the vicinity of Fire Support Base Cunningham, the 1st Platoon of Company M came under intense automatic weapons fire and a grenade attack from a well concealed enemy force. As the center of the column was pinned down, the leading squad moved to outflank the enemy. Pfc. Wilson, acting as squad leader of the rear squad, skillfully maneuvered his men to form a base of fire and act as a blocking force. In the ensuing fire fight, both his machine gunner and assistant machine gunner were seriously wounded and unable to operate their weapons. Realizing the urgent need to bring the weapon into operation again, Pfc. Wilson, followed by another marine and with complete disregard for his safety, fearlessly dashed across the fire-swept terrain to recover the weapon. As they reached the machinegun, an enemy soldier stepped from behind a tree and threw a grenade toward the 2 marines. Observing the grenade fall between himself and the other marine, Pfc. Wilson, fully realizing the inevitable result of his actions, shouted to his companion and unhesitating threw himself on the grenade, absorbing the full force of the explosion with his own body. His heroic actions inspired his platoon members to maximum effort as they aggressively attacked and defeated the enemy. Pfc. Wilson's indomitable courage, inspiring valor and selfless devotion to duty upheld the highest traditions of the Marine Corps and the U.S. Naval Service. He gallantly gave his life for his country.

*WINDER, DAVID F.

Rank and organization: Private First Class, U.S. Army, Headquarters and Headquarters Company, 3d Battalion, 1st Infantry, 11th Infantry Brigade, American Division. *Place and date:* Republic of Vietnam, 13 May 1970. *Entered service at:* Columbus, Ohio. *Born:* 10 August 1946, Edinboro, Pa. *Citation:* Pfc. Winder distinguished himself while serving in the Republic of Vietnam as a senior medical aidman with Company A. After moving through freshly cut rice paddies in search of a suspected company-size enemy force, the unit started a thorough search of the area. Suddenly they were engaged with intense automatic weapons and rocket propelled grenade fire by a well entrenched enemy force. Several friendly soldiers fell wounded in the initial contact and the unit was pinned down. Responding instantly to the cries of his wounded comrades, Pfc. Winder began maneuvering aross approximately 100 meters of open, bullet-swept terrain toward the nearest casualty. Unarmed and crawling most of the distance, he was wounded by enemy fire before reaching his comrades. Despite his wounds and with great effort, Pfc. Winder reached the first casualty and administered medical aid. As he continued to crawl across the open terrain toward a second wounded soldier he was forced to stop when wounded a second time. Aroused by the cries of an injured comrade for aid, Pfc. Winder's great determination and sense of duty impelled him to move forward once again, despite his wounds, in a courageous attempt to reach and assist the injured man. After struggling to within 10 meters of the man, Pfc. Winder was mortally wounded. His dedication and sacrifice inspired his unit to initiate an aggressive counterassault which led to the defeat of the enemy. Pfc. Winder's conspicuous gallantry and intrepidity in action at the cost of his life were in keeping with the highest traditions of the military service and reflect great credit on him, his unit and the U.S. Army.

*WORLEY, KENNETH L.

Rank and organization: Lance Corporal, U.S. Marine Corps, 3d Battalion, 7th Marines, 1st Marine Division (Rein), FMF. *Place and date:* Bo Ban, Quang Nam Province, Republic of Vietnam, 12 August 1968. *Entered service at:* Fresno, Calif. *Born:* 27 April 1948, Farmington, N. Mex. *Citation:* For conspicuous gallantry and intrepidity at the risk of his life above and beyond the call of duty while serving as a machine gunner with Company L, 3d Battalion, in action against enemy forces. After establishing a night ambush position in a house in the Bo Ban, Hamlet of Quang Nam Province, security was set up and the remainder of the patrol members retired until their respective watch. During the early morning hours the marines were abruptly awakened by the platoon leader's warning that "grenades" had landed in the house. Fully realizing the inevitable result of his actions, L/Cpl. Worley, in a valiant act of heroism, instantly threw himself upon the grenade nearest him and his comrades, absorbing with his body, the full and tremendous force of the explosion. Through his extraordinary initiative and inspiring valor in the face of almost certain death, he saved his comrades from serious injury and possible loss of life although 5 of his fellow marines incurred minor wounds as the other grenades exploded. L/Cpl. Worley's gallant actions upheld the highest traditions of the Marine Corps and the U.S. Naval Service. He gallantly gave his life for his country.

WRIGHT, RAYMOND R.

Rank and organization: Specialist Fourth Class, U.S. Army, Company A, 3d Battalion, 60th Infantry, 9th Infantry Division. *Place and date:* Ap Bac Zone, Republic of Vietnam, 2 May 1967. *Entered service at:* Moriah, N.Y. *Born:* 5 December 1945, Moriah, N.Y. *Citation:* For conspicuous gallantry and intrepidity at the risk of his life above and beyond the call of duty. While serving as a rifleman with Company A, Sp4c. Wright distinguished himself during a combat patrol in an area where an enemy ambush had occurred earlier. Sp4c. Wright's unit suddenly came under intense automatic weapons and small-arms fire from an enemy bunker system protected by numerous snipers in nearby trees. Despite the heavy enemy fire, Sp4c. Wright and another soldier leaped to the top of a dike to assault the position. Armed with a rifle and several grenades, he and his comrade exposed themselves to intense fire from the bunkers as they charged the nearest one. Sp4c. Wright raced to the bunker, threw in a grenade, killing its occupant. The 2 soldiers then ran through a hail of fire to the second bunker. While his comrade covered him with his machinegun, Sp4c. Wright charged the bunker and succeeded in killing its occupant with a grenade. A third bunker contained an automatic rifleman who had pinned down much of the friendly platoon. While his comrade again covered him with machinegun fire, Sp4c. Wright charged in and killed the enemy rifleman with a grenade. The 2 soldiers worked their way through the remaining bunkers, knocking out 4 of them. Throughout their furious assault, Sp4c. Wright and his comrade had been almost continuously exposed to intense sniper fire from the treeline as the enemy desperately sought to stop their attack. Overcoming stubborn resistance from the bunker system, the men advanced into the treeline forcing the snipers to retreat, giving immediate chase, and driving the enemy away from the friendly unit so that it advanced across the open area without further casualty. When his ammunition was exhausted, Sp4c. Wright returned to his unit to assist in the evacuation of the wounded. This 2-man assault had driven an enemy platoon from a well prepared position, accounted for numerious enemy casualties, and averted further friendly casualties. Sp4c. Wright's extraordinary heroism, courage, and indomitable fighting spirit saved the lives of many of his comrades and inflicted serious damage on the enemy. His acts were in keeping with the highest traditions of the military service and reflect great credit upon himself and the U.S. Army.

*YABES, MAXIMO

Rank and organization: First Sergeant, U.S. Army, Company A, 4th Battalion, 9th Infantry, 25th Infantry Division. *Place and date:* Near Phu Hoa Dong, Republic of Vietnam, 26 February 1967. *Entered service at:* Eugene, Oreg. *Born:* 29 January 1932, Lodi, Calif. *Citation:* For conspicuous gallantry and intrepidity at the risk of his life above and beyond the call of duty. 1st Sgt.Yabes distinguished himself with Company A, which was providing security for a land clearing operation. Early in the morning the company suddenly came under intense automatic weapons and mortar fire followed by a battalion sized assault from 3 sides. Penetrating the defensive perimeter the enemy advanced on the company command post bunker. The command post received increasingly heavy fire and was in danger of being overwhelmed. When several enemy grenades landed within the command post, 1st Sgt. Yabes shouted a warning and used his body as a shield to protect others in the bunker. Although painfully wounded by numerous grenade fragments, and despite the vicious enemy fire on the bunker, he remained there to provide covering fire and enable the others in the command group to relocate. When the command group had reached a new position, 1st Sgt. Yabes moved through a withering hail of enemy fire to another bunker 50 meters away. There he secured a grenade launcher from a fallen comrade and fired point blank into the attacking Viet Cong stopping further penetration of the perimeter. Noting 2 wounded men helpless in the fire swept area, he moved them to a safer position where they could be given medical treatment. He resumed his accurate and effective fire killing several enemy soldiers and forcing others to withdraw from the vicinity of the command post. As the battle continued, he observed an enemy machinegun within the perimeter which threatened the whole position. On his own, he dashed across the exposed area, assaulted the machinegun, killed the crew, destroyed the weapon, and fell mortally wounded. 1st Sgt. Yabes' valiant and selfless actions saved the lives of many of his fellow soldiers and inspired his comrades to effectively repel the enemy assault. His indomitable fighting spirit, extraordinary courage and intrepidity at the cost of his life are in the highest military traditions and reflect great credit upon himself and the Armed Forces of his country.

*YANO, RODNEY J. T.

Rank and organization: Sergeant First Class, U.S. Army, Air Cavalry Troop, 11th Armored Cavalry Regiment. *Place and date:* Near Bien Hao, Republic of Vietnam, 1 Janaury 1969. *Entered service at:* Honolulu, Hawaii. *Born:* 13 December 1943, Kealakekua Kona, Hawaii. *Citation:* Sfc. Yano distinguished himself while serving with the Air Cavalry Troop. Sfc. Yano was performing the duties of crew chief aboard the troop's command-and-control helicopter during action against enemy forces entrenched in dense jungle. From an exposed position in the face of intense small arms and antiaircraft fire he delivered suppressive fire upon the enemy forces and marked their positions with smoke and white phosphorous grenades, thus enabling his troop commander to direct accurate and effective artillery fire against the hostile emplacements. A grenade, exploding prematurely, covered him with burning phosphorous, and left him severely wounded. Flaming fragments within the helicopter caused supplies and ammunition to detonate. Dense white smoke filled the aircraft, obscuring the pilot's vision and causing him to lose control. Although having the use of only 1 arm and being partially blinded by the initial explosion, Sfc. Yano completely disregarded his welfare and began hurling blazing ammunition from the helicopter. In so doing he inflicted additional wounds upon himself, yet he persisted until the danger was past. Sfc. Yano's indomitable courage and profound concern for his comrades averted loss of life and additional injury to the rest of the crew. By his conspicuous gallantry at the cost of his life, in the highest traditions of the military service, Sfc. Yano has reflected great credit on himself, his unit, and the U.S. Army.

*YNTEMA, GORDON DOUGLAS

Rank and organization: Sergeant, U.S. Army, Company D, 5th Special Forces Group (Airborne). *Place and date:* Near Thong Binh, Republic of Vietnam, 16–18 January 1968. *Entered service at:* Detroit, Mich. *Born:* 26 June 1945, Bethesda, Md. *Citation:* For conspicuous gallantry and intrepidity in action at the risk of his life and above and beyond the call of duty. Sgt. Yntema, U.S. Army, distinguished himself while assigned to Detachment A–431, Company D. As part of a larger force of civilian irregulars from Camp Cai Cai, he accompanied 2 platoons to a blocking position east of the village of Thong Binh, where they became heavily engaged in a small-arms fire fight with the Viet Cong. Assuming control of the force when the Vietnamese commander was seriously wounded, he advanced his troops to within 50 meters of the enemy bunkers. After a fierce 30 minute fire fight, the enemy forced Sgt. Yntema to withdraw his men to a trench in order to afford them protection and still perform their assigned blocking mission. Under cover of machinegun fire, approximately 1 company of Viet Cong maneuvered into a position which pinned down the friendly platoons from 3 sides. A dwindling ammunition supply, coupled with a Viet Cong mortar barrage which inflicted heavy losses on the exposed friendly troops, caused many of the irregulars to withdraw. Seriously wounded and ordered to withdraw himself, Sgt. Yntema refused to leave his fallen comrades. Under withering small arms and machinegun fire, he carried the wounded Vietnamese commander and a mortally wounded American Special Forces advisor to a small gully 50 meters away in order to shield them from the enemy fire. Sgt. Yntema then continued to repulse the attacking Viet Cong attempting to overrun his position until, out of ammunition and surrounded, he was offered the opportunity to surrender. Refusing, Sgt. Yntema stood his ground, using his rifle as a club to fight the approximately 15 Viet Cong attempting his capture. His resistance was so fierce that the Viet Cong were forced to shoot in order to overcome him. Sgt. Yntema's personal bravery in the face of insurmountable odds and supreme self-sacrifice were in keeping with the highest traditions of the military service and reflect the utmost credit upon himself, the 1st Special Forces, and the U.S. Army.

YOUNG, GERALD O.

Rank and organization: Captain, U.S. Air Force, 37th ARS Da Nang AFB, Republic of Vietnam. *Place and date:* Khesanh, 9 November 1967. *Entered service at:* Colorado Springs, Colo. *Born:* 9 May 1930, Chicago, Ill. *Citation:* For conspicuous gallantry and intrepidity at the risk of his life above and beyond the call of duty. Capt. Young distinguished himself while serving as a helicopter rescue crew commander. Capt. Young was flying escort for another helicopter attempting the night rescue of an Army ground reconnaissance team in imminent danger of death or capture. Previous attempts had resulted in the loss of 2 helicopters to hostile ground fire. The endangered team was positioned on the side of a steep slope which required unusual airmanship on the part of Capt. Young to effect pickup. Heavy automatic weapons fire from the surrounding enemy severely damaged 1 rescue helicopter, but it was able to extract 3 of the team. The commander of this aircraft recommended to Capt. Young that further rescue attempts be abandoned because it was not possible to suppress the concentrated fire from enemy automatic weapons. With full knowledge of the danger involved, and the fact that supporting helicopter gunships were low on fuel and ordnance, Capt. Young hovered under intense fire until the remaining survivors were aboard. As he maneuvered the aircraft for takeoff, the enemy appeared at point-blank range and raked the aircraft with automatic weapons fire. The aircraft crashed, inverted, and burst into flames. Capt. Young escaped through a window of the burning aircraft. Disregarding serious burns, Capt. Young aided one of the wounded men and attempted to lead the hostile forces away from his position. Later, despite intense pain from his burns, he declined to accept rescue because he had observed hostile forces setting up automatic weapons positions to entrap any rescue aircraft. For more than 17 hours he evaded the enemy until rescue aircraft could be brought into the area. Through his extraordinary heroism, aggressiveness, and concern for his fellow man, Capt. Young reflected the highest credit upon himself, the U.S. Air Force, and the Armed Forces of his country.

*YOUNG, MARVIN R.

Rank and organization: Staff Sergeant, U.S. Army, Company C, 1st Battalion, (Mechanized), 5th Infantry, 25th Infantry Division. *Place and date:* Near Ben Cui, Republic of Vietnam, 21 August 1968. *Entered service at:* Odessa, Tex. *Born:* 11 May 1947, Alpine, Tex. *Citation:* For conspicuous gallantry and intrepidity in action at the risk of his life above and beyond the call of duty. S/Sgt. Young distinguished himself at the cost of his life while serving as a squad leader with Company C. While conducting a reconnaissance mission in the vicinity of Ben Cui, Company C was suddenly engaged by an estimated regimental-size force of the North Vietnamese Army. During the initial volley of fire the point element of the 1st Platoon was pinned down, sustaining several casualties, and the acting platoon leader was killed. S/Sgt. Young unhesitatingly assumed command of the platoon and immediately began to organize and deploy his men into a defensive position in order to repel the attacking force. As a human wave attack advanced on S/Sgt. Young's platoon, he moved from position to position, encouraging and directing fire on the hostile insurgents while exposing himself to the hail of enemy bullets. After receiving orders to withdraw to a better defensive position, he remained behind to provide covering fire for the withdrawal. Observing that a small element of the point squad was unable to extract itself from its position, and completely disregarding his personal safety, S/Sgt. Young began moving toward their position, firing as he maneuvered. When halfway to their position he sustained a critical head injury, yet he continued his mission and ordered the element to withdraw. Remaining with the squad as it fought its way to the rear, he was twice seriously wounded in the arm and leg. Although his leg was badly shattered, S/Sgt. Young refused assistance that would have slowed the retreat of his comrades, and he ordered them to continue their withdrawal while he provided protective covering fire. With indomitable courage and heroic self-sacrifice, he continued his self-assigned mission until the enemy force engulfed his position. By his gallantry at the cost of his life are in the highest traditions of the military service, S/Sgt. Young has reflected great credit upon himself, his unit, and the U.S. Army.

ZABITOSKY, FRED WILLIAM

Rank and organization: Sergeant First Class (then S/Sgt.), U.S. Army, 5th Special Forces Group (Airborne). *Place and date:* Republic of Vietnam, 19 February 1968. *Entered service at:* Trenton, N.J. *Born:* 27 October 1942, Trenton, N.J. *Citation:* For conspicuous gallantry and intrepidity in action at the risk of his life above and beyond the call of duty. Sfc. Zabitosky, U.S. Army, distinguished himself while serving as an assistant team leader of a 9-man Special Forces long-range reconnaissance patrol. Sfc. Zabitosky's patrol was operating deep within enemy controlled territory when they were attacked by a numerically superior North Vietnamese Army unit. Sfc. Zabitosky rallied his team members, deployed them into defensive positions, and, exposing himself to concentrated enemy automatic weapons fire, directed their return fire. Realizing the gravity of the situation, Sfc. Zabitosky ordered his patrol to move to a landing zone for helicopter extraction while he covered their withdrawal with rifle fire and grenades. Rejoining the patrol under increasing enemy pressure, he positioned each man in a tight perimeter defense and continually moved from man to man, encouraging them and controlling their defensive fire. Mainly due to his example, the outnumbered patrol maintained its precarious position until the arrival of tactical air support and a helicopter extraction team. As the rescue helicopters arrived, the determined North Vietnamese pressed their attack. Sfc. Zabitosky repeatedly exposed himself to their fire to adjust suppressive helicopter gunship fire around the landing zone. After boarding 1 of the rescue helicopters, he positioned himself in the door delivering fire on the enemy as the ship took off. The helicopter was engulfed in a hail of bullets and Sfc. Zabitosky was thrown from the craft as it spun out of control and crashed. Recovering consciousness, he ignored his extremely painful injuries and moved to the flaming wreckage. Heedless of the danger of exploding ordnance and fuel, he pulled the severely wounded pilot from the searing blaze and made repeated attempts to rescue his patrol members but was driven back by the intense heat. Despite his serious burns and crushed ribs, he carried and dragged the unconscious pilot through a curtain of enemy fire to within 10 feet of a hovering rescue helicopter before collapsing. Sfc. Zabitosky's extraordinary heroism and devotion to duty were in keeping with the highest traditions of the military service and reflect great credit upon himself, his unit, and the U.S. Army.

KOREA

(KOREAN CONFLICT)

*ABRELL, CHARLES G.

Rank and organization: Corporal, U.S. Marine Corps, Company E, 2d Battalion, 1st Marines, 1st Marine Division (Rein). *Place and date:* Hangnyong, Korea, 10 June 1951. *Entered service at:* Terre Haute, Ind. *Born:* 12 August 1931, Terre Haute, Ind. *Citation:* For conspicuous gallantry and intrepidity at the risk of his life above and beyond the call of duty while serving as a fire team leader in Company E, in action against enemy aggressor forces. While advancing with his platoon in an attack against well-concealed and heavily fortified enemy hill positions, Cpl. Abrell voluntarily rushed forward through the assaulting squad which was pinned down by a hail of intense and accurate automatic-weapons fire from a hostile bunker situated on commanding ground. Although previously wounded by enemy handgrenade fragments, he proceeded to carry out a bold, singlehanded attack against the bunker, exhorting his comrades to follow him. Sustaining 2 additional wounds as he stormed toward the emplacement, he resolutely pulled the pin from a grenade clutched in his hand and hurled himself bodily into the bunker with the live missile still in his grasp. Fatally wounded in the resulting explosion which killed the entire enemy guncrew within the stronghold, Cpl. Abrell, by his valiant spirit of selfsacrifice in the face of certain death, served to inspire all his comrades and contributed directly to the success of his platoon in attaining its objective. His superb courage and heroic initiative sustain and enhance the highest traditions of the U.S. Naval Service. He gallantly gave his life for his country.

ADAMS, STANLEY T.

Rank and organization: Master Sergeant (then Sfc.), U.S. Army, Company A, 19th Infantry Regiment. *Place and date:* Near Sesim-ni, Korea, 4 February 1951. *Entered service at:* Olathe, Kans. *Born:* 9 May 1922, DeSoto, Kans. *G.O. No.:* 66, 2 August 1951. *Citation:* M/Sgt. Adams, Company A, distinguished himself by conspicuous gallantry and intrepidity above and beyond the call of duty in action against an enemy. At approximately 0100 hours, M/Sgt. Adams' platoon, holding an outpost some 200 yards ahead of his company, came under a determined attack by an estimated 250 enemy troops. Intense small-arms, machinegun, and mortar fire from 3 sides pressed the platoon back against the main line of resistance. Observing approximately 150 hostile troops silhouetted against the skyline advancing against his platoon, M/Sgt. Adams leaped to his feet, urged his men to fix bayonets, and he, with 13 members of his platoon, charged this hostile force with indomitable courage. Within 50 yards of the enemy M/Sgt. Adams was knocked to the ground when pierced in the leg by an enemy bullet. He jumped to his feet and, ignoring his wound, continued on to close with the enemy when he was knocked down 4 times from the concussion of grenades which had bounced off his body. Shouting orders he charged the enemy positions and engaged them in hand-to-hand combat where man after man fell before his terrific onslaught with bayonet and rifle butt. After nearly an hour of vicious action M/Sgt. Adams and his comrades routed the fanatical foe, killing over 50 and forcing the remainder to withdraw. Upon receiving orders that his battalion was moving back he provided cover fire while his men withdrew. M/Sgt. Adams' superb leadership, incredible courage, and consummate devotion to duty so inspired his comrades that the enemy attack was completely thwarted, saving his battalion from possible disaster. His sustained personal bravery and indomitable fighting spirit against overwhelming odds reflect the utmost glory upon himself and uphold the finest traditions of the infantry and the military service.

BARBER, WILLIAM E.

Rank and organization: Captain, U.S. Marine Corps, commanding officer, Company F, 2d Battalion, 7th Marines, 1st Marine Division (Rein). *Place and date:* Chosin Reservoir area, Korea, 28 November to 2 December 1950. *Entered service at:* West Liberty, Ky. *Born:* 30 November 1919, Dehart, Ky. *Citation:* For conspicuous gallantry and intrepidity at the risk of his life above and beyond the call of duty as commanding officer of Company F in action against enemy aggressor forces. Assigned to defend a 3-mile mountain pass along the division's main supply line and commanding the only route of approach in the march from Yudam-ni to Hagaru-ri, Capt. Barber took position with his battle-weary troops and, before nightfall, had dug in and set up a defense along the frozen, snow-covered hillside. When a force of estimated regimental strength savagely attacked during the night, inflicting heavy casualties and finally surrounding his position following a bitterly fought 7-hour conflict, Capt. Barber, after repulsing the enemy, gave assurance that he could hold if supplied by airdrops and requested permission to stand fast when orders were received by radio to fight his way back to a relieving force after 2 reinforcing units had been driven back under fierce resistance in their attempts to reach the isolated troops. Aware that leaving the position would sever contact with the 8,000 marines trapped at Yudam-ni and jeopardize their chances of joining the 3,000 more awaiting their arrival in Hagaru-ri for the continued drive to the sea, he chose to risk loss of his command rather than sacrifice more men if the enemy seized control and forced a renewed battle to regain the position, or abandon his many wounded who were unable to walk. Although severely wounded in the leg in the early morning of the 29th, Capt. Barber continued to maintain personal control, often moving up and down the lines on a stretcher to direct the defense and consistently encouraging and inspiring his men to supreme efforts despite the staggering opposition. Waging desperate battle throughout 5 days and 6 nights of repeated onslaughts launched by the fanatical aggressors, he and his heroic command accounted for approximately 1,000 enemy dead in this epic stand in bitter subzero weather, and when the company was relieved, only 82 of his original 220 men were able to walk away from the position so valiantly defended against insuperable odds. His profound faith and courage, great personal valor, and unwavering fortitude were decisive factors in the successful withdrawal of the division from the deathtrap in the Chosin Reservoir sector and reflect the highest credit upon Capt. Barber, his intrepid officers and men, and the U.S. Naval Service.

*BARKER, CHARLES H.

Rank and organization: Private First Class (then Pvt.), U.S. Army, Company K, 17th Infantry Regiment, 7th Infantry Division. *Place and date:* Near Sokkogae, Korea, 4 June 1953. *Entered service at:* Pickens County, S.C. *Born:* 12 April 1935, Pickens County, S.C. *G.O. No.:* 37, 7 June 1955. *Citation:* Pfc. Barker, a member of Company K, distinguished himself by conspicuous gallantry and indomitable courage above and beyond the call of duty in action against the enemy. While participating in a combat patrol engaged in screening an approach to "Pork-Chop Outpost," Pfc. Barker and his companions surprised and engaged an enemy group digging emplacements on the slope. Totally unprepared, the hostile troops sought cover. After ordering Pfc. Barker and a comrade to lay down a base of fire, the patrol leader maneuvered the remainder of the platoon to a vantage point on higher ground. Pfc. Barker moved to an open area firing his rifle and hurling grenades on the hostile positions. As enemy action increased in volume and intensity, mortar bursts fell on friendly positions, ammunition was in critical supply, and the platoon was ordered to withdraw into a perimeter defense preparatory to moving back to the outpost. Voluntarily electing to cover the retrograde movement, he gallantly maintained a defense and was last seen in close hand-to-hand combat with the enemy. Pfc. Barker's unflinching courage, consummate devotion to duty, and supreme sacrifice enabled the patrol to complete the mission and effect an orderly withdrawal to friendly lines, reflecting lasting glory upon himself and upholding the highest traditions of the military service.

*BAUGH, WILLIAM B.

Rank and organization: Private First Class, U.S. Marine Corps, Company G, 3d Battalion, 1st Marine, 1st Marine Division (Rein). *Place and date:* Along road from Koto-ri to Hagaru-ri, Korea, 29 November 1950. *Entered service at:* Harrison, Ohio. *Born:* 7 July 1930, McKinney, Ky. *Citation:* For conspicuous gallantry and intrepidity at the risk of his life above and beyond the call of duty while serving as a member of an antitank assault squad attached to Company G, during a nighttime enemy attack against a motorized column. Acting instantly when a hostile handgrenade landed in his truck as he and his squad prepared to alight and assist in the repulse of an enemy force delivering intense automatic-weapons and grenade fire from deeply entrenched and well-concealed roadside positions, Pfc. Baugh quickly shouted a warning to the other men in the vehicle and, unmindful of his personal safety, hurled himself upon the deadly missile, thereby saving his comrades from serious injury or possible death. Sustaining severe wounds from which he died a short time afterward, Pfc. Baugh, by his superb courage and valiant spirit of self-sacrifice, upheld the highest traditions of the U.S. Naval Service. He gallantly gave his life for his country.

*BENFORD, EDWARD C.

Rank and organization: Hospital Corpsman Third Class, U.S. Navy, attached to a company in the 1st Marine Division. *Place and date:* Korea, 5 September 1952. *Entered service at:* Philadelphia, Pa. *Born:* 15 January 1931, Staten Island, N.Y. *Citation:* For gallantry and intrepidity at the risk of his life above and beyond the call of duty while serving in operations against enemy aggressor forces. When his company was subjected to heavy artillery and mortar barrages, followed by a determined assault during the hours of darkness by an enemy force estimated at battalion strength, HC3c. Benford resolutely moved from position to position in the face of intense hostile fire, treating the wounded and lending words of encouragement. Leaving the protection of his sheltered position to treat the wounded when the platoon area in which he was working was attacked from both the front and rear, he moved forward to an exposed ridge line where he observed 2 marines in a large crater. As he approached the 2 men to determine their condition, an enemy soldier threw 2 grenades into the crater while 2 other enemy charged the position. Picking up a grenade in each hand, HC3c. Benford leaped out of the crater and hurled himself against the onrushing hostile soldiers, pushing the grenades against their chests and killing both the attackers. Mortally wounded while carrying out this heroic act, HC3c. Benford, by his great personal valor and resolute spirit of self-sacrifice in the face of almost certain death, was directly responsible for saving the lives of his 2 comrades. His exceptional courage reflects the highest credit upon himself and enhances the finest traditions of the U.S. Naval Service. He gallantly gave his life for others.

*BENNETT, EMORY L.

Rank and organization: Private First Class, U.S. Army, Company B, 15th Infantry Regiment, 3d Infantry Division. *Place and date:* Near Sobangsan, Korea, 24 June 1951. *Entered service at:* Cocoa, Fla. *Born:* 20 December 1929, New Smyrna Beach, Fla. *G.O. No.:* 11, 1 February 1952. *Citation:* Pfc. Bennett a member of Company B, distinguished himself by conspicuous gallantry and intrepidity at the risk of his life above and beyond the call of duty in action against an armed enemy of the United Nations. At approximately 0200 hours, 2 enemy battalions swarmed up the ridge line in a ferocious banzai charge in an attempt to dislodge Pfc. Bennett's company from its defensive positions. Meeting the challenge, the gallant defenders delivered destructive retaliation, but the enemy pressed the assault with fanatical determination and the integrity of the perimeter was imperiled. Fully aware of the odds against him, Pfc. Bennett unhesitatingly left his foxhole, moved through withering fire, stood within full view of the enemy, and, employing his automatic rifle, poured crippling fire into the ranks of the onrushing assailants, inflicting numerous casualties. Although wounded, Pfc. Bennett gallantly maintained his 1-man defense and the attack was momentarily halted. During this lull in battle, the company regrouped for counterattack, but the numerically superior foe soon infiltrated into the position. Upon orders to move back, Pfc. Bennett voluntarily remained to provide covering fire for the withdrawing elements, and, defying the enemy, continued to sweep the charging foe with devastating fire until mortally wounded. His willing self-sacrifice and intrepid actions saved the position from being overrun and enabled the company to effect an orderly withdrawal. Pfc. Bennett's unflinching courage and consummate devotion to duty reflect lasting glory on himself and the military service.

BLEAK, DAVID B.

Rank and organization: Sergeant, U.S. Army, Medical Company, 223d Infantry Regiment, 40th Infantry Division. *Place and date:* Vicinity of Minari-gol, Korea, 14 June 1952. *Entered service at:* Shelley, Idaho. *Born:* 27 February 1932, Idaho Falls, Idaho. *G.O. No.:* 83, 2 November 1953. *Citation:* Sgt. Bleak, a member of the medical company, distinguished himself by conspicuous gallantry and indomitable courage above and beyond the call of duty in action against the enemy. As a medical aidman, he volunteered to accompany a reconnaissance patrol committed to engage the enemy and capture a prisoner for interrogation. Forging up the rugged slope of the key terrain, the group was subjected to intense automatic weapons and small-arms fire and suffered several casualties. After administering to the wounded, he continued to advance with the patrol. Nearing the military crest of the hill, while attempting to cross the fire-swept area to attend the wounded, he came under hostile fire from a small group of the enemy concealed in a trench. Entering the trench he closed with the enemy, killed 2 with bare hands and a third with his trench knife. Moving from the emplacement, he saw a concussion grenade fall in front of a companion and, quickly shifting his position, shielded the man from the impact of the blast. Later, while ministering to the wounded, he was struck by a hostile bullet but, despite the wound, he undertook to evacuate a wounded comrade. As he moved down the hill with his heavy burden, he was attacked by 2 enemy soldiers with fixed bayonets. Closing with the aggressors, he grabbed them and smacked their heads together, then carried his helpless comrade down the hill to safety. Sgt. Bleak's dauntless courage and intrepid actions reflect utmost credit upon himself and are in keeping with the honored traditions of the military service.

*BRITTIN, NELSON V.

Rank and organization: Sergeant First Class, U.S. Army, Company I, 19th Infantry Regiment. *Place and date:* Vicinity of Yonggong-ni, Korea, 7 March 1951. *Entered service at:* Audubon, N.J. *Birth:* Audubon, N.J. *G.O. No.:* 12, 1 February 1952. *Citation:* Sfc. Brittin, a member of Company I, distinguished himself by conspicuous gallantry and intrepidity above and beyond the call of duty in action. Volunteering to lead his squad up a hill, with meager cover against murderous fire from the enemy, he ordered his squad to give him support and, in the face of withering fire and bursting shells, he tossed a grenade at the nearest enemy position. On returning to his squad, he was knocked down and wounded by an enemy grenade. Refusing medical attention, he replenished his supply of grenades and returned, hurling grenades into hostile positions and shooting the enemy as they fled. When his weapon jammed, he leaped without hesitation into a foxhole and killed the occupants with his bayonet and the butt of his rifle. He continued to wipe out foxholes and, noting that his squad had been pinned down, he rushed to the rear of a machinegun position, threw a grenade into the nest, and ran around to its front, where he killed all 3 occupants with his rifle. Less than 100 yards up the hill, his squad again came under vicious fire from another camouflaged, sandbagged, machinegun nest well-flanked by supporting riflemen. Sfc. Brittin again charged this new position in an aggressive endeavor to silence this remaining obstacle and ran direct into a burst of automatic fire which killed him instantly. In his sustained and driving action, he had killed 20 enemy soldiers and destroyed 4 automatic weapons. The conspicuous courage, consummate valor, and noble self-sacrifice displayed by Sfc. Brittin enabled his inspired company to attain its objective and reflect the highest glory on himself and the heroic traditions of the military service.

*BROWN, MELVIN L.

Rank and organization: Private First Class, U.S. Army, Company D, 8th Engineer Combat Battalion. *Place and date:* Near Kasan, Korea, 4 September 1950. *Entered service at:* Erie, Pa. *Birth:* Mahaffey, Pa.

G.O. No.: 11, 16 February 1951. *Citation:* Pfc. Brown, Company D, distinguished himself by conspicuous gallantry and intrepidity above and beyond the call of duty in action against the enemy. While his platoon was securing Hill 755 (the Walled City), the enemy, using heavy automatic weapons and small arms, counterattacked. Taking a position on a 50-foot-high wall he delivered heavy rifle fire on the enemy. His ammunition was soon expended and although wounded, he remained at his post and threw his few grenades into the attackers causing many casualties. When his supply of grenades was exhausted his comrades from nearby foxholes tossed others to him and he left his position, braving a hail of fire, to retrieve and throw them at the enemy. The attackers continued to assault his position and Pfc. Brown, weaponless, drew his entrenching tool from his pack and calmly waited until they 1 by 1 peered over the wall, delivering each a crushing blow upon the head. Knocking 10 or 12 enemy from the wall, his daring action so inspired his platoon that they repelled the attack and held their position. Pfc. Brown's extraordinary heroism, gallantry, and intrepidity reflect the highest credit upon himself and was in keeping with the honored traditions of the military service. Reportedly missing in action and officially killed in action, September 5, 1950.

BURKE, LLOYD L.

Rank and organization: First Lieutenant, U.S. Army, Company G, 5th Cavalry Regiment, 1st Cavalry Division. *Place and date:* Near Chong-dong, Korea, 28 October 1951. *Entered service at:* Stuttgart, Ark. *Born:* 29 September 1924, Tichnor, Ark. *G.O. No.:* 43. *Citation:* 1st Lt. Burke, distinguished himself by conspicuous gallantry and outstanding courage above and beyond the call of duty in action against the enemy. Intense enemy fire had pinned down leading elements of his company committed to secure commanding ground when 1st Lt. Burke left the command post to rally and urge the men to follow him toward 3 bunkers impeding the advance. Dashing to an exposed vantage point he threw several grenades at the bunkers, then, returning for an M1 rifle and adapter, he made a lone assault, wiping out the position and killing the crew. Closing on the center bunker he lobbed grenades through the opening and, with his pistol, killed 3 of its occupants attempting to surround him. Ordering his men forward he charged the third emplacement, catching several grenades in midair and hurling them back at the enemy. Inspired by his display of valor his men stormed forward, overran the hostile position, but were again pinned down by increased fire. Securing a light machinegun and 3 boxes of ammunition, 1st Lt. Burke dashed through the impact area to an open knoll, set up his gun and poured a crippling fire into the ranks of the enemy, killing approximately 75. Although wounded, he ordered more ammunition, reloading and destroying 2 mortar emplacements and a machinegun position with his accurate fire. Cradling the weapon in his arms he then led his men forward, killing some 25 more of the retreating enemy and securing the objective. 1st Lt. Burke's heroic action and daring exploits inspired his small force of 35 troops. His unflinching courage and outstanding leadership reflect the highest credit upon himself, the infantry, and the U.S. Army.

*BURRIS, TONY K.

Rank and organization: Sergeant First Class, U.S. Army, Company L, 38th Infantry Regiment, 2d Infantry Division. *Place and date:* Vicinity of Mundung-ni, Korea 8 and 9 October 1951. *Entered service at:* Blanchard, Okla. *Birth:* Blanchard, Okla. *G.O. No.:* 84, 5 September 1952. *Citation:* Sfc. Burris, a member of Company L, distinguished himself by conspicuous gallantry and outstanding courage above and beyond the call of duty. On 8 October, when his company encountered intense fire from an entrenched hostile force, Sfc. Burris charged forward alone, throwing grenades into the position and destroying approximately 15 of the enemy. On the following day, spearheading a renewed assault on enemy positions on the next ridge, he was wounded by machinegun fire but continued the assault, reaching the crest of the ridge ahead of his unit and sustaining a second wound. Calling for a 57mm. recoilless rifle team, he deliberately exposed himself to draw hostile fire and reveal the enemy position. The enemy machinegun emplacement was destroyed. The company then moved forward and prepared to assault other positions on the ridge line. Sfc. Burris, refusing evacuation and submitting only to emergency treatment, joined the unit in its renewed attack but fire from hostile emplacement halted the advance. Sfc. Burris rose to his feet, charged forward and destroyed the first emplacement with its heavy machinegun and crew of 6 men. Moving out to the next emplacement, and throwing his last grenade which destroyed this position, he fell mortally wounded by enemy fire. Inspired by his consummate gallantry, his comrades renewed a spirited assault which overran enemy positions and secured Hill 605, a strategic position in the battle for "Heartbreak Ridge," Sfc. Burris' indomitable fighting spirit, outstanding heroism, and gallant self-sacrifice reflect the highest glory upon himself, the infantry and the U.S. Army.

CAFFERATA, HECTOR A., JR.

Rank and organization: Private, U.S. Marine Corps Reserve, Company F, 2d Battalion, 7th Marines, 1st Marine Division (Rein). *Place and date:* Korea, 28 November 1950. *Entered service at:* Dover, N.J. *Born:* 4 November 1929, New York, N.Y. *Citation:* For conspicuous gallantry and intrepidity at the risk of his life above and beyond the call of duty while serving as a rifleman with Company F, in action against enemy aggressor forces. When all the other members of his fire team became casualties, creating a gap in the lines, during the initial phase of a vicious attack launched by a fanatical enemy of regimental strength against his company's hill position, Pvt. Cafferata waged a lone battle with grenades and rifle fire as the attack gained momentum and the enemy threatened penetration through the gap and endangered the integrity of the entire defensive perimeter. Making a target of himself under the devastating fire from automatic weapons, rifles, grenades, and mortars, he maneuvered up and down the line and delivered accurate and effective fire against the onrushing force, killing 15, wounding many more, and forcing the others to withdraw so that reinforcements could move up and consolidate the position. Again fighting desperately against a renewed onslaught later that same morning when a hostile grenade landed in a shallow entrenchment occupied by wounded marines, Pvt. Cafferata rushed into the gully under heavy fire, seized the deadly missile in his right hand and hurled it free of his comrades before it detonated, severing part of 1 finger and seriously wounding him in the right hand and arm. Courageously ignoring the intense pain, he stanchly fought on until he was struck by a sniper's bullet and forced to submit to evacuation for medical treatment. Stouthearted and indomitable, Pvt. Cafferata, by his fortitude, great personal valor, and dauntless perseverance in the face of almost certain death, saved the lives of several of his fellow marines and contributed essentially to the success achieved by his company in maintaining its defensive position against tremendous odds. His extraordinary heroism throughout was in keeping with the highest traditions of the U.S. Naval Service.

*CHAMPAGNE, DAVID B.

Rank and organization: Corporal, U.S. Marine Corps, Company A, 1st Battalion, 7th Marines, 1st Marine Division (Rein). *Place and date:* Korea, 28 May 1952. *Entered service at:* Wakefield, R.I. *Born:* 13 November 1932, Waterville, Md. *Citation:* For conspicuous gallantry and intrepidity at the risk of his life above and beyond the call of duty while serving as a fire team leader of Company A, in action against enemy aggressor forces. Advancing with his platoon in the initial assault of the company against a strongly fortified and heavily defended hill position, Cpl. Champagne skillfully led his fire team through a veritable hail of intense enemy machinegun, small-arms, and grenade fire, overrunning trenches and a series of almost impregnable bunker positions before reaching the crest of the hill and placing his men in defensive positions. Suffering a painful leg wound while assisting in repelling the ensuing hostile counterattack, which was launched under cover of a murderous hail of mortar and artillery fire, he steadfastly refused evacuation and fearlessly continued to control his fire team. When the enemy counterattack increased in intensity, and a hostile grenade landed in the midst of the fire team, Cpl. Champagne unhesitatingly seized the deadly missile and hurled it in the direction of the approaching enemy. As the grenade left his hand, it exploded, blowing off his hand and throwing him out of the trench. Mortally wounded by enemy mortar fire while in this exposed position, Cpl. Champagne, by his valiant leadership, fortitude, and gallant spirit of self-sacrifice in the face of almost certain death, undoubtedly saved the lives of several of his fellow marines. His heroic actions served to inspire all who observed him and reflect the highest credit upon himself and the U.S. Naval Service. He gallantly gave his life for his country.

CHARETTE, WILLIAM R.

Rank and organization: Hospital Corpsman Third Class, U.S. Navy, Medical Corpsman serving with a marine rifle company. *Place and date:* Korea, 27 March 1953. *Entered service at:* Ludington, Michigan. *Birth:* Ludington, Mich. *Citation:* For conspicuous gallantry and intrepidity at the risk of his life above and beyond the call of duty in action against enemy agressor forces during the early morning hours. Participating in a fierce encounter with a cleverly concealed and well-entrenched enemy force occupying positions on a vital and bitterly contested outpost far in advance of the main line of resistance, HC3c. Charette repeatedly and unhesitatingly moved about through a murderous barrage of hostile small-arms and mortar fire to render assistance to his wounded comrades. When an enemy grenade landed within a few feet of a marine he was attending, he immediately threw himself upon the stricken man and absorbed the entire concussion of the deadly missile with his body. Although sustaining painful facial wounds, and undergoing shock from the intensity of the blast which ripped the helmet and medical aid kit from his person, HC3c. Charette resourcefully improvised emergency bandages by tearing off part of his clothing, and gallantly continued to administer medical aid to the wounded in his own unit and to those in adjacent platoon areas as well. Observing a seriously wounded comrade whose armored vest had been torn from his body by the blast from an exploding shell, he selflessly removed his own battle vest and placed it upon the helpless man although fully aware of the added jeopardy to himself. Moving to the side of another casualty who was suffering excruciating pain from a serious leg wound, HC3c. Charette stood upright in the trench line and exposed himself to a deadly hail of enemy fire in order to lend more effective aid to the victim and to alleviate his anguish while being removed to a position of safety. By his indomitable courage and inspiring efforts in behalf of his wounded comrades, HC3c. Charette was directly responsible for saving many lives. His great personal valor reflects the highest credit upon himself and enhances the finest traditions of the U.S. Naval Service.

*CHARLTON, CORNELIUS H.

Rank and organization: Sergeant, U.S. Army, Company C, 24th Infantry Regiment, 25th Infantry Division. *Place and date:* Near Chipo-ri, Korea, 2 June 1951. *Entered service at:* Bronx, N.Y. *Born:* 24 July 1929, East Gulf, W. Va. *G.O. No.:* 30, 19 March 1952. *Citation:* Sgt. Charlton, a member of Company C, distinguished himself by conspicuous gallantry and intrepidity above and beyond the call of duty in action against the enemy. His platoon was attacking heavily defended hostile positions on commanding ground when the leader was wounded and evacuated. Sgt. Charlton assumed command, rallied the men, and spearheaded the assault against the hill. Personally eliminating 2 hostile positions and killing 6 of the enemy with his rifle fire and grenades, he continued up the slope until the unit suffered heavy casualties and became pinned down. Regrouping the men he led them forward only to be again hurled back by a shower of grenades. Despite a severe chest wound, Sgt. Charlton refused medical attention and led a third daring charge which carried to the crest of the ridge. Observing that the remaining emplacement which had retarded the advance was situated on the reverse slope, he charged it alone, was again hit by a grenade but raked the position with a devastating fire which eliminated it and routed the defenders. The wounds received during his daring exploits resulted in his death but his indomitable courage, superb leadership, and gallant self-sacrifice reflect the highest credit upon himself, the infantry, and the military service.

*CHRISTIANSON, STANLEY R.

Rank and organization: Private First Class, U.S. Marine Corps, Company E, 2d Battalion, 1st Marines, 1st Marine Division (Rein). *Place and date:* Seoul, Korea, 29 September 1950. *Entered service at:* Mindoro, Wis. *Born:* 24 January 1925, Mindoro, Wis. *Citation:* For conspicuous gallantry and intrepidity at the risk of his life above and beyond the call of duty while serving with Company E, in action against enemy aggressor forces at Hill 132, in the early morning hours. Manning 1 of the several listening posts covering approaches to the platoon area when the enemy commenced the attack, Pfc. Christianson quickly sent another marine to alert the rest of the platoon. Without orders, he remained in his position and, with full knowledge that he would have slight chance of escape, fired relentlessly at oncoming hostile troops attacking furiously with rifles, automatic weapons, and incendiary grenades. Accounting for 7 enemy dead in the immediate vicinity before his position was overrun and he himself fatally struck down, Pfc. Christianson, by his superb courage, valiant fighting spirit, and devotion to duty, was responsible for allowing the rest of the platoon time to man positions, build up a stronger defense on that flank, and repel the attack with 41 of the enemy destroyed, many more wounded, and 3 taken prisoner. His self-sacrificing actions in the face of overwhelming odds sustain and enhance the finest traditions of the U.S. Naval Service. Pfc. Christianson gallantly gave his life for his country.

*COLLIER, GILBERT G.

Rank and organization: Sergeant (then Cpl.), U.S. Army, Company F, 223d Infantry Regiment, 40th Infantry Division. *Place and date:* Near Tutayon, Korea, 19–20 July 1953. *Entered service at:* Tichnor, Ark. *Born:* 30 December 1930, Hunter, Ark. *G.O. No.:* 3, 12 January 1955. *Citation:* Sgt. Collier, a member of Company F, distinguished himself by conspicuous gallantry and indomitable courage above and beyond the call of duty in action against the enemy. Sgt. Collier was pointman and assistant leader of a combat patrol committed to make contact with the enemy. As the patrol moved forward through the darkness, he and his commanding officer slipped and fell from a steep, 60-foot cliff and were injured. Incapacitated by a badly sprained ankle which prevented immediate movement, the officer ordered the patrol to return to the safety of friendly lines. Although suffering from a painful back injury, Sgt. Collier elected to remain with his leader, and before daylight they managed to crawl back up and over the mountainous terrain to the opposite valley where they concealed themselves in the brush until nightfall, then edged toward their company positions. Shortly after leaving the daylight retreat they were ambushed and, in the ensuing fire fight, Sgt. Collier killed 2 hostile soldiers, received painful wounds, and was separated from his companion. Then, ammunition expended, he closed in hand-to-hand combat with 4 attacking hostile infantrymen, killing, wounding, and routing the foe with his bayonet. He was mortally wounded during this action, but made a valiant attempt to reach and assist his leader in a desperate effort to save his comrade's life without regard for his own personal safety. Sgt.

Collier's unflinching courage, consummate devotion to duty, and gallant selfcsacrifice reflect lasting ·glory upon himself and uphold the noble traditions of the military service.

*COLLIER, JOHN W.

Rank and organization: Corporal, U.S. Army, Company C, 27th Infantry Regiment. *Place and date:* Near Chindong-ni, Korea, 19 September 1950. *Entered service at:* Worthington, Ky. *Born:* 3 April 1929, Worthington, Ky. *G.O. No.:* 86, 2 August 1951. *Citation:* Cpl. Collier, Company C, distinguished himself by conspicuous gallantry and intrepidity above and beyond the call of duty in action. While engaged in an assault on a strategic ridge strongly defended by a fanatical enemy, the leading elements of his company encountered intense automatic weapons and grenade fire. Cpl. Collier and 3 comrades volunteered and moved forward to neutralize an enemy machinegun position which was hampering the company's advance, but they were twice repulsed. On the third attempt, Cpl. Collier, despite heavy enemy fire and grenade barrages, moved to an exposed position ahead of his comrades, assaulted and detroyed the machinegun nest, killing at least 4 enemy soldiers. As he returned down the rocky, fire-swept hill and joined his squad, an enemy grenade landed in their midst. Shouting a warning to his comrades, he, selflessly and unhesitatingly, threw himself upon the grenade and smothered its explosion with his body. This intrepid action saved his comrades from death or injury. Cpl. Collier's supreme, personal bravery, consummate gallantry, and noble self-sacrifice reflect untold glory upon himself and uphold the honored traditions of the military service.

COMMISKEY, HENRY A., Sr.

Rank and organization: First Lieutenant (then 2d Lt.), U.S. Marine Corps, Company C, 1st Battalion, 1st Marines, 1st Marine Division (Rein). *Place and date:* Near Yongdungp'o, Korea, 20 September 1950. *Entered service at:* Hattiesburg, Miss. *Birth:* 10 January 1927, Hattiesburg, Miss. *Citation:* For conspicuous gallantry and intrepidity at the risk of his life above and beyond the call of duty while serving as a platoon leader in Company C, in action against enemy aggressor forces. Directed to attack hostile forces well dug in on Hill 85, 1st Lt. Commiskey, spearheaded the assault, charging up the steep slopes on the run. Coolly disregarding the heavy enemy machinegun and small-arms fire, he plunged on well forward of the rest of his platoon and was the first man to reach the crest of the objective. Armed only with a pistol, he jumped into a hostile machinegun emplacement occupied by 5 enemy troops and quickly disposed of 4 of the soldiers with his aut ·matic pistol. Grappling with the fifth, 1st Lt. Commiskey knocked him to the ground and held him until he could obtain a weapon from another member of his platoon and killed the last of the enemy guncrew. Continuing his bold assault, he moved to the next emplacement, killed 2 more of the enemy and then led his platoon toward the rear nose of the hill to rout the remainder of the hostile troops and destroy them as they fled from their positions. His valiant leadership and courageous fighting spirit served to inspire the men of his company to heroic endeavor in seizing the objective and reflect the highest credit upon 1st Lt. Commiskey and the U.S. Naval Service.

*COURSEN, SAMUEL S.

Rank and organization: First Lieutenant, U.S. Army, Company C, 5th Cavalry Regiment. *Place and date:* Near Kaesong, Korea, 12 October 1950. *Entered service at:* Madison, N.J. *Born:* 4 August 1926, Madison, N.J. *G.O. No.:* 57, 2 August 1951. *Citation:* 1st Lt. Coursen distinguished himself by conspicuous gallantry and intrepidity above and beyond the call of duty in action. While Company C was attacking Hill 174 under heavy enemy small-arms fire, his platoon received enemy fire from close range. The platoon returned the fire and continued to advance. During this phase 1 his men moved into a well-camouflaged emplacement, which was thought to be unoccupied, and was wounded by the enemy who were hidden within the emplacement. Seeing the soldier in difficulty he rushed to the man's aid and, without regard for his personal safety, engaged the enemy in hand-to-hand combat in an effort to protect his wounded comrade until he himself was killed. When his body was recovered after the battle 7 enemy dead were found in the emplacement. As the result of 1st Lt. Coursen's violent struggle several of the enemies' heads had been crushed with his rifle. His aggressive and intrepid actions saved the life of the wounded man, eliminated the main position of the enemy roadblock, and greatly inspired the men in his command. 1st Lt. Coursen's extraordinary heroism and intrepidity reflect the highest credit on himself and are in keeping with the honored traditions of the military service.

*CRAIG, GORDON M.

Rank and organization: Corporal, U.S. Army, Reconnaissance Company, 1st Cavalry Division. *Place and date:* Near Kasan, Korea, 10 September 1950. *Entered service at:* Brockton, Mass. *Born:* 3 August 1929, Brockton, Mass. *G.O. No.:* 23, 25 April 1951. *Citation:* Cpl. Craig, 16th Reconnaissance Company, distinguished himself by conspicuous gallantry and intrepidity above and beyond the call of duty in action against the enemy. During the attack on a strategic enemy-held hill his company's advance was subjected to intense hostile grenade, mortar, and small-arms fire. Cpl. Craig and 4 comrades moved forward to eliminate an enemy machinegun nest that was hampering the company's advance. At that instance an enemy machine gunner hurled a handgrenade at the advancing men. Without hesitating or attempting to seek cover for himself, Cpl. Craig threw himself on the grenade and smothered its burst with his body. His intrepid and selfless act, in which he unhesitantly gave his life for his comrades, inspired them to attack with such ferocity that they annihilated the enemy machinegun crew, enabling the company to continue its attack. Cpl. Craig's noble self-sacrifice reflects the highest credit upon himself and upholds the esteemed traditions of the military service.

CRUMP, JERRY K.

Rank and organization: Corporal, U.S. Army, Company L, 7th Infantry Regiment, 3d Infantry Division. *Place and date:* Near Chorwon, Korea, 6 and 7 September 1951. *Entered service at:* Forest City, N.C. *Born:* 18 February 1933, Charlotte, N.C. *G.O. No.:* 68, 11 July 1952. *Citation:* Cpl. Crump, a member of Company L, distinguished himself by conspicuous gallantry and outstanding courage above and beyond the call of duty in action against the enemy. During the night a numerically superior hostile force launched an assault against his platoon on Hill 284, overrunning friendly positions and swarming into the sector. Cpl. Crump repeatedly exposed himself to deliver effective fire into the ranks of the assailants, inflicting numerous casualties. Observing 2 enemy soldiers endeavoring to capture a friendly machinegun, he charged and killed both with his bayonet, regaining control of the weapon. Returning to his position, now occupied by 4 of his wounded comrades, he continued his accurate fire into enemy troops surrounding his emplacement. When a hostile soldier hurled a grenade into the position, Cpl. Crump immediately flung himself over the missile, absorbing the blast with his body and saving his comrades from death or serious injury. His aggressive actions had so inspired his comrades that a spirited counterattack drove the enemy from the perimeter. Cpl. Crump's heroic devotion to duty, indomitable fighting spirit, and willingness to sacrifice himself to save his comrades reflect the highest credit upon himself, the infantry and the U.S. Army.

*DAVENPORT, JACK A.

Rank and organization: Corporal, U.S. Marine Corps, Company G, 3d Battalion, 5th Marines, 1st Marine Division (Rein). *Place and date:* Vicinity of Songnae-Dong, Korea, 21 September 1951. *Entered service at:* Mission, Kans. *Born:* 7 September 1931, Kansas City, Mo. *Citation:* For conspicuous gallantry and intrepidity at the risk of his life above and beyond the call of duty while serving as a squad leader in Company G, in action against enemy aggressor forces, early in the morning. While expertly directing the defense of his position during a probing attack by hostile forces attempting to infiltrate the area, Cpl. Davenport, acting quickly when an enemy grenade fell into the foxhole which he was occupying with another marine, skillfully located the deadly projectile in the dark and, undeterred by the personal risk involved, heroically threw himself over the live missile, thereby saving his companion from serious injury or possible death. His cool and resourceful leadership were contributing factors in the successful repulse of the enemy attack and his superb courage and admirable spirit of self-sacrifice in the face of almost certain death enhance and sustain the highest traditions of the U.S. Naval Service. Cpl. Davenport gallantly gave his life for his country.

*DAVIS, GEORGE ANDREW, Jr.

Rank and organization: Major, U.S. Air Force, CO, 334th Fighter Squadron, 4th Fighter Group, 5th Air Force. *Place and date:* Near Sinuiju-Yalu River area, Korea, 10 February 1952. *Entered service at:* Lubbock, Tex. *Born:* 1 December 1920, Dublin, Tex. *Citation:* Maj. Davis distinguished himself by conspicuous gallantry and intrepidity at the risk of his life above and beyond the call of duty. While leading a flight of 4 F-86 Saberjets on a combat aerial patrol mission near the Manchurian border, Maj. Davis' element leader ran out of oxygen and was forced to retire from the flight with his wingman accompanying him. Maj. Davis and the remaining F-86's continued the mission and sighted a formation of approximately 12 enemy MIG-15 aircraft speeding southward toward an area where friendly fighter-bombers were conducting low level operations against the Communist lines of communications. With selfless disregard for the numerical superiority of the enemy, Maj. Davis positioned his 2 aircraft, then dove at the MIG formation. While speeding through the formation from the rear, he singled out a MIG–15 and destroyed it with a concentrated burst of fire. Although he was now under continuous fire from the enemy fighters to his rear, Maj. Davis sustained his attack. He fired at another MIG–15 which, bursting into smoke and flames, went into a vertical dive. Rather than maintain his superior speed and evade the enemy fire being concentrated on him, he elected to reduce his speed and sought out still a third MIG–15. During this latest attack his aircraft sustained a direct hit, went out of control, then crashed into a mountain 30 miles south of the Yalu River. Maj. Davis' bold attack completely disrupted the enemy formation, permitting the friendly fighter-bombers to successfully complete their interdiction mission. Maj. Davis, by his indomitable fighting spirit, heroic aggressiveness, and superb courage in engaging the enemy against formidable odds exemplified valor at its highest.

DAVIS, RAYMOND G.

Rank and organization: Lieutenant Colonel, U.S. Marine Corps, commanding officer, 1st Battalion, 7th Marines, 1st Marine Division (Rein). *Place and date:* Vicinity Hagaru-ri, Korea, 1 through 4 December 1950. *Entered service at:* Atlanta, Ga. *Born:* 13 January 1915, Fitzgerald, Ga. *Citation:* For conspicuous gallantry and intrepidity at the risk of his life above and beyond the call of duty as commanding officer of the 1st Battalion, in action against enemy aggressor forces. Although keenly aware that the operation involved breaking through a surrounding enemy and advancing 8 miles along primitive icy trails in the bitter cold with every passage disputed by a savage and determined foe, Lt. Col. Davis boldly led his battalion into the attack in a daring attempt to relieve a beleaguered rifle company and to seize, hold, and defend a vital mountain pass controlling the only route available for 2 marine regiments in danger of being cut off by numerically superior hostile forces during their redeployment to the port of Hungnam. When the battalion immediately encountered strong opposition from entrenched enemy forces commanding high ground in the path of the advance, he promptly spearheaded his unit in a fierce attack up the steep, ice-covered slopes in the face of withering fire and, personally leading the assault groups in a hand-to-hand encounter, drove the hostile troops from their positions, rested his men, and reconnoitered the area under enemy fire to determine the best route for continuing the mission. Always in the thick of the fighting Lt. Col. Davis led his battalion over 3 successive ridges in the deep snow in continuous attacks against the enemy and, constantly inspiring and encouraging his men throughout the night, brought his unit to a point within 1,500 yards of the surrounded rifle company by daybreak. Although knocked to the ground when a shell fragment struck his helmet and 2 bullets pierced his clothing, he arose and fought his way forward at the head of his men until he reached the isolated marines. On the following morning, he bravely led his battalion in securing the vital mountain pass from a strongly entrenched and numerically superior hostile force, carrying all his wounded with him, including 22 litter cases and numerous ambulatory patients. Despite repeated savage and heavy assaults by the enemy, he stubbornly held the vital terrain until the 2 regiments of the division had deployed through the pass and, on the morning of 4 December, led his battalion into Hagaru-ri intact. By his superb leadership, outstanding courage, and brilliant tactical ability, Lt. Col. Davis was directly instrumental in saving the beleagured rifle company from complete annihilation and enabled the 2 marine regiments to escape possible destruction. His valiant devotion to duty and unyielding fighting spirit in the face of almost insurmountable odds enhance and sustain the highest traditions of the U.S. Naval Service.

DEAN, WILLIAM F.

Rank and organization: Major General, U.S. Army, commanding general, 24th Infantry Division. *Place and date:* Taejon, Korea, 20 and 21 July 1950. *Entered service at:* California. *Born:* 1 August 1899, Carlyle, Ill. *G.O. No.:* 7, 16 February 1951. *Citation:* Maj. Gen. Dean distinguished himself by conspicuous gallantry and intrepidity at the repeated risk of his life above and beyond the call of duty. In command of a unit suddenly relieved from occupation duties in Japan and as yet untried in combat, faced with a ruthless and determined enemy, highly trained and overwhelmingly superior in numbers, he felt it his duty to take action which to a man of his military experience and knowledge was clearly apt to result in his death. He personally and alone attacked an enemy tank while armed only with a handgrenade. He also directed the fire of his tanks from an exposed position with neither cover nor concealment while under observed artillery and small-arm fire. When the town of Taejon was finally overrun he refused to insure his own safety by leaving with the leading elements but remained behind organizing his retreating forces, directing stragglers, and was last seen assisting the wounded to a place of safety. These actions indicate that Maj. Gen. Dean felt it necessary to sustain the courage and resolution of his troops by examples of excessive gallantry committed always at the threatened portions of his frontlines. The magnificent response of his unit to this willing and cheerful sacrifice, made with full knowledge of its certain cost, is history. The success of this phase of the campaign is in large measure due to Maj. Gen. Dean's heroic leadership, courageous and loyal devotion to his men, and his complete disregard for personal safety.

*DESIDERIO, REGINALD B.

Rank and organization: Captain, U.S. Army, commanding officer, Company E, 27th Infantry Regiment, 25th Infantry Division. *Place and date:* Near Ipsok, Korea, 27 November 1950. *Entered service at:* Gilroy, Calif. *Born:* 12 September 1918, Clairton, Pa. *G.O. No.:* 58, 2 August 1951. *Citation:* Capt. Desiderio distinguished himself by conspicuous gallantry and intrepidity at the repeated risk of his life above and beyond the call of duty. His company was given the mission of defending the command post of a task force against an enemy breakthrough. After personal reconnaissance during darkness and under intense enemy fire, he placed his men in defensive positions to repel an attack. Early in the action he was wounded, but refused evacuation and despite enemy fire continued to move among his men checking their positions and making sure that each element was prepared to receive the next attack. Again wounded, he continued to direct his men. By his inspiring leadership he encouraged them to hold their position. In the subsequent fighting when the fanatical enemy succeeded in penetrating the position, he personally charged them with carbine, rifle, and grenades, inflicting many casualties until he himself was mortally wounded. His men, spurred on by his intrepid example, repelled this final attack. Capt. Desiderio's heroic leadership, courageous and loyal devotion to duty, and his complete disregard for personal safety reflect the highest honor on him and are in keeping with the esteemed traditions of the U.S. Army.

*DEWERT, RICHARD DAVID

Rank and organization: Hospital Corpsman, U.S. Navy. Hospital Corpsman attached to Marine infantry company, 1st Marine Division. *Place and date:* Korea, 5 April 1951. *Entered service at:* Taunton, Mass. *Birth:* Taunton, Mass. *Citation:* For conspicuous gallantry and intrepidity at the risk of his life above and beyond the call of duty while serving as a HC, in action against enemy aggressor forces. When a fire team from the point platoon of his company was pinned down by a deadly barrage of hostile automatic weapons fired and suffered many casualties, HC Dewert rushed to the assistance of 1 of the more seriously wounded and, despite a painful leg wound sustained while dragging the stricken marine to safety, steadfastly refused medical treatment for himself and immediately dashed back through the fire-swept area to carry a second wounded man out of the line of fire. Undaunted by the mounting hail of devastating enemy fire, he bravely moved forward a third time and received another serious wound in the shoulder after discovering that a wounded marine had already died. Still persistent in his refusal to submit to first aid, he resolutely answered the call of a fourth stricken comrade and, while rendering medical assistance, was himself mortally wounded by a burst of enemy fire. His courageous initiative, great personal valor, and heroic spirit of self-sacrifice in the face of overwhelming odds reflect the highest credit upon HC Dewert and enhance the finest traditions of the U.S. Naval Service. He gallantly gave his life for his country.

DEWEY, DUANE E.

Rank and organization: Corporal, U.S. Marine Corps Reserve, Company E, 2d Battalion, 5th Marines, 1st Marine Division (Rein). *Place and date:* Near Panmunjon, Korea, 16 April 1952. *Entered service at:* Muskegon, Mich. *Born:* 16 November 1931, Grand Rapids, Mich. *Citation:* For conspicuous gallantry and intrepidity at the risk of his life above and beyond the call of duty while serving as a gunner in a machinegun platoon of Company E, in action against enemy aggressor forces. When an enemy grenade landed close to his position while he and his assistant gunner were receiving medical attention for their wounds during a fierce night attack by numerically superior hostile forces, Cpl. Dewey, although suffering intense pain, immediately pulled the corpsman to the ground and, shouting a warning to the other marines around him, bravely smothered the deadly missile with his body, personally absorbing the full force of the explosion to save his comrades from possible injury or death. His indomitable courage, outstanding initiative, and valiant efforts in behalf of others in the face of almost certain death reflect the highest credit upon Cpl. Dewey and enhance the finest traditions of the U.S. Naval Service.

DODD, CARL H.

Rank and organization: First Lieutenant (then 2d Lt.), U.S. Army, Company E, 5th Infantry Regiment, 24th Infantry Division. *Place and date:* Near Subuk, Korea, 30 and 31 January 1951. *Entered service at:* Kenvir, Ky. *Born:* 21 April 1925, Evarts, Ky. *G.O. No.:* 37, 4 June 1951. *Citation:* 1st Lt. Dodd, Company E, distinguished himself by conspicuous gallantry and intrepidity above and beyond the call of duty in action against the enemy. First Lt. Dodd, given the responsibility of spearheading an attack to capture Hill 256, a key terrain feature defended by a well-armed, crafty foe who had withstood several previous assaults, led his platoon forward over hazardous terrain under hostile small-arms, mortar, and artillery fire from well-camouflaged enemy emplacements which reached such intensity that his men faltered. With utter disregard for his safety, 1st Lt. Dodd moved among his men, reorganized and encouraged them, and then singlehandedly charged the first hostile machinegun nest, killing or wounding all its occupants. Inspired by his incredible courage, his platoon responded magnificiently and, fixing bayonets and throwing grenades, closed on the enemy and wiped out every hostile position as it moved relentlessly onward to its initial objective. Securing the first series of enemy positions, 1st Lt. Dodd again reorganized his platoon and led them across a narrow ridge and onto Hill 256. Firing his rifle and throwing grenades, he advanced at the head of his platoon despite the intense concentrated hostile fire which was brought to bear on their narrow avenue of approach. When his platoon was still 200 yards from the objective he moved ahead and with his last grenade destroyed an enemy mortar killing the crew. Darkness then halted the advance but at daybreak 1st Lt. Dodd, again boldly advancing ahead of his unit, led the platoon through a dense fog against the remaining hostile positions. With bayonet and grenades he continued to set pace without regard for the danger to his life, until he and his troops had eliminated the last of the defenders and had secured the final objective. First Lt. Dodd's superb leadership and extraordinary heroism inspired his men to overcome this strong enemy defense reflecting the highest credit upon himself and upholding the esteemed traditions of the military service.

*DUKE, RAY E.

Rank and organization: Sergeant First Class, U.S. Army, Company C, 21st Infantry Regiment, 24th Infantry Division. *Place and date:* Near Mugok, Korea, 26 April 1951. *Entered service at:* Whitwell (Marion County), Tenn. *Born:* 9 May 1923, Whitwell, Tenn. *G.O. No.:* 20, 19 March 1954. *Citation:* Sfc. Duke, a member of Company C, distinguished himself by conspicuous gallantry and outstanding courage above and beyond the call of duty in action against the enemy. Upon learning that several of his men were isolated and heavily engaged in an area yielded by his platoon when ordered to withdraw, he led a small force in a daring assault which recovered the position and the beleaguered men. Another enemy attack in strength resulted in numerous casualties but Sfc. Duke, although wounded by mortar fragments, calmly moved along his platoon line to coordinate fields of fire and to urge his men to hold firm in the bitter encounter. Wounded a second time he received first aid and returned to his position. When the enemy again attacked shortly after dawn, despite his wounds, Sfc. Duke repeatedly braved withering fire to insure maximum defense of each position. Threatened with annihilation and with mounting casualties, the platoon was again ordered to withdraw when Sfc. Duke was wounded a third time in both legs and was unable to walk. Realizing that he was impeding the progress of 2 comrades who were carrying him from the hill, he urged them to leave him and seek safety. He was last seen pouring devastating fire into the ranks of the onrushing assailants. The consummate courage, superb leadership, and heroic actions of Sfc. Duke, displayed during intensive action against overwhelming odds, reflect the highest credit upon himself, the infantry, and the U.S. Army.

*EDWARDS, JUNIOR D.

Rank and organization: Sergeant First Class, U.S. Army, Company E, 23d Infantry Regiment, 2d Infantry Division. *Place and date:* Near Changbong-ni, Korea, 2 January 1951. *Entered service at:* Indianola, Iowa. *Born:* 7 October 1926, Indianola, Iowa. *G.O. No.:* 13, 1 February 1952. *Citation:* Sfc. Edwards, Company E, distinguished himself by conspicuous gallantry and intrepidity above and beyond the call of duty in action against the enemy. When his platoon, while assisting in the defense of a strategic hill, was forced out of its position and came under vicious raking fire from an enemy machinegun set up on adjacent high ground, Sfc. Edwards individually charged the hostile emplacement, throwing grenades as he advanced. The enemy withdrew but returned to deliver devastating fire when he had expended his ammunition. Securing a fresh supply of grenades, he again charged the emplacement, neutralized the weapon and killed the crew, but was forced back by hostile small-arms fire. When the enemy emplaced another machinegun and resumed fire, Sfc. Edwards again renewed his supply of grenades, rushed a third time through a vicious hail of fire, silenced this second gun and annihilated its crew. In this third daring assault he was mortally wounded but his indomitable courage and successful action enabled his platoon to regain and hold the vital strongpoint. Sfc. Edwards' consummate valor and gallant self-sacrifice reflect the utmost glory upon himself and are in keeping with the esteemed traditions of the infantry and military service.

*ESSEBAGGER, JOHN, Jr.

Rank and organization: Corporal, U.S. Army, Company A, 7th Infantry Regiment, 3d Infantry Division. *Place and date:* Near Popsu-dong, Korea, 25 April 1951. *Entered service at:* Holland, Mich. *Born:* 29 October 1928, Holland, Mich. *G.O. No.:* 61, 24 April 1952. *Citation:* Cpl. Essebagger, a member of Company A, distinguished himself by conspicuous gallantry and outstanding courage above and beyond the call of duty in action against the enemy. Committed to effect a delaying action to cover the 3d Battalion's withdrawal through Company A, Cpl. Essebagger, a member of 1 of 2 squads maintaining defensive positions in key terrain and defending the company's right flank, had participated in repulsing numerous attacks. In a frenzied banzai charge the numerically superior enemy seriously threatened the security of the planned route of withdrawal and isolation of the small force. Badly shaken, the grossly outnumbered detachment started to fall back and Cpl. Essebagger, realizing the impending danger, voluntarily remained to provide security for the withdrawal. Gallantly maintaining a 1-man stand, Cpl. Essebagger raked the menacing hordes with crippling fire and, with the foe closing on the position, left the comparative safety of his shelter and advanced in the face of overwhelming odds, firing his weapon and hurling grenades to disconcert the enemy and afford time for displacement of friendly elements to more tenable positions. Scorning the withering fire and bursting shells, Cpl. Essebagger continued to move forward, inflicting destruction upon the fanatical foe until he was mortally wounded. Cpl. Essebagger's intrepid action and supreme sacrifice exacted a heavy toll in enemy dead and wounded, stemmed the onslaught, and enabled the retiring squads to reach safety. His valorous conduct and devotion to duty reflected lasting glory upon himself and was in keeping with the noblest traditions of the infantry and the U.S. Army.

*FAITH, DON C., JR.

Rank and organization: Lieutenant Colonel, U.S. Army, commanding officer, 1st Battalion, 32d Infantry Regiment, 7th Infantry Division. *Place and date:* Vicinity Hagaru-ri, Northern Korea, 27 November to 1 December 1950. *Entered service at:* Washington, Ind. *Born:* 26 August 1918, Washington, Ind. *G.O. No.:* 59, 2 August 1951. *Citation:* Lt. Col. Faith, commanding 1st Battalion, distinguished himself conspicuously by gallantry and intrepidity in action above and beyond the call of duty in the area of the Chosin Reservoir. When the enemy launched a fanatical attack against his battalion, Lt. Col. Faith unhesitatingly exposed himself to heavy enemy fire as he moved about directing the action. When the enemy penetrated the positions, Lt. Col. Faith personally led counterattacks to restore the position. During an attack by his battalion to effect a junction with another U.S. unit, Lt. Col. Faith reconnoitered the route for, and personally directed, the first elements of his command across the ice-covered reservoir and then directed the movement of his vehicles which were loaded with wounded until all of his command had passed through the enemy fire. Having completed this he crossed the reservoir himself. Assuming command of the force his unit had joined he was given the mission of attacking to join friendly elements to the south. Lt. Col. Faith, although physically exhausted in the bitter cold, organized and launched an attack which was soon stopped by enemy fire. He ran forward under enemy small-arms and automatic weapons fire, got his men on their feet and personally led the fire attack as it blasted its way through the enemy ring. As they came to a hairpin curve, enemy fire from a roadblock again pinned the column down. Lt. Col. Faith organized a group of men and directed their attack on the enemy positions on the right flank. He then placed himself at the head of another group of men and in the face of direct enemy fire led an attack on the enemy roadblock, firing his pistol and throwing grenades. When he had reached a position approximately 30 yards from the roadblock he was mortally wounded, but continued to direct the attack until the roadblock was overrun. Throughout the 5 days of action Lt. Col. Faith gave no thought to his safety and did not spare himself. His presence each time in the position of greatest danger was an inspiration to his men. Also, the damage he personally inflicted firing from his position at the head of his men was of material assistance on several occasions. Lt. Col. Faith's outstanding gallantry and noble self-sacrifice above and beyond the call of duty reflect the highest honor on him and are in keeping with the highest traditions of the U.S. Army. (This award supersedes the prior award of the Silver Star (First Oak Leaf Cluster) as announced in G.O. No. 32, Headquarters X Corps, dated 23 February 1951, for gallantry in action on 27 November 1950.)

*GARCIA, FERNANDO LUIS

Rank and organization: Private First Class, U.S. Marine Corps, Company I, 3d Battalion, 5th Marines, 1st Marine Division (Rein). *Place and date:* Korea, 5 September 1952. *Entered service at:* San Juan, P.R. *Born:* 14 October 1929, Utuado, P.R. *Citation:* For conspicuous gallantry and intrepidity at the risk of his life above and beyond the call of duty while serving as a member of Company I, in action against enemy aggressor forces. While participating in the defense of a combat outpost located more than 1 mile forward of the main line of resistance during a savage night attack by a fanatical enemy force employing grenades, mortars, and artillery, Pfc. Garcia, although suffering painful wounds, moved through the intense hail of hostile fire to a supply point to secure more handgrenades. Quick to act when a hostile grenade landed nearby, endangering the life of another marine, as well as his own, he unhesitatingly chose to sacrifice himself and immediately threw his body upon the deadly missile, receiving the full impact of the explosion. His great personal valor and cool decision in the face of almost certain death sustain and enhance the finest traditions of the U.S. Naval Service. He gallantly gave his life for his country.

*GEORGE, CHARLES

Rank and organization: Private First Class, U.S. Army, Company C, 179th Infantry Regiment, 45th Infantry Division. *Place and date:* Near Songnae-dong, Korea, 30 November 1952. Entered service at: Whittier, N.C. *Born:* 23 August 1932, Cherokee, N.C. *G.O. No.:* 19, 18 March 1954. *Citation:* Pfc. George, a member of Company C, distinguished himself by conspicuous gallantry and outstanding courage above and beyond the call of duty in action against the enemy on the night of 30 November 1952. He was a member of a raiding party committed to engage the enemy and capture a prisoner for interrogation. Forging up the rugged slope of the key terrain feature, the group was subjected to intense mortar and machinegun fire and suffered several casualties. Throughout the advance, he fought valiantly and, upon reaching the crest of the hill, leaped into the trenches and closed with the enemy in hand-to-hand combat. When friendly troops were ordered to move back upon completion of the assignment, he and 2 comrades remained to cover the withdrawal. While in the process of leaving the trenches a hostile soldier hurled a grenade into their midst. Pfc. George shouted a warning to 1 comrade, pushed the other soldier out of danger, and, with full knowledge of the consequences, unhesitatingly threw himself upon the grenade, absorbing the full blast of the explosion. Although seriously wounded in this display of valor, he refrained from any outcry which would divulge the position of his companions. The 2 soldiers evacuated him to the forward aid station and shortly thereafter he succumbed to his wound. Pfc. George's indomitable courage, consummate devotion to duty, and willing self-sacrifice reflect the highest credit upon himself and uphold the finest traditions of the military service.

*GILLILAND, CHARLES L.

Rank and organization: Corporal (then Pfc.), U.S. Army, Company I, 7th Infantry Regiment, 3d Infantry Division. *Place and date:* Near Tongmang-ni, Korea, 25 April 1951. *Entered service at:* Yellville (Marion County), Ark. *Born:* 24 May 1933, Mountain Home, Ark. *G.O. No.:* 2, 11 January 1955. *Citation:* Cpl. Gilliland, a member of Company I, distinguished himself by conspicuous gallantry and outstanding courage above and beyond the call of duty in action against the enemy. A numerically superior hostile force launched a coordinated assault against his company perimeter, the brunt of which was directed up a defile covered by his automatic rifle. His assistant was killed by enemy fire but Cpl. Gilliland, facing the full force of the assault, poured a steady fire into the foe which stemmed the onslaught. When 2 enemy soldiers escaped his raking fire and infiltrated the sector, he leaped from his foxhole, overtook and killed them both with his pistol. Sustaining a serious head wound in this daring exploit, he refused medical attention and returned to his emplacement to continue his defense of the vital defile. His unit was ordered back to new defensive positions but Cpl. Gilliland volunteered to remain to cover the withdrawal and hold the enemy at bay. His heroic actions and indomitable devotion to duty prevented the enemy from completely overrunning his company positions. Cpl. Gilliland's incredible valor and supreme sacrifice reflect lasting glory upon himself and are in keeping with the honored traditions of the military service.

*GOMEZ, EDWARD

Rank and organization: Private First Class, U.S. Marine Corps, Reserve, Company E, 2d Battalion, 1st Marines, 1st Marine Division (Rein). *Place and date:* Korea, Hill 749, 14 September 1951. *Entered service at:* Omaha, Nebr. *Born:* 10 August 1932, Omaha, Nebr. *Citation:* For conspicuous gallantry and intrepidity at the risk of his life above and beyond the call of duty while serving as an ammunition bearer in Company E, in action against enemy aggressor forces. Bolding advancing with his squad in support of a group of riflemen assaulting a series of strongly fortified and bitterly defended hostile positions on Hill 749, Pfc. Gomez consistently exposed himself to the withering barrage to keep his machinegun supplied with ammunition during the drive forward to seize the objective. As his squad deployed to meet an imminent counterattack, he voluntarily moved down an abandoned trench to search for a new location for the gun and, when a hostile grenade landed between himself and his weapon, shouted a warning to those around him as he grasped the activated charge in his hand. Determined to save his comrades, he unhesitatingly chose to sacrifice himself and, diving into the ditch with the deadly missile, absorbed the shattering violence of the explosion in his body. By his stouthearted courage, incomparable valor, and decisive spirit of self-sacrifice, Pfc. Gomez inspired the others to heroic efforts in subsequently repelling the outnumbering foe, and his valiant conduct throughout sustained and enhanced the finest traditions of the U.S. Naval Service. He gallantly gave his life for his country.

*GOODBLOOD, CLAIR

Rank and organization: Corporal, U.S. Army, Company D, 7th Infantry Regiment. *Place and date:* Near Popsu-dong, Korea, 24 and 25 April 1951. *Entered service at:* Burnham, Maine. *Born:* 18 September 1929, Fort Kent, Maine. *G.O. No.:* 14, 1 February 1952. *Citation:* Cpl. Goodblood, a member of Company D, distinguished himself by conspicuous gallantry and intrepidity at the risk of his life above and beyond the call of duty in action against an armed enemy of the United Nations. Cpl. Goodblood, a machine gunner, was attached to Company B in defensive positions on thickly wooded key terrain under attack by a ruthless foe. In bitter fighting which ensued, the numerically superior enemy infiltrated the perimeter, rendering the friendly positions untenable. Upon order to move back, Cpl. Goodblood voluntarily remained to cover the withdrawal and, constantly vulnerable to heavy fire, inflicted withering destruction on the assaulting force. Seeing a grenade lobbed at his position, he shoved his assistant to the ground and flinging himself upon the soldier attempted to shield him. Despite his valorous act both men were wounded. Rejecting aid for himself, he ordered the ammunition bearer to evacuate the injured man for medical treatment. He fearlessly maintained his 1-man defense, sweeping the onrushing assailants with fire until an enemy banzai charge carried the hill and silenced his gun. When friendly elements regained the commanding ground, Cpl. Goodblood's body was found lying beside his gun and approximately 100 hostile dead lay in the wake of his field of fire. Through his unflinching courage and willing self-sacrifice the onslaught was retarded, enabling his unit to withdraw, regroup, and resecure the strongpoint. Cpl. Goodblood's inspirational conduct and devotion to duty reflect lasting glory on himself and are in keeping with the noble traditions of the military service.

*GUILLEN, AMBROSIO

Rank and organization: Staff Sergeant, U.S. Marine Corps, Company F, 2d Battalion, 7th Marines, 1st Marine Division (Rein). *Place and date:* Near Songuch-on, Korea, 25 July 1953. *Entered service at:* El Paso, Tex. *Born:* 7 December 1929, La Junta, Colo. *Citation:* For conspicuous gallantry and intrepidity at the risk of his life above and beyond the call of duty while serving as a platoon sergeant of Company F in action against enemy aggressor forces. Participating in the defense of an outpost forward of the main line of resistance, S/Sgt. Guillen maneuvered his platoon over unfamiliar terrain in the face of hostile fire and placed his men in fighting positions. With his unit pinned down when the outpost was attacked under cover of darkness by an estimated force of 2 enemy battalions supported by mortar and artillery fire, he deliberately exposed himself to the heavy barrage and attacks to direct his men in defending their positions and personally supervise the treatment and evacuation of the wounded. Inspired by his leadership, the platoon quickly rallied and engaged the enemy in fierce hand-to-hand combat. Although critically wounded during the course of the battle, S/Sgt. Guillen refused medical aid and continued to direct his men throughout the remainder of the engagement until the enemy was defeated and thrown into disorderly retreat. Succumbing to his wounds within a few hours, S/Sgt. Guillen, by his outstanding courage and indomitable fighting spirit, was directly responsible for the success of his platoon in repelling a numerically superior enemy force. His personal valor reflects the highest credit upon himself and enhances the finest traditions of the U.S. Naval Service. He gallantly gave his life for his country.

*HAMMOND, FRANCIS C.

Rank and organization: Hospital Corpsman, U.S. Navy, attached as a medical corpsman to 1st Marine Division. *Place and date:* Korea, 26–27 March 1953. *Entered service at:* Alexandria, Va. *Birth:* Alexandria, Va. *Citation:* For conspicuous gallantry and intrepidity at the risk of his life above and beyond the call of duty as a HC serving with the 1st Marine Division in action against enemy aggressor forces on the night of 26–27 March 1953. After reaching an intermediate objective during a counterattack against a heavily entrenched and numerically superior hostile force occupying ground on a bitterly contested outpost far in advance of the main line of resistance, HC Hammond's platoon was subjected to a murderous barrage of hostile mortar and artillery fire, followed by a vicious assault by onrushing enemy troops. Resolutely advancing through the veritable curtain of fire to aid his stricken comrades, HC Hammond moved among the stalwart garrison of marines and, although critically wounded himself, valiantly continued to administer aid to the other wounded throughout an exhausting 4-hour period. When the unit was ordered to withdraw, he skillfully directed the evacuation of casualties and remained in the fire-swept area to assist the corpsmen of the relieving unit until he was struck by a round of enemy mortar fire and fell, mortally wounded. By his exceptional fortitude, inspiring initiative and self-sacrificing efforts, HC Hammond undoubtedly saved the lives of many marines. His great personal valor in the face of overwhelming odds enhances and sustains the finest traditions of the U.S. Naval Service. He gallantly gave his life for his country.

*HAMMOND, LESTER, Jr.

Rank and organization: Corporal, U.S. Army, Company A, 187th Airborne Regimental Combat Team. *Place and date:* Near Kumwha, Korea, 14 August 1952. *Entered service at:* Quincy, Ill. *Born:* 25 March 1931, Wayland, Mo. *G.O. No.:* 63, 17 August 1953. *Citation:* Cpl.

Hammond, a radio operator with Company A, distinguished himself by conspicuous gallantry and outstanding courage above and beyond the call of duty in action against the enemy. Cpl. Hammond was a member of a 6 man reconnaissance patrol which had penetrated approximately 3,500 yards into enemy-held territory. Ambushed and partially surrounded by a large hostile force, the small group opened fire, then quickly withdrew up a narrow ravine in search of protective cover. Despite a wound sustained in the initial exchange of fire and imminent danger of being overrun by the numerically superior foe, he refused to seek shelter and, remaining in an exposed place, called for artillery fire to support a defensive action. Constantly vulnerable to enemy observation and action, he coordinated and directed crippling fire on the assailants, inflicting heavy casualties and repulsing several attempts to overrun friendly positions. Although wounded a second time, he remained steadfast and maintained his stand until mortally wounded. His indomitable fighting spirit set an inspiring example of valor to his comrades and, through his actions, the onslaught was stemmed, enabling a friendly platoon to reach the beleaguered patrol, evacuate the wounded, and effect a safe withdrawal to friendly lines. Cpl. Hammond's unflinching courage and consummate devotion to duty reflect lasting glory on himself and uphold the finest traditions of the military service.

*HANDRICH, MELVIN O.

Rank and organization: Master Sergeant, U.S. Army, Company C, 5th Infantry Regiment. *Place and date:* Near Sobuk San Mountain, Korea, 25 and 26 August 1950. *Entered service at:* Manawa, Wis. *Born:* 26 January 1919, Manawa, Wis. *G.O. No.:* 60, 2 August 1951. *Citation:* M/Sgt. Handrich, Company C, distinguished himself by conspicuous gallantry and intrepidity above and beyond the call of duty in action. His company was engaged in repulsing an estimated 150 enemy who were threatening to overrun its position. Near midnight on 25 August, a hostile group over 100 strong attempted to infiltrate the company perimeter. M/Sgt. Handrich, despite the heavy enemy fire, voluntarily left the comparative safety of the defensive area and moved to a forward position where he could direct mortar and artillery fire upon the advancing enemy. He remained at this post for 8 hours directing fire against the enemy who often approached to within 50 feet of his position. Again, on the morning of 26 August, another strong hostile force made an attempt to overrun the company's position. With complete disregard for his safety, M/Sgt. Handrich rose to his feet and from this exposed position fired his rifle and directed mortar and artillery fire on the attackers. At the peak of this action he observed elements of his company preparing to withdraw. He perilously made his way across fire-swept terrain to the defense area where, by example and forceful leadership, he reorganized the men to continue the fight. During the action M/Sgt. Handrich was severely wounded. Refusing to take cover or be evacuated, he returned to his forward position and continued to direct the company's fire. Later a determined enemy attack overran M/Sgt. Handrich's position and he was mortally wounded. When the position was retaken, over 70 enemy dead were counted in the area he had so intrepidly defended. M/Sgt. Handrich's sustained personal bravery, consummate courage, and gallant self-sacrifice reflect untold glory upon himself and the heroic traditions of the military service.

*HANSON, JACK G.

Rank and organization: Private First Class, U.S. Army, Company F, 31st Infantry Regiment. *Place and date:* Near Pachi-dong, Korea, 7 June 1951. *Entered service at:* Galveston, Tex. *Born:* 18 September 1930, Escaptawpa, Miss. *G.O. No.:* 15, 1 February 1952. *Citation:* Pfc. Hanson, a machine gunner with the 1st Platoon, Company F, distinguished himself by conspicuous gallantry and intrepidity at the risk of his life above and beyond the call of duty in action against an armed enemy of the United Nations. The company, in defensive positions on two strategic hills separated by a wide saddle, was ruthlessly attacked at approximately 0300 hours, the brunt of which centered on the approach to the divide within range of Pfc. Hanson's machinegun. In the initial phase of the action, 4 riflemen were wounded and evacuated and the numerically superior enemy, advancing under cover of darkness, infiltrated and posed an imminent threat to the security of the command post and weapons platoon. Upon orders to move to key terrain above and to the right of Pfc. Hanson's position, he voluntarily remained to provide protective fire for the withdrawal. Subsequent to the retiring elements fighting a rearguard action to the new location, it was learned that Pfc. Hanson's assistant gunner and 3 riflemen had been wounded and had crawled to safety, and that he was maintaining a lone-man defense. After the 1st Platoon reorganized, counterattacked, and resecured its original positions at approximately 0530 hours, Pfc. Hanson's body was found lying in front of his emplacement, his machinegun ammunition expended, his empty pistol in his right hand, and a machete with blood on the blade in his left hand, and approximately 22 enemy dead lay in the wake of his action. Pfc. Hanson's consummate valor, inspirational conduct, and willing self-sacrifice enabled the company to contain the enemy and regain the commanding ground, and reflect lasting glory on himself and the noble traditions of the military service.

*HARTELL, LEE R.

Rank and organization: First Lieutenant, U.S. Army, Battery A, 15th Field Artillery Battalion, 2d Infantry Division. *Place and date:* Near Kobangsan-ni, Korea, 27 August 1951. *Entered service at:* Danbury, Conn. *Birth:* Philadelphia, Pa. *G.O. No.:* 16, 1 February 1952. *Citation:* 1st. Lt. Hartell, a member of Battery A, distinguished himself by conspicuous gallantry and intrepidity at the risk of his life above and beyond the call of duty in action against an armed enemy of the United Nations. During the darkness of early morning, the enemy launched a ruthless attack against friendly positions on a rugged mountainous ridge. 1st Lt. Hartell, attached to Company B, 9th Infantry Regiment, as forward observer, quickly moved his radio to an exposed vantage on the ridge line to adjust defensive fires. Realizing the tactical advantage of illuminating the area of approach, he called for flares and then directed crippling fire into the onrushing assailants. At this juncture a large force of hostile troops swarmed up the slope in a banzai charge and came within 10 yards of 1st Lt. Hartell's position. 1st Lt. Hartell sustained a severe hand wound in the ensuing encounter, but grasped the microphone with his other hand and maintained his magnificent stand until the front and left flank of the company were protected by a close-in wall of withering fire, causing the fanatical foe to disperse and fall back momentarily. After the numerically superior enemy overran an outpost and was closing on his position, 1st Lt. Hartell, in a final radio call, urged the friendly elements to fire both batteries continuously. Although mortally wounded, 1st Lt. Hartell's intrepid actions contributed significantly to stemming the onslaught and enabled his company to maintain the strategic strongpoint. His consummate valor and unwavering devotion to duty reflect lasting glory on himself and uphold the noble traditions of the military service.

HARVEY, RAYMOND

Rank and organization: Captain, U.S. Army, Company C, 17th Infantry Regiment. *Place and date:* Vicinity of Taemi-Dong, Korea, 9 March 1951. *Entered service at:* Pasadena, Calif. *Born:* 1 March 1920, Ford City, Pa. *G.O. No.:* 67, 2 August 1951. *Citation:* Capt. Harvey, Company C, distinguished himself by conspicuous gallantry and intrepidity above and beyond the call of duty in action. When his company was pinned down by a barrage of automatic weapons fire from numerous well-entrenched emplacements, imperiling accomplishment of its mission, Capt. Harvey braved a hail of fire and exploding grenades to advance to the first enemy machinegun nest, killing its crew with grenades. Rushing to the edge of the next emplacement, he killed its crew with carbine fire. He then moved the 1st Platoon forward until it was again halted by a curtain of automatic fire from well-fortified hostile positions. Disregarding the hail of fire, he personally charged and neutralized a third emplacement. Miraculously escaping death from intense crossfire, Capt. Harvey continued to lead the assault. Spotting an enemy pillbox well camouflaged by logs, he moved close enough to sweep the emplacement with carbine fire and throw grenades through the openings, annihilating its 5 occupants. Though wounded he then turned to order the company forward, and, suffering agonizing pain, he continued to direct the reduction of the remaining hostile positions, refusing evacuation until assured that the mission would be accomplished. Capt. Harvey's valorous and intrepid actions served as an inspiration to his company, reflecting the utmost glory upon himself and upholding the heroic traditions of the military service.

*HENRY, FREDERICK F.

Rank and organization: First Lieutenant, U.S. Army, Company F, 28th Infantry Regiment. *Place and date:* Vicinity of Am-Dong, Korea, 1 September 1950. *Entered service at:* Clinton, Okla. *Birth:* Vian, Okla. *G.O. No.:* 8, 16 February 1951. *Citation:* 1st Lt. Henry, Company F, distinguished himself by conspicuous gallantry and intrepidity above and beyond the call of duty in action. His platoon was holding a strategic ridge near the town when they were attacked by a superior enemy force, supported by heavy mortar and artillery fire. Seeing his platoon disorganized by this fanatical assault, he left his foxhole and moving along the line ordered his men to stay in place and keep firing. Encouraged by this heroic action the platoon reformed a defensive line and rained devastating fire on the enemy, checking its advance. Enemy fire had knocked out all communications and 1st Lt. Henry was unable to determine whether or not the main line of resistance was altered to this heavy attack. On his own initiative, although severely wounded, he decided to hold his position as long as possible and ordered the wounded evacuated and their weapons and ammunition brought to him. Establishing a 1-man defensive position, he ordered the platoon's withdrawal and despite his wound and with complete disregard for himself remained behind to cover the movement. When last seen he was singlehandedly firing all available weapons so effectively that he caused an estimated 50 enemy casualties. His ammunition was soon expended and his position overrun, but this intrepid action saved the platoon and halted the enemy's advance until the main line of resistance was prepared to throw back the attack. 1st Lt. Henry's outstanding gallantry and noble self-sacrifice above and beyond the call of duty reflect the highest honor on him and are in keeping with the esteemed traditions of the U.S. Army.

HERNANDEZ, RODOLFO P.

Rank and organization: Corporal, U.S. Army, Company G, 187th Airborne Regimental Combat Team. *Place and date:* Near Wontong-ni, Korea, 31 May 1951. *Entered service at:* Fowler, Calif. *Born:* 14 April 1931, Colton, Calif. *G.O. No.:* 40, 21 April 1962. *Citation:* Cpl. Hernandez, a member of Company G, distinguished himself by conspicuous gallantry and intrepidity above and beyond the call of duty in action against the enemy. His platoon, in defensive positions on Hill 420, came under ruthless attack by a numerically superior and fanatical hostile force, accompanied by heavy artillery, mortar, and machinegun fire which inflicted numerous casualties on the platoon. His comrades were forced to withdraw due to lack of ammunition but Cpl. Hernandez, although wounded in an exchange of grenades, continued to deliver deadly fire into the ranks of the onrushing assailants until a ruptured cartridge rendered his rifle inoperative. Immediately leaving his position, Cpl. Hernandez rushed the enemy armed only with rifle and bayonet. Fearlessly engaging the foe, he killed 6 of the enemy before falling unconscious from grenade, bayonet, and bullet wounds but his heroic action momentarily halted the enemy advance and enabled his unit to counterattack and retake the lost ground. The indomitable fighting spirit, outstanding courage, and tenacious devotion to duty clearly demonstrated by Cpl. Hernandez reflect the highest credit upon himself, the infantry, and the U.S. Army.

HUDNER, THOMAS JEROME, JR.

Rank and organization: Lieutenant (jg.) U.S. Navy, pilot in Fighter Squadron 32, attached to U.S.S. *Leyte. Place and date:* Chosin Reservoir area of Korea, 4 December 1950. *Entered service at:* Fall River, Mass. *Born:* 31 August 1924, Fall River, Mass. *Citation.* For conspicuous gallantry and intrepidity at the risk of his life above and beyond the call of duty as a pilot in Fighter Squadron 32, while attempting to rescue a squadron mate whose plane struck by antiaircraft fire and trailing smoke, was forced down behind enemy lines. Quickly maneuvering to circle the downed pilot and protect him from enemy troops infesting the area, Lt. (jg.) Hudner risked his life to save the injured flier who was trapped alive in the burning wreckage. Fully aware of the extreme danger in landing on the rough mountainous terrain, and the scant hope of escape or survival in subzero temperature, he put his plane down skillfully in a deliberate wheels-up landing in the presence of enemy troops. With his bare hands, he packed the fuselage with snow to keep the flames away from the pilot and struggled to pull him free. Unsuccessful in this, he returned to his crashed aircraft and radioed other airborne planes, requesting that a helicopter be dispatched with an ax and fire extinguisher. He then remained on the spot despite the continuing danger from enemy action and, with the assistance of the rescue pilot, renewed a desperate but unavailing battle against time, cold, and flames. Lt. (jg.) Hudner's exceptionally valiant action and selfless devotion to a shipmate sustain and enhance the highest traditions of the U.S. Naval Service.

INGMAN, EINAR H., JR.

Rank and organization: Sergeant (then Cpl.), U.S. Army, Company E, 17th Infantry Regiment, 7th Infantry Division. *Place and date:* Near Maltari, Korea, 26 February 1951. *Entered service at:* Tomahawk, Wis. *Born:* 6 October 1929, Milwaukee, Wis. *G.O. No.:* 68, 2 August 1951. *Citation:* Sgt. Ingman, a member of Company E, distinguished himself by conspicuous gallantry and intrepidity above and beyond the call of duty in action against the enemy. The 2 leading squads of the assault platoon of his company, while attacking a strongly fortified ridge held by the enemy, were pinned down by withering fire and both squad leaders and several men were wounded. Cpl. Ingman assumed command, reorganized and combined the 2 squads, then moved from 1 position to another, designating fields of fire and giving advice and encouragement to the men. Locating an enemy machinegun position that was raking his men with devastating fire he charged it alone, threw a grenade into the position, and killed the remaining crew with rifle fire. Another enemy machinegun opened fire approximately 15 yards away and inflicted additional casualties to the group and stopped the attack. When Cpl. Ingman charged the second position he was hit by grenade fragments and a hail of fire which seriously wounded him about the face and neck and knocked him to the ground. With incredible courage and stamina, he arose instantly and, using only his rifle, killed the entire guncrew before falling unconscious from his wounds. As a result of the singular action by Cpl. Ingman the defense of the enemy was broken, his squad secured its objective, and more than 100 hostile troops abandoned their weapons and fled in disorganized retreat. Cpl. Ingman's indomitable courage, extraordinary heroism, and superb leadership reflect the highest credit on himself and are in keeping with the esteemed traditions of the infantry and the U.S. Army.

*JECELIN, WILLIAM R.

Rank and organization: Sergeant, U.S. Army, Company C, 35th Infantry Regiment, 25th Infantry Division. *Place and date:* Near Saga, Korea, 19 September 1950. *Entered service at:* Baltimore, Md. *Birth:*

Baltimore, Md. *G.O. No.:* 24, 25 April 1951. *Citation:* Sgt. Jecelin, Company C, distinguished himself by conspicuous gallantry and intrepidity above and beyond the call of duty in action against the enemy. His company was ordered to secure a prominent, sawtoothed ridge from a well-entrenched and heavily armed enemy. Unable to capture the objective in the first attempt, a frontal and flanking assault was launched. He led his platoon through heavy enemy fire and bursting shells, across ricefields and rocky terrain, in direct frontal attack on the ridge in order to draw fire away from the flanks. The unit advanced to the base of the cliff, where intense, accurate hostile fire stopped the attack. Realizing that an assault was the only solution, Sgt. Jecelin rose from his position firing his rifle and throwing grenades as he called on his men to follow him. Despite the intense enemy fire this attack carried to the crest of the ridge where the men were forced to take cover. Again he rallied his men and stormed the enemy strongpoint. With fixed bayonets they charged into the face of antitank fire and engaged the enemy in hand-to-hand combat. After clubbing and slashing this force into submission the platoon was forced to take cover from direct frontal fire of a self-propelled gun. Refusing to be stopped he leaped to his feet and through sheer personal courage and fierce determination led his men in a new attack. At this instant a well-camouflaged enemy soldier threw a grenade at the remaining members of the platoon. He immediately lunged and covered the grenade with his body, absorbing the full force of the explosion to save those around him. This incredible courage and willingness to sacrifice himself for his comrades so imbued them with fury that they completely eliminated the enemy force. Sgt. Jecelin's heroic leadership and outstanding gallantry reflect the highest credit upon himself and uphold the esteemed traditions of the military service.

*JOHNSON, JAMES E.

Rank and organization: Sergeant, U.S. Marine Corps, Company J, 3d Battalion, 7th Marines, 1st Marine Division (Rein). *Place and date:* Yudam-ni, Korea, 2 December 1950 (declared missing in action on 2 December 1950, and killed in action as of 2 November 1953). *Entered service at:* Washington, D.C. *Born:* 1 January 1926, Pocatello, Idaho. *Citation:* For conspicuous gallantry and intrepidity at the risk of his life above and beyond the call of duty while serving as a squad leader in a provisional rifle platoon composed of artillerymen and attached to Company J, in action against enemy aggressor forces. Vastly outnumbered by a well-entrenched and cleverly concealed enemy force wearing the uniforms of friendly troops and attacking his platoon's open and unconcealed positions, Sgt. Johnson unhesitatingly took charge of his platoon in the absence of the leader and, exhibiting great personal valor in the face of a heavy barrage of hostile fire, coolly proceeded to move about among his men, shouting words of encouragement and inspiration and skillfully directing their fire. Ordered to displace his platoon during the fire fight, he immediately placed himself in an extremely hazardous position from which he could provide covering fire for his men. Fully aware that his voluntary action meant either certain death or capture to himself, he courageously continued to provide effective cover for his men and was last observed in a wounded condition singlehandedly engaging enemy troops in close handgrenade and hand-tolhand fighting. By his valiant and inspiring leadership, Sgt. Johnson was directly responsible for the successful completion of the platoon's displacement and the saving of many lives. His dauntless fighting spirit and unfaltering devotion to duty in the face of terrific odds reflect the highest credit upon himself and the U.S. Naval Service.

*JORDAN, MACK A.

Rank and organization: Private First Class, U.S. Army, Company K, 21st Infantry Regiment, 24th Infantry Division. *Place and date:* Near Kumsong, Korea, 15 November 1951. *Entered service at:* Collins, Miss. *Born:* 8 December 1928, Collins, Miss. *G.O. No.:* 3, 8 January 1953. *Citation:* Pfc. Jordan, a member of Company K, distinguished himself by conspicuous gallantry and indomitable courage above and beyond the call of duty in action against the enemy. As a squad leader of the 3d Platoon, he was participating in a night attack on key terrain against a fanatical hostile force when the advance was halted by intense small-arms and automatic-weapons fire and a vicious barrage of handgrenades. Upon orders for the platoon to withdraw and reorganize, Pfc. Jordan voluntarily remained behind to provide covering fire. Crawling toward an enemy machinegun emplacement, he threw 3 grenades and neutralized the gun. He then rushed the position delivering a devastating hail of fire, killing several of the enemy and forcing the remainder to fall back to new positions. He courageously attempted to move forward to silence another machinegun but, before he could leave his position, the ruthless foe hurled explosives down the hill and in the ensuing blast both legs were severed. Despite mortal wounds, he continued to deliver deadly fire and held off the assailants until the platoon returned. Pfc. Jordan's unflinching courage and gallant self-sacrifice reflect lasting glory upon himself and uphold the noble traditions of the infantry and the military service.

*KANELL, BILLIE G.

Rank and organization: Private, U.S. Army, Company I, 35th Infantry Regiment, 25th Infantry Division. *Place and date:* Near Pyongyang, Korea, 7 September 1951. *Entered service at:* Poplar Bluff, Mo. *Born:* 26 June 1931, Poplar Bluff, Mo. *G.O. No.:* 57, 13 June 1952. *Citation:* Pvt. Kanell, a member of Company I, distinguished himself by conspicuous gallantry and outstanding courage above and beyond the call of duty in action against the enemy. A numerically superior hostile force had launched a fanatical assault against friendly positions, supported by mortar and artillery fire, when Pvt. Kanell stood in his emplacement exposed to enemy observation and action and delivered accurate fire into the ranks of the assailants. An enemy grenade was hurled into his emplacement and Pvt. Kanell threw himself upon the grenade, absorbing the blast with his body to protect 2 of his comrades from serious injury and possible death. A few seconds later another grenade was thrown into the emplacement and, although seriously wounded by the first missile, he summoned his waning strength to roll toward the second grenade and used his body as a shield to again protect his comrades. He was mortally wounded as a result of his heroic actions. His indomitable courage, sustained fortitude against overwhelming odds, and gallant self-sacrifice reflect the highest credit upon himself, the infantry, and the U.S. Army.

*KAUFMAN, LOREN R.

Rank and organization: Sergeant First Class, U.S. Army, Company G, 9th Infantry Regiment. *Place and date:* Near Yongsan, Korea, 4 and 5 September 1950. *Entered service at:* The Dalles, Oreg. *Born:* 27 July 1923, The Dalles, Oreg. *G.O. No.:* 61, 2 August 1951. *Citation:* Sfc. Kaufman distinguished himself by conspicuous gallantry and intrepidity above and beyond the call of duty in action. On the night of 4 September the company was in a defensive position on 2 adjoining hills. His platoon was occupying a strong point 2 miles away protecting the battalion flank. Early on 5 September the company was attacked by an enemy battalion and his platoon was ordered to reinforce the company. As his unit moved along a ridge it encountered a hostile encircling force. Sfc. Kaufman, running forward, bayoneted the lead scout and engaged the column in a rifle and grenade assault. His quick vicious attack so surprised the enemy that they retreated in confusion. When his platoon joined the company he discovered that the enemy had taken commanding ground and pinned the company down in a draw. Without hesitation Sfc. Kaufman charged the enemy lines firing his rifle and throwing grenades. During the action, he bayoneted 2 enemy and seizing an unmanned machinegun, delivered deadly fire on the defenders. Following this encounter the company regrouped and resumed the attack. Leading the assault he reached the ridge, destroyed a hostile machinegun position, and routed the remaining enemy. Pursuing the hostile troops he bayoneted 2 more and then rushed a mortar position shooting the gunners. Remnants of the enemy fled to a village and Sfc. Kaufman led a patrol into the town, dispersed them, and burned the buildings. The dauntless courage and resolute intrepid leadership of Sfc. Kaufman were directly responsible for the success of his company in regaining its positions, reflecting distinct credit upon himself and upholding the esteemed traditions of the military service.

*KELLY, JOHN D.

Rank and organization: Private First Class, U.S. Marine Corps, Company C, 1st Battalion, 7th Marines, 1st Marine Division (Rein). *Place and date:* Korea, 28 May 1952. *Entered service at:* Homestead, Pa. *Born:* 8 July 1928, Youngstown, Ohio. *Citation:* For conspicuous gallantry and intrepidity at the risk of his life above and beyond the call of duty while serving as a radio operator of Company C, in action against enemy aggressor forces. With his platoon pinned down by a numerically superior enemy force employing intense mortar, artillery, small-arms and grenade fire, Pfc. Kelly requested permission to leave his radio in the care of another man and to participate in an assault on enemy key positions. Fearlessly charging forward in the face of a murderous hail of machinegun fire and handgrenades, he initiated a daring attack against a hostile strongpoint and personally neutralized the position, killing 2 of the enemy. Unyielding in the fact of heavy odds, he continued forward and singlehandedly assaulted a machinegun bunker.

Although painfully wounded, he bravely charged the bunker and destroyed it, killing 3 of the enemy. Courageously continuing his 1-man assault, he again stormed forward in a valiant attempt to wipe out a third bunker and boldly delivered pointblank fire into the aperture of the hostile emplacement. Mortally wounded by enemy fire while carrying out this heroic action, Pfc. Kelly, by his great personal valor and aggressive fighting spirit, inspired his comrades to sweep on, overrun and secure the objective. His extraordinary heroism in the face of almost certain death reflects the highest credit upon himself and enhances the finest traditions of the U.S. Naval Service. He gallantly gave his life for his country.

*KELSO, JACK WILLIAM

Rank and organization: Private First Class, U.S. Marine Corps, Company I, 3d Battalion, 7th Marines, 1st Marine Division (Rein). *Place and date:* Korea, 2 October 1952. *Entered service at:* Caruthers, Calif. *Born:* 23 January 1934, Madera, Calif. *Citation:* For conspicuous gallantry and intrepidity at the risk of his life above and beyond the call of duty while serving as a rifleman of Company I, in action against enemy aggressor forces. When both the platoon commander and the platoon sergeant became casualties during the defense of a vital outpost against a numerically superior enemy force attacking at night under cover of intense small-arms, grenade, and mortar fire, Pfc. Kelso bravely exposed himself to the hail of enemy fire in a determined effort to reorganize the unit and to repel the onrushing attackers. Forced to seek cover, along with 4 other marines, in a nearby bunker which immediately came under attack, he unhesitatingly picked up an enemy grenade which landed in the shelter, rushed out into the open and hurled it back at the enemy. Although painfully wounded when the grenade exploded as it left his hand, and again forced to seek the protection of the bunker when the hostile fire became more intensified, Pfc. Kelso refused to remain in his position of comparative safety and moved out into the fire-swept area to return the enemy fire, thereby permitting the pinned-down marines in the bunker to escape. Mortally wounded while providing covering fire for his comrades, Pfc. Kelso, by his valiant fighting spirit, aggressive determination, and self-sacrificing efforts in behalf of others, served to inspire all who observed him. His heroic actions sustain and enhance the highest traditions of the U.S. Naval Service. He gallantly gave his life for his country.

KENNEMORE, ROBERT S.

Rank and organization: Staff Sergeant, U.S. Marine Corps, Company E, 2d Battalion, 7th Marines, 1st Marine Division (Rein). *Place and date:* North of Yudam-ni, Korea, 27 and 28 November 1950. *Entered service at:* Greenville, S.C. *Born:* 21 June 1920, Greenville, S.C. *Citation:* For conspicuous gallantry and intrepidity at the risk of his life above and beyond the call of duty as leader of a machinegun section in Company E, in action against enemy aggressor forces. With the company's defensive perimeter overrun by a numerically superior hostile force during a savage night attack north of Yudam-ni and his platoon commander seriously wounded, S/Sgt. Kennemore unhesitatingly assumed command, quickly reorganized the unit and directed the men in consolidating the position. When an enemy grenade landed in the midst of a machinegun squad, he bravely placed his foot on the missile and, in the face of almost certain death, personally absorbed the full force of the explosion to prevent injury to his fellow marines. By his indomitable courage, outstanding leadership and selfless efforts in behalf of his comrades, S/Sgt. Kennemore was greatly instrumental in driving the enemy from the area and upheld the highest traditions of the U.S. Naval Service.

*KILMER, JOHN E.

Rank and organization: Hospital Corpsman, U.S. Navy, attached to duty as a medical corpsman with a Marine rifle company in the 1st Marine Division. *Place and date:* Korea, 13 August 1952. *Entered service at:* Houston, Tex. *Born:* 15 August 1930, Highland Park, Ill. *Citation:* For conspicous gallantry and intrepidity at the risk of his life above and beyond the call of duty in action against enemy aggressor forces. With his company engaged in defending a vitally important hill position well forward of the main line of resistance during an assault by large concentrations of hostile troops, HC Kilmer repeatedly braved intense enemy mortar, artillery, and sniper fire to move from 1 position to another, administering aid to the wounded and expediting their evacuation. Painfully wounded himself when struck by mortar fragments while moving to the aid of a casualty, he persisted in his efforts and inched his way to the side of the stricken marine through a hail of enemy shells falling around him. Undaunted by the devastating hostile fire, he skillfully administered first aid to his comrade and, as another mounting barrage of enemy fire shattered the immediate area, unhesitatingly shielded the wounded man with his body. Mortally wounded by flying shrapnel while carrying out this heroic action, HC Kilmer, by his great personal valor and gallant spirit of self-sacrifice in saving the life of a comrade, served to inspire all who observed him. His unyielding devotion to duty in the face of heavy odds reflects the highest credit upon himself and enhances the finest traditions of the U.S. Naval Service. He gallantly gave his life for another.

*KNIGHT, NOAH O.

Rank and organization: Private First Class, U.S. Army, Company F, 7th Infantry Regiment, 3d Infantry Division. *Place and date:* Near Kowang-San, Korea, 23 and 24 November 1951. *Entered service at:* Jefferson, S.C. *Born:* 27 October 1929, Chesterfield County, S.C. *G.O. No.:* 2, 7 January 1953. *Citation:* Pfc. Knight, a member of Company F, distinguished himself by conspicuous gallantry and indomitable courage above and beyond the call of duty in action against the enemy. He occupied a key position in the defense perimeter when waves of enemy troops passed through their own artillery and mortar concentrations and charged the company position. Two direct hits from an enemy emplacement demolished his bunker and wounded him. Disregarding personal safety, he moved to a shallow depression for a better firing vantage. Unable to deliver effective fire from his defilade position, he left his shelter, moved through heavy fire in full view of the enemy and, firing into the ranks of the relentless assailants, inflicted numerous casualties, momentarily stemming the attack. Later during another vicious onslaught, he observed an enemy squad infiltrating the position and, counterattacking, killed or wounded the entire group. Expending the last of his ammunition, he discovered 3 enemy soldiers entering the friendly position with demolition charges. Realizing the explosives would enable the enemy to exploit the breach, he fearlessly rushed forward and disabled 2 assailants with the butt of his rifle when the third exploded a demolition charge killing the 3 enemy soldiers and mortally wounding Pfc. Knight. Pfc. Knight's supreme sacrifice and consummate devotion to duty reflect lasting glory on himself and uphold the noble traditions of the military service.

*KOELSCH, JOHN KELVIN.

Rank and organization: Lieutenant (jg.), U.S. Navy, Navy helicopter rescue unit. *Place and date:* North Korea, 3 July 1951. *Entered service at:* Los Angeles, Calif. *Birth:* London, England. *Citation:* For conspicuous gallantry and intrepidity at the risk of his life above and beyond the call of duty while serving with a Navy helicopter rescue unit. Although darkness was rapidly approaching when information was received that a marine aviator had been shot down and was trapped by the enemy in mountainous terrain deep in hostile territory, Lt. (jg.) Koelsch voluntarily flew a helicopter to the reported position of the downed airman in an attempt to effect a rescue. With an almost solid overcast concealing everything below the mountain peaks, he descended in his unarmed and vulnerable aircraft without the accompanying fighter escort to an extremely low altitude beneath the cloud level and began a systematic search. Despite the increasingly intense enemy fire, which struck his helicopter on 1 occasion, he persisted in his mission until he succeeded in locating the downed pilot, who was suffering from serious burns on the arms and legs. While the victim was being hoisted into the aircraft, it was struck again by an accurate burst of hostile fire and crashed on the side of the mountain. Quickly extricating his crewmen and the aviator from the wreckage, Lt. (jg.) Koelsch led them from the vicinity in an effort to escape from hostile troops, evading the enemy forces for 9 days and rendering such medical attention as possible to his severely burned companion until all were captured. Up to the time of his death while still a captive of the enemy, Lt. (jg.) Koelsch steadfastly refused to aid his captors in any manner and served to inspire his fellow prisoners by his fortitude and consideration for others. His great personal valor and heroic spirit of self-sacrifice throughout sustain and enhance the finest traditions of the U.S. Naval Service.

KOUMA, ERNEST R.

Rank and organization: Master Sergeant (then Sfc.) U.S. Army, Company A, 72d Tank Battalion. *Place and date:* Vicinity of Agok, Korea, 31 August and 1 September 1950. *Entered service at:* Dwight, Nebr. *Born:* 23 November 1919, Dwight, Nebr. *G.O. No.:* 38, 4 June 1951. *Citation:* M/Sgt. Kouma, a tank commander in Company A, distinguished himself by conspicuous gallantry and intrepidity at the risk of his life above and beyond the call of duty in action against the enemy. His unit was engaged in supporting infantry elements on the Naktong River front. Near midnight on 31 August, a hostile force estimated at 500 crossed the river and launched a fierce attack against the infantry positions, inflicting heavy casualties. A withdrawal was ordered and his armoured unit was given the mission of covering the movement until a secondary position could be established. The enemy assault overran 2 tanks, destroyed 1 and forced another to withdraw. Suddenly M/Sgt. Kouma discovered that his tank was the only obstacle in the path of the hostile onslaught. Holding his ground, he gave fire orders to his crew and remained in position throughout the night, fighting off repeated enemy attacks. During 1 fierce assault, the enemy surrounded his tank and he leaped from the armored turret, exposing himself to a hail of hostile fire, manned the .50 caliber machinegun mounted on the rear deck, and delivered pointblank fire into the fanatical foe. His machinegun emptied, he fired his pistol and threw grenades to keep the enemy from his tank. After more than 9 hours of constant combat and close-in fighting, he withdrew his vehicle to friendly lines. During the withdrawal through 8 miles of hostile territory, M/Sgt. Kouma continued to inflict casualties upon the enemy and exhausted his ammunition in destroying 3 hostile machinegun positions. During this action, M/Sgt. Kouma killed an estimated 250 enemy soldiers. His magnificent stand allowed the infantry sufficient time to reestablish defensive positions. Rejoining his company, although suffering intensely from his wounds, he attempted to resupply his tank and return to the battle area. While being evacuated for medical treatment, his courage was again displayed when he requested to return to the front. M/Sgt. Kouma's superb leadership, heroism, and intense devotion to duty reflect the highest credit on himself and uphold the esteemed traditions of the U.S. Army.

*KRZYZOWSKI, EDWARD C.

Rank and organization: Captain, U.S. Army, Company B, 9th Infantry Regiment, 2d Infantry Division. *Place and date:* Near Tondul, Korea, from 31 August to 3 September 1951. *Entered service at:* Cicero, Ill. *Born:* 16 January 1914, Chicago, Ill. *G.O. No.:* 56, 12 June 1952. *Citation:* Capt. Krzyzowski, distinguished himself by conspicuous gallantry and indomitable courage above and beyond the call of duty in action against the enemy as commanding officer of Company B. Spearheading an assault against strongly defended Hill 700, his company came under vicious crossfire and grenade attack from enemy bunkers. Creeping up the fire-swept hill, he personally eliminated 1 bunker with his grenades and wiped out a second with carbine fire. Forced to retire to more tenable positions for the night, the company, led by Capt. Krzyzowski, resumed the attack the following day, gaining several hundred yards and inflicting numerous casualties. Overwhelmed by the numerically superior hostile force, he ordered his men to evacuate the wounded and move back. Providing protective fire for their safe withdrawal, he was wounded again by grenade fragments, but refused evacuation and continued to direct the defense. On 3 September, he led his valiant unit in another assault which overran several hostile positions, but again the company was pinned down by murderous fire. Courageously advancing alone to an open knoll to plot mortar concentrations against the hill, he was killed instantly by an enemy sniper's fire. Capt. Krzyzowski's consummate fortitude, heroic leadership, and gallant self-sacrifice, so clearly demonstrated throughout 3 days of bitter combat, reflect the highest credit and lasting glory on himself, the infantry, and the U.S. Army.

*KYLE, DARWIN K.

Rank and organization: Second Lieutenant, U.S. Army, Company K, 7th Infantry Regiment, 3d Infantry Division. *Place and date:* Near Kamil-ni, Korea, 16 February 1951. *Entered service at:* Racine, W. Va. *Born:* 1 June 1918, Jenkins, Ky. *G.O. No.:* 17, 1 February 1952. *Citation:* 2d Lt. Kyle, distinguished himself by conspicuous gallantry and intrepidity above and beyond the call of duty in action against the enemy. When his platoon had been pinned down by intense fire, he completely exposed himself to move among and encourage his men to continue the advance against enemy forces strongly entrenched on Hill 185. Inspired by his courageous leadership, the platoon resumed the advance but was again pinned down when an enemy machinegun opened fire, wounding 6 of the men. 2d Lt. Kyle immediately charged the hostile emplacement alone, engaged the crew in hand-to-hand combat, killing all 3. Continuing on toward the objective, his platoon suddenly received an intense automatic-weapons fire from a well-concealed hostile position on its right flank. Again leading his men in a daring bayonet charge against this position, firing his carbine and throwing grenades, 2d Lt. Kyle personally destroyed 4 of the enemy before he was killed by a burst from an enemy submachinegun. The extraordinary heroism and outstanding leadership of 2d Lt. Kyle, and his gallant self-sacrifice, reflect the highest credit upon himself and are in keeping with the esteemed traditions of the military service.

LEE, HUBERT L.

Rank and organization: Master Sergeant, U.S. Army, Company I, 23d Infantry Regiment, 2d Infantry Division. *Place and date:* Near Ip-o-ri, Korea, 1 February 1951. *Entered service at:* Leland, Miss. *Born:* 2 February 1915, Arburg, Mo. *G.O. No.:* 21, 5 February 1952. *Citation:* M/Sgt. Lee, a member of Company I, distinguished himself by conspicuous gallantry and intrepidity above and beyond the call of duty in action against the enemy. When his platoon was forced from its position by a numerically superior enemy force, and his platoon leader wounded, M/Sgt. Lee assumed command, regrouped the remnants of his unit, and led them in repeated assaults to regain the position. Within 25 yards of his objective he received a leg wound from grenade fragments, but refused assistance and continued the attack. Although forced to withdraw 5 times, each time he regrouped his remaining men and renewed the assault. Moving forward at the head of his small group in the fifth attempt, he was struck by an exploding grenade, knocked to the ground, and seriously wounded in both legs. Still refusing assistance, he advanced by crawling, rising to his knees to fire, and urging his men to follow. While thus directing the final assault he was wounded a third time, by small-arms fire. Persistently continuing to crawl forward, he directed his men in a final and successful attack which regained the vital objective. His intrepid leadership and determination led to the destruction of 83 of the enemy and withdrawal of the remainder, and was a vital factor in stopping the enemy attack.

M/Sgt. Lee's indomitable courage, consummate valor, and outstanding leadership reflect the highest credit upon himself and are in keeping with the finest traditions of the infantry and the U.S. Army.

*LIBBY, GEORGE D.

Rank and organization: Sergeant, U.S. Army, Company C, 3d Engineer Combat Battalion, 24th Infantry Division. *Place and date:* Near Taejon, Korea, 20 July 1950. *Entered service at:* Waterbury, Conn. *Birth:* Bridgton, Maine. *G.O. No.:* 62, 2 August 1951. *Citation:* Sgt. Libby distinguished himself by conspicuous gallantry and intrepidity above and beyond the call of duty in action. While breaking through an enemy encirclement, the vehicle in which he was riding approached an enemy roadblock and encountered devastating fire which disabled the truck, killing or wounding all the passengers except Sgt. Libby. Taking cover in a ditch Sgt. Libby engaged the enemy and despite the heavy fire crossed the road twice to administer aid to his wounded comrades. He then hailed a passing M–5 artillery tractor and helped the wounded aboard. The enemy directed intense small-arms fire at the driver, and Sgt. Libby, realizing that no one else could operate the vehicle, placed himself between the driver and the enemy thereby shielding him while he returned the fire. During this action he received several wounds in the arms and body. Continuing through the town the tractor made frequent stops and Sgt. Libby helped more wounded aboard. Refusing first aid, he continued to shield the driver and return the fire of the enemy when another roadblock was encountered. Sgt. Libby received additional wounds but held his position until he lost consciousness. Sgt. Libby's sustained, heroic actions enabled his comrades to reach friendly lines. His dauntless courage and gallant self-sacrifice reflect the highest credit upon himself and uphold the esteemed traditions of the U.S. Army.

*LITTLETON, HERBERT A.

Rank and organization: Private First Class, U.S. Marine Corps Reserve, Company C, 1st Battalion, 7th Marines, 1st Marine Division (Rein). *Place and date:* Chungchon, Korea, 22 April 1951. *Entered service at:* Blackhawk, S. Dak. *Born:* 1 July 1930, Mena, Ark. *Citation:* For conspicuous gallantry and intrepidity at the risk of his life above and beyond the call of duty while serving as a radio operator with an artillery forward observation team of Company C, in action against enemy aggressor forces. Standing watch when a well-concealed and numerically superior enemy force launched a violent night attack from nearby positions against his company, Pfc. Littleton quickly alerted the forward observation team and immediately moved into an advantageous position to assist in calling down artillery fire on the hostile force. When an enemy handgrenade was thrown into his vantage point shortly after the arrival of the remainder of the team, he unhesitatingly hurled himself on the deadly missile, absorbing its full, shattering impact in his body. By his prompt action and heroic spirit of self-sacrifice, he saved the other members of his team from serious injury or death and enabled them to carry on the vital mission which culminated in the repulse of the hostile attack. His indomitable valor in the face of almost certain death reflects the highest credit upon Pfc. Littleton and the U.S. Naval Service. He gallantly gave his life for his country.

Rank and organization: Sergeant, U.S. Army, Company M, 38th Infantry Regiment, 2d Infantry Division. *Place and date:* Near Hoengsong, Korea, 12 February 1951. *Entered service at:* Kansas City, Mo. *Born:* 10 December 1923, Kansas City, Mo. *G.O. No.:* 18, 1 February 1952. *Citation:* Sgt. Long, a member of Company M, distinguished himself by conspicuous gallantry and intrepidity above and beyond the call of duty in action against an armed enemy of the United Nations. When Company M, in a defensive perimeter on Hill 300, was viciously attacked by a numerically superior hostile force at approximately 0300 hours and ordered to withdraw, Sgt. Long, a forward observer for the mortar platoon, voluntarily remained at his post to provide cover by directing mortar fire on the enemy. Maintaining radio contact with his platoon, Sgt. Long coolly directed accurate mortar fire on the advancing foe. He continued firing his carbine and throwing handgrenades until his position was surrounded and he was mortally wounded. Sgt. Long's inspirational, valorous action halted the onslaught, exacted a heavy toll of enemy casualties, and enabled his company to withdraw, reorganize, counterattack, and regain the hill strongpoint. His unflinching courage and noble self-sacrifice reflect the highest credit on himself and are in keeping with the honored traditions of the military service.

*LOPEZ, BALDOMERO

Rank and organization: First Lieutenant, U.S. Marine Corps, Company A, 1st Battalion, 5th Marines, 1st Marine Division (Rein). *Place and date:* During Inchon invasion in Korea, 15 September 1950. *Entered service at:* Tampa, Fla. *Born:* 23 August 1925, Tampa, Fla. *Citation:* For conspicuous gallantry and intrepidity at the risk of his life above and beyond the call of duty as a rifle platoon commander of Company A, in action against enemy aggressor forces. With his platoon 1st Lt. Lopez was engaged in the reduction of immediate enemy beach defenses after landing with the assault waves. Exposing himself to hostile fire, he moved forward alongside a bunker and prepared to throw a handgrenade into the next pillbox whose fire was pinning down that sector of the beach. Taken under fire by an enemy automatic weapon and hit in the right shoulder and chest as he lifted his arm to throw, he fell backward and dropped the deadly missile. After a moment, he turned and dragged his body forward in an effort to retrieve the grenade and throw it. In critical condition from pain and loss of blood, and unable to grasp the handgrenade firmly enough to hurl it, he chose to sacrifice himself rather than endanger the lives of his men and, with a sweeping motion of his wounded right arm, cradled the grenade under him and absorbed the full impact of the explosion. His exceptional courage, fortitude, and devotion to duty reflect the highest credit upon 1st Lt. Lopez and the U.S. Naval Service. He gallantly gave his life for his country.

*LORING, CHARLES J., Jr.

Rank and organization: Major, U.S. Air Force, 80th Fighter-Bomber Squadron, 8th Fighter-Bomber Wing. *Place and date:* Near Sniper

Ridge, North Korea, 22 November 1952. *Entered service at:* Portland, Maine. *Born:* 2 October 1918, Portland, Maine. *Citation:* Maj. Loring distinguished himself by conspicuous gallantry and intrepidity at the risk of his life above and beyond the call of duty. While leading a flight of 4 F–80 type aircraft on a close support mission, Maj. Loring was briefed by a controller to dive-bomb enemy gun positions which were harassing friendly ground troops. After verifying the location of the target, Maj. Loring rolled into his dive bomb run. Throughout the run, extremely accurate ground fire was directed on his aircraft. Disregarding the accuracy and intensity of the ground fire, Maj. Loring aggressively continued to press the attack until his aircraft was hit. At approximately 4,000 feet, he deliberately altered his course and aimed his diving aircraft at active gun emplacements concentrated on a ridge northwest of the briefed target, turned his aircraft 45 degrees to the left, pulled up in a deliberate, controlled maneuver, and elected to sacrifice his life by diving his aircraft directly into the midst of the enemy emplacements. His selfless and heroic action competely destroyed the enemy gun emplacement and eliminated a dangerous threat to United Nations ground forces. Maj. Loring's noble spirit, superlative courage, and conspicuous self-sacrifice in inflicting maximum damage on the enemy exemplified valor of the highest degree and his actions were in keeping with the finest traditions of the U.S. Air Force.

*LYELL, WILLIAM F.

Rank and organization: Corporal, U.S. Army, Company F, 17th Infantry Regiment, 7th Infantry Division. *Place and date:* Near Chup'a-ri, Korea, 31 August 1951. *Entered service at:* Old Hickory, Tenn. *Birth:* Hickman County, Tenn. *G.O. No.:* 4, 9 January 1953. *Citation:* Cpl. Lyell, a member of Company F, distinguished himself by conspicuous gallantry and outstanding courage above and beyond the call of duty in action against the enemy. When his platoon leader was killed, Cpl. Lyell assumed command and led his unit in an assault on strongly fortified enemy positions located on commanding terrain. When his platoon came under vicious, raking fire which halted the forward movement, Cpl. Lyell seized a 57mm. recoilless rifle and unhesitatingly moved ahead to a suitable firing position from which he delivered deadly accurate fire completely destroying an enemy bunker, killing its occupants. He then returned to his platoon and was resuming the assault when the unit was again subjected to intense hostile fire from 2 other bunkers. Disregarding his personal safety, armed with grenades he charged forward hurling grenades into 1 of the enemy emplacements, and although painfully wounded in this action he pressed on destroying the bunker and killing 6 of the foe. He then continued his attack against a third enemy position, throwing grenades as he ran forward, annihilating 4 enemy soldiers. He then led his platoon to the north slope of the hill where positions were occupied from which effective fire was delivered against the enemy in support of friendly troops moving up. Fearlessly exposing himself to enemy fire, he continuously moved about directing and encouraging his men until he was mortally wounded by enemy mortar fire. Cpl. Lyell's extraordinary heroism, indomitable courage, and aggressive leadership reflect great credit on himself and are in keeping with the highest traditions of the military service.

*MARTINEZ, BENITO

Rank and organization: Corporal, U.S. Army, Company A, 27th Infantry Regiment, 25th Infantry Division. *Place and date:* Near Satae-ri, Korea, 6 September 1952. *Entered service at:* Fort Hancock, Tex. *Born:* 21 March 1931, Fort Hancock, Tex. *G.O. No.:* 96, 29 December 1953. *Citation:* Cpl. Martinez, a machine gunner with Company A, distinguished himself by conspicuous gallantry and outstanding courage above and beyond the call of duty in action against the enemy. While manning a listening post forward of the main line of resistance, his position was attacked by a hostile force of reinforced company strength. In the bitter fighting which ensued, the enemy infiltrated the defense perimeter and, realizing that encirclement was imminent, Cpl. Martinez elected to remain at his post in an attempt to stem the onslaught. In a daring defense, he raked the attacking troops with crippling fire, inflicting numerous casualties. Although contacted by sound power phone several times, he insisted that no attempt be made to rescue him because of the danger involved. Soon thereafter, the hostile forces rushed the emplacement, forcing him to make a limited withdrawal with only an automatic rifle and pistol to defend himself. After a courageous 6-hour stand and shortly before dawn, he called in for the last time, stating that the enemy was converging on his position. His magnificent stand enabled friendly elements to reorganize, attack, and regain the key terrain. Cpl. Martinez' incredible valor and supreme sacrifice reflect lasting glory upon himself and are in keeping with the honored traditions of the military service.

*MATTHEWS, DANIEL P.

Rank and organization: Sergeant, U.S. Marine Corps, Company F, 2d Battalion, 7th Marines, 1st Marine Division (Rein). *Place and date:* Vegas Hill, Korea, 28 March 1953. *Entered service at:* Van Nuys, Calif. *Born:* 31 December 1931, Van Nuys, Calif. *Award presented:* 29 March 1954. *Citation:* For conspicuous gallantry and intrepidity at the risk of his life above and beyond the call of duty while serving as a squad leader of Company F, in action against enemy aggressor forces. Participating in a counterattack against a firmly entrenched and well concealed hostile force which had repelled 6 previous assaults on a vital enemy-held outpost far forward of the main line of resistance, Sgt. Matthews fearlessly advanced in the attack until his squad was pinned down by a murderous sweep of fire from an enemy machinegun located on the peak of the outpost. Observing that the deadly fire prevented a corpsman from removing a wounded man lying in an open area fully exposed to the brunt of the devastating gunfire, he worked his way to the base of the hostile machinegun emplacement, leaped onto the rock fortification surrounding the gun and, taking the enemy by complete surprise, singlehandedly charged the hostile emplacement with his rifle. Although severely wounded when the enemy brought a withering hail of fire to bear upon him, he gallantly continued his valiant 1-man assault and, firing his rifle with deadly effectiveness, succeeded in killing 2 of the enemy, routing a third, and completely silencing the enemy weapon, thereby enabling his comrades to evacuate the stricken marine to a safe position. Succumbing to his wounds before aid could reach him, Sgt. Matthews, by his indomitable fighting spirit, courageous initiative, and resolute determination in the face of almost certain death, served to inspire all who observed him and was directly instrumental in saving the life of his wounded comrade. His great personal valor reflects the highest credit upon himself and enhances the finest traditions of the U.S. Naval Service. He gallantly gave his life for his country.

*MAUSERT, FREDERICK W., III

Rank and organization: Sergeant, U.S. Marine Corps, Company B, 1st Battalion, 7th Marines, 1st Marine Division (Rein.) *Place and date:* Songnap-yong, Korea, 12 September 1951. *Entered service at:* Dresher, Pa. *Born:* 2 May 1930, Cambridge, N.Y. *Citation:* For conspicuous gallantry and intrepidity at the risk of his life above and beyond the call of duty while serving as a squad leader in Company B, in action against enemy aggressor forces. With his company pinned down and suffering heavy casualties under murderous machinegun, rifle, artillery, and mortar fire laid down from heavily fortified, deeply entrenched hostile strongholds on Hill 673, Sgt. Mausert unhesitatingly left his covered position and ran through a heavily mined and fire-swept area to bring back 2 critically wounded men to the comparative safety of the lines. Staunchly refusing evacuation despite a painful head wound sustained during his voluntary act, he insisted on remaining with his squad and, with his platoon ordered into the assault moments later, took the point position and led his men in a furious bayonet charge against the first of a literally impregnable series of bunkers. Stunned and knocked to the ground when another bullet struck his helmet, he regained his feet and resumed his drive, personally silencing the machinegun and leading his men in eliminating several other emplacements in the area. Promptly reorganizing his unit for a renewed fight to the final objective on top of the ridge, Sgt. Mausert boldly left his position when the enemy's fire gained momentum and, making a target of himself, boldy advanced alone into the face of the machinegun, drawing the fire away from his men and enabling them to move into position to assault. Again severely wounded when the enemy's fire found its mark, he still refused aid and continued spearheading the assault to the topmost machinegun nest and bunkers, the last bulwark of the fanatic aggressors. Leaping into the wall of fire, he destroyed another machinegun with grenades before he was mortally wounded by bursting grenades and machinegun fire. Stouthearted and indomitable, Sgt. Mausert, by his fortitude, great personal valor, and extraordinary heroism in the face of almost certain death, had inspired his men to sweep on, overrun and finally secure the objective. His unyielding courage throughout reflects the highest credit upon himself and the U.S. Naval Service. He gallantly gave his life for his country.

*McGOVERN, ROBERT M.

Rank and organization: First Lieutenant, U.S. Army, Company A, 5th Cavalry Regiment, 1st Cavalry Division. *Place and date:* Near Kamyangjan-ni, Korea, 30 January 1951. *Entered service at:* Washington, D.C. *Birth:* Washington, D.C. *G.O. No.:* 2, 8 January 1952. *Citation:* 1st Lt. McGovern, a member of Company A, distinguished himself by conspicuous gallantry and intrepidity at the risk of life above and beyond the call of duty in action against an armed enemy of the United Nations. As 1st Lt. McGovern led his platoon up a slope to engage hostile troops emplaced in bunker-type pillboxes with connecting trenches, the unit came under heavy machinegun and rifle fire from the crest of the hill, approximately 75 yards distant. Despite a wound sustained in this initial burst of withering fire, 1st Lt. McGovern, assured the men of his ability to continue on and urged them forward. Forging up the rocky incline, he fearlessly led the platoon to within several yards of its objective when the ruthless foe threw and rolled a vicious barrage of handgrenades on the group and halted the advance. Enemy fire increased in volume and intensity and 1st Lt. McGovern, realizing that casualties were rapidly increasing and the morale of his men badly shaken, hurled back several grenades before they exploded. Then, disregarding his painful wound and weakened condition, he charged a machinegun emplacement which was raking his position with flanking fire. When he was within 10 yards of the position a burst of fire ripped the carbine from his hands, but, undaunted, he continued his lone-man assault and, firing his pistol and throwing grenades, killed 7 hostile soldiers before falling mortally wounded in front of the gun he had silenced. 1st Lt. McGovern's incredible display of valor imbued his men with indomitable resolution to avenge his death. Fixing bayonets and throwing grenades, they charged with such ferocity that hostile positions were overrun and the enemy routed from the hill. The inspirational leadership, unflinching courage, and intrepid actions of 1st Lt. McGovern reflected utmost glory on himself and the honored tradition of the military services.

McLAUGHLIN, ALFORD L.

Rank and organization: Private First Class, U.S. Marine Corps, Company L, 3d Battalion, 5th Marines, 1st Marine Division (Rein.) *Place and date:* Korea, 4 and 5 September 1952. *Entered service at:* Leeds, Ala. *Born:* 18 March 1928, Leeds, Ala. *Citation:* For conspicuous gallantry and intrepidity at the risk of his life above and beyond the call of duty while serving as a machine gunner of Company L, in action against enemy aggressor forces on the night of 4–5 September 1952. Volunteering for his second continuous tour of duty on a strategic combat outpost far in advance of the main line of resistance, Pfc. McLaughlin, although operating under a barrage of enemy artillery and mortar fire, set up plans for the defense of his position which proved decisive in the successful defense of the outpost. When hostile forces attacked in battalion strength during the night, he maintained a constant flow of devastating fire upon the enemy, alternately employing 2 machineguns, a carbine, and handgrenades. Although painfully wounded, he bravely fired the machineguns from the hip until his hands became blistered by the extreme heat from the weapons and, placing the guns on the ground to allow them to cool, continued to defend the position with his carbine and grenades. Standing up in full view, he shouted words of encouragement to his comrades above the din of battle and, throughout a series of fanatical enemy attacks, sprayed the surrounding area with deadly fire, accounting for an estimated 150 enemy dead and 50 wounded. By his indomitable courage, superb leadership, and valiant fighting spirit in the face of overwhelming odds, Pfc. McLaughlin served to inspire his fellow marines in their gallant stand against the enemy and was directly instrumental in preventing the vital outpost from falling into the hands of a determined and numerically superior hostile force. His outstanding heroism and unwavering devotion to duty reflect the highest credit upon himself and enhance the finest traditions of the U.S. Naval Service.

*MENDONCA, LEROY A.

Rank and organization: Sergeant, U.S. Army, Company B, 7th Infantry Regiment, 3d Infantry Division. *Place and date:* Near Chich-on, Korea, 4 July 1951. *Entered service at:* Honolulu, T.H. *Birth:* Honolulu, T.H. *G.O. No.:* 83, 3 September 1952. *Citation:* Sgt. LeRoy A. Mendonca, distinguished himself by conspicuous gallantry above and beyond the call of duty in action against the enemy. After his platoon, in an exhaustive fight, had captured Hill 586, the newly won positions were assaulted during the night by a numerically superior enemy force. When the 1st Platoon positions were outflanked and under great pressure and the platoon was ordered to withdraw to a secondary line of defense, Sgt. Mendonca voluntarily remained in an exposed position and covered the platoon's withdrawal. Although under murderous enemy fire, he fired his weapon and hurled grenades at the onrushing enemy until his supply of ammunition was exhausted. He fought on, clubbing with his rifle and using his bayonet until he was mortally wounded. After the action it was estimated that Sgt. Mendonca had accounted for 37 enemy casualties. His daring actions stalled the crushing assault, protecting the platoon's withdrawal to secondary positions, and enabling the entire unit to repel the enemy attack and retain possession of the vital hilltop position. Sgt. Mendonca's extraordinary gallantry and exemplary valor are in keeping with the highest traditions of the U.S. Army.

MILLETT, LEWIS L.

Rank and organization: Captain, U.S. Army, Company E, 27th Infantry Regiment. *Place and date:* Vicinity of Soam-Ni, Korea, 7 February 1951. *Entered service at:* Mechanic Falls, Maine. *Born:* 15 December 1920, Mechanic Falls, Maine. *G.O. No.:* 69, 2 August 1951. *Citation:* Capt. Millett, Company E, distinguished himself by conspicuous gallantry and intrepidity above and beyond the call of duty in action. While personally leading his company in an attack against a strongly held position he noted that the 1st Platoon was pinned down by small-arms, automatic, and antitank fire. Capt. Millett ordered the 3d Platoon forward, placed himself at the head of the 2 platoons, and, with fixed bayonet, led the assault up the fire-swept hill. In the fierce charge Capt. Millett bayoneted 2 enemy soldiers and boldly continued on, throwing grenades, clubbing and bayoneting the enemy, while urging his men forward by shouting encouragement. Despite vicious opposing fire, the whirlwind hand-to-hand assault carried to the crest of the hill. His dauntless leadership and personal courage so inspired his men that they stormed into the hostile position and used their bayonets with such lethal effect that the enemy fled in wild disorder. During this fierce onslaught Capt. Millett was wounded by grenade fragments but refused evacuation until the objective was taken and firmly secured. The superb leadership, conspicuous courage, and consummate devotion to duty demonstrated by Capt. Millett were directly responsible for the successful accomplishment of a hazardous mission and reflect the highest credit on himself and the heroic traditions of the military service.

*MITCHELL, FRANK N.

Rank and organization: First Lieutenant, U.S. Marine Corps, Company A, 1st Battalion, 7th Marines, 1st Marine Division (Rein). *Place and date:* Near Hansan-ni, Korea, 26 November 1950. *Entered service at:* Roaring Springs, Tex. *Born:* 18 August 1921, Indian Gap, Tex. *Citation:* For conspicuous gallantry and intrepidity at the risk of his life above and beyond the call of duty as leader of a rifle platoon of Company A, in action against enemy aggressor forces. Leading his platoon in point position during a patrol by his company through a thickly wooded and snow-covered area in the vicinity of Hansan-ni, 1st Lt. Mitchell acted immediately when the enemy suddenly opened fire at pointblank range, pinning down his forward elements and inflicting numerous casualties in his ranks. Boldly dashing to the front under blistering fire from automatic weapons and small arms, he seized an automatic rifle from one of the wounded men and effectively trained it against the attackers and, when his ammunition was expended, picked up and hurled grenades with deadly accuracy, at the same time directing and encouraging his men in driving the outnumbering enemy from his position. Maneuvering to set up a defense when the enemy furiously counterattacked to the front and left flank, 1st Lt. Mitchell, despite wounds sustained early in the action, reorganized his platoon under the devastating fire, and spearheaded a fierce hand-to-hand struggle to repulse the onslaught. Asking for volunteers to assist in searching for and evacuating the wounded, he personally led a party of litter bearers through the hostile lines in growing darkness and, although suffering intense pain from multiple wounds, stormed ahead and waged a singlehanded battle against the enemy, successfully covering the withdrawal of his men before he was fatally struck down by a burst of small-arms fire. Stouthearted and indomitable in the face of tremendous odds, 1st Lt. Mitchell, by his fortitude, great personal valor and extraordinary heroism, saved the lives of several marines and inflicted heavy casualties among the aggressors. His unyielding courage throughout reflects the highest credit upon himself and the U.S. Naval Service. He gallantly gave his life for his country.

MIYAMURA, HIROSHI H.

Rank and organization: Corporal, U.S. Army, Company H, 7th Infantry Regiment, 3rd Infantry Division. *Place and date:* Near Taejon-ni, Korea, 24 and 25 April 1951. *Entered service at:* Gallup, N. Mex. *Birth:* Gallup, N. Mex. *G.O. No.:* 85, 4 November 1953. *Citation:* Cpl. Miyamura, a member of Company H, distinguished himself by conspicuous gallantry and intrepidity above and beyond the call of duty in action against the enemy. On the night of 24 April, Company H was occupying a defensive position when the enemy fanatically attacked threatening to overrun the position. Cpl. Miyamura, a machinegun

218

squad leader, aware of the imminent danger to his men unhesitatingly
jumped from his shelter wielding his bayonet in close hand-to-hand
combat killing approximately 10 of the enemy. Returning to his position, he administered first aid to the wounded and directed their
evacuation. As another savage assault hit the line, he manned his
machinegun and delivered withering fire until his ammunition was expended. He ordered the squad to withdraw while he stayed behind to
render the gun inoperative. He then bayoneted his way through infiltrated enemy soldiers to a second gun emplacement and assisted in its
operation. When the intensity of the attack necessitated the withdrawal
of the company Cpl. Miyamura ordered his men to fall back while he
remained to cover their movement. He killed more than 50 of the
enemy before his ammunition was depleted and he was severely
wounded. He maintained his magnificent stand despite his painful
wounds, continuing to repel the attack until his position was overrun.
When last seen he was fighting ferociously against an overwhelming
number of enemy soldiers. Cpl. Miyamura's indomitable heroism and
consummate devotion to duty reflect the utmost glory on himself and
uphold the illustrious traditions on the military service.

MIZE, OLA L.

Rank and organization: Master Sergeant (then Sgt.), U.S. Army,
Company K, 15th Infantry Regiment, 3d Infantry Division. *Place and
date:* Near Surang-ni, Korea, 10 to 11 June 1953. *Entered service at:*
Gadsden, Ala. *Born:* 28 August 1931, Marshall County, Ala. *G.O. No.:*
70, 24 September 1954. *Citation:* M/Sgt. Mize, a member of Company
K, distinguished himself by conspicuous gallantry and outstanding courage above and beyond the call of duty in action against the enemy.
Company K was committed to the defense of "Outpost Harry", a
strategically valuable position, when the enemy launched a heavy attack. Learning that a comrade on a friendly listening post had been
wounded he moved through the intense barrage, accompanied by a
medical aid man, and rescued the wounded soldier. On returning to
the main position he established an effective defense system and inflicted heavy casualties against attacks from determined enemy assault
forces which had penetrated into trenches within the outpost area.
During his fearless actions he was blown down by artillery and grenade
blasts 3 times but each time he dauntlessly returned to his position,
tenaciously fighting and successfully repelling hostile attacks. When
enemy onslaughts ceased he took his few men and moved from bunker
to bunker, firing through apertures and throwing grenades at the foe,
neutralizing their positions. When an enemy soldier stepped out behind
a comrade, prepared to fire, M/Sgt. Mize killed him, saving the life of
his fellow soldier. After rejoining the platoon, moving from man to
man, distributing ammunition, and shouting words of encouragement
he observed a friendly machinegun position overrun. He immediately
fought his way to the position, killing 10 of the enemy and dispersing
the remainder. Fighting back to the command post, and finding several
friendly wounded there, he took a position to protect them. Later,
securing a radio, he directed friendly artillery fire upon the attacking
enemy's routes of approach. At dawn he helped regroup for a counterattack which successfully drove the enemy from the outpost. M/Sgt.

Mize's valorous conduct and unflinching courage reflect lasting glory upon himself and uphold the noble traditions of the military service.

*MONEGAN, WALTER C., JR.

Rank and organization: Private First Class, U.S. Marine Corps, Company F, 2d Battalion, 1st Marines, 1st Marine Division (Rein). *Place and date:* Near Sosa-ri, Korea, 17 and 20 September 1950. *Entered service at:* Seattle, Wash. *Born:* 25 December 1930, Melrose, Mass. *Citation:* For conspicuous gallantry and intrepidity at the risk of his life above and beyond the call of duty while serving as a rocket gunner attached to Company F, and in action against enemy aggressor forces. Dug in on a hill overlooking the main Seoul highway when 6 enemy tanks threatened to break through the battalion position during a predawn attack on 17 September, Pfc. Monegan promptly moved forward with his bazooka, under heavy hostile automatic weapons fire and engaged the lead tank at a range of less than 50 yards. After scoring a direct hit and killing the sole surviving tankman with his carbine as he came through the escape hatch, he boldly fired 2 more rounds of ammunition at the oncoming tanks, disorganizing the attack and enabling our tank crews to continue blasting with their 90-mm guns. With his own and an adjacent company's position threatened by annihilation when an overwhelming enemy tank-infantry force bypassed the area and proceeded toward the battalion command post during the early morning of September 20, he seized his rocket launcher and, in total darkness, charged down the slope of the hill where the tanks had broken through. Quick to act when an illuminating shell lit the area, he scored a direct hit on one of the tanks as hostile rifle and automatic-weapons fire raked the area at close range. Again exposing himself, he fired another round to destroy a second tank and, as the rear tank turned to retreat, stood upright to fire and was fatally struck down by hostile machinegun fire when another illuminating shell silhouetted him against the sky. Pfc. Monegan's daring initiative, gallant fighting spirit and courageous devotion to duty were contributing factors in the success of his company in repelling the enemy, and his self-sacrificing efforts throughout sustain and enhance the highest traditions of the U.S. Naval Service. He gallantly gave his life for his country.

*MORELAND, WHITT L.

Rank and organization: Private First Class, U.S. Marine Corps Reserve, Company C, 1st Battalion, 5th Marines, 1st Marine Division (Rein). *Place and date:* Kwagch'i-Dong, Korea, 29 May 1951. *Entered service at:* Austin, Tex. *Born:* 7 March 1930, Waco, Tex. *Citation:* For conspicuous gallantry and intrepidity at the risk of his life above and beyond the call of duty while serving as an intelligence scout attached to Company C, in action against enemy aggressor forces. Voluntarily accompanying a rifle platoon in a daring assault against a strongly defended enemy hill position, Pfc. Moreland delivered accurate rifle fire on the hostile emplacement and thereby aided materially in seizing the objective. After the position had been secured, he unhesitatingly led a party forward to neutralize an enemy bunker which he had observed some 400 meters beyond, and moving boldly through a fire-swept area, almost reached the hostile emplacement when the enemy launched a volley of handgrenades on his group. Quick to act despite the personal danger involved, he kicked several of the grenades off the ridge line where they exploded harmlessly and, while attempting to kick away another, slipped and fell near the deadly missile. Aware that the sputtering grenade would explode before he could regain his feet and dispose of it, he shouted a warning to his comrades, covered the missile with his body and absorbed the full blast of the explosion, but in saving his companions from possible injury or death, was mortally wounded. His heroic initiative and valiant spirit of self-sacrifice in the face of certain death reflect the highest credit upon Pfc. Moreland and the U.S. Naval Service. He gallantly gave his life for his country.

*MOYER, DONALD R.

Rank and organization: Sergeant First Class, U.S. Army, Company E, 35th Infantry Regiment. *Place and date:* Near Seoul, Korea, 20 May 1951. *Entered service at:* Keego Harbor, Oakland, Mich. *Born:* 15 April 1930, Pontiac, Mich. *G.O. No.:* 19, 1 February 1952. *Citation:* Sfc. Moyer assistant platoon leader, Company E, distinguished himself by conspicuous gallantry and intrepidity at the risk of his life above and beyond the call of duty in action against an armed enemy of the United Nations. Sfc. Moyer's platoon was committed to attack and secure commanding terrain stubbornly defended by a numerically superior hostile force emplaced in well-fortified positions. Advancing up the rocky hill, the leading elements came under intense automatic-weapons, small-arms, and grenade fire, wounding the platoon leader and platoon sergeant. Sfc. Moyer, realizing the success of the mission was imperiled, rushed to the head of the faltering column, assumed command and urged the men forward. Inspired by Sfc. Moyer's unflinching courage, the troops responded magnificently, but as they reached the final approaches to the rugged crest of the hill, enemy fire increased in volume and intensity and the fanatical foe showered the platoon with grenades. Undaunted, the valiant group forged ahead, and as they neared the top of the hill, the enemy hurled a grenade into their midst. Sfc. Moyer, fully aware of the odds against him, unhesitatingly threw himself on the grenade, absorbing the full blast of the explosion with his body. Although mortally wounded in this fearless display of valor, Sfc. Moyer's intrepid act saved several of his comrades from death or serious injury, and his inspirational leadership and consummate devotion to duty contributed significantly to the subsequent seizure of the enemy stronghold and reflect lasting glory on himself and the noble traditions of the military service.

MURPHY, RAYMOND G.

Rank and organization: Second Lieutenant, U.S. Marine Corps Reserve, Company A, 1st Battalion, 5th Marines, 1st Marine Division (Rein). *Place and date:* Korea, 3 February 1953. *Entered service at:* Pueblo, Colo. *Born:* 14 January 1930, Pueblo, Colo. *Citation:* For conspicuous gallantry and intrepidity at the risk of his life above and beyond the call of duty as a platoon commander of Company A, in action against enemy aggressor forces. Although painfully wounded by fragments from an enemy mortar shell while leading his evacuation platoon in support of assault units attacking a cleverly concealed and well-entrenched hostile force occupying commanding ground, 2d Lt. Murphy steadfastly refused medical aid and continued to lead his men up a hill through a withering barrage of hostile mortar and small-arms fire, skillfully maneuvering his force from one position to the next and shouting words of encouragement. Undeterred by the increasing intense enemy fire, he immediately located casualties as they fell and made several trips up and down the fire-swept hill to direct evacuation teams to the wounded, personally carrying many of the stricken marines to safety. When reinforcements were needed by the assaulting elements, 2d Lt. Murphy employed part of his unit as support and, during the ensuing battle, personally killed 2 of the enemy with his pistol. With all the wounded evacuated and the assaulting units beginning to disengage, he remained behind with a carbine to cover the movement of friendly forces off the hill and, though suffering intense pain from his previous wounds, seized an automatic rifle to provide more firepower when the enemy reappeared in the trenches. After reaching the base of the hill, he organized a search party and again ascended the slope for a final check on missing marines, locating and carrying the bodies of a machinegun crew back down the hill. Wounded a second time while conducting the entire force to the line of departure through a continuing barrage of enemy small-arms, artillery, and mortar fire, he again refused medical assistance until assured that every one of his men, including all casualties, had preceded him to the main lines. His resolute and inspiring leadership, exceptional fortitude, and great personal valor reflect the highest credit upon 2d Lt. Murphy and enhance the finest traditions of the U.S. Naval Service.

MYERS, REGINALD R.

Rank and organization: Major, U.S. Marine Corps, 3d Battalion, 1st Marines, 1st Marine Division, (Rein). *Place and date:* Near Hagaru-ri, Korea, 29 November 1950. *Entered service at:* Boise, Idaho. *Born:* 26 November 1919, Boise, Idaho. *Citation:* For conspicuous gallantry and intrepidity at the risk of his life above and beyond the call of duty as executive officer of the 3d Battalion, in action against enemy aggressor forces. Assuming command of a composite unit of Army and Marine service and headquarters elements totaling approximately 250 men, during a critical stage in the vital defense of the strategically important military base at Hagaru-ri, Maj. Myers immediately initiated a determined and aggressive counterattack against a well-entrenched and cleverly concealed enemy force numbering an estimated 4,000. Severely handicapped by a lack of trained personnel and experienced leaders in his valiant efforts to regain maximum ground prior to daylight, he persisted in constantly exposing himself to intense, accurate, and sustained hostile fire in order to direct and supervise the employment of his men and to encourage and spur them on in pressing the attack. Inexorably moving forward up the steep, snow-covered slope with his depleted group in the face of apparently insurmountable odds, he concurrently directed artillery and mortar fire with superb skill and although losing 170 of his men during 14 hours of raging combat in subzero temperatures, continued to reorganize his unit and spearhead the attack which resulted in 600 enemy killed and 500 wounded. By his exceptional and valorous leadership throughout, Maj. Myers contributed directly to the success of his unit in restoring the perimeter. His resolute spirit of self-sacrifice and unfaltering devotion to duty enhance and sustain the highest traditions of the U.S. Naval Service.

*OBREGON, EUGENE ARNOLD

Rank and organization: Private First Class, U.S. Marine Corps, Company G, 3d Battalion, 5th Marines, 1st Marine Division (Rein). *Place and date:* Seoul, Korea, 26 September 1950. *Entered service at:* Los Angeles, Calif. *Born:* 12 November 1930, Los Angeles, Calif. *Citation:* For conspicuous gallantry and intrepidity at the risk of his life above and beyond the call of duty while serving with Company G, in action against enemy aggressor forces. While serving as an ammunition carrier of a machinegun squad in a marine rifle company which was temporarily pinned down by hostile fire, Pfc. Obregon observed a fellow marine fall wounded in the line of fire. Armed only with a pistol, he unhesitating dashed from his covered position to the side of the casualty. Firing his pistol with 1 hand as he ran, he grasped his comrade by the arm with his other hand and, dispite the great peril to himself dragged him to the side of the road. Still under enemy fire, he was bandaging the man's wounds when hostile troops of approximately platoon strength began advancing toward his position. Quickly seizing the wounded marine's carbine, he placed his own body as a shield in front of him and lay there firing accurately and effectively into the hostile group until he himself was fatally wounded by enemy machinegun fire. By his courageous fighting spirit, fortitude, and loyal devotion to duty, Pfc. Obregon enabled his fellow marines to rescue the wounded man and aided essentially in repelling the attack, thereby sustaining and enhancing the highest traditions of the U.S. Naval Service. He gallantly gave his life for his country.

O'BRIEN, GEORGE H., JR.

Rank and organization: Second Lieutenant, U.S. Marine Corps Reserve, Company H, 3d Battalion, 7th Marines, 1st Marine Division (Rein). *Place and date:* Korea, 27 October, 1952. *Entered service at:* Big Spring, Tex. *Born:* 10 September 1926, Fort Worth, Tex. *Citation:* For conspicuous gallantry and intrepidity at the risk of his life above and beyond the call of duty as a rifle platoon commander of Company H, in action against enemy aggressor forces. With his platoon subjected to an intense mortar and artillery bombardment while preparing to assault a vitally important hill position on the main line of resistance which had been overrun by a numerically superior enemy force on the preceding night, 2d Lt. O'Brien leaped from his trench when the attack signal was given and, shouting for his men to follow, raced across an exposed saddle and up the enemy-held hill through a virtual hail of deadly small-arms, artillery, and mortar fire. Although shot through the arm and thrown to the ground by hostile automatic-weapons fire as he neared the well-entrenched enemy position, he bravely regained his feet, waved his men onward, and continued to spearhead the assault, pausing only long enough to go to the aid of a wounded marine. Encountering the enemy at close range, he proceeded to hurl handgrenades into the bunkers and, utilizing his carbine to best advantage in savage hand-to-hand combat, succeeded in killing at least 3 of the enemy. Struck down by the concussion of grenades on 3 occasions during the subsequent action, he steadfastly refused to be evacuated for medical treatment and continued to lead his platoon in the assault for a period of nearly 4 hours, repeatedly encouraging his men and maintaining superb direction of the unit. With the attack halted, he set up a defense with his remaining forces to prepare for a counterattack, personally checking each position, attending to the wounded and expediting their evacuation. When a relief of the position was effected by another unit, he remained to cover the withdrawal and to assure that no wounded were left behind. By his exceptionally daring and forceful leadership in the face of overwhelming odds, 2d Lt. O'Brien served as a constant source of inspiration to all who observed him and was greatly instrumental in the recapture of a strategic position on the main line of resistance. His indomitable determination and valiant fighting spirit reflect the highest credit upon himself and enhance the finest traditions of the U.S. Naval Service.

*OUELLETTE, JOSEPH R.

Rank and organization: Private First Class, U.S. Army, Company H, 9th Infantry Regiment, 2d Infantry Division. *Place and date:* Near Yongsan, Korea, from 31 August to 3 September 1950. *Entered service at:* Lowell, Mass. *Birth:* Lowell, Mass. *G.O. No.:* 25, 25 April 1951. *Citation:* Pfc. Ouellette distinguished himself by conspicuous gallantry and intrepidity in action against the enemy in the Makioug-Chang River salient. When an enemy assault cut off and surrounded his unit, he voluntarily made a reconnaissance of a nearby hill under intense enemy fire to locate friendly troop positions and obtain information of the enemy's strength and location. Finding that friendly troops were not on the hill, he worked his way back to his unit under heavy fire. Later, when an airdrop of water was made outside the perimeter, he again braved enemy fire in an attempt to retrieve water for his unit. Finding the dropped cans broken and devoid of water, he returned to his unit. His heroic attempt greatly increased his comrades' morale. When ammunition and grenades ran low, Pfc. Ouellette again slipped out of the perimeter to collect these from the enemy dead. After collecting grenades he was attacked by an enemy soldier. He killed this enemy in hand-to-hand combat, gathered up the ammunition, and returned to his unit. When the enemy attacked on 3 September, they assaulted his position with grenades. On 6 occasions Pfc. Ouellette leaped from his foxhole to escape exploding grenades. In doing so, he had to face enemy small-arms fire. He continued his resistance, despite a severe wound, until he lost his life. The extraordinary heroism and intrepidity displayed by Pfc. Ouellette reflect the highest credit on himself and are in keeping with the esteemed traditions of the military service.

*PAGE, JOHN U. D.

Rank and organization: Lieutenant Colonel, U.S. Army, X Corps Artillery, while attached to the 52d Transportation Truck Battalion. *Place and date:* Near Chosin Reservoir, Korea, 29 November to 10 December 1950. *Entered service at:* St Paul, Minn. *Born:* 8 February 1904, Malahi Island, Luzon, Philippine Islands. *G.O. No.:* 21, 25 April 1957. *Citation:* Lt. Col. Page, a member of X Corps Artillery, distinguished himself by conspicuous gallantry and intrepidity in action above and beyond the call of duty in a series of exploits. On 29 November, Lt. Col. Page left X Corps Headquarters at Hamhung with the mission of establishing traffic control on the main supply route to 1st Marine Division positions and those of some Army elements on the Chosin Reservoir plateau. Having completed his mission Lt. Col. Page was free to return to the safety of Hamhung but chose to remain on the plateau to aid an isolated signal station, thus being cut off with elements of the marine division. After rescuing his jeep driver by breaking up an ambush near a destroyed bridge Lt. Col. Page reached the lines of a surrounded marine garrison at Koto-ri. He then voluntarily developed and trained a reserve force of assorted army troops trapped with the marines. By exemplary leadership and tireless devotion he made an effective tactical unit available. In order that casualties might be evacuated, an airstrip was improvised on frozen ground partly outside of the Koto-ri defense perimeter which was continually under enemy attack. During 2 such attacks, Lt. Col. Page exposed himself on the airstrip to direct fire on the enemy, and twice mounted the rear deck of a tank, manning the machinegun on the turret to drive the enemy back into a no man's land. On 3 December while being flown low over enemy lines in a light observation plane, Lt. Col. Page dropped handgrenades on Chinese positions and sprayed foxholes with automatic fire from his carbine. After 10 days of constant fighting the marine and army units in the vicinity of the Chosin Reservoir had succeeded in gathering at the edge of the plateau and Lt. Col. Page was flown to Hamhung to arrange for artillery support of the beleaguered troops attempting to break out. Again Lt. Col. Page refused an opportunity to remain in safety and returned to give every assistance to his comrades. As the column slowly moved south Lt. Col. Page joined the rear guard. When it neared the entrance to a narrow pass it came under frequent attacks on both flanks. Mounting an abandoned tank Lt. Col. Page manned the machinegun, braved heavy return fire, and covered the passing vehicles until the danger diminished. Later when another attack threatened his section of the convoy, then in the middle of the pass, Lt. Col. Page took a machinegun to the hillside and delivered effective counterfire, remaining exposed while men and vehicles passed through the ambuscade. On the night of 10 December the convoy reached the botton of the pass but was halted by a strong enemy force at the front and on both flanks. Deadly small-arms fire poured into the column. Realizing the danger to the column as it lay motionless, Lt. Col. Page fought his way to the head of the column and plunged forward into the heart of the hostile position. His intrepid action so surprised the enemy that their ranks became disordered and suffered heavy casualties. Heedless of his safety, as he had been throughout the preceding 10 days, Lt. Col. Page remained forward, fiercely engaging the enemy singlehanded until mortally wounded. By his valiant and aggressive spirit Lt. Col. Page enabled friendly forces to stand off the enemy. His outstanding courage, unswerving devotion to duty, and supreme self-sacrifice reflect great credit upon Lt. Col. Page and are in the highest tradition of the military service.

*PENDLETON, CHARLES F.

Rank and organization: Corporal. U.S. Army, Company D, 15th Infantry Regiment, 3d Infantry Division. *Place and date:* Near Choo Gung-Dong, Korea, 16 and 17 July 1953. *Entered service at:* Fort Worth, Tex. *Born:* 26 September 1931, Camden, Tenn. *Citation:* Cpl. Pendleton, a machine gunner with Company D, distinguished himself by conspicuous gallantry and indomitable courage above and beyond the call of duty in action against the enemy. After consolidating and establishing a defensive perimeter on a key terrain feature, friendly elements were attacked by a large hostile force. Cpl. Pendleton delivered deadly accurate fire into the approaching troops, killing approximately 15 and disorganizing the remainder with grenades. Unable to protect the flanks because of the narrow confines of the trench, he removed the machinegun from the tripod and, exposed to enemy observation, positioned it on his knee to improve his firing vantage. Observing a hostile infantryman jumping into the position, intent on throwing a grenade at his comrades, he whirled about and killed the attacker, then inflicted such heavy casualties on the enemy force that they retreated to regroup. After reorganizing, a second wave of hostile soldiers moved forward in an attempt to overrun the position and, later, when a hostile grenade landed nearby, Cpl. Pendleton quickly retrieved and hurled it back at the foe. Although he was burned by the hot shells ejecting from his weapon, and he was wounded by a grenade, he refused evacuation and continued to fire on the assaulting force. As enemy action increased in tempo, his machinegun was destroyed by a grenade but, undaunted, he grabbed a carbine and continued his heroic defense until mortally wounded by a mortar burst. Cpl. Pendleton's unflinching courage, gallant self-sacrifice, and consummate devotion to duty reflect lasting glory upon himself and uphold the finest traditions of the military service.

*PHILLIPS, LEE H.

Rank and organization: Corporal, U.S. Marine Corps, Company F, 2d Battalion, 7 Marines, 1st Marine Division (Rein). *Place and date:* Korea, 4 November 1950. *Entered service at:* Ben Hill, Ga. *Born:* 3 February 1930, Stockbridge, Ga. Cpl. Phillips was killed in action 27 November 1950. *Citation:* For conspicuous gallantry and intrepidity at the risk of his life above and beyond the call of duty while serving as a squad leader of Company E, in action against enemy aggressor forces. Assuming the point position in the attack against a strongly defended and well-entrenched numerically superior enemy force occupying a vital hill position which had been unsuccessfully assaulted on 5 separate occasions by units of the Marine Corps and other friendly forces, Cpl. Phillips fearlessly led his men in a bayonet charge up the precipitous slope under a deadly hail of hostile mortar, small-arms, and machinegun fire. Quickly rallying his squad when it was pinned down by a heavy and accurate mortar barrage, he continued to lead his men through the bombarded area and, although only 5 members were left in the casualty ridden unit, gained the military crest of the hill where he was immediately subjected to an enemy counterattack. Although greatly outnumbered by an estimated enemy squad, Cpl. Phillips boldly engaged the hostile force with handgrenades and rifle fire and, exhorting his gallant group of marines to follow him, stormed forward to completely overwhelm the enemy. With only 3 men now left in his squad, he proceeded to spearhead an assault on the last remaining strongpoint which was defended by 4 of the enemy on a rocky and almost inaccessible portion of the hill position. Using 1 hand to climb up the extremely hazardous precipice, he hurled grenades with the other and, with 2 remaining comrades, succeeded in annihilating the pocket of resistance and in consolidating the position. Immediately subjected to a sharp counterattack by an estimated enemy squad, he skillfully directed the fire of his men and employed his own weapon with deadly effectiveness to repulse the numerically superior hostile force. By his valiant leadership, indomitable fighting spirit and resolute determination in the face of heavy odds, Cpl. Phillips served to inspire all who observed him and was directly responsible for the destruction of the enemy stronghold. His great personal valor reflects the highest credit upon himself and enhances and sustains the finest traditions of the U.S. Naval Service.

*PILILAAU, HERBERT K.

Rank and organization: Private First Class, U.S. Army, Company C, 23d Infantry Regiment, 2nd Infantry Division. *Place and date:* Near Pia-ri, Korea, 17 September 1951. *Entered service at:* Oahu, T.H. *Born:* 10 October 1928, Waianae, Oahu, T.H. *G.O. No.:* 58, 18 June 1952. *Citation:* Pfc. Pililaau, a member of Company C, distinguished himself by conspicuous gallantry and outstanding courage above and beyond the call of duty in action against the enemy. The enemy sent wave after wave of fanatical troops against his platoon which held a key terrain feature on "Heartbreak Ridge." Valiantly defending its position, the unit repulsed each attack until ammunition became practically exhausted and it was ordered to withdraw to a new position. Voluntarily remaining behind to cover the withdrawal, Pfc. Pililaau fired his automatic weapon into the ranks of the assailants, threw all his grenades and, with ammunition exhausted, closed with the foe in hand-to-hand combat, courageously fighting with his trench knife and bare fists until finally overcome and mortally wounded. When the position was subsequently retaken, more than 40 enemy dead were counted in the area he had so valiantly defended. His heroic devotion to duty, indomitable fighting spirit, and gallant self-sacrifice reflect the highest credit upon himself, the infantry, and the U.S. Army.

PITTMAN, JOHN A.

Rank and organization: Sergeant, U.S. Army, Company C, 23d Infantry Regiment, 2d Infantry Division. *Place and date:* Near Kujang-dong, Korea, 26 November 1950. *Entered service at:* Carrolton, Miss. *Born:* 15 October 1928, Carrolton, Miss. *G.O. No.:* 39, 4 June 1951. *Citation:* Sgt. Pittman, distinguished himself by conspicuous gallantry and intrepidity above and beyond the call of duty in action against the enemy. He volunteered to lead his squad in a counterattack to regain commanding terrain lost in an earlier engagement. Moving aggressively forward in the face of intense artillery, mortar, and small-arms fire he was wounded by mortar fragments. Disregarding his wounds he continued to lead and direct his men in a bold advance against the hostile standpoint. During this daring action, an enemy grenade was thrown in the midst of his squad endangering the lives of his comrades. Without hesitation, Sgt. Pittman threw himself on the grenade and absorbed its burst with his body. When a medical aid man reached him, his first request was to be informed as to how many of his men were hurt. This intrepid and selfless act saved several of his men from death or serious injury and was an inspiration to the entire command. Sgt. Pittman's extraordinary heroism reflects the highest credit upon himself and is in keeping with the esteemed traditions of the military service.

*POMEROY, RALPH E.

Rank and organization: Private First Class, U.S. Army, Company E, 31st Infantry Regiment, 7th Infantry Division. *Place and date:* Near Kumhwa, Korea, 15 October 1952. *Entered service at:* Quinwood, W. Va. *Born:* 26 March 1930, Quinwood, W. Va. *G.O. No.:* 97, 30 December 1953. *Citation:* Pfc. Pomeroy, a machine gunner with Company E, distinguished himself by conspicuous gallantry and indomitable courage above and beyond the call of duty in action against the enemy. While his comrades were consolidating on a key terrain feature, he manned a machinegun at the end of a communication trench on the forward slope to protect the platoon flank and prevent a surprise attack. When the enemy attacked through a ravine leading directly to his firing position, he immediately opened fire on the advancing troops inflicting a heavy toll in casualties and blunting the assault. At this juncture the enemy directed intense concentrations of artillery and mortar fire on his position in an attempt to neutralize his gun. Despite withering fire and bursting shells, he maintained his heroic stand and poured crippling fire into the ranks of the hostile force until a mortar burst severely wounded him and rendered the gun mount inoperable. Quickly removing the hot, heavy weapon, he cradled it in his arms and, moving forward with grim determination, raked the attacking forces with a hail of fire. Although wounded a second time he pursued his relentless course until his ammunition was expended within 10 feet of the foe and then, using the machinegun as a club, he courageously closed with the enemy in hand-to-hand combat until mortally wounded. Pfc. Pomeroy's consummate valor, inspirational actions and supreme sacrifice enabled the platoon to contain the attack and maintain the integrity of the perimeter, reflecting lasting glory upon himself and upholding the noble traditions of the military service.

*PORTER, DONN F.

Rank and organization: Sergeant, U.S. Army, Company G, 14th Infantry Regiment, 25th Infantry Division. *Place and date:* Near Mundung-ni Korea, 7 September 1952. *Entered service at:* Baltimore, Md. *Born:* 1 March 1931, Sewickley, Pa. *G.O. No.:* 64, 18 August 1953. *Citation:* Sgt. Porter, a member of Company G, distinguished himself by conspicuous gallantry and outstanding courage above and beyond the call of duty in action against the enemy. Advancing under cover of intense mortar and artillery fire, 2 hostile platoons attacked a combat outpost commanded by Sgt. Porter, destroyed communications, and killed 2 of his 3-man crew. Gallantly maintaining his position, he poured deadly accurate fire into the ranks of the enemy, killing 15 and dispersing the remainder. After falling back under a hail of fire, the determined foe reorganized and stormed forward in an attempt to overrun the outpost. Without hesitation, Sgt. Porter jumped from his position with bayonet fixed and, meeting the onslaught and in close combat, killed 6 hostile soldiers and routed the attack. While returning to the outpost, he was killed by an artillery burst, but his courageous actions forced the enemy to break off the engagement and thwarted a surprise attack on the main line of resistance. Sgt. Porter's incredible display of valor, gallant self-sacrifice, and consummate devotion to duty reflect the highest credit upon himself and uphold the noble traditions of the military service.

*POYNTER, JAMES I.

Rank and organization: Sergeant, U.S. Marine Corps Reserve, Company A, 1st Battalion, 7th Marines, 1st Marine Division (Rein). *Place and date:* Near Sudong, Korea, 4 November 1950. *Entered service at:* Downey, Calif. *Born:* 1 December 1916, Bloomington, Ill. *Citation:* For conspicuous gallantry and intrepidity at the risk of his life above and beyond the call of duty while serving as a squad leader in a rifle platoon of Company A, in action against enemy aggressor forces during the defense of Hill 532, south of Sudong, Korea. When a vastly outnumbering, well-concealed hostile force launched a sudden, vicious counterattack against his platoon's hasty defensive position, Sgt. Poynter displayed superb skill and courage in leading his squad and directing its fire against the onrushing enemy. With his ranks critically depleted by casualties and he himself critically wounded as the onslaught gained momentum and the hostile force surrounded his position, he siezed his bayonet and engaged in bitter hand-to-hand combat as the breakthrough continued. Observing 3 machineguns closing in at a distance of 25 yards, he dashed from his position and, grasping handgrenades from fallen marines as he ran, charged the emplacements in rapid succession, killing the crews of 2 and putting the other out of action before he fell, mortally wounded. By his self-sacrificing and valiant conduct, Sgt. Poynter inspired the remaining members of his squad to heroic endeavor in bearing down upon and repelling the disorganized enemy, thereby enabling the platoon to move out of the trap to a more favorable tactical position. His indomitable fighting spirit, fortitude, and great personal valor maintained in the face of overwhelming odds sustain and enhance the finest traditions of the U.S. Naval Service. He gallantly gave his life for his country.

*RAMER, GEORGE H.

Rank and organization: Second Lieutenant, U.S. Marine Corps Reserve, Company I, 3d Battalion, 7th Marines, 1st Marine Division (Rein). *Place and date:* Korea, 12 September 1951. *Entered service at:* Lewisburg, Pa. *Born:* 27 March 1927, Meyersdale, Pa. *Citation:* For conspicuous gallantry and intrepidity at the risk of his life above and beyond the call of duty as leader of the 3d Platoon in Company I, in action against enemy aggressor forces. Ordered to attack and seize hostile positions atop a hall, vigorously defended by well-entrenched enemy forces delivering massed small-arms mortar, and machinegun fire, 2d Lt. Ramer fearlessly led his men up the steep slopes and, although he and the majority of his unit were wounded during the ascent, boldly continued to spearhead the assault. With the terrain becoming more precipitous near the summit and the climb more perilous as the hostile forces added grenades to the devastating hail of fire, he stanchly carried the attack to the top, personally annihilated 1 enemy bunker with grenade and carbine fire and captured the objective with his remaining 8 men. Unable to hold the position against an immediate, overwhelming hostile counterattack, he ordered his group to withdraw and singlehandedly fought the enemy to furnish cover for his men and for the evacuation of 3 fatally wounded marines. Severely wounded a second time, 2d Lt. Ramer refused aid when his men returned to help him and, after ordering them to seek shelter, courageously manned his post until the hostile troops overran his position and he fell mortally wounded. His indomitable fighting spirit, inspiring leadership and unselfish concern for others in the face of death, reflect the highest credit upon 2d Lt. Ramer and the U.S. Naval Service. He gallantly gave his life for his country.

*RED CLOUD, MITCHELL, JR.

Rank and organization: Corporal, U.S. Army, Company E, 19th Infantry Regiment, 24th Infantry Division. *Place and date:* Near Chonghyon, Korea, 5 November 1950. *Entered service at:* Merrilan, Wis. *Born:* 2 July 1924, Hatfield, Wis. *G.O. No.:* 26, 25 April 1951. *Citation:* Cpl. Red Cloud, Company E, distinguished himself by conspicuous gallantry and intrepidity above and beyond the call of duty in action against the enemy. From his position on the point of a ridge immediately in front of the company command post he was the first to detect the approach of the Chinese Communist forces and give the alarm as the enemy charged from a brush-covered area less than 100 feet from him. Springing up he delivered devastating pointblank automatic rifle fire into the advancing enemy. His accurate and intense fire checked this assault and gained time for the company to consolidate its defense. With utter fearlessness he maintained his firing position until severely wounded by enemy fire. Refusing assistance he pulled himself to his feet and wrapping his arm around a tree continued his deadly fire again, until he was fatally wounded. This heroic act stopped the enemy from overrunning his company's position and gained time for reorganization and evacuation of the wounded. Cpl. Red Cloud's dauntless courage and gallant self-sacrifice reflects the highest credit upon himself and upholds the esteemed traditions of the U.S. Army.

*REEM, ROBERT DALE

Rank and organization: Second Lieutenant, U.S. Marine Corps, Company H, 3d Battalion, 7th Marines, 1st Marine Division (Rein). *Place and date:* Vicinity Chinhung-ni, Korea, 6 November 1950. *Entered service at:* Elizabethtown, Pa. *Born:* 20 October 1925, Lancaster, Pa. *Citation:* For conspicuous gallantry and intrepidity at the risk of his life above and beyond the call of duty as a platoon commander in

Company H, in action against enemy aggressor forces. Grimly determined to dislodge a group of heavy enemy infantry units occupying well-concealed and strongly fortified positions on commanding ground overlooking unprotected terrain. 2d Lt. Reem moved slowly forward up the side of the ridge with his platoon in the face of a veritable hail of shattering hostile machinegun, grenade, and rifle fire. Three times repulsed by a resolute enemy force in achieving his objective, and pinned down by the continuing fury of hostile fire, he rallied and regrouped the heroic men in his depleted and disorganized platoon in preparation for a fourth attack. Issuing last-minute orders to his non-commissioned officers when an enemy grenade landed in a depression of the rocky ground in which the group was standing, 2d Lt. Reem unhesitatingly chose to sacrifice himself and, springing upon the deadly missile, absorbed the full impact of the explosion in his body, thus protecting others from serious injury and possible death. Stouthearted and indomitable, he readily yielded his own chance of survival that his subordinate leaders might live to carry on the fight against a fanatic enemy. His superb courage, cool decisiveness, and valiant spirit of self-sacrifice in the face of certain death reflect the highest credit upon 2d Lt. Reem and the U.S. Naval Service. He gallantly gave his life for his country.

RODRIGUEZ, JOSEPH C.

Rank and organization: Sergeant (then Pfc.), U.S. Army, Company F, 17th Infantry Regiment, 7th Infantry Division. *Place and date:* Near Munye-ri, Korea, 21 May 1951. *Entered service at:* California. *Born:* 14 November 1928, San Bernardino, Calif. *G.O. No.:* 22, 5 February 1952. *Citation:* Sgt. Rodriguez, distinguished himself by conspicuous gallantry and intrepidity at the risk of his life above and beyond the call of duty in action against an armed enemy of the United Nations. Sgt. Rodriguez, an assistant squad leader of the 2d Platoon, was participating in an attack against a fanatical hostile force occupying well-fortified positions on rugged commanding terrain, when his squad's advance was halted within approximately 60 yards by a withering barrage of automatic weapons and small-arms fire from 5 emplacements directly to the front and right and left flanks, together with grenades which the enemy rolled down the hill toward the advancing troops. Fully aware of the odds against him, Sgt. Rodriguez leaped to his feet, dashed 60 yards up the fire-swept slope, and, after lobbing grenades into the first foxhole with deadly accuracy, ran around the left flank, silenced an automatic weapon with 2 grenades and continued his whirlwind assault to the top of the peak, wiping out 2 more foxholes and then, reaching the right flank, he tossed grenades into the remaining emplacement, destroying the gun and annihilating its crew. Sgt. Rodriguez' intrepid actions exacted a toll of 15 enemy dead and, as a result of his incredible display of valor, the defense of the opposition was broken, and the enemy routed, and the strategic strongpoint secured. His unflinching courage under fire and inspirational devotion to duty reflect highest credit on himself and uphold the honored traditions of the military service.

ROSSER, RONALD E.

Rank and organization: Corporal, U.S. Army, Heavy Mortar Company, 38th Infantry Regiment, 2d Infantry Division. *Place and date:* Vicinity of Ponggilli, Korea, 12 January 1952. *Entered service at:* Crooksville, Ohio. *Born:* 24 October 1929, Columbus, Ohio. *G.O. No.:* 67, 7 July 1952. *Citation:* Cpl. Rosser, distinguished himself by conspicuous gallantry above and beyond the call of duty. While assaulting heavily fortified enemy hill positions, Company L, 38th Infantry Regiment, was stopped by fierce automatic-weapons, small-arms, artillery, and mortar fire. Cpl. Rosser, a forward observer was with the lead platoon of Company L, when it came under fire from 2 directions. Cpl. Rosser turned his radio over to his assistant and, disregarding the enemy fire, charged the enemy positions armed with only carbine and a grenade. At the first bunker, he silenced its occupants with a burst from his weapon. Gaining the top of the hill, he killed 2 enemy soldiers, and then went down the trench, killing 5 more as he advanced. He then hurled his grenade into a bunker and shot 2 other soldiers as they emerged. Having exhausted his ammunition, he returned through the enemy fire to obtain more ammunition and grenades and charged the hill once more. Calling on others to follow him, he assaulted 2 more enemy bunkers. Although those who attempted to join him became casualties, Cpl. Rosser once again exhausted his ammunition, obtained a new supply, and returning to the hilltop a third time hurled grenades into the enemy positions. During this heroic action Cpl. Rosser singlehandedly killed at least 13 of the enemy. After exhausting his ammunition he accompanied the withdrawing platoon, and though himself wounded, made several trips across open terrain still under enemy fire to help remove other men injured more seriously than himself. This outstanding soldier's courageous and selfless devotion to duty is worthy of emulation by all men. He has contributed magnificently to the high traditions of the military service.

*SCHOONOVER, DAN D.

Rank and organization: Corporal, U.S. Army, Company A, 13th Engineer Combat Battalion, 7th Infantry Division. *Place and date:* Near Sokkogae, Korea, 8 to 10 July 1953. *Entered service at:* Boise, Idaho. *Born:* 8 October 1933, Boise, Idaho. *G.O. No.:* 5, 14 January 1955. *Citation:* Cpl. Schoonover, distinguished himself by conspicuous gallantry and outstanding courage above and beyond the call of duty in action against the enemy. He was in charge of an engineer demolition squad attached to an infantry company which was committed to dislodge the enemy from a vital hill. Realizing that the heavy fighting and intense enemy fire made it impossible to carry out his mission, he voluntarily employed his unit as a rifle squad and, forging up the steep barren slope, participated in the assault on hostile positions. When an artillery round exploded on the roof of an enemy bunker, he courageously ran forward and leaped into the position, killing 1 hostile infantryman and taking another prisoner. Later in the action, when friendly forces were pinned down by vicious fire from another enemy bunker, he dashed through the hail of fire, hurled grenades in the nearest aperture, then ran to the doorway and emptied his pistol,

232

killing the remainder of the enemy. His brave action neutralized the position and enabled friendly troops to continue their advance to the crest of the hill. When the enemy counterattacked he constantly exposed himself to the heavy bombardment to direct the fire of his men and to call in an effective artillery barrage on hostile forces. Although the company was relieved early the following morning, he voluntarily remained in the area, manned a machinegun for several hours, and subsequently joined another assault on enemy emplacements. When last seen he was operating an automatic rifle with devastating effect until mortally wounded by artillery fire. Cpl. Schoonover's heroic leadership during 2 days of heavy fighting, superb personal bravery, and willing self-sacrifice inspired his comrades and saved many lives, reflecting lasting glory upon himself and upholding the honored traditions of the military service.

SCHOWALTER, EDWARD R., Jr.

Rank and organization: First Lieutenant, U.S. Army, Company A, 31st Infantry Regiment, 7th Infantry Division. *Place and date:* Near Kumhwa, Korea, 14 October 1952. *Entered service at:* Metairie, La. *Born:* 24 December 1927, New Orleans, La. *G.O. No.:* 6, 28 January 1954. *Citation:* 1st Lt. Schowalter, commanding, Company A, distinguished himself by conspicuous gallantry and indomitable courage above and beyond the call of duty in action against the enemy. Committed to attack and occupy a key-approach to the primary objective, the 1st Platoon of his company came under heavy vicious small-arms, grenade, and mortar fire within 50 yards of the enemy-held strongpoint, halting the advance and inflicting several casualties. The 2d Platoon moved up in support at this juncture, and although wounded, 1st Lt. Schowalter continued to spearhead the assault. Nearing the objective he was severely wounded by a grenade fragment but, refusing medical aid, he led his men into the trenches and began routing the enemy from the bunkers with grenades. Suddenly from a burst of fire from a hidden cove off the trench he was again wounded. Although suffering from his wounds, he refused to relinquish command and continued issuing orders and encouraging his men until the commanding ground was secured and then he was evacuated. 1st Lt. Schowalter's unflinching courage, extraordinary heroism, and inspirational leadership reflect the highest credit upon himself and are in keeping with the highest traditions of the military service.

*SEBILLE, LOUIS J.

Rank and organization: Major, U.S. Air Force, 67th Fighter-Bomber Squadron, 18th Fighter-Bomber Group, 5th Air Force. *Place and date:* Near Hanchang, Korea, 5 August 1950. *Entered service at:* Chicago, Ill. *Born:* 21 November 1915, Harbor Beach, Mich. *Citation:* Maj. Sebille, distinguished himself by conspicuous gallantry and intrepidity at the risk of his life above and beyond the call of duty. During an attack on a camouflaged area containing a concentration of enemy troops, artillery, and armored vehicles, Maj. Sebille's F-51 aircraft was severely damaged by antiaircraft fire. Although fully cognizant of the short period he could remain airborne, he deliberately ignored the possibility of survival by abandoning the aircraft or by crash landing, and continued his attack against the enemy forces threatening the security of friendly ground troops. In his determination to inflict maximum damage upon the enemy, Maj. Sebille again exposed himself to the intense fire of enemy gun batteries and dived on the target to his death. The superior leadership, daring, and selfless devotion to duty which he displayed in the execution of an extremely dangerous mission were an inspiration to both his subordinates and superiors and reflect the highest credit upon himself, the U.S. Air Force, and the armed forces of the United Nations.

*SHEA, RICHARD T., JR.

Rank and organization: First Lieutenant, U.S. Army, Company A, 17th Infantry Regiment, 7th Infantry Division. *Place and date:* Near Sokkogae, Korea, 6 to 8 July 1953. *Entered service at:* Portsmouth, Va. *Born:* 3 January 1927, Portsmouth, Va. *G.O. No.:* 38, 8 June 1955. *Citation:* 1st Lt. Shea, executive officer, Company A, distinguished himself by conspicuous gallantry and indomitable courage above and beyond the call of duty in action against the enemy. On the night of 6 July, he was supervising the reinforcement of defensive positions when the enemy attacked with great numerical superiority. Voluntarily proceeding to the area most threatened, he organized and led a counterattack and, in the bitter fighting which ensued, closed with and killed 2 hostile soldiers with his trench knife. Calmly moving among the men, checking positions, steadying and urging the troops to hold firm, he fought side by side with them throughout the night. Despite heavy losses, the hostile force pressed the assault with determination, and at dawn made an all-out attempt to overrun friendly elements. Charging forward to meet the challenge, 1st Lt. Shea and his gallant men drove back the hostile troops. Elements of Company G joined the defense on the afternoon of 7 July, having lost key personnel through casualties. Immediately integrating these troops into his unit, 1st Lt. Shea rallied a group of 20 men and again charged the enemy. Although wounded in this action, he refused evacuation and continued to lead the counterattack. When the assaulting element was pinned down by heavy machinegun fire, he personally rushed the emplacement and, firing his carbine and lobbing grenades with deadly accuracy, neutralized the weapon and killed 3 of the enemy. With forceful leadership and by his heroic example, 1st Lt. Shea coordinated and directed a holding action throughout the night and the following morning. On 8 July, the enemy attacked again. Despite additional wounds, he launched a determined counterattack and was last seen in close hand-to-hand combat with the enemy. 1st Lt. Shea's inspirational leadership and unflinching courage set an illustrious example of valor to the men of his regiment, reflecting lasting glory upon himself and upholding the noble traditions of the military service.

*SHUCK, WILLIAM E., JR.

Rank and organization: Staff Sergeant, U.S. Marine Corps, Company G, 3d Battalion, 7th Marines, 1st Marine Division (Rein). *Place and date:* Korea, 3 July 1952. *Entered service at:* Cumberland, Md. *Born:* 16 August 1926, Cumberland, Md. *Citation:* For conspicuous gallantry and intrepidity at the risk of his life above and beyond the call of duty

234

while serving as a squad leader of Company G, in action against enemy aggressor forces. When his platoon was subjected to a devastating barrage of enemy small-arms, grenade, artillery, and mortar fire during an assault against strongly fortified hill positions well forward of the main line of resistance, S/Sgt. Shuck, although painfully wounded, refused medical attention and continued to lead his machinegun squad in the attack. Unhesitatingly assuming command of a rifle squad when the leader became a casualty, he skillfully organized the 2 squads into an attacking force and led 2 more daring assaults upon the hostile positions. Wounded a second time, he steadfastly refused evacuation and remained in the foremost position under heavy fire until assured that all dead and wounded were evacuated. Mortally wounded by an enemy sniper bullet while voluntarily assisting in the removal of the last casualty, S/Sgt. Shuck, by his fortitude and great personal valor in the face of overwhelming odds, served to inspire all who observed him. His unyielding courage throughout reflects the highest credit upon himself and the U.S. Naval Service. He gallantly gave his life for his country.

SIMANEK, ROBERT E.

Rank and organization: Private First Class, U.S. Marine Corps, Company F, 2d Battalion, 5th Marines, 1st Marine Division (Rein). *Place and date:* Korea, 17 August 1952. *Entered service at:* Detroit, Mich. *Born:* 26 April 1930, Detroit, Mich. *Citation:* For conspicuous gallantry and intrepidity at the risk of his life above and beyond the call of duty while serving with Company F, in action against enemy aggressor forces. While accompanying a patrol en route to occupy a combat outpost forward of friendly lines, Pfc. Simanek exhibited a high degree of courage and a resolute spirit of self-sacrifice in protecting the lives of his fellow marines. With his unit ambushed by an intense concentration of enemy mortar and small-arms fire, and suffering heavy casualties, he was forced to seek cover with the remaining members of the patrol in a nearby trench line. Determined to save his comrades when a hostile grenade was hurled into their midst, he unhesitatingly threw himself on the deadly missile absorbing the shattering violence of the exploding charge in his body and shielding his fellow marines from serious injury or death. Gravely wounded as a result of his heroic action, Pfc. Simanek, by his daring initiative and great personal valor in the face of almost certain death, served to inspire all who observed him and upheld the highest traditions of the U.S. Naval Service.

*SITMAN, WILLIAM S.

Rank and organization: Sergeant First Class, U.S. Army, Company M, 23d Infantry Regiment, 2d Infantry Division. *Place and date:* Near Chipyong-ni, Korea, 14 February 1951. *Entered service at:* Bellwood, Pa. *Birth:* Bellwood, Pa. *G.O. No.:* 20, 1 February 1952. *Citation:* Sfc. Sitman distinguished himself by conspicuous gallantry and intrepidity above and beyond the call of duty in action against an armed enemy of the United Nations. Sfc. Sitman, a machinegun section leader of Company M, was attached to Company I, under attack by a numerically superior hostile force. During the encounter when an enemy grenade knocked out his machinegun, a squad from Company I, immediately emplaced a light machinegun and Sfc. Sitman and his men remained to provide security for the crew. In the ensuing action, the enemy lobbed a grenade into the position and Sfc. Sitman, fully aware of the odds against him, selflessly threw himself on it, absorbing the full force of the explosion with his body. Although mortally wounded in this fearless display of valor, his intrepid act saved 5 men from death or serious injury, and enabled them to continue inflicting withering fire on the ruthless foe throughout the attack. Sfc. Sitman's noble self-sacrifice and consummate devotion to duty reflect lasting glory on himself and uphold the honored traditions of the military service.

SITTER, CARL L.

Rank and organization: Captain, U.S. Marine Corps, Company G, 3d Battalion, 1st Marines, 1st Marine Division (Rein). *Place and date:* Hagaru-ri, Korea, 29 and 30 November 1950. *Entered service at:* Pueblo, Colo. *Born:* 2 December 1921, Syracuse, Mo. *Citation:* For conspicuous gallantry and intrepidity at the risk of his life above and beyond the call of duty as commanding officer of Company G, in action against enemy aggressor forces. Ordered to break through enemy-infested territory to reinforce his battalion the morning of 29 November, Capt. Sitter continuously exposed himself to enemy fire as he led his company forward and, despite 25 percent casualties suffered in the furious action, succeeded in driving through to his objective. Assuming the responsibility of attempting to seize and occupy a strategic area occupied by a hostile force of regiment strength deeply entrenched on a snow-covered hill commanding the entire valley southeast of the town, as well as the line of march of friendly troops withdrawing to the south, he reorganized his depleted units the following morning and boldly led them up the steep, frozen hillside under blistering fire, encouraging and redeploying his troops as casualties occured and directing forward platoons as they continued the drive to the top of the ridge. During the night when a vastly outnumbering enemy launched a sudden, vicious counterattack, setting the hill ablaze with mortar, machinegun, and automatic-weapons fire and taking a heavy toll in troops, Capt. Sitter visited each foxhole and gun position, coolly deploying and integrating reinforcing units consisting of service personnel unfamiliar with infantry tactics into a coordinated combat team and instilling in every man the will and determination to hold his position at all costs. With the enemy penetrating his lines in repeated counterattacks which often required hand-to-hand combat, and, on one occasion infiltrating to the command post with handgrenades, he fought gallantly with his men in repulsing and killing the fanatic attackers in each encounter. Painfully wounded in the face, arms, and chest by bursting grenades, he stanchly refused to be evacuated and continued to fight on until a successful defense of the area was assured with a loss to the enemy of more than 50 percent dead, wounded, and captured. His valiant leadership, superb tactics, and great personal valor throughout 36 hours of bitter combat reflect the highest credit upon Capt. Sitter and the U.S. Naval Service.

*SKINNER, SHERROD E., JR.

Rank and organization: Second Lieutenant, U.S. Marine Corps Reserve, Battery F, 2d Battalion, 11th Marines, 1st Marine Division

(Rein). *Place and date:* Korea, 26 October 1952. *Entered service at:* East Lansing, Mich. *Born:* 29 October 1929, Hartford, Conn. *Citation:* For conspicuous gallantry and intrepidity at the risk of his life above and beyond the call of duty as an artillery forward observer of Battery F, in action against enemy aggressor forces on the night of 26 October 1952. When his observation post in an extremely critical and vital sector of the main line of resistance was subjected to a sudden and fanatical attack by hostile forces, supported by a devastating barrage of artillery and mortar fire which completely severed communication lines connecting the outpost with friendly firing batteries, 2d Lt. Skinner, in a determined effort to hold his position, immediately organized and directed the surviving personnel in the defense of the outpost, continuing to call down fire on the enemy by means of radio alone until his equipment became damaged beyond repair. Undaunted by the intense hostile barrage and the rapidly-closing attackers, he twice left the protection of his bunker in order to direct accurate machinegun fire and to replenish the depleted supply of ammunition and grenades. Although painfully wounded on each occasion, he steadfastly refused medical aid until the rest of the men received treatment. As the ground attack reached its climax, he gallantly directed the final defense until the meager supply of ammunition was exhausted and the position overrun. During the 3 hours that the outpost was occupied by the enemy, several grenades were thrown into the bunker which served as protection for 2d Lt. Skinner and his remaining comrades. Realizing that there was no chance for other than passive resistance, he directed his men to feign death even though the hostile troops entered the bunker and searched their persons. Later, when an enemy grenade was thrown between him and 2 other survivors, he immediately threw himself on the deadly missile in an effort to protect the others, absorbing the full force of the explosion and sacrificing his life for his comrades. By his indomitable fighting spirit, superb leadership, and great personal valor in the face of tremendous odds, 2d Lt. Skinner served to inspire his fellow marines in their heroic stand against the enemy and upheld the highest traditions of the U.S. Naval Service. He gallantly gave his life for his country.

*SMITH, DAVID M.

Rank and organization: Private First Class, U.S. Army, Company E, 9th Infantry Regiment, 2d Infantry Division. *Place and date:* Near Yongsan, Korea, 1 September 1950. *Entered service at:* Livingston, Ky. *Born:* 10 November 1926, Livingston, Ky. *G.O. No.:* 78, 21 August 1952. *Citation:* Pfc. Smith, distinguished himself by conspicuous gallantry and outstanding courage above and beyond the call of duty in action. Pfc. Smith was a gunner in the mortar section of Company E, emplaced in rugged mountainous terrain and under attack by a numerically superior hostile force. Bitter fighting ensued and the enemy overran forward elements, infiltrated the perimeter, and rendered friendly positions untenable. The mortar section was ordered to withdraw, but the enemy had encircled and closed in on the position. Observing a grenade lobbed at his emplacement, Pfc. Smith shouted a warning to his comrades and, fully aware of the odds against him, flung himself upon it and smothered the explosion with his body. Although mortally wounded in this display of valor, his intrepid act saved 5 men from death or serious injury. Pfc. Smith's inspirational conduct and supreme sacrifice reflect lasting glory on himself and are in keeping with the noble traditions of the infantry of the U.S. Army.

*SPEICHER, CLIFTON T.

Rank and organization: Corporal, U.S. Army, Company F, 223d Infantry Regiment, 40th Infantry Division. *Place and date:* Near Minarigol, Korea, 14 June 1952. *Entered service at:* Gray, Pa. *Born:* 25 March 1931, Gray, Pa. *G.O. No.:* 65, 19 August 1953. *Citation:* Cpl. Speicher distinguished himself by conspicuous gallantry and indomitable courage above and beyond the call of duty in action against the enemy. While participating in an assault to secure a key terrain feature, Cpl. Speicher's squad was pinned down by withering small-arms, mortar, and machinegun fire. Although already wounded he left the comparative safety of his position, and made a daring charge against the machinegun emplacement. Within 10 yards of the goal, he was again wounded by small-arms fire but continued on, entered the bunker, killed 2 hostile soldiers with his rifle, a third with his bayonet, and silenced the machinegun. Inspired by this incredible display of valor, the men quickly moved up and completed the mission. Dazed and shaken, he walked to the foot of the hill where he collapsed and died. Cpl. Speicher's consummate sacrifice and unflinching devotion to duty reflect lasting glory upon himself and uphold the noble traditions of the military service.

STONE, JAMES L.

Rank and organization: First Lieutenant, U.S. Army, Company E, 8th Cavalry Regiment, 1st Cavalry Division. *Place and date:* Near Sokkogae, Korea, 21 and 22 November 1951. *Entered service at:* Houston, Tex. *Born:* 27 December 1922, Pine Bluff, Ark. *G.O. No.:* 82, 20 October 1953. *Citation:* 1st Lt. Stone, distinguished himself by conspicuous gallantry and indomitable courage above and beyond the call of duty in action against the enemy. When his platoon, holding a vital outpost position, was attacked by overwhelming Chinese forces, 1st Lt. Stone stood erect and exposed to the terrific enemy fire calmly directed his men in the defense. A defensive flamethrower failing to function, he personally moved to its location, further exposing himself, and personally repaired the weapon. Throughout a second attack, 1st Lt. Stone; though painfully wounded, personally carried the only remaining light machinegun from place to place in the position in order to bring fire upon the Chinese advancing from 2 directions. Throughout he continued to encourage and direct his depleted platoon in its hopeless defense. Although again wounded, he continued the fight with his carbine, still exposing himself as an example to his men. When this final overwhelming assault swept over the platoon's position his voice could still be heard faintly urging his men to carry on, until he lost consciousness. Only because of this officer's driving spirit and heroic action was the platoon emboldened to make its brave but hopeless last ditch stand.

*STORY, LUTHER H.

Rank and organization: Private First Class, U.S. Army, Company A, 9th Infantry Regiment, 2d Infantry Division. *Place and date:* Near Agok, Korea, 1 September 1950. *Entered service at:* Georgia. *Born:* 20 July 1931, Buena Vista, Ga. *G.O. No.:* 70, 2 August 1951. *Citation:* Pfc. Story, distinguished himself by conspicuous gallantry and intrepidity above and beyond the call of duty in action. A savage daylight attack by elements of 3 enemy divisions penetrated the thinly held lines of the 9th Infantry. Company A beat off several banzai attacks but was bypassed and in danger of being cut off and surrounded. Pfc. Story, a weapons squad leader, was heavily engaged in stopping the early attacks and had just moved his squad to a position overlooking the Naktong River when he observed a large group of the enemy crossing the river to attack Company A. Seizing a machinegun from his wounded gunner he placed deadly fire on the hostile column killing or wounding an estimated 100 enemy soldiers. Facing certain encirclement the company commander ordered a withdrawal. During the move Pfc. Story noticed the apporach of an enemy truck loaded with troops and towing an ammunition trailer. Alerting his comrades to take cover he fearlessly stood in the middle of the road, throwing grenades into the truck. Out of grenades he crawled to his squad, gathered up additional grenades and again attacked the vehicle. During the withdrawal the company was attacked by such superior numbers that it was forced to deploy in a ricefield. Pfc. Story was wounded in this action, but, disregarding his wounds, rallied the men about him and repelled the attack. Realizing that his wounds would hamper his comrades he refused to retire to the next position but remained to cover the company's withdrawal. When last seen he was firing every weapon available and fighting off another hostile assault. Private Story's extraordinary heroism, aggressive leadership, and supreme devotion to duty reflect the highest credit upon himself and were in keeping with the esteemed traditions of the military service.

*SUDUT, JEROME A.

Rank and organization: Second Lieutenant, U.S. Army, Company B, 27th Infantry Regiment, 25th Infantry Division. *Place and date:* Near Kumhwa, Korea, 12 September 1951. *Entered service at:* Wisconsin. *Birth:* Wausau, Wis. *G.O. No.:* 31, 21 March 1952. *Citation:* 2d Lt. Sudut distinguished himself by conspicuous gallantry above and beyond the call of duty in action against the enemy. His platoon, attacking heavily fortified and strategically located hostile emplacements, had been stopped by intense fire from a large bunker containing several firing posts. Armed with submachinegun, pistol, and grenades, 2d Lt. Sudut charged the emplacement alone through vicious hostile fire, killing 3 of the occupants and dispersing the remainder. Painfully wounded, he returned to reorganize his platoon, refused evacuation and led his men in a renewed attack. The enemy had returned to the bunker by means of connecting trenches from other emplacements and the platoon was again halted by devastating fire. Accompanied by an automatic-rifleman, 2d Lt. Sudut again charged into close-range fire to eliminate the position. When the rifleman was wounded, 2d Lt. Sudut seized his weapon and continued alone, killing 3 of the 4 remaining occupants. Though mortally wounded and his ammunition exhausted, he jumped into the emplacement and killed the remaining enemy soldier with his trench knife. His singlehanded assaults so inspired his comrades that they continued the attack and drove the enemy from the hill, securing the objective. 2d Lt. Sudut's consummate fighting spirit, outstanding leadership, and gallant self-sacrifice are in keeping with the finest traditions of the infantry and the U.S. Army.

*THOMPSON, WILLIAM.

Rank and organization: Private First Class, U.S. Army, 24th Company M, 24th Infantry Regiment, 25th Infantry Division. *Place and date:* Near Haman, Korea, 6 August 1950. *Entered service at:* Bronx, N.Y. *Birth:* New York, N.Y. *G.O. No.:* 63, 2 August 1951. *Citation:* Pfc. Thompson, distinguished himself by conspicuous gallantry and intrepidity above and beyond the call of duty in action against the enemy. While his platoon was reorganizing under cover of darkness, fanatical enemy forces in overwhelming strength launched a surprise attack on the unit. Pfc. Thompson set up his machinegun in the path of the onslaught and swept the enemy with withering fire, pinning them down momentarily thus permitting the remainder of his platoon to withdraw to a more tenable position. Although hit repeatedly by grenade fragments and small-arms fire, he resisted all efforts of his comrades to induce him to withdraw, steadfastly remained at his machinegun and continued to deliver deadly, accurate fire until mortally wounded by an enemy grenade. Pfc. Thompson's dauntless courage and gallant self-sacrifice reflect the highest credit on himself and uphold the esteemed traditions of military service.

*TURNER, CHARLES W.

Rank and organization: Sergeant First Class, U.S. Army, 2d Reconnaissance Company, 2d Infantry Division. *Place and date:* Near Yongsan, Korea, 1 September 1950. *Entered service at:* Massachusetts. *Birth:* Boston, Mass. *G.O. No.:* 10, 16 February 1951. *Citation:* Sfc. Turner distinguished himself by conspicuous gallantry and intrepidity above and beyond the call of duty in action against the enemy. A large enemy force launched a mortar and automatic weapon supported assault against his platoon. Sfc. Turner, a section leader, quickly organized his unit for defense and then observed that the attack was directed at the tank section 100 yards away. Leaving his secured section he dashed through a hail of fire to the threatened position and, mounting a tank, manned the exposed turret machinegun. Disregarding the intense enemy fire he calmly held this position delivering deadly accurate fire and pointing out targets for the tank's 75mm. gun. His action resulted in the destruction of 7 enemy machinegun nests. Although severely wounded he remained at the gun shouting encouragement to his comrades. During the action the tank received over 50 direct hits; the periscopes and antenna were shot away and 3 rounds hit the machinegun mount. Despite this fire he remained at his post until a burst of enemy fire cost him his life. This intrepid and heroic performance enabled the platoon to withdraw and later launch an attack which routed the enemy. Sfc. Turner's valor and example reflect the highest credit upon himself and are in keeping with the esteemed traditions of the U.S. Army.

VAN WINKLE, ARCHIE

Rank and organization: Staff Sergeant, U.S. Marine Corps Reserve, Company B, 1st Battalion, 7th Marines, 1st Marine Division (Rein). *Place and date:* Vicinity of Sudong, Korea, 2 November 1950. *Entered service at:* Arlington, Wash. *Born:* 17 March 1925, Juneau, Alaska. *Citation:* For conspicuous gallantry and intrepidity at the risk of his life above and beyond the call of duty while serving as a platoon sergeant in Company B, in action against enemy aggressor forces. Immediately rallying the men in his area after a fanatical and numerically superior enemy force penetrated the center of the line under cover of darkness and pinned down the platoon with a devastating barrage of deadly automatic weapons and grenade fire, S/Sgt. Van Winkle boldly spearheaded a determined attack through withering fire against hostile frontal positions and, though he and all the others who charged with him were wounded, succeeded in enabling his platoon to gain the fire superiority and the opportunity to reorganize. Realizing that the left-flank squad was isolated from the rest of the unit, he rushed through 40 yards of fierce enemy fire to reunite his troops despite an elbow wound which rendered 1 of his arms totally useless. Severely wounded a second time when a direct hit in the chest from a hostile handgrenade caused serious and painful wounds, he stanchly refused evacuation and continued to shout orders and words of encouragement to his depleted and battered platoon. Finally carried from his position unconscious from shock and from loss of blood, S/Sgt. Van Winkle served to inspire all who observed him to heroic efforts in successfully repulsing the enemy attack. His superb leadership, valiant fighting spirit, and unfaltering devotion to duty in the face of heavy odds reflect the highest credit upon himself and the U.S. Naval Service.

*VITTORI, JOSEPH

Rank and organization: Corporal, U.S. Marine Corps Reserve, Company F, 2d Battalion, 1st Marines, 1st Marine Division (Rein). *Place and date:* Hill 749, Korea, 15 and 16 September 1951. *Entered service at:* Beverly, Mass. *Born:* 1 August 1929, Beverly, Mass. *Citation:* For conspicuous gallantry and intrepidity at the risk of his life above and beyond the call of duty while serving as an automatic-rifleman in Company F, in action against enemy aggressor forces. With a forward platoon suffering heavy casualties and forced to withdraw under a vicious enemy counterattack as his company assaulted strong hostile forces entrenched on Hill 749, Cpl. Vittori boldly rushed through the withdrawing troops with 2 other volunteers from his reserve platoon and plunged directly into the midst of the enemy. Overwhelming them in a fierce hand-to-hand struggle, he enabled his company to consolidate its positions to meet further imminent onslaughts. Quick to respond to an urgent call for a rifelman to defend a heavy machinegun positioned on the extreme point of the northern flank and virtually isolated from the remainder of the unit when the enemy again struck in force during the night, he assumed position under the devastating barrage and, fighting a singlehanded battle, leaped from 1 flank to the other, covering each foxhole in turn as casualties continued to mount, manning a machinegun when the gunner was struck down and making repeated trips through the heaviest shellfire to replenish ammunition. With the situation becoming extremely critical, reinforcing units to the rear pinned down under the blistering attack and foxholes left practically void by dead and wounded for a distance of 100 yards, Cpl. Vittori continued his valiant stand, refusing to give ground as the enemy penetrated to within feet of his position, simulating strength in the line and denying the foe physical occupation of the ground. Mortally wounded by the enemy machinegun and rifle bullets while persisting in his magnificent defense of the sector where approximately 200 enemy dead were found the following morning, Cpl. Vittori, by his fortitude, stouthearted courage, and great personal valor, had kept the point position intact despite the tremendous odds and undoubtedly prevented the entire battalion position from collapsing. His extraordinary heroism throughout the furious nightlong battle reflects the highest credit upon himself and the U.S. Naval Service. He gallantly gave his life for his country.

*WALMSLEY, JOHN S., JR.

Rank and organization: Captain, U.S. Air Force, 8th Bombardment Squadron, 3d Bomb Group. *Place and date:* Near Yangdok, Korea, 14 September 1951. *Entered service at:* Baltimore, Md. *Born:* 7 January 1920, Baltimore, Md. *Citation:* Capt. Walmsley, distinguished himself by conspicuous gallantry and intrepidity at the risk of his life above and beyond the call of duty. While flying a B-26 aircraft on a night combat mission with the objective of developing new tactics, Capt. Walmsley sighted an enemy supply train which had been assigned top priority as a target of opportunity. He immediately attacked, producing a strike which disabled the train, and, when his ammunition was expended, radioed for friendly aircraft in the area to complete destruction of the target. Employing the searchlight mounted on his aircraft, he guided another B-26 aircraft to the target area, meanwhile constantly exposing himself to enemy fire. Directing an incoming B-26 pilot, he twice boldly alined himself with the target, his searchlight illuminating the area, in a determined effort to give the attacking aircraft full visibility. As the friendly aircraft prepared for the attack, Capt. Walmsley descended into the valley in a low level run over the target with searchlight blazing, selflessly exposing himself to vicious enemy antiaircraft fire. In his determination to inflict maximum damage on the enemy, he refused to employ evasive tactics and valiantly pressed forward straight through an intense barrage, thus insuring complete destruction of the enemy's vitally needed war cargo. While he courageously pressed his attack Capt. Walmsley's plane was hit and crashed into the surrounding mountains, exploding upon impact. His heroic initiative and daring aggressiveness in completing this important mission in the face of overwhelming opposition and at the risk of his life, reflects the highest credit upon himself and the U.S. Air Force.

*WATKINS, LEWIS G.

Rank and organization: Staff Sergeant, U.S. Marine Corps, Company I, 3d Battalion, 7th Marines, 1st Marine Division (Rein). *Place and date:* Korea, 7 October 1952. *Entered service at:* Seneca, S.C. *Born:* 6 June 1925, Seneca, S.C. *Citation:* For conspicuous gallantry and intrepidity at the risk of his life above and beyond the call of duty while serving as a guide of a rifle platoon of Company I, in action against enemy aggressor forces during the hours of darkness on the morning of 7 October 1952. With his platoon assigned the mission of retaking an outpost which had been overrun by the enemy earlier in the night, S/Sgt. Watkins skillfully led his unit in the assault up the designated hill. Although painfully wounded when a well-entrenched hostile force at the crest of the hill engaged the platoon with intense small-arms and grenade fire, he gallantly continued to lead his men. Obtaining an automatic rifle from 1 of the wounded men, he assisted in pinning down an enemy machinegun holding up the assault. When an enemy grenade landed among S/Sgt. Watkins and several other marines while they were moving forward through a trench on the hill crest, he immediately pushed his companions aside, placed himself in a position to shield them and picked up the deadly missile in an attempt to throw it outside the trench. Mortally wounded when the grenade exploded in his hand, S/Sgt. Watkins, by his great personal valor in the face of almost certain death, saved the lives of several of his comrades and contributed materially to the success of the mission. His extraordinary heroism, inspiring leadership, and resolute spirit of self-sacrifice reflect the highest credit upon himself and enhance the finest traditions of the U.S. Naval Service. He gallantly gave his life for his country.

*WATKINS, TRAVIS E.

Rank and organization: Master Sergeant, U.S. Army, Company H, 9th Infantry Regiment, 2d Infantry Division. *Place and date:* Near Yongsan, Korea, 31 August through 3 September 1950. *Entered service at:* Texas. *Birth:* Waldo, Ark. *G.O. No.:* 9, 16 February 1951. *Citation:* M/Sgt. Watkins distinguished himself by conspicuous gallantry and intrepidity above and beyond the call of duty in action against the enemy. When an overwhelming enemy force broke through and isolated 30 men of his unit, he took command, established a perimeter defense and directed action which repelled continuous, fanatical enemy assaults. With his group completely surrounded and cut off, he moved from foxhole to foxhole exposing himself to enemy fire, giving instructions and offering encouragement to his men. Later when the need for ammunition and grenades became critical he shot 2 enemy soldiers 50 yards outside the perimeter and went out alone for their ammunition and weapons. As he picked up their weapons he was attacked by 3 others and wounded. Returning their fire he killed all 3 and gathering up the weapons of the 5 enemy dead returned to his amazed comrades. During a later assault, 6 enemy soldiers gained a defiladed spot and began to throw grenades into the perimeter making it untenable. Realizing the desperate situation and disregarding his wound he rose from his foxhole to engage them with rifle fire. Although immediately hit by a burst from an enemy machinegun he continued to fire until he had killed the grenade throwers. With this threat eliminated he collapsed and despite being paralyzed from the waist down, encouraged his men to hold on. He refused all food, saving it for his comrades, and when it became apparent that help would not arrive in time to hold the position ordered his men to escape to friendly lines. Refusing evacuation as his hopeless condition would burden his comrades, he remained in his position and cheerfully wished them luck. Through his aggressive leadership and intrepid actions, this small force destroyed nearly 500 of the enemy before abandoning their position. M/Sgt. Watkins' sustained personal bravery and noble self-sacrifice reflect the highest glory upon himself and is in keeping with the esteemed traditions of the U.S. Army.

WEST, ERNEST E.

Rank and organization: Private First Class, U.S. Army, Company L, 14th Infantry Regiment, 25th Infantry Division. *Place and date:* Near Sataeri, Korea, 12 October 1952. *Entered service at:* Wurtland, Ky. *Born:* 2 September 1931, Russell, Ky. *G.O. No.:* 7, 29 January 1954. *Citation:* Pfc. West distinguished himself by conspicuous gallantry above and beyond the call of duty in action against the enemy. He voluntarily accompanied a contingent to locate and destroy a reported enemy outpost. Nearing the objective, the patrol was ambushed and suffered numerous casualities. Observing his wounded leader lying in an exposed position, Pfc. West ordered the troops to withdraw, then braved intense fire to reach and assist him. While attempting evacuation, he was attacked by 3 hostile soldiers employing grenades and small-arms fire. Quickly shifting his body to shelter the officer, he killed the assailants with his rifle, then carried the helpless man to safety. He was critically wounded and lost an eye in this action, but courageously returned through withering fire and bursting shells to assist the wounded. While evacuating 2 comrades, he closed with and killed 3 more of the foe. Pfc. West's indomitable spirit, consummate valor, and intrepid actions inspired all who observed him, reflect the highest credit on himself, and uphold the honored traditions of the military service.

WILSON, BENJAMIN F.

Rank and organization: First Lieutenant (then M/Sgt.), U.S. Army, Company I, 31st Infantry Regiment, 7th Infantry Division. *Place and date:* Near Hwach'on-Myon, Korea, 5 June 1951. *Entered service at:* Vashon, Wash. *Birth:* Vashon, Wash. *G.O. No.:* 69, 23 September 1954. *Citation:* 1st Lt. Wilson distinguished himself by conspicuous gallantry and indomitable courage above and beyond the call of duty in action against the enemy. Company I was committed to attack and secure commanding terrain stubbornly defended by a numerically superior hostile force emplaced in well-fortified positions. When the spearheading element was pinned down by withering hostile fire, he dashed forward and, firing his rifle and throwing grenades, neutralized the position denying the advance and killed 4 enemy soldiers manning submachineguns. After the assault platoon moved up, occupied the position, and a base of fire was established, he led a bayonet attack which reduced the objective and killed approximately 27 hostile soldiers. While friendly forces were consolidating the newly won gain, the enemy launched a counterattack and 1st Lt. Wilson, realizing the imminent threat of being overrun, made a determined lone-man charge, killing 7 and wounding 2 of the enemy, and routing the remainder in disorder. After the position was organized, he led an assault carrying to approximately 15 yards of the final objective, when enemy fire halted the advance. He ordered the platoon to withdraw and, although painfully wounded in this action, remained to provide covering fire. During an ensuing counterattack, the commanding officer and 1st Platoon leader became casualties. Unhesitatingly, 1st Lt. Wilson charged the enemy ranks and fought valiantly, killing 3 enemy soldiers with his rifle before it was wrested from his hands, and annihilating 4 others with his entrenching tool. His courageous delaying action enabled his comrades to reorganize and effect an orderly withdrawal. While directing evacuation of the wounded, he suffered a second wound, but elected to remain on the position until assured that all of the men had reached safety. 1st Lt. Wilson's sustained valor and intrepid actions reflect utmost credit upon himself and uphold the honored traditions of the military service.

WILSON, HAROLD E.

Rank and organization: Technical Sergeant, U.S. Marine Corps Reserve, Company G, 3d Battalion, 1st Marines, 1st Marine Division (Rein). *Place and date:* Korea, 23-24 April 1951. *Entered service at:* Birmingham, Ala. *Born:* 5 December 1921, Birmingham, Ala. *Citation:* For gallantry and intrepidity at the risk of his life above and beyond the call of duty while serving as platoon sergeant of a rifle platoon attached to Company G, in action against enemy aggressor forces on the night of 23-24 April 1951. When the company outpost was overrun by the enemy while his platoon, firing from hastily constructed foxholes, was engaged in resisting the brunt of a fierce mortar, machinegun, grenade, and small-arms attack launched by hostile forces from high ground under cover of darkness, T/Sgt. Wilson braved intense fire to assist the survivors back into the line and to direct the treatment of casualties. Although twice wounded by gunfire, in the right arm and the left leg, he refused medical aid for himself and continued to move about among his men, shouting words of encouragement. After receiving further wounds in the head and shoulder as the attack increased in intensity, he again insisted upon remaining with his unit. Unable to use either arm to fire, and with mounting casualties among our forces, he resupplied his men with rifles and ammunition taken from the wounded. Personally reporting to his company commander on several occasions, he requested and received additional assistance when the enemy attack became even more fierce and, after placing the reinforcements in strategic positions in the line, directed effective fire until blown off his feet by the bursting of a hostile mortar round in his face. Dazed and suffering from concussion, he still refused medical aid and, despite weakness from loss of blood, moved from foxhole to foxhole, directing fire, resupplying ammunition, rendering first aid, and encouraging his men. By his heroic actions in the face of almost certain death, when the unit's ability to hold the disadvantageous position was doubtful, he instilled confidence in his troops, inspiring them to rally repeatedly and turn back the furious assaults. At dawn, after the final attack had been repulsed, he personally accounted for each man in his platoon before walking unassisted ½ mile to the aid station where he submitted to treatment. His outstanding courage, initiative, and skilled leadership in the face of overwhelming odds were contributing factors in the success of his company's mission and reflect the highest credit upon T/Sgt. Wilson and the U.S. Naval Service.

*WILSON, RICHARD G.

Rank and organization: Private First Class, U.S. Army, Co. I, Medical Company, 187th Airborne Infantry Regiment. *Place and date:* Opari, Korea, 21 October 1950. *Entered service at:* Cape Girardeau, Mo. *Born:* 19 August 1931, Marion, Ill. *G.O. No.:* 64, 2 August 1951. *Citation:* Pfc. Wilson distinguished himself by conspicuous gallantry and intrepidity above and beyond the call of duty in action. As medical aid man attached to Company I, he accompanied the unit during a reconnaissance in force through the hilly country near Opari. The main body of the company was passing through a narrow valley flanked on 3 sides by high hills when the enemy laid down a barrage of mortar, automatic-weapons and small-arms fire. The company suffered a large number of casualties from the intense hostile fire while fighting its way out of the ambush. Pfc. Wilson proceeded at once to move among the wounded and administered aid to them oblivious of the danger to himself, constantly exposing himself to hostile fire. The company commander ordered a withdrawal as the enemy threatened to encircle and isolate the company. As his unit withdrew Private Wilson assisted wounded men to safety and assured himself that none were left behind. After the company had pulled back he learned that a comrade previously thought dead had been seen to be moving and attempting to crawl to safety. Despite the protests of his comrades, unarmed and facing a merciless enemy, Pfc. Wilson returned to the dangerous position in search of his comrade. Two days later a patrol found him lying beside the man he returned to aid. He had been shot several times while trying to shield and administer aid to the wounded man. Pfc. Wilson's superb personal bravery, consummate courage and willing self-sacrifice for his comrades reflect untold glory upon himself and uphold the esteemed traditions of the military service.

*WINDRICH, WILLIAM G.

Rank and organization: Staff Sergeant, U.S. Marine Corps, Company I, 3d Battalion, 5th Marines, 1st Marine Division (Rein). *Place and date:* Vicinity of Yudam-ni, Korea, 1 December 1950. *Entered service at:* Hammond, Ind. *Born:* 14 May 1921, Chicago, Ill. *Citation:* For conspicuous gallantry and intrepidity at the risk of his life above and beyond the call of duty as a platoon sergeant of Company I, in action against enemy aggressor forces the night of 1 December 1950. Promptly organizing a squad of men when the enemy launched a sudden, vicious counterattack against the forward elements of his company's position, rendering it untenable, S/Sgt. Windrich, armed with a carbine, spearheaded the assault to the top of the knoll immediately confronting the overwhelming forces and, under shattering hostile automatic-weapons, mortar, and grenade fire, directed effective fire to hold back the attackers and cover the withdrawal of our troops to commanding ground. With 7 of his men struck down during the furious action and himself wounded in the head by a bursting grenade, he made his way to his company's position and, organizing a small group of volunteers, returned with them to evacuate the wounded and dying from the frozen hillside, stanchly refusing medical attention himself. Immediately redeploying the remainder of his troops, S/Sgt. Windrich placed them on the left flank of the defensive sector before the enemy again attacked in force. Wounded in the leg during the bitter fight that followed, he bravely fought on with his men, shouting words of encouragement and directing their fire until the attack was repelled. Refusing evacuation although unable to stand, he still continued to direct his platoon in setting up defensive positions until weakened by the bitter cold, excessive loss of blood, and severe pain, he lapsed into unconsciousness and died. His valiant leadership, fortitude, and courageous fighting spirit against tremendous odds served to inspire others to heroic endeavor in holding the objective and reflect the highest credit upon S/Sgt. Windrich and the U.S. Naval Service. He gallantly gave his life for his country.

and wounded him in the face and shoulder. Refusing to be evacuated, Pfc. Young remained in position and continued to fire at the enemy until wounded a second time. As he awaited first aid near the company command post the enemy attempted an enveloping movement. Disregarding medical treatment he took an exposed position and firing with deadly accuracy killed 5 of the enemy. During this action he was again hit by hostile fire which knocked him to the ground and destroyed his helmet. Later when supporting tanks moved forward, Pfc. Young, his wounds still unattended, directed tank fire which destroyed 3 enemy gun positions and enabled the company to advance. Wounded again by an enemy mortar burst, and while aiding several of his injured comrades, he demanded that all others be evacuated first. Throughout the course of this action the leadership and combative instinct displayed by Pfc. Young exerted a profound influence on the conduct of the company. His aggressive example affected the whole course of the action and was responsible for its success. Pfc. Young's dauntless courage and intrepidity reflect the highest credit upon himself and uphold the esteemed traditions of the U.S. Army.

WORLD WAR
II

ADAMS, LUCIAN

Rank and organization: Staff Sergeant, U.S. Army, 30th Infantry, 3d Infantry Division. *Place and date:* Near St. Die, France, 28 October 1944. *Entered service at:* Port Arthur, Tex. *Birth:* Port Arthur, Tex. *G.O. No.:* 20, 29 March 1945. *Citation:* For conspicuous gallantry and intrepidity at risk of life above and beyond the call of duty on 28 October 1944, near St. Die, France. When his company was stopped in its effort to drive through the Mortagne Forest to reopen the supply line to the isolated third battalion, S/Sgt. Adams braved the concentrated fire of machineguns in a lone assault on a force of German troops. Although his company had progressed less than 10 yards and had lost 3 killed and 6 wounded, S/Sgt. Adams charged forward dodging from tree to tree firing a borrowed BAR from the hip. Despite intense machinegun fire which the enemy directed at him and rifle grenades which struck the trees over his head showering him with broken twigs and branches, S/Sgt. Adams made his way to within 10 yards of the closest machinegun and killed the gunner with a handgrenade. An enemy soldier threw handgrenades at him from a position only 10 yards distant; however, S/Sgt. Adams dispatched him with a single burst of BAR fire. Charging into the vortex of the enemy fire, he killed another machinegunner at 15 yards range with a handgrenade and forced the surrender of 2 supporting infantrymen. Although the remainder of the German group concentrated the full force of its automatic weapons fire in a desparate effort to knock him out, he proceeded through the woods to find and exterminate 5 more of the enemy. Finally, when the third German machinegun opened up on him at a range of 20 yards, S/Sgt. Adams killed the gunner with BAR fire. In the course of the action, he personally killed 9 Germans, eliminated 3 enemy machineguns, vanquished a specialized force which was armed with automatic weapons and grenade launchers, cleared the woods of hostile elements, and reopened the severed supply lines to the assault companies of his battalion.

*AGERHOLM, HAROLD CHRIST

Rank and organization: Private First Class, U.S. Marine Corps Reserve. *Born:* 29 January 1925, Racine, Wis. *Accredited to:* Wisconsin. *Citation:* For conspicuous gallantry and intrepidity at the risk of his life above and beyond the call of duty while serving with the 4th Battalion, 10th Marines, 2d Marine Division, in action against enemy Japanese forces on Saipan, Marianas Islands, 7 July 1944. When the enemy launched a fierce, determined counterattack against our positions and overran a neighboring artillery battalion, Pfc. Agerholm immediately volunteered to assist in the efforts to check the hostile attack and evacuate our wounded. Locating and appropriating an abandoned ambulance jeep, he repeatedly made extremely perilous trips under heavy rifle and mortar fire and single-handedly loaded and evacuated approximately 45 casualties, working tirelessly and with utter disregard for his own safety during a gruelling period of more than 3 hours. Despite intense, persistent enemy fire, he ran out to aid 2 men whom he believed to be wounded marines but was himself mortally wounded by a Japanese sniper while carrying out his hazardous mission. Pfc. Agerholm's brilliant initiative, great personal valor and self-sacrificing efforts in the face of almost certain death reflect the highest credit upon himself and the U.S. Naval Service. He gallantly gave his life for his country.

ANDERSON, BEAUFORT T.

Rank and organization: Technical Sergeant, U.S. Army, 381st Infantry, 96th Infantry Division. *Place and date:* Okinawa, 13 April 1945. *Entered service at:* Soldiers Grove, Wis. *Birth:* Eagle, Wis. *G.O. No.:* 63, 27 June 1946. *Citation:* He displayed conspicuous gallantry and intrepidity above and beyond the call of duty. When a powerfully conducted predawn Japanese counterattack struck his unit's flank, he ordered his men to take cover in an old tomb, and then, armed only with a carbine, faced the onslaught alone. After emptying 1 magazine at pointblank range into the screaming attackers, he seized an enemy mortar dud and threw it back among the charging Japs, killing several as it burst. Securing a box of mortar shells, he extracted the safety pins, banged the bases upon a rock to arm them and proceeded alternately to hurl shells and fire his piece among the fanatical foe, finally forcing them to withdraw. Despite the protests of his comrades, and bleeding profusely from a severe shrapnel wound, he made his way to his company commander to report the action. T/Sgt. Anderson's intrepid conduct in the face of overwhelming odds accounted for 25 enemy killed and several machineguns and knee mortars destroyed, thus singlehandedly removing a serious threat to the company's flank.

*ANDERSON, RICHARD BEATTY

Rank and organization: Private First Class, U.S. Marine Corps. *Born:* 26 June 1921, Tacoma, Wash. *Accredited to:* Washington. *Citation:* For conspicuous gallantry and intrepidity at the risk of his life above and beyond the call of duty while serving with the 4th Marine Division during action against enemy Japanese forces on Roi Island, Kwajalein Atoll, Marshall Islands, 1 February 1944. Entering a shell crater occupied by 3 other marines, Pfc. Anderson was preparing to throw a grenade at an enemy position when it slipped from his hands and rolled toward the men at the bottom of the hole. With insufficient time to retrieve the armed weapon and throw it, Pfc. Anderson fearlessly chose to sacrifice himself and save his companions by hurling his body upon the grenade and taking the full impact of the explosion. His personal valor and exceptional spirit of loyalty in the face of almost certain death were in keeping with the highest traditions of the U.S. Naval Service. He gallantly gave his life for his country.

*ANTOLAK, SYLVESTER

Rank and organization: Sergeant, U.S. Army, Company B, 15th Infantry, 3d Infantry Division. *Place and date:* Near Cisterna di Littoria, Italy, 24 May 1944. *Entered service at:* St. Clairsville, Ohio. *Birth:* St. Clairsville, Ohio. *G.O. No.:* 89, 19 October 1945. *Citation:* Near Cisterna di Littoria, Italy, he charged 200 yards over flat, coverless terrain to destroy an enemy machinegun nest during the second day of the offensive which broke through the German cordon of steel around the Anzio beachhead. Fully 30 yards in advance of his squad, he ran into withering enemy machinegun, machine-pistol and rifle fire. Three times he was struck by bullets and knocked to the ground, but each time he struggled to his feet to continue his relentless advance. With one shoulder deeply gashed and his right arm shattered, he continued to rush directly into the enemy fire concentration with his submachinegun wedged under his uninjured arm until within 15 yards of the enemy strongpoint, where he opened fire at deadly close range, killing 2 Germans and forcing the remaining 10 to surrender. He reorganized his men and, refusing to seek medical attention so badly needed, chose to lead the way toward another strongpoint 100 yards distant. Utterly disregarding the hail of bullets concentrated upon him, he had stormed ahead nearly three-fourths of the space between strongpoints when he was instantly killed by hostile enemy fire. Inspired by his example, his squad went on to overwhelm the enemy troops. By his supreme sacrifice, superb fighting courage, and heroic devotion to the attack, Sgt.

Antolak was directly responsible for eliminating 20 Germans, capturing an enemy machinegun, and clearing the path for his company to advance.

ANTRIM, RICHARD NOTT

Rank and organization: Commander, U.S. Navy. *Place and date:* Makassar, Celebes, Netherlands East Indies, April 1942. *Entered service at:* Indiana. *Born:* 17 December 1907, Peru, Ind. *Citation:* For conspicuous gallantry and intrepidity at the risk of his life above and beyond the call of duty while interned as a prisoner of war of the enemy Japanese in the city of Makassar, Celebes, Netherlands East Indies, in April 1942. Acting instantly on behalf of a naval officer who was subjected to a vicious clubbing by a frenzied Japanese guard venting his insane wrath upon the helpless prisoner, Comdr. (then Lt.) Antrim boldly intervened, attempting to quiet the guard and finally persuading him to discuss the charges against the officer. With the entire Japanese force assembled and making extraordinary preparations for the threatened beating, and with the tension heightened by 2,700 Allied prisoners rapidly closing in, Comdr. Antrim courageously appealed to the fanatic enemy, risking his own life in a desperate effort to mitigate the punishment. When the other had been beaten unconscious by 15 blows of a hawser and was repeatedly kicked by 3 soldiers to a point beyond which he could not survive, Comdr. Antrim gallantly stepped forward and indicated to the perplexed guards that he would take the remainder of the punishment, throwing the Japanese completely off balance in their amazement and eliciting a roar of acclaim from the suddenly inspired Allied prisoners. By his fearless leadership and valiant concern for the welfare of another, he not only saved the life of a fellow officer and stunned the Japanese into sparing his own life but also brought about a new respect for American officers and men and a great improvement in camp living conditions. His heroic conduct throughout reflects the highest credit upon Comdr. Antrim and the U.S. Naval Service.

ATKINS, THOMAS E.

Rank and organization: Private First Class, U.S. Army, Company A, 127th Infantry, 32d Infantry Division. *Place and date:* Villa Verde Trail, Luzon, Philippine Islands, 10 March 1945. *Entered service at:* Campobello, S.C. *Birth:* Campobello, S.C. *G.O. No.:* 95, 30 October 1945. *Citation:* He fought gallantly on the Villa Verde Trail, Luzon, Philippine Islands. With 2 companions he occupied a position on a ridge outside the perimeter defense established by the 1st Platoon on a high hill. At about 3 a.m., 2 companies of Japanese attacked with rifle and machinegun fire, grenades, TNT charges, and land mines, severely wounding Pfc. Atkins and killing his 2 companions. Despite the intense hostile fire and pain from his deep wound, he held his ground and returned heavy fire. After the attack was repulsed, he remained in his precarious position to repel any subsequent assaults instead of returning to the American lines for medical treatment. An enemy machinegun, set up within 20 yards of his foxhole, vainly attempted to drive him off or silence his gun. The Japanese repeatedly made fierce attacks, but for 4 hours Pfc. Atkins determinedly remained in his foxhole, bearing the brunt of each assault and maintaining steady and accurate fire until each charge was repulsed. At 7 a.m., 13 enemy dead lay in front of his position; he had fired 400 rounds, all he and his 2 dead companions possessed, and had used 3 rifles until each had jammed too badly for further operation. He withdrew during a lull to secure a rifle and more ammunition, and was persuaded to remain for medical treatment. While waiting, he saw a Japanese within the perimeter and, seizing a nearby rifle, killed him. A few minutes later, while lying on a litter, he discovered an enemy group moving up behind the platoon's lines. Despite his severe wound, he sat up, delivered heavy rifle fire against the group and forced them to withdraw. Pfc. Atkins' superb bravery and his fearless determination to hold his post against the main force of repeated enemy attacks, even though painfully wounded, were major factors in enabling his comrades to maintain their lines against a numerically superior enemy force.

*BAILEY, KENNETH D.

Rank and organization: Major, U.S. Marine Corps. *Born:* 21 October 1910, Pawnee, Okla. *Appointed from:* Illinois. *Other Navy awards:* Silver Star Medal. *Citation:* For extraordinary courage and heroic conduct above and beyond the call of duty as Commanding Officer of Company C, 1st Marine Raider Battalion, during the enemy Japanese attack on Henderson Field, Guadalcanal, Solomon Islands, on 12–13 September 1942. Completely reorganized following the severe engagement of the night before, Maj. Bailey's company, within an hour after taking its assigned position as reserve battalion between the main line and the coveted airport, was threatened on the right flank by the penetration of the enemy into a gap in the main line. In addition to repulsing this threat, while steadily improving his own desperately held position, he used every weapon at his command to cover the forced withdrawal of the main line before a hammering assault by superior enemy forces. After rendering invaluable service to the battalion commander in stemming the retreat, reorganizing the troops and extending the reverse position to the left, Maj. Bailey, despite a severe head wound, repeatedly led his troops in fierce hand-to-hand combat for a period of 10 hours. His great personal valor while exposed to constant and merciless enemy fire, and his indomitable fighting spirit inspired his troops to heights of heroic endeavor which enabled them to repulse the enemy and hold Henderson Field. He gallantly gave his life in the service of his country.

*BAKER, ADDISON E. (Air Mission)

Rank and organization: Lieutenant Colonel, U.S. Army Air Corps, 93d Heavy Bombardment Group. *Place and date:* Ploesti Raid, Rumania, 1 August 1943. *Entered service at:* Akron, Ohio. *Born:* 1 January 1907, Chicago, Ill. *G.O. No.:* 20, 11 March 1944. *Citation:* For conspicuous gallantry and intrepidity above and beyond the call of duty in action with the enemy on 1 August 1943. On this date he led his command, the 93d Heavy Bombardment Group, on a daring low-level attack against enemy oil refineries and installations at Ploesti, Rumania. Approaching the target, his aircraft was hit by a large caliber antiaircraft shell, seriously damaged and set on fire. Ignoring the fact he was flying over terrain suitable for safe landing, he refused to jeopardize the mission by breaking up the lead formation and continued unswervingly to lead his group to the target upon which he dropped his bombs with devastating effect. Only then did he leave formation, but his valiant attempts to gain sufficient altitude for the crew to escape by parachute were unavailing and his aircraft crashed in flames after his successful efforts to avoid other planes in formation. By extraordinary flying skill, gallant leadership and intrepidity, Lt. Col. Baker rendered outstanding, distinguished, and valorous service to our Nation.

*BAKER, THOMAS A.

Rank and organization: Sergeant, U.S. Army, Company A, 105th Infantry, 27th Infantry Division. *Place and date:* Saipan, Mariana Islands, 19 June to 7 July 1944. *Entered service at:* Troy, N.Y. *Birth:* Troy, N.Y. *G.O. No.:* 35, 9 May 1945. *Citation:* For conspicuous gallantry and intrepidity at the risk of his life above and beyond the call of duty at Saipan, Mariana Islands, 19 June to 7 July 1944. When his entire company was held up by fire from automatic weapons and small-arms fire from strongly fortified enemy positions that commanded the view of the company, Sgt. (then Pvt.) Baker voluntarily took a bazooka and dashed alone to within 100 yards of the enemy. Through heavy rifle and machinegun fire that was directed at him by the enemy, he knocked out the strongpoint, enabling his company to assault the ridge. Some days later while his company advanced across the open field flanked with obstructions and places of concealment for the enemy, Sgt. Baker again voluntarily took up a position in the rear to protect the company against surprise attack and came upon 2 heavily fortified enemy pockets manned by 2 officers and 10 enlisted men which had been bypassed. Without regard for such superior numbers, he unhesitatingly attacked and killed all of them. Five hundred yards farther, he discovered 6 men of the enemy who had concealed themselves behind our lines and destroyed all of them. On 7 July 1944, the perimeter of which Sgt. Baker was a part was attacked from 3 sides by from 3,000 to 5,000 Japanese. During the early stages of this attack, Sgt. Baker was seriously wounded but he insisted on remaining in the line and fired at the enemy at ranges sometimes as close as 5 yards until his ammunition ran out. Without ammunition and with his own weapon battered to uselessness from hand-to-hand combat, he was carried about 50 yards to the rear by a comrade, who was then himself wounded. At this point Sgt. Baker refused to be moved any farther stating that he preferred to be left to die rather than risk the lives of any more of his friends. A short time later, at his request, he was placed in a sitting position against a small tree. Another comrade, withdrawing, offered assistance. Sgt. Baker refused, insisting that he be left alone and be given a soldier's pistol with its remaining 8 rounds of ammunition. When last seen alive, Sgt. Baker was propped against a tree, pistol in hand, calmly facing the foe. Later Sgt. Baker's body was found in the same position, gun empty, with 8 Japanese lying dead before him. His deeds were in keeping with the highest traditions of the U.S. Army.

BARFOOT, VAN T.

Rank and organization: Second Lieutenant, U.S. Army, 157th Infantry, 45th Infantry Division. *Place and date:* Near Carano, Italy, 23 May 1944. *Entered service at:* Carthage, Miss. *Birth:* Edinburg, Miss. *G.O. No.:* 79, 4 October 1944. *Citation:* For conspicuous gallantry and intrepidity at the risk of life above and beyond the call of duty on 23 May 1944, near Carano, Italy. With his platoon heavily engaged during an assault against forces well entrenched on commanding ground, 2d Lt. Barfoot (then Tech. Sgt.) moved off alone upon the enemy left flank. He crawled to the proximity of 1 machinegun nest and made a direct hit on it with a handgrenade, killing 2 and wounding 3 Germans. He continued along the German defense line to another machinegun emplacement, and with his tommygun killed 2 and captured 3 soldiers. Members of another enemy machinegun crew then abandoned their position and gave themselves up to Sgt. Barfoot. Leaving the prisoners for his support squad to pick up, he proceeded to mop up positions in the immediate area, capturing more prisoners and bringing his total count to 17. Later that day, after he had reorganized his men and consolidated the newly captured ground, the enemy launched a fierce armored counterattack directly at his platoon positions. Securing a bazooka, Sgt. Barfoot took up an exposed position directly in front of 3 advancing Mark VI tanks. From a distance of 75 yards his first shot destroyed the track of the leading tank, effectively disabling it, while the other 2 changed direction toward the flank. As the crew of the disabled tank dismounted, Sgt. Barfoot killed 3 of them with his tommygun. He continued onward into enemy terrain and destroyed a recently abandoned German fieldpiece with a demolition charge placed in the breech. While returning to his platoon position, Sgt. Barfoot, though greatly fatigued by his herculean efforts, assisted 2 of his seriously wounded men 1,700 yards to a position of safety. Sgt. Barfoot's extraordinary heroism, demonstration of magnificent valor, and aggressive determination in the face of pointblank fire are a perpetual inspiration to his fellow soldiers.

BARRETT, CARLTON W.

Rank and organization: Private, U.S. Army, 18th Infantry, 1st Infantry Division. *Place and date:* Near St. Laurent-sur-Mer, France, 6 June 1944. *Entered service at:* Albany, N.Y. *Birth:* Fulton, N.Y. *G.O. No.:* 78, 2 October 1944. *Citation:* For gallantry and intrepidity at the risk of his life above and beyond the call of duty on 6 June 1944, in the vicinity of St. Laurent-sur-Mer, France. On the morning of D-day Pvt. Barrett, landing in the face of extremely heavy enemy fire, was forced to wade ashore through neck-deep water. Disregarding the personal danger, he returned to the surf again and again to assist his floundering comrades and save them from drowning. Refusing to remain pinned down by the intense barrage of small-arms and mortar fire poured at the landing points, Pvt. Barrett, working with fierce determination, saved many lives by carrying casualties to an evacuation boat lying offshore. In addition to his assigned mission as guide, he carried dispatches the length of the fire-swept beach; he assisted the wounded; he calmed the shocked; he arose as a leader in the stress of the occasion. His coolness and his dauntless daring courage while constantly risking his life during a period of many hours had an inestimable effect on his comrades and is in keeping with the highest traditions of the U.S. Army.

BASILONE, JOHN

Rank and organization: Sergeant, U.S. Marine Corps. *Born:* 4 November 1916, Buffalo, N.Y. *Accredited to:* New Jersey. *Other Navy award:* Navy Cross. *Citation:* For extraordinary heroism and conspicuous gallantry in action against enemy Japanese forces, above and beyond the call of duty, while serving with the 1st Battalion, 7th Marines, 1st Marine Division in the Lunga Area. Guadalcanal, Solomon Islands, on 24 and 25 October 1942. While the enemy was hammering at the Marines' defensive positions, Sgt. Basilone, in charge of 2 sections of heavy machineguns, fought valiantly to check the savage and determined assault. In a fierce frontal attack with the Japanese blasting his guns with grenades and mortar fire, one of Sgt. Basilone's sections, with its guncrews, was put out of action, leaving only 2 men able to carry on. Moving an extra gun into position, he placed it in action, then, under continual fire, repaired another and personally manned it, gallantly holding his line until replacements arrived. A little later, with ammunition critically low and the supply lines cut off, Sgt. Basilone, at great risk of his life and in the face of continued enemy attack, battled his way through hostile lines with urgently needed shells for his gunners, thereby contributing in large measure to the virtual annihilation of a Japanese regiment. His great personal valor and courageous initiative were in keeping with the highest traditions of the U.S. Naval Service.

*BAUER, HAROLD WILLIAM

Rank and organization: Lieutenant Colonel, U.S. Marine Corps. *Born:* 20 November 1908. Woodruff, Kans. *Appointed from:* Nebraska. *Citation:* For extraordinary heroism and conspicuous courage as Squadron Commander of Marine Fighting Squadron 212 in the South Pacific Area during the period 10 May to 14 November 1942. Volunteering to pilot a fighter plane in defense of our positions on Guadalcanal, Lt. Col. Bauer participated in 2 air battles against enemy bombers and fighters outnumbering our force more than 2 to 1, boldly engaged the enemy and destroyed 1 Japanese bomber in the engagement of 28 September and shot down 4 enemy fighter planes in flames on 3 October, leaving a fifth smoking badly. After successfully leading 26 planes on an over-water ferry flight of more than 600 miles on 16 October, Lt. Col. Bauer, while circling to land, sighted a squadron of enemy planes attacking the U.S.S. *McFarland*. Undaunted by the formidable opposition and with valor above and beyond the call of duty, he engaged the entire squadron and, although alone and his fuel supply nearly exhausted, fought his plane so brilliantly that 4 of the Japanese planes were destroyed before he was forced down by lack of fuel. His intrepid fighting spirit and distinctive ability as a leader and an airman, exemplified in his splendid record of combat achievement, were vital factors in the successful operations in the South Pacific Area.

*BAUSELL, LEWIS KENNETH

Rank and organization: Corporal, U.S. Marine Corps. *Born:* 17 April 1924, Pulaski, Va. *Accredited to:* District of Columbia. *Citation:* For conspicuous gallantry and intrepidity at the risk of his life above and beyond the call of duty while serving with the 1st Battalion, 5th Marines, 1st Marine Division, during action against enemy Japanese forces on Peleliu Island, Palau Group, 15 September 1944. Valiantly placing himself at the head of his squad, Cpl. Bausell led the charge forward against a hostile pillbox which was covering a vital sector of the beach and, as the first to reach the emplacement, immediately started firing his automatic into the aperture while the remainder of his men closed in on the enemy. Swift to act, as a Japanese grenade was hurled into their midst, Cpl. Bausell threw himself on the deadly weapon, taking the full blast of the explosion and sacrificing his own life to save his men. His unwavering loyalty and inspiring courage reflect the highest credit upon Cpl. Bausell and the U.S. Naval Service. He gallantly gave his life for his country.

*BEAUDOIN, RAYMOND O.

Rank and organization: First Lieutenant, U.S. Army, Company F, 119th Infantry, 30th Infantry Division. *Place and date:* Hamelin, Germany, 6 April 1945. *Entered service at:* Holyoke, Mass. *Birth:* Holyoke, Mass. *G.O. No.:* 9, 25 January 1946. *Citation:* He was leading the 2d Platoon of Company F over flat, open terrain to Hamelin, Germany, when the enemy went into action with machineguns and automatic weapons, laying down a devastating curtain of fire which pinned his unit to the ground. By rotating men in firing positions he made it possible for his entire platoon to dig in, defying all the while the murderous enemy fire to encourage his men and to distribute ammunition. He then dug in himself at the most advanced position, where he kept up a steady fire, killing 6 hostile soldiers, and directing his men in inflicting heavy casualties on the numerically superior opposing force. Despite these defensive measures, however, the position of the platoon became more precarious, for the enemy had brought up strong reinforcements and was preparing a counterattack. Three men, sent back at intervals to obtain ammunition and reinforcements, were killed by sniper fire. To relieve his command from the desperate situation, 1st Lt. Beaudoin decided to make a 1-man attack on the most damaging enemy sniper nest 90 yards to the right flank, and thereby divert attention from the runner who would attempt to pierce the enemy's barrier of bullets and secure help. Crawling over completely exposed ground, he relentlessly advanced, undeterred by 8 rounds of bazooka fire which threw mud and stones over him or by rifle fire which ripped his uniform. Ten yards from the enemy position he stood up and charged. At point-blank range he shot and killed 2 occupants of the nest; a third, who tried to bayonet him, he overpowered and killed with the butt of his carbine; and the fourth adversary was cut down by the platoon's rifle fire as he attempted to flee. He continued his attack by running toward a dugout, but there he was struck and killed by a burst from a machinegun. By his intrepidity, great fighting skill, and supreme devotion to his responsibility for the well-being of his platoon, 1st Lt.

Beaudoin singlehandedly accomplished a mission that enabled a messenger to secure help which saved the stricken unit and made possible the decisive defeat of the German forces.

BELL, BERNARD P.

Rank and organization: Technical Sergeant, U.S. Army, Company I, 142d Infantry, 36th Infantry Division. *Place and date:* Mittelwihr, France, 18 December 1944. *Entered service at:* New York, N.Y. *Birth:* Grantsville, W. Va. *G.O. No.:* 73, 30 August 1945. *Citation:* For fighting gallantly at Mittelwihr, France. On the morning of 18 December 1944, he led a squad against a schoolhouse held by enemy troops. While his men covered him, he dashed toward the building, surprised 2 guards at the door and took them prisoner without firing a shot. He found that other Germans were in the cellar. These he threatened with handgrenades, forcing 26 in all to emerge and surrender. His squad then occupied the building and prepared to defend it against powerful enemy action. The next day, the enemy poured artillery and mortar barrages into the position, disrupting communications which T/Sgt. Bell repeatedly repaired under heavy small-arms fire as he crossed dangerous terrain to keep his company commander informed of the squad's situation. During the day, several prisoners were taken and other Germans killed when hostile forces were attracted to the schoolhouse by the sound of captured German weapons fired by the Americans. At dawn the next day the enemy prepared to assault the building. A German tank fired round after round into the structure, partially demolishing the upper stories. Despite this heavy fire, T/Sgt. Bell climbed to the second floor and directed artillery fire which forced the hostile tank to withdraw. He then adjusted mortar fire on large forces of enemy foot soldiers attempting to reach the American position and, when this force broke and attempted to retire, he directed deadly machinegun and rifle fire into their disorganized ranks. Calling for armored support to blast out the German troops hidden behind a wall, he unhesitatingly exposed himself to heavy small-arms fire to stand beside a friendly tank and tell its occupants where to rip holes in walls protecting approaches to the school building. He then trained machineguns on the gaps and mowed down all hostile troops attempting to cross the openings to get closer to the school building. By his intrepidity and bold, aggressive leadership, T/Sgt. Bell enabled his 8-man squad to drive back approximately 150 of the enemy, killing at least 87 and capturing 42. Personally, he killed more than 20 and captured 33 prisoners.

BENDER, STANLEY

Rank and organization: Staff Sergeant, U.S. Army, Company E, 7th Infantry, 3d Infantry Division. *Place and date:* Near La Lande, France, 17 August 1944. *Entered service at:* Chicago, Ill. *Born:* 31 October 1909, Carlisle, W. Va. *G.O. No.:* 7, 1 February 1945. *Citation:* For conspicuous gallantry and intrepidity at risk of life above and beyond the call of duty. On 17 August 1944, near La Lande, France, he climbed on top of a knocked-out tank, in the face of withering machinegun fire which had halted the advance of his company, in an effort to locate the source of this fire. Although bullets ricocheted off the turret at his feet, he nevertheless remained standing upright in full view of the enemy for over 2 minutes. Locating the enemy machine-guns on a knoll 200 yards away, he ordered 2 squads to cover him and led his men down an irrigation ditch, running a gauntlet of intense machinegun fire, which completely blanketed 50 yards of his advance and wounded 4 of his men. While the Germans hurled handgrenades at the ditch, he stood his ground until his squad caught up with him, then advanced alone, in a wide flanking approach, to the rear of the knoll. He walked deliberately a distance of 40 yards, without cover, in full view of the Germans and under a hail of both enemy and friendly fire, to the first machinegun and knocked it out with a single short burst. Then he made his way through the strongpoint, despite bursting handgrenades, toward the second machinegun, 25 yards distant, whose 2-man crew swung the machinegun around and fired two bursts at him, but he walked calmly through the fire and, reaching the edge of the emplacement, dispatched the crew. Signaling his men to rush the rifle pits, he then walked 35 yards further to kill an enemy rifleman and returned to lead his squad in the destruction of the 8 remaining Germans in the strongpoint. His audacity so inspired the remainder of the assault company that the men charged out of their positions, shouting and yelling, to overpower the enemy roadblock and sweep into town, knocking out 2 antitank guns, killing 37 Germans and capturing 26 others. He had sparked and led the assault company in an attack which overwhelmed the enemy, destroying a roadblock, taking a town, seizing intact 3 bridges over the Maravenne River, and capturing commanding terrain which dominated the area.

*BENJAMIN, GEORGE, JR.

Rank and organization: Private First Class, U.S. Army, Company A, 306th Infantry, 77th Infantry Division. *Place and date:* Leyte, Philippine Islands, 21 December 1944. *Entered service at:* Carney's Point, N.J. *Birth:* Philadelphia, Pa. *G.O. No.:* 49, 28 June 1945. *Citation:* He was a radio operator, advancing in the rear of his company as it engaged a well-defended Japanese strongpoint holding up the progress of the entire battalion. When a rifle platoon supporting a light tank hesitated in its advance, he voluntarily and with utter disregard for personal safety left his comparatively secure position and ran across bullet-whipped terrain to the tank, waving and shouting to the men of the platoon to follow. Carrying his bulky radio and armed only with a pistol, he fearlessly penetrated intense machinegun and rifle fire to the enemy position, where he killed 1 of the enemy in a foxhole and moved on to annihilate the crew of a light machinegun. Heedless of the terrific fire now concentrated on him, he continued to spearhead the assault, killing 2 more of the enemy and exhorting the other men to advance, until he fell mortally wounded. After being evacuated to an aid station, his first thought was still of the American advance. Overcoming great pain he called for the battalion operations officer to report the location of enemy weapons and valuable tactical information he had secured in his heroic charge. The unwavering courage, the unswerving devotion to the task at hand, the aggressive leadership of Pfc. Benjamin were a source of great and lasting inspiration to his comrades and were to a great extent responsible for the success of the battalion's mission.

BENNETT, EDWARD A.

Rank and organization: Corporal, U.S. Army, Company B, 358th Infantry, 90th Infantry Division. *Place and date:* Heckhuscheid, Germany, 1 February 1945. *Entered service at:* Middleport, Ohio. *Birth:* Middleport, Ohio. *G.O. No.:* 95, 30 October 1945. *Citation:* He was advancing with Company B across open ground to assault Heckhuscheid, Germany, just after dark when vicious enemy machinegun fire from a house on the outskirts of the town pinned down the group and caused several casualties. He began crawling to the edge of the field in an effort to flank the house, persisting in this maneuver even when the hostile machinegunners located him by the light of burning buildings and attempted to cut him down as he made for the protection of some trees. Reaching safety, he stealthily made his way by a circuitous route to the rear of the building occupied by the German gunners. With his trench knife he killed a sentry on guard there and then charged into the darkened house. In a furious hand-to-hand struggle he stormed about a single room which harbored 7 Germans. Three he killed with rifle fire, another he clubbed to death with the butt of his gun, and the 3 others he dispatched with his .45 caliber pistol. The fearless initiative, stalwart combat ability, and outstanding gallantry of Cpl. Bennett eliminated the enemy fire which was decimating his company's ranks and made it possible for the Americans to sweep all resistance from the town.

*BENNION, MERVYN SHARP

Rank and organization: Captain, U.S. Navy. *Born:* 5 May 1887, Vernon, Utah. *Appointed from:* Utah. *Citation:* For conspicuous devotion to duty, extraordinary courage, and complete disregard of his own life, above and beyond the call of duty, during the attack on the Fleet in Pearl Harbor, by Japanese forces on 7 December 1941. As Commanding Officer of the U.S.S. *West Virginia*, after being mortally wounded, Capt. Bennion evidenced apparent concern only in fighting and saving his ship, and strongly protested against being carried from the bridge.

*BERRY, CHARLES JOSEPH

Rank and organization: Corporal, U.S. Marine Corps. *Born:* 10 July 1923, Lorain, Ohio. *Accredited to:* Ohio. *Citation:* For conspicuous gallantry and intrepidity at the risk of his life above and beyond the call of duty as member of a machinegun crew, serving with the 1st Battalion, 26th Marines, 5th Marine Division, in action against enemy Japanese forces during the seizure of Iwo Jima in the Volcano Islands, on 3 March 1945. Stationed in the front lines, Cpl. Berry manned his weapon with alert readiness as he maintained a constant vigil with other members of his guncrew during the hazardous night hours. When infiltrating Japanese soldiers launched a surprise attack shortly after midnight in an attempt to overrun his position, he engaged in a pitched handgrenade duel, returning the dangerous weapons with prompt and deadly accuracy until an enemy grenade landed in the foxhole. Determined to save his comrades, he unhesitatingly chose to sacrifice himself and immediately dived on the deadly missile, absorbing the shattering violence of the exploding charge in his own body and protecting the others from serious injury. Stouthearted and indomitable, Cpl. Berry fearlessly yielded his own life that his fellow marines might carry on the relentless battle against a ruthless enemy and his superb valor and unfaltering devotion to duty in the face of certain death reflect the highest credit upon himself and upon the U.S. Naval Service. He gallantly gave his life for his country.

BERTOLDO, VITO R.

Rank and organization: Master Sergeant, U.S. Army, Company A, 242d Infantry, 42d Infantry Division. *Place and date:* Hatten, France, 9–10 January 1945. *Entered service at:* Decatur, Ill. *Born:* 1 December 1916, Decatur, Ill. *G.O. No.:* 5, 10 January 1946. *Citation:* He fought with extreme gallantry while guarding 2 command posts against the assault of powerful infantry and armored forces which had overrun the battalion's main line of resistance. On the close approach of enemy soldiers, he left the protection of the building he defended and set up his gun in the street, there to remain for almost 12 hours driving back attacks while in full view of his adversaries and completely exposed to 88-mm., machinegun and small-arms fire. He moved back inside the command post, strapped his machinegun to a table and covered the main approach to the building by firing through a window, remaining steadfast even in the face of 88-mm. fire from tanks only 75 yards away. One shell blasted him across the room, but he returned to his weapon. When 2 enemy personnel carriers led by a tank moved toward his position, he calmly waited for the troops to dismount and then, with the tank firing directly at him, leaned out of the window and mowed down the entire group of more than 20 Germans. Some time later, removal of the command post to another building was ordered. M/Sgt. Bertoldo voluntarily remained behind, covering the withdrawal of his comrades and maintaining his stand all night. In the morning he carried his machinegun to an adjacent building used as the command post of another battalion and began a day-long defense of that position. He broke up a heavy attack, launched by a self-propelled 88-mm. gun covered by a tank and about 15 infantrymen. Soon afterward another 88-mm. weapon moved up to within a few feet of his position, and, placing the muzzle of its gun almost inside the building, fired into the room, knocking him down and seriously wounding others. An American bazooka team set the German weapon afire, and M/Sgt. Bertoldo went back to his machinegun dazed as he was and killed several of the hostile troops as they attempted to withdraw. It was decided to evacuate the command post under the cover of darkness, but before the plan could be put into operation the enemy began an intensive assault supported by fire from their tanks and heavy guns. Disregarding the devastating barrage, he remained at his post and hurled white phosphorous grenades into the advancing enemy troops until they broke and retreated. A tank less than 50 yards away fired at his stronghold, destroyed the machinegun and blew him across the room again but he once more returned to the bitter fight and, with a rifle, singlehandedly covered the withdrawal of his fellow soldiers when the post was finally abandoned. With inspiring bravery and intrepidity M/Sgt. Bertoldo withstood the attack of vastly superior forces for more than 48 hours without rest or relief, time after time escaping death only by the slightest margin while killing at least 40 hostile soldiers and wounding many more during his grim battle against the enemy hordes.

BEYER, ARTHUR O.

Rank and organization: Corporal, U.S. Army, Company C, 603d Tank Destroyer Battalion. *Place and date:* Near Arloncourt, Belgium, 15 January 1945. *Entered service at:* St. Ansgar, Iowa. *Born:* 20 May 1909, Rock Township, Mitchell County, Iowa. *G.O. No.:* 73, 30 August 1945. *Citation:* He displayed conspicuous gallantry in action. His platoon, in which he was a tank-destroyer gunner, was held up by antitank, machinegun, and rifle fire from enemy troops dug in along a ridge about 200 yards to the front. Noting a machinegun position in this defense line, he fired upon it with his 76-mm. gun killing 1 man and silencing the weapon. He dismounted from his vehicle and, under direct enemy observation, crossed open ground to capture the 2 remaining members of the crew. Another machinegun, about 250 yards to the left, continued to fire on him. Through withering fire, he advanced on the position. Throwing a grenade into the emplacement, he killed 1 crewmember and again captured the 2 survivors. He was subjected to concentrated small-arms fire but, with great bravery, he worked his way a quarter mile along the ridge, attacking hostile soldiers in their foxholes with his carbine and grenades. When he had completed his self-imposed mission against powerful German forces, he had destroyed 2 machinegun positions, killed 8 of the enemy and captured 18 prisoners, including 2 bazooka teams. Cpl. Beyer's intrepid action and unflinching determination to close with and destroy the enemy eliminated the German defense line and enabled his task force to gain its objective.

*BIANCHI, WILLIBALD C.

Rank and organization: First Lieutenant, U.S. Army, 45th Infantry, Philippine Scouts. *Place and date:* Near Bagac, Bataan Province, Philippine Islands, 3 February 1942. *Entered service at:* New Ulm, Minn. *Birth:* New Ulm, Minn. *G.O. No.:* 11, 5 March 1942. *Citation:* For conspicuous gallantry and intrepidity above and beyond the call of duty in action with the enemy on 3 February 1942, near Bagac, Province of Bataan, Philippine Islands. When the rifle platoon of another company was ordered to wipe out 2 strong enemy machinegun nests, 1st Lt. Bianchi voluntarily and of his own initiative, advanced with the platoon leading part of the men. When wounded early in the action by 2 bullets through the left hand, he did not stop for first aid but discarded his rifle and began firing a pistol. He located a machinegun nest and personally silenced it with grenades. When wounded the second time by 2 machinegun bullets through the chest muscles, 1st Lt. Bianchi climbed to the top of an American tank, manned its antiaircraft machinegun, and fired into strongly held enemy position until knocked completely off the tank by a third severe wound.

BIDDLE, MELVIN E.

Rank and organization: Private First Class, U.S. Army, Company B, 517th Parachute Infantry Regiment. *Place and date:* Near Soy, Belgium, 23–24 December 1944. *Entered service at:* Anderson, Ind. *Birth:*

Daleville, Ind. *G.O. No.:* 95, 30 October 1945. *Citation:* He displayed conspicuous gallantry and intrepidity in action against the enemy near Soy, Belgium, on 23 and 24 December 1944. Serving as lead scout during an attack to relieve the enemy-encircled town of Hotton, he aggressively penetrated a densely wooded area, advanced 400 yards until he came within range of intense enemy rifle fire, and within 20 yards of enemy positions killed 3 snipers with unerring marksmanship. Courageously continuing his advance an additional 200 yards, he discovered a hostile machinegun position and dispatched its 2 occupants. He then located the approximate position of a well-concealed enemy machinegun nest, and crawling forward threw handgrenades which killed two Germans and fatally wounded a third. After signaling his company to advance, he entered a determined line of enemy defense, coolly and deliberately shifted his position, and shot 3 more enemy soldiers. Undaunted by enemy fire, he crawled within 20 yards of a machinegun nest, tossed his last handgrenade into the position, and after the explosion charged the emplacement firing his rifle. When night fell, he scouted enemy positions alone for several hours and returned with valuable information which enabled our attacking infantry and armor to knock out 2 enemy tanks. At daybreak he again led the advance and, when flanking elements were pinned down by enemy fire, without hesitation made his way toward a hostile machinegun position and from a distance of 50 yards killed the crew and 2 supporting riflemen. The remainder of the enemy, finding themselves without automatic weapon support, fled panic stricken. Pfc. Biddle's intrepid courage and superb daring during his 20-hour action enabled his battalion to break the enemy grasp on Hotton with a minimum of casualties.

*BIGELOW, ELMER CHARLES

Rank and organization: Watertender First Class, U.S. Naval Reserve. *Born:* 12 July 1920, Hebron, Ill. *Accredited to:* Illinois. *Citation:* For conspicuous gallantry and intrepidity at the risk of his life above and beyond the call of duty while serving on board the U.S.S. *Fletcher* during action against enemy Japanese forces off Corregidor Island in the Philippines, 14 February 1945. Standing topside when an enemy shell struck the *Fletcher*, Bigelow, acting instantly as the deadly projectile exploded into fragments which penetrated the No. 1 gun magazine and set fire to several powder cases, picked up a pair of fire extinguishers and rushed below in a resolute attempt to quell the raging flames. Refusing to waste the precious time required to don rescue-breathing apparatus, he plunged through the blinding smoke billowing out of the magazine hatch and dropped into the blazing compartment. Despite the acrid, burning powder smoke which seared his lungs with every agonizing breath, he worked rapidly and with instinctive sureness and succeeded in quickly extinguishing the fires and in cooling the cases and bulkheads, thereby preventing further damage to the stricken ship. Although he succumbed to his injuries on the following day, Bigelow, by his dauntless valor, unfaltering skill and prompt action in the critical emergency, had averted a magazine explosion which undoubtedly would have left his ship wallowing at the mercy of the furiously pounding Japanese guns on Corregidor, and his heroic spirit of self-sacrifice in the face of almost certain death enhanced and sustained the highest traditions of the U.S. Naval Service. He gallantly gave his life in the service of his country.

BJORKLUND, ARNOLD L.

Rank and organization: First Lieutenant, U.S. Army, 36th Infantry Division. *Place and date:* Near Altavilla, Italy, 13 September 1943. *Entered service at:* Seattle, Wash. *Birth:* Clinton, Wash. *G.O. No.:* 73, 6 September 1944. *Citation:* For conspicuous gallantry and intrepidity at the risk of life above and beyond the call of duty in action with the enemy near Altavilla, Italy, 13 September 1943. When his company attacked a German position on Hill 424, the first platoon, led by 1st Lt. Bjorklund, moved forward on the right flank to the slope of the hill where it was pinned down by a heavy concentration of machinegun and rifle fire. Ordering his men to give covering fire, with only 3 handgrenades, he crept and crawled forward to a German machinegun position located on a terrace along the forward slope. Approaching within a few yards of the position, and while continuously exposed to enemy fire, he hurled 1 grenade into the nest, destroyed the gun and killed 3 Germans. Discovering a second machinegun 20 yards to the right on a higher terrace, he moved under intense enemy fire to a point within a few yards and threw a second grenade into this position, destroying it and killing 2 more Germans. The first platoon was then able to advance 150 yards further up the slope to the crest of the hill, but was again stopped by the fire from a heavy enemy mortar on the reverse slope. 1st Lt. Bjorklund located the mortar and worked his way under little cover to within 10 yards of its position and threw his third grenade, destroying the mortar, killing 2 of the Germans, and forcing the remaining 3 to flee. His actions permitted the platoon to take its objective.

BLOCH, ORVILLE EMIL

Rank and organization: First Lieutenant, U.S. Army, Company E, 338th Infantry, 85th Infantry Division. *Place and date:* Near Firenzuola, Italy, 22 September 1944. *Entered service at:* Streeter, N. Dak. *Birth:* Big Falls, Wis. *G.O. No.:* 9, 10 February 1945. *Citation:* For conspicuous gallantry and intrepidity at risk of life above and beyond the call of duty. 1st Lt. Bloch undertook the task of wiping out 5 enemy machinegun nests that had held up the advance in that particular sector for 1 day. Gathering 3 volunteers from his platoon, the patrol snaked their way to a big rock, behind which a group of 3 buildings and 5 machinegun nests were located. Leaving the 3 men behind the rock, he attacked the first machinegun nest alone charging into furious automatic fire, kicking over the machinegun, and capturing the machinegun crew of 5. Pulling the pin from a grenade, he held it ready in his hand and dashed into the face of withering automatic fire toward this second enemy machinegun nest located at the corner of an adjacent building 15 yards distant. When within 20 feet of the machinegun he hurled the grenade, wounding the machinegunner, the other 2 members of the crew fleeing into a door of the house. Calling one of his volunteer group to accompany him, they advanced to the opposite end of the house, there contacting a machinegun crew of 5 running toward this house. 1st Lt. Bloch and his men opened fire on the enemy crew, forcing them to abandon this machinegun and ammunition and flee into the same house. Without a moment's hesitation, 1st Lt. Bloch, unassisted, rushed through the door into a hail of small-arms fire, firing his carbine from the hip, and captured the 7 occupants, wounding 3 of them. 1st Lt. Bloch with his men then proceeded to a third house where they discovered an abandoned enemy machinegun and detected another enemy machinegun nest at the next corner of the building. The crew of 6 spotted 1st Lt. Bloch the instant he saw them. Without a moment's hesitation he dashed toward them. The enemy fired pistols wildly in his direction and vanished through a door of the house, 1st Lt. Bloch following them through the door, firing his carbine from the hip, wounding 2 of the enemy and capturing 6. Altogether 1st Lt. Bloch had singlehandedly captured 19 prisoners, wounding 6 of them and eliminating a total of 5 enemy machinegun nests. His gallant and heroic actions saved his company many casualties and permitted them to continue the attack with new inspiration and vigor.

BOLDEN, PAUL L.

Rank and organization: Staff Sergeant, U.S. Army, Company I, 120th Infantry, 30th Infantry Division. *Place and date:* Petit-Coo, Belgium, 23 December 1944. *Entered service at:* Madison, Ala. *Birth:* Hobbes Island, Iowa. *G.O. No.:* 73, 30 August 1945. *Citation:* He voluntarily attacked a formidable enemy strongpoint in Petit-Coo, Belgium, on 23 December, 1944, when his company was pinned down by extremely heavy automatic and small-arms fire coming from a house 200 yards to the front. Mortar and tank artillery shells pounded the unit, when S/Sgt. Bolden and a comrade, on their own initiative, moved forward into a hail of bullets to eliminate the ever-increasing fire from the German position. Crawling ahead to close with what they knew was a powerfully armed, vastly superior force, the pair reached the house and took up assault positions, S/Sgt. Bolden under a window, his comrade across the street where he could deliver covering fire. In rapid succession, S/Sgt. Bolden hurled a fragmentation grenade and a white phosphorous grenade into the building; and then, fully realizing that he faced tremendous odds, rushed to the door, threw it open and fired into 35 SS troopers who were trying to reorganize themselves after the havoc wrought by the grenades. Twenty Germans died under fire of his submachinegun before he was struck in the shoulder, chest, and stomach by part of a burst which killed his comrade across the street. He withdrew from the house, waiting for the surviving Germans to come out and surrender. When none appeared in the doorway, he summoned his ebbing strength, overcame the extreme pain he suffered and boldly walked back into the house, firing as he went. He had killed the remaining 15 enemy soldiers when his ammunition ran out. S/Sgt. Bolden's heroic advance against great odds, his fearless assault, and his magnificent display of courage in reentering the building where he had been severely wounded cleared the path for his company and insured the success of its mission.

BOLTON, CECIL H.

Rank and organization: First Lieutenant, U.S. Army, Company E, 413th Infantry, 104th Infantry Division. *Place and date:* Mark River, Holland, 2 November 1944. *Entered service at:* Huntsville, Ala. *Birth:* Crawfordsville, Fla. *G.O. No.:* 74, 1 September 1945. *Citation:* As leader of the weapons platoon of Company E, 413th Infantry, on the night of 2 November 1944, he fought gallantly in a pitched battle which followed the crossing of the Mark River in Holland. When 2 machineguns pinned down his company, he tried to eliminate, with mortar fire, their grazing fire which was inflicting serious casualties and preventing the company's advance from an area rocked by artillery shelling. In the moonlight it was impossible for him to locate accurately the enemy's camouflaged positions; but he continued to direct fire until wounded severely in the legs and rendered unconscious by a German shell. When he recovered consciousness he instructed his unit and then crawled to the forward rifle platoon positions. Taking a two-man bazooka team on his voluntary mission, he advanced chest deep in chilling water along a canal toward 1 enemy machinegun. While the bazooka team covered him, he approached alone to within 15 yards of the hostile emplacement in a house. He charged the remaining distance and killed the 2 gunners with handgrenades. Returning to his men he led them through intense fire over open ground to assault the second German machinegun. An enemy sniper who tried to block the way was dispatched, and the trio pressed on. When discovered by the machinegun crew and subjected to direct fire, 1st Lt. Bolton killed 1 of the 3 gunners with carbine fire, and his 2 comrades shot the others. Continuing to disregard his wounds, he led the bazooka team toward an 88-mm. artillery piece which was having telling effect on the American ranks, and approached once more through icy canal water until he could dimly make out the gun's silhouette. Under his fire direction, the two soldiers knocked out the enemy weapon with rockets. On the way back to his own lines he was again wounded. To prevent his men being longer subjected to deadly fire, he refused aid and ordered them back to safety, painfully crawling after them until he reached his lines, where he collapsed. 1st Lt. Bolton's heroic assaults in the face of vicious fire, his inspiring leadership, and continued aggressiveness even through suffering from serious wounds, contributed in large measure to overcoming strong enemy resistance and made it possible for his battalion to reach its objective.

BONG, RICHARD I. (Air Mission)

Rank and organization: Major, U.S. Army Air Corps. *Place and date:* Over Borneo and Leyte, 10 October to 15 November 1944. *Entered service at:* Poplar, Wis. *Birth:* Poplar, Wis. *G.O. No.:* 90, 8 December 1944. *Citation:* For conspicuous gallantry and intrepidity in action above and beyond the call of duty in the Southwest Pacific area from 10 October to 15 November 1944. Though assigned to duty as gunnery instructor and neither required nor expected to perform combat duty, Maj. Bong voluntarily and at his own urgent request engaged in repeated combat missions, including unusually hazardous sorties over Balikpapan, Borneo, and in the Leyte area of the Philippines. His aggressiveness and daring resulted in his shooting down 8 enemy airplanes during this period.

*BONNYMAN, ALEXANDER, Jr.

Rank and organization: First Lieutenant, U.S. Marine Corps Reserves. *Born:* 2 May 1910, Atlanta, Ga. *Accredited to:* New Mexico. *Citation:* For conspicuous gallantry and intrepidity at the risk of his life above and beyond the call of duty as Executive Officer of the 2d Battalion Shore Party, 8th Marines, 2d Marine Division, during the assault against enemy Japanese-held Tarawa in the Gilbert Islands, 20–22 November 1943. Acting on his own initiative when assault troops were pinned down at the far end of Betio Pier by the overwhelming fire of Japanese shore batteries, 1st Lt. Bonnyman repeatedly defied the blasting fury of the enemy bombardment to organize and lead the besieged men over the long, open pier to the beach and then, voluntarily obtaining flame throwers and demolitions, organized his pioneer shore party into assault demolitionists and directed the blowing of several hostile installations before the close of D-day. Determined to effect an opening in the enemy's strongly organized defense line the following day, he voluntarily crawled approximately 40 yards forward of our lines and placed demolitions in the entrance of a large Japanese emplacement as the initial move in his planned attack against the heavily garrisoned, bombproof installation which was stubbornly resisting despite the destruction early in the action of a large number of Japanese who had been inflicting heavy casualties on our forces and holding up our advance. Withdrawing only to replenish his ammunition, he led his men in a renewed assault, fearlessly exposing himself to the merciless slash of hostile fire as he stormed the formidable bastion, directed the placement of demolition charges in both entrances and seized the top of the bombproof position, flushing more than 100 of the enemy who were instantly cut down, and effecting the annihilation of approximately 150 troops inside the emplacement. Assailed by additional Japanese after he had gained his objective, he made a heroic stand on the edge of the structure, defending his strategic position with indomitable determination in the face of the desperate charge and killing 3 of the enemy before he fell, mortally wounded. By his dauntless fighting spirit, unrelenting aggressiveness and forceful leadership throughout 3 days of unremitting, violent battle, 1st Lt. Bonnyman had inspired his men to heroic effort, enabling them to beat off the counterattack and break the back of hostile resistance in that sector for an immediate gain of 400 yards with no further casualties to our forces in this zone. He gallantly gave his life for his country.

*BOOKER, ROBERT D.

Rank and organization: Private, U.S. Army, 34th Infantry Division. *Place and date:* Near Fondouk, Tunisia, 9 April 1943. *Entered service at:* Callaway, Nebr. *Born:* 11 July 1920, Callaway, Nebr. *G.O. No.:* 34, 25 April 1944. *Citation:* For conspicuous gallantry and intrepidity at risk of life above and beyond the call of duty in action. On 9 April 1943 in the vicinity of Fondouk, Tunisia, Pvt. Booker, while engaged in action against the enemy, carried a light machinegun and a box of ammunition over 200 yards of open ground. He continued to advance despite the fact that 2 enemy machineguns and several mortars were using him as an individual target. Although enemy artillery also began to register on him, upon reaching his objective he immediately commenced firing. After being wounded he silenced 1 enemy machinegun and was beginning to fire at the other when he received a second mortal wound. With his last remaining strength he encouraged the members of his squad and directed their fire. Pvt. Booker acted without regard for his own safety. His initiative and courage against insurmountable odds are an example of the highest standard of self-sacrifice and fidelity to duty.

*BORDELON, WILLIAM JAMES

Rank and organization: Staff Sergeant, U.S. Marine Corps. *Born:* 25 December 1920, San Antonio, Tex. *Accredited to:* Texas. *Citation:* For valorous and gallant conduct above and beyond the call of duty as a member of an assault engineer platoon of the 1st Batallion, 18th Marines, tactically attached to the 2d Marine Division, in action against the Japanese-held atoll of Tarawa in the Gilbert Islands on 20 November 1943. Landing in the assault waves under withering enemy fire which killed all but 4 of the men in his tractor, S/Sgt. Bordelon hurriedly made demolition charges and personally put 2 pillboxes out of action. Hit by enemy machinegun fire just as a charge exploded in his hand while assaulting a third position, he courageously remained in action and, although out of demolition, provided himself with a rifle and furnished fire coverage for a group of men scaling the seawall. Disregarding his own serious condition, he unhesitatingly went to the aid of one of his demolition men, wounded and calling for help in the water, rescuing this man and another who had been hit by enemy fire while attempting to make the rescue. Still refusing first aid for himself, he again made up demolition charges and singlehandedly assaulted a fourth Japanese machinegun position but was instantly killed when caught in a final burst of fire from the enemy. S/Sgt. Bordelon's great personal valor during a critical phase of securing the limited beachhead was a contributing factor in the ultimate occupation of the island, and his heroic determination throughout 3 days of violent battle reflects the highest credit upon the U.S. Naval Service. He gallantly gave his life for his country.

*BOYCE, GEORGE W. G., Jr.

Rank and organization: Second Lieutenant, U.S. Army, 112th Cavalry Regimental Combat Team. *Place and date:* Near Afua, New Guinea, 23 July 1944. *Entered service at:* Town of Cornwall, Orange County, N.Y. *Birth:* New York City, N.Y. *G.O. No.:* 25, 7 April 1945. *Citation:* For conspicuous gallantry and intrepidity at risk of his life above and beyond the call of duty near Afua, New Guinea, on 23 July 1944. 2d Lt. Boyce's troop, having been ordered to the relief of another unit surrounded by superior enemy forces, moved out, and upon gaining contact with the enemy, the two leading platoons deployed and built up a firing line. 2d Lt. Boyce was ordered to attack with his platoon and make the main effort on the right of the troop. He launched his attack but after a short advance encountered such intense rifle, machinegun, and mortar fire that the forward movement of his platoon was temporarily halted. A shallow depression offered a route of advance and he worked his squad up this avenue of approach in order to close with the enemy. He was promptly met by a volley of handgrenades, 1 falling between himself and the men immediately following. Realizing at once that the explosion would kill or wound several of his men, he promptly threw himself upon the grenade and smothered the blast with his own body. By thus deliberately sacrificing his life to save those of his men, this officer exemplified the highest traditions of the U.S. Armed Forces.

BOYINGTON, GREGORY

Rank and organization: Major, U.S. Marine Corps Reserve, Marine Squadron 214. *Place and date:* Central Solomons area, from 12 September 1943 to 3 January 1944. *Entered service at:* Washington. *Born:* 4 December 1912, Coeur D'Alene, Idaho. *Other Navy award:* Navy Cross. *Citation:* For extraordinary heroism and valiant devotion to duty as commanding officer of Marine Fighting Squadron 214 in action against enemy Japanese forces in the Central Solomons area from 12 September 1943 to 3 January 1944. Consistently outnumbered throughout successive hazardous flights over heavily defended hostile territory, Maj. Boyington struck at the enemy with daring and courageous persistence, leading his squadron into combat with devastating results to Japanese shipping, shore installations, and aerial forces. Resolute in his efforts to inflict crippling damage on the enemy, Maj. Boyington led a formation of 24 fighters over Kahili on 17 October and, persistently circling the airdrome where 60 hostile aircraft were grounded, boldly challenged the Japanese to send up planes. Under his brilliant command, our fighters shot down 20 enemy craft in the ensuing action without the loss of a single ship. A superb airman and determined fighter against overwhelming odds, Maj. Boyington personally destroyed 26 of the many Japanese planes shot down by his squadron and, by his forceful leadership, developed the combat readiness in his command which was a distinctive factor in the Allied aerial achievements in this vitally strategic area.

BRILES, HERSCHEL F.

Rank and organization: Staff Sergeant, U.S. Army, Co. C, 899th Tank Destroyer Battalion. *Place and date:* Near Scherpenseel, Germany, 20 November 1944. *Entered service at:* Fort Des Moines, Iowa. *Birth:* Colfax, Iowa. *G.O. No.:* 77, 10 September 1945. *Citation:* He was leading a platoon of destroyers across an exposed slope near Scherpenseel, Germany, on 20 November 1944, when they came under heavy enemy artillery fire. A direct hit was scored on 1 of the vehicles, killing 1 man, seriously wounding 2 others, and setting the destroyer afire. With a comrade, S/Sgt. Briles left the cover of his own armor and raced across ground raked by artillery and small-arms fire to the rescue of the men in the shattered destroyer. Without hesitation, he lowered himself into the burning turret, removed the wounded and then extinguished the fire. From a position he assumed the next morning, he observed hostile infantrymen advancing. With his machinegun, he poured such deadly fire into the enemy ranks that an entire pocket of 55 Germans surrendered, clearing the way for a junction between

American units which had been held up for 2 days. Later that day, when another of his destroyers was hit by a concealed enemy tank, he again left protection to give assistance. With the help of another soldier, he evacuated two wounded under heavy fire and, returning to the burning vehicle, braved death from exploding ammunition to put out the flames. By his heroic initiative and complete disregard for personal safety, S/Sgt. Briles was largely responsible for causing heavy enemy casualties, forcing the surrender of 55 Germans, making possible the salvage of our vehicles, and saving the lives of wounded comrades.

BRITT, MAURICE L.

Rank and organization: Captain (then Lieutenant), U.S. Army, 3d Infantry Division. *Place and date:* North of Mignano, Italy, 10 November 1943. *Entered service at:* Lonoke, Ark. *Born:* 29 June 1919, Carlisle, Ark. *G.O. No.:* 23, 24 March 1944. *Citation:* For conspicuous gallantry and intrepidity at the risk of his life above and beyond the call of duty. Disdaining enemy handgrenades and close-range machine pistol, machinegun, and rifle, Lt. Britt inspired and led a handful of his men in repelling a bitter counterattack by approximately 100 Germans against his company positions north of Mignano, Italy, the morning of 10 November 1943. During the intense fire fight, Lt. Britt's canteen and field glasses were shattered; a bullet pierced his side; his chest, face, and hands were covered with grenade wounds. Despite his wounds, for which he refused to accept medical attention until ordered to do so by his battalion commander following the battle, he personally killed 5 and wounded an unknown number of Germans, wiped out one enemy machinegun crew, fired 5 clips of carbine and an undetermined amount of M1 rifle ammunition, and threw 32 fragmentation grenades. His bold, aggressive actions, utterly disregarding superior enemy numbers, resulted in capture of 4 Germans, 2 of them wounded, and enabled several captured Americans to escape. Lt. Britt's undaunted courage and prowess in arms were largely responsible for repulsing a German counterattack which, if successful, would have isolated his battalion and destroyed his company.

*BROSTROM, LEONARD C.

Rank and organization: Private First Class, U.S. Army, Company F, 17th Infantry, 7th Infantry Division. *Place and date:* Near Dagami, Leyte, Philippine Islands, 28 October 1944. *Entered service at:* Preston, Idaho. *Birth:* Preston, Idaho. *G.O. No.:* 104, 15 November 1945. *Citation:* He was a rifleman with an assault platoon which ran into powerful resistance near Dagami, Leyte, Philippine Islands, on 28 October 1944. From pillboxes, trenches, and spider holes, so well camouflaged that they could be detected at no more than 20 yards, the enemy poured machinegun and rifle fire, causing severe casualties in the platoon. Realizing that a key pillbox in the center of the strong point would have to be knocked out if the company were to advance, Pfc. Bostrom, without orders and completely ignoring his own safety, ran forward to attack the pillbox with grenades. He immediately became the prime target for all the riflemen in the area, as he rushed to the rear of the pillbox and tossed grenades through the entrance. Six enemy soldiers left a trench in a bayonet charge against the heroic

American, but he killed 1 and drove the others off with rifle fire. As he threw more grenades from his completely exposed position he was wounded several times in the abdomen and knocked to the ground. Although suffering intense pain and rapidly weakening from loss of blood, he slowly rose to his feet and once more hurled his deadly missles at the pillbox. As he collapsed, the enemy began fleeing from the fortification and were killed by riflemen of his platoon. Pfc. Brostrom died while being carried from the battlefield, but his intrepidity and unhesitating willingness to sacrifice himself in a 1-man attack against overwhelming odds enabled his company to reorganize against attack, and annihilate the entire enemy position.

BROWN, BOBBIE E.

Rank and organization: Captain, U.S. Army, Company C, 18th Infantry, 1st Infantry Division. *Place and date:* Crucifix Hill, Aachen, Germany, 8 October 1944. *Entered service at:* Atlanta, Ga. *Born:* 2 September 1903, Dublin, Ga. *G.O. No.:* 74, 1 September 1945. *Citation:* He commanded Company C, 18th Infantry Regiment, on 8 October 1944, when it, with the Ranger Platoon of the 1st Battalion, attacked Crucifix Hill, a key point in the enemy's defense of Aachen, Germany. As the leading rifle platoon assaulted the first of many pillboxes studding the rising ground, heavy fire from a flanking emplacement raked it. An intense artillery barrage fell on the American troops which had been pinned down in an exposed position. Seeing that the pillboxes must be neutralized to prevent the slaughter of his men, Capt. Brown obtained a pole charge and started forward alone toward the first pillbox, about 100 yards away. Hugging the ground while enemy bullets whipped around him, he crawled and then ran toward the aperture of the fortification, rammed his explosive inside and jumped back as the pillbox and its occupants were blown up. He rejoined the assault platoon, secured another pole charge, and led the way toward the next pillbox under continuous artillery mortar, automatic, and small-arms fire. He again ran forward and placed his charge in the enemy fortification, knocking it out. He then found that fire from a third pillbox was pinning down his company; so he returned to his men, secured another charge, and began to creep and crawl toward the hostile emplacement. With heroic bravery he disregarded opposing fire and worked ahead in the face of bullets streaming from the pillbox. Finally reaching his objective, he stood up and inserted his explosive, silencing the enemy. He was wounded by a mortar shell but refused medical attention and, despite heavy hostile fire, moved swiftly among his troops exhorting and instructing them in subduing powerful opposition. Later, realizing the need for information of enemy activity beyond the hill, Capt. Brown went out alone to reconnoiter. He observed possible routes of enemy approach and several times deliberately drew enemy fire to locate gun emplacements. Twice more, on this self-imposed mission, he was wounded; but he succeeded in securing information which led to the destruction of several enemy guns and enabled his company to throw back 2 powerful counterattacks with heavy losses. Only when Company C's position was completely secure did he permit treatment of his 3 wounds. By his indomitable courage, fearless leadership, and outstanding skill as a soldier, Capt. Brown contributed in great measure to the taking of Crucifix Hill, a vital link in the American line encircling Aachen.

BULKELEY, JOHN DUNCAN

Rank and organization: Lieutenant Commander, Commander of Motor Torpedo Boat Squadron 3, U.S. Navy. *Place and date:* Philippine waters, 7 December 1941 to 10 April 1942. *Entered service at:* Texas. *Born:* 19 August 1911, New York, N.Y. *Other awards:* Navy Cross, Distinguished Service Cross, Silver Star, Legion of Merit. *Citation:* For extraordinary heroism, distinguished service, and conspicuous gallantry above and beyond the call of duty as commander of Motor Torpedo Boat Squadron 3, in Philippine waters during the period 7 December 1941 to 10 April 1942. The remarkable achievement of Lt. Comdr. Bulkeley's command in damaging or destroying a notable number of Japanese enemy planes, surface combatant and merchant ships, and in dispersing landing parties and land-based enemy forces during the 4 months and 8 days of operation without benefit of repairs, overhaul, or maintenance facilities for his squadron, is believed to be without precedent in this type of warfare. His dynamic forcefulness and daring in offensive action, his brilliantly planned and skillfully executed attacks, supplemented by a unique resourcefulness and ingenuity, characterize him as an outstanding leader of men and a gallant and intrepid seaman. These qualities coupled with a complete disregard for his own personal safety reflect great credit upon him and the Naval Service.

BURKE, FRANK (also known as FRANCIS X. BURKE)

Rank and organization: First Lieutenant, U.S. Army, 15th Infantry, 3d Infantry Division. *Place and date:* Nuremberg, Germany, 17 April 1945. *Entered service at:* Jersey City, N.J. *Born:* 29 September 1918, New York, N.Y. *G.O. No.:* 4, 9 January 1946. *Citation:* He fought with extreme gallantry in the streets of wartorn Nuremberg, Germany, where the 1st Battalion, 15th Infantry, was engaged in rooting out fanatical defenders of the citadel of Nazism. As battalion transportation officer he had gone forward to select a motor-pool site, when, in a desire to perform more than his assigned duties and participate in the fight, he advanced beyond the lines of the forward riflemen. Detecting a group of about 10 Germans making preparations for a local counterattack, he rushed back to a nearby American company, secured a light machinegun with ammunition, and daringly opened fire on this superior force, which deployed and returned his fire with machine pistols, rifles, and rocket launchers. From another angle a German machinegun tried to blast him from his emplacement, but 1st Lt. Burke killed this guncrew and drove off the survivors of the unit he had originally attacked. Giving his next attention to enemy infantrymen in ruined buildings, he picked up a rifle dashed more than 100 yards through intense fire and engaged the Germans from behind an abandoned tank. A sniper nearly hit him from a cellar only 20 yards away, but he dispatched this adversary by running directly to the basement window, firing a full clip into it and then plunging through the darkened aperture to complete the job. He withdrew from the fight only long enough to replace his jammed rifle and secure grenades, then reengaged the Germans. Finding his shots ineffective, he pulled the pins from 2 grenades, and, holding 1 in each hand, rushed the enemy-held building, hurling his missiles just as the enemy threw a potato masher grenade at him. In the triple explosion the Germans were wiped out and 1st Lt. Burke was dazed; but he emerged from the shower of debris that engulfed him, recovered his rifle, and went on to kill 3 more Germans and meet the charge of a machine pistolman, whom he cut down with 3 calmly delivered shots. He then retired toward the American lines and there assisted a platoon in a raging, 30-minute fight against formidable armed hostile forces. This enemy group was repulsed, and the intrepid fighter moved to another friendly group which broke the power of a German unit armed with a 20-mm. gun in a fierce fire fight. In 4 hours of heroic action, 1st Lt. Burke singlehandedly killed 11 and wounded 3 enemy soldiers and took a leading role in engagements in which an additional 29 enemy were killed or wounded. His extraordinary bravery and superb fighting skill were an inspiration to his comrades, and his entirely voluntary mission into extremely dangerous territory hastened the fall of Nuremberg, in his battalion's sector.

*BURR, ELMER J.

Rank and organization: First Sergeant, U.S. Army, Company I, 127th Infantry, 32d Infantry Division. *Place and date:* Buna, New Guinea, 24 December 1942. *Entered service at:* Menasha, Wis. *Birth:* Neenah, Wis. *G.O. No.:* 66, 11 Oct. 1943. *Citation:* For conspicuous gallantry and intrepidity in action above and beyond the call of duty. During an attack near Buna, New Guinea, on 24 December 1942, 1st Sgt. Burr saw an enemy grenade strike near his company commander. Instantly and with heroic self-sacrifice he threw himself upon it, smothering the explosion with his body. 1st Sgt. Burr thus gave his life in saving that of his commander.

BURR, HERBERT H.

Rank and organization: Staff Sergeant, U.S. Army, Company C, 41st Tank Battalion, 11th Armored Division. *Place and date:* Near Dorr-moschel, Germany, 19 March 1945. *Entered service at:* Kansas City, Mo. *Birth:* St. Joseph, Mo. *G.O. No.:* 73, 30 August 1945. *Citation:* He displayed conspicuous gallantry during action when the tank in which he was bow gunner was hit by an enemy rocket, which severely wounded the platoon sergeant and forced the remainder of the crew to abandon the vehicle. Deafened, but otherwise unhurt, S/Sgt. Burr immediately climbed into the driver's seat and continued on the mission of entering the town to reconnoiter road conditions. As he rounded a turn he encountered an 88-mm. antitank gun at pointblank range. Realizing that he had no crew, no one to man the tank's guns, he heroically chose to disregard his personal safety in a direct charge on the German weapon. At considerable speed he headed straight for the loaded gun, which was fully manned by enemy troops who had only to pull the lanyard to send a shell into his vehicle. So unexpected and daring was his assault that he was able to drive his tank completely over the gun, demolishing it and causing its crew to flee in confusion. He then skillfully sideswiped a large truck, overturned it, and wheeling his lumbering vehicle, returned to his company. When medical personnel who had been summoned to treat the wounded sergeant could not locate him, the valiant soldier ran through a hail of sniper fire to direct them to his stricken comrade. The bold, fearless determination of S/Sgt. Burr, his skill and courageous devotion to duty, resulted in the completion of his mission in the face of seemingly impossible odds.

BURT, JAMES M.

Rank and organization: Captain, U.S. Army, Company B, 66th Armored Regiment, 2d Armored Division. *Place and date:* Near Wurselen, Germany, 13 October 1944. *Entered service at:* Lee, Mass. *Birth:* Hinsdale, Mass. *G.O. No.:* 95, 30 October 1945. *Citation:* Capt. James M. Burt was in command of Company B, 66th Armored Regiment on the western outskirts of Wurselen, Germany, on 13 October 1944, when his organization participated in a coordinated infantry-tank attack destined to isolate the large German garrison which was tenaciously defending the city of Aachen. In the first day's action, when infantrymen ran into murderous small-arms and mortar fire, Capt. Burt dismounted from his tank about 200 yards to the rear and moved forward on foot beyond the infantry positions, where, as the enemy concentrated a tremendous volume of fire upon him, he calmly motioned his tanks into good firing positions. As our attack gained momentum, he climbed aboard his tank and directed the action from the rear deck, exposed to hostile volleys which finally wounded him painfully in the face and neck. He maintained his dangerous post despite pointblank self-propelled gunfire until friendly artillery knocked out these enemy weapons, and then proceeded to the advanced infantry scouts' positions to deploy his tanks for the defense of the gains which had been made. The next day, when the enemy counterattacked, he left cover and went 75 yards through heavy fire to assist the infantry battalion commander who was seriously wounded. For the next 8 days, through rainy, miserable weather and under constant, heavy shelling, Capt. Burt held the combined forces together, dominating and controlling the critical situation through the sheer force of his heroic example. To direct artillery fire, on 15 October, he took his tank 300 yards into the enemy lines, where he dismounted and remained for 1 hour giving accurate data to friendly gunners. Twice more that day he went into enemy territory under deadly fire on reconnaissance. In succeeding days he never faltered in his determination to defeat the strong German forces opposing him. Twice the tank in which he was riding was knocked out by enemy action, and each time he climbed aboard another vehicle and continued the fight. He took great risks to rescue wounded comrades and inflicted prodigious destruction on enemy personnel and materiel even though suffering from the wounds he received in the battle's opening phase. Capt. Burt's intrepidity and disregard of personal safety were so complete that his own men and the infantry who attached themselves to him were inspired to overcome the wretched and extremely hazardous conditions which accompanied one of the most bitter local actions of the war. The victory achieved closed the Aachen gap.

BUSH, RICHARD EARL

Rank and organization: Corporal, U.S. Marine Corps Reserve, 1st Battalion, 4th Marines, 6th Marine Division. *Place and date:* Mount Yaetake on Okinawa, Ryukyu Islands, 16 April 1945. *Entered service at:* Kentucky. *Born:* 23 December 1923, Glasgow, Ky. *Citation:* For conspicuous gallantry and intrepidity at the risk of his life above and beyond the call of duty as a squad leader serving with the 1st Battalion, 4th Marines, 6th Marine Division, in action against enemy Japanese forces, during the final assault against Mount Yaetake on Okinawa, Ryukyu Islands, 16 April 1945. Rallying his men forward with indomitable determination, Cpl. Bush boldly defied the slashing fury of concentrated Japanese artillery fire pouring down from the gun-studded mountain fortress to lead his squad up the face of the rocky precipice, sweep over the ridge, and drive the defending troops from their deeply entrenched position. With his unit, the first to break through to the inner defense of Mount Yaetake, he fought relentlessly in the forefront of the action until seriously wounded and evacuated with others under protecting rocks. Although prostrate under medical treatment when a Japanese handgrenade landed in the midst of the group, Cpl. Bush, alert and courageous in extremity as in battle, unhesitatingly pulled the deadly missile to himself and absorbed the shattering violence of the exploding charge in his body, thereby saving his fellow marines from severe injury or death despite the certain peril to his own life. By his valiant leadership and aggressive tactics in the face of savage opposition, Cpl. Bush contributed materially to the success of the sustained drive toward the conquest of this fiercely defended outpost of the Japanese Empire. His constant concern for the welfare of his men, his resolute spirit of self-sacrifice, and his unwavering devotion to duty throughout the bitter conflict enhance and sustain the highest traditions of the U.S. Naval Service.

BUSH, ROBERT EUGENE

Rank and organization: Hospital Apprentice First Class, U.S. Naval Reserve, serving as Medical Corpsman with a rifle company, 2d Battalion, 5th Marines, 1st Marine Division. *Place and date:* Okinawa Jima, Ryukyu Islands, 2 May 1945. *Entered service at:* Washington. *Born:* 4 October 1926, Tacoma, Wash. Citation: For conspicuous gallantry and intrepidity at the risk of his life above and beyond the call of duty while serving as Medical Corpsman with a rifle company, in action against enemy Japanese forces on Okinawa Jima, Ryukyu Islands, 2 May 1945. Fearlessly braving the fury of artillery, mortar, and machinegun fire from strongly entrenched hostile positions, Bush constantly and unhesitatingly moved from 1 casualty to another to attend the wounded falling under the enemy's murderous barrages. As the attack passed over a ridge top, Bush was advancing to administer blood plasma to a marine officer lying wounded on the skyline when the Japanese launched a savage counterattack. In this perilously exposed position, he resolutely maintained the flow of lifegiving plasma. With the bottle held high in 1 hand, Bush drew his pistol with the other and fired into the enemy's ranks until his ammunition was expended. Quickly seizing a discarded carbine, he trained his fire on the

Japanese charging pointblank over the hill, accounting for 6 of the enemy despite his own serious wounds and the loss of 1 eye suffered during his desperate battle in defense of the helpless man. With the hostile force finally routed, he calmly disregarded his own critical condition to complete his mission, valiantly refusing medical treatment for himself until his officer patient had been evacuated, and collapsing only after attempting to walk to the battle aid station. His daring initiative, great personal valor, and heroic spirit of self-sacrifice in service of others reflect great credit upon Bush and enhance the finest traditions of the U.S. Naval Service.

*BUTTS, JOHN E.

Rank and organization: Second Lieutenant, U.S. Army, Co. E, 60th Infantry, 9th Infantry Division. *Place and date:* Normandy, France, 14, 16, and 23 June 1944. *Entered service at:* Buffalo, N.Y. *Birth:* Medina, N.Y. *G.O. No.:* 58, 19 July 1945. *Citation:* Heroically led his platoon against the enemy in Normandy, France, on 14, 16, and 23 June 1944. Although painfully wounded on the 14th near Orglandes and again on the 16th while spearheading an attack to establish a bridgehead across the Douve River, he refused medical aid and remained with his platoon. A week later, near Flottemanville Hague, he led an assault on a tactically important and stubbornly defended hill studded with tanks, antitank guns, pillboxes, and machinegun emplacements, and protected by concentrated artillery and mortar fire. As the attack was launched, 2d Lt. Butts, at the head of his platoon, was critically wounded by German machinegun fire. Although weakened by his injuries, he rallied his men and directed 1 squad to make a flanking movement while he alone made a frontal assault to draw the hostile fire upon himself. Once more he was struck, but by grim determination and sheer courage continued to crawl ahead. When within 10 yards of his objective, he was killed by direct fire. By his superb courage, unflinching valor and inspiring actions, 2d Lt. Butts enabled his platoon to take a formidable strong point and contributed greatly to the success of his battalion's mission.

*CADDY, WILLIAM ROBERT

Rank and organization: Private First Class, U.S. Marine Corps Reserve. *Born:* 8 August 1925, Quincy, Mass. *Accredited to:* Massachusetts. *Citation:* For conspicuous gallantry and intrepidity at the risk of his life above and beyond the call of duty while serving as a rifleman with Company I, 3d Battalion, 26th Marines, 5th Marine Division, in action against enemy Japanese forces during the seizure of Iwo Jima in the Volcano Islands, 3 March 1945. Consistently aggressive, Pfc Caddy boldly defied shattering Japanese machinegun and small-arms fire to move forward with his platoon leader and another marine during the determined advance of his company through an isolated sector and, gaining the comparative safety of a shell hole, took temporary cover with his comrades. Immediately pinned down by deadly sniper fire from a well-concealed position, he made several unsuccessful attempts to again move forward and then, joined by his platoon leader, engaged the enemy in a fierce exchange of handgrenades until a Japanese grenade fell beyond reach in the shell hole. Fearlessly disregarding all personal danger, Pfc. Caddy instantly dived on the deadly missile, absorbing the exploding charge in his own body and protecting the others from serious injury. Stouthearted and indomitable, he unhesitatingly yielded his own life that his fellow marines might carry on the relentless battle against a fanatic enemy. His dauntless courage and valiant spirit of self-sacrifice in the face of certain death reflect the highest credit upon Pfc. Caddy and upon the U.S. Naval Service. He gallantly gave his life for his comrades.

*CALLAGHAN, DANIEL JUDSON

Rank and organization: Rear Admiral, U.S. Navy. *Born:* 26 July 1892, San Francisco, Calif. *Appointed from:* California. *Entered service at:* Oakland, Calif. *Other Navy award:* Distinguished Service Medal. *Citation:* For extraordinary heroism and conspicuous intrepidity above and beyond the call of duty during action against enemy Japanese forces off Savo Island on the night of 12–13 November 1942. Although out-balanced in strength and numbers by a desperate and determined enemy, Rear Adm. Callaghan, with ingenious tactical skill and superb coordination of the units under his command, led his forces into battle against tremendous odds, thereby contributing decisively to the rout of a powerful invasion fleet, and to the consequent frustration of a formidable Japanese offensive. While faithfully directing close-range operations in the face of furious bombardment by superior enemy fire power, he was killed on the bridge of his flagship. His courageous initiative, inspiring leadership, and judicious foresight in a crisis of grave responsibility were in keeping with the finest traditions of the U.S. Naval Service. He gallantly gave his life in the defense of his country.

CALUGAS, JOSE

Rank and organization: Sergeant, U.S. Army, Battery B, 88th Field Artillery, Philippine Scouts. *Place and date:* At Culis, Bataan Province, Philippine Islands, 16 January 1942. *Entered service at:* Fort Stotsenburg, Philippine Islands. *Born:* 29 December 1907, Barrio Tagsing, Leon, Iloilo, Philippine Islands. *G.O. No.:* 10, 24 February 1942. *Citation:* The action for which the award was made took place near Culis, Bataan Province, Philippine Islands, on 16 January 1942. A battery gun position was bombed and shelled by the enemy until 1 gun was put out of commission and all the cannoneers were killed or wounded. Sgt. Calugas, a mess sergeant of another battery, voluntarily and without orders ran 1,000 yards across the shell-swept area to the gun position. There he organized a volunteer squad which placed the gun back in commission and fired effectively against the enemy, although the position remained under constant and heavy Japanese artillery fire.

*CANNON, GEORGE HAM

Rank and organization: First Lieutenant, U.S. Marine Corps. *Born:* 5 November 1915, Webster Groves, Mo. *Entered service at:* Michigan. *Citation:* For distinguished conduct in the line of his profession, extraordinary courage and disregard of his own condition during the bombardment of Sand Island, Midway Islands, by Japanese forces on 7 December 1941. 1st Lt. Cannon, Battery Commander of Battery H,

6th Defense Battalion, Fleet Marine Force, U.S. Marine Corps, was at his command post when he was mortally wounded by enemy shellfire. He refused to be evacuated from his post until after his men who had been wounded by the same shell were evacuated, and directed the reorganization of his command post until forcibly removed. As a result of his utter disregard of his own condition he died from loss of blood.

*CAREY, ALVIN P.

Rank and organization: Staff Sergeant, U.S. Army, 38th Infantry, 2d Infantry Division. *Place and date:* Near Plougastel, Brittany, France, 23 August 1944. *Entered service at:* Laughlinstown, Pa. *Born:* 16 August 1916, Lycippus, Pa. *G.O. No.:* 37, 11 May 1945. *Citation:* For conspicuous gallantry and intrepidity at the risk of his life, above and beyond the call of duty, on 23 August 1944. S/Sgt. Carey, leader of a machinegun section, was advancing with his company in the attack on the strongly held enemy hill 154, near Plougastel, Brittany, France. The advance was held up when the attacking units were pinned down by intense enemy machinegun fire from a pillbox 200 yards up the hill. From his position covering the right flank, S/Sgt. Carey displaced his guns to an advanced position and then, upon his own initiative, armed himself with as many handgrenades as he could carry and without regard for his personal safety started alone up the hill toward the pillbox. Crawling forward under its withering fire, he proceeded 150 yards when he met a German rifleman whom he killed with his carbine. Continuing his steady forward movement until he reached grenade-throwing distance, he hurled his grenades at the pillbox opening in the face of intense enemy fire which wounded him mortally. Undaunted, he gathered his strength and continued his grenade attack until one entered and exploded within the pillbox, killing the occupants and putting their guns out of action. Inspired by S/Sgt. Carey's heroic act, the riflemen quickly occupied the position and overpowered the remaining enemy resistance in the vicinity.

*CAREY, CHARLES F., JR.

Rank and organization: Technical Sergeant, U.S. Army, 379th Infantry, 100th Infantry Division. *Place and date:* Rimling, France, 8-9 January 1945. *Entered service at:* Cheyenne, Wyo. *Birth:* Canadian, Okla. *G.O. No.:* 53, July 1945. *Citation:* He was in command of an antitank platoon when about 200 enemy infantrymen and 12 tanks attacked his battalion, overrunning part of its position. After losing his guns, T/Sgt. Carey, acting entirely on his own initiative, organized a patrol and rescued 2 of his squads from a threatened sector, evacuating those who had been wounded. He organized a second patrol and advanced against an enemy-held house from which vicious fire issued, preventing the free movement of our troops. Covered by fire from his patrol, he approached the house, killed 2 snipers with his rifle, and threw a grenade in the door. He entered alone and a few minutes later emerged with 16 prisoners. Acting on information he furnished, the American forces were able to capture an additional 41 Germans in adjacent houses. He assembled another patrol, and, under covering fire, moved to within a few yards of an enemy tank and damaged it with a rocket. As the crew attempted to leave their burning vehicle, he calmly shot them with his rifle, killing 3 and wounding a fourth. Early in the morning of 9 January, German infantry moved into the western part of the town and encircled a house in which T/Sgt. Carey had previously posted a squad. Four of the group escaped to the attic. By maneuvering an old staircase against the building, T/Sgt. Carey was able to rescue these men. Later that day, when attempting to reach an outpost, he was struck down by sniper fire. The fearless and aggressive leadership of T/Sgt. Carey, his courage in the face of heavy fire from superior enemy forces, provided an inspiring example for his comrades and materially helped his battalion to withstand the German onslaught.

CARR, CHRIS (name legally changed from CHRISTOS H. KARABERIS, under which name the medal was awarded)

Rank and organization: Sergeant, U.S. Army, Company L, 337th Infantry, 85th Infantry Division. *Place and date:* Near Guignola, Italy, 1-2 October 1944. *Entered service at:* Manchester, N.H. *Birth:* Manchester, N.H. *G.O. No.:* 97, 1 November 1945. *Citation:* Leading a squad of Company L, he gallantly cleared the way for his company's approach along a ridge toward its objective, the Casoni di Remagna. When his platoon was pinned down by heavy fire from enemy mortars, machineguns, machine pistols, and rifles, he climbed in advance of his squad on a maneuver around the left flank to locate and eliminate the enemy gun positions. Undeterred by deadly fire that ricocheted off the barren rocky hillside, he crept to the rear of the first machinegun and charged, firing his submachinegun. In this surprise attack he captured 8 prisoners and turned them over to his squad before striking out alone for a second machinegun. Discovered in his advance and subjected to direct fire from the hostile weapon, he leaped to his feet and ran forward, weaving and crouching, pouring automatic fire into the emplacement that killed 4 of its defenders and forced the surrender of a lone survivor. He again moved forward through heavy fire to attack a third machinegun. When close to the emplacement, he closed with a nerve-shattering shout and burst of fire. Paralyzed by his whirlwind attack, all 4 gunners immediately surrendered. Once more advancing aggressively in the face of a thoroughly alerted enemy, he approached a point of high ground occupied by 2 machineguns which were firing on his company on the slope below. Charging the first of these weapons, he killed 4 of the crew and captured 3 more. The 6 defenders of the adjacent position, cowed by the savagery of his assault, immediately gave up. By his 1-man attack, heroically and voluntarily undertaken in the face of tremendous risks, Sgt. Karaberis captured 5 enemy machinegun positions, killed 8 Germans, took 22 prisoners, cleared the ridge leading to his company's objective, and drove a deep wedge into the enemy line, making it possible for his battalion to occupy important, commanding ground.

*CARSWELL, HORACE S., Jr. (Air Mission)

Rank and organization: Major, 308th Bombardment Group, U.S. Army Air Corps. *Place and date:* Over South China Sea, 26 October 1944. *Entered service at:* San Angelo, Tex. *Birth:* Fort Worth, Tex. *G.O. No.:* 14, 4 February 1946. *Citation:* He piloted a B-24 bomber in a one-plane strike against a Japanese convoy in the South China Sea on the night of 26 October 1944. Taking the enemy force of 12 ships escorted by at least 2 destroyers by surprise, he made 1 bombing run at 600 feet, scoring a near miss on 1 warship and escaping without drawing fire. He circled, and fully realizing that the convoy was thoroughly alerted and would meet his next attack with a barrage of antiaircraft fire, began a second low-level run which culminated in 2 direct hits on a large tanker. A hail of steel from Japanese guns, riddled the bomber, knocking out 2 engines, damaging a third, crippling the hydraulic system, puncturing 1 gasoline tank, ripping uncounted holes in the aircraft, and wounding the copilot; but by magnificent display of flying skill, Maj. Carswell controlled the plane's plunge toward the sea and carefully forced it into a halting climb in the direction of the China shore. On reaching land, where it would have been possible to abandon the staggering bomber, one of the crew discovered that his parachute had been ripped by flak and rendered useless; the pilot, hoping to cross mountainous terrain and reach a base, continued onward until the third engine failed. He ordered the crew to bail out while he struggled to maintain altitude, and, refusing to save himself, chose to remain with his comrade and attempt a crash landing. He died when the airplane struck a mountainside and burned. With consummate gallantry and intrepidity, Maj. Carswell gave his life in a supreme effort to save all members of his crew. His sacrifice, far beyond that required of him, was in keeping with the traditional bravery of America's war heroes.

CASAMENTO, ANTHONY

Rank and organization: Corporal, Company D, First Battalion, Fifth Marines, First Marine Division. *Place and date:* Guadalcanal, Solomon Islands. *Entered service at:* Brooklyn, New York. *Date and place of birth:* 16 November 1920, Brooklyn, New York. For conspicuous gallantry and intrepidity at the risk of his life above and beyond the call of duty while serving with Company "D," First Battalion, Fifth Marines, First Marine Division on Guadalcanal, British Solomon Islands, in action against the enemy Japanese forces on 1 November 1942. Serving as a leader of a machine gun section, Corporal Casamento directed his unit to advance along a ridge near the Matanikau River where they engaged the enemy. He positioned his section to provide covering fire for two flanking units and to provide direct support for the main force of his company which was behind him. During the course of this engagement, all members of his section were either killed or severely wounded and he himself suffered multiple, grievous wounds. Nonetheless, Corporal Casamento continued to provide critical supporting fire for the attack and in defense of his position. Following the loss of all effective personnel, he set up, loaded, and manned his unit's machine gun, tenaciously holding the enemy forces at bay. Corporal Casamento single-handedly engaged and destroyed one machine gun emplacement to his front and took under fire the other emplacement on the flank. Despite the heat and ferocity of the engagement, he continued to man his weapon and repeatedly repulsed multiple assaults by the enemy forces, thereby protecting the flanks of the adjoining companies and holding his position until the arrival of his main attacking force. Corporal Casamento's courageous fighting spirit, heroic conduct, and unwavering dedication to duty reflected great credit upon himself and were in keeping with the highest traditions of the Marine Corps and the United States Naval Service.

*CASTLE, FREDERICK W. (Air Mission)

Rank and organization: Brigadier General, Assistant Commander, 4th Bomber Wing, U.S. Army Air Corps. *Place and date:* Germany, 24 December 1944. *Entered service at:* Mountain Lake, N.J. *Born:* 14 October 1908, Manila, P.I. *G.O. No.* 22, 28 February 1947. *Citation:* He was air commander and leader of more than 2,000 heavy bombers in a strike against German airfields on 24 December 1944. En route to the target, the failure of 1 engine forced him to relinquish his place at the head of the formation. In order not to endanger friendly troops on the ground below, he refused to jettison his bombs to gain speed maneuverability. His lagging, unescorted aircraft became the target of numerous enemy fighters which ripped the left wing with cannon shells, set the oxygen system afire, and wounded 2 members of the crew. Repeated attacks started fires in 2 engines, leaving the Flying Fortress in imminent danger of exploding. Realizing the hopelessness of the situation, the bail-out order was given. Without regard for his personal safety he gallantly remained alone at the controls to afford all other crewmembers an opportunity to escape. Still another attack exploded gasoline tanks in the right wing, and the bomber plunged earthward, carrying Gen. Castle to his death. His intrepidity and willing sacrifice of his life to save members of the crew were in keeping with the highest traditions of the military service.

CHAMBERS, JUSTICE M.

Rank and organization: Colonel, U.S. Marine Corps Reserve, 3rd Assault Battalion Landing Team, 25th Marines, 4th Marine Division. *Place and date:* On Iwo Jima, Volcano Islands, from 19 to 22 February

1945. *Entered service at:* Washington, D.C. *Born:* 2 February 1908, Huntington, W. Va. *Citation:* For conspicuous gallantry and intrepidity at the risk of his life above and beyond the call of duty as commanding officer of the 3d Assault Battalion Landing Team, 25th Marines, 4th Marine Division, in action against enemy Japanese forces on Iwo Jima, Volcano Islands, from 19 to 22 February 1945. Under a furious barrage of enemy machinegun and small-arms fire from the commanding cliffs on the right, Col. Chambers (then Lt. Col.) landed immediately after the initial assault waves of his battalion on D-day to find the momentum of the assault threatened by heavy casualties from withering Japanese artillery, mortar rocket, machinegun, and rifle fire. Exposed to relentless hostile fire, he coolly reorganized his battle-weary men, inspiring them to heroic efforts by his own valor and leading them in an attack on the critical, impregnable high ground from which the enemy was pouring an increasing volume of fire directly onto troops ashore as well as amphibious craft in succeeding waves. Constantly in the frontlines encouraging his men to push forward against the enemy's savage resistance, Col. Chambers led the 8-hour battle to carry the flanking ridge top and reduce the enemy's fields of aimed fire, thus protecting the vital foothold gained. In constant defiance of hostile fire while reconnoitering the entire regimental combat team zone of action, he maintained contact with adjacent units and forwarded vital information to the regimental commander. His zealous fighting spirit undiminished despite terrific casualties and the loss of most of his key officers, he again reorganized his troops for renewed attack against the enemy's main line of resistance and was directing the fire of the rocket platoon when he fell, critically wounded. Evacuated under heavy Japanese fire, Col. Chambers, by forceful leadership, courage, and fortitude in the face of staggering odds, was directly instrumental in insuring the success of subsequent operations of the 5th Amphibious Corps on Iwo Jima, thereby sustaining and enhancing the finest traditions of the U.S. Naval Service.

*CHELI, RALPH (Air Mission)

Rank and organization: Major, U.S. Army Air Corps. *Place and date:* Near Wewak, New Guinea, 18 August 1943. *Entered service at:* Brooklyn, N.Y. *Birth:* San Francisco, Calif. *G.O. No.:* 72, 28 October 1943. *Citation:* For conspicuous gallantry and intrepidity above and beyond the call of duty in action with the enemy. While Maj. Cheli was leading his squadron in a dive to attack the heavily defended Dagua Airdrome, intercepting enemy aircraft centered their fire on his plane, causing it to burst into flames while still 2 miles from the objective. His speed would have enabled him to gain necessary altitude to parachute to safety, but this action would have resulted in his formation becoming disorganized and exposed to the enemy. Although a crash was inevitable, he courageously elected to continue leading the attack in his blazing plane. From a minimum altitude, the squadron made a devastating bombing and strafing attack on the target. The mission completed, Maj. Cheli instructed his wingman to lead the formation and crashed into the sea.

CHILDERS, ERNEST

Rank and organization: Second Lieutenant, U.S. Army, 45th Infantry Division. *Place and date:* At Oliveto, Italy, 22 September 1943. *Entered service at:* Tulsa, Okla. *Birth:* Broken Arrow, Okla. *G.O. No.:* 30, 8 April 1944. *Citation:* For conspicuous gallantry and intrepidity at risk of life above and beyond the call of duty in action on 22 September 1943, at Oliveto, Italy. Although 2d Lt. Childers previously had just suffered a fractured instep he, with 8 enlisted men, advanced up a hill toward enemy machinegun nests. The group advanced to a rock wall overlooking a cornfield and 2d Lt. Childers ordered a base of fire laid across the field so that he could advance. When he was fired upon by 2 enemy snipers from a nearby house he killed both of them. He moved behind the machinegun nests and killed all occupants of the nearer one. He continued toward the second one and threw rocks into it. When the 2 occupants of the nest raised up, he shot 1. The other was killed by 1 of the 8 enlisted men. 2d Lt. Childers continued his advance toward a house farther up the hill, and singlehanded, captured an enemy mortar observer. The exceptional leadership, initiative, calmness under fire, and conspicuous gallantry displayed by 2d Lt. Childers were an inspiration to his men.

CHOATE, CLYDE L.

Rank and organization: Staff Sergeant, U.S. Army, Company C, 601st Tank Destroyer Battalion. *Place and date:* Near Bruyeres, France, 25 October 1944. *Entered service at:* Anna, Ill. *Born:* 28 June 1920, West Frankfurt, Ill. *G.O. No.:* 75, 5 September 1945. *Citation:* He commanded a tank destroyer near Bruyeres, France, on 25 October 1944. Our infantry occupied a position on a wooded hill when, at dusk, an enemy Mark IV tank and a company of infantry attacked, threatening to overrun the American position and capture a command post 400 yards to the rear. S/Sgt. Choate's tank destroyer, the only weapon available to oppose the German armor, was set afire by 2 hits. Ordering his men to abandon the destroyer, S/Sgt. Choate reached comparative safety. He returned to the burning destroyer to search for comrades possibly trapped in the vehicle risking instant death in an explosion which was imminent and braving enemy fire which ripped his jacket and tore the helmet from his head. Completing the search and seeing the tank and its supporting infantry overrunning our infantry in their shallow foxholes, he secured a bazooka and ran after the tank, dodging from tree to tree and passing through the enemy's loose skirmish line. He fired a rocket from a distance of 20 yards, immobilizing the tank but leaving it able to spray the area with cannon and machinegun fire. Running back to our infantry through vicious fire, he secured another rocket, and, advancing against a hail of machinegun and small-arms fire reached a position 10 yards from the tank. His second shot shattered the turret. With his pistol he killed 2 of the crew as they emerged from the tank; and then running to the crippled Mark IV while enemy infantry sniped at him, he dropped a grenade inside the tank and completed its destruction. With their armor gone, the enemy infantry became disorganized and was driven back. S/Sgt. Choate's great daring in assaulting an enemy tank singlehanded, his determination to follow the vehicle after it had passed his position, and his skill and crushing thoroughness in the attack prevented the enemy from capturing a battalion command post and turned a probable defeat into a tactical success.

*CHRISTENSEN, DALE ELDON

Rank and organization: Second Lieutenant, U.S. Army, Troop E, 112th Cavalry Regiment. *Place and date:* Driniumor River, New Guinea, 16–19 July 1944. *Entered service at:* Gray, Iowa. *Birth:* Cameron Township, Iowa. *G.O. No.:* 36, 10 May 1945. *Citation:* For conspicuous gallantry and intrepidity at the risk of his life above and beyond the call of duty along the Driniumor River, New Guinea, from 16–19 July 1944. 2d Lt. Christensen repeatedly distinguished himself by conspicuous gallantry above and beyond the call of duty in the continuous heavy fighting which occurred in this area from 16–19 July. On 16 July, his platoon engaged in a savage fire fight in which much damage was caused by 1 enemy machinegun effectively placed. 2d Lt. Christensen ordered his men to remain under cover, crept forward under fire, and at a range of 15 yards put the gun out of action with handgrenades. Again, on 19 July, while attacking an enemy position strong in mortars and machineguns, his platoon was pinned to the ground by intense fire. Ordering his men to remain under cover, he crept forward alone to locate definitely the enemy automatic weapons and the best direction from which to attack. Although his rifle was struck by enemy fire and knocked from his hands he continued his reconnaissance, located 5 enemy machineguns, destroyed 1 with handgrenades, and rejoined his platoon. He then led his men to the point selected for launching the attack and, calling encouragement, led the charge. This assault was successful and the enemy was driven from the positions with a loss of 4 mortars and 10 machineguns and leaving many dead on the field. On 4 August 1944, near Afua, Dutch New Guinea, 2d Lt. Christensen was killed in action about 2 yards from his objective while leading his platoon in an attack on an enemy machinegun position. 2d Lt. Christensen's leadership, intrepidity, and repeatedly demonstrated gallantry in action at the risk of his life, above and beyond the call of duty, exemplify the highest traditions of the U.S. Armed Forces.

*CHRISTIAN, HERBERT F.

Rank and organization: Private, U.S. Army, 15th Infantry, 3d Infantry Division. *Place and date:* Near Valmontone, Italy, 2-3 June 1944. *Entered service at:* Steubenville, Ohio. *Birth:* Byersville, Ohio. *G.O. No.:* 43, 30 May 1945. *Citation:* For conspicuous gallantry and intrepidity at risk of life above and beyond the call of duty. On 2-3 June 1944, at 1 a.m., Pvt. Christian elected to sacrifice his life in order that his comrades might extricate themselves from an ambush. Braving massed fire of about 60 riflemen, 3 machineguns, and 3 tanks from positions only 30 yards distant, he stood erect and signaled to the patrol to withdraw. The whole area was brightly illuminated by enemy flares. Although his right leg was severed above the knee by cannon fire, Pvt. Christian advanced on his left knee and the bloody stump of his right thigh, firing his submachinegun. Despite excruciating pain,

Pvt. Christian continued on his self-assigned mission. He succeeded in distracting the enemy and enabled his 12 comrades to escape. He killed 3 enemy soldiers almost at once. Leaving a trail of blood behind him, he made his way forward 20 yards, halted at a point within 10 yards of the enemy, and despite intense fire killed a machine-pistol man. Reloading his weapon, he fired directly into the enemy position. The enemy appeared enraged at the success of his ruse, concentrated 20-mm. machinegun, machine-pistol and rifle fire on him, yet he refused to seek cover. Maintaining his erect position, Pvt. Christian fired his weapon to the very last. Just as he emptied his submachinegun, the enemy bullets found their mark and Pvt. Christian slumped forward dead. The courage and spirit of self-sacrifice displayed by this soldier were an inspiration to his comrades and are in keeping with the highest traditions of the armed forces.

*CICCHETTI, JOSEPH J.

Rank and organization: Private First Class, U.S. Army, Company A, 148th Infantry, 37th Infantry Division. *Place and date:* South Manila, Luzon, Philippine Islands, 9 February 1945. *Entered service at:* Waynesburg, Ohio. *Birth:* Waynesburg, Ohio. *G.O. No.:* 115, 8 December 1945. *Citation:* He was with troops assaulting the first important line of enemy defenses. The Japanese had converted the partially destroyed Manila Gas Works and adjacent buildings into a formidable system of mutually supporting strongpoints from which they were concentrating machinegun, mortar, and heavy artillery fire on the American forces. Casualties rapidly mounted, and the medical aid men, finding it increasingly difficult to evacuate the wounded, called for volunteer litter bearers. Pfc. Cicchetti immediately responded, organized a litter team and skillfully led it for more than 4 hours in rescuing 14 wounded men, constantly passing back and forth over a 400-yard route which was the impact area for a tremendous volume of the most intense enemy fire. On 1 return trip the path was blocked by machinegun fire, but Pfc. Cicchetti deliberately exposed himself to draw the automatic fire which he neutralized with his own rifle while ordering the rest of the team to rush past to safety with the wounded. While gallantly continuing his work, he noticed a group of wounded and helpless soldiers some distance away and ran to their rescue although the enemy fire had increased to new fury. As he approached the casualties, he was struck in the head by a shell fragment, but with complete disregard for his gaping wound he continued to his comrades, lifted 1 and carried him on his shoulders 50 yards to safety. He then collapsed and died. By his skilled leadership, indomitable will, and dauntless courage, Pfc. Cicchetti saved the lives of many of his fellow soldiers at the cost of his own.

CLARK, FRANCIS J.

Rank and organization: Technical Sergeant, U.S. Army, Company K, 109th Infantry, 28th Infantry Division. *Place and date:* Near Kalborn, Luxembourg, 12 September 1944; near Sevenig, Germany, 17 September 1944. *Entered service at:* Salem, N.Y. *Birth:* Whitehall, N.Y. *G.O. No.:* 77, 10 September 1945. *Citation:* He fought gallantly in Luxembourg and Germany. On 12 September 1944, Company K began fording the Our River near Kalborn, Luxembourg, to take high ground on the opposite bank. Covered by early morning fog, the 3d Platoon, in which T/Sgt. Clark was squad leader, successfully negotiated the crossing; but when the 2d Platoon reached the shore, withering automatic and small-arms fire ripped into it, eliminating the platoon leader and platoon sergeant and pinning down the troops in the open. From his comparatively safe position, T/Sgt. Clark crawled alone across a field through a hail of bullets to the stricken troops. He led the platoon to safety and then unhesitatingly returned into the fireswept area to rescue a wounded soldier, carrying him to the American line while hostile gunners tried to cut him down. Later, he led his squad and men of the 2d Platoon in dangerous sorties against strong enemy positions to weaken them by lightning-like jabs. He assaulted an enemy machinegun with handgrenades, killing 2 Germans. He roamed the front and flanks, dashing toward hostile weapons, killing and wounding an undetermined number of the enemy, scattering German patrols and, eventually, forcing the withdrawal of a full company of Germans heavily armed with automatic weapons. On 17 September, near Sevenig, Germany, he advanced alone against an enemy machinegun, killed the gunner and forced the assistant to flee. The Germans counterattacked, and heavy casualties were suffered by Company K. Seeing that 2 platoons lacked leadership, T/Sgt. Clark took over their command and moved among the men to give encouragement. Although wounded on the morning of 18 September, he refused to be evacuated and took up a position in a pillbox when night came. Emerging at daybreak, he killed a German soldier setting up a machinegun not more than 5 yards away. When he located another enemy gun, he moved up unobserved and killed 2 Germans with rifle fire. Later that day he voluntarily braved small-arms fire to take food and water to members of an isolated platoon. T/Sgt. Clark's actions in assuming command when leadership was desperately needed, in launching attacks and beating off counterattacks, in aiding his stranded comrades, and in fearlessly facing powerful enemy fire, were strikingly heroic examples and put fighting heart into the hardpressed men of Company K.

COLALILLO, MIKE

Rank and organization: Private First Class, U.S. Army, Company C, 398th Infantry, 100th Infantry Division. *Place and date:* Near Untergriesheim, Germany, 7 April 1945. *Entered service at:* Duluth, Minn. *Birth:* Hibbing, Minn. *G.O. No.:* 4, 9 January 1946. *Citation:* He was pinned down with other members of his company during an attack against strong enemy positions in the vicinity of Untergriesheim, Germany. Heavy artillery, mortar, and machinegun fire made any move hazardous when he stood up, shouted to the company to follow, and ran forward in the wake of a supporting tank, firing his machine pistol. Inspired by his example, his comrades advanced in the face of savage enemy fire. When his weapon was struck by shrapnel and rendered useless, he climbed to the deck of a friendly tank, manned an exposed machinegun on the turret of the vehicle, and, while bullets rattled about him, fired at an enemy emplacement with such devastating accuracy that he killed or wounded at least 10 hostile soldiers and destroyed their machinegun. Maintaining his extremely dangerous post as the tank forged ahead, he blasted 3 more positions, destroyed another machinegun emplacement and silenced all resistance in his area, killing at least 3 and wounding an undetermined number of riflemen as they fled. His machinegun eventually jammed; so he secured a submachinegun from the tank crew to continue his attack on foot. When our armored forces exhausted their ammunition and the order to withdraw was given, he remained behind to help a seriously wounded comrade over several hundred yards of open terrain rocked by an intense enemy artillery and mortar barrage. By his intrepidity and inspiring courage Pfc. Colallilo gave tremendous impetus to his company's attack, killed or wounded 25 of the enemy in bitter fighting, and assisted a wounded soldier in reaching the American lines at great risk of his own life.

*COLE, DARRELL SAMUEL

Rank and organization: Sergeant, U.S. Marine Corps Reserve. *Born:* 20 July 1920, Flat River, Mo. *Entered service at:* Esther, Mo. *Other Navy award:* Bronze Star Medal. *Citation:* For conspicuous gallantry and intrepidity at the risk of his life above and beyond the call of duty while serving as leader of a Machinegun Section of Company B, 1st Battalion, 23d Marines, 4th Marine Division, in action against enemy Japanese forces during the assault on Iwo Jima in the Volcano Islands, 19 February 1945. Assailed by a tremendous volume of small-arms, mortar and artillery fire as he advanced with 1 squad of his section in the initial assault wave, Sgt. Cole boldly led his men up the sloping beach toward Airfield No. 1 despite the blanketing curtain of flying shrapnel and, personally destroying with handgrenades 2 hostile emplacements which menaced the progress of his unit, continued to move forward until a merciless barrage of fire emanating from 3 Japanese pillboxes halted the advance. Instantly placing his 1 remaining machinegun in action, he delivered a shattering fusillade and succeeded in silencing the nearest and most threatening emplacement before his weapon jammed and the enemy, reopening fire with knee mortars and grenades, pinned down his unit for the second time. Shrewdly gaging the tactical situation and evolving a daring plan of counterattack, Sgt. Cole, armed solely with a pistol and 1 grenade, cooly advanced alone to the hostile pillboxes. Hurling his 1 grenade at the enemy in sudden, swift attack, he quickly withdrew, returned to his own lines for additional grenades and again advanced, attacked, and withdrew. With enemy guns still active, he ran the gauntlet of slashing fire a third time to complete the total destruction of the Japanese strong point and the annihilation of the defending garrison in this final assault. Although instantly killed by an enemy grenade as he returned to his squad, Sgt. Cole had eliminated a formidable Japanese position, thereby enabling his company to storm the remaining fortifications, continue the advance, and seize the objective. By his dauntless initiative, unfaltering courage, and indomitable determination during a critical period of action, Sgt. Cole served as an inspiration to his comrades, and his stouthearted leadership in the face of almost certain death sustained and enhanced the highest tradition of the U.S. Naval Service. He gallantly gave his life for his country.

*COLE, ROBERT G.

Rank and organization: Lieutenant Colonel, U.S. Army, 101st Airborne Division. *Place and date:* Near Carentan, France, 11 June 1944. *Entered service at:* San Antonio, Tex. *Birth:* Fort Sam Houston, Tex. *G.O. No.:* 79, 4 October 1944. *Citation:* For gallantry and intrepidity at the risk of his own life, above and beyond the call of duty on 11 June 1944, in France. Lt. Col. Cole was personally leading his battalion in forcing the last 4 bridges on the road to Carentan when his entire unit was suddenly pinned to the ground by intense and withering enemy rifle, machinegun, mortar, and artillery fire placed upon them from well-prepared and heavily fortified positions within 150 yards of the foremost elements. After the devastating and unceasing enemy fire had for over 1 hour prevented any move and inflicted numerous casualties, Lt. Col. Cole, observing this almost hopeless situation, courageously issued orders to assault the enemy positions with fixed bayonets. With utter disregard for his own safety and completely ignoring the enemy fire, he rose to his feet in front of his battalion and with drawn pistol shouted to his men to follow him in the assault. Catching up a fallen man's rifle and bayonet, he charged on and led the remnants of his battalion across the bullet-swept open ground and into the enemy position. His heroic and valiant action in so inspiring his men resulted in the complete establishment of our bridgehead across the Douve River. The cool fearlessness, personal bravery, and outstanding leadership displayed by Lt. Col. Cole reflect great credit upon himself and are worthy of the highest praise in the military service.

CONNOR, JAMES P.

Rank and organization: Sergeant, U.S. Army, 7th Infantry, 3d Infantry Division. *Place and date:* Cape Cavalaire, southern France, 15 August 1944. *Entered service at:* Wilmington, Del. *Birth:* Wilmington, Del. *G.O. No.:* 18, 15 March 1945. *Citation:* For conspicuous gallantry and intrepidity at risk of life above and beyond the call of duty. On 15 August 1944 Sgt. Connor, through sheer grit and determination, led his platoon in clearing an enemy vastly superior in numbers and firepower from strongly entrenched positions on Cape Cavalaire, removing a grave enemy threat to his division during the amphibious landing in southern France, and thereby insured safe and uninterrupted landings for the huge volume of men and materiel which followed. His battle patrol landed on "Red Beach" with the mission of destroying the strongly fortified enemy positions on Cape Cavalaire with utmost speed. From the peninsula the enemy had commanding observation and seriously menaced the vast landing operations taking place. Though knocked down and seriously wounded in the neck by a hanging mine which killed his platoon lieutenant, Sgt. Connor refused medical aid and with his driving spirit practically carried the platoon across several thousand yards of mine-saturated beach through intense fire from mortars, 20-mm. flak guns, machineguns, and snipers. En route to the Cape he personally shot and killed 2 snipers. The platoon sergeant was killed and Sgt. Connor became platoon leader. Receiving a second wound, which lacerated his shoulder and back, he again refused evacuation, expressing determination to carry on until physically unable to continue. He reassured and prodded the hesitating men of his decimated platoon forward through almost impregnable mortar concentrations. Again emphasizing the prevalent urgency of their mission, he impelled his men toward a group of buildings honeycombed with enemy snipers and machineguns. Here he received his third grave wound, this time in the leg, felling him in his tracks. Still resolved to carry on, he relinquished command only after his attempts proved that it was physically impossible to stand. Nevertheless, from his prone position, he gave the orders and directed his men in assaulting the enemy. Infused with Sgt. Connor's dogged determination, the platoon, though reduced to less than one-third of its original 36 men, outflanked and rushed the enemy with such furiousness that they killed 7, captured 40, seized 3 machineguns and considerable other materiel, and took all their assigned objectives, successfully completing their mission. By his repeated examples of tenaciousness and indomitable spirit Sgt. Connor transmitted his heroism to his men until they became a fighting team which could not be stopped.

COOLEY, RAYMOND H.

Rank and organization: Staff Sergeant, U.S. Army, Company B, 27th Infantry, 25th Infantry Division. *Place and date:* Near Lumboy, Luzon, Philippine Islands, 24 February 1945. *Entered service at:* Richard City, Tenn. *Born:* 7 May 1914, Dunlap, Tenn. *G.O. No.:* 77, 10 September 1945. *Citation:* He was a platoon guide in an assault on a camouflaged entrenchment defended by machineguns, rifles, and mortars. When his men were pinned down by 2 enemy machineguns, he voluntarily advanced under heavy fire to within 20 yards of 1 of the guns and attacked it with a handgrenade. The enemy, however, threw the grenade back at him before it could explode. Arming a second grenade, he held it for several seconds of the safe period and then hurled it into the enemy position, where it exploded instantaneously, destroying the gun and crew. He then moved toward the remaining gun, throwing grenades into enemy foxholes as he advanced. Inspired by his actions, 1 squad of his platoon joined him. After he had armed another grenade and was preparing to throw it into the second machinegun position, 6 enemy soldiers rushed at him. Knowing he could not dispose of the armed grenade without injuring his comrades, because of the intermingling in close combat of the men of his platoon and the enemy in the melee which ensued, he deliberately covered the grenade with his body and was severely wounded as it exploded. By his heroic actions, S/Sgt. Cooley not only silenced a machinegun and so inspired his fellow soldiers that they pressed the attack and destroyed the remaining enemy emplacements, but also, in complete disregard of his own safety, accepted certain injury and possible loss of life to avoid wounding his comrades.

COOLIDGE, CHARLES H.

Rank and organization: Technical Sergeant, U.S. Army, Company M, 141st Infantry, 36th Infantry Division. *Place and date:* East of Belmont sur Buttant, France, 24–27 October 1944. *Entered service at:* Signal Mountain, Tenn. *Birth:* Signal Mountain, Tenn. *G.O. No.:* 53, July 1945. *Citation:* Leading a section of heavy machineguns supported by

1 platoon of Company K, he took a position near Hill 623, east of Belmont sur Buttant, France, on 24 October 1944, with the mission of covering the right flank of the 3d Battalion and supporting its action. T/Sgt. Coolidge went forward with a sergeant of Company K to reconnoiter positions for coordinating the fires of the light and heavy machineguns. They ran into an enemy force in the woods estimated to be an infantry company. T/Sgt. Coolidge, attempting to bluff the Germans by a show of assurance and boldness called upon them to surrender, whereupon the enemy opened fire. With his carbine, T/Sgt. Coolidge wounded 2 of them. There being no officer present with the force, T/Sgt. Coolidge at once assumed command. Many of the men were replacements recently arrived; this was their first experience under fire. T/Sgt. Coolidge, unmindful of the enemy fire delivered at close range, walked along the position, calming and encouraging his men and directing their fire. The attack was thrown back. Through 25 and 26 October the enemy launched repeated attacks against the position of this combat group but each was repulsed due to T/Sgt. Coolidge's able leadership. On 27 October, German infantry, supported by 2 tanks, made a determined attack on the position. The area was swept by enemy small-arms, machinegun, and tank fire. T/Sgt. Coolidge armed himself with a bazooka and advanced to within 25 yards of the tanks. His bazooka failed to function and he threw it aside. Securing all the handgrenades he could carry, he crawled forward and inflicted heavy casualties on the advancing enemy. Finally it became apparent that the enemy, in greatly superior force, supported by tanks, would overrun the position. T/Sgt. Coolidge, displaying great coolness and courage, directed and conducted an orderly withdrawal, being himself the last to leave the position. As a result of T/Sgt. Coolidge's heroic and superior leadership, the mission of this combat group was accomplished throughout 4 days of continuous fighting against numerically superior enemy troops in rain and cold and amid dense woods.

*COURTNEY, HENRY ALEXIUS, Jr.

Rank and organization: Major, U.S. Marine Corps Reserve. *Born:* 6 January 1916, Duluth, Minn. *Appointed from:* Minnesota. *Citation:* For conspicuous gallantry and intrepidity at the risk of his life above and beyond the call of duty as Executive Officer of the 2d Battalion, 22d Marines, 6th Marine Division, in action against enemy Japanese forces on Okinawa Shima in the Ryukyu Islands, 14 and 15 May 1945. Ordered to hold for the night in static defense behind Sugar Loaf Hill after leading the forward elements of his command in a prolonged fire fight, Maj. Courtney weighed the effect of a hostile night counterattack against the tactical value of an immediate marine assault, resolved to initiate the assault, and promptly obtained permission to advance and seize the forward slope of the hill. Quickly explaining the situation to his small remaining force, he declared his personal intention of moving forward and then proceeded on his way, boldly blasting nearby cave positions and neutralizing enemy guns as he went. Inspired by his courage, every man followed without hesitation, and together the intrepid marines braved a terrific concentration of Japanese gunfire to skirt the hill on the right and reach the reverse slope. Temporarily halting, Maj. Courtney sent guides to the rear for more ammunition and possible replacements. Subsequently reinforced by 26 men and an LVT load of grenades, he determined to storm the crest of the hill and crush any planned counterattack before it could gain sufficient momentum to effect a breakthrough. Leading his men by example rather than by command, he pushed ahead with unrelenting aggressiveness, hurling grenades into cave openings on the slope with devastating effect. Upon reaching the crest and observing large numbers of Japanese forming for action less than 100 yards away, he instantly attacked, waged a furious battle and succeeded in killing many of the enemy and in forcing the remainder to take cover in the caves. Determined to hold, he ordered his men to dig in and, coolly disregarding the continuous hail of flying enemy shrapnel to rally his weary troops, tirelessly aided casualties and assigned his men to more advantageous positions. Although instantly killed by a hostile mortar burst while moving among his men, Maj. Courtney, by his astute military acumen, indomitable leadership and decisive action in the face of overwhelming odds, had contributed essentially to the success of the Okinawa campaign. His great personal valor throughout sustained and enhanced the highest traditions of the U.S. Naval Service. He gallantly gave his life for his country.

*COWAN, RICHARD ELLER

Rank and organization: Private First Class, U.S. Army, Company M, 23d Infantry, 2d Infantry Division. *Place and date:* Near Krinkelter Wald, Belgium, 17 December 1944. *Entered service at:* Wichita, Kans. *Birth:* Lincoln, Nebr. *G.O. No.:* 48, 23 June 1945. *Citation:* He was a heavy machinegunner in a section attached to Company I in the vicinity of Krinkelter Wald, Belgium, 17 December 1944, when that company was attacked by a numerically superior force of German infantry and tanks. The first 6 waves of hostile infantrymen were repulsed with heavy casualties, but a seventh drive with tanks killed or wounded all but 3 of his section, leaving Pvt. Cowan to man his gun, supported by only 15 to 20 riflemen of Company I. He maintained his position, holding off the Germans until the rest of the shattered force had set up a new line along a firebreak. Then, unaided, he moved his machinegun and ammunition to the second position. At the approach of a Royal Tiger tank, he held his fire until about 80 enemy infantrymen supporting the tank appeared at a distance of about 150 yards. His first burst killed or wounded about half of these infantrymen. His position was rocked by an 88-mm. shell when the tank opened fire, but he continued to man his gun, pouring deadly fire into the Germans when they again advanced. He was barely missed by another shell. Fire from three machineguns and innumerable small arms struck all about him; an enemy rocket shook him badly, but did not drive him from his gun. Infiltration by the enemy had by this time made the position untenable, and the order was given to withdraw. Pvt. Cowan was the last man to leave, voluntarily covering the withdrawal of his remaining comrades. His heroic actions were entirely responsible for allowing the remaining men to retire successfully from the scene of their last-ditch stand.

CRAFT, CLARENCE B.

Rank and organization: Private, First Class, U.S. Army, Company G, 382d Infantry, 96th Infantry Division. *Place and date:* Hen Hill, Okinawa, Ryukyu Islands, 31 May 1945. *Entered service at:* Santa Ana, Calif. *Birth:* San Bernardino, Calif. *G.O. No.:* 97, 1 November 1945. *Citation:* He was a rifleman when his platoon spearheaded an attack on Hen Hill, the tactical position on which the entire Naha-Shuri-Yonaburu line of Japanese defense on Okinawa, Ryukyu Islands, was hinged. For 12 days our forces had been stalled, and repeated, heavy assaults by 1 battalion and then another had been thrown back by the enemy with serious casualties. With 5 comrades, Pfc. Craft was dispatched in advance of Company G to feel out the enemy resistance. The group had proceeded only a short distance up the slope when rifle and machinegun fire, coupled with a terrific barrage of grenades, wounded 3 and pinned down the others. Against odds that appeared suicidal, Pfc. Craft launched a remarkable 1-man attack. He stood up in full view of the enemy and began shooting with deadly marksmanship wherever he saw a hostile movement. He steadily advanced up the hill, killing Japanese soldiers with rapid fire, driving others to cover in their strongly disposed trenches, unhesitatingly facing alone the strength that had previously beaten back attacks in battalion strength. He reached the crest of the hill, where he stood silhouetted against the sky while quickly throwing grenades at extremely short range into the enemy positions. His extraordinary assault lifted the pressure from his company for the moment, allowing members of his platoon to comply with his motions to advance and pass him more grenades. With a chain of his comrades supplying him while he stood atop the hill, he furiously hurled a total of 2 cases of grenades into a main trench and other positions on the reverse slope of Hen Hill, meanwhile directing the aim of his fellow soldiers who threw grenades from the slope below him. He left his position, where grenades from both sides were passing over his head and bursting on either slope, to attack the main enemy trench as confusion and panic seized the defenders. Straddling the excavation, he pumped rifle fire into the Japanese at pointblank range, killing many and causing the others to flee down the trench. Pursuing them, he came upon a heavy machinegun which was still creating havoc in the American ranks. With rifle fire and a grenade he wiped out this position. By this time the Japanese were in complete rout and American forces were swarming over the hill. Pfc. Craft continued down the central trench to the mouth of a cave where many of the enemy had taken cover. A satchel charge was brought to him, and he tossed it into the cave. It failed to explode. With great daring, the intrepid fighter retrieved the charge from the cave, relighted the fuse and threw it back, sealing up the Japs in a tomb. In the local action, against tremendously superior forces heavily armed with rifles, machineguns, mortars, and grenades, Pfc. Craft killed at least 25 of the enemy; but his contribution to the campaign on Okinawa was of much more far-reaching consequence for Hen Hill was the key to the entire defense line, which rapidly crumbled after his utterly fearless and heroic attack.

*CRAIG, ROBERT

Rank and organization: Second Lieutenant, U.S. Army, 15th Infantry, 3d Infantry Division. *Place and date:* Near Favoratta, Sicily, 11 July 1943. *Entered service at:* Toledo, Ohio. *Birth:* Scotland. *G.O. No.:* 41, 26 May 1944. *Citation:* For conspicuous gallantry and intrepidity at the risk of life, above and beyond the call of duty, on 11 July 1943, at Favoratta, Sicily. 2d Lt. Craig voluntarily undertook the perilous task of locating and destroying a hidden enemy machinegun which had halted the advance of his company. Attempts by 3 other officers to locate the weapon had resulted in failure, with each officer receiving wounds. 2d Lt. Craig located the gun and snaked his way to a point within 35 yards of the hostile position before being discovered. Charging headlong into the furious automatic fire, he reached the gun, stood over it, and killed the 3 crew members with his carbine. With this obstacle removed, his company continued its advance. Shortly thereafter, while advancing down the forward slope of a ridge, 2d Lt. Craig and his platoon, in a position devoid of cover and concealment, encountered the fire of approximately 100 enemy soldiers. Electing to sacrifice himself so that his platoon might carry on the battle, he ordered his men to withdraw to the cover of the crest while he drew the enemy fire to himself. With no hope of survival, he charged toward the enemy until he was within 25 yards of them. Assuming a kneeling position, he killed 5 and wounded 3 enemy soldiers. While the hostile force concentrated fire on him, his platoon reached the cover of the crest. 2d Lt. Craig was killed by enemy fire, but his intrepid action so inspired his men that they drove the enemy from the area, inflicting heavy casualties on the hostile force.

*CRAIN, MORRIS E.

Rank and organization: Technical Sergeant, U.S. Army, Company E, 141st Infantry, 36th Infantry Division. *Place and date:* Haguenau, France, 13 March 1945. *Entered service at:* Paducah, Ky. *Birth:* Bandana, Ky. *G.O. No.:* 18, 13 February 1946. *Citation:* He led his platoon against powerful German forces during the struggle to enlarge the bridgehead across the Moder River. With great daring and aggressiveness he spearheaded the platoon in killing 10 enemy soldiers, capturing 12 more and securing its objective near an important road junction. Although heavy concentrations of artillery, mortar, and self-propelled gunfire raked the area, he moved about among his men during the day, exhorting them to great efforts and encouraging them to stand firm. He carried ammunition and maintained contact with the company command post, exposing himself to deadly enemy fire. At nightfall the enemy barrage became more intense and tanks entered the fray to cover foot troops while they bombarded our positions with grenades and rockets. As buildings were blasted by the Germans, the Americans fell back from house to house. T/Sgt. Crain deployed another platoon which had been sent to his support and then rushed through murderous tank and small-arms fire to the foremost house, which was being defended by 5 of his men. With the enemy attacking from an adjoining room and a tank firing pointblank at the house, he ordered the men to withdraw while he remained in the face of almost certain death to hold the position. Although shells were crashing through the walls and bullets were hitting all around him, he held his ground and with accurate fire from his submachinegun killed 3 Germans. He was killed when the building was destroyed by the enemy. T/Sgt. Crain's outstanding valor and intrepid leadership enabled his platoon to organize a new defense, repel the attack and preserve the hard-won bridgehead.

*CRAW, DEMAS T.

Rank and organization: Colonel, U.S. Army Air Corps. *Place and date:* Near Port Lyautey, French Morocco, 8 November 1942. *Entered service at:* Michigan. *Born:* 9 April 1900, Traverse City, Mich. *G.O. No.:* 11, 4 March 1943. *Citation:* For conspicuous gallantry and intrepidity in action above and beyond the call of duty. On 8 November 1942, near Port Lyautey, French Morocco, Col. Craw volunteered to accompany the leading wave of assault boats to the shore and pass through the enemy lines to locate the French commander with a view to suspending hostilities. This request was first refused as being too dangerous but upon the officer's insistence that he was qualified to undertake and accomplish the mission he was allowed to go. Encountering heavy fire while in the landing boat and unable to dock in the river because of shell fire from shore batteries, Col. Craw, accompanied by 1 officer and 1 soldier, succeeded in landing on the beach at Mehdia Plage under constant low-level strafing from 3 enemy planes. Riding in a bantam truck toward French headquarters, progress of the party was hindered by fire from our own naval guns. Nearing Port Lyautey, Col. Craw was instantly killed by a sustained burst of machinegun fire at pointblank range from a concealed position near the road.

CRAWFORD, WILLIAM J.

Rank and organization: Private, U.S. Army, 36th Infantry Division. *Place and date:* Near Altavilla, Italy, 13 September 1943. *Entered service at:* Pueblo, Colo. *Birth:* Pueblo, Colo. *G.O. No.:* 57, 20 July 1944. *Citation:* For conspicuous gallantry and intrepidity at risk of life above and beyond the call of duty in action with the enemy near Altavilla, Italy, 13 September 1943. When Company I attacked an enemy-held position on Hill 424, the 3d Platoon, in which Pvt. Crawford was a squad scout, attacked as base platoon for the company. After reaching the crest of the hill, the platoon was pinned down by intense enemy machinegun and small-arms fire. Locating 1 of these guns, which was dug in on a terrace on his immediate front, Pvt. Crawford, without orders and on his own initiative, moved over the hill under enemy fire to a point within a few yards of the gun emplacement and singlehandedly destroyed the machinegun and killed 3 of the crew with a handgrenade, thus enabling his platoon to continue its advance. When the platoon, after reaching the crest, was once more delayed by enemy fire, Pvt. Crawford again, in the face of intense fire, advanced directly to the front midway between 2 hostile machinegun nests located on a higher terrace and emplaced in a small ravine. Moving first to the left, with a handgrenade he destroyed 1 gun emplacement and killed the crew; he then worked his way, under continuous fire, to the other and with 1 grenade and the use of his rifle, killed 1 enemy and forced the remainder to flee. Seizing the enemy machinegun, he fired on the withdrawing Germans and facilitated his company's advance.

CREWS, JOHN R.

Rank and organization: Staff Sergeant, U.S. Army, Company F, 253d Infantry, 63d Infantry Division. *Place and date:* Near Lobenbacherhof, Germany, 8 April 1945. *Entered service at:* Bowlegs, Okla. *Birth:* Golden, Okla. *Citation:* He displayed conspicuous gallantry and intrepidity at the risk of his life above and beyond the call of duty on 8 April 1945 near Lobenbacherhof, Germany. As his company was advancing toward the village under heavy fire, an enemy machinegun and automatic rifle with rifle support opened upon it from a hill on the right flank. Seeing that his platoon leader had been wounded by their fire, S/Sgt. Crews, acting on his own initiative, rushed the strongpoint with 2 men of his platoon. Despite the fact that 1 of these men was killed and the other was badly wounded, he continued his advance up the hill in the face of terrific enemy fire. Storming the well-dug-in position singlehandedly, he killed 2 of the crew of the machinegun at pointblank range with his M1 rifle and wrested the gun from the hands of the German whom he had already wounded. He then with his rifle charged the strongly emplaced automatic rifle. Although badly wounded in the thigh by crossfire from the remaining enemy, he kept on and silenced the entire position with his accurate and deadly rifle fire. His actions so unnerved the remaining enemy soldiers that 7 of them surrendered and the others fled. His heroism caused the enemy to concentrate on him and permitted the company to move forward into the village.

*CROMWELL, JOHN PHILIP

Rank and organization: Captain, U.S. Navy. *Born:* 11 September 1901, Henry, Ill. *Appointed from:* Illinois. *Other Navy award:* Legion of Merit. *Citation:* For conspicuous gallantry and intrepidity at the risk of his life above and beyond the call of duty as Commander of a Submarine Coordinated Attack Group with Flag in the U.S.S. *Sculpin*, during the 9th War Patrol of that vessel in enemy-controlled waters off Truk Island, 19 November 1943. Undertaking this patrol prior to the launching of our first large-scale offensive in the Pacific, Capt. Cromwell, alone of the entire Task Group, possessed secret intelligence information of our submarine strategy and tactics, scheduled Fleet movements and specific attack plans. Constantly vigilant and precise in carrying out his secret orders, he moved his underseas flotilla inexorably forward despite savage opposition and established a line of submarines to southeastward of the main Japanese stronghold at Truk. Cool and undaunted as the submarine, rocked and battered by Japanese depth charges, sustained terrific battle damage and sank to an excessive depth, he authorized the *Sculpin* to surface and engage the enemy in a gunfight, thereby providing an opportunity for the crew to abandon ship. Determined to sacrifice himself rather than risk capture and subsequent danger of revealing plans under Japanese torture or use of drugs, he stoically remained aboard the mortally wounded vessel as she plunged to her death. Preserving the security of his mission, at the cost of his own life, he had served his country as he had served the Navy, with deep integrity and an uncompromising devotion to duty. His great moral courage in the face of certain death adds new luster to the traditions of the U.S. Naval Service. He gallantly gave his life for his country.

CURREY, FRANCIS S.

Rank and organization: Sergeant, U.S. Army, Company K, 120th Infantry, 30th Infantry Division. *Place and date:* Malmedy, Belgium, 21 December 1944. *Entered service at:* Hurleyville, N.Y. *Birth:* Loch Sheldrake, N.Y. *G.O. No.:* 69, 17 August 1945. *Citation:* He was an automatic rifleman with the 3d Platoon defending a strong point near Malmedy, Belgium, on 21 December 1944, when the enemy launched a powerful attack. Overrunning tank destroyers and antitank guns located near the strong point, German tanks advanced to the 3d Platoon's position, and, after prolonged fighting, forced the withdrawal of this group to a nearby factory. Sgt. Currey found a bazooka in the building and crossed the street to secure rockets meanwhile enduring intense fire from enemy tanks and hostile infantrymen who had taken up a position at a house a short distance away. In the face of small-arms, machinegun, and artillery fire, he, with a companion, knocked out a tank with 1 shot. Moving to another position, he observed 3 Germans in the doorway of an enemy-held house. He killed or wounded all 3 with his automatic rifle. He emerged from cover and advanced alone to within 50 yards of the house, intent on wrecking it with rockets. Covered by friendly fire, he stood erect, and fired a shot which knocked down half of 1 wall. While in this forward position, he observed 5 Americans who had been pinned down for hours by fire from the house and 3 tanks. Realizing that they could not escape until the enemy tank and infantry guns had been silenced, Sgt. Currey crossed the street to a vehicle, where he procured an armful of antitank grenades. These he launched while under heavy enemy fire, driving the tankmen from the vehicles into the house. He then climbed onto a halftrack in full view of the Germans and fired a machinegun at the house. Once again changing his position, he manned another machinegun whose crew had been killed; under his covering fire the 5 soldiers were able to retire to safety. Deprived of tanks and with heavy infantry casualties, the enemy was forced to withdraw. Through his extensive knowledge of weapons and by his heroic and repeated braving of murderous enemy fire, Sgt. Currey was greatly responsible for inflicting heavy losses in men and material on the enemy, for rescuing 5 comrades, 2 of whom were wounded, and for stemming an attack which threatened to flank his battalion's position.

DAHLGREN, EDWARD C.

Rank and organization: Second Lieutenant (then Sergeant), U.S. Army, Company E, 142d Infantry, 36th Infantry Division. *Place and date:* Oberhoffen, France, 11 February 1945. *Entered service at:* Portland, Maine. *Birth:* Perham, Maine. *G.O. No.:* 77, 10 September 1945. *Citation:* He led the 3d Platoon to the rescue of a similar unit which had been surrounded in an enemy counterattack at Oberhoffen, France. As he advanced along a street, he observed several Germans crossing a field about 100 yards away. Running into a barn, he took up a position in a window and swept the hostile troops with submachinegun fire, killing 6, wounding others, and completely disorganizing the group. His platoon then moved forward through intermittent sniper fire and made contact with the beseiged Americans. When the 2 platoons had been reorganized, Sgt. Dahlgren continued to advance along the street until he drew fire from an enemy-held house. In the face of machine-pistol and rifle fire, he ran toward the building, hurled a grenade through the door, and blasted his way inside with his gun. This aggressive attack so rattled the Germans that all 8 men who held the strongpoint immediately surrendered. As Sgt. Dahlgren started toward the next house, hostile machinegun fire drove him to cover. He secured rifle grenades, stepped to an exposed position, and calmly launched his missiles from a difficult angle until he had destroyed the machinegun and killed its 2 operators. He moved to the rear of the house and suddenly came under the fire of a machinegun emplaced in a barn. Throwing a grenade into the structure, he rushed the position, firing his weapon as he ran; within, he overwhelmed 5 Germans. After reorganizing his unit he advanced to clear hostile riflemen from the building where he had destroyed the machinegun. He entered the house by a window and trapped the Germans in the cellar, where he tossed grenades into their midst, wounding several and forcing 10 more to surrender. While reconnoitering another street with a comrade, he heard German voices in a house. An attack with rifle grenades drove the hostile troops to the cellar. Sgt. Dahlgren entered the building, kicked open the cellar door, and, firing several bursts down the stairway, called for the trapped enemy to surrender. Sixteen soldiers filed out with their hands in the air. The bold leadership and magnificent courage displayed by Sgt. Dahlgren in his heroic attacks were in a large measure responsible for repulsing an enemy counterattack and saving an American platoon from great danger.

DALESSONDRO, PETER J.

Rank and organization: Technical Sergeant, U.S. Army, Company E, 39th Infantry, 9th Infantry Division. *Place and date:* Near Kalterherberg, Germany, 22 December 1944. *Entered service at:* Watervliet, N.Y. *Born:* 19 May 1918, Watervliet, N.Y. *G.O. No.:* 73, 30 August, 1945. *Citation:* He was with the 1st Platoon holding an important road junction on high ground near Kalterherberg, Germany, on 22 December 1944. In the early morning hours, the enemy after laying down an intense artillery and mortar barrage, followed through with an all-out attack that threatened to overwhelm the position. T/Sgt. Dalessondro, seeing that his men were becoming disorganized, braved the intense fire to move among them with words of encouragement. Advancing to a fully exposed observation post, he adjusted mortar fire upon the attackers, meanwhile firing upon them with his rifle and encouraging his men in halting and repulsing the attack. Later in the day the enemy launched a second determined attack. Once again, T/Sgt. Dalessondro, in the face of imminent death, rushed to his forward position and immediately called for mortar fire. After exhausting his rifle ammunition, he crawled 30 yards over exposed ground to secure a light machinegun, returned to his position, and fired upon the enemy at almost pointblank range until the gun jammed. He managed to get the gun to fire 1 more burst, which used up his last round, but with these bullets he killed 4 German soldiers who were on the verge of murdering an aid man and 2 wounded soldiers in a nearby foxhole. When the enemy had almost surrounded him, he remained alone, steadfastly facing almost certain death or capture, hurling grenades and calling for mortar fire closer and closer to his outpost as he covered the withdrawal of his platoon to a second line of defense. As the German hordes swarmed about him, he was last heard calling for a barrage, saying, "OK, mortars, let me have it—right in this position!" The gallantry and intrepidity shown by T/Sgt. Dalessondro against an overwhelming enemy attack saved his company from complete rout.

DALY, MICHAEL J.

Rank and organization: Captain (then Lieutenant), U.S. Army, Company A, 15th Infantry, 3d Infantry Division. *Place and date:* Nuremberg, Germany, 18 April 1945. *Entered service at:* Southport, Conn. *Born:* 15 September 1924, New York, N.Y. *G.O. No.:* 77, 10 September 1945. *Citation:* Early in the morning of 18 April 1945, he led his company through the shell-battered, sniper-infested wreckage of Nuremberg, Germany. When blistering machinegun fire caught his unit in an exposed position, he ordered his men to take cover, dashed forward alone, and, as bullets whined about him, shot the 3-man gun-crew with his carbine. Continuing the advance at the head of his company, he located an enemy patrol armed with rocket launchers which threatened friendly armor. He again went forward alone, secured a vantage point and opened fire on the Germans. Immediately he became the target for concentrated machine-pistol and rocket fire, which blasted the rubble about him. Calmly, he continued to shoot at the patrol until he had killed all 6 enemy infantrymen. Continuing boldly far in front of his company, he entered a park, where as his men advanced, a German machinegun opened up on them without warning. With his carbine, he killed the gunner; and then, from a completely exposed position, he directed machinegun fire on the remainder of the crew until all were dead. In a final duel, he wiped out a third machinegun emplacement with rifle fire at a range of 10 yards. By fearlessly engaging in 4 singlehanded fire fights with a desperate, powerfully armed enemy, Lt. Daly, voluntarily taking all major risks himself and protecting his men at every opportunity, killed 15 Germans, silenced 3 enemy machineguns and wiped out an entire enemy patrol. His heroism during the lone bitter struggle with fanatical enemy forces was an inspiration to the valiant Americans who took Nuremberg.

*DAMATO, ANTHONY PETER

Rank and organization: Corporal, U.S. Marine Corps. *Born:* 28 March 1922, Shenandoah, Pa. *Accredited to:* Pennsylvania. *Citation:* For conspicuous gallantry and intrepidity at the risk of his life above and beyond the call of duty while serving with an assault company in action against enemy Japanese forces on Engebi Island, Eniwetok Atoll, Marshall Islands, on the night of 19–20 February 1944. Highly vulnerable to sudden attack by small, fanatical groups of Japanese still at large despite the efficient and determined efforts of our forces to clear the area, Cpl. Damato lay with 2 comrades in a large foxhole in his company's defense perimeter which had been dangerously thinned by the forced withdrawal of nearly half of the available men. When 1 of the enemy approached the foxhole undetected and threw in a handgrenade, Cpl. Damato desperately groped for it in the darkness. Realizing the imminent peril to all 3 and fully aware of the consequences of his act, he unhesitatingly flung himself on the grenade and, although instantly killed as his body absorbed the explosion, saved the lives of his 2 companions. Cpl. Damato's splendid initiative, fearless conduct and valiant sacrifice reflect great credit upon himself and the U.S. Naval Service. He gallantly gave his life for his comrades.

*DAVID, ALBERT LeROY

Rank and organization: Lieutenant, Junior Grade, U.S. Navy. *Born:* 18 July 1902, Maryville, Mo. *Accredited to:* Missouri. *Other Navy award:* Navy Cross with gold star. *Citation:* For conspicuous gallantry and intrepidity at the risk of his life above and beyond the call of duty while attached to the U.S.S. *Pillsbury* during the capture of an enemy German submarine off French West Africa, 4 June 1944. Taking a vigorous part in the skillfully coordinated attack on the German *U–505* which climaxed a prolonged search by the Task Group, Lt. (then Lt., jg.) David boldly led a party from the *Pillsbury* in boarding the hostile submarine as it circled erratically at 5 or 6 knots on the surface. Fully aware that the U-boat might momentarily sink or be blown up by exploding demolition and scuttling charges, he braved the added danger of enemy gunfire to plunge through the conning tower hatch and, with his small party, exerted every effort to keep the ship afloat and to assist the succeeding and more fully equipped salvage parties in making the *U–505* seaworthy for the long tow across the Atlantic to a U.S. port. By his valiant service during the first successful boarding and capture of an enemy man-o-war on the high seas by the U.S. Navy since 1815, Lt. David contributed materially to the effectiveness of our Battle of the Atlantic and upheld the highest traditions of the U.S. Naval Service.

DAVIS, CHARLES W.

Rank and organization: Major, U.S. Army, 25th Infantry Division. *Place and date:* Guadalcanal Island, 12 January 1943. *Entered service at:* Montgomery, Ala. *Birth:* Gordo, Ala. *G.O. No.:* 40, 17 July 1943. *Citation:* For distinguishing himself conspicuously by gallantry and intrepidity at the risk of his life above and beyond the call of duty in action with the enemy on Guadalcanal Island. On 12 January 1943, Maj. Davis (then Capt.), executive officer of an infantry battalion, volunteered to carry instructions to the leading companies of his battalion which had been caught in crossfire from Japanese machineguns. With complete disregard for his own safety, he made his way to the trapped units, delivered the instructions, supervised their execution, and remained overnight in this exposed position. On the following day, Maj. Davis again volunteered to lead an assault on the Japanese position which was holding up the advance. When his rifle jammed at its first shot, he drew his pistol and, waving his men on, led the assault over the top of the hill. Electrified by this action, another body of soldiers followed and seized the hill. The capture of this position broke

Japanese resistance and the battalion was then able to proceed and secure the corps objective. The courage and leadership displayed by Maj. Davis inspired the entire battalion and unquestionably led to the success of its attack.

*DAVIS, GEORGE FLEMING

Rank and organization: Commander, U.S. Navy. *Born:* 23 March 1911, Manila, Philippine Islands. *Accredited to:* Philippine Islands. *Other Navy awards:* Silver Star Medal, Legion of Merit. *Citation:* For conspicuous gallantry and intrepidity at the risk of his life and beyond the call of duty as Commanding Officer of the U.S.S. *Walke* engaged in a detached mission in support of minesweeping operations to clear the waters for entry of our heavy surface and amphibious forces preparatory to the invasion of Lingayen Gulf, Luzon, Philippine Islands, 6 January 1945. Operating without gun support of other surface ships when 4 Japanese suicide planes were detected flying low overland to attack simultaneously, Comdr. Davis boldly took his position in the exposed wings of the bridge and directed control to pick up the leading plane and open fire. Alert and fearless as the *Walke's* deadly fire sent the first target crashing into the water and caught the second as it passed close over the bridge to plunge into the sea of portside, he remained steadfast in the path of the third plane plunging swiftly to crash the after end of the bridge structure. Seriously wounded when the craft struck, drenched with gasoline and immediately enveloped in flames, he conned the *Walke* in the midst of the wreckage; he rallied his command to heroic efforts; he exhorted his officers and men to save the ship and, still on his feet, saw the barrage from his guns destroy the fourth suicide bomber. With the fires under control and the safety of the ship assured, he consented to be carried below. Succumbing several hours later, Comdr. Davis by his example of valor and his unhesitating self-sacrifice, steeled the fighting spirit of his command into unyielding purpose in completing a vital mission. He gallantly gave his life in the service of his country.

*DEALEY, SAMUEL DAVID

Rank and organization: Commander, U.S. Navy. *Born:* 13 September 1906, Dallas, Tex. *Appointed from:* Texas. *Other Navy awards:* Navy Cross with 3 Gold Stars, Silver Star Medal. *Citation:* For conspicuous gallantry and intrepidity at the risk of his life above and beyond the call of duty as Commanding Officer of the U.S.S. *Harder* during her 5th War Patrol in Japanese-controlled waters. Floodlighted by a bright moon and disclosed to an enemy destroyer escort which bore down with intent to attack, Comdr. Dealey quickly dived to periscope depth and waited for the pursuer to close range, then opened fire, sending the target and all aboard down in flames with his third torpedo. Plunging deep to avoid fierce depth charges, he again surfaced and, within 9 minutes after sighting another destroyer, had sent the enemy down tail first with a hit directly amidship. Evading detection, he penetrated the confined waters off Tawi Tawi with the Japanese Fleet base 6 miles away and scored death blows on 2 patrolling destroyers in quick succession. With his ship heeled over by concussion from the first exploding target and the second vessel nose-diving in a blinding detonation, he cleared the area at high speed. Sighted by a large hostile fleet force on the following day, he swung his bow toward the lead destroyer for another "down-the-throat" shot, fired 3 bow tubes and promptly crash-dived to be terrifically rocked seconds later by the exploding ship as the *Harder* passed beneath. This remarkable record of 5 vital Japanese destroyers sunk in 5 short-range torpedo attacks attests the valiant fighting spirit of Comdr. Dealey and his indomitable command.

DeBLANC, JEFFERSON JOSEPH

Rank and organization: Captain, U.S. Marine Corps Reserve, Marine Fighting Squadron 112. *Place and date:* Off Kolombangara Island in the Solomons group, 31 January 1943. *Entered service at:* Louisiana. *Born:* 15 February 1921, Lockport, La. *Citation:* For conspicuous gallantry and intrepidity at the risk of his life above and beyond the call of duty as leader of a section of 6 fighter planes in Marine Fighting Squadron 112, during aerial operations against enemy Japanese forces off Kolombangara Island in the Solomons group, 31 January 1943. Taking off with his section as escort for a strike force of dive bombers and torpedo planes ordered to attack Japanese surface vessels, 1st Lt. DeBlanc led his flight directly to the target area where, at 14,000 feet, our strike force encountered a large number of Japanese Zeros protecting the enemy's surface craft. In company with the other fighters, 1st Lt. DeBlanc instantly engaged the hostile planes and aggressively countered their repeated attempts to drive off our bombers, persevering in his efforts to protect the diving planes and waging fierce combat until, picking up a call for assistance from the dive bombers, under attack by enemy float planes at 1,000 feet, he broke off his engagement with the Zeros, plunged into the formation of float planes and disrupted the savage attack, enabling our dive bombers and torpedo planes to complete their runs on the Japanese surface disposition and withdraw without further incident. Although his escort mission was fulfilled upon the safe retirement of the bombers, 1st Lt. DeBlanc courageously remained on the scene despite a rapidly diminishing fuel supply and, boldly challenging the enemy's superior number of float planes, fought a valiant battle against terrific odds, seizing the tactical advantage and striking repeatedly to destroy 3 of the hostile aircraft and to disperse the remainder. Prepared to maneuver his damaged plane back to base, he had climbed aloft and set his course when he discovered 2 Zeros closing in behind. Undaunted, he opened fire and blasted both Zeros from the sky in a short, bitterly fought action which resulted in such hopeless damage to his own plane that he was forced to bail out at a perilously low altitude atop the trees on enemy-held Kolombangara. A gallant officer, a superb airman, and an indomitable fighter, 1st Lt. DeBlanc had rendered decisive assistance during a critical stage of operations, and his unwavering fortitude in the face of overwhelming opposition reflects the highest credit upon himself and adds new luster to the traditions of the U.S. Naval Service.

*DeFRANZO, ARTHUR F.

Rank and organization: Staff Sergeant, U.S. Army, 1st Infantry Division. *Place and date:* Near Vaubadon, France, 10 June 1944. *Entered service at:* Saugus, Mass. *Birth:* Saugus, Mass. *G.O. No.:* 1, 4 January

1945. *Citation:* For conspicuous gallantry and intrepidity at the risk of his life, above and beyond the call of duty, on 10 June 1944, near Vaubadon, France. As scouts were advancing across an open field, the enemy suddenly opened fire with several machine-guns and hit 1 of the men. S/Sgt. DeFranzo courageously moved out in the open to the aid of the wounded scout and was himself wounded but brought the man to safety. Refusing aid, S/Sgt. DeFranzo reentered the open field and led the advance upon the enemy. There were always at least 2 machine-guns bringing unrelenting fire upon him, but S/Sgt. DeFranzo kept going forward, firing into the enemy and 1 by 1 the enemy emplacements became silent. While advancing he was again wounded, but continued on until he was within 100 yards of the enemy position and even as he fell, he kept firing his rifle and waving his men forward. When his company came up behind him, S/Sgt. DeFranzo, despite his many severe wounds, suddenly raised himself and once more moved forward in the lead of his men until he was again hit by enemy fire. In a final gesture of indomitable courage, he threw several grenades at the enemy machinegun position and completely destroyed the gun. In this action, S/Sgt. DeFranzo lost his life, but by bearing the brunt of the enemy fire in leading the attack, he prevented a delay in the assault which would have been of considerable benefit to the foe, and he made possible his company's advance with a minimum of casualties. The extraordinary heroism and magnificent devotion to duty displayed by S/Sgt. DeFranzo was a great inspiration to all about him, and is in keeping with the highest traditions of the armed forces.

*DeGLOPPER, CHARLES N.

Rank and organization: Private First Class, U.S. Army, Co. C, 325th Glider Infantry, 82d Airborne Division. *Place and date:* Merderet River at la Fiere, France, 9 June 1944. *Entered service at:* Grand Island, N.Y. *Birth:* Grand Island, N.Y. *G.O. No.:* 22, 28 February 1946. *Citation:* He was a member of Company C, 325th Glider Infantry, on 9 June 1944 advancing with the forward platoon to secure a bridgehead across the Merderet River at La Fiere, France. At dawn the platoon had penetrated an outer line of machineguns and riflemen, but in so doing had become cut off from the rest of the company. Vastly superior forces began a decimation of the stricken unit and put in motion a flanking maneuver which would have completely exposed the American platoon in a shallow roadside ditch where it had taken cover. Detecting this danger, Pfc. DeGlopper volunteered to support his comrades by fire from his automatic rifle while they attempted a withdrawal through a break in a hedgerow 40 yards to the rear. Scorning a concentration of enemy automatic weapons and rifle fire, he walked from the ditch onto the road in full view of the Germans, and sprayed the hostile positions with assault fire. He was wounded, but he continued firing. Struck again, he started to fall; and yet his grim determination and valiant fighting spirit could not be broken. Kneeling in the roadway, weakened by his grievous wounds, he leveled his heavy weapon against the enemy and fired burst after burst until killed outright. He was successful in drawing the enemy action away from his fellow soldiers, who continued the fight from a more advantageous position and established the first bridgehead over the Merderet. In the area where he made his intrepid stand his comrades later found the ground strewn with dead Germans and many machineguns and automatic weapons which he had knocked out of action. Pfc. DeGlopper's gallant sacrifice and unflinching heroism while facing unsurmountable odds were in great measure responsible for a highly important tactical victory in the Normandy Campaign.

*DELEAU, EMILE, JR.

Rank and organization: Sergeant, U.S. Army, Company A, 142d Infantry, 36th Infantry Division. *Place and date:* Oberhoffen, France, 1–2 February 1945. *Entered service at:* Blaine, Ohio. *Birth:* Lansing, Ohio. *G.O. No.:* 60, 25 July 1945. *Citation:* He led a squad in the night attack on Oberhoffen, France, where fierce house-to-house fighting took place. After clearing 1 building of opposition, he moved his men toward a second house from which heavy machine-gun fire came. He courageously exposed himself to hostile bullets and, firing his submachinegun as he went, advanced steadily toward the enemy position until close enough to hurl grenades through a window, killing 3 Germans and wrecking their gun. His progress was stopped by heavy rifle and machinegun fire from another house. Sgt. Deleau dashed through the door with his gun blazing. Within, he captured 10 Germans. The squad then took up a position for the night and awaited daylight to resume the attack. At dawn of 2 February Sgt. Deleau pressed forward with his unit, killing 2 snipers as he advanced to a point where machine-gun fire from a house barred the way. Despite vicious small-arms fire, Sgt. Deleau ran across an open area to reach the rear of the building, where he destroyed 1 machinegun and killed its 2 operators with a grenade. He worked to the front of the structure and located a second machinegun. Finding it impossible to toss a grenade into the house from his protected position, he fearlessly moved away from the building and was about to hurl his explosive when he was instantly killed by a burst from the gun he sought to knock out. With magnificent courage and daring aggressiveness, Sgt. Deleau cleared 4 well-defended houses of Germans, inflicted severe losses on the enemy and at the sacrifice of his own life aided his battalion to reach its objective with a minimum of casualties.

DERVISHIAN, ERNEST H.

Rank and organization: Second Lieutenant, U.S. Army, 34th Infantry Division. *Place and date:* Near Cisterna, Italy, 23 May 1944. *Entered service at:* Richmond, Va. *Birth:* Richmond, Va. *G.O. No.:* 3, 8 January 1945. *Citation:* For conspicuous gallantry and intrepidity at risk of life above and beyond the call of duty on 23 May 1944, in the vicinity of Cisterna, Italy. 2d Lt. Dervishian (then Tech. Sgt.) and 4 members of his platoon found themselves far ahead of their company after an aggressive advance in the face of enemy artillery and sniper fire. Approaching a railroad embankment, they observed a force of German soldiers hiding in dugouts. 2d Lt. Dervishian, directing his men to cover him, boldly moved forward and firing his carbine forced 10 Germans to surrender. His men then advanced and captured 15 more Germans occupying adjacent dugouts. The prisoners were returned to the rear to be picked up by advancing units. From the railroad embankment, 2d Lt. Dervishian and his men then observed 9 Germans who were fleeing across a ridge. He and his men opened fire and 3 of the enemy were wounded. As his men were firing, 2d Lt. Dervishian, unnoticed, fearlessly dashed forward alone and captured all of the fleeing enemy before his companions joined him on the ridge. At this point 4 other men joined 2d Lt. Dervishian's group. An attempt was made to send the 4 newly arrived men along the left flank of a large, dense vineyard that lay ahead, but murderous machinegun fire forced them back. Deploying his men, 2d Lt. Dervishian moved to the front of his group and led the advance into the vineyard. He and his men suddenly became pinned down by a machinegun firing at them at a distance of 15 yards. Feigning death while the hostile weapon blazed away at him, 2d Lt. Dervishian assaulted the position during a halt in the firing, using a handgrenade and carbine fire, and forced the 4 German crewmembers to surrender. The 4 men on the left flank were now ordered to enter the vineyard but encountered machinegun fire which killed 1 soldier and wounded another. At this moment the enemy intensified the fight by throwing potato-masher grenades at the valiant band of American soldiers within the vineyard. 2d Lt. Dervishian ordered his men to withdraw; but instead of following, jumped into the machinegun position he had just captured and opened fire with the enemy weapon in the direction of the second hostile machinegun nest. Observing movement in a dugout 2 or 3 yards to the rear, 2d Lt. Dervishian seized a machine-pistol. Simultaneously blazing away at the entrance to the dugout to prevent its occupants from firing and firing his machinegun at the other German nest, he forced 5 Germans in each position to surrender. Determined to rid the area of all Germans, 2d Lt. Dervishian continued his advance alone. Noticing another machinegun position beside a house, he picked up an abandoned machine-pistol and forced 6 more Germans to surrender by spraying their position with fire. Unable to locate additional targets in the vicinity, 2d Lt. Dervishian conducted these prisoners to the rear. The prodigious courage and combat skill exhibited by 2d Lt. Dervishian are exemplary of the finest traditions of the U.S. Armed Forces.

*DIAMOND, JAMES H.

Rank and organization: Private First Class, U.S. Army, Company D, 21st Infantry, 24th Infantry Division. *Place and date:* Mintal, Mindanao, Philippine Islands, 8–14 May 1945. *Entered service at:* Gulfport, Miss. *Birth:* New Orleans, La. *G.O. No.:* 23, 6 March 1946. *Citation:* As a member of the machinegun section, he displayed extreme gallantry and intrepidity above and beyond the call of duty. When a Japanese sniper rose from his foxhole to throw a grenade into their midst, this valiant soldier charged and killed the enemy with a burst from his submachine-gun; then, by delivering sustained fire from his personal arm and simultaneously directing the fire of 105-mm. and .50 caliber weapons upon the enemy pillboxes immobilizing this and another machinegun section, he enabled them to put their guns into action. When 2 infantry companies established a bridgehead, he voluntarily assisted in evacuating the wounded under heavy fire; and then, securing an abandoned vehicle, transported casualties to the rear through mortar and artillery fire so intense as to render the vehicle inoperative and despite the fact he was suffering from a painful wound. The following day he again volunteered, this time for the hazardous job of repairing a bridge under heavy enemy fire. On 14 May 1945, when leading a patrol to evacuate casualties from his battalion, which was cut off, he ran through a virtual hail of Japanese fire to secure an abandoned machine gun. Though mortally wounded as he reached the gun, he succeeded in drawing sufficient fire upon himself so that the remaining members of the patrol could reach safety. Pfc. Diamond's indomitable spirit, constant disregard of danger, and eagerness to assist his comrades, will ever remain a symbol of selflessness and heroic sacrifice to those for whom he gave his life.

*DIETZ, ROBERT H.

Rank and organization: Staff Sergeant, U.S. Army, Company A, 38th Armored Infantry Battalion, 7th Armored Division. *Place and date:* Kirchain, Germany, 29 March 1945. *Entered service at:* Kingston, N.Y. *Birth:* Kingston, N.Y. *G.O. No.:* 119, 17 December 1945. *Citation:* He was a squad leader when the task force to which his unit was attached encountered resistance in its advance on Kirchain, Germany. Between the town's outlying buildings 300 yards distant, and the stalled armored column were a minefield and 2 bridges defended by German rocket-launching teams and riflemen. From the town itself came heavy small-arms fire. Moving forward with his men to protect engineers while they removed the minefield and the demolition charges attached to the bridges, S/Sgt. Dietz came under intense fire. On his own initiative he advanced alone, scorning the bullets which struck all around him, until he was able to kill the bazooka team defending the first bridge. He continued ahead and had killed another bazooka team, bayoneted an enemy soldier armed with a panzerfaust and shot 2 Germans when he was knocked to the ground by another blast of another panzerfaust. He quickly recovered, killed the man who had fired at him and then jumped into waist-deep water under the second bridge to disconnect the demolition charges. His work was completed; but as he stood up to signal that the route was clear he was killed by another enemy volley from the left flank. S/Sgt. Dietz by his intrepidity and valiant effort on his self-imposed mission, singlehandedly opened the road for the capture of Kirchain and left with his comrades an inspiring example of gallantry in the face of formidable odds.

DOOLITTLE, JAMES H. (Air Mission)

Rank and organization: Brigadier General, U.S. Army. Air Corps. *Place and date:* Over Japan. *Entered service at:* Berkeley, Calif. *Birth:* Alameda, Calif. *G.O. No.:* 29, 9 June 1942. *Citation:* For conspicuous leadership above the call of duty, involving personal valor and intrepidity at an extreme hazard to life. With the apparent certainty of being forced to land in enemy territory or to perish at sea, Gen. Doolittle personally led a squadron of Army bombers, manned by volunteer crews, in a highly destructive raid on the Japanese mainland.

DOSS, DESMOND T.

Rank and organization: Private First Class, U.S. Army, Medical Detachment, 307th Infantry, 77th Infantry Division. *Place and date:*

Desmond T. Doss, C.M.H.   *Oct. 12, 1945*

Near Urasoe-Mura, Okinawa, Ryukyu Islands, 29 April–21 May 1945. *Entered service at:* Lynchburg, Va. *Birth:* Lynchburg, Va. *G.O. No.:* 97, 1 November 1945. *Citation:* He was a company aid man when the 1st Battalion assaulted a jagged escarpment 400 feet high. As our troops gained the summit, a heavy concentration of artillery, mortar and machinegun fire crashed into them, inflicting approximately 75 casualties and driving the others back. Pfc. Doss refused to seek cover and remained in the fire-swept area with the many stricken, carrying them 1 by 1 to the edge of the escarpment and there lowering them on a rope-supported litter down the face of a cliff to friendly hands. On 2 May, he exposed himself to heavy rifle and mortar fire in rescuing a wounded man 200 yards forward of the lines on the same escarpment; and 2 days later he treated 4 men who had been cut down while assaulting a strongly defended cave, advancing through a shower of grenades to within 8 yards of enemy forces in a cave's mouth, where he dressed his comrades' wounds before making 4 separate trips under fire to evacuate them to safety. On 5 May, he unhesitatingly braved enemy shelling and small-arms fire to assist an artillery officer. He applied bandages, moved his patient to a spot that offered protection from small-arms fire and, while artillery and mortar shells fell close by, painstakingly administered plasma. Later that day, when an American was severely wounded by fire from a cave, Pfc. Doss crawled to him where he had fallen 25 feet from the enemy position, rendered aid, and carried him 100 yards to safety while continually exposed to enemy fire. On 21 May, in a night attack on high ground near Shuri, he remained in exposed territory while the rest of his company took cover, fearlessly risking the chance that he would be mistaken for an infiltrating Japanese and giving aid to the injured until he was himself seriously wounded in the legs by the explosion of a grenade. Rather than call another aid man from cover, he cared for his own injuries and waited 5 hours before litter bearers reached him and started carrying him to cover. The trio was caught in an enemy tank attack and Pfc. Doss, seeing a more critically wounded man nearby, crawled off the litter and directed the bearers to give their first attention to the other man. Awaiting the litter bearers' return, he was again struck, this time suffering a compound fracture of 1 arm. With magnificent fortitude he bound a rifle stock to his shattered arm as a splint and then crawled 300 yards over rough terrain to the aid station. Through his outstanding bravery and unflinching determination in the face of desperately dangerous conditions Pfc. Doss saved the lives of many soldiers. His name became a symbol throughout the 77th Infantry Division for outstanding gallantry far above and beyond the call of duty.

DROWLEY, JESSE R.

Rank and organization: Staff Sergeant, U.S. Army, Americal Infantry Division. *Place and date:* Bougainville, Solomon Islands, 30 January 1944. *Entered service at:* Spokane, Wash. *Birth:* St. Charles, Mich. *G.O. No.:* 73, 6 September 1944. *Citation:* For gallantry and intrepidity at the risk of his life above and beyond the call of duty in action with the enemy at Bougainville, Solomon Islands, 30 January 1944. S/Sgt. Drowley, a squad leader in a platoon whose mission during an attack was to remain under cover while holding the perimeter defense and acting as a reserve for assaulting echelon, saw 3 members of the assault company fall badly wounded. When intense hostile fire prevented aid from reaching the casualties, he fearlessly rushed forward to carry the wounded to cover. After rescuing 2 men, S/Sgt. Drowley discovered an enemy pillbox undetected by assaulting tanks that was inflicting heavy casualties upon the attacking force and was a chief obstacle to the success of the advance. Delegating the rescue of the third man to an assistant, he ran across open terrain to 1 of the tanks. Signaling to the crew, he climbed to the turret, exchanged his weapon for a submachinegun and voluntarily rode the deck of the tank directing it toward the pillbox by tracer fire. The tank, under constant heavy enemy fire, continued to within 20 feet of the pillbox where S/Sgt. Drowley received a severe bullet wound in the chest. Refusing to return for medical treatment, he remained on the tank and continued to direct its progress until the enemy box was definitely located by the crew. At this point he again was wounded by small-arms fire, losing his left eye and falling to the ground. He remained alongside the tank until the pillbox had been completely demolished and another directly behind the first destroyed. S/Sgt. Drowley, his voluntary mission successfully accomplished, returned alone for medical treatment.

DUNHAM, RUSSELL E.

Rank and organization: Technical Sergeant, U.S. Army, Company I, 30th Infantry, 3d Infantry Division. *Place and date:* Near Kayserberg, France, 8 January 1945. *Entered service at:* Brighton Ill. *Born:* 23 February 1920, East Carondelet, Ill. *G.O. No.: 37,* 11 May 1945. *Citation:* For conspicuous gallantry and intrepidity at risk of life above and beyond the call of duty. At about 1430 hours on 8 January 1945, during an attack on Hill 616, near Kayserberg, France, T/Sgt. Dunham singlehandedly assaulted 3 enemy machineguns. Wearing a white robe made of a mattress cover, carrying 12 carbine magazines and with a dozen handgrenades snagged in his belt, suspenders, and buttonholes, T/Sgt. Dunham advanced in the attack up a snow-covered hill under fire from 2 machineguns and supporting riflemen. His platoon 35 yards behind him, T/Sgt. Dunham crawled 75 yards under heavy direct fire toward the timbered emplacement shielding the left machinegun. As he jumped to his feet 10 yards from the gun and charged forward, machinegun fire tore through his camouflage robe and a rifle bullet seared a 10-inch gash across his back sending him spinning 15 yards down hill into the snow. When the indomitable sergeant sprang to his feet to renew his 1-man assault, a German egg grenade landed beside him. He kicked it aside, and as it exploded 5 yards away, shot and killed the German machinegunner and assistant gunner. His carbine empty, he jumped into the emplacement and hauled out the third member of the gun crew by the collar. Although his back wound was causing him excruciating pain and blood was seeping through his white coat, T/Sgt. Dunham proceeded 50 yards through a storm of automatic and rifle fire to attack the second machinegun. Twenty-five yards from the emplacement he hurled 2 grenades, destroying the gun and its crew; then fired down into the supporting foxholes with his carbine, dispatching and dispersing the enemy riflemen. Although his coat was so thoroughly bloodsoaked that he was a conspicuous target against the white landscape, T/Sgt. Dunham again advanced ahead of his platoon in an assault on enemy positions farther up the hill. Coming under machinegun fire from 65 yards to his front, while rifle grenades exploded 10 yards from his position, he hit the ground and crawled forward. At 15 yards range, he jumped to his feet, staggered a few paces toward the timbered machinegun emplacement and killed the crew with handgrenades. An enemy rifleman fired at pointblank range, but missed him. After killing the rifleman, T/Sgt. Dunham drove others from their foxholes with grenades and carbine fire. Killing 9 Germans—wounding 7 and capturing 2—firing about 175 rounds of carbine ammunition, and expending 11 grenades, T/Sgt. Dunham, despite a painful wound, spearheaded a spectacular and successful diversionary attack.

DUNLAP, ROBERT HUGO

Rank and organization: Captain, U.S. Marine Corps Reserve, Company C, 1st Battalion, 26th Marines, 5th Marine Division. *Place and date:* On Iwo Jima, Volcano Islands, 20 and 21 February 1945. *Entered service at:* Illinois. *Born:* 19 October 1920, Abingdon, Ill. *Citation:* For conspicuous gallantry and intrepidity at the risk of his life above and beyond the call of duty as commanding officer of Company C, 1st Battalion, 26th Marines, 5th Marine Division, in action against enemy Japanese forces during the seizure of Iwo Jima in the Volcano Islands, on 20 and 21 February, 1945. Defying uninterrupted blasts of Japanese artillery, mortar, rifle and machinegun fire, Capt. Dunlap led his troops in a determined advance from low ground uphill toward the steep cliffs from which the enemy poured a devastating rain of shrapnel and bullets, steadily inching forward until the tremendous volume of enemy fire from the caves located high to his front temporarily halted his progress. Determined not to yield, he crawled alone approximately 200 yards forward of his front lines, took observation at the base of the cliff 50 yards from Japanese lines, located the enemy gun positions and returned to his own lines where he relayed the vital information to supporting artillery and naval gunfire units. Persistently disregarding his own personal safety, he then placed himself in an exposed vantage point to direct more accurately the supporting fire and, working without respite for 2 days and 2 nights under constant enemy fire, skillfully directed a smashing bombardment against the almost impregnable Japanese positions despite numerous obstacles and heavy marine casualties. A brilliant leader, Capt. Dunlap inspired his men to heroic efforts during this critical phase of the battle and by his cool decision, indomitable fighting spirit, and daring tactics in the face of fanatic opposition greatly accelerated the final decisive defeat of Japanese countermeasures in his sector and materially furthered the continued advance of his company. His great personal valor and gallant spirit of self-sacrifice throughout the bitter hostilities reflect the highest credit upon Capt. Dunlap and the U.S. Naval Service.

*DUTKO, JOHN W.

Rank and organization: Private First Class, U.S. Army, 3d Infantry Division. *Place and date:* Near Ponte Rotto, Italy, 23 May 1944. *Entered service at:* Riverside, N.J. *Birth:* Dilltown, Pa. *G.O. No.:* 80, 5

October 1944. *Citation:* For conspicuous gallantry and intrepidity at risk of life above and beyond the call of duty, on 23 May 1944, near Ponte Rotto, Italy. Pfc. Dutko left the cover of an abandoned enemy trench at the height of an artillery concentration in a singlehanded attack upon 3 machine-guns and an 88-mm. mobile gun. Despite the intense fire of these 4 weapons which were aimed directly at him, Pfc. Dutko ran 100 yards through the impact area, paused momentarily in a shell crater, and then continued his 1-man assault. Although machinegun bullets kicked up the dirt at his heels, and 88-mm. shells exploded within 30 yards of him, Pfc. Dutko nevertheless made his way to a point within 30 yards of the first enemy machinegun and killed both gunners with a handgrenade. Although the second machinegun wounded him, knocking him to the ground, Pfc. Dutko regained his feet and advanced on the 88-mm. gun, firing his Browning automatic rifle from the hip. When he came within 10 yards of this weapon he killed its 5-man crew with 1 long burst of fire. Wheeling on the machinegun which had wounded him, Pfc. Dutko killed the gunner and his assistant. The third German machinegun fired on Pfc. Dutko from a position 20 yards distant wounding him a second time as he proceeded toward the enemy weapon in a half run. He killed both members of its crew with a single burst from his Browning automatic rifle, continued toward the gun and died, his body falling across the dead German crew.

*DYESS, AQUILLA JAMES

Rank and organization: Lieutenant Colonel, U.S. Marine Corps Reserve. *Born:* 11 January 1909, Augusta, Ga. *Appointed from:* Georgia. *Citation:* For conspicuous gallantry and intrepidity at the risk of his life above and beyond the call of duty as Commanding Officer of the 1st Battalion, 24th Marines (Rein), 4th Marine Division, in action against enemy Japanese forces during the assault on Namur Island, Kwajalein Atoll, Marshall Islands, 1 and 2 February 1944. Undaunted by severe fire from automatic Japanese weapons, Lt. Col. Dyess launched a powerful final attack on the second day of the assault, unhesitatingly posting himself between the opposing lines to point out objectives and avenues of approach and personally leading the advancing troops. Alert, and determined to quicken the pace of the offensive against increased enemy fire, he was constantly at the head of advance units, inspiring his men to push forward until the Japanese had been driven back to a small center of resistance and victory assured. While standing on the parapet of an anti-tank trench directing a group of infantry in a flanking attack against the last enemy position, Lt. Col. Dyess was killed by a burst of enemy machinegun fire. His daring and forceful leadership and his valiant fighting spirit in the face of terrific opposition were in keeping with the highest traditions of the U.S. Naval Service. He gallantly gave his life for his country.

EDSON, MERRITT AUSTIN

Rank and organization: Colonel, U.S. Marine Corps. *Born:* 25 April 1897, Rutland, Vt. *Appointed from:* Vermont. *Other Navy awards:* Navy Cross with Gold Star, Silver Star Medal, Legion of Merit with Gold Star. *Citation:* For extraordinary heroism and conspicuous intrepidity above and beyond the call of duty as Commanding Officer of the 1st Marine Raider Battalion, with Parachute Battalion attached, during action against enemy Japanese forces in the Solomon Islands on the night of 13–14 September 1942. After the airfield on Guadacanal had been seized from the enemy on 8 August, Col. Edson, with a force of 800 men, was assigned to the occupation and defense of a ridge dominating the jungle on either side of the airport. Facing a formidable Japanese attack which, augmented by infiltration, had crashed through our front lines, he, by skillful handling of his troops, successfully withdrew his forward units to a reserve line with minimum casualties. When the enemy, in a subsequent series of violent assaults, engaged our force in desperate hand-to-hand combat with bayonets, rifles, pistols, grenades, and knives, Col. Edson, although continuously exposed to hostile fire throughout the night, personally directed defense of the reserve position against a fanatical foe of greatly superior numbers. By his astute leadership and gallant devotion to duty, he enabled his men, despite severe losses, to cling tenaciously to their position on the vital ridge, thereby retaining command not only of the Guadalcanal airfield, but also of the 1st Division's entire offensive installations in the surrounding area.

EHLERS, WALTER D.

Rank and organization: Staff Sergeant, U.S. Army, 18th Infantry, 1st Infantry Division. *Place and date:* Near Goville, France, 9–10 June 1944. *Entered service at:* Manhattan, Kans. *Birth:* Junction City, Kans. *G.O. No.:* 91, 19 December 1944. *Citation:* For conspicuous gallantry and intrepidity at the risk of his life above and beyond the call of duty on 9–10 June 1944, near Goville, France. S/Sgt. Ehlers, always acting as the spearhead of the attack, repeatedly led his men against heavily defended enemy strong points exposing himself to deadly hostile fire whenever the situation required heroic and courageous leadership. Without waiting for an order, S/Sgt. Ehlers, far ahead of his men, led his squad against a strongly defended enemy strong point, personally killing 4 of an enemy patrol who attacked him en route. Then crawling forward under withering machinegun fire, he pounced upon the guncrew and put it out of action. Turning his attention to 2 mortars protected by the crossfire of 2 machineguns, S/Sgt. Ehlers led his men through this hail of bullets to kill or put to flight the enemy of the mortar section, killing 3 men himself. After mopping up the mortar positions, he again advanced on a machinegun, his progress effectively covered by his squad. When he was almost on top of the gun he leaped to his feet and, although greatly outnumbered, he knocked out the position singlehanded. The next day, having advanced deep into enemy territory, the platoon of which S/Sgt. Ehlers was a member, finding itself in an untenable position as the enemy brought increased mortar, machinegun, and small-arms fire to bear on it, was ordered to withdraw. S/Sgt. Ehlers, after his squad had covered the withdrawal of the remainder of the platoon, stood up and by continuous fire at the semicircle of enemy placements, diverted the bulk of the heavy hostile fire on himself, thus permitting the members of his own squad to withdraw. At this point, though wounded himself, he carried his wounded automatic rifleman to safety and then returned fearlessly over the shell-swept field to retrieve the automatic rifle which he was unable to carry previously. After having his wound treated, he refused to be evacuated, and returned to lead his squad. The intrepid leadership, indomitable courage, and fearless aggressiveness displayed by S/Sgt. Ehlers in the face of overwhelming enemy forces serve as an inspiration to others.

*ELROD, HENRY TALMAGE

Rank and organization: Captain, U.S. Marine Corps. *Born:* 27 September 1905, Rebecca, Ga. *Entered service at:* Ashburn, Ga. *Citation:* For conspicuous gallantry and intrepidity at the risk of his life above and beyond the call of duty while attached to Marine Fighting Squadron 211, during action against enemy Japanese land, surface and aerial units at Wake Island, 8 to 23 December 1941. Engaging vastly superior forces of enemy bombers and warships on 9 and 12 December, Capt. Elrod shot down 2 of a flight of 22 hostile planes and, executing repeated bombing and strafing runs at extremely low altitude and close range, succeeded in inflicting deadly damage upon a large Japanese vessel, thereby sinking the first major warship to be destroyed by small-caliber bombs delivered from a fighter-type aircraft. When his plane was disabled by hostile fire and no other ships were operative, Capt. Elrod assumed command of 1 flank of the line set up in defiance of the enemy landing and, conducting a brilliant defense, enabled his men to hold their positions and repulse intense hostile fusillades to provide covering fire for unarmed ammunition carriers. Capturing an automatic weapon during 1 enemy rush in force, he gave his own firearm to 1 of his men and fought on vigorously against the Japanese. Responsible in a large measure for the strength of his sector's gallant resistance, on 23 December, Capt. Elrod led his men with bold aggressiveness until he fell, mortally wounded. His superb skill as a pilot, daring leadership and unswerving devotion to duty distinguished him among the defenders of Wake Island, and his valiant conduct reflects the highest credit upon himself and the U.S. Naval Service. He gallantly gave his life for his country.

*ENDL, GERALD L.

Rank and organization: Staff Sergeant, U.S. Army, 32d Infantry Division. *Place and date:* Near Anamo, New Guinea, 11 July 1944. *Entered service at:* Janesville, Wis. *Birth:* Ft. Atkinson, Wis. *G.O. No.:* 17, 13 March 1945. *Citation:* For conspicuous gallantry and intrepidity at the risk of his life above and beyond the call of duty near Anamo, New Guinea, on 11 July 1944. S/Sgt. Endl was at the head of the leading platoon of his company advancing along a jungle trail when enemy troops were encountered and a fire fight developed. The enemy attacked in force under heavy rifle, machinegun, and grenade fire. His platoon leader wounded, S/Sgt. Endl immediately assumed command and deployed his platoon on a firing line at the fork in the trail toward which the enemy attack was directed. The dense jungle terrain greatly restricted vision and movement, and he endeavored to penetrate down the trail toward an open clearing of Kunai grass. As he advanced, he detected the enemy, supported by at least 6 light and 2 heavy machineguns, attempting an enveloping movement around both flanks. His commanding officer sent a second platoon to move up on the left flank of the position, but the enemy closed in rapidly, placing our force in imminent danger of being isolated and annihilated. Twelve members of his platoon were wounded, 7 being cut off by the enemy. Realizing that if his platoon were forced farther back, these 7 men would be hopelessly trapped and at the mercy of a vicious enemy, he resolved to advance at all cost, knowing it meant almost certain death, in an effort to rescue his comrades. In the face of extremely heavy fire he went forward alone and for a period of approximately 10 minutes engaged the enemy in a heroic close-range fight, holding them off while his men crawled forward under cover to evacuate the wounded and to withdraw. Courageously refusing to abandon 4 more wounded men who were lying along the trail, 1 by 1 he brought them back to safety. As he was carrying the last man in his arms he was struck by a heavy burst of automatic fire and was killed. By his persistent and daring self-sacrifice and on behalf of his comrades, S/Sgt. Endl made possible the successful evacuation of all but 1 man, and enabled the 2 platoons to withdraw with their wounded and to reorganize with the rest of the company.

*EPPERSON, HAROLD GLENN

Rank and organization: Private First Class, U.S. Marine Corps Reserve. *Born:* 14 July 1923, Akron, Ohio. *Accredited to:* Ohio. *Citation:* For conspicuous gallantry and intrepidity at the risk of his life above and beyond the call of duty while serving with the 1st Battalion, 6th Marines, 2d Marine Division, in action against enemy Japanese forces on the Island of Saipan in the Marianas, on 25 June 1944. With his machinegun emplacement bearing the full brunt of a fanatic assault initiated by the Japanese under cover of predawn darkness, Pfc. Epperson manned his weapon with determined aggressiveness, fighting furiously in the defense of his battalion's position and maintaining a steady stream of devastating fire against rapidly infiltrating hostile troops to aid materially in annihilating several of the enemy and in breaking the abortive attack. Suddenly a Japanese soldier, assumed to be dead, sprang up and hurled a powerful handgrenade into the emplacement. Determined to save his comrades, Pfc. Epperson unhesitatingly chose to sacrifice himself and, diving upon the deadly missile, absorbed the shattering violence of the exploding charge in his own body. Stouthearted and indomitable in the face of certain death, Pfc. Epperson fearlessly yielded his own life that his able comrades might carry on the relentless battle against a ruthless enemy. His superb valor and unfaltering devotion to duty throughout reflect the highest credit upon himself and upon the U.S. Naval Service. He gallantly gave his life for his country.

ERWIN, HENRY E. (Air Mission)

Rank and organization: Staff Sergeant, U.S. Army Air Corps, 52d Bombardment Squadron, 29th Bombardment Group, 20th Air Force. *Place and date:* Koriyama, Japan, 12 April 1945. *Entered service at:* Bessemer, Ala. *Born:* 8 May 1921, Adamsville, Ala. *G.O. No.:* 44, 6 June 1945. *Citation:* He was the radio operator of a B–29 airplane leading a group formation to attack Koriyama, Japan. He was charged with the additional duty of dropping phosphoresce smoke bombs to aid in assembling the group when the launching point was reached. Upon entering the assembly area, aircraft fire and enemy fighter opposition was encountered. Among the phosphoresce bombs launched by S/Sgt. Erwin, 1 proved faulty, exploding in the launching chute, and shot back into the interior of the aircraft, striking him in the face. The burning phosphoresce obliterated his nose and completely blinded him. Smoke filled the plane, obscuring the vision of the pilot. S/Sgt. Erwin realized that the aircraft and crew would be lost if the burning bomb remained in the plane. Without regard for his own safety, he picked it up and feeling his way, instinctively, crawled around the gun turret and headed for the copilot's window. He found the navigator's table obstructing his passage. Grasping the burning bomb between his forearm and body, he unleashed the spring lock and raised the table. Struggling through the narrow passage he stumbled forward into the smoke-filled pilot's compartment. Groping with his burning hands, he located the window and threw the bomb out. Completely aflame, he fell back upon the floor. The smoke cleared, the pilot, at 300 feet, pulled the plane out of its dive. S/Sgt. Erwin's gallantry and heroism above and beyond the call of duty saved the lives of his comrades.

*EUBANKS, RAY E.

Rank and organization: Sergeant, U.S. Army, Company D, 503d Parachute Infantry. *Place and date:* At Noemfoor Island, Dutch New Guinea, 23 July 1944. *Entered service at:* LaGrange, N.C. *Born:* 6 February 1922, Snow Hill, N.C. *G.O. No.:* 20, 29 March 1945. *Citation:* For conspicuous gallantry and intrepidity at the risk of his life above and beyond the call of duty at Noemfoor Island, Dutch New Guinea, 23 July 1944. While moving to the relief of a platoon isolated by the enemy, his company encountered a strong enemy position supported by machinegun, rifle, and mortar fire. Sgt. Eubanks was ordered to make an attack with 1 squad to neutralize the enemy by fire in order to assist the advance of his company. He maneuvered his squad to within 30 yards of the enemy where heavy fire checked his advance. Directing his men to maintain their fire, he and 2 scouts worked their way forward up a shallow depression to within 25 yards of the enemy. Directing the scouts to remain in place, Sgt. Eubanks armed himself with an automatic rifle and worked himself forward over terrain swept by intense fire to within 15 yards of the enemy position when he opened fire with telling effect. The enemy, having located his position, concentrated their fire with the result that he was wounded and a bullet rendered his rifle useless. In spite of his painful wounds he immediately charged the enemy and using his weapon as a club killed 4 of the enemy before he was himself again hit and killed. Sgt. Eubanks' heroic action, courage, and example in leadership so inspired his men that their advance was successful. They killed 45 of the enemy and drove the remainder from the position, thus effecting the relief of our beleaguered troops.

*EVANS, ERNEST EDWIN

Rank and organization: Commander, U.S. Navy. *Born:* 13 August 1908, Pawnee, Okla. *Accredited to:* Oklahoma. *Other Navy awards:*

Navy Cross, Bronze Star Medal. *Citation:* For conspicuous gallantry and intrepidity at the risk of his life above and beyond the call of duty as commanding officer of the U.S.S. *Johnston* in action against major units of the enemy Japanese fleet during the battle off Samar on 25 October 1944. The first to lay a smokescreen and to open fire as an enemy task force, vastly superior in number, firepower and armor, rapidly approached. Comdr. Evans gallantly diverted the powerful blasts of hostile guns from the lightly armed and armored carriers under his protection, launching the first torpedo attack when the *Johnston* came under straddling Japanese shellfire. Undaunted by damage sustained under the terrific volume of fire, he unhesitatingly joined others of his group to provide fire support during subsequent torpedo attacks against the Japanese and, outshooting and outmaneuvering the enemy as he consistently interposed his vessel between the hostile fleet units and our carriers despite the crippling loss of engine power and communications with steering aft, shifted command to the fantail, shouted steering orders through an open hatch to men turning the rudder by hand and battled furiously until the *Johnston*, burning and shuddering from a mortal blow, lay dead in the water after 3 hours of fierce combat. Seriously wounded early in the engagement, Comdr. Evans, by his indomitable courage and brilliant professional skill, aided materially in turning back the enemy during a critical phase of the action. His valiant fighting spirit throughout this historic battle will venture as an inspiration to all who served with him.

EVERHART, FORREST E.

Rank and organization: Technical Sergeant, U.S. Army, Company H, 359th Infantry, 90th Infantry Division. *Place and date:* Near Kerling, France, 12 November 1944. *Entered service at:* Texas City, Tex. *Birth:* Bainbridge, Ohio. *G.O. No.:* 77, 10 September 1945. *Citation:* He commanded a platoon that bore the brunt of a desperate enemy counterattack near Korling, France, before dawn on 12 November 1944. When German tanks and self-propelled guns penetrated his left flank and overwhelming infantry forces threatened to overrun the 1 remaining machine-gun in that section, he ran 400 yards through woods churned by artillery and mortar concentrations to strengthen the defense. With the 1 remaining gunner, he directed furious fire into the advancing hordes until they swarmed close to the position. He left the gun, boldly charged the attackers and, after a 15-minute exchange of handgrenades, forced them to withdraw leaving 30 dead behind. He recrossed the fire-swept terrain to his then threatened right flank, exhorted his men and directed murderous fire from the single machine-gun at that position. There, in the light of bursting mortar shells, he again closed with the enemy in a handgrenade duel and, after a fierce 30-minute battle, forced the Germans to withdraw leaving another 20 dead. The gallantry and intrepidity of T/Sgt. Everhart in rallying his men and refusing to fall back in the face of terrible odds were highly instrumental in repelling the fanatical enemy counterattack directed at the American bridgehead across the Moselle River.

*FARDY, JOHN PETER

Rank and organization: Corporal, U.S. Marine Corps. *Born:* 8 August 1922, Chicago, Ill. *Accredited to:* Illinois. *Citation:* For conspicuous gallantry and intrepidity at the risk of his life above and beyond the call of duty as a squad leader, serving with Company C, 1st Battalion, 1st Marines, 1st Marine Division, in action against enemy Japanese forces on Okinawa Shima in the Ryukyu Islands, 7 May 1945. When his squad was suddenly assailed by extremely heavy small-arms fire from the front during a determined advance against strongly fortified, fiercely defended Japanese positions, Cpl. Fardy temporarily deployed his men along a nearby drainage ditch. Shortly thereafter, an enemy grenade fell among the marines in the ditch. Instantly throwing himself upon the deadly missile, Cpl. Fardy absorbed the exploding blast in his own body, thereby protecting his comrades from certain and perhaps fatal injuries. Concerned solely for the welfare of his men, he willingly relinquished his own hope of survival that his fellow marines might live to carry on the fight against a fanatic enemy. A stouthearted leader and indomitable fighter, Cpl. Fardy, by his prompt decision and resolute spirit of self-sacrifice in the face of certain death, had rendered valiant service, and his conduct throughout reflects the highest credit upon himself and the U.S. Naval Service. He gallantly gave his life for his country.

*FEMOYER, ROBERT E. (Air Mission)

Rank and organization: Second Lieutenant, 711th Bombing Squadron, 447th Bomber Group, U.S. Army Air Corps. *Place and date:* Over Merseburg, Germany, 2 November 1944. *Entered service at:* Jacksonville, Fla. *Born:* 31 October 1921, Huntington, W. Va. *G.O. No.:* 35, 9 May 1945. *Citation:* For conspicuous gallantry and intrepidity at the risk of his life above and beyond the call of duty near Merseburg, Germany, on 2 November 1944. While on a mission, the bomber, of which 2d Lt. Femoyer was the navigator, was struck by 3 enemy antiaircraft shells. The plane suffered serious damage and 2d Lt. Femoyer was severely wounded in the side and back by shell fragments which penetrated his body. In spite of extreme pain and great loss of blood he refused an offered injection of morphine. He was determined to keep his mental faculties clear in order that he might direct his plane out of danger and so save his comrades. Not being able to arise from the floor, he asked to be propped up in order to enable him to see his charts and instruments. He successfully directed the navigation of his lone bomber for 2½ hours so well it avoided enemy flak and returned to the field without further damage. Only when the plane had arrived in the safe area over the English Channel did he feel that he had accomplished his objective; then, and only then, he permitted an injection of a sedative. He died shortly after being removed from the plane. The heroism and self-sacrifice of 2d Lt. Femoyer are in keeping with the highest traditions of the U.S. Army.

FIELDS, JAMES H.

Rank and organization: First Lieutenant, U.S. Army, 10th Armored Infantry, 4th Armored Division. *Place and date:* Rechicourt, France, 27

September 1944. *Entered service at:* Houston, Tex. *Birth:* Caddo, Tex. *G.O. No.:* 13, 27 February 1945. *Citation:* For conspicuous gallantry and intrepidity at risk of life above and beyond the call of duty, at Rechicourt, France. On 27 September 1944, during a sharp action with the enemy infantry and tank forces, 1st Lt. Fields personally led his platoon in a counterattack on the enemy position. Although his platoon had been seriously depleted, the zeal and fervor of his leadership was such as to inspire his small force to accomplish their mission in the face of overwhelming enemy opposition. Seeing that 1 of the men had been wounded, he left his slit trench and with complete disregard for his personal safety attended the wounded man and administered first aid. While returning to his slit trench he was seriously wounded by a shell burst, the fragments of which cut through his face and head, tearing his teeth, gums, and nasal passage. Although rendered speechless by his wounds, 1st Lt. Fields refused to be evacuated and continued to lead his platoon by the use of hand signals. On 1 occasion, when 2 enemy machineguns had a portion of his unit under deadly crossfire, he left his hole, wounded as he was, ran to a light machinegun, whose crew had been knocked out, picked up the gun, and fired it from his hip with such deadly accuracy that both the enemy gun positions were silenced. His action so impressed his men that they found new courage to take up the fire fight, increasing their firepower, and exposing themselves more than ever to harass the enemy with additional bazooka and machinegun fire. Only when his objective had been taken and the enemy scattered did 1st Lt. Fields consent to be evacuated to the battalion command post. At this point he refused to move further back until he had explained to his battalion commander by drawing on paper the position of his men and the disposition of the enemy forces. The dauntless and gallant heroism displayed by 1st Lt. Fields were largely responsible for the repulse of the enemy forces and contributed in a large measure to the successful capture of his battalion objective during this action. His eagerness and determination to close with the enemy and to destroy him was an inspiration to the entire command, and are in the highest traditions of the U.S. Armed Forces.

FINN, JOHN WILLIAM

Rank and organization: Lieutenant, U.S. Navy. *Place and date:* Naval Air Station, Kaneohe Bay, Territory of Hawaii, 7 December 1941. *Entered service at:* California. *Born:* 23 July 1909, Los Angeles, Calif. *Citation:* For extraordinary heroism distinguished service, and devotion above and beyond the call of duty. During the first attack by Japanese airplanes on the Naval Air Station, Kaneohe Bay, on 7 December 1941, Lt. Finn promptly secured and manned a .50-caliber machinegun mounted on an instruction stand in a completely exposed section of the parking ramp, which was under heavy enemy machinegun strafing fire. Although painfully wounded many times, he continued to man this gun and to return the enemy's fire vigorously and with telling effect throughout the enemy strafing and bombing attacks and with complete disregard for his own personal safety. It was only by specific orders that he was persuaded to leave his post to seek medical attention. Following first-aid treatment, although obviously suffering much pain and moving with great difficulty, he returned to the squadron area and actively supervised the rearming of returning planes. His extraordinary heroism and conduct in this action were in keeping with the highest traditions of the U.S. Naval Service.

FISHER, ALMOND E.

Rank and organization: Second Lieutenant, U.S. Army, Company E, 157th Infantry, 45th Infantry Division. *Place and date:* Near Grammont, France, 12-13 September 1944. *Entered service at:* Brooklyn, N.Y. *Birth:* Hume, N.Y. *G.O. No:* 32, 23 April 1945. *Citation:* For conspicuous gallantry and intrepidity at the risk of his life above and beyond the call of duty on the night of 12–13 September 1944, near Grammont, France. In the darkness of early morning, 2d Lt. Fisher was leading a platoon of Company E, 157th Infantry, in single column to the attack of a strongly defended hill position. At 2:30 A.M., the forward elements were brought under enemy machinegun fire from a distance of not more than 20 yards. Working his way alone to within 20 feet of the gun emplacement, he opened fire with his carbine and killed the entire guncrew. A few minutes after the advance was resumed, heavy machinegun fire was encountered from the left flank. Again crawling forward alone under withering fire, he blasted the gun and crew from their positions with handgrenades. After a halt to replenish ammunition, the advance was again resumed and continued for 1 hour before being stopped by intense machinegun and rifle fire. Through the courageous and skillfull leadership of 2d Lt. Fisher, the pocket of determined enemy resistance was rapidly obliterated. Spotting an emplaced machine pistol a short time later, with 1 of his men he moved forward and destroyed the position. As the advance continued the fire fight became more intense. When a bypassed German climbed from his foxhole and attempted to tear an M1 rifle from the hands of 1 of his men, 2d Lt. Fisher whirled and killed the enemy with a burst from his carbine. About 30 minutes later the platoon came under the heavy fire of machineguns from across an open field. 2d Lt. Fisher, disregarding the terrific fire, moved across the field with no cover or concealment to within range, knocked the gun from the position and killed or wounded the crew. Still under heavy fire he returned to his platoon and continued the advance. Once again heavy fire was encountered from a machinegun directly in front. Calling for handgrenades, he found only 2 remaining in the entire platoon. Pulling the pins and carrying a grenade in each hand, he crawled toward the gun emplacement, moving across areas devoid of cover and under intense fire to within 15 yards when he threw the grenades, demolished the gun and killed the guncrew. With ammunition low and daybreak near, he ordered his men to dig in and hold the ground already won. Under constant fire from the front and from both flanks, he moved among them directing the preparations for the defense. Shortly after the ammunition supply was replenished, the Germans launched a last determined effort against the depleted group. Attacked by superior numbers from the front, right, and left flank, and even from the rear, the platoon, in bitter hand-to-hand engagements drove back the enemy at every point. Wounded in both feet by close-range machine pistol fire early in the battle, 2d Lt. Fisher refused medical attention. Unable to walk, he crawled from man to man encouraging them and checking each position. Only after the fighting had subsided did 2d Lt. Fisher crawl 300 yards to the aid station from which he was evacuated. His extraordinary heroism, magnificent valor, and aggressive determination in the face of pointblank enemy fire is an inspiration to his organization and reflects the finest traditions of the U.S. Armed Forces.

*FLAHERTY, FRANCIS C.

Rank and organization: Ensign, U.S. Naval Reserve. *Born:* 15 March 1919, Charlotte, Mich. *Accredited to:* Michigan. *Citation:* For conspicuous devotion to duty and extraordinary courage and complete disregard of his own life, above and beyond the call of duty, during the attack on the Fleet in Pearl Harbor, by Japanese forces on 7 December 1941. When it was seen that the U.S.S. *Oklahoma* was going to capsize and the order was given to abandon ship, Ens. Flaherty remained in a turret, holding a flashlight so the remainder of the turret crew could see to escape, thereby sacrificing his own life.

*FLEMING, RICHARD E.

Rank and organization: Captain, U.S. Marine Corps Reserve. *Born:* 2 November 1917, St. Paul, Minn. *Appointed from:* Minnesota. *Citation:* For extraordinary heroism and conspicuous intrepidity above and beyond the call of duty as Flight Officer, Marine Scout-Bombing Squadron 241, during action against enemy Japanese forces in the battle of Midway on 4 and 5 June 1942. When his Squadron Commander was shot down during the initial attack upon an enemy aircraft carrier, Capt. Fleming led the remainder of the division with such fearless determination that he dived his own plane to the perilously low altitude of 400 feet before releasing his bomb. Although his craft was riddled by 179 hits in the blistering hail of fire that burst upon him from Japanese fighter guns and antiaircraft batteries, he pulled out with only 2 minor wounds inflicted upon himself. On the night of 4 June, when the squadron commander lost his way and became separated from the others, Capt. Fleming brought his own plane in for a safe landing at its base despite hazardous weather conditions and total darkness. The following day, after less than 4 hours' sleep, he led the second division of his squadron in a coordinated glide-bombing and dive-bombing assault upon a Japanese battleship. Undeterred by a fateful approach glide, during which his ship was struck and set afire, he grimly pressed home his attack to an altitude of 500 feet, released his bomb to score a near miss on the stern of his target, then crashed to the sea in flames. His dauntless perseverance and unyielding devotion to duty were in keeping with the highest traditions of the U.S. Naval Service.

FLUCKEY, EUGENE BENNETT

Rank and organization: Commander, U.S. Navy, Commanding U.S.S. *Barb. Place and date:* Along coast of China, 19 December 1944 to 15 February 1945. *Entered service at:* Illinois. *Born:* 5 October 1913, Washington, D.C. *Other Navy award:* Navy Cross with 3 Gold Stars. *Citation:* For conspicuous gallantry and intrepidity at the risk of his life above and beyond the call of duty as commanding officer of the U.S.S.

Barb during her 11th war patrol along the east coast of China from 19 December 1944 to 15 February 1945. After sinking a large enemy ammunition ship and damaging additional tonnage during a running 2-hour night battle on 8 January, Comdr. Fluckey, in an exceptional feat of brilliant deduction and bold tracking on 25 January, located a concentration of more than 30 enemy ships in the lower reaches of Nankuan Chiang (Mamkwan Harbor). Fully aware that a safe retirement would necessitate an hour's run at full speed through the uncharted, mined, and rock-obstructed waters, he bravely ordered, "Battle station—torpedoes!" In a daring penetration of the heavy enemy screen, and riding in 5 fathoms of water, he launched the *Barb's* last forward torpedoes at 3,000-yard range. Quickly bringing the ship's stern tubes to bear, he turned loose 4 more torpedoes into the enemy, obtaining 8 direct hits on 6 of the main targets to explode a large ammunition ship and cause inestimable damage by the resultant flying shells and other pyrotechnics. Clearing the treacherous area at high speed, he brought the *Barb* through to safety and 4 days later sank a large Japanese freighter to complete a record of heroic combat achievement, reflecting the highest credit upon Comdr. Fluckey, his gallant officers and men, and the U.S. Naval Service.

FOSS, JOSEPH JACOB

Rank and organization: Captain, U.S. Marine Corps Reserve, Marine Fighting Squadron 121, 1st Marine Aircraft Wing. *Place and date:* Over Guadalcanal, 9 October to 19 November 1942, 15 and 23 January 1943. *Entered service at:* South Dakota. *Born:* 17 April 1915, Sioux Falls, S. Dak. *Citation:* For outstanding heroism and courage above and beyond the call of duty as executive officer of Marine Fighting Squadron 121, 1st Marine Aircraft Wing, at Guadalcanal. Engaging in almost daily combat with the enemy from 9 October to 19 November 1942, Capt. Foss personally shot down 23 Japanese planes and damaged others so severely that their destruction was extremely probable. In addition, during this period, he successfully led a large number of escort missions, skillfully covering reconnaissance, bombing, and photographic planes as well as surface craft. On 15 January 1943, he added 3 more enemy planes to his already brilliant successes for a record of aerial combat achievement unsurpassed in this war. Boldly searching out an approaching enemy force on 25 January, Capt. Foss led his 8 F4F Marine planes and 4 Army P-38's into action and, undaunted by tremendously superior numbers, intercepted and struck with such force that 4 Japanese fighters were shot down and the bombers were turned back without releasing a single bomb. His remarkable flying skill, inspiring leadership, and indomitable fighting spirit were distinctive factors in the defense of strategic American positions on Guadalcanal.

*FOSTER, WILLIAM ADELBERT

Rank and organization: Private First Class, U.S. Marine Corps Reserve. *Born:* 17 February 1915, Cleveland, Ohio. *Accredited to:* Ohio. *Citation:* For conspicuous gallantry and intrepidity at the risk of his life above and beyond the call of duty while serving as a rifleman with the 3d Battalion, 1st Marines, 1st Marine Division, in action against enemy Japanese forces on Okinawa Shima in the Ryukyu Chain 2 May 1945. Dug in with another marine on the point of the perimeter defense after waging a furious assault against a strongly fortified Japanese position, Pfc. Foster and his comrade engaged in a fierce handgrenade duel with infiltrating enemy soldiers. Suddenly an enemy grenade landed beyond reach in the foxhole. Instantly diving on the deadly missile, Pfc. Foster absorbed the exploding charge in his own body, thereby protecting the other marine from serious injury. Although mortally wounded as a result of his heroic action, he quickly rallied, handed his own remaining 2 grenades to his comrade and said, "Make them count." Stouthearted and indomitable, he had unhesitatingly relinquished his own chance of survival that his fellow marine might carry on the relentless fight against a fanatic enemy, and his dauntless determination, cool decision and valiant spirit of self-sacrifice in the face of certain death reflect the highest credit upon Pfc. Foster and upon the U.S. Naval Service. He gallantly gave his life in the service of his country.

*FOURNIER, WILLIAM G.

Rank and organization: Sergeant, U.S. Army, Company M, 35th Infantry, 25th Infantry Division. *Place and date:* Mount Austen, Guadalcanal, Solomon Islands, 10 January 1943. *Entered service at:* Winterport, Maine. *Birth:* Norwich, Conn. *G.O. No.:* 28, 5 June 1943. *Citation:* For gallantry and intrepidity above and beyond the call of duty. As leader of a machinegun section charged with the protection of other battalion units, his group was attacked by a superior number of Japanese, his gunner killed, his assistant gunner wounded, and an adjoining guncrew put out of action. Ordered to withdraw from this hazardous position, Sgt. Fournier refused to retire but rushed forward to the idle gun and, with the aid of another soldier who joined him, held up the machinegun by the tripod to increase its field action. They opened fire and inflicted heavy casualties upon the enemy. While so engaged both these gallant soldiers were killed, but their sturdy defensive was a decisive factor in the following success of the attacking battalion.

*FOWLER, THOMAS W.

Rank and organization: Second Lieutenant, U.S. Army, 1st Armored Division. *Place and date:* Near Carano, Italy, 23 May 1944. *Entered service at:* Wichita Falls, Tex. *Birth:* Wichita Falls, Tex. *G.O. No.:* 84, 28 October, 1944. *Citation:* For conspicuous gallantry and intrepidity at risk of life above and beyond the call of duty, on 23 May 1944, in the vicinity of Carano, Italy. In the midst of a full-scale armored-infantry attack, 2d Lt. Fowler, while on foot, came upon 2 completely disorganized infantry platoons held up in their advance by an enemy minefield. Although a tank officer, he immediately reorganized the infantry. He then made a personal reconnaissance through the minefield, clearing a path as he went, by lifting the antipersonnel mines out of the ground with his hands. After he had gone through the 75-yard belt of deadly explosives, he returned to the infantry and led them through the minefield, a squad at a time. As they deployed, 2d Lt. Fowler, despite small-arms fire and the constant danger of antipersonnel mines, made a reconnaissance into enemy territory in search of a route to continue the advance. He then returned through the minefield and, on foot, he led the tanks through the mines into a position from which they could best support the infantry. Acting as scout 300 yards in front of the infantry, he led the 2 platoons forward until he had gained his objective, where he came upon several dug-in enemy infantrymen. Having taken them by surprise, 2d Lt. Fowler dragged them out of their foxholes and sent them to the rear; twice, when they resisted, he threw handgrenades into their dugouts. Realizing that a dangerous gap existed between his company and the unit to his right, 2d Lt. Fowler decided to continue his advance until the gap was filled. He reconnoitered to his front, brought the infantry into position where they dug in and, under heavy mortar and small-arms fire, brought his tanks forward. A few minutes later, the enemy began an armored counterattack. Several Mark VI tanks fired their cannons directly on 2d Lt. Fowler's position. One of his tanks was set afire. With utter disregard for his own life, with shells bursting near him, he ran directly into the enemy tank fire to reach the burning vehicle. For a half-hour, under intense strafing from the advancing tanks, although all other elements had withdrawn, he remained in his forward position, attempting to save the lives of the wounded tank crew. Only when the enemy tanks had almost overrun him, did he withdraw a short distance where he personally rendered first aid to 9 wounded infantrymen in the midst of the relentless incoming fire. 2d Lt. Fowler's courage, his ability to estimate the situation and to recognize his full responsibility as an officer in the Army of the United States, exemplify the high traditions of the military service for which he later gave his life.

*FRYAR, ELMER E.

Rank and organization: Private, U.S. Army, Company E, 511th Parachute Infantry, 11th Airborne Division. *Place and date:* Leyte, Philippine Islands, 8 December 1944. *Entered service at:* Denver, Colo. *Birth:* Denver, Colo. *G.O. No.:* 35, 9 May 1945. *Citation:* For conspicuous gallantry and intrepidity at the risk of his life above and beyond the call of duty. Pvt. Fryar's battalion encountered the enemy strongly entrenched in a position supported by mortars and automatic weapons. The battalion attacked, but in spite of repeated efforts was unable to take the position. Pvt. Fryar's company was ordered to cover the battalion's withdrawal to a more suitable point from which to attack, but the enemy launched a strong counterattack which threatened to cut off the company. Seeing an enemy platoon moving to outflank his company, he moved to higher ground and opened heavy and accurate fire. He was hit, and wounded, but continuing his attack he drove the enemy back with a loss of 27 killed. While withdrawing to overtake his squad, he found a seriously wounded comrade, helped him to the rear, and soon overtook his platoon leader, who was assisting another wounded. While these 4 were moving to rejoin their platoon, an enemy sniper appeared and aimed his weapon at the platoon leader. Pvt. Fryar instantly sprang forward, received the full burst of automatic fire in his own body and fell mortally wounded. With his remaining strength he threw a handgrenade and killed the sniper. Pvt. Fryar's indomitable fighting spirit and extraordinary gallantry above and beyond the call of duty contributed outstandingly to the success of the battalion's withdrawal and its subsequent attack and defeat of the enemy. His heroic action in unhesitatingly giving his own life for his comrade in arms exemplifies the highest tradition of the U.S. Armed Forces.

FUNK, LEONARD A., JR.

Rank and organization: First Sergeant, U.S. Army, Company C, 508th Parachute Infantry, 82d Airborne Division. *Place and date:* Holzheim, Belgium, 29 January 1945. *Entered service at:* Wilkinsburg, Pa. *Birth:* Braddock Township, Pa. *G.O. No.:* 75, 5 September 1945. *Citation:* He distinguished himself by gallant, intrepid actions against the enemy. After advancing 15 miles in a driving snowstorm, the American force prepared to attack through waist-deep drifts. The company executive officer became a casualty, and 1st Sgt. Funk immediately assumed his duties, forming headquarters soldiers into a combat unit for an assault in the face of direct artillery shelling and harassing fire from the right flank. Under his skillfull and courageous leadership, this miscellaneous group and the 3d Platoon attacked 15 houses, cleared them, and took 30 prisoners without suffering a casualty. The fierce drive of Company C quickly overran Holzheim, netting some 80 prisoners, who were placed under a 4-man guard, all that could be spared, while the rest of the understrength unit went about mopping up isolated points of resistance. An enemy patrol, by means of a ruse, succeeded in capturing the guards and freeing the prisoners, and had begun preparations to attack Company C from the rear when 1st Sgt. Funk walked around the building and into their midst. He was ordered to surrender by a German officer who pushed a machine pistol into his stomach. Although overwhelmingly outnumbered and facing almost certain death, 1st Sgt. Funk, pretending to comply with the order, began slowly to unsling his submachinegun from his shoulder and then, with lightning motion, brought the muzzle into line and riddled the German officer. He turned upon the other Germans, firing and shouting to the other Americans to seize the enemy's weapons. In the ensuing fight 21 Germans were killed, many wounded, and the remainder captured. 1st Sgt. Funk's bold action and heroic disregard for his own safety were directly responsible for the recapture of a vastly superior enemy force, which, if allowed to remain free, could have taken the widespread units of Company C by surprise and endangered the entire attack plan.

FUQUA, SAMUEL GLENN

Rank and organization: Captain, U.S. Navy, U.S.S. *Arizona*. *Place and date:* Pearl Harbor, Territory of Hawaii, 7 December 1941. *Entered service at:* Laddonia, Mo. *Born:* 15 October 1899, Laddonia Mo. *Citation:* For distinguished conduct in action, outstanding heroism, and utter disregard of his own safety above and beyond the call of duty during the attack on the Fleet in Pearl Harbor, by Japanese forces on 7 December 1941. Upon the commencement of the attack, Lt. Comdr. Fuqua rushed to the quarterdeck of the U.S.S. *Arizona* to which he was attached where he was stunned and knocked down by the explosion of a large bomb which hit the quarterdeck, penetrated several decks, and started a severe fire. Upon regaining consciousness, he began to direct the fighting of the fire and the rescue of wounded and injured personnel. Almost immediately there was a tremendous explosion forward, which made the ship appear to rise out of the water, shudder, and settle down by the bow rapidly. The whole forward part of the ship was enveloped in flames which were spreading rapidly, and wounded and burned men were pouring out of the ship to the quarterdeck. Despite these conditions, his harrowing experience, and severe enemy bombing and strafing, at the time, Lt. Comdr. Fuqua continued to direct the fighting of fires in order to check them while the wounded and burned could be taken from the ship and supervised the rescue of these men in such an amazingly calm and cool manner and with such excellent judgment that it inspired everyone who saw him and undoubtedly resulted in the saving of many lives. After realizing the ship could not be saved and that he was the senior surviving officer aboard, he directed it to be abandoned, but continued to remain on the quarterdeck and directed abandoning ship and rescue of personnel until satisfied that all personnel that could be had been saved, after which he left his ship with the boatload. The conduct of Lt. Comdr. Fuqua was not only in keeping with the highest traditions of the naval service but characterizes him as an outstanding leader of men.

GALER, ROBERT EDWARD

Rank and organization: Major, U.S. Marine Corps, Marine Fighter Sqdn. 244. *Place:* Solomon Islands Area. *Entered service at:* Washington. *Born:* 23 October 1913, Seattle, Wash. *Other Navy awards:* Navy Cross, Distinguished Flying Cross. *Citation:* For conspicuous heroism and courage above and beyond the call of duty as leader of a marine fighter squadron in aerial combat with enemy Japanese forces in the Solomon Islands area. Leading his squadron repeatedly in daring and aggressive raids against Japanese aerial forces, vastly superior in numbers, Maj. Galer availed himself of every favorable attack opportunity, individually shooting down 11 enemy bomber and fighter aircraft over a period of 29 days. Though suffering the extreme physical strain attendant upon protracted fighter operations at an altitude above 25,000 feet, the squadron under his zealous and inspiring leadership shot down a total of 27 Japanese planes. His superb airmanship, his outstanding skill and personal valor reflect great credit upon Maj. Galer's gallant fighting spirit and upon the U.S. Naval Service.

*GALT, WILLIAM WYLIE

Rank and organization: Captain, U.S. Army, 168th Infantry, 34th Infantry Division. *Place and date:* At Villa Crocetta, Italy, 29 May 1944. *Entered service at:* Stanford, Mont. *Birth:* Geyser, Mont. *G.O. No.:* 7, 1 February 1945. *Citation:* For conspicuous gallantry and intrepidity above and beyond the call of duty. Capt. Galt, Battalion S-3, at a particularly critical period following 2 unsuccessful attacks by his battalion, of his own volition went forward and ascertained just how critical the situation was. He volunteered, at the risk of his life, personally to lead the battalion against the objective. When the lone remaining tank destroyer refused to go forward, Capt. Galt jumped on the tank destroyer and ordered it to precede the attack. As the tank destroyer moved forward, followed by a company of riflemen, Capt. Galt manned the .30-caliber machinegun in the turret of the tank destroyer, located and directed fire on an enemy 77-mm. antitank gun, and destroyed it. Nearing the enemy positions, Capt. Galt stood fully exposed in the turret, ceaselessly firing his machinegun and tossing handgrenades into the enemy zigzag series of trenches despite the hail of sniper and machinegun bullets ricocheting off the tank destroyer. As the tank destroyer moved, Capt. Galt so maneuvered it that 40 of the enemy were trapped in one trench. When they refused to surrender, Capt. Galt pressed the trigger of the machinegun and dispatched every one of them. A few minutes later an 88-mm. shell struck the tank destroyer and Capt. Galt fell mortally wounded across his machinegun. He had personally killed 40 Germans and wounded many more. Capt. Galt pitted his judgment and superb courage against overwhelming odds, exemplifying the highest measure of devotion to his country and the finest traditions of the U.S. Army.

*GAMMON, ARCHER T.

Rank and organization: Staff Sergeant, U.S. Army, Company A, 9th Armored Infantry Battalion, 6th Armored Division. *Place and date:* Near Bastogne, Belgium, 11 January 1945. *Entered service at:* Roanoke, Va. *Born:* 11 September 1918, Chatham, Va. *G.O. No.:* 18, 13 February 1946. *Citation:* He charged 30 yards through hip-deep snow to knock out a machinegun and its 3-man crew with grenades, saving his platoon from being decimated and allowing it to continue its advance from an open field into some nearby woods. The platoon's advance through the woods had only begun when a machinegun supported by riflemen opened fire and a Tiger Royal tank sent 88-mm. shells screaming at the unit from the left flank. S/Sgt. Gammon, disregarding all thoughts of personal safety, rushed forward, then cut to the left, crossing the width of the platoon's skirmish line in an attempt to get within grenade range of the tank and its protecting foot troops. Intense fire was concentrated on him by riflemen and the machinegun emplaced near the tank. He charged the automatic weapon, wiped out its crew of 4 with grenades, and, with supreme daring, advanced to within 25 yards of the armored vehicle, killing 2 hostile infantrymen with rifle fire as he moved forward. The tank had started to withdraw, backing a short distance, then firing, backing some more, and then stopping to blast out another round, when the man whose singlehanded relentless attack had put the ponderous machine on the defensive was struck and instantly killed by a direct hit from the Tiger Royal's heavy gun. By his intrepidity and extreme devotion to the task of driving the enemy back no matter what the odds, S/Sgt. Gammon cleared the woods of German forces, for the tank continued to withdraw, leaving open the path for the gallant squad leader's platoon.

GARCIA, MARCARIO

Rank and organization: Staff Sergeant, U.S. Army, Company B, 22d Infantry, 4th Infantry Division. *Place and date:* Near Grosshau, Germany, 27 November 1944. *Entered service at:* Sugarland, Tex. *Born:* 20 January 1920, Villa de Castano, Mexico. *G.O. No.:* 74, 1 September 1945. *Citation:* While an acting squad leader of Company B, 22d Infantry, on 27 November 1944, near Grosshau, Germany, he single-handedly assaulted 2 enemy machinegun emplacements. Attacking prepared positions on a wooded hill, which could be approached only through meager cover, his company was pinned down by intense machinegun fire and subjected to a concentrated artillery and mortar barrage. Although painfully wounded, he refused to be evacuated and on his own initiative crawled forward alone until he reached a position near an enemy emplacement. Hurling grenades, he boldly assaulted the position, destroyed the gun, and with his rifle killed 3 of the enemy who attempted to escape. When he rejoined his company, a second machinegun opened fire and again the intrepid soldier went forward, utterly disregarding his own safety. He stormed the position and destroyed the gun, killed 3 more Germans, and captured 4 prisoners. He fought on with his unit until the objective was taken and only then did he permit himself to be removed for medical care. S/Sgt. (then private) Garcia's conspicuous heroism, his inspiring, courageous conduct, and his complete disregard for his personal safety wiped out 2 enemy emplacements and enabled his company to advance and secure its objective.

GARMAN, HAROLD A.

Rank and organization: Private, U.S. Army, Company B, 5th Medical Battalion, 5th Infantry Division. *Place and date:* Near Montereau, France, 25 August 1944. *Entered service at:* Albion, Ill. *Born:* 26 February 1918, Fairfield, Ill. *G.O. No.:* 20, 29 March 1945. *Citation:* For conspicuous gallantry and intrepidity at the risk of his life above and beyond the call of duty. On 25 August 1944, in the vicinity of Montereau, France, the enemy was sharply contesting any enlargement of the bridgehead which our forces had established on the northern bank of the Seine River in this sector. Casualties were being evacuated to the southern shore in assault boats paddled by litter bearers from a medical battalion. Pvt. Garman, also a litter bearer in this battalion, was working on the friendly shore carrying the wounded from the boats to waiting ambulances. As 1 boatload of wounded reached midstream, a German machinegun suddenly opened fire upon it from a commanding position on the northern bank 100 yards away. All of the men in the boat immediately took to the water except 1 man who was so badly wounded he could not rise from his litter. Two other patients who were unable to swim because of their wounds clung to the sides of the boat. Seeing the extreme danger of these patients, Pvt. Garman without a moment's hesitation plunged into the Seine. Swimming directly into a hail of machinegun bullets, he rapidly reached the assault boat and then while still under accurately aimed fire towed the boat with great effort to the southern shore. This soldier's moving heroism not only saved the lives of the three patients but so inspired his comrades that additional assault boats were immediately procured and the evacuation of the wounded resumed. Pvt. Garman's great courage and his heroic devotion to the highest tenets of the Medical Corps may be written with great pride in the annals of the corps.

GARY, DONALD ARTHUR

Rank and organization: Lieutenant, Junior Grade, U.S. Navy, U.S.S. *Franklin. Place and date:* Japanese Home Islands near Kobe, Japan, 19 March 1945. *Entered service at:* Ohio. *Born:* 23 July 1903, Findlay, Ohio. *Citation:* For conspicuous gallantry and intrepidity at the risk of his life above and beyond the call of duty as an engineering officer attached to the U.S.S. *Franklin* when that vessel was fiercely attacked by enemy aircraft during the operations against the Japanese Home Islands near Kobe, Japan, 19 March 1945. Stationed on the third deck when the ship was rocked by a series of violent explosions set off in her own ready bombs, rockets, and ammunition by the hostile attack, Lt. (jg.) Gary unhesitatingly risked his life to assist several hundred men trapped in a messing compartment filled with smoke, and with no apparent egress. As the imperiled men below decks became increasingly panic stricken under the raging fury of incessant explosions, he confidently assured them he would find a means of effecting their release and, groping through the dark, debris-filled corridors, ultimately discovered an escapeway. Stanchly determined, he struggled back to the messing compartment 3 times despite menacing flames, flooding water, and the ominous threat of sudden additional explosions, on each occasion calmly leading his men through the blanketing pall of smoke until the last one had been saved. Selfless in his concern for his ship and his fellows, he constantly rallied others about him, repeatedly organized and led firefighting parties into the blazing inferno on the flight deck and, when firerooms 1 and 2 were found to be inoperable, entered the No. 3 fireroom and directed the raising of steam in 1 boiler in the face of extreme difficulty and hazard. An inspiring and courageous leader, Lt. (jg.) Gary rendered self-sacrificing service under the most perilous conditions and, by his heroic initiative, fortitude, and valor, was responsible for the saving of several hundred lives. His conduct throughout reflects the highest credit upon himself and upon the U.S. Naval Service.

GERSTUNG, ROBERT E.

Rank and organization: Technical Sergeant, U.S. Army, Company H, 313th Infantry, 79th Infantry Division. *Place and date:* Siegfried Line near Berg, Germany, 19 December 1944. *Entered service at:* Chicago, Ill. *Born:* 6 August 1915, Chicago, Ill. *G.O. No.:* 75, 5 September 1945. *Citation:* On 19 December 1944 he was ordered with his heavy machinegun squad to the support of an infantry company attacking the outer defense of the Siegfried Line near Berg, Germany. For 8 hours he maintained a position made almost untenable by the density of artillery and mortar fire concentrated upon it and the proximity of enemy troops who threw handgrenades into the emplacement. While all other members of his squad became casualties, he remained at his gun. When he ran out of ammunition, he fearlessly dashed across bullet-swept, open terrain to secure a new supply from a disabled friendly tank. A fierce barrage pierced the water jacket of his gun, but he continued to fire until the weapon overheated and jammed. Instead of withdrawing, he crawled 50 yards across coverless ground to another of his company's machineguns which had been silenced when its entire crew was killed. He continued to man this gun, giving support vitally needed by the infantry. At one time he came under direct fire from a hostile tank, which shot the glove from his hand with an armor-piercing shell but could not drive him from his position or stop his shooting. When the American forces were ordered to retire to their original positions, he remained at his gun, giving the only covering fire. Finally withdrawing, he cradled the heavy weapon in his left arm, slung a belt of ammunition over his shoulder, and walked to the rear, loosing small bursts at the enemy as he went. One hundred yards from safety, he was struck in the leg by a mortar shell; but, with a supreme effort, he crawled the remaining distance, dragging along the gun which had served him and his comrades so well. By his remarkable perseverence, indomitable courage, and heroic devotion to his task in the face of devastating fire, T/Sgt. Gerstung gave his fellow soldiers powerful support in their encounter with formidable enemy forces.

*GIBSON, ERIC G.

Rank and organization: Technician Fifth Grade, U.S. Army, 3d Infantry Division. *Place and date:* Near Isola Bella, Italy, 28 January 1944. *Entered service at:* Chicago, Ill. *Birth:* Nysund, Sweden. *G.O. No.:* 74, 11 September 1944. *Citation:* For conspicuous gallantry and intrepidity at risk of life above and beyond the call of duty. On 28 January 1944, near Isola Bella, Italy, Tech. 5th Grade Gibson, company cook, led a squad of replacements through their initial baptism of fire, destroyed four enemy positions, killed 5 and captured 2 German soldiers, and secured the left flank of his company during an attack on a strongpoint. Placing himself 50 yards in front of his new men, Gibson advanced down the wide stream ditch known as the Fossa Femminamorta, keeping pace with the advance of his company. An enemy soldier allowed Tech. 5th Grade Gibson to come within 20 yards of his concealed position and then opened fire on him with a machine pistol. Despite the stream of automatic fire which barely missed him, Gibson charged the position, firing his submachinegun every few steps. Reaching the position, Gibson fired point-blank at his opponent, killing him. An artillery concentration fell in and around the ditch; the concussion from one shell knocked him flat. As he got to his feet Gibson was fired on by two soldiers armed with a machine pistol and a rifle from a position only 75 yards distant. Gibson immediately raced toward the foe. Halfway to the position a machinegun opened fire on him. Bullets came within inches of his body, yet Gibson never paused in his forward movement. He killed one and captured the other soldier. Shortly after, when he was fired upon by a heavy machinegun 200 yards down the ditch, Gibson crawled back to his squad and ordered it to lay down a base of fire while he flanked the emplacement. Despite all warning, Gibson crawled 125 yards through an artillery concentration and the cross fire of 2 machineguns which showered dirt over his body, threw 2 handgrenades into the emplacement and charged it with his submachinegun, killing 2 of the enemy and capturing a third. Before leading his men around a bend in the stream ditch, Gibson went forward alone to reconnoiter. Hearing an exchange of machine pistol and submachinegun fire, Gibson's squad went forward to find that its leader had run 35 yards toward an outpost, killed the machine pistol man, and had himself been killed while firing at the Germans.

*GILMORE, HOWARD WALTER

Rank and organization: Commander, U.S. Navy. *Born:* 29 September 1902, Selma, Ala. *Appointed from:* Louisiana. *Other Navy award:* Navy Cross with one gold star. *Citation:* For distinguished gallantry and valor above and beyond the call of duty as commanding officer of the U.S.S. *Growler* during her Fourth War Patrol in the Southwest Pacific from 10 January to 7 February 1943. Boldly striking at the enemy in spite of continuous hostile air and anti-submarine patrols, Comdr. Gilmore sank one Japanese freighter and damaged another by torpedo fire, successfully evading severe depth charges following each attack. In the darkness of night on 7 February, an enemy gunboat closed range and prepared to ram the *Growler*. Comdr. Gilmore daringly maneuvered to avoid the crash and rammed the attacker instead, ripping into her port side at 17 knots and bursting wide her plates. In the terrific fire of the sinking gunboat's heavy machineguns, Comdr. Gilmore calmly gave the order to clear the bridge, and refusing safety for himself, remained on deck while his men preceded him below. Struck down by the fusillade of bullets and having done his utmost against the enemy, in his final living moments, Comdr. Gilmore gave his last order to the officer of the deck, "Take her down." The *Growler* dived; seriously damaged but under control, she was brought safely to port by her well-trained crew inspired by the courageous fighting spirit of their dead captain.

*GONSALVES, HAROLD

Rank and organization: Private First Class, U.S. Marine Corps Reserve. *Born:* 28 January 1926, Alameda, Calif. *Accredited to:* California. *Citation:* For conspicuous gallantry and intrepidity at the risk of his life above and beyond the call of duty while serving as Acting Scout Sergeant with the 4th Battalion, 15th Marines, 6th Marine Division, during action against enemy Japanese forces on Okinawa Shima in the Ryukyu Chain, 15 April 1945. Undaunted by the powerfully organized opposition encountered on Motobu Peninsula during the fierce assault waged by his battalion against the Japanese stronghold at Mount Yaetake, Pfc. Gonsalves repeatedly braved the terrific enemy bombardment to aid his forward observation team in directing well-placed artillery fire. When his commanding officer determined to move into the front lines in order to register a more effective bombardment in the enemy's defensive position, he unhesitatingly advanced uphill with the officer and another Marine despite a slashing barrage of enemy mortar and rifle fire. As they reached the front and a Japanese grenade fell close within the group, instantly Pfc. Gonsalves dived on the deadly missile, absorbing the exploding charge in his own body and thereby protecting the others from serious and perhaps fatal wounds. Stouthearted and indomitable, Pfc. Gonsalves readily yielded his own chances of survival that his fellow marines might carry on the relentless battle against a fanatic enemy and his cool decision, prompt action and valiant spirit of self-sacrifice in the face of certain death reflect the highest credit upon himself and upon the U.S. Naval Service.

*GONZALES, DAVID M.

Rank and organization: Private First Class, U.S. Army, Company A, 127th Infantry, 32d Infantry Division. *Place and date:* Villa Verde Trail, Luzon, Philippine Islands, 25 April 1945. *Entered service at:* Pacoima, Calif. *Birth:* Pacoima, Calif. *G.O. No.:* 115, 8 December 1945. *Citation:* He was pinned down with his company. As enemy fire swept the area, making any movement extremely hazardous, a 500-pound bomb smashed into the company's perimeter, burying 5 men with its explosion. Pfc. Gonzales, without hesitation, seized an entrenching tool and under a hail of fire crawled 15 yards to his entombed comrades, where his commanding officer, who had also rushed forward, was beginning to dig the men out. Nearing his goal, he saw the officer struck and instantly killed by machinegun fire. Undismayed, he set to work swiftly and surely with his hands and the entrenching tool while enemy sniper and machinegun bullets struck all about him. He succeeded in digging one of the men out of the pile of rock and sand. To dig faster he stood up regardless of the greater danger from so exposing himself. He extricated a second man, and then another. As he completed the liberation of the third, he was hit and mortally wounded, but the comrades for whom he so gallantly gave his life were safely evacuated. Pfc. Gonzales' valiant and intrepid conduct exemplifies the highest tradition of the military service.

GORDON, NATHAN GREEN

Rank and organization: Lieutenant, U.S. Navy, commander of Catalina patrol plane. *Place and date:* Bismarck Sea, 15 February 1944. *Entered service at:* Arkansas. *Born:* 4 September 1916, Morrilton, Ark. *Citation:* For extraordinary heroism above and beyond the call of duty as commander of a Catalina patrol plane in rescuing personnel of the U.S. Army 5th Air Force shot down in combat over Kavieng Harbor in the Bismarck Sea, 15 February 1944. On air alert in the vicinity of Vitu Islands, Lt. (then Lt. jg.) Gordon unhesitatingly responded to a report of the crash and flew boldly into the harbor, defying close-range fire from enemy shore guns to make 3 separate landings in full view of the Japanese and pick up 9 men, several of them injured. With his cumbersome flying boat dangerously overloaded, he made a brilliant takeoff despite heavy swells and almost total absence of wind and set a course for base, only to receive the report of another group stranded in a rubber liferaft 600 yards from the enemy shore. Promptly turning back, he again risked his life to set his plane down under direct fire of the heaviest defenses of Kavieng and take aboard 6 more survivors, coolly making his fourth dexterous takeoff with 15 rescued officers and men. By his exceptional daring, personal valor, and incomparable airmanship under most perilous conditions, Lt. Gordon prevented certain death or capture of our airmen by the Japanese.

*GOTT, DONALD J. (Air Mission)

Rank and organization: First Lieutenant, U.S. Army Air Corps, 729th Bomber Squadron, 452d Bombardment Group. *Place and date:* Saarbrucken, Germany, 9 November 1944. *Entered service at:* Arnett, Okla. *Born:* 3 June 1923, Arnett, Okla. *G.O. No.:* 38, 16 May 1945.

Citation: On a bombing run upon the marshaling yards at Saarbrucken a B–17 aircraft piloted by 1st. Lt. Gott was seriously damaged by antiaircraft fire. Three of the aircraft's engines were damaged beyond control and on fire; dangerous flames from the No. 4 engine were leaping back as far as the tail assembly. Flares in the cockpit were ignited and a fire raged therein, which was further increased by free-flowing fluid from damaged hydraulic lines. The interphone system was rendered useless. In addition to these serious mechanical difficulties the engineer was wounded in the leg and the radio operator's arm was severed below the elbow. Suffering from intense pain, despite the application of a tourniquet, the radio operator fell unconscious. Faced with the imminent explosion of his aircraft, and death to his entire crew, mere seconds before bombs away on the target, 1st. Lt. Gott and his copilot conferred. Something had to be done immediately to save the life of the wounded radio operator. The lack of a static line and the thought that his unconscious body striking the ground in unknown territory would not bring immediate medical attention forced a quick decision. 1st. Lt. Gott and his copilot decided to fly the flaming aircraft to friendly territory and then attempt to crash land. Bombs were released on the target and the crippled aircraft proceeded alone to Allied-controlled territory. When that had been reached, 1st. Lt. Gott had the copilot personally inform all crewmembers to bail out. The copilot chose to remain with 1st. Lt. Gott in order to assist in landing the bomber. With only one normally functioning engine, and with the danger of explosion much greater, the aircraft banked into an open field, and when it was at an altitude of 100 feet it exploded, crashed, exploded again and then disintegrated. All 3 crewmembers were instantly killed. 1st. Lt. Gott's loyalty to his crew, his determination to accomplish the task set forth to him, and his deed of knowingly performing what may have been his last service to his country was an example of valor at its highest.

*GRABIARZ, WILLIAM J.

Rank and organization: Private First Class, U.S. Army. Troop E, 5th Cavalry, 1st Cavalry Division. *Place and date:* Manila, Luzon, Philippine Islands, 23 February 1945. *Entered service at:* Buffalo, N.Y. *Birth:* Buffalo, N.Y. *G.O. No.:* 115, 8 December 1945. *Citation:* He was a scout when the unit advanced with tanks along a street in Manila, Luzon, Philippine Islands. Without warning, enemy machinegun and rifle fire from concealed positions in the Customs building swept the street, striking down the troop commander and driving his men to cover. As the officer lay in the open road, unable to move and completely exposed to the point-blank enemy fire, Pfc. Grabiarz voluntarily ran from behind a tank to carry him to safety, but was himself wounded in the shoulder. Ignoring both the pain in his injured useless arm and his comrades' shouts to seek the cover which was only a few yards distant, the valiant rescuer continued his efforts to drag his commander out of range. Finding this impossible, he rejected the opportunity to save himself and deliberately covered the officer with his own body to form a human shield, calling as he did so for a tank to maneuver into position between him and the hostile emplacement. The enemy riddled him with concentrated fire before the tank could interpose itself. Our troops found that he had been successful in preventing bullets from striking his leader, who survived. Through his magnificent sacrifice in gallantly giving his life to save that of his commander, Pfc. Grabiarz provided an outstanding and lasting inspiration to his fellow soldiers.

*GRAY, ROSS FRANKLIN

Rank and organization: Sergeant, U.S. Marine Corps Reserve. *Born:* 1 August 1920, Marvel Valley, Ala. *Accredited to:* Alabama. *Citation:* For conspicuous gallantry and intrepidity at the risk of his life above and beyond the call of duty as a Platoon Sergeant attached to Company A, 1st Battalion, 25th Marines, 4th Marine Division, in action against enemy Japanese forces on Iwo Jima, Volcano Islands, 21 February 1945. Shrewdly gaging the tactical situation when his platoon was held up by a sudden barrage of hostile grenades while advancing toward the high ground northeast of Airfield No. 1, Sgt. Gray promptly organized the withdrawal of his men from enemy grenade range, quickly moved forward alone to reconnoiter and discovered a heavily mined area extending along the front of a strong network of emplacements joined by covered trenches. Although assailed by furious gunfire, he cleared a path leading through the minefield to one of the fortifications, then returned to the platoon position and, informing his leader of the serious situation, volunteered to initiate an attack under cover of 3 fellow marines. Alone and unarmed but carrying a huge satchel charge, he crept up on the Japanese emplacement, boldly hurled the short-fused explosive and sealed the entrance. Instantly taken under machinegun fire from a second entrance to the same position, he unhesitatingly braved the increasingly vicious fusillades to crawl back for another charge, returned to his objective and blasted the second opening, thereby demolishing the position. Repeatedly covering the ground between the savagely defended enemy fortifications and his platoon area, he systematically approached, attacked and withdrew under blanketing fire to destroy a total of 6 Japanese positions, more than 25 troops and a quantity of vital ordnance gear and ammunition. Stouthearted and indomitable, Sgt. Gray had singlehandedly overcome a strong enemy garrison and had completely disarmed a large minefield before finally rejoining his unit. By his great personal valor, daring tactics and tenacious perseverance in the face of extreme peril, he had contributed materially to the fulfillment of his company mission. His gallant conduct throughout enhanced and sustained the highest traditions of the U.S. Naval Service.

GREGG, STEPHEN R.

Rank and organization: Second Lieutenant, U.S. Army, 143d Infantry, 36th Infantry Division. *Place and date:* Near Montelimar, France, 27 August 1944. *Entered service at:* Bayonne, N.J. *Birth:* New York, N.Y. *G.O. No.:* 31, 17 April 1945. *Citation:* For conspicuous gallantry and intrepidity at risk of life above and beyond the call of duty on 27 August 1944, in the vicinity of Montelimar, France. As his platoon advanced upon the enemy positions, the leading scout was fired upon and 2d Lt. Gregg (then a Tech. Sgt.) immediately put his machineguns into action to cover the advance of the riflemen. The

Germans, who were at close range, threw handgrenades at the riflemen, killing some and wounding 7. Each time a medical aid man attempted to reach the wounded, the Germans fired at him. Realizing the seriousness of the situation, 2d Lt. Gregg took 1 of the light .30 caliber machineguns, and firing from the hip, started boldly up the hill with the medical aid man following him. Although the enemy was throwing handgrenades at him, 2d Lt. Gregg remained and fired into the enemy positions while the medical aid man removed the 7 wounded men to safety. When 2d Lt. Gregg had expended all his ammunition, he was covered by 4 Germans who ordered him to surrender. Since the attention of most of the Germans had been diverted by watching this action, friendly riflemen were able to maneuver into firing positions. One, seeing 2d Lt. Gregg's situation, opened fire on his captors. The 4 Germans hit the ground and thereupon 2d Lt. Gregg recovered a machine pistol from one of the Germans and managed to escape to his other machinegun positions. He manned a gun, firing at his captors, killed 1 of them and wounded the other. This action so discouraged the Germans that the platoon was able to continue its advance up the hill to achieve its objective. The following morning, just prior to daybreak, the Germans launched a strong attack, supported by tanks, in an attempt to drive Company L from the hill. As these tanks moved along the valley and their foot troops advanced up the hill, 2d Lt. Gregg immediately ordered his mortars into action. During the day, by careful observation, he was able to direct effective fire on the enemy, inflicting heavy casualties. By late afternoon he had directed 600 rounds when his communication to the mortars was knocked out. Without hesitation he started checking his wires, although the area was under heavy enemy small-arms and artillery fire. When he was within 100 yards of his mortar position, 1 of his men informed him that the section had been captured and the Germans were using the mortars to fire on the company. 2d Lt. Gregg with this man and another nearby rifleman started for the gun position where he could see 5 Germans firing his mortars. He ordered the 2 men to cover him, crawled up, threw a handgrenade into the position, and then charged it. The handgrenade killed 1, injured 2; 2d Lt. Gregg took the other 2 prisoners, and put his mortars back into action.

*GRUENNERT, KENNETH E.

Rank and organization: Sergeant, U.S. Army, Company L, 127th Infantry, 32d Infantry Division. *Place and date:* Near Buna, New Guinea, 24 December 1942. *Entered service at:* Helenville, Wis. *Birth:* Helenville, Wis. *G.O. No.:* 66, 11 October 1943. *Citation:* For conspicuous gallantry and intrepidity in action above and beyond the call of duty. On 24 December 1942, near Buna, New Guinea, Sgt. Gruennert was second in command of a platoon with a mission to drive through the enemy lines to the beach 600 yards ahead. Within 150 yards of the objective, the platoon encountered 2 hostile pillboxes. Sgt. Gruennert advanced alone on the first and put it out of action with handgrenades and rifle fire, killing 3 of the enemy. Seriously wounded in the shoulder, he bandaged his wound under cover of the pillbox, refusing to withdraw to the aid station and leave his men. He then, with undiminished daring, and under extremely heavy fire, attacked the second pillbox. As he neared it he threw grenades which forced the enemy out where they were easy targets for his platoon. Before the leading elements of his platoon could reach him he was shot by enemy snipers. His inspiring valor cleared the way for his platoon which was the first to attain the beach in this successful effort to split the enemy position.

*GURKE, HENRY

Rank and organization: Private First Class, U.S. Marine Corps. *Born:* 6 November 1922, Neche, N. Dak. *Accredited to:* North Dakota. *Citation:* For extraordinary heroism and courage above and beyond the call of duty while attached to the 3d Marine Raider Battalion during action against enemy Japanese forces in the Solomon Islands area on 9 November 1943. While his platoon was engaged in the defense of a vital road block near Empress Augusta Bay on Bougainville Island. Pfc. Gurke, in company with another Marine, was delivering a fierce stream of fire against the main vanguard of the Japanese. Concluding from the increasing ferocity of grenade barrages that the enemy was determined to annihilate their small, 2-man foxhole, he resorted to a bold and desperate measure for holding out despite the torrential hail of shells. When a Japanese grenade dropped squarely into the foxhole, Pfc. Gurke, mindful that his companion manned an automatic weapon of superior fire power and therefore could provide more effective resistance, thrust him roughly aside and flung his own body over the missile to smother the explosion. With unswerving devotion to duty and superb valor, Pfc. Gurke sacrificed himself in order that his comrade might live to carry on the fight. He gallantly gave his life in the service of his country.

HALL, GEORGE J.

Rank and organization: Staff Sergeant, U.S. Army, 135th Infantry, 34th Infantry Division. *Place and date:* Near Anzio, Italy, 23 May 1944. *Entered service at:* Boston, Mass. *Born:* 9 January 1921, Stoneham, Mass. *G.O. No.:* 24, 6 April 1945. *Citation:* For conspicuous gallantry and intrepidity at risk of life above and beyond the call of duty. Attacking across flat, open terrain under direct enemy observation, S/Sgt. Hall's company was pinned down by grazing fire from 3 enemy machineguns and harassing sniper fire. S/Sgt. Hall volunteered to eliminate these obstacles in the path of advance. Crawling along a plowed furrow through furious machinegun fire, he made his way to a point within handgrenade range of 1 of the enemy positions. He pounded the enemy with 4 handgrenades, and when the smoke had died away, S/Sgt. Hall and 2 dead Germans occupied the position, while 4 of the enemy were crawling back to our lines as prisoners. Discovering a quantity of German potato-masher grenades in the position, S/Sgt. Hall engaged the second enemy nest in a deadly exchange of grenades. Each time he exposed himself to throw a grenade the Germans fired machinegun bursts at him. The vicious duel finally ended in S/Sgt. Hall's favor with 5 of the enemy surrendered and 5 others lay dead. Turning his attention to the third machinegun, S/Sgt. Hall left his position and crawled along a furrow, the enemy firing frantically in an effort to halt him. As he neared his final objective, an enemy artillery concentration fell on the area, and S/Sgt. Hall's right leg was severed by a shellburst. With 2 enemy machineguns eliminated, his company was able to flank the third and continue its advance without incurring excessive casualties. S/Sgt. Hall's fearlessness, his determined fighting spirit, and his prodigious combat skill exemplify the heroic tradition of the American Infantryman.

*HALL, LEWIS

Rank and organization: Technician Fifth Grade, U.S. Army, Company M, 35th Infantry, 25th Infantry Division. *Place and date:* Mount Austen, Guadalcanal, Solomon Islands, 10 January 1943. *Entered service at:* Obetz, Rural Station 7, Columbus, Ohio. *Born:* 1895, Bloom, Ohio. *G.O. No.:* 28, 5 June 1943. *Citation:* For gallantry and intrepidity above and beyond the call of duty. As leader of a machinegun squad charged with the protection of other battalion units, his group was attacked by a superior number of Japanese, his gunner killed, his assistant gunner wounded, and an adjoining guncrew put out of action. Ordered to withdraw from his hazardous position, he refused to retire but rushed forward to the idle gun and with the aid of another soldier who joined him and held up the machinegun by the tripod to increase its field of action he opened fire and inflicted heavy casualties upon the enemy. While so engaged both these gallant soldiers were killed, but their sturdy defense was a decisive factor in the following success of the attacking battalion.

HALL, WILLIAM E.

Rank and organization: Lieutenant, Junior Grade, U.S. Naval Reserve. *Place and date:* Coral Sea, 7 and 8 May 1942. *Entered service at:* Utah. *Born:* 31 October 1913, Storrs, Utah. *Citation:* For extreme courage and conspicuous heroism in combat above and beyond the call of duty as pilot of a scouting plane in action against enemy Japanese forces in the Coral Sea on 7 and 8 May 1942. In a resolute and determined attack on 7 May, Lt. (jg.) Hall dived his plane at an enemy Japanese aircraft carrier, contributing materially to the destruction of that vessel. On 8 May, facing heavy and fierce fighter opposition, he again displayed extraordinary skill as an airman and the aggressive spirit of a fighter in repeated and effectively executed counterattacks against a superior number of enemy planes in which 3 enemy aircraft were destroyed. Though seriously wounded in this engagement, Lt. (jg.) Hall, maintaining the fearless and indomitable tactics pursued throughout these actions, succeeded in landing his plane safe.

*HALLMAN, SHERWOOD H.

Rank and organization: Staff Sergeant, U.S. Army, 175th Infantry, 29th Infantry Division. *Place and date:* Brest, Brittany, France, 13 September 1944. *Entered service at:* Spring City, Pa. *Birth:* Spring City, Pa. *G.O. No.:* 31, 17 April 1945. *Citation:* For conspicuous gallantry and intrepidity at risk of his life above and beyond the call of duty. On 13 September 1944, in Brittany, France, the 2d Battalion in its attack on the fortified city of Brest was held up by a strongly defended enemy position which had prevented its advance despite repeated attacks extending over a 3-day period. Finally, Company F advanced to within several hundred yards of the enemy position but was again halted by intense fire. Realizing that the position must be neutralized without delay, S/Sgt. Hallman ordered his squad to cover his movements with fire while he advanced alone to a point from which he could make the assault. Without hesitating, S/Sgt. Hallman leaped over a hedgerow into a sunken road, the central point of the German defenses which was known to contain an enemy machinegun position and at least 30 enemy riflemen. Firing his carbine and hurling grenades, S/Sgt. Hallman, unassisted, killed or wounded 4 of the enemy, then ordered the remainder to surrender. Immediately, 12 of the enemy surrendered and the position was shortly secured by the remainder of his company. Seeing the surrender of this position, about 75 of the enemy in the vicinity surrendered, yielding a defensive organization which the battalion with heavy supporting fires had been unable to take. This single heroic act on the part of S/Sgt. Hallman resulted in the immediate advance of the entire battalion for a distance of 2,000 yards to a position from which Fort Keranroux was captured later the same day. S/Sgt. Hallman's fighting determination and intrepidity in battle exemplify the highest tradition of the U.S. Armed Forces.

*HALYBURTON, WILLIAM DAVID, Jr.

Rank and organization: Pharmacist's Mate Second Class, U.S. Naval Reserve. *Born:* 2 August 1924, Canton, N.C. *Accredited to:* North Carolina. *Citation:* For conspicuous gallantry and intrepidity at the risk of his life above and beyond the call of duty while serving with a Marine Rifle Company in the 2d Battalion, 5th Marines, 1st Marine Division, during action against enemy Japanese forces on Okinawa Shima in the Ryukyu Chain, 10 May 1945. Undaunted by the deadly accuracy of Japanese counterfire as his unit pushed the attack through a strategically important draw, Halyburton unhesitatingly dashed across the draw and up the hill into an open fireswept field where the company advance squad was suddenly pinned down under a terrific concentration of mortar, machinegun and sniper fire with resultant severe casualties. Moving steadily forward despite the enemy's merciless barrage, he reached the wounded marine who lay farthest away and was rendering first aid when his patient was struck for the second time by a Japanese bullet. Instantly placing himself in the direct line of fire, he shielded the fallen fighter with his own body and staunchly continued his ministrations although constantly menaced by the slashing fury of shrapnel and bullets falling on all sides. Alert, determined and completely unselfish in his concern for the helpless marine, he persevered in his efforts until he himself sustained mortal wounds and collapsed, heroically sacrificing himself that his comrade might live. By his outstanding valor and unwavering devotion to duty in the face of tremendous odds, Halyburton sustained and enhanced the highest traditions of the U.S. Naval Service. He gallantly gave his life in the service of his country.

HAMILTON, PIERPONT M.

Rank and organization: Major, U.S. Army Air Corps. *Place and date:* Near Port Lyautey, French Morocco, 8 November 1942. *Entered ser-

vice at: New York, N.Y. *Born:* 3 August 1898, Tuxedo Park, N.Y. *G.O. No.:* 4, 23 January 1943. *Citation:* For conspicuous gallantry and intrepidity in action above and beyond the call of duty. On 8 November 1942, near Port Lyautey, French Morocco, Lt. Col. Hamilton volunteered to accompany Col. Demas Craw on a dangerous mission to the French commander, designed to bring about a cessation of hostilities. Driven away from the mouth of the Sebou River by heavy shelling from all sides, the landing boat was finally beached at Mehdia Plage despite continuous machinegun fire from 3 low-flying hostile planes. Driven in a light truck toward French headquarters, this courageous mission encountered intermittent firing, and as it neared Port Lyautey a heavy burst of machinegun fire was delivered upon the truck from pointblank range, killing Col. Craw instantly. Although captured immediately, after this incident, Lt. Col. Hamilton completed the mission.

*HAMMERBERG, OWEN FRANCIS PATRICK

Rank and organization: Boatswain's Mate Second Class, U.S. Navy. *Born:* 31 May 1920, Daggett, Mich. *Accredited to:* Michigan. *Citation:* For conspicuous gallantry and intrepidity at the risk of his life above and beyond the call of duty as a diver engaged in rescue operations at West Loch, Pearl Harbor, 17 February 1945. Aware of the danger when 2 fellow divers were hopelessly trapped in a cave-in of steel wreckage while tunneling with jet nozzles under an LST sunk in 40 feet of water and 20 feet of mud. Hammerberg unhesitatingly went overboard in a valiant attempt to effect their rescue despite the certain hazard of additional cave-ins and the risk of fouling his lifeline on jagged pieces of steel imbedded in the shifting mud. Washing a passage through the original excavation, he reached the first of the trapped men, freed him from the wreckage and, working desperately in pitch-black darkness, finally effected his release from fouled lines, thereby enabling him to reach the surface. Wearied but undaunted after several hours of arduous labor, Hammerberg resolved to continue his struggle to wash through the oozing submarine, subterranean mud in a determined effort to save the second diver. Venturing still farther under the buried hulk, he held tenaciously to his purpose, reaching a place immediately above the other man just as another cave-in occurred and a heavy piece of steel pinned him crosswise over his shipmate in a position which protected the man beneath from further injury while placing the full brunt of terrific pressure on himself. Although he succumbed in agony 18 hours after he had gone to the aid of his fellow divers, Hammerberg, by his cool judgment, unfaltering professional skill and consistent disregard of all personal danger in the face of tremendous odds, had contributed effectively to the saving of his 2 comrades. His heroic spirit of self-sacrifice throughout enhanced and sustained the highest traditions of the U.S. Naval Service. He gallantly gave his life in the service of his country.

*HANSEN, DALE MERLIN

Rank and organization: Private, U.S. Marine Corps. *Born:* 13 December 1922, Wisner, Nebr. *Accredited to:* Nebraska. *Citation:* For conspicuous gallantry and intrepidity at the risk of his life above and beyond the call of duty while serving with Company E, 2d Battalion, 1st Marines, 1st Marine Division, in action against enemy Japanese forces on Okinawa Shima in the Ryukyu Chain, 7 May 1945. Cool and courageous in combat, Pvt. Hansen unhesitatingly took the initiative during a critical stage of the action and, armed with a rocket launcher, crawled to an exposed position where he attacked and destroyed a strategically located hostile pillbox. With his weapon subsequently destroyed by enemy fire, he seized a rifle and continued his 1-man assault. Reaching the crest of a ridge, he leaped across, opened fire on 6 Japanese and killed 4 before his rifle jammed. Attacked by the remaining 2 Japanese, he beat them off with the butt of his rifle and then climbed back to cover. Promptly returning with another weapon and supply of grenades, he fearlessly advanced, destroyed a strong mortar position and annihilated 8 more of the enemy. In the forefront of battle throughout this bitterly waged engagement, Pvt. Hansen, by his indomitable determination, bold tactics and complete disregard of all personal danger, contributed essentially to the success of his company's mission and to the ultimate capture of this fiercely defended outpost of the Japanese Empire. His great personal valor in the face of extreme peril reflects the highest credit upon himself and the U.S. Naval Service.

*HANSON, ROBERT MURRAY

Rank and organization: First Lieutenant, U.S. Marine Corps Reserve. *Born:* 4 February 1920, Lucknow, India. *Accredited to:* Massachusetts. *Other Navy awards:* Navy Cross, Air Medal. *Citation:* For conspicuous gallantry and intrepidity at the risk of his life and above and beyond the call of duty as fighter pilot attached to Marine Fighting Squadron 215 in action against enemy Japanese forces at Bougainville Island, 1 November 1943; and New Britain Island, 24 January 1944. Undeterred by fierce opposition, and fearless in the face of overwhelming odds, 1st Lt. Hanson fought the Japanese boldly and with daring aggressiveness. On 1 November, while flying cover for our landing operations at Empress Augusta Bay, he dauntlessly attacked 6 enemy torpedo bombers, forcing them to jettison their bombs and destroying 1 Japanese plane during the action. Cut off from his division while deep in enemy territory during a high cover flight over Simpson Harbor on 24 January, 1st Lt. Hanson waged a lone and gallant battle against hostile interceptors as they were orbiting to attack our bombers and, striking with devastating fury, brought down 4 Zeroes and probably a fifth. Handling his plane superbly in both pursuit and attack measures, he was a master of individual air combat, accounting for a total of 25 Japanese aircraft in this theater of war. His great personal valor and invincible fighting spirit were in keeping with the highest traditions of the U.S. Naval Service.

*HARMON, ROY W.

Rank and organization: Sergeant, U.S. Army, Company C, 362d Infantry, 91st Infantry Division. *Place and date:* Near Casaglia, Italy, 12 July 1944. *Entered service at:* Pixley, Calif. *Birth:* Talala, Okla. *G.O. No.:* 83, 2 October 1945. *Citation:* He was an acting squad leader when heavy machinegun fire from enemy positions, well dug in on commanding ground and camouflaged by haystacks, stopped his company's advance and pinned down 1 platoon where it was exposed to almost certain annihilation. Ordered to rescue the beleaguered platoon by neutralizing the German automatic fire, he led his squad forward along a draw to the right of the trapped unit against 3 key positions which poured murderous fire into his helpless comrades. When within range, his squad fired tracer bullets in an attempt to set fire to the 3 haystacks which were strung out in a loose line directly to the front, 75, 150, and 250 yards away. Realizing that this attack was ineffective, Sgt. Harmon ordered his squad to hold their position and voluntarily began a 1-man assault. Carrying white phosphorus grenades and a submachinegun, he skillfully took advantage of what little cover the terrain afforded and crept to within 25 yards of the first position. He set the haystack afire with a grenade, and when 2 of the enemy attempted to flee from the inferno, he killed them with his submachinegun. Crawling toward the second machinegun emplacement, he attracted fire and was wounded; but he continued to advance and destroyed the position with handgrenades, killing the occupants. He then attacked the third machinegun, running to a small knoll, then crawling over ground which offered no concealment or cover. About halfway to his objective, he was again wounded. But he struggled ahead until within 20 yards of the machinegun nest, where he raised himself to his knees to throw a grenade. He was knocked down by direct enemy fire. With a final, magnificent effort, he again arose, hurled the grenade and fell dead, riddled by bullets. His missile fired the third position, destroying it. Sgt. Harmon's extraordinary heroism, gallantry, and self-sacrifice saved a platoon from being wiped out, and made it possible for his company to advance against powerful enemy resistance.

*HARR, HARRY R.

Rank and organization: Corporal, U.S. Army, Company D, 124th Infantry, 31st Infantry Division. *Place and date:* Near Maglamin, Mindanao, Philippine Islands, 5 June 1945. *Entered service at:* East Freedom, Pa. *Birth:* Pine Croft, Pa. *G.O. No.:* 28, 28 March 1946. *Citation:* He displayed conspicuous gallantry and intrepidity. In a fierce counterattack, the Japanese closed in on his machinegun emplacement, hurling handgrenades, 1 of which exploded under the gun, putting it out of action and wounding 2 of the crew. While the remaining gunners were desperately attempting to repair their weapon another grenade landed squarely in the emplacement. Quickly realizing he could not safely throw the unexploded missile from the crowded position, Cpl. Harr unhesitatingly covered it with his body to smother the blast. His supremely courageous act, which cost him his life, saved 4 of his comrades and enabled them to continue their mission.

HARRELL, WILLIAM GEORGE

Rank and organization: Sergeant, U.S. Marine Corps, 1st Battalion, 28th Marines, 5th Marine Division. *Place and date:* Iwo Jima, Volcano Islands, 3 March 1945. *Entered service at:* Mercedes, Tex. *Born:* 26 June 1922, Rio Grande City, Tex. *Citation:* For conspicuous gallantry and intrepidity at the risk of his life above and beyond the call of duty as leader of an assault group attached to the 1st Battalion, 28th

Marines, 5th Marine Division during hand-to-hand combat with enemy Japanese at Iwo Jima, Volcano Islands, on 3 March 1945. Standing watch alternately with another marine in a terrain studded with caves and ravines, Sgt. Harrell was holding a position in a perimeter defense around the company command post when Japanese troops infiltrated our lines in the early hours of dawn. Awakened by a sudden attack, he quickly opened fire with his carbine and killed 2 of the enemy as they emerged from a ravine in the light of a star shellburst. Unmindful of his danger as hostile grenades fell closer, he waged a fierce lone battle until an exploding missile tore off his left hand and fractured his thigh. He was vainly attempting to reload the carbine when his companion returned from the command post with another weapon. Wounded again by a Japanese who rushed the foxhole wielding a saber in the darkness, Sgt. Harrell succeeded in drawing his pistol and killing his opponent and then ordered his wounded companion to a place of safety. Exhausted by profuse bleeding but still unbeaten, he fearlessly met the challenge of 2 more enemy troops who charged his position and placed a grenade near his head. Killing 1 man with his pistol, he grasped the sputtering grenade with his good right hand, and, pushing it painfully toward the crouching soldier, saw his remaining assailant destroyed but his own hand severed in the explosion. At dawn Sgt. Harrell was evacuated from a position hedged by the bodies of 12 dead Japanese, at least 5 of whom he had personally destroyed in his self-sacrificing defense of the command post. His grim fortitude, exceptional valor, and indomitable fighting spirit against almost insurmountable odds reflect the highest credit upon himself and enhance the finest traditions of the U.S. Naval Service.

*HARRIS, JAMES L.

Rank and organization: Second Lieutenant, U.S. Army, 756th Tank Battalion. *Place and date:* At Vagney, France, 7 October 1944. *Entered service at:* Hillsboro, Tex. *Birth:* Hillsboro, Tex. *G.O. No.:* 32, 23 April 1945. *Citation:* For conspicuous gallantry and intrepidity at risk of life above and beyond the call of duty on 7 October 1944, in Vagney, France. At 9 p.m. an enemy raiding party, comprising a tank and 2 platoons of infantry, infiltrated through the lines under cover of mist and darkness and attacked an infantry battalion command post with handgrenades, retiring a short distance to an ambush position on hearing the approach of the M4 tank commanded by 2d Lt. Harris. Realizing the need for bold aggressive action, 2d Lt. Harris ordered his tank to halt while he proceeded on foot, fully 10 yards ahead of his 6-man patrol and armed only with a service pistol, to probe the darkness for the enemy. Although struck down and mortally wounded by machine-gun bullets which penetrated his solar plexus, he crawled back to his tank, leaving a trail of blood behind him, and, too weak to climb inside it, issued fire orders while lying on the road between the 2 contending armored vehicles. Although the tank which he commanded was destroyed in the course of the fire fight, he stood the enemy off until friendly tanks, preparing to come to his aid, caused the enemy to withdraw and thereby lose an opportunity to kill or capture the entire battalion command personnel. Suffering a second wound, which severed his leg at the hip, in the course of this tank duel, 2d Lt. Harris refused aid until after a wounded member of his crew had been carried to safety. He died before he could be given medical attention.

*HASTINGS, JOE R.

Rank and organization: Private First Class, U.S. Army, Company C, 386th Infantry, 97th Infantry Division. *Place and date:* Drabenderhohe, Germany, 12 April 1945. *Entered service at:* Magnolia, Ohio. *Birth:* Malvern, Ohio. *G.O. No.:* 101, 8 November 1945. *Citation:* He fought gallantly during an attack against strong enemy forces defending Drabenderhohe, Germany, from the dug-in positions on commanding ground. As squad leader of a light machinegun section supporting the advance of the 1st and 3d Platoons, he braved direct rifle, machinegun, 20-mm., and mortar fire, some of which repeatedly missed him only by inches, and rushed forward over 350 yards of open, rolling fields to reach a position from which he could fire on the enemy troops. From this vantage point he killed the crews of a 20-mm. gun and a machinegun, drove several enemy riflemen from their positions, and so successfully shielded the 1st Platoon, that it had time to reorganize and remove its wounded to safety. Observing that the 3d Platoon to his right was being met by very heavy 40-mm. and machinegun fire, he ran 150 yards with his gun to the leading elements of that unit, where he killed the crew of the 40-mm. gun. As spearhead of the 3d Platoon's attack, he advanced, firing his gun held at hip height, disregarding the bullets that whipped past him, until the assault had carried 175 yards to the objective. In this charge he and the riflemen he led killed or wounded many of the fanatical enemy and put 2 machineguns out of action. Pfc. Hastings, by his intrepidity, outstanding leadership, and unrelenting determination to wipe out the formidable German opposition, cleared the path for his company's advance into Drabenderhohe. He was killed 4 days later while again supporting the 3d Platoon.

*HAUGE, LOUIS JAMES, Jr.

Rank and organization: Corporal, U.S. Marine Corps Reserve. *Born:* 12 December 1924, Ada, Minn. *Accredited to:* Minnesota. *Citation:* For conspicuous gallantry and intrepidity at the risk of his life above and beyond the call of duty as leader of a machinegun squad serving with Company C, 1st Battalion, 1st Marines, 1st Marine Division, in action against enemy Japanese forces on Okinawa Shima in the Ryukyu Chain on 14 May 1945. Alert and aggressive during a determined assault against a strongly fortified Japanese hill position, Cpl. Hauge boldly took the initiative when his company's left flank was pinned down under a heavy machinegun and mortar barrage with resultant severe casualties and, quickly locating the 2 machineguns which were delivering the uninterrupted stream of enfilade fire, ordered his squad to maintain a covering barrage as he rushed across an exposed area toward the furiously blazing enemy weapons. Although painfully wounded as he charged the first machinegun, he launched a vigorous singlehanded grenade attack, destroyed the entire hostile gun position and moved relentlessly forward toward the other emplacement despite his wounds and the increasingly heavy Japanese fire. Undaunted by the savage opposition, he again hurled his deadly grenades with unerring aim and succeeded in demolishing the second enemy gun before he fell under the slashing fury of Japanese sniper fire. By his ready grasp of the critical situation and his heroic 1-man assault tactics, Cpl. Hauge had eliminated 2 strategically placed enemy weapons, thereby releasing the besieged troops from an overwhelming volume of hostile fire and enabling his company to advance. His indomitable fighting spirit and decisive valor in the face of almost certain death reflect the highest credit upon Cpl. Hauge and the U.S. Naval Service. He gallantly gave his life in the service of his country.

HAWK, JOHN D.

Rank and organization: Sergeant, U.S. Army, Company E, 359th Infantry, 90th Infantry Division. *Place and date:* Near Chambois, France, 20 August 1944. *Entered service at:* Bremerton, Wash. *Birth:* San Francisco, Calif. *G.O. No.:* 55, 13 July 1945. *Citation:* He manned a light machinegun on 20 August 1944, near Chambois, France, a key point in the encirclement which created the Falaise Pocket. During an enemy counterattack, his position was menaced by a strong force of tanks and infantry. His fire forced the infantry to withdraw, but an artillery shell knocked out his gun and wounded him in the right thigh. Securing a bazooka, he and another man stalked the tanks and forced them to retire to a wooded section. In the lull which followed, Sgt. Hawk reorganized 2 machinegun squads and, in the face of intense enemy fire, directed the assembly of 1 workable weapon from 2 damaged guns. When another enemy assault developed, he was forced to pull back from the pressure of spearheading armor. Two of our tank destroyers were brought up. Their shots were ineffective because of the terrain until Sgt. Hawk, despite his wound, boldly climbed to an exposed position on a knoll where, unmoved by fusillades from the enemy, he became a human aiming stake for the destroyers. Realizing that his shouted fire directions could not be heard above the noise of battle, he ran back to the destroyers through a concentration of bullets and shrapnel to correct the range. He returned to his exposed position, repeating this performance until 2 of the tanks were knocked out and a third driven off. Still at great risk, he continued to direct the destroyers' fire into the Germans' wooded position until the enemy came out and surrendered. Sgt. Hawk's fearless initiative and heroic conduct, even while suffering from a painful wound, was in large measure responsible for crushing 2 desperate attempts of the enemy to escape from the Falaise Picket and for taking more than 500 prisoners.

*HAWKINS, WILLIAM DEAN

Rank and organization: First Lieutenant, U.S. Marine Corps. *Born:* 19 April 1914, Fort Scott, Kans. *Appointed from:* El Paso, Tex. *Citation:* For valorous and gallant conduct above and beyond the call of duty as commanding officer of a Scout Sniper Platoon attached to the Assault Regiment in action against Japanese-held Tarawa in the Gilbert Island, 20 and 21 November 1943. The first to disembark from the jeep lighter, 1st Lt. Hawkins unhesitatingly moved forward under heavy enemy fire at the end of the Betio Pier, neutralizing emplacements in coverage of troops assaulting the main beach positions. Fearlessly leading his men on to join the forces fighting desperately to gain a beachhead, he repeatedly risked his life throughout the day and night to direct and lead attacks on pillboxes and installations with grenades and demolitions. At dawn on the following day, 1st Lt. Hawkins resumed the dangerous mission of clearing the limited beachhead of Japanese resistance, personally initiating an assault on a hostile position fortified by 5 enemy machineguns, and, crawling forward in the face of withering fire, boldly fired point-blank into the loopholes and completed the destruction with grenades. Refusing to withdraw after being seriously wounded in the chest during this skirmish, 1st Lt. Hawkins steadfastly carried the fight to the enemy, destroying 3 more pillboxes before he was caught in a burst of Japanese shellfire and mortally wounded. His relentless fighting spirit in the face of formidable opposition and his exceptionally daring tactics served as an inspiration to his comrades during the most crucial phase of the battle and reflect the highest credit upon the U.S. Naval Service. He gallantly gave his life for his country.

HAWKS, LLOYD C.

Rank and organization: Private First Class, U.S. Army, Medical Detachment, 30th Infantry, 3d Infantry Division. *Place and date:* Near Carano, Italy, 30 January 1944. *Entered service at:* Park Rapids, Minn. *Born:* 13 January 1911, Becker, Minn. *G.O. No.:* 5, 15 January 1945. *Citation:* For gallantry and intrepidity at risk of life above and beyond the call of duty. On 30 January 1944, at 3 p.m., near Carano, Italy, Pfc. Hawks braved an enemy counterattack in order to rescue 2 wounded men who, unable to move, were lying in an exposed position within 30 yards of the enemy. Two riflemen, attempting the rescue, had been forced to return to their fighting holes by extremely severe enemy machinegun fire, after crawling only 10 yards toward the casualties. An aid man, whom the enemy could plainly identify as such, had been critically wounded in a similar attempt. Pfc. Hawks, nevertheless, crawled 50 yards through a veritable hail of machinegun bullets and flying mortar fragments to a small ditch, administered first aid to his fellow aid man who had sought cover therein, and continued toward the 2 wounded men 50 yards distant. An enemy machinegun bullet penetrated his helmet, knocking it from his head, momentarily stunning him. Thirteen bullets passed through his helmet as it lay on the ground within 6 inches of his body. Pfc. Hawks, crawled to the casualties, administered first aid to the more seriously wounded man and dragged him to a covered position 25 yards distant. Despite continuous automatic fire from positions only 30 yards away and shells which exploded within 25 yards, Pfc. Hawks returned to the second man and administered first aid to him. As he raised himself to obtain bandages from his medical kit his right hip was shattered by a burst of machinegun fire and a second burst splintered his left forearm. Displaying dogged determination and extreme self-control, Pfc. Hawks, despite severe pain and his dangling left arm, completed the task of bandaging the remaining casualty and with superhuman effort dragged him to the same depression to which he had brought the first man. Finding insufficient cover for 3 men at this point, Pfc. Hawks crawled 75 yards in an effort to regain his company, reaching the ditch in which his fellow aid man was lying.

*HEDRICK, CLINTON M.

Rank and organization: Technical Sergeant, U.S. Army, Company I, 194th Glider Infantry, 17th Airborne Division. *Place and date:* Near Lembeck, Germany, 27-28 March 1945. *Entered service at:* Riverton, W. Va. *Birth:* Cherrygrove, W. Va. *G.O. No.:* 89, 19 October 1945. *Citation:* He displayed extraordinary heroism and gallantry in action on 27-28 March 1945, in Germany. Following an airborne landing near Wesel, his unit was assigned as the assault platoon for the assault on Lembeck. Three times the landing elements were pinned down by intense automatic weapons fire from strongly defended positions. Each time, T/Sgt. Hedrick fearlessly charged through heavy fire, shooting his automatic rifle from his hip. His courageous action so inspired his men that they reduced the enemy positions in rapid succession. When 6 of the enemy attempted a surprise, flanking movement, he quickly turned and killed the entire party with a burst of fire. Later, the enemy withdrew across a moat into Lembeck Castle. T/Sgt. Hedrick, with utter disregard for his own safety, plunged across the drawbridge alone in pursuit. When a German soldier, with hands upraised, declared the garrison wished to surrender, he entered the castle yard with 4 of his men to accept the capitulation. The group moved through a sally port, and was met by fire from a German self-propelled gun. Although mortally wounded, T/Sgt. Hedrick fired at the enemy gun and covered the withdrawal of his comrades. He died while being evacuated after the castle was taken. His great personal courage and heroic leadership contributed in large measure to the speedy capture of Lembeck and provided an inspiring example to his comrades.

HENDRIX, JAMES R.

Rank and organization: Private, U.S. Army, Company C, 53d Armored Infantry Battalion, 4th Armored Division. *Place and date:* Near Assenois, Belgium, 26 December 1944. *Entered service at:* Lepanto, Ark. *Birth:* Lepanto, Ark. *G.O. No.:* 74, 1 September 1945. *Citation:* On the night of 26 December 1944, near Assenois, Belgium, he was with the leading element engaged in the final thrust to break through to the besieged garrison at Bastogne when halted by a fierce combination of artillery and small-arms fire. He dismounted from his halftrack and advanced against two 88-mm. guns, and, by the ferocity of his rifle fire, compelled the guncrews to take cover and then to surrender. Later in the attack he again left his vehicle, voluntarily, to aid 2 wounded soldiers, helpless and exposed to intense machinegun fire. Effectively silencing 2 hostile machineguns, he held off the enemy by his own fire until the wounded men were evacuated. Pvt. Hendrix again distinguished himself when he hastened to the aid of still another soldier who was trapped in a burning halftrack. Braving enemy sniper fire and exploding mines and ammunition in the vehicle, he extricated the wounded man and extinguished his flaming clothing, thereby saving the life of his fellow soldier. Pvt. Hendrix, by his superb courage and heroism, exemplified the highest traditions of the military service.

344

*HENRY, ROBERT T.

Rank and organization: Private, U.S. Army, 16th Infantry, 1st Infantry Division. *Place and date:* Luchem, Germany, 3 December 1944. *Entered service at:* Greenville, Miss. *Birth:* Greenville, Miss. *G.O. No.:* 45, 12 June 1945. *Citation:* Near Luchem, Germany, he volunteered to attempt the destruction of a nest of 5 enemy machineguns located in a bunker 150 yards to the flank which had stopped the advance of his platoon. Stripping off his pack, overshoes, helmet, and overcoat, he sprinted alone with his rifle and handgrenades across the open terrain toward the enemy emplacement. Before he had gone half the distance he was hit by a burst of machinegun fire. Dropping his rifle, he continued to stagger forward until he fell mortally wounded only 10 yards from the enemy emplacement. His singlehanded attack forced the enemy to leave the machineguns. During this break in hostile fire the platoon moved forward and overran the position. Pvt. Henry, by his gallantry and intrepidity and utter disregard for his own life, enabled his company to reach its objective, capturing this key defense and 70 German prisoners.

HERRERA, SILVESTRE S.

Rank and organization: Private First Class, U.S. Army, Company E, 142d Infantry, 36th Infantry Division. *Place and date:* Near Mertzwiller, France, 15 March 1945. *Entered service at:* Phoenix, Ariz. *Birth:* El Paso, Tex. *G.O. No.:* 75, 5 September 1945. *Citation:* He advanced with a platoon along a wooded road until stopped by heavy enemy machinegun fire. As the rest of the unit took cover, he made a 1-man frontal assault on a strongpoint and captured 8 enemy soldiers. When the platoon resumed its advance and was subjected to fire from a second emplacement beyond an extensive minefield, Pvt. Herrera again moved forward, disregarding the danger of exploding mines, to attack the position. He stepped on a mine and had both feet severed; but, despite intense pain and unchecked loss of blood, he pinned down the enemy with accurate rifle fire while a friendly squad captured the enemy gun by skirting the minefield and rushing in from the flank. The magnificent courage, extraordinary heroism, and willing self-sacrifice displayed by Pvt. Herrera resulted in the capture of 2 enemy strongpoints and the taking of 8 prisoners.

HERRING, RUFUS G.

Rank and organization: Lieutenant, U.S. Naval Reserve, LCI (G) 449. *Place and date:* Iwo Jima, 17 February 1945. *Entered service at:* North Carolina. *Born:* 11 June 1921, Roseboro, N.C. *Citation:* For conspicuous gallantry and intrepidity at the risk of his life above and beyond the call of duty as commanding officer of LCI (G) 449 operating as a unit of LCI (G) Group 8, during the pre-invasion attack on Iwo Jima on 17 February 1945. Boldly closing the strongly fortified shores under the devastating fire of Japanese coastal defense guns, Lt. (then Lt. (jg.)) Herring directed shattering barrages of 40-mm. and 20-mm. gunfire against hostile beaches until struck down by the enemy's savage counterfire which blasted the *449's* heavy guns and whipped her decks into sheets of flame. Regaining consciousness despite profuse bleeding he was again critically wounded when a Japanese mortar crashed the conning station, instantly killing or fatally wounding most of the officers and leaving the ship wallowing without navigational control. Upon recovering the second time, Lt. Herring resolutely climbed down to the pilothouse and, fighting against his rapidly waning strength, took over the helm, established communication with the engineroom, and carried on valiantly until relief could be obtained. When no longer able to stand, he propped himself against empty shell cases and rallied his men to the aid of the wounded; he maintained position in the firing line with his 20-mm. guns in action in the face of sustained enemy fire, and conned his crippled ship to safety. His unwavering fortitude, aggressive perseverance, and indomitable spirit against terrific odds reflect the highest credit upon Lt. Herring and uphold the highest traditions of the U.S. Naval Service.

*HILL, EDWIN JOSEPH

Rank and organization: Chief Boatswain, U.S. Navy. *Born:* 4 October 1894, Philadelphia, Pa. *Accredited to:* Pennsylvania. *Citation:* For distinguished conduct in the line of his profession, extraordinary courage, and disregard of his own safety during the attack on the Fleet in Pearl Harbor, by Japanese forces on 7 December 1941. During the height of the strafing and bombing, Chief Boatswain Hill led his men of the line-handling details of the U.S.S. *Nevada* to the quays, cast off the lines and swam back to his ship. Later, while on the forecastle, attempting to let go the anchors, he was blown overboard and killed by the explosion of several bombs.

HORNER, FREEMAN V.

Rank and organization: Staff Sergeant, U.S. Army, Company K, 119th Infantry, 30th Infantry Division. *Place and date:* Wurselen, Germany, 16 November 1944. *Entered service at:* Shamokin, Pa. *Birth:* Mount Carmel, Pa. *G.O. No.:* 95, 30 October 1945. *Citation:* S/Sgt. Horner and other members of his company were attacking Wurselen, Germany, against stubborn resistance on 16 November 1944, when machinegun fire from houses on the edge of the town pinned the attackers in flat, open terrain 100 yards from their objective. As they lay in the field, enemy artillery observers directed fire upon them, causing serious casualties. Realizing that the machineguns must be eliminated in order to permit the company to advance from its precarious position, S/Sgt. Horner voluntarily stood up with his submachinegun and rushed into the teeth of concentrated fire, burdened by a heavy load of ammunition and handgrenades. Just as he reached a position of seeming safety, he was fired on by a machinegun which had remained silent up until that time. He coolly wheeled in his fully exposed position while bullets barely missed him and killed 2 hostile gunners with a single, devastating burst. He turned to face the fire of the other 2 machineguns, and dodging fire as he ran, charged the 2 positions 50 yards away. Demoralized by their inability to hit the intrepid infantryman, the enemy abandoned their guns and took cover in the cellar of the house they occupied. S/Sgt. Horner burst into the building, hurled 2 grenades down the cellar stairs, and called for the Germans to surrender. Four men gave up to him. By his extraordinary courage,

S/Sgt. Horner destroyed 3 enemy machinegun positions, killed or captured 7 enemy, and cleared the path for his company's successful assault on Wurselen.

HOWARD, JAMES H. (Air Mission)

Rank and organization: Lieutenant Colonel, U.S. Army Air Corps. *Place and date:* Over Oschersleben, Germany, 11 January 1944. *Entered service at:* St Louis, Mo. *Birth:* Canton, China. *G.O. No.:* 45, 5 June 1944. *Citation:* For conspicuous gallantry and intrepidity above and beyond the call of duty in action with the enemy near Oschersleben, Germany, on 11 January 1944. On that day Col. Howard was the leader of a group of P-51 aircraft providing support for a heavy bomber formation on a long-range mission deep in enemy territory. As Col. Howard's group met the bombers in the target area the bomber force was attacked by numerous enemy fighters. Col. Howard, with his group, and at once engaged the enemy and himself destroyed a German ME. 110. As a result of this attack Col. Howard lost contact with his group, and at once returned to the level of the bomber formation. He then saw that the bombers were being heavily attacked by enemy airplanes and that no other friendly fighters were at hand. While Col. Howard could have waited to attempt to assemble his group before engaging the enemy, he chose instead to attack singlehanded a formation of more than 30 German airplanes. With utter disregard for his own safety he immediately pressed home determined attacks for some 30 minutes, during which time he destroyed 3 enemy airplanes and probably destroyed and damaged others. Toward the end of this engagement 3 of his guns went out of action and his fuel supply was becoming dangerously low. Despite these handicaps and the almost insuperable odds against him, Col. Howard continued his aggressive action in an attempt to protect the bombers from the numerous fighters. His skill, courage, and intrepidity on this occasion set an example of heroism which will be an inspiration to the U.S. Armed Forces.

HUFF, PAUL B.

Rank and organization: Corporal, U.S. Army, 509th Parachute Infantry Battalion. *Place and date:* Near Carano, Italy, 8 February 1944. *Entered service at:* Cleveland, Tenn. *Birth:* Cleveland, Tenn. *G.O. No.:* 41, 26 May 1944. *Citation:* For conspicuous gallantry and intrepidity at risk of life above and beyond the call of duty, in action on 8 February 1944, near Carano, Italy. Cpl. Huff volunteered to lead a 6-man patrol with the mission of determining the location and strength of an enemy unit which was delivering fire on the exposed right flank of his company. The terrain over which he had to travel consisted of exposed, rolling ground, affording the enemy excellent visibility. As the patrol advanced, its members were subjected to small arms and machinegun fire and a concentration of mortar fire, shells bursting within 5 to 10 yards of them and bullets striking the ground at their feet. Moving ahead of his patrol, Cpl. Huff drew fire from 3 enemy machineguns and a 20-mm. weapon. Realizing the danger confronting his patrol, he advanced alone under deadly fire through a minefield and arrived at a point within 75 yards of the nearest machinegun position. Under direct fire from the rear machinegun, he crawled the remaining 75 yards to the closest emplacement, killed the crew with his submachinegun and destroyed the gun. During this act he fired from a kneeling position which drew fire from other positions, enabling him to estimate correctly the strength and location of the enemy. Still under concentrated fire, he returned to his patrol and led his men to safety. As a result of the information he gained, a patrol in strength sent out that afternoon, 1 group under the leadership of Cpl. Huff, succeeded in routing an enemy company of 125 men, killing 27 Germans and capturing 21 others, with a loss of only 3 patrol members. Cpl. Huff's intrepid leadership and daring combat skill reflect the finest traditions of the American infantryman.

*HUGHES, LLOYD H. (Air Mission)

Rank and organization: Second Lieutenant, U.S. Army Air Corps, 564th Bomber Squadron, 389th Bomber Group, 9th Air Force. *Place and date:* Ploesti Raid, Rumania, 1 August 1943. *Entered service at:* San Antonio, Tex. *Born:* 12 July 1921, Alexandria, La. *G.O. No.:* 17, 26 February 1944. *Citation:* For conspicuous gallantry in action and intrepidity at the risk of his life above and beyond the call of duty. On 1 August 1943, 2d Lt. Hughes served in the capacity of pilot of a heavy bombardment aircraft participating in a long and hazardous minimum-altitude attack against the Axis oil refineries of Ploesti, Rumania, launched from the northern shores of Africa. Flying in the last formation to attack the target, he arrived in the target area after previous flights had thoroughly alerted the enemy defenses. Approaching the target through intense and accurate antiaircraft fire and dense balloon barrages at dangerously low altitude, his plane received several direct hits from both large and small caliber antiaircraft guns which seriously damaged his aircraft, causing sheets of escaping gasoline to stream from the bomb bay and from the left wing. This damage was inflicted at a time prior to reaching the target when 2d Lt. Hughes could have made a forced landing in any of the grain fields readily available at that time. The target area was blazing with burning oil tanks and damaged refinery installations from which flames leaped high above the bombing level of the formation. With full knowledge of the consequences of entering this blazing inferno when his airplane was profusely leaking gasoline in two separate locations, 2d Lt. Hughes, motivated only by his high conception of duty which called for the destruction of his assigned target at any cost, did not elect to make a forced landing or turn back from the attack. Instead, rather than jeopardize the formation and the success of the attack, he unhesitatingly entered the blazing area and dropped his bomb load with great precision. After successfully bombing the objective, his aircraft emerged from the conflagration with the left wing aflame. Only then did he attempt a forced landing, but because of the advanced stage of the fire enveloping his aircraft the plane crashed and was consumed. By 2d Lt. Hughes' heroic decision to complete his mission regardless of the consequences in utter disregard of his own life, and by his gallant and valorous execution of this decision, he has rendered a service to our country in the defeat of our enemies which will everlastingly be outstanding in the annals of our Nation's history.

*HUTCHINS, JOHNNIE DAVID

Rank and organization: Seaman First Class, U.S. Naval Reserve. *Born:* 4 August 1922, Weimer, Tex. *Accredited to:* Texas. *Citation:* For extraordinary heroism and conspicuous valor above and beyond the call of duty while serving on board a Landing Ship, Tank, during the assault on Lae, New Guinea, 4 September 1943. As the ship on which Hutchins was stationed approached the enemy-occupied beach under a veritable hail of fire from Japanese shore batteries and aerial bombardment, a hostile torpedo pierced the surf and bore down upon the vessel with deadly accuracy. In the tense split seconds before the helmsman could steer clear of the threatening missile, a bomb struck the pilot house, dislodged him from his station, and left the stricken ship helplessly exposed. Fully aware of the dire peril of the situation, Hutchins, although mortally wounded by the shattering explosion, quickly grasped the wheel and exhausted the last of his strength in maneuvering the vessel clear of the advancing torpedo. Still clinging to the helm, he eventually succumbed to his injuries, his final thoughts concerned only with the safety of his ship, his final efforts expended toward the security of his mission. He gallantly gave his life in the service of his country.

*JACHMAN, ISADORE S.

Rank and organization: Staff Sergeant, U.S. Army, Company B, 513th Parachute Infantry Regiment. *Place and date:* Flamierge, Belgium, 4 January 1945. *Entered service at:* Baltimore, Md. *Birth:* Berlin, Germany. *G.O. No.:* 25, 9 June 1950. *Citation:* For conspicuous gallantry and intrepidity above and beyond the call of duty at Flamierge, Belgium, on 4 January 1945, when his company was pinned down by enemy artillery, mortar, and small-arms fire, 2 hostile tanks attacked the unit, inflicting heavy casualties. S/Sgt. Jachman, seeing the desperate plight of his comrades, left his place of cover and with total disregard for his own safety dashed across open ground through a hail of fire and seizing a bazooka from a fallen comrade advanced on the tanks, which concentrated their fire on him. Firing the weapon alone, he damaged one and forced both to retire. S/Sgt. Jachman's heroic action, in which he suffered fatal wounds, disrupted the entire enemy attack, reflecting the highest credit upon himself and the parachute infantry.

JACKSON, ARTHUR J.

Rank and organization: Private First Class, U.S. Marine Corps, 3d Battalion, 7th Marines, 1st Marine Division. *Place and date:* Island of Peleliu in the Palau group, 18 September 1944. *Entered service at:* Oregon. *Born:* 18 October 1924, Cleveland, Ohio. *Citation:* For conspicuous gallantry and intrepidity at the risk of his life above and beyond the call of duty while serving with the 3d Battalion, 7th Marines, 1st Marine Division, in action against enemy Japanese forces on the Island of Peleliu in the Palau group, 18 September 1944. Boldly taking the initiative when his platoon's left flank advance was held up by the fire of Japanese troops concealed in strongly fortified positions, Pfc. Jackson unhesitatingly proceeded forward of our lines and, courageously defying the heavy barrages, charged a large pillbox housing approximately 35 enemy soldiers. Pouring his automatic fire into the opening of the fixed installation to trap the occupying troops, he hurled white phosphorus grenades and explosive charges brought up by a fellow marine, demolishing the pillbox and killing all of the enemy. Advancing alone under the continuous fire from other hostile emplacements, he employed similar means to smash 2 smaller positions in the immediate vicinity. Determined to crush the entire pocket of resistance although harassed on all sides by the shattering blasts of Japanese weapons and covered only by small rifle parties, he stormed 1 gun position after another, dealing death and destruction to the savagely fighting enemy in his inexorable drive against the remaining defenses, and succeeded in wiping out a total of 12 pillboxes and 50 Japanese soldiers. Stouthearted and indomitable despite the terrific odds. Pfc. Jackson resolutely maintained control of the platoon's left flank movement throughout his valiant 1-man assault and, by his cool decision and relentless fighting spirit during a critical situation, contributed essentially to the complete annihilation of the enemy in the southern sector of the island. His gallant initiative and heroic conduct in the face of extreme peril reflect the highest credit upon Pfc. Jackson and the U.S. Naval Service.

JACOBSON, DOUGLAS THOMAS

Rank and organization: Private First Class, U.S. Marine Corps Reserve, 3d Battalion, 23d Marines, 4th Marine Division. *Place and date:* Iwo Jima, Volcano Islands, 26 February 1945. *Entered service at:* New York. *Born:* 25 November 1925, Rochester, N.Y. *Citation:* For conspicuous gallantry and intrepidity at the risk of his life above and beyond the call of duty while serving with the 3d Battalion, 23d Marines, 4th Marine Division, in combat against enemy Japanese forces during the seizure of Iwo Jima in the Volcano Island, 26 February 1945. Promptly destroying a stubborn 20-mm. antiaircraft gun and its crew after assuming the duties of a bazooka man who had been killed, Pfc. Jacobson waged a relentless battle as his unit fought desperately toward the summit of Hill 382 in an effort to penetrate the heart of Japanese cross-island defense. Employing his weapon with ready accuracy when his platoon was halted by overwhelming enemy fire on 26 February, he first destroyed 2 hostile machinegun positions, then attacked a large blockhouse, completely neutralizing the fortification before dispatching the 5-man crew of a second pillbox and exploding the installation with a terrific demolitions blast. Moving steadily forward, he wiped out an earth-covered rifle emplacement and, confronted by a cluster of similar emplacements which constituted the perimeter of enemy defenses in his assigned sector, fearlessly advanced, quickly reduced all 6 positions to a shambles, killed 10 of the enemy, and enabled our forces to occupy the strong point. Determined to widen the breach thus forced, he volunteered his services to an adjacent assault company, neutralized a pillbox holding up its advance, opened fire on a Japanese tank pouring a steady stream of bullets on 1 of our supporting tanks, and smashed the enemy tank's gun turret in a brief but furious action culminating in a singlehanded assault against still another blockhouse and the subsequent neutralization of its firepower. By his dauntless skill and valor, Pfc. Jacobson destroyed a total of 16 enemy positions and annihilated approximately 75 Japanese, thereby contributing essentially to the success of his division's operations against this fanatically defended outpost of the Japanese Empire. His gallant conduct in the face of tremendous odds enhanced and sustained the highest traditions of the U.S. Naval Service.

*JERSTAD, JOHN L. (Air Mission)

Rank and organization: Major, U.S. Army Air Corps, 9th Air Force. *Place and date:* Ploesti Raid, Rumania, 1 August 1943. *Entered service at:* Racine, Wis. *Born:* 12 February 1918, Racine, Wis. *G.O. No.:* 72, 28 October 1943. *Citation:* For conspicuous gallantry and intrepidity above and beyond the call of duty. On 1 August 1943, he served as pilot of the lead aircraft in his group in a daring low-level attack against enemy oil refineries and installations at Ploesti, Rumania. Although he had completed more than his share of missions and was no longer connected with this group, so high was his conception of duty that he volunteered to lead the formation in the correct belief that his participation would contribute materially to success in this attack. Maj. Jerstad led the formation into attack with full realization of the extreme hazards involved and despite withering fire from heavy and light antiaircraft guns. Three miles from the target his airplane was hit, badly damaged, and set on fire. Ignoring the fact that he was flying over a field suitable for a forced landing, he kept on the course. After the bombs of his aircraft were released on the target, the fire in his ship became so intense as to make further progress impossible and he crashed into the target area. By his voluntary acceptance of a mission he knew was extremely hazardous, and his assumption of an intrepid course of action at the risk of life over and above the call of duty, Maj. Jerstad set an example of heroism which will be an inspiration to the U.S. Armed Forces.

*JOHNSON, ELDEN H.

Rank and organization: Private, U.S. Army, 15th Infantry, 3d Infantry Division. *Place and date:* Near Valmontone, Italy, 3 June 1944. *Entered service at:* East Weymouth, Mass. *Birth:* Bivalue, N.J. *G.O. No.:* 38, 16 May 1945. *Citation:* For conspicuous gallantry and intrepidity at risk of life above and beyond the call of duty. Pvt. Johnson elected to sacrifice his life in order that his comrades might extricate themselves from an ambush. Braving the massed fire of about 60 riflemen, 3 machineguns, and 3 tanks from positions only 25 yards distant, he stood erect and signaled his patrol leader to withdraw. The whole area was brightly illuminated by enemy flares. Then, despite 20-mm. machineguns, machine pistol, and rifle fire directed at him, Pvt. Johnson advanced beyond the enemy in a slow deliberate walk. Firing his automatic rifle from the hip, he succeeded in distracting the enemy and enabled his 12 comrades to escape. Advancing to within 5 yards of a machinegun, emptying his weapon, Pvt. Johnson killed its crew. Standing in full view of the enemy he reloaded and turned on the riflemen to the left, firing directly into their positions. He either killed or wounded 4 of them. A burst of machinegun fire tore into Pvt. Johnson and he dropped to his knees. Fighting to the very last, he steadied himself on his knees and sent a final burst of fire crashing into another German. With that he slumped forward dead. Pvt. Johnson had willingly given his life in order that his comrades might live. These acts on the part of Pvt. Johnson were an inspiration to the entire command and are in keeping with the highest traditions of the armed forces.

JOHNSON, LEON W. (Air Mission)

Rank and organization: Colonel, U.S. Army Air Corps, 44th Bomber Group, 9th Air Force. *Place and date:* Ploesti Raid, Rumania, 1 August 1943. *Entered service at:* Moline, Kans. *Born:* 13 September 1904, Columbia, Mo. *G.O. No.:* 54, 7 September 1943. *Citation:* For conspicuous gallantry in action and intrepidity at the risk of his life above and beyond the call of duty on 1 August 1943. Col. Johnson, as commanding officer of a heavy bombardment group, let the formation of the aircraft of his organization constituting the fourth element of the mass low-level bombing attack of the 9th U.S. Air Force against the vitally important enemy target of the Ploesti oil refineries. While proceeding to the target on this 2,400-mile flight, his element became separated from the leading elements of the mass formation in maintaining the formation of the unit while avoiding dangerous cumulous cloud conditions encountered over mountainous territory. Though temporarily lost, he reestablished contact with the third element and continued on the mission with this reduced force to the prearranged point of attack, where it was discovered that the target assigned to Col. Johnson's group had been attacked and damaged by a preceding element. Though having lost the element of surprise upon which the safety and success of such a daring form of mission in heavy bombardment aircraft so strongly depended, Col. Johnson elected to carry out his planned low-level attack despite the thoroughly alerted defenses, the destructive antiaircraft fire, enemy fighter airplanes, the imminent danger of exploding delayed action bombs from the previous element, of oil fires and explosions, and of intense smoke obscuring the target. By his gallant courage, brilliant leadership, and superior flying skill, Col. Johnson so led his formation as to destroy totally the important refining plants and installations which were the object of his mission. Col. Johnson's personal contribution to the success of this historic raid, and the conspicuous gallantry in action, and intrepidity at the risk of his life above and beyond the call of duty demonstrated by him on this occasion constitute such deeds of valor and distinguished service as have during our Nation's history formed the finest traditions of our Armed Forces.

*JOHNSON, LEROY

Rank and organization: Sergeant, U.S. Army, Company K, 126th Infantry, 32d Infantry Division. *Place and date:* Near Limon, Leyte, Philippine Islands, 15 December 1944. *Entered service at:* Oakdale, La. *Birth:* Caney Creek, La. *G.O. No.:* 83, 2 October 1945. *Citation:* He was squad leader of a 9-man patrol sent to reconnoiter a ridge held by a well-entrenched enemy force. Seeing an enemy machinegun position, he ordered his men to remain behind while he crawled to within 6 yards of the gun. One of the enemy crew jumped up and prepared to man the weapon. Quickly withdrawing, Sgt. Johnson rejoined his patrol and reported the situation to his commanding officer. Ordered to destroy the gun, which covered the approaches to several other enemy positions, he chose 3 other men, armed them with hand grenades, and led them to a point near the objective. After taking partial cover behind a log, the men had knocked out the gun and begun an assault when hostile troops on the flank hurled several grenades. As he started for cover, Sgt. Johnson saw 2 unexploded grenades which had fallen near his men. Knowing that his comrades would be wounded or killed by the explosion, he deliberately threw himself on the grenades and received their full charge in his body. Fatally wounded by the blast, he died soon afterward. Through his outstanding gallantry in sacrificing his life for his comrades, Sgt. Johnson provided a shining example of the highest traditions of the U.S. Army.

JOHNSON, OSCAR G.

Rank and organization: Sergeant, U.S. Army, Company B, 363d Infantry, 91st Infantry Division. *Place and date:* Near Scarperia, Italy, 16–18 September 1944. *Entered service at:* Foster City, Mich. *Birth:* Foster City, Mich. *G.O. No.:* 58, 19 July 1945. *Citation:* (then Pfc.) He practically singlehanded protected the left flank of his company's position in the offensive to break the German's gothic line. Company B was the extreme left assault unit of the corps. The advance was stopped by heavy fire from Monticelli Ridge, and the company took cover behind an embankment. Sgt. Johnson, a mortar gunner, having expended his ammunition, assumed the duties of a rifleman. As leader of a squad of 7 men he was ordered to establish a combat post 50 yards to the left of the company to cover its exposed flank. Repeated enemy counterattacks, supported by artillery, mortar, and machinegun fire from the high ground to his front, had by the afternoon of 16 September killed or wounded all his men. Collecting weapons and ammunition from his fallen comrades, in the face of hostile fire, he held his exposed position and inflicted heavy casualties upon the enemy, who several times came close enough to throw handgrenades. On the night of 16–17 September, the enemy launched his heaviest attack on Company B, putting his greatest pressure against the lone defender of the left flank. In spite of mortar fire which crashed about him and machine-gun bullets which whipped the crest of his shallow trench, Sgt. Johnson stood erect and repulsed the attack with grenades and small-arms fire. He remained awake and on the alert throughout the night, frustrating all attempts at infiltration. On 17 September, 25 German soldiers surrendered to him. Two men, sent to reinforce him that afternoon, were caught in a devastating mortar and artillery barrage. With no thought of his own safety, Sgt. Johnson rushed to the shellhole where they lay half buried and seriously wounded, covered their position by his fire, and assisted a Medical Corpsman in rendering aid. That night he secured their removal to the rear and remained on watch until his company was relieved. Five companies of a German paratroop regiment had been repeatedly committed to the attack on Company B without success. Twenty dead Germans were found in front of his position. By his heroic stand and utter disregard for personal safety, Sgt. Johnson was in a large measure responsible for defeating the enemy's attempts to turn the exposed left flank.

JOHNSTON, WILLIAM J.

Rank and organization: Private First Class, U.S. Army, Company G, 180th Infantry, 45th Infantry Division. *Place and date:* Near Padiglione, Italy, 17–19 February 1944. *Entered service at:* Colchester, Conn. *Birth:* Trenton, N.J. *G.O. No.:* 73, 6 September 1944. *Citation:* For conspicuous gallantry and intrepidity at risk of life above and beyond the call of duty in action against the enemy. On 17 February 1944, near Padiglione, Italy, he observed and fired upon an attacking force of approximately 80 Germans, causing at least 25 casualties and forcing withdrawal of the remainder. All that day he manned his gun without relief, subject to mortar, artillery, and sniper fire. Two Germans individually worked so close to his position that his machinegun was ineffective, whereupon he killed 1 with his pistol, the second with a rifle taken from another soldier. When a rifleman protecting his gun position was killed by a sniper, he immediately moved the body and relocated the machinegun in that spot in order to obtain a better field of fire. He volunteered to cover the platoon's withdrawal and was the last man to leave that night. In his new position he maintained an all-night vigil, the next day causing 7 German casualties. On the afternoon of the 18th, the organization on the left flank having been forced to withdraw, he again covered the withdrawal of his own organization. Shortly thereafter, he was seriously wounded over the heart, and a passing soldier saw him trying to crawl up the embankment. The soldier aided him to resume his position behind the machinegun which was soon heard in action for about 10 minutes. Though reported killed, Pfc. Johnston was seen returning to the American lines on the morning of 19 February slowly and painfully working his way back from his overrun position through enemy lines. He gave valuable information of new enemy dispositions. His heroic determination to destroy the enemy and his disregard of his own safety aided immeasurably in halting a strong enemy attack, caused an enormous amount of enemy casualties, and so inspired his fellow soldiers that they fought for and held a vitally important position against greatly superior forces.

*JONES, HERBERT CHARPOIT

Rank and organization: Ensign, U.S. Naval Reserve. *Born:* 1 December 1918, Los Angeles, Calif. *Accredited to:* California. *Citation:* For conspicuous devotion to duty, extraordinary courage, and complete disregard of his own life, above and beyond the call of duty, during the attack on the Fleet in Pearl Harbor, by Japanese forces on 7 December 1941. Ens. Jones organized and led a party, which was supplying ammunition to the antiaircraft battery of the U.S.S. *California* after the mechanical hoists were put out of action when he was fatally wounded by a bomb explosion. When 2 men attempted to take him from the area which was on fire, he refused to let them do so, saying in words to the effect, "Leave me alone! I am done for. Get out of here before the magazines go off."

*JULIAN, JOSEPH RODOLPH

Rank and organization: Platoon Sergeant, U.S. Marine Corps Reserve. *Born:* 3 April 1918, Sturbridge, Mass. *Accredited to:* Massachusetts. *Citation:* For conspicuous gallantry and intrepidity at the risk of his life above and beyond the call of duty as a P/Sgt. serving with the 1st Battalion, 27th Marines, 5th Marine Division, in action against enemy Japanese forces during the seizure of Iwo Jima in the Volcano Islands, 9 March 1945. Determined to force a breakthrough when Japanese troops occupying trenches and fortified positions on the left front laid down a terrific machinegun and mortar barrage in a desperate effort to halt his company's advance, P/Sgt. Julian quickly established his platoon's guns in strategic supporting positions, and then, acting on his own initiative, fearlessly moved forward to execute a 1-man assault on the nearest pillbox. Advancing alone, he hurled deadly demolitions and white phosphorus grenades into the emplacement, killing 2 of the enemy and driving the remaining 5 out into the adjoining trench system. Seizing a discarded rifle, he jumped into the trench and dispatched the 5 before they could make an escape. Intent on wiping out all resistance, he obtained more explosives and, accompanied by another marine, again charged the hostile fortifications and knocked out 2 more cave positions. Immediately thereafter, he launched a bazooka attack unassisted, firing 4 rounds into the 1 remaining pillbox and completely destroying it before he fell, mortally wounded by a vicious burst of enemy fire. Stouthearted and indomitable, P/Sgt. Julian consistently disregarded all personal danger and, by his bold decision, daring tactics, and relentless fighting spirit during a critical phase of the battle, contributed materially to the continued advance of his company and to the success of his division's operations in the sustained drive toward the conquest of this fiercely defended outpost of the Japanese Empire. His outstanding valor and unfaltering spirit of self-sacrifice throughout the bitter conflict sustained and enhanced the highest traditions of the U.S. Naval Service. He gallantly gave his life for his country.

*KANDLE, VICTOR L.

Rank and organization: First Lieutenant, U.S. Army, 15th Infantry, 3d Infantry Division. *Place and date:* Near La Forge, France, 9 October 1944. *Entered service at:* Redwood City, Calif. *Birth:* Roy, Wash. *G.O. No.:* 37, 11 May 1945. *Citation:* For conspicuous gallantry and intrepidity at risk of his life above and beyond the call of duty. On 9 October 1944, at about noon, near La Forge, France, 1st Lt. Kandle, while leading a reconnaissance patrol into enemy territory, engaged in a duel at pointblank range with a German field officer and killed him. Having already taken 5 enemy prisoners that morning, he led a skeleton platoon of 16 men, reinforced with a light machinegun squad, through fog and over precipitous mountain terrain to fall on the rear of a German quarry stronghold which had checked the advance of an infantry battalion for 2 days. Rushing forward, several yards ahead of his assault elements, 1st Lt. Kandle fought his way into the heart of the enemy strongpoint, and, by his boldness and audacity, forced the Germans to surrender. Harassed by machinegun fire from a position which he had bypassed in the dense fog, he moved to within 15 yards of the enemy, killed a German machinegunner with accurate rifle fire and led his men in the destruction of another machinegun crew and its rifle security elements. Finally, he led his small force against a fortified house held by 2 German officers and 30 enlisted men. After establishing a base of fire, he rushed forward alone through an open clearing in full view of the enemy, smashed through a barricaded door, and forced all 32 Germans to surrender. His intrepidity and bold leadership resulted in the capture or killing of 3 enemy officers and 54 enlisted men, the destruction of 3 enemy strongpoints, and the seizure of enemy positions which had halted a battalion attack.

KANE, JOHN R. (Air Mission)

Rank and organization: Colonel, U.S. Army Air Corps, 9th Air Force. *Place and date:* Ploetsi Raid, Rumania, 1 August 1943. *Entered service at:* Shreveport, La. *Birth:* McGregor, Tex. *G.O. No.:* 54, 9 August 1943. *Citation:* For conspicuous gallantry in action and intrepidity at the risk of his life above and beyond the call of duty on 1 August 1943. On this date he led the third element of heavy bombardment aircraft in a mass low-level bombing attack against the vitally important enemy target of the Ploesti oil refineries. En route to the target, which necessitated a round-trip flight of over 2,400 miles, Col. Kane's element became separated from the leading portion of the massed formation in avoiding dense and dangerous cumulous cloud conditions over mountainous terrain. Rather than turn back from such a vital mission he elected to proceed to his target. Upon arrival at the target area it was discovered that another group had apparently missed its target and had previously attacked and damaged the target assigned to Col. Kane's element. Despite the thoroughly warned defenses, the intensive antiaircraft fire, enemy fighter airplanes, extreme hazards on a low-level attack of exploding delayed action bombs from the previous element, of oil fires and explosions and dense smoke over the target area, Col. Kane elected to lead his formation into the attack. By his gallant courage, brilliant leadership, and superior flying skill, he and the formation under his command successfully attacked this vast refinery so essential to our enemies' war effort. Through his conspicuous gallantry in this most hazardous action against the enemy, and by his intrepidity at the risk of his life above and beyond the call of duty, Col. Kane personally contributed vitally to the success of this daring mission and thereby rendered most distinguished service in the furtherance of the defeat of our enemies.

KEARBY, NEEL E. (Air Mission)

Rank and organization: Colonel, U.S. Army Air Corps. *Place and date:* Near Wewak, New Guinea, 11 October 1943. *Entered service at:* Dallas, Tex. *Birth:* Wichita Falls, Tex. *G.O. No.:* 3, 6 January 1944. *Citation:* For conspicuous gallantry and intrepidity above and beyond the call of duty in action with the enemy, Col. Kearby volunteered to lead a flight of 4 fighters to reconnoiter the strongly defended enemy base at Wewak. Having observed enemy installations and reinforcements at 4 airfields, and secured important tactical information, he saw an enemy fighter below him, made a diving attack and shot it down in flames. The small formation then sighted approximately 12 enemy bombers accompanied by 36 fighters. Although his mission had been completed, his fuel was running low, and the numerical odds were 12 to 1, he gave the signal to attack. Diving into the midst of the enemy airplanes he shot down 3 in quick succession. Observing 1 of his comrades with 2 enemy fighters in pursuit, he destroyed both enemy aircraft. The enemy broke off in large numbers to make a multiple attack on his airplane but despite his peril he made one more pass before seeking cloud protection. Coming into the clear, he called his flight together and led them to a friendly base. Col. Kearby brought down 6 enemy aircraft in this action, undertaken with superb daring after his mission was completed.

*KEATHLEY, GEORGE D.

Rank and organization: Staff Sergeant, U.S. Army, 85th Infantry Division. *Place and date:* Mt. Altuzzo, Italy, 14 September 1944. *Entered service at:* Lamesa, Tex. *Birth:* Olney, Tex. *G.O. No.:* 20, 29 March 1945. *Citation:* For conspicuous gallantry and intrepidity at risk of life above and beyond the call of duty, in action on the western ridge of Mount Altuzzo, Italy. After bitter fighting his company had advanced to within 50 yards of the objective, where it was held up due to intense enemy sniper, automatic, small-arms, and mortar fire. The enemy launched 3 desperate counterattacks in an effort to regain their former positions, but all 3 were repulsed with heavy casualties on both sides. All officers and noncommissioned officers of the 2d and 3d platoons of Company B had become casualties, and S/Sgt. Keathley, guide of the 1st platoon, moved up and assumed command of both the 2d and 3d platoons, reduced to 20 men. The remnants of the 2 platoons were dangerously low on ammunition, so S/Sgt. Keathley, under deadly small-arms and mortar fire, crawled from 1 casualty to another, collecting their ammunition and administering first aid. He then visited each man of his 2 platoons, issuing the precious ammunition he had collected from the dead and wounded, and giving them words of encouragement. The enemy now delivered their fourth counterattack, which was approximately 2 companies in strength. In a furious charge they attacked from the front and both flanks, throwing handgrenades, firing automatic weapons, and assisted by a terrific mortar barrage. So strong was the enemy counterattack that the company was given up for lost. The remnants of the 2d and 3d platoons of Company B were now looking to S/Sgt. Keathley for leadership. He shouted his orders precisely and with determination and the men responded with all that was in them. Time after time the enemy tried to drive a wedge into S/Sgt. Keathley's position and each time they were driven back, suffering huge casualties. Suddenly an enemy handgrenade hit and exploded near S/Sgt. Keathley, inflicting a mortal wound in his left side. However, hurling defiance at the enemy, he rose to his feet. Taking his left hand away from his wound and using it to steady his rifle, he fired and killed an attacking enemy soldier, and continued shouting orders to his men. His heroic and intrepid action so inspired his men that they fought with incomparable determination and viciousness. For 15 minutes S/Sgt. Keathley continued leading his men and effectively firing his rifle. He could have sought a sheltered spot and perhaps saved his life, but instead he elected to set an example for his men and make every possible effort to hold his position. Finally, friendly artillery fire helped to force the enemy to withdraw, leaving behind many of their number either dead or seriously wounded. S/Sgt. Keathley died a few moments later. Had it not been for his indomitable courage and incomparable heroism, the remnants of 3 rifle platoons of Company B might well have been annihilated by the overwhelming enemy attacking force. His actions were in keeping with the highest traditions of the military service.

*KEFURT, GUS

Rank and organization: Staff Sergeant, U.S. Army, Company K, 15th Infantry, 3d Infantry Division. *Place and date:* Near Bennwihr, France, 23–24 December 1944. *Entered service at:* Youngstown, Ohio. *Birth:* Greenville, Pa. *Citation:* He distinguished himself by conspicuous gallantry and intrepidity above and beyond the call of duty on 23 and 24 December 1944, near Bennwihr, France. Early in the attack S/Sgt. Kefurt jumped through an opening in a wall to be confronted by about 15 Germans. Although outnumbered he opened fire, killing 10 and capturing the others. During a seesaw battle which developed he effectively adjusted artillery fire on an enemy tank close to his position although exposed to small-arms fire. When night fell he maintained a 3-man outpost in the center of the town in the middle of the German positions and successfully fought off several hostile patrols attempting to penetrate our lines. Assuming command of his platoon the following morning he led it in hand-to-hand fighting through the town until blocked by a tank. Using rifle grenades he forced surrender of its crew and some supporting infantry. He then continued his attack from house to house against heavy machinegun and rifle fire. Advancing against a strongpoint that was holding up the company, his platoon was subjected to a strong counterattack and infiltration to its rear. Suffering heavy casualties in their exposed position the men remained there due to S/Sgt. Kefurt's personal example of bravery, determination and leadership. He constantly exposed himself to fire by going from man to man to direct fire. During this time he killed approximately 15 of the enemy at close range. Although severely wounded in the leg he refused first aid and immediately resumed fighting. When the forces to his rear were pushed back 3 hours later, he refused to be evacuated, but, during several more counterattacks moved painfully about under intense small-arms and mortar fire, stiffening the resistance of his platoon by encouraging individual men and by his own fire until he was killed. As a result of S/Sgt. Kefurt's gallantry the position was maintained.

*KELLEY, JONAH E.

Rank and organization: Staff Sergeant, U.S. Army, 311th Infantry, 78th Infantry Division. *Place and date:* Kesternich, Germany, 30–31 January 1945. *Entered service at:* Keyser, W. Va. *Birth:* Roda, W. Va. *G.O. No.:* 77, 10 September 1945. *Citation:* In charge of the leading squad of Company E, he heroically spearheaded the attack in furious house-to-house fighting. Early on 30 January, he led his men through intense mortar and small-arms fire in repeated assaults on barricaded houses. Although twice wounded, once when struck in the back, the second time when a mortar shell fragment passed through his left hand and rendered it practically useless, he refused to withdraw and continued to lead his squad after hasty dressings had been applied. His serious wounds forced him to fire his rifle with 1 hand, resting it on rubble or over his left forearm. To blast his way forward with handgrenades, he set aside his rifle to pull the pins with his teeth while grasping the missiles with his good hand. Despite these handicaps, he created tremendous havoc in the enemy ranks. He rushed 1 house, killing 3 of the enemy and clearing the way for his squad to advance. On approaching the next house, he was fired upon from an upstairs window. He killed the sniper with a single shot and similarly accounted for another enemy soldier who ran from the cellar of the house. As darkness came, he assigned his men to defensive positions, never leaving them to seek medical attention. At dawn the next day, the squad resumed the attack, advancing to a point where heavy automatic and small-arms fire stalled them. Despite his wounds, S/Sgt. Kelley moved out alone, located an enemy gunner dug in under a haystack and killed him with rifle fire. He returned to his men and found that a German machine-gun, from a well-protected position in a neighboring house, still held up the advance. Ordering the squad to remain in comparatively safe positions, he valiantly dashed into the open and attacked the position singlehandedly through a hail of bullets. He was hit several times and fell to his knees when within 25 yards of his objective; but he summoned his waning strength and emptied his rifle into the machinegun nest, silencing the weapon before he died. The superb courage, aggressiveness, and utter disregard for his own safety displayed by S/Sgt. Kelley inspired the men he led and enabled them to penetrate the last line of defense held by the enemy in the village of Kesternich.

*KELLEY, OVA A.

Rank and organization: Private, U.S. Army, Company A, 382d Infantry, 96th Infantry Division. *Place and date:* Leyte, Philippine Islands, 8 December 1944. *Entered service at:* Norwood, Mo. *Birth:* Norwood, Mo. *G.O. No.:* 89, 19 October 1945. *Citation:* For conspicuous gallantry and intrepidity at the risk of his life above and beyond the call of duty. Before dawn, near the edge of the enemy-held Buri airstrip, the company was immobilized by heavy, accurate rifle and machinegun fire from hostile troops entrenched in bomb craters and a ditch less than 100 yards distant. The company commander ordered a mortar concentration which destroyed 1 machinegun but failed to dislodge the main body of the enemy. At this critical moment Pvt. Kelley, on his own initiative, left his shallow foxhole with an armload of handgrenades and began a 1-man assault on the foe. Throwing his missiles with great accuracy, he moved forward, killed or wounded 5 men, and forced the remainder to flee in a disorganized route. He picked up a M1 rifle and emptied its clip at the running Japanese, killing 3. Discarding this weapon, he took a carbine and killed 3 more of the enemy. Inspired by his example, his comrades followed him in a charge which destroyed the entire enemy force of 34 enlisted men and 2 officers and captured 2 heavy and 1 light machineguns. Pvt. Kelley continued to press the attack on to an airstrip, where sniper fire wounded him so grievously that he died 2 days later. His outstanding courage, aggressiveness, and initiative in the face of grave danger was an inspiration to his entire company and led to the success of the attack.

KELLY, CHARLES E.

Rank and organization: Corporal, U.S. Army, Company L, 143d Infantry, 36th Infantry Division. *Place and date:* Near Altavilla, Italy, 13 September 1943. *Entered service at:* Pittsburgh, Pa. *Birth:* Pittsburgh, Pa. *G.O. No.:* 13, 18 February 1944. *Citation:* For conspicuous gallantry and intrepidity at risk of life above and beyond the call of duty. On 13 September 1943, near Altavilla, Italy, Cpl. Kelly voluntarily joined a patrol which located and neutralized enemy machinegun positions. After this hazardous duty he volunteered to establish contact with a battalion of U.S. infantry which was believed to be located on Hill 315, a mile distant. He traveled over a route commanded by enemy observation and under sniper, mortar, and artillery fire; and later he returned with the correct information that the enemy occupied Hill 315 in organized positions. Immediately thereafter Cpl. Kelly, again a volunteer patrol member, assisted materially in the destruction of 2 enemy machinegun nests under conditions requiring great skill and courage. Having effectively fired his weapon until all the ammunition was exhausted, he secured permission to obtain more at an ammunition dump. Arriving at the dump, which was located near a storehouse on the extreme flank of his regiment's position, Cpl. Kelly found that the Germans were attacking ferociously at this point. He obtained his ammunition and was given the mission of protecting the rear of the storehouse. He held his position throughout the night. The following morning the enemy attack was resumed. Cpl. Kelly took a position at an open window of the storehouse. One machine gunner had been killed at this position and several other soldiers wounded. Cpl. Kelly delivered continuous aimed and effective fire upon the enemy with his automatic rifle until the weapon locked from overheating. Finding another automatic rifle, he again directed effective fire upon the enemy until this weapon also locked. At this critical point, with the enemy threatening to overrun the position, Cpl. Kelly picked up 60-mm. mortar shells, pulled the safety pins, and used the shells as grenades, killing at least 5 of the enemy. When it became imperative that the house be evacuated, Cpl. Kelly, despite his sergeant's injunctions, volunteered to hold the position until the remainder of the detachment could withdraw. As the detachment moved out, Cpl. Kelly was observed deliberately loading and firing a rocket launcher from the window. He was successful in covering the withdrawal of the unit, and later in joining his own organization. Cpl. Kelly's fighting determination and intrepidity in battle exemplify the highest traditions of the U.S. Armed Forces.

*KELLY, JOHN D.

Rank and organization: Technical Sergeant (then Corporal), U.S. Army, Company E, 314th Infantry, 79th Infantry Division. *Place and date:* Fort du Roule, Cherbourg, France, 25 June 1944. *Entered service at:* Cambridge Springs, Pa. *Birth:* Venango Township, Pa. *G.O. No.:* 6, 24 January 1945. *Citation:* For conspicuous gallantry and intrepidity at the risk of his life above and beyond the call of duty. On 25 June 1944, in the vicinity of Fort du Roule, Cherbourg, France, when Cpl. Kelly's unit was pinned down by heavy enemy machinegun fire emanating from a deeply entrenched strongpoint on the slope leading up to the fort, Cpl. Kelly volunteered to attempt to neutralize the strongpoint. Arming himself with a pole charge about 10 feet long and with 15 pounds of explosive affixed, he climbed the slope under a withering blast of machinegun fire and placed the charge at the strongpoint's base. The subsequent blast was ineffective, and again, alone and unhesitatingly, he braved the slope to repeat the operation. This second blast blew off the ends of the enemy guns. Cpl. Kelly then climbed the slope a third time to place a pole charge at the strongpoint's rear entrance. When this had been blown open he hurled handgrenades inside the position, forcing survivors of the enemy guncrews to come out and surrender. The gallantry, tenacity of purpose, and utter disregard for personal safety displayed by Cpl. Kelly were an incentive to his comrades and worthy of emulation by all.

KELLY, THOMAS J.

Rank and organization: Corporal, U.S. Army, Medical Detachment, 48th Armored Infantry Battalion, 7th Armored Division. *Place and date:* Alemert, Germany, 5 April 1945. *Entered service at:* Brooklyn, N.Y. *Birth:* Brooklyn, N.Y. *G.O. No.:* 97, 1 November 1945. *Citation:* He was an aid man with the 1st Platoon of Company C during an attack on the town of Alemert, Germany. The platoon, committed in a flanking maneuver, had advanced down a small, open valley overlooked by wooded slopes hiding enemy machineguns and tanks, when the attack was stopped by murderous fire that inflicted heavy casualties in the American ranks. Ordered to withdraw, Cpl. Kelly reached safety with uninjured remnants of the unit, but, on realizing the extent of casualties suffered by the platoon, voluntarily retraced his steps and began evacuating his comrades under direct machinegun fire. He was forced to crawl, dragging the injured behind him for most of the 300 yards separating the exposed area from a place of comparative safety. Two other volunteers who attempted to negotiate the hazardous route with him were mortally wounded, but he kept on with his herculean task after dressing their wounds and carrying them to friendly hands. In all, he made 10 separate trips through the brutal fire, each time bringing out a man from the death trap. Seven more casualties who were able to crawl by themselves he guided and encouraged in escaping from the hail of fire. After he had completed his heroic, self-imposed task and was near collapse from fatigue, he refused to leave his platoon until the attack had been resumed and the objective taken. Cpl. Kelly's gallantry and intrepidity in the face of seemingly certain death saved the lives of many of his fellow soldiers and was an example of bravery under fire.

*KEPPLER, REINHARDT JOHN

Rank and organization: Boatswain's Mate First Class, U.S. Navy. *Born:* 22 January 1918, Ralston, Wash. *Accredited to:* Washington. *Other Navy award:* Navy Cross. *Citation:* For extraordinary heroism and distinguished courage above and beyond the call of duty while serving aboard the U.S.S. *San Francisco* during action against enemy Japanese forces in the Solomon Islands, 12–13 November 1942. When a hostile torpedo plane, during a daylight air raid, crashed on the after machinegun platform, Keppler promptly assisted in removal of the dead and, by his capable supervision of the wounded, undoubtedly helped save the lives of several shipmates who otherwise might have perished. That night, when the ship's hangar was set afire during the great battle off Savo Island, he bravely led a hose into the starboard side of the stricken area and there, without assistance and despite frequent hits from terrific enemy bombardment, eventually brought the fire under control. Later, although mortally wounded, he labored valiantly in the midst of bursting shells, persistently directing firefighting operations and administering to wounded personnel until he finally collapsed from loss of blood. His great personal valor, maintained with utter disregard of personal safety, was in keeping with the highest traditions of the U.S. Naval Service. He gallantly gave his life for his country.

KERSTETTER, DEXTER J.

Rank and organization: Private First Class, U.S. Army, Company C, 130th Infantry, 33d Infantry Division. *Place and date:* Near Galiano, Luzon, Philippine Islands, 13 April 1945. *Entered service at:* Centralia, Wash. *Birth:* Centralia, Wash. *G.O. No.:* 97, 1 November 1945. *Citation:* He was with his unit in a dawn attack against hill positions approachable only along a narrow ridge paralleled on each side by steep cliffs which were heavily defended by enemy mortars, machineguns, and rifles in well-camouflaged spider holes and tunnels leading to caves. When the leading element was halted by intense fire that inflicted 5 casualties, Pfc. Kerstetter passed through the American line with his squad. Placing himself well in advance of his men, he grimly worked his way up the narrow steep hogback, meeting the brunt of enemy action. With well-aimed shots and rifle-grenade fire, he forced the Japs to take cover. He left the trail and moving down a cliff that offered only precarious footholds, dropped among 4 Japs at the entrance to a cave, fired his rifle from his hip and killed them all. Climbing back to the trail, he advanced against heavy enemy machinegun, rifle, and mortar fire to silence a heavy machinegun by killing its crew of 4 with rifle fire and grenades. He expended his remaining ammunition and grenades on a group of approximately 20 Japs, scattering them, and returned to his squad for more ammunition and first aid for his left hand, which had been blistered by the heat from his rifle. Resupplied, he guided a fresh platoon into a position from which a concerted attack could be launched, killing 3 hostile soldiers on the way. In all, he dispatched 16 Japs that day. The hill was taken and held against the enemy's counterattacks, which continued for 3 days. Pfc. Kerstetter's dauntless and gallant heroism was largely responsible for the capture of this key enemy position, and his fearless attack in the face of great odds was an inspiration to his comrades in their dangerous task.

*KESSLER, PATRICK L.

Rank and organization: Private First Class, U.S. Army, Company K, 30th Infantry, 3d Infantry Division. *Place and date:* Near Ponte Rotto, Italy, 23 May 1944. *Entered service at:* Middletown, Ohio. *Birth:* Middletown, Ohio. *G.O. No.:* 1, 4 January 1945. *Citation:* For conspicuous gallantry and intrepidity at risk of life above and beyond the call of duty. Pfc. Kessler, acting without orders, raced 50 yards through a hail of machinegun fire, which had killed 5 of his comrades and halted the advance of his company, in order to form an assault group to destroy the machinegun. Ordering 3 men to act as a base of fire, he left the cover of a ditch and snaked his way to a point within 50 yards of the enemy machinegun before he was discovered, whereupon he plunged headlong into the furious chain of automatic fire. Reaching a spot within 6 feet of the emplacement he stood over it and killed both the gunner and his assistant, jumped into the gun position, overpowered and captured a third German after a short struggle. The remaining member of the crew escaped, but Pfc. Kessler wounded him as he ran. While taking his prisoner to the rear, this soldier saw 2 of his comrades killed as they assaulted an enemy strongpoint, fire from which had already killed 10 men in the company. Turning his prisoner over to another man, Pfc. Kessler crawled 35 yards to the side of 1 of the casualties, relieved him of his BAR and ammunition and continued on toward the strongpoint, 125 yards distant. Although 2 machineguns concentrated their fire directly on him and shells exploded within 10 yards, bowling him over, Pfc. Kessler crawled 75 yards, passing through an antipersonnel minefield to a point within 50 yards of the enemy and engaged the machineguns in a duel. When an artillery shell burst within a few feet of him, he left the cover of a ditch and advanced upon the position in a slow walk, firing his BAR from the hip. Although the enemy poured heavy machinegun and small-arms fire at him, Pfc. Kessler succeeded in reaching the edge of their position, killed the gunners, and captured 13 Germans. Then, despite continuous shelling, he started to the rear. After going 25 yards, Pfc. Kessler was fired upon by 2 snipers only 100 yards away. Several of his prisoners took advantage of this opportunity and attempted to escape; however, Pfc. Kessler hit the ground, fired on either flank of his prisoners, forcing them to cover, and then engaged the 2 snipers in a fire fight, and captured them. With this last threat removed, Company K continued its advance, capturing its objective without further opposition. Pfc. Kessler was killed in a subsequent action.

*KIDD, ISAAC CAMPBELL

Rank and organization: Rear Admiral, U.S. Navy. *Born:* 26 March 1884, Cleveland, Ohio. *Appointed from:* Ohio. *Citation:* For conspicuous devotion to duty, extraordinary courage and complete disregard of his own life, during the attack on the Fleet in Pearl Harbor, by Japanese forces on 7 December 1941. Rear Adm. Kidd immediately went to the bridge and, as Commander Battleship Division One, courageously discharged his duties as Senior Officer Present Afloat until the U.S.S. *Arizona*, his Flagship, blew up from magazine explosions and a direct bomb hit on the bridge which resulted in the loss of his life.

*KIMBRO, TRUMAN

Rank and organization: Technician Fourth Grade, U.S. Army, Company C, 2d Engineer Combat Battalion, 2d Infantry Division. *Place and date:* Near Rocherath, Belgium, 19 December 1944. *Entered service at:* Houston, Tex. *Birth:* Madisonville, Tex. *G.O. No.:* 42, 24 May 1945.

Citation: On 19 December 1944, as scout, he led a squad assigned to the mission of mining a vital crossroads near Rocherath, Belgium. At the first attempt to reach the objective, he discovered it was occupied by an enemy tank and at least 20 infantrymen. Driven back by withering fire, Technician 4th Grade Kimbro made 2 more attempts to lead his squad to the crossroads but all approaches were covered by intense enemy fire. Although warned by our own infantrymen of the great danger involved, he left his squad in a protected place and, laden with mines, crawled alone toward the crossroads. When nearing his objective he was severely wounded, but he continued to drag himself forward and laid his mines across the road. As he tried to crawl from the objective his body was riddled with rifle and machinegun fire. The mines laid by his act of indomitable courage delayed the advance of enemy armor and prevented the rear of our withdrawing columns from being attacked by the enemy.

*KINER, HAROLD G.

Rank and organization: Private, U.S. Army, Company F, 117th Infantry, 30th Infantry Division. *Place and date:* Near Palenberg, Germany, 2 October 1944. *Entered service at:* Enid, Okla. *Birth:* Aline, Okla. *G.O. No.:* 48, 23 June 1945. With 4 other men, he was leading in a frontal assault 2 October 1944, on a Siegfried Line pillbox near Palenberg, Germany. Machinegun fire from the strongly defended enemy position 25 yards away pinned down the attackers. The Germans threw handgrenades, 1 of which dropped between Pvt. Kiner and 2 other men. With no hesitation, Private Kiner hurled himself upon the grenade, smothering the explosion. By his gallant action and voluntary sacrifice of his own life, he saved his 2 comrades from serious injury or death.

*KINGSLEY, DAVID R. (Air Mission)

Rank and organization: Second Lieutenant, U.S. Army Air Corps, 97th Bombardment Group, 15th Air Force. *Place and date:* Ploesti Raid, Rumania, 23 June 1944. *Entered service at.* Portland, Oreg. *Birth:* Oregon. *G.O. No.:* 26, 9 April 1945. *Citation:* For conspicuous gallantry and intrepidity in action at the risk of life above and beyond the call of duty, 23 June 1944 near Ploesti, Rumania, while flying as bombardier of a B-17 type aircraft. On the bomb run 2d Lt. Kingsley's aircraft was severely damaged by intense flak and forced to drop out of formation but the pilot proceeded over the target and 2d Lt. Kingsley successfully dropped his bombs, causing severe damage to vital installations. The damaged aircraft, forced to lose altitude and to lag behind the formation, was aggressively attacked by 3 ME-109 aircraft, causing more damage to the aircraft and severely wounding the tail gunner in the upper arm. The radio operator and engineer notified 2d Lt. Kingsley that the tail gunner had been wounded and that assistance was needed to check the bleeding. 2d Lt. Kingsley made his way back to the radio room, skillfully applied first aid to the wound, and succeeded in checking the bleeding. The tail gunner's parachute harness and heavy clothes were removed and he was covered with blankets, making him as comfortable as possible. Eight ME-109 aircraft again aggressively attacked 2d Lt. Kingsley's aircraft and the ball turret gunner was wounded by 20-mm. shell fragments. He went forward to the radio room to have 2d Lt. Kingsley administer first aid. A few minutes later when the pilot gave the order to prepare to bail out, 2d Lt. Kingsley immediately began to assist the wounded gunners in putting on their parachute harness. In the confusion the tail gunner's harness, believed to have been damaged, could not be located in the bundle of blankets and flying clothes which had been removed from the wounded men. With utter disregard for his own means of escape, 2d Lt. Kingsley unhesitatingly removed his parachute harness and adjusted it to the wounded tail gunner. Due to the extensive damage caused by the accurate and concentrated 20-mm. fire by the enemy aircraft the pilot gave the order to bail out, as it appeared that the aircraft would disintegrate at any moment. 2d Lt. Kingsley aided the wounded men in bailing out and when last seen by the crewmembers he was standing on the bomb bay catwalk. The aircraft continued to fly on automatic pilot for a short distance, then crashed and burned. His body was later found in the wreckage. 2d Lt. Kingsley by his gallant heroic action was directly responsible for saving the life of the wounded gunner.

*KINSER, ELBERT LUTHER

Rank and organization: Sergeant, U.S. Marine Corps Reserve. *Born:* 21 October 1922, Greeneville, Tenn. *Accredited to:* Tennessee. *Citation:* For conspicuous gallantry and intrepidity at the risk of his life above and beyond the call of duty while acting as leader of a Rifle Platoon, serving with Company I, 3d Battalion, 1st Marines, 1st Marine Division, in action against Japanese forces on Okinawa Shima in the Ryukyu Chain, 4 May 1945. Taken under sudden, close attack by hostile troops entrenched on the reverse slope while moving up a strategic ridge along which his platoon was holding newly won positions, Sgt. Kinser engaged the enemy in a fierce handgrenade battle. Quick to act when a Japanese grenade landed in the immediate vicinity, Sgt. Kinser unhesitatingly threw himself on the deadly missile, absorbing the full charge of the shattering explosion in his own body and thereby protecting his men from serious injury and possible death. Stouthearted and indomitable, he had yielded his own chance of survival that his comrades might live to carry on the relentless battle against a fanatic enemy. His courage, cool decision and valiant spirit of self-sacrifice in the face of certain death sustained and enhanced the highest traditions of the U.S. Naval Service. He gallantly gave his life for his country.

KISTERS, GERRY H.

Rank and organization: Second Lieutenant (then Sergeant), U.S. Army, 2d Armored Division. *Place and date:* Near Gagliano, Sicily, 31 July 1943. *Entered service at:* Bloomington, Ind. *Birth:* Salt Lake City, Utah. *G.O. No.:* 13, 18 February 1944. *Citation:* On 31 July 1943, near Gagliano, Sicily, a detachment of 1 officer and 9 enlisted men, including Sgt. Kisters, advancing ahead of the leading elements of U.S. troops to fill a large crater in the only available vehicle route through Gagliano, was taken under fire by 2 enemy machine-guns. Sgt. Kisters and the officer, unaided and in the face of intense small-arms fire, advanced on the nearest machinegun emplacement and succeeded in capturing the gun and its crew of 4. Although the greater part of the remaining small-arms fire was now directed on the captured machinegun position, Sgt. Kisters voluntarily advanced alone toward the second gun emplacement. While creeping forward, he was struck 5 times by enemy bullets, receiving wounds in both legs and his right arm. Despite the wounds, he continued to advance on the enemy, and captured the second machinegun after killing 3 of its crew and forcing the fourth member to flee. The courage of this soldier and his unhesitating willingness to sacrifice his life, if necessary, served as an inspiration to the command.

KNAPPENBERGER, ALTON W.

Rank and organization: Private First Class, U.S. Army, 3d Infantry Division. *Place and date:* Near Cisterna di Littoria, Italy, 1 February 1944. *Entered service at:* Spring Mount, Pa. *Birth:* Cooperstown, Pa. *G.O. No.:* 41, 26 May 1944. *Citation:* For conspicuous gallantry and intrepidity at the risk of his life above and beyond the call of duty in action involving actual conflict with the enemy, on 1 February 1944 near Cisterna di Littoria, Italy. When a heavy German counterattack was launched against his battalion, Pfc. Knappenberger crawled to an exposed knoll and went into position with his automatic rifle. An enemy machinegun 85 yards away opened fire, and bullets struck within 6 inches of him. Rising to a kneeling position, Pfc. Knappenberger opened fire on the hostile crew, knocked out the gun, killed 2 members of the crew, and wounded the third. While he fired at this hostile position, 2 Germans crawled to a point within 20 yards of the knoll and threw potato-masher grenades at him, but Pfc. Knappenberger killed them both with 1 burst from his automatic rifle. Later, a second machinegun opened fire upon his exposed position from a distance of 100 yards, and this weapon also was silenced by his well-aimed shots. Shortly thereafter, an enemy 20-mm. antiaircraft gun directed fire at him, and again Pfc. Knappenberger returned fire to wound 1 member of the hostile crew. Under tank and artillery shellfire, with shells bursting within 15 yards of him, he held his precarious position and fired at all enemy infantrymen armed with machine pistols and machineguns which he could locate. When his ammunition supply became exhausted, he crawled 15 yards forward through steady machinegun fire, removed rifle clips from the belt of a casualty, returned to his position and resumed firing to re l an assaulting German platoon armed with automatic weapons. Fii 'y, his ammunition supply being completely exhausted, he rejoined is company. Pfc. Knappenberger's intrepid action disrupted the enemy attack for over 2 hours.

*KNIGHT, JACK L.

Rank and organization: First Lieutenant, U.S. Army, 124th Cavalry Regiment, Mars Task Force. *Place and date:* Near Loi-Kang, Burma, 2 February 1945. *Entered service at:* Weatherford, Tex. *Birth:* Garner, Tex. *G.O. No.:* 44, 6 June 1945. *Citation:* He led his cavalry troop against heavy concentrations of enemy mortar, artillery, and small-arms fire. After taking the troop's objective and while making preparations for a defense, he discovered a nest of Japanese pillboxes and fox-holes to the right front. Preceding his men by at least 10 feet, he immediately led an attack. Singlehandedly he knocked out 2 enemy pillboxes and killed the occupants of several foxholes. While attempting to knock out a third pillbox, he was struck and blinded by an enemy grenade. Although unable to see, he rallied his platoon and continued forward in the assault on the remaining pillboxes. Before the task was completed he fell mortally wounded. 1st Lt. Knight's gallantry and intrepidity were responsible for the successful elimination of most of the Jap positions and served as an inspiration to officers and men of his troop.

*KNIGHT, RAYMOND L. (Air Mission)

Rank and organization: First Lieutenant, U.S. Army Air Corps. *Place and date:* In Northern Po Valley, Italy, 24–25 April 1945. *Entered service at:* Houston, Tex. *Birth:* Texas. *G.O. No.:* 81, 24 September 1945. *Citation:* He piloted a fighter-bomber aircraft in a series of low-level strafing missions, destroying 14 grounded enemy aircraft and leading attacks which wrecked 10 others during a critical period of the Allied drive in northern Italy. On the morning of 24 April, he volunteered to lead 2 other aircraft against the strongly defended enemy airdrome at Ghedi. Ordering his fellow-pilots to remain aloft, he skimmed the ground through a deadly curtain of antiaircraft fire to reconnoiter the field, locating 8 German aircraft hidden beneath heavy camouflage. He rejoined his flight, briefed them by radio, and then led them with consummate skill through the hail of enemy fire in a low-level attack, destroying 5 aircraft, while his flight accounted for 2 others. Returning to his base, he volunteered to lead 3 other aircraft in reconnaissance of Bergamo airfield, an enemy base near Ghedi and 1 known to be equally well defended. Again ordering his flight to remain out of range of antiaircraft fire, 1st Lt. Knight flew through an exceptionally intense barrage, which heavily damaged his Thunderbolt, to observe the field at minimum altitude. He discovered a squadron of enemy aircraft under heavy camouflage and led his flight to the assault. Returning alone after this strafing, he made 10 deliberate passes against the field despite being hit by antiaircraft fire twice more, destroying 6 fully loaded enemy twin-engine aircraft and 2 fighters. His skillfully led attack enabled his flight to destroy 4 other twin-engine aircraft and a fighter plane. He then returned to his base in his seriously damaged plane. Early the next morning, when he again attacked Bergamo, he sighted an enemy plane on the runway. Again he led 3 other American pilots in a blistering low-level sweep through vicious antiaircraft fire that damaged his plane so severely that it was virtually nonflyable. Three of the few remaining enemy twin-engine aircraft at that base were destroyed. Realizing the critical need for aircraft in his unit, he declined to parachute to safety over friendly territory and unhesitatingly attempted to return his shattered plane to his home field. With great skill and strength, he flew homeward until caught by treacherous air conditions in the Appennines Mountains, where he crashed and was killed. The gallant action of 1st Lt. Knight eliminated the German aircraft which were poised to wreak havoc on Allied forces pressing to establish the first firm bridgehead across the Po

River; his fearless daring and voluntary self-sacrifice averted possible heavy casualties among ground forces and the resultant slowing on the German drive culminated in the collapse of enemy resistance in Italy.

*KRAUS, RICHARD EDWARD

Rank and organization: Private First Class, U.S. Marine Corps Reserve. *Born:* 24 November 1925, Chicago, Ill. *Accredited to:* Minnesota. *Citation:* For conspicuous gallantry and intrepidity at the risk of his life above and beyond the call of duty while serving with the 8th Amphibious Tractor Battalion, Fleet Marine Force, in action against enemy Japanese forces on Peleliu, Palau Islands, on 5 October 1944. Unhesitatingly volunteering for the extremely hazardous mission of evacuating a wounded comrade from the front lines, Pfc. Kraus and 3 companions courageously made their way forward and successfully penetrated the lines for some distance before the enemy opened with an intense, devastating barrage of handgrenades which forced the stretcher party to take cover and subsequently abandon the mission. While returning to the rear, they observed 2 men approaching who appeared to be marines and immediately demanded the password. When, instead of answering, 1 of the 2 Japanese threw a handgrenade into the midst of the group, Pfc. Kraus heroically flung himself upon the grenade and, covering it with his body, absorbed the full impact of the explosion and was instantly killed. By his prompt action and great personal valor in the face of almost certain death, he saved the lives of his 3 companions, and his loyal spirit of self-sacrifice reflects the highest credit upon himself and the U.S. Naval Service. He gallantly gave his life for his comrades.

*KROTIAK, ANTHONY L.

Rank and organization: Private First Class, U.S. Army, Company I, 148th Infantry, 37th Infantry Division. *Place and date:* Balete Pass, Luzon, Philippine Islands, 8 May 1945. *Entered service at:* Chicago, Ill. *Born:* 15 August 1915, Chicago, Ill. *G.O. No.:* 18, 13 February 1946. *Citation:* He was an acting squad leader, directing his men in consolidating a newly won position on Hill B when the enemy concentrated small-arms fire and grenades upon him and 4 others, driving them to cover in an abandoned Japanese trench. A grenade thrown from above landed in the center of the group. Instantly pushing his comrades aside and jamming the grenade into the earth with his rifle butt, he threw himself over it, making a shield of his body to protect the other men. The grenade exploded under him, and he died a few minutes later. By his extraordinary heroism in deliberately giving his life to save those of his comrades, Pfc. Krotiak set an inspiring example of utter devotion and self-sacrifice which reflects the highest traditions of the military service.

*LA BELLE, JAMES DENNIS

Rank and organization: Private First Class, U.S. Marine Corps Reserve. *Born:* 22 November 1925, Columbia Heights, Minn. *Accredited to:* Minnesota. *Citation:* For conspicuous gallantry and intrepidity at the risk of his life above and beyond the call of duty while attached to the 27th Marines, 5th Marine Division, in action against enemy Japanese forces during the seizure of Iwo Jima in the Volcano Islands, 8 March 1945. Filling a gap in the front lines during a critical phase of the battle, Pfc. LaBelle had dug into a foxhole with 2 other marines and, grimly aware of the enemy's persistent attempts to blast a way through our lines with handgrenades, applied himself with steady concentration to maintaining a sharply vigilant watch during the hazardous night hours. Suddenly a hostile grenade landed beyond reach in his foxhole. Quickly estimating the situation, he determined to save the others if possible, shouted a warning, and instantly dived on the deadly missile, absorbing the exploding charge in his own body and thereby protecting his comrades from serious injury. Stouthearted and indomitable, he had unhesitatingly relinquished his own chance of survival that his fellow marines might carry on the relentless fight against a fanatic enemy. His dauntless courage, cool decision and valiant spirit of self-sacrifice in the face of certain death reflect the highest credit upon Pfc. LaBelle and upon the U.S. Naval Service. He gallantly gave his life in the service of his country.

LAWLEY, WILLIAM R., Jr. (Air Mission)

Rank and organization: First Lieutenant, U.S. Army Air Corps, 364th Bomber Squadron, 305th Bomber Group. *Place and date:* Over Europe, 20 February 1944. *Entered service at:* Birmingham, Ala. *Born:* 23 August 1920, Leeds, Ala. *G.O. No.:* 64, 8 August 1944. *Citation:* For conspicuous gallantry and intrepidity in action above and beyond the call of duty, 20 February 1944, while serving as pilot of a B–17 aircraft on a heavy bombardment mission over enemy-occupied continental Europe. Coming off the target he was attacked by approximately 20 enemy fighters, shot out of formation, and his plane severely crippled. Eight crewmembers were wounded, the copilot was killed by a 20-mm. shell. One engine was on fire, the controls shot away, and 1st Lt. Lawley seriously and painfully wounded about the face. Forcing the copilot's body off the controls, he brought the plane out of a steep dive, flying with his left hand only. Blood covered the instruments and windshield and visibility was impossible. With a full bomb load the plane was difficult to maneuver and bombs could not be released because the racks were frozen. After the order to bail out had been given, 1 of the waist gunners informed the pilot that 2 crewmembers were so severely wounded that it would be impossible for them to bail out. With the fire in the engine spreading, the danger of an explosion was imminent. Because of the helpless condition of his wounded crewmembers 1st Lt. Lawley elected to remain with the ship and bring them to safety if it was humanly possible, giving the other crewmembers the option of bailing out. Enemy fighters again attacked but by using masterful evasive action he managed to lose them. One engine again caught on fire and was extinguished by skillful flying. 1st Lt. Lawley remained at his post, refusing first aid until he collapsed from sheer exhaustion caused by loss of blood, shock, and the energy he had expended in keeping control of his plane. He was revived by the bombardier and again took over the controls. Coming over the English coast 1 engine ran out of gasoline and had to be feathered. Another engine started to burn and continued to do so until a successful crash landing was made on a small fighter base. Through his heroism and ex-

ceptional flying skill 1st Lt. Lawley rendered outstanding distinguished
and valorous service to our Nation.

LAWS, ROBERT E.

Rank and organization: Staff Sergeant, U.S. Army, Company G,
169th Infantry, 43d Infantry Division. *Place and date:* Pangasinan
Province, Luzon, Philippine Islands, 12 January 1945. *Entered service
at:* Altoona, Pa. *Birth:* Altoona, Pa. *G.O. No.:* 77, 10 September 1945.
Citation: He led the assault squad when Company G attacked enemy
hill positions. The enemy force, estimated to be a reinforced infantry
company, was well supplied with machineguns, ammunition, grenades,
and blocks of TNT and could be attacked only across a narrow ridge
70 yards long. At the end of this ridge an enemy pillbox and rifle positions were set in rising ground. Covered by his squad, S/Sgt. Laws
traversed the hogback through vicious enemy fire until close to the
pillbox, where he hurled grenades at the fortification. Enemy grenades
wounded him, but he persisted in his assault until 1 of his missiles
found its mark and knocked out the pillbox. With more grenades,
passed to him by members of his squad who had joined him, he led the
attack on the entrenched riflemen. In the advance up the hill, he suffered additional wounds in both arms and legs, about the body and in
the head, as grenades and TNT charges exploded near him. Three Japs
rushed him with fixed bayonets, and he emptied the magazine of his
machine pistol at them, killing 2. He closed in hand-to-hand combat
with the third, seizing the Jap's rifle as he met the onslaught. The 2 fell
to the ground and rolled some 50 or 60 feet down a bank. When the
dust cleared the Jap lay dead and the valiant American was climbing
up the hill with a large gash across the head. He was given first aid and
evacuated from the area while his squad completed the destruction of
the enemy position. S/Sgt. Laws' heroic actions provided great inspiration to his comrades, and his courageous determination, in the face of
formidable odds and while suffering from multiple wounds, enabled
them to secure an important objective with minimum casualties.

LEE, DANIEL W.

Rank and organization: First Lieutenant, U.S. Army, Troop A, 117th
Cavalry Reconnaissance Squadron. *Place and date:* Montreval, France,
2 September 1944. *Entered service at:* Alma, Ga. *Born:* 23 June 1919,
Alma, Ga. *G.O. No.:* 14, 4 February 1946. *Citation:* 1st Lt. (then 2d
Lt.) Daniel W. Lee was leader of Headquarters Platoon, Troop A,
117th Cavalry Reconnaissance Squadron, Mechanized, at Montreval,
France, on 2 September 1944, when the Germans mounted a strong
counterattack, isolating the town and engaging its outnumbered defenders in a pitched battle. After the fight had raged for hours and our
forces had withstood heavy shelling and armor-supported infantry attacks, 2d Lt. Lee organized a patrol to knock out mortars which were
inflicting heavy casualties on the beleaguered reconnaissance troops.
He led the small group to the edge of the town, sweeping enemy
riflemen out of position on a ridge from which he observed 7 Germans
manning 2 large mortars near an armored halftrack about 100 yards
down the reverse slope. Armed with a rifle and grenades, he left his
men on the high ground and crawled to within 30 yards of the mortars,

where the enemy discovered him and unleased machine-pistol fire which shattered his right thigh. Scorning retreat, bleeding and suffering intense pain, he dragged himself relentlessly forward. He killed 5 of the enemy with rifle fire, and the others fled before he reached their position. Fired on by an armored car, he took cover behind the German halftrack and there found a panzerfaust with which to neutralize this threat. Despite his wounds, he inched his way toward the car through withering machinegun fire, maneuvered into range, and blasted the vehicle with a round from the rocket launcher, forcing it to withdraw. Having cleared the slope of hostile troops, he struggled back to his men, where he collapsed from pain and loss of blood. 2d Lt. Lee's outstanding gallantry, willing risk of life, and extreme tenacity of purpose in coming to grips with the enemy, although suffering from grievous wounds, set an example of bravery and devotion to duty in keeping with the highest traditions of the military service.

LEIMS, JOHN HAROLD

Rank and organization: Second Lieutenant, U.S. Marine Corps Reserve, Company B, 1st Battalion, 9th Marines, 3d Marine Division. *Place and date:* Iwo Jima, Volcano Islands, 7 March 1945. *Entered service at:* Chicago, Ill. *Born:* 8 June 1921, Chicago, Ill. *Citation:* For conspicuous gallantry and intrepidity at the risk of his life above and beyond the call of duty as commanding officer of Company B, 1st Battalion, 9th Marines, 3d Marine Division, in action against enemy Japanese forces on Iwo Jima in the Volcano Islands, 7 March 1945. Launching a surprise attack against the rock-imbedded fortifications of a dominating Japanese hill position, 2d Lt. Leims spurred his company forward with indomitable determination and, skillfully directing his assault platoons against the cave-emplaced enemy troops and heavily fortified pillboxes, succeeded in capturing the objective in the late afternoon. When it became apparent that his assault platoons were cut off in this newly won position, approximately 400 yards forward of adjacent units and lacked all communication with the command post, he personally advanced and laid telephone lines across the isolating expanse of open, fire-swept terrain. Ordered to withdraw his command after he had joined his forward platoons he immediately complied, adroitly effecting the withdrawal of his troops without incident. Upon arriving at the rear, he was informed that several casualties had been left at the abandoned ridge position beyond the frontlines. Although suffering acutely from the strain and exhaustion of battle, he instantly went forward despite darkness and the slashing fury of hostile machinegun fire, located and carried to safety 1 seriously wounded marine and then, running the gauntlet of enemy fire for the third time that night, again made his tortuous way into the bullet-riddled deathtrap and rescued another of his wounded men. A dauntless leader, concerned at all times for the welfare of his men, 2d Lt. Leims soundly maintained the coordinated strength of his battle-wearied company under extremely difficult conditions and, by his bold tactics, sustained aggressiveness, and heroic disregard of all personal danger, contributed essentially to the success of his division's operations against this vital Japanese base. His valiant conduct in the face of fanatic opposition sustains and enhances the highest traditions of the U.S. Naval Service.

*LEONARD, TURNEY W.

Rank and organization: First Lieutenant, U.S. Army, Company C, 893d Tank Destroyer Battalion. *Place and date:* Kommerscheidt, Germany, 4–6 November 1944. *Entered service at:* Dallas, Tex. *Birth:* Dallas, Tex. *G.O. No.:* 74, 1 September 1945. *Citation:* He displayed extraordinary heroism while commanding a platoon of mobile weapons at Kommerscheidt, Germany, on 4, 5, and 6 November 1944. During the fierce 3-day engagement, he repeatedly braved overwhelming enemy fire in advance of his platoon to direct the fire of his tank destroyer from exposed, dismounted positions. He went on lone reconnaissance missions to discover what opposition his men faced, and on 1 occasion, when fired upon by a hostile machinegun, advanced alone and eliminated the enemy emplacement with a handgrenade. When a strong German attack threatened to overrun friendly positions, he moved through withering artillery, mortar, and small-arms fire, reorganized confused infantry units whose leaders had become casualties, and exhorted them to hold firm. Although wounded early in battle, he continued to direct fire from his advanced position until he was disabled by a high-explosive shell which shattered his arm, forcing him to withdraw. He was last seen at a medical aid station which was subsequently captured by the enemy. By his superb courage, inspiring leadership, and indomitable fighting spirit, 1st Lt. Leonard enabled our forces to hold off the enemy attack and was personally responsible for the direction of fire which destroyed 6 German tanks.

*LESTER, FRED FAULKNER

Rank and organization: Hospital Apprentice First Class, U.S. Navy. *Born:* 29 April 1926, Downers Grove, Ill. *Accredited to:* Illinois. *Citation:* For conspicuous gallantry and intrepidity at the risk of his life above and beyond the call of duty while serving as a Medical Corpsman with an Assault Rifle Platoon, attached to the 1st Battalion, 22d Marines, 6th Marine Division, during action against enemy Japanese forces on Okinawa Shima in the Ryukyu Chain, 8 June 1945. Quick to spot a wounded marine lying in an open field beyond the front lines following the relentless assault against a strategic Japanese hill position, Lester unhesitatingly crawled toward the casualty under a concentrated barrage from hostile machineguns, rifles, and grenades. Torn by enemy rifle bullets as he inched forward, he stoically disregarded the mounting fury of Japanese fire and his own pain to pull the wounded man toward a covered position. Struck by enemy fire a second time before he reached cover, he exerted tremendous effort and succeeded in pulling his comrade to safety where, too seriously wounded himself to administer aid, he instructed 2 of his squad in proper medical treatment of the rescued marine. Realizing that his own wounds were fatal, he staunchly refused medical attention for himself and, gathering his fast-waning strength with calm determination, coolly and expertly directed his men in the treatment of 2 other wounded marines, succumbing shortly thereafter. Completely selfless in his concern for the welfare of his fighting comrades, Lester, by his indomitable spirit, outstanding valor, and competent direction of others, had saved the life of 1 who otherwise must have perished and had contributed to the safety of countless others. Lester's fortitude in the face of certain death sustains and enhances the highest traditions of the U.S. Naval Service. He gallantly gave his life for his country.

*LINDSEY, DARRELL R. (Air Mission)

Rank and organization: Captain, U.S. Army Air Corps. *Place and date:* L'Isle Adam railroad bridge over the Seine in occupied France, 9 August 1944. *Entered service at:* Storm Lake, Iowa. *Birth:* Jefferson, Iowa. *G.O. No.:* 43, 30 May 1945. *Citation:* On 9 August 1944, Capt. Lindsey led a formation of 30 B–26 medium bombers in a hazardous mission to destroy the strategic enemy held L'Isle Adam railroad bridge over the Seine in occupied France. With most of the bridges over the Seine destroyed, the heavily fortified L'Isle Adam bridge was of inestimable value to the enemy in moving troops, supplies, and equipment to Paris. Capt. Lindsey was fully aware of the fierce resistance that would be encountered. Shortly after reaching enemy territory the formation was buffeted with heavy and accurate antiaircraft fire. By skillful evasive action, Capt. Lindsey was able to elude much of the enemy flak, but just before entering the bombing run his B–26 was peppered with holes. During the bombing run the enemy fire was even more intense, and Capt. Lindsey's right engine received a direct hit and burst into flames. Despite the fact that his ship was hurled out of formation by the violence of the concussion, Capt. Lindsey brilliantly maneuvered back into the lead position without disrupting the flight. Fully aware that the gasoline tanks might explode at any moment, Capt. Lindsey gallantly elected to continue the perilous bombing run. With fire streaming from his right engine and his right wing half enveloped in flames, he led his formation over the target upon which the bombs were dropped with telling effect. Immediately after the objective was attacked, Capt. Lindsey gave the order for the crew to parachute from the doomed aircraft. With magnificent coolness and superb pilotage, and without regard for his own life, he held the swiftly descending airplane in a steady glide until the members of the crew could jump to safety. With the right wing completely enveloped in flames and an explosion of the gasoline tank imminent, Capt. Lindsey still remained unperturbed. The last man to leave the stricken plane was the bombardier, who offered to lower the wheels so that Capt. Lindsey might escape from the nose. Realizing that this might throw the aircraft into an uncontrollable spin and jeopardize the bombardier's chances to escape, Capt. Lindsey refused the offer. Immediately after the bombardier had bailed out, and before Capt. Lindsey was able to follow, the right gasoline tank exploded. The aircraft sheathed in fire, went into a steep dive and was seen to explode as it crashed. All who are living today from this plane owe their lives to the fact that Capt. Lindsey remained cool and showed supreme courage in this emergency.

LINDSEY, JAKE W.

Rank and organization: Technical Sergeant, U.S. Army, 16th Infantry, 1st Infantry Division. *Place and date:* Near Hamich, Germany, 16 November 1944. *Entered service at:* Lucedale, Miss. *Birth:* Isney, Ala. *G.O. No.:* 43, 30 May 1945. *Citation:* For gallantry and intrepidity at the risk of his life above and beyond the call of duty on 16 November 1944, in Germany. T/Sgt. Lindsey assumed a position about 10 yards to the front of his platoon during an intense enemy infantry-tank counterattack, and by his unerringly accurate fire destroyed 2 enemy machinegun nests, forced the withdrawal of 2 tanks, and effectively halted enemy flanking patrols. Later, although painfully wounded, he engaged 8 Germans, who were reestablishing machinegun positions, in hand-to-hand combat, killing 3, capturing 3, and causing the other 2 to flee. By his gallantry, T/Sgt. Lindsey secured his unit's position, and reflected great credit upon himself and the U.S. Army.

*LINDSTROM, FLOYD K.

Rank and organization: Private First Class, U.S. Army, 3d Infantry Division. *Place and date:* Near Mignano, Italy, 11 November 1943. *Entered service at:* Colorado Springs, Colo. *Birth:* Holdredge, Nebr. *G.O. No.:* 32, 20 April 1944. *Citation:* For conspicuous gallantry and intrepidity at risk of life above and beyond the call of duty. On 11 November 1943, this soldier's platoon was furnishing machinegun support for a rifle company attacking a hill near Mignano, Italy, when the enemy counterattacked, forcing the riflemen and half the machinegun platoon to retire to a defensive position. Pfc. Lindstrom saw that his small section was alone and outnumbered 5 to 1, yet he immediately deployed the few remaining men into position and opened fire with his single gun. The enemy centered fire on him with machinegun, machine pistols, and grenades. Unable to knock out the enemy nest from his original position, Pfc. Lindstrom picked up his own heavy machinegun and staggered 15 yards up the barren, rocky hillside to a new position, completely ignoring enemy small-arms fire which was striking all around him. From this new site, only 10 yards from the enemy machinegun, he engaged it in an intense duel. Realizing that he could not hit the hostile gunners because they were behind a large rock, he charged uphill under a steady stream of fire, killed both gunners with his pistol and dragged their gun down to his own men, directing them to employ it against the enemy. Disregarding heavy rifle fire, he returned to the enemy machinegun nest for 2 boxes of ammunition, came back and resumed withering fire from his own gun. His spectacular performance completely broke up the German counterattack. Pfc. Lindstrom demonstrated aggressive spirit and complete fearlessness in the face of almost certain death.

*LLOYD, EDGAR H.

Rank and organization: First Lieutenant, U.S. Army, Company E, 319th Infantry, 80th Infantry Division. *Place and date:* Near Pompey, France, 14 September 1944. *Entered service at:* Blytheville, Ark. *Birth:* Blytheville, Ark. *G.O. No.:* 25, 7 April 1945. *Citation:* For conspicuous gallantry and intrepidity at the risk of his life above and beyond the call of duty. On 14 September 1944, Company E, 319th Infantry, with which 1st Lt. Lloyd was serving as a rifle platoon leader, was assigned the mission of expelling an estimated enemy force of 200 men from a heavily fortified position near Pompey, France. As the attack progressed, 1st Lt. Lloyd's platoon advanced to within 50 yards of the enemy position where they were caught in a withering machinegun and rifle crossfire which inflicted heavy casualties and momentarily disorganized the platoon. With complete disregard for his own safety, 1st Lt. Lloyd leaped to his feet and led his men on a run into the raking fire, shouting encouragement to them. He jumped into the first enemy machine-gun position, knocked out the gunner with his fist, dropped a grenade, and jumped out before it exploded. Still shouting encouragement he went from 1 machinegun nest to another, pinning the enemy down with submachinegun fire until he was within throwing distance, and then destroyed them with handgrenades. He personally destroyed 5 machineguns and many of the enemy, and by his daring leadership and conspicuous bravery inspired his men to overrun the enemy positions and accomplish the objective in the face of seemingly insurmountable odds. His audacious determination and courageous devotion to duty exemplify the highest traditions of the military forces of the United States.

*LOBAUGH, DONALD R.

Rank and organization: Private, U.S. Army, 127th Infantry, 32d Infantry Division. *Place and date:* Near Afua, New Guinea, 22 July 1944. *Entered service at:* Freeport, Pa. *Birth:* Freeport, Pa. *G.O. No.:* 31, 17 April 1945. *Citation:* For conspicuous gallantry and intrepidity at the risk of his life above and beyond the call of duty near Afua, New Guinea, on 22 July 1944. While Pvt. Lobaugh's company was withdrawing from its position on 21 July, the enemy attacked and cut off approximately 1 platoon of our troops. Tne platoon immediately occupied, organized, and defended a position, which it held throughout the night. Early on 22 July, an attempt was made to effect its withdrawal, but during the preparation therefor, the enemy emplaced a machinegun, protected by the fire of rifles and automatic weapons, which blocked the only route over which the platoon could move. Knowing that it was the key to the enemy position, Pfc. Lobaugh volunteered to attempt to destroy this weapon, even though in order to reach it he would be forced to work his way about 30 yards over ground devoid of cover. When part way across this open space he threw a handgrenade, but exposed himself in the act and was wounded. Heedless of his wound, he boldly rushed the emplacement, firing as he advanced. The enemy concentrated their fire on him, and he was struck repeatedly, but he continued his attack and killed 2 more before he was himself slain. Pfc. Lobaugh's heroic actions inspired his comrades to press the attack, and to drive the enemy from the position with heavy losses. His fighting determination and intrepidity in battle exemplify the highest traditions of the U.S. Armed Forces.

LOGAN, JAMES M.

Rank and organization: Sergeant, U.S. Army, 36th Infantry Division. *Place and date:* Near Salerno, Italy, 9 September 1943. *Entered service at:* Luling, Tex. *Birth:* McNeil, Tex. *G.O. No.:* 54, 5 July 1944. *Citation:* For conspicuous gallantry and intrepidity at risk of life above and beyond the call of duty in action involving actual conflict on 9 September 1943 in the vicinity of Salerno, Italy. As a rifleman of an infantry company, Sgt. Logan landed with the first wave of the assault echelon on the beaches of the Gulf of Salerno, and after his company had advanced 800 yards inland and taken positions along the forward bank of an irrigation canal, the enemy began a serious counterattack from positions along a rock wall which ran parallel with the canal about 200 yards further inland. Voluntarily exposing himself to the fire of a machinegun located along the rock wall, which sprayed the ground so close to him that he was splattered with dirt and rock splinters from the impact of the bullets, Sgt. Logan killed the first 3 Germans as they came through a gap in the wall. He then attacked the machinegun. As he dashed across the 200 yards of exposed terrain a withering stream of fire followed his advance. Reaching the wall, he crawled along the base, within easy reach of the enemy crouched along the opposite side, until he reached the gun. Jumping up, he shot the 2 gunners down, hurdled the wall, and seized the gun. Swinging it around, he immediately opened fire on the enemy with the remaining ammunition, raking their flight and inflicting further casualties on them as they fled. After smashing the machinegun over the rocks, Sgt. Logan captured an enemy officer and private who were attempting to sneak away. Later in the morning, Sgt. Logan went after a sniper hidden in a house about 150 yards from the company. Again the intrepid Sgt. ran a gauntlet of fire to reach his objective. Shooting the lock off the door, Sgt. Logan kicked it in and shot the sniper who had just reached the bottom of the stairs. The conspicuous gallantry and intrepidity which characterized Sgt. Logan's exploits proved a constant inspiration to all the men of his company, and aided materially in insuring the success of the beachhead at Salerno.

LOPEZ, JOSE M.

Rank and organization: Sergeant, U.S. Army, 23d Infantry, 2d Infantry Division. *Place and date:* Near Krinkelt, Belgium, 17 December 1944. *Entered service at:* Brownsville, Tex. *Birth:* Mission, Tex. *G.O. No.:* 47, 18 June 1945. *Citation:* On his own initiative, he carried his heavy machinegun from Company K's right flank to its left, in order to protect that flank which was in danger of being overrun by advancing enemy infantry supported by tanks. Occupying a shallow hole offering no protection above his waist, he cut down a group of 10 Germans. Ignoring enemy fire from an advancing tank, he held his position and cut down 25 more enemy infantry attempting to turn his flank. Glancing to his right, he saw a large number of infantry swarming in from the front. Although dazed and shaken from enemy artillery fire which had crashed into the ground only a few yards away, he realized that his position soon would be outflanked. Again, alone, he carried his machinegun to a position to the right rear of the sector; enemy tanks and infantry were forcing a withdrawal. Blown over backward by the concussion of enemy fire, he immediately reset his gun and continued his fire. Singlehanded he held off the German horde until he was satisfied his company had effected its retirement. Again he loaded his gun on his back and in a hail of small-arms fire he ran to a point where a few of his comrades were attempting to set up another defense against the onrushing enemy. He fired from this position until his ammunition was exhausted. Still carrying his gun, he fell back with his small group to Krinkelt. Sgt. Lopez's gallantry and intrepidity, on seemingly suicidal missions in which he killed at least 100 of the enemy, were almost solely responsible for allowing Company K to avoid being enveloped, to withdraw successfully and to give other forces coming up in support time to build a line which repelled the enemy drive.

LUCAS, JACKLYN HAROLD

Rank and organization: Private First Class, U.S. Marine Corps Reserve, 1st Battalion, 26th Marines, 5th Marine Division. *Place and date:* Iwo Jima, Volcano Islands, 20 February 1945. *Entered service at:* Norfolk, Va. *Born:* 14 February 1928, Plymouth, N.C. *Citation:* For conspicuous gallantry and intrepidity at the risk of his life above and beyond the call of duty while serving with the 1st Battalion, 26th Marines, 5th Marine Division, during action against enemy Japanese forces on Iwo Jima, Volcano Islands, 20 February 1945. While creeping through a treacherous, twisting ravine which ran in close proximity to a fluid and uncertain frontline on D-plus-1 day, Pfc. Lucas and 3 other men were suddenly ambushed by a hostile patrol which savagely attacked with rifle fire and grenades. Quick to act when the lives of the small group were endangered by 2 grenades which landed directly in front of them, Pfc. Lucas unhesitatingly hurled himself over his comrades upon 1 grenade and pulled the other under him, absorbing the whole blasting forces of the explosions in his own body in order to shield his companions from the concussion and murderous flying fragments. By his inspiring action and valiant spirit of self-sacrifice, he not only protected his comrades from certain injury or possible death but also enabled them to rout the Japanese patrol and continue the advance. His exceptionally courageous initiative and loyalty reflect the highest credit upon Pfc. Lucas and the U.S. Naval Service.

*LUMMUS, JACK

Rank and organization: First Lieutenant, U.S. Marine Corps Reserve. *Born:* 22 October 1915, Ennie, Tex. *Appointed from:* Texas. *Citation:* For conspicuous gallantry and intrepidity at the risk of his life above and beyond the call of duty as leader of a Rifle Platoon attached to the 2d Battalion, 27th Marines, 5th Marine Division, in action against enemy Japanese forces on Iwo Jima in the Volcano Islands, 8 March 1945. Resuming his assault tactics with bold decision after fighting without respite for 2 days and nights, 1st Lt. Lummus slowly advanced his platoon against an enemy deeply entrenched in a network of mutually supporting positions. Suddenly halted by a terrific concentration of hostile fire, he unhesitatingly moved forward of his front lines in an effort to neutralize the Japanese position. Although knocked to the ground when an enemy grenade exploded close by, he immediately recovered himself and, again moving forward despite the intensified barrage, quickly located, attacked, and destroyed the occupied emplacement. Instantly taken under fire by the garrison of a supporting pillbox and further assailed by the slashing fury of hostile rifle fire, he fell under the impact of a second enemy grenade but, courageously disregarding painful shoulder wounds, staunchly continued his heroic 1-man assault and charged the second pillbox, annihilating all the occupants. Subsequently returning to his platoon position, he fearlessly traversed his lines under fire, encouraging his men to advance and directing the fire of supporting tanks against other stubbornly holding Japanese emplacements. Held up again by a devastating barrage, he again moved into the open, rushed a third heavily fortified installation and killed the defending troops. Determined to crush all resistance, he led his men indomitably, personally attacking foxholes and spider traps with his carbine and systematically reducing the fanatic opposition, until, stepping on a land mine, he sustained fatal wounds. By his outstanding valor, skilled tactics, and tenacious perseverance in the face of overwhelming odds, 1st Lt. Lummus had inspired his stouthearted marines to continue the relentless drive northward, thereby contributing materially to the success of his regimental mission. His dauntless leadership and unwavering devotion to duty throughout sustain and enhance the highest traditions of the U.S. Naval Service. He gallantly gave his life in the service of his country.

MABRY, GEORGE L., JR.

Rank and organization: Lieutenant Colonel, U.S. Army, 2d Battalion, 8th Infantry, 4th Infantry Division. *Place and date:* Hurtgen Forest near Schevenhutte, Germany, 20 November 1944. *Entered service at:* Sumter, S.C. *Birth:* Sumter, S.C. *G.O. No.:* 77, September 1945. *Citation:* He was commanding the 2d Battalion, 8th Infantry, in an attack through the Hurtgen Forest near Schevenhutte, Germany, on 20 November 1944. During the early phases of the assault, the leading elements of his battalion were halted by a minefield and immobilized by heavy hostile fire. Advancing alone into the mined area, Col. Mabry established a safe route of passage. He then moved ahead of the foremost scouts, personally leading the attack, until confronted by a boobytrapped double concertina obstacle. With the assistance of the scouts, he disconnected the explosives and cut a path through the wire. Upon moving through the opening, he observed 3 enemy in foxholes whom he captured at bayonet point. Driving steadily forward he paced the assault against 3 log bunkers which housed mutually supported automatic weapons. Racing up a slope ahead of his men, he found the initial bunker deserted, then pushed on to the second where he was suddenly confronted by 9 onrushing enemy. Using the butt of his rifle, he felled 1 adversary and bayoneted a second, before his scouts came to his aid and assisted him in overcoming the others in hand-to-hand combat. Accompanied by the riflemen, he charged the third bunker under pointblank small-arms fire and led the way into the fortification from which he prodded 6 enemy at bayonet point. Following the consolidation of this area, he led his battalion across 300 yards of fire-swept terrain to seize elevated ground upon which he established a defensive position which menaced the enemy on both flanks, and provided his regiment a firm foothold on the approach to the Cologne Plain. Col. Mabry's superlative courage, daring, and leadership in an operation of major importance exemplify the finest characteristics of the military service.

MacARTHUR, DOUGLAS

Rank and organization: General, U.S. Army, commanding U.S. Army Forces in the Far East. *Place and date:* Bataan Peninsula, Philippine Islands. *Entered service at:* Ashland, Wis. *Birth:* Little Rock, Ark. *G.O.*

No.: 16, 1 April 1942. *Citation:* For conspicuous leadership in preparing the Philippine Islands to resist conquest, for gallantry and intrepidity above and beyond the call of duty in action against invading Japanese forces, and for the heroic conduct of defensive and offensive operations on the Bataan Peninsula. He mobilized, trained, and led an army which has received world acclaim for its gallant defense against a tremendous superiority of enemy forces in men and arms. His utter disregard of personal danger under heavy fire and aerial bombardment, his calm judgment in each crisis, inspired his troops, galvanized the spirit of resistance of the Filipino people, and confirmed the faith of the American people in their Armed Forces.

MacGILLIVARY, CHARLES A.

Rank and organization: Sergeant, U.S. Army, Company I, 71st Infantry, 44th Infantry Division. *Place and date:* Near Woelfling, France, 1 January 1945. *Entered service at:* Boston, Mass. *Birth:* Charlottetown, Prince Edward Island, Canada. *G.O. No.:* 77, 10 September 1945. *Citation:* He led a squad when his unit moved forward in darkness to meet the threat of a breakthrough by elements of the 17th German Panzer Grenadier Division. Assigned to protect the left flank, he discovered hostile troops digging in. As he reported this information, several German machineguns opened fire, stopping the American advance. Knowing the position of the enemy, Sgt. MacGillivary volunteered to knock out 1 of the guns while another company closed in from the right to assault the remaining strong points. He circled from the left through woods and snow, carefully worked his way to the emplacement and shot the 2 camouflaged gunners at a range of 3 feet as other enemy forces withdrew. Early in the afternoon of the same day, Sgt. MacGillivary was dispatched on reconnaissance and found that Company I was being opposed by about 6 machineguns reinforcing a company of fanatically fighting Germans. His unit began an attack but was pinned down by furious automatic and small-arms fire. With a clear idea of where the enemy guns were placed, he voluntarily embarked on a lone combat patrol. Skillfully taking advantage of all available cover, he stalked the enemy, reached a hostile machinegun and blasted its crew with a grenade. He picked up a submachinegun from the battlefield and pressed on to within 10 yards of another machinegun, where the enemy crew discovered him and feverishly tried to swing their weapon into line to cut him down. He charged ahead, jumped into the midst of the Germans and killed them with several bursts. Without hesitation, he moved on to still another machinegun, creeping, crawling, and rushing from tree to tree, until close enough to toss a grenade into the emplacement and close with its defenders. He dispatched this crew also, but was himself seriously wounded. Through his indomitable fighting spirit, great initiative, and utter disregard for personal safety in the face of powerful enemy resistance, Sgt. MacGillivary destroyed four hostile machineguns and immeasurably helped his company to continue on its mission with minimum casualties.

*MAGRATH, JOHN D.

Rank and organization: Private First Class, U.S. Army, Company G, 85th Infantry, 10th Mountain Division. *Place and date:* Near Castel d'Aiano, Italy, 14 April 1945. *Entered service at:* East Norwalk, Conn. *Birth:* East Norwalk, Conn. *G.O. No.:* 71, 17 July 1946. *Citation:* He displayed conspicuous gallantry and intrepidity above and beyond the call of duty when his company was pinned down by heavy artillery, mortar, and small-arms fire, near Castel d'Aiano, Italy. Volunteering to act as a scout, armed with only a rifle, he charged headlong into withering fire, killing 2 Germans and wounding 3 in order to capture a machinegun. Carrying this enemy weapon across an open field through heavy fire, he neutralized 2 more machinegun nests; he then circled behind 4 other Germans, killing them with a burst as they were firing on his company. Spotting another dangerous enemy position to this right, he knelt with the machinegun in his arms and exchanged fire with the Germans until he had killed 2 and wounded 3. The enemy now poured increased mortar and artillery fire on the company's newly won position. Pfc. Magrath fearlessly volunteered again to brave the shelling in order to collect a report of casualties. Heroically carrying out this task, he made the supreme sacrifice—a climax to the valor and courage that are in keeping with highest traditions of the military service.

*MANN, JOE E.

Rank and organization: Private First Class, U.S. Army, Company H, 502d Parachute Infantry, 101st Airborne Division. *Place and date:* Best, Holland, 18 September 1944. *Entered service at:* Seattie, Wash. *Birth:* Rearden, Wash. *G.O. No.:* 73, 30 August 1945. *Citation:* He distinguished himself by conspicuous gallantry above and beyond the call of duty. On 18 September 1944, in the vicinity of Best, Holland, his platoon, attempting to seize the bridge across the Wilhelmina Canal, was surrounded and isolated by an enemy force greatly superior in personnel and firepower. Acting as lead scout, Pfc. Mann boldly crept to within rocket-launcher range of an enemy artillery position and, in the face of heavy enemy fire, destroyed an 88-mm. gun and an ammunition dump. Completely disregarding the great danger involved, he remained in his exposed position, and, with his M1 rifle, killed the enemy one by one until he was wounded 4 times. Taken to a covered position, he insisted on returning to a forward position to stand guard during the night. On the following morning the enemy launched a concerted attack and advanced to within a few yards of the position, throwing handgrenades as they approached. One of these landed within a few feet of Pfc. Mann. Unable to raise his arms, which were bandaged to his body, he yelled "grenade" and threw his body over the grenade, and as it exploded, died. His outstanding gallantry above and beyond the call of duty and his magnificent conduct were an everlasting inspiration to his comrades for whom he gave his life.

*MARTIN, HARRY LINN

Rank and organization: First Lieutenant, U.S. Marine Corps Reserve. *Born:* 4 January 1911, Bucyrus, Ohio. *Appointed from:* Ohio. *Citation:*

For conspicuous gallantry and intrepidity at the risk of his life above and beyond the call of duty as platoon leader attached to Company C, 5th Pioneer Battalion, 5th Marine Division, in action against enemy Japanese forces on Iwo Jima, Volcano Islands, 26 March 1945. With his sector of the 5th Pioneer Battalion bivouac area penetrated by a concentrated enemy attack launched a few minutes before dawn, 1st Lt. Martin instantly organized a firing line with the marines nearest his foxhole and succeeded in checking momentarily the headlong rush of the Japanese. Determined to rescue several of his men trapped in positions overrun by the enemy, he defied intense hostile fire to work his way through the Japanese to the surrounded marines. Although sustaining 2 severe wounds, he blasted the Japanese who attempted to intercept him, located his beleaguered men and directed them to their own lines. When 4 of the infiltrating enemy took possession of an abandoned machinegun pit and subjected his sector to a barrage of handgrenades, 1st Lt. Martin, alone and armed only with a pistol, boldly charged the hostile position and killed all of its occupants. Realizing that his few remaining comrades could not repulse another organized attack, he called to his men to follow and then charged into the midst of the strong enemy force, firing his weapon and scattering them until he fell, mortally wounded by a grenade. By his outstanding valor, indomitable fighting spirit and tenacious determination in the face of overwhelming odds, 1st Lt. Martin permanently disrupted a coordinated Japanese attack and prevented a greater loss of life in his own and adjacent platoons. His inspiring leadership and unswerving devotion to duty reflect the highest credit upon himself and the U.S. Naval Service. He gallantly gave his life in the service of his country.

*MARTINEZ, JOE P.

Rank and organization: Private, U.S. Army, Company K, 32d Infantry, 7th Infantry Division. *Place and date:* On Attu, Aleutians, 26 May 1943. *Entered service at:* Ault, Colo. *Birth:* Taos, N. Mex. *G.O. No.:* 71, 27 October 1943. *Citation:* For conspicuous gallantry and intrepidity above and beyond the call of duty in action with the enemy. Over a period of several days, repeated efforts to drive the enemy from a key defensive position high in the snow-covered precipitous mountains between East Arm Holtz Bay and Chichagof Harbor had failed. On 26 May 1943, troop dispositions were readjusted and a trial coordinated attack on this position by a reinforced battalion was launched. Initially successful, the attack hesitated. In the face of severe hostile machinegun, rifle, and mortar fire, Pvt. Martinez, an automatic rifleman, rose to his feet and resumed his advance. Occasionally he stopped to urge his comrades on. His example inspired others to follow. After a most difficult climb, Pvt. Martinez eliminated resistance from part of the enemy position by BAR fire and handgrenades, thus assisting the advance of other attacking elements. This success only partially completed the action. The main Holtz-Chichagof Pass rose about 150 feet higher, flanked by steep rocky ridges and reached by a snow-filled defile. Passage was barred by enemy fire from either flank and from tiers of snow trenches in front. Despite these obstacles, and knowing of their existence, Pvt. Martinez again led the troops on and up, personally silencing several trenches with BAR fire and ultimately reaching the pass itself. Here, just below the knifelike rim of the pass, Pvt. Martinez encountered a final enemy-occupied trench and as he was engaged in firing into it he was mortally wounded. The pass, however, was taken, and its capture was an important preliminary to the end of organized hostile resistance on the island.

*MASON, LEONARD FOSTER

Rank and organization: Private First Class, U.S. Marine Corps. *Born:* 2 February 1920, Middleborough, Ky. *Accredited to:* Ohio. *Citation:* For conspicuous gallantry and intrepidity at the risk of his life above and beyond the call of duty as an automatic rifleman serving with the 2d Battalion, 3d Marines, 3d Marine Division, in action against enemy Japanese forces on the Asan-Adelup Beachhead, Guam, Marianas Islands on 22 July 1944. Suddenly taken under fire by 2 enemy machineguns not more than 15 yards away while clearing out hostile positions holding up the advance of his platoon through a narrow gully, Pfc. Mason, alone and entirely on his own initiative, climbed out of the gully and moved parallel to it toward the rear of the enemy position. Although fired upon immediately by hostile riflemen from a higher position and wounded repeatedly in the arm and shoulder, Pfc. Mason grimly pressed forward and had just reached his objective when hit again by a burst of enemy machinegun fire, causing a critical wound to which he later succumbed. With valiant disregard for his own peril, he persevered, clearing out the hostile position, killing 5 Japanese, wounding another and then rejoining his platoon to report the results of his action before consenting to be evacuated. His exceptionally heroic act in the face of almost certain death enabled his platoon to accomplish its mission and reflects the highest credit upon Pfc. Mason and the U.S. Naval Service. He gallantly gave his life for his country.

*MATHIES, ARCHIBALD (Air Mission)

Rank and organization: Sergeant, U.S. Army Air Corps, 510th Bomber Squadron, 351st Bomber Group. *Place and date:* Over Europe, 20 February 1944. *Entered service at:* Pittsburgh, Pa. *Born:* 3 June 1918, Scotland. *G.O. No.:* 52, 22 June 1944. *Citation:* For conspicuous gallantry and intrepidity at risk of life above and beyond the call of duty in action against the enemy in connection with a bombing mission over enemy-occupied Europe on 20 February 1944. The aircraft on which Sgt. Mathies was serving as engineer and ball turret gunner was attacked by a squadron of enemy fighters with the result that the copilot was killed outright, the pilot wounded and rendered unconscious, the radio operator wounded and the plane severely damaged. Nevertheless, Sgt. Mathies and other members of the crew managed to right the plane and fly it back to their home station, where they contacted the control tower and reported the situation. Sgt. Mathies and the navigator volunteered to attempt to land the plane. Other members of the crew were ordered to jump, leaving Sgt. Mathies and the navigator aboard. After observing the distressed aircraft from another plane, Sgt. Mathies' commanding officer decided the damaged plane could not be landed by the inexperienced crew and ordered them to abandon it and parachute to safety. Demonstrating unsurpassed courage and heroism, Sgt. Mathies and the navigator replied that the pilot was still alive but could not be moved and they would not desert him. They were then told to attempt a landing. After two unsuccessful efforts, the plane crashed into an open field in a third attempt to land. Sgt. Mathies, the navigator, and the wounded pilot were killed.

*MATHIS, JACK W. (Air Mission)

Rank and organization: First Lieutenant, U.S. Army Air Corps, 359th Bomber Squadron, 303d Bomber Group. *Place and date:* Over Vegesack, Germany, 18 March 1943. *Entered service at:* San Angelo, Tex. *Born:* 25 September 1921, San Angelo, Tex. *G.O. No.:* 38, 12 July 1943. *Citation:* For conspicuous gallantry and intrepidity above and beyond the call of duty in action with the enemy over Vegesack, Germany, on 18 March 1943. 1st Lt. Mathis, as leading bombardier of his squadron, flying through intense and accurate antiaircraft fire, was just starting his bomb run, upon which the entire squadron depended for accurate bombing, when he was hit by the enemy antiaircraft fire. His right arm was shattered above the elbow, a large wound was torn in his side and abdomen, and he was knocked from his bomb sight to the rear of the bombardier's compartment. Realizing that the success of the mission depended upon him, 1st Lt. Mathis, by sheer determination and willpower, though mortally wounded, dragged himself back to his sights, released his bombs, then died at his post of duty. As the result of this action the airplanes of his bombardment squadron placed their bombs directly upon the assigned target for a perfect attack against the enemy. 1st Lt. Mathis' undaunted bravery has been a great inspiration to the officers and men of his unit.

MAXWELL, ROBERT D.

Rank and organization: Technician Fifth Grade, U.S. Army, 7th Infantry, 3d Infantry Division. *Place and date:* Near Besancon, France, 7 September 1944. *Entered service at:* Larimer County, Colo. *Birth:* Boise, Idaho. *G.O. No.:* 24, 6 April 1945. *Citation:* For conspicuous gallantry and intrepidity at risk of life above and beyond the call of duty on 7 September 1944, near Besancon, France. Technician 5th Grade Maxwell and 3 other soldiers, armed only with .45 caliber automatic pistols, defended the battalion observation post against an overwhelming onslaught by enemy infantrymen in approximately platoon strength, supported by 20-mm. flak and machinegun fire, who had infiltrated through the battalion's forward companies and were attacking the observation post with machinegun, machine pistol, and grenade fire at ranges as close as 10 yards. Despite a hail of fire from automatic weapons and grenade launchers, Technician 5th Grade Maxwell aggressively fought off advancing enemy elements and, by his calmness, tenacity, and fortitude, inspired his fellows to continue the unequal struggle. When an enemy handgrenade was thrown in the midst of his squad, Technician 5th Grade Maxwell unhesitatingly hurled himself squarely upon it, using his blanket and his unprotected body to absorb the full force of the explosion. This act of instantaneous heroism permanently maimed Technician 5th Grade Maxwell, but saved the lives of his comrades in arms and facilitated maintenance of vital military communications during the temporary withdrawal of the battalion's forward headquarters.

*MAY, MARTIN O.

Rank and organization: Private First Class, U.S. Army, 307th Infantry, 77th Infantry Division. *Place and date:* Iegusuku-Yama, Ie Shima, Ryukyu Islands, 19–21 April 1945. *Entered service at:* Phillipsburg, N.J. *Birth:* Phillipsburg, N.J. *G.O. No.:* 9, 25 January 1946. *Citation:* He gallantly maintained a 3-day stand in the face of terrible odds when American troops fought for possession of the rugged slopes of Iegusuku-Yama on Ie Shima, Ryukyu Islands. After placing his heavy machinegun in an advantageous yet vulnerable position on a ridge to support riflemen, he became the target of fierce mortar and small arms fire from counterattacking Japanese. He repulsed this assault by sweeping the enemy with accurate bursts while explosions and ricocheting bullets threw blinding dust and dirt about him. He broke up a second counterattack by hurling grenades into the midst of the enemy forces, and then refused to withdraw, volunteering to maintain his post and cover the movement of American riflemen as they reorganized to meet any further hostile action. The major effort of the enemy did not develop until the morning of 21 April. It found Pfc. May still supporting the rifle company in the face of devasting rifle, machinegun, and mortar fire. While many of the friendly troops about him became casualties, he continued to fire his machinegun until he was severely wounded and his gun rendered useless by the burst of a mortar shell. Refusing to withdraw from the violent action, he blasted fanatical Japanese troops with handgrenades until wounded again, this time mortally. By his intrepidity and the extreme tenacity with which he held firm until death against overwhelming forces, Pfc. May killed at least 16 Japanese, was largely responsible for maintaining the American lines, and inspired his comrades to efforts which later resulted in complete victory and seizure of the mountain stronghold.

MAYFIELD, MELVIN

Rank and organization: Corporal, U.S. Army, Company D, 20th Infantry, 6th Infantry Division. *Place and date:* Cordillera Mountains, Luzon, Philippine Islands, 29 July 1945. *Entered service at:* Nashport, Ohio. *Birth:* Salem, W. Va. *G.O. No.:* 49, 31 May 1946. *Citation:* He displayed conspicuous gallantry and intrepidity above and beyond the call of duty while fighting in the Cordillera Mountains of Luzon, Philippine Islands. When 2 Filipino companies were pinned down under a torrent of enemy fire that converged on them from a circular ridge commanding their position, Cpl. Mayfield, in a gallant single-handed effort to aid them, rushed from shellhole to shellhole until he reached 4 enemy caves atop the barren fire-swept hill. With grenades and his carbine, he assaulted each of the caves while enemy fire pounded about him. However, before he annihilated the last hostile redoubt, a machinegun bullet destroyed his weapon and slashed his left hand. Disregarding his wound, he secured more grenades and dauntlessly charged again into the face of pointblank fire to help destroy a hostile observation post. By his gallant determination and heroic leadership, Cpl. Mayfield inspired the men to eliminate all remaining pockets of resistance in the area and to press the advance against the enemy.

McCALL, THOMAS E.

Rank and organization: Staff Sergeant, U.S. Army, Company F, 143d Infantry, 36th Infantry Division. *Place and date:* Near San Angelo, Italy, 22 January 1944. *Entered service at:* Veedersburg, Ind. *Birth:* Burton, Kans. *G.O. No.:* 31, 17 April 1945. *Citation:* For conspicuous gallantry and intrepidity at risk of life above and beyond the call of duty. On 22 January 1944, Company F had the mission of crossing the Rapido River in the vicinity of San Angelo, Italy, and attacking the well-prepared German positions to the west. For the defense of these positions the enemy had prepared a network of machinegun positions covering the terrain to the front with a pattern of withering machinegun fire, and mortar and artillery positions zeroed in on the defilade areas. S/Sgt. McCall commanded a machinegun section that was to provide added fire support for the riflemen. Under cover of darkness, Company F advanced to the river crossing site and under intense enemy mortar, artillery, and machinegun fire crossed an ice-covered bridge which was continually the target for enemy fire. Many casualties occurred on reaching the west side of the river and reorganization was imperative. Exposing himself to the deadly enemy machinegun and small-arms fire that swept over the flat terrain, S/Sgt. McCall, with unusual calmness, encouraged and welded his men into an effective fighting unit. He then led them forward across the muddy, exposed terrain. Skillfully he guided his men through a barbed-wire entanglement to reach a road where he personally placed the weapons of his two squads into positions of vantage, covering the battalion's front. A shell landed near one of the positions, wounding the gunner, killing the assistant gunner, and destroying the weapon. Even though enemy shells were falling dangerously near, S/Sgt. McCall crawled across the treacherous terrain and rendered first aid to the wounded man, dragging him into a position of cover with the help of another man. The gunners of the second machinegun had been wounded from the fragments of an enemy shell, leaving S/Sgt. McCall the only remaining member of his machinegun section. Displaying outstanding aggressiveness, he ran forward with the weapon on his hip, reaching a point 30 yards from the enemy, where he fired 2 bursts of fire into the nest, killing or wounding all of the crew and putting the gun out of action. A second machinegun now opened fire upon him and he rushed its position, firing his weapon from the hip, killing 4 of the guncrew. A third machinegun, 50 yards in rear of the first two, was delivering a tremendous volume of fire upon our troops. S/Sgt. McCall spotted its position and valiantly went toward it in the face of overwhelming enemy fire. He was last seen courageously moving forward on the enemy position, firing his machinegun from his hip. S/Sgt. McCall's intrepidity and unhesitating willingness to sacrifice his life exemplify the highest traditions of the Armed Forces.

McCAMPBELL, DAVID

Rank and organization: Commander, U.S. Navy, Air Group 15. *Place and date:* First and second battles of the Philippine Sea, 19 June 1944. *Entered service at:* Florida. *Born:* 16 January 1910, Bessemer, Ala. *Other Navy awards:* Navy Cross, Silver Star, Legion of Merit, Distinguished Flying Cross with 2 Gold Stars, Air Medal. *Citation:* For conspicuous gallantry and intrepidity at the risk of his life above and beyond the call of duty as commander, Air Group 15, during combat against enemy Japanese aerial forces in the first and second battles of the Philippine Sea. An inspiring leader, fighting boldly in the face of terrific odds, Comdr. McCampbell led his fighter planes against a force of 80 Japanese carrier-based aircraft bearing down on our fleet on 19 June 1944. Striking fiercely in valiant defense of our surface force, he personally destroyed 7 hostile planes during this single engagement in which the outnumbering attack force was utterly routed and virtually annihilated. During a major fleet engagement with the enemy on 24 October, Comdr. McCampbell, assisted by but 1 plane, intercepted and daringly attacked a formation of 60 hostile land-based craft approaching our forces. Fighting desperately but with superb skill against such overwhelming airpower, he shot down 9 Japanese planes and, completely disorganizing the enemy group, forced the remainder to abandon the attack before a single aircraft could reach the fleet. His great personal valor and indomitable spirit of aggression under extremely perilous combat conditions reflect the highest credit upon Comdr. McCampbell and the U.S. Naval Service.

McCANDLESS, BRUCE

Rank and organization: Commander, U.S. Navy, U.S.S. *San Francisco. Place and date:* Battle off Savo Island, 12–13 November 1942. *Entered service at:* Colorado. *Born:* 12 August 1911, Washington, D.C. *Other Navy award:* Silver Star. *Citation:* For conspicuous gallantry and exceptionally distinguished service above and beyond the call of duty as communication officer of the U.S.S. *San Francisco* in combat with enemy Japanese forces in the battle off Savo Island, 12–13 November 1942. In the midst of a violent night engagement, the fire of a determined and desperate enemy seriously wounded Lt. Comdr. McCandless and rendered him unconscious, killed or wounded the admiral in command, his staff, the captain of the ship, the navigator, and all other personnel on the navigating and signal bridges. Faced with the lack of superior command upon his recovery, and displaying superb initiative, he promptly assumed command of the ship and ordered her course and gunfire against an overwhelmingly powerful force. With his superiors in other vessels unaware of the loss of their admiral, and challenged by his great responsibility, Lt. Comdr. McCandless boldly continued to engage the enemy and to lead our column of following vessels to a great victory. Largely through his brilliant seamanship and great courage, the *San Francisco* was brought back to port, saved to fight again in the service of her country.

*McCARD, ROBERT HOWARD

Rank and organization: Gunnery Sergeant, U.S. Marine Corps. *Born:* 25 November 1918, Syracuse, N.Y. *Accredited to:* New York. *Citation:* For conspicuous gallantry and intrepidity at the risk of his life above and beyond the call of duty while serving as platoon sergeant of Company A, 4th Tank Battalion, 4th Marine Division, during the battle for enemy Japanese-held Saipan, Marianas Islands, on 16 June 1944. Cut off from the other units of his platoon when his tank was put out of action by a battery of enemy 77-mm. guns, G/Sgt. McCard carried on resolutely, bringing all the tank's weapons to bear on the enemy, until the severity of hostile fire caused him to order his crew out of the escape hatch while he courageously exposed himself to enemy guns by hurling handgrenades, in order to cover the evacuation of his men. Seriously wounded during this action and with his supply of grenades exhausted, G/Sgt. McCard then dismantled one of the tank's machine-guns and faced the Japanese for the second time to deliver vigorous fire into their positions, destroying 16 of the enemy but sacrificing himself to insure the safety of his crew. His valiant fighting spirit and supreme loyalty in the face of almost certain death reflect the highest credit upon G/Sgt. McCard and the U.S. Naval Service. He gallantly gave his life for his country.

McCARTER, LLOYD G.

Rank and organization: Private, U.S. Army, 503d Parachute Infantry Regiment. *Place and date:* Corregidor, Philippine Islands, 16–19 February 1945. *Entered service at:* Tacoma, Wash. *Born:* 11 May 1917, St. Maries, Idaho. *G.O. No.:* 77, 10 September 1945. *Citation:* He was a scout with the regiment which seized the fortress of Corregidor, Philippine Islands. Shortly after the initial parachute assault on 16 February 1945, he crossed 30 yards of open ground under intense enemy fire, and at point-blank range silenced a machinegun with handgrenades. On the afternoon of 18 February he killed 6 snipers. That evening, when a large force attempted to bypass his company, he voluntarily moved to an exposed area and opened fire. The enemy attacked his position repeatedly throughout the night and was each time repulsed. By 2 o'clock in the morning, all the men about him had been wounded; but shouting encouragement to his comrades and defiance at the enemy, he continued to bear the brunt of the attack, fearlessly exposing himself to locate enemy soldiers and then pouring heavy fire on them. He repeatedly crawled back to the American line to secure more ammunition. When his submachinegun would no longer operate, he seized an automatic rifle and continued to inflict heavy casualties. This weapon, in turn, became too hot to use and, discarding it, he continued with an M1 rifle. At dawn the enemy attacked with renewed intensity. Completely exposing himself to hostile fire, he stood erect to locate the most dangerous enemy positions. He was seriously wounded; but, though he had already killed more than 30 of the enemy, he refused to evacuate until he had pointed out immediate objectives for attack. Through his sustained and outstanding heroism in the face of grave and obvious danger, Pvt. McCarter made outstanding contributions to the success of his company and to the recapture of Corregidor.

McCARTHY, JOSEPH JEREMIAH

Rank and organization: Captain, U.S. Marine Corps Reserve, 2d Battalion, 24th Marines, 4th Marine Division. *Place and date:* Iwo Jima, Volcano Islands, 21 February 1945. *Entered service at:* Illinois. *Born:* 10 August 1911, Chicago, Ill. *Citation:* For conspicuous gallantry and intrepidity at the risk of his life above and beyond the call of duty as commanding officer of a rifle company attached to the 2d Battalion,

24th Marines, 4th Marine Division, in action against enemy Japanese forces during the seizure of Iwo Jima, Volcano Islands, on 21 February 1945. Determined to break through the enemy's cross-island defenses, Capt. McCarthy acted on his own initiative when his company advance was held up by uninterrupted Japanese rifle, machinegun, and high-velocity 47-mm. fire during the approach to Motoyama Airfield No. 2. Quickly organizing a demolitions and flamethrower team to accompany his picked rifle squad, he fearlessly led the way across 75 yards of fire-swept ground, charged a heavily fortified pillbox on the ridge of the front and, personally hurling handgrenades into the emplacement as he directed the combined operations of his small assault group, completely destroyed the hostile installation. Spotting 2 Japanese soldiers attempting an escape from the shattered pillbox, he boldly stood upright in full view of the enemy and dispatched both troops before advancing to a second emplacement under greatly intensified fire and then blasted the strong fortifications with a well-planned demolitions attack. Subsequently entering the ruins, he found a Japanese taking aim at 1 of our men and, with alert presence of mind, jumped the enemy, disarmed and shot him with his own weapon. Then, intent on smashing through the narrow breach, he rallied the remainder of his company and pressed a full attack with furious aggressiveness until he had neutralized all resistance and captured the ridge. An inspiring leader and indomitable fighter, Capt. McCarthy consistently disregarded all personal danger during the fierce conflict and, by his brilliant professional skill, daring tactics, and tenacious perseverance in the face of overwhelming odds, contributed materially to the success of his division's operations against this savagely defended outpost of the Japanese Empire. His cool decision and outstanding valor reflect the highest credit upon Capt. McCarthy and enhance the finest traditions of the U.S. Naval Service.

McCOOL, RICHARD MILES, JR.

Rank and organization: Lieutenant, U.S. Navy, U.S.S. *LSC(L)(3)122. Place and date:* Off Okinawa, 10 and 11 June 1945. *Entered service at:* Oklahoma. *Born:* 4 January 1922, Tishomingo, Okla. *Citation:* For conspicuous gallantry and intrepidity at the risk of his life above and beyond the call of duty as commanding officer of the U.S.S. *LSC(L)(3)122* during operations against enemy Japanese forces in the Ryukyu chain, 10 and 11 June 1945. Sharply vigilant during hostile air raids against Allied ships on radar picket duty off Okinawa on 10 June, Lt. McCool aided materially in evacuating all survivors from a sinking destroyer which had sustained mortal damage under the devasting attacks. When his own craft was attacked simultaneously by 2 of the enemy's suicide squadron early in the evening of 11 June, he instantly hurled the full power of his gun batteries against the plunging aircraft, shooting down the first and damaging the second before it crashed his station in the conning tower and engulfed the immediate area in a mass of flames. Although suffering from shrapnel wounds and painful burns, he rallied his concussion-shocked crew and initiated vigorous firefighting measures and then proceeded to the rescue of several trapped in a blazing compartment, subsequently carrying 1 man to safety despite the excruciating pain of additional severe burns. Unmindful of all personal danger, he continued his efforts without respite until aid arrived from other ships and he was evacuated. By his staunch leadership, capable direction, and indomitable determination throughout the crisis, Lt. McCool saved the lives of many who otherwise might have perished and contributed materially to the saving of his ship for further combat service. His valiant spirit of self-sacrifice in the face of extreme peril sustains and enhances the highest traditions of the U.S. Naval Service.

McGAHA, CHARLES L.

Rank and organization: Master Sergeant, U.S. Army, Company G, 35th Infantry, 25th Infantry Division. *Place and date:* Near Lupao, Luzon, Philippine Islands, 7 February 1945. *Entered service at:* Crosby, Tenn. *Birth:* Crosby, Tenn. *G.O. No.:* 30, 2 April 1946. *Citation:* He displayed conspicuous gallantry and intrepidity. His platoon and 1 other from Company G were pinned down in a roadside ditch by heavy fire from 5 Japanese tanks supported by 10 machineguns and a platoon of riflemen. When 1 of his men fell wounded 40 yards away, he unhesitatingly crossed the road under a hail of bullets and moved the man 75 yards to safety. Although he had suffered a deep arm wound, he returned to his post. Finding the platoon leader seriously wounded, he assumed command and rallied his men. Once more he braved the enemy fire to go to the aid of a litter party removing another wounded soldier. A shell exploded in their midst, wounding him in the shoulder and killing 2 of the party. He picked up the remaining man, carried him to cover, and then moved out in front deliberately to draw the enemy fire while the American forces, thus protected, withdrew to safety. When the last man had gained the new position, he rejoined his command and there collapsed from loss of blood and exhaustion. M/Sgt. McGaha set an example of courage and leadership in keeping with the highest traditions of the service.

McGARITY, VERNON

Rank and organization: Technical Sergeant, U.S. Army, Company L, 393d Infantry, 99th Infantry Division. *Place and date:* Near Krinkelt, Belgium, 16 December 1944. *Entered service at:* Model, Tenn. *Born:* 1 December 1921, Right, Tenn. *G.O. No.:* 6, 11 January 1946. *Citation:* He was painfully wounded in an artillery barrage that preceded the powerful counteroffensive launched by the Germans near Krinkelt, Belgium, on the morning of 16 December 1944. He made his way to an aid station, received treatment, and then refused to be evacuated, choosing to return to his hard-pressed men instead. The fury of the enemy's great Western Front offensive swirled about the position held by T/Sgt. McGarity's small force, but so tenaciously did these men fight on orders to stand firm at all costs that they could not be dislodged despite murderous enemy fire and the breakdown of their communications. During the day the heroic squad leader rescued 1 of his friends who had been wounded in a forward position, and throughout the night he exhorted his comrades to repulse the enemy's attempts at infiltration. When morning came and the Germans attacked with tanks and infantry, he braved heavy fire to run to an advantageous position where he immobilized the enemy's lead tank with a round from a rocket launcher. Fire from his squad drove the attacking infantrymen back, and 3 supporting tanks withdrew. He rescued, under heavy fire, another wounded American, and then directed devastating fire on a light cannon which had been brought up by the hostile troops to clear resistance from the area. When ammunition began to run low, T/Sgt. McGarity, remembering an old ammunition hole about 100 yards distant in the general direction of the enemy, braved a concentration of hostile fire to replenish his unit's supply. By circuitous route the enemy managed to emplace a machinegun to the rear and flank of the squad's position, cutting off the only escape route. Unhesitatingly, the gallant soldier took it upon himself to destroy this menace singlehandedly. He left cover, and while under steady fire from the enemy, killed or wounded all the hostile gunners with deadly accurate rifle fire and prevented all attempts to re-man the gun. Only when the squad's last round had been fired was the enemy able to advance and capture the intrepid leader and his men. The extraordinary bravery and extreme devotion to duty of T/Sgt. McGarity supported a remarkable delaying action which provided the time necessary for assembling reserves and forming a line against which the German striking power was shattered.

*McGEE, WILLIAM D.

Rank and organization: Private, U.S. Army, Medical Detachment, 304th Infantry, 76th Infantry Division. *Place and date:* Near Mulheim, Germany, 18 March 1945. *Entered service at:* Indianapolis, Ind. *Birth:* Indianapolis, Ind. *G.O. No.:* 21, 26 February 1946. *Citation:* A medical aid man, he made a night crossing of the Moselle River with troops endeavoring to capture the town of Mulheim. The enemy had retreated in the sector where the assault boats landed, but had left the shore heavily strewn with antipersonnel mines. Two men of the first wave attempting to work their way forward detonated mines which wounded them seriously, leaving them bleeding and in great pain beyond the reach of their comrades. Entirely on his own initiative, Pvt. McGee entered the minefield, brought out 1 of the injured to comparative safety, and had returned to rescue the second victim when he stepped on a mine and was severely wounded in the resulting explosion. Although suffering intensely and bleeding profusely, he shouted orders that none of his comrades was to risk his life by entering the death-sown field to render first aid that might have saved his life. In making the supreme sacrifice, Pvt. McGee demonstrated a concern for the well-being of his fellow soldiers that transcended all considerations for his own safety and a gallantry in keeping with the highest traditions of the military service.

*McGILL, TROY A.

Rank and organization: Sergeant, U.S. Army, Troop G, 5th Cavalry Regiment, 1st Cavalry Division. *Place and date:* Los Negros Islands, Admiralty Group, 4 March 1944. *Entered service at:* Ada, Okla. *Birth:* Knoxville, Tenn. *G.O. No.:* 74, 11 September 1944. *Citation:* For conspicuous gallantry and intrepidity above and beyond the call of duty in action with the enemy at Los Negros Island, Admiralty Group, on 4 March 1944. In the early morning hours Sgt. McGill, with a squad of 8 men, occupied a revetment which bore the brunt of a furious attack by approximately 200 drink-crazed enemy troops. Although covered by crossfire from machineguns on the right and left flank he could receive no support from the remainder of our troops stationed at his rear. All members of the squad were killed or wounded except Sgt. McGill and another man, whom he ordered to return to the next revetment. Courageously resolved to hold his position at all cost, he fired his weapon until it ceased to function. Then, with the enemy only 5 yards away, he charged from his foxhole in the face of certain death and clubbed the enemy with his rifle in hand-to-hand combat until he was killed. At dawn 105 enemy dead were found around his position. Sgt. McGill's intrepid stand was an inspiration to his comrades and a decisive factor in the defeat of a fanatical enemy.

*McGRAW, FRANCIS X.

Rank and organization: Private First Class, U.S. Army, Company H, 26th Infantry, 1st Infantry Division. *Place and date:* Near Schevenhutte, Germany, 19 November 1944. *Entered service at:* Camden, N.J. *Birth:* Philadelphia, Pa. *G.O. No.:* 92, 25 October 1945. *Citation:* He manned a heavy machinegun emplaced in a foxhole near Schevenhutte, Germany, on 19 November 1944, when the enemy launched a fierce counterattack. Braving an intense hour-long preparatory barrage, he maintained his stand and poured deadly accurate fire into the advancing foot troops until they faltered and came to a halt. The hostile forces brought up a machinegun in an effort to dislodge him but were frustrated when he lifted his gun to an exposed but advantageous position atop a log, courageously stood up in his foxhole and knocked out the enemy weapon. A rocket blasted his gun from position, but he retrieved it and continued firing. He silenced a second machinegun and then made repeated trips over fireswept terrain to replenish his ammunition supply. Wounded painfully in this dangerous task, he disregarded his injury and hurried back to his post, where his weapon was showered with mud when another rocket barely missed him. In the midst of the battle, with enemy troops taking advantage of his predicament to press forward, he calmly cleaned his gun, put it back into action and drove off the attackers. He continued to fire until his ammunition was expended, when, with a fierce desire to close with the enemy, he picked up a carbine, killed 1 enemy soldier, wounded another and engaged in a desperate fire-fight with a third until he was mortally wounded by a burst from a machine pistol. The extraordinary heroism and intrepidity displayed by Pvt. McGraw inspired his comrades to great efforts and was a major factor in repulsing the enemy attack.

*McGUIRE, THOMAS B., JR. (Air Mission)

Rank and organization: Major, U.S. Army Air Corps, 13th Air Force. *Place and date:* Over Luzon, Philippine Islands, 25–26 December 1944. *Entered service at:* Sebring, Fla.. *Birth:* Ridgewood, N.J. *G.O. No.:* 24, 7 March 1946. *Citation:* He fought with conspicuous gallantry and intrepidity over Luzon, Philippine Islands. Voluntarily, he led a squadron of 15 P–38's as top cover for heavy bombers striking Mabalacat Airdrome, where his formation was attacked by 20 aggressive Japanese

fighters. In the ensuing action he repeatedly flew to the aid of embattled comrades, driving off enemy assaults while himself under attack
and at times outnumbered 3 to 1, and even after his guns jammed,
continuing the fight by forcing a hostile plane into his wingman's line
of fire. Before he started back to his base he had shot down 3 Zeros.
The next day he again volunteered to lead escort fighters on a mission
to strongly defended Clark Field. During the resultant engagement he
again exposed himself to attacks so that he might rescue a crippled
bomber. In rapid succession he shot down 1 aircraft, parried the attack
of 4 enemy fighters, 1 of which he shot down, singlehandedly engaged
3 more Japanese, destroying 1, and then shot down still another, his
38th victory in aerial combat. On 7 January 1945, while leading a
voluntary fighter sweep over Los Negros Island, he risked an extremely
hazardous maneuver at low altitude in an attempt to save a fellow flyer
from attack, crashed, and was reported missing in action. With gallant
initiative, deep and unselfish concern for the safety of others, and
heroic determination to destroy the enemy at all costs, Maj. McGuire
set an inspiring example in keeping with the highest traditions of the
military service.

McKINNEY, JOHN R.

Rank and organization: Sergeant (then Private), U.S. Army, Company A, 123d Infantry, 33d Infantry Division. *Place and date:* Tayabas
Province, Luzon, Philippine Islands, 11 May 1945. *Entered service at:*
Woodcliff, Ga. *Birth:* Woodcliff, Ga. *G.O. No.:* 14, 4 February 1946.
Citation: He fought with extreme gallantry to defend the outpost which
had been established near Dingalan Bay. Just before daybreak approximately 100 Japanese stealthily attacked the perimeter defense, concentrating on a light machinegun position manned by 3 Americans. Having completed a long tour of duty at this gun, Pvt. McKinney was resting a few paces away when an enemy soldier dealt him a glancing blow
on the head with a saber. Although dazed by the stroke, he seized his
rifle, bludgeoned his attacker, and then shot another assailant who was
charging him. Meanwhile, 1 of his comrades at the machinegun had
been wounded and his other companion withdrew carrying the injured
man to safety. Alone, Pvt. McKinney was confronted by 10 infantrymen who had captured the machinegun with the evident intent
of reversing it to fire into the perimeter. Leaping into the emplacement, he shot 7 of them at pointblank range and killed 3 more with his
rifle butt. In the melee the machinegun was rendered inoperative, leaving him only his rifle with which to meet the advancing Japanese, who
hurled grenades and directed knee mortar shells into the perimeter. He
warily changed position, secured more ammunition, and reloading repeatedly, cut down waves of the fanatical enemy with devastating fire
or clubbed them to death in hand-to-hand combat. When assistance arrived, he had thwarted the assault and was in complete control of the
area. Thirty-eight dead Japanese around the machinegun and 2 more
at the side of a mortar 45 yards distant was the amazing toll he had exacted singlehandedly. By his indomitable spirit, extraordinary fighting
ability, and unwavering courage in the face of tremendous odds, Pvt.
McKinney saved his company from possible annihilation and set an example of unsurpassed intrepidity.

*McTUREOUS, ROBERT MILLER, Jr.

Rank and organization: Private, U.S. Marine Corps. *Born:* 26 March 1924, Altoona, Fla. *Accredited to:* Florida. *Citation:* For conspicuous gallantry and intrepidity at the risk of his life above and beyond the call of duty, while serving with the 3d Battalion, 29th Marines, 6th Marine Division, during action against enemy Japanese forces on Okinawa in the Ryukyu Chain, 7 June 1945. Alert and ready for any hostile counteraction following his company's seizure of an important hill objective, Pvt. McTureous was quick to observe the plight of company stretcher bearers who were suddenly assailed by slashing machine-gun fire as they attempted to evacuate wounded at the rear of the newly won position. Determined to prevent further casualties, he quickly filled his jacket with handgrenades and charged the enemy-occupied caves from which the concentrated barrage was emanating. Coolly disregarding all personal danger as he waged his furious 1-man assault, he smashed grenades into the cave entrances, thereby diverting the heaviest fire from the stretcher bearers to his own person and, resolutely returning to his own lines under a blanketing hail of rifle and machinegun fire to replenish his supply of grenades, dauntlessly continued his systematic reduction of Japanese strength until he himself sustained serious wounds after silencing a large number of the hostile guns. Aware of his own critical condition and unwilling to further endanger the lives of his comrades, he stoically crawled a distance of 200 yards to a sheltered position within friendly lines before calling for aid. By his fearless initiative and bold tactics, Pvt. McTureous had succeeded in neutralizing the enemy fire, killing 6 Japanese troops and effectively disorganizing the remainder of the savagely defending garrison. His outstanding valor and heroic spirit of self-sacrifice during a critical stage of operations reflect the highest credit upon himself and the U.S. Naval Service.

*McVEIGH, JOHN J.

Rank and organization: Sergeant, U.S. Army, Company H, 23d Infantry, 2d Infantry Division. *Place and date:* Near Brest, France, 29 August 1944. *Entered service at:* Philadelphia, Pa. *Birth:* Philadelphia, Pa. *G.O. No.:* 24, 6 April 1945. *Citation:* For conspicuous gallantry and intrepidity at risk of his life above and beyond the call of duty near Brest, France, on 29 August 1944. Shortly after dusk an enemy counterattack of platoon strength was launched against 1 platoon of Company G, 23d Infantry. Since the Company G platoon was not dug in and had just begun to assume defensive positions along a hedge, part of the line sagged momentarily under heavy fire from small arms and 2 flak guns, leaving a section of heavy machineguns holding a wide frontage without rifle protection. The enemy drive moved so swiftly that German riflemen were soon almost on top of 1 machine-gun position. Sgt. McVeigh, heedless of a tremendous amount of small-arms and flak fire directed toward him, stood up in full view of the enemy and directed the fire of his squad on the attacking Germans until his position was almost overrun. He then drew his trench knife, and singlehanded charged several of the enemy. In a savage hand-to-hand struggle, Sgt. McVeigh killed 1 German with the knife, his only weapon, and was advancing on 3 more of the enemy when he was shot down and killed with small-arms fire at point-blank range. Sgt. Mc-Veigh's heroic act allowed the 2 remaining men in his squad to concentrate their machine-gun fire on the attacking enemy and then turn their weapons on the 3 Germans in the road, killing all 3. Fire from this machinegun and the other gun of the section was almost entirely responsible for stopping this enemy assault, and allowed the rifle platoon to which it was attached time to reorganize, assume positions on and hold the high ground gained during the day.

*McWHORTER, WILLIAM A.

Rank and organization: Private First Class, U.S. Army, Company M, 126th Infantry, 32d Infantry Division. *Place and date:* Leyte, Philippine Islands, 5 December 1944. *Entered service at:* Liberty, S.C. *Birth:* Liberty, S.C. *G.O. No.:* 82, 27 September 1945. *Citation:* He displayed gallantry and intrepidity at the risk of his life above and beyond the call of duty while engaged in operations against the enemy. Pfc. McWhorter, a machine gunner, was emplaced in a defensive position with 1 assistant when the enemy launched a heavy attack. Manning the gun and opening fire, he killed several members of an advancing demolition squad, when 1 of the enemy succeeded in throwing a fused demolition charge in the entrenchment. Without hesitation and with complete disregard for his own safety, Pfc. McWhorter picked up the improvised grenade and deliberately held it close to his body, bending over and turning away from his companion. The charge exploded, killing him instantly, but leaving his assistant unharmed. Pfc. McWhorter's outstanding heroism and supreme sacrifice in shielding a comrade reflect the highest traditions of the military service.

MEAGHER, JOHN

Rank and organization: Technical Sergeant, U.S. Army, Company E, 305th Infantry, 77th Infantry Division. *Place and date:* Near Ozato, Okinawa, 19 June 1945. *Entered service at:* Jersey City, N.J. *Birth:* Jersey City, N.J. *G.O. No.:* 60, 26 June 1946. *Citation:* He displayed conspicuous gallantry and intrepidity above and beyond the call of duty. In the heat of the fight, he mounted an assault tank, and, with bullets splattering about him, designated targets to the gunner. Seeing an enemy soldier carrying an explosive charge dash for the tank treads, he shouted fire orders to the gunner, leaped from the tank, and bayonetted the charging soldier. Knocked unconscious and his rifle destroyed, he regained consciousness, secured a machinegun from the tank, and began a furious 1-man assault on the enemy. Firing from his hip, moving through vicious crossfire that ripped through his clothing, he charged the nearest pillbox, killing 6. Going on amid the hail of bullets and grenades, he dashed for a second enemy gun, running out of ammunition just as he reached the position. He grasped his empty gun by the barrel and in a violent onslaught killed the crew. By his fearless assaults T/Sgt. Meagher singlehandedly broke the enemy resistance, enabling his platoon to take its objective and continue the advance.

MERLI, GINO J.

Rank and organization: Private First Class, U.S. Army, 18th Infantry, 1st Infantry Division. *Place and date:* Near Sars la Bruyere, Belgium, 4–5 September 1944. *Entered service at:* Peckville, Pa. *Birth:* Scranton, Pa. *G.O. No.:* 64, 4 August 1945. *Citation:* He was serving as a machine gunner in the vicinity of Sars la Bruyere, Belgium, on the night of 4–5 September 1944, when his company was attacked by a superior German force. Its position was overrun and he was surrounded when our troops were driven back by overwhelming numbers and firepower. Disregarding the fury of the enemy fire concentrated on him he maintained his position, covering the withdrawal of our riflemen and breaking the force of the enemy pressure. His assistant machine gunner was killed and the position captured; the other 8 members of the section were forced to surrender. Pfc. Merli slumped down beside the dead assistant gunner and feigned death. No sooner had the enemy group withdrawn then he was up and firing in all directions. Once more his position was taken and the captors found 2 apparently lifeless bodies. Throughout the night Pfc. Merli stayed at his weapon. By daybreak the enemy had suffered heavy losses, and as our troops launched an assault, asked for a truce. Our negotiating party, who accepted the German surrender, found Pfc. Merli still at his gun. On the battlefield lay 52 enemy dead, 19 of whom were directly in front of the gun. Pfc. Merli's gallantry and courage, and the losses and confusion that he caused the enemy, contributed materially to our victory.

*MERRELL, JOSEPH F.

Rank and organization: Private, U.S. Army, Company I, 15th Infantry, 3d Infantry Division. *Place and date:* Near Lohe, Germany, 18 April 1945. *Entered service at:* Staten Island, N.Y. *Birth:* Staten Island, N.Y. *G.O. No.:* 21, 26 February 1946. *Citation:* He made a gallant, 1-man attack against vastly superior enemy forces near Lohe, Germany. His unit, attempting a quick conquest of hostile-hill positions that would open the route to Nuremberg before the enemy could organize his defense of that city, was pinned down by brutal fire from rifles, machine pistols, and 2 heavy machineguns. Entirely on his own initiative, Pvt. Merrell began a singlehanded assault. He ran 100 yards through concentrated fire, barely escaping death at each stride, and at point-blank range engaged 4 German machine pistolmen with his rifle, killing all of them while their bullets ripped his uniform. As he started forward again, his rifle was smashed by a sniper's bullet, leaving him armed only with 3 grenades. But he did not hesitate. He zigzagged 200 yards through a hail of bullets to within 10 yards of the first machinegun, where he hurled 2 grenades and then rushed the position ready to fight with his bare hands if necessary. In the emplacement he seized a Luger pistol and killed what Germans had survived the grenade blast. Rearmed, he crawled toward the second machinegun located 30 yards away, killing 4 Germans in camouflaged foxholes on the way, but himself receiving a critical wound in the abdomen. And yet he went on, staggering, bleeding, disregarding bullets which tore through the folds of his clothing and glanced off his helmet. He threw his last grenade into the machinegun nest and stumbled on to wipe out the crew. He had completed this self-appointed task when a machine pistol burst killed him instantly. In his spectacular 1-man attack Pvt. Merrell killed 6 Germans in the first machinegun emplacement, 7 in the next, and an additional 10 infantrymen who were astride his path to the weapons which would have decimated his unit had he not assumed the burden of the assault and stormed the enemy positions with utter fearlessness, intrepidity of the highest order, and a willingness to sacrifice his own life so that his comrades could go on to victory.

*MESSERSCHMIDT, HAROLD O.

Rank and organization: Sergeant, U.S. Army, Company L, 30th Infantry, 3d Infantry Division. *Place and date:* Near Radden, France, 17 September 1944. *Entered service at:* Chester, Pa. *Birth:* Grier City, Pa. *G.O. No.:* 71, 17 July 1946. *Citation:* He displayed conspicuous gallantry and intrepidity above and beyond the call of duty. Braving machinegun, machine pistol, and rifle fire, he moved fearlessly and calmly from man to man along his 40-yard squad front, encouraging each to hold against the overwhelming assault of a fanatical foe surging up the hillside. Knocked to the ground by a burst from an enemy automatic weapon, he immediately jumped to his feet, and ignoring his grave wounds, fired his submachinegun at the enemy that was now upon them, killing 5 and wounding many others before his ammunition was spent. Virtually surrounded by a frenzied foe and all of his squad now casualties, he elected to fight alone, using his empty submachine-gun as a bludgeon against his assailants. Spotting 1 of the enemy about to kill a wounded comrade, he felled the German with a blow of his weapon. Seeing friendly reinforcements running up the hill, he continued furiously to wield his empty gun against the foe in a new attack, and it was thus that he made the supreme sacrifice. Sgt. Messerschmidt's sustained heroism in hand-to-hand combat with superior enemy forces was in keeping with the highest traditions of the military service.

*METZGER, WILLIAM E., JR. (Air Mission)

Rank and organization: Second Lieutenant, U.S. Army Air Corps, 729th Bomber Squadron 452d Bombardment Group. *Place and date:* Saarbrucken, Germany, 9 November 1944. *Entered service at:* Lima, Ohio. *Born:* 9 February 1922, Lima, Ohio. *G.O. No.:* 38, 16 May 1945. *Citation:* On a bombing run upon the marshaling yards at Saar-brucken, Germany, on 9 November 1944, a B-17 aircraft on which 2d Lt. Metzger was serving as copilot was seriously damaged by antiair-craft fire. Three of the aircraft's engines were damaged beyond control and on fire; dangerous flames from the No. 4 engine were leaping back as far as the tail assembly. Flares in the cockpit were ignited and a fire roared therein which was further increased by free-flowing fluid from damaged hydraulic lines. The interphone system was rendered useless. In addition to these serious mechanical difficulties the engineer was wounded in the leg and the radio operator's arm was severed below the elbow. Suffering from intense pain, despite the application of a tourniquet, the radio operator fell unconscious. Faced with the imminent explosion of his aircraft and death to his entire crew, mere seconds before bombs away on the target, 2d Lt. Metzger and his pilot conferred. Something had to be done immediately to save the life of the wounded radio operator. The lack of a static line and the thought that his unconscious body striking the ground in unknown territory would not bring immediate medical attention forced a quick decision. 2d Lt. Metzger and his pilot decided to fly the flaming aircraft to friendly territory and then attempt to crash land. Bombs were released on the target and the crippled aircraft proceeded along to Allied-controlled territory. When that had been reached 2d Lt. Metzger personally informed all crewmembers to bail out upon the suggestion of the pilot. 2d Lt. Metzger chose to remain with the pilot for the crash landing in order to assist him in this emergency. With only 1 normally functioning engine and with the danger of explosion much greater, the aircraft banked into an open field, and when it was at an altitude of 100 feet it exploded, crashed, exploded again, and then disintegrated. All 3 crewmembers were instantly killed. 2d Lt. Metzger's loyalty to his crew, his determination to accomplish the task set forth to him, and his deed of knowingly performing what may have been his last service to his country was an example of valor at its highest.

MICHAEL, EDWARD S. (Air Mission)

Rank and organization: First Lieutenant, U.S. Army Air Corps, 364th Bomber Squadron, 305th Bomber Group. *Place and date:* Over Germany, 11 April 1944. *Entered service at:* Chicago, Ill. *Born:* 2 May 1918, Chicago, Ill. *G.O. No.:* 5, 15 January 1945. *Citation:* For conspicuous gallantry and intrepidity above and beyond the call of duty while serving as pilot of a B–17 aircraft on a heavy-bombardment mission to Germany, 11 April 1944. The group in which 1st Lt. Michael was flying was attacked by a swarm of fighters. His plane was singled out and the fighters pressed their attacks home recklessly, completely disregarding the Allied fighter escort and their own intense flak. His plane was riddled from nose to tail with exploding cannon shells and knocked out of formation, with a large number of fighters following it down, blasting it with cannon fire as it descended. A cannon shell exploded in the cockpit, wounded the copilot, wrecked the instruments, and blew out the side window. 1st Lt. Michael was seriously and painfully wounded in the right thigh. Hydraulic fluid filmed over the windshield making visibility impossible, and smoke filled the cockpit. The controls failed to respond and 3,000 feet were lost before he succeeded in leveling off. The radio operator informed him that the whole bomb bay was in flames as a result of the explosion of 3 cannon shells, which had ignited the incendiaries. With a full load of incendiaries in the bomb bay and a considerable gas load in the tanks, the danger of fire enveloping the plane and the tanks exploding seemed imminent. When the emergency release lever failed to function, 1st Lt. Michael at once gave the order to bail out and 7 of the crew left the plane. Seeing the bombardier firing the navigator's gun at the enemy planes, 1st Lt. Michael ordered him to bail out as the plane was liable to explode any minute. When the bombardier looked for his parachute he found that it had been riddled with 20-mm. fragments and was useless. 1st Lt. Michael, seeing the ruined parachute, realized that if the plane was abandoned the bombardier would perish and decided that the only chance would be a crash landing. Completely disregarding his own painful and profusely bleeding wounds, but thinking only of the safety of the remaining crewmembers, he gallantly evaded the enemy, using violent evasive action despite the battered condition of his plane. After the plane had been under sustained enemy attack for fully 45 minutes, 1st Lt. Michael finally lost the persistent fighters in a cloud bank. Upon emerging, an accurate barrage of flak caused him to come down to treetop level where flak towers poured a continuous rain of fire on the plane. He continued into France, realizing that at any moment a crash landing might have to be attempted, but trying to get as far as possible to increase the escape possibilities if a safe landing could be achieved. 1st Lt. Michael flew the plane until he became exhausted from the loss of blood, which had formed on the floor in pools, and he lost consciousness. The copilot succeeded in reaching England and sighted an RAF field near the coast. 1st Lt. Michael finally regained consciousness and insisted upon taking over the controls to land the plane. The undercarriage was useless; the bomb bay doors were jammed open; the hydraulic system and altimeter were shot out. In addition, there was no airspeed indicator, the ball turret was jammed with the guns pointing downward, and the flaps would not respond. Despite these apparently insurmountable obstacles, he landed the plane without mishap.

*MICHAEL, HARRY J.

Rank and organization: Second Lieutenant, U.S. Army, Company L, 318th Infantry, 80th Infantry Division. *Place and date:* Near Neiderzerf, Germany, 14 March 1945. *Entered service at:* Milford, Ind. *Birth:* Milford, Ind. *G.O. No.:* 18, 13 February 1946. *Citation:* He was serving as a rifle platoon leader when his company began an assault on a wooded ridge northeast of the village of Neiderzerf, Germany, early on 13 March 1945. A short distance up the side of the hill, 2d Lt. Michael, at the head of his platoon, heard the click of an enemy machinegun bolt. Quietly halting the company, he silently moved off into the woods and discovered 2 enemy machineguns and crews. Executing a sudden charge, he completely surprised the enemy and captured the guns and crews. At daybreak, enemy voices were heard in the thick woods ahead. Leading his platoon in a flanking movement, they charged the enemy with handgrenades and, after a bitter fight, captured 25 members of an SS mountain division, 3 artillery pieces, and 20 horses. While his company was establishing its position, 2d Lt. Michael made 2 personal reconnaissance missions of the wood on his left flank. On his first mission he killed 2, wounded 4, and captured 6 enemy soldiers singlehandedly. On the second mission he captured 7 prisoners. During the afternoon he led his platoon on a frontal assault of a line of enemy pillboxes, successfully capturing the objective, killing 10 and capturing 30 prisoners. The following morning the company was subjected to sniper fire and 2d Lt. Michael, in an attempt to find the hidden sniper, was shot and killed. The inspiring leadership and heroic aggressiveness displayed by 2d Lt. Michael upheld the highest traditions of the military service.

2.

*MILLER, ANDREW

Rank and organization: Staff Sergeant, U.S. Army, Company G, 377th Infantry, 95th Infantry Division. *Place and date:* From Woippy, France, through Metz to Kerprich Hemmersdorf, Germany, 16–29 November 1944. *Entered service at:* Two Rivers, Wis. *Birth:* Manitowoc, Wis. *G.O. No.:* 74, 1 September 1945. *Citation:* For performing a series of heroic deeds from 16–29 November 1944, during his company's relentless drive from Woippy, France, through Metz to Kerprich Hemmersdorf, Germany. As he led a rifle squad on 16 November at Woippy, a crossfire from enemy machineguns pinned down his unit. Ordering his men to remain under cover, he went forward alone, entered a building housing 1 of the guns and forced 5 Germans to surrender at bayonet point. He then took the second gun singlehandedly by hurling grenades into the enemy position, killing 2, wounding 3 more, and taking 2 additional prisoners. At the outskirts of Metz the next day, when his platoon, confused by heavy explosions and the withdrawal of friendly tanks, retired, he fearlessly remained behind armed with an automatic rifle and exchanged bursts with a German machinegun until he silenced the enemy weapon. His quick action in covering his comrades gave the platoon time to regroup and carry on the fight. On 19 November S/Sgt. Miller led an attack on large enemy barracks. Covered by his squad, he crawled to a barracks window, climbed in and captured 6 riflemen occupying the room. His men, and then the entire company, followed through the window, scoured the building, and took 75 prisoners. S/Sgt. Miller volunteered, with 3 comrades, to capture Gestapo officers who were preventing the surrender of German troops in another building. He ran a gauntlet of machinegun fire and was lifted through a window. Inside, he found himself covered by a machine pistol, but he persuaded the 4 Gestapo agents confronting him to surrender. Early the next morning, when strong hostile forces punished his company with heavy fire, S/Sgt. Miller assumed the task of destroying a well-placed machinegun. He was knocked down by a rifle grenade as he climbed an open stairway in a house, but pressed on with a bazooka to find an advantageous spot from which to launch his rocket. He discovered that he could fire only from the roof, a position where he would draw tremendous enemy fire. Facing the risk, he moved into the open, coolly took aim and scored a direct hit on the hostile emplacement, wreaking such havoc that the enemy troops became completely demoralized and began surrendering by the score. The following day, in Metz, he captured 12 more prisoners and silenced an enemy machinegun after volunteering for a hazardous mission in advance of his company's position. On 29 November, as Company G climbed a hill overlooking Kerprich Hemmersdorf, enemy fire pinned the unit to the ground. S/Sgt. Miller, on his own initiative, pressed ahead with his squad past the company's leading element to meet the surprise resistance. His men stood up and advanced deliberately, firing as they went. Inspired by S/Sgt. Miller's leadership, the platoon followed, and then another platoon arose and grimly closed with the Germans. The enemy action was smothered, but at the cost of S/Sgt. Miller's life. His tenacious devotion to the attack, his gallant choice to expose himself to enemy action rather than endanger his men, his limitless bravery, assured the success of Company G.

MILLS, JAMES H.

Rank and organization: Private, U.S. Army, Company F, 15th Infantry, 3d Infantry Division. *Place and date:* Near Cisterna di Littoria, Italy, 24 May 1944. *Entered service at:* Fort Meade, Fla. *Birth:* Fort Meade, Fla. *G.O. No.:* 87, 14 November 1944. *Citation:* For conspicuous gallantry and intrepidity at risk of life above and beyond the call of duty. Pvt. Mills, undergoing his baptism of fire, preceded his platoon down a draw to reach a position from which an attack could be launched against a heavily fortified strongpoint. After advancing about 300 yards, Pvt. Mills was fired on by a machinegun only 5 yards distant. He killed the gunner with 1 shot and forced the surrender of the assistant gunner. Continuing his advance, he saw a German soldier in a camouflaged position behind a large bush pulling the pin of a potato-masher grenade. Covering the German with his rifle, Pvt. Mills forced him to drop the grenade and captured him. When another enemy soldier attempted to throw a handgrenade into the draw, Pvt. Mills killed him with 1 shot. Brought under fire by a machinegun, 2 machine pistols, and 3 rifles at a range of only 50 feet, he charged headlong into the furious chain of automatic fire shooting his M1 from the hip. The enemy was completely demoralized by Pvt. Mills' daring charge, and when he reached a point within 10 feet of their position, all 6 surrendered. As he neared the end of the draw, Pvt. Mills was brought under fire by a machinegunner 20 yards distant. Despite the fact that he had absolutely no cover, Pvt. Mills killed the gunner with 1 shot. Two enemy soldiers near the machinegunner fired wildly at Pvt. Mills and then fled. Pvt. Mills fired twice, killing 1 of the enemy. Continuing on to the position, he captured a fourth soldier. When it became apparent that an assault on the strongpoint would in all probability cause heavy casualties on the platoon, Pvt. Mills volunteered to cover the advance down a shallow ditch to a point within 50 yards of the objective. Standing on the bank in full view of the enemy less than 100 yards away, hc shouted and fired his rifle directly into the position. His ruse worked exactly as planned. The enemy centered his fire on Pvt. Mills. Tracers passed within inches of his body, rifle and machine-pistol bullets ricocheted off the rocks at his feet. Yet he stood there firing until his rifle was empty. Intent on covering the movement of his platoon, Pvt. Mills jumped into the draw, reloaded his weapon, climbed out again, and continued to lay down a base of fire. Repeating this action 4 times, he enabled his platoon to reach the designated spot undiscovered, from which position it assaulted and overwhelmed the enemy, capturing 22 Germans and taking the objective without casualties.

*MINICK, JOHN W.

Rank and organization: Staff Sergeant, U.S. Army, Company I, 121st Infantry, 8th Infantry Division. *Place and date:* Near Hurtgen, Germany, 21 November 1944. *Entered service at:* Carlisle, Pa. *Birth:* Wall, Pa. *Citation:* He displayed conspicuous gallantry and intrepidity at the risk of his own life, above and beyond the call of duty, in action involving actual conflict with the enemy on 21 November 1944, near Hurtgen, Germany. S/Sgt. Minick's battalion was halted in its advance by extensive minefields, exposing troops to heavy concentrations of enemy artillery and mortar fire. Further delay in the advance would result in numerous casualties and a movement through the minefield was essential. Voluntarily, S/Sgt. Minick led 4 men through hazardous barbed wire and debris, finally making his way through the minefield for a distance of 300 yards. When an enemy machinegun opened fire, he signalled his men to take covered positions, edged his way alone toward the flank of the weapon and opened fire, killing 2 members of the guncrew and capturing 3 others. Moving forward again, he encountered and engaged singlehandedly an entire company killing 20 Germans and capturing 20, and enabling his platoon to capture the remainder of the hostile group. Again moving ahead and spearheading his battalion's advance, he again encountered machinegun fire. Crawling forward toward the weapon, he reached a point from which he knocked the weapon out of action. Still another minefield had to be crossed. Undeterred, S/Sgt. Minick advanced forward alone through constant enemy fire and while thus moving, detonated a mine and was instantly killed.

*MINUE, NICHOLAS

Rank and organization: Private, U.S. Army, Company A, 6th Armored Infantry, 1st Armored Division. *Place and date:* Near Medjez-el-Bab, Tunisia, 28 April 1943. *Entered service at:* Carteret, N.J. *Birth:* Sedden, Poland. *G.O. No.:* 24, 25 March 1944. *Citation:* For distinguishing himself conspicuously by gallantry and intrepidity at the loss of his life above and beyond the call of duty in action with the enemy on 28 April 1943, in the vicinity of Medjez-el-Bab, Tunisia. When the advance of the assault elements of Company A was held up by flanking fire from an enemy machinegun nest, Pvt. Minue voluntarily, alone, and unhesitatingly, with complete disregard of his own welfare, charged the enemy entrenched position with fixed bayonet. Pvt. Minue assaulted the enemy under a withering machinegun and rifle fire, killing approximately 10 enemy machinegunners and riflemen. After completely destroying this position, Pvt. Minue continued forward, routing enemy riflemen from dugout positions until he was fatally wounded. The courage, fearlessness and aggressiveness displayed by Pvt. Minue in the face of inevitable death was unquestionably the factor that gave his company the offensive spirit that was necessary for advancing and driving the enemy from the entire sector.

*MONTEITH, JIMMIE W., Jr.

Rank and organization: First Lieutenant, U.S. Army, 16th Infantry, 1st Infantry Division. *Place and date:* Near Colleville-sur-Mer, France, 6 June 1944. *Entered service at:* Richmond, Va. *Born:* 1 July 1917, Low Moor, Va. *G.O. No.:* 20, 29 March 1945. *Citation:* For conspicuous gallantry and intrepidity above and beyond the call of duty on 6 June 1944, near Colleville-sur-Mer, France. 1st Lt. Monteith landed with the initial assault waves on the coast of France under heavy enemy fire. Without regard to his own personal safety he continually moved up and down the beach reorganizing men for further assault.

He then led the assault over a narrow protective ledge and across the flat, exposed terrain to the comparative safety of a cliff. Retracing his steps across the field to the beach, he moved over to where 2 tanks were buttoned up and blind under violent enemy artillery and machine-gun fire. Completely exposed to the intense fire, 1st Lt. Monteith led the tanks on foot through a minefield and into firing positions. Under his direction several enemy positions were destroyed. He then rejoined his company and under his leadership his men captured an advantageous position on the hill. Supervising the defense of his newly won position against repeated vicious counterattacks, he continued to ignore his own personal safety, repeatedly crossing the 200 or 300 yards of open terrain under heavy fire to strengthen links in his defensive chain. When the enemy succeeded in completely surrounding 1st Lt. Monteith and his unit and while leading the fight out of the situation, 1st Lt. Monteith was killed by enemy fire. The courage, gallantry, and intrepid leadership displayed by 1st Lt. Monteith is worthy of emulation.

MONTGOMERY, JACK C.

Rank and organization: First Lieutenant, U.S. Army, 45th Infantry Division. *Place and date:* Near Padiglione, Italy, 22 February 1944. *Entered service at:* Sallisaw, Okla. *Birth:* Long, Okla. *G.O. No.:* 5, 15 January 1945. *Citation:* For conspicuous gallantry and intrepidity at risk of life above and beyond the call of duty on 22 February 1944, near Padiglione, Italy. Two hours before daybreak a strong force of enemy infantry established themselves in 3 echelons at 50 yards, 100 yards, and 300 yards, respectively, in front of the rifle platoons commanded by 1st Lt. Montgomery. The closest position, consisting of 4 machineguns and 1 mortar, threatened the immediate security of the platoon position. Seizing an M1 rifle and several handgrenades, 1st Lt. Montgomery crawled up a ditch to within handgrenade range of the enemy. Then climbing boldly onto a little mound, he fired his rifle and threw his grenades so accurately that he killed 8 of the enemy and captured the remaining 4. Returning to his platoon, he called for artillery fire on a house, in and around which he suspected that the majority of the enemy had entrenched themselves. Arming himself with a carbine, he proceeded along the shallow ditch, as withering fire from the riflemen and machinegunners in the second position was concentrated on him. He attacked this position with such fury that 7 of the enemy surrendered to him, and both machineguns were silenced. Three German dead were found in the vicinity later that morning. 1st Lt. Montgomery continued boldly toward the house, 300 yards from his platoon position. It was now daylight, and the enemy observation was excellent across the flat open terrain which led to 1st Lt. Montgomery's objective. When the artillery barrage had lifted, 1st Lt. Montgomery ran fearlessly toward the strongly defended position. As the enemy started streaming out of the house, 1st Lt. Montgomery, unafraid of treacherous snipers, exposed himself daringly to assemble the surrendering enemy and send them to the rear. His fearless, aggressive, and intrepid actions that morning, accounted for a total of 11 enemy dead, 32 prisoners, and an unknown number of wounded. That night, while aiding an adjacent unit to repulse a counterattack, he was struck by mortar fragments and seriously wounded. The selflessness and courage exhibited by 1st Lt. Montgomery in alone attacking 3 strong enemy positions inspired his men to a degree beyond estimation.

*MOON, HAROLD H., JR.

Rank and organization: Private, U.S. Army, Company G, 34th Infantry, 24th Infantry Division. *Place and date:* Pawig, Leyte, Philippine Islands, 21 October 1944. *Entered service at:* Gardena, Calif. *Birth:* Albuquerque, N. Mex. *G.O. No.:* 104, 15 November 1945. *Citation:* He fought with conspicuous gallantry and intrepidity when powerful Japanese counterblows were being struck in a desperate effort to annihilate a newly won beachhead. In a forward position, armed with a submachinegun, he met the brunt of a strong, well-supported night attack which quickly enveloped his platoon's flanks. Many men in nearby positions were killed or injured, and Pvt. Moon was wounded as his foxhole became the immediate object of a concentration of mortar and machinegun fire. Nevertheless, he maintained his stand, poured deadly fire into the enemy, daringly exposed himself to hostile fire time after time to exhort and inspire what American troops were left in the immediate area. A Japanese officer, covered by machinegun fire and hidden by an embankment, attempted to knock out his position with grenades, but Pvt. Moon, after protracted and skillful maneuvering, killed him. When the enemy advanced a light machinegun to within 20 yards of the shattered perimeter and fired with telling effects on the remnants of the platoon, he stood up to locate the gun and remained exposed while calling back range corrections to friendly mortars which knocked out the weapon. A little later he killed 2 Japanese as they charged an aid man. By dawn his position, the focal point of the attack for more than 4 hours, was virtually surrounded. In a fanatical effort to reduce it and kill its defender, an entire platoon charged with fixed bayonets. Firing from a sitting position, Pvt. Moon calmly emptied his magazine into the advancing horde, killing 18 and repulsing the attack. In a final display of bravery, he stood up to throw a grenade at a machinegun which had opened fire on the right flank. He was hit and instantly killed, falling in the position from which he had not been driven by the fiercest enemy action. Nearly 200 dead Japanese were found within 100 yards of his foxhole. The continued tenacity, combat sagacity, and magnificent heroism with which Pvt. Moon fought on against overwhelming odds contributed in a large measure to breaking up a powerful enemy threat and did much to insure our initial successes during a most important operation.

✓ MORGAN, JOHN C. (Air Mission)

Rank and organization: Second Lieutenant, U.S. Army Air Corps, 326th Bomber Squadron, 92d Bomber Group. *Place and date:* Over Europe, 28 July 1943. *Entered service at:* London, England. *Born:* 24 August 1914, Vernon, Tex. *G.O. No.:* 85, 17 December 1943. *Citation:* For conspicuous gallantry and intrepidity above and beyond the call of duty, while participating on a bombing mission over enemy-occupied continental Europe, 28 July 1943. Prior to reaching the German coast on the way to the target, the B–17 airplane in which 2d Lt.

Morgan was serving as copilot was attacked by a large force of enemy fighters, during which the oxygen system to the tail, waist, and radio gun positions was knocked out. A frontal attack placed a cannon shell through the windshield, totally shattering it, and the pilot's skull was split open by a .303 caliber shell, leaving him in a crazed condition. The pilot fell over the steering wheel, tightly clamping his arms around it. 2d Lt. Morgan at once grasped the controls from his side and, by sheer strength, pulled the airplane back into formation despite the frantic struggles of the semiconscious pilot. The interphone had been destroyed, rendering it impossible to call for help. At this time the top turret gunner fell to the floor and down through the hatch with his arm shot off at the shoulder and a gaping wound in his side. The waist, tail, and radio gunners had lost consciousness from lack of oxygen and, hearing no fire from their guns, the copilot believed they had bailed out. The wounded pilot still offered desperate resistance in his crazed attempts to fly the airplane. There remained the prospect of flying to and over the target and back to a friendly base wholly unassisted. In the face of this desperate situation, 2d Lt. Officer Morgan made his decision to continue the flight and protect any members of the crew who might still be in the ship and for 2 hours he flew in formation with one hand at the controls and the other holding off the struggling pilot before the navigator entered the steering compartment and relieved the situation. The miraculous and heroic performance of 2d Lt. Morgan on this occasion resulted in the successful completion of a vital bombing mission and the safe return of his airplane and crew.

*MOSKALA, EDWARD J.

Rank and organization: Private First Class, U.S. Army, Company C, 383d Infantry, 96th Infantry Division. *Place and date:* Kakazu Ridge, Okinawa, Ryukyu Islands, 9 April 1945. *Entered service at:* Chicago, Ill. *Born:* 6 November 1921, Chicago, Ill. *G.O. No.:* 21, 26 February 1946. *Citation:* He was the leading element when grenade explosions and concentrated machinegun and mortar fire halted the unit's attack on Kakazu Ridge, Okinawa, Ryukyu Islands. With utter disregard for his personal safety, he charged 40 yards through withering, grazing fire and wiped out 2 machinegun nests with well-aimed grenades and deadly accurate fire from his automatic rifle. When strong counterattacks and fierce enemy resistance from other positions forced his company to withdraw, he voluntarily remained behind with 8 others to cover the maneuver. Fighting from a critically dangerous position for 3 hours, he killed more than 25 Japanese before following his surviving companions through screening smoke down the face of the ridge to a gorge where it was discovered that one of the group had been left behind, wounded. Unhesitatingly, Pvt. Moskala climbed the bullet-swept slope to assist in the rescue, and, returning to lower ground, volunteered to protect other wounded while the bulk of the troops quickly took up more favorable positions. He had saved another casualty and killed 4 enemy infiltrators when he was struck and mortally wounded himself while aiding still another disabled soldier. With gallant initiative, unfaltering courage, and heroic determination to destroy the enemy, Pvt. Moskala gave his life in his complete devotion to his company's mission and his comrades' well-being. His intrepid conduct provided a lasting inspiration for those with whom he served.

*MOWER, CHARLES E.

Rank and organization: Sergeant, U.S. Army, Company A, 34th Infantry, 24th Infantry Division. *Place and date:* Near Capoocan, Leyte, Philippine Islands, 3 November 1944. *Entered service at:* Chippewa Falls, Wis. *Birth:* Chippewa Falls, Wis. *G.O. No.:* 17, 11 February 1946. *Citation:* He was an assistant squad leader in an attack against strongly defended enemy positions on both sides of a stream running through a wooded gulch. As the squad advanced through concentrated fire, the leader was killed and Sgt. Mower assumed command. In order to bring direct fire upon the enemy, he had started to lead his men across the stream, which by this time was churned by machinegun and rifle fire, but he was severely wounded before reaching the opposite bank. After signaling his unit to halt, he realized his own exposed position was the most advantageous point from which to direct the attack, and stood fast. Half submerged, gravely wounded, but refusing to seek shelter or accept aid of any kind, he continued to shout and signal to his squad as he directed it in the destruction of 2 enemy machineguns and numerous riflemen. Discovering that the intrepid man in the stream was largely responsible for the successful action being taken against them, the remaining Japanese concentrated the full force of their firepower upon him, and he was killed while still urging his men on. Sgt. Mower's gallant initiative and heroic determination aided materially in the successful completion of his squad's mission. His magnificent leadership was an inspiration to those with whom he served.

*MULLER, JOSEPH E.

Rank and organization: Sergeant, U.S. Army, Company B, 305th Infantry, 77th Infantry Division. *Place and date:* Near Ishimmi, Okinawa, Ryukyu Islands, 15–16 May 1945. *Entered service at:* New York, N.Y. *Birth:* Holyoke, Mass. *G.O. No.:* 71, 17 July 1946. *Citation:* He displayed conspicuous gallantry and intrepidity above and beyond the call of duty. When his platoon was stopped by deadly fire from a strongly defended ridge, he directed men to points where they could cover his attack. Then through the vicious machinegun and automatic fire, crawling forward alone, he suddenly jumped up, hurled his grenades, charged the enemy, and drove them into the open where his squad shot them down. Seeing enemy survivors about to man a machinegun, he fired his rifle at point-blank range, hurled himself upon them, and killed the remaining 4. Before dawn the next day, the enemy counterattacked fiercely to retake the position. Sgt. Muller crawled forward through the flying bullets and explosives, then leaping to his feet, hurling grenades and firing his rifle, he charged the Japs and routed them. As he moved into his foxhole shared with 2 other men, a lone enemy, who had been feigning death, threw a grenade. Quickly seeing the danger to his companions, Sgt. Muller threw himself over it and smothered the blast with his body. Heroically sacrificing his life to save his comrades, he upheld the highest traditions of the military service.

*MUNEMORI, SADAO S.

Rank and organization: Private First Class, U.S. Army, Company A, 100th Infantry Battalion, 442d Combat Team. *Place and date:* Near

Seravezza, Italy, 5 April 1945. *Entered service at:* Los Angeles, Calif. *Birth:* Los Angeles, Calif. *G.O. No.:* 24, 7 March 1946. *Citation:* He fought with great gallantry and intrepidity near Seravezza, Italy. When his unit was pinned down by grazing fire from the enemy's strong mountain defense and command of the squad devolved on him with the wounding of its regular leader, he made frontal, 1-man attacks through direct fire and knocked out 2 machineguns with grenades. Withdrawing under murderous fire and showers of grenades from other enemy emplacements, he had nearly reached a shell crater occupied by 2 of his men when an unexploded grenade bounced on his helmet and rolled toward his helpless comrades. He arose into the withering fire, dived for the missile and smothered its blast with his body. By his swift, supremely heroic action Pfc. Munemori saved 2 of his men at the cost of his own life and did much to clear the path for his company's victorious advance.

*MUNRO, DOUGLAS ALBERT

Rank and organization: Signalman First Class, U.S. Coast Guard. *Born:* 11 October 1919, Vancouver, British Columbia. *Accredited to:* Washington. *Citation:* For extraordinary heroism and conspicuous gallantry in action above and beyond the call of duty as Petty Officer in Charge of a group of 24 Higgins boats, engaged in the evacuation of a battalion of marines trapped by enemy Japanese forces at Point Cruz, Guadalcanal, on 27 September 1942. After making preliminary plans for the evacuation of nearly 500 beleaguered marines, Munro, under constant strafing by enemy machineguns on the island, and at great risk of his life, daringly led 5 of his small craft toward the shore. As he closed the beach, he signaled the others to land, and then in order to draw the enemy's fire and protect the heavily loaded boats, he valiantly placed his craft with its 2 small guns as a shield between the beachhead and the Japanese. When the perilous task of evacuation was nearly completed, Munro was instantly killed by enemy fire, but his crew, 2 of whom were wounded, carried on until the last boat had loaded and cleared the beach. By his outstanding leadership, expert planning, and dauntless devotion to duty, he and his courageous comrades undoubtedly saved the lives of many who otherwise would have perished. He gallantly gave his life for his country.

MURPHY, AUDIE L.

Rank and organization: Second Lieutenant, U.S. Army, Company B, 15th Infantry, 3d Infantry Division. *Place and date:* Near Holtzwihr, France, 26 January 1945. *Entered service at:* Dallas, Tex. *Birth:* Hunt Co' nty, near Kingston, Tex. *G.O. No.:* 65, 9 August 1945. *Citation:* 2d Lt. Murphy commanded Company B, which was attacked by 6 tanks and waves of infantry. 2d Lt. Murphy ordered his men to withdraw to prepared positions in a woods, while he remained forward at his command post and continued to give fire directions to the artillery by telephone. Behind him, to his right, 1 of our tank destroyers received a direct hit and began to burn. Its crew withdrew to the woods. 2d Lt. Murphy continued to direct artillery fire which killed large numbers of the advancing enemy infantry. With the enemy tanks abreast of his position, 2d Lt. Murphy climbed on the burning tank destroyer, which was in danger of blowing up at any moment, and employed its .50 caliber machinegun against the enemy. He was alone and exposed to German fire from 3 sides, but his deadly fire killed dozens of Germans and caused their infantry attack to waver. The enemy tanks, losing infantry support, began to fall back. For an hour the Germans tried every available weapon to eliminate 2d Lt. Murphy, but he continued to hold his position and wiped out a squad which was trying to creep up unnoticed on his right flank. Germans reached as close as 10 yards, only to be mowed down by his fire. He received a leg wound, but ignored it and continued the singlehanded fight until his ammunition was exhausted. He then made his way to his company, refused medical attention, and organized the company in a counterattack which forced the Germans to withdraw. His directing of artillery fire wiped out many of the enemy; he killed or wounded about 50. 2d Lt. Murphy's indomitable courage and his refusal to give an inch of ground saved his company from possible encirclement and destruction, and enabled it to hold the woods which had been the enemy's objective.

*MURPHY, FREDERICK C.

Rank and organization: Private First Class, U.S. Army, Medical Detachment, 259th Infantry, 65th Infantry Division. *Place and date:* Siegfried Line at Saarlautern, Germany, 18 March 1945. *Entered service at:* Weymouth, Mass. *Birth:* Boston, Mass. *G.O. No.:* 21, 26 February 1946. *Citation:* An aid man, he was wounded in the right shoulder soon after his comrades had jumped off in a dawn attack 18 March 1945, against the Siegfried Line at Saarlautern, Germany. He refused to withdraw for treatment and continued forward, administering first aid under heavy machinegun, mortar, and artillery fire. When the company ran into a thickly sown antipersonnel minefield and began to suffer more and more casualties, he continued to disregard his own wound and unhesitatingly braved the danger of exploding mines, moving about through heavy fire and helping the injured until he stepped on a mine which severed one of his feet. In spite of his grievous wounds, he struggled on with his work, refusing to be evacuated and crawling from man to man administering to them while in great pain and bleeding profusely. He was killed by the blast of another mine which he had dragged himself across in an effort to reach still another casualty. With indomitable courage, and unquenchable spirit of self-sacrifice and supreme devotion to duty which made it possible for him to continue performing his tasks while barely able to move, Pfc. Murphy saved many of his fellow soldiers at the cost of his own life.

MURRAY, CHARLES P., JR.

Rank and organization: First Lieutenant, U.S. Army, Company C, 30th Infantry, 3d Infantry Division. *Place and date:* Near Kaysersberg, France, 16 December 1944. *Entered service at:* Wilmington, N.C. *Birth:* Baltimore, Md. *G.O. No.:* 63, 1 August 1945. *Citation:* For commanding Company C, 30th Infantry, displaying supreme courage and heroic initiative near Kaysersberg, France, on 16 December 1944, while leading a reinforced platoon into enemy territory. Descending into a valley beneath hilltop positions held by our troops, he observed a force of 200 Germans pouring deadly mortar, bazooka, machinegun, and smalliarms fire into an American battalion occupying the crest of the ridge. The enemy's position in a sunken road, though hidden from the ridge, was open to a flank attack by 1st Lt. Murray's patrol but he hesitated to commit so small a force to battle with the superior and strongly disposed enemy. Crawling out ahead of his troops to a vantage point, he called by radio for artillery fire. His shells bracketed the German force, but when he was about to correct the range his radio went dead. He returned to his patrol, secured grenades and a rifle to launch them and went back to his self-appointed outpost. His first shots disclosed his position; the enemy directed heavy fire against him as he methodically fired his missiles into the narrow defile. Again he returned to his patrol. With an automatic rifle and ammunition, he once more moved to his exposed position. Burst after burst he fired into the enemy, killing 20, wounding many others, and completely disorganizing its ranks, which began to withdraw. He prevented the removal of 3 German mortars by knocking out a truck. By that time a mortar had been brought to his support. 1st Lt. Murray directed fire of this weapon, causing further casualties and confusion in the German ranks. Calling on his patrol to follow, he then moved out toward his original objective, possession of a bridge and construction of a roadblock. He captured 10 Germans in foxholes. An eleventh, while pretending to surrender, threw a grenade which knocked him to the ground, inflicting 8 wounds. Though suffering and bleeding profusely, he refused to return to the rear until he had chosen the spot for the block and had seen his men correctly deployed. By his singlehanded attack on an overwhelming force and by his intrepid and heroic fighting, 1st Lt. Murray stopped a counterattack, established an advance position against formidable odds, and provided an inspiring example for the men of his command.

*NELSON, WILLIAM L.

Rank and organization: Sergeant, U.S. Army, 60th Infantry, 9th Infantry Division. *Place and date:* At Djebel Dardys, Northwest of Sedjenane, Tunisia, 24 April 1943. *Entered service at:* Middletown, Del. *Birth:* Dover, Del. *G.O. No.:* 85, 17 December 1943. *Citation:* For conspicuous gallantry and intrepidity at risk of life, above and beyond the call of duty in action involving actual conflict. On the morning of 24 April 1943, Sgt. Nelson led his section of heavy mortars to a forward position where he placed his guns and men. Under intense enemy artillery, mortar, and small-arms fire, he advanced alone to a chosen observation position from which he directed the laying of a concentrated mortar barrage which successfully halted an initial enemy counterattack. Although mortally wounded in the accomplishment of his mission, and with his duty clearly completed, Sgt. Nelson crawled to a still more advanced observation point and continued to direct the fire of his section. Dying of handgrenade wounds and only 50 yards from the enemy, Sgt. Nelson encouraged his section to continue their fire and by doing so they took a heavy toll of enemy lives. The skill which Sgt. Nelson displayed in this engagement, his courage, and self-sacrificing devotion to duty and heroism resulting in the loss of his life, was a priceless inspiration to our Armed Forces and were in keeping with the highest tradition of the U.S. Army.

NEPPEL, RALPH G.

Rank and organization: Sergeant, U.S. Army, Company M, 329th Infantry, 83d Infantry Division. *Place and date:* Birgel, Germany, 14 December 1944. *Entered service at:* Glidden, Iowa. *Birth:* Willey, Iowa. *G.O. No.:* 77, 10 September 1945. *Citation:* He was leader of a machinegun squad defending an approach to the village of Birgel, Germany, on 14 December 1944, when an enemy tank, supported by 20 infantrymen, counterattacked. He held his fire until the Germans were within 100 yards and then raked the foot soldiers beside the tank, killing several of them. The enemy armor continued to press forward, and, at the pointblank range of 30 yards, fired a high-velocity shell into the American emplacement, wounding the entire squad. Sgt. Neppel, blown 10 yards from his gun, had 1 leg severed below the knee and suffered other wounds. Despite his injuries and the danger from the onrushing tank and infantry, he dragged himself back to his position on his elbows, remounted his gun and killed the remaining enemy riflemen. Stripped of its infantry protection, the tank was forced to withdraw. By his superb courage and indomitable fighting spirit, Sgt. Neppel inflicted heavy casualties on the enemy and broke a determined counterattack.

NETT, ROBERT P.

Rank and organization: Captain (then Lieutenant), U.S. Army, Company E, 305th Infantry, 77th Infantry Division. *Place and date:* Near Cognon, Leyte, Philippine Islands, 14 December 1944. *Entered service at:* Lynchburg, Va. *Birth:* New Haven, Conn. *G.O. No.:* 16, 8 February 1946. *Citation:* He commanded Company E in an attack against a reinforced enemy battalion which had held up the American advance for 2 days from its entrenched positions around a 3-story concrete building. With another infantry company and armored vehicles, Company E advanced against heavy machinegun and other automatic weapons fire with Lt. Nett spearheading the assault against the strongpoint. During the fierce hand-to-hand encounter which ensued, he killed 7 deeply entrenched Japanese with his rifle and bayonet and, although seriously wounded, gallantly continued to lead his men forward, refusing to relinquish his command. Again he was severely wounded, but, still unwilling to retire, pressed ahead with his troops to assure the capture of the objective. Wounded once more in the final assault, he calmly made all arrangements for the resumption of the advance, turned over his command to another officer, and then walked unaided to the rear for medical treatment. By his remarkable courage in continuing forward through sheer determination despite successive wounds, Lt. Nett provided an inspiring example for his men and was instrumental in the capture of a vital strongpoint.

*NEW, JOHN DURY

Rank and organization: Private First Class, U.S. Marine Corps. *Born:* 12 August 1924, Mobile, Ala. *Accredited to:* Alabama. *Citation:* For conspicuous gallantry and intrepidity at the risk of his life above and beyond the call of duty while serving with the 2d Battalion, 7th Marines, 1st Marine Division, in action against enemy Japanese forces on Peleliu Island, Palau Group, 25 September 1944. When a Japanese soldier emerged from a cave in a cliff directly below an observation post and suddenly hurled a grenade into the position from which 2 of our men were directing mortar fire against enemy emplacements, Pfc. New instantly perceived the dire peril to the other marines and, with utter disregard for his own safety, unhesitatingly flung himself upon the grenade and absorbed the full impact of the explosion, thus saving the lives of the 2 observers. Pfc. New's great personal valor and selfless conduct in the face of almost certain death reflect the highest credit upon himself and the U.S. Naval Service. He gallantly gave his life for his country.

NEWMAN, BERYL R.

Rank and organization: First Lieutenant, U.S. Army, 133d Infantry, 34th Infantry Division. *Place and date:* Near Cisterna, Italy, 26 May 1944. *Entered service at:* Baraboo, Wis. *Birth:* Baraboo, Wis. *G.O. No.:* 5, 15 January 1945. *Citation:* For conspicuous gallantry and intrepidity above and beyond the call of duty on 26 May 1944. Attacking the strongly held German Anzio-Nettuno defense line near Cisterna, Italy, 1st Lt. Newman, in the lead of his platoon, was suddenly fired upon by 2 enemy machineguns located on the crest of a hill about 100 yards to his front. The 4 scouts with him immediately hit the ground, but 1st Lt. Newman remained standing in order to see the enemy positions and his platoon then about 100 yards behind. Locating the enemy nests, 1st Lt. Newman called back to his platoon and ordered 1 squad to advance to him and the other to flank the enemy to the right. Then, still standing upright in the face of the enemy machinegun fire, 1st Lt. Newman opened up with his tommygun on the enemy nests. From this range, his fire was not effective in covering the advance of his squads, and 1 squad was pinned down by the enemy fire. Seeing that his squad was unable to advance, 1st Lt. Newman, in full view of the enemy gunners and in the face of their continuous fire, advanced alone on the enemy nests. He returned their fire with his tommygun and succeeded in wounding a German in each of the nests. The remaining 2 Germans fled from the position into a nearby house. Three more enemy soldiers then came out of the house and ran toward a third machinegun. 1st Lt. Newman, still relentlessly advancing toward them, killed 1 before he reached the gun, the second before he could fire it. The third fled for his life back into the house. Covering his assault by firing into the doors and windows of the house, 1st Lt. Newman, boldly attacking by himself, called for the occupants to surrender to him. Gaining the house, he kicked in the door and went inside. Although armed with rifles and machine pistols, the 11 Germans there, apparently intimidated, surrendered to the lieutenant without further resistance, 1st Lt. Newman, singlehanded, had silenced 3 enemy machineguns, wounded 2 Germans, killed 2 more, and took 11 prisoners. This demonstration of sheer courage, bravery, and willingness to close with the enemy even in the face of such heavy odds, instilled into these green troops the confidence of veterans and reflects the highest traditions of the U.S. Armed Forces.

*NININGER, ALEXANDER R., Jr.

Rank and organization: Second Lieutenant, U.S. Army, 57th Infantry, Philippine Scouts. *Place and date:* Near Abucay, Bataan, Philippine Islands, 12 January 1942. *Entered service at:* Fort Lauderdale, Fla. *Birth:* Gainesville, Ga. *G.O. No.:* 9, 5 February 1942. *Citation:* For conspicuous gallantry and intrepidity above and beyond the call of duty in action with the enemy near Abucay, Bataan, Philippine Islands, on 12 January 1942. This officer, though assigned to another company not then engaged in combat, voluntarily attached himself to Company K, same regiment, while that unit was being attacked by enemy force superior in firepower. Enemy snipers in trees and foxholes had stopped a counterattack to regain part of position. In hand-to-hand fighting which followed, 2d Lt. Nininger repeatedly forced his way to and into the hostile position. Though exposed to heavy enemy fire, he continued to attack with rifle and handgrenades and succeeded in destroying several enemy groups in foxholes and enemy snipers. Although wounded 3 times, he continued his attacks until he was killed after pushing alone far within the enemy position. When his body was found after recapture of the position, 1 enemy officer and 2 enemy soldiers lay dead around him.

*O'BRIEN, WILLIAM J.

Rank and organization: Lieutenant Colonel, U.S. Army, 1st Battalion, 105th Infantry, 27th Infantry Division. *Place and date:* At Saipan, Marianas Islands, 20 June through 7 July 1944. *Entered service at:* Troy, N.Y. *Birth:* Troy, N.Y. *G.O. No.:* 35, 9 May 1945. *Citation:* For conspicuous gallantry and intrepidity at the risk of his life above and beyond the call of duty at Saipan, Marianas Islands, from 20 June through 7 July 1944. When assault elements of his platoon were held up by intense enemy fire, Lt. Col. O'Brien ordered 3 tanks to precede the assault companies in an attempt to knock out the strongpoint. Due to direct enemy fire the tanks' turrets were closed, causing the tanks to lose direction and to fire into our own troops. Lt. Col. O'Brien, with complete disregard for his own safety, dashed into full view of the enemy and ran to the leader's tank, and pounded on the tank with his pistol butt to attract 2 of the tank's crew and, mounting the tank fully exposed to enemy fire, Lt. Col. O'Brien personally directed the assault until the enemy strongpoint had been liquidated. On 28 June 1944, while his platoon was attempting to take a bitterly defended high ridge in the vicinity of Donnay, Lt. Col. O'Brien arranged to capture the ridge by a double envelopment movement of 2 large combat battalions. He personally took control of the maneuver. Lt. Col. O'Brien crossed 1,200 yards of sniper-infested underbrush alone to arrive at a point where 1 of his platoons was being held up by the enemy. Leaving some men to contain the enemy he personally led 4 men into a narrow ravine behind, and killed or drove off all the Japanese manning that strongpoint. In this action he captured 5 machineguns and one 77-mm. fieldpiece. Lt. Col. O'Brien then organized the 2 platoons for night defense and against repeated counterattacks directed them. Meanwhile he managed to hold ground. On 7 July 1944 his battalion and another battalion were attacked by an overwhelming enemy force estimated at between 3,000 and 5,000 Japanese. With bloody hand-to-hand fighting in progress everywhere, their forward positions were finally overrun by the sheer weight of the enemy numbers. With many casualties and ammunition running low, Lt. Col. O'Brien refused to leave the front lines. Striding up and down the lines, he fired at the enemy with a pistol in each hand and his presence there bolstered the spirits of the men, encouraged them in their fight and sustained them in their heroic stand. Even after he was seriously wounded, Lt. Col. O'Brien refused to be evacuated and after his pistol ammunition was exhausted, he manned a .50 caliber machinegun, mounted on a jeep, and continued firing. When last seen alive he was standing upright firing into the Jap hordes that were then enveloping him. Some time later his body was found surrounded by enemy he had killed. His valor was consistent with the highest traditions of the service.

O'CALLAHAN, JOSEPH TIMOTHY

Rank and organization: Commander (Chaplain Corps), U.S. Naval Reserve, U.S.S. *Franklin. Place and date:* Near Kobe, Japan, 19 March 1945. *Entered service at:* Massachusetts. *Born:* 14 May 1904, Boston, Mass. *Citation:* For conspicuous gallantry and intrepidity at the risk of his life above and beyond the call of duty while serving as chaplain on board the U.S.S. *Franklin* when that vessel was fiercely attacked by enemy Japanese aircraft during offensive operations near Kobe, Japan, on 19 March 1945. A valiant and forceful leader, calmly braving the perilous barriers of flame and twisted metal to aid his men and his ship, Lt. Comdr. O'Callahan groped his way through smoke-filled corridors to the open flight deck and into the midst of violently exploding bombs, shells, rockets, and other armament. With the ship rocked by incessant explosions, with debris and fragments raining down and fires raging in ever-increasing fury, he ministered to the wounded and dying, comforting and encouraging men of all faiths; he organized and led firefighting crews into the blazing inferno on the flight deck; he directed the jettisoning of live ammunition and the flooding of the magazine; he manned a hose to cool hot, armed bombs rolling dangerously on the listing deck, continuing his efforts, despite searing, suffocating smoke which forced men to fall back gasping and imperiled others who replaced them. Serving with courage, fortitude, and deep spiritual strength, Lt. Comdr. O'Callahan inspired the gallant officers and men of the *Franklin* to fight heroically and with profound faith in the face of almost certain death and to return their stricken ship to port.

OGDEN, CARLOS C.

Rank and organization: First Lieutenant, U.S. Army, Company K, 314th Infantry, 79th Infantry Division. *Place and date:* Near Fort du Roule, France, 25 June 1944. *Entered service at:* Fairmont, Ill. *Born:* 19 May 1917, Borton, Ill. *G.O. No.:* 49, 28 June 1945. *Citation:* On the morning of 25 June 1944, near Fort du Roule, guarding the approaches to Cherbourg, France, 1st Lt. Ogden's company was pinned down by fire from a German 88-mm. gun and 2 machineguns. Arming himself with an M1 rifle, a grenade launcher, and a number of rifle and handgrenades, he left his company in position and advanced alone, under fire, up the slope toward the enemy emplacements. Struck on the head and knocked down by a glancing machinegun bullet, 1st Lt. Ogden, in spite of his painful wound and enemy fire from close range, continued up the hill. Reaching a vantage point, he silenced the 88-mm. gun with a well-placed rifle grenade and then, with handgrenades, knocked out the 2 machineguns, again being painfully wounded. 1st Lt. Ogden's heroic leadership and indomitable courage in alone silencing these enemy weapons inspired his men to greater effort and cleared the way for the company to continue the advance and reach its objectives.

O'HARE, EDWARD HENRY

Rank and organization: Lieutenant, U.S. Navy. *Born:* 13 March 1914, St. Louis, Mo. *Entered service at:* St. Louis, Mo. *Other Navy awards:* Navy Cross, Distinguished Flying Cross with 1 gold star. *Citation:* For conspicuous gallantry and intrepidity in aerial combat, at grave risk of his life above and beyond the call of duty, as section leader and pilot of Fighting Squadron 3 on 20 February 1942. Having lost the assistance of his teammates, Lt. O'Hare interposed his plane between his ship and an advancing enemy formation of 9 attacking twin-engined heavy bombers. Without hesitation, alone and unaided, he repeatedly attacked this enemy formation, at close range in the face of intense combined machinegun and cannon fire. Despite this concentrated opposition, Lt. O'Hare, by his gallant and courageous action, his extremely skillful marksmanship in making the most of every shot of his limited amount of ammunition, shot down 5 enemy bombers and severely damaged a sixth before they reached the bomb release point. As a result of his gallant action—one of the most daring, if not the most daring, single action in the history of combat aviation—he undoubtedly saved his carrier from serious damage.

O'KANE, RICHARD HETHERINGTON

Rank and organization: Commander, U.S. Navy, commanding U.S.S. *Tang. Place and date:* Vicinity Philippine Islands, 23 and 24 October 1944. *Entered service at:* New Hampshire. *Born:* 2 February 1911, Dover, N.H. *Citation:* For conspicuous gallantry and intrepidity at the risk of his life above and beyond the call of duty as commanding officer of the U.S.S. *Tang* operating against 2 enemy Japanese convoys on 23 and 24 October 1944, during her fifth and last war patrol. Boldly maneuvering on the surface into the midst of a heavily escorted convoy, Comdr. O'Kane stood in the fusillade of bullets and shells from all directions to launch smashing hits on 3 tankers, coolly swung his ship to fire at a freighter and, in a split-second decision, shot out of the path of an onrushing transport, missing it by inches. Boxed in by blazing tankers, a freighter, transport, and several destroyers, he blasted 2 of the targets with his remaining torpedoes and, with pyrotechnics bursting on all sides, cleared the area. Twenty-four hours later, he again made contact with a heavily escorted convoy steaming to support the Leyte campaign with reinforcements and supplies and with crated planes piled high on each unit. In defiance of the enemy's relentless fire, he closed the concentration of ship and in quick succession sent 2 torpedoes each into the first and second transports and an adjacent tanker, finding his mark with each torpedo in a series of violent explosions at less than 1,000-yard range. With ships bearing down from all sides, he charged the enemy at high speed, exploding the tanker in a burst of flame, smashing the transport dead in the water, and blasting the destroyer with a mighty roar which rocked the *Tang* from stem to stern. Expending his last 2 torpedoes into the remnants of a once powerful convoy before his own ship went down, Comdr. O'Kane, aided by his gallant command, achieved an illustrious record of heroism in combat, enhancing the finest traditions of the U.S. Naval Service.

*OLSON, ARLO L.

Rank and organization: Captain, U.S. Army, 15th Infantry, 3d Infantry Division. *Place and date:* Crossing of the Volturno River, Italy, 13 October 1943. *Entered service at:* Toronto, S. Dak. *Birth:* Greenville, Iowa. *G.O. No.:* 71, 31 August 1944. *Citation:* For conspicuous gallantry and intrepidity at the risk of his life above and beyond the call of duty. On 13 October 1943, when the drive across the Volturno River began, Capt. Olson and his company spearheaded the advance of the regiment through 30 miles of mountainous enemy territory in 13 days. Placing himself at the head of his men, Capt. Olson waded into the chest-deep water of the raging Volturno River and despite point-blank machine-gun fire aimed directly at him made his way to the opposite bank and threw 2 handgrenades into the gun position, killing the crew. When an enemy machinegun 150 yards distant opened fire on his company, Capt. Olson advanced upon the position in a slow, deliberate walk. Although 5 German soldiers threw handgrenades at him from a range of 5 yards, Capt. Olson dispatched them all, picked up a machine pistol and continued toward the enemy. Advancing to within 15 yards of the position he shot it out with the foe, killing 9 and seizing the post. Throughout the next 13 days Capt. Olson led combat patrols, acted as company No. 1 scout and maintained unbroken contact with the enemy. On 27 October 1943, Capt. Olson conducted a platoon in attack on a strongpoint, crawling to within 25 yards of the enemy and then charging the position. Despite continuous machinegun fire which barely missed him, Capt. Olson made his way to the gun and killed the crew with his pistol. When the men saw their leader make this desperate attack they followed him and overran the position. Continuing the advance, Capt. Olson led his company to the next objective at the summit of Monte San Nicola. Although the company to his right was forced to take cover from the furious automatic and small arms fire, which was directed upon him and his men with equal intensity, Capt. Olson waved his company into a skirmish line and despite the fire of a machinegun which singled him out as its sole target led the assault which drove the enemy away. While making a reconnaissance for defensive positions, Capt. Olson was fatally wounded. Ignoring his severe pain, this intrepid officer completed his reconnaissance, supervised the location of his men in the best defense positions, refused medical aid until all of his men had been cared for, and died as he was being carried down the mountain.

*OLSON, TRUMAN O.

Rank and organization: Sergeant, U.S. Army, Company B, 7th Infantry, 3d Infantry Division. *Place and date:* Near Cisterna di Littoria, Italy, 30–31 January 1944. *Entered service at:* Cambridge, Wis. *Birth:* Christiana, Wis. *G.O. No.:* 6, 24 January 1945. *Citation:* For conspicuous gallantry and intrepidity above and beyond the call of duty. Sgt. Olson, a light machine gunner, elected to sacrifice his life to save his company from annihilation. On the night of 30 January 1944, after a 16-hour assault on entrenched enemy positions in the course of which over one-third of Company B became casualties, the survivors dug in behind a horseshoe elevation, placing Sgt. Olson and his crew, with the 1 available machinegun, forward of their lines and in an exposed position to bear the brunt of the expected German counterattack. Although he had been fighting without respite, Sgt. Olson stuck grimly to his post all night while his guncrew was cut down, 1 by 1, by accurate and overwhelming enemy fire. Weary from over 24 hours of continuous battle and suffering from an arm wound, received during the night engagement, Sgt. Olson manned his gun alone, meeting the full force of an all-out enemy assault by approximately 200 men supported by mortar and machinegun fire which the Germans launched at daybreak on the morning of 31 January. After 30 minutes of fighting, Sgt. Olson was mortally wounded, yet, knowing that only his weapons stood between his company and complete destruction, he refused evacuation. For an hour and a half after receiving his second and fatal wound he continued to fire his machinegun, killing at least 20 of the enemy, wounding many more, and forcing the assaulting German elements to withdraw.

ORESKO, NICHOLAS

Rank and organization: Master Sergeant, U.S. Army, Company C, 302d Infantry, 94th Infantry Division. *Place and date:* Near Tettington, Germany, 23 January 1945. *Entered service at:* Bayonne, N.J. *Birth:* Bayonne, N.J. *G.O. No.:* 95, 30 October 1945. *Citation:* M/Sgt. Oresko was a platoon leader with Company C, in an attack against strong enemy positions. Deadly automatic fire from the flanks pinned down his unit. Realizing that a machinegun in a nearby bunker must be eliminated, he swiftly worked ahead alone, braving bullets which struck about him, until close enough to throw a grenade into the German position. He rushed the bunker and, with pointblank rifle fire, killed all the hostile occupants who survived the grenade blast. Another machinegun opened up on him, knocking him down and seriously wounding him in the hip. Refusing to withdraw from the battle, he placed himself at the head of his platoon to continue the assault. As withering machinegun and rifle fire swept the area, he struck out alone in advance of his men to a second bunker. With a grenade, he crippled the dug-in machinegun defending this position and then wiped out the troops manning it with his rifle, completing his second self-imposed, 1-man attack. Although weak from loss of blood, he refused to be evacuated until assured the mission was successfully accomplished. Through quick thinking, indomitable courage, and unswerving devotion to the attack in the face of bitter resistance and while wounded, M/Sgt.

Oresko killed 12 Germans, prevented a delay in the assault, and made it possible for Company C to obtain its objective with minimum casualties.

*OWENS, ROBERT ALLEN

Rank and organization: Sergeant, U.S. Marine Corps. *Born:* 13 September 1920, Greenville, S.C. *Accredited to:* South Carolina. *Citation:* For conspicuous gallantry and intrepidity at the risk of his life above and beyond the call of duty while serving with a marine division, in action against enemy Japanese forces during extremely hazardous landing operations at Cape Torokina, Bougainville, Solomon Islands, on 1 November 1943. Forced to pass within disastrous range of a strongly protected, well-camouflaged Japanese 75-mm. regimental gun strategically located on the beach, our landing units were suffering heavy losses in casualties and boats while attempting to approach the beach, and the success of the operations was seriously threatened. Observing the ineffectiveness of marine rifle and grenade attacks against the incessant, devastating fire of the enemy weapon and aware of the urgent need for prompt action, Sgt. Owens unhesitatingly determined to charge the gun bunker from the front and, calling on 4 of his comrades to assist him, carefully placed them to cover the fire of the 2 adjacent hostile bunkers. Choosing a moment that provided a fair opportunity for passing these bunkers, he immediately charged into the mouth of the steadily firing cannon and entered the emplacement through the fire port, driving the guncrew out of the rear door and insuring their destruction before he himself was wounded. Indomitable and aggressive in the face of almost certain death, Sgt. Owens silenced a powerful gun which was of inestimable value to the Japanese defense and, by his brilliant initiative and heroic spirit of self-sacrifice, contributed immeasurably to the success of the vital landing operations. His valiant conduct throughout reflects the highest credit upon himself and the U.S. Naval Service.

*OZBOURN, JOSEPH WILLIAM

Rank and organization: Private, U.S. Marine Corps. *Born:* 24 October 1919, Herrin, Ill. *Accredited to:* Illinois. *Citation:* For conspicuous gallantry and intrepidity at the risk of his life above and beyond the call of duty as a Browning Automatic Rifleman serving with the 1st Battalion, 23d Marines, 4th Marine Division, during the battle for enemy Japanese-held Tinian Island, Marianas Islands, 30 July 1944. As a member of a platoon assigned the mission of clearing the remaining Japanese troops from dugouts and pillboxes along a tree line, Pvt. Ozbourn, flanked by 2 men on either side, was moving forward to throw an armed handgrenade into a dugout when a terrific blast from the entrance severely wounded the 4 men and himself. Unable to throw the grenade into the dugout and with no place to hurl it without endangering the other men, Pvt. Ozbourn unhesitatingly grasped it close to his body and fell upon it, sacrificing his own life to absorb the full impact of the explosion, but saving his comrades. His great personal valor and unwavering loyalty reflect the highest credit upon Pvt. Ozbourn and the U.S. Naval Service. He gallantly gave his life for his country.

PAIGE, MITCHELL

Rank and organization: Platoon Sergeant, U.S. Marine Corps. *Place and date:* Solomon Islands, 26 October 1942. *Entered service at:* Pennsylvania. *Born:* 31 August 1918, Charleroi, Pa. *Citation:* For extraordinary heroism and conspicuous gallantry in action above and beyond the call of duty while serving with a company of marines in combat against enemy Japanese forces in the Solomon Islands on 26 October 1942. When the enemy broke through the line directly in front of his position, P/Sgt. Paige, commanding a machinegun section with fearless determination, continued to direct the fire of his gunners until all his men were either killed or wounded. Alone, against the deadly hail of Japanese shells, he fought with his gun and when it was destroyed, took over another, moving from gun to gun, never ceasing his withering fire against the advancing hordes until reinforcements finally arrived. Then, forming a new line, he dauntlessly and aggressively led a bayonet charge, driving the enemy back and preventing a breakthrough in our lines. His great personal valor and unyielding devotion to duty were in keeping with the highest traditions of the U.S. Naval Service.

*PARLE, JOHN JOSEPH

Rank and organization: Ensign, U.S. Naval Reserve. *Born:* 26 May 1920, Omaha, Nebr. *Accredited to:* Nebraska. *Citation:* For valor and courage above and beyond the call of duty as Officer-in-Charge of Small Boats in the U.S.S. LST *375* during the amphibious assault on the island of Sicily, 9–10 July 1943. Realizing that a detonation of explosives would prematurely disclose to the enemy the assault about to be carried out, and with full knowledge of the peril involved, Ens. Parle unhesitatingly risked his life to extinguish a smoke pot accidentally ignited in a boat carrying charges of high explosives, detonating fuses and ammunition. Undaunted by fire and blinding smoke, he entered the craft, quickly snuffed out a burning fuse, and after failing in his desperate efforts to extinguish the fire pot, finally seized it with both hands and threw it over the side. Although he succumbed a week later from smoke and fumes inhaled, Ens. Parle's heroic self-sacrifice prevented grave damage to the ship and personnel and insured the security of a vital mission. He gallantly gave his life in the service of his country.

*PARRISH, LAVERNE

Rank and organization: Technician 4th Grade, U.S. Army, Medical Detachment, 161st Infantry, 25th Infantry Division. *Place and date:* Binalonan, Luzon, Philippine Islands, 18–24 January 1945. *Entered service at:* Ronan, Mont. *Birth:* Knox City, Mo. *G.O. No.:* 55, 13 July 1945. *Citation:* He was medical aid man with Company C during the fighting in Binalonan, Luzon, Philippine Islands. On the 18th, he observed 2 wounded men under enemy fire and immediately went to their rescue. After moving 1 to cover, he crossed 25 yards of open ground to administer aid to the second. In the early hours of the 24th, his company, crossing an open field near San Manuel, encountered intense enemy fire and was ordered to withdraw to the cover of a ditch.

While treating the casualties, Technician Parrish observed 2 wounded still in the field. Without hesitation he left the ditch, crawled forward under enemy fire, and in 2 successive trips brought both men to safety. He next administered aid to 12 casualties in the same field, crossing and recrossing the open area raked by hostile fire. Making successive trips, he then brought 3 wounded in to cover. After treating nearly all of the 37 casualties suffered by his company, he was mortally wounded by mortar fire, and shortly after was killed. The indomitable spirit, intrepidity, and gallantry of Technician Parrish saved many lives at the cost of his own.

*PEASE, HARL, JR. (Air Mission)

Rank and organization: Captain, U.S. Army Air Corps, Heavy Bombardment Squadron. *Place and date:* Near Rabaul, New Britain, 6–7 August 1942. *Entered service at:* Plymouth, N.H. *Birth:* Plymouth, N.H. *G.O. No.:* 59, 4 November 1942. *Citation:* For conspicuous gallantry and intrepidity above and beyond the call of duty in action with the enemy on 6–7 August 1942. When 1 engine of the bombardment airplane of which he was pilot failed during a bombing mission over New Guinea, Capt. Pease was forced to return to a base in Australia. Knowing that all available airplanes of his group were to participate the next day in an attack on an enemy-held airdrome near Rabaul, New Britain, although he was not scheduled to take part in this mission, Capt. Pease selected the most serviceable airplane at this base and prepared it for combat, knowing that it had been found and declared unserviceable for combat missions. With the members of his combat crew, who volunteered to accompany him, he rejoined his squadron at Port Moresby, New Guinea, at 1 a.m. on 7 August, after having flown almost continuously since early the preceding morning. With only 3 hours' rest, he took off with his squadron for the attack. Throughout the long flight to Rabaul, New Britain, he managed by skillful flying of his unserviceable airplane to maintain his position in the group. When the formation was intercepted by about 30 enemy fighter airplanes before reaching the target, Capt. Pease, on the wing which bore the brunt of the hostile attack, by gallant action and the accurate shooting by his crew, succeeded in destroying several Zeros before dropping his bombs on the hostile base as planned, this in spite of continuous enemy attacks. The fight with the enemy pursuit lasted 25 minutes until the group dived into cloud cover. After leaving the target, Capt. Pease's aircraft fell behind the balance of the group due to unknown difficulties as a result of the combat, and was unable to reach this cover before the enemy pursuit succeeded in igniting 1 of his bomb bay tanks. He was seen to drop the flaming tank. It is believed that Capt. Pease's airplane and crew were subsequently shot down in flames, as they did not return to their base. In voluntarily performing this mission Capt. Pease contributed materially to the success of the group, and displayed high devotion to duty, valor, and complete contempt for personal danger. His undaunted bravery has been a great inspiration to the officers and men of his unit.

*PEDEN, FORREST E.

Rank and organization: Technician 5th Grade, U.S. Army, Battery C, 10th Field Artillery Battalion, 3d Infantry Division. *Place and date:* Near Biesheim, France, 3 February 1945. *Entered service at:* Wathena, Kans. *Birth:* St. Joseph, Mo. *G.O. No.:* 18, 13 February 1946. *Citation:* He was a forward artillery observer when the group of about 45 infantrymen with whom he was advancing was ambushed in the uncertain light of a waning moon. Enemy forces outnumbering the Americans by 4 to 1 poured withering artillery, mortar, machinegun, and small-arms fire into the stricken unit from the flanks, forcing our men to seek the cover of a ditch which they found already occupied by enemy foot troops. As the opposing infantrymen struggled in hand-to-hand combat, Technician Peden courageously went to the assistance of 2 wounded soldiers and rendered first aid under heavy fire. With radio communications inoperative, he realized that the unit would be wiped out unless help could be secured from the rear. On his own initiative, he ran 800 yards to the battalion command post through a hail of bullets which pierced his jacket and there secured 2 light tanks to go to the relief of his hard-pressed comrades. Knowing the terrible risk involved, he climbed upon the hull of the lead tank and guided it into battle. Through a murderous concentration of fire the tank lumbered onward, bullets and shell fragments ricocheting from its steel armor within inches of the completely exposed rider, until it reached the ditch. As it was about to go into action it was turned into a flaming pyre by a direct hit which killed Technician Peden. However, his intrepidity and gallant sacrifice was not in vain. Attracted by the light from the burning tank, reinforcements found the beleaguered Americans and drove off the enemy.

*PENDLETON, JACK J.

Rank and organization: Staff Sergeant, U.S. Army, Company I, 120th Infantry, 30th Infantry Division. *Place and date:* Bardenberg, Germany, 12 October 1944. *Entered service at:* Yakima, Wash. *Birth:* Sentinel Butte, N. Dak. *G.O. No.:* 24, 6 April 1945. *Citation:* For conspicuous gallantry and intrepidity at the risk of his life above and beyond the call of duty on 12 October 1944. When Company I was advancing on the town of Bardenberg, Germany, they reached a point approximately two-thirds of the distance through the town when they were pinned down by fire from a nest of enemy machineguns. This enemy strong point was protected by a lone machinegun strategically placed at an intersection and firing down a street which offered little or no cover or concealment for the advancing troops. The elimination of this protecting machinegun was imperative in order that the stronger position it protected could be neutralized. After repeated and unsuccessful attempts had been made to knock out this position, S/Sgt. Pendleton volunteered to lead his squad in an attempt to neutralize this strongpoint. S/Sgt. Pendleton started his squad slowly forward, crawling about 10 yards in front of his men in the advance toward the enemy gun. After advancing approximately 130 yards under the withering fire, S/Sgt. Pendleton was seriously wounded in the leg by a burst from the gun he was assaulting. Disregarding his grievous wound, he ordered his men to remain where they were, and with a supply of handgrenades he slowly and painfully worked his way forward alone. With no hope of surviving the veritable hail of machinegun fire which he deliberately drew onto himself, he succeeded in advancing to within 10 yards of the enemy position when he was instantly killed by a burst from the enemy gun. By deliberately diverting the attention of the enemy machine gunners upon himself, a second squad was able to advance, undetected, and with the help of S/Sgt. Pendleton's squad, neutralized the lone machinegun, while another platoon of his company advanced up the intersecting street and knocked out the machinegun nest which the first gun had been covering. S/Sgt. Pendleton's sacrifice enabled the entire company to continue the advance and complete their mission at a critical phase of the action.

*PEREGORY, FRANK D.

Rank and organization: Technical Sergeant, U.S. Army, Company K, 116th Infantry, 29th Infantry Division. *Place and date:* Grandcampe, France, 8 June 1944. *Entered service at:* Charlottesville, Va. *Born:* 10 April 1915, Esmont, Va. *G.O. No.:* 43, 30 May 1945. *Citation:* On 8 June 1944, the 3d Battalion of the 116th Infantry was advancing on the strongly held German defenses at Grandcampe, France, when the leading elements were suddenly halted by decimating machinegun fire from a firmly entrenched enemy force on the high ground overlooking the town. After numerous attempts to neutralize the enemy position by supporting artillery and tank fire had proved ineffective, T/Sgt. Peregory, on his own initiative, advanced up the hill under withering fire, and worked his way to the crest where he discovered an entrenchment leading to the main enemy fortifications 200 yards away. Without hesitating, he leaped into the trench and moved toward the emplacement. Encountering a squad of enemy riflemen, he fearlessly attacked them with handgrenades and bayonet, killed 8 and forced 3 to surrender. Continuing along the trench, he singlehandedly forced the surrender of 32 more riflemen, captured the machine gunners, and opened the way for the leading elements of the battalion to advance and secure its objective. The extraordinary gallantry and aggressiveness displayed by T/Sgt. Peregory are exemplary of the highest tradition of the armed forces.

*PEREZ, MANUEL, JR.

Rank and organization: Private First Class, U.S. Army, Company A, 511th Parachute Infantry, 11th Airborne Division. *Place and date:* Fort William McKinley, Luzon, Philippine Islands, 13 February 1945. *Entered service at:* Chicago, Ill. *Born:* 3 March 1923 Oklahoma City, Okla. *G.O. No.:* 124, 27 December 1945. *Citation:* He was lead scout for Company A, which had destroyed 11 of 12 pillboxes in a strongly fortified sector defending the approach to enemy-held Fort William McKinley on Luzon, Philippine Islands. In the reduction of these pillboxes, he killed 5 Japanese in the open and blasted others in pillboxes with grenades. Realizing the urgent need for taking the last emplacement, which contained 2 twin-mount .50-caliber dual-purpose machineguns, he took a circuitous route to within 20 yards of the position, killing 4 of the enemy in his advance. He threw a grenade into the pillbox, and, as the crew started withdrawing through a tunnel just to the rear of the emplacement, shot and killed 4 before exhausting his clip. He had reloaded and killed 4 more when an escaping Japanese threw his rifle with fixed bayonet at him. In warding off this thrust, his own rifle was knocked to the ground. Seizing the Jap rifle, he continued firing, killing 2 more of the enemy. He rushed the remaining Japanese, killed 3 of them with the butt of the rifle and entered the pillbox, where he bayoneted the 1 surviving hostile soldier. Singlehandedly, he killed 18 of the enemy in neutralizing the position that had held up the advance of his entire company. Through his courageous determination and heroic disregard of grave danger, Pfc. Perez made possible the successful advance of his unit toward a valuable objective and provided a lasting inspiration for his comrades.

*PETERS, GEORGE J.

Rank and organization: Private, U.S. Army, Company G, 507th Parachute Infantry, 17th Airborne Division. *Place and date:* Near Fluren, Germany, 24 March 1945. *Entered service at:* Cranston, R.I. *Birth:* Cranston, R.I. *G.O. No.:* 16, 8 February 1946. *Citation:* Pvt. Peters, a platoon radio operator with Company G, made a descent into Germany near Fluren, east of the Rhine. With 10 others, he landed in a field about 75 yards from a German machinegun supported by riflemen, and was immediately pinned down by heavy, direct fire. The position of the small unit seemed hopeless with men struggling to free themselves of their parachutes in a hail of bullets that cut them off from their nearby equipment bundles, when Pvt. Peters stood up without orders and began a 1-man charge against the hostile emplacement armed only with a rifle and grenades. His singlehanded assault immediately drew the enemy fire away from his comrades. He had run halfway to his objective, pitting rifle fire against that of the machinegun, when he was struck and knocked to the ground by a burst. Heroically, he regained his feet and struggled onward. Once more he was torn by bullets, and this time he was unable to rise. With gallant devotion to his self-imposed mission, he crawled directly into the fire that had mortally wounded him until close enough to hurl grenades which knocked out the machinegun, killed 2 of its operators, and drove protecting riflemen from their positions into the safety of a woods. By his intrepidity and supreme sacrifice, Pvt. Peters saved the lives of many of his fellow soldiers and made it possible for them to reach their equipment, organize, and seize their first objective.

*PETERSON, GEORGE

Rank and organization: Staff Sergeant, U.S. Army, Company K, 18th Infantry, 1st Infantry Division. *Place and date:* Near Eisern, Germany, 30 March 1945. *Entered service at:* Brooklyn, N.Y. *Birth:* Brooklyn, N.Y. *G.O. No.:* 88, 17 October 1945. *Citation:* He was an acting platoon sergeant with Company K, near Eisern, Germany. When his company encountered an enemy battalion and came under heavy small-arms, machinegun, and mortar fire, the 2d Platoon was given the mission of flanking the enemy positions while the remaining units attacked frontally. S/Sgt. Peterson crept and crawled to a position in the lead and motioned for the 2d Platoon to follow. A mortar shell fell close by and severely wounded him in the legs, but, although bleeding and suffering intense pain, he refused to withdraw and continued forward. Two hostile machineguns went into action at close range. Braving this grazing fire, he crawled steadily toward the guns and worked his way alone to a shallow draw, where, despite the hail of bullets, he raised himself to his knees and threw a grenade into the nearest machinegun nest, silencing the weapon and killing or wounding all its crew. The second gun was immediately turned on him, but he calmly and deliberately threw a second grenade which rocked the position and killed all 4 Germans who occupied it. As he continued forward he was spotted by an enemy rifleman, who shot him in the arm. Undeterred, he crawled some 20 yards until a third machinegun opened fire on him. By almost superhuman effort, weak from loss of blood and suffering great pain, he again raised himself to his knees and fired a grenade from his rifle, killing 3 of the enemy guncrew and causing the remaining one to flee. With the first objective seized, he was being treated by the company aid man when he observed 1 of his outpost men seriously wounded by a mortar burst. He wrenched himself from the hands of the aid man and began to crawl forward to assist his comrade, whom he had almost reached when he was struck and fatally wounded by an enemy bullet. S/Sgt. Peterson, by his gallant, intrepid actions, unrelenting fighting spirit, and outstanding initiative, silenced 3 enemy machineguns against great odds and while suffering from severe wounds, enabling his company to advance with minimum casualties.

*PETERSON, OSCAR VERNER

Rank and organization: Chief Watertender, U.S. Navy. *Born:* 27 August 1899, Prentice, Wis. *Accredited to:* Wisconsin. *Citation:* For extraordinary courage and conspicuous heroism above and beyond the call of duty while in charge of a repair party during an attack on the U.S.S. *Neosho* by enemy Japanese aerial forces on 7 May 1942. Lacking assistance because of injuries to the other members of his repair party and severely wounded himself, Peterson, with no concern for his own life, closed the bulkhead stop valves and in so doing received additional burns which resulted in his death. His spirit of self sacrifice and loyalty, characteristic of a fine seaman, was in keeping with the highest traditions of the U.S. Naval Service. He gallantly gave his life in the service of his country.

*PETRARCA, FRANK J.

Rank and organization: Private First Class, U.S. Army, Medical Detachment, 145th Infantry, 37th Infantry Division. *Place and date:* At Horseshoe Hill, New Georgia, Solomon Islands, 27 July 1943. *Entered service at:* Cleveland, Ohio. *Birth:* Cleveland, Ohio. *G.O. No.:* 86, 23 December 1943. *Citation:* For conspicuous gallantry and intrepidity in action above and beyond the call of duty. Pfc. Petrarca advanced with the leading troop element to within 100 yards of the enemy fortifications where mortar and small-arms fire caused a number of casualties. Singling out the most seriously wounded, he worked his way to the aid of Pfc. Scott, lying within 75 yards of the enemy, whose wounds were so serious that he could not even be moved out of the direct line of fire. Pfc. Petrarca fearlessly administered first aid to Pfc. Scott and 2 other soldiers and shielded the former until his death. On 29 July 1943, Pfc. Petrarca, during an intense mortar barrage, went to the aid of his sergeant who had been partly buried in a foxhole under the debris of a shell explosion, dug him out, restored him to consciousness and caused his evacuation. On 31 July 1943 and against the warning of a fellow soldier, he went to the aid of a mortar fragment casualty where his path over the crest of a hill exposed him to enemy observation from only 20 yards distance. A target for intense knee mortar and automatic fire, he resolutely worked his way to within 2 yards of his objective where he was mortally wounded by hostile mortar fire. Even on the threshold of death he continued to display valor and contempt for the foe; raising himself to his knees, this intrepid soldier shouted defiance at the enemy, made a last attempt to reach his wounded comrade and fell in glorious death.

PHARRIS, JACKSON CHARLES

Rank and organization: Lieutenant, U.S. Navy, U.S.S. *California. Place and date:* Pearl Harbor, Territory of Hawaii, 7 December 1941. *Entered service at:* California. *Born:* 26 June 1912, Columbus, Ga. *Citation:* For conspicuous gallantry and intrepidity at the risk of his life above and beyond the call of duty while attached to the U.S.S. *California* during the surprise enemy Japanese aerial attack on Pearl Harbor, Territory of Hawaii, 7 December 1941. In charge of the ordnance repair party on the third deck when the first Japanese torpedo struck almost directly under his station, Lt. (then Gunner) Pharris was stunned and severely injured by the concussion which hurled him to the overhead and back to the deck. Quickly recovering, he acted on his own initiative to set up a hand-supply ammunition train for the anti-aircraft guns. With water and oil rushing in where the port bulkhead had been torn up from the deck, with many of the remaining crewmembers overcome by oil fumes, and the ship without power and listing heavily to port as a result of a second torpedo hit, Lt. Pharris ordered the shipfitters to counterflood. Twice rendered unconscious by the nauseous fumes and handicapped by his painful injuries, he persisted in his desperate efforts to speed up the supply of ammunition and at the same time repeatedly risked his life to enter flooding compartments and drag to safety unconscious shipmates who were gradually being submerged in oil. By his inspiring leadership, his valiant efforts and his extreme loyalty to his ship and her crew, he saved many of his shipmates from death and was largely responsible for keeping the *California* in action during the attack. His heroic conduct throughout this first eventful engagement of World War II reflects the highest credit upon Lt. Pharris and enhances the finest traditions of the U.S. Naval Service.

*PHELPS, WESLEY

Rank and organization: Private, U.S. Marine Corps Reserve. *Born:* 12 June 1923, Neafus, Ky. *Accredited to:* Kentucky. *Citation:* For conspicuous gallantry and intrepidity at the risk of his life above and beyond the call of duty while serving with the 3d Battalion, 7th Marines, 1st Marine Division, in action against enemy Japanese forces on Peleliu Island, Palau Group, during a savage hostile counterattack on the night of 4 October 1944. Stationed with another marine in an advanced position when a Japanese handgrenade landed in his foxhole, Pfc. Phelps instantly shouted a warning to his comrade and rolled over on the deadly bomb, absorbing with his own body the full, shattering impact of the exploding charge. Courageous and indomitable, Pfc. Phelps fearlessly gave his life that another might be spared serious injury, and his great valor and heroic devotion to duty in the face of certain death reflect the highest credit upon himself and the U.S. Naval Service. He gallantly gave his life for his country.

*PHILLIPS, GEORGE

Rank and organization: Private, U.S. Marine Corps Reserve. *Born:* 14 July 1926, Rich Hill, Mo. *Entered service at:* Labadie, Mo. *Citation:* For conspicuous gallantry and intrepidity at the risk of his life above and beyond the call of duty while serving with the 2d Battalion, 28th Marines, 5th Marine Division, in action against enemy Japanese forces during the seizure of Iwo Jima in the Volcano Islands, on 14 March 1945. Standing the foxhole watch while other members of his squad rested after a night of bitter handgrenade fighting against infiltrating Japanese troops, Pvt. Phillips was the only member of his unit alerted when an enemy handgrenade was tossed into their midst. Instantly shouting a warning, he unhesitatingly threw himself on the deadly missile, absorbing the shattering violence of the exploding charge in his own body and protecting his comrades from serious injury. Stouthearted and indomitable, Pvt. Phillips willingly yielded his own life that his fellow marines might carry on the relentless battle against a fanatic enemy. His superb valor and unfaltering spirit of self-sacrifice in the face of certain death reflect the highest credit upon himself and upon the U.S. Naval Service. He gallantly gave his life for his country.

PIERCE, FRANCIS JUNIOR

Rank and organization: Pharmacist's Mate First Class, U.S. Navy, serving with 2d Battalion, 24th Marines, 4th Marine Division. *Place and date:* Iwo Jima, 15 and 16 March 1945. *Entered service at:* Iowa. *Born:* 7 December 1924, Earlville, Iowa. *Citation:* For conspicuous gallantry and intrepidity at the risk of his life above and beyond the call of duty while attached to the 2d Battalion, 24th Marines, 4th Marine Division, during the Iwo Jima campaign, 15 and 16 March 1945. Almost continuously under fire while carrying out the most dangerous volunteer assignments, Pierce gained valuable knowledge of the terrain and disposition of troops. Caught in heavy enemy rifle and machinegun fire which wounded a corpsman and 2 of the 8 stretcher bearers who were carrying 2 wounded marines to a forward aid station on 15 March, Pierce quickly took charge of the party, carried the newly wounded men to a sheltered position, and rendered first aid. After directing the evacuation of 3 of the casualties, he stood in the open to draw the enemy's fire and, with his weapon blasting, enabled the litter bearers to reach cover. Turning his attention to the other 2 casualties, he was attempting to stop the profuse bleeding of 1 man when a Japanese fired from a cave less than 20 yards away and wounded his patient again. Risking his own life to save his patient, Pierce deliberately exposed himself to draw the attacker from the cave and destroyed him with the last of his ammunition. Then lifting the wounded man to his back, he advanced unarmed through deadly rifle fire across 200 feet of open terrain. Despite exhaustion and in the face of warnings against such a suicidal mission, he again traversed the same fire-swept path to rescue the remaining marine. On the following morning, he led a combat patrol to the sniper nest and, while aiding a striken marine, was seriously wounded. Refusing aid for himself, he directed treatment for the casualty, at the same time maintaining protective fire for his comrades. Completely fearless, completely devoted to the care of his patients, Pierce inspired the entire battalion. His valor in the face of extreme peril sustains and enhances the finest traditions of the U.S. Naval Service.

*PINDER, JOHN J., JR.

Rank and organization: Technician Fifth Grade, U.S. Army, 16th Infantry, 1st Infantry Division. *Place and date:* Near Colleville-sur-Mer, France, 6 June 1944. *Entered service at:* Burgettstown, Pa. *Birth:* McKees Rocks, Pa. *G.O. No.:* 1, 4 January 1945. *Citation:* For conspicuous gallantry and intrepidity above and beyond the call of duty on 6 June 1944, near Colleville-sur-Mer, France. On D-day, Technician 5th Grade Pinder landed on the coast 100 yards off shore under devastating enemy machinegun and artillery fire which caused severe casualties among the boatload. Carrying a vitally important radio, he struggled towards shore in waist-deep water. Only a few yards from his craft he was hit by enemy fire and was gravely wounded. Technician 5th Grade Pinder never stopped. He made shore and delivered the radio. Refusing to take cover afforded, or to accept medical attention for his wounds, Technician 5th Grade Pinder, though terribly weakened by loss of blood and in fierce pain, on 3 occasions went into the fire-swept surf to salvage communication equipment. He recovered many vital parts and equipment, including another workable radio. On the 3rd trip he was again hit, suffering machinegun bullet wounds in the legs. Still this valiant soldier would not stop for rest or medical attention. Remaining exposed to heavy enemy fire, growing steadily weaker, he aided in establishing the vital radio communication on the beach. While so engaged this dauntless soldier was hit for the third time and killed. The indomitable courage and personal bravery of Technician 5th Grade Pinder was a magnificent inspiration to the men with whom he served.

POPE, EVERETT PARKER

Rank and organization: Captain, U.S. Marine Corps, Company C, 1st Battalion, 1st Marines, 1st Marine Division. *Place and date:* Peleliu Island, Palau group, 19–20 September 1944. *Entered service at:* Massachusetts. *Born:* 16 July 1919, Milton, Mass. *Citation:* For conspicuous gallantry and intrepidity at the risk of his life above and beyond the call of duty while serving as commanding officer of Company C, 1st Battalion, 1st Marines, 1st Marine Division, during action against enemy Japanese forces on Peleliu Island, Palau group, on 19–20 September 1944. Subjected to pointblank cannon fire which caused heavy casualties and badly disorganized his company while assaulting a steep coral hill, Capt. Pope rallied his men and gallantly led them to the summit in the face of machinegun, mortar, and sniper fire. Forced by widespread hostile attack to deploy the remnants of his company thinly in order to hold the ground won, and with his machineguns out of order and insufficient water and ammunition, he remained on the exposed hill with 12 men and 1 wounded officer, determined to hold through the night. Attacked continuously with grenades, machineguns, and rifles from 3 sides, he and his valiant men fiercely beat back or destroyed the enemy, resorting to hand-to-hand combat as the supply of ammunition dwindled, and still maintaining his lines with his 8 remaining riflemen when daylight brought more deadly fire and he was ordered to withdraw. His valiant leadership against devastating odds while protecting the units below from heavy Japanese attack reflects the highest credit upon Capt. Pope and the U.S. Naval Service.

*POWER, JOHN VINCENT

Rank and organization: First Lieutenant, U.S. Marine Corps. *Born:* 20 November 1918, Worcester, Mass. *Appointed from:* Massachusetts. *Citation:* For conspicuous gallantry and intrepidity at the risk of his life above and beyond the call of duty as platoon leader, attached to the 4th Marine Division, during the landing and battle of Namur Island, Kwajalein Atoll, Marshall Islands, 1 February 1944. Severely wounded in the stomach while setting a demolition charge on a Japanese pillbox, 1st Lt. Power was steadfast in his determination to remain in action. Protecting his wound with his left hand and firing with his right, he courageously advanced as another hostile position was taken under attack, fiercely charging the opening made by the explosion and emptying his carbine into the pillbox. While attempting to reload and continue the attack, 1st Lt. Power was shot again in the stomach and head and collapsed in the doorway. His exceptional valor, fortitude and indomitable fighting spirit in the face of withering enemy fire were in keeping with the highest traditions of the U.S. Naval Service. He gallantly gave his life for his country.

*POWERS, JOHN JAMES

Rank and organization: Lieutenant, U.S. Navy. *Born:* 13 July 1912, New York City, N.Y. *Accredited to:* New York. *Other Navy award:* Air Medal with 1 gold star. *Citation:* For distinguished and conspicuous gallantry and intrepidity at the risk of his life above and beyond the call of duty, while pilot of an airplane of Bombing Squadron 5, Lt. Powers participated, with his squadron, in 5 engagements with Japanese forces in the Coral Sea area and adjacent waters during the period 4 to 8 May 1942. Three attacks were made on enemy objectives at or near Tulagi on 4 May. In these attacks he scored a direct hit which instantly demolished a large enemy gunboat or destroyer and is credited with 2 close misses, 1 of which severely damaged a large aircraft tender, the other damaging a 20,000-ton transport. He fearlessly strafed a gunboat, firing all his ammunition into it amid intense antiaircraft fire. This gunboat was then observed to be leaving a heavy oil slick in its wake and later was seen beached on a nearby island. On 7 May, an attack was launched against an enemy airplane carrier and other units of the enemy's invasion force. He fearlessly led his attack section of 3 Douglas Dauntless dive bombers, to attack the carrier. On this occasion he dived in the face of heavy antiaircraft fire, to an altitude well below the safety altitude, at the risk of his life and almost certain damage to his own plane, in order that he might positively obtain a hit in a vital part of the ship, which would insure her complete destruction. This bomb hit was noted by many pilots and observers to cause a tremendous explosion engulfing the ship in a mass of flame, smoke, and debris. The ship sank soon after. That evening, in his capacity as Squadron Gunnery Officer, Lt. Powers gave a lecture to the squadron on point-of-aim and diving technique. During this discourse he advocated low release point in order to insure greater accuracy; yet he stressed the danger not only from enemy fire and the resultant low pull-out, but from own bomb blast and bomb fragments. Thus his low-dive bombing attacks were deliberate and premeditated, since he well knew and realized the dangers of such tactics, but went far beyond the call of duty in order to further the cause which he knew to be right. The next morning, 8 May, as the pilots of the attack group left the ready room to man planes, his indomitable spirit and leadership were well expressed in his own words, "Remember the folks back home are counting on us. I am going to get a hit if I have to lay it on their flight deck." He led his section of dive bombers down to the target from an altitude of 18,000 feet, through a wall of bursting antiaircraft shells and into the face of enemy fighter planes. Again, completely disregarding the safety altitude and without fear or concern for his safety, Lt. Powers courageously pressed home his attack, almost to the very deck of an enemy carrier and did not release his bomb until he was sure of a direct hit. He was last seen attempting recovery from his dive at the extremely low altitude of 200 feet, and amid a terrific barrage of shell and bomb fragments, smoke, flame and debris from the stricken vessel.

POWERS, LEO J.

Rank and organization: Private First Class, U.S. Army, 133d Infantry, 34th Infantry Division. *Place and date:* Northwest of Cassino, Italy, 3 February 1944. *Entered service at:* Alder Gulch, Mont. *Birth:* Anselmo, Nebr. *G.O. No.:* 5, 15 January 1945. *Citation:* For conspicuous gallantry and intrepidity at risk of life above and beyond the call of duty. On 3 February 1944, this soldier's company was assigned the mission of capturing Hill 175, the key enemy strong point northwest of Cassino, Italy. The enemy, estimated to be at least 50 in strength, supported by machineguns emplaced in 3 pillboxes and mortar fire from behind the hill, was able to pin the attackers down and inflict 8 casualties. The company was unable to advance, but Pfc. Powers, a rifleman in 1 of the assault platoons, on his own initiative and in the face of the terrific fire, crawled forward to assault 1 of the enemy pillboxes which he had spotted. Armed with 2 handgrenades and well aware that if the enemy should see him it would mean almost certain death, Pfc. Powers crawled up the hill to within 15 yards of the enemy pillbox. Then standing upright in full view of the enemy gunners in order to throw his grenade into the small opening in the roof, he tossed a grenade into the pillbox. At this close, the grenade entered the pillbox, killed 2 of the occupants and 3 or 4 more fled the position, probably wounded. This enemy gun silenced, the center of the line was able to move forward again, but almost immediately came under machinegun fire from a second enemy pillbox on the left flank. Pfc. Powers, however, had located this pillbox, and crawled toward it, with absolutely no cover if the enemy should see him. Raising himself in full view of the enemy gunners about 15 feet from the pillbox, Pfc. Powers threw his grenade into the pillbox, silencing this gun, killing another German and probably wounding 3 or 4 more who fled. Pfc. Powers, still acting on his own initiative, commenced crawling toward the third enemy pillbox in the face of heavy machine-pistol and machinegun fire. Skillfully availing himself of the meager cover and concealment, Pfc. Powers crawled up to within 10 yards of this pillbox, fully exposed himself to the enemy gunners, stood upright and tossed the 2 grenades into the small opening in the roof of the pillbox. His grenades killed 2 of the enemy and 4 more, all wounded, came out and surrendered to Pfc. Powers, who was now unarmed. Pfc. Powers had worked his way over the entire company front, and against tremendous odds had singlehandedly broken the backbone of this heavily defended and strategic enemy position, and enabled his regiment to advance into the city of Cassino. Pfc. Powers' fighting determination and intrepidity in battle exemplify the highest traditions of the U.S. Armed Forces.

PRESTON, ARTHUR MURRAY

Rank and organization: Lieutenant, U.S. Navy Reserve, Torpedo Boat Squadron 33. *Place and date:* Wasile Bay, Halmahera Island, 16 September 1944. *Entered service at:* Maryland. *Born:* 1 November 1913, Washington, D.C. *Citation:* For conspicuous gallantry and intrepidity at the risk of his life above and beyond the call of duty as commander, Motor Torpedo Boat Squadron 33, while effecting the rescue of a Navy pilot shot down in Wasile Bay, Halmahera Island, less than 200 yards from a strongly defended Japanese dock and supply area, 16 September 1944. Volunteering for a perilous mission unsuccessfully attempted by the pilot's squadron mates and a PBY plane, Lt. Comdr. (then Lieutenant) Preston led PT-489 and PT-363 through 60 miles of restricted, heavily mined waters. Twice turned back while running the gauntlet of fire from powerful coastal defense guns guarding the 11-mile strait at the entrance to the bay, he was again turned back by furious fire in the immediate area of the downed airman. Aided by an aircraft smokescreen, he finally succeeded in reaching his objective and, under vicious fire delivered at 150-yard range, took the pilot aboard and cleared the area, sinking a small hostile cargo vessel with 40-mm. fire during retirement. Increasingly vulnerable when covering aircraft were forced to leave because of insufficient fuel, Lt. Comdr. Preston raced PT boats 489 and 363 at high speed for 20 minutes through shell-splashed water and across minefields to safety. Under continuous fire for 2½ hours, Lt. Comdr. Preston successfully achieved a mission considered suicidal in its tremendous hazards, and brought his boats through without personnel casualties and with but superficial damage from shrapnel. His exceptional daring and great personal valor enhance the finest traditions of the U.S. Naval Service.

428

*PRUSSMAN, ERNEST W.

Rank and organization: Private First Class, U.S. Army, 13th Infantry, 8th Infantry Division. *Place and date:* Near Les Coates, Brittany, France, 8 September 1944. *Entered service at:* Brighton, Mass. *Birth:* Baltimore, Md. *G.O. No.:* 31, 17 April 1945. Citation: For conspicuous gallantry and intrepidity at risk of life above and beyond the call of duty on 8 September 1944, near Les Coates, Brittany, France. When the advance of the flank companies of 2 battalions was halted by intense enemy mortar, machinegun, and sniper fire from a fortified position on his left, Pfc. Prussman maneuvered his squad to assault the enemy fortifications. Hurdling a hedgerow, he came upon 2 enemy riflemen whom he disarmed. After leading his squad across an open field to the next hedgerow, he advanced to a machinegun position, destroyed the gun, captured its crew and 2 riflemen. Again advancing ahead of his squad in the assault, he was mortally wounded by an enemy rifleman, but as he fell to the ground he threw a handgrenade, killing his opponent. His superb leadership and heroic action at the cost of his life so demoralized the enemy that resistance at this point collapsed, permitting the 2 battalions to continue their advance.

*PUCKET, DONALD D. (Air Mission)

Rank and organization: First Lieutenant, U.S. Army Air Corps, 98th Bombardment Group. *Place and date:* Ploesti Raid, Rumania, 9 July 1944. *Entered service at:* Boulder, Colo. *Birth:* Longmont, Colo. *G.O. No.:* 48, 23 June 1945. *Citation:* He took part in a highly effective attack against vital oil installation in Ploesti, Rumania, on 9 July 1944. Just after "bombs away," the plane received heavy and direct hits from antiaircraft fire. One crewmember was instantly killed and 6 others severely wounded. The airplane was badly damaged, 2 were knocked out, the control cables cut, the oxygen system on fire, and the bomb bay flooded with gas and hydraulic fluid. Regaining control of his crippled plane, 1st Lt. Pucket turned its direction over to the copilot. He calmed the crew, administered first aid, and surveyed the damage. Finding the bomb bay doors jammed, he used the hand crank to open them to allow the gas to escape. He jettisoned all guns and equipment but the plane continued to lose altitude rapidly. Realizing that it would be impossible to reach friendly territory he ordered the crew to abandon ship. Three of the crew, uncontrollable from fright or shock, would not leave. 1st Lt. Pucket urged the others to jump. Ignoring their entreaties to follow, he refused to abandon the 3 hysterical men and was last seen fighting to regain control of the plane. A few moments later the flaming bomber crashed on a mountainside. 1st Lt. Pucket, unhesitatingly and with supreme sacrifice, gave his life in his courageous attempt to save the lives of 3 others.

RAMAGE, LAWSON PATERSON

Rank and organization: Commander, U.S. Navy, U.S.S. *Parche. Place and date:* Pacific, 31 July 1944. *Entered service at:* Vermont. *Born:* 19 January 1920, Monroe Bridge, Mass. *Citation:* For conspicuous gallantry and intrepidity at the risk of his life above and beyond the call of duty as commanding officer of the U.S.S. *Parche* in a predawn attack on a Japanese convoy, 31 July 1944. Boldly penetrating the screen of a heavily escorted convoy, Comdr. Ramage launched a perilous surface attack by delivering a crippling stern shot into a freighter and quickly following up with a series of bow and stern torpedoes to sink the leading tanker and damage the second one. Exposed by the light of bursting flares and bravely defiant of terrific shellfire passing close overhead, he struck again, sinking a transport by two forward reloads. In the mounting fury of fire from the damaged and sinking tanker, he calmly ordered his men below, remaining on the bridge to fight it out with an enemy now disorganized and confused. Swift to act as a fast transport closed in to ram, Comdr. Ramage daringly swung the stern of the speeding *Parche* as she crossed the bow of the onrushing ship, clearing by less than 50 feet but placing his submarine in a deadly crossfire from escorts on all sides and with the transport dead ahead. Undaunted, he sent 3 smashing "down the throat" bow shots to stop the target, then scored a killing hit as a climax to 46 minutes of violent action with the *Parche* and her valiant fighting company retiring victorious and unscathed.

*RAY, BERNARD J.

Rank and organization: First Lieutenant, U.S. Army, Company F, 8th Infantry, 4th Infantry Division. *Place and date:* Hurtgen Forest near Schevenhutte, Germany, 17 November 1944. *Entered service at:* Baldwin, N.Y. *Birth:* Brooklyn, N.Y. *G.O. No.:* 115, 8 December 1945. *Citation:* He was platoon leader with Company F, 8th Infantry, on 17 November 1944, during the drive through the Hurtgen Forest near Schevenhutte, Germany. The American forces attacked in wet, bitterly cold weather over rough, wooded terrain, meeting brutal resistance from positions spaced throughout the forest behind minefields and wire obstacles. Small arms, machinegun, mortar, and artillery fire caused heavy casualties in the ranks when Company F was halted by a concertina-type wire barrier. Under heavy fire, 1st Lt. Ray reorganized his men and prepared to blow a path through the entanglement, a task which appeared impossible of accomplishment and from which others tried to dissuade him. With implacable determination to clear the way, he placed explosive caps in his pockets, obtained several bangalore torpedoes, and then wrapped a length of highly explosive primer cord about his body. He dashed forward under direct fire, reached the barbed wire and prepared his demolition charge as mortar shells, which were being aimed at him alone, came steadily nearer his completely exposed position. He had placed a torpedo under the wire and was connecting it to a charge he carried when he was severely wounded by a bursting mortar shell. Apparently realizing that he would fail in his self-imposed mission unless he completed it in a few moments, he made a supremely gallant decision. With the primer cord still wound about his body and the explosive caps in his pocket, he completed a hasty wiring system and unhesitatingly thrust down on the handle of the charger, destroying himself with the wire barricade in the resulting blast. By the deliberate sacrifice of his life, 1st Lt. Ray enabled his company to continue its attack, resumption of which was of positive significance in gaining the approaches to the Cologne Plain.

*REESE, JAMES W.

Rank and organization: Private, U.S. Army, 26th Infantry, 1st Infantry Division. *Place and date:* At Mt. Vassillio, Sicily, 5 August 1943. *Entered service at:* Chester, Pa. *Birth:* Chester, Pa. *G.O. No.:* 85, 17 December 1943. *Citation:* For conspicuous gallantry and intrepidity at the risk of life, above and beyond the call of duty in action involving actual conflict with the enemy. When the enemy launched a counterattack which threatened the position of his company, Pvt. Reese, as the acting squad leader of a 60-mm. mortar squad, displaying superior leadership on his own initiative, maneuvered his squad forward to a favorable position, from which, by skillfully directing the fire of his weapon, he caused many casualties in the enemy ranks, and aided materially in repulsing the counterattack. When the enemy fire became so severe as to make his position untenable, he ordered the other members of his squad to withdraw to a safer position, but declined to seek safety for himself. So as to bring more effective fire upon the enemy, Pvt. Reese, without assistance, moved his mortar to a new position and attacked an enemy machinegun nest. He had only 3 rounds of ammunition but secured a direct hit with his last round, completely destroying the nest and killing the occupants. Ammunition being exhausted, he abandoned the mortar, seized a rifle and continued to advance, moving into an exposed position overlooking the enemy. Despite a heavy concentration of machinegun, mortar, and artillery fire, the heaviest experienced by his unit throughout the entire Sicilian campaign, he remained at this position and continued to inflict casualties upon the enemy until he was killed. His bravery, coupled with his gallant and unswerving determination to close with the enemy, regardless of consequences and obstacles which he faced, are a priceless inspiration to our armed forces.

*REESE, JOHN N., JR.

Rank and organization: Private First Class, U.S. Army, Company B, 148th Infantry, 37th Infantry Division. *Place and date:* Paco Railroad Station, Manila, Philippine Islands, 9 February 1945. *Entered service at:* Pryor, Okla. *Birth:* Muskogee, Okla. *G.O. No.:* 89, 19 October 1945. *Citation:* He was engaged in the attack on the Paco Railroad Station, which was strongly defended by 300 determined enemy soldiers with machineguns and rifles, supported by several pillboxes, 3 20-mm. guns, 1 37-mm. gun and heavy mortars. While making a frontal assault across an open field, his platoon was halted 100 yards from the station by intense enemy fire. On his own initiative he left the platoon, accompanied by a comrade, and continued forward to a house 60 yards from the objective. Although under constant enemy observation, the 2 men remained in this position for an hour, firing at targets of opportunity, killing more than 35 Japanese and wounding many more. Moving closer to the station and discovering a group of Japanese replacements attempting to reach pillboxes, they opened heavy fire, killed more than 40 and stopped all subsequent attempts to man the emplacements. Enemy fire became more intense as they advanced to within 20 yards of the station. From that point Pfc. Reese provided effective covering fire and courageously drew enemy fire to himself while his companion killed 7 Japanese and destroyed a 20-mm. gun and heavy machinegun with handgrenades. With their ammunition running low, the 2 men started to return to the American lines, alternately providing covering fire for each other as they withdrew. During this movement, Pfc. Reese was killed by enemy fire as he reloaded his rifle. The intrepid team, in 2½ hours of fierce fighting, killed more than 82 Japanese, completely disorganized their defense and paved the way for subsequent complete defeat of the enemy at this strong point. By his gallant determination in the face of tremendous odds, aggressive fighting spirit, and extreme heroism at the cost of his life, Pfc. Reese materially aided the advance of our troops in Manila and providing a lasting inspiration to all those with whom he served.

*REEVES, THOMAS JAMES

Rank and organization: Radio Electrician (Warrant Officer) U.S. Navy. *Born:* 9 December 1895, Thomaston, Conn. *Accredited to:* Connecticut. *Citation:* For distinguished conduct in the line of his profession, extraordinary courage and disregard of his own safety during the attack on the Fleet in Pearl Harbor, by Japanese forces on 7 December 1941. After the mechanized ammunition hoists were put out of action in the U.S.S. *California*, Reeves, on his own initiative, in a burning passageway, assisted in the maintenance of an ammunition supply by hand to the antiaircraft guns until he was overcome by smoke and fire, which resulted in his death.

*RICKETTS, MILTON ERNEST

Rank and organization: Lieutenant, U.S. Navy. *Born:* 5 August 1913, Baltimore, Md. *Appointed from:* Maryland. *Citation:* For extraordinary and distinguished gallantry above and beyond the call of duty as Officer-in-Charge of the Engineering Repair Party of the U.S.S. *Yorktown* in action against enemy Japanese forces in the Battle of the Coral Sea on 8 May 1942. During the severe bombarding of the *Yorktown* by enemy Japanese forces, an aerial bomb passed through and exploded directly beneath the compartment in which Lt. Ricketts' battle station was located, killing, wounding or stunning all of his men and mortally wounding him. Despite his ebbing strength, Lt. Ricketts promptly opened the valve of a near-by fireplug, partially led out the firehose and directed a heavy stream of water into the fire before dropping dead beside the hose. His courageous action, which undoubtedly prevented the rapid spread of fire to serious proportions, and his unflinching devotion to duty were in keeping with the highest traditions of the U.S. Naval Service. He gallantly gave his life for his country.

*RIORDAN, PAUL F.

Rank and organization: Second Lieutenant, U.S. Army, 34th Infantry Division. *Place and date:* Near Cassino, Italy, 3-8 February 1944. *Entered service at:* Kansas City, Mo. *Birth:* Charles City, Iowa. *G.O. No.:* 74, 11 September 1944. *Citation:* For conspicuous gallantry and intrepidity above and beyond the call of duty. In the attack on the approaches to the city of Cassino on 3 February 1944, 2d Lt. Riordan led 1 of the assault platoons. Attacking Hill 175, his command was pinned down by enemy machinegun fire from the hill and from a pill-box about 45 yards to the right of the hill. In the face of intense fire, 2d Lt. Riordan moved out in full view of the enemy gunners to reach a position from where he could throw a handgrenade into the pillbox. Then, getting to his knees, he hurled the grenade approximately 45 yards, scoring a direct hit. The grenade killed 1 and wounded the other 2 Germans in the nest and silenced the gun. Another soldier then cleaned out the enemy pillboxes on the hill itself, and the company took its objective. Continuing the assault into Cassino itself on 8 February 1944, 2d Lt. Riordan and his platoon were given the mission of taking the city jailhouse, one of the enemy's several strongpoints. Again 2d Lt. Riordan took the lead and managed to get through the ring of enemy fire covering the approaches and reached the building. His platoon, however, could not get through the intense fire and was cut off. 2d Lt. Riordan, aware that his men were unable to follow, determined to carry on singlehanded, but the numerically superior enemy force was too much for him to overcome, and he was killed by enemy small-arms fire after disposing of at least 2 of the defenders. 2d Lt. Riordan's bravery and extraordinary heroism in the face of almost certain death were an inspiration to his men and exemplify the highest traditions of the U.S. Armed Forces.

*ROAN, CHARLES HOWARD

Rank and organization: Private First Class, U.S. Marine Corps Reserve. *Born:* 16 August 1923, Claude, Tex. *Accredited to:* Texas. *Citation:* For conspicuous gallantry and intrepidity at the risk of his life above and beyond the call of duty while serving with the 2d Battalion, 7th Marines, 1st Marine Division, in action against enemy Japanese forces on Peleliu, Palau Islands, 18 September 1944. Shortly after his leader ordered a withdrawal upon discovering that the squad was partly cut off from their company as a result of the rapid advance along an exposed ridge during an aggressive attack on the strongly entrenched enemy, Pfc. Roan and his companions were suddenly engaged in a furious exchange of handgrenades by Japanese forces emplaced in a cave on higher ground and to the rear of the squad. Seeking protection with 4 other marines in a depression in the rocky, broken terrain, Pfc. Roan was wounded by an enemy grenade which fell close to their position and, immediately realizing the eminent peril to his comrades when another grenade landed in the midst of the group, unhesitatingly flung himself upon it, covering it with his body and absorbing the full impact of the explosion. By his prompt action and selfless conduct in the face of almost certain death, he saved the lives of 4 men. His great personal valor reflects the highest credit upon himself and the U.S. Naval Service. He gallantly gave his life for his comrades.

*ROBINSON, JAMES E., Jr.

Rank and organization: First Lieutenant, U.S. Army, Battery A, 861st Field Artillery Battalion, 63d Infantry Division. *Place and date:* Near Untergriesheim, Germany, 6 April 1945. *Entered service at:* Waco, Tex. *Birth:* Toledo, Ohio. *G.O. No.:* 117, 11 December 1945. *Citation:* He was a field artillery forward observer attached to Company A, 253d Infantry, near Untergriesheim, Germany, on 6 April 1945. Eight hours of desperate fighting over open terrain swept by German machinegun, mortar, and small-arms fire had decimated Company A, robbing it of its commanding officer and most of its key enlisted personnel when 1st Lt. Robinson rallied the 23 remaining uninjured riflemen and a few walking wounded, and, while carrying his heavy radio for communication with American batteries, led them through intense fire in a charge against the objective. Ten German infantrymen in foxholes threatened to stop the assault, but the gallant leader killed them all at point-blank range with rifle and pistol fire and then pressed on with his men to sweep the area of all resistance. Soon afterward he was ordered to seize the defended town of Kressbach. He went to each of the 19 exhausted survivors with cheering words, instilling in them courage and fortitude, before leading the little band forward once more. In the advance he was seriously wounded in the throat by a shell fragment, but, despite great pain and loss of blood, he refused medical attention and continued the attack, directing supporting artillery fire even though he was mortally wounded. Only after the town had been taken and he could no longer speak did he leave the command he had inspired in victory and walk nearly 2 miles to an aid station where he died from his wound. By his intrepid leadership 1st Lt. Robinson was directly responsible for Company A's accomplishing its mission against tremendous odds.

RODRIGUEZ, CLETO

Rank and organization: Technical Sergeant (then Private), U.S. Army, Company B, 148th Infantry, 37th Infantry Division. *Place and date:* Paco Railroad Station, Manila, Philippine Islands, 9 February 1945. *Entered service at:* San Antonio, Tex. *Birth:* San Marcos, Tex. *G.O. No.:* 97, 1 November 1945. *Citation:* He was an automatic rifleman when his unit attacked the strongly defended Paco Railroad Station during the battle for Manila, Philippine Islands. While making a frontal assault across an open field, his platoon was halted 100 yards from the station by intense enemy fire. On his own initiative, he left the platoon, accompanied by a comrade, and continued forward to a house 60 yards from the objective. Although under constant enemy observation, the 2 men remained in this position for an hour, firing at targets of opportunity, killing more than 35 hostile soldiers and wounding many more. Moving closer to the station and discovering a group of Japanese replacements attempting to reach pillboxes, they opened heavy fire, killed more than 40 and stopped all subsequent attempts to man the emplacements. Enemy fire became more intense as they advanced to within 20 yards of the station. Then, covered by his companion, Pvt. Rodriguez boldly moved up to the building and threw 5 grenades through a doorway killing 7 Japanese, destroying a 20-mm. gun and wrecking a heavy machinegun. With their ammunition running low, the 2 men started to return to the American lines, alternately providing covering fire for each other's withdrawal. During this movement, Pvt. Rodriguez' companion was killed. In 2½ hours of fierce fighting the intrepid team killed more than 82 Japanese, completely disorganized their defense, and paved the way for the subsequent overwhelming defeat of the enemy at this strongpoint. Two days later,

434

Pvt. Rodriguez again enabled his comrades to advance when he single-handedly killed 6 Japanese and destroyed a well-placed 20-mm. gun. By his outstanding skill with his weapons, gallant determination to destroy the enemy, and heroic courage in the face of tremendous odds, Pvt. Rodriguez, on 2 occasions, materially aided the advance of our troops in Manila.

*ROEDER, ROBERT E.

Rank and organization: Captain, U.S. Army, Company G, 350th Infantry, 88th Infantry Division. *Place and date:* Mt. Battaglia, Italy, 27–28 September 1944. *Entered service at:* Summit Station, Pa. *Birth:* Summit Station, Pa. *G.O. No.:* 31, 17 April 1945. *Citation:* For conspicuous gallantry and intrepidity at risk of life above and beyond the call of duty. Capt. Roeder commanded his company in defense of the strategic Mount Battaglia. Shortly after the company had occupied the hill, the Germans launched the first of a series of determined counterattacks to regain this dominating height. Completely exposed to ceaseless enemy artillery and small-arms fire, Capt. Roeder constantly circulated among his men, encouraging them and directing their defense against the persistent enemy. During the sixth counterattack, the enemy, by using flamethrowers and taking advantage of the fog, succeeded in overrunning the position. Capt. Roeder led his men in a fierce battle at close quarters, to repulse the attack with heavy losses to the Germans. The following morning, while the company was engaged in repulsing an enemy counterattack in force, Capt. Roeder was seriously wounded and rendered unconscious by shell fragments. He was carried to the company command post, where he regained consciousness. Refusing medical treatment, he insisted on rejoining his men. Although in a weakened condition, Capt. Roeder dragged himself to the door of the command post and, picking up a rifle, braced himself in a sitting position. He began firing his weapon, shouted words of encouragement, and issued orders to his men. He personally killed 2 Germans before he himself was killed instantly by an exploding shell. Through Capt. Roeder's able and intrepid leadership his men held Mount Battaglia against the aggressive and fanatical enemy attempts to retake this important and strategic height. His valorous performance is exemplary of the fighting spirit of the U.S. Army.

*ROOKS, ALBERT HAROLD

Rank and organization: Captain, U.S. Navy. *Born:* 29 December 1891, Colton, Wash. *Appointed from:* Washington. *Citation:* For extraordinary heroism, outstanding courage, gallantry in action and distinguished service in the line of his profession, as Commanding Officer of the U.S.S. *Houston* during the period 4 to 27 February 1942, while in action with superior Japanese enemy aerial and surface forces. While proceeding to attack an enemy amphibious expedition, as a unit in a mixed force, *Houston* was heavily attacked by bombers; after evading 4 attacks, she was heavily hit in a fifth attack, lost 60 killed and had 1 turret wholly disabled. Capt. Rooks made his ship again seaworthy and sailed within 3 days to escort an important reinforcing convoy from Darwin to Koepang, Timor, Netherlands East Indies. While so engaged, another powerful air attack developed which by

Houston's marked efficiency was fought off without much damage to the convoy. The commanding general of all forces in the area thereupon canceled the movement and Capt. Rooks escorted the convoy back to Darwin. Later, while in a considerable American-British-Dutch force engaged with an overwhelming force of Japanese surface ships, *Houston* with H.M.S. *Exeter* carried the brunt of the battle, and her fire alone heavily damaged 1 and possibly 2 heavy cruisers. Although heavily damaged in the actions, Capt. Rooks succeeded in disengaging his ship when the flag officer commanding broke off the action and got her safely away from the vicinity, whereas one-half of the cruisers were lost.

*ROOSEVELT, THEODORE, JR.

Rank and organization: Brigadier General, U.S. Army. *Place and date:* Normandy Invasion, 6 June 1944. *Entered service at:* Oyster Bay, N.Y. *Birth:* Oyster Bay, N.Y. *G.O. No.:* 77, 28 September 1944. *Citation:* For gallantry and intrepidity at the risk of his life above and beyond the call of duty on 6 June 1944, in France. After 2 verbal requests to accompany the leading assault elements in the Normandy invasion had been denied, Brig. Gen. Roosevelt's written request for this mission was approved and he landed with the first wave of the forces assaulting the enemy-held beaches. He repeatedly led groups from the beach, over the seawall and established them inland. His valor, courage, and presence in the very front of the attack and his complete unconcern at being under heavy fire inspired the troops to heights of enthusiasm and self-sacrifice. Although the enemy had the beach under constant direct fire, Brig. Gen. Roosevelt moved from one locality to another, rallying men around him, directed and personally led them against the enemy. Under his seasoned, precise, calm, and unfaltering leadership, assault troops reduced beach strong points and rapidly moved inland with minimum casualties. He thus contributed substantially to the successful establishment of the beachhead in France.

ROSS, DONALD KIRBY

Rank and organization: Machinist, U.S. Navy, U.S.S. *Nevada*. *Place and date:* Pearl Harbor, Territory of Hawaii, 7 December 1941. *Entered service at:* Denver, Colo. *Born:* 8 December 1910, Beverly, Kans. *Citation:* For distinguished conduct in the line of his profession, extraordinary courage and disregard of his own life during the attack on the Fleet in Pearl Harbor, Territory of Hawaii, by Japanese forces on 7 December 1941. When his station in the forward dynamo room of the U.S.S. *Nevada* became almost untenable due to smoke, steam, and heat, Machinist Ross forced his men to leave that station and performed all the duties himself until blinded and unconscious. Upon being rescued and resuscitated, he returned and secured the forward dynamo room and proceeded to the after dynamo room where he was later again rendered unconscious by exhaustion. Again recovering consciousness he returned to his station where he remained until directed to abandon it.

ROSS, WILBURN K.

Rank and organization: Private, U.S. Army, Company G, 350th Infantry, 3d Infantry Division. *Place and date:* Near St. Jacques, France, 30 October 1944. *Entered service at:* Strunk, Ky. *Birth:* Strunk, Ky. *G.O. No.:* 30, 14 April 1945. *Citation:* For conspicuous gallantry and intrepidity at risk of life above and beyond the call of duty near St. Jacques, France. At 11:30 a.m. on 30 October 1944, after his company had lost 55 out of 88 men in an attack on an entrenched, full-strength German company of elite mountain troops, Pvt. Ross placed his light machinegun 10 yards in advance of the foremost supporting riflemen in order to absorb the initial impact of an enemy counterattack. With machinegun and small-arms fire striking the earth near him, he fired with deadly effect on the assaulting force and repelled it. Despite the hail of automatic fire and the explosion of rifle grenades within a stone's throw of his position, he continued to man his machinegun alone, holding off 6 more German attacks. When the eighth assault was launched, most of his supporting riflemen were out of ammunition. They took positions in echelon behind Pvt. Ross and crawled up, during the attack, to extract a few rounds of ammunition from his machinegun ammunition belt. Pvt. Ross fought on virtually without assistance and, despite the fact that enemy grenadiers crawled to within 4 yards of his position in an effort to kill him with handgrenades, he again directed accurate and deadly fire on the hostile force and hurled it back. After expending his last rounds, Pvt. Ross was advised to withdraw to the company command post, together with 8 surviving riflemen, but, as more ammunition was expected, he declined to do so. The Germans launched their last all-out attack, converging their fire on Pvt. Ross in a desperate attempt to destroy the machinegun which stood between them and a decisive breakthrough. As his supporting riflemen fixed bayonets for a last-ditch stand, fresh ammunition arrived and was brought to Pvt. Ross just as the advance assault elements were about to swarm over his position. He opened murderous fire on the oncoming enemy; killed 40 and wounded 10 of the attacking force; broke the assault singlehandedly, and forced the Germans to withdraw. Having killed or wounded at least 58 Germans in more than 5 hours of continuous combat and saved the remnants of his company from destruction, Pvt. Ross remained at his post that night and the following day for a total of 36 hours. His actions throughout this engagement were an inspiration to his comrades and maintained the high traditions of the military service.

ROUH, CARLTON ROBERT

Rank and organization: First Lieutenant, U.S. Marine Corps Reserve, 1st Battalion, 5th Marines, 1st Marine Division. *Place and date:* Peleliu Island, Palau group, 15 September 1944. *Entered service at:* New Jersey. *Born:* 11 May 1919, Lindenwold, N.J. *Citation:* For conspicuous gallantry and intrepidity at the risk of his life above and beyond the call of duty while attached to the 1st Battalion, 5th Marines, 1st Marine Division, during action against enemy Japanese forces on Peleliu Island, Palau group, 15 September 1944. Before permitting his men to use an enemy dugout as a position for an 81-mm. mortar observation post, 1st Lt. Rouh made a personal reconnaissance of the pillbox and, upon entering, was severely wounded by Japanese rifle fire from within. Emerging from the dugout, he was immediately assisted by 2 marines to a less exposed area but, while receiving first aid, was further endangered by an enemy grenade which was thrown into their midst. Quick to act in spite of his weakened condition, he lurched to a crouching position and thrust both men aside, placing his own body between them and the grenade and taking the full blast of the explosion himself. His exceptional spirit of loyalty and self-sacrifice in the face of almost certain death reflects the highest credit upon 1st Lt. Rouh and the U.S. Naval Service.

RUDOLPH, DONALD E.

Rank and organization: Second Lieutenant, U.S. Army, Company E, 20th Infantry, 6th Infantry Division. *Place and date:* Munoz, Luzon, Philippine Islands, 5 February 1945. *Entered service at:* Minneapolis, Minn. *Birth:* South Haven, Minn. *G.O. No.:* 77, 10 September 1945. *Citation:* 2d Lt. Rudolph (then T/Sgt.) was acting as platoon leader at Munoz, Luzon, Philippine Islands. While administering first aid on the battlefield, he observed enemy fire issuing from a nearby culvert. Crawling to the culvert with rifle and grenades, he killed 3 of the enemy concealed there. He then worked his way across open terrain toward a line of enemy pillboxes which had immobilized his company. Nearing the first pillbox, he hurled a grenade through its embrasure and charged the position. With his bare hands he tore away the wood and tin covering, then dropped a grenade through the opening, killing the enemy gunners and destroying their machinegun. Ordering several riflemen to cover his further advance, 2d Lt. Rudolph seized a pick mattock and made his way to the second pillbox. Piercing its top with the mattock, he dropped a grenade through the hole, fired several rounds from his rifle into it and smothered any surviving enemy by sealing the hole and the embrasure with earth. In quick succession he attacked and neutralized 6 more pillboxes. Later, when his platoon was attacked by an enemy tank, he advanced under covering fire, climbed to the top of the tank and dropped a white phosphorus grenade through the turret, destroying the crew. Through his outstanding heroism, superb courage, and leadership, and complete disregard for his own safety, 2d Lt. Rudolph cleared a path for an advance which culminated in one of the most decisive victories of the Philippine campaign.

*RUHL, DONALD JACK

Rank and organization: Private First Class, U.S. Marine Corps Reserve. *Born:* 2 July 1923, Columbus, Mont. *Accredited to:* Montana. *Citation:* For conspicuous gallantry and intrepidity at the risk of his life above and beyond the call of duty while serving as a rifleman in an assault platoon of Company E, 28th Marines, 5th Marine Division, in action against enemy Japanese forces on Iwo Jima, Volcano Islands, from 19 to 21 February 1945. Quick to press the advantage after 8 Japanese had been driven from a blockhouse on D-day, Pfc. Ruhl singlehandedly attacked the group, killing 1 of the enemy with his bayonet and another by rifle fire in his determined attempt to an-

438

nihilate the escaping troops. Cool and undaunted as the fury of hostile resistance steadily increased throughout the night, he voluntarily left the shelter of his tank trap early in the morning of D-day plus 1 and moved out under a tremendous volume of mortar and machinegun fire to rescue a wounded marine lying in an exposed position approximately 40 yards forward of the line. Half pulling and half carrying the wounded man, he removed him to a defiladed position, called for an assistant and a stretcher and, again running the gauntlet of hostile fire, carried the casualty to an aid station some 300 yards distant on the beach. Returning to his platoon, he continued his valiant efforts, volunteering to investigate and apparently abandoned Japanese gun emplacement 75 yards forward of the right flank during consolidation of the front lines, and subsequently occupying the position through the night to prevent the enemy from repossessing the valuable weapon. Pushing forward in the assault against the vast network of fortifications surrounding Mt. Suribachi the following morning, he crawled with his platoon guide to the top of a Japanese bunker to bring fire to bear on enemy troops located on the far side of the bunker. Suddenly a hostile grenade landed between the 2 marines. Instantly Pfc. Ruhl called a warning to his fellow marine and dived on the deadly missile, absorbing the full impact of the shattering explosion in his own body and protecting all within range from the danger of flying fragments although he might easily have dropped from his position on the edge of the bunker to the ground below. An indomitable fighter, Pfc. Ruhl rendered heroic service toward the defeat of a ruthless enemy, and his valor, initiative and unfaltering spirit of self-sacrifice in the face of almost certain death sustain and enhance the highest traditions of the U.S. Naval Service. He gallantly gave his life for his country.

RUIZ, ALEJANDRO R. RENTERIA

Rank and organization: Private First Class, U.S. Army, 165th Infantry, 27th Infantry Division. *Place and date:* Okinawa, Ryukyu Islands, 28 April 1945. *Entered service at:* Carlsbad, N. Mex. *Birth:* Loving, N. Mex. *G.O. No.:* 60, 26 June 1946. *Citation:* When his unit was stopped by a skillfully camouflaged enemy pillbox, he displayed conspicuous gallantry and intrepidity above and beyond the call of duty. His squad, suddenly brought under a hail of machinegun fire and a vicious grenade attack, was pinned down. Jumping to his feet, Pfc. Ruiz seized an automatic rifle and lunged through the flying grenades and rifle and automatic fire for the top of the emplacement. When an enemy soldier charged him, his rifle jammed. Undaunted, Pfc. Ruiz whirled on his assailant and clubbed him down. Then he ran back through bullets and grenades, seized more ammunition and another automatic rifle, and again made for the pillbox. Enemy fire now was concentrated on him, but he charged on, miraculously reaching the position, and in plain view he climbed to the top. Leaping from 1 opening to another, he sent burst after burst into the pillbox, killing 12 of the enemy and completely destroying the position. Pfc. Ruiz's heroic conduct, in the face of overwhelming odds, saved the lives of many comrades and eliminated an obstacle that long would have checked his unit's advance.

*SADOWSKI, JOSEPH J.

Rank and organization: Sergeant, U.S. Army, 37th Tank Battalion, 4th Armored Division. *Place and date:* Valhey, France, 14 September 1944. *Entered service at:* Perth Amboy, N.J. *Birth:* Perth Amboy, N.J. *G.O. No.:* 32, 23 April 1945. *Citation:* For conspicuous gallantry and intrepidity at the risk of his life above and beyond the call of duty at Valhey, France. On the afternoon of 14 September 1944, Sgt. Sadowski as a tank commander was advancing with the leading elements of Combat Command A, 4th Armored Division, through an intensely severe barrage of enemy fire from the streets and buildings of the town of Valhey. As Sgt. Sadowski's tank advanced through the hail of fire, it was struck by a shell from an 88-mm. gun fired at a range of 20 yards. The tank was disabled and burst into flames. The suddenness of the enemy attack caused confusion and hesitation among the crews of the remaining tanks of our forces. Sgt. Sadowski immediately ordered his crew to dismount and take cover in the adjoining buildings. After his crew had dismounted, Sgt. Sadowski discovered that 1 member of the crew, the bow gunner, had been unable to leave the tank. Although the tank was being subjected to a withering hail of enemy small-arms, bazooka, grenade, and mortar fire from the streets and from the windows of adjacent buildings, Sgt. Sadowski unhesitatingly returned to his tank and endeavored to pry up the bow gunner's hatch. While engaged in this attempt to rescue his comrade from the burning tank, he was cut down by a stream of machinegun fire which resulted in his death. The gallant and noble sacrifice of his life in the aid of his comrade, undertaken in the face of almost certain death, so inspired the remainder of the tank crews that they pressed forward with great ferocity and completely destroyed the enemy forces in this town without further loss to themselves. The heroism and selfless devotion to duty displayed by Sgt. Sadowski, which resulted in his death, inspired the remainder of his force to press forward to victory, and reflect the highest tradition of the armed forces.

*SARNOSKI, JOSEPH R. (Air Mission)

Rank and organization: Second Lieutenant, U.S. Army Air Corps, 43rd Bomber Group, *Place and date:* Over Buka Area, Solomon Islands, 16 June 1943. *Entered service at:* Simpson, Pa. *Born:* 30 January 1915, Simpson, Pa. *G.O. No.:* 85, 17 December 1943. *Citation:* For conspicuous gallantry and intrepidity in action above and beyond the call of duty. On 16 June 1943, 2d Lt. Sarnoski volunteered as bombardier of a crew on an important photographic mapping mission covering the heavily defended Buka area, Solomon Islands. When the mission was nearly completed, about 20 enemy fighters intercepted. At the nose guns, 2d Lt. Sarnoski fought off the first attackers, making it possible for the pilot to finish the plotted course. When a coordinated frontal attack by the enemy extensively damaged his bomber, and seriously injured 5 of the crew, 2d Lt. Sarnoski, though wounded, continued firing and shot down 2 enemy planes. A 20-millimeter shell which burst in the nose of the bomber knocked him into the catwalk under the cockpit. With indomitable fighting spirit, he crawled back to his post and kept on firing until he collapsed on his guns. 2d Lt. Sarnoski by resolute defense of his aircraft at the price of his life, made possible the completion of a vitally important mission.

*SAYERS, FOSTER J.

Rank and organization: Private First Class, U.S. Army, Company L, 357th Infantry, 90th Infantry Division. *Place and date:* Near Thionville, France, 12 November 1944. *Entered service at:* Howard, Pa. *Birth:* Marsh Creek, Pa. *G.O. No.:* 89, 19 October 1945. *Citation:* He displayed conspicuous gallantry above and beyond the call of duty in combat on 12 November 1944, near Thionville, France. During an attack on strong hostile forces entrenched on a hill he fearlessly ran up the steep approach toward his objective and set up his machinegun 20 yards from the enemy. Realizing it would be necessary to attract full attention of the dug-in Germans while his company crossed an open area and flanked the enemy, he picked up his gun, charged through withering machinegun and rifle fire to the very edge of the emplacement, and there killed 12 German soldiers with devastating close-range fire. He took up a position behind a log and engaged the hostile infantry from the flank in an heroic attempt to distract their attention while his comrades attained their objective at the crest of the hill. He was killed by the very heavy concentration of return fire; but his fearless assault enabled his company to sweep the hill with minimum of casualties, killing or capturing every enemy soldier on it. Pfc. Sayers' indomitable fighting spirit, aggressiveness, and supreme devotion to duty live on as an example of the highest traditions of the military service.

SCHAEFER, JOSEPH E.

Rank and organization: Staff Sergeant, U.S. Army, Company I, 18th Infantry, 1st Infantry Division. *Place and date:* Near Stolberg, Germany, 24 September 1944. *Entered service at:* Long Island, N.Y. *Birth:* New York, N.Y. *G.O. No.:* 71, 22 August 1945. *Citation:* He was in charge of a squad of the 2d Platoon in the vicinity of Stolberg, Germany, early in the morning of 24 September 1944, when 2 enemy companies supported by machineguns launched an attack to seize control of an important crossroads which was defended by his platoon. One American squad was forced back, another captured, leaving only S/Sgt. Schaefer's men to defend the position. To shift his squad into a house which would afford better protection, he crawled about under heavy small-arms and machinegun fire, instructed each individual, and moved to the building. A heavy concentration of enemy artillery fire scored hits on his strong point. S/Sgt. Schaefer assigned his men to positions and selected for himself the most dangerous one at the door. With his M1 rifle, he broke the first wave of infantry thrown toward the house. The Germans attacked again with grenades and flame throwers but were thrown back a second time, S/Sgt. Schaefer killing and wounding several. Regrouped for a final assault, the Germans approached from 2 directions. One force drove at the house from the front, while a second group advanced stealthily along a hedgerow. Recognizing the threat, S/Sgt. Schaefer fired rapidly at the enemy before him, killing or wounding all 6; then, with no cover whatever, dashed to the hedgerow and poured deadly accurate shots into the second group, killing 5, wounding 2 others, and forcing the enemy to withdraw. He scoured the area near his battered stronghold and captured 10 prisoners. By this time the rest of his company had begun a counterattack; he moved forward to assist another platoon to regain its position. Remaining in the lead, crawling and running in the face of heavy fire, he overtook the enemy, and liberated the American squad captured earlier in the battle. In all, single-handed and armed only with his rifle, he killed between 15 and 20 Germans, wounded at least as many more, and took 10 prisoners. S/Sgt. Schaefer's indomitable courage and his determination to hold his position at all costs were responsible for stopping an enemy break-through.

SCHAUER, HENRY

Rank and organization: Private First Class, U.S. Army, 3d Infantry Division. *Place and date:* Near Cisterna di Littoria, Italy, 23–24 May 1944. *Entered service at:* Scobey, Mont. *Born:* 9 October 1918, Clinton, Okla. *G.O. No.:* 83, 27 October 1944. *Citation:* For conspicuous gallantry and intrepidity at risk of life above and beyond the call of duty. On 23 May 1944, at 12 noon, Pfc. (now T/Sgt.) Schauer left the cover of a ditch to engage 4 German snipers who opened fire on the patrol from its rear. Standing erect he walked deliberately 30 yards toward the enemy, stopped amid the fire from 4 rifles centered on him, and with 4 bursts from his BAR, each at a different range, killed all of the snipers. Catching sight of a fifth sniper waiting for the patrol behind a house chimney, Pfc. Schauer brought him down with another burst. Shortly after, when a heavy enemy artillery concentration and 2 machineguns temporarily halted the patrol, Pfc. Schauer again left cover to engage the enemy weapons singlehanded. While shells exploded within 15 yards, showering dirt over him, and strings of grazing German tracer bullets whipped past him at chest level, Pfc. Schauer knelt, killed the 2 gunners of the machinegun only 60 yards from him with a single burst from his BAR, and crumpled 2 other enemy soldiers who ran to man the gun. Inserting a fresh magazine in his BAR, Pfc. Schauer shifted his body to fire at the other weapon 500 yards distant and emptied his weapon into the enemy crew, killing all 4 Germans. Next morning, when shells from a German Mark VI tank and a machinegun only 100 yards distant again forced the patrol to seek cover, Pfc. Schauer crawled toward the enemy machinegun, stood upright only 80 yards from the weapon as its bullets cut the surrounding ground, and 4 tank shells fired directly at him burst within 20 yards. Raising his BAR to his shoulder, Pfc. Schauer killed the 4 members of the German machinegun crew with 1 burst of fire.

SCHONLAND, HERBERT EMERY

Rank and organization: Commander, U.S. Navy, U.S.S. *San Francisco. Place and date:* Savo Island, 12–13 November 1943. *Entered service at:* Maine. *Born:* 7 September 1900, Portland, Maine. *Citation:* For extreme heroism and courage above and beyond the call of duty as damage control officer of the U.S.S. *San Francisco* in action against greatly superior enemy forces in the battle off Savo Island, 12–13 November 1942. In the same violent night engagement in which all of his superior officers were killed or wounded, Lt. Comdr. Schonland was fighting valiantly to free the *San Francisco* of large quantities of water flooding the second deck compartments through numerous shell-holes caused by enemy fire. Upon being informed that he was commanding officer, he ascertained that the conning of the ship was being efficiently handled, then directed the officer who had taken over that task to continue while he himself resumed the vitally important work of maintaining the stability of the ship. In water waist deep, he carried on his efforts in darkness illuminated only by hand lanterns until water in flooded compartments had been drained or pumped off and water-tight integrity had again been restored to the *San Francisco*. His great personal valor and gallant devotion to duty at great peril to his own life were instrumental in bringing his ship back to port under her own power, saved to fight again in the service of her country.

*SCHWAB, ALBERT EARNEST

Rank and organization: Private First Class, U.S. Marine Corps Reserve. *Born:* 17 July 1920, Washington, D.C. *Entered service at:* Tulsa, Okla. *Citation:* For conspicuous gallantry and intrepidity at the risk of his life above and beyond the call of duty as a flamethrower operator in action against enemy Japanese forces on Okinawa Shima in the Rykuyu Islands, 7 May 1945. Quick to take action when his company was pinned down in a valley and suffered resultant heavy casualties under blanketing machinegun fire emanating from a high ridge to the front, Pfc. Schwab, unable to flank the enemy emplacement because of steep cliffs on either side, advanced up the face of the ridge in bold defiance of the intense barrage and, skillfully directing the fire of his flamethrower, quickly demolished the hostile gun position, thereby enabling his company to occupy the ridge. Suddenly a second enemy machinegun opened fire, killing and wounding several marines with its initial bursts. Estimating with split-second decision the tactical difficulties confronting his comrades, Pfc. Schwab elected to continue his 1-man assault despite a diminished supply of fuel for his flamethrower. Cool and indomitable, he moved forward in the face of a direct concentration of hostile fire, relentlessly closed the enemy position and attacked. Although severely wounded by a final vicious blast from the enemy weapon, Pfc. Schwab had succeeded in destroying 2 highly strategic Japanese gun positions during a critical stage of the operation and, by his dauntless, singlehanded efforts, had materially furthered the advance of his company. His aggressive initiative, outstanding valor and professional skill throughout the bitter conflict sustain and enhance the highest traditions of the U.S. Naval Service.

*SCOTT, NORMAN

Rank and organization: Rear Admiral, U.S. Navy. *Born:* 10 August 1889, Indianapolis, Ind. *Appointed from:* Indiana. *Citation:* For extraordinary heroism and conspicuous intrepidity above and beyond the call of duty during action against enemy Japanese forces off Savo Island on the night of 11–12 October and again on the night of 12–13 November 1942. In the earlier action, intercepting a Japanese Task Force intent upon storming our island positions and landing reinforcements at Guadalcanal, Rear Adm. Scott, with courageous skill and superb coordination of the units under his command, destroyed 8 hostile vessels and put the others to flight. Again challenged, a month later, by the return of a stubborn and persistent foe, he led his force into a desperate battle against tremendous odds, directing close-range operations against the invading enemy until he himself was killed in the furious bombardment by their superior firepower. On each of these occasions his dauntless initiative, inspiring leadership and judicious foresight in a crisis of grave responsibility contributed decisively to the rout of a powerful invasion fleet and to the consequent frustration of a formidable Japanese offensive. He gallantly gave his life in the service of his country.

*SCOTT, ROBERT R.

Rank and organization: Machinist's Mate First Class, U.S. Navy. *Born:* 13 July 1915, Massillon, Ohio. *Accredited to:* Ohio. *Citation:* For conspicuous devotion to duty, extraordinary courage and complete disregard of his own life, above and beyond the call of duty, during the attack on the Fleet in Pearl Harbor by Japanese forces on 7 December 1941. The compartment, in the U.S.S. *California*, in which the air compressor, to which Scott was assigned as his battle station, was flooded as the result of a torpedo hit. The remainder of the personnel evacuated that compartment but Scott refused to leave, saying words to the effect "This is my station and I will stay and give them air as long as the guns are going."

SCOTT, ROBERT S.

Rank and organization: Captain (then Lieutenant), U.S. Army, 172d Infantry, 43d Infantry Division. *Place and date:* Near Munda Air Strip, New Georgia, Solomon Islands, 29 July 1943. *Entered service at:* Santa Fe, N. Mex. *Birth:* Washington, D.C. *G.O. No.:* 81, 14 October 1944. *Citation:* For conspicuous gallantry and intrepidity at the risk of his life above and beyond the call of duty near Munda Airstrip, New Georgia, Solomon Islands, on 29 July 1943. After 27 days of bitter fighting, the enemy held a hilltop salient which commanded the approach to Munda Airstrip. Our troops were exhausted from prolonged battle and heavy casualties, but Lt. Scott advanced with the leading platoon of his company to attack the enemy position, urging his men forward in the face of enemy rifle and enemy machinegun fire. He had pushed forward alone to a point midway across the barren hilltop within 75 yards of the enemy when the enemy launched a desperate counterattack, which if successful would have gained undisputed possession of the hill. Enemy riflemen charged out on the plateau, firing and throwing grenades as they moved to engage our toops. The company withdrew, but Lt. Scott, with only a blasted tree stump for cover, stood his ground against the wild enemy assault. By firing his carbine and throwing the grenades in his possession he momentarily stopped the enemy advance, using the brief respite to obtain more grenades. Disregarding small-arms fire and exploding grenades aimed at him, suffering a bullet wound in the left hand and a painful shrapnel wound in the head after his carbine had been shot from his hand, he threw grenade after grenade with devastating accuracy until the beaten enemy withdrew. Our troops, inspired to renewed effort by Lt. Scott's intrepid stand and incomparable courage, swept across the plateau to capture the hill, and from this strategic position 4 days later captured Munda Airstrip.

SHEA, CHARLES W.

Rank and organization: Second Lieutenant, U.S. Army, Company F, 350th Infantry, 88th Infantry Division. *Place and date:* Near Mount Damiano, Italy, 12 May 1944. *Entered service at:* New York, N.Y. *Birth:* New York, NY. *G.O. No.:* 4, 12 January 1945. *Citation:* For conspicuous gallantry and intrepidity at risk of life above and beyond the call of duty, on 12 May 1944, near Mount Damiano, Italy. As 2d Lt. Shea and his company were advancing toward a hill occupied by the enemy, 3 enemy machineguns suddenly opened fire, inflicting heavy casualties upon the company and halting its advance. 2d Lt. Shea immediately moved forward to eliminate these machinegun nests in order to enable his company to continue its attack. The deadly hail of machinegun fire at first pinned him down, but, boldly continuing his advance, 2d Lt. Shea crept up to the first nest. Throwing several hand grenades, he forced the 4 enemy soldiers manning this position to surrender, and disarming them, he sent them to the rear. He then crawled to the second machinegun position, and after a short fire fight forced 2 more German soldiers to surrender. At this time, the third machinegun fired at him, and while deadly small arms fire pitted the earth around him, 2d Lt. Shea crawled toward the nest. Suddenly he stood up and rushed the emplacement and with well-directed fire from his rifle, he killed all 3 of the enemy machine gunners. 2d Lt. Shea's display of personal valor was an inspiration to the officers and men of his company.

*SHERIDAN, CARL V.

Rank and organization: Private First Class, U.S. Army, Company K, 47th Infantry, 9th Infantry Division. *Place and date:* Frenzenberg Castle, Weisweiler, Germany, 26 November 1944. *Entered service at:* Baltimore, Md. *Birth:* Baltimore, Md. *G.O. No.:* 43, 30 May 1945. *Citation:* Attached to the 2d Battalion of the 47th Infantry on 26 November 1944, for the attack on Frenzenberg Castle, in the vicinity of Weisweiler, Germany, Company K, after an advance of 1,000 yards through a shattering barrage of enemy artillery and mortar fire, had captured 2 buildings in the courtyard of the castle but was left with an effective fighting strength of only 35 men. During the advance, Pfc. Sheridan, acting as a bazooka gunner, had braved the enemy fire to stop and procure the additional rockets carried by his ammunition bearer who was wounded. Upon rejoining his company in the captured buildings, he found it in a furious fight with approximately 70 enemy paratroopers occupying the castle gate house. This was a solidly built stone structure surrounded by a deep water-filled moat 20 feet wide. The only approach to the heavily defended position was across the courtyard and over a drawbridge leading to a barricaded oaken door. Pfc. Sheridan, realizing that his bazooka was the only available weapon with sufficient power to penetrate the heavy oak planking, with complete disregard for his own safety left the protection of the buildings and in the face of heavy and intense small-arms and grenade fire, crossed the courtyard to the drawbridge entrance where he could bring direct fire to bear against the door. Although handicapped by the lack of an assistant, and a constant target for the enemy fire that burst around him, he skillfully and effectively handled his awkward weapon to place two well-aimed rockets into the structure. Observing that the door was only weakened, and realizing that a gap must be made for a successful assault, he loaded his last rocket, took careful aim, and blasted a hole through the heavy planks. Turning to his company he shouted, "Come on, let's get them!" With his .45 pistol blazing, he charged into the gaping entrance and was killed by the withering fire that met him. The final assault on Frezenberg Castle was made through the gap which Pfc. Sheridan gave his life to create.

*SHOCKLEY, WILLIAM R.

Rank and organization: Private First Class, U.S. Army, Company L, 128th Infantry, 32d Infantry Division. *Place and date:* Villa Verde Trail, Luzon, Philippine Islands, 31 March 1945. *Entered service at:* Selma, Calif. *Birth:* Bokoshe, Okla. *G.O. No.:* 89, 19 October 1945. *Citation:* He was in position with his unit on a hill when the enemy, after a concentration of artillery fire, launched a counterattack.. He maintained his position under intense enemy fire and urged his comrades to withdraw, saying that he would "remain to the end" to provide cover. Although he had to clear two stoppages which impeded the reloading of his weapon, he halted one enemy charge. Hostile troops then began moving in on his left flank, and he quickly shifted his gun to fire on them. Knowing that the only route of escape was being cut off by the enemy, he ordered the remainder of his squad to withdraw to safety and deliberately remained at his post. He continued to fire until he was killed during the ensuing enemy charge. Later, 4 Japanese were found dead in front of his position. Pfc. Shockley, facing certain death, sacrificed himself to save his fellow soldiers, but the heroism and gallantry displayed by him enabled his squad to reorganize and continue its attack.

SHOMO, WILLIAM A. (Air Mission)

Rank and organization: Major, U.S. Army Air Corps, 82d Tactical Reconnaissance Squadron. *Place and date:* Over Luzon, Philippine Islands, 11 January 1945. *Entered service at:* Westmoreland County, Pa. *Birth:* Jeannette, Pa. *G.O. No.:* 25, 7 April 1945. *Citation:* For conspicuous gallantry and intrepidity at the risk of his life above and beyond the call of duty. Maj. Shomo was lead pilot of a flight of 2 fighter planes charged with an armed photographic and strafing mission against the Aparri and Laoag airdromes. While en route to the objective, he observed an enemy twin engine bomber, protected by 12 fighters, flying about 2,500 feet above him and in the opposite direction. Although the odds were 13 to 2, Maj. Shomo immediately ordered an attack. Accompanied by his wingman he closed on the enemy formation in a climbing turn and scored hits on the leading plane of the third element, which exploded in midair. Maj. Shomo then attacked the second element from the left side of the formation and shot another fighter down in flames. When the enemy formed for counterattack, Maj. Shomo moved to the other side of the formation and hit a third fighter which exploded and fell. Diving below the bomber, he put a burst into its underside and it crashed and burned. Pulling up from this pass he encountered a fifth plane firing head on and destroyed it. He next dived upon the first element and shot down the lead plane; then diving to 300 feet in pursuit of another fighter he caught it with his initial burst and it crashed in flames. During this action his wingman had shot down 3 planes, while the 3 remaining enemy fighters had fled into a cloudbank and escaped. Maj. Shomo's extraordinary gallantry and intrepidity in attacking such a far superior force and destroying 7 enemy aircraft in one action is unparalleled in the southwest Pacific area.

*SHOUP, CURTIS F.

Rank and organization: Staff Sergeant, U.S. Army, Company I, 346th Infantry, 87th Infantry Division. *Place and date:* Near Tillet, Belgium, 7 January 1945. *Entered service at:* Buffalo, N.Y. *Birth:* Napenoch, N.Y. *G.O. No.:* 60, 25 July 1945. *Citation:* On 7 January 1945, near Tillet, Belgium, his company attacked German troops on rising ground. Intense hostile machinegun fire pinned down and threatened to annihilate the American unit in an exposed position where frozen ground made it impossible to dig in for protection. Heavy mortar and artillery fire from enemy batteries was added to the storm of destruction falling on the Americans. Realizing that the machinegun must be silenced at all costs, S/Sgt. Shoup, armed with an automatic rifle, crawled to within 75 yards of the enemy emplacement. He found that his fire was ineffective from this position, and completely disregarding his own safety, stood up and grimly strode ahead into the murderous stream of bullets, firing his low-held weapon as he went. He was hit several times and finally was knocked to the ground. But he struggled to his feet and staggered forward until close enough to hurl a grenade, wiping out the enemy machinegun nest with his dying action. By his heroism, fearless determination, and supreme sacrifice, S/Sgt. Shoup eliminated a hostile weapon which threatened to destroy his company and turned a desperate situation into victory.

SHOUP, DAVID MONROE

Rank and organization: Colonel, U.S. Marine Corps, commanding officer of all Marine Corps troops on Betio Island, Tarawa Atoll, and Gilbert Islands, from 20 to 22 November 1943. *Entered service at:* Indiana. *Born:* 30 December 1904, Tippecanoe, Ind. *Citation:* For conspicuous gallantry and intrepidity at the risk of his life above and beyond the call of duty as commanding officer of all Marine Corps troops in action against enemy Japanese forces on Betio Island, Tarawa Atoll, Gilbert Islands, from 20 to 22 November 1943. Although severely shocked by an exploding enemy shell soon after landing at the pier and suffering from a serious, painful leg wound which had become infected, Col. Shoup fearlessly exposed himself to the terrific and relentless artillery, machinegun, and rifle fire from hostile shore emplacements. Rallying his hesitant troops by his own inspiring heroism, he gallantly led them across the fringing reefs to charge the heavily fortified island and reinforce our hard-pressed, thinly held lines. Upon arrival on shore, he assumed command of all landed troops and, working without rest under constant, withering enemy fire during the next 2 days, conducted smashing attacks against unbelievably strong and fanatically defended Japanese positions despite innumerable obstacles and heavy casualties. By his brilliant leadership, daring tactics, and selfless devotion to duty, Col. Shoup was largely responsible for the final decisive defeat of the enemy, and his indomitable fighting spirit reflects great credit upon the U.S. Naval Service.

SIGLER, FRANKLIN EARL

Rank and organization: Private, U.S. Marine Corps Reserve, 2d Battalion, 26th Marines, 5th Marine Division. *Place and date:* Iwo Jima, Volcano Islands, 14 March 1945. *Entered service at:* New Jersey. *Born:* 6 November 1924, Glen Ridge, N.J. *Citation:* For conspicuous gallantry and intrepidity at the risk of his life above and beyond the call of duty while serving with the 2d Battalion, 26th Marines, 5th Marine Division, in action against enemy Japanese forces during the seizure of Iwo Jima in the Volcano Islands on 14 March 1945. Voluntarily taking command of his rifle squad when the leader became a casualty, Pvt. Sigler fearlessly led a bold charge against an enemy gun installation which had held up the advance of his company for several days and, reaching the position in advance of the others, assailed the emplacement with handgrenades and personally annihilated the entire crew. As additional Japanese troops opened fire from concealed tunnels and caves above, he quickly scaled the rocks leading to the attacking guns, surprised the enemy with a furious 1-man assault and, although severely wounded in the encounter, deliberately crawled back to his squad position where he steadfastly refused evacuation, persistently directing heavy machinegun and rocket barrages on the Japanese cave entrances. Undaunted by the merciless rain of hostile fire during the intensified action, he gallantly disregarded his own painful wounds to aid casualties, carrying 3 wounded squad members to safety behind the lines and returning to continue the battle with renewed determination until ordered to retire for medical treatment. Stouthearted and indomitable in the face of extreme peril, Pvt. Sigler, by his alert initiative, unfaltering leadership, and daring tactics in a critical situation, effected the release of his besieged company from enemy fire and contributed essentially to its further advance against a savagely fighting enemy. His superb valor, resolute fortitude, and heroic spirit of self-sacrifice throughout reflect the highest credit upon Pvt. Sigler and the U.S. Naval Service.

SILK, EDWARD A.

Rank and organization: First Lieutenant, U.S. Army, Company E, 398th Infantry, 100th Infantry Division. *Place and date:* Near St. Pravel, France, 23 November 1944. *Entered service at:* Johnstown, Pa. *Born:* 8 June 1916, Johnstown, Pa. *G.O. No.:* 97, 1 November 1945. *Citation:* 1st Lt. Edward A. Silk commanded the weapons platoon of Company E, 398th Infantry, on 23 November 1944, when the end battalion was assigned the mission of seizing high ground overlooking Moyenmoutier, France, prior to an attack on the city itself. His company jumped off in the lead at dawn and by noon had reached the edge of a woods in the vicinity of St. Pravel where scouts saw an enemy sentry standing guard before a farmhouse in a valley below. One squad, engaged in reconnoitering the area, was immediately pinned down by intense machinegun and automatic-weapons fire from within the house. Skillfully deploying his light machinegun section, 1st Lt. Silk answered enemy fire, but when 15 minutes had elapsed with no slackening of resistance, he decided to eliminate the strong point by a 1-man attack. Running 100 yards across an open field to the shelter of a low stone wall directly in front of the farmhouse, he fired into the door and windows with his carbine; then, in full view of the enemy, vaulted the wall and dashed 50 yards through a hail of bullets to the left side of the house, where he hurled a grenade through a window, silencing a machinegun and killing 2 gunners. In attempting to move to the right side of the house he drew fire from a second machinegun emplaced in the woodshed. With magnificent courage he rushed this position in the face of direct fire and succeeded in neutralizing the weapon and killing the 2 gunners by throwing grenades into the structure. His supply of grenades was by now exhausted, but undaunted, he dashed back to the side of the farmhouse and began to throw rocks through a window, demanding the surrender of the remaining enemy. Twelve Germans, overcome by his relentless assault and confused by his unorthodox methods, gave up to the lone American. By his gallant willingness to assume the full burden of the attack and the intrepidity with which he carried out his extremely hazardous mission, 1st Lt. Silk enabled his battalion to continue its advance and seize its objective.

SJOGREN, JOHN C.

Rank and organization: Staff Sergeant, U.S. Army, Company I, 160th Infantry, 40th Infantry Division. *Place and date:* Near San Jose Hacienda, Negros, Philippine Islands, 23 May 1945. *Entered service at:* Rockford, Mich. *Birth:* Rockford, Mich. *G.O. No.:* 97, 1 November 1945. *Citation:* He led an attack against a high precipitous ridge defended by a company of enemy riflemen, who were entrenched in spider holes and supported by well-sealed pillboxes housing automatic weapons with interlocking bands of fire. The terrain was such that only 1 squad could advance at one time; and from a knoll atop a ridge a pillbox covered the only approach with automatic fire. Against this enemy stronghold, S/Sgt. Sjogren led the first squad to open the assault. Deploying his men, he moved forward and was hurling grenades when he saw that his next in command, at the opposite flank, was gravely wounded. Without hesitation he crossed 20 yards of exposed terrain in the face of enemy fire and exploding dynamite charges, moved the man to cover and administered first aid. He then worked his way forward and, advancing directly into the enemy fire, killed 8 Japanese in spider holes guarding the approach to the pillbox. Crawling to within a few feet of the pillbox while his men concentrated their bullets on the fire port, he began dropping grenades through the narrow firing slit. The enemy immediately threw 2 or 3 of these unexploded grenades out, and fragments from one wounded him in the hand and back. However, by hurling grenades through the embrasure faster then the enemy could return them, he succeeded in destroying the occupants. Despite his wounds, he directed his squad to follow him in a systematic attack on the remaining positions, which he eliminated in like manner, taking tremendous risks, overcoming bitter resistance, and never hesitating in his relentless advance. To silence one of the pillboxes, he wrenched a light machinegun out through the embrasure as it was firing before blowing up the occupants with handgrenades. During this action, S/Sgt. Sjogren, by his heroic bravery, aggressiveness, and skill as a soldier, singlehandedly killed 43 enemy soldiers and destroyed 9 pillboxes, thereby paving the way for his company's successful advance.

SKAGGS, LUTHER, JR.

Rank and organization: Private First Class, U.S. Marine Corps Reserve, 3d Battalion, 3d Marines, 3d Marine Division. *Place and date:* Asan-Adelup beachhead, Guam, Marianas Islands, 21–22 July 1944. *Entered service at:* Kentucky. *Born:* 3 March 1923, Henderson, Ky. *Citation:* For conspicuous gallantry and intrepidity at the risk of his life above and beyond the call of duty while serving as squad leader with a mortar section of a rifle company in the 3d Battalion, 3d Marines, 3d Marine Division, during action against enemy Japanese forces on the Asan-Adelup beachhead, Guam, Marianas Islands, 21–22 July 1944. When the section leader became a casualty under a heavy mortar barrage shortly after landing, Pfc. Skaggs promptly assumed command and led the section through intense fire for a distance of 200 yards to a position from which to deliver effective coverage of the assault on a strategic cliff. Valiantly defending this vital position against strong enemy counterattacks during the night, Pfc. Skaggs was critically wounded when a Japanese grenade lodged in his foxhole and exploded, shattering the lower part of one leg. Quick to act, he applied an improvised tourniquet and, while propped up in his foxhole, gallantly returned the enemy's fire with his rifle and handgrenades for a period of 8 hours, later crawling unassisted to the rear to continue the fight until the Japanese had been annihilated. Uncomplaining and calm throughout this critical period, Pfc. Skaggs served as a heroic example of courage and fortitude to other wounded men and, by his courageous leadership and inspiring devotion to duty, upheld the high traditions of the U.S. Naval Service.

SLATON, JAMES D.

Rank and organization: Corporal, U.S. Army, 157th Infantry, 45th Infantry Division. *Place and date:* Near Oliveto, Italy, 23 September 1943. *Entered service at:* Gulfport, Miss. *Born:* 2 April 1912, Laurel, Miss. *G.O. No.:* 44, 30 May 1944. *Citation:* For conspicuous gallantry and intrepidity at the risk of life above and beyond the call of duty in action with the enemy in the vicinity of Oliveto, Italy, on 23 September 1943. Cpl. Slaton was lead scout of an infantry squad which had been committed to a flank to knock out enemy resistance which had succeeded in pinning 2 attacking platoons to the ground. Working ahead of his squad, Cpl. Slaton crept upon an enemy machinegun nest and, assaulting it with his bayonet, succeeded in killing the gunner. When his bayonet stuck, he detached it from the rifle and killed another gunner with rifle fire. At that time he was fired upon by a machinegun to his immediate left. Cpl. Slaton then moved over open ground under constant fire to within throwing distance, and on his second try scored a direct hit on the second enemy machinegun nest, killing 2 enemy gunners. At that time a third machinegun fired on him

100 yards to his front, and Cpl. Slaton killed both of these enemy gunners with rifle fire. As a result of Cpl. Slaton's heroic action in immobilizing 3 enemy machinegun nests with bayonet, grenade, and rifle fire, the 2 rifle platoons which were receiving heavy casualties from enemy fire were enabled to withdraw to covered positions and again take the initiative. Cpl. Slaton withdrew under mortar fire on order of his platoon leader at dusk that evening. The heroic actions of Cpl. Slaton were far above and beyond the call of duty and are worthy of emulation.

*SMITH, FURMAN L.

Rank and organization: Private, U.S. Army, 135th Infantry, 34th Infantry Division. *Place and date:* Near Lanuvio, Italy, 31 May 1944. *Entered service at:* Central, S.C. *Birth:* Six Miles, S.C. *G.O. No.:* 6, 24 January 1945. *Citation:* For conspicuous gallantry and intrepidity at the risk of his life above and beyond the call of duty. In its attack on a strong point, an infantry company was held up by intense enemy fire. The group to which Pvt. Smith belonged was far in the lead when attacked by a force of 80 Germans. The squad leader and 1 other man were seriously wounded and other members of the group withdrew to the company position, but Pvt. Smith refused to leave his wounded comrades. He placed them in the shelter of shell craters and then alone faced a strong enemy counterattack, temporarily checking it by his accurate rifle fire at close range, killing and wounding many of the foe. Against overwhelming odds, he stood his ground until shot down and killed, rifle in hand.

SMITH, JOHN LUCIAN

Rank and organization: Major, U.S. Marine Corps, Marine Fighting Squadron 223, *Place and date:* In the Solomon Islands area, August–September 1942. *Entered service at:* Oklahoma. *Born:* 26 December 1914, Lexington, Okla. *Other Navy award:* Legion of Merit. *Citation:* For conspicuous gallantry and heroic achievement in aerial combat above and beyond the call of duty as commanding officer of Marine Fighting Squadron 223 during operations against enemy Japanese forces in the Solomon Islands area, August–September 1942. Repeatedly risking his life in aggressive and daring attacks, Maj. Smith led his squadron against a determined force, greatly superior in numbers, personally shooting down 16 Japanese planes between 21 August and 15 September 1942. In spite of the limited combat experience of many of the pilots of this squadron, they achieved the notable record of a total of 83 enemy aircraft destroyed in this period, mainly attributable to the thorough training under Maj. Smith and to his intrepid and inspiring leadership. His bold tactics and indomitable fighting spirit, and the valiant and zealous fortitude of the men of his command not only rendered the enemy's attacks ineffective and costly to Japan, but contributed to the security of our advance base. His loyal and courageous devotion to duty sustains and enhances the finest traditions of the U.S. Naval Service.

SMITH, MAYNARD H. (Air Mission)		*Born: 5/19/1911*

Rank and organization: Sergeant, U.S. Army Air Corps, 423d Bombardment Squadron, 306th Bomber Group. *Place and date:* Over Europe, 1 May 1943. *Entered service at:* Cairo, Mich. *Born:* 1911, ~~Cairo,~~ *CARO*, Mich. *G.O. No.:* 38, 12 July 1943. *Citation:* For conspicuous gallantry and intrepidity in action above and beyond the call of duty. The aircraft of which Sgt. Smith was a gunner was subjected to intense enemy antiaircraft fire and determined fighter airplane attacks while returning from a mission over enemy-occupied continental Europe on 1 May 1943. The airplane was hit several times by antiaircraft fire and cannon shells of the fighter airplanes, 2 of the crew were seriously wounded, the aircraft's oxygen system shot out, and several vital control cables severed when intense fires were ignited simultaneously in the radio compartment and waist sections. The situation became so acute that 3 of the crew bailed out into the comparative safety of the sea. Sgt. Smith, then on his first combat mission, elected to fight the fire by himself, administered first aid to the wounded tail gunner, manned the waist guns, and fought the intense flames alternately. The escaping oxygen fanned the fire to such intense heat that the ammunition in the radio compartment began to explode, the radio, gun mount, and camera were melted, and the compartment completely gutted. Sgt. Smith threw the exploding ammunition overboard, fought the fire until all the firefighting aids were exhausted, manned the workable guns until the enemy fighers were driven away, further administered first aid to his wounded comrade, and then by wrapping himself in protecting cloth, completely extinguished the fire by hand. This soldier's gallantry in action, undaunted bravery, and loyalty to his aircraft and fellow crewmembers, without regard for his own personal safety, is an inspiration to the U.S. Armed Forces.

SODERMAN, WILLIAM A.

Rank and organization: Private First Class, U.S. Army, Company K, 9th Infantry, 2d Infantry Division. *Place and date:* Near Rocherath, Belgium, 17 December 1944. *Entered service at:* West Haven, Conn. *Birth:* West Haven, Conn. *G.O. No.:* 97, 1 November 1945. *Citation:* Armed with a bazooka, he defended a key road junction near Rocherath, Belgium, on 17 December 1944, during the German Ardennes counteroffensive. After a heavy artillery barrage had wounded and forced the withdrawal of his assistant, he heard enemy tanks approaching the position where he calmly waited in the gathering darkness of early evening until the 5 Mark V tanks which made up the hostile force were within pointblank range. He then stood up, completely disregarding the firepower that could be brought to bear upon him, and launched a rocket into the lead tank, setting it afire and forcing its crew to abandon it as the other tanks pressed on before Pfc. Soderman could reload. The daring bazookaman remained at his post all night under severe artillery, mortar, and machinegun fire, awaiting the next onslaught, which was made shortly after dawn by 5 more tanks. Running along a ditch to meet them, he reached an advantageous point and there leaped to the road in full view of the tank gunners, deliberately aimed his weapon and disabled the lead tank.

The other vehicles, thwarted by a deep ditch in their attempt to go around the crippled machine, withdrew. While returning to his post Pfc. Soderman, braving heavy fire to attack an enemy infantry platoon from close range, killed at least 3 Germans and wounded several others with a round from his bazooka. By this time, enemy pressure had made Company K's position untenable. Orders were issued for withdrawal to an assembly area, where Pfc. Soderman was located when he once more heard enemy tanks approaching. Knowing that elements of the company had not completed their disengaging maneuver and were consequently extremely vulnerable to an armored attack, he hurried from his comparatively safe position to meet the tanks. Once more he disabled the lead tank with a single rocket, his last; but before he could reach cover, machinegun bullets from the tank ripped into his right shoulder. Unarmed and seriously wounded he dragged himself along a ditch to the American lines and was evacuated. Through his unfaltering courage against overwhelming odds, Pfc. Soderman contributed in great measure to the defense of Rocherath, exhibiting to a superlative degree the intrepidity and heroism with which American soldiers met and smashed the savage power of the last great German offensive.

SORENSON, RICHARD KEITH

Rank and organization: Private, U.S. Marine Corps Reserve, 4th Marine Division. *Place and date:* Namur Island, Kwajalein Atoll, Marshall Islands, 1–2 February 1944. *Entered service at:* Minnesota. *Born:* 28 August 1924, Anoka, Minn. *Citation:* For conspicuous gallantry and intrepidity at the risk of his life above and beyond the call of duty while serving with an assault battalion attached to the 4th Marine Division during the battle of Namur Island, Kwajalein Atoll, Marshall Islands, on 1–2 February 1944. Putting up a brave defense against a particularly violent counterattack by the enemy during invasion operations, Pvt. Sorenson and 5 other marines occupying a shellhole were endangered by a Japanese grenade thrown into their midst. Unhesitatingly, and with complete disregard for his own safety, Pvt. Sorenson hurled himself upon the deadly weapon, heroically taking the full impact of the explosion. As a result of his gallant action, he was severely wounded, but the lives of his comrades were saved. His great personal valor and exceptional spirit of self-sacrifice in the face of almost certain death were in keeping with the highest traditions of the U.S. Naval Service.

*SPECKER, JOE C.

Rank and organization: Sergeant, U.S. Army, 48th Engineer Combat Battalion. *Place and date:* At Mount Porchia, Italy, 7 January 1944. *Entered service at:* Odessa, Mo. *Birth:* Odessa, Mo. *G.O. No.:* 56, 12 July 1944. *Citation:* For conspicuous gallantry and intrepidity at risk of life, above and beyond the call of duty, in action involving actual conflict. On the night of 7 January 1944, Sgt. Specker, with his company, was advancing up the slope of Mount Porchia, Italy. He was sent forward on reconnaissance and on his return he reported to his company commander the fact that there was an enemy machinegun nest and several well-placed snipers directly in the path and awaiting the company. Sgt. Specker requested and was granted permission to place 1 of his machineguns in a position near the enemy machinegun. Voluntarily and alone he made his way up the mountain with a machinegun and a box of ammunition. He was observed by the enemy as he walked along and was severely wounded by the deadly fire directed at him. Though so seriously wounded that he was unable to walk, he continued to drag himself over the jagged edges of rock and rough terrain until he reached the position at which he desired to set up his machinegun. He set up the gun so well and fired so accurately that the enemy machine0gun nest was silenced and the remainder of the snipers forced to retire, enabling his platoon to obtain their objective. Sgt. Specker was found dead at his gun. His personal bravery, self-sacrifice, and determination were an inspiration to his officers and fellow soldiers.

SPURRIER, JUNIOR J.

Rank and organization: Staff Sergeant, U.S. Army, Company G, 134th Infantry, 35th Infantry Division. *Place and date:* Achain, France, 13 November 1944. *Entered service at:* Riggs, Ky. *Birth:* Russell County, Ky. *G.O. No.:* 18, 15 March 1945. *Citation:* For conspicuous gallantry and intrepidity at risk of his life above and beyond the call of duty in action against the enemy at Achain, France, on 13 November 1944. At 2 p.m., Company G attacked the village of Achain from the east. S/Sgt. Spurrier armed with a BAR passed around the village and advanced alone. Attacking from the west, he immediately killed 3 Germans. From this time until dark, S/Sgt. Spurrier, using at different times his BAR and M1 rifle, American and German rocket launchers, a German automatic pistol, and handgrenades, continued his solitary attack against the enemy regardless of all types of small-arms and automatic-weapons fire. As a result of his heroic actions he killed an officer and 24 enlisted men and captured 2 officers and 2 enlisted men. His valor has shed fresh honor on the U.S. Armed Forces.

*SQUIRES, JOHN C.

Rank and organization: Sergeant (then Private First Class), U.S. Army, Company A, 30th Infantry, 3d Infantry Division. *Place and date:* Near Padiglione, Italy, 23–24 April 1944. *Entered service at:* Louisville, Ky. *Birth:* Louisville, Ky. *G.O. No.:* 78, 2 October 1944. *Citation:* For conspicuous gallantry and intrepidity at risk of life above and beyond the call of duty. At the start of his company's attack on strongly held enemy positions in and around Spaccasassi Creek, near Padiglione, Italy, on the night of 23–24 April 1944, Pfc. Squires, platoon messenger, participating in his first offensive action, braved intense artillery, mortar, and antitank gun fire in order to investigate the effects of an antitank mine explosion on the leading platoon. Despite shells which burst close to him, Pfc. Squires made his way 50 yards forward to the advance element, noted the situation, reconnoitered a new route of advance and informed his platoon leader of the casualties sustained and the alternate route. Acting without orders, he rounded up stragglers, organized a group of lost men into a squad and led them forward. When the platoon reached Spaccasassi Creek and established an outpost, Pfc. Squires, knowing that almost all of the noncommissioned officers were casualties, placed 8 men in position of his own volition, disregarding enemy machinegun, machine-pistol, and grenade fire which covered the creek draw. When his platoon had been reduced to 14 men, he brought up reinforcements twice. On each trip he went through barbed wire and across an enemy minefield, under intense artillery and mortar fire. Three times in the early morning the outpost was counterattacked. Each time Pfc. Squires ignored withering enemy automatic fire and grenades which struck all around him, and fired hundreds of rounds of rifle, Browning automatic rifle, and captured German Spandau machinegun ammunition at the enemy, inflicting numerous casualties and materially aiding in repulsing the attacks. Following these fights, he moved 50 yards to the south end of the outpost and engaged 21 German soldiers in individual machinegun duels at point-blank range, forcing all 21 enemy to surrender and capturing 13 more Spandau guns. Learning the function of this weapon by questioning a German officer prisoner, he placed the captured guns in position and instructed other members of his platoon in their operation. The next night when the Germans attacked the outpost again he killed 3 and wounded more Germans with captured potato-masher grenades and fire from his Spandau gun. Pfc. Squires was killed in a subsequent action.

*STEIN, TONY

Rank and organization: Corporal, U.S. Marine Corps Reserve. *Born:* 30 September 1921, Dayton, Ohio. *Accredited to:* Ohio. *Citation:* For conspicuous gallantry and intrepidity at the risk of his life above and beyond the call of duty while serving with Company A, 1st Battalion, 28th Marines, 5th Marine Division, in action against enemy Japanese forces on Iwo Jima, in the Volcano Islands, 19 February 1945. The first man of his unit to be on station after hitting the beach in the initial assault, Cpl. Stein, armed with a personally improvised aircraft-type weapon, provided rapid covering fire as the remainder of his platoon attempted to move into position. When his comrades were stalled by a concentrated machinegun and mortar barrage, he gallantly stood upright and exposed himself to the enemy's view, thereby drawing the hostile fire to his own person and enabling him to observe the location of the furiously blazing hostile guns. Determined to neutralize the strategically placed weapons, he boldly charged the enemy pillboxes 1 by 1 and succeeded in killing 20 of the enemy during the furious singlehanded assault. Cool and courageous under the merciless hail of exploding shells and bullets which fell on all sides, he continued to deliver the fire of his skillfully improvised weapon at a tremendous rate of speed which rapidly exhausted his ammunition. Undaunted, he removed his helmet and shoes to expedite his movements and ran back to the beach for additional ammunition, making a total of 8 trips under intense fire and carrying or assisting a wounded man back each time. Despite the unrelenting savagery and confusion of battle, he rendered prompt assistance to his platoon whenever the unit was in position, directing the fire of a half-track against a stubborn pillbox until he had effected the ultimate destruction of the Japanese fortification. Later in the day, although his weapon was twice shot from his hands, he personally covered the withdrawal of his platoon to the company position.

Stouthearted and indomitable, Cpl. Stein, by his aggressive initiative, sound judgment, and unwavering devotion to duty in the face of terrific odds, contributed materially to the fulfillment of his mission, and his outstanding valor throughout the bitter hours of conflict sustains and enhances the highest traditions of the U.S. Naval Service.

STREET, GEORGE LEVICK, III

Rank and organization: Commander, U.S. Navy, U.S.S. *Tirante. Place and date:* Harbor of Quelpart Island, off the coast of Korea, 14 April 1945. *Entered service at:* Virginia. *Born:* 27 July 1913, Richmond, Va. *Other Navy awards:* Navy Cross, Silver Star with 1 Gold Star. *Citation:* For conspicuous gallantry and intrepidity at the risk of his life above and beyond the call of duty as commanding officer of the U.S.S. *Tirante* during the first war patrol of that vessel against enemy Japanese surface forces in the harbor of Quelpart Island, off the coast of Korea, on 14 April 1945. With the crew at surface battle stations, Comdr. (then Lt. Comdr.) Street approached the hostile anchorage from the south within 1,200 yards of the coast to complete a reconnoitering circuit of the island. Leaving the 10-fathom curve far behind, he penetrated the mined and shoal-obstructed waters of the restricted harbor despite numerous patroling vessels and in defiance of 5 shore-based radar stations and menacing aircraft. Prepared to fight it out on the surface if attacked, Comdr. Street went into action, sending 2 torpedoes with deadly accuracy into a large Japanese ammunition ship and exploding the target in a mountainous and blinding glare of white flames. With the *Tirante* instantly spotted by the enemy as she stood out plainly in the flare of light, he ordered the torpedo data computer set up while retiring and fired his last 2 torpedoes to disintegrate in quick succession the leading frigate and a similar flanking vessel. Clearing the gutted harbor at emergency full speed ahead, he slipped undetected along the shoreline, diving deep as a pursuing patrol dropped a pattern of depth charges at the point of submergence. His illustrious record of combat achievement during the first war patrol of the *Tirante* characterizes Comdr. Street as a daring and skilled leader and reflects the highest credit upon himself, his valiant command, and the U.S. Naval Service.

*STRYKER, STUART S.

Rank and organization: Private First Class, U.S. Army, Company E, 513th Parachute Infantry, 17th Airborne Division. *Place and date:* Near Wesel, Germany, 24 March 1945. *Entered service at:* Portland, Oreg. *Birth:* Portland, Oreg. *G.O. No.:* 117, 11 December 1945. *Citation:* He was a platoon runner, when the unit assembled near Wesel, Germany, after a descent east of the Rhine. Attacking along a railroad, Company E reached a point about 250 yards from a large building used as an enemy headquarters and manned by a powerful force of Germans with rifles, machineguns, and 4 field pieces. One platoon made a frontal assault but was pinned down by intense fire from the house after advancing only 50 yards. So badly stricken that it could not return the raking fire, the platoon was at the mercy of German machine gunners when Pfc. Stryker voluntarily left a place of comparative safety, and, armed with a carbine, ran to the head of the unit. In full view of the enemy and under constant fire, he exhorted the men to get to their feet and follow him. Inspired by his fearlessness, they rushed after him in a desperate charge through an increased hail of bullets. Twenty-five yards from the objective the heroic soldier was killed by the enemy fusilades. His gallant and wholly voluntary action in the face of overwhelming firepower, however, so encouraged his comrades and diverted the enemy's attention that other elements of the company were able to surround the house, capturing more than 200 hostile soldiers and much equipment, besides freeing 3 members of an American bomber crew held prisoner there. The intrepidity and unhesitating self-sacrifice of Pfc. Stryker were in keeping with the highest traditions of the military service.

SWETT, JAMES ELMS

Rank and organization: First Lieutenant, U.S. Marine Corps Reserve, Marine Fighting Squadron 221, with Marine Aircraft Group 12, 1st Marine Aircraft Wing. *Place and date:* Solomon Islands area, 7 April 1943. *Entered service at:* California. *Born:* 15 June 1920, Seattle, Wash. *Other Navy award:* Distinguished Flying Cross with 1 Gold Star. *Citation:* For extraordinary heroism and personal valor above and beyond the call of duty, as division leader of Marine Fighting Squadron 221 with Marine Aircraft Group 12, 1st Marine Aircraft Wing, in action against enemy Japanese aerial forces in the Solomons Islands area, 7 April 1943. In a daring flight to intercept a wave of 150 Japanese planes, 1st Lt. Swett unhesitatingly hurled his 4-plane division into action against a formation of 15 enemy bombers and personally exploded 3 hostile planes in midair with accurate and deadly fire during his dive. Although separated from his division while clearing the heavy concentration of antiaircraft fire, he boldly attacked 6 enemy bombers, engaged the first 4 in turn and, unaided, shot down all in flames. Exhausting his ammunition as he closed the fifth Japanese bomber, he relentlessly drove his attack against terrific opposition which partially disabled his engine, shattered the windscreen and slashed his face. In spite of this, he brought his battered plane down with skillful precision in the water off Tulagi without further injury. The superb airmanship and tenacious fighting spirit which enabled 1st Lt. Swett to destroy 7 enemy bombers in a single flight were in keeping with the highest traditions of the U.S. Naval Service.

*TERRY, SEYMOUR W.

Rank and organization: Captain, U.S. Army, Company B, 382d Infantry, 96th Infantry Division. *Place and date:* Zebra Hill, Okinawa, Ryukyu Islands, 11 May 1945. *Entered service at:* Little Rock, Ark. *Birth:* Little Rock, Ark. *G.O. No.:* 23, 6 March 1946. *Citation:* 1st Lt. Terry was leading an attack against heavily defended Zebra Hill when devastating fire from 5 pillboxes halted the advance. He braved the hail of bullets to secure satchel charges and white phosphorus grenades, and then ran 30 yards directly at the enemy with an ignited charge to the first stronghold, demolished it, and moved on to the other pillboxes, bombarding them with his grenades and calmly cutting down their defenders with rifle fire as they attempted to escape. When he had finished this job by sealing the 4 pillboxes with explosives, he had killed 20 Japanese and destroyed 3 machineguns. The advance was again held up by an intense grenade barrage which inflicted several casualties. Locating the source of enemy fire in trenches on the reverse slope of the hill, 1st Lt. Terry, burdened by 6 satchel charges, launched a 1-man assault. He wrecked the enemy's defenses by throwing explosives into their positions and himself accounted for 10 of the 20 hostile troops killed when his men overran the area. Pressing forward again toward a nearby ridge, his 2 assault platoons were stopped by slashing machinegun and mortar fire. He fearlessly ran across 100 yards of fire-swept terrain to join the support platoon and urge it on in a flanking maneuver. This thrust, too, was halted by stubborn resistance. 1st Lt. Terry began another 1-man drive, hurling grenades upon the strongly entrenched defenders until they fled in confusion, leaving 5 dead behind them. Inspired by this bold action, the support platoon charged the retreating enemy and annihilated them. Soon afterward, while organizing his company to repulse a possible counterattack, the gallant company commander was mortally wounded by the burst of an enemy mortar shell. By his indomitable fighting spirit, brilliant leadership, and unwavering courage in the face of tremendous odds, 1st Lt. Terry made possible the accomplishment of his unit's mission and set an example of heroism in keeping with the highest traditions of the military service.

*THOMAS, HERBERT JOSEPH

Rank and organization: Sergeant, U.S. Marine Corps Reserve. *Born:* 8 February 1918, Columbus, Ohio. *Accredited to:* West Virginia. *Citation:* For extraordinary heroism and conspicuous gallantry above and beyond the call of duty while serving with the 3d Marines, 3d Marine Division, in action against enemy Japanese forces during the battle at the Koromokina River, Bougainville Islands, Solomon Islands, on 7 November 1943. Although several of his men were struck by enemy bullets as he led his squad through dense jungle undergrowth in the face of severe hostile machinegun fire, Sgt. Thomas and his group fearlessly pressed forward into the center of the Japanese position and destroyed the crews of 2 machineguns by accurate rifle fire and grenades. Discovering a third gun more difficult to approach, he carefully placed his men closely around him in strategic positions from which they were to charge after he had thrown a grenade into the emplacement. When the grenade struck vines and fell back into the midst of the group, Sgt. Thomas deliberately flung himself upon it to smother the explosion, valiantly sacrificing his life for his comrades. Inspired by his selfless action, his men unhesitatingly charged the enemy machinegun and, with fierce determination, killed the crew and several other nearby-defenders. The splendid initiative and extremely heroic conduct of Sgt. Thomas in carrying out his prompt decision with full knowledge of his fate reflect great credit upon himself and the U.S. Naval Service. He gallantly gave his life for his country.

*THOMAS, WILLIAM H.

Rank and organization: Private First Class, U.S. Army, 149th Infantry, 38th Infantry Division. *Place and date:* Zambales Mountains, Luzon, Philippine Islands, 22 April 1945. *Entered service at:* Ypsilanti,

Mich. *Birth:* Wynne, Ark. *G.O. No.:* 81, 24 September 1945. *Citation:* He was a member of the leading squad of Company B, which was attacking along a narrow, wooded ridge. The enemy strongly entrenched in camouflaged emplacements on the hill beyond directed heavy fire and hurled explosive charges on the attacking riflemen. Pfc. Thomas, an automatic rifleman, was struck by 1 of these charges, which blew off both his legs below the knees. He refused medical aid and evacuation, and continued to fire at the enemy until his weapon was put out of action by an enemy bullet. Still refusing aid, he threw his last 2 grenades. He destroyed 3 of the enemy after suffering the wounds from which he died later that day. The effective fire of Pfc. Thomas prevented the repulse of his platoon and assured the capture of the hostile position. His magnificent courage and heroic devotion to duty provided a lasting inspiration for his comrades.

*THOMASON, CLYDE

Rank and organization: Sergeant, U.S. Marine Corps Reserve. *Born:* 23 May 1914, Atlanta, Ga. *Accredited to:* Georgia. *Citation:* For conspicuous heroism and intrepidity above and beyond the call of duty during the Marine Raider Expedition against the Japanese-held island of Makin on 17–18 August 1942. Leading the advance element of the assault echelon, Sgt. Thomason disposed his men with keen judgment and discrimination and, by his exemplary leadership and great personal valor, exhorted them to like fearless efforts. On 1 occasion, he dauntlessly walked up to a house which concealed an enemy Japanese sniper, forced in the door and shot the man before he could resist. Later in the action, while leading an assault on an enemy position, he gallantly gave his life in the service of his country. His courage and loyal devotion to duty in the face of grave peril were in keeping with the finest traditions of the U.S. Naval Service.

THOMPSON, MAX

Rank and organization: Sergeant, U.S. Army, Company K, 18th Infantry, 1st Infantry Division. *Place and date:* Near Haaren, Germany, 18 October 1944. *Entered service at:* Prescott, Ariz. *Birth:* Bethel, N.C. *G.O. No.:* 47, 18 June 1945. *Citation:* On 18 October 1944, Company K, 18th Infantry, occupying a position on a hill near Haaren, Germany, was attacked by an enemy infantry battalion supported by tanks. The assault was preceded by an artillery concentration, lasting an hour, which inflicted heavy casualties on the company. While engaged in moving wounded men to cover, Sgt. Thompson observed that the enemy had overrun the positions of the 3d Platoon. He immediately attempted to stem the enemy's advance singlehandedly. He manned an abandoned machinegun and fired on the enemy until a direct hit from a hostile tank destroyed the gun. Shaken and dazed, Sgt. Thompson picked up an automatic rifle and although alone against the enemy force which was pouring into the gap in our lines, he fired burst after burst, halting the leading elements of the attack and dispersing those following. Throwing aside his automatic rifle, which had jammed, he took up a rocket gun, fired on a light tank, setting it on fire. By evening the enemy had been driven from the greater part of the captured position but still held 3 pillboxes. Sgt. Thompson's squad was assigned the task of dislodging the enemy from these emplacements. Darkness having fallen and finding that fire of his squad was ineffective from a distance, Sgt. Thompson crawled forward alone to within 20 yards of 1 of the pillboxes and fired grenades into it. The Germans holding the emplacement concentrated their fire upon him. Though wounded, he held his position fearlessly, continued his grenade fire, and finally forced the enemy to abandon the blockhouse. Sgt. Thompson's courageous leadership inspired his men and materially contributed to the clearing of the enemy from his last remaining hold on this important hill position.

*THORNE, HORACE M.

Rank and organization: Corporal, U.S. Army, Troop D, 89th Cavalry Reconnaissance Squadron, 9th Armored Division. *Place and date:* Near Grufflingen, Belgium, 21 December 1944. *Entered service at:* Keyport, N.J. *Birth:* Keansburg, N.J. *G.O. No.:* 80, 19 September 1945. *Citation:* He was the leader of a combat patrol on 21 December 1944, near Grufflingen, Belgium, with the mission of driving German forces from dug-in positions in a heavily wooded area. As he advanced his light machinegun, a German Mark III tank emerged from the enemy position and was quickly immobilized by fire from American light tanks supporting the patrol. Two of the enemy tankmen attempted to abandon their vehicle but were killed by Cpl. Thorne's shots before they could jump to the ground. To complete the destruction of the tank and its crew, Cpl. Thorne left his covered position and crept forward alone through intense machinegun fire until close enough to toss 2 grenades into the tank's open turret, killing 2 more Germans. He returned across the same fire-beaten zone as heavy mortar fire began falling in the area, seized his machinegun and, without help, dragged it to the knocked-out tank and set it up on the vehicle's rear deck. He fired short rapid bursts into the enemy positions from his advantageous but exposed location, killing or wounding 8. Two enemy machinegun crews abandoned their positions and retreated in confusion. His gun jammed; but rather than leave his self-chosen post he attempted to clear the stoppage; enemy small-arms fire, concentrated on the tank, killed him instantly. Cpl. Thorne, displaying heroic initiative and intrepid fighting qualities, inflicted costly casualties on the enemy and insured the success of his patrol's mission by the sacrifice of his life.

*THORSON, JOHN F.

Rank and organization: Private First Class, U.S. Army, Company G, 17th Infantry, 7th Infantry Division. *Place and date:* Dagami, Leyte, Philippine Islands, 28 October 1944. *Entered service at:* Armstrong, Iowa. *Birth:* Armstrong, Iowa. *G.O. No.:* 58, 19 July 1945. *Citation:* He was an automatic rifleman on 28 October 1944, in the attack on Dagami, Leyte, Philippine Islands. A heavily fortified enemy position consisting of pillboxes and supporting trenches held up the advance of his company. His platoon was ordered to out-flank and neutralize the strong point. Voluntarily moving well out in front of his group, Pvt. Thorson came upon an enemy fire trench defended by several hostile riflemen and, disregarding the intense fire directed at him, attacked singlehanded. He was seriously wounded and fell about 6 yards from the trench. Just as the remaining 20 members of the platoon reached him, 1 of the enemy threw a grenade into their midst. Shouting a warning and making a final effort, Pvt. Thorson rolled onto the grenade and smothered the explosion with his body. He was instantly killed, but his magnificent courage and supreme self-sacrifice prevented the injury and possible death of his comrades, and remain with them as a lasting inspiration.

*TIMMERMAN, GRANT FREDERICK

Rank and organization: Sergeant, U.S. Marine Corps. *Born:* 14 February 1919, Americus, Kans. *Accredited to:* Kansas. *Other Navy award:* Bronze Star Medal. *Citation:* For conspicuous gallantry and intrepidity at the risk of his life above and beyond the call of duty as tank commander serving with the 2d Battalion, 6th Marines, 2d Marine Division, during action against enemy Japanese forces on Saipan, Marianas Islands, on 8 July 1944. Advancing with his tank a few yards ahead of the infantry in support of a vigorous attack on hostile positions, Sgt. Timmerman maintained steady fire from his antiaircraft sky mount machinegun until progress was impeded by a series of enemy trenches and pillboxes. Observing a target of opportunity, he immediately ordered the tank stopped and, mindful of the danger from the muzzle blast as he prepared to open fire with the 75-mm., fearlessly stood up in the exposed turret and ordered the infantry to hit the deck. Quick to act as a grenade, hurled by the Japanese, was about to drop into the open turret hatch, Sgt. Timmerman unhesitatingly blocked the opening with his body holding the grenade against his chest and taking the brunt of the explosion. His exception valor and loyalty in saving his men at the cost of his own life reflect the highest credit upon Sgt. Timmerman and the U.S. Naval Service. He gallantly gave his life in the service of his country.

*TOMICH, PETER

Rank and organization: Chief Watertender, U.S. Navy. *Born:* 3 June 1893, Prolog, Austria. *Accredited to:* New Jersey. *Citation:* For distinguished conduct in the line of his profession, and extraordinary courage and disregard of his own safety, during the attack on the Fleet in Pearl Harbor by the Japanese forces on 7 December 1941. Although realizing that the ship was capsizing, as a result of enemy bombing and torpedoing, Tomich remained at his post in the engineering plant of the U.S.S. *Utah*, until he saw that all boilers were secured and all fireroom personnel had left their stations, and by so doing lost his own life.

TOMINAC, JOHN J.

Rank and organization: First Lieutenant, U.S. Army, Company I, 15th Infantry, 3d Infantry Division. *Place and date:* Saulx de Vesoul, France, 12 September 1944. *Entered service at:* Conemaugh, Pa. *Birth:* Conemaugh, Pa. *G.O. No.:* 20, 29 March 1945. *Citation:* For conspicuous gallantry and intrepidity at risk of life above and beyond the call of duty on 12 September 1944, in an attack on Saulx de Vesoul, France. 1st Lt. Tominac charged alone over 50 yards of exposed terrain onto an enemy roadblock to dispatch a 3-man crew of German machine gunners with a single burst from his Thompson machinegun. After smashing the enemy outpost, he led 1 of his squads in the annihilation of a second hostile group defended by mortar, machinegun, automatic pistol, rifle and grenade fire, killing about 30 of the enemy. Reaching the suburbs of the town, he advanced 50 yards ahead of his men to reconnoiter a third enemy position which commanded the road with a 77-mm. SP gun supported by infantry elements. The SP gun opened fire on his supporting tank, setting it afire with a direct hit. A fragment from the same shell painfully wounded 1st Lt. Tominac in the shoulder, knocking him to the ground. As the crew abandoned the M-4 tank, which was rolling down hill toward the enemy, 1st Lt. Tominac picked himself up and jumped onto the hull of the burning vehicle. Despite withering enemy machinegun, mortar, pistol, and sniper fire, which was ricocheting off the hull and turret of the M-4, 1st Lt. Tominac climbed to the turret and gripped the 50-caliber antiaircraft machinegun. Plainly silhouetted against the sky, painfully wounded, and with the tank burning beneath his feet, he directed bursts of machinegun fire on the roadblock, the SP gun, and the supporting German infantrymen, and forced the enemy to withdraw from his prepared position. Jumping off the tank before it exploded, 1st Lt. Tominac refused evacuation despite his painful wound. Calling upon a sergeant to extract the shell fragments from his shoulder with a pocketknife, he continued to direct the assault, led his squad in a handgrenade attack against a fortified position occupied by 32 of the enemy armed with machineguns, machine pistols, and rifles, and compelled them to surrender. His outstanding heroism and exemplary leadership resulted in the destruction of 4 successive enemy defensive positions, surrender of a vital sector of the city Saulx de Vesoul, and the death or capture of at least 60 of the enemy.

*TOWLE, JOHN R.

Rank and organization: Private, U.S. Army, Company C, 504th Parachute Infantry, 82d Airborne Division. *Place and date:* Near Oosterhout, Holland, 21 September 1944. *Entered service at:* Cleveland, Ohio. *Birth:* Cleveland, Ohio. *G.O. No.:* 18, 15 March 1945. *Citation:* For conspicuous gallantry and intrepidity at the risk of life above and beyond the call of duty on 21 September 1944, near Oosterhout, Holland. The rifle company in which Pvt. Towle served as rocket launcher gunner was occupying a defensive position in the west sector of the recently established Nijmegen bridgehead when a strong enemy force of approximately 100 infantry supported by 2 tanks and a half-track formed for a counterattack. With full knowledge of the disastrous consequences resulting not only to his company but to the entire bridgehead by an enemy breakthrough, Pvt. Towle immediately and without orders left his foxhole and moved 200 yards in the face of intense small-arms fire to a position on an exposed dike roadbed. From this precarious position Pvt. Towle fired his rocket launcher at and hit both tanks to his immediate front. Armored skirting on both tanks prevented penetration by the projectiles, but both vehicles withdrew slightly damaged. Still under intense fire and fully exposed to the enemy, Pvt. Towle then engaged a nearby house which 9 Germans had entered and were using as a strongpoint and with 1 round killed all 9.

Hurriedly replenishing his supply of ammunition, Pvt. Towle, motivated only by his high conception of duty which called for the destruction of the enemy at any cost, then rushed approximately 125 yards through grazing enemy fire to an exposed position from which he could engage the enemy half-track with his rocket launcher. While in a kneeling position preparatory to firing on the enemy vehicle, Pvt. Towle was mortally wounded by a mortar shell. By his heroic tenacity, at the price of his life, Pvt. Towle saved the lives of many of his comrades and was directly instrumental in breaking up the enemy counterattack.

TREADWELL, JACK L.

Rank and organization: Captain, U.S. Army, Company F, 180th Infantry, 45th Infantry Division. *Place and date:* Near Nieder-Wurzbach, Germany, 18 March 1945. *Entered service at:* Snyder, Okla. *Birth:* Ashland, Ala. *G.O. No.:* 79, 14 September 1945. *Citation:* Capt. Treadwell (then 1st Lt.), commanding officer of Company F, near Nieder-Wurzbach, Germany, in the Siegfried line, singlehandedly captured 6 pillboxes and 18 prisoners. Murderous enemy automatic and rifle fire with intermittent artillery bombardments had pinned down his company for hours at the base of a hill defended by concrete fortifications and interlocking trenches. Eight men sent to attack a single point had all become casualties on the bare slope when Capt. Treadwell, armed with a submachinegun and handgrenades, went forward alone to clear the way for his stalled company. Over the terrain devoid of cover and swept by bullets, he fearlessly advanced, firing at the aperture of the nearest pillbox and, when within range, hurling grenades at it. He reached the pillbox, thrust the muzzle of his gun through the port, and drove 4 Germans out with their hands in the air. A fifth was found dead inside. Waving these prisoners back to the American line, he continued under terrible, concentrated fire to the next pillbox and took it in the same manner. In this fort he captured the commander of the hill defenses, whom he sent to the rear with the other prisoners. Never slackening his attack, he then ran across the crest of the hill to a third pillbox, traversing this distance in full view of hostile machinegunners and snipers. He was again successful in taking the enemy position. The Germans quickly fell prey to his further rushes on 3 more pillboxes in the confusion and havoc caused by his whirlwind assaults and capture of their commander. Inspired by the electrifying performance of their leader, the men of Company F stormed after him and overwhelmed resistance on the entire hill, driving a wedge into the Siegfried line and making it possible for their battalion to take its objective. By his courageous willingness to face nearly impossible odds and by his overwhelming one-man offensive, Capt. Treadwell reduced a heavily fortified, seemingly impregnable enemy sector.

*TRUEMPER, WALTER E. (Air Mission)

Rank and organization: Second Lieutenant, U.S. Army Air Corps, 510th Bomber Squadron, 351st Bomber Group. *Place and date:* Over Europe, 20 February 1944. *Entered service at:* Aurora, Ill. *Born:* 31 October 1918, Aurora, Ill. *G.O. No.:* 52, 22 June 1944. *Citation:* For conspicuous gallantry and intrepidity at risk of life above and beyond the call of duty in action against the enemy in connection with a bombing mission over enemy-occupied Europe on 20 February 1944. The aircraft on which 2d Lt. Truemper was serving as navigator was attacked by a squadron of enemy fighters with the result that the copilot was killed outright, the pilot wounded and rendered unconscious, the radio operator wounded and the plane severely damaged. Nevertheless, 2d Lt. Truemper and other members of the crew managed to right the plane and fly it back to their home station, where they contacted the control tower and reported the situation. 2d Lt. Truemper and the engineer volunteered to attempt to land the plane. Other members of the crew were ordered to jump, leaving 2d Lt. Truemper and the engineer aboard. After observing the distressed aircraft from another plane, 2d Lt. Truemper's commanding officer decided the damaged plane could not be landed by the inexperienced crew and ordered them to abandon it and parachute to safety. Demonstrating unsurpassed courage and heroism, 2d Lt. Truemper and the engineer replied that the pilot was still alive but could not be moved and that they would not desert him. They were then told to attempt a landing. After 2 unsuccessful efforts their plane crashed into an open field in a third attempt to land. 2d Lt. Truemper, the engineer, and the wounded pilot were killed.

*TURNER, DAY G.

Rank and organization: Sergeant, U.S. Army, Company B, 319th Infantry, 80th Infantry Division. *Place and date:* At Dahl, Luxembourg, 8 January 1945. *Entered service at:* Nescopek, Pa. *Birth:* Berwick, Pa. *G.O. No.:* 49, 28 June 1945. *Citation:* He commanded a 9-man squad with the mission of holding a critical flank position. When overwhelming numbers of the enemy attacked under cover of withering artillery, mortar, and rocket fire, he withdrew his squad into a nearby house, determined to defend it to the last man. The enemy attacked again and again and were repulsed with heavy losses. Supported by direct tank fire, they finally gained entrance, but the intrepid sergeant refused to surrender although 5 of his men were wounded and 1 was killed. He boldly flung a can of flaming oil at the first wave of attackers, dispersing them, and fought doggedly from room to room, closing with the enemy in fierce hand-to-hand encounters. He hurled handgrenade for handgrenade, bayoneted 2 fanatical Germans who rushed a doorway he was defending and fought on with the enemy's weapons when his own ammunition was expended. The savage fight raged for 4 hours, and finally, when only 3 men of the defending squad were left unwounded, the enemy surrendered. Twenty-five prisoners were taken, 11 enemy dead and a great number of wounded were counted. Sgt. Turner's valiant stand will live on as a constant inspiration to his comrades. His heroic, inspiring leadership, his determination and courageous devotion to duty exemplify the highest tradition of the military service.

TURNER, GEORGE B.

Rank and organization: Private First Class, U.S. Army, Battery C, 499th Armored Field Artillery Battalion, 14th Armored Division. *Place and date:* Philippsbourg, France, 3 January 1945. *Entered service at:*

464

Los Angeles, Calif. *Born:* 27 June 1899, Longview, Tex. *G.O. No.:* 79, 14 September 1945. *Citation:* At Phillippsbourg, France, he was cut off from his artillery unit by an enemy armored infantry attack. Coming upon a friendly infantry company withdrawing under the vicious onslaught, he noticed 2 German tanks and approximately 75 supporting foot soldiers advancing down the main street of the village. Seizing a rocket launcher, he advanced under intense small-arms and cannon fire to meet the tanks and, standing in the middle of the road, fired at them, destroying 1 and disabling the second. From a nearby half-track he then dismounted a machinegun, placed it in the open street and fired into the enemy infantrymen, killing or wounding a great number and breaking up the attack. In the American counterattack which followed, 2 supporting tanks were disabled by an enemy antitank gun. Firing a light machinegun from the hip, Pfc. Turner held off the enemy so that the crews of the disabled vehicles could extricate themselves. He ran through a hail of fire to one of the tanks which had burst into flames and attempted to rescue a man who had been unable to escape; but an explosion of the tank's ammunition frustrated his effort and wounded him painfully. Refusing to be evacuated, he remained with the infantry until the following day, driving off an enemy patrol with serious casualties, assisting in capturing a hostile strong point, and voluntarily and fearlessly driving a truck through heavy enemy fire to deliver wounded men to the rear aid station. The great courage displayed by Pfc. Turner and his magnificently heroic initiative contributed materially to the defense of the French town and inspired the troops about him.

*VALDEZ, JOSE F.

Rank and organization: Private First Class, U.S. Army, Company B, 7th Infantry, 3d Infantry Division. *Place and date:* Near Rosenkrantz, France, 25 January 1945. *Entered service at:* Pleasant Grove, Utah. *Birth:* Governador, N. Mex. *G.O. No.:* 16, 8 February 1946. *Citation:* He was on outpost duty with 5 others when the enemy counterattacked with overwhelming strength. From his position near some woods 500 yards beyond the American lines he observed a hostile tank about 75 yards away, and raked it with automatic rifle fire until it withdrew. Soon afterward he saw 3 Germans stealthily approaching through the woods. Scorning cover as the enemy soldiers opened up with heavy automatic weapons fire from a range of 30 yards, he engaged in a fire fight with the attackers until he had killed all 3. The enemy quickly launched an attack with 2 full companies of infantrymen, blasting the patrol with murderous concentrations of automatic and rifle fire and beginning an encircling movement which forced the patrol leader to order a withdrawal. Despite the terrible odds, Pfc. Valdez immediately volunteered to cover the maneuver, and as the patrol 1 by 1 plunged through a hail of bullets toward the American lines, he fired burst after burst into the swarming enemy. Three of his companions were wounded in their dash for safety and he was struck by a bullet that entered his stomach and, passing through his body, emerged from his back. Overcoming agonizing pain, he regained control of himself and resumed his firing position, delivering a protective screen of bullets until all others of the patrol were safe.

By field telephone he called for artillery and mortar fire on the Germans and corrected the range until he had shells falling within 50 yards of his position. For 15 minutes he refused to be dislodged by more than 200 of the enemy; then, seeing that the barrage had broken the counter attack, he dragged himself back to his own lines. He died later as a result of his wounds. Through his valiant, intrepid stand and at the cost of his own life, Pfc. Valdez made it possible for his comrades to escape, and was directly responsible for repulsing an attack by vastly superior enemy forces.

URBAN, MATT

Rank and organization: Lieutenant Colonel (then Captain), 2d Battalion, 60th Infantry Regiment, 9th Infantry Division, World War II. *Place and date:* Renouf, France, 14 June to 3 September 1944. *Entered service at:* Fort Bragg, North Carolina, 2 July 1941. *Date and place of birth:* 25 August 1919, Buffalo, New York. Lieutenant Colonel (then Captain) Matt Urban, 112-22-2414, United States Army, who distinguished himself by a series of bold, heroic actions, exemplified by singularly outstanding combat leadership, personal bravery, and tenacious devotion to duty, during the period 14 June to 3 September 1944 while assigned to the 2d Battalion, 60th Infantry Regiment, 9th Infantry Division. On 14 June, Captain Urban's company, attacking at Renouf, France, encountered heavy enemy small arms and tank fire. The enemy tanks were unmercifully raking his unit's positions and inflicting heavy casualties. Captain Urban, realizing that his company was in imminent danger of being decimated, armed himself with a bazooka. He worked his way with an ammo carrier through hedgerows, under a continuing barrage of fire, to a point near the tanks. He brazenly exposed himself to the enemy fire and, firing the bazooka, destroyed both tanks. Responding to Captain Urban's action, his company moved forward and routed the enemy. Later that same day, still in the attack near Orglandes, Captain Urban was wounded in the leg by direct fire from a 37mm tank-gun. He refused evacuation and continued to lead his company until they moved into defensive positions for the night. At 0500 hours the next day, still in the attack near Orglandes, Captain Urban, though badly wounded, directed his company in another attack. One hour later he was again wounded. Suffering from two wounds, one serious, he was evacuated to England. In mid-July, while recovering from his wounds, he learned of his unit's severe losses in the hedgerows of Normandy. Realizing his unit's need for battle-tested leaders, he voluntarily left the hospital and hitchhiked his way back to his unit hear St. Lo, France. Arriving at the 2d Battalion Command Post at

1130 hours, 25 July, he found that his unit had jumped-off at 1100 hours in the first attack of "Operation Cobra." Still limping from his leg wound, Captain Urban made his way forward to retake command of his company. He found his company held up by strong enemy opposition. Two supporting tanks had been destroyed and another, intact but with no tank commander or gunner, was not moving. He located a lieutenant in charge of the support tanks and directed a plan of attack to eliminate the enemy strong-point. The lieutenant and a sergeant were immediately killed by the heavy enemy fire when they tried to mount the tank. Captain Urban, though physically hampered by his leg wound and knowing quick action had to be taken, dashed through the scathing fire and mounted the tank. With enemy bullets ricocheting from the tank, Captain Urban ordered the tank forward and, completely exposed to the enemy fire, manned the machine gun and placed devastating fire on the enemy. His action, in the face of enemy fire, galvanized the battalion into action and they attacked and destroyed the enemy position. On 2 August, Captain Urban was wounded in the chest by shell fragments and, disregarding the recommendation of the Battalion Surgeon, again refused evacuation. On 6 August, Captain Urban became the commander of the 2d Battalion. On 15 August, he was again wounded but remained with his unit. On 3 September, the 2d Battalion was given the mission of establishing a crossing-point on the Meuse River near Heer, Belgium. The enemy planned to stop the advance of the allied Army by concentrating heavy forces at the Meuse. The 2d Battalion, attacking toward the crossing-point, encountered fierce enemy artillery, small arms and mortar fire which stopped the attack. Captain Urban quickly moved from his command post to the lead position of the battalion. Reorganizing the attacking elements, he personally led a charge toward the enemy's strong-point. As the charge moved across the open terrain, Captain Urban was seriously wounded in the neck. Although unable to talk above a whisper from the paralyzing neck wound, and in danger of losing his life, he refused to be evacuated until the enemy was routed and his battalion had secured the crossing-point on the Meuse River. Captain Urban's personal leadership, limitless bravery, and repeated extraordinary exposure to enemy fire served as an inspiration to his entire battalion. His valorous and intrepid actions reflect the utmost credit on him and uphold the noble traditions of the United States Army.

*VANCE, LEON R., Jr (Air Mission)

Rank and organization: Lieutenant Colonel, U.S. Army Corps, 489th Bomber Group. *Place and date:* Over Wimereaux, France, 5 June 1944. *Entered service at:* Garden City, N.Y. *Born:* 11 August 1916, Enid, Okla. *G.O. No.:* 1, 4 January 1945. *Citation:* For conspicuous gallantry and intrepidity above and beyond the call of duty on 5 June 1944, when he led a Heavy Bombardment Group, in an attack against defended enemy coastal positions in the vicinity of Wimereaux, France. Approaching the target, his aircraft was hit repeatedly by antiaircraft fire which seriously crippled the ship, killed the pilot, and wounded several members of the crew, including Lt. Col. Vance, whose right foot was practically severed. In spite of his injury, and with 3 engines lost to the flak, he led his formation over the target, bombing it successfully. After applying a tourniquet to his leg with the aid of the radar operator, Lt. Col. Vance, realizing that the ship was approaching a stall altitude with the 1 remaining engine failing, struggled to a semi-upright position beside the copilot and took over control of the ship. Cutting the power and feathering the last engine he put the aircraft in glide sufficiently steep to maintain his airspeed. Gradually losing altitude, he at last reached the English coast, whereupon he ordered all members of the crew to bail out as he knew they would all safely make land. But he received a message over the interphone system which led him to believe 1 of the crewmembers was unable to jump due to injuries; so he made the decision to ditch the ship in the channel, thereby giving this man a chance for life. To add further to the danger of ditching the ship in his crippled condition, there was a 500-pound bomb hung up in the bomb bay. Unable to climb into the seat vacated by the copilot, since his foot, hanging on to his leg by a few tendons, had becomed lodged behind the copilot's seat, he nevertheless made a successful ditching while lying on the floor using only aileron and elevators for control and the side window of the cockpit for visual reference. On coming to rest in the water the aircraft commenced to sink rapidly with Lt. Col. Vance pinned in the cockpit by the upper turret which had crashed in during the landing. As it was settling beneath the waves an explosion occurred which threw Lt. Col. Vance clear of the wreckage. After clinging to a piece of floating wreckage until he could muster enough strength to inflate his life vest he began searching for the crewmember whom he believed to be aboard. Failing to find anyone he began swimming and was found approximately 50 minutes later by an Air-Sea Rescue craft. By his extraordinary flying skill and gallant leadership, despite his grave injury, Lt. Col. Vance led his formation to a successful bombing of the assigned target and returned the crew to a point where they could bail out with safety. His gallant and valorous decision to ditch the aircraft in order to give the crewmember he believed to be aboard a chance for life exemplifies the highest traditions of the U.S. Armed Forces.

VANDEGRIFT, ALEXANDER ARCHER

Rank and organization: Major General, U.S. Marine Corps, commanding officer of the 1st Marine Division. *Place and date:* Solomon Islands, 7 August to 9 December 1942. *Entered service at:* Virginia. *Born:* 13 March 1887, Charlottesville, Va. *Citation:* For outstanding and heroic accomplishment above and beyond the call of duty as commanding officer of the 1st Marine Division in operations against enemy Japanese forces in the Solomon Islands during the period 7 August to 9 December 1942. With the adverse factors of weather, terrain, and disease making his task a difficult and hazardous undertaking, and with his command eventually including sea, land, and air forces of Army, Navy, and Marine Corps, Maj. Gen. Vandegrift achieved marked success in commanding the initial landings of the U.S. forces in the Solomon Islands and in their subsequent occupation. His tenacity, courage, and resourcefulness prevailed against a strong, determined, and experienced enemy, and the gallant fighting spirit of the men under his inspiring leadership enabled them to withstand aerial, land, and sea bombardment, to surmount all obstacles, and leave a disorganized and ravaged enemy. This dangerous but vital mission, accomplished at the constant risk of his life, resulted in securing a valuable base for further operations of our forces against the enemy, and its successful completion reflects great credit upon Maj. Gen. Vandegrift, his command, and the U.S. Naval Service.

*VAN NOY, JUNIOR

Rank and organization: Private, U.S. Army, Headquarters Company, Shore Battalion, Engineer Boat and Shore Regiment. *Place and date:* Near Finschafen, New Guinea, 17 October 1943. *Entered service at:* Preston, Idaho. *Birth:* Grace, Idaho. *G.O. No.:* 17, 26 February 1944. *Citation:* For conspicuous gallantry and intrepidity above and beyond the call of duty in action with the enemy near Finschafen, New Guinea, on 17 October 1943. When wounded late in September, Pvt. Van Noy declined evacuation and continued on duty. On 17 October 1943 he was gunner in charge of a machinegun post only 5 yards from the water's edge when the alarm was given that 3 enemy barges loaded with troops were approaching the beach in the early morning darkness. One landing barge was sunk by Allied fire, but the other 2 beached 10 yards from Pvt. Van Noy's emplacement. Despite his exposed position, he poured a withering hail of fire into the debarking enemy troops. His loader was wounded by a grenade and evacuated. Pvt. Van Noy, also grievously wounded, remained at his post, ignoring calls of nearby soldiers urging him to withdraw, and continued to fire with deadly accuracy. He expended every round and was found, covered with wounds dead beside his gun. In this action Pvt. Van Noy killed at least half of the 39 enemy taking part in the landing. His heroic tenacity at the price of his life not only saved the lives of many of his comrades, but enabled them to annihilate the attacking detachment.

*VAN VALKENBURGH, FRANKLIN

Rank and organization: Captain, U.S. Navy. *Born:* 5 April 1888, Minneapolis, Minn. *Appointed from:* Wisconsin. *Citation:* For conspicuous devotion to duty, extraordinary courage and complete disregard of his own life, during the attack on the Fleet in Pearl Harbor, T.H., by Japanese forces on 7 December 1941. As commanding officer of the U.S.S. *Arizona*, Capt. Van Valkenburgh gallantly fought his ship until the U.S.S. *Arizona* blew up from magazine explosions and a direct bomb hit on the birdge which resulted in the loss of his life.

*VAN VOORHIS, BRUCE AVERY

Rank and organization: Lieutenant Commander, U.S. Navy. *Born:* 29 January 1908, Aberdeen, Wash. *Appointed from:* Nevada. *Citation:* For conspicuous gallantry and intrepidity at the risk of his life above and beyond the call of duty as Squadron Commander of Bombing Squadron 102 and as Plane Commander of a PB4Y-1 Patrol Bomber operating against the enemy on Japanese-held Greenwich Island during the battle of the Solomon Islands, 6 July 1943. Fully aware of the limited chance of surviving an urgent mission, voluntarily undertaken to prevent a surprise Japanese attack against our forces, Lt. Comdr. Van Voorhis took off in total darkness on a perilous 700-mile flight without escort or support. Successful in reaching his objective despite treacherous and varying winds, low visibility and difficult terrain, he fought a lone but relentless battle under fierce antiaircraft fire and overwhelming aerial opposition. Forced lower and lower by pursuing planes, he coolly persisted in his mission of destruction. Abandoning all chance of a safe return he executed 6 bold, ground-level attacks to demolish the enemy's vital radio station, installations, antiaircraft guns and crews with bombs and machinegun fire, and to destroy 1 fighter plane in the air and 3 on the water. Caught in his own bomb blast, Lt. Comdr. Van Voorhis crashed into the lagoon off the beach, sacrificing himself in a singlehanded fight against almost insuperable odds, to make a distinctive contribution to our continued offensive in driving the Japanese from the Solomons and, by his superb daring, courage and resoluteness of purpose, enhanced the finest traditions of the U.S. Naval Service. He gallantly gave his life for his country.

*VIALE, ROBERT M.

Rank and organization: Second Lieutenant, U.S. Army, Company K, 148th Infantry, 37th Infantry Division. *Place and date:* Manila, Luzon, Philippine Islands, 5 February 1945. *Entered service at:* Ukiah, Calif. *Birth:* Bayside, Calif. *G.O. No.:* 92, 25 October 1945. *Citation:* He displayed conspicuous gallantry and intrepidity above and beyond the call of duty. Forced by the enemy's detonation of prepared demolitions to shift the course of his advance through the city, he led the 1st platoon toward a small bridge, where heavy fire from 3 enemy pillboxes halted the unit. With 2 men he crossed the bridge behind screening grenade smoke to attack the pillboxes. The first he knocked out himself while covered by his men's protecting fire; the other 2 were silenced by 1 of his companions and a bazooka team which he had called up. He suffered a painful wound in the right arm during the action. After his entire platoon had joined him, he pushed ahead through mortar fire and encircling flames. Blocked from the only escape route by an enemy machinegun placed at a street corner, he entered a nearby building with his men to explore possible means of reducing the emplacement. In 1 room he found civilians huddled together, in another, a small window placed high in the wall and reached by a ladder. Because of the relative positions of the window, ladder, and enemy emplacement, he decided that he, being left-handed, could better hurl a grenade than 1 of his men who had made an unsuccessful attempt. Grasping an armed grenade, he started up the ladder. His wounded right arm weakened, and, as he tried to steady himself, the grenade fell to the floor. In the 5 seconds before the grenade would explode, he dropped down, recovered the grenade and looked for a place to dispose of it safely. Finding no way to get rid of the grenade without exposing his own men or the civilians to injury or death, he turned to the wall, held it close to his body and bent over it as it exploded. 2d Lt. Viale died in a few minutes, but his heroic act saved the lives of others.

*VILLEGAS, YSMAEL R.

Rank and organization: Staff Sergeant, U.S. Army, Company F, 127th Infantry, 32d Infantry Division. *Place and date:* Villa Verde Trail, Luzon, Philippine Islands, 20 March 1945. *Entered service at:* Casa Blanca, Calif. *Birth:* Casa Blanca, Calif. *G.O. No.:* 89, 19 October 1945. *Citation:* He was a squad leader when his unit, in a forward position, clashed with an enemy strongly entrenched in connected caves and foxholes on commanding ground. He moved boldly from man to man, in the face of bursting grenades and demolition charges, through heavy machinegun and rifle fire, to bolster the spirit of his comrades. Inspired by his gallantry, his men pressed forward to the crest of the hill. Numerous enemy riflemen, refusing to flee, continued firing from their foxholes. S/Sgt. Villegas, with complete disregard for his own safety and the bullets which kicked up the dirt at his feet, charged an enemy position, and, firing at point-blank range killed the Japanese in a foxhole. He rushed a second foxhole while bullets missed him by inches, and killed 1 more of the enemy. In rapid succession he charged a third, a fourth, a fifth foxhole, each time destroying the enemy within. The fire against him increased in intensity, but he pressed onward to attack a sixth position. As he neared his goal, he was hit and killed by enemy fire. Through his heroism and indomitable fighting spirit, S/Sgt. Villegas, at the cost of his life, inspired his men to a determined attack in which they swept the enemy from the field.

VLUG, DIRK J.

Rank and organization: Private First Class, U.S. Army, 126th Infantry, 32d Infantry Division. *Place and date:* Near Limon, Leyte, Philippine Islands, 15 December 1944. *Entered service at:* Grand Rapids, Mich. *Birth:* Maple Lake, Minn. *G.O. No.:* 60, 26 June 1946. *Citation:* He displayed conspicuous gallantry and intrepidity above and beyond the call of duty when an American roadblock on the Ormoc Road was attacked by a group of enemy tanks. He left his covered position, and with a rocket launcher and 6 rounds of ammunition, advanced alone under intense machinegun and 37-mm. fire. Loading singlehandedly, he destroyed the first tank, killing its occupants with a single round. As the crew of the second tank started to dismount and attack him, he killed 1 of the foe with his pistol, forcing the survivors to return to their vehicle, which he then destroyed with a second round. Three more hostile tanks moved up the road, so he flanked the first and eliminated it, and then, despite a hail of enemy fire, pressed forward again to destroy another. With his last round of ammunition he struck the remaining vehicle, causing it to crash down a steep embankment. Through his sustained heroism in the face of superior forces, Pfc. Vlug alone destroyed 5 enemy tanks and greatly facilitated successful accomplishment of his battalion's mission.

VOSLER, FORREST T. (Air Mission)

Rank and organization: Technical Sergeant, U.S. Army Air Corps, 358th Bomber Squadron, 303d Bomber Group. *Place and date:* Over Bremen, Germany, 20 December 1943. *Entered service at:* Rochester, N.Y. *Born:* 29 July 1923, Lyndonville, N.Y. *G.O. No.:* 73, 6 September 1944. *Citation:* For conspicuous gallantry in action against the enemy above and beyond the call of duty while serving as a radio operator-air gunner on a heavy bombardment aircraft in a mission over Bremen, Germany, on 20 December 1943. After bombing the target, the aircraft in which T/Sgt. Vosler was serving was severely damaged by antiaircraft fire, forced out of formation, and immediately subjected to repeated vicious attacks by enemy fighters. Early in the engagement a 20-mm. cannon shell exploded in the radio compartment, painfully wounding T/Sgt. Vosler in the legs and thighs. At about the same time a direct hit on the tail of the ship seriously wounded the tail gunner and rendered the tail guns inoperative. Realizing the great need for firepower in protecting the vulnerable tail of the ship, T/Sgt. Vosler, with grim determination, kept up a steady stream of deadly fire. Shortly thereafter another 20-mm. enemy shell exploded, wounding T/Sgt. Vosler in the chest and about the face. Pieces of metal lodged in both eyes, impairing his vision to such an extent that he could only distinguish blurred shapes. Displaying remarkable tenacity and courage, he kept firing his guns and declined to take first-aid treatment. The radio equipment had been rendered inoperative during the battle, and when the pilot announced that he would have to ditch, although unable to see and working entirely by touch, T/Sgt. Vosler finally got the set operating and sent out distress signals despite several lapses into unconsciousness. When the ship ditched, T/Sgt. Vosler managed to get out on the wing by himself and hold the wounded tail gunner from slipping off until the other crewmembers could help them into the dinghy. T/Sgt. Vosler's actions on this occasion were an inspiration to all serving with him. The extraordinary courage, coolness, and skill he displayed in the face of great odds, when handicapped by injuries that would have incapacitated the average crewmember, were outstanding.

WAHLEN, GEORGE EDWARD

Rank and organization: Pharmacist's Mate Second Class, U.S. Navy, serving with 2d Battalion, 26th Marines, 5th Marine Division. *Place and date:* Iwo Jima, Volcano Islands group, 3 March 1945. *Entered ser-*

vice at: Utah. *Born:* 8 August 1924, Ogden, Utah. *Citation:* For conspicuous gallantry and intrepidity at the risk of his life above and beyond the call of duty while serving with the 2d Battalion, 26th Marines, 5th Marine Division, during action against enemy Japanese forces on Iwo Jima in the Volcano group on 3 March 1945. Painfully wounded in the bitter action on 26 February, Wahlen remained on the battlefield, advancing well forward of the frontlines to aid a wounded marine and carrying him back to safety despite a terrific concentration of fire. Tireless in his ministrations, he consistently disregarded all danger to attend his fighting comrades as they fell under the devastating rain of shrapnel and bullets, and rendered prompt assistance to various elements of his combat group as required. When an adjacent platoon suffered heavy casualties, he defied the continuous pounding of heavy mortars and deadly fire of enemy rifles to care for the wounded, working rapidly in an area swept by constant fire and treating 14 casualties before returning to his own platoon. Wounded again on 2 March, he gallantly refused evacuation, moving out with his company the following day in a furious assault across 600 yards of open terrain and repeatedly rendering medical aid while exposed to the blasting fury of powerful Japanese guns. Stouthearted and indomitable, he persevered in his determined efforts as his unit waged fierce battle and, unable to walk after sustaining a third agonizing wound, resolutely crawled 50 yards to administer first aid to still another fallen fighter. By his dauntless fortitude and valor, Wahlen served as a constant inspiration and contributed vitally to the high morale of his company during critical phases of this strategically important engagement. His heroic spirit of self-sacrifice in the face of overwhelming enemy fire upheld the highest traditions of the U.S. Naval Service.

WAINWRIGHT, JONATHAN M.

Rank and organization: General, Commanding U.S. Army Forces in the Philippines. *Place and date:* Philippine Islands, 12 March to 7 May 1942. *Entered service at:* Skaneateles, N.Y. *Birth:* Walla Walla, Wash. *G.O. No.:* 80, 19 September 1945. *Citation:* Distinguished himself by intrepid and determined leadership against greatly superior enemy forces. At the repeated risk of life above and beyond the call of duty in his position, he frequented the firing line of his troops where his presence provided the example and incentive that helped make the gallant efforts of these men possible. The final stand on beleaguered Corregidor, for which he was in an important measure personally responsible, commanded the admiration of the Nation's allies. It reflected the high morale of American arms in the face of overwhelming odds. His courage and resolution were a vitally needed inspiration to the then sorely pressed freedom-loving peoples of the world.

*WALKER, KENNETH N. (Air Mission)

Rank and organization: Brigadier General, U.S. Army Air Corps, Commander of V Bomber Command. *Place and date:* Rabaul, New Britain, 5 January 1943. *Entered service at:* Colorado. *Birth:* Cerrillos, N. Mex. *G.O. No.:* 13, 11 March 1943. *Citation:* For conspicuous leadership above and beyond the call of duty involving personal valor and intrepidity at an extreme hazard to life. As commander of the 5th

Bomber Command during the period from 5 September 1942, to 5 January 1943, Brig. Gen. Walker repeatedly accompanied his units on bombing missions deep into enemy-held territory. From the lessons personally gained under combat conditions, he developed a highly efficient technique for bombing when opposed by enemy fighter airplanes and by antiaircraft fire. On 5 January 1943, in the face of extremely heavy antiaircraft fire and determined opposition by enemy fighters, he led an effective daylight bombing attack against shipping in the harbor at Rabaul, New Britain, which resulted in direct hits on 9 enemy vessels. During this action his airplane was disabled and forced down by the attack of an overwhelming number of enemy fighters.

*WALLACE, HERMAN C.

Rank and organization: Private First Class, U.S. Army, Company B, 301st Engineer Combat Battalion, 76th Infantry Division. *Place and date:* Near Prumzurley, Germany, 27 February 1945. *Entered service at:* Lubbock, Tex. *Birth:* Marlow, Okla. *G.O. No.:* 92, 25 October 1945. *Citation:* He displayed conspicuous gallantry and intrepidity. While helping clear enemy mines from a road, he stepped on a well-concealed S-type antipersonnel mine. Hearing the characteristic noise indicating that the mine had been activated and, if he stepped aside, would be thrown upward to explode above ground and spray the area with fragments, surely killing 2 comrades directly behind him and endangering other members of his squad, he deliberately placed his other foot on the mine even though his best chance for survival was to fall prone. Pvt. Wallace was killed when the charge detonated, but his supreme heroism at the cost of his life confined the blast to the ground and his own body and saved his fellow soldiers from death or injury.

WALSH, KENNETH AMBROSE

Rank and organization: First Lieutenant, pilot in Marine Fighting Squadron 124, U.S. Marine Corps. *Place and date:* Solomon Islands area, 15 and 30 August 1943. *Entered service at:* New York. *Born:* 24 November 1916, Brooklyn, N.Y. *Other Navy awards:* Distinguished Flying Cross with 5 Gold Stars. *Citation:* For extraordinary heroism and intrepidity above and beyond the call of duty as a pilot in Marine Fighting Squadron 124 in aerial combat against enemy Japanese forces in the Solomon Islands area. Determined to thwart the enemy's attempt to bomb Allied ground forces and shipping at Vella Lavella on 15 August 1943, 1st Lt. Walsh repeatedly dived his plane into an enemy formation outnumbering his own division 6 to 1 and, although his plane was hit numerous times, shot down 2 Japanese dive bombers and 1 fighter. After developing engine trouble on 30 August during a vital escort mission, 1st Lt. Walsh landed his mechanically disabled plane at Munda, quickly replaced it with another, and proceeded to rejoin his flight over Kahili. Separated from his escort group when he encountered approximately 50 Japanese Zeros, he unhesitatingly attacked, striking with relentless fury in his lone battle against a powerful force. He destroyed 4 hostile fighters before cannon shellfire forced him to make a dead-stick landing off Vella Lavella where he was later picked up. His valiant leadership and his daring skill as a flier served as a source of confidence and inspiration to his fellow pilots and reflect the highest credit upon the U.S. Naval Service.

*WALSH, WILLIAM GARY

Rank and organization: Gunnery Sergeant, U.S. Marine Corps Reserve. *Born:* 7 April 1922, Roxbury, Mass. *Accredited to:* Massachusetts. *Citation:* For extraordinary gallantry and intrepidity at the risk of his life above and beyond the call of duty as leader of an assault platoon, attached to Company G, 3d Battalion, 27th Marines, 5th Marine Division, in action against enemy Japanese forces at Iwo Jima, Volcano Islands, on 27 February 1945. With the advance of his company toward Hill 362 disrupted by vicious machinegun fire from a forward position which guarded the approaches to this key enemy stronghold, G/Sgt. Walsh fearlessly charged at the head of his platoon against the Japanese entrenched on the ridge above him, utterly oblivious to the unrelenting fury of hostile automatic weapons fire and handgrenades employed with fanatic desperation to smash his daring assault. Thrown back by the enemy's savage resistance, he once again led his men in a seemingly impossible attack up the steep, rocky slope, boldly defiant of the annihilating streams of bullets which saturated the area. Despite his own casualty losses and the overwhelming advantage held by the Japanese in superior numbers and dominant position, he gained the ridge's top only to be subjected to an intense barrage of handgrenades thrown by the remaining Japanese staging a suicidal last stand on the reverse slope. When 1 of the grenades fell in the midst of his surviving men, huddled together in a small trench, G/Sgt. Walsh, in a final valiant act of complete self-sacrifice, instantly threw himself upon the deadly bomb, absorbing with his own body the full and terrific force of the explosion. Through his extraordinary initiative and inspiring valor in the face of almost certain death, he saved his comrades from injury and possible loss of life and enabled his company to seize and hold this vital enemy position. He gallantly gave his life for his country.

*WARD, JAMES RICHARD

Rank and organization: Seaman First Class, U.S. Navy. *Born:* 10 September 1921, Springfield, Ohio. *Entered service at:* Springfield, Ohio. *Citation:* For conspicuous devotion to duty, extraordinary courage and complete disregard of his life, above and beyond the call of duty, during the attack on the Fleet in Pearl Harbor by Japanese forces on 7 December 1941. When it was seen that the U.S.S. *Oklahoma* was going to capsize and the order was given to abandon ship, Ward remained in a turret holding a flashlight so the remainder of the turret crew could see to escape, thereby sacrificing his own life.

WARE, KEITH L.

Rank and organization: Lieutenant Colonel, U.S. Army, 1st Battalion, 15th Infantry, 3d Infantry Division. *Place and date:* Near Sigolsheim, France, 26 December 1944. *Entered service at:* Glendale, Calif. *Born:* 23 November 1915, Denver, Colo. *G.O. No.:* 47, 18 June 1945. *Citation:* Commanding the 1st Battalion attacking a strongly held enemy position on a hill near Sigolsheim, France, on 26 December 1944, found that 1 of his assault companies had been stopped and forced to dig in by a concentration of enemy artillery, mortar, and machinegun fire. The company had suffered casualties in attempting to take the hill. Realizing that his men must be inspired to new courage, Lt. Col. Ware went forward 150 yards beyond the most forward elements of his command, and for 2 hours reconnoitered the enemy positions, deliberately drawing fire upon himself which caused the enemy to disclose his dispositions. Returning to his company, he armed himself with an automatic rifle and boldly advanced upon the enemy, followed by 2 officers, 9 enlisted men, and a tank. Approaching an enemy machinegun, Lt. Col. Ware shot 2 German riflemen and fired tracers into the emplacement, indicating its position to his tank, which promptly knocked the gun out of action. Lt. Col. Ware turned his attention to a second machinegun, killing 2 of its supporting riflemen and forcing the others to surrender. The tank destroyed the gun. Having expended the ammunition for the automatic rifle, Lt. Col. Ware took up an M1 rifle, killed a German rifleman, and fired upon a third machinegun 50 yards away. His tank silenced the gun. Upon his approach to a fourth machinegun, its supporting riflemen surrendered and his tank disposed of the gun. During this action Lt. Col. Ware's small assault group was fully engaged in attacking enemy positions that were not receiving his direct and personal attention. Five of his party of 11 were casualties and Lt. Col. Ware was wounded, but refused medical attention until this important hill position was cleared of the enemy and securely occupied by his command.

*WARNER, HENRY F.

Rank and organization: Corporal, U.S. Army, Antitank Company, 2d Battalion, 26th Infantry, 1st Infantry Division. *Place and date:* Near Dom Butgenbach, Belgium, 20–21 December 1944. *Entered service at:* Troy, N.C. *Born:* 23 August 1923, Troy, N.C. *G.O. No.:* 48, 23 June 1945. *Citation:* Serving as 57-mm. antitank gunner with the 2d Battalion, he was a major factor in stopping enemy tanks during heavy attacks against the battalion position near Dom Butgenbach, Belgium, on 20–21 December 1944. In the first attack, launched in the early morning of the 20th, enemy tanks succeeded in penetrating parts of the line. Cpl. Warner, disregarding the concentrated cannon and machinegun fire from 2 tanks bearing down on him, and ignoring the imminent danger of being overrun by the infantry moving under tank cover, destroyed the first tank and scored a direct and deadly hit upon the second. A third tank approached to within 5 yards of his position while he was attempting to clear a jammed breach lock. Jumping from his gun pit, he engaged in a pistol duel with the tank commander standing in the turret, killing him and forcing the tank to withdraw. Following a day and night during which our forces were subjected to constant shelling, mortar barrages, and numerous unsuccessful infantry attacks, the enemy struck in great force on the early morning of the 21st. Seeing a Mark IV tank looming out of the mist and heading toward his position, Cpl. Warner scored a direct hit. Disregarding his injuries, he endeavored to finish the loading and again fire at the tank, whose motor was now aflame, when a second machinegun burst killed him. Cpl. Warner's gallantry and intrepidity at the risk of life above and beyond the call of duty contributed materially to the successful defense against the enemy attacks.

WATSON, WILSON DOUGLAS

Rank and organization: Private, U.S. Marine Corps Reserve, 2d Battalion, 9th Marines, 3d Marine Division. *Place and date:* Iwo Jima, Volcano Islands, 26 and 27 February 1945. *Entered service at:* Arkansas. *Born:* 18 February 1921, Tuscumbia, Ala. *Citation:* For conspicuous gallantry and intrepidity at the risk of his life above and beyond the call of duty as automatic rifleman serving with the 2d Battalion, 9th Marines, 3d Marine Division, during action against enemy Japanese forces on Iwo Jima, Volcano Islands, 26 and 27 February 1945. With his squad abruptly halted by intense fire from enemy fortifications in the high rocky ridges and crags commanding the line of advance, Pvt. Watson boldly rushed 1 pillbox and fired into the embrasure with his weapon, keeping the enemy pinned down singlehandedly until he was in a position to hurl in a grenade, and then running to the rear of the emplacement to destroy the retreating Japanese and enable his platoon to take its objective. Again pinned down at the foot of a small hill, he dauntlessly scaled the jagged incline under fierce mortar and machinegun barrages and, with his assistant BAR man, charged the crest of the hill, firing from his hip. Fighting furiously against Japanese troops attacking with grenades and knee mortars from the reverse slope, he stood fearlessly erect in his exposed position to cover the hostile entrenchments and held the hill under savage fire for 15 minutes, killing 60 Japanese before his ammunition was exhausted and his platoon was able to join him. His courageous initiative and valiant fighting spirit against devastating odds were directly responsible for the continued advance of his platoon, and his inspiring leadership throughout this bitterly fought action reflects the highest credit upon Pvt. Watson and the U.S. Naval Service.

*WAUGH, ROBERT T.

Rank and organization: First Lieutenant, U.S. Army, 339th Infantry, 85th Infantry Division. *Place and date:* Near Tremensucli, Italy, 11–14 May 1944. *Entered service at:* Augusta, Maine. *Birth:* Ashton, R.I. *G.O. No.:* 79, 4 October 1944. *Citation:* For conspicuous gallantry and intrepidity at risk of life above and beyond the call of duty in action with the enemy. In the course of an attack upon an enemy-held hill on 11 May, 1st Lt. Waugh personally reconnoitered a heavily mined area before entering it with his platoon. Directing his men to deliver fire on 6 bunkers guarding this hill, 1st Lt. Waugh advanced alone against them, reached the first bunker, threw phosphorus grenades into it and as the defenders emerged, killed them with a burst from his tommygun. He repeated this process on the 5 remaining bunkers, killing or capturing the occupants. On the morning of 14 May, 1st Lt. Waugh ordered his platoon to lay a base of fire on 2 enemy pillboxes located on a knoll which commanded the only trail up the hill. He then ran to the first pillbox, threw several grenades into it, drove the defenders into the open, and killed them. The second pillbox was next taken by this intrepid officer by similar methods. The fearless actions of 1st Lt. Waugh broke the Gustav Line at that point, neutralizing 6 bunkers and 2 pillboxes and he was personally responsible for the death of 30 of the enemy and the capture of 25 others. He was later killed in action in Itri, Italy, while leading his platoon in an attack.

WAYBUR, DAVID C.

Rank and organization: First Lieutenant, U.S. Army, 3d Reconnaissance Troop, 3d Infantry Division. *Place and date:* Near Agrigento, Sicily, 17 July 1943. *Entered service at:* Piedmont, Calif. *Birth:* Oakland, Calif. *G.O. No.:* 69, 21 October 1943. *Citation:* For conspicuous gallantry and intrepidity at the risk of life above and beyond the call of duty in action involving actual conflict with the enemy. Commander of a reconnaissance platoon, 1st Lt. Waybur volunteered to lead a 3-vehicle patrol into enemy-held territory to locate an isolated Ranger unit. Proceeding under cover of darkness, over roads known to be heavily mined, and strongly defended by road blocks and machinegun positions, the patrol's progress was halted at a bridge which had been destroyed by enemy troops and was suddenly cut off from its supporting vehicles by 4 enemy tanks. Although hopelessly outnumbered and out-gunned, and himself and his men completely exposed, he quickly dispersed his vehicles and ordered his gunners to open fire with their .30 and .50 caliber machineguns. Then, with ammunition exhausted, 3 of his men hit and himself seriously wounded, he seized his .45 caliber Thompson submachinegun and standing in the bright moonlight directly in the line of fire, alone engaged the leading tank at 30 yards and succeeded in killing the crewmembers, causing the tank to run onto the bridge and crash into the stream bed. After dispatching 1 of the men for aid he rallied the rest to cover and withstood the continued fire of the tanks till the arrival of aid the following morning.

*WEICHT, ELLIS R.

Rank and organization: Sergeant, U.S. Army, Company F, 142d Infantry, 36th Infantry Division. *Place and date:* St. Hippolyte, France, 3 December 1944. *Entered service at:* Bedford, Pa. *Birth:* Clearville, Pa. *G.O. No.:* 58, 19 July 1945. *Citation:* For commanding an assault squad in Company F's attack against the strategically important Alsatian town of St. Hippolyte on 3 December 1944. He aggressively led his men down a winding street, clearing the houses of opposition as he advanced. Upon rounding a bend, the group was suddenly brought under the fire of 2 machineguns emplaced in the door and window of a house 100 yards distant. While his squad members took cover, Sgt. Weicht moved rapidly forward to a high rock wall and, fearlessly exposing himself to the enemy action, fired 2 clips of ammunition from his rifle. His fire proving ineffective, he entered a house opposite the enemy gun position, and, firing from a window, killed the 2 hostile gunners. Continuing the attack, the advance was again halted when two 20-mm. guns opened fire on the company. An artillery observer ordered friendly troops to evacuate the area and then directed artillery fire upon the gun positions. Sgt. Weicht remained in the shelled area and continued to fire on the hostile weapons. When the barrage lifted and the enemy soldiers attempted to remove their gun, he killed 2 crewmembers and forced the others to flee. Sgt. Weicht continued to lead his squad forward until he spotted a road block approximate 125 yards away. Moving to the second floor of a nearby house and firing from a window, he killed 3 and wounded several of the enemy. Instantly becoming a target for heavy and direct fire, he disregarded personal safety to continue his fire, with unusual effectiveness, until he was killed by a direct hit from an antitank gun.

*WETZEL, WALTER C.

Rank and organization: Private First Class, U.S. Army, 13th Infantry, 8th Infantry Division. *Place and date:* Birken, Germany, 3 April 1945. *Entered service at:* Roseville, Mich. *Birth:* Huntington, W. Va. *G.O. No.:* 21, 26 February 1946. *Citation:* Pfc. Wetzel, an acting squad leader with the Antitank Company of the 13th Infantry, was guarding his platoon's command post in a house at Birken, Germany, during the early morning hours of 3 April 1945, when he detected strong enemy forces moving in to attack. He ran into the house, alerted the occupants and immediately began defending the post against heavy automatic weapons fire coming from the hostile troops. Under cover of darkness the Germans forced their way close to the building where they hurled grenades, 2 of which landed in the room where Pfc. Wetzel and the others had taken up firing positions. Shouting a warning to his fellow soldiers, Pfc. Wetzel threw himself on the grenades and, as they exploded, absorbed their entire blast, suffering wounds from which he died. The supreme gallantry of Pfc. Wetzel saved his comrades from death or serious injury and made it possible for them to continue the defense of the command post and break the power of a dangerous local counterthrust by the enemy. His unhesitating sacrifice of his life was in keeping with the U.S. Army's highest traditions of bravery and heroism.

WHITELEY, ELI

Rank and organization: First Lieutenant, U.S. Army, Company L, 15th Infantry, 3d Infantry Division. *Place and date:* Sigolsheim, France, 27 December 1944. *Entered service at:* Georgetown, Tex. *Birth:* Florence, Tex. *G.O. No.:* 79, 14 September 1945. *Citation:* While leading his platoon on 27 December 1944, in savage house-to-house fighting through the fortress town of Sigolsheim, France, he attacked a building through a street swept by withering mortar and automatic weapons fire. He was hit and severely wounded in the arm and shoulder; but he charged into the house alone and killed its 2 defenders. Hurling smoke and fragmentation grenades before him, he reached the next house and stormed inside, killing 2 and capturing 11 of the enemy. He continued leading his platoon in the extremely dangerous task of clearing hostile troops from strong points along the street until he reached a building held by fanatical Nazi troops. Although suffering from wounds which had rendered his left arm useless, he advanced on this strongly defended house, and after blasting out a wall with bazooka fire, charged through a hail of bullets. Wedging his submachinegun under his uninjured arm, he rushed into the house through the hole torn by his rockets, killed 5 of the enemy and forced the remaining 12 to surrender. As he emerged to continue his fearless attack, he was again hit and critically wounded. In agony and with 1 eye pierced by a shell fragment, he shouted for his men to follow him to the next house. He was determined to stay in the fighting, and remained at the head of his platoon until forcibly evacuated. By his disregard for personal safety, his aggressiveness while suffering from severe wounds, his determined leadership and superb courage, 1st Lt. Whiteley killed 9 Germans, captured 23 more and spearheaded an attack which cracked the core of enemy resistance in a vital area.

WHITTINGTON, HULON B.

Rank and organization: Sergeant, U.S. Army, 41st Armored Infantry, 2d Armored Division. *Place and date:* Near Grimesnil, France, 29 July 1944. *Entered service at:* Bastrop, La. *Born:* 9 July 1921, Bogalusa, La. *G.O. No.:* 32, 23 April 1945. *Citation:* For conspicuous gallantry and intrepidity at the risk of life above and beyond the call of duty. On the night of 29 July 1944, near Grimesnil, France, during an enemy armored attack, Sgt. Whittington, a squad leader, assumed command of his platoon when the platoon leader and platoon sergeant became missing in action. He reorganized the defense and, under fire, courageously crawled between gun positions to check the actions of his men. When the advancing enemy attempted to penetrate a roadblock, Sgt. Whittington, completely disregarding intense enemy action, mounted a tank and by shouting through the turret, directed it into position to fire pointblank at the leading Mark V German tank. The destruction of this vehicle blocked all movement of the remaining enemy column consisting of over 100 vehicles of a Panzer unit. The blocked vehicles were then destroyed by handgrenades, bazooka, tank, and artillery fire and large numbers of enemy personnel were wiped out by a bold and resolute bayonet charge inspired by Sgt. Whittington. When the medical aid man had become a casualty, Sgt. Whittington personally administered first aid to his wounded men. The dynamic leadership, the inspiring example, and the dauntless courage of Sgt. Whittington, above and beyond the call of duty, are in keeping with the highest traditions of the military service.

WIEDORFER, PAUL J.

Rank and organization: Staff Sergeant (then Private), U.S. Army, Company G, 318th Infantry, 80th Infantry Division. *Place and date:* Near, Chaumont, Belgium, 25 December 1944. *Entered service at:* Baltimore, Md. *Birth:* Baltimore, Md. *G.O. No.:* 45, 12 June 1945. *Citation:* He alone made it possible for his company to advance until its objective was seized. Company G had cleared a wooded area of snipers, and 1 platoon was advancing across an open clearing toward another wood when it was met by heavy machinegun fire from 2 German positions dug in at the edge of the second wood. These positions were flanked by enemy riflemen. The platoon took cover behind a small ridge approximately 40 yards from the enemy position. There was no other available protection and the entire platoon was pinned down by the German fire. It was about noon and the day was clear, but the terrain extremely difficult due to a 3-inch snowfall the night before over ice-covered ground. Pvt. Wiedorfer, realizing that the platoon advance could not continue until the 2 enemy machinegun nests were destroyed, voluntarily charged alone across the slippery open ground with no protecting cover of any kind. Running in a crouched position, under a hail of enemy fire, he slipped and fell in the snow, but quickly rose and continued forward with the enemy concentrating automatic and small-arms fire on him as he advanced. Miraculously escaping injury, Pvt. Wiedorfer reached a point some 10 yards from the first machinegun emplacement and hurled a handgrenade into it. With his rifle he killed the remaining Germans, and, without hesitation, wheeled to the right and attacked the second emplacement. One of the enemy was wounded by his fire and the other 6 immediately surrendered. This heroic action by 1 man enabled the platoon to advance from behind its protecting ridge and continue successfully to reach its objective. A few minutes later, when both the platoon leader and the platoon sergeant were wounded, Pvt. Wiedorfer assumed command of the platoon, leading it forward with inspired energy until the mission was accomplished.

*WIGLE, THOMAS W.

Rank and organization: Second Lieutenant, U.S. Army, Company K, 135th Infantry, 34th Infantry Division. *Place and date:* Monte Frassino, Italy, 14 September 1944. *Entered service at:* Detroit, Mich. *Birth:* Indianapolis, Ind. *G.O. No.:* 8, 7 February 1945. *Citation:* For conspicuous gallantry and intrepidity at the risk of life above and beyond the call of duty in the vicinity of Monte Frassino, Italy. The 3d Platoon, in attempting to seize a strongly fortified hill position protected by 3 parallel high terraced stone walls, was twice thrown back by the withering crossfire. 2d Lt. Wigle, acting company executive, observing that the platoon was without an officer, volunteered to command it on the next attack. Leading his men up the bare, rocky slopes through intense and concentrated fire, he succeeded in reaching the first of the stone walls. Having himself boosted to the top and perching there in full view of the enemy, he drew and returned their fire while his men helped each other up and over. Following the same method, he successfully negotiated the second. Upon reaching the top of the third wall, he faced 3 houses which were the key point of the enemy defense. Ordering his men to cover him, he made a dash through a hail of machine-pistol fire to reach the nearest house. Firing his carbine as he entered, he drove the enemy before him out of the back door and into the second house. Following closely on the heels of the foe, he drove them from this house into the third where they took refuge in the cellar. When his men rejoined him, they found him mortally wounded on the cellar stairs which he had started to descend to force the surrender of the enemy. His heroic action resulted in the capture of 36 German soldiers and the seizure of the strongpoint.

WILBUR, WILLIAM H.

Rank and organization: Colonel, U.S. Army, Western Task Force, North Africa. *Place and date:* Fedala, North Africa, 8 November 1942. *Entered service at:* Palmer, Mass. *Birth:* Palmer, Mass. *G.O. No.:* 2, 13 January 1943. *Citation:* For conspicuous gallantry and intrepidity in action above and beyond the call of duty. Col. Wilbur prepared the plan for making contact with French commanders in Casablanca and obtaining an armistice to prevent unnecessary bloodshed. On 8 November 1942, he landed at Fedala with the leading assault waves where opposition had developed into a firm and continuous defensive line across his route of advance. Commandeering a vehicle, he was driven toward the hostile defenses under incessant fire, finally locating a French officer who accorded him passage through the forward positions. He then proceeded in total darkness through 16 miles of enemy-occupied country intermittently subjected to heavy bursts of fire, and accomplished his mission by delivering his letters to appropriate French officials in Casablanca. Returning toward his command, Col. Wilbur detected a hostile battery firing effectively on our troops. He took charge of a platoon of American tanks and personally led them in an attack and capture of the battery. From the moment of landing until the cessation of hostile resistance, Col. Wilbur's conduct was voluntary and exemplary in its coolness and daring.

*WILKIN, EDWARD G.

Rank and organization: Corporal, U.S. Army, Company C, 157th Infantry, 45th Infantry Division. *Place and date:* Siegfried Line in Germany, 18 March 1945. *Entered service at:* Longmeadow, Mass. *Birth:* Burlington, Vt. *G.O. No.:* 119, 17 December 1945. *Citation:* He spearheaded his unit's assault of the Siegfried Line in Germany. Heavy fire from enemy riflemen and camouflaged pillboxes had pinned down his comrades when he moved forward on his own initiative to reconnoiter a route of advance. He cleared the way into an area studded with pillboxes, where he repeatedly stood up and walked into vicious enemy fire, storming 1 fortification after another with automatic rifle fire and grenades, killing enemy troops, taking prisoners as the enemy defense became confused, and encouraging his comrades by his heroic example. When halted by heavy barbed wire entanglements, he secured bangalore torpedoes and blasted a path toward still more pillboxes, all the time braving bursting grenades and mortar shells and direct rifle and automatic-weapons fire. He engaged in fierce fire fights, standing in the open while his adversaries fought from the protection of concrete emplacements, and on 1 occasion pursued enemy soldiers across an open field and through interlocking trenches, disregarding the crossfire from 2 pillboxes until he had penetrated the formidable line 200 yards in advance of any American element. That night, although terribly fatigued, he refused to rest and insisted on distributing rations and supplies to his comrades. Hearing that a nearby company was suffering heavy casualties, he secured permission to guide litter bearers and assist them in evacuating the wounded. All that night he remained in the battle area on his mercy missions, and for the following 2 days he continued to remove casualties, venturing into enemy-held territory, scorning cover and braving devastating mortar and artillery bombardments. In 3 days he neutralized and captured 6 pillboxes singlehandedly, killed at least 9 Germans, wounded 13, took 13 prisoners, aided in the capture of 14 others, and saved many American lives by his fearless performance as a litter bearer. Through his superb fighting skill, dauntless courage, and gallant, inspiring actions, Cpl. Wilkin contributed in large measure to his company's success in cracking the Siegfried Line. One month later he was killed in action while fighting deep in Germany.

482

*WILKINS, RAYMOND H. (Air Mission)

Rank and organization: Major, U.S. Army Air Corps. *Place and date:* Near Rabaul, New Britain, 2 November 1943. *Entered service at:* Portsmouth, Va. *Born:* 28 September 1917, Portsmouth, Va. *G.O. No.:* 23, 24 March 1944. *Citation:* For conspicuous gallantry and intrepidity above and beyond the call of duty in action with the enemy near Rabaul, New Britain, on 2 November 1943. Leading his squadron in an attack on shipping in Simpson Harbor, during which intense antiaircraft fire was expected, Maj. Wilkins briefed his squadron so that his airplane would be in the position of greatest risk. His squadron was the last of 3 in the group to enter the target area. Smoke from bombs dropped by preceding aircraft necessitated a last-second revision of tactics on his part, which still enabled his squadron to strike vital shipping targets, but forced it to approach through concentrated fire, and increased the danger of Maj. Wilkins' left flank position. His airplane was hit almost immediately, the right wing damaged, and control rendered extremely difficult. Although he could have withdrawn, he held fast and led his squadron into the attack. He strafed a group of small harbor vessels, and then, at low level, attacked an enemy destroyer. His 1,000 pound bomb struck squarely amidships, causing the vessel to explode. Although antiaircraft fire from this vessel had seriously damaged his left vertical stabilizer, he refused to deviate from the course. From below-masthead height he attacked a transport of some 9,000 tons, scoring a hit which engulfed the ship in flames. Bombs expended, he began to withdraw his squadron. A heavy cruiser barred the path. Unhesitatingly, to neutralize the cruiser's guns and attract its fire, he went in for a strafing run. His damaged stabilizer was completely shot off. To avoid swerving into his wing planes he had to turn so as to expose the belly and full wing surfaces of his plane to the enemy fire; it caught and crumpled his left wing. Now past control, the bomber crashed into the sea. In the fierce engagement Maj. Wilkins destroyed 2 enemy vessels, and his heroic self-sacrifice made possible the safe withdrawal of the remaining planes of his squadron.

*WILL, WALTER J.

Rank and organization: First Lieutenant, U.S. Army, Company K, 18th Infantry, 1st Infantry Division. *Place and date:* Near Eisern, Germany, 30 March 1945. *Entered service at:* West Winfield, N.Y. *Birth:* Pittsburgh, Pa. *G.O. No.:* 88, 17 October 1945. *Citation:* He displayed conspicuous gallantry during an attack on powerful enemy positions. He courageously exposed himself to withering hostile fire to rescue 2 wounded men and then, although painfully wounded himself, made a third trip to carry another soldier to safety from an open area. Ignoring the profuse bleeding of his wound, he gallantly led men of his platoon forward until they were pinned down by murderous flanking fire from 2 enemy machineguns. He fearlessly crawled alone to within 30 feet of the first enemy position, killed the crew of 4 and silenced the gun with accurate grenade fire. He continued to crawl through intense enemy fire to within 20 feet of the second position where he leaped to his feet, made a lone, ferocious charge and captured the gun and its 9-man crew. Observing another platoon pinned down by 2 more German machineguns, he led a squad on a flanking approach and, rising to his knees in the face of direct fire, coolly and deliberately lobbed 3 grenades at the Germans, silencing 1 gun and killing its crew. With tenacious aggressiveness, he ran toward the other gun and knocked it out with grenade fire. He then returned to his platoon and led it in a fierce, inspired charge, forcing the enemy to fall back in confusion. 1st Lt. Will was mortally wounded in this last action, but his heroic leadership, indomitable courage, and unflinching devotion to duty live on as a perpetual inspiration to all those who witnessed his deeds.

WILLIAMS, HERSHEL WOODROW

Rank and organization: Corporal, U.S. Marine Corps Reserve, 21st Marines, 3d Marine Division. *Place and date:* Iwo Jima, Volcano Islands, 23 February 1945. *Entered service at:* West Virginia. *Born:* 2 October 1923, Quiet Dell, W. Va. *Citation:* For conspicuous gallantry and intrepidity at the risk of his life above and beyond the call of duty as demolition sergeant serving with the 21st Marines, 3d Marine Division, in action against enemy Japanese forces on Iwo Jima, Volcano Islands, 23 February 1945. Quick to volunteer his services when our tanks were maneuvering vainly to open a lane for the infantry through the network of reinforced concrete pillboxes, buried mines, and black volcanic sands, Cpl. Williams daringly went forward alone to attempt the reduction of devastating machinegun fire from the unyielding positions. Covered only by 4 riflemen, he fought desperately for 4 hours under terrific enemy small-arms fire and repeatedly returned to his own lines to prepare demolition charges and obtain serviced flamethrowers, struggling back, frequently to the rear of hostile emplacements, to wipe out 1 position after another. On 1 occasion, he daringly mounted a pillbox to insert the nozzle of his flamethrower through the air vent, killing the occupants and silencing the gun; on another he grimly charged enemy riflemen who attempted to stop him with bayonets and destroyed them with a burst of flame from his weapon. His unyielding determination and extraordinary heroism in the face of ruthless enemy resistance were directly instrumental in neutralizing one of the most fanatically defended Japanese strong points encountered by his regiment and aided vitally in enabling his company to reach its objective. Cpl. Williams' aggressive fighting spirit and valiant devotion to duty throughout this fiercely contested action sustain and enhance the highest traditions of the U.S. Naval Service.

*WILLIAMS, JACK

Rank and organization: Pharmacist's Mate Third Class, U.S. Naval Reserve. *Born:* 18 October 1924, Harrison, Ark. *Accredited to:* Arkansas. *Citation:* For conspicuous gallantry and intrepidity at the risk of his life above and beyond the call of duty while serving with the 3d Battalion, 28th Marines, 5th Marine Division, during the occupation of Iwo Jima, Volcano Islands, 3 March 1945. Gallantly going forward on the frontlines under intense enemy small-arms fire to assist a marine wounded in a fierce grenade battle, Williams dragged the man to a shallow depression and was kneeling, using his own body as a screen from the sustained fire as he administered first aid, when struck in the abdomen and groin 3 times by hostile rifle fire. Momentarily stunned,

484

he quickly recovered and completed his ministration before applying battle dressings to his own multiple wounds. Unmindful of his own urgent need for medical attention, he remained in the perilous fire-swept area to care for another marine casualty. Heroically completing his task despite pain and profuse bleeding, he then endeavored to make his way to the rear in search of adequate aid for himself when struck down by a Japanese sniper bullet which caused his collapse. Succumbing later as a result of his self-sacrificing service to others, Williams, by his courageous determination, unwavering fortitude and valiant performance of duty, served as an inspiring example of heroism, in keeping with the highest traditions of the U.S. Naval Service. He gallantly gave his life for his country.

*WILLIS, JOHN HARLAN

Rank and organization: Pharmacist's Mate First Class, U.S. Navy. *Born:* 10 June 1921, Columbia, Tenn. *Accredited to:* Tennessee. *Citation:* For conspicuous gallantry and intrepidity at the risk of his life above and beyond the call of duty as Platoon Corpsman serving with the 3d Battalion, 27th Marines, 5th Marine Division, during operations against enemy Japanese forces on Iwo Jima, Volcano Islands, 28 February 1945. Constantly imperiled by artillery and mortar fire from strong and mutually supporting pillboxes and caves studding Hill 362 in the enemy's cross-island defenses, Willis resolutely administered first aid to the many marines wounded during the furious close-in fighting until he himself was struck by shrapnel and was ordered back to the battle-aid station. Without waiting for official medical release, he quickly returned to his company and, during a savage hand-to-hand enemy counterattack, daringly advanced to the extreme frontlines under mortar and sniper fire to aid a marine lying wounded in a shell-hole. Completely unmindful of his own danger as the Japanese intensified their attack, Willis calmly continued to administer blood plasma to his patient, promptly returning the first hostile grenade which landed in the shell-hole while he was working and hurling back 7 more in quick succession before the ninth 1 exploded in his hand and instantly killed him. By his great personal valor in saving others at the sacrifice of his own life, he inspired his companions, although terrifically outnumbered, to launch a fiercely determined attack and repulse the enemy force. His exceptional fortitude and courage in the performance of duty reflect the highest credit upon Willis and the U.S. Naval Service. He gallantly gave his life for his country.

*WILSON, ALFRED L.

Rank and organization: Technician Fifth Grade, U.S. Army, Medical Detachment, 328th Infantry, 26th Infantry Division. *Place and date:* Near Bezange la Petite, France, 8 November 1944. *Entered service at:* Fairchance, Pa. *Birth:* Fairchance, Pa. *G.O. No.:* 47, 18 June 1945. *Citation:* He volunteered to assist as an aid man a company other than his own, which was suffering casualties from constant artillery fire. He administered to the wounded and returned to his own company when a shellburst injured a number of its men. While treating his comrades he was seriously wounded, but refused to be evacuated by litter bearers sent to relieve him. In spite of great pain and loss of blood, he continued to administer first aid until he was too weak to stand. Crawling from 1 patient to another, he continued his work until excessive loss of blood prevented him from moving. He then verbally directed unskilled enlisted men in continuing the first aid for the wounded. Still refusing assistance himself, he remained to instruct others in dressing the wounds of his comrades until he was unable to speak above a whisper and finally lapsed into unconsciousness. The effects of his injury later caused his death. By steadfastly remaining at the scene without regard for his own safety, Cpl. Wilson through distinguished devotion to duty and personal sacrifice helped to save the lives of at least 10 wounded men.

WILSON, LOUIS HUGH, JR.

Rank and organization: Captain, U.S. Marine Corps, Commanding Rifle Company, 2d Battalion, 9th Marines, 3d Marine Division. *Place and date:* Fonte Hill, Guam, 25–26 July 1944. *Entered service at:* Mississippi. *Born:* 11 February 1920, Brandon, Miss. *Citation:* For conspicuous gallantry and intrepidity at the risk of his life above and beyond the call of duty as commanding officer of a rifle company attached to the 2d Battalion, 9th Marines, 3d Marine Division, in action against enemy Japanese forces at Fonte Hill, Guam, 25–26 July 1944. Ordered to take that portion of the hill within his zone of action, Capt. Wilson initiated his attack in midafternoon, pushed up the rugged, open terrain against terrific machinegun and rifle fire for 300 yards and successfully captured the objective. Promptly assuming command of other disorganized units and motorized equipment in addition to his own company and 1 reinforcing platoon, he organized his night defenses in the face of continuous hostile fire and, although wounded 3 times during this 5-hour period, completed his disposition of men and guns before retiring to the company command post for medical attention. Shortly thereafter, when the enemy launched the first of a series of savage counterattacks lasting all night, he voluntarily rejoined his beseiged units and repeatedly exposed himself to the merciless hail of shrapnel and bullets, dashing 50 yards into the open on 1 occasion to rescue a wounded marine lying helpless beyond the frontlines. Fighting fiercely in hand-to-hand encounters, he led his men in furiously waged battle for approximately 10 hours, tenaciously holding his line and repelling the fanatically renewed counterthrusts until he succeeded in crushing the last efforts of the hard-pressed Japanese early the following morning. Then organizing a 17-man patrol, he immediately advanced upon a strategic slope essential to the security of his position and, boldly defying intense mortar, machinegun, and rifle fire which struck down 13 of his men, drove relentlessly forward with the remnants of his patrol to seize the vital ground. By his indomitable leadership, daring combat tactics, and valor in the face of overwhelming odds, Capt. Wilson succeeded in capturing and holding the strategic high ground in his regimental sector, thereby contributing essentially to the success of his regimental mission and to the annihilation of 350 Japanese troops. His inspiring conduct throughout the critical periods of this decisive action sustains and enhances the highest traditions of the U.S. Naval Service.

*WILSON, ROBERT LEE

Rank and organization: Private First Class, U.S. Marine Corps. *Born:* 24 May 1921, Centralia, Ill. *Accredited to:* Illinois. *Citation:* For conspicuous gallantry and intrepidity at the risk of his life above and beyond the call of duty while serving with the 2d Battalion, 6th Marines, 2d Marine Division, during action against enemy Japanese forces at Tinian Island, Marianas Group, on 4 August 1944. As 1 of a group of marines advancing through heavy underbrush to neutralize isolated points of resistance, Pfc. Wilson daringly preceded his companions toward a pile of rocks where Japanese troops were supposed to be hiding. Fully aware of the danger involved, he was moving forward while the remainder of the squad, armed with automatic rifles, closed together in the rear when an enemy grenade landed in the midst of the group. Quick to act, Pfc. Wilson cried a warning to the men and unhesitatingly threw himself on the grenade, heroically sacrificing his own life that the others might live and fulfill their mission. His exceptional valor, his courageous loyalty and unwavering devotion to duty in the face of grave peril reflect the highest credit upon Pfc. Wilson and the U.S. Naval Service. He gallantly gave his life for his country.

WISE, HOMER L.

Rank and organization: Staff Sergeant, U.S. Army, Company L, 142d Infantry, 36th Infantry Division. *Place and date:* Magliano, Italy, 14 June 1944. *Entered service at:* Baton Rouge, La. *Birth:* Baton Rouge, La. *G.O. No.:* 90, 8 December 1944. *Citation:* While his platoon was pinned down by enemy small-arms fire from both flanks, he left his position of comparative safety and assisted in carrying 1 of his men, who had been seriously wounded and who lay in an exposed position, to a point where he could receive medical attention. The advance of the platoon was resumed but was again stopped by enemy frontal fire. A German officer and 2 enlisted men, armed with automatic weapons, threatened the right flank. Fearlessly exposing himself, he moved to a position from which he killed all 3 with his submachinegun. Returning to his squad, he obtained an M1 rifle and several antitank grenades, then took up a position from which he delivered accurate fire on the enemy holding up the advance. As the battalion moved forward it was again stopped by enemy frontal and flanking fire. He procured an automatic rifle and, advancing ahead of his men, neutralized an enemy machinegun with his fire. When the flanking fire became more intense he ran to a nearby tank and exposing himself on the turret, restored a jammed machinegun to operating efficiency and used it so effectively that the enemy fire from an adjacent ridge was materially reduced, thus permitting the battalion to occupy its objective.

*WITEK, FRANK PETER

Rank and organization: Private First Class, U.S. Marine Corps Reserve. *Born:* December 1921, Derby, Conn. *Accredited to:* Illinois. *Citation:* For conspicuous gallantry and intrepidity at the risk of his life above and beyond the call of duty while serving with the 1st Battalion, 9th Marines, 3d Marine Division, during the Battle of Finegayen at Guam, Marianas, on 3 August 1944. When his rifle platoon was halted by heavy surprise fire from well-camouflaged enemy positions, Pfc. Witek daringly remained standing to fire a full magazine from his automatic at point-blank range into a depression housing Japanese troops, killing 8 of the enemy and enabling the greater part of his platoon to take cover. During his platoon's withdrawal for consolidation of lines, he remained to safeguard a severely wounded comrade, courageously returning the enemy's fire until the arrival of stretcher bearers, and then covering the evacuation by sustained fire as he moved backward toward his own lines. With his platoon again pinned down by a hostile machinegun, Pfc. Witek, on his own initiative, moved forward boldly to the reinforcing tanks and infantry, alternately throwing handgrenades and firing as he advanced to within 5 to 10 yards of the enemy position, and destroying the hostile machinegun emplacement and an additional 8 Japanese before he himself was struck down by an enemy rifleman. His valiant and inspiring action effectively reduced the enemy's firepower, thereby enabling his platoon to attain its objective, and reflects the highest credit upon Pfc. Witek and the U.S. Naval Service. He gallantly gave his life for his country.

*WOODFORD, HOWARD E.

Rank and organization: Staff Sergeant, U.S. Army, Company I, 130th Infantry, 33d Infantry Division. *Place and date:* Near Tabio, Luzon, Philippine Islands, 6 June 1945. *Entered service at:* Barberton, Ohio. *Birth:* Barberton, Ohio. *G.O. No.:* 14, 4 February 1946. *Citation:* He volunteered to investigate the delay in a scheduled attack by an attached guerrilla battalion. Reaching the line of departure, he found that the lead company, in combat for the first time, was immobilized by intense enemy mortar, machinegun, and rifle fire which had caused casualties to key personnel. Knowing that further failure to advance would endanger the flanks of adjacent units, as well as delay capture of the objective, he immediately took command of the company, evacuated the wounded, reorganized the unit under fire, and prepared to attack. He repeatedly exposed himself to draw revealing fire from the Japanese strongpoints, and then moved forward with a 5-man covering force to determine exact enemy positions. Although intense enemy machinegun fire killed 2 and wounded his other 3 men, S/Sgt. Woodford resolutely continued his patrol before returning to the company. Then, against bitter resistance, he guided the guerrillas up a barren hill and captured the objective, personally accounting for 2 hostile machinegunners and courageously reconnoitering strong defensive positions before directing neutralizing fire. After organizing a perimeter defense for the night, he was given permission by radio to return to his battalion, but, feeling that he was needed to maintain proper control, he chose to remain with the guerrillas. Before dawn the next morning the enemy launched a fierce suicide attack with mortars, grenades, and small-arms fire, and infiltrated through the perimeter. Though wounded by a grenade, S/Sgt. Woodford remained at his post calling for mortar support until bullets knocked out his radio. Then, seizing a rifle he began working his way around the perimeter, encouraging the men until he reached a weak spot where 2 guerrillas had been killed. Filling this gap himself, he fought off the enemy. At daybreak he was found dead in his foxhole, but 37 enemy dead were lying in and around his position. By his daring, skillful, and inspiring leadership, as well as by his gallant determination to search out and kill the enemy, S/Sgt. Woodford led an inexperienced unit in capturing and securing a vital objective, and was responsible for the successful continuance of a vitally important general advance.

YOUNG, CASSIN

Rank and organization: Commander, U.S. Navy. *Born:* 6 March 1894, Washington, D.C. *Appointed from:* Wisconsin. *Other Navy award:* Navy Cross. *Citation:* For distinguished conduct in action, outstanding heroism and utter disregard of his own safety, above and beyond the call of duty, as commanding officer of the U.S.S. *Vestal*, during the attack on the Fleet in Pearl Harbor, Territory of Hawaii, by enemy Japanese forces on 7 December 1941. Comdr. Young proceeded to the bridge and later took personal command of the 3-inch antiaircraft gun. When blown overboard by the blast of the forward magazine explosion of the U.S.S. *Arizona*, to which the U.S.S. *Vestal* was moored, he swam back to his ship. The entire forward part of the U.S.S. *Arizona* was a blazing inferno with oil afire on the water between the 2 ships; as a result of several bomb hits, the U.S.S. *Vestal* was afire in several places, was settling and taking on a list. Despite severe enemy bombing and strafing at the time, and his shocking experience of having been blown overboard, Comdr. Young, with extreme coolness and calmness, moved his ship to an anchorage distant from the U.S.S. *Arizona*, and subsequently beached the U.S.S. *Vestal* upon determining that such action was required to save his ship.

*YOUNG, RODGER W.

Rank and organization: Private, U.S. Army, 148th Infantry, 37th Infantry Division. *Place and date:* On New Georgia, Solomon Islands, 31 July 1943. *Entered service at:* Clyde, Ohio. *Birth:* Tiffin, Ohio. *G.O. No.:* 3, 6 January 1944. *Citation:* On 31 July 1943, the infantry company of which Pvt. Young was a member, was ordered to make a limited withdrawal from the battle line in order to adjust the battalion's position for the night. At this time, Pvt. Young's platoon was engaged with the enemy in a dense jungle where observation was very limited. The platoon suddenly was pinned down by intense fire from a Japanese machinegun concealed on higher ground only 75 yards away. The initial burst wounded Pvt. Young. As the platoon started to obey the order to withdraw, Pvt. Young called out that he could see the enemy emplacement, whereupon he started creeping toward it. Another burst from the machinegun wounded him the second time. Despite the wounds, he continued his heroic advance, attracting enemy fire and answering with rifle fire. When he was close enough to his objective, he began throwing handgrenades, and while doing so was hit again and killed. Pvt. Young's bold action in closing with this Japanese pillbox and thus diverting its fire, permitted his platoon to disengage itself, without loss, and was responsible for several enemy casualties.

ZEAMER, JAY JR. (Air Mission)

Rank and organization: Major, U.S. Army Air Corps. *Place and date:* Over Buka area, Solomon Islands, 16 June 1943. *Entered service at:*

Machias, Maine. *Birth:* Carlisle, Pa. *G.O. No.:* 1, 4 January 1944. *Citation:* On 16 June 1943, Maj. Zeamer (then Capt.) volunteered as pilot of a bomber on an important photographic mapping mission covering the formidably defended area in the vicinity of Buka, Solomon Islands. While photographing the Buka airdrome, his crew observed about 20 enemy fighters on the field, many of them taking off. Despite the certainty of a dangerous attack by this strong force, Maj. Zeamer proceeded with his mapping run, even after the enemy attack began. In the ensuing engagement, Maj. Zeamer sustained gunshot wounds in both arms and legs, 1 leg being broken. Despite his injuries, he maneuvered the damaged plane so skillfully that his gunners were able to fight off the enemy during a running fight which lasted 40 minutes. The crew destroyed at least 5 hostile planes, of which Maj. Zeamer himself shot down 1. Although weak from loss of blood, he refused medical aid until the enemy had broken combat. He then turned over the controls, but continued to exercise command despite lapses into unconsciousness, and directed the flight to a base 580 miles away. In this voluntary action, Maj. Zeamer, with superb skill, resolution, and courage, accomplished a mission of great value.

*ZUSSMAN, RAYMOND

Rank and organization: Second Lieutenant, U.S. Army, 756th Tank Battalion. *Place and date:* Noroy le Bourg, France, 12 September 1944. *Entered service at:* Detroit, Mich. *Birth:* Hamtramck, Mich. *G.O. No.:* 42, 24 May 1945. *Citation:* On 12 September 1944, 2d Lt. Zussman was in command of 2 tanks operating with an infantry company in the attack on enemy forces occupying the town of Noroy le Bourg, France. At 7 p.m., his command tank bogged down. Throughout the ensuing action, armed only with a carbine, he reconnoitered alone on foot far in advance of his remaining tank and the infantry. Returning only from time to time to designate targets, he directed the action of the tank and turned over to the infantry the numerous German soldiers he had caused to surrender. He located a road block and directed his tanks to destroy it. Fully exposed to fire from enemy positions only 50 yards distant, he stood by his tank directing its fire. Three Germans were killed and 8 surrendered. Again he walked before his tank, leading it against an enemy-held group of houses, machinegun and small-arms fire kicking up dust at his feet. The tank fire broke the resistance and 20 enemy surrendered. Going forward again alone he passed an enemy-occupied house from which Germans fired on him and threw grenades in his path. After a brief fire fight, he signaled his tank to come up and fire on the house. Eleven German soldiers were killed and 15 surrendered. Going on alone, he disappeared around a street corner. The fire of his carbine could be heard and in a few minutes he reappeared driving 30 prisoners before him. Under 2d Lt. Zussman's heroic and inspiring leadership, 18 enemy soldiers were killed and 92 captured.

SPECIAL ACT OF CONGRESS

*MITCHELL, WILLIAM

AN ACT Authorizing the President of the United States to award posthumously in the name of Congress a Medal of Honor to William Mitchell.

Be it enacted by the Senate and House of Representatives of the United States of America in Congress assembled, That the President of the United States is requested to cause a gold medal to be struck, with suitable emblems, devices and inscriptions, to be presented to the late William Mitchell, formerly a Colonel, United States Army, in recognition of his outstanding pioneer service and foresight in the field of American military aviation.

SEC. 2. When the medal provided for in section 1 of this Act shall have been struck, the President shall transmit the same to William Mitchell, Junior, son of the said William Mitchell, to be presented to him in the name of the people of the United States.

SEC. 3. A sufficient sum of money to carry this Act into effect is hereby authorized to be appropriated, out of money in the Treasury not otherwise appropriated.

Approved August 8, 1946. Private Law 884.

MEDALS OF HONOR AWARDED
TO UNKNOWNS

On Armistice Day, 1921, the Medal of Honor was pinned to the flag-draped coffin of the American Unknown Soldier by President Harding during services at the Arlington National Cemetery. A special bill was passed by Congress permitting the award to an unknown as "typifying the gallantry and intrepidity, at the risk of life above and beyond the call of duty, or our beloved heroes who made the supreme sacrifice, in the World War." Medals of Honor were also awarded by special legislation to the unknown soldiers of Belgium, Great Britain, France, Italy, and Rumania.

BELGIUM

* * * By virtue of the authority vested by law in the President of the United States, the Congressional Medal of Honor, emblem of the highest military ideals and virtues, is bestowed in the name of the Congress of the United States upon the unknown, unidentified Belgian soldier in a desire to add all that is possible to the imperishable glory won by the soldiers of Belgium who fought as comrades of the Amer-

ican soldiers during the World War, and to commemorate with them the deeds of the nations associated with the United States of America, by paying this tribute to their unknown dead (A.G. 220.523) (War Department General Orders, No. 52, 1 Dec. 1922, Sec. I).

GREAT BRITAIN AND FRANCE

* * * By virtue of an act of Congress approved 4 March 1921, the Medal of Honor, emblem of highest ideals and virtues, is bestowed in the name of the Congress of the United States upon the unknown, unidentified British soldier and French soldier buried, respectively, in Westminster Abbey and Arc de Triomphe.

Whereas Great Britain and France, two of the Allies of the United States in the World War, have lately done honor to the unknown dead of their armies by placing with fitting ceremony the body of an unknown, unidentified soldier, respectively, in Westminster Abbey and in the Arc de Triomphe; and

Whereas animated by the same spirit of comradeship in which we of the American forces fought alongside these Allies, we desire to add whatever we can to the imperishable glory won by the deeds of our Allies and commemorated in part by this tribute to their unknown dead: Now, therefore,

Be it enacted by the Senate and House of Representatives of the United States of America in Congress assembled, That the President of the United States of America be, and he hereby is, authorized to bestow with appropriate ceremonies, military and civil, the Congressional Medal of Honor upon the unknown, unidentified British soldier buried in Westminster Abbey, London, England, and upon the unknown, unidentified French soldier buried in the Arc de Triomphe, Paris, France (A.G. 220.523) (War Department General Orders, No. 52, 1 Dec. 1922, Sec. II).

ITALY

* * * By virtue of a joint resolution of Congress, approved 12 October 1921, the Medal of Honor, emblem of highest ideals and virtues, is bestowed in the name of the Congress of the United States upon the unknown, unidentified Italian soldier to be buried in the National Monument to Victor Emanuel II, in Rome.

Whereas the Congress has authorized the bestowal of the Congressional Medal of Honor upon unknown, unidentified British and French soldiers buried in Westminster Abbey, London, England, and the Arc de Triomphe, Paris, France, respectively, who fought beside our soldiers in the recent war; and

Whereas, animated by the same spirit of friendship toward the soldiers of Italy who also fought as comrades of the American soldiers during the World War, we desire to add whatever we can to the imperishable glory won by their deeds and to participate in paying tribute to their unknown dead: Now, therefore, be it

Resolved by the Senate and House of Representatives of the United States of America in Congress assembled, That the President of the United States be, and he is hereby, authorized to bestow, with appropriate ceremonies, military and civil, the Congressional Medal of Honor upon the unknown, unidentified Italian soldier to be buried in the National Monument to Victor Emanuel II, in Rome, Italy (A.G. 220.523) (War Department General Orders, No. 52, 1 Dec. 1922, Sec. III).

RUMANIA

* * * By virtue of the authority vested by law in the President of the United States, the Congressional Medal of Honor, emblem of the highest military ideals and virtues, is bestowed in the name of the Congress of the United States upon the unknown, unidentified Rumanian soldier in a desire to add all that is possible to the imperishable glory won by the soldiers of Rumania who fought as comrades of the American soldiers during the World War, and to commemorate with them the deeds of the nations associated with the United States of America, by paying this tribute to their unknown dead (A.G. 220.52, 17 May 1923) (War Department General Orders, No. 22, 6 June 1923).

UNITED STATES

* * * By virtue of an act of Congress approved 24 August 1921, the Medal of Honor, emblem of highest ideals and virtues is bestowed in the name of the Congress of the United States upon the unknown American, typifying the gallantry and intrepidity, at the risk of life above and beyond the call of duty, of our beloved heroes who made the supreme sacrifice in the World War. They died in order that others might live (293.8, A.G.O.) (War Department General Orders, No. 59, 13 Dec. 1921, sec. I).

AN ACT To authorize the President to award the Medal of Honor to the unknown American who lost his life while serving overseas in the armed forces of the United States during the Second World War.

Be it enacted by the Senate and House of Representatives of the United States of America in Congress assembled, That the President is hereby authorized and directed to award, in the name of Congress, a Medal of Honor to the unknown American who lost his life while serving overseas in the armed forces of the United States during the Second World War, and who will lie buried in the Memorial Amphitheater of the National Cemetery at Arlington, Virginia, as authorized by the Act of June 24, 1946, Public Law 429, Seventy-ninth Congress.

Approved March 9, 1948. Public Law 438, 80th Congress.

AN ACT To authorize the President to award the Medal of Honor to the unknown American who lost his life while serving overseas in the Armed Forces of the United States during the Korean conflict.

Be it enacted by the Senate and House of Representatives of the United States of America in Congress assembled, That the President is hereby authorized and directed to award, in the name of the Congress, a Medal of Honor to the unknown American who lost his life while serving overseas in the Armed Forces of the United States during the Korean conflict, and who will lie buried in the Memorial Ampitheater of the National Cemetery at Arlington, Virginia, as authorized by the Act of August 3, 1956, Public Law 975, Eighty-fourth Congress.

Approved August 31, 1957. Public Law 85–251.

AN ACT To authorize the President to award the Medal of Honor to the unknown American who lost his life while serving in the Armed Forces of the United States in Southeast Asia during the Vietnam era and who has been selected to be buried in the Memorial Amphitheater at Arlington National Cemetery.

Be it enacted by the Senate and House of Representatives of the United States of America in Congress assembled, That the President may award, and present in the name of Congress, the Medal of Honor to the unknown American who lost his life while serving in Southeast Asia during the Vietnam era as a member of the Armed Forces of the United States and who has been selected to lie buried in the Memorial Amphitheater of the National Cemetery at Arlington, Virginia, as authorized by section 9 of the National Cemeteries Act of 1973 (Public Law 93-43).

Approved May 25, 1984. Public Law 98-301, 98th Congress.

INTERIM 1920 TO 1940

BADDERS, WILLIAM

Rank and organization: Chief Machinist's Mate, U.S. Navy. *Place and date:* At sea following sinking of the U.S.S. *Squalus*, 13 May 1939. *Entered service at:* Indianapolis, Ind. *Born:* 16 September 1900, Harrisburg, Ill. *Other Navy awards:* Navy Cross, Navy-Marine Corps Medal. *Citation:* For extraordinary heroism in the line of his profession during the rescue and salvage operations following the sinking of the U.S.S. *Squalus* on 13 May 1939. During the rescue operations, Badders, as senior member of the rescue chamber crew, made the last extremely hazardous trip of the rescue chamber to attempt to rescue any possible survivors in the flooded after portion of the *Squalus*. He was fully aware of the great danger involved in that if he and his assistant became incapacitated, there was no way in which either could be rescued. During the salvage operations, Badders made important and difficult dives under the most hazardous conditions. His outstanding performance of duty contributed much to the success of the operations and characterizes conduct far above and beyond the ordinary call of duty.

BENNETT, FLOYD

Rank and organization: Machinist, U.S. Navy. *Born:* 25 October 1890, Warrensburg, N.Y. *Accredited to:* New York. *Other Navy award:* Distinguished Service Medal. *Citation:* For distinguishing himself conspicuously by courage and intrepidity at the risk of his life as a member of the Byrd Arctic Expedition and thus contributing largely to the success of the first heavier-than-air flight to the North Pole and return.

BREAULT, HENRY

Rank and organization: Torpedoman Second Class, U.S. Navy. *Born:* 14 October, 1900, Putnam, Conn. *Accredited to:* Vermont. *G.O. No.:* 125, 20 February 1924. *Citation:* For heroism and devotion to duty while serving on board the U.S. submarine *O–5* at the time of the sinking of that vessel. On the morning of 28 October 1923, the *O–5* collided with the steamship *Abangarez* and sank in less than a minute. When the collision occurred, Breault was in the torpedo room. Upon reaching the hatch, he saw that the boat was rapidly sinking. Instead of jumping overboard to save his own life, he returned to the torpedo room to the rescue of a shipmate whom he knew was trapped in the boat, closing the torpedo room hatch on himself. Breault and Brown remained trapped in this compartment until rescued by the salvage party 31 hours later. (Medal presented by President Coolidge at the White House on 8 March 1924.)

BYRD, RICHARD EVELYN, Jr.

Rank and organization: Commander, U.S. Navy. *Born:* 25 October 1888, Winchester, Va. *Appointed from:* Virginia. *Other Navy awards:* Navy Cross, Distinguished Service Medal, Legion of Merit with gold star, Distinguished Flying Cross. *Citation:* For distinguishing himself conspicuously by courage and intrepidity at the risk of his life, in demonstrating that it is possible for aircraft to travel in continuous flight from a now inhabited portion of the earth over the North Pole and return.

*CHOLISTER, GEORGE ROBERT

Rank and organization: Boatswain's Mate First Class, U.S. Navy. *Born:* 18 December 1898, Camden, N.J. *Accredited to:* New Jersey. (Awarded by Special Act of Congress 3 February 1933.) *Citation:* For extraordinary heroism in the line of his profession on the occasion of a fire on board the U.S.S. *Trenton.* At 3:35 on the afternoon of 20 October 1924, while the *Trenton* was preparing to fire trial installation shots from the two 6-inch guns in the forward twin mount of that vessel, 2 charges of powder ignited. Twenty men were trapped in the twin mount. Four died almost immediately and 10 later from burns and inhalation of flames and gases. The 6 others were severely injured. Cholister, without thought of his own safety, on seeing that the charge of powder from the left gun was ignited, jumped for the right charge and endeavored to put it in the immersion tank. The left charge burst into flame and ignited the right charge before Cholister could accomplish his purpose. He fell unconscious while making a supreme effort to save his shipmates and died the following day.

*CORRY, WILLIAM MERRILL, Jr.

Rank and organization: Lieutenant Commander, U.S. Navy. *Place and date:* Near Hartford, Conn., 2 October 1920. *Born:* 5 October 1889, Quincy, Fla. *Accredited to:* Florida. *Other Navy award:* Navy Cross. *Citation:* For heroic service in attempting to rescue a brother officer from a flame-enveloped airplane. On 2 October 1920, an airplane in which Lt. Comdr. Corry was a passenger crashed and burst into flames. He was thrown 30 feet clear of the plane and, though injured, rushed back to the burning machine and endeavored to release the pilot. In so doing he sustained serious burns, from which he died 4 days later.

CRANDALL, ORSON L.

Rank and organization: Chief Boatswain's Mate, U.S. Navy. *Place and date:* At sea following sinking of U.S.S. *Squalus,* 13 May 1939. *Born:* 2 February 1903, St. Joseph, Mo. *Entered service at:* Connecticut. *Citation:* For extraordinary heroism in the line of his profession as a master diver throughout the rescue and salvage operations following the sinking of the U.S.S. *Squalus* on 23 May 1939. His leadership and devotion to duty in directing diving operations and in making important and difficult dives under the most hazardous conditions characterize conduct far above and beyond the ordinary call of duty.

*DREXLER, HENRY CLAY

Rank and organization: Ensign, U.S. Navy. *Born:* 7 August 1901, Braddock, Pa. *Accredited to:* Pennsylvania. (Awarded by Special Act of Congress, 3 February 1933.) *Other Navy award:* Navy Cross. *Citation:* For extraordinary heroism in the line of his profession on the occasion of a fire on board the U.S.S. *Trenton.* At 3:35 on the afternoon of 20 October 1924, while the *Trenton* was preparing to fire trial installation shots from the two 6-inch guns in the forward twin mount of that vessel, 2 charges of powder ignited. Twenty men were trapped in the twin mount. Four died almost immediately and 10 later from burns and inhalation of flame and gases. The 6 others were severely injured. Ens. Drexler, without thought of his own safety, on seeing that the charge of powder for the left gun was ignited, jumped for the right charge and endeavored to put it in the immersion tank. The left charge burst into flame and ignited the right charge before Ens. Drexler could accomplish his purpose. He met his death while making a supreme effort to save his shipmates.

EADIE, THOMAS

Rank and organization: Chief Gunner's Mate, U.S. Navy. *Place and date:* Off Provincetown, Mass., 18 December 1927. *Entered service at:* Rhode Island. *Born:* 7 April 1887, Scotland. *Other Navy award:* Navy Cross. *Citation:* For display of extraordinary heroism in the line of his profession above and beyond the call of duty on 18 December 1927, during the diving operations in connection with the sinking of the U.S.S. *S-4* with all on board, as a result of a collision off Prividence-town, Mass. On this occasion when Michels, Chief Torpedoman, U.S. Navy, while attempting to connect an airline to the submarine at a depth of 102 feet became seriously fouled, Eadie, under the most adverse diving conditions, deliberately, knowingly, and willingly took his own life in his hands by promptly descending to the rescue in response to the desperate need of his companion diver. After 2 hours of extremely dangerous and heartbreaking work, by his cool, calculating, and skillful labors, he succeeded in his mission and brought Michels safely to the surface.

EDWARDS, WALTER ATLEE

Rank and organization: Lieutenant Commander, U.S. Navy. *Place and date:* Sea of Marmora, Turkey, 16 December 1922. *Born:* 8 November 1886, Philadelphia, Pa. *Accredited to:* Pennsylvania. *G.O. No.:* 123, 4 February 1924. (Medal presented by President Coolidge at the White House on 2 February 1924.) *Other Navy award:* Navy Cross. *Citation:* For heroism in rescuing 482 men, women and children from the French military transport *Vinh-Long,* destroyed by fire in the Sea of Marmora, Turkey, on 16 December 1922. Lt. Comdr. Edwards, commanding the U.S.S. *Bainbridge,* placed his vessel alongside the bow of the transport and, in spite of several violent explosions which occurred on the burning vessel, maintained his ship in that position until all who were alive were taken on board. Of a total of 495 on board, 482 were rescued by his coolness, judgment and professional skill, which were combined with a degree of heroism that must reflect new glory on the U.S. Navy.

GREELY, ADOLPHUS W.

Rank and organization: Major General, U.S. Army, retired. *Place and date:* ———. *Entered service at:* Louisiana. *Born:* 27 March 1844, Newburyport, Mass. *G.O. No.:* 3, W.D., 1935. Act of Congress, 21 March 1935. *Citation:* For his life of splendid public service, begun on 27 March 1844, having enlisted as a private in the U.S. Army on 26 July 1861, and by successive promotions was commissioned as major general 10 February 1906, and retired by operation of law on his 64th birthday.

HUBER, WILLIAM RUSSEL

Rank and organization: Machinist's Mate, U.S. Navy. *Place and date:* Aboard the U.S.S. *Bruce* at the Naval Shipyard, Norfolk, Va., 11 June 1928. *Entered service at:* Pennsylvania. *Birth:* Harrisburg, Pa. *Citation:* For display of extraordinary heroism in the line of his profession on 11 June 1928, after a boiler accident on the U.S.S. *Bruce*, then at the Naval Shipyard, Norfolk, Va. Immediately on becoming aware of the accident, Huber without hesitation and in complete disregard of his own safety, entered the steamfilled fireroom and at grave risk to his life succeeded by almost superhuman efforts in carrying Charles H. Byran to safety. Although having received severe and dangerous burns about the arms and neck, he descended with a view toward rendering further assistance. The great courage, grit, and determination displayed by Huber on this occasion characterized conduct far above and beyond the call of duty.

*HUTCHINS, CARLTON BARMORE

Rank and organization: Lieutenant, U.S. Navy. *Place and date:* Off California Coast, 2 February 1938. *Born:* 12 September 1904, Albany, N.Y. *Accredited to:* New York. *Citation:* For extraordinary heroism as the pilot of the U.S. Navy Seaplane PBY-2 No. 0463 (11-P-3) while engaged in tactical exercises with the U.S. Fleet on 2 February 1938. Although his plane was badly damaged, Lt. Hutchins remained at the controls endeavoring to bring the damaged plane to a safe landing and to afford an opportunity for his crew to escape by parachutes. His cool, calculated conduct contributed principally to the saving of the lives of all who survived. His conduct on this occasion was above and beyond the call of duty.

LINDBERGH, CHARLES A.

Rank and organization: Captain, U.S. Army Air Corps Reserve. *Place and date:* From New York City to Paris, France, 20–21 May 1927. *Entered service at:* Little Falls, Minn. *Born:* 4 February 1902, Detroit, Mich. *G.O. No.:* 5, W.D., 1928; act of Congress 14 December 1927. *Citation:* For displaying heroic courage and skill as a navigator, at the risk of his life, by his nonstop flight in his airplane, the *Spirit of St. Louis*, from New York City to Paris, France, 20–21 May 1927, by which Capt. Lindbergh not only achieved the greatest individual triumph of any American citizen but demonstrated that travel across the ocean by aircraft was possible.

McDONALD, JAMES HARPER

Rank and organization: Chief Metalsmith, U.S. Navy. *Place and date:* Area at sea of sinking of the U.S.S. *Squalus*, 23 May 1939. *Entered service at:* Washington, D.C. *Born:* 15 July 1900, Scotland. *Citation:* For extraordinary heroism in the line of his profession as a master diver throughout the rescue and salvage operations following the sinking of the U.S.S. *Squalus* on 23 May 1939. His leadership, masterly skill, general efficiency, and untiring devotion to duty in directing diving operations, and in making important and difficult dives under the most hazardous conditions, characterize conduct far above and beyond the ordinary call of duty.

MIHALOWSKI, JOHN

Rank and organization: Torpedoman First Class, U.S. Navy. *Place and date:* Area at sea of the sinking of the U.S.S. *Squalus*, 23 May 1939. *Entered service at:* Massachusetts. *Born:* 12 August 1910, Worcester, Mass. *Citation:* For extraordinary heroism in the line of his profession during the rescue and salvage operations following the sinking of the U.S.S. *Squalus* on 23 May 1939. Mihalowski, as a member of the rescue chamber crew, made the last extremely hazardous trip of the rescue chamber to attempt the rescue of any possible survivors in the flooded after portion of the *Squalus*. He was fully aware of the great danger involved, in that, if he and the other member of the crew became incapacitated, there was no way in which either could be rescued. During the salvage operations Mihalowski made important and difficult dives under the most hazardous conditions. His outstanding performance of duty contributed much to the success of the operations and characterizes conduct far above and beyond the ordinary call of duty.

RYAN, THOMAS JOHN

Rank and organization: Ensign, U.S. Navy. *Place and date:* Yokohama, Japan, 1 September 1923. *Entered service at:* Louisiana. *Born:* 5 August 1901, New Orleans, La. *Citation:* For heroism in effecting the rescue of a woman from the burning Grand Hotel, Yokohama, Japan, on 1 September 1923. Following the earthquake and fire which occurred in Yokohama on 1 September, Ens. Ryan, with complete disregard for his own life, extricated a woman from the Grand Hotel, thus saving her life. His heroic conduct upon this occasion reflects the greatest credit on himself and on the U.S. Navy, of which he is a part. (Medal presented by President Coolidge at the White House on 15 March 1924.)

SMITH, ALBERT JOSEPH

Rank and organization: Private, U.S. Marine Corps. *Place and date:* Marine Barracks, Naval Air Station, Pensacola, Fla., 11 February 1921. *Entered service at:* Michigan. *Born:* 31 July 1898, Calumet, Mich. *G.O. No.:* 72, 29 September 1921. *Citation:* At about 7:30 a.m. on the morning of 11 February 1921, Pvt. Smith, while on duty as a sentry, rescued Plen M. Phelps, late machinist's mate second class, U.S. Navy, from a burning seaplane which had fallen near his post, gate No. 1, Marine Barracks, Naval Air Station, Pensacola, Fla. Despite the explosion of the gravity gasoline tank, with total disregard of personal safety, he pushed himself to a position where he could reach Phelps, who was pinned beneath the burning wreckage, and rescued him from the burning plane, in the performance of which he sustained painful burns about the head, neck and both hands.

SECOND
NICARAGUAN CAMPAIGN

Soon after the withdrawal of the Legation Guard in 1925, the worst civil war in the history of Nicaragua broke out. Long-continued disorder and clashes between opposing political factions had caused a general state of demoralization throughout the country. Lawlessness, banditry and sporadic revolutions hampered normal business activities and civil administration. American aid was necessary to protect the lives and property of our citizens and was requested by interested foreign powers for their nationals.

Under the State Department's program of intervention, Naval vessels were kept in Nicaraguan waters and detachments of marines and sailors were landed. The plan involved the tremendous task of creating a nonpolitical constabulary, of establishing and controlling zones of neutrality, and of maintaining law and order generally toward a restoration of peace.

With the help of the Marine Brigade and the Marine Aviation Squadron which rendered valuable service in keeping up communications with remote posts as well as delivering emergency supplies and evacuating the wounded, the Guardia Nacional gained strength and efficiency, Nicaraguan officers were given every opportunity to gain experience and, by the end of 1932, the last of the American officers retired from the Guardia Nacional and the United States shifted the responsibility for maintaining order to the Nicaraguan Government.

SCHILT, CHRISTIAN FRANK

Rank and organization: First Lieutenant, U.S. Marine Corps. *Place and date:* Quilali, Nicaragua, 6, 7 and 8 January 1928. *Entered service at:* Illinois. *Born:* 1 March 1895, Richland County, Ill. *Other Navy awards:* Distinguished Service Medal, Legion of Merit, Distinguished Flying Cross with 1 gold star. *Citation:* During the progress of an insurrection at Quilali, Nicaragua, 6, 7, and 8 January 1928, 1st Lt. Schilt, then a member of a marine expedition which had suffered severe losses in killed and wounded, volunteered under almost impossible conditions to evacuate the wounded by air and transport a relief commanding officer to assume charge of a very serious situation. 1st Lt. Schilt bravely undertook this dangerous and important task and, by taking off a total of 10 times in the rough, rolling street of a partially burning village, under hostile infantry fire on each occasion, succeeded in accomplishing his mission, thereby actually saving 3 lives and bringing supplies and aid to others in desperate need.

TRUESDELL, DONALD LeROY (Name officially changed to Truesdale)

Rank and organization: Corporal, U.S. Marine Corps. *Place and date:* Vicinity Constancia, near Coco River, northern Nicaragua, 24 April 1932. *Entered service at:* South Carolina. *Born:* 8 August 1906, Lugoff, S.C. *Citation:* Cpl. Truesdale was second in command of a Guardia Nacional Patrol in active operations against armed bandit forces in the vicinity of Constancia, near Coco River, northern Nicaragua, on 24 April 1932. While the patrol was in formation on the trail searching for a bandit group with which contact had just previously been made, a rifle grenade fell from its carrier and struck a rock, igniting the detonator. Several men close to the grenade at the time were in danger. Cpl. Truesdale, who was several yards away, could easily have sought cover and safety for himself. Knowing full well the grenade would explode within 2 or 3 seconds, he rushed for the grenade, grasped it in his right hand, and attempted to throw it away from the patrol. The grenade exploded in his hand blowing it off and inflicting serious multiple wounds about his body. Cpl. Truesdale, in taking the full shock of the explosion himself, saved the members of the patrol from loss of life or serious injury.

HAITIAN CAMPAIGN
1919 TO 1920

After the trouble in 1915, there was a period of comparative peace in the Haiti Republic, a period of road construction, general improvements and public works under the direction of the Gendarmerie. Active resistance to the system in operation provided an opening for Charlemagne Peralte, a Caco chief, to foment trouble. He organized groups of bandits and they, with the peasants forced to join his band, launched a series of attacks on the Gendarmerie. In northern Haiti many of the peasants fled to the towns for protection, abandoning their land and thus producing serious food shortages.

The Marine Brigade, requested to cooperate in suppressing the uprising, carried on an intensive campaign which was climaxed by one of the most daring exploits in Marine Corps history to that date. By a clever ruse, 2d Lt. Herman H. Hanneken was able to slip past the bandit outposts and finally gained entrance to Charlemagne's headquarters at the top of a distant hill. When the bandit chief became suspicious and his followers closed in with their arms ready, 2d Lt. Hanneken went into action. Supported by Cpl. Button who opened fire on the Caco guards, he succeeded in killing the leader and, with the group dispersed, repelled several Caco attacks throughout the night. He then took Charlemagne's body back to Grande Riviere for positive identification. Both these Marines received the Medal of Honor for their gallant action.

By the end of June in the following year, thousands of outlaws, constituting almost one-fifth of the population, had been captured or had surrendered, and the duty of policing the country was gradually shifted back to the Gendarmerie.

BUTTON, WILLIAM ROBERT

Rank and organization: Corporal, U.S. Marine Corps. *Entered service at:* St. Louis, Mo. *Born:* 3 December 1895, St. Louis, Mo. *G.O. No.:* 536, 10 June 1920. *Citation:* For extraordinary heroism and conspicuous gallantry and intrepidity in actual conflict with the enemy near Grande Riviere, Republic of Haiti, on the night of 31 October–1 November 1919, resulting in the death of Charlemagne Peralte, the supreme bandit chief in the Republic of Haiti, and the killing, capture and dispersal of about 1,200 of his outlaw followers. Cpl. William R. Button not only distinguished himself by his excellent judgment and leadership but also unhesitatingly exposed himself to great personal danger when the slightest error would have forfeited not only his life but the lives of the detachments of Gendarmerie under his command. The successful termination of his mission will undoubtedly prove of untold value to the Republic of Haiti.

HANNEKEN, HERMAN HENRY

Rank and organization: Second Lieutenant, U.S. Marine Corps. *Place and date:* Near Grande Riviere, Republic of Haiti, 31 October–1 November 1919. *Entered service at:* St. Louis, Mo. *Born:* 23 June 1893, St. Louis, Mo. *G.O. No.:* 536, 10 June 1920. *Other Navy awards:* Navy Cross with 1 gold star, Silver Star, Legion of Merit. *Citation:* For extraordinary heroism and conspicuous gallantry and intrepidity in actual conflict with the enemy near Grande Riviere, Republic of Haiti, on the night of 31 October–1 November 1919, resulting in the death of Charlemagne Peralte, the supreme bandit chief in the Republic of Haiti, and the killing, capture, and dispersal of about 1,200 of his outlaw followers. 2d Lt. Hanneken not only distinguished himself by his excellent judgment and leadership but also unhesitatingly exposed himself to great personal danger when the slightest error would have forfeited not only his life but the lives of the detachments of gendarmerie under his command. The successful termination of his mission will undoubtedly prove of untold value to the Republic of Haiti.

WORLD WAR
I

leave out

ADKINSON, JOSEPH B.

Rank and organization: Sergeant, U.S. Army, Company C, 119th Infantry, 30th Division. *Place and date:* Near Bellicourt, France, 29 September 1918. *Entered service at:* Memphis, Tenn. *Born:* 4 January 1892, Egypt, Tenn. *G.O. No.:* 59, W.D., 1919. *Citation:* When murderous machinegun fire at a range of 50 yards had made it impossible for his platoon to advance, and had caused the platoon to take cover, Sgt. Adkinson alone, with the greatest intrepidity, rushed across the 50 yards of open ground directly into the face of the hostile machinegun, kicked the gun from the parapet into the enemy trench, and at the point of the bayonet captured the 3 men manning the gun. The gallantry and quick decision of this soldier enabled the platoon to resume its advance.

ALLEX, JAKE

Rank and organization: Corporal, U.S. Army, Company H, 131st Infantry, 33d Division. *Place and date:* At Chipilly Ridge, France, 9 August 1918. *Entered service at:* Chicago, Ill. *Born:* 13 July 1887, Prizren, Serbia. *G.O. No.:* 44, W.D., 1919. *Citation:* At a critical point in the action, when all the officers with his platoon had become casualties, Cpl. Allex took command of the platoon and led it forward until the advance was stopped by fire from a machinegun nest. He then advanced alone for about 30 yards in the face of intense fire and attacked the nest. With his bayonet he killed 5 of the enemy, and when it was broken, used the butt of his rifle, capturing 15 prisoners.

ALLWORTH, EDWARD C.

Rank and organization: Captain, U.S. Army, 60th Infantry, 5th Division. *Place and date:* At Clery-le-Petit, France, 5 November 1918. *Entered service at:* Corvallis, Oreg. *Born:* 6 July 1887, Crawford, Wash. *G.O. No.:* 16, W.D., 1919. *Citation:* While his company was crossing the Meuse River and canal at a bridgehead opposite Clery-le-Petit, the bridge over the canal was destroyed by shell fire and Capt. Allworth's command became separated, part of it being on the east bank of the canal and the remainder on the west bank. Seeing his advance units making slow headway up the steep slope ahead, this officer mounted the canal bank and called for his men to follow. Plunging in he swam across the canal under fire from the enemy, followed by his men. Inspiring his men by his example of gallantry, he led them up the slope, joining his hard-pressed platoons in front. By his personal leadership he forced the enemy back for more than a kilometer, overcoming machinegun nests and capturing 100 prisoners, whose number exceeded that of the men in his command. The exceptional courage and leadership displayed by Capt. Allworth made possible the reestablishment of a bridgehead over the canal and the successful advance of other troops.

ANDERSON, JOHANNES S.

Rank and organization: First Sergeant, U.S. Army, Company B, 132d Infantry, 33d Division. *Place and date:* At Consenvoye, France, 8 October 1918. *Entered service at:* Chicago, Ill. *Birth:* Finland. *G.O. No.:* 16, W.D., 1919. *Citation:* While his company was being held up by intense artillery and machinegun fire, 1st Sgt. Anderson, without aid, voluntarily left the company and worked his way to the rear of the nest that was offering the most stubborn resistance. His advance was made through an open area and under constant hostile fire, but the mission was successfully accomplished, and he not only silenced the gun and captured it, but also brought back with him 23 prisoners.

*BAESEL, ALBERT E.

Rank and organization: Second Lieutenant, U.S. Army, 148th Infantry, 37th Division. *Place and date:* Near Ivoiry, France, 27 September 1918. *Entered service at:* Berea, Ohio. *Born:* 1892, Berea, Ohio. *G.O. No.:* 43, W.D., 1922. *Citation:* Upon hearing that a squad leader of his platoon had been severely wounded while attempting to capture an enemy machinegun nest about 200 yards in advance of the assault line and somewhat to the right, 2d Lt. Baesel requested permission to go to the rescue of the wounded corporal. After thrice repeating his request and permission having been reluctantly given, due to the heavy artillery, rifle, and machinegun fire, and heavy deluge of gas in which the company was at the time, accompanied by a volunteer, he worked his way forward, and reaching the wounded man, placed him upon his shoulders and was instantly killed by enemy fire.

BALCH, JOHN HENRY

Rank and organization: Pharmacist's Mate First Class, U.S. Navy. *Place and date:* Vierzy, France, and Somme-Py, France, 19 July and 5 October 1918. *Entered service at:* Kansas City, Mo. *Born:* 2 January 1896, Edgerton, Kans. *Citation:* For gallantry and intrepidity at the risk of his life above and beyond the call of duty, with the 6th Regiment, U.S. Marines, in action at Vierzy, on 19 July 1918. Balch unhesitatingly and fearlessly exposed himself to terrific machinegun and high-explosive fire to succor the wounded as they fell in the attack, leaving his dressing station voluntarily and keeping up the work all day and late into the night unceasingly for 16 hours. Also in the action at Somme-Py on 5 October 1918, he exhibited exceptional bravery in establishing an advanced dressing station under heavy shellfire.

BARGER, CHARLES D.

Rank and organization: Private First Class, U.S. Army, Company L, 354th Infantry, 89th Division. *Place and date:* Near Bois-de-Bantheville, France, 31 October 1918. *Entered service at:* Stotts City, Mo. *Birth:* Mount Vernon, Mo. *G.O. No.:* 20, W.D., 1919. *Citation:* Learning that 2 daylight patrols had been caught out in No Man's Land and were unable to return, Pfc. Barger and another stretcher bearer upon their own initiative made 2 trips 500 yards beyond our lines, under constant machinegun fire, and rescued 2 wounded officers.

*BARKELEY, DAVID B.

Rank and organization: Private, U.S. Army, Company A, 356th Infantry, 89th Division. *Place and date:* Near Pouilly, France, 9 November 1918. *Entered service at:* San Antonio, Tex. *Birth:* Laredo, Tex. *G.O. No.:* 20, W.D., 1919. *Citation:* When information was desired as to the enemy's position on the opposite side of the Meuse River, Pvt. Barkeley, with another soldier, volunteered without hesitation and swam the river to reconnoiter the exact location. He succeeded in reaching the opposite bank, despite the evident determination of the enemy to prevent a crossing. Having obtained his information, he again entered the water for his return, but before his goal was reached, he was seized with cramps and drowned.

BARKLEY, JOHN L.

Rank and organization: Private First Class, U.S. Army, Company K, 4th Infantry, 3d Division. *Place and date:* Near Cunel, France, 7 October 1918. *Entered service at:* Blairstown, Mo. *Born:* 28 August 1895, Blairstown, Mo. *G.O. No.:* 44, W.D., 1919. *Citation:* Pfc. Barkley, who was stationed in an observation post half a kilometer from the German line, on his own initiative repaired a captured enemy machinegun and mounted it in a disabled French tank near his post. Shortly afterward, when the enemy launched a counterattack against our forces, Pfc. Barkley got into the tank, waited under the hostile barrage until the enemy line was abreast of him and then opened fire, completely breaking up the counterattack and killing and wounding a large number of the enemy. Five minutes later an enemy 77-millimeter gun opened fire on the tank pointblank. One shell struck the drive wheel of the tank, but this soldier nevertheless remained in the tank and after the barrage ceased broke up a second enemy counterattack, thereby enabling our forces to gain and hold Hill 25.

BART, FRANK J.

Rank and organization: Private, U.S. Army, Company C, 9th Infantry, 2d Division. *Place and date:* Near Medeah Ferme, France, 3 October 1918. *Entered service at:* Newark, N.J. *Birth:* New York, N.Y. *G.O. No.:* 16, W.D., 1919. *Citation:* Pvt. Bart, being on duty as a company runner, when the advance was held up by machinegun fire voluntarily picked up an automatic rifle, ran out ahead of the line, and silenced a hostile machinegun nest, killing the German gunners. The advance then continued, and when it was again hindered shortly afterward by another machinegun nest this courageous soldier repeated his bold exploit by putting the second machinegun out of action.

*BLACKWELL, ROBERT L.

Rank and organization: Private, U.S. Army, Company K, 119th Infantry, 30th Division. *Place and date:* Near St. Souplet, France, 11 October 1918. *Entered service at:* Hurdle Mills, N.C. *Birth:* Person County, N.C. *G.O. No.:* 13, W.D., 1919. *Citation:* When his platoon was almost surrounded by the enemy and his platoon commander asked for volunteers to carry a message calling for reinforcements, Pvt. Blackwell volunteered for this mission, well knowing the extreme danger connected with it. In attempting to get through the heavy shell and machinegun fire this gallant soldier was killed.

*BLECKLEY, ERWIN R. (Air Mission)

Rank and organization: Second Lieutenant, U.S. Army Air Corps, 130th Field Artillery, observer 50th Aero Squadron, Air Service. *Place and date:* Near Binarville, France, 6 October 1918. *Entered service at:* Wichita, Kans. *Birth:* Wichita, Kans. *G.O. No.:* 56, W.D., 1922. *Citation:* 2d Lt. Bleckley, with his pilot, 1st Lt. Harold E. Goettler, Air Service, left the airdrome late in the afternoon on their second trip to drop supplies to a battalion of the 77th Division, which had been cut off by the enemy in the Argonne Forest. Having been subjected on the first trip to violent fire from the enemy, they attempted on the second trip to come still lower in order to get the packages even more precisely on the designated spot. In the course of his mission the plane was brought down by enemy rifle and machinegun fire from the ground, resulting in fatal wounds to 2d Lt. Bleckley, who died before he could be taken to a hospital. In attempting and performing this mission 2d Lt. Bleckley showed the highest possible contempt of personal danger, devotion to duty, courage, and valor.

BOONE, JOEL THOMPSON

Rank and organization: Lieutenant (Medical Corps), U.S. Navy. *Place and date:* Vicinity Vierzy, France, 19 July 1918. *Entered service at:* St. Clair, Pa. *Born:* 2 August 1889, St. Clair, Pa. *Citation:* For extraordinary heroism, conspicuous gallantry, and intrepidity while serving with the 6th Regiment, U.S. Marines, in actual conflict with the enemy. With absolute disregard for personal safety, ever conscious and mindful of the suffering fallen, Surg. Boone, leaving the shelter of a ravine, went forward onto the open field where there was no protection and despite the extreme enemy fire of all calibers, through a heavy mist of gas, applied dressings and first aid to wounded marines. This occurred southeast of Vierzy, near the cemetery, and on the road south from that town. When the dressings and supplies had been exhausted, he went through a heavy barrage of large-caliber shells, both high explosive and gas, to replenish these supplies, returning quickly with a sidecar load, and administered them in saving the lives of the wounded. A second trip, under the same conditions and for the same purpose, was made by Surg. Boone later that day.

BRADLEY, WILLIS WINTER, JR.

Rank and organization: Commander, U.S. Navy. *Born:* 28 June 1884, Ransomville, N.Y. *Appointed from:* North Dakota. *Citation:* For extraordinary heroism and devotion to duty while serving on the U.S.S. *Pittsburgh*, at the time of an accidental explosion of ammunition on that vessel. On 23 July 1917, some saluting cartridge cases were being reloaded in the after casemate: through an accident an explosion occurred. Comdr. Bradley (then Lieutenant), who was about to enter the casemate, was blown back by the explosion and rendered momentarily unconscious, but while still dazed, crawled into the casemate to extinguish burning materials in dangerous proximity to a considerable amount of powder, thus preventing further explosions.

BRONSON, DEMING

Rank and organization: First Lieutenant, U.S. Army, Company H, 364th Infantry, 91st Division. *Place and date:* Near Eclisfontaine, France, 26–27 September 1918. *Entered service at:* Seattle, Wash. *Born:* 8 July 1894, Rhinelander, Wis. *G.O. No.:* 12 W.D., 1929. *Citation:* For conspicuous gallantry and intrepidity above and beyond the call of duty in action with the enemy. On the morning of 26 September, during the advance of the 364th Infantry, 1st Lt. Bronson was struck by an exploding enemy handgrenade, receiving deep cuts on his face and the back of his head. He nevertheless participated in the action which resulted in the capture of an enemy dugout from which a great number of prisoners were taken. This was effected with difficulty and under extremely hazardous conditions because it was necessary to advance without the advantage of cover and, from an exposed position, throw handgrenades and phosphorous bombs to compel the enemy to surrender. On the afternoon of the same day he was painfully wounded in the left arm by an enemy rifle bullet, and after receiving first aid treatment he was directed to the rear. Disregarding these instructions, 1st Lt. Bronson remained on duty with his company through the night although suffering from severe pain and shock. On the morning of 27 September, his regiment resumed its attack, the object being the village of Eclisfontaine. Company H, to which 1st Lt. Bronson was assigned, was left in support of the attacking line, Company E being in the line. He gallantly joined that company in spite of his wounds and engaged with it in the capture of the village. After the capture he remained with Company E and participated with it in the capture of an enemy machinegun, he himself killing the enemy gunner. Shortly after this encounter the company was compelled to retire due to the heavy enemy artillery barrage. During this retirement 1st Lt. Bronson, who was the last man to leave the advanced position, was again wounded in both arms by an enemy high-explosive shell. He was then assisted to cover by another officer who applied first aid. Although bleeding profusely and faint from the loss of blood, 1st Lt. Bronson remained with the survivors of the company throughout the night of the second day, refusing to go to the rear for treatment. His conspicuous gallantry and spirit of self-sacrifice were a source of great inspiration to the members of the entire command.

CALL, DONALD M.

Rank and organization: Corporal, U.S. Army, 344th Battalion, Tank Corps. *Place and date:* Near Varennes, France, 26 September 1918. *Entered service at:* France. *Born:* 29 November 1892, New York, N.Y. *G.O. No.:* 13, W.D., 1919. *Citation:* During an operation against enemy machinegun nests west of Varennes, Cpl. Call was in a tank with an officer when half of the turret was knocked off by a direct artillery hit. Choked by gas from the high-explosive shell, he left the tank and took cover in a shellhole 30 yards away. Seeing that the officer did not follow, and thinking that he might be alive, Cpl. Call returned to the tank under intense machinegun and shell fire and carried the officer over a mile under machinegun and sniper fire to safety.

CANN, TEDFORD H.

Rank and organization: Seaman, U.S. Navy. *Born:* 3 September 1897, Bridgeport, Conn. *Accredited to:* New York. *G.O. No.:* 366, 1918. *Citation:* For courageous conduct while serving on board the U.S.S. *May*, 5 November 1917. Cann found a leak in a flooded compartment and closed it at the peril of his life, thereby unquestionably saving the ship.

*CHILES, MARCELLUS H.

Rank and organization: Captain, U.S. Army, 356th Infantry, 89th Division. *Place and date:* Near Le Champy Bas, France, 3 November 1918. *Entered service at:* Denver, Colo. *Birth:* Eureka Springs, Ark. *G.O. No.:* 20, W.D., 1919. *Citation:* When his battalion, of which he had just taken command, was halted by machinegun fire from the front and left flank, he picked up the rifle of a dead soldier and, calling on his men to follow led the advance across a stream, waist deep, in the face of the machinegun fire. Upon reaching the opposite bank this gallant officer was seriously wounded in the abdomen by a sniper, but before permitting himself to be evacuated he made complete arrangements for turning over his command to the next senior officer, and under the inspiration of his fearless leadership his battalion reached its objective. Capt. Chiles died shortly after reaching the hospital.

*COLYER, WILBUR E.

Rank and organization: Sergeant, U.S. Army, Company A, 1st Engineers, 1st Division. *Place and date:* Near Verdun, France, 9 October 1918. *Entered service at:* South Ozone, Long Island, N.Y. *Birth:* Brooklyn, N.Y. *G.O. No.:* 20, W.D., 1919. *Citation:* Volunteering with 2 other soldiers to locate machinegun nests, Sgt. Colyer advanced on the hostile positions to a point where he was half surrounded by the nests, which were in ambush. He killed the gunner of one gun with a captured German grenade and then turned this gun on the other nests, silencing all of them before he returned to his platoon. He was later killed in action.

*COSTIN, HENRY G.

Rank and organization: Private, U.S. Army, Company H, 115th Infantry, 29th Division. *Place and date:* Near Bois-de-Consenvoye, France, 8 October 1918. *Entered service at:* Baltimore, Md. *Birth:* Baltimore, Md. *G.O. No.:* 34, W.D., 1919. *Citation:* When the advance of his platoon had been held up by machinegun fire and a request was made for an automatic rifle team to charge the nest, Pvt. Costin was the first to volunteer. Advancing with his team, under terrific fire of enemy artillery, machineguns, and trench mortars, he continued after all his comrades had become casualties and he himself had been seriously wounded. He operated his rifle until he collapsed. His act resulted in the capture of about 100 prisoners and several machineguns. He succumbed from the effects of his wounds shortly after the accomplishment of his heroic deed.

COVINGTON, JESSE WHITFIELD

Rank and organization: Ship's Cook Third Class, U.S. Navy. *Place and date:* At sea aboard the U.S.S. *Stewart*, 17 April 1918. *Entered service at:* California. *Born:* 16 September 1889, Haywood, Tenn. *G.O. No.:* 403, 1918. *Citation:* For extraordinary heroism following internal explosion of the *Florence H.* The sea in the vicinity of wreckage was covered by a mass of boxes of smokeless powder, which were repeatedly exploding. Jesse W. Covington, of the U.S.S. *Stewart*, plunged overboard to rescue a survivor who was surrounded by powder boxes and too exhausted to help himself, fully realizing that similar powder boxes in the vicinity were continually exploding and that he was thereby risking his life in saving the life of this man.

CUKELA, LOUIS (Army Medal)

Rank and organization: Sergeant, U.S. Marine Corps, 66th Company, 5th Regiment. *Place and date:* Near Villers-Cotterets, France, 18 July 1918. *Entered service at:* Minneapolis, Minn. *Born:* 1 May 1888, Sebenes, Austria. *G.O. No.:* 34, W.D., 1919. (Also received Navy Medal of Honor.) *Citation:* When his company, advancing through a wood, met with strong resistance from an enemy strong point, Sgt. Cukela crawled out from the flank and made his way toward the German lines in the face of heavy fire, disregarding the warnings of his comrades. He succeeded in getting behind the enemy position and rushed a machinegun emplacement, killing or driving off the crew with his bayonet. With German handgrenades he then bombed out the remaining portion of the strong point, capturing 4 men and 2 damaged machineguns.

CUKELA, LOUIS (Navy Medal)

Rank and organization: Sergeant, U.S. Marine Corps, 66th Company, 5th Regiment. *Born:* 1 May 1888, Sebenes, Austria. *Accredited to:* Minnesota. (Also received Army Medal of Honor.) *Citation:* For extraordinary heroism while serving with the 66th Company, 5th Regiment, during action in the Forest de Retz, near Viller-Cottertes, France, 18 July 1918. Sgt. Cukela advanced alone against an enemy strong point that was holding up his line. Disregarding the warnings of his comrades, he crawled out from the flank in the face of heavy fire and worked his way to the rear of the enemy position. Rushing a machinegun emplacement, he killed or drove off the crew with his bayonet, bombed out the remaining part of the strong point with German handgrenades and captured 2 machineguns and 4 men.

*DILBOY, GEORGE

Rank and organization: Private First Class, U.S. Army, Company H, 103d Infantry, 26th Division. *Place and date:* Near Belleau, France, 18 July 1918. *Entered service at:* Keene, N.H. *Birth:* Greece. *G.O. No.:* 13, W.D., 1919. *Citation:* After his platoon had gained its objective along a railroad embankment, Pfc. Dilboy, accompanying his platoon leader to reconnoiter the ground beyond, was suddenly fired upon by an enemy machinegun from 100 yards. From a standing position on the railroad track, fully exposed to view, he opened fire at once, but failing to silence the gun, rushed forward with his bayonet fixed, through a wheat field toward the gun emplacement, falling within 25 yards of the gun with his right leg nearly severed above the knee and with several bullet holes in his body. With undaunted courage he continued to fire into the emplacement from a prone position, killing 2 of the enemy and dispersing the rest of the crew.

DONALDSON, MICHAEL A.

Rank and organization: Sergeant, U.S. Army, Company I, 165th Infantry, 42d Division. *Place and date:* At Sommerance-Landres-et St. Georges Road, France, 14 October 1918. *Entered service at:* Haverstraw, N.Y. *Born:* 1884, Haverstraw, N.Y. *G.O. No.:* 9, W.D., 1923. *Citation:* The advance of his regiment having been checked by intense machinegun fire of the enemy, who were entrenched on the crest of a hill before Landres-et St. Georges, his company retired to a sunken road to reorganize their position, leaving several of their number wounded near the enemy lines. Of his own volition, in broad daylight and under direct observation of the enemy and with utter disregard for his own safety, he advanced to the crest of the hill, rescued one of his wounded comrades, and returned under withering fire to his own lines, repeating his splendidly heroic act until he had brought in all the men, 6 in number.

F

DONOVAN, WILLIAM JOSEPH

Rank and organization: Lieutenant Colonel, U.S. Army, 165th Infantry, 42d Division. *Place and date:* Near Landres-et-St. Georges, France, 14–15 October 1918. *Entered service at:* Buffalo, N.Y. *Born:* 1 January 1883, Buffalo, N.Y. *G.O., No.:* 56, W.D., 1922. *Citation:* Lt. Col. Donovan personally led the assaulting wave in an attack upon a very strongly organized position, and when our troops were suffering heavy casualties he encouraged all near him by his example, moving among his men in exposed positions, reorganizing decimated platoons, and accompanying them forward in attacks. When he was wounded in the leg by machine-gun bullets, he refused to be evacuated and continued with his unit until it withdrew to a less exposed position.

DOZIER, JAMES C.

Rank and organization: First Lieutenant, U.S. Army, Company G, 118th Infantry, 30th Division. *Place and date:* Near Montbrehain, France, 8 October 1918. *Entered service at:* Rock Hill, S.C. *Born:* 17 February 1885, Galivants Ferry, N.C. *G.O. No.:* 16, W.D., 1919. *Citation:* In command of 2 platoons, 1st. Lt. Dozier was painfully wounded in the shoulder early in the attack, but he continued to lead his men, displaying the highest bravery and skill. When his command was held up by heavy machinegun fire, he disposed his men in the best cover available and with a soldier continued forward to attack a machinegun nest. Creeping up to the position in the face of intense fire, he killed the entire crew with handgrenades and his pistol and a little later captured a number of Germans who had taken refuge in a dugout nearby.

*DUNN, PARKER F.

Rank and organization: Private First Class, U.S. Army, Company A, 312th Infantry, 78th Division. *Place and date:* Near Grand-Pre, France, 23 October 1918. *Entered service at:* Albany, N.Y. *Birth:* Albany, N.Y. *G.O. No.:* 49, W.D., 1922. *Citation:* When his battalion commander found it necessary to send a message to a company in the attacking line and hesitated to order a runner to make the trip because of the extreme danger involved, Pfc. Dunn, a member of the intelligence section, volunteered for the mission. After advancing but a short distance across a field swept by artillery and machinegun fire, he was wounded, but continued on and fell wounded a second time. Still undaunted, he persistently attempted to carry out his mission until he was killed by a machinegun bullet before reaching the advance line.

EDWARDS, DANIEL R.

Rank and organization: Private First Class, U.S. Army, Company C, 3d Machine Gun Battalion, 1st Division. *Place and date:* Near Soissons, France, 18 July 1918. *Entered service at:* Bruceville, Tex. *Born:* 9 April 1897, Moorville, Tex. *G.O. No.:* 14, W.D., 1923. *Citation:* Reporting for duty from hospital where he had been for several weeks under treatment for numerous and serious wounds and although suffering intense pain from a shattered arm, he crawled alone into an enemy trench for the purpose of capturing or killing enemy soldiers known to be concealed therein. He killed 4 of the men and took the remaining 4 men prisoners; while conducting them to the rear one of the enemy was killed by a high explosive enemy shell which also completely shattered 1 of Pfc. Edwards' legs, causing him to be immediately evacuated to the hospital. The bravery of Pfc. Edwards, now a tradition in his battalion because of his previous gallant acts, again caused the morale of his comrades to be raised to high pitch.

EGGERS, ALAN LOUIS

Rank and organization: Sergeant, U.S. Army, Machine Gun Company, 107th Infantry, 27th Division. *Place and date:* Near Le Catelet, France, 29 September 1918. *Entered service at:* Summit, N.J. *Birth:* Saranac Lake, N.Y. *G.O. No.:* 20, W.D., 1919. *Citation:* Becoming separated from their platoon by a smoke barrage, Sgt. Eggers, Sgt. John C. Latham and Cpl. Thomas E. O'Shea took cover in a shell hole well within the enemy's lines. Upon hearing a call for help from an American tank, which had become disabled 30 yards from them, the 3 soldiers left their shelter and started toward the tank, under heavy fire from German machineguns and trench mortars. In crossing the fireswept area Cpl. O'Shea was mortally wounded, but his companions, undeterred, proceeded to the tank, rescued a wounded officer, and assisted 2 wounded soldiers to cover in a sap of a nearby trench. Sgt. Eggers and Sgt. Latham then returned to the tank in the face of the violent fire, dismounted a Hotchkiss gun, and took it back to where the wounded men were, keeping off the enemy all day by effective use of the gun and later bringing it, with the wounded men, back to our lines under cover of darkness.

ELLIS, MICHAEL B.

Rank and organization: Sergeant, U.S. Army, Company C, 28th Infantry, 1st Division. *Place and date:* Near Exermont, France, 5 October 1918. *Entered service at:* East St. Louis, Ill. *Born:* 28 October 1894, St. Louis, Mo. *G.O. No.:* 74, W.D., 1919. *Citation:* During the entire day's engagement he operated far in advance of the first wave of his company, voluntarily undertaking most dangerous missions and singlehandedly attacking and reducing machinegun nests. Flanking one emplacement, he killed 2 of the enemy with rifle fire and captured 17 others. Later he singlehandedly advanced under heavy fire and captured 27 prisoners, including 2 officers and 6 machineguns, which had been holding up the advance of the company. The captured officers indicated the locations of 4 other machineguns, and he in turn captured these, together with their crews, at all times showing marked heroism and fearlessness.

FORREST, ARTHUR J.

Rank and organization: Sergeant, U.S. Army, Company D, 354th Infantry, 89th Division. *Place and date:* Near Remonville, France, 1 November 1918. *Entered service at:* Hannibal, Mo. *Birth:* St. Louis, Mo. *G.O. No.:* 50, W.D., 1919. *Citation:* When the advance of his company was stopped by bursts of fire from a nest of 6 enemy machineguns, without being discovered, he worked his way singlehanded to a point within 50 yards of the machinegun nest. Charging, singlehanded, he drove out the enemy in disorder, thereby protecting the advance platoon from annihilating fire, and permitting the resumption of the advance of his company.

FOSTER, GARY EVANS

Rank and organization: Sergeant, U.S. Army, Company F, 118th Infantry, 30th Division. *Place and date:* Near Montbrehain, France, 8 October 1918. *Entered service at:* Inman, S.C. *Birth:* Spartanburg, S.C. *G.O. No.:* 16, W.D., 1919. *Citation:* When his company was held up by violent machinegun fire from a sunken road, Sgt. Foster with an officer went forward to attack the hostile machinegun nests. The officer was wounded, but Sgt. Foster continued on alone in the face of the heavy fire and by effective use of handgrenades and his pistol killed several of the enemy and captured 18.

FUNK, JESSE N.

Rank and organization: Private First Class, U.S. Army, Company L, 354th Infantry, 89th Division. *Place and date:* Near Bois-de-Bantheville, France, 31 October 1918. *Entered service at:* Calhan, Colo. *Born:* 20 August 1888, New Hampton, Mo. *G.O. No.:* 20, W.D., 1919. *Citation:* Learning that 2 daylight patrols had been caught out in No Man's Land and were unable to return, Pfc. Funk and another stretcher bearer, upon their own initiative, made 2 trips 500 yards beyond our lines, under constant machinegun fire, and rescued 2 wounded officers.

FURLONG, HAROLD A.

Rank and organization: First Lieutenant, U.S. Army, 353d Infantry, 89th Division. *Place and date:* Near Bantheville, France, 1 November 1918. *Entered service at:* Detroit, Mich. *Birth:* Pontiac, Mich. *G.O. No.:* 16, W.D., 1919. *Citation:* Immediately after the opening of the attack in the Bois-de-Bantheville, when his company was held up by severe machinegun fire from the front, which killed his company commander and several soldiers, 1st. Lt. Furlong moved out in advance of the line with great courage and coolness, crossing an open space several hundred yards wide. Taking up a position behind the line of the machineguns, he closed in on them, one at a time, killing a number of the enemy with his rifle, putting 4 machinegun nests out of action, and driving 20 German prisoners into our lines.

GAFFNEY, FRANK

Rank and organization: Private First Class, U.S. Army, Company G, 108th Infantry, 27th Division. *Place and date:* Near Ronssoy, France, 29 September 1918. *Entered service at:* Niagara Falls, N.Y. *Birth:* Buffalo, N.Y. *G.O. No.:* 20, W.D., 1919. *Citation:* Pfc. Gaffney, an automatic rifleman, pushing forward alone, after all the other members of his squad had been killed, discovered several Germans placing a heavy machinegun in position. He killed the crew, captured the gun, bombed several dugouts, and, after killing 4 more of the enemy with his pistol, held the position until reinforcements came up, when 80 prisoners were captured.

*GOETTLER, HAROLD ERNEST (Air Mission)

Rank and organization: First Lieutenant, pilot, U.S. Army Air Corps, 50th Aero Squadron, Air Service. *Place and date:* Near Binarville, France, 6 October 1918. *Entered service at:* Chicago, Ill. *Born:* 21 July 1890, Chicago, Ill. *G.O. No.:* 56, W.D., 1922. *Citation:* 1st. Lt. Goettler, with his observer, 2d Lt. Erwin R. Bleckley, 130th Field Artillery, left the airdrome late in the afternoon on their second trip to drop supplies to a battalion of the 77th Division which had been cut off by the enemy in the Argonne Forest. Having been subjected on the first trip to violent fire from the enemy, they attempted on the second trip to come still lower in order to get the packages even more precisely on the designated spot. In the course of this mission the plane was brought down by enemy rifle and machinegun fire from the ground, resulting in the instant death of 1st. Lt. Goettler. In attempting and performing this mission 1st. Lt. Goettler showed the highest possible contempt of personal danger, devotion to duty, courage and valor.

GRAVES, ORA

Rank and organization: Seaman, U.S. Navy. *Born:* 26 July 1896, Los Animas, Colo. *Accredited to:* Nebraska. *G.O. No.:* 366, 1918. *Citation:* For extraordinary heroism on 23 July 1917, while the U.S.S. *Pittsburgh* was proceding to Buenos Aires, Argentina. A 3-inch saluting charge exploded, causing the death of C. T. Lyles, seaman. Upon the explosion, Graves was blown to the deck, but soon recovered and discovered burning waste on the deck. He put out the burning waste while the casemate was filled with clouds of smoke, knowing that there was more powder there which might explode.

GREGORY, EARL D.

Rank and organization: Sergeant, U.S. Army, Headquarters Company, 116th Infantry, 29th Division. *Place and date:* At Bois-de-Consenvoye, north of Verdun, France, 8 October 1918. *Entered service at:* Chase City, Va. *Birth:* Chase City, Va. *G.O. No.:* 34, W.D., 1919. *Citation:* With the remark "I will get them," Sgt. Gregory seized a rifle and a trench-mortar shell, which he used as a handgrenade, left his detachment of the trench-mortar platoon, and advancing ahead of the infantry, captured a machinegun and 3 of the enemy. Advancing still farther from the machinegun nest, he captured a 7.5-centimeter mountain howitzer and, entering a dugout in the immediate vicinity, singlehandedly captured 19 of the enemy.

GUMPERTZ, SYDNEY G.

Rank and organization: First Sergeant, U.S. Army, Company E, 132d Infantry, 33d Division. *Place and date:* In the Bois-de-Forges, France, 29 September 1918. *Entered service at:* Chicago, Ill. *Born:* 24 October 1879, San Raphael, Calif. *G.O. No.:* 16, W.D., 1919. *Citation:* When the advancing line was held up by machinegun fire, 1st Sgt. Gumpertz left the platoon of which he was in command and started with 2 other soldiers through a heavy barrage toward the machinegun nest. His 2 companions soon became casualties from bursting shells, but 1st Sgt. Gumpertz continued on alone in the face of direct fire from the machinegun, jumped into the nest and silenced the gun, capturing 9 of the crew.

*HALL, THOMAS LEE

Rank and organization: Sergeant, U.S. Army, Company G, 118th Infantry, 30th Division. *Place and date:* Near Montbrehain, France, 8 October 1918. *Entered service at:* Fort Mill, S.C. *Birth:* Fort Mill, S.C., *G.O. No.:* 50, W.D., 1919. *Citation:* Having overcome 2 machinegun nests under his skillful leadership, Sgt. Hall's platoon was stopped 800 yards from its final objective by machinegun fire of particular intensity. Ordering his men to take cover in a sunken road, he advanced alone on the enemy machinegun post and killed 5 members of the crew with his bayonet and thereby made possible the further advance of the line. While attacking another machinegun nest later in the day this gallant soldier was mortally wounded.

HAMMANN, CHARLES HAZELTINE

Rank and organization: Ensign, U.S. Naval Reserve Fleet. *Born:* 16 March 1892, Baltimore, Md. *Appointed from:* Maryland. *Citation:* For extraordinary heroism as a pilot of a seaplane on 21 August 1918, when with 3 other planes Ens. Hammann took part in a patrol and attacked a superior force of enemy land planes. In the course of the engagement which followed the plane of Ens. George M. Ludlow was shot down and fell in the water 5 miles off Pola. Ens. Hammann immediately dived down and landed on the water close alongside the disabled machine, where he took Ludlow on board. Although his machine was not designed for the double load to which it was subjected, and although there was danger of attack by Austrian planes, he made his way to Porto Corsini.

HATLER, M. WALDO

Rank and organization: Sergeant, U.S. Army, Company B, 356th Infantry, 89th Division. *Place and date:* Near Pouilly, France, 8 November 1918. *Entered service at:* Neosho, Mo. *Born:* 6 January 1894, Bolivar, Mo. *G.O. No.:* 74, W.D., 1919. *Citation:* When volunteers were called for to secure information as to the enemy's position on the opposite bank of the Meuse River, Sgt. Hatler was the first to offer his services for this dangerous mission. Swimming across the river, he succeeded in reaching the German lines, after another soldier, who had started with him, had been seized with cramps and drowned in midstream. Alone he carefully and courageously reconnoitered the enemy's positions, which were held in force, and again successfully swam the river, bringing back information of great value.

HAYDEN, DAVID E.

Rank and organization: Hospital Apprentice First Class, U.S. Navy, serving with the 2d Battalion, 6th Regiment, U.S. Marines. *Place and date:* Thiaucourt, France, 15 September 1918. *Entered service at:* Texas. *Born:* 2 October 1897 Florence, Tex. *Citation:* For gallantry and intrepidity at the risk of his life above and beyond the call of duty. During the advance, when Cpl. Creed was mortally wounded while crossing an open field swept by machinegun fire, Hayden unhesitatingly ran to his assistance and, finding him so severely wounded as to require immediate attention, disregarded his own personal safety to dress the wound under intense machinegun fire, and then carried the wounded man back to a place of safety.

HAYS, GEORGE PRICE

Rank and organization: First Lieutenant, U.S. Army 10th Field Artillery, 3d Division. *Place and date:* Near Greves Farm, France, 14–15 July 1918. *Entered service at:* Okarche, Oklahoma. *Born:* 27 September 1892, China. *G.O. No.:* 34, W.D., 1919. *Citation:* At the very outset of the unprecedented artillery bombardment by the enemy, his line of communication was destroyed beyond repair. Despite the hazard attached to the mission of runner, he immediately set out to establish contact with the neighboring post of command and further establish liaison with 2 French batteries, visiting their position so frequently that he was mainly responsible for the accurate fire therefrom. While thus engaged, 7 horses were shot under him and he was severely wounded. His activity under most severe fire was an important factor in checking the advance of the enemy.

*HERIOT, JAMES D.

Rank and organization: Corporal, U.S. Army, Company I, 118th Infantry, 30th Division. *Place and date:* At Vaux-Andigny, France, 12 October 1918. *Entered service at:* Providence, S.C. *Birth:* Providence, S.C. *G.O. No.:* 13, W.D., 1919. *Citation:* Cpl. Heriot, with 4 other soldiers, organized a combat group and attacked an enemy machine-gun nest which had been inflicting heavy casualties on his company. In the advance 2 of his men were killed, and because of the heavy fire from all sides the remaining 2 sought shelter. Unmindful of the hazard attached to his mission, Cpl. Heriot, with fixed bayonet, alone charged the machinegun, making his way through the fire for a distance of 30 yards and forcing the enemy to surrender. During this exploit he received several wounds in the arm, and later in the same day, while charging another nest, he was killed.

HILL, RALYN M.

Rank and organization: Corporal, U.S. Army, Company H, 129th Infantry, 33d Division. *Place and date:* Near Donnevoux, France, 7 October 1918. *Entered service at:* Oregon, Ill. *Born:* 6 May 1899, Lindenwood, Ill. *G.O. No.:* 34, W.D., 1919. *Citation:* Seeing a French airplane fall out of control on the enemy side of the Meuse River with its pilot injured, Cpl. Hill voluntarily dashed across the footbridge to the side of the wounded man and, taking him on his back, started back to his lines. During the entire exploit he was subjected to murderous fire of enemy machineguns and artillery, but he successfully accomplished his mission and brought his man to a place of safety, a distance of several hundred yards.

HILTON, RICHMOND H.

Rank and organization: Sergeant, U.S. Army, Company M, 118th Infantry, 30th Division. *Place and date:* At Brancourt, France, 11 October 1918. *Entered service at:* Westville, S.C. *Born:* 8 October 1898,

Westville, S.C. *G.O. No.:* 16, W.D., 1919. *Citation:* While Sgt. Hilton's company was advancing through the village of Brancourt it was held up by intense enfilading fire from a machinegun. Discovering that this fire came from a machinegun nest among shell holes at the edge of the town, Sgt. Hilton, accompanied by a few other soldiers, but well in advance of them, pressed on toward this position, firing with his rifle until his ammunition was exhausted, and then with his pistol, killing 6 of the enemy and capturing 10. In the course of this daring exploit he received a wound from a bursting shell, which resulted in the loss of his arm.

HOFFMAN, CHARLES F. (Army Medal)

Rank and organization: Gunnery Sergeant, U.S. Marine Corps, 49th Company, 5th Regiment, 2d Division, (Name changed to Ernest August Janson, see p. 444.) *Place and date:* Near Chateau-Thierry, France, 6 June 1918. *Entered service at:* Brooklyn, N.Y. *Born:* 17 August 1878, New York, N.Y. *G.O. No.:* 34, W.D., 1919. (Also received Navy Medal of Honor.) *Citation:* Immediately after the company to which he belonged had reached its objective on Hill 142, several hostile counterattacks were launched against the line before the new position had been consolidated. G/Sgt. Hoffman was attempting to organize a position on the north slope of the hill when he saw 12 of the enemy, armed with 5 light machineguns, crawling toward his group. Giving the alarm, he rushed the hostile detachment, bayoneted the 2 leaders, and forced the others to flee, abandoning their guns. His quick action, initiative, and courage drove the enemy from a position from which they could have swept the hill with machinegun fire and forced the withdrawal of our troops.

HOLDERMAN, NELSON M.

Rank and organization: Captain, U.S. Army, 307th Infantry, 77th Division. *Place and date:* Northeast of Binarville, in the forest of Argonne, France, 2–8 October 1918. *Entered service at:* Santa Ana, Calif. *Birth:* Trumbell, Nebr. *G.O. No.:* 11, W.D., 1921. *Citation:* Capt. Holderman commanded a company of a battalion which was cut off and surrounded by the enemy. He was wounded on 4, 5, and 7 October, but throughout the entire period, suffering great pain and subjected to fire of every character, he continued personally to lead and encourage the officers and men under his command with unflinching courage and with distinguished success. On 6 October, in a wounded condition, he rushed through enemy machinegun and shell fire and carried 2 wounded men to a place of safety.

*INGRAM, OSMOND K.

Rank and organization: Gunner's Mate First Class, U.S. Navy. *Born:* 4 August 1887, Alabama. *Accredited to:* Alabama. *Citation:* For extraordinary heroism in the presence of the enemy on the occasion of the torpedoing of the *Cassin*, on 15 October 1917. While the *Cassin* was searching for the submarine, Ingram sighted the torpedo coming, and realizing that it might strike the ship aft in the vicinity of the depth charges, ran aft with the intention of releasing the depth charges before the torpedo could reach the *Cassin*. The torpedo struck the ship before he could accomplish his purpose and Ingram was killed by the explosion. The depth charges exploded immediately afterward. His life was sacrificed in an attempt to save the ship and his shipmates, as the damage to the ship would have been much less if he had been able to release the depth charges.

IZAC, EDOUARD VICTOR MICHEL

Rank and organization: Lieutenant, U.S. Navy. *Place and date:* Aboard German submarine *U–90* as prisoner of war, 21 May 1918. *Entered service at:* Illinois. *Born:* 18 December 1891, Cresco, Howard County, Iowa. *Citation:* When the U.S.S. *President Lincoln* was attacked and sunk by the German submarine *U–90*, on 21 May 1918, Lt. Izac was captured and held as a prisoner on board the *U–90* until the return of the submarine to Germany, when he was confined in the prison camp. During his stay on the *U–90* he obtained information of the movements of German submarines which was so important that he determined to escape, with a view to making this information available to the U.S. and Allied Naval authorities. In attempting to carry out this plan, he jumped through the window of a rapidly moving train at the imminent risk of death, not only from the nature of the act itself but from the fire of the armed German soldiers who were guarding him. Having been recaptured and reconfined, Lt. Izac made a second and successful attempt to escape, breaking his way through barbed-wire fences and deliberately drawing the fire of the armed guards in the hope of permitting others to escape during the confusion. He made his way through the mountains of southwestern Germany, having only raw vegetables for food, and at the end, swam the River Rhine during the night in the immediate vicinity of German sentries.

JANSON, ERNEST AUGUST (Navy Medal)

Rank and organization: Gunnery Sergeant, U.S. Marine Corps, 49th Company. (Served under name of Charles F. Hoffman, see p. 443.) *Born:* 17 August 1878, New York, N.Y. *Accredited to:* New York. (Also received Army Medal of Honor.) *Citation:* For conspicuous gallantry and intrepidity above and beyond the call of duty in action with the enemy near Chateau-Thierry, France, 6 June 1918. Immediately after the company to which G/Sgt. Janson belonged, had reached its objective on Hill 142, several hostile counterattacks were launched against the line before the new position had been consolidated. G/Sgt. Janson was attempting to organize a position on the north slope of the hill when he saw 12 of the enemy, armed with 5 light machineguns, crawling toward his group. Giving the alarm, he rushed the hostile detachment, bayoneted the 2 leaders, and forced the others to flee, abandoning their guns. His quick action, initiative and courage drove the enemy from a position from which they could have swept the hill with machinegun fire and forced the withdrawal of our troops.

JOHNSTON, HAROLD I.

Rank and organization: Sergeant (then Private First Class), U.S. Army, Company A, 356th Infantry, 89th Division. *Place and date:* Near Pouilly, France, 9 November 1918. *Entered service at:* Chicago, Ill. *Birth:* Kendell, Kans. *G.O. No.:* 20, W.D., 1919. *Citation:* When information was desired as to the enemy's position on the opposite side of the Meuse River, Sgt. Johnston, with another soldier, volunteered without hesitation and swam the river to reconnoiter the exact location of the enemy. He succeeded in reaching the opposite bank, despite the evident determination of the enemy to prevent a crossing. Having obtained his information, he again entered the water for his return. This was accomplished after a severe struggle which so exhausted him that he had to be assisted from the water, after which he rendered his report of the exploit.

KARNES, JAMES E.

Rank and organization: Sergeant, U.S. Army, Company D, 117th Infantry, 30th Division. *Place and date:* Near Estrees, France, 8 October 1918. *Entered service at:* Knoxville, Tenn. *Born:* 1889, Arlington, Tenn. *G.O. No.:* 50, W.D., 1919. *Citation:* During an advance, his company was held up by a machinegun, which was enfilading the line. Accompanied by another soldier, he advanced against this position and succeeded in reducing the nest by killing 3 and capturing 7 of the enemy and their guns.

KATZ, PHILLIP C.

Rank and organization: Sergeant, U.S. Army, Company C, 363d Infantry, 91st Division. *Place and date:* Near Eclisfontaine, France, 26 September 1918. *Entered service at:* San Francisco, Calif. *Birth:* San Francisco, Calif. *G.O. No.:* 16, W.D., 1919. *Citation:* After his company had withdrawn for a distance of 200 yards on a line with the units on its flanks, Sgt. Katz learned that one of his comrades had been left wounded in an exposed position at the point from which the withdrawal had taken place. Voluntarily crossing an area swept by heavy machinegun fire, he advanced to where the wounded soldier lay and carried him to a place of safety.

KAUFMAN, BENJAMIN

Rank and organization: First Sergeant, U.S. Army, Company K, 308th Infantry, 77th Division. *Place and date:* In the forest of Argonne, France, 4 October 1918. *Entered service at:* Brooklyn, N.Y. *Born:* 10 March 1894, Buffalo, N.Y. *G.O. No.:* 50, W.D., 1919. *Citation:* He took out a patrol for the purpose of attacking an enemy machinegun which had checked the advance of his company. Before reaching the gun he became separated from his patrol and a machinegun bullet shattered his right arm. Without hesitation he advanced on the gun alone, throwing grenades with his left hand and charging with an empty pistol, taking one prisoner and scattering the crew, bringing the gun and prisoner back to the first-aid station.

KELLY, JOHN JOSEPH (Army Medal)

Rank and organization: Private, U.S. Marine Corps, 78th Company, 6th Regiment, 2d Division. *Place and date:* At Blanc Mont Ridge, France, 3 October 1918. *Entered service at:* Chicago, Ill. *Born:* 24 June 1898, Chicago, Ill. *G.O. No.:* 16, W.D., 1919. (Also received Navy Medal of Honor.) *Citation:* Pvt. Kelly ran through our own barrage 100 yards in advance of the front line and attacked an enemy machinegun nest, killing the gunner with a grenade, shooting another member of the crew with his pistol, and returning through the barrage with 8 prisoners.

KELLY, JOHN JOSEPH (Navy Medal)

Rank and organization: Private, U.S. Marine Corps, 78th Company, 6th Regiment. *Born:* 24 June 1898, Chicago, Ill. *Accredited to:* Illinois. (Also received Army Medal of Honor.) *Citation:* For conspicuous gallantry and intrepidity above and beyond the call of duty while serving with the 78th Company, 6th Regiment, 2d Division, in action with the enemy at Blanc Mont Ridge, France, 3 October 1918. Pvt. Kelly ran through our own barrage a hundred yards in advance of the front line and attacked an enemy machinegun nest, killing the gunner with a grenade, shooting another member of the crew with his pistol, and returning through the barrage with 8 prisoners.

*KOCAK, MATEJ (Army Medal)

Rank and organization: Sergeant, U.S. Marine Corps, 66th Company, 5th Regiment, 2d Division. *Place and date:* Near Soissons, France, 18 July 1918. *Entered service at:* New York, N.Y. *Born:* 31 December 1882, Gbely (Slovakia), Austria. *G.O. No.:* 34, W.D., 1919. (Also received Navy Medal of Honor.) *Citation:* When the advance of his battalion was checked by a hidden machinegun nest, he went forward alone, unprotected by covering fire from his own men, and worked in between the German positions in the face of fire from enemy covering detachments. Locating the machinegun nest, he rushed it and with his bayonet drove off the crew. Shortly after this he organized 25 French colonial soldiers who had become separated from their company and led them in attacking another machinegun nest, which was also put out of action.

*KOCAK, MATEJ (Navy Medal)

Rank and organization: Sergeant, U.S. Marine Corps. *Born:* 31 December 1882, Gbely (Slovakia), Austria. *Accredited to:* New York. (Also received Army Medal of Honor.) *Citation:* For extraordinary heroism while serving with the 66th Company, 5th Regiment, 2d Division, in action in the Viller-Cottertes section, south of Soissons, France, 18 July 1918. When a hidden machinegun nest halted the advance of his battalion, Sgt. Kocak went forward alone unprotected by covering fire and worked his way in between the German positions in the face of heavy enemy fire. Rushing the enemy position with his bayonet, he drove off the crew. Later the same day, Sgt. Kocak organized French colonial soldiers who had become separated from their company and led them in an attack on another machinegun nest which was also put out of action.

LATHAM, JOHN CRIDLAND

Rank and organization: Sergeant, U.S. Army, Machine Gun Company, 107th Infantry, 27th Division. *Place and date:* Near Le Catelet, France, 29 September 1918. *Entered service at:* Rutherford, N.J. *Born:* 3 March 1888, Windemere, England. *G.O. No.:* 20, W.D., 1919. *Citation:* Becoming separated from their platoon by a smoke barrage, Sgt.

Latham, Sgt. Alan L. Eggers, and Cpl. Thomas E. O'Shea took cover in a shellhole well within the enemy's lines. Upon hearing a call for help from an American tank which had become disabled 30 yards from them, the 3 soldiers left their shelter and started toward the tank under heavy fire from German machineguns and trench mortars. In crossing the fire-swept area, Cpl. O'Shea was mortally wounded, but his companions, undeterred, proceeded to the tank, rescued a wounded officer, and assisted 2 wounded soldiers to cover in the sap of a nearby trench. Sgts. Latham and Eggers then returned to the tank in the face of the violent fire, dismounted a Hotchkiss gun, and took it back to where the wounded men were, keeping off the enemy all day by effective use of the gun and later bringing it with the wounded men back to our lines under cover of darkness.

*LEMERT, MILO

Rank and organization: First Sergeant, U.S. Army, Company G, 119th Infantry, 30th Division. *Place and date:* Near Bellicourt, France, 29 September 1918. *Entered service at:* Crossville, Tenn. *Birth:* Marshalltown, Iowa. *G.O. No.:* 59, W.D., 1919. *Citation:* Seeing that the left flank of his company was held up, he located the enemy machinegun emplacement, which had been causing heavy casualties. In the face of heavy fire he rushed it singlehanded, killing the entire crew with grenades. Continuing along the enemy trench in advance of the company, he reached another emplacement, which he also charged, silencing the gun with grenades. A third machinegun emplacement opened up on him from the left and with similar skill and bravery he destroyed this also. Later, in company with another sergeant, he attacked a fourth machinegun nest, being killed as he reached the parapet of the emplacement. His courageous action in destroying in turn 4 enemy machinegun nests prevented many casualties ar.'ong his company and very materially aided in achieving the objective.

LOMAN, BERGER

Rank and organization: Private, U.S. Army, Company H, 132d Infantry, 33d Division. *Place and date:* Near Consenvoye, France, 9 October 1918. *Entered service at:* Chicago, Ill. *Born:* 24 August 1886, Bergen, Norway. *G.O. No.:* 16, W.D., 1919. *Citation:* When his company had reached a point within 100 yards of its objective, to which it was advancing under terrific machinegun fire, Pvt. Loman voluntarily and unaided made his way forward after all others had taken shelter from the direct fire of an enemy machinegun. He crawled to a flank position of the gun and, after killing or capturing the entire crew, turned the machinegun on the retreating enemy.

*LUKE, FRANK, JR. (Air Mission)

Rank and organization: Second Lieutenant, U.S. Army Air Corps, 27th Aero Squadron, 1st Pursuit Group, Air Service. *Place and date:* Near Murvaux, France, 29 September 1918. *Entered service at:* Phoenix, Ariz. *Born:* 19 May 1897, Phoenix, Ariz. *G.O. No.:* 59, W.D., 1919. *Citation:* After having previously destroyed a number of enemy aircraft within 17 days he voluntarily started on a patrol after German observation balloons. Though pursued by 8 German planes which were protecting the enemy balloon line, he unhesitatingly attacked and shot down in flames 3 German balloons, being himself under heavy fire from ground batteries and the hostile planes. Severely wounded, he descended to within 50 meters of the ground, and flying at this low altitude near the town of Murvaux opened fire upon enemy troops, killing 6 and wounding as many more. Forced to make a landing and surrounded on all sides by the enemy, who called upon him to surrender, he drew his automatic pistol and defended himself gallantly until he fell dead from a wound in the chest.

LYLE, ALEXANDER GORDON

Rank and organization: Lieutenant Commander (Dental Corps), U.S. Navy. *Born:* 12 November 1889, Gloucester, Mass. *Appointed from:* Massachusetts. *Other Navy award:* Legion of Merit. *Citation:* For extraordinary heroism and devotion to duty while serving with the 5th Regiment, U.S. Marine Corps. Under heavy shellfire, on 23 April 1918, on the French Front, Lt. Comdr. Lyle rushed to the assistance of Cpl. Thomas Regan, who was seriously wounded, and administered such effective surgical aid while bombardment was still continuing, as to save the life of Cpl. Regan.

MacKENZIE, JOHN

Rank and organization: Chief Boatswain's Mate, U.S. Navy. *Born:* 7 July 1886, Bridgeport, Conn. *Accredited to:* Massachusetts. *G.O. No.:* 391, 1918. *Citation:* For extraordinary heroism while serving on board the U.S.S. *Remlik*, on the morning of 17 December 1917, when the *Remlik* encountered a heavy gale. During this gale, there was a heavy sea running. The depth charge box on the taffrail aft, containing a Sperry depth charge, was washed overboard, the depth charge itself falling inboard and remaining on deck. MacKenzie, on his own initiative, went aft and sat down on the depth charge, as it was impracticable to carry it to safety until the ship was headed up into the sea. In acting as he did, MacKenzie exposed his life and prevented a serious accident to the ship and probable loss of the ship and the entire crew.

MADISON, JAMES JONAS

Rank and organization: Lieutenant Commander, U.S. Naval Reserve Force. *Born:* 20 May 1884, Jersey City, N.J. *Appointed from:* Mississippi. *Citation:* For exceptionally heroic service in a position of great responsibility as commanding officer of the U.S.S. *Ticonderoga*, when, on 4 October 1918, that vessel was attacked by an enemy submarine and was sunk after a prolonged and gallant resistance. The submarine opened fire at a range of 500 yards, the first shots taking effect on the bridge and forecastle, 1 of the 2 forward guns of the *Ticonderoga* being disabled by the second shot. The fire was returned and the fight continued for nearly 2 hours. Lt. Comdr. Madison was severely wounded early in the fight, but caused himself to be placed in a chair on the bridge and continued to direct the fire and to maneuver the ship. When the order was finally given to abandon the sinking ship, he became unconscious from loss of blood, but was lowered into a lifeboat and was saved, with 31 others, out of a total number of 236 on board.

MALLON, GEORGE H.

Rank and organization: Captain, U.S. Army, 132d Infantry, 33d Division. *Place and date:* In the Bois-de-Forges, France, 26 September 1918. *Entered service at:* Minneapolis, Minn. *Born:* 15 June 1877, Ogden, Kans. *G.O. No.:* 16, W.D., 1919. *Citation:* Becoming separated from the balance of his company because of a fog, Capt. Mallon, with 9 soldiers, pushed forward and attacked 9 active hostile machineguns, capturing all of them without the loss of a man. Continuing on through the woods, he led his men in attacking a battery of four 155-millimeter howitzers, which were in action, rushing the position and capturing the battery and its crew. In this encounter Capt. Mallon personally attacked 1 of the enemy with his fists. Later, when the party came upon 2 more machineguns, this officer sent men to the flanks while he rushed forward directly in the face of the fire and silenced the guns, being the first one of the party to reach the nest. The exceptional gallantry and determination displayed by Capt. Mallon resulted in the capture of 100 prisoners, 11 machineguns, four 155-millimeter howitzers and 1 antiaircraft gun.

MANNING, SIDNEY E.

Rank and organization: Corporal, U.S. Army Company G, 167th Infantry, 42d Division. *Place and date:* Near Breuvannes, France, 28 July 1918. *Entering service at:* Flomaton, Ala. *Born:* 17 July 1892, Butler County, Ala. *G.O. No.:* 44, W.D., 1919. *Citation:* When his platoon commander and platoon sergeant had both become casualties soon after the beginning of an assault on strongly fortified heights overlooking the Ourcq River, Cpl. Manning took command of his platoon, which was near the center of the attacking line. Though himself severely wounded he led forward the 35 men remaining in the platoon and finally succeeded in gaining a foothold on the enemy's position, during which time he had received more wounds and all but 7 of his men had fallen. Directing the consolidation of the position, he held off a large body of the enemy only 50 yards away by fire from his automatic rifle. He declined to take cover until his line had been entirely consolidated with the line of the platoon on the front when he dragged himself to shelter, suffering from 9 wounds in all parts of the body.

McGUNIGAL, PATRICK

Rank and organization: Shipfitter First Class, U.S. Navy. *Born:* 30 May 1876, Hubbard, Ohio. *Accredited to:* Ohio. *G.O. No.:* 341, 1917. *Citation:* For extraordinary heroism while attached to the *Huntington*. On the morning of 17 September 1917, while the U.S.S. *Huntington* was passing through the war zone, a kite balloon was sent up with Lt. (jg.) H. W. Hoyt, U.S. Navy, as observer. When the balloon was about 400 feet in the air, the temperature suddenly dropped, causing the balloon to descend about 200 feet, when it was struck by a squall. The balloon was hauled to the ship's side, but the basket trailed in the water and the pilot was submerged. McGunigal, with great daring, climbed down the side of the ship, jumped to the ropes leading to the basket, and cleared the tangle enough to get the pilot out of them. He then helped the pilot to get clear, put a bowline around him, and enabled him to be hauled to the deck. A bowline was lowered to McGunigal and he was taken safely aboard.

McMURTRY, GEORGE G.

Rank and organization: Captain, U.S. Army, 308th Infantry, 77th Division. *Place and date:* At Charlevaux, in the forest of Argonne, France, 2–8 October 1918. *Entered service at:* New York, N.Y. *Born:* 6 November 1876, Pittsburgh, Pa. *G.O. No.:* 118, W.D., 1918. *Citation:* Commanded a battalion which was cut off and surrounded by the enemy and although wounded in the knee by shrapnel on 4 October and suffering great pain, he continued throughout the entire period to encourage his officers and men with a resistless optimism that contributed largely toward preventing panic and disorder among the troops, who were without food, cut off from communication with our lines. On 4 October during a heavy barrage, he personally directed and supervised the moving of the wounded to shelter before himself seeking shelter. On 6 October he was again wounded in the shoulder by a German grenade, but continued personally to organize and direct the defense against the German attack on the position until the attack was defeated. He continued to direct and command his troops, refusing relief, and personally led his men out of the position after assistance arrived before permitting himself to be taken to the hospital on 8 October. During this period the successful defense of the position was due largely to his efforts.

*MESTROVITCH, JAMES I.

Rank and organization: Sergeant, U.S. Army, Company C, 111th Infantry, 28th Division. *Place and date:* At Fismette, France, 10 August 1918. *Entered service at:* Pittsburgh, Pa. *Birth:* Montenegro. *G.O. No.:* 20, W.D., 1919. *Citation:* Seeing his company commander lying wounded 30 yards in front of the line after his company had withdrawn to a sheltered position behind a stone wall, Sgt. Mestrovitch voluntarily left cover and crawled through heavy machinegun and shell fire to where the officer lay. He took the officer upon his back and crawled to a place of safety, where he administered first-aid treatment, his exceptional heroism saving the officer's life.

MILES, L. WARDLAW

Rank and organization: Captain, U.S. Army, 308th Infantry, 77th Division. *Place and date:* Near Revillon, France, 14 September 1918. *Entered service at:* Princeton, N.J. *Born:* 23 March 1873, Baltimore, Md. *G.O. No.:* 44, W.D., 1919. *Citation:* Volunteered to lead his company in a hazardous attack on a commanding trench position near the Aisne Canal, which other troops had previously attempted to take without success. His company immediately met with intense machinegun fire, against which it had no artillery assistance, but Capt. Miles preceded the first wave and assisted in cutting a passage through the enemy's wire entanglements. In so doing he was wounded 5 times by machinegun bullets, both legs and 1 arm being fractured, whereupon he ordered himself placed on a stretcher and had himself carried forward to the enemy trench in order that he might encourage and direct his company, which by this time had suffered numerous casualties.

Under the inspiration of this officer's indomitable spirit his men held the hostile position and consolidated the front line after an action lasting 2 hours, at the conclusion of which Capt. Miles was carried to the aid station against his will.

*MILLER, OSCAR F.

Rank and organization: Major, U.S. Army, 361st Infantry, 91st Division. *Place and date:* Near Gesnes, France, 28 September 1918. *Entered service at:* Los Angeles, Calif. *Birth:* Franklin County, Ark. *G.O. No.:* 16, W.D. 1919. *Citation:* After 2 days of intense physical and mental strain, during which Maj. Miller had led his battalion in the front line of the advance through the forest of Argonne, the enemy was met in a prepared position south of Gesnes. Though almost exhausted, he energetically reorganized his battalion and ordered an attack. Upon reaching open ground the advancing line began to waver in the face of machinegun fire from the front and flanks and direct artillery fire. Personally leading his command group forward between his front-line companies, Maj. Miller inspired his men by his personal courage, and they again pressed on toward the hostile position. As this officer led the renewed attack he was shot in the right leg, but he nevertheless staggered forward at the head of his command. Soon afterwards he was again shot in the right arm, but he continued the charge, personally cheering his troops on through the heavy machinegun fire. Just before the objective was reached he received a wound in the abdomen, which forced him to the ground, but he continued to urge his men on, telling them to push on to the next ridge and leave him where he lay. He died from his wounds a few days later.

MORELOCK, STERLING

Rank and organization: Private, U.S. Army, Company M, 28th Infantry, 1st Division. *Place and date:* Near Exermont, France, 4 October 1918. *Entered service at:* Oquawka, Ill. *Birth:* Silver Run, Md. *G.O. No.:* 43, W.D., 1922. *Citation:* While his company was being held up by heavy enemy fire, Pvt. Morelock, with 3 other men who were acting as runners at company headquarters, voluntarily led them as a patrol in advance of his company's frontline through an intense rifle, artillery, and machinegun fire and penetrated a woods which formed the German frontline. Encountering a series of 5 hostile machinegun nests, containing from 1 to 5 machineguns each, with his patrol he cleaned them all out, gained and held complete mastery of the situation until the arrival of his company commander with reinforcements, even though his entire party had become casualties. He rendered first aid to the injured and evacuated them by using stretcher bearers 10 German prisoners whom he had captured. Soon thereafter his company commander was wounded and while dressing his wound Pvt. Morelock was very severely wounded in the hip, which forced his evacuation. His heroic action and devotion to duty were an inspiration to the entire regiment.

NEIBAUR, THOMAS C.

Rank and organization: Private, U.S. Army, Company M, 107th Infantry, 42d Division. *Place and date:* Near Landres-et-St. Georges,

France, 16 October 1918. *Entered service at:* Sugar City, Idaho. *Born:* 17 May 1898, Sharon, Idaho. *G.O. No.:* 118, W.D., 1918. *Citation:* On the afternoon of 16 October 1918, when the Cote-de-Chatillion had just been gained after bitter fighting and the summit of that strong bulwark in the Kriemhilde Stellung was being organized, Pvt. Neibaur was sent out on patrol with his automatic rifle squad to enfilade enemy machinegun nests. As he gained the ridge he set up his automatic rifle and was directly thereafter wounded in both legs by fire from a hostile machinegun on his flank. The advance wave of the enemy troops, counterattacking, had about gained the ridge, and although practically cut off and surrounded, the remainder of his detachment being killed or wounded, this gallant soldier kept his automatic rifle in operation to such effect that by his own efforts and by fire from the skirmish line of his company, at least 100 yards in his rear, the attack was checked. The enemy wave being halted and lying prone, 4 of the enemy attacked Pvt. Neibaur at close quarters. These he killed. He then moved alone among the enemy lying on the ground about him, in the midst of the fire from his own lines, and by coolness and gallantry captured 11 prisoners at the point of his pistol and, although painfully wounded, brought them back to our lines. The counterattack in full force was arrested to a large extent by the single efforts of this soldier, whose heroic exploits took place against the skyline in full view of his entire battalion.

O'NEIL, RICHARD W.

Rank and organization: Sergeant, U.S. Army, Company D, 165th Infantry, 42d Division. *Place and date:* On the Ourcq River, France, 30 July 1918. *Entered service at:* New York, N.Y. *Birth:* New York, N.Y. *G.O. No.:* 30, W.D., 1921. *Citation:* In advance of an assaulting line, he attacked a detachment of about 25 of the enemy. In the ensuing hand-to-hand encounter he sustained pistol wounds, but heroically continued in the advance, during which he received additional wounds; but, with great physical effort, he remained in active command of his detachment. Being again wounded, he was forced by weakness and loss of blood to be evacuated, but insisted upon being taken first to the battalion commander in order to transmit to him valuable information relative to enemy positions and the disposition of our men.

ORMSBEE, FRANCIS EDWARD, Jr.

Rank and organization: Chief Machinist's Mate, U.S. Navy. *Born:* 30 April 1892, Providence, R.I. *Accredited to:* Florida. *G.O. No.:* 436, 1918. *Citation:* For extraordinary heroism while attached to the Naval Air Station, Pensacola, Fla., on 25 September 1918. While flying with Ens. J. A. Jova, Ormsbee saw a plane go into a tailspin and crash about three-quarters of a mile to the right. Having landed near by, Ormsbee lost no time in going overboard and made for the wreck, which was all under water except the 2 wing tips. He succeeded in partially extricating the gunner so that his head was out of water, and held him in this position until the speedboat arrived. Ormsbee then made a number of desperate attempts to rescue the pilot, diving into the midst of the tangled wreckage although cut about the hands, but was too late to save his life.

*OSBORNE, WEEDON E.

Rank and organization: Lieutenant, Junior Grade, (Dental Corps), U.S. Navy. *Born:* 13 November 1892, Chicago, Ill. *Appointed from:* Illinois. *Citation:* For extraordinary heroism while attached to the 6th Regiment, U.S. Marines, in actual conflict with the enemy and under fire during the advance on Bouresche, France, on 6 June 1918. In the hottest of the fighting when the marines made their famous advance on Bouresche at the southern edge of Belleau Wood, Lt (jg.). Osborne threw himself zealously into the work of rescuing the wounded. Extremely courageous in the performance of this perilous task, he was killed while carrying a wounded officer to a place of safety.

*O'SHEA, THOMAS E.

Rank and organization: Corporal, U.S. Army, Machine Gun Company, 107th Infantry, 27th Division. *Place and date:* Near Le Catelet, France, 29 September 1918. *Entered service at:* Summit, N.J. *Birth:* New York, N.Y. *G.O. No.:* 20, W.D., 1919. *Citation:* Becoming separated from their platoon by a smoke barrage, Cpl. O'Shea, with 2 other soldiers, took cover in a shell hole well within the enemy's lines. Upon hearing a call for help from an American tank, which had become disabled 30 yards from them, the 3 soldiers left their shelter and started toward the tank under heavy fire from German machineguns and trench mortars. In crossing the fire-swept area Cpl. O'Shea was mortally wounded and died of his wounds shortly afterwards.

PARKER, SAMUEL I.

Rank and organization: Second Lieutenant, U.S. Army, Company K, 28th Infantry, 1st Division. *Place and date:* Near Soissons, France, 18–19 July 1918. *Entered service at:* Monroe, N.C. *Birth:* Monroe, N.C. *G.O. No.:* 1, W.D. 1937. *Citation:* For conspicuous gallantry and intrepidity above and beyond the call of duty. During the attack the 2d and 3d Battalions of the 28th Infantry were merged, and after several hours of severe fighting, successfully established a frontline position. In so doing, a gap was left between the right flank of the French 153d Division on their left and the left flank of the 28th Infantry, exposing the left flank to a terrific enfilade fire from several enemy machineguns located in a rock quarry on high ground. 2d Lt. Parker, observing this serious situation, ordered his depleted platoon to follow him in an attack upon the strong point. Meeting a disorganized group of French Colonials wandering leaderlessly about, he persuaded them to join his platoon. This consolidated group followed 2d Lt. Parker through direct enemy rifle and machinegun fire to the crest of the hill, and rushing forward, took the quarry by storm, capturing 6 machineguns and about 40 prisoners. The next day when the assault was continued, 2d Lt. Parker in command of the merged 2d and 3d Battalions was in support of the 1st Battalion. Although painfully wounded in the foot, he refused to be evacuated and continued to lead his command until the objective was reached. Seeing that the assault battalion was subjected to heavy enfilade fire due to a gap between it and the French on its left, 2d Lt. Parker led his battalion through this heavy fire up on the line to the left of the 1st Battalion and thereby closed the gap, remaining in command of his battalion until the newly established lines of the 28th Infantry were thoroughly consolidated. In supervising the consolidation of the new position, 2d Lt. Parker was compelled to crawl about on his hands and knees on account of his painful wound. His conspicuous gallantry and spirit of self-sacrifice were a source of great inspiration to the members of the entire command.

PECK, ARCHIE A.

Rank and organization: Private, U.S. Army, Company A, 307th Infantry, 77th Division. *Place and date:* In the Argonne Forest, France, 6 October 1918. *Entered service at:* Hornell, N.Y. *Birth:* Tyrone, N.Y. *G.O. No.:* 16, W.D., 1919. *Citation:* While engaged with 2 other soldiers on patrol duty, he and his comrades were subjected to the direct fire of an enemy machinegun, at which time both his companions were wounded. Returning to his company, he obtained another soldier to accompany him to assist in bringing in the wounded men. His assistant was killed in the exploit, but he continued on, twice returning safely bringing in both men, being under terrific machinegun fire during the entire journey.

*PERKINS, MICHAEL J.

Rank and organization: Private First Class, U.S. Army, Company D, 101st Infantry, 26th Division. *Place and date:* At Belieu Bois, France, 27 October 1918. *Entered service at:* Boston, Mass. *Birth:* Boston, Mass. *G.O. No.:* 34, W.D. 1919. *Citation:* He, voluntarily and alone, crawled to a German "pill box" machinegun emplacement, from which grenades were being thrown at his platoon. Awaiting his opportunity, when the door was again opened and another grenade thrown, he threw a bomb inside, bursting the door open, and then, drawing his trench knife, rushed into the emplacement. In a hand-to-hand struggle he killed or wounded several of the occupants and captured about 25 prisoners, at the same time silencing 7 machineguns.

PETTY, ORLANDO HENDERSON

Rank and organization: Lieutenant (Medical Corps), USNRF. *Born:* 20 February 1874, Harrison, Ohio. *Appointed from:* Pennsylvania. *Citation:* For extraordinary heroism while serving with the 5th Regiment, U.S. Marines, in France during the attack in the Boise de Belleau, 11 June 1918. While under heavy fire of high explosive and gas shells in the town of Lucy, where his dressing station was located, Lt. Petty attended to and evacuated the wounded under most trying conditions. Having been knocked to the ground by an exploding gas shell which tore his mask, Lt. Petty discarded the mask and courageously continued his work. His dressing station being hit and demolished, he personally helped carry Capt. Williams, wounded, through the shellfire to a place of safety.

*PIKE, EMORY J.

Rank and organization: Lieutenant Colonel, U.S. Army, Division Machinegun Officer, 82d Division. *Place and date:* Near Vandieres, France, 15 September 1918. *Entered service at:* Des Moines, Iowa.

Birth: Columbia City, Iowa. *G.O. No.:* 16, W.D., 1919. *Citation:* Having gone forward to reconnoiter new machinegun positions, Lt. Col. Pike offered his assistance in reorganizing advance infantry units which had become disorganized during a heavy artillery shelling. He succeeded in locating only about 20 men, but with these he advanced and when later joined by several infantry platoons rendered inestimable service in establishing outposts, encouraging all by his cheeriness, in spite of the extreme danger of the situation. When a shell had wounded one of the men in the outpost, Lt. Col. Pike immediately went to his aid and was severely wounded himself when another shell burst in the same place. While waiting to be brought to the rear, Lt. Col. Pike continued in command, still retaining his jovial manner of encouragement, directing the reorganization until the position could be held. The entire operation was carried on under terrific bombardment, and the example of courage and devotion to duty, as set by Lt. Col. Pike, established the highest standard of morale and confidence to all under his charge. The wounds he received were the cause of his death.

POPE, THOMAS A.

Rank and organization: Corporal, U.S. Army, Company E, 131st Infantry, 33d Division. *Place and date:* At Hamel, France, 4 July 1918. *Entered service at:* Chicago, Ill. *Birth:* Chicago, Ill. *G.O. No.:* 44, W.D., 1919. *Citation:* His company was advancing behind the tanks when it was halted by hostile machinegun fire. Going forward alone, he rushed a machinegun nest, killed several of the crew with his bayonet, and, standing astride his gun, held off the others until reinforcements arrived and captured them.

*PRUITT, JOHN HENRY (Army Medal)

Rank and organization: Corporal, U.S. Marine Corps, 78th Company, 6th Regiment, 2d Division. *Place and date:* At Blanc Mont Ridge, France, 3 October 1918. *Entered service at:* Phoenix, Ariz. *Born:* 4 October 1896, Fayettesville, Ark. *G.O. No.:* 62, W.D., 1919. (Also received Navy Medal of Honor.) *Citation:* Cpl. Pruitt singlehanded attacked 2 machineguns, capturing them and killing 2 of the enemy. He then captured 40 prisoners in a dugout nearby. This gallant soldier was killed soon afterward by shellfire while he was sniping at the enemy.

*PRUITT, JOHN HENRY (Navy Medal)

Rank and organization: Corporal, U.S. Marine Corps. *Born:* 4 October 1896, Fayettesville, Ark. *Accredited to:* Arizona. (Also received Army Medal of Honor.) *Citation:* For extraordinary gallantry and intrepidity above and beyond the call of duty while serving with the 78th Company, 6th Regiment, 2d Division, in action with the enemy at Blanc Mont Ridge, France, 3 October 1918. Cpl. Pruitt, singlehanded attacked 2 machineguns, capturing them and killing 2 of the enemy. He then captured 40 prisoners in a dugout nearby. This gallant soldier was killed soon afterward by shellfire while he was sniping the enemy.

REGAN, PATRICK

Rank and organization: Second Lieutenant, U.S. Army, 115th Infantry, 29th Division. *Place and date:* At the Bois-de-Consenvoye,

France, 8 October 1918. *Entered service at:* Los Angeles, Calif. *Birth:* Middleboro, Mass. *G.O. No.:* 50, W.D., 1919. *Citation:* While leading his platoon against a strong enemy machinegun nest which had held up the advance of 2 companies, 2d Lt. Regan divided his men into 3 groups, sending 1 group to either flank, and he himself attacking with an automatic rifle team from the front. Two of the team were killed outright, while 2d Lt. Regan and the third man were seriously wounded, the latter unable to advance. Although severely wounded, 2d Lt. Regan dashed with empty pistol into the machinegun nest, capturing 30 Austrian gunners and 4 machineguns. This gallant deed permitted the companies to advance, avoiding a terrific enemy fire. Despite his wounds, he continued to lead his platoon forward until ordered to the rear by his commanding officer.

RICKENBACKER, EDWARD V. (Air Mission)

Rank and organization: First Lieutenant, U.S. Army Air Corps, 94th Aero Squadron, Air Service. *Place and date:* Near Billy, France, 25 September 1918. *Entered service at:* Columbus, Ohio. *Born:* 8 October 1890, Columbus, Ohio. *G.O. No.:* 2, W.D., 1931. *Citation:* For conspicuous gallantry and intrepidity above and beyond the call of duty in action against the enemy near Billy, France, 25 September 1918. While on a voluntary patrol over the lines, 1st Lt. Rickenbacker attacked 7 enemy planes (5 type Fokker, protecting two type Halberstadt). Disregarding the odds against him, he dived on them and shot down one of the Fokkers out of control. He then attacked one of the Halberstadts and sent it down also.

ROBB, GEORGE S.

Rank and organization: First Lieutenant, U.S. Army, 369th Infantry, 93d Division. *Place and date:* Near Sechault, France, 29–30 September 1918. *Entered service at:* Salina, Kans. *Born:* 18 May 1887, Assaria, Kans. *G.O. No.:* 16, W.D., 1919. *Citation:* While leading his platoon in the assault 1st Lt. Robb was severely wounded by machinegun fire, but rather than go to the rear for proper treatment he remained with his platoon until ordered to the dressing station by his commanding officer. Returning within 45 minutes, he remained on duty throughout the entire night, inspecting his lines and establishing outposts. Early the next morning he was again wounded, once again displaying his remarkable devotion to duty by remaining in command of his platoon. Later the same day a bursting shell added 2 more wounds, the same shell killing his commanding officer and 2 officers of his company. He then assumed command of the company and organized its position in the trenches. Displaying wonderful courage and tenacity at the critical times, he was the only officer of his battalion who advanced beyond the town, and by clearing machinegun and sniping posts contributed largely to the aid of his battalion in holding their objective. His example of bravery and fortitude and his eagerness to continue with his mission despite severe wounds set before the enlisted men of his command a most wonderful standard of morale and self-sacrifice.

*ROBERTS, HAROLD W.

Rank and organization: Corporal, U.S. Army Company A, 344th Battalion, Tank Corps. *Place and date:* In the Montrebeau Woods, France, 4 October 1918. *Entered service at:* San Francisco, Calif. *Birth:* San Francisco, Calif. *G.O. No.:* 16, W.D., 1919. *Citation:* Cpl. Roberts, a tank driver, was moving his tank into a clump of bushes to afford protection to another tank which had become disabled. The tank slid into a shell hole, 10 feet deep, filled with water, and was immediately submerged. Knowing that only 1 of the 2 men in the tank could escape, Cpl. Roberts said to the gunner, "Well, only one of us can get out, and out you go," whereupon he pushed his companion through the back door of the tank and was himself drowned.

ROBINSON, ROBERT GUY

Rank and organization: Gunnery Sergeant, U.S. Marine Corps, 1st Marine Aviation Force *Place and date:* Pittham, Belgium, 14 October 1918. *Entered service at:* Chicago, Ill. *Born:* 30 April 1896, New York, N.Y. *Citation:* For extraordinary heroism as observer in the 1st Marine Aviation Force at the front in France. In company with planes from Squadron 218, Royal Air Force, conducting an air raid on 8 October 1918, G/Sgt. Robinson's plane was attacked by 9 enemy scouts. In the fight which followed, he shot down 1 of the enemy planes. In a later air raid over Pittham, Belgium, on 14 October 1918, his plane and 1 other became separated from their formation on account of motor trouble and were attacked by 12 enemy scouts. Acting with conspicuous gallantry and intrepidity in the fight which ensued, G/Sgt. Robinson, after shooting down 1 of the enemy planes, was struck by a bullet which carried away most of his elbow. At the same time his gun jammed. While his pilot maneuvered for position, he cleared the jam with one hand and returned to the fight. Although his left arm was useless, he fought off the enemy scouts until he collapsed after receiving 2 more bullet wounds, one in the stomach and one in the thigh.

SAMPLER, SAMUEL M.

Rank and organization: Corporal, U.S. Army, Company H, 142d Infantry, 36th Division. *Place and date:* Near St. Etienne, France, 8 October 1918. *Entered service at:* Altus, Okla. *Birth:* Decatur, Tex. *G.O. No.:* 59, W.D., 1919. *Citation:* His company having suffered severe casualties during an advance under machinegun fire, was finally stopped. Cpl. Sampler detected the position of the enemy machineguns on an elevation. Armed with German handgrenades, which he had picked up, he left the line and rushed forward in the face of heavy fire until he was near the hostile nest, where he grenaded the position. His third grenade landed among the enemy, killing 2, silencing the machineguns, and causing the surrender of 28 Germans, whom he sent to the rear as prisoners. As a result of his act the company was immediately enabled to resume the advance.

SANDLIN, WILLIE

Rank and organization: Sergeant, U.S. Army, Company A, 132d Infantry, 33d Division. *Place and date:* At Bois-de-Forges, France, 26

September 1918. *Entered service at:* Hyden, Ky. *Birth:* Jackson, Ky. *G.O. No.:* 16, W.D., 1919. *Citation:* He showed conspicuous gallantry in action by advancing alone directly on a machinegun nest which was holding up the line with its fire. He killed the crew with a grenade and enabled the line to advance. Later in the day he attacked alone and put out of action 2 other machinegun nests, setting a splendid example of bravery and coolness to his men.

*SAWELSON, WILLIAM

Rank and organization: Sergeant, U.S. Army, Company M, 312th Infantry, 78th Division. *Place and date:* At Grand-Pre, France, 26 October, 1918. *Entered service at:* Harrison, N.J. *Born:* 5 August 1895, Newark, N.J. *G.O. No.:* 16, W.D., 1919. *Citation:* Hearing a wounded man in a shell hole some distance away calling for water, Sgt. Sawelson, upon his own initiative, left shelter and crawled through heavy machinegun fire to where the man lay, giving him what water he had in his canteen. He then went back to his own shell hole, obtained more water, and was returning to the wounded man when he was killed by a machinegun bullet.

SCHAFFNER, DWITE H.

Rank and organization: First Lieutenant, U.S. Army, 306th Infantry, 77th Division. *Place and date:* Near St. Hubert's Pavillion, Boureuilles, France, 28 September 1918. *Entered service at:* Falls Creek, Pa. *Birth:* Arroya, Pa. *G.O. No.:* 15, W.D., 1923. *Citation:* He led his men in an attack on St. Hubert's Pavillion through terrific enemy machinegun, rifle, and artillery fire and drove the enemy from a strongly held entrenched position after hand-to-hand fighting. His bravery and contempt for danger inspired his men, enabling them to hold fast in the face of 3 determined enemy counterattacks. His company's position being exposed to enemy fire from both flanks, he made 3 efforts to locate an enemy machinegun which had caused heavy casualties. On his third reconnaissance he discovered the gun position and personally silenced the gun, killing or wounding the crew. The third counterattack made by the enemy was initiated by the appearance of a small detachment in advance of the enemy attacking wave. When almost within reach of the American front line the enemy appeared behind them, attacking vigorously with pistols, rifles, and handgrenades, causing heavy casualties in the American platoon. 1st Lt. Schaffner mounted the parapet of the trench and used his pistol and grenades killing a number of enemy soldiers, finally reaching the enemy officer leading the attacking forces, a captain, shooting and mortally wounding the latter with his pistol, and dragging the captured officer back to the company's trench, securing from him valuable information as to the enemy's strength and position. The information enabled 1st Lt. Schaffner to maintain for 5 hours the advanced position of his company despite the fact that it was surrounded on 3 sides by strong enemy forces. The undaunted bravery, gallant soldierly conduct, and leadership displayed by 1st Lt. Schaffner undoubtedly saved the survivors of the company from death or capture.

SCHMIDT, OSCAR, JR.

Rank and organization: Chief Gunner's Mate, U.S. Navy. *Place and date:* At sea, 9 October 1918. *Entered service at:* Pennsylvania. *Born:* 25 March 1896, Philadelphia, Pa. *G.O. No.:* 450, 1919. *Citation:* For gallant conduct and extraordinary heroism while attached to the U.S.S. *Chestnut Hill,* on the occasion of the explosion and subsequent fire on board the U.S. submarine chaser *219.* Schmidt, seeing a man, whose legs were partly blown off, hanging on a line from the bow of the *219,* jumped overboard, swam to the sub chaser and carried him from the bow to the stern where a member of the *219's* crew helped him land the man on the afterdeck of the submarine. Schmidt then endeavored to pass through the flames amidships to get another man who was seriously burned. This he was unable to do, but when the injured man fell overboard and drifted to the stern of the chaser Schmidt helped him aboard.

SEIBERT, LLOYD M.

Rank and organization: Sergeant, U.S. Army, Company F, 364th Infantry, 91st Division. *Place and date:* Near Epinonville, France, 26 September 1918. *Entered service at:* Salinas, Calif. *Birth:* Caledonia, Mich. *G.O. No.:* 445, W.D., 1919. *Citation:* Suffering from illness, Sgt. Seibert remained with his platoon and led his men with the highest courage and leadership under heavy shell and machinegun fire. With 2 other soldiers he charged a machinegun emplacement in advance of their company, he himself killing one of the enemy with a shotgun and capturing 2 others. In this encounter he was wounded, but he nevertheless continued in action, and when a withdrawal was ordered he returned with the last unit, assisting a wounded comrade. Later in the evening he volunteered and carried in wounded until he fainted from exhaustion.

SIEGEL, JOHN OTTO

Rank and organization· Boatswain's Mate Second Class, U.S. Navy. *Born:* 21 April 1890, Milwaukee, Wis. *Accredited to:* New Jersey. *Citation:* For extraordinary heroism while serving on board the *Mohawk* in performing a rescue mission aboard the schooner *Hjeltenaes* which was in flames on 1 November 1918. Going aboard the blazing vessel, Siegel rescued 2 men from the crew's quarters and went back the third time. Immediately after he had entered the crew's quarters, a steam pipe over the door bursted, making it impossible for him to escape. Siegel was overcome with smoke and fell to the deck, being finally rescued by some of the crew of the *Mohawk* who carried him out and rendered first aid.

*SKINKER, ALEXANDER R.

Rank and organization: Captain, U.S. Army, 138th Infantry, 35th Division. *Place and date:* At Cheppy, France, 26 September 1918. *Entered service at:* St. Louis, Mo. *Birth:* St. Louis, Mo. *G.O. No.:* 13, W.D., 1919. *Citation:* Unwilling to sacrifice his men when his company was held up by terrific machinegun fire from iron pill boxes in the Hindenburg Line, Capt. Skinker personally led an automatic rifleman and a carrier in an attack on the machineguns. The carrier was killed instantly, but Capt. Skinker seized the ammunition and continued through an opening in the barbed wire, feeding the automatic rifle until he, too, was killed.

SLACK, CLAYTON K.

Rank and organization: Private, U.S. Army, Company D, 124th Machine Gun Battalion, 33d Division. *Place and date:* Near Consenvoye, France, 8 October 1918. *Entered service at:* Madison, Wis. *Born:* 23 February 1896, Plover, Wis. *G.O. No.:* 16, W.D., 1919. *Citation:* Observing German soldiers under cover 50 yards away on the left flank, Pvt. Slack, upon his own initiative, rushed them with his rifle and, singlehanded, captured 10 prisoners and 2 heavy-type machineguns, thus saving his company and neighboring organizations from heavy casualties.

*SMITH, FRED E.

Rank and organization: Lieutenant Colonel, U.S. Army, 308th Infantry, 77th Division. *Place and date:* Near Binarville, France, 29 September 1918. *Entered service at:* Bartlett, N. Dak. *Birth:* Rockford, Ill. *G.O. No.:* 49, W.D., 1922. *Citation:* When communication from the forward regimental post of command to the battalion leading the advance had been interrupted temporarily by the infiltration of small parties of the enemy armed with machineguns, Lt. Col. Smith personally led a party of 2 other officers and 10 soldiers, and went forward to reestablish runner posts and carry ammunition to the front line. The guide became confused and the party strayed to the left flank beyond the outposts of supporting troops, suddenly coming under fire from a group of enemy machineguns only 50 yards away. Shouting to the other members of his party to take cover this officer, in disregard of his danger, drew his pistol and opened fire on the German guncrew. About this time he fell, severely wounded in the side, but regaining his footing, he continued to fire on the enemy until most of the men in his party were out of danger. Refusing first-aid treatment he then made his way in plain view of the enemy to a handgrenade dump and returned under continued heavy machinegun fire for the purpose of making another attack on the enemy emplacements. As he was attempting to ascertain the exact location of the nearest nest, he again fell, mortally wounded.

*STOCKHAM, FRED W. (Army Medal)

Rank and organization: Gunnery Sergeant, U.S. Marine Corps, 96th Company, 2d Battalion, 6th Regiment. *Place and date:* In Bois-de-Belleau, France, 13–14 June 1918. *Entered service at:* New York, N.Y. *Birth:* Detroit, Mich. *G.O. No.:* —. *Citation:* During an intense enemy bombardment with high explosive and gas shells which wounded or killed many members of the company, G/Sgt. Stockham, upon noticing that the gas mask of a wounded comrade was shot away, without hesitation, removed his own gas mask and insisted upon giving it to the wounded man, well knowing that the effects of the gas would be fatal to himself. He continued with undaunted courage and valor to direct and assist in the evacuation of the wounded, until he himself collapsed from the effects of gas, dying as a result thereof a few days later. His courageous conduct undoubtedly saved the lives of many of his wounded comrades and his conspicuous gallantry and spirit of self-sacrifice were a source of great inspiration to all who served with him.

SULLIVAN, DANIEL AUGUSTUS JOSEPH

Rank and organization: Ensign, U.S. Naval Reserve Force. *Born:* 31 July 1884, Charleston, S.C. *Appointed from:* South Carolina. *Citation:* For extraordinary heroism as an officer of the U.S.S. *Cristabel* in conflict with an enemy submarine on 21 May 1918. As a result of the explosion of a depth bomb dropped near the submarine, the *Christabel* was so badly shaken that a number of depth charges which had been set for firing were thrown about the deck and there was imminent danger that they would explode. Ens. Sullivan immediately fell on the depth charges and succeeded in securing them, thus saving the ship from disaster, which would inevitably have caused great loss of life.

*TALBOT, RALPH

Rank and organization: Second Lieutenant, U.S. Marine Corps. *Born:* 6 January 1897, South Weymouth, Mass. *Appointed from:* Connecticut. *Citation:* For exceptionally meritorious service and extraordinary heroism while attached to Squadron C, 1st Marine Aviation Force, in France. 2d Lt. Talbot participated in numerous air raids into enemy territory. On 8 October 1918, while on such a raid, he was attacked by 9 enemy scouts, and in the fight that followed shot down an enemy plane. Also, on 14 October 1918, while on a raid over Pittham, Belgium, 2d Lt. Talbot and another plane became detached from the formation on account of motor trouble and were attacked by 12 enemy scouts. During the severe fight that followed, his plane shot down 1 of the enemy scouts. His observer was shot through the elbow and his gun jammed. 2d Lt. Talbot maneuvered to gain time for his observer to clear the jam with one hand, and then returned to the fight. The observer fought until shot twice, once in the stomach and once in the hip and then collapsed, 2d Lt. Talbot attacked the nearest enemy scout with his front guns and shot him down. With his observer unconscious and his motor failing, he dived to escape the balance of the enemy and crossed the German trenches at an altitude of 50 feet, landing at the nearest hospital to leave his observer, and then returning to his aerodrome.

TALLEY, EDWARD R.

Rank and organization: Sergeant, U.S. Army, Company L, 117th Infantry, 30th Division. *Place and date:* Near Ponchaux, France, 7 October 1918. *Entered service at:* Russellville, Tenn. *Born:* 8 September 1890, Russellville, Tenn. *G.O. No.:* 50, W.D., 1919. *Citation:* Undeterred by seeing several comrades killed in attempting to put a hostile machinegun nest out of action, Sgt. Talley attacked the position singlehanded. Armed only with a rifle, he rushed the nest in the face of intense enemy fire, killed or wounded at least 6 of the crew, and silenced the gun. When the enemy attempted to bring forward another gun and ammunition he drove them back by effective fire from his rifle.

THOMPSON, JOSEPH H.

Rank and organization: Major, U.S. Army, 110th Infantry, 28th Division. *Place and date:* Near Apremont, France, 1 October 1918. *Entered service at:* Beaver Falls, Pa. *Born:* 26 September 1871, Kilkeel, County Down, Ireland. *G.O. No.:* 21, W.D., 1925. *Citation:* Counterattacked by 2 regiments of the enemy, Maj. Thompson encouraged his battalion in the front line of constantly braving the hazardous fire of machineguns and artillery. His courage was mainly responsible for the heavy repulse of the enemy. Later in the action, when the advance of his assaulting companies was held up by fire from a hostile machinegun nest and all but 1 of the 6 assaulting tanks were disabled, Maj. Thompson, with great gallantry and coolness, rushed forward on foot 3 separate times in advance of the assaulting line, under heavy machinegun and antitank-gun fire, and led the 1 remaining tank to within a few yards of the enemy machinegun nest, which succeeded in reducing it, thereby making it possible for the infantry to advance.

TURNER, HAROLD L.

Rank and organization: Corporal, U.S. Army, Company F, 142d Infantry, 36th Division. *Place and date:* Near St. Etienne, France, 8 October 1918. *Entered service at:* Seminole, Okla. *Born:* 5 May 1898, Aurora, Mo. *G.O. No.:* 59, W.D., 1919. *Citation:* After his platoon had started the attack Cpl. Turner assisted in organizing a platoon consisting of the battalion scouts, runners, and a detachment of Signal Corps. As second in command of this platoon he fearlessly led them forward through heavy enemy fire, continually encouraging the men. Later he encountered deadly machinegun fire which reduced the strength of his command to but 4 men, and these were obliged to take shelter. The enemy machinegun emplacement, 25 yards distant, kept up a continual fire from 4 machineguns. After the fire had shifted momentarily, Cpl. Turner rushed forward with fixed bayonet and charged the position alone, capturing the strong point with a complement of 50 Germans and 4 machineguns. His remarkable display of courage and fearlessness was instrumental in destroying the strong point, the fire from which had blocked the advance of his company.

*TURNER, WILLIAM B.

Rank and organization: First Lieutenant, U.S. Army 105th Infantry, 27th Division. *Place and date:* Near Ronssoy, France, 27 September 1918. *Entered service at:* Garden City, N.Y. *Birth:* Boston, Mass. *G.O. No.:* 81, W.D., 1919. *Citation:* He led a small group of men to the attack, under terrific artillery and machinegun fire, after they had become separated from the rest of the company in the darkness. Singlehanded he rushed an enemy machinegun which had suddenly opened fire on his group and killed the crew with his pistol. He then pressed forward to another machinegun post 25 yards away and had killed 1 gunner himself by the time the remainder of his detachment arrived and put the gun out of action. With the utmost bravery he continued to lead his men over 3 lines of hostile trenches, cleaning up each one as they advanced, regardless of the fact that he had been wounded 3 times, and killed several of the enemy in hand-to-hand encounters. After his pistol ammunition was exhausted, this gallant officer seized the rifle of a dead soldier, bayoneted several members of a machinegun crew, and shot the other. Upon reaching the fourth-line trench, which was his objective, 1st Lt. Turner captured it with the 9 men remaining in his group and resisted a hostile counterattack until he was finally surrounded and killed.

UPTON, FRANK MONROE

Rank and organization: Quartermaster, U.S. Navy. *Born:* 29 April 1896, Loveland, Colo. *Accredited to:* Colorado. *G.O. No.:* 403, 1918. *Citation:* For extraordinary heroism following internal explosion of the *Florence H*, on 17 April 1918. The sea in the vicinity of wreckage was covered by a mass of boxes of smokeless powder, which were repeatedly exploding. Frank M. Upton, of the U.S.S. *Stewart*, plunged overboard to rescue a survivor who was surrounded by powder boxes and too exhausted to help himself. Fully realizing the danger from continual explosion of similar powder boxes in the vicinity, he risked his life to save the life of this man.

VALENTE, MICHAEL

Rank and organization: Private, U.S. Army, Company D, 107th Infantry, 27th Division. *Place and date:* East of Ronssoy, France, 29 September 1918. *Entered service at:* Ogdensburg, N.Y. *Born:* 5 February 1895, Cassino, Italy. *G.O. No.:* 16, W.D., 1929. *Citation:* For conspicuous gallantry and intrepidity above and beyond the call of duty in action with the enemy during the operations against the Hindenburg line, east of Ronssoy, France, 29 September 1918. Finding the advance of his organization held up by a withering enemy machinegun fire, Pvt. Valente volunteered to go forward. With utter disregard of his own personal danger, accompanied by another soldier, Pvt. Valente rushed forward through an intense machinegun fire directly upon the enemy nest, killing 2 and capturing 5 of the enemy and silencing the gun. Discovering another machinegun nest close by which was pouring a deadly fire on the American forces, preventing their advance, Pvt. Valente and his companion charged upon this strong point, killing the gunner and putting this machinegun out of action. Without hesitation they jumped into the enemy's trench, killed 2 and captured 16 German soldiers. Pvt. Valente was later wounded and sent to the rear.

VAN IERSEL, LUDOVICUS M. M.

Rank and organization: Sergeant, U.S. Army, Company M, 9th Infantry, 2d Division. *Place and date:* At Mouzon, France, 9 November 1918. *Entered service at:* Glen Rock, N.J. *Birth:* Holland. *G.O. No.:* 34, W.D., 1919. *Citation:* While a member of the reconnaissance patrol, sent out at night to ascertain the condition of a damaged bridge, Sgt. Van Iersel volunteered to lead a party across the bridge in the face of heavy machinegun and rifle fire from a range of only 75 yards. Crawling alone along the debris of the ruined bridge he came upon a trap, which gave away and precipitated him into the water. In spite of the swift current he succeeded in swimming across the stream and found a lodging place among the timbers on the opposite bank. Disregarding the enemy fire, he made a careful investigation of the hostile position by which the bridge was defended and then returned to the other bank of the river, reporting this valuable information to the battalion commander.

VILLEPIGUE, JOHN C.

Rank and organization: Corporal, U.S. Army, Company M, 118th Infantry, 30th Division. *Place and date:* At Vaux-Andigny, France, 15 October 1918. *Entered service at:* Camden, S.C. *Born:* 29 March 1896, Camden, S.C. *G.O. No.:* 16, W.D., 1919. *Citation:* Having been sent out with 2 other soldiers to scout through the village of Vaux-Andigny, he met with strong resistance from enemy machinegun fire, which killed 1 of his men and wounded the other. Continuing his advance without aid 500 yards in advance of his platoon and in the face of machinegun and artillery fire he encountered 4 of the enemy in a dugout, whom he attacked and killed with a handgrenade. Crawling forward to a point 150 yards in advance of his first encounter, he rushed a machinegun nest, killing 4 and capturing 6 of the enemy and taking 2 light machineguns. After being joined by his platoon he was severely wounded in the arm.

WAALER, REIDAR

Rank and organization: Sergeant, U.S. Army, Company A, 105th Machine-Gun Battalion, 27th Division. *Place and date:* Near Ronssoy, France, 27 September 1918. *Entered service at:* New York, N.Y. *Birth:* Norway. *G.O. No.:* 5, W.D., 1920. *Citation:* In the face of heavy artillery and machinegun fire, he crawled forward to a burning British tank, in which some of the crew were imprisoned, and succeeded in rescuing 2 men. Although the tank was then burning fiercely and contained ammunition which was likely to explode at any time, this soldier immediately returned to the tank and, entering it, made a search for the other occupants, remaining until he satisfied himself that there were no more living men in the tank.

WARD, CALVIN JOHN

Rank and organization: Private, U.S. Army, Company D, 117th Infantry, 30th Division. *Place and date:* Near Estrees, France, 8 October 1918. *Entered service at:* Morristown, Tenn. *Born:* October 1898, Green County, Tenn. *G.O. No.:* 16, W.D., 1919. *Citation:* During an advance, Pvt. Ward's company was held up by a machinegun, which was enfilading the line. Accompanied by a noncommissioned officer, he advanced against this post and succeeded in reducing the nest by killing 3 and capturing 7 of the enemy and their guns.

WEST, CHESTER H.

Rank and organization: First Sergeant, U.S. Army, Company D, 363d Infantry, 91st Division. *Place and date:* Near Bois-de-Cheppy, France, 26 September 1918. *Entered service at:* Los Banos, Calif. *Birth:* Fort Collins, Colo. *G.O. No.:* 34, W.D., 1919. *Citation:* While making his way through a thick fog with his automatic rifle section, his advance was halted by direct and unusual machinegun fire from 2 guns. Without aid, he at once dashed through the fire and, attacking the nest, killed 2 of the gunners, 1 of whom was an officer. This prompt and decisive hand-to-hand encounter on his part enabled his company to advance farther without the loss of a man.

WHITTLESEY, CHARLES W.

Rank and organization: Major, U.S. Army, 308th Infantry, 77th Division. *Place and date:* Northeast of Binarville, in the forest of Argonne, France, 2–7 October 1918. *Entered service at:* Pittsfield, Mass. *Birth:* Florence, Wis. *G.O. No.:* 118, W.D., 1918. *Citation:* Although cut off for 5 days from the remainder of his division, Maj. Whittlesey maintained his position, which he had reached under orders received for an advance, and held his command, consisting originally of 46 officers and men of the 308th Infantry and of Company K of the 307th Infantry, together in the face of superior numbers of the enemy during the 5 days. Maj. Whittlesey and his command were thus cut off, and no rations or other supplies reached him, in spite of determined efforts which were made by his division. On the 4th day Maj. Whittlesey received from the enemy a written proposition to surrender, which he treated with contempt, although he was at the time out of rations and had suffered a loss of about 50 percent in killed and wounded of his command and was surrounded by the enemy.

*WICKERSHAM, J. HUNTER

Rank and organization: Second Lieutenant, U.S. Army, 353d Infantry, 89th Division. *Place and date:* Near Limey, France, 12 September 1918. *Entered service at:* Denver, Colo. *Birth:* New York, N.Y. *G.O. No.:* 16, W.D., 1919. *Citation:* Advancing with his platoon during the St. Mihiel offensive, he was severely wounded in 4 places by the bursting of a high-explosive shell. Before receiving any aid for himself he dressed the wounds of his orderly, who was wounded at the same time. He then ordered and accompanied the further advance of his platoon, although weakened by the loss of blood. His right hand and arm being disabled by wounds, he continued to fire his revolver with his left hand until, exhausted by loss of blood, he fell and died from his wounds before aid could be administered.

*WOLD, NELS

Rank and organization: Private, U.S. Army, Company I, 138th Infantry, 35th Division. *Place and date:* Near Cheppy, France, 26 September 1918. *Entered service at:* Minnewaukan, N. Dak. *Birth:* Winger, Minn. *G.O. No.:* 16, W.D., 1919. *Citation:* He rendered most gallant service in aiding the advance of his company, which had been held up by machinegun nests, advancing, with 1 other soldier, and silencing the guns, bringing with him, upon his return, 11 prisoners. Later the same day he jumped from a trench and rescued a comrade who was about to be shot by a German officer, killing the officer during the exploit. His actions were entirely voluntary, and it was while attempting to rush a 5th machinegun nest that he was killed. The advance of his company was mainly due to his great courage and devotion to duty.

WOODFILL, SAMUEL

Rank and organization: First Lieutenant, U.S. Army, 60th Infantry, 5th Division. *Place and date:* At Cunel, France, 12 October 1918. *Entered service at:* Bryantsburg, Ind. *Birth:* Jefferson County, Ind. *G.O. No.:* 16, W.D., 1919. *Citation:* While he was leading his company against the enemy, his line came under heavy machinegun fire, which threatened to hold up the advance. Followed by 2 soldiers at 25 yards, this officer went out ahead of his first line toward a machinegun nest and worked his way around its flank, leaving the 2 soldiers in front. When he got within 10 yards of the gun it ceased firing, and 4 of the enemy appeared, 3 of whom were shot by 1st Lt. Woodfill. The fourth, an officer, rushed at 1st Lt. Woodfill, who attempted to club the officer with his rifle. After a hand-to-hand struggle, 1st Lt. Woodfill killed the officer with his pistol. His company thereupon continued to advance, until shortly afterwards another machinegun nest was encountered. Calling on his men to follow, 1st Lt. Woodfill rushed ahead of his line in the face of heavy fire from the nest, and when several of the enemy appeared above the nest he shot them, capturing 3 other members of the crew and silencing the gun. A few minutes later this officer for the third time demonstrated conspicuous daring by charging another machinegun position, killing 5 men in one machinegun pit with his rifle. He then drew his revolver and started to jump into the pit, when 2 other gunners only a few yards away turned their gun on him. Failing to kill them with his revolver, he grabbed a pick lying nearby and killed both of them. Inspired by the exceptional courage displayed by this officer, his men pressed on to their objective under severe shell and machinegun fire.

YORK, ALVIN C.

Rank and organization: Corporal, U.S. Army, Company G, 328th Infantry, 82d Division. *Place and date:* Near Chatel-Chehery, France, 8 October 1918. *Entered service at:* Pall Mall, Tenn. *Born:* 13 December 1887, Fentress County, Tenn. *G.O. No.:* 59, W.D., 1919. *Citation:* After his platoon had suffered heavy casualties and 3 other noncommissioned officers had become casualties, Cpl. York assumed command. Fearlessly leading 7 men, he charged with great daring a machinegun nest which was pouring deadly and incessant fire upon his platoon. In this heroic feat the machinegun nest was taken, together with 4 officers and 128 men and several guns.

DOMINICAN CAMPAIGN

United States intervention in the Dominican Republic was necessitated by one of the periodic revolutions in that area of political and economic instability. Anticipating the probability of violent reaction against our citizens, the American Minister, on 3 May 1916, requested additional naval vessels.

Fighting between the contending political factions reached a climax on 5 May and, when it became impossible to postpone armed intervention, the *Prairie* and *Castine* landed two companies of marines who were immediately sent in to protect the American and Haitian Legations. An additional detachment of sailors landed and seized Fort San Geronimo to be held as a base for the forces ashore.

Under the existing conditions of governmental and economic demoralization, an American Military Government carried out the policy proclaimed in the "Roosevelt Corollary" of 1904, to protect our own interests and to insure the efficient financial administration of the Republic's obligations abroad.

GLOWIN, JOSEPH ANTHONY

Rank and organization: Corporal, U.S. Marine Corps. *Born:* 14 March 1892, Detroit, Mich. *Accredited to:* Michigan. *G.O. No.:* 244, 30 October 1916. *Citation:* During an engagement at Guayacanas on 3 July 1916, Cpl. Glowin participated in action against a considerable force of rebels on the line of march.

WILLIAMS, ERNEST CALVIN

Rank and organization: First Lieutenant, U.S. Marine Corps. *Born:* 2 August 1887, Broadwell, Ill. *Accredited to:* Illinois. *G.O. No.:* 289, 27 April 1917. *Other Navy award:* Navy Cross. *Citation:* In action against hostile forces at San Francisco de Macoris, Dominican Republic, 29 November 1916. With only a dozen men available, 1st Lt. Williams rushed the gate of the fortress. With 8 of his party wounded by rifle fire of the defenders, he pressed on with the 4 remaining men, threw himself against the door just as it was being closed by the Dominicans and forced an entry. Despite a narrow escape from death at the hands of a rifleman, he and his men disposed of the guards and within a few minutes had gained control of the fort and the hundred prisoners confined there.

WINANS, ROSWELL

Rank and organization: Brigadier General (then First Sergeant), U.S. Marine Corps. *Place and date:* Guayacanas, Dominican Republic, 3

July 1916. *Entered service at:* Washington. *Born:* 9 December 1887, Brookville, Ind. *G.O. No.:* 244, 30 October 1916. *Citation:* During an engagement at Guavacanas on 3 July 1916, 1st Sgt. Winans participated in action against a considerable force of rebels on the line of march. During a running fight of 1,200 yards, our forces reached the enemy entrenchments and Cpl. Joseph A. Gowin, U.S.M.C., placed the machinegun, of which he had charge, behind a large log across the road and immediately opened fire on the trenches. He was struck once but continued firing his gun, but a moment later he was again struck and had to be dragged out of the position into cover. 1st Sgt. Winans, U.S.M.C., then arrived with a Colt's gun which he placed in a most exposed position, coolly opened fire on the trenches and when the gun jammed, stood up and repaired it under fire. All the time Glowin and Winans were handling their guns they were exposed to a very heavy fire which was striking into the logs and around the men, 7 men being wounded and 1 killed within 20 feet. 1st Sgt. Winans continued firing his gun until the enemy had abandoned the trenches.

INTERIM 1915 TO 1916

CARY, ROBERT W.

Rank and organization: Lieutenant Commander, U.S. Navy, U.S.S. *San Diego. Place and date:* Aboard U.S.S. *San Diego*, 21 January 1915. *Entered service at:* Buncston, Mo. *Birth:* Kansas City, Mo. *Citation:* For extraordinary heroism in the line of his profession on the occasion of an explosion on board the U.S.S. *San Diego*, 21 January 1915. Lt. Comdr. Cary (then Ensign), U.S. Navy, an observer on duty in the firerooms of the U.S.S. *San Diego*, commenced to take the half-hourly readings of the steam pressure at every boiler. He had read the steam and air pressure on No. 2 boiler and was just stepping through the electric watertight door into No. 1 fireroom when the boilers in No. 2 fireroom exploded. Ens. Cary stopped and held open the doors which were being closed electrically from the bridge, and yelled to the men in No. 2 fireroom to escape through these doors, which 3 of them did. Ens. Cary's action undoubtedly saved the lives of these men. He held the doors probably a minute with the escaping steam from the ruptured boilers around him. His example of coolness did much to keep the men in No. 1 fireroom at their posts hauling fires, although 5 boilers in their immediate vicinity had exploded and boilers Nos. 1 and 3 apparently had no water in them and were likely to explode any instant. When these fires were hauled under Nos. 1 and 3 boilers, Ens. Cary directed the men in this fireroom into the bunker, for they well knew the danger of these 2 boilers exploding. During the entire time Ens. Cary was cool and collected and showed an abundance of nerve under the most trying circumstances. His action on this occasion was above and beyond the call of duty.

CRILLEY, FRANK WILLIAM

Rank and organization: Chief Gunner's Mate, U.S. Navy. *Born:* 13 September 1883, Trenton, N.J. *Accredited to:* Pennsylvania. (19 November 1928). *Citation:* For display of extraordinary heroism in the line of his profession above and beyond the call of duty during the diving operations in connection with the sinking in a depth of water 304 feet, of the U.S.S. *F-4* with all on board, as a result of loss of depth control, which occurred off Honolulu, T.H., on 25 March 1915. On 17 April 1915, William F. Loughman, chief gunner's mate, U.S. Navy, who had descended to the wreck and had examined one of the wire hawsers attached to it, upon starting his ascent, and when at a depth of 250 feet beneath the surface of the water, had his lifeline and air hose so badly fouled by this hawser that he was unable to free himself; he could neither ascend nor descend. On account of the length of time that Loughman had already been subjected to the great pressure due to the depth of water, and of the uncertainty of the additional time he would have to be subjected to this pressure before he could be brought to the surface, it was imperative that steps be taken at once to clear him. Instantly, realizing the desperate case of his comrade, Crilley volunteered to go to his aid, immediately donned a diving suit and descended. After a lapse of time of 2 hours and 11 minutes, Crilley was brought to the surface, having by a superb exhibition of skill, coolness, endurance and fortitude, untangled the snarl of lines and cleared his imperiled comrade, so that he was brought, still alive, to the surface.

JONES, CLAUD ASHTON

Rank and organization: Commander, U.S. Navy. *Born:* 7 October 1885, Fire Creek, W.Va. *Accredited to:* West Virginia. (1 August 1932.) *Citation:* For extraordinary heroism in the line of his profession as a senior engineer officer on board the U.S.S. *Memphis*, at a time when the vessel was suffering total destruction from a hurricane while anchored off Santo Domingo City, 29 August 1916. Lt. Jones did everything possible to get the engines and boilers ready, and if the elements that burst upon the vessel had delayed for a few minutes, the engines would have saved the vessel. With boilers and steampipes bursting about him in clouds of scalding steam, with thousands of tons of water coming down upon him and in almost complete darkness, Lt. Jones nobly remained at his post as long as the engines would turn over, exhibiting the most supreme unselfish heroism which inspired the officers and men who were with him. When the boilers exploded, Lt. Jones, accompanied by 2 of his shipmates, rushed into the firerooms and drove the men there out, dragging some, carrying others to the engineroom, where there was air to be breathed instead of steam. Lt. Jones' action on this occasion was above and beyond the call of duty.

*RUD, GEORGE WILLIAM

Rank and organization: Chief Machinist's Mate, U.S. Navy. *Born:* 7 October 1883, Minneapolis, Minn. *Accredited to:* Minnesota. (1 August 1932.) *Citation:* For extraordinary heroism in the line of his profession while attached to the U.S.S. *Memphis*, at a time when that vessel was suffered total destruction from a hurricane while anchored off Santo Domingo City, 29 August 1916. C.M.M. Rud took his station in the engineroom and remained at his post amidst scalding steam and the rushing of thousands of tons of water into his department, receiving serious burns from which he immediately died.

SMITH, EUGENE P.

Rank and organization: Chief Watertender, U.S. Navy. *Born:* 8 August 1871, Truney, Ill. *Accredited to:* California. *G.O. No.:* 189, 8 February 1916. *Citation:* Attached to U.S.S. *Decatur;* for several times entering compartments on board of *Decatur* immediately following an explosion on board that vessel, 9 September 1915, and locating and rescuing injured shipmates.

SMITH, WILHELM

Rank and organization: Gunner's Mate First Class, U.S. Navy. *Born:* 10 April 1870, Germany. *Accredited to:* New York. *G.O. No.:* 202, 6 April 1916. *Citation:* On board the U.S.S. *New York;* for entering a compartment filled with gases and rescuing a shipmate on 24 January 1916.

TRINIDAD, TELESFORO

Rank and organization: Fireman Second Class, U.S. Navy. *Born:* 25 November 1890, New Washington Capig, Philippine Islands. *Accredited to:* Philippine Islands. *G.O. No.:* 142, 1 April 1915. *Citation:* For extraordinary heroism in the line of his profession at the time of the boiler explosion on board the U.S.S. *San Diego,* 21 January 1915. Trinidad was driven out of fireroom No. 2 by the explosion, but at once returned and picked up R. E. Daly, fireman, second class, whom he saw to be injured, and proceeded to bring him out. While coming into No. 4 fireroom, Trinidad was just in time to catch the explosion in No. 3 fireroom, but without consideration for his own safety, passed Daly on and then assisted in rescuing another injured man from No. 3 fireroom. Trinidad was himself burned about the face by the blast from the explosion in No. 3 fireroom.

WILLEY, CHARLES H.

Rank and organization: Machinist, U.S. Navy. *Place and date:* Off Santo Domingo City, Santo Domingo, 29 August 1916. *Entered service at:* Massachusetts. *Born:* 31 March 1889, East Boston, Mass. *G.O. No.:*—1 August 1932. *Citation:* For extraordinary heroism in the line of his profession while serving on board the U.S.S. *Memphis,* at a time when that vessel was suffering total destruction from a hurricane while anchored off Santo Domingo City, 29 August 1916. Machinist Willey took his station in the engineer's department and remained at his post of duty amidst scalding steam and the rush of thousands of tons of water into his department as long as the engines would turn, leaving only when ordered to leave. When the boilers exploded, he assisted in getting the men out of the fireroom and carrying them into the engineroom, where there was air instead of steam to breathe. Machinist Willey's conduct on this occasion was above and beyond the call of duty.

HAITIAN CAMPAIGN
1915

In 1915, our peacetime diplomacy was supported by the Navy in settling disorders at Port au Prince in Haiti. Rear Admiral Caperton alleviated the situation temporarily by landing marines and sailors from his flagship *Washington*, with reinforcements from our naval station at Guantanamo Bay. A forthcoming election pointed to more serious internal strife, and six additional ships were sent to Haiti, increasing the complement of marine officers and men to some 2,000.

In various parts of the country, native Cacos had been terrorizing the people and interrupting railroad connections, communications, and water and food supply. Efforts to control them by peaceable means were for the most part unsuccessful, and several encounters brought the marines into active combat with the troublesome group, particularly at Fort Liberte and Fort Riviere. The latter engagement developed into a sharp hand-to-hand battle with weapons, clubs, and rocks and continued in ferocity until the last Caco had fallen.

A treaty ratified in November provided for the organization of a local Gendarmerie under marine supervision for preserving law and order.

BUTLER, SMEDLEY DARLINGTON (Second Award)

Rank and organization: Major, U.S. Marine Corps. *Born:* 30 July 1881, West Chester, Pa. *Appointed from:* Pennsylvania. *Other Navy awards:* Second Medal of Honor, Distinguished Service Medal. *Citation:* As Commanding Officer of detachments from the 5th, 13th, 23d Companies and the marine and sailor detachment from the U.S.S. *Connecticut*, Maj. Butler led the attack on Fort Riviere, Haiti, 17 November 1915. Following a concentrated drive, several different detachments of marines gradually closed in on the old French bastion fort in an effort to cut off all avenues of retreat for the Caco bandits. Reaching the fort on the southern side where there was a small opening in the wall, Maj. Butler gave the signal to attack and marines from the 15th Company poured through the breach, engaged the Cacos in hand-to-hand combat, took the bastion and crushed the Caco resistance. Throughout this perilous action, Maj. Butler was conspicuous for his bravery and forceful leadership.

DALY, DANIEL JOSEPH (Second Award)

Rank and organization: Gunnery Sergeant, U.S. Marine Corps. *Born:* Glen Cove, Long Island, N.Y., 11 November 1873. *Accredited to:* New York. *Other Navy awards:* Second Medal of Honor, Navy Cross. *Citation:* Serving with the 15th Company of Marines on 22 October 1915,

G/Sgt. Daly was one of the company to leave Fort Liberte, Haiti, for a 6-day reconnaissance. After dark on the evening of 24 October, while crossing the river in a deep ravine, the detachment was suddenly fired upon from 3 sides by about 400 Cacos concealed in bushes about 100 yards from the fort. The marine detachment fought its way forward to a good position, which it maintained during the night, although subjected to a continuous fire from the Cacos. At daybreak the marines, in 3 squads, advanced in 3 different directions, surprising and scattering the Cacos in all directions. G/Sgt. Daly fought with exceptional gallantry against heavy odds throughout this action.

GROSS, SAMUEL

Rank and organization: Private, U.S. Marine Corps, 23d Co. (Real name is Marguiles, Samuel.) *Born:* 9 May 1891, Philadelphia, Pa. *Accredited to:* Pennsylvania. *Citation:* In company with members of the 5th, 13th, 23d Companies and the marine and sailor detachment from the U.S.S. *Connecticut*, Gross participated in the attack on Fort Riviere, Haiti, 17 November 1915. Following a concentrated drive, several different detachments of marines gradually closed in on the old French bastion fort in an effort to cut off all avenues of retreat for the Caco bandits. Approaching a breach in the wall which was the only entrance to the fort, Gross was the second man to pass through the breach in the face of constant fire from the Cacos and, thereafter, for a 10-minute period, engaged the enemy in desperate hand-to-hand combat until the bastion was captured and Caco resistance neutralized.

IAMS, ROSS LINDSEY

Rank and organization: Sergeant, U.S. Marine Corps, 5th Co. *Born:* 5 May 1879, Graysville, Pa. *Accredited to:* Pennsylvania. *Citation:* In company with members of the 5th, 13th, 23d Companies and marine and sailor detachment from the U.S.S. *Connecticut*, Sgt. Iams participated in the attack on Fort Riviere, Haiti, 17 November 1915. Following a concentrated drive, several different detachments of marines gradually closed in on the old French bastion fort in an effort to cut off all avenues of retreat for the Caco bandits. Approaching a breach in the wall which was the only entrance to the fort, Sgt. Iams unhesitatingly jumped through the breach despite constant fire from the Cacos and engaged the enemy in a desperate hand-to-hand combat until the bastion was captured and Caco resistance neutralized.

OSTERMANN, EDWARD ALBERT

Rank and organization: First Lieutenant, U.S. Marine Corps, 15th Company of Marines (mounted). *Place and date:* Vicinity Fort Liberte, Haiti, 24 October 1915. *Entered service at:* Ohio. *Born:* 1883, Columbus, Ohio. *Citation:* In company with members of the 15th Company of Marines, all mounted, 1st Lt. Ostermann left Fort Liberte, Haiti, for a 6-day reconnaissance. After dark on the evening of 24 October 1915, while crossing the river in a deep ravine, the detachment was suddenly fired upon from 3 sides by about 400 Cacos concealed in bushes about 100 yards from the fort. The marine detachment fought its way forward to a good position, which it maintained during the night, although subjected to a continuous fire from the Cacos. At daybreak, 1st Lt. Ostermann, in command of 1 of the 3 squads which advanced in 3 different directions, led his men forward, surprising and scattering the Cacos, and aiding in the capture of Fort Dipitie.

UPSHUR, WILLIAM PETERKIN

Rank and organization: Captain, U.S. Marine Corps. *Born:* 28 October 1881, Richmond, Va. *Appointed from:* Virginia. *Citation:* In company with members of the 15th Company of Marines, all mounted, Capt. Upshur left Fort Liberte, Haiti, for a 6-day reconnaissance. After dark on the evening of 24 October 1915, while crossing the river in a deep ravine, the detachment was suddenly fired upon from 3 sides by about 400 Cacos concealed in bushes about 100 yards from the fort. The marine detachment fought its way forward to a good position, which it maintained during the night, although subjected to a continuous fire from the Cacos. At daybreak, Capt. Upshur, in command of one of the 3 squads which advanced in 3 different directions led his men forward, surprising and scattering the Cacos, and aiding in the capture of Fort Dipitie.

MEXICAN CAMPAIGN

(VERA CRUZ)

On April 6, 1914, an incident occurred at Tampico boat landing in Mexico which sent the Navy on a diplomatic mission. While a boat from the U.S.S. *Dolphin* was obtaining supplies, the crew in charge of Commander Earle was arrested and marched through the streets under guard. Part of the men were taken from the boat itself flying the American flag.

Rear Admiral Mayo demanded a formal disavowal of this inexcusable affront. Mexican authorities refused to apologize or to comply with the demand to salute the American flag.

On 20 April, President Wilson delivered an address at a joint session of the two houses of Congress on "The situation in our dealings with General Victoriano Huerta at Mexico City." As a part of his remarks, the President said: " * * * I therefore come to ask your approval that I should use the armed forces of the United States in such ways and to such an extent as may be necessary to obtain from Gen. Huerta and his adherents the fullest recognition of the rights and dignity of the United States even amidst the distressing conditions now unhappily obtaining in Mexico.

"There can in what we do be no thought of aggression or of selfish aggrandizement. We seek to maintain the dignity and authority of the United States only because we wish always to keep our great influence unimpaired for the uses of liberty, both in the United States and wherever else it may be employed for the benefit of mankind."

On 22 April, Congress approved the employment of armed forces and disclaimed any hostility to the Mexican people or any purpose to make war upon Mexico.

Accordingly, Adm. Fletcher landed a regiment of marines from the *Prairie*, *Utah* and *Florida* together with a seaman battalion from the latter ship. These forces, augmented by seamen from the *Utah* as the engagement developed, seized the customhouse and other vital facilities near the water front. Marines and bluejackets advanced into the city despite street fighting and sniper fire.

Mexican troops firing from the naval school near the pier were taken under fire by naval vessels. The end of the first day found only about one-half of the city cleared of the Mexican forces.

During the night Adm. Fletcher took personal command ashore with additional forces landed, and Marine regiments under Lt. Col. Wendell C. Neville and Maj. Albertus W. Catlin resumed the difficult work of clearing their sector of snipers shooting from windows and the tops of buildings.

By noon of the third day, buildings had been searched, firearms confiscated and strong outposts established along the sandhills to the sea. Before Army detachments were sent to Vera Cruz to take over occupation of the city, 15 Americans had been killed and 56 wounded.

ANDERSON, EDWIN A.

Rank and organization: Captain, U.S. Navy. *Born:* 16 July 1860, Wilmington, N.C. *Accredited to:* North Carolina. *G.O. No.:* 177, 4 December 1915. *Other Navy award:* Distinguished Service Medal. *Citation:* For extraordinary heroism in battle, engagement of Vera Cruz, 22 April 1914, in command of the 2d Seaman Regiment. Marching his regiment across the open space in front of the Naval Academy and other buildings, Capt. Anderson unexpectedly met a heavy fire from riflemen, machineguns and 1-pounders, which caused part of his command to break and fall back, many casualties occurring amongst them at the time. His indifference to the heavy fire, to which he himself was exposed at the head of his regiment, showed him to be fearless and courageous in battle.

BADGER, OSCAR CHARLES

Rank and organization: Ensign, U.S. Navy. *Born:* 26 June 1890, Washington, D.C. *Accredited to:* District of Columbia. *G.O. No.:* 177, 4 December 1915. *Other Navy Award:* Navy Cross. *Citation:* For distinguished conduct in battle, engagements of Vera Cruz, 21 and 22 April

1914. Ens. Badger was in both days' fighting at the head of his company, and was eminent and conspicuous in his conduct, leading his men with skill and courage.

BEASLEY, HARRY C.

Rank and organization: Seaman, U.S. Navy. *Born:* 1 November 1888, Ohio. *Accredited to:* Ohio. *G.O. No.:* 101, 15 June 1914. *Citation:* On board the U.S.S. *Florida* for extraordinary heroism in the line of his profession during the seizure of Vera Cruz, Mexico, 21 April 1914.

BERKELEY, RANDOLPH CARTER

Rank and organization: Major, U.S. Marine Corps. *Born:* 9 January 1875, Staunton, Va. *Appointed from:* Washington, D.C. *G.O. No.:* 177, 4 December 1915. *Other Navy awards:* Navy Cross, Distinguished Service Medal. *Citation:* For distinguished conduct in battle, engagements of Vera Cruz, 21 and 22 April 1914. Maj. Berkeley was eminent and conspicuous in command of his battalion; was in the fighting of both days, and exhibited courage and skill in leading his men through action. His cool judgment and courage, and his skill in handling his men in encountering and overcoming the machinegun and rifle fire down Cinco de Mayo and parallel streets account for the small percentage of the losses of marines under his command.

BISHOP, CHARLES FRANCIS

Rank and organization: Quartermaster Second Class, U.S. Navy. *Born:* 2 August 1898, Pittsburgh, Pa. *Accredited to:* Pennsylvania. *G.O. No.:* 101, 15 June 1914. *Citation:* On board the U.S.S. *Florida* for extraordinary heroism in the line of his profession during the seizure of Vera Cruz, Mexico, 21 April 1914.

BRADLEY, GEORGE

Rank and organization: Chief Gunner's Mate, U.S. Navy. *Born:* 5 December 1881, New York, N.Y. *Accredited to:* Rhode Island. *G.O. No.:* 117, 13 September 1923. *Citation:* For meritorious service under fire on the occasion of the landing of the American naval forces at Vera Cruz in 1914. C.G. Bradley was then attached to the U.S.S. *Utah*, as a chief gunner's mate, and was in charge of the ammunition party and special details at Vera Cruz. (Medal presented by President Coolidge at the White House on 4 October 1923.)

BUCHANAN, ALLEN

Rank and organization: Lieutenant Commander, U.S. Navy. *Born:* 22 December 1876, Evansville, Ind. *Accredited to:* Indiana. *G.O. No.:* 177, 4 December 1915. *Other Navy award:* Navy Cross. *Citation:* For distinguished conduct in battle, engagements of Vera Cruz, 21 and 22 April 1914. In command of the 1st Seaman Regiment, Lt. Cmdr. Buchanan was in both days' fighting and almost continually under fire from soon after landing, about noon of the 21st, until we were in possession of the city, about noon of the 22d. His duties required him to be at points of great danger in directing his officers and men, and he exhibited conspicuous courage, coolness, and skill in his conduct of the fighting. Upon his courage and skill depended, in great measure, success or failure. His responsibilities were great, and he met them in a manner worthy of commendation.

BUTLER, SMEDLEY DARLINGTON (First Award)

Rank and organization: Major, U.S. Marine Corps. *Born:* 30 July 1881, West Chester, Pa. *Appointed from:* Pennsylvania. *G.O. No.:* 177, 4 December 1915. *Other Navy awards:* Second Medal of Honor, Distinguished Service Medal. *Citation:* For distinguished conduct in battle, engagement of Vera Cruz, 22 April 1914. Maj. Butler was eminent and conspicuous in command of his battalion. He exhibited courage and skill in leading his men through the action of the 22d and in the final occupation of the city.

CASTLE, GUY WILKINSON STUART

Rank and organization: Lieutenant, U.S. Navy. *Born:* 8 February 1880. *Appointed from:* Wisconsin. *G.O. No.:* 177, 4 December 1915. *Citation:* For distinguished conduct in battle, engagements of Vera Cruz, 21 and 22 April 1914. Eminent and conspicuous in command of his battalion, Lt. Castle was in the fighting of both days, and exhibited courage and skill in leading his men through action. In seizing the customhouse, he encountered for many hours the heaviest and most pernicious concealed fire of the entire day, but his courage and coolness under trying conditions were marked.

CATLIN, ALBERTUS WRIGHT

Rank and organization: Major, U.S. Marine Corps. *Born:* 1 December 1868, Gowanda, N.Y. *Appointed from:* Minnesota. *G.O. No.:* 177, 4 December 1915. *Citation:* For distinguished conduct in battle, engagement of Vera Cruz, 22 April 1914. Eminent and conspicuous in command of his battalion, Maj. Catlin exhibited courage and skill in leading his men through the action of the 22d and in the final occupation of the city.

COURTS, GEORGE McCALL

Rank and organization: Lieutenant, Junior Grade, U.S. Navy. *Born:* 16 February 1888, Washington, D.C. *Accredited to:* District of Columbia. *G.O. No.:* 177, 4 December 1915. *Citation:* For distinguished conduct in battle, engagements of Vera Cruz, 21 and 22 April 1914. Under fire, Lt.(jg.) Courts was eminent and conspicuous in the performance of his duties. He had well qualified himself by thorough study during his years of duty in Mexico to deal with the conditions of this engagement, and his services were of great value. He twice volunteered and passed in an open boat through the zone of fire to convey important orders to the *Chester*, then under a severe fire.

CREGAN, GEORGE

Rank and organization: Coxswain, U.S. Navy. *Place and date:* On board the U.S.S. *Florida*, at Vera Cruz, Mexico, 21 April 1914. *Entered service at:* New York. *Born:* 11 December 1885, New York, N.Y. *G.O. No.:* 101, 15 June 1914. *Citation:* On board the U.S.S. *Florida*, for extraordinary heroism in the line of his profession during the seizure of Vera Cruz, Mexico, 21 April 1914. Cregan was ashore when he volunteered for an assault detail under Ens. George Maus Lowry on the Vera Cruz Customhouse under enemy fire both in the alley between the customhouse and warehouse and the assault over objective's walls. During the move up the alley, he tended a wounded comrade, J. F. Schumaker holding a compress with one hand and firing with the other.

DECKER, PERCY A.

Rank and organization: Boatswain's Mate Second Class, U.S. Navy. *Born:* 4 August 1890, New York, N.Y. *Accredited to:* New York. *G.O. No.:* 101, 15 June 1914. *Citation:* On board the U.S.S. *Florida* during the seizure of Vera Cruz, Mexico, 21 April 1914; for extraordinary heroism in the line of his profession during the seizure of Vera Cruz, Mexico.

DeSOMER, ABRAHAM

Rank and organization: Lieutenant, U.S. Navy, U.S.S. *Utah. Place and date:* Vera Cruz, Mexico, 21 and 22 April 1914. *Entered service at:* Wisconsin. *Birth:* Milwaukee, Wis. *Citation:* On board the U.S.S. *Utah,* for extraordinary heroism in the line of his profession during the seizure of Vera Cruz, Mexico, 21 and 22 April 1914.

DRUSTRUP, NIELS

Rank and organization: Lieutenant, U.S. Navy. *Born:* 17 October 1876, Denmark. *Accredited to:* Pennsylvania. *G.O. No.:* 131, 17 July 1924. *Citation:* For meritorious service under fire on the occasion of landing of the naval forces at Vera Cruz, Mexico, on 21 April 1914. For several hours Lt. Drustrup was in charge of an advanced barricade under a heavy fire, and not only displayed utmost ability as a leader of men but also exerted a great steadying influence on the men around him. Lt. Drustrup was then attached to the U.S.S. *Utah* as a chief turret captain.

DYER, JESSE FARLEY

Rank and organization: Captain, U.S. Marine Corps. *Born:* 2 December 1877, St. Paul, Minn. *Appointed from:* Minnesota. *G.O. No.:* 177, 4 December 1915. *Citation:* For distinguished conduct in battle, engagements of Vera Cruz, 21 and 22 April 1914; was in both days fighting at the head of his company, and was eminent and conspicuous in his conduct, leading his men with skill and courage.

ELLIOTT, MIDDLETON STUART

Rank and organization: Surgeon, U.S. Navy. *Born:* 16 October 1872, Beaufort, S.C. *Accredited to:* South Carolina. *G.O. No.:* 177, 4 December 1915. *Citation:* For distinguished conduct in battle, engagements of Vera Cruz, 21 and 22 April 1914. Surg. Elliott was eminent and conspicuous in the efficient establishment and operation of the base hospital, and in his cool judgment and courage in supervising first aid stations on the firing line and removing the wounded.

FLETCHER, FRANK FRIDAY

Rank and organization: Rear Admiral, U.S. Navy. *Born:* 23 November 1855, Oskaloosa, Iowa. *Accredited to:* Iowa. *G.O. No.:* 177, 4 December 1915. *Citation:* For distinguished conduct in battle, engagements of Vera Cruz, 21 and 22 April 1914. Under fire, Rear Adm. Fletcher was eminent and conspicuous in the performance of his duties; was senior officer present at Vera Cruz, and the landing and the operations of the landing force were carried out under his orders and directions. In connection with these operations, he was at times on shore and under fire.

FLETCHER, FRANK JACK

Rank and organization: Lieutenant, U.S. Navy. *Place and date:* Vera Cruz, Mexico, 21 and 22 April 1914. *Entered service at:* Iowa. *Born:* 29 April 1885, Marshalltown, Iowa. *G.O. No.:* 177, 4 December 1915. *Citation:* For distinguished conduct in battle, engagements of Vera Cruz, 21 and 22 April 1914. Under fire, Lt. Fletcher was eminent and conspicuous in performance of his duties. He was in charge of the *Esperanze* and succeeded in getting on board over 350 refugees, many of them after the conflict had commenced. Although the ship was under fire, being struck more than 30 times, he succeeded in getting all the refugees placed in safety. Lt. Fletcher was later placed in charge of the train conveying refugees under a flag of truce. This was hazardous duty, as it was believed that the track was mined, and a small error in dealing with the Mexican guard of soldiers might readily have caused a conflict, such a conflict at one time being narrowly averted. It was greatly due to his efforts in establishing friendly relations with the Mexican soldiers that so many refugees succeeded in reaching Vera Cruz from the interior.

FOSTER, PAUL FREDERICK

Rank and organization: Ensign, U.S. Navy. *Place and date:* Vera Cruz, Mexico, 21 and 22 April 1914. *Entered service at:* Kansas. *Birth:* Wichita, Kans. *G.O. No.:* 177, 4 December 1915. *Citation:* For distinguished conduct in battle, engagements of Vera Cruz, 21 and 22 April 1914. In both days' fighting at the head of his company, Ens. Foster was eminent and conspicuous in his conduct, leading his men with skill and courage.

FRAZER, HUGH CARROLL

Rank and organization: Ensign, U.S. Navy. *Place and date:* Vera Cruz, Mexico, 22 April 1914. *Entered service at:* West Virginia. *Birth:* Martinsburg, W. Va. *G.O. No.:* 177, 4 December 1915. *Citation:* For extraordinary heroism in battle, engagement of Vera Cruz, 22 April 1914. During this engagement, Ens. Frazer ran forward to rescue a wounded man, exposing himself to hostile fire and that of his own men. Having accomplished the mission, he returned at once to his position in line.

FRYER, ELI THOMPSON

Rank and organization: Captain, U.S. Marine Corps. *Born:* 22 August 1878, Hightstown, N.J. *Appointed from:* New Jersey. *G.O. No.:* 177, 4 December 1915. *Citation:* For distinguished conduct in battle, engagements of Vera Cruz, 21 and 22 April 1914. In both days' fighting at the head of his company, Captain Fryer was eminent and conspicuous in his conduct, leading his men with skill and courage.

GAUJOT, JULIEN E.

Rank and organization: Captain, Troop K, 1st U.S. Cavalry. *Place and date:* At Aqua Prieta, Mexico, 13 April 1911. *Entered service at:* Williamson, W. Va. *Birth:* Keweenaw, Mich. *Date of issue:* 23 November 1912. *Citation:* Crossed the field of fire to obtain the permission of the rebel commander to receive the surrender of the surrounded forces of Mexican Federals and escort such forces, together with 5 Americans held as prisoners, to the American line.

GISBURNE, EDWARD A.

Rank and organization: Electrician Third Class, U.S. Navy. *Born:* 14 June 1892, Providence, R.I. *Accredited to:* Massachusetts. *G.O. No.:* 101, 15 June 1914. *Citation:* On board the U.S.S. *Florida* during the seizure of Vera Cruz, Mexico, 21 and 22 April 1914, and for extraordinary heroism in the line of his profession during this action.

GRADY, JOHN

Rank and organization: Lieutenant, U.S. Navy. *Born:* 25 December 1872, Canada. *Appointed from:* Massachusetts. *G.O. No.:* 177, 4 December 1915. *Other Navy award:* Navy Cross. *Citation:* For distinguished conduct in battle, engagement of Vera Cruz, 22 April 1914. During the second day's fighting, the service performed by Lt. Grady, in command of the 2d Regiment, Artillery, was eminent and conspicuous. From necessarily exposed positions, he shelled the enemy from the strongest position.

HARNER, JOSEPH GABRIEL

Rank and organization: Boatswain's Mate Second Class, U.S. Navy. *Born:* 19 February 1889, Louisville, Ohio. *Accredited to:* Ohio. *G.O. No.:* 101, 15 June 1914. *Citation:* On board the U.S.S. *Florida,* for extraordinary heroism in the line of his profession during the seizure of Vera Cruz, Mexico, 21 April 1914.

HARRISON, WILLIAM KELLY

Rank and organization: Commander, U.S. Navy. *Born:* 30 July 1870, Waco, Tex. *Accredited to:* Texas. *G.O. No.:* 177, 4 December 1915. *Citation:* For distinguished conduct in battle, engagements of Vera Cruz, 21 and 22 April 1914. During this period, Comdr. Harrison brought his ship into the inner harbor during the nights of the 21st and 22d without the assistance of a pilot or navigational lights, and was in a position on the morning of the 22d to use his guns with telling effect at a critical time.

HARTIGAN, CHARLES CONWAY

Rank and organization: Lieutenant, U.S. Navy. *Born:* 13 September 1882, Norwich, N.Y. *Accredited to:* New York. *G.O. No.:* 177, 4 December 1915. *Citation:* For distinguished conduct in battle, engagement of Vera Cruz, 22 April 1914. During the second day's fighting the service performed by him was eminent and conspicuous. He was conspicuous for the skillful handling of his company under heavy rifle and machinegun fire, for which conduct he was commended by his battalion commander.

HILL, WALTER NEWELL

Rank and organization: Captain, U.S. Marine Corps. *Born:* 29 September 1881, Haverhill, Mass. *Appointed from:* Massachusetts. *G.O. No.:* 177, 4 December 1915. *Citation:* For distinguished conduct in battle, engagements of Vera Cruz, 21 and 22 April 1914. Capt. Hill was in both days' fighting at the head of his company, and was eminent and conspicuous in his conduct, leading his men with skill and courage.

HUGHES, JOHN ARTHUR

Rank and organization: Captain, U.S. Marine Corps. *Born:* 2 November 1880, New York, N.Y. *Accredited to:* New York. G.O. No.: 177, 4 December 1915. *Other Navy award:* Navy Cross. *Citation:* For distinguished conduct in battle, engagements of Vera Cruz, 21 and 22 April 1914. Capt. Hughes was in both days' fighting at the head of his company, and was eminent and conspicuous in his conduct, leading his men with skill and courage.

HUSE, HENRY McLAREN PINCKNEY

Rank and organization: Captain, U.S. Navy. *Born:* 8 December 1858, U.S. Military Academy, West Point, N.Y. *Appointed from:* New York. *G.O. No.:* 177, 4 December 1915. *Citation:* For distinguished conduct in battle, engagements of Vera Cruz, 21 and 22 April 1914. Under fire, Capt. Huse was eminent and conspicuous in the performance of his duties; was indefatigable in his labors of a most important character, both with the division commander in directing affairs and in his efforts on shore to get in communication with the Mexican authorities to avoid needlessly prolonging the conflict.

INGRAM, JONAS HOWARD

Rank and organization: Lieutenant, Junior Grade, U.S. Navy. *Born:* 15 October 1886, Jeffersonville, Ind. *Accredited to:* Indiana. *G.O. No.:* 177, 4 December 1915. *Other Navy awards:* Navy Cross, Distinguished Service Medal with gold stars in lieu of 2 additional DSM's. *Citation:* For distinguished conduct in battle, engagement of Vera Cruz, 22 April 1914. During the second day's fighting the service performed by him was eminent and conspicuous. He was conspicuous for skillful and efficient handling of the artillery and machineguns of the Arkansas battalion, for which he was specially commended in reports.

JARRETT, BERRIE H.

Rank and organization: Seaman, U.S. Navy. *Born:* 10 June 1894, Baltimore, Md. *Accredited to:* Maryland. *G.O. No.:* 116, 19 August 1914. *Citation:* On board the U.S.S. *Florida* Jarrett displayed extraordinary heroism in the line of his profession during the seizure of Vera Cruz, Mexico, 21 April 1914.

JOHNSTON, RUFUS ZENAS

Rank and organization: Lieutenant Commander, U.S. Navy. *Born:* 7 June 1874, Lincolnton, N.C. *Accredited to:* North Carolina. *G.O. No.:* 177, 4 December 1915. *Other Navy award:* Navy Cross. *Citation:* For distinguished conduct in battle, engagement of Vera Cruz, 22 April 1914; was regimental adjutant, and eminent and conspicuous in his conduct. He exhibited courage and skill in leading his men through the action of the 22d and in the final occupation of the city.

LANGHORNE, CARY DeVALL

Rank and organization: Surgeon, U.S. Navy. *Born:* 14 May 1873, Lynchburg, Va. *Accredited to:* Virginia. *G.O. No.:* 177, 4 December 1915. *Citation:* For extraordinary heroism in battle, engagement of Vera Cruz, 22 April 1914. Surg. Langhorne carried a wounded man from the front of the Naval Academy while under heavy fire.

LANNON, JAMES PATRICK

Rank and organization: Lieutenant, U.S. Navy. *Born:* 12 October 1878, Alexandria, Va. *Accredited to:* Virginia. *G.O. No.:* 177, 4 December 1915. *Other Navy award:* Navy Cross. *Citation:* For extraordinary heroism in battle, engagement of Vera Cruz, 22 April 1914. Lt. Lannon assisted a wounded man under heavy fire, and after returning to his battalion was himself desperately wounded.

LOWRY, GEORGE MAUS

Rank and organization: Ensign, U.S. Navy. *Place and date:* Vera Cruz, Mexico, 21–22 April 1914. *Entered service at:* Pennsylvania. *Birth:* Eve, Pa. *G.O. No.:* 177, 4 December 1915. *Citation:* For distinguished conduct in battle, engagements of Vera Cruz, 21–22 April 1914; Ens. Lowry was in both days' fighting at the head of his company, and was eminent and conspicuous in his conduct, leading his men with skill and courage.

McCLOY, JOHN (Second Award)

Rank and organization: Chief Boatswain, U.S. Navy. *Born:* 3 January 1876, Brewster, N.Y. *Accredited to:* New York. *G.O. No.:* 177, 4 December 1915. *Other Navy awards:* Second Medal of Honor, Navy, Cross. *Citation:* For heroism in leading 3 picket launches along Vera Cruz sea front, drawing Mexican fire and enabling cruisers to save our men on shore, 22 April 1914. Though wounded, he gallantly remained at his post.

562

McDONNELL, EDWARD ORRICK

Rank and organization: Ensign, U.S. Navy. *Born:* 13 November
1891, Baltimore, Md. *Accredited to:* Maryland. *G.O. No.:* 177, 4
December 1915. *Citation:* For extraordinary heroism in battle, engagements of Vera Cruz, 21 and 22 April 1914. Posted on the roof of the
Terminal Hotel and landing, Ens. McDonnell established a signal station there day and night, maintaining communication between troops
and ships. At this exposed post he was continually under fire. One man
was killed and 3 wounded at his side during the 2 days' fighting. He
showed extraordinary heroism and striking courage and maintained his
station in the highest degree of efficiency. All signals got through,
largely due to his heroic devotion to duty.

McNAIR, FREDERICK VALLETTE, Jr.

Rank and organization: Lieutenant, U.S. Navy. *Born:* 13 March,
1882, Maryland. *Appointed at large. G.O. No.:* 177, 4 December 1915.
Other Navy award: Navy Cross. *Citation:* For distinguished conduct in
battle engagement of Vera Cruz, 22 April 1914. Lt. McNair was
eminent and conspicuous in command of his battalion. He exhibited
courage and skill in leading his men through the action of the 22d and
in the final occupation of the city.

MOFFETT, WILLIAM A.

Rank and organization: Commander, U.S. Navy. *Entered service at:*
Charleston, S.C. *Born:* 31 October 1869, Charleston, S.C. *G.O. No.:*
177, 4 December 1915. *Other Navy award:* Distinguished Service
Medal. *Citation:* For distinguished conduct in battle, engagements of
Vera Cruz, 21 and 22 April 1914. Comdr. Moffett brought his ship
into the inner harbor during the nights of the 21st and 22d without the
assistance of a pilot or navigational lights, and was in a position on the
morning of the 22d to use his guns at a critical time with telling effect.
His skill in mooring his ship at night was especially noticeable. He
placed her nearest to the enemy and did most of the firing and
received most of the hits.

NEVILLE, WENDELL CUSHING

Rank and organization: Lieutenant Colonel, U.S. Marine Corps.
Born: 12 May 1870, Portsmouth, Va. *Appointed from:* Virginia. *G.O.
No.:* 177, 4 December 1915. *Other Navy award:* Distinguished Service
Medal. *Citation:* For distinguished conduct in battle engagements of
Vera Cruz 21 and 22 April 1914. In command of the 2d Regiment
Marines, Lt. Col. Neville was in both days' fighting and almost continually under fire from soon after landing, about noon on the 21st,
until we were in possession of the city, about noon of the 22d. His duties required him to be at points of great danger in directing his officers and men, and he exhibited conspicuous courage, coolness, and
skill in his conduct of the fighting. Upon his courage and skill depended, in great measure, success or failure. His responsibilities were
great and he met them in a manner worthy of commendation.

NICKERSON, HENRY NEHEMIAH

Rank and organization: Boatswain's Mate Second Class, U.S. Navy, U.S.S. *Utah. Place and date:* Vera Cruz, Mexico, 21 April 1914. *Entered service at:* West Virginia. *Birth:* Edgewood, W. Va. *Citation:* On board the U.S.S. *Utah,* Nickerson showed extraordinary heroism in the line of his profession during the seizure of Vera Cruz, Mexico, 21 April 1914.

NORDSIEK, CHARLES LUERS

Rank and organization: Ordinary Seaman, U.S. Navy. *Born:* 19 April 1896, New York, N.Y. *Accredited to:* New York. *G.O. No.:* 101, 15 June 1914. *Citation:* On board the U.S.S. *Florida,* Nordsiek showed extraordinary heroism in the line of his profession during the seizure of Vera Cruz, Mexico, 21 and 22 April 1914.

REID, GEORGE CROGHAN

Rank and organization: Major, U.S. Marine Corps. *Born:* 9 December 1876, Lorain, Ohio. *Appointed from:* Ohio. *G.O. No.:* 177, 4 December 1915. *Citation:* For distinguished conduct in battle, engagements of Vera Cruz, 21 and 22 April 1914; was eminent and conspicuous in command of his battalion; was in the righting of both days and exhibited courage and skill in leading his men through action. His cool judgment and courage and his skill in handling his men in encountering and overcoming the machinegun and rifle fire down Cinco de Mayo and parallel streets account for the small percentage of the losses of marines under his command.

RUSH, WILLIAM REES

Rank and organization: Captain, U.S. Navy. *Born:* 19 September 1857, Philadelphia, Pa. *Accredited to:* Pennsylvania. *G.O. No.:* 177, 4 December 1915. *Other Navy award:* Distinguished Service Medal. *Citation:* For distinguished conduct in battle, engagements of Vera Cruz, 21 and 22 April 1914. In command of the naval brigade, Capt. Rush was in both days' fighting and almost continually under fire from soon after landing, about noon on the 21st, until we were in possession of the city, about noon of the 22d. His duties required him to be at points of great danger in directing his officers and men, and he exhibited conspicuous courage, coolness and skill in his conduct of the fighting. Upon his courage and skill depended in great measure success or failure. His responsibilities were great, and he met them in a manner worthy of commendation.

SCHNEPEL, FRED JURGEN

Rank and organization: Ordinary Seaman, U.S. Navy. *Born:* 24 February 1892, New York, N.Y. *Accredited to:* New York. *G.O. No.:* 101, 15 June 1914. *Citation:* On board the U.S.S. *Florida,* Schnepel showed extraordinary heroism in the line of his profession during the seizure of Vera Cruz, Mexico, 21 and 22 April 1914.

SEMPLE, ROBERT

Rank and organization: Chief Gunner, U.S. Navy. *Born:* 18 August 1887, Pittsburgh, Pa. *Accredited to:* Pennsylvania. *G.O. No.:* 120, 10 January 1924. *Other Navy award:* Navy Cross. *Citation:* For meritorious service under fire on the occasion of the landing of the American naval forces at Vera Cruz on 21 April 1914. C.G. Semple was then attached to the U.S.S. *Florida* as a chief turret captain.

SINNETT, LAWRENCE C.

Rank and organization: Seaman, U.S. Navy. *Born:* 4 April 1888, Burnt House, W. Va. *Accredited to:* Pennsylvania. *G.O. No.:* 101, 15 June 1914. *Citation:* On board the U.S.S. *Florida*, Sinnett showed extraordinary heroism in the line of his profession during the seizure of Vera Cruz, Mexico, 21 April 1914.

STATON, ADOLPHUS

Rank and organization: Lieutenant, U.S. Navy. *Place and date:* Vera Cruz, Mexico, 22 April 1914. *Entered service at:* North Carolina. *Born:* 28 August 1879, Tarboro, N.C. *Citation:* For distinguished conduct in battle, engagement of Vera Cruz, 22 April 1914; was eminent and conspicuous in command of his battalion. He exhibited courage and skill in leading his men through the action of the 22d and in the final occupation of the city.

STICKNEY, HERMAN OSMAN

Rank and organization: Commander, U.S. Navy. *Born:* 10 December 1867, Pepperell, Mass. *Accredited to:* Massachusetts. *G.O. No.:* 177, 4 December 1915. *Other Navy award:* Navy Cross. *Citation:* For distinguished conduct in battle, engagements of Vera Cruz, 21 and 22 April 1914. Comdr. Stickney covered the landing of the 21st with the guns of the *Prairie*, and throughout the attack and occupation, rendered important assistance to our forces on shore with his 3-inch battery.

TOWNSEND, JULIUS CURTIS

Rank and organization: Lieutenant, U.S. Navy. *Born:* 22 February 1881, Athens, Mo. *Entered service at:* Athens, Mo. *G.O. No.:* 177, 4 December 1915. *Citation:* For distinguished conduct in battle, engagement of Vera Cruz, 22 April 1914. Lt. Townsend was eminent and conspicuous in command of his battalion. He exhibited courage and skill in leading his men through the action of the 22d and in the final occupation of the city.

WAINWRIGHT, RICHARD, Jr.

Rank and organization: Lieutenant, U.S. Navy. *Born:* 15 September 1881, Washington, D.C. *Accredited to:* District of Columbia. *G.O. No.:* 177, 4 December 1915. *Citation:* For distinguished conduct in battle, engagements of Vera Cruz, 21 and 22 April 1914. Lt. Wainwright was eminent and conspicuous in command of his battalion; was in the fighting of both days, and exhibited courage and skill in leading his men through action. In seizing the customhouse, he encountered for many hours the heaviest and most pernicious concealed fire of the entire day, but his courage and coolness under trying conditions were marked.

WALSH, JAMES A.

Rank and organization: Seaman, U.S. Navy. *Born:* 24 July 1897, New York, N.Y. *Entered service at:* New York, N.Y. *G.O. No.:* 101, 15 June 1914. *Citation:* On board the U.S.S. *Florida;* for extraordinary heroism in the line of his profession during the seizure of Vera Cruz, Mexico, 21 and 22 April 1914.

WILKINSON, THEODORE STARK, Jr.

Rank and organization: Ensign, U.S. Navy. *Born:* 22 December 1888, Annapolis, Md. *Appointed from:* Louisiana. *G.O. No.:* 177, 4 December 1915. *Other Navy award:* Distinguished Service Medal with gold stars in lieu of 2 additional DSM's. *Citation:* For distinguished conduct in battle, engagements of Vera Cruz, 21 and 22 April 1914. Ens. Wilkinson was in both days' fighting at the head of his company and was eminent and conspicuous in his conduct, leading his men with skill and courage.

ZUIDERVELD, WILLIAM

Rank and organization: Hospital Apprentice First Class, U.S. Navy. *Place and date:* Vera Cruz, Mexico, 21 April 1914. *Entered service at:* Michigan. *Birth:* Michigan. *G.O. No.:* 116, 9 August 1914. *Citation:* On board the U.S.S. *Florida,* Zuiderveld showed extraordinary heroism in the line of his profession during the seizure of Vera Cruz, Mexico, 21 April 1914.

ACTION AGAINST OUTLAWS PHILIPPINES 1911

CATHERWOOD, JOHN HUGH

Rank and organization: Ordinary Seaman, U.S. Navy. *Born:* 7 August 1888, Springfield, Ill. *Accredited to:* Illinois. *G.O. No.:* 138, 13 December 1911. *Citation:* While attached to the U.S.S. *Pampang,* Catherwood was one of a shore party moving in to capture Mundang, on the island of Basilan, Philippine Islands, on the morning of 24 September 1911. Advancing with the scout party to reconnoiter a group of nipa huts close to the trail, Catherwood unhesitatingly entered the open area before the huts, where his party was suddenly taken under point-blank fire and charged by approximately 20 enemy Moros coming out from inside the native huts and from other concealed positions. Struck down almost instantly by the outlaws' deadly fire, Catherwood, although unable to rise, rallied to the defense of his leader and fought desperately to beat off the hostile attack. By his valiant effort under fire and in the face of great odds, Catherwood contributed materially toward the destruction and rout of the enemy.

HARRISON, BOLDEN REUSH

Rank and organization: Seaman, U.S. Navy. *Born:* 26 April 1886, Savannah, Tenn. *Accredited to:* Tennessee. *G.O. No.:* 138, 13 December 1911. *Citation:* While attached to the U.S.S. *Pampang,* Harrison was one of a shore party moving in to capture Mundang, on the island of Basilan, Philippine Islands, on 24 September 1911. Harrison instantly responded to the calls for help when the advance scout party investigating a group of nipa huts close to the trail, was suddenly taken under point-blank fire and rushed by approximately 20 enemy Moros attacking from inside the huts and from other concealed positions. Armed with a double-barreled shotgun, he concentrated his blasting fire on the outlaws, destroying 3 of the Moros and assisting in the rout of the remainder. By his aggressive charging of the enemy under heavy fire and in the face of great odds, Harrison contributed materially to the success of the engagement.

McGUIRE, FRED HENRY

Rank and organization: Hospital Apprentice, U.S. Navy. *Born:* 7 November 1890, Gordonville, Mo. *Entered service at:* Gordonville, Mo. *G.O. No.:* 138, 13 December 1911. *Citation:* While attached to the U.S.S. *Pampang,* McGuire was one of a shore party moving in to capture Mundang, on the island of Basilan, Philippine Islands, on the morning of 24 September 1911. Ordered to take station within 100 yards of a group of nipa huts close to the trail, McGuire advanced and stood guard as the leader and his scout party first searched the surrounding deep grasses, then moved into the open area before the huts. Instantly enemy Moros opened point-blank fire on the exposed men and approximately 20 Moros charged the small group from inside the huts and from other concealed positions. McGuire, responding to the calls for help, was one of the first on the scene. After emptying his rifle into the attackers, he closed in with rifle, using it as a club to wage fierce battle until his comrades arrived on the field, when he rallied to the aid of his dying leader and other wounded. Although himself wounded, McGuire ministered tirelessly and efficiently to those who had been struck down, thereby saving the lives of 2 who otherwise might have succumbed to enemy-inflicted wounds.

HENRECHON, GEORGE FRANCIS

Rank and organization: Machinist's Mate Second Class, U.S. Navy. *Born:* 22 November 1885, Hartford, Conn. *Accredited to:* California. *G.O. No.:* 138, 13 December 1911. *Citation:* While attached to the U.S.S. *Pampang,* Henrechon was one of a shore party moving in to capture Mundang, Philippine Islands, on 24 September 1911. Ordered to take station within 100 yards of a group of nipa huts close to the trail, Henrechon advanced and stood guard as the leader and his scout party first searched the surrounding deep grasses, then moved into the open area before the huts. Instantly enemy Moros opened point-blank fire on the exposed men and approximately 20 Moros rushed the small group from inside the huts and from other concealed positions. Henrechon, responding to the calls for help, was one of the first on the scene. When his rifle jammed after the first shot, he closed in with rifle, using it as a club to break the stock over the head of the nearest Moro and then, drawing his pistol, started in pursuit of the fleeing outlaws. Henrechon's aggressive charging of the enemy under heavy fire and in the face of great odds contributed materially to the success of the engagement.

VOLZ, JACOB

Rank and organization: Carpenter's Mate Third Class, U.S. Navy. *Place and date:* Island of Basilan, Philippine Islands, 24 September 1911. *Entered service at:* Nebraska. *Birth:* Sutton, Nebr. *G.O. No.:* 138, 13 December 1911. *Citation:* While attached to the U.S.S. *Pampang,* Volz was one of a shore party moving in to capture Mundang, on the island of Basilan, Philippine Islands, on 24 September 1911. Investigating a group of nipa huts close to the trail, the advance scout party was suddenly taken under point-blank fire and rushed by approximately 20 enemy Moros attacking from inside the huts and other concealed positions. Volz responded instantly to calls for help and, finding all members of the scout party writhing on the ground but still fighting, he blazed his rifle into the outlaws with telling effect, destroying several of the Moros and assisting in the rout of the remainder. By his aggressive charging of the enemy under heavy fire and in the face of great odds, Volz contributed materially to the success of the engagement.

INTERIM 1901 TO 1910

BEHNE, FREDERICK

Rank and organization: Fireman First Class, U.S. Navy. *Born:* 3 October 1873, Lodi, N.J. *Accredited to:* New Jersey. *G.O. No.:* 182, 20 March 1905. *Citation:* On board the U.S.S. *Iowa*, 25 January 1905. Following the blowing out of the manhole plate of boiler D of that vessel, Behne displayed extraordinary heroism in the resulting action.

BEHNKE, HEINRICH

Rank and organization: Seaman First Class, U.S. Navy. *Born:* 10 April 1882, Germany. *Accredited to:* Washington, D.C. *G.O. No.:* 182, 20 March 1905. *Citation:* While serving aboard the U.S.S. *Iowa*, Behnke displayed extraordinary heroism at the time of the blowing out of the manhole plate of boiler D on board that vessel, 25 January 1905.

BJORKMAN, ERNEST H.

Rank and organization: Ordinary Seaman, U.S. Navy. *Born:* 25 April 1881, Malmo, Sweden. *Accredited to:* New York. *G.O. No.:* 145, 26 December 1903. *Citation:* On board the U.S.S. *Leyden*, 21 January 1903, Bjorkman displayed heroism at the time of the wreck of that vessel.

BOERS, EDWARD WILLIAM

Rank and organization: Seaman, U.S. Navy. *Born:* 10 March 1884, Cincinnati, Ohio. *Accredited to:* Kentucky. *G.O. No.:* 13, 5 January 1906. *Citation:* On board the U.S.S. *Bennington*, 21 July 1905. Following the explosion of a boiler of that vessel, Boers displayed extraordinary heroism in the resulting action.

BONNEY, ROBERT EARL

Rank and organization: Chief Watertender, U.S. Navy, U.S.S. *Hopkins. Place and date:* Aboard U.S.S. *Hopkins*, 14 February 1910. *Entered service at:* Nashville, Tenn. *Birth:* Tennessee. *Citation:* While serving on board the U.S.S. *Hopkins*, Bonney displayed extraordinary heroism in the line of his profession on the occasion of the accident to one of the boilers of that vessel, 14 February 1910.

BREEMAN, GEORGE

Rank and organization: Seaman, U.S. Navy. *Born:* 15 September 1880, Passaic, N.J. *Accredited to:* New Jersey. *G.O. No.:* 21, 5 May 1906. *Citation:* Breeman displayed heroism in the line of his profession while serving on board the U.S.S. *Kearsarge* at the time of the accidental ignition of powder charges in the forward 13-inch turret.

BRESNAHAN, PATRICK FRANCIS

Rank and organization: Watertender, U.S. Navy. *Born:* 1 May 1872, Peabody, Mass. *Accredited to:* Vermont. *G.O. No.:* 182, 20 March 1905. *Citation:* Serving on board the U.S.S. *Iowa* for extraordinary heroism at the time of the blowing out of the manhole plate of boiler D on board that vessel, 25 January 1905.

BROCK, GEORGE F.

Rank and organization: Carpenter's Mate Second Class, U.S. Navy. *Born:* 18 October 1872, Cleveland, Ohio. *Accredited to:* California. *G.O. No.:* 13, 5 January 1906. *Citation:* Serving on board the U.S.S. *Bennington* for extraordinary heroism displayed at the time of the explosion of that vessel at San Diego, Calif., 21 July 1905.

CAHEY, THOMAS

Rank and organization: Seaman, U.S. Navy. *Born:* 13 April 1870, Bellfast, Ireland. *Accredited to:* New York. *G.O. No.:* 85, 22 March 1902. *Citation:* On board the U.S.S. *Petrel* for heroism and gallantry, fearlessly exposing his own life to danger in saving others on the occasion of the fire on board that vessel, 31 March 1901.

CLARY, EDWARD ALVIN

Rank and organization: Watertender, U.S. Navy. *Born:* 6 May 1883, Foxport, Ky. *Accredited to:* Kentucky. *G.O. No.:* 59, 23 March 1910. *Citation:* On board the U.S.S. *Hopkins* for extraordinary heroism in the line of his profession on the occasion of the accident to one of the boilers of that vessel, 14 February 1910.

CLAUSEY, JOHN J.

Rank and organization: Chief Gunner's Mate, U.S. Navy. *Born:* 16 May 1875, San Francisco, Calif. *Accredited to:* California. *G.O. No.:* 13, 5 January 1906. *Citation:* On board the U.S.S. *Bennington* for extraordinary heroism displayed at the time of the explosion of a boiler of that vessel at San Diego, Calif., 21 July 1905.

CORAHORGI, DEMETRI

Rank and organization: Fireman First Class, U.S. Navy. *Place and date:* Aboard U.S.S. *Iowa*, 25 January 1905. *Entered service at:* New York. *Born:* 3 January 1880, Trieste, Austria. *G.O. No.:* 182, 20 March 1905. *Citation:* Serving on board the U.S.S. *Iowa* for extraordinary heroism at the time of the blowing out of the manhole plate of boiler D on board that vessel, 25 January 1905.

COX, ROBERT EDWARD

Rank and organization: Chief Gunner's Mate, U.S. Navy. *Born:* 22 December 1855, St. Albans, W. Va. *Accredited to:* West Virginia. *G.O. No.:* 43, 14 April 1921. (Medal presented by President Harding.) *Citation:* For extraordinary heroism on U.S.S. *Missouri* 13 April, 1904. While at target practice off Pensacola, Fla., an accident occurred in the after turret of the *Missouri* whereby the lives of 5 officers and 28 men were lost. The ship was in imminent danger of destruction by explosion, and the prompt action of C.G. Cox and 2 gunners' mates caused the fire to be brought under control, and the loss of the Missouri, together with her crew, was averted.

CRONAN, WILLIE

Rank and organization: Boatswain's Mate, U.S. Navy. *Born:* 23 October 1883, Chicago, Ill. *Accredited to:* Illinois. *G.O. No.:* 13, 5 January 1906. *Citation:* Serving on board the U.S.S. *Bennington*, for extraordinary heroism displayed at the time of the explosion of a boiler of that vessel at San Diego, Calif., 21 July 1905.

DAVIS, RAYMOND E.

Rank and organization: Quartermaster Third Class, U.S. Navy. *Place and date:* On board the U.S.S. *Bennington*, 21 July 1905. *Entered service at:* Puget Sound, Wash. *Born:* 19 September 1885, Mankato, Minn. *G.O. No.:* 13, 5 January 1906. *Citation:* Serving on board the U.S.S. *Bennington*, for extraordinary heroism displayed at the time of the explosion of a boiler of that vessel at San Diego, Calif., 21 July 1905.

FADDEN, HARRY D.

Rand and organization: Coxswain, U.S. Navy. *Born:* 17 September 1882, Oregon. *Accredited to:* Washington. *G.O. No.:* 138, 31 July 1903. *Citation:* On board the U.S.S. *Adams*, for gallantry, rescuing O. C. Hawthorne, landsman for training, from drowning at sea, 30 June 1903.

FLOYD, EDWARD

Rank and organization: Boilermaker, U.S. Navy. *Born:* 21 February 1850, Ireland. *Accredited to:* South Carolina. *G.O. No.:* 182, 20 March 1905. *Citation:* Serving on board the U.S.S. *Iowa*, for extraordinary heroism at the time of the blowing out of the manhole plate of boiler D on board that vessel, 25 January 1905.

FREDERICKSEN, EMIL

Rank and organization: Watertender, U.S. Navy. (Biography not available.) *G.O. No.:* 13, 5 January 1906. *Citation:* Serving on board the U.S.S. *Benington*, for extraordinary heroism displayed at the time of the explosion of a boiler of that vessel at San Diego, Calif., 21 July 1905.

GIRANDY, ALPHONSE

Rank and organization: Seaman, U.S. Navy. *Born:* 21 January 1868, Guadaloupe, West Indies. *Accredited to:* Pennsylvania. *G.O. No.:* 85, 22 March 1902. *Citation:* Serving on board the U.S.S. *Petrel*, for heroism and gallantry, fearlessly exposing his own life to danger for the saving of others, on the occasion of the fire on board that vessel, 31 March 1901.

GOWAN, WILLIAM HENRY

Rank and organization: Boatswain's Mate, U.S. Navy. *Born:* 2 June 1884, Rye, New York. *Accredited to:* New York. *G.O. No.:* 18, 19

March 1909. *Citation:* For bravery and extraordinary heroism displayed by him during a conflagration in Coquimbo, Chile, 20 January 1909.

GRBITCH, RADE

Rank and organization: Seaman, U.S. Navy. *Born:* 24 December 1870, Austria. *Accredited to:* Illinois. *G.O. No.:* 13, 5 January 1906. *Citation:* On board the U.S.S. *Bennington,* for extraordinary heroism displayed at the time of the explosion of a boiler of that vessel at San Diego, Calif., 21 July 1905.

HALLING, LUOVI

Rank and organization: Boatswain's Mate First Class, U.S. Navy. *Born:* 7 August 1867, Stockholm, Sweden. *Accredited to:* New York. *G.O. No.:* 172, 4 October 1904. *Citation:* Serving on board the U.S.S. *Missouri,* for heroism in attempting to rescue from drowning Cecil C. Young, ordinary seaman, 15 September 1904.

HELMS, JOHN HENRY

Rank and organization: Sergeant, U.S. Marine Corps. *Born:* 16 March 1874, Chicago, Ill. *Accredited to:* Illinois. *G.O. No.:* 35, 23 March 1901. *Citation:* Serving on board the U.S.S. *Chicago,* for heroism in rescuing Ishi Tomizi, ship's cook, from drowning at Montevideo, Uruguay, 10 January 1901.

HILL, FRANK E.

Rank and organization: Ship's Cook First Class, U.S. Navy. *Born:* 31 July 1880, La Grange, Ind. *Accredited to:* Indiana. *G.O. No.:* 13, 5 January 1906. *Citation:* On board the U.S.S. *Bennington,* for extraordinary heroism displayed at the time of the explosion of a boiler of that vessel at San Diego, Calif., 21 July 1905.

HOLTZ, AUGUST

Rank and organization: Chief Watertender, U.S. Navy. *Born:* 12 February 1871, St. Louis, Mo. *Entered service at:* St. Louis, Mo. *G.O. No.:* 83, 4 October 1910. *Citation:* On board the U.S.S. *North Dakota,* for extraordinary heroism in the line of his profession during the fire on board that vessel, 8 September 1910.

JOHANNESSEN, JOHANNES J.

Rank and organization: Chief Watertender, U.S. Navy. *Born:* 13 May 1872, Bodo, Norway. *Enlisted at:* Yokohama, Japan. *G.O. No.:* 182, 20 March 1905. *Citation:* Serving on board the U.S.S. *Iowa,* for extraordinary heroism at the time of the blowing out of the manhole plate of boiler D on board that vessel, 25 January 1905.

KING, JOHN

Rank and organization: Watertender, U.S. Navy. *Born:* 7 February 1865, Ireland. *Accredited to:* New York. *G.O. No.:* 72, 6 December 1901. Second award. *Citation:* On board the U.S.S. *Vicksburg,* for heroism in the line of his profession at the time of the accident to the boilers, 29 May 1901.

G.O. No.: 40, 19 October 1909. *Citation:* Watertender, serving on board the U.S.S. *Salem*, for extraordinary heroism in the line of his profession on the occasion of the accident to one of the boilers of that vessel, 13 September 1909.

KLEIN, ROBERT

Rank and organization: Chief Carpenter's Mate, U.S. Navy. *Born:* 11 November 1884, Gerdonen, Germany. *Enlisted at:* Marseilles, France. *G.O. No.:* 173, 6 October 1904. *Citation:* Serving on board the U.S.S. *Raleigh*, for heroism in rescuing shipmates overcome in double bottoms by fumes of turpentine, 25 January 1904.

LIPSCOMB, HARRY

Rank and organization: Watertender, U.S. Navy. *Born:* 2 April 1878, Washington, D.C. *Accredited to:* Washington, D.C. *G.O. No.:* 83, 4 October 1910. *Citation:* On board the U.S.S. *North Dakota*, for extraordinary heroism in the line of his profession during the fire on board that vessel, 8 September 1910.

MONSSEN, MONS

Rank and organization. Chief Gunner's Mate, U.S. Navy. *Born:* 20 January 1867, Norway. *G.O. No.:* 160, 26 May 1904. *Citation:* Serving on board the U.S.S. *Missouri*, for extraordinary heroism in entering a burning magazine through the scuttle and endeavoring to extinguish the fire by throwing water with his hands until a hose was passed to him, 13 April 1904.

NELSON, OSCAR FREDERICK

Rank and organization: Machinist's Mate First Class, U.S. Navy. *Born:* 5 November 1881, Minneapolis, Minn. *Accredited to:* Minnesota. *G.O. No.:* 13, 5 January 1906. *Citation:* Serving on board the U.S.S. *Bennington*, for extraordinary heroism displayed at the time of the explosion of a boiler of that vessel at San Diego, Calif., 21 July 1905.

NORDSTROM, ISIDOR

Rank and organization: Chief Boatswain, U.S. Navy. *Born:* 24 May 1876, Goteborg, Sweden. *Accredited to:* New York. *G.O. No.:* 142, 4 December 1924. *Citation:* For gallant conduct upon the occasion of the disastrous fire of accidentally ignited powder charges, which occurred in the forward turret of the U.S.S. *Kearsage* during target practice on 13 April 1906. Chief Boatswain Nordstrom, then chief boatswain's mate was among the first to enter the turret in order to assist in bringing out the injured.

PETERS, ALEXANDER

Rank and organization: Boatswain's Mate First Class, U.S. Navy. *Born:* 16 November 1869, Russia. *Accredited to:* Pennsylvania. *G.O. No.:* 172, 4 October 1904. *Citation:* For heroism in attempting to rescue from drowning Cecil C. Young, ordinary seaman, 15 September 1904, while serving on board the U.S.S. *Missouri*.

PFEIFER, LOUIS FRED

Rank and organization: Private, U.S. Marine Corps. (Served as Theis, Louis F., during first enlistment.) *Born:* 19 June 1876, Philadelphia, Pa. *Accredited to:* New Jersey. *G.O. No.:* 85, 22 March 1902. *Citation:* Serving on board the U.S.S. *Petrel;* for heroism and gallantry, fearlessly exposing his own life to danger for the saving of the others on the occasion of the fire on board that vessel, 31 March 1901.

QUICK, JOSEPH

Rank and organization: Coxswain, U.S. Navy. *Place and date:* Yokohama, Japan, 27 April 1902. *Entered service at:* New York. *Birth:* New York. *G.O. No.:* 93, 7 July 1902. *Citation:* For heroism in rescuing Walenty Wisnieroski, Machinist Second Class, from drowning at Yokohama, Japan, 27 April 1902, while serving on board the U.S.S. *Yorktown.*

REID, PATRICK

Rank and organization: Chief Watertender, U.S. Navy. *Born:* 17 June 1875, Dublin, Ireland. *Accredited to:* New York. *G.O. No.:* 83, 4 October 1910. *Citation:* For extraordinary heroism in the line of his profession during the fire on board the U.S.S. *North Dakota* where Reid was serving, 8 September 1910.

ROBERTS, CHARLES CHURCH

Rank and organization: Machinist's Mate First Class, U.S. Navy. *Born:* 6 March 1882, Newton, Mass. *Accredited to:* Illinois. *G.O. No.:* 83, 4 October 1910. *Citation:* Serving on board the U.S.S. *North Dakota;* for extraordinary heroism in the line of his profession during the fire on board that vessel, 8 September 1910.

SCHEPKE, CHARLES S.

Rank and organization: Gunner's Mate First Class, U.S. Navy. *Born:* 26 December 1878, New York, N.Y. *Accredited to:* New York. *G.O. No.:* 160, 26 May 1904. *Citation:* For extraordinary heroism while serving on the U.S.S. *Missouri* in remaining by a burning magazine and assisting to extinguish the fire, 13 April 1904.

SCHMIDT, OTTO DILLER

Rank and organization: Seaman, U.S. Navy. *Born:* 10 August 1884, Blair, Nebr. *Accredited to:* Nebraska. *G.O. No.:* 13, 5 January 1906. *Citation:* While serving on board the U.S.S. *Bennington* for extraordinary heroism displayed at the time of the explosion of a boiler of that vessel at San Diego, Calif., 21 July 1905.

SHACKLETTE, WILLIAM SIDNEY

Rank and organization: Hospital Steward, U.S. Navy. *Born:* 17 May 1880, Delaplane, Va. *Accredited to:* Virginia. *G.O. No.:* 13, 5 January 1906. *Citation:* For extraordinary heroism while serving on the U.S.S. *Bennington* at the time of the explosion of a boiler of that vessel at San Diego, Calif., 21 July 1905.

SNYDER, WILLIAM E.

Rank and organization: Chief Electrician, U.S. Navy. *Born:* 24 February 1883, South Bethlehem, Pa. *Accredited to:* Pennsylvania. *G.O. No.:* 58, 2 March 1910. *Citation:* Serving on board the U.S.S. *Birmingham*, for extraordinary heroism, rescuing G. H. Kephart, seaman, from drowning at Hampton Roads, Va., 4 January 1910.

STANTON, THOMAS

Rank and organization: Chief Machinist's Mate, U.S. Navy. *Born:* 11 August 1869, Ireland. *Accredited to:* New York. *G.O. No.:* 83, 4 October 1910. *Citation:* For extraordinary heroism in the line of his profession during the fire on board the U.S.S. *North Dakota*, 8 September 1910.

STUPKA, LODDIE

Rank and organization: Fireman First Class, U.S. Navy. *Born:* 4 March 1878, Cleveland, Ohio. *Accredited to:* Ohio. *G.O. No.:* 145, 26 December 1903. *Citation:* Serving on board the U.S.S. *Leyden;* for heroism at the time of the wreck of that vessel, 21 January 1903.

TEYTAND, AUGUST P.

Rank and organization: Quartermaster Third Class, U.S. Navy. *Born:* 6 April 1878, Santa Cruz, West Indies. *Accredited to:* New Jersey. *G.O. No.:* 145, 26 December 1903. *Citation:* For heroism while serving on board the U.S.S. *Leyden* at the time of the wreck of that vessel, 21 January 1903.

WALSH, MICHAEL

Rank and organization: Chief Machinist, U.S. Navy. *Born:* 27 July 1858, Newport, R.I. *Accredited to:* Rhode Island. *G.O. No.:* 145, 26 December 1903. *Citation:* Serving on board the U.S.S. *Leyden;* for heroism at the time of the wreck of that vessel, 21 January 1903.

WESTA, KARL

Rank and organization: Chief Machinist's Mate, U.S. Navy. *Born:* 8 April 1875, Norway. *Accredited to:* New York. *G.O. No.:* 83, 4 October 1910. *Citation:* On board the U.S.S. *North Dakota;* for extraordinary heroism in the line of his profession during the fire on board that vessel, 8 September 1910.

WHEELER, GEORGE HUBER

Rank and organization: Shipfitter First Class, U.S. Navy. *Born:* 26 September 1881, Charleston, S.C. *Accredited to:* South Carolina. *G.O. No.:* 18, 19 March 1909. *Citation:* For bravery and extraordinary heroism displayed by him during a conflagration in Coquimbo, Chile, 20 January 1909.

CHINA RELIEF EXPEDITION
BOXER REBELLION

Our interests in the Far East which date back to the Revolution were intensified by acquisition of Pacific possessions in 1898 and 1899. During this period of our occupation with the Spanish-American War, European nations had inaugurated policies in China jeopardizing the freedom of trade in the Orient and threatening to lead to dismemberment of China itself.

As the nineteenth century drew to a close, the weakening Manchu Dynasty was faced with the choice of continuing to protect foreigners in China or of remaining in power on the side of the "Boxers," societies originally organized in patriotic protest against foreign aggression. In 1900 a series of outrages against all "foreign devils" culminated in the siege of the British legation at Peking where many alien residents had taken refuge.

The Imperial Government refused to take action and the American minister appealed to the Navy. As a result, the U.S.S. *Newark* placed ashore a contingent of marines and three bluejackets as a legation guard. These men with another detachment of marines, soldiers, and sailors joined with troops of other western nations in the gallant defense of the Peking legations against the Boxers until the arrival of the Allied Army in August.

ADAMS, JOHN MAPES

Rank and organization: Sergeant, U.S. Marine Corps. *Born:* 11 October 1871, Haverhill, Mass. *Accredited to:* Massachusetts. *G.O. No.:* 55, 19 July 1901. *Citation:* In the presence of the enemy during the battle near Tientsin, China, 13 July 1900, Adams distinguished himself by meritorious conduct.

ADRIANCE, HARRY CHAPMAN

Rank and organization: Corporal, U.S. Marine Corps. *Born:* 27 October 1864, Oswego, N.Y. *Accredited to:* Massachusetts. *G.O. No.:* 55, 19 July 1901. *Citation:* In the presence of the enemy during the battle near Tientsin, China, 13 July 1900, Adriance distinguished himself by meritorious conduct.

ALLEN, EDWARD

Rank and organization: Boatswain's Mate First Class, U.S. Navy. *Born:* 4 December 1859, Amsterdam, Holland. *Accredited to:* New York. *G.O. No.:* 55, 19 July 1901. *Citation:* Fighting with the relief expedition of the Allied forces on 13, 20, 21, and 22 June 1900, Allen distinguished himself by meritorious conduct.

APPLETON, EDWIN NELSON

Rank and organization: Corporal, U.S. Marine Corps. *Born:* 29 August 1876, Brooklyn, N.Y. *Accredited to:* New York. G.O. No.: 84, 22 March 1902. *Citation:* In action against the enemy at Tientsin, China, 20 June 1900. Crossing the river in a small boat while under heavy enemy fire, Appleton assisted in destroying buildings occupied by the enemy.

BOYDSTON, ERWIN JAY

Rank and organization: Private, U.S. Marine Corps. *Born:* 22 April, 1875, Deer Creek, Colo. *Accredited to:* California. *G.O. No.:* 55, 19 July 1901. *Citation:* In the presence of the enemy at Peking, China, 21 July to 17 August 1900. Under a heavy fire from the enemy during this period, Boydston assisted in the erection of barricades.

BREWSTER, ANDRE W.

Rank and organization: Captain, 9th U.S. Infantry. *Place and date:* At Tientsin, China, 13 July 1900. *Entered service at:* Philadelphia, Pa.

Birth: Hoboken, N.J. *Date of issue:* 15 September 1903. *Citation:* While under fire rescued 2 of his men from drowning.

BURNES, JAMES

Rank and organization: Private, U.S. Marine Corps. *Born:* 14 January 1870, Worcester, Mass. *Accredited to:* California. *G.O. No.:* 84, 22 March 1902. *Citation:* In action against the enemy at Tientsin, China, 20 June 1900. Crossing the river in a small boat with 3 other men while under a heavy fire from the enemy, Burnes assisted in destroying buildings occupied by hostile forces.

CAMPBELL, ALBERT RALPH

Rank and organization: Private, U.S. Marine Corps. *Born:* 8 April 1875, Williamsport, Pa. *Accredited to:* Pennsylvania. *G.O. No.:* 55, 19 July 1901. *Citation:* In action at Tientsin, China, 21 June 1900. During the advance on Tientsin, Campbell distinguished himself by his conduct.

CARR, WILLIAM LOUIS

Rank and organization: Private, U.S. Marine Corps. *Born:* 1 April 1875, Peabody, Mass. *Accredited to:* Massachusetts. *G.O. No.:* 55, 19 July 1901. *Citation:* In action at Peking, China, 21 July to 17 August 1900. Throughout this action and in the presence of the enemy, Carr distinguished himself by his conduct.

CHATHAM, JOHN PURNELL

Rank and organization: Gunner's Mate Second Class, U.S. Navy. *Born:* 2 July 1872, Warchester, Md. *Accredited to:* Maryland. *G.O. No.:* 55, 19 July 1901. *Citation:* In action with the relief expedition of the Allied Forces in China, 13, 20, 21 and 22 June 1900. During this period and in the presence of the enemy, Chatham distinguished himself by his conduct.

CLANCY, JOSEPH

Rank and organization: Chief Boatswain's Mate, U.S. Navy. *Born:* 29 September 1863, New York, N.Y. *G.O. No.:* 55, 19 July 1901. *Citation:* In action with the relief expedition of the Allied forces in China, 13, 20, 21 and 22 June 1900. During this period and in the presence of the enemy, Clancy distinguished himself by his conduct.

COONEY, JAMES

Rank and organization: Private, U.S. Marine Corps. *Born:* 27 July 1860, Limerick, Ireland. *Accredited to:* Massachusetts. *G.O. No.:* 55, 19 July 1901. *Citation:* In the presence of the enemy during the battle near Tientsin, China, 13 July 1900, Cooney distinguished himself by meritorious conduct.

DAHLGREN, JOHN OLOF

Rank and organization: Corporal, U.S. Marine Corps. *Born:* 14 September 1872, Kahliwar, Sweden. *Accredited to:* California. *G.O. No.:* 55, 19 July 1901. *Citation:* In the presence of the enemy during the battle of Peking, China, 20 June to 16 July 1900, Dahlgren distinguished himself by meritorious conduct.

DALY, DANIEL JOSEPH (First Award)

Rank and organization: Private, U.S. Marine Corps. *Born:* 11 November 1873, Glen Cove, Long Island, N.Y. *Accredited to:* New York. *G.O. No.:* 55, 19 July 1901. *Other Navy Awards:* Second Medal of Honor, Navy Cross. *Citation:* In the presence of the enemy during the battle of Peking, China, 14 August 1900, Daly distinguished himself by meritorious conduct.

*FISHER, HARRY

Rank and organization: Private, U.S. Marine Corps. *Born:* 20 October 1874, McKeesport, Pa. *Accredited to:* Pennsylvania. *G.O. No.:* 55, 19 July 1901. *Citation:* Served in the presence of the enemy at the battle of Peking, China, 20 June to 16 July 1900. Assisting in the erection of barricades during the action, Fisher was killed by the heavy fire of the enemy.

FOLEY, ALEXANDER JOSEPH

Rank and organization: Sergeant, U.S. Marine Corps. *Born:* 19 February 1866, Heckersville, Pa. *Accredited to:* Pennsylvania. *G.O. No.: 55, 19 July 1901. Citation:* In the presence of the enemy in the battle near Tientsin, China, 13 July 1900, Foley distinguished himself by meritorious conduct.

FRANCIS, CHARLES ROBERT

Rank and organization: Private, U.S. Marine Corps. *Born:* 19 May 1875, Doylestown, Pa. *Accredited to:* Pennsylvania. *G.O. No.: 55*, 19 July 1901. *Citation:* In the presence of the enemy during the battle near Tientsin, China, 21 June 1900, Francis distinguished himself by meritorious conduct.

GAIENNIE, LOUIS RENE

Rank and organization: Private, U.S. Marine Corps. *Born:* 9 June 1878, St. Louis, Mo. *Entered service at:* St. Louis, Mo. *G.O. No.:* 55, 19 July 1901. *Citation:* In the presence of the enemy during the action at Peking, China, 21 July to 17 August 1900, Gaiennie distinguished himself by meritorious conduct.

HAMBERGER, WILLIAM F.

Rank and organization: Chief Carpenter's Mate, U.S. Navy. *Born:* 5 August 1870, Newark, N.J. *Accredited to:* New Jersey. *G.O. No.:* 55, 19 July 1901. *Citation:* Fighting with the relief expedition of the Allied forces on 13, 20, 21 and 22 June 1900, Hamberger distinguished himself by meritorious conduct.

HANFORD, BURKE

Rank and organization: Machinist First Class, U.S. Navy. *Born:* 17 December 1872, Toledo, Ohio. *Accredited to:* Ohio. *G.O. No.:* 55, 19 July 1901. *Citation:* Served with the relief expedition of the Allied forces in China on 13, 20, 21 and 22 June 1900. In the presence of the enemy during this period, Hanford distinguished himself by meritorious conduct.

HANSEN, HANS A.

Rank and organization: Seaman, U.S. Navy. *Born:* 16 April 1872, Germany. *Accredited to:* California. *G.O. No.:* 55, 19 June 1901. *Citation:* Served with the relief expedition of the Allied forces in China on 13, 20, 21 and 22 June 1900. In the presence of the enemy during this period, Hansen distinguished himself by meritorious conduct.

HEISCH, HENRY WILLIAM

Rank and organization: Private, U.S. Marine Corps. *Born:* 10 June 1872, Latendorf, Germany. *Accredited to:* California. *G.O. No.:* 84, 22 March 1902. *Citation:* In action against the enemy at Tientsin, China, 20 June 1900. Crossing the river in a small boat while under heavy fire, Heisch assisted in destroying buildings occupied by the enemy.

HOLYOKE, WILLIAM E.

Rank and organization: Boatswain's Mate First Class, U.S. Navy. *Born:* 13 March 1868, Groveton, N.H. *Accredited to:* Illinois. *G.O. No.:* 55, 19 July 1901. *Citation:* In action with the relief expedition of the allied forces in China, 13, 20, 21 and 22 June 1900. During this period and in the presence of the enemy, Holyoke distinguished himself by meritorious conduct.

HORTON, WILLIAM CHARLIE

Rank and organization: Private, U.S. Marine Corps. *Place and date:* Peking, China, 21 July to 17 August 1900. *Entered service at:* Pennsylvania. *Born:* 21 July 1876, Chicago, Ill. *G.O. No.:* 55, 19 July 1901. *Citation:* In action against the enemy at Peking, China, 21 July to 17 August 1900. Although under heavy fire from the enemy, Horton assisted in the erection of barricades.

HUNT, MARTIN

Rank and organization: Private, U.S. Marine Corps. *Born:* 9 July 1873, County of Mayo, Ireland. *Accredited to:* Massachusetts. *G.O. No.:* 55, 19 July 1901. *Citation:* In the presence of the enemy during the battle of Peking, China, 20 June to 16 July 1900, Hunt distinguished himself by meritorious conduct.

KATES, THOMAS WILBUR

Rank and organization: Private, U.S. Marine Corps. *Born:* 7 May 1865, Shelby Center, N.Y. *Accredited to:* New York. *G.O. No.:* 55, 19 July 1901. *Citation:* In the presence of the enemy during the advance on Tientsin, China, 21 June 1900, Kates distinguished himself by meritorious conduct.

KILLACKEY, JOSEPH

Rank and organization: Landsman, U.S. Navy. *Born:* 21 January 1897, Cork County, Ireland. *Accredited to:* Pennsylvania. *G.O. No.:* 55, 19 July 1901. *Citation:* In action with the relief expedition of the Allied forces in China, 13, 20, 21 and 22 June 1900. During this period and in the presence of the enemy, Killackey distinguished himself by meritorious conduct.

LAWTON, LOUIS B.

Rank and organization: First Lieutenant, 9th U.S. Infantry. *Place and date:* At Tientsin, China, 13 July 1900. *Entered service at:* Auburn, N.Y. *Birth:* Independence, Iowa. *Date of issue:* 11 March 1902. *Citation:* Carried a message and guided reinforcements across a wide and fireswept space, during which he was thrice wounded.

MATHIAS, CLARENCE EDWARD

Rank and organization: Private, U.S. Marine Corps. *Born:* 12 December 1876, Royalton, Pa. *Accredited to:* Pennsylvania. *G.O. No.:* 55, 19 July 1901. *Citation:* In the presence of the enemy during the advance on Tientsin, China, 13 July 1900, Mathias distinguished himself by meritorious conduct.

McALLISTER, SAMUEL

Rank and organization: Ordinary Seaman, U.S. Navy. *Born:* 23 January 1869, Belfast, Ireland. *Accredited to:* California. *G.O. No.:* 84, 22 March 1902. *Citation:* In action against the enemy at Tientsin, China, 20 June 1900. Crossing the river in a small boat while under heavy enemy fire, McAllister assisted in destroying buildings occupied by the enemy.

McCLOY, JOHN (First Award)

Rank and organization: Coxswain, U.S. Navy. *Born:* 3 January 1876, Brewsters, N.Y. *Accredited to:* New York. *G.O. No.:* 55, 19 July 1901. *Other Navy award:* Second Medal of Honor. *Citation:* In action with the relief expedition of the Allied forces in China, 13, 20, 21, and 22 June 1900. During this period and in the presence of the enemy, Coxswain McCloy distinguished himself by meritorious conduct.

MITCHELL, JOSEPH

Rank and organization: Gunner's Mate First Class, U.S. Navy. *Born:* 27 November 1876, Philadelphia, Pa. *Accredited to:* Pennsylvania. *G.O. No.:* 55, 19 July 1901. *Citation:* In the presence of the enemy during the battle of Peking, China, 12 July 1900, Mitchell distinguished himself by meritorious conduct.

MOORE, ALBERT

Rank and organization: Private, U.S. Marine Corps. *Born:* 25 December 1862, Merced, Calif. *Accredited to:* California. *G.O. No.:* 55, 19 July 1901. *Citation:* In the presence of the enemy during the battle of Peking, China, 21 July to 17 August 1900. Although under a heavy fire from the enemy, Moore assisted in the erection of barricades.

MURPHY, JOHN ALPHONSUS

Rank and organization: Drummer, U.S. Marine Corps. *Born:* 26 February 1881, New York, N.Y. *Accredited to:* Washington, D.C. *G.O. No.:* 55, 19 July 1901. *Citation:* In the presence of the enemy during the action at Peking, China, 21 July to 17 August 1900, Murphy distinguished himself by meritorious conduct.

MURRAY, WILLIAM H.

Rank and organization: Private, U.S. Marine Corps. *Born:* 3 June 1876, Brooklyn, N.Y. *Accredited to:* New York. *G.O. No.:* 55, 19 July 1901. *Citation:* In the presence of the enemy during the action at Peking, China, 21 July to 17 August 1900. During this period, Murray distinguished himself by meritorious conduct. (Served as Henry W. Davis.)

ORNDOFF, HARRY WESTLEY

Rank and organization: Private, U.S. Marine Corps. *Born:* 9 November 1872, Sandusky, Ohio. *Accredited to:* California. *G.O. No.:* 55, 19 July 1901. *Citation:* In action with the relief expedition of the Allied forces in China, 13, 20, 21, and 22 June 1900. During this period and in the presence of the enemy, Orndoff distinguished himself by meritorious conduct.

PETERSEN, CARL EMIL

Rank and organization: Chief Machinist, U.S. Navy. *Place and date:* Peking, China, 28 June to 17 August 1900. *Entered service at:* New Jersey. *Born:* 24 August 1875, Hamburg, Germany. *G.O. No.:* 55, 19 July 1901. *Citation:* In the presence of the enemy during the action at Peking, China, 28 June to 17 August 1900. During this period Chief Machinist Petersen distinguished himself by meritorious conduct.

PHILLIPS, REUBEN JASPER

Rank and organization: Corporal, U.S. Marine Corps. *Born:* 28 July 1874, Cambria, Calif. *Accredited to:* California. *G.O. No.:* 55, 19 July 1901. *Citation:* In action with the relief expedition of the Allied forces in China during the battles of 13, 20, 21 and 22 June 1900. Throughout this period and in the presence of the enemy, Phillips distinguished himself by meritorious conduct.

PRESTON, HERBERT IRVING

Rank and organization: Private, U.S. Marine Corps. *Born:* 6 August 1876, Berkeley, N.J. *Accredited to:* New Jersey *G.O. No.:* 55, 19 July 1901. *Citation:* In the presence of the enemy during the action at Peking, China, 21 July to 17 August 1900. Throughout this period, Preston distinguished himself by meritorious conduct.

ROSE, GEORGE

Rank and organization: Seaman, U.S. Navy. *Born:* 28 February 1880, Stamford, Conn. *Accredited to:* Connecticut. *G.O. No.:* 55, 19 July 1901. *Citation:* In the presence of the enemy during the battles at Peking, China, 13, 20, 21 and 22 June 1900. Throughout this period, Rose distinguished himself by meritorious conduct. While stationed as a crewmember of the U.S.S. *Newark*, he was part of its landing force that went ashore off Taku, China. On 31 May 1900, he was in a party of 6 under John McCloy (MH) which took ammunition from the *Newark* to Tientsin. On 10 June 1900, he was one of a party that carried dispatches from LaFa to Yongstsum at night. On the 13th he was one of a few who fought off a large force of the enemy saving the main baggage train from destruction. On the 20th and 21st he was engaged in heavy fighting against the Imperial Army being always in the first rank. On the 22d he showed gallantry in the capture of the Siku Arsenal. He volunteered to go to the nearby village which was occupied by the enemy to secure medical supplies urgently required. The party brought back the supplies carried by newly taken prisoners.

RYAN, FRANCIS T.

Rank and organization: Coxswain, U.S. Navy. *Born:* 6 April 1868, Massachusetts. *Accredited to:* Massachusetts. *G.O. No.:* 55, 19 July 1901. *Citation:* In action with the relief expedition of the Allied forces in China during the battles of 13, 20, 21 and 22 June 1900. Throughout this period and in the presence of the enemy, Ryan distinguished himself by meritorious conduct.

SCANNELL, DAVID JOHN

Rank and organization: Private, U.S. Marine Corps. *Born:* 30 March 1875, Boston, Mass. *Accredited to:* Massachusetts. *G.O. No.:* 55, 19 July 1901. *Citation:* In the presence of the enemy during the action at Peking, China, 21 July to 17 August 1900. Throughout this period, Scannell distinguished himself by meritorious conduct.

SEACH, WILLIAM

Rank and organization: Ordinary Seaman, U.S. Navy. *Place and date:* China 13, 20, 21, and 22 June 1900. *Entered service at:* Massachusetts. *Born:* 23 May 1877, London, England. *G.O. No.:* 55, 19 July 1901. *Citation:* In action with the relief expedition of the Allied forces in China during the battles of 13, 20, 21 and 22 June 1900. June 13: Seach and 6 others were cited for their courage in repulsing an attack by 300 Chinese Imperialist soldiers and Boxer militants with a bayonet charge, thus thwarting a planned massive attack on the entire force. June 20: During a day-long battle, Seach ran across an open clearing, gained cover, and cleaned out nests of Chinese snipers. June 21: During a surprise sabre attack by Chinese cavalrymen, Seach was cited for defending gun emplacements. June 22: Seach and others breached the wall of a Chinese fort, fought their way to the enemy's guns, and turned the cannon upon the defenders of the fort. Throughout this period and in the presence of the enemy, Seach distinguished himself by meritorious conduct.

SILVA, FRANCE

Rank and organization: Private, U.S. Marine Corps. *Born:* 8 May 1876, Haywards, Calif. *Accredited to:* California. *G.O. No.:* 55, 19 July 1901. *Citation:* In the presence of the enemy during the action at Peking, China, 28 June to 17 August 1900./Throughout this period, Silva distinguished himself by meritorious conduct.

SMITH, FRANK ELMER

Rank and organization: Oiler, U.S. Navy. *Born:* 22 August 1864, Boston, Mass. *Accredited to:* Virginia. *G.O. No.:* 55, 19 July 1901. *Citation:* In action with the relief expedition of the Allied Forces in China during the battles of 13, 20, 21, and 22 June 1900. Throughout

this period and in the presence of the enemy, Smith distinguished himself by meritorious conduct.

SMITH, JAMES

Rank and organization: Landsman, U.S. Navy. *Born:* 2 September
1880, New York. *Accredited to:* New York. *G.O. No.:* 55, 19 July
1901. *Citation:* In action with the relief expedition of the Allied forces
in China during the battles of 13, 20, 21, and 22 June 1900.
Throughout this period and in the presence of the enemy, Smith distinguished himself by meritorious conduct.

STANLEY, ROBERT HENRY

Rank and organization: Hospital Apprentice, U.S. Navy. *Place and
date:* China, 13, 20, 21, and 22 June 1900. *Entered service:* Aboard
U.S.S. *Vermont. Born:* 2 May 1881, Brooklyn, N.Y. *Accredited to:*
New York. *G.O. No.:* 55, 19 July 1901. *Citation:* For distinguished
conduct in the presence of the enemy in volunteering and carrying
messages under fire at Peking, China, 12 July 1900.

STEWART, PETER

Rank and organization: Gunnery Sergeant, U.S. Marine Corps. *Born:*
17 February 1858, Airdrie, Scotland. *Accredited to:* Washington, D.C.
G.O. No.: 55, 19 July 1901. *Citation:* In action with the relief expedition of the Allied forces in China during the battles of 13, 20, 21, and
22 June 1900. Throughout this period and in the presence of the
enemy, Stewart distinguished himself by meritorious conduct.

SUTTON, CLARENCE EDWIN

Rank and organization: Sergeant, U.S. Marine Corps. *Born:* 18
February 1871, Middlesex County, Va. *Accredited to:* Washington,
D.C. *G.O. No.:* 55, 19 July 1901. *Citation:* In action during the battle
near Tientsin, China, 13 July 1900. Although under heavy fire from
the enemy, Sutton assisted in carrying a wounded officer from the field
of battle.

THOMAS, KARL

Rank and organization: Coxswain, U.S. Navy. *Born:* 17 March 1871,
Germany. *Accredited to:* New York. *G.O. No.:* 55, 19 July 1901. *Citation:* In action with the relief expedition of the Allied forces in China,
13, 20, 21, and 22 June 1900. During this period and in the presence
of the enemy, Thomas distinguished himself by meritorious conduct.

TITUS, CALVIN PEARL

Rank and organization: Musician, U.S. Army, Company E, 14th U.S.
Infantry. *Place and date:* At Peking, China, 14 August 1900. *Entered
service at:* Iowa. *Birth:* Vinton, Iowa. *Date of issue:* 11 March 1902.
Citation: Gallant and daring conduct in the presence of his colonel and
other officers and enlisted men of his regiment; was first to scale the
wall of the city.

TORGERSON, MARTIN T.

Rank and organization: Gunner's Mate Third Class, U.S. Navy. *Born:* 7 November 1875, Oleesen, Norway. *Accredited to:* Virginia. *G.O. No.:* 55, 19 July 1901. *Citation:* In action with the relief expedition of the Allied Forces in China, 13, 20, 21, and 22 June 1900. During this period and in the presence of the enemy, Torgerson distinguished himself by meritorious conduct.

UPHAM, OSCAR J.

Rank and organization: Private, U.S. Marine Corps. *Born:* 14 January 1871, Toledo, Ohio. *Accredited to:* Illinois. *G.O. No.:* 55, 19 July 1901. *Citation:* In the presence of the enemy at Peking, China, 21 July to 17 August 1900. Although under a heavy fire from the enemy during this period, Upham assisted in the erection of barricades.

*VON SCHLICK, ROBERT H.

Rank and organization: Private, Company C, 9th U.S. Infantry. *Place and date:* At Tientsin, China, 13 July 1900. *Entered service at:* San Francisco, Calif. *Birth:* Germany. *Date of issue:* Unknown. *Citation:* Although previously wounded while carrying a wounded comrade to a place of safety, rejoined his command, which partly occupied an exposed position upon a dike, remaining there after his command had been withdrawn, singly keeping up the fire, and obliviously presenting himself as a conspicuous target until he was literally shot off his position by the enemy.

WALKER, EDWARD ALEXANDER

Rank and organization: Sergeant, U.S. Marine Corps. *Born:* 2 October 1864, Huntley, Scotland. *Accredited to:* New York. *G.O. No.:* 55, 19 July 1901. *Citation:* In the presence of the enemy during the battle of Peking, China, 20 June to 16 July 1900. Throughout this period, Walker distinguished himself by meritorious conduct.

WESTERMARK, AXEL

Rank and organization: Seaman, U.S. Navy. *Born:* 8 April 1875, Finland. *Accredited to:* California. *G.O. No.:* 55, 19 July 1901. *Citation:* In the presence of the enemy during the battle of Peking, China, 28 June to 17 August 1900. Throughout this period, Westermark distinguished himself by meritorious conduct.

WILLIAMS, JAY

Rank and organization: Coxswain, U.S. Navy. *Born:* 23 September 1872, Orland, Ind. *Accredited to:* Ohio. *G.O. No.:* 55, 19 July 1901. *Citation:* In action with the relief expedition of the Allied forces in China, 13, 20, 21 and 22 June 1900. During this period and in the presence of the enemy, Williams distinguished himself by meritorious conduct.

YOUNG, FRANK ALBERT

Rank and organization: Private, U.S. Marine Corps. *Born:* 22 June 1876, Milwaukee, Wis. *Accredited to:* Wisconsin. *G.O. No.:* 55, 19 July

1901. *Citation:* In the presence of the enemy during the battle of Peking, China, 20 June to 16 July 1900. Throughout this period, Young distinguished himself by meritorious conduct.

ZION, WILLIAM

Rank and organization: Private, U.S. Marine Corps. *Born:* 23 October 1872, Knightstown, Ind. *Accredited to:* California. *G.O. No.:* 55, 19 July 1901. *Citation:* In the presence of the enemy during the battle of Peking, China, 21 July to 17 August 1900. Throughout this period, Zion distinguished himself by meritorious conduct.

PHILIPPINE INSURRECTION

Incident to the acquisition of the Philippines, insurgent forces caused a critical situation by carrying out unprovoked attacks in the vicinity of Manila, and organized an uprising within the city itself. The *insurrectos*, in the assumption that independence would result from the overthrow of Spanish rule, expressed their dissatisfaction by creating hotbeds of rebellion throughout the archipelago.

The Navy's role in suppressing the guerrilla fighting, known as the "Philippine Insurrection," consisted of transport and artillery operations in support of Marine and Army forces, as well as extensive patrols in coastal waters and gunboat excursions up the rivers to support the troops ashore.

The massacre of men of Company C, 9th Infantry, by savage Moros on the island of Samar, on 28 September 1901, initiated months of perilous jungle fighting by Marines before the rebellious forces were driven from their cliff defenses along the Sohoton River.

ANDERS, FRANK L.

Rank and organization: Corporal, U.S. Army, Company B, 1st North Dakota Volunteer Infantry. *Place and date:* At San Miguel de Mayumo, Luzon, Philippine Islands, 13 May 1899. *Entered service at:* Fargo, N. Dak. *Birth:* Fort Lincoln, Dakota Territory. *Date of issue:* 3 March 1906. *Citation:* With 11 other scouts, without waiting for the supporting battalion to aid them or to get into a position to do so, charged over a distance of about 150 yards and completely routed about 300 of the enemy who were in line and in a position that could only be carried by a frontal attack.

BATSON, MATTHEW A.

Rank and organization: First Lieutenant, 4th U.S. Cavalry. *Place and date:* At Calamba, Luzon, Philippine Islands, 26 July 1899. *Entered service at:* Carbondale, Ill. *Birth:* Anna, Ill. *Date of issue:* 8 March 1902. *Citation:* Swam the San Juan River in the face of the enemy's fire and drove him from his entrenchments.

BEARSS, HIRAM IDDINGS

Rank and organization: Colonel, U.S. Marine Corps. *Born:* 13 April 1875, Peru, Ind. *Appointed from:* Indiana. *Other Navy award:* Distinguished Service Medal. *Citation:* For extraordinary heroism and eminent and conspicuous conduct in battle at the junction of the Cadacan and Sohoton Rivers, Samar, Philippine Islands, 17 November 1901. Col. Bearss (then Capt.), second in command of the columns upon their uniting ashore in the Sohoton River region, made a surprise attack on the fortified cliffs and completely routed the enemy, killing 30 and capturing and destroying the powder magazine, 40 lantacas (guns), rice, food and cuartels. Due to his courage, intelligence, discrimination and zeal, he successfully led his men up the cliffs by means of bamboo ladders to a height of 200 feet. The cliffs were of soft stone of volcanic origin, in the nature of pumice, and were honeycombed with caves. Tons of rocks were suspended in platforms held in position by vine cables (known as bejuco) in readiness to be precipitated upon people below. After driving the insurgents from their position which was almost impregnable, being covered with numerous trails lined with poison spears, pits, etc., he led his men across the river, scaled the cliffs on the opposite side, and destroyed the camps there. Col. Bearss and the men under his command overcame incredible difficulties and dangers in destroying positions which, according to reports from old prisoners, had taken 3 years to perfect, were held as a final rallying point, and were never before penetrated by white troops. Col. Bearss also rendered distinguished public service in the presence of the enemy at Quinapundan River, Samar, Philippine Islands, on 19 January 1902.

BELL, HARRY

Rank and organization: Captain, 36th Infantry, U.S. Volunteers. *Place and date:* Near Porac, Luzon, Philippine Islands, 17 October 1899. *Entered service at:* Minneapolis, Minn. *Born:* 21 September 1860, Milwaukee, Wis. *Date of issue:* 8 March 1902. *Citation:* Led a successful charge against a superior force, capturing and dispersing the enemy and relieving other members of his regiment from a perilous position.

BELL, J. FRANKLIN

Rank and organization: Colonel, 36th Infantry, U.S. Volunteers. *Place and date:* Near Porac, Luzon, Philippine Islands, 9 September 1899. *Entered service at:* Shelbyville, Ky. *Born:* 9 January 1856, Shelbyville, Ky. *Date of issue:* 11 December 1899. *Citation:* While in advance of his regiment charged 7 insurgents with his pistol and compelled the surrender of the captain and 2 privates under a close fire from the remaining insurgents concealed in a bamboo thicket.

BICKHAM, CHARLES G.

Rank and organization: First Lieutenant, 27th U.S. Infantry. *Place and date:* At Bayong, near Lake Lanao, Mindanao, Philippine Islands, 2 May 1902. *Entered service at:* Dayton, Ohio. *Birth:* Dayton, Ohio. *Date of issue:* 28 April 1904. *Citation:* Crossed a fire-swept field, in close range of the enemy, and brought a wounded soldier to a place of shelter.

BIEGLER, GEORGE W.

Rank and organization: Captain, 28th Infantry, U.S. Volunteers. *Place and date:* Near Loac, Luzon, Philippine Islands, 21 October 1900. *Entered service at:* Terre Haute, Ind. *Birth:* Terre Haute, Ind. *Date of issue:* 11 March 1902. *Citation:* With but 19 men resisted and at close quarters defeated 300 of the enemy.

BIRKHIMER, WILLIAM E.

Rank and organization: Captain, 3d U.S. Artillery. *Place and date:* At San Miguel de Mayumo, Luzon, Philippine Islands, 13 May 1899. *Entered service at:* Iowa. *Birth:* Somerset, Ohio. *Date of issue:* 15 July 1902. *Citation:* With 12 men charged and routed 300 of the enemy.

BOEHLER, OTTO

Rank and organization: Private, Company I, 1st North Dakota Volunteer Infantry. *Place and date:* Near San Isidro, Philippine Islands, 16 May 1899. *Entered service at:* Wahpeton, N. Dak. *Birth:* Germany. *Date of issue:* 17 May 1906. *Citation:* With 21 other scouts charged across a burning bridge, under heavy fire, and completely routed 600 of the enemy who were entrenched in a strongly fortified position.

BUCKLEY, HOWARD MAJOR

Rank and organization: Private, U.S. Marine Corps. *Born:* 23 January 1868, Croton Falls, N.Y. *Accredited to:* New York. *G.O. No.:* 55, 19 July 1901. *Citation:* For distinguished conduct in the presence of the enemy in battle while with the Eighth Army Corps on 25, 27, 29 March, and 4 April 1899.

BYRNE, BERNARD A.

Rank and organization: Captain, 6th U.S. Infantry. *Place and date:* At Bobong, Negros, Philippine Islands, 19 July 1899. *Entered service at:* Washington, D.C. *Birth:* Newport Barracks, Va. *Date of issue:* 15 July 1902. *Citation:* Most distinguished gallantry in rallying his men on the bridge after the line had been broken and pushed back.

CARSON, ANTHONY J.

Rank and organization: Corporal, Company H, 43d Infantry, U.S. Volunteers. *Place and date:* At Catubig, Samar, Philippine Islands, 15–19 April 1900. *Entered service at:* Malden, Mass. *Birth:* Boston, Mass. *Date of issue:* 4 January 1906. *Citation:* Assumed command of a detachment of the company which had survived an overwhelming attack of the enemy, and by his bravery and untiring efforts and the exercise of extraordinary good judgment in the handling of his men successfully withstood for 2 days the attacks of a large force of the enemy, thereby saving the lives of the survivors and protecting the wounded until relief came.

CAWETZKA, CHARLES

Rank and organization: Private, Company F, 30th Infantry, U.S. Volunteers. *Place and date:* Near Sariaya, Luzon, Philippine Islands, 23 August 1900. *Entered service at:* Wayne, Mich. *Birth:* Detroit, Mich. *Date of issue:* 14 March 1902. *Citation:* Singlehanded, he defended a disabled comrade against a greatly superior force of the enemy.

CECIL, JOSEPHUS S.

Rank and organization: First Lieutenant, 19th U.S. Infantry. *Place and date:* At Bud-Dajo, Jolo, Philippine Islands, 7 March 1906. *Entered service at:* New River, Tenn. *Birth:* New River, Tenn. *Date of issue:* Unknown. *Citation:* While at the head of the column about to assault the first cotta under a superior fire at short range personally carried to a sheltered position a wounded man and the body of one who was killed beside him.

CONDON, CLARENCE M.

Rank and organization: Sergeant, Battery G, 3d U.S. Artillery. *Place and date:* Near Calulut, Luzon, Philippine Islands, 5 November 1899. *Entered service at:* ———. *Birth:* South Brooksville, Maine. *Date of issue:* 11 March 1902. *Citation:* While in command of a detachment of 4 men, charged and routed 40 entrenched insurgents, inflicting on them heavy loss.

DAVIS, CHARLES P.

Rank and organization: Private, Company G, 1st North Dakota Volunteer Infantry. *Place and date:* Near San Isidro, Philippine Islands, 16 May 1899. *Entered service at:* Valley City, N. Dak. *Birth:* Long Prairie, Minn. *Date of issue:* 28 April 1906. *Citation:* With 21 other scouts charged across a burning bridge, under heavy fire, and completely routed 600 of the enemy who were entrenched in a strongly fortified position.

DOWNS, WILLIS H.

Rank and organization: Private, Company H, 1st North Dakota Volunteer Infantry. *Place and date:* At San Miguel de Mayumo, Luzon, Philippine Islands, 13 May 1899. *Entered service at:* Jamestown, N. Dak. *Birth:* Mount Carmel, Conn. *Date of issue:* 16 February 1906. *Citation:* With 11 other scouts, without waiting for the supporting battalion to aid them or to get into a position to do so, charged over a distance of about 150 yards and completely routed about 300 of the enemy who were in line and in a position that could only be carried by a frontal attack.

EPPS, JOSEPH L.

Rank and organization: Private, Company B, 33d Infantry, U.S. Volunteers. *Place and date:* At Vigan Luzon, Philippine Islands, 4 December 1899. *Entered service at:* Oklahoma Indian Territory. *Birth:* Jamestown, Mo. *Date of issue:* 7 February 1902. *Citation:* Discovered a party of insurgents inside a wall, climbed to the top of the wall, covered them with his gun, and forced them to stack arms and surrender.

FERGUSON, ARTHUR M.

Rank and organization: First Lieutenant, 36th Infantry, U.S. Volunteers. *Place and date:* Near Porac, Luzon, Philippine Islands, 28 September 1899. *Entered service at:* Burlington, Kans. *Birth:* Coffey County, Kans. *Date of issue:* 8 March 1902. *Citation:* Charged alone a body of the enemy and captured a captain.

FISHER, FREDERICK THOMAS

Rank and organization: Gunner's Mate First Class, U.S. Navy. *Born:* 3 June 1872, England. *Accredited to:* California. *G.O. No.:* 55, 19 July 1901. *Citation:* On board the U.S.S. *Philadelphia*, Samoa, Philippine Islands, 1 April 1899. Serving in the presence of the enemy on this date, Fisher distinguished himself by his conduct.

FITZ, JOSEPH

Rank and organization: Ordinary Seaman, U.S. Navy. *Born:* 24 May 1886, Austria. *Accredited to:* Iowa. *G.O. No.:* 19, 1 May 1906. *Citation:* On board the U.S.S. *Pampanga*, Mount Dajo Jolo, Philippine Islands, 8 March 1906. Serving in the presence of the enemy on this date, Fitz displayed bravery and extraordinary heroism.

FORBECK, ANDREW P.

Rank and organization: Seaman, U.S. Navy. *Born:* 29 August 1879, New York. *Accredited to:* New York. *G.O. No.:* 55, 19 July 1901. *Citation:* For distinguished conduct in the presence of the enemy during the battle of Katbalogan, Samar, Philippine Islands, 16 July 1900.

FORSTERER, BRUNO ALBERT

Rank and organization: Sergeant, U.S. Marine Corps. *Born:* 14 July 1869, Koenigsberg, Germany. *Accredited to:* Massachusetts. *G.O. No.:* 55, 19 July 1901. *Citation:* For distinguished conduct in the presence of the enemy at Samoa, Philippine Islands, 1 April 1899.

FUNSTON, FREDERICK

Rank and organization: Colonel, 20th Kansas Volunteer Infantry. *Place and date:* At Rio Grande de la Pampanga, Luzon, Philippine Islands, 27 April 1899. *Entered service at:* Iola, Kans. *Birth:* Springfield, Ohio. *Date of issue:* 14 February 1900. *Citation:* Crossed the river on a raft and by his skill and daring enabled the general commanding to carry the enemy's entrenched position on the north bank of the river and to drive him with great loss from the important strategic position of Calumpit.

GALBRAITH, ROBERT

Rank and organization: Gunner's Mate Third Class, U.S. Navy. *Born:* 17 February 1880, Brooklyn, N.Y. *Accredited to:* New York. *G.O. No.:* 531, 21 November 1900. *Citation:* For extraordinary heroism and gallantry while under fire of the enemy at El Pardo, Cebu, Philippine Islands, 12 and 13 September 1899.

GALT, STERLING A.

Rank and organization: Artificer, Company F, 36th Infantry, U.S. Volunteers. *Place and date:* At Bamban, Luzon, Philippine Islands, 9 November 1899. *Entered service at:* Pawneytown, Md. *Birth:* Pawneytown, Md. *Date of issue:* 30 April 1902. *Citation:* Distinguished bravery and conspicuous gallantry in action against insurgents.

GAUJOT, ANTOINE A.

Rank and organization: Corporal, Company M, 27th Infantry, U.S. Volunteers. *Place and date:* At San Mateo, Philippine Islands, 19 December 1899. *Entered service at:* Williamson, W. Va. *Birth:* Keweenaw, Mich. *Date of issue:* 15 February 1911. *Citation:* Attempted under a heavy fire of the enemy to swim a river for the purpose of obtaining and returning with a canoe.

GEDEON, LOUIS

Rank and organization: Private, Company G, 19th U.S. Infantry. *Place and date:* At Mount Amia, Cebu, Philippine Islands, 4 February 1900. *Entered service at:* Pittsburgh, Pa. *Birth:* Pittsburgh, Pa. *Date of issue:* 10 March 1902. *Citation:* Singlehanded, defended his mortally wounded captain from an overwhelming force of the enemy.

GIBSON, EDWARD H.

Rank and organization: Sergeant, Company M, 27th Infantry, U.S. Volunteers. *Place and date:* At San Mateo, Philippine Islands, 19 December 1899. *Entered service at:* Boston, Mass. *Birth:* Boston, Mass. *Date of issue:* Unknown. *Citation:* Attempted under a heavy fire of the enemy to swim a river for the purpose of obtaining and returning with a canoe.

GILLENWATER, JAMES R.

Rank and organization: Corporal, Company A, 36th Infantry, U.S. Volunteers. *Place and date:* Near Porac, Luzon, Philippine Islands, 3 September 1899. *Entered service at:* Rye Cove, Va. *Birth:* Rye Cove, Va. *Date of issue:* 15 March 1902. *Citation:* While on a scout drove off a superior force of insurgents and with the assistance of 1 comrade brought from the field of action the bodies of 2 comrades, 1 killed and the other severely wounded.

GREER, ALLEN J.

Rank and organization: Second Lieutenant, U.S. Army, 4th U.S. Infantry. *Place and date:* Near Majada, Laguna Province, Philippine Islands, 2 July 1901. *Entered service at:* Memphis, Tenn. *Birth:* Memphis, Tenn. *Date of issue:* 10 March 1902. *Citation:* Charged alone an insurgent outpost with his pistol, killing 1, wounding 2, and capturing 3 insurgents with their rifles and equipment.

GROVE, WILLIAM R.

Rank and organization: Lieutenant Colonel, 36th Infantry, U.S. Volunteers. *Place and date:* Near Porac, Luzon, Philippine Islands, 9 September 1899. *Entered service at:* Denver, Colo. *Birth:* Montezuma, Iowa. *Date of issue:* 16 July 1902. *Citation:* In advance of his regiment, rushed to the assistance of his colonel, charging, pistol in hand, 7 insurgents, and compelling surrender of all not killed or wounded.

HARVEY, HARRY

Rank and organization: Sergeant, U.S. Marine Corps. *Born:* 4 June 1873, New York, N.Y. *Accredited to:* New Jersey. *G.O. No.:* 55, 19 July 1901. *Citation:* Served in battle against the enemy at Benictican, 16 February 1900. Throughout this action and in the presence of the enemy, Harvey distinguished himself by meritorious conduct.

HAYES, WEBB C.

Rank and organization: Lieutenant Colonel, 31st Infantry, U.S. Volunteers. *Place and date:* At Vigan, Luzon, Philippine Islands, 4 December 1899. *Entered service at:* Fremont, Ohio. *Born:* 20 March 1856, Cincinnati, Ohio. *Date of issue:* 17 December 1902. *Citation:* Pushed through the enemy's lines alone, during the night, from the beach to the beleaguered force at Vigan, and returned the following morning to report the condition of affairs to the Navy and secure assistance.

HENDERSON, JOSEPH

Rank and organization: Sergeant, Troop B, 6th U.S. Cavalry. *Place and date:* At Patian Island, Philippine Islands, 2 July 1909. *Entered service at:* Leavenworth, Kans. *Birth:* Leavenworth, Kans. *Date of issue:* Unknown. *Citation:* While in action against hostile Moros, voluntarily advanced alone, in the face of a heavy fire, to within about 15 yards of the hostile position and refastened to a tree a block and tackle used in checking the recoil of a mountain gun.

HIGH, FRANK C.

Rank and organization: Private, U.S. Army, Company G, 2d Oregon Volunteer Infantry. *Place and date:* Near San Isidro, Philippine Islands, 16 May 1899. *Entered service at:* Picard, Calif. *Birth:* Yolo County, Calif. *Date of issue:* Unknown. *Citation:* With 21 other scouts charged across a burning bridge, under heavy fire, and completely routed 600 of the enemy who were entrenched in a strongly fortified position.

HULBERT, HENRY LEWIS

Rank and organization: Private, U.S. Marine Corps. *Born:* 12 January 1867, Kingston-upon-Hull, England. *Accredited to:* California. *G.O. No.:* 55, 19 July 1901. *Other Navy award:* Navy Cross. *Citation:* For distinguished conduct in the presence of the enemy at Samoa, Philippine Islands, 1 April 1899.

HUNTSMAN, JOHN A.

Rank and organization: Sergeant, Company E, 36th Infantry, U.S. Volunteers. *Place and date:* At Bamban, Luzon, Philippine Islands, 9 November 1899. *Entered service at:* Lawrence, Kans. *Birth:* Oskaloosa County, Iowa. *Date of issue:* Unknown. *Citation:* For distinguished bravery and conspicuous gallantry in action against insurgents.

JENSEN, GOTFRED

Rank and organization: Private, Company D, 1st North Dakota Volunteer Infantry. *Place and date:* At San Miguel de Mayumo, Luzon, Philippine Islands, 13 May 1899. *Entered service at:* Devils Lake, N. Dak. *Birth:* Denmark. *Date of issue:* 6 June 1906. *Citation:* With 11 other scouts, without waiting for the supporting battalion to aid them or to get into a position to do so, charged over a distance of about 150 yards and completely routed about 300 of the enemy, who were in line and in a position that could only be carried by a frontal attack.

JOHNSTON, GORDON

Rank and organization: First Lieutenant, U.S. Signal Corps. *Place and date:* At Mount Bud Dajo, Jolo, Philippine Islands, 7 March 1906. *Entered service at:* Birmingham, Ala. *Born:* 25 May 1874, Charlotte, N.C. *Date of issue:* 7 November 1910. *G.O. No.:* 207. *Citation:* Voluntarily took part in and was dangerously wounded during an assault on the enemy's works.

KENNEDY, JOHN T.

Rank and organization: Second Lieutenant, U.S. Army, 6th U.S. Cavalry. *Place and date:* At Patian Island, Philippine Islands, 4 July 1909. *Entered service at:* Orangeburg, S.C. *Birth:* Hendersonville, S.C. *Date of issue:* Unknown. *Citation:* While in action against hostile Moros, he entered with a few enlisted men the mouth of a cave occupied by a desperate enemy, this act having been ordered after he had volunteered several times. In this action 2d Lt. Kennedy was severely wounded.

KILBOURNE, CHARLES E.

Rank and organization: First Lieutenant, U.S. Volunteer Signal Corps. *Place and date:* At Paco Bridge, Philippine Islands, 5 February 1899. *Entered service at:* Portland, Oreg. *Birth:* Fort Myer, Va. *Date of issue:* 6 May 1905. *Citation:* Within a range of 250 yards of the enemy and in the face of a rapid fire climbed a telegraph pole at the east end of the bridge and in full view of the enemy coolly and carefully repaired a broken telegraph wire, thereby reestablishing telegraphic communication to the front.

KINNE, JOHN B.

Rank and organization: Private, Company B, 1st North Dakota Infantry. *Place and date:* Near San Isidro, Philippine Islands, 16 May 1889. *Entered service at:* Fargo, N. Dak. *Birth:* Beloit, Wis. *Date of issue:* 17 May 1906. *Citation:* With 21 other scouts charged across a burning bridge, under heavy fire, and completely routed 600 of the enemy who were entrenched in a strongly fortified position.

LEAHY, CORNELIUS J.

Rank and organization: Private, Company A, 36th Infantry, U.S. Volunteers. *Place and date:* Near Porac, Luzon, Philippine Islands, 3 September 1899. *Entered service at:* San Francisco, Calif. *Birth:* Ireland. *Date of issue:* 3 May 1902. *Citation:* Distinguished gallantry in action in driving off a superior force and with the assistance of 1 comrade brought from the field of action the bodies of 2 comrades, 1 killed and the other severely wounded, this while on a scout.

2. LEONARD, JOSEPH

Rank and organization: Private, U.S. Marine Corps. (Enlisted as Joseph Melvin). *Born:* 28 August 1876, Cohoes, N.Y. *Accredited to:* New York. *G.O. No.:* 55, 19 July 1901. *Citation:* For distinguished conduct in the presence of the enemy in battles, while with the Eighth Army Corps on 25, 27, and 29 March, and on 4 April 1899.

*LOGAN, JOHN A.

Rank and organization: Major, 33d Infantry, U.S. Volunteers. *Place and date:* At San Jacinto, Philippine Islands, 11 November 1899. *Entered service at:* Youngstown, Ohio. *Born:* 24 July 1865, Carbondale, Ill. *Date of issue:* 3 May 1902. *Citation:* For most distinguished gallantry in leading his battalion upon the entrenchments of the enemy, on which occasion he fell mortally wounded.

LONGFELLOW, RICHARD M.

Rank and organization: Private, Company A, 1st North Dakota Volunteer Infantry. *Place and date:* Near San Isidro, Philippine Islands, 16 May 1899. *Entered service at:* Mandan, N. Dak. *Birth:* Logan County, Ill, *Date of issue:* Unknown. *Citation:* With 21 other scouts charged across a burning bridge, under heavy fire, and completely routed 600 of the enemy who were entrenched in a strongly fortified position.

LYON, EDWARD E.

Rank and organization: Private, Company B, 2d Oregon Volunteer Infantry. *Place and date:* At San Miguel de Mayumo, Luzon, Philippine Islands, 13 May 1899. *Entered service at:* Amboy, Wash. *Birth:* Hixton, Wis. *Date of issue:* 24 January 1906. *Citation:* With 11 other scouts, without waiting for the supporting battalion to aid them or to get into position to do so, charged over a distance of about 150 yards and completely routed about 300 of the enemy, who were in line and in a position that could only be carried by a frontal attack.

MACLAY, WILLIAM P.

Rank and organization: Private, Company A, 43d Infantry, U.S. Volunteers. *Place and date:* At Hilongas, Leyte, Philippine Islands, 6 May 1900. *Entered service at:* Altoona, Pa. *Birth:* Spruce Creek, Pa. *Date of issue:* 11 March 1902. *Citation:* Charged an occupied bastion, saving the life of an officer in a hand-to-hand combat and destroying the enemy.

MATHEWS, GEORGE W.

Rank and organization: Assistant Surgeon, 36th Infantry, U.S. Volunteers. *Place and date:* Near Labo, Luzon, Philippine Islands, 29 October 1899. *Entered service at:* Worcester, Mass. *Birth:* Worcester, Mass. *Date of issue:* 14 March 1902. *Citation:* While in attendance upon the wounded and under a severe fire from the enemy, seized a carbine and beat off an attack upon wounded officers and men under his charge.

McCONNELL, JAMES

Rank and organization: Private, Company B, 33d Infantry, U.S. Volunteers. *Place and date:* At Vigan, Luzon, Philippine Islands, 4 December 1899. *Entered service at:* Detroit, Mich. *Birth:* Syracuse, N.Y. *Date of issue:* 1 October 1902. *Citation:* Fought for hours lying between 2 dead comrades, notwithstanding his hat was pierced, his clothing plowed through by bullets, and his face cut and bruised by flying gravel.

McGRATH, HUGH J.

Rank and organization: Captain, 4th U.S. Cavalry. *Place and date:* At Calamba, Luzon, Philippine Islands, 26 July 1899. *Entered service at:* Eau Claire, Wis. *Birth:* Fond du Lac, Wis. *Date of issue:* 29 April 1902. *Citation:* Swam the San Juan River in the face of the enemy's fire and drove him from his entrenchments.

McNALLY, MICHAEL JOSEPH

Rank and organization: Sergeant, U.S. Marine Corps. *Born:* 29 June 1860, New York, N.Y. *Accredited to:* California. *G.O. No.:* 55, 19 July 1901. *Citation:* For distinguished conduct in the presence of the enemy at Samoa, Philippine Islands, 1 April 1899.

MILLER, ARCHIE

Rank and organization: First Lieutenant, 6th U.S. Cavalry. *Place and date:* At Patian Island, Philippine Islands, 2 July 1909. *Entered service at:* St. Louis, Mo. *Birth:* Fort Sheridan, Ill. *Date of issue:* Unknown. *Citation:* While in action against hostile Moros, when the machinegun detachment, having been driven from its position by a heavy fire, 1 member being killed, did, with the assistance of an enlisted man, place the machinegun in advance of its former position at a distance of about 20 yards from the enemy, in accomplishing which he was obliged to splice a piece of timber to one leg of the gun tripod, all the while being under a heavy fire, and the gun tripod being several times struck by bullets.

MORAN, JOHN E.

Rank and organization: Captain, Company L, 37th Infantry, U.S. Volunteers. *Place and date:* Near Mabitac, Laguna, Luzon, Philippine Islands, 17 September 1900. *Entered service at:* Cascade County, Mont. *Born:* 23 August 1856, Vernon, Windham County, Vt. *Date of issue:* 10 June 1910. *Citation:* After the attacking party had become demoralized, fearlessly led a small body of troops under a severe fire and through water waist deep in the attack against the enemy.

MOSHER, LOUIS C.

Rank and organization: Second Lieutenant, Philippine Scouts. *Place and date:* At Gagsak Mountain, Jolo, Philippine Islands, 11 June 1913. *Entered service at:* Brockton, Mass. *Birth:* Westport, Mass. *Date of issue:* Unknown. *Citation:* Voluntarily entered a cleared space within about 20 yards of the Moro trenches under a furious fire from them and carried a wounded soldier of his company to safety at the risk of his own life.

MULLIN, HUGH P.

Rank and organization: Seaman, U.S. Navy. *Born:* 20 March 1878, Richmond, Ill. *Accredited to:* Illinois. *G.O. No.:* 537, 8 January 1900. *Citation:* On board the U.S.S. *Texas* during the coaling of that vessel at Hampton Roads, Va., 11 November 1899. Jumping overboard while wearing a pair of heavy rubber boots and at great risk to himself, Mullin rescued Alfred Kosminski, apprentice, second class, who fell overboard, by supporting him until he was safely hauled from the water.

NISPEROS, JOSE B.

Rank and organization: Private, 34th Company, Philippine Scouts. *Place and date:* At Lapurap, Basilan, Philippine Islands, 24 September 1911. *Entered service at:* San Fernandos Union, P.I. *Birth:* San Fernandos Union, P.I. *Date of issue:* Unknown. Citation: Having been badly wounded (his left arm was broken and lacerated and he had received several spear wounds in the body so that he could not stand) continued to fire his rifle with one hand until the enemy was repulsed, thereby aiding materially in preventing the annihilation of his party and the mutilation of their bodies.

NOLAN, JOSEPH A.

Rank and organization: Artificer, Company B, 45th Infantry, U.S. Volunteers. *Place and date:* At Labo, Luzon, Philippine Islands, 29 May 1900. *Entered service at:* South Bend, Ind. *Birth:* Elkhart, Ind. *Date of issue:* 14 March 1902. *Citation:* Voluntarily left shelter and at great personal risk passed the enemy's lines and brought relief to besieged comrades.

PARKER, JAMES

Rank and organization: Lieutenant Colonel, 45th Infantry, U.S. Volunteers. *Place and date:* At Vigan, Luzon, Philippine Islands, 4 December 1899. *Entered service at:* Newark, N.J. *Birth:* Newark, N.J. *Date of issue:* 8 March 1902. *Citation:* While in command of a small garrison repulsed a savage night attack by overwhelming numbers of the enemy, fighting at close quarters in the dark for several hours.

PIERCE, CHARLES H.

Rank and organization: Private, Company I, 22d U.S. Infantry. *Place and date:* Near San Isidro, Luzon, Philippine Islands, 19 October 1899. *Entered service at:* Delaware City, Del. *Birth:* Cecil County, Md. *Date of issue:* 10 March 1902. *Citation:* Held a bridge against a superior force of the enemy and fought, though severely wounded, until the main body came up to cross.

PORTER, DAVID DIXON

Rank and organization: Colonel, U.S. Marine Corps. *Born:* 29 April 1877, Washington, D.C. *Appointed from:* District of Columbia. *Citation:* For extraordinary heroism and eminent and conspicuous conduct in battle at the junction of the Cadacan and Sohoton Rivers, Samar, Philippine Islands, 17 November 1901. In command of the columns upon their uniting ashore in the Sohoton Region, Col. Porter (then Capt.) made a surprise attack on the fortified cliffs and completely routed the enemy, killing 30 and capturing and destroying the powder magazine, 40 lantacas (guns), rice, food and cuartels. Due to his courage, intelligence, discrimination and zeal, he successfully led his men up the cliffs by means of bamboo ladders to a height of 200 feet. The cliffs were of soft stone of volcanic origin, in the nature of pumice and were honeycombed with caves. Tons of rocks were suspended in platforms held in position by vines and cables (known as bejuco) in readiness to be precipitated upon people below. After driving the insurgents from their position which was almost impregnable, being covered with numerous trails lined with poisoned spears, pits, etc., Col. Porter led his men across the river, scaled the cliffs on the opposite side, and destroyed the camps there. He and the men under his command overcame incredible difficulties and dangers in destroying positions which, according to reports from old prisoners, had taken 3 years to perfect, were held as a final rallying post, and were never before penetrated by white troops. Col. Porter also rendered distinguished public service in the presence of the enemy at Quinapundan River, Samar, Philippine Islands, on 26 October 1901.

PRENDERGAST, THOMAS FRANCIS

Rank and organization: Corporal, U.S. Marine Corps. *Born:* 2 April 1871, Waterford, Ireland. *Accredited to:* Massachusetts. *G.O. No.:* 55, 19 July 1901. *Citation:* For distinguished conduct in the presence of the enemy in battle while with the Eighth Army Corps, 25, 27, 29 March, and 5 April 1899.

QUINN, PETER H.

Rank and organization: Private, Company L, 4th U.S. Cavalry. *Place and date:* At San Miguel de Mayumo, Luzon, Philippine Islands, 13 May 1899. *Entered service at: San Francisco, Calif. Birth:* San Francisco, Calif. *Date of issue:* 6 June 1906. *Citation:* With 11 other scouts, without waiting for the supporting battalion to aid them or to get into a position to do so, charged over a distance of about 150 yards and completely routed about 300 of the enemy who were in line and in a position that could only be carried by a frontal attack.

RAY, CHARLES W.

Rank and organization: Sergeant, Company I, 22d U.S. Infantry. *Place and date:* Near San Isidro, Luzon, Philippine Islands, 19 October 1899. *Entered service at:* St. Louis, Mo. *Birth:* Pensacola, Yancey County, N.C. *Date of issue:* 18 April 1902. *Citation:* Most distinguished gallantry in action. Captured a bridge with the detachment he commanded and held it against a superior force of the enemy, thereby enabling an army to come up and cross.

ROBERTSON, MARCUS W.

Rank and organization: Private, Company B, 2d Oregon Volunteer Infantry. *Place and date:* Near San Isidro, Philippine Islands, 16 May 1899. *Entered service at:* Hood River, Oreg. *Birth:* Flintville, Wis. *Date of issue:* 28 April 1906. *Citation:* With 21 other scouts charged across a burning bridge, under heavy fire, and completely routed 600 of the enemy who were entrenched in a strongly fortified position.

ROSS, FRANK F.

Rank and organization: Private, Company H, 1st North Dakota Volunteer Infantry. *Place and date:* Near San Isidro, Philippine Islands, 16 May 1899. *Entered service at:* Langdon, N. Dak. *Birth:* Avon, Ill. *Date of issue:* 6 June 1906. *Citation:* With 21 other scouts charged across a burning bridge, under heavy fire, and completely routed 600 of the enemy who were entrenched in a strongly fortified position.

SAGE, WILLIAM H.

Rank and organization: Captain, 23d U.S. Infantry. *Place and date:* Near Zapote River, Luzon, Philippine Islands, 13 June 1899. *Entered service at:* Binghamton, N.Y. *Birth:* Centerville, N.Y. *Date of issue:* 24 July 1902. *Citation:* With 9 men volunteered to hold an advanced position and held it against a terrific fire of the enemy estimated at 1,000 strong. Taking a rifle from a wounded man, and cartridges from the belts of others, Capt. Sage himself killed 5 of the enemy.

SCHROEDER, HENRY F.

Rank and organization: Sergeant, Company L, 16th U.S. Infantry. *Place and date:* At Carig, Philippine Islands, 14 September 1900. *Entered service at:* Chicago, Ill. *Birth:* Chicago, Ill. *Date of issue:* 10 March 1902. *Citation:* With 22 men defeated 400 insurgents, killing 36 and wounding 90.

SHANAHAN, PATRICK

Rank and organization: Chief Boatswain's Mate, U.S. Navy. *Born:* 6 November 1867, Ireland. *Accredited to:* New York. *G.O. No.:* 534, 29 November 1899. *Citation:* On board the U.S.S. *Alliance*, 28 May 1899. Displaying heroism, Shanahan rescued William Steven, quartermaster, first class, from drowning.

SHAW, GEORGE C.

Rank and organization: First Lieutenant, 27th U.S. Infantry. *Place and date:* At Fort Pitacus, Lake Lanao, Mindanao, Philippine Islands, 4 May 1903. *Entered service at:* Washington, D.C. *Birth:* Pontiac, Mich. *Date of issue:* 9 June 1904. *Citation:* For distinguished gallantry in leading the assault and, under a heavy fire from the enemy, maintaining alone his position on the parapet after the first 3 men who followed him there had been killed or wounded, until a foothold was gained by others and the capture of the place assured.

SHELTON, GEORGE M.

Rank and organization: Private, Company I, 23d U.S. Infantry. *Place and date:* At La Paz, Leyte, Philippine Islands, 26 April 1900. *Entered service at:* Bellington, Tex. *Birth:* Brownwood, Tex. *Date of issue:* 10 March 1902. *Citation:* Advanced alone under heavy fire of the enemy and rescued a wounded comrade.

SHIELS, GEORGE F.

Rank and organization: Surgeon, U.S. Volunteers. *Place and date:* At Tuliahan River, Philippine Islands, 25 March 1899. *Entered service at:* California. *Birth:* California. *Date of issue:* 22 November 1906. *Citation:* Voluntarily exposed himself to the fire of the enemy and went with 4 men to the relief of 2 native Filipinos lying wounded about 150 yards in front of the lines and personally carried one of them to a place of safety.

SLETTELAND, THOMAS

Rank and organization: Private, Company C, 1st North Dakota Infantry. *Place and date:* Near Paete, Luzon, Philippine Islands, 12 April 1899. *Entered service at:* Grafton, N. Dak. *Birth:* Norway. *Date of issue:* 11 March 1902. *Citation:* Singlehanded and alone defended his dead and wounded comrades against a greatly superior force of the enemy.

STEWART, GEORGE E.

Rank and organization: Second Lieutenant, 19th U.S. Infantry. *Place and date:* At Passi, Island of Panay, Philippine Islands, 26 November

1899. *Entered service at:* New York, N.Y. *Birth:* New South Wales. *Date of issue:* 26 June 1900. *Citation:* While crossing a river in face of the enemy, this officer plunged in and at the imminent risk of his own life saved from drowning an enlisted man of his regiment.

STOKES, JOHN

Rank and organization: Chief Master-at-Arms, U.S. Navy. *Born:* 12 June 1871, New York, N.Y. *Accredited to:* New York. *G.O. No.:* 525, 29 July 1899. *Citation:* On board the U.S.S. *New York* off the coast of Jamaica, 31 March 1899. Showing gallant conduct, Stokes jumped overboard and assisted in the rescue of Peter Mahoney, watertender, U.S. Navy.

STOLTENBERG, ANDREW V.

Rank and organization: Gunner's Mate Second Class, U.S. Navy. *Born:* Boto, Norway. *Accredited to:* California. *G.O. No.:* 55, 29 July 1899. *Citation:* For distinguished conduct in the presence of the enemy in battle at Katbalogan, Samar, Philippine Islands, 16 July 1900.

STRAUB, PAUL F.

Rank and organization: Surgeon. 36th Infantry, U.S. Volunteers. *Place and date:* At Alos, Zambales, Luzon, Philippine Islands, 21 December 1899. *Entered service at:* Iowa. *Birth:* Germany. *Date of issue:* 6 October 1906. *Citation:* Voluntarily exposed himself to a hot fire from the enemy in repelling with pistol fire an insurgent attack and at great risk of his own life went under fire to the rescue of a wounded officer and carried him to a place of safety.

THORDSEN, WILLIAM GEORGE

Rank and organization: Coxswain, U.S. Navy. *Born:* 2 April 1879, Fredericstadt, Germany. *Accredited to:* New York. *G.O. No.:* 6, 15 August 1900. *Citation.* For heroism and gallantry under fire of the enemy at Hilongas, Philippine Islands, 6 May 1900.

TREMBLEY, WILLIAM B.

Rank and organization: Private, Company B, 20th Kansas Volunteer Infantry. *Place and date:* At Calumpit, Luzon, Philippine Islands, 27 April 1899. *Entered service at:* Kansas City, Kans. *Birth:* Johnson, Kans. *Date of issue:* 11 March 1902. *Citation:* Swam the Rio Grande de Pampanga in face of the enemy's fire and fastened a rope to the occupied trenches, thereby enabling the crossing of the river and the driving of the enemy from his fortified position.

VAN SCHAICK, LOUIS J.

Rank and organization: First Lieutenant, 4th U.S. Infantry. *Place and date:* Near Nasugbu, Batangas, Philippine Islands, 23 November 1901. *Entered service at:* Cobleskill, N.Y. *Birth:* Cobleskill, N.Y. *G.O. No.:* 33, 1913. *Date of issue:* Unknown. *Citation:* While in pursuit of a band of insurgents was the first of his detachment to emerge from a canyon, and seeing a column of insurgents and fearing they might turn and dispatch his men as they emerged one by one from the canyon, galloped forward and closed with the insurgents, thereby throwing them into confusion until the arrival of others of the detachment.

WALKER, FRANK O.

Rank and organization: Private, Company F, 46th Infantry, U.S. Volunteers. *Place and date:* Near Taal, Luzon, Philippine Islands, 18 January 1900. *Entered service at:* Burlington, Mass. *Birth:* South Boston, Mass. *Date of issue:* 11 March 1902. *Citation:* Under heavy fire of the enemy he rescued a dying comrade who was sinking beneath the water.

WALLACE, GEORGE W.

Rank and organization: Second Lieutenant, 9th U.S. Infantry. *Place and date:* At Tinuba, Luzon, Philippine Islands, 4 March 1900. *Entered service at:* Denver, Colo. *Birth:* Fort Riley, Kans. *Date of issue:* 25 June 1900. *Citation:* With another officer and a native Filipino, was shot at from an ambush, the other officer falling severely wounded. 2d Lt. Wallace fired in the direction of the enemy, put them to rout, removed the wounded officer from the path, returned to the town, a mile distant, and summoned assistance from his command.

WEAVER, AMOS

Rank and organization: Sergeant, Company F, 36th Infantry, U.S. Volunteers. *Place and date:* Between Calubus and Malalong, Philippine Islands, 5 November 1899. *Entered service at:* San Francisco, Calif. *Born:* 13 June 1869, Niles Township, Delaware County, Ind. *Date of issue:* 15 March 1902. *Citation:* Alone and unaided, charged a body of 15 insurgents, dislodging them, killing 4 and wounding several.

WELD, SETH L.

Rank and organization: Corporal, Company L, 8th U.S. Infantry. *Place and date:* At La Paz, Leyte, Philippine Islands, 5 December 1906. *Entered service at:* Altamont, Tenn. *Birth:* Sandy Hook, Md. *Date of issue:* 20 October 1908. *Citation:* With his right arm cut open with a bolo, went to the assistance of a wounded constabulary officer and a fellow soldier who were surrounded by about 40 Pulajanes, and, using his disabled rifle as a club, beat back the assailants and rescued his party.

WETHERBY, JOHN C.

Rank and organization: Private, Company L, 4th U.S. Infantry. *Place and date:* Near Imus, Luzon, Philippine Islands, 20 November 1899. *Entered service at:* Martinsville, Ind. *Birth:* Morgan County, Ind. *Date of issue:* 25 April 1902. *Citation:* While carrying important orders on the battlefield, was desperately wounded and, being unable to walk, crawled far enough to deliver his orders.

WHITE, EDWARD

Rank and organization: Private, Company B, 20th Kansas Volunteer Infantry. *Place and date:* At Calumpit, Luzon, Philippine Islands, 27 April 1899. *Entered service at:* Kansas City, Kans. *Birth:* Seneca, Kans. *Date of issue:* 11 March 1902. *Citation:* Swam the Rio Grande de Pampanga in face of the enemy's fire and fastened a rope to occupied trenches, thereby enabling the crossing of the river and the driving of the enemy from his fortified position.

WILSON, ARTHUR H.

Rank and organization: Second Lieutenant, 6th U.S. Cavalry. *Place and date:* At Patian Island, Philippine Islands, 4 July 1909. *Entered service at:* Springfield, Ill. *Birth:* Springfield, Ill. *Date of issue:* Unknown. *Citation:* While in action against hostile Moros, when, it being necessary to secure a mountain gun in position by rope and tackle, voluntarily with the assistance of an enlisted man, carried the rope forward and fastened it, being all the time under heavy fire of the enemy at short range.

WAR WITH SPAIN

BAKER, BENJAMIN F.

Rank and organization: Coxswain, U.S. Navy. *Born:* 12 March 1862, Dennisport, Mass. *G.O. No.:* 521, 7 July 1899. *Citation:* On board the U.S.S. *Nashville* during the cutting of the cable leading from Cienfuegos, Cuba, 11 May 1898. Facing the heavy fire of the enemy, Baker set an example of extraordinary bravery and coolness throughout this action.

BAKER, EDWARD L., JR.

Rank and organization: Sergeant Major, 10th U.S. Cavalry. *Place and date:* At Santiago, Cuba, 1 July 1898. *Entered service at:* ———. *Birth:* Laramie County, Wyo. *Date of issue:* 3 July 1902. *Citation:* Left cover and, under fire, rescued a wounded comrade from drowning.

BARROW, DAVID D.

Rank and organization: Seaman, U.S. Navy. *Born:* 22 October 1877, Reelsboro, N.C. *Entered service at:* Norfolk, Va. *G.O. No.:* 521, 7 July 1899. *Citation:* On board the U.S.S. *Nashville* during the cutting of the cable leading from Cienfuegos, Cuba, 11 May 1898. Facing the heavy fire of the enemy, Barrow set an example of extraordinary bravery and coolness throughout this action.

BELL, DENNIS

Rank and organization: Private, Troop H, 10th U.S. Cavalry. *Place and date:* At Tayabacoa, Cuba, 30 June 1898. *Entered service at:* Washington, D.C. *Birth:* Washington, D.C. *Date of issue:* 23 June 1899. *Citation:* Voluntarily went ashore in the face of the enemy and aided in the rescue of his wounded comrades; this after several previous attempts at rescue had been frustrated.

BENNETT, JAMES H.

Rank and organization: Chief Boatswain's Mate, U.S. Navy. *Born:* 11 August 1877, New York, N.Y. *Accredited to:* New York. *G.O. No.:* 521, 7 July 1899. *Citation:* On board the U.S.S. *Marblehead* during the cutting of the cable leading from Cienfuegos, Cuba, 11 May 1898. Facing the heavy fire of the enemy, Bennett set an example of extraordinary bravery and coolness throughout this action.

BERG, GEORGE

Rank and organization: Private, Company C, 17th U.S. Infantry. *Place and date:* At El Caney, Cuba, 1 July 1898. *Entered service at:* ———. *Birth:* Wayne County, Ill. *Date of issue:* Unknown. *Citation:* Gallantly assisted in the rescue of the wounded from in front of the lines and while under heavy fire of the enemy.

BEYER, ALBERT

Rank and organization: Coxswain, U.S. Navy. *Born:* 13 June 1859, Hanover, Germany. *Entered service at:* Boston, Mass. *G.O. No.:* 521, 7 July 1899. *Citation:* On board the U.S.S. *Nashville* during the cutting of the cable leading from Cienfuegos, Cuba, 11 May 1898. Facing the heavy fire of the enemy, Beyer set an example of extraordinary bravery and coolness throughout this action.

BLUME, ROBERT

Rank and organization: Seaman, U.S. Navy. *Born:* 19 November 1868, Pittsburgh, Pa. *Accredited to:* New Jersey. *G.O. No.:* 521, 7 July 1899. *Citation:* On board the U.S.S. *Nashville* during the cutting of the cable leading from Cienfuegos, Cuba, 11 May 1898. Facing the heavy fire of the enemy, Blume set an example of extraordinary bravery and coolness throughout this action.

BRADY, GEORGE F.

Rank and organization: Chief Gunner's Mate, U.S. Navy. *Born:* 7 September 1867, Ireland. *Accredited to:* New York. *G.O. No.:* 497, 3 September 1899. *Citation:* On board the torpedo boat *Winslow* during the actions at Cardenas, Cuba, 11 May 1898. Conspicuously gallant during this period, Brady, by his energy in assisting to sustain fire, his efforts to repair the steering gear and his promptness in maintaining watertight integrity, was largely instrumental in saving the vessel.

BRIGHT, GEORGE WASHINGTON

Rank and organization: Coal Passer, U.S. Navy. *Born:* 27 December 1874, Norfolk, Va. *Accredited to:* Virginia. *G.O. No.:* 521, 7 July 1899. *Citation:* On board the U.S.S. *Nashville* during the cutting of the cable leading from Cienfuegos, Cuba, 11 May 1898. Facing the heavy fire of the enemy, Bright set an example of extraordinary bravery and coolness throughout this action.

BROOKIN, OSCAR

Rank and organization: Private, Company C, 17th U.S. Infantry. *Place and date:* At El Caney, Cuba, 1 July 1898. *Entered service at:* Green County, Ohio. *Birth:* Byron, Wis. *Date of issue:* 21 June 1899. *Citation:* Gallantly assisted in the rescue of the wounded from in front of the lines and under heavy fire from the enemy.

BUZZARD, ULYSSES G.

Rank and organization: Corporal, Company C, 17th U.S. Infantry. *Place and date:* At El Caney, Cuba, 1 July 1898. *Entered service at:* ―――. *Birth:* Armstrong, Pa. *Date of issue:* 24 June 1899. *Citation:* Gallantly assisted in the rescue of the wounded from in front of the lines and under heavy fire from the enemy.

CAMPBELL, DANIEL

Rank and organization: Private, U.S. Marine Corps. *Born:* 26 October 1874, Prince Edward Island, Canada. *Accredited to:* Massachusetts. *G.O. No.:* 521, 7 July 1899. *Citation:* On board the U.S.S. *Marblehead* during the cutting of the cable leading from Cienfuegos, Cuba, 11 May 1898. Facing the heavy fire of the enemy, Campbell set an example of extraordinary bravery and coolness throughout this action.

CANTRELL, CHARLES P.

Rank and organization: Private, Company F, 10th U.S. Infantry. *Place and date:* At Santiago, Cuba, 1 July 1898. *Entered service at:* Nashville, Tenn. *Born:* 13 February 1874, Smithville, Tenn. *Date of issue:* 22 June 1899. *Citation:* Gallantly assisted in the rescue of the wounded from in front of the lines and under heavy fire from the enemy.

CARTER, JOSEPH E.

Rank and organization: Blacksmith, U.S. Navy. *Born:* 15 August 1875, Manchester, England. *Accredited:* North Dakota. *G.O. No.:* 521, 7 July 1899. *Citation:* On board the U.S.S. *Marblehead* during the operation of cutting the cable leading from Cienfuegos, Cuba, 11 May 1898. Facing the heavy fire of the enemy, Carter set an example of extraordinary bravery and coolness throughout this action.

CAVANAUGH, THOMAS

Rank and organization: Fireman First Class, U.S. Navy. *Born:* 10 May 1869, Ireland. *Accredited to:* New York. *G.O. No.:* 503, 12 December 1898. *Citation:* On board the U.S.S. *Potomac* during the passage of that vessel from Cat Island to Nassau, 14 November 1898. Volunteering to enter the fireroom which was filled with steam, Cavanaugh, after repeated attempts, succeeded in reaching the auxiliary valve and opening it, thereby relieving the vessel from further danger.

CHADWICK, LEONARD

Rank and organization: Apprentice First Class, U.S. Navy. *Born:* 24 November 1878, Middletown, Del. *Accredited to:* Delaware. *G.O. No.:* 521, 7 July 1899. *Citation:* On board the U.S.S. *Marblehead* during the operation of cutting the cable leading from Cienfuegos, Cuba, 11 May 1898. Facing the heavy fire of the enemy, Chadwick set an example of extraordinary bravery and coolness throughout this period.

CHARETTE, GEORGE

Rank and organization: Gunner's Mate First Class, U.S. Navy. *Entered service at:* Lowell, Mass. *Born:* 6 June 1867, Lowell, Mass. *G.O. No.:* 529, 2 November 1899. *Citation:* In connection with the sinking of the U.S.S. *Merrimac* at the entrance to the harbor of Santiago de Cuba, 2 June 1898. Despite heavy fire from the Spanish batteries, Charette displayed extraordinary heroism throughout this operation.

CHURCH, JAMES ROBB

Rank and organization: Assistant Surgeon, 1st U.S. Volunteer Cavalry. *Place and date:* At Las Guasimas, Cuba, 24 June 1898. *Entered service at:* Washington, D.C. *Birth:* Chicago, Ill. *Date of issue:* 10 January 1906. *Citation:* In addition to performing gallantly the duties pertaining to his position, voluntarily and unaided carried several seriously wounded men from the firing line to a secure position in the rear, in each instance being subjected to a very heavy fire and great exposure and danger.

CLAUSEN, CLAUS KRISTIAN

Rank and organization: Coxswain, U.S. Navy. *Born:* 9 December 1869, Denmark. *Accredited to:* New York. *G.O. No.:* 529, 2 November 1899. *Citation:* In connection with the sinking of the U.S.S. *Merrimac* at the entrance to the harbor of Santiago de Cuba, 2 June 1898. Despite heavy fire from the Spanish batteries, Clausen displayed extraordinary heroism throughout this operation.

COONEY, THOMAS C.

Rank and organization: Chief Machinist, U.S. Navy. *Born:* 18 July 1853, Westport, Nova Scotia. *Accredited to:* New Jersey. *G.O. No.:* 497, 3 September 1898. *Citation:* On board the U.S. Torpedo Boat *Winslow* during the action at Cardenas, Cuba, 11 May 1898. Following the piercing of the boiler by an enemy shell, Cooney, by his gallantry and promptness in extinguishing the resulting flames, saved the boiler tubes from burning out.

CROUSE, WILLIAM ADOLPHUS

Rank and organization: Watertender, U.S. Navy. *Born:* 22 October 1866, Tannettsburg, Pa. *Accredited to:* Pennsylvania. *G.O. No.:* 502, 14 December 1898. *Citation:* On board the U.S.S. *Concord* off Cavite, Manila Bay, P.I., 21 May 1898. Following the blowing out of a lower manhole plate joint on boiler B of that vessel, Crouse hauled the fires in the hot, vapor-filled atmosphere which necessitated the playing of water into the fireroom from a hose.

CUMMINS, ANDREW J.

Rank and organization: Sergeant, Company F, 10th U.S. Infantry. *Place and date:* At Santiago, Cuba, 1 July 1898. *Entered service at:* ———. *Birth:* Alexandria, Ind. *Date of issue:* 22 June 1899. *Citation:* Gallantly assisted in the rescue of the wounded from in front of the lines and under heavy fire of the enemy.

DAVIS, JOHN

Rank and organization: Gunner's Mate Third Class, U.S. Navy. *Place and date:* On board U.S.S. *Marblehead* at Cienfuegos, Cuba, 11 May 1898. *Entered service at:* New York, N.Y. *Born:* 28 October 1878, Germany. *G.O. No.:* 521, 7 July 1899. *Citation:* On board the U.S.S. *Marblehead*, during the operation of cutting the cable leading from Cienfuegos, Cuba, 11 May 1898. Facing the heavy fire of the enemy, Davis set an example of extraordinary bravery and coolness throughout this action.

DEIGNAN, OSBORN

Rank and organization: Coxswain, U.S. Navy. *Born:* 24 February 1873, Sheart, Iowa. *Accredited to:* Iowa. *G.O. No.:* 529, 2 November 1899. *Citation:* In connection with the sinking of the U.S.S. *Merrimac* at the entrance to the harbor of Santiago de Cuba, 2 June 1898. Despite heavy fire from the Spanish batteries, Deignan displayed extraordinary heroism throughout this operation.

DE SWAN, JOHN F.

Rank and organization: Private, Company H, 21st U.S. Infantry. *Place and date:* At Santiago, Cuba, 1 July 1898. *Entered service at:* Philadelphia, Pa. *Birth:* Philadelphia, Pa. *Date of issue:* 22 June 1899. *Citation:* Gallantly assisted in the rescue of the wounded from in front of the lines and under heavy fire from the enemy.

DOHERTY, THOMAS M.

Rank and organization: Corporal, Company H, 21st U.S. Infantry. *Place and date:* At Santiago, Cuba, 1 July 1898. *Entered service at:* Newcastle, Maine. *Birth:* Ireland. *Date of issue:* 22 June 1899. *Citation:* Gallantly assisted in the rescue of the wounded from in front of the lines and while under heavy fire from the enemy.

DORAN, JOHN J.

Rank and organization: Boatswain's Mate Second Class, U.S. Navy. *Born:* Massachusetts. *Accredited to:* Massachusetts. *G.O. No.:* 521, 7

July 1899. *Citation:* On board the U.S.S. *Marblehead* during the operation of cutting the cable leading from Cienfuegos, Cuba, 11 May 1898. Facing the heavy fire of the enemy, Doran set an example of extraordinary bravery and coolness throughout this action.

DURNEY, AUSTIN J.

Rank and organization: Blacksmith, U.S. Navy. *Born:* 26 November 1867, Philadelphia, Pa. *Entered service at:* Woodland, Mo. *G.O. No.:* 521, 7 July 1899. *Citation:* On board the U.S.S. *Nashville* during the operation of cutting the cable leading from Cienfuegos, Cuba, 11 May 1898. Facing the heavy fire of the enemy, Durney set an example of extraordinary bravery and coolness throughout this action.

EGLIT, JOHN

Rank and organization: Seaman, U.S. Navy. *Born:* 17 October 1874, Finland. *Accredited to:* New York. *G.O. No.:* 521, 7 July 1899. *Citation:* On board the U.S.S. *Nashville* during the operation of cutting the cable leading from Cienfuegos, Cuba, 11 May 1898. Facing the heavy fire of the enemy, Eglit set an example of extraordinary bravery and coolness throughout this action.

EHLE, JOHN WALTER

Rank and organization: Fireman First Class, U.S. Navy. *Born:* 11 May 1873, Kearney, Nebr. *Accredited to:* Nebraska. *G.O. No.:* 502 14 December 1898. *Citation:* On board the U.S.S. *Concord* off Cavite, Manila Bay, Philippine Islands, 21 May 1898. Following the blowing out of a lower manhole plate joint on boiler B of that vessel, Ehle assisted in hauling the fires in the hot, vapor-filled atmosphere which necessitated the playing of water into the fireroom from a hose.

ERICKSON, NICK

Rank and organization: Coxswain, U.S. Navy. *Born:* 18 July 1870, Finland. *Accredited to:* New York. *G.O. No.:* 521, 7 July 1899. *Citation:* On board the U.S.S. *Marblehead* during the operation of cutting the cable leading from Cienfuegos, Cuba, 11 May 1898. Facing the heavy fire of the enemy, Erickson set an example of extraordinary bravery and coolness throughout this action.

FIELD, OSCAR WADSWORTH

Rank and organization: Private, U.S. Marine Corps. *Born:* 6 October 1873, Jersey City, N.J. *Accredited to:* New York. *G.O. No.:* 521, 7 July 1899. *Citation:* On board the U.S.S. *Nashville* during the operation of cutting the cable leading from Cienfuegos, Cuba, 11 May 1898. Facing the heavy fire of the enemy, Field set an example of extraordinary bravery and coolness throughout this action.

FITZGERALD, JOHN

Rank and organization: Private, U.S. Marine Corps. *Born:* 17 March 1873, Limerick, Ireland. *Accredited to:* New York. *G.O. No.:* 92, 8 December 1910. *Citation:* For heroism and gallantry in action at Cuzco, Cuba, 14 June 1898.

FOSS, HERBERT LOUIS

Rank and organization: Seaman, U.S. Navy. *Born:* 12 October 1871, Belfast, Maine. *Accredited to:* Maine. *G.O. No.:* 521, 7 July 1899. *Citation:* On board the U.S.S. *Marblehead* during the operation of cutting the cable leading from Cienfuegos, Cuba, 11 May 1898. Facing the heavy fire of the enemy, Foss set an example of extraordinary bravery and coolness throughout this action.

FOURNIA, FRANK O.

Rank and organization: Private, Company H, 21st U.S. Infantry. *Place and date:* At Santiago, Cuba, 1 July 1898. *Entered service at:* Plattsburg, N.Y. *Birth:* Rome, N.Y. *Date of issue:* 22 June 1899. *Citation:* Gallantly assisted in the rescue of the wounded from in front of the lines and while under heavy fire of the enemy.

FRANKLIN, JOSEPH JOHN

Rank and organization: Private, U.S. Marine Corps. *Born:* 18 June 1870, Buffalo, N.Y. *Accredited to:* New York. *G.O. No.:* 521, 7 July 1899. *Citation:* On board the U.S.S. *Nashville* during the operation of cutting the cable leading from Cienfuegos, Cuba, 11 May 1898. Facing the heavy fire of the enemy, Franklin set an example of extraordinary bravery and coolness throughout this action.

GAUGHAN, PHILIP

Rank and organization: Sergeant, U.S. Marine Corps. *Born:* 17 March 1865, Belmullet, Ireland. *Accredited to:* Pennsylvania. *G.O. No.:* 521, 7 July 1899. *Citation:* On board the U.S.S. *Nashville* during the operation of cutting the cable leading from Cienfuegos, Cuba, 11 May 1898. Facing the heavy fire of the enemy, Gaughan set an example of extraordinary bravery and coolness throughout this action.

GIBBONS, MICHAEL

Rank and organization: Oiler, U.S. Navy. *Born:* Ireland. *Accredited to:* New York. *G.O. No.:* 521, 7 July 1899. *Citation:* On board the U.S.S. *Nashville* during the operation of cutting the cable leading from Cienfugos, Cuba, 11 May 1898. Facing the heavy fire of the enemy, Gibbons set an example of extraordinary bravery and coolness throughout this action.

GILL, FREEMAN

Rank and organization: Gunner's Mate First Class, U.S. Navy. *Born:* 5 September 1851, Boston, Mass. *Accredited to:* Massachusetts. *G.O. No.:* 55, 19 July 1901. *Citation:* On board the U.S.S. *Marblehead* during the operation of cutting the cable leading from Cienfuegos, Cuba, 11 May 1898. Facing the heavy fire of the enemy, Gill set an example of extraordinary bravery and coolness throughout this action.

GRAVES, THOMAS J.

Rank and organization: Private, Company C, 17th U.S. Infantry. *Place and date:* At El Caney, Cuba, 1 July 1898. *Entered service at:* Millville, Ind. *Birth:* Milton, Ind. *Date of issue:* 22 June 1899. *Citation:* Gallantly assisted in the rescue of the wounded from in front of the lines and under heavy fire from the enemy.

HARDAWAY, BENJAMIN F.

Rank and organization: First Lieutenant, 17th U.S. Infantry. *Place and date:* At El Caney, Cuba, 1 July 1898. *Entered service at:* ———. *Birth:* Benleyville, Ky. *Date of issue:* 21 June 1899. *Citation:* Gallantly assisted in the rescue of the wounded from in front of the lines and under heavy fire from the enemy.

HART, WILLIAM

Rank and organization: Machinist First Class, U.S. Navy. *Born:* 9 June 1866, Massachusetts. *Accredited to:* Massachusetts. *G.O. No.:* 521, 7 July 1899. *Citation:* On board the U.S.S. *Marblehead* during the operation of cutting the cable leading from Cienfuegos, Cuba, 11 May 1898. Facing the heavy fire of the enemy, Hart set an example of extraordinary bravery and coolness throughout this action.

HEARD, JOHN W.

Rank and organization: First Lieutenant, 3d U.S. Cavalry. *Place and date:* At Mouth of Manimani River, west of Bahia Honda, Cuba, 23 July 1898. *Entered service at:* Mississippi. *Birth:* Mississippi. *Date of issue:* 21 June 1899. *Citation:* After 2 men had been shot down by Spaniards while transmitting orders to the engine-room on the *Wanderer*, the ship having become disabled, this officer took the position held by them and personally transmitted the orders, remaining at his post until the ship was out of danger.

HENDRICKSON, HENRY

Rank and organization: Seaman, U.S. Navy. *Born:* 12 March 1862, Germany. *G.O. No.:* 521, 7 July 1899. *Citation:* On board the U.S.S. *Marblehead* during the operation of cutting the cable leading from Cienfuegos, Cuba, 11 May 1898. Facing the heavy fire of the enemy, Hendrickson displayed extraordinary bravery and coolness throughout this action.

HILL, FRANK

Rank and organization: Private, U.S. Marine Corps. *Born:* 13 August 1864, Hartford, Conn. *Accredited to:* Connecticut. *G.O. No.:* 521, 7 July 1899. *Citation:* On board the U.S.S. *Nashville* during the operation of cutting the cable leading from Cienfuegos, Cuba, 11 May 1898. Facing the heavy fire of the enemy, Hill displayed extraordinary bravery and coolness throughout this action.

HOBAN, THOMAS

Rank and organization: Coxswain, U.S. Navy. *Born:* 11 September 1872, New York, N.Y. *Accredited to:* New York. *G.O. No.:* 521, 7 July 1899. *Citation:* On board the U.S.S. *Nashville* during the operation of cutting the cable leading from Cienfuegos, Cuba, 11 May 1898. Facing the heavy fire of the enemy, Hoban displayed extraordinary bravery and coolness throughout this action.

HOBSON, RICHMOND PEARSON

Rank and organization: Lieutenant, U.S. Navy. *Born:* 17 August 1870, Greensboro, Ala. *Accredited to:* New York. (Medal presented by President, 29 April 1933.) *Citation:* In connection with the sinking of the U.S.S. *Merrimac* at the entrance to the fortified harbor of Santiago de Cuba, 3 June 1898. Despite persistent fire from the enemy fleet and fortifications on shore, Lt. Hobson distinguished himself by extraordinary courage and carried out this operation at the risk of his own personal safety.

HULL, JAMES, L.

Rank and organization: Fireman First Class, U.S. Navy. *Born:* 27 November 1873, Patoka, Ill. *Accredited to:* Illinois. *G.O. No.:* 502, 14 December 1898. *Citation:* On board the U.S.S. *Concord* off Cavite, Manila Bay, Philippine Islands, 21 May 1898. Following the blowing out of a lower manhole plate joint on boiler B of that vessel, Hull assisted in hauling the fires in the hot, vapor-filled atmosphere, which necessitated the playing of water into the fireroom from a hose.

ITRICH, FRANZ ANTON

Rank and organization: Chief Carpenter's Mate, U.S. Navy. *Born:* 26 November 1853, Gross Katz, Germany. *Accredited to:* California. *G.O. No.:* 13, 5 December 1900. *Citation:* On board the U.S.S. *Petrel*, Manila, Philippine Islands, 1 May 1898. Serving in the presence of the enemy, Itrich displayed heroism during the action.

JARDINE, ALEXANDER

Rank and organization: Fireman First Class, U.S. Navy. *Born:* 19 March 1873, Inverness, Scotland. *Accredited to:* Ohio. *G.O. No.:* 503, 13 December 1898. *Citation:* On board the U.S.S. *Potomac* during the passage of that vessel from Cat Island to Nassau, 14 November 1898. Volunteering to enter the fireroom which was filled with steam, Jardine, after repeated attempts, succeeded in reaching the auxiliary valve and opening it, thereby relieving the vessel from further danger.

JOHANSON, JOHN P.

Rank and organization: Seaman, U.S. Navy. *Born:* 22 January 1865, Sweden. *Accredited to:* Maryland. *G.O. No.:* 529, 21 November 1899. *Citation:* On board the U.S.S. *Marblehead* during the operation of cutting the cable leading from Cienfuegos, Cuba, 11 May 1898. Facing the heavy fire of the enemy, Johanson set an example of extraordinary bravery and coolness throughout this action.

JOHANSSON, JOHAN J.

Rank and organization: Ordinary Seaman, U.S. Navy. *Born:* 12 May 1870, Sweden. *Accredited to:* New York. *G.O. No.:* 521, 7 July 1899. *Citation:* On board the U.S.S. *Nashville* during the operation of cutting the cable leading from Cienfuegos, Cuba, 11 May 1898. Facing the heavy fire of the enemy, Johansson set an example of extraordinary bravery and coolness throughout this action.

JOHNSEN, HANS

Rank and organization: Chief Machinist, U.S. Navy. *Born:* 3 January 1865, Sandnes, Norway. *Accredited to:* Pennsylvania. *G.O. No.:* 497, 3 September 1898. *Citation:* On board the torpedo boat *Winslow* during the action at Cardenas, Cuba, 11 May 1898. Showing great presence of mind, Johnsen turned off the steam from the engine which had been wrecked by a shell bursting in the cylinder.

JOHNSON, PETER

Rank and organization: Fireman First Class, U.S. Navy. *Born:* 29 December 1857, Sumerland, England. *Accredited to:* Pennsylvania. *G.O. No.:* 167, 27 August 1904. *Citation:* On board the U.S.S. *Vixen* on the night of 28 May 1898. Following the explosion of the lower front manhole gasket of boiler A of the vessel, Johnson displayed great coolness and self-possession in entering the fireroom.

KEARNEY, MICHAEL

Rank and organization: Private, U.S. Marine Corps. *Born:* 4 October 1874, Newmarket, Ireland. *Accredited to:* Massachusetts. *G.O. No.:* 521, 7 July 1899. *Citation:* On board the U.S.S. *Nashville* during the operation of cutting the cable leading from Cienfuegos, Cuba, 11 May 1898. Facing the heavy fire of the enemy, Kearney set an example of extraordinary bravery and coolness throughout this action.

KEEFER, PHILIP B.

Rank and organization: Coppersmith, U.S. Navy. *Born:* 4 September 1875, Washington, D.C. *Accredited to:* District of Columbia. *G.O. No.:* 501, 14 December 1898. *Citation:* On board the U.S.S. *Iowa* off Santiago de Cuba, 20 July 1898. Following the blow-out of a manhole gasket of that vessel which caused the fireroom to be filled with live steam and the floor plates to be covered with boiling water, Keefer showed courageous and zealous conduct in hauling fires from 2 furnaces of boiler B.

KELLER, WILLIAM

Rank and organization: Private, Company F, 10th U.S. Infantry. *Place and date:* At Santiago de Cuba, 1 July 1898. *Entered service at:* Buffalo, N.Y. *Birth:* Buffalo, N.Y. *Date of issue:* 22 June 1899. *Citation:* Gallantly assisted in the rescue of the wounded from in front of the lines and under heavy fire of the enemy.

KELLY, FRANCIS

Rank and organization: Watertender, U.S. Navy. *Born:* 28 March 1879, Boston, Mass. *Accredited to:* Massachusetts. *G.O. No.:* 529, 2 November 1899. *Citation:* In connection with the sinking of the U.S.S. *Merrimac* at the entrance to the harbor of Santiago de Cuba, 2 June 1898. Despite heavy fire from the Spanish batteries, Kelly displayed extraordinary heroism throughout this operation.

KELLY, THOMAS

Rank and organization: Private, Company H, 21st U.S. Infantry. *Place and date:* At Santiago de Cuba, 1 July 1898. *Entered service at:* New York, N.Y. *Birth:* Ireland. *Date of issue:* 22 June 1899. *Citation:* Gallantly assisted in the rescue of the wounded from in front of the lines and while under heavy fire from the enemy.

KRAMER, FRANZ

Rank and organization: Seaman, U.S. Navy. *Born:* 20 January 1865, Germany. *G.O. No.:* 521, 7 July 1899. *Citation:* On board the U.S.S. *Marblehead* during the operation of cutting the cable leading from Cienfuegos, Cuba, 11 May 1898. Facing the heavy fire of the enemy, Kramer set an example of extraordinary bravery and coolness throughout this action.

KRAUSE, ERNEST

Rank and organization: Coxswain, U.S. Navy. *Born:* 3 July 1866, Germany. *Accredited to:* New York. *G.O. No.:* 521, 7 July 1899. *Citation:* On board the U.S.S. *Nashville* during the operation of cutting the cable leading from Cienfuegos, Cuba, 11 May 1898. Facing the heavy fire of the enemy, Krause displayed extraordinary bravery and coolness throughout this action.

KUCHNEISTER, HERMANN WILLIAM

Rank and organization: Private, U.S. Marine Corps. *Born:* Hamburg, Germany. *Accredited to:* New York. *G.O. No.:* 521, 7 July 1899. *Citation:* On board the U.S.S. *Marblehead* during the operation of cutting the cable leading from Cienfuegos, Cuba, 11 May 1898. Facing the heavy fire of the enemy, Kuchneister displayed extraordinary bravery and coolness throughout this action.

LEE, FITZ

Rank and organization: Private, Troop M, 10th U.S. Cavalry. *Place and date:* At Tayabacoa, Cuba, 30 June 1898. *Entered service at:* Dinwiddie County, Va. *Birth:* Dinwiddie County, Va. *Date of issue:* 23 June 1899. *Citation:* Voluntarily went ashore in the face of the enemy and aided in the rescue of his wounded comrades; this after several previous attempts had been frustrated.

LEVERY, WILLIAM

Rank and organization: Apprentice First Class, U.S. Navy. *Born:* 3 June 1879, Pennsylvania. *Accredited to:* Pennsylvania. *G.O. No.:* 521, 7 July 1899. *Citation:* On board the U.S.S. *Marblehead* during the operation of cutting the cable leading from Cienfuegos, Cuba, 11 May 1898. Facing the heavy fire of the enemy, Levery displayed extraordinary bravery and coolness throughout this action.

MacNEAL, HARRY LEWIS

Rank and organization: Private, U.S. Marine Corps. *Born:* 22 March 1875, Philadelphia, Pa. *Accredited to:* Pennsylvania. *G.O. No.:* 526, 9 August 1899. *Citation:* On board the U.S.S. *Brooklyn* during action at the Battle of Santiago de Cuba, 3 July 1898. Braving the fire of the enemy, MacNeal displayed gallantry throughout this action.

MAGER, GEORGE FREDERICK

Rank and organization: Apprentice First Class, U.S. Navy. *Born:* 23 February 1875, Philipsburg, N.J. *Accredited to:* New Jersey. *G.O. No.:* 529, 2 November 1899. *Citation:* On board the U.S.S. *Marblehead* during the operation of cutting the cable leading from Cienfuegos, Cuba, 11 May 1898. Facing the heavy fire of the enemy, Mager displayed extraordinary bravery and coolness throughout this action.

MAHONEY, GEORGE

Rank and organization: Fireman First Class, U.S. Navy. *Born:* 15 January 1865, Worcester, Mass. *Accredited to:* Pennsylvania. *G.O. No.:* 167, 27 August 1904. *Citation:* On board the U.S.S. *Vixen* on the night of 28 May 1898. Following the explosion of the lower front manhole gasket of boiler A of that vessel, Mahoney displayed great coolness and self-possession in entering the fireroom.

MAXWELL, JOHN

Rank and organization: Fireman Second Class, U.S. Navy. *Born:* 21 June 1841, Ireland. *G.O. No.:* 521, 7 July 1899. *Citation:* On board the U.S.S. *Marblehead* during the operation of cutting the cable leading from Cienfuegos, Cuba, 11 May 1898. Facing the heavy fire of the enemy, Maxwell displayed extraordianry bravery and coolness throughout this action.

MEREDITH, JAMES

Rank and organization: Private, U.S. Marine Corps. (Name changed to Patrick F. Ford, Jr.) *Born:* 11 April 1872, Omaha, Nebr. *Accredited to:* Virginia. *G.O. No.:* 521, 7 July 1899. *Citation:* On board the U.S.S. *Marblehead* during the operation of cutting the cable leading from Cienfuegos, Cuba, 11 May 1898. Facing the heavy fire of the enemy, Meredith displayed extraordinary bravery and coolness throughout this action.

MEYER, WILLIAM

Rank and organization: Carpenter's Mate Third Class, U.S. Navy. *Born:* 22 June 1863, Germany. *Accredited to:* Illinois. *G.O. No.:* 521, 7 July 1899. *Citation:* On board the U.S.S. *Nashville* during the operation of cutting the cable leading from Cienfuegos, Cuba, 11 May 1898. Facing the heavy fire of the enemy, Meyer displayed extraordinary bravery and coolness through this action.

MILLER, HARRY HERBERT

Rank and organization: Seaman, U.S. Navy. *Place and date:* On board the U.S.S. *Nashville*, Cienfuegos, Cuba, 11 May 1898. *Entered service at:* Massachusetts. *Born:* 4 May 1879, Noel Shore, Hants County, Nova Scotia. *G.O. No.:* 521, 7 July 1899. *Citation:* On board the U.S.S. *Nashville*, during the operation of cutting the cable leading from Cienfuegos, Cuba, 11 May 1898. Facing the heavy fire of the enemy,

Miller displayed extraordinary bravery and coolness throughout this action.

MILLER, WILLARD

Rank and organization: Seaman, U.S. Navy. *Born:* 5 June 1877, Noel Shore, Hants County, Nova Scotia, *Accredited to:* Massachusetts. *G.O. No.:* 521, 7 July 1899. *Citation:* On board the U.S.S. *Nashville* during the operation of cutting the cable leading from Cienfuegos, Cuba, 11 May 1898. Facing the heavy fire of the enemy, Miller displayed extraordinary bravery and coolness throughout this action.

MILLS, ALBERT L.

Rank and organization: Captain and Assistant Adjutant General, U.S. Volunteers. *Place and date:* Near Santiago, Cuba, 1 July 1898. *Entered service at:* New York, N.Y. *Birth:* New York, N.Y. *Date of issue:* 9 July 1902. *Citation:* Distinguished gallantry in encouraging those near him by his bravery and coolness after being shot through the head and entirely without sight.

MONTAGUE, DANIEL

Rank and organization: Chief Master-at-Arms, U.S. Navy. *Born:* 22 October 1867, Wicklow, Ireland. *G.O. No.:* 529, 2 November 1899. *Citation:* In connection with the sinking of the U.S.S. *Merrimac* at the entrance to the harbor of Santiago de Cuba, 2 June 1898. Despite heavy fire from the Spanish batteries, Montague displayed extraordinary heroism throughout this operation.

MORIN, WILLIAM H.

Rank and organization: Boatswain's Mate Second Class, U.S. Navy. *Born:* 23 May 1869, England. *G.O. No.:* 500, 14 December 1898. *Citation:* On board the U.S.S. *Marblehead* at the approaches to Caimanera, Guantanamo Bay, Cuba, 26 and 27 July 1898. Displaying heroism, Morin took part in the perilous work of sweeping for and disabling 27 contact mines during this period.

MULLER, FREDERICK

Rank and organization: Mate, U.S. Navy. *Born:* 29 March 1861, Copenhagen, Denmark. *Accredited to:* Massachusetts. *G.O. No.:* 45, 30 April 1901. *Citation:* On board the U.S.S. *Wompatuck*, Manzanillo, Cuba, 30 June 1898. Serving under the fire of the enemy, Muller displayed heroism and gallantry during this period.

MURPHY, JOHN EDWARD

Rank and organization: Coxswain, U.S. Navy. *Born:* 1869, Ireland. *Accredited to:* New York. *G.O. No.:* 529, 2 November 1899. *Citation:* In connection with the sinking of the U.S.S. *Merrimac* at the entrance to the harbor of Santiago de Cuba, 2 June 1898. Despite heavy fire from the Spanish shore batteries, Murphy displayed extraordinary heroism throughout this operation.

NASH, JAMES J.

Rank and organization: Private, Company F, 10th U.S. Infantry. *Place and date:* At Santiago, Cuba, 1 July 1898. *Entered service at:* Louisville, Ky. *Birth:* Louisville, Ky. *Date of issue:* 22 June 1899. *Citation:* Gallantly assisted in the rescue of the wounded from in front of the lines and under heavy fire from the enemy.

NEE, GEORGE H.

Rank and organization: Private, Company H, 21st U.S. Infantry. *Place and date:* At Santiago, Cuba, 1 July 1898. *Entered service at:* Boston, Mass. *Birth:* Boston, Mass. *Date of issue:* 22 June 1899. *Citation:* Gallantly assisted in the rescue of the wounded from in front of the lines and under heavy fire from the enemy.

NELSON, LAURITZ

Rank and organization: Sailmaker's Mate, U.S. Navy. *Born:* 26 March 1860, Norway. *G.O. No.:* 521, 7 July 1899. *Citation:* On board the U.S.S. *Nashville* during the operation of cutting the cable leading from Cienfuegos, Cuba, 11 May 1898. Facing the heavy fire of the enemy, Nelson displayed extraordinary bravery and coolness throughout this action.

OAKLEY, WILLIAM

Rank and organization: Gunner's Mate Second Class, U.S. Navy. *Born:* 8 August 1860, Colchester, England. *Accredited to:* New York. *G.O. No.:* 521, 7 July 1899. *Citation:* On board the U.S.S. *Marblehead* during the operation of cutting the cable leading from Cienfuegos, Cuba, 11 May 1898. Facing the heavy fire of the enemy, Oakley displayed extraordinary bravery and coolness throughout this period.

OLSEN, ANTON

Rank and organization: Ordinary Seaman, U.S. Navy. *Born:* 26 April 1867, Norway. *Accredited to:* Massachusetts. *G.O. No.:* 529, 2 November 1899. *Citation:* On board the U.S.S. *Marblehead* during the operation of cutting the cable leading from Cienfuegos, Cuba, 11 May 1898. Facing the heavy fire of the enemy, Olsen displayed extraordinary bravery and coolness throughout this period.

PARKER, POMEROY

Rank and organization: Private, U.S. Marine Corps. *Born:* 17 March 1874, Gates County, N.C. *Accredited to:* North Carolina. *G.O. No.:* 521, 7 July 1899. *Citation:* On board the U.S.S. *Nashville* during the operation of cutting the cable leading from Cienfuegos, Cuba, 11 May 1898. Facing the heavy fire of the enemy, Parker displayed extraordinary bravery and coolness throughout this action.

PENN, ROBERT

Rank and organization: Fireman First Class, U.S. Navy. *Born:* 10 October 1872, City Point, Va. *Accredited to:* Virginia. *G.O. No.:* 501, 14 December 1898. *Citation:* On board the U.S.S. *Iowa* off Santiago de Cuba, 20 July 1898. Performing his duty at the risk of serious scalding at the time of the blowing out of the manhole gasket on board the vessel, Penn hauled the fire while standing on a board thrown across a coal bucket 1 foot above the boiling water which was still blowing from the boiler.

PFISTERER, HERMAN

Rank and organization: Musician, Company H, 21st U.S. Infantry. *Place and date:* At Santiago, Cuba, 1 July 1898. *Entered service at:* New York, N.Y. *Birth:* Brooklyn, N.Y. *Date of issue:* 22 June 1899. *Citation:* Gallantly assisted in the rescue of the wounded from in front of the lines and under heavy fire from the enemy.

PHILLIPS, GEORGE F.

Rank and organization: Machinist First Class, U.S. Navy. *Born:* 9 March 1864, Boston, Mass. *Accredited to:* New York. *G.O. No.:* 529, 2 November 1899. *Citation:* In connection with the sinking of the U.S.S. *Merrimac* at the entrance to the harbor of Santiago de Cuba, 2 June 1898. Despite heavy fire from the Spanish shore batteries, Phillips displayed extraordinary heroism throughout this operation.

POLOND, ALFRED

Rank and organization: Private, Company F, 10th U.S. Infantry. *Place and date:* At Santiago, Cuba, 1 July 1898. *Entered service at:* Lapeer, Mich. *Birth:* Lapeer, Mich. *Date of issue:* 22 June 1899. *Citation:* Gallantly assisted in the rescue of the wounded from in front of the lines and while under heavy fire of the enemy.

QUICK, JOHN HENRY

Rank and organization: Sergeant, U.S. Marine Corps. *Born:* 20 June 1870, Charleston, W. Va. *Accredited to:* Pennsylvania, *G.O. No.:* 504, 13 December 1898. *Other Navy award:* Navy Cross. *Citation:* In action during the battle of Cuzco, Cuba, 14 June 1898. Distinguishing himself during this action, Quick signaled the U.S.S. *Dolphin* on 3 different occasions while exposed to a heavy fire from the enemy.

QUINN, ALEXANDER M.

Rank and organization: Sergeant, Company A, 13th U.S. Infantry. *Place and date:* At Santiago, Cuba, 1 July 1898. *Entered service at:* Philadelphia, Pa. *Birth:* Passaic, N.J. *Date of issue:* 22 June 1899. *Citation:* Gallantly assisted in the rescue of the wounded from in front of the lines and under heavy fire from the enemy.

RESSLER, NORMAN W.

Rank and organization: Corporal, Company D, 17th U.S. Infantry. *Place and date:* At El Caney, Cuba, 1 July 1898. *Entered service at:* Dalmatia, Pa. *Birth:* Dalmatia, Pa. *Date of issue:* 21 August 1899. *Citation:* Gallantly assisted in the rescue of the wounded from in front of the lines and under heavy fire of the enemy.

RILLEY, JOHN PHILLIP

Rank and organization: Landsman, U.S. Navy. *Born:* 22 January 1877, Allentown, Pa. *Accredited to:* Massachusetts. *G.O. No.:* 521, July

1899. *Citation:* On board the U.S.S. *Nashville* during the operation of cutting the cable leading from Cienfuegos, Cuba, 11 May 1898. Facing the heavy fire of the enemy, Rilley displayed extraordinary bravery and coolness throughout this action.

ROBERTS, CHARLES D.

Rank and organization: Second Lieutenant, U.S. Army, 17th U.S. Infantry. *Place and date:* At El Caney, Cuba, 1 July 1898. *Entered service at:* Fort D. A. Russell, Wyo. *Birth:* Fort D. A. Russell, Wyo. *Date of issue:* 21 June 1899. *Citation:* Gallantly assisted in the rescue of the wounded from in front of the lines under heavy fire of the enemy.

RUSSELL, HENRY P.

Rank and organization: Landsman, U.S. Navy. *Born:* 10 June 1878, Quebec, Canada. *Accredited to:* New York. *G.O. No.:* 521, 7 July 1899. *Citation:* On board the U.S.S. *Marblehead* during the operation of cutting the cable leading from Cienfuegos, Cuba, 11 May 1898. Facing the heavy fire of the enemy, Russell displayed extraordinary bravery and coolness throughout this action.

SCOTT, JOSEPH FRANCIS

Rank and organization: Private, U.S. Marine Corps. *Born:* 4 June 1864, Boston, Mass. *Accredited to:* Massachusetts. *G.O. No.:* 521, 7 July 1899. *Citation:* On board the U.S.S. *Nashville* during the operation of cutting the cable leading from Cienfuegos, Cuba, 11 May 1898. Facing the heavy fire of the enemy, Scott displayed extraordinary bravery and coolness throughout this action.

SHEPHERD, WARREN J.

Rank and organization: Corporal, Company D, 17th U.S. Infantry. *Place and date:* At El Caney, Cuba, 1 July 1898. *Entered service at:* Westover, Pa. *Birth:* Cherry Tree, Pa. *Date of issue:* 21 August 1899. *Citation:* Gallantly assisted in the rescue of the wounded from in front of the lines under heavy fire from the enemy.

SPICER, WILLIAM

Rank and organization: Gunner's Mate First Class, U.S. Navy. *Born:* 28 May 1864, England. *Accredited to:* New York. *G.O. No.:* 500, 14 December 1898. *Citation:* On board the U.S.S. *Marblehead* at the approaches to Caimanera, Guantanamo Bay, Cuba, 26 and 27 July 1898. Displaying heroism, Spicer took part in the perilous work of sweeping for and disabling 27 contact mines during this period.

SULLIVAN, EDWARD

Rank and organization: Private, U.S. Marine Corps. *Born:* 16 May 1870, Cork, Ireland. *Accredited to:* Massachusetts. *G.O. No.:* 521, 7 July 1899. *Citation:* On board the U.S.S. *Marblehead* during the operation of cutting the cable leading from Cienfuegos, Cuba, 11 May 1898. Facing the heavy fire of the enemy, Sullivan displayed extraordinary bravery and coolness throughout this action.

SUNDQUIST, AXEL

Rank and organization: Chief Carpenter's Mate, U.S. Navy. *Born:* 26 May 1867, Furland, Russia. *Accredited to:* Pennsylvania. *G.O. No.:* 500, 19 December 1898. *Citation:* On board the U.S.S. *Marblehead* at the approaches to Caimanera, Guantanamo Bay, Cuba, 26 and 27 July 1898. Displaying heroism, Sundquist took part in the perilous work of sweeping for and disabling 27 contact mines during this period.

SUNDQUIST, GUSTAV A.

Rank and organization: Ordinary Seaman, U.S. Navy. *Born:* 4 June 1879, Sweden. *Accredited to:* New York. *G.O. No.:* 529, 2 November 1899. *Citation:* On board the U.S.S. *Nashville* during the operation of cutting the cable leading from Cienfuegos, Cuba, 11 May 1898. Facing the heavy fire of the enemy, Sundquist displayed extraordinary bravery and coolness throughout this action.

THOMPKINS, WILLIAM H.

Rank and organization: Private, Troop G, 10th U.S. Cavalry. *Place and date:* At Tayabacoa, Cuba, 30 June 1898. *Entered service at:* Paterson, N.J. *Birth:* Paterson, N.J. *Date of issue:* 23 June 1899. *Citation:* Voluntarily went ashore in the face of the enemy and aided in the rescue of his wounded comrades; this after several previous attempts at rescue had been frustrated.

TRIPLETT, SAMUEL

Rank and organization: Ordinary Seaman, U.S. Navy. *Born:* 18 December 1869, Chenokeeke, Kans. *Accredited to:* New York. *G.O. No.:* 500, 14 December 1898. *Citation:* On board the U.S.S. *Marblehead* at the approaches to Caimanera, Guantanamo Bay, Cuba, 26 and 27 July 1898. Displaying heroism, Triplett took part in the perilous work of sweeping for and disabling 27 contact mines during this period.

VADAS, ALBERT

Rank and organization: Seaman, U.S. Navy. (Named changed to Wadas, Albert.) Born: 26 March 1876, Austria-Hungary. *Accredited to:* New York. *G.O. No.:* 521, 7 July 1899. *Citation:* On board the U.S.S. *Marblehead* during the operation of cutting the cable leading from Cienfuegos, Cuba, 11 May 1898. Facing the heavy fire of the enemy, Vadas displayed extraordinary bravery and coolness throughout this period.

VAN ETTEN, HUDSON

Rank and organization: Seaman, U.S. Navy. *Born:* 17 May 1874, Port Jervis, N.J. *Accredited to:* New Jersey. *G.O. No.:* 521, 7 July 1899. *Citation:* On board the U.S.S. *Nashville* during the operation of cutting the cable leading from Cienfuegos, Cuba, 11 May 1898. Facing the heavy fire of the enemy, Van Etten displayed extraordinary bravery and coolness throughout this period.

VOLZ, ROBERT

Rank and organization: Seaman, U.S. Navy. *Born:* 31 January 1875, San Francisco, Calif. *Accredited to:* Virginia. *G.O. No.:* 521, 7 July

1899. *Citation:* On board the U.S.S. *Nashville* during the operation of cutting the cable leading from Cienfuegos, Cuba, 11 May 1898. Facing the heavy fire of the enemy, Volz displayed extraordinary bravery and coolness throughout this period.

WANTON, GEORGE H. (First black man to receive Medal of Honor)

Rank and organization: Private, Troop M, 10th U.S. Cavalry. *Place and date:* At Tayabacoa, Cuba, 30 June 1898. *Entered service at:* Paterson, N.J. *Birth:* Paterson, N.J. *Date of issue:* 23 June 1899. *Citation:* Voluntarily went ashore in the face of the enemy and aided in the rescue of his wounded comrades; this after several previous attempts at rescue had been frustrated.

WELBORN, IRA C.

Rank and organization: Second Lieutenant, 9th U.S. Infantry. *Place and date:* At Santiago, Cuba, 2 July 1898. *Entered service at:* Mico, Miss. *Birth:* Mico, Miss. *Date of issue:* 21 June 1899. *Citation:* Voluntarily left shelter and went, under fire, to the aid of a private of his company who was wounded.

WENDE, BRUNO

Rank and organization: Private, Company C, 17th U.S. Infantry. *Place and date:* At El Caney, Cuba, 1 July 1898. *Entered service at:* Canton, Ohio. *Birth:* Germany. *Date of issue:* 22 June 1899. *Citation:* Gallantly assisted in the rescue of the wounded from in front of the lines and under heavy fire from the enemy.

WEST, WALTER SCOTT

Rank and organization: Private, U.S. Marine Corps. *Born:* 13 March 1872, Bradford, N.H. *Accredited to:* New Hampshire. *G.O. No.:* 521, 7 July 1899. *Citation:* On board the U.S.S. *Marblehead* during the operation of cutting the cable leading from Cienfuegos, Cuba, 11 May 1898. Facing the heavy fire of the enemy, West displayed extraordinary bravery and coolness throughout this action.

WILKE, JULIUS A. R.

Rank and organization: Boatswain's Mate First Class, U.S. Navy. *Born:* 14 November 1860, Germany. *Accredited to:* New York. *G.O. No.:* 521, 7 July 1899. *Citation:* On board the U.S.S. *Marblehead* during the operation of cutting the cable leading from Cienfuegos, Cuba, 11 May 1898. Facing the heavy fire of the enemy, Wilke displayed extraordinary bravery and coolness throughout this action.

WILLIAMS, FRANK

Rank and organization: Seaman, U.S. Navy. *Born:* 19 October 1872, Germany. *Accredited to:* New York. *G.O. No.:* 521, 7 July 1899. *Citation:* On board the U.S.S. *Marblehead* during the operation of cutting the cable leading from Cienfuegos, Cuba, 11 May 1898. Facing the heavy fire of the enemy, Williams displayed extraordinary bravery and coolness throughout this period.

INTERIM 1871 TO 1898

AHERN, WILLIAM

Rank and organization: Watertender, U.S. Navy. *Born:* 1861, Ireland. *Accredited to:* New York. *G.O. No.:* 482, 1 November 1897. *Citation:* On board the U.S.S. *Puritan* at the time of the collapse of one of the crown sheets of boiler E of that vessel, 1 July 1897. Wrapped in wet cloths to protect his face and arms, Ahern entered the fireroom, crawled over the tops of the boilers and closed the auxiliary stop valve, disconnecting boiler E and removing the danger of disabling the other boilers.

ANDERSON, WILLIAM

Rank and organization: Coxswain, U.S. Navy. *Born:* 1852, Sweden. *Accredited to:* New York. *Citation:* On board the U.S.S. *Powhatan*, 28 June 1878. Acting courageously, Anderson rescued from drowning W. H. Moffatt, first class boy.

ATKINS, DANIEL

Rank and organization: Ship's Cook, First Class, U.S. Navy. *Born:* 1867, Brunswick, Va. *Accredited to:* Virginia. *G.O. No.:* 489, 20 May 1898. *Citation:* On board the U.S.S. *Cushing*, 11 February 1898. Showing gallant conduct, Atkins attempted to save the life of the late Ens. Joseph C. Breckenridge, U.S. Navy, who fell overboard at sea from that vessel on this date.

AUER, JOHN F.

Rank and organization: Ordinary Seaman Apprentice, U.S. Navy. *Born:* 1866, New York. *Accredited to:* New York. Citation: On board the U.S.S. *Lancaster*, Marseille, France, 20 November 1883. Jumping overboard, Auer rescued from drowning a French lad who had fallen into the sea from a stone pier astern of the ship.

BARRETT, EDWARD

Rank and organization: Second Class Fireman, U.S. Navy. *Born:* 1855, Philadelphia, Pa. *Accredited to:* Pennsylvania. *G.O. No.:* 326, 18 October 1884. *Citation:* On board the U.S.S. *Alaska* at Callao Bay, Peru, 14 September 1881. Following the rupture of the stop-valve chamber, Barrett courageously hauled the fires from under the boiler of that vessel.

BELPITT, W. H.

Rank and organization: Captain of the Afterguard, U.S. Navy. *Born:* 1859, Sydney, Australia. (Letter No. 126, 27 October 1884, LCDR

Iverson, U.S. Navy.) *Citation:* On board the U.S.S. *Monocacy*, Foochow, China, 7 October 1884. Jumping overboard from that vessel on the morning of this date, Belpitt sustained, until picked up, a Chinaman who had been thrown into the water by the capsizing of a canoe.

BENSON, JAMES

Rank and organization: Seaman, U.S. Navy. *Born:* 1845, Denmark. *Enlisted at:* Yokohama, Japan. *G.O. No.:* 180, 10 October 1872. *Citation:* On board the U.S.S. *Ossipee*, 20 June 1872. Risking his life, Benson leaped into the sea while the ship was going at a speed of 4 knots and endeavored to save John K. Smith, landsman, of the same vessel, from drowning.

BRADLEY, ALEXANDER   *Cornelius Bonner*

Rank and organization: Landsman, U.S. Navy. *Born:* 1854, Boston, Mass. *Accredited to:* Massachusetts. *G.O. No.:* 180, 10 October 1872. *Citation:* On board the U.S.S. *Wachusett* off Cowes, 7 August 1872. Jumping overboard into a strong tideway, Bradley attempted to save Philip Cassidy, landsman, of the U.S.S. *Wabash*, from drowning.

BUCHANAN, DAVID M.

Rank and organization: Apprentice, U.S. Navy. *Born:* 1862, Philadelphia, Pa. *Accredited to:* Pennsylvania. *G.O. No.:* 246, 22 July 1879. *Citation:* On board the U.S.S. *Saratoga* off Battery, New York Harbor, 15 July 1879. On the morning of this date, Robert Lee Robey, apprentice, fell overboard from the after part of the ship into the tide which was running strong ebb at the time and, not being an expert swimmer, was in danger of drowning. Instantly springing over the rail after him, Buchanan never hesitated for an instant to remove even a portion of his clothing. Both men were picked up by the ship's boat following this act of heroism.

CHANDRON, AUGUST

Rank and organization: Seaman Apprentice, Second Class, U.S. Navy. *Born:* 1866, France. *Accredited to:* New York. (Letter, Capt. N. Judlow, U.S. Navy, No. 8326B; 21 November 1885.) *Citation:* On board the U.S.S. *Quinnebaug*, Alexandria, Egypt, on the morning of 21 November 1885. Jumping overboard from that vessel, Chandron, with the aid of Hugh Miller, boatswain's mate, rescued William Evans, ordinary seaman, from drowning.

CONNOLLY, MICHAEL

Rank and organization: Ordinary Seaman, U.S. Navy. *Born:* 1855, Boston, Mass. *Accredited to:* Massachusetts. *G.O. No.:* 218, 24 August 1876. *Citation:* On board the U.S.S. *Plymouth*, Halifax Harbor, Nova Scotia, 7 August 1876. Acting gallantly, Connolly succeeding in rescuing a citizen from drowning on this date.

COREY, WILLIAM

Rank and organization: Landsman, U.S. Navy. *Born:* 1853, New York, N.Y. *Accredited to:* New York. *G.O. No.:* 215, 9 August 1876. *Citation:* On board the U.S.S. *Plymouth*, Navy Yard, New York, 26

July 1876. Showing heroic conduct, Corey endeavored to save the life of one of the crew of that ship who had fallen overboard from aloft.

COSTELLO, JOHN

Rank and organization: Ordinary Seaman, U.S. Navy. *Born:* 1850, Rouses Point, N.Y. *Accredited to:* New York. *G.O. No.:* 214, 27 July 1876. *Citation:* On board the U.S.S. *Hartford,* Philadelphia, Pa., 16 July 1876. Showing gallantry, Costello rescued from drowning a landsman of that vessel.

COURTNEY, HENRY C.

Rank and organization: Seaman, U.S. Navy. *Born:* 1856, Springfield, Ill. *Accredited to:* Illinois. *G.O. No.:* 326, 18 October 1884. *Citation:* On board the U.S. Training Ship *Portsmouth,* Washington Navy Yard, 7 February 1882. Jumping overboard from that vessel, Courtney assisted in rescuing Charles Taliaferro, jack-of-the-dust, from drowning.

CRAMEN, THOMAS

Rank and organization: Boatswain's Mate, U.S. Navy. *Born:* 1848, Ireland. *Accredited to:* Massachusetts. *G.O. No.:* 326, 18 October 1884. *Citation:* On board the U.S.S. *Portsmouth,* Washington Navy Yard, 7 February 1882. Jumping overboard from that vessel, Cramen rescued Charles Taliaferro, jack-of-the-dust, from drowning.

CREELMAN, WILLIAM J.

Rank and organization: Landsman, U.S. Navy. *Born:* 1874, Brooklyn, N.Y. *Accredited to:* New York. *Citation:* Attached to the U.S.S. *Maine,* February 1897. Distinguishing himself, Creelman showed extraordinary heroism in the line of his profession during an attempt to save life at sea.

CUTTER, GEORGE W.

Rank and organization: Landsman, U.S. Navy. *Born:* 1849, Philadelphia, Pa. *Accredited to:* Pennsylvania. *G.O. No.:* 176, 9 July 1872. *Citation:* On board the U.S.S. *Powhatan,* Norfolk, Va., 27 May 1872. Jumping overboard on this date, Cutter aided in saving one of the crew of that vessel from drowning.

DAVIS, JOHN

Rank and organization: Ordinary Seaman, U.S. Navy. *Born:* 1854, Kingslow, Jamaica. *G.O. No.:* 326, 18 October 1884. *Citation:* On board the U.S.S. *Trenton,* Toulon, France, February 1881. Jumping overboard, Davis rescued Augustus Ohlensen, coxswain, from drowning.

DAVIS, JOSEPH H.

Rank and organization: Landsman, U.S. Navy. *Entered service at:* Philadelphia, Pa. *Born:* 22 July 1860, Philadelphia, Pa. (Letter, Mate J. W. Baxter, U.S. Navy, No. 8985; 25 January 1886.) *Citation:* On board the U.S. Receiving Ship *Dale* off the Wharf at Norfolk, Va., 22 January 1886. Jumping overboard from the ferryboat, Davis rescued from drowning John Norman, ordinary seaman.

DEMPSEY, JOHN

Rank and organization: Seaman, U.S. Navy. *Born:* 1848, Ireland. *Accredited to:* Massachusetts. *Citation:* On board the U.S.S. *Kearsarge* at Shanghai, China, 23 January 1875. Displaying gallant conduct, Dempsey jumped overboard from the *Kearsarge* and rescued from drowning one of the crew of that vessel.

DENEEF, MICHAEL

Rank and organization: Captain of the Top, U.S. Navy. *Born:* 1851, Massachusetts. *Accredited to:* Massachusetts. *G.O. No.:* 201, 18 January 1876. *Citation:* On board the U.S.S. *Swatara* at Para, Brazil, 1 December 1875. Displaying gallant conduct, Deneef jumped overboard and rescued one of the crew of that vessel from drowning.

DENHAM, AUSTIN

Rank and organization: Seaman, U.S. Navy. *Born:* 1849, England. *Accredited to:* New York. *G.O. No.:* 176, 9 July 1872. *Citation:* On board the U.S.S. *Kansas* near Greytown, Nicaragua, 12 April 1872. Displaying great coolness and self-possession at the time Comdr. A. F. Crosman and others were drowned, Denham, by heroism and personal exertion, prevented greater loss of life.

EILERS, HENRY A.

Rank and organization: Gunner's Mate, U.S. Navy. *Born:* 1871, Newark, N.J. *Accredited to:* New Jersey. *G.O. No.:* 404, 22 November 1892. *Citation:* On board the U.S.S. *Philadelphia* during the sham attack on Fort McHenry, Baltimore, Md., 17 September 1892. Displaying extraordinary heroism in the line of his profession on this occasion, Eilers remained at his post in the magazine and stamped out the burning particles of a prematurely exploded cartridge which had blown down the chute.

ELMORE, WALTER

Rank and organization: Landsman, U.S. Navy. *Born:* 1857, England. *Enlisted at:* Toulon, France. *Citation:* On board the U.S.S. *Gettysburg;* for jumping overboard and saving from drowning Wallace Febrey, landsman, while that vessel was under way at sea in latitude 36 degrees 58 minutes north, longitude 3 degrees 44 minutes east, 1 October 1878.

ENRIGHT, JOHN

Rank and organization: Landsman, U.S. Navy. *Born:* 1864, Lynn, Mass. *Accredited to:* Massachusetts. *Citation:* On board the U.S.S. *Ranger* off Ensenada, Mexico, 18 January 1886. Jumping overboard from that vessel, Enright rescued John Bell, ordinary seaman, and George Svensson, ordinary seaman, from drowning.

EVERETTS, JOHN

Rank and organization: Gunner's Mate, Third Class, U.S. Navy. *Born:* 25 August 1873, Therold, Canada. *Accredited to:* New York. *G.O. No.:* 489, 20 May 1898. *Citation:* Serving on board the U.S.S.

Cushing, 11 February 1898, Everetts displayed gallant conduct in attempting to save the life of the late Ens. Joseph C. Breckinridge, U.S. Navy, who fell overboard at sea from that vessel.

FASSEUR, ISAAC L.

Rank and organization: Ordinary Seaman, U.S. Navy. *Born:* 1860, Holland. Biography not available. *Citation:* Serving on board the U.S.S. *Lackawanna,* 13 June 1884, at Callao, Peru, Fasseur rescued William Cruise, who had fallen overboard, from drowning.

FLANNAGAN, JOHN

Rank and organization: Boatswain's Mate, U.S. Navy. *Born:* 1852, Ireland. *Accredited to:* New York. *Citation:* Serving on board the U.S.S. *Supply,* Flannagan rescued from drowning David Walsh, seaman, of Le Havre, France, 26 October 1878.

FOWLER, CHRISTOPHER

Rank and organization: Quartermaster, U.S. Navy. *Born:* 1850, New York. *Accredited to:* New York. *Citation:* Served on board the U.S.S. *Fortune* off Point Zapotitlan, Mexico, 11 May 1874. On the occasion of the capsizing of one of the boats of the *Fortune* and the drowning of a portion of the boat's crew, Fowler displayed gallant conduct.

GIDDING, CHARLES

Rank and organization: Seaman, U.S. Navy. *Born:* 1853, Bangor, Maine. *Accredited to:* Maine. *G.O. No.:* 215, 9 August 1876. *Citation:* Serving on board the U.S.S. *Plymouth,* Gidding showed heroic conduct in trying to save the life of one of the crew of that ship, who had fallen overboard from aloft at the Navy Yard, New York, 26 July 1876.

GILLICK, MATTHEW

Rank and organization: Boatswain's Mate, U.S. Navy. *Born:* 1852, Providence, R.I. *Accredited to:* Rhode Island. *G.O. No.:* 326, 18 October 1884. *Citation:* Serving on board the U.S.S. *Lancaster* at Marseille, France, 20 November 1883. Jumping overboard from the *Lancaster,* Gillick rescued from drowning a French lad who had fallen into the sea from a stone pier astern of the ship.

HANDRAN, JOHN

Rank and organization: Seaman, U.S. Navy. *Born:* 1852, Massachusetts. *Accredited to:* Massachusetts. *G.O. No.:* 206, 15 February 1876. *Citation:* For gallant conduct while serving on board the U.S.S. *Franklin* at Lisbon, Portugal, 9 January 1876. Jumping overboard, Handran rescued from drowning one of the crew of that vessel.

HARRINGTON, DAVID

Rank and organization: First Class Fireman, U.S. Navy. *Born:* 1856, Washington, D.C. *Accredited to:* Washington, D.C. *G.O. No.:* 326, 18 October 1884. *Citation:* Served on board the U.S.S. *Tallapoosa* at the time of the sinking of that vessel, on the night of 21 August 1884. Remaining at his post of duty in the fireroom until the fires were put out by the rising waters, Harrington opened the safety valves when the water was up to his waist.

HAYDEN, JOHN

Rank and organization: Apprentice, U.S. Navy. *Born:* 1863, Washington, D.C. *Accredited to:* Washington, D.C. *G.O. No.:* 246, 22 July 1879. *Citation:* On board the U.S. Training Ship *Saratoga.* On the morning of 15 July 1879, while the *Saratoga* was anchored off the Battery, in New York Harbor, R. L. Robey, apprentice, fell overboard. As the tide was running strong ebb, the man, not being an expert swimmer, was in danger of drowning. David M. Buchanan, apprentice, instantly, without removing any of his clothing, jumped after him. Stripping himself, Hayden stood coolly watching the 2 in the water, and when he thought his services were required, made a dive from the rail and came up alongside them and rendered assistance until all 3 were picked up by a boat from the ship.

HILL, GEORGE

Rank and organization: Chief Quarter Gunner, U.S. Navy. *Born:* 1844, England. *Entered service at:* New York, N.Y. *G.O. No.:* 176, 9 July 1872. *Citation:* Serving on board the U.S.S. *Kansas*, Hill displayed great coolness and self-possession at the time Comdr. A. F. Crosman and others were drowned, near Greytown, Nicaragua, 12 April 1872, and by extraordinary heroism and personal exertion, prevented greater loss of life.

HILL, WILLIAM L.

Rank and organization: Captain of the Top, U.S. Navy. *Born:* 1856, Brooklyn, N.Y. *Accredited to:* New York. *G.O. No.:* 326, 18 October 1884. *Citation:* Serving on board the U.S. Training Ship *Minnesota* at Newport, R.I., 22 June 1881, Hill jumped overboard and sustained William Mulcahy, third class boy, who had fallen overboard, until picked up by a steam launch.

HOLT, GEORGE

Rank and organization: Quarter Gunner, U.S. Navy. *Born:* 1840, Kentucky. *Accredited to:* Kentucky. *G.O. No.:* 180, 10 October 1872. *Citation:* On board the U.S.S. *Plymouth*, Hamburg Harbor, 3 July 1871. Jumping overboard at the imminent risk of his life, Holt, with a comrade, rescued from drowning one of a party who was thrown from a shore boat into a 4-knot, running tide while the boat was coming alongside the ship.

HORTON, JAMES

Rank and organization: Captain of the Top, U.S. Navy. *Born:* 1850, Boston, Mass. *Accredited to:* Massachusetts. *G.O. No.:* 326, 18 October 1884. *Citation:* Serving on board the U.S.S. *Constitution*, at sea, 13 February 1879, Horton showed courageous conduct in going over the stern during a heavy gale and cutting the fastenings of the ship's rudder chains.

JOHNSON, JOHN

Rank and organization: Seaman, U.S. Navy. *Born:* 1839, Philadelphia, Pa. *Accredited to:* Pennsylvania. *G.O. No.:* 176, 9 July 1872. *Cita-

tion: Serving on board the U.S.S. *Kansas* near Greytown, Nicaragua, 12 April 1872, Johnson displayed great coolness and self-possession at the time Comdr. A. F. Crosman and others were drowned and, by extraordinary heroism and personal exertion, prevented greater loss of life.

JOHNSON, WILLIAM

Rank and organization: Cooper, U.S. Navy. *Born:* 1855, St. Vincent, West Indies. *Accredited to:* New York. *G.O. No.:* 326, 18 October 1884. *Citation:* Serving on board the U.S.S. *Adams* at the Navy Yard, Mare Island, Calif., 14 November 1879, Johnson rescued Daniel W. Kloppen, a workman, from drowning.

KERSEY, THOMAS

Rank and organization: Ordinary Seaman, U.S. Navy. *Born:* 1847, St. Johns, Newfoundland. *Accredited to:* Massachusetts. *G.O. No.:* 215, 9 August 1876. *Citation:* Serving on board the U.S.S. *Plymouth* at the Navy Yard, New York, 26 July 1876, Kersey displayed bravery and presence of mind in rescuing from drowning one of the crew of that vessel.

KING, HUGH

Rank and organization: Ordinary Seaman, U.S. Navy. *Born:* 1845, Ireland. *Accredited to:* New York. *G.O. No.:* 176, 9 July 1872. *Citation:* On board the U.S.S. *Iroquois*, Delaware River, 7 September 1871. Jumping overboard at the imminent risk of his life, King rescued one of the crew of that vessel from drowning.

KYLE, PATRICK J.

Rank and organization: Landsman, U.S. Navy. *Born:* 1855, Ireland. *Accredited to:* Massachusetts. *Citation:* For rescuing from drowning a shipmate from the U.S.S. *Quinnebaug*, at Port Mahon, Minorca, 13 March 1879.

LAKIN, THOMAS

Rank and organization: Seaman, U.S. Navy. *Born:* 1840, New York. *Accredited to:* New York. *Citation:* Serving on board the U.S.S. *Narragansett* at the Navy Yard, Mare Island, Calif., November 1874, jumping overboard, Lakin displayed gallant conduct by rescuing 2 men of that ship from drowning.

LAVERTY, JOHN

Rank and organization: First Class Fireman, U.S. Navy. *Born:* 1849, Ireland. *Accredited to:* California. *G.O. No.:* 326, 18 October 1884. *Citation:* Serving on board the U.S.S. *Alaska* at Callao Bay, Peru, 14 September 1881. Following the rupture of the stop-valve chamber on that vessel, Laverty hauled the fires from under the boiler,

LEJEUNE, EMILE

Rank and organization: Seaman, U.S. Navy. *Born:* 1853, France. *Accredited to:* New York. *G.O. No.:* 212, 9 June 1876. *Citation:* Serving on board the U.S.S. *Plymouth*, Lejeune displayed gallant conduct in rescuing a citizen from drowning at Port Royal, S.C., 6 June 1876.

LOW, GEORGE

Rank and organization: Seaman, U.S. Navy. *Born:* 1847, Canada. *Accredited to:* New York. *G.O. No.:* 326, 18 October 1884. *Citation:* For jumping overboard from the U.S.S. *Tennessee* at New Orleans, La., 15 February 1881, and sustaining, until picked up by a boat's crew, N. P. Petersen, gunner's mate, who had fallen overboard.

LUCY, JOHN

Rank and organization: Second Class Boy, U.S. Navy. *Born:* 1859, New York, N.Y. *Accredited to:* New York. *G.O. No.:* 214, 27 July 1876. *Citation:* Displayed heroic conduct while serving on board the U.S. Training Ship *Minnesota* on the occasion of the burning of Castle Garden at New York, 9 July 1876.

MADDIN, EDWARD

Rank and organization: Ordinary Seaman, U.S. Navy. *Born:* 1852, Newfoundland. *Accredited to:* Massachusetts. *G.O. No.:* 206, 15 February 1876. *Citation:* Serving on board the U.S.S. *Franklin* at Lisbon, Portugal, 9 January 1876. Displaying gallant conduct, Maddin jumped overboard and rescued one of the crew of that vessel from drowning.

MAGEE, JOHN W.

Rank and organization: Second Class Fireman, U.S. Navy. *Born:* 1859, Maryland. *Accredited to:* Maryland. *G.O. No.:* 326, 18 October 1884. *Citation:* Serving on board the U.S.S. *Tallapoosa* during the sinking of that vessel on the night of 21 August 1884. During this period, Magee remained at his post of duty in the fireroom until the fires were put out by the rising waters.

MANNING, HENRY J.

Rank and organization: Quartermaster, U.S. Navy. *Born:* 1859, New Haven, Conn. *Accredited to:* Connecticut. *G.O. No.:* 326, 18 October 1884. *Citation:* Serving on board the U.S. Training Ship *New Hampshire*, off Newport, R.I., 4 January 1882. Jumping overboard, Manning endeavored to rescue Jabez Smith, second class musician, from drowning.

MATTHEWS, JOSEPH

Rank and organization: Captain of the Top, U.S. Navy. *Born:* 1849, Malta. *Accredited to:* Pennsylvania. *G.O. No.:* 326, 18 October 1884. *Citation:* For courageous conduct in going over the stern of the U.S.S. *Constitution* at sea, 13 February 1879, during a heavy gale, and cutting the fastenings of the ship's rudder chains.

McCARTON, JOHN

Rank and organization: Ship's Printer, U.S. Navy. *Born:* 1847, Brooklyn, N.Y. *Accredited to:* New York. *G.O. No.:* 326, 18 October 1884. *Citation:* For jumping overboard from the U.S. Training Ship *New Hampshire* off Coasters Harbor Island, near Newport, R.I., 4 January 1882, and endeavoring to rescue Jabez Smith, second class musician, from drowning.

MILLER, HUGH

12.

Rank and organization: Boatswain's Mate, U.S. Navy. *Born:* 1859, Philadelphia, Pa. *Accredited to:* Pennsylvania. (Letter Capt. N. Judlow, U.S. Navy, No. 8326/B; 21 November 1885.) *Citation:* For jumping overboard from the U.S.S. *Quinnebaug,* at Alexandria, Egypt, on the morning of 21 November 1885 and assisting in saving a shipmate from drowning.

MILLMORE, JOHN

Rank and organization: Ordinary Seaman, U.S. Navy. *Born:* 1860, New York, N.Y. *Accredited to:* New York. *G.O. No.:* 326, 18 October 1884. *Citation:* Serving on board the U.S.S. *Essex,* Millmore rescued from drowning John W. Powers, ordinary seaman, serving on the same vessel with him, at Monrovia, Liberia, 31 October 1877.

MITCHELL, THOMAS

Rank and organization: Landsman, U.S. Navy. *Born:* 1857, New York, N.Y. *Accredited to:* New York. *G.O. No.:* 326, 18 October 1884. *Citation:* Serving on board the U.S.S. *Richmond,* Mitchell rescued from drowning, M. F. Caulan, first class boy, serving with him on the same vessel, at Shanghai, China, 17 November 1879.

MOORE, FRANCIS

Rank and organization: Boatswain's Mate, U.S. Navy. *Born:* 1858, New York. *Accredited to:* New York. *G.O. No.:* 326, 18 October 1884. *Citation:* For jumping overboard from the U.S. Training Ship *Portsmouth,* at the Washington Navy Yard, 23 January 1882, and endeavoring to rescue Thomas Duncan, carpenter and calker, who had fallen overboard.

MOORE, PHILIP

Rank and organization: Seaman, U.S. Navy. *Born:* 1853, Newfoundland. *Accredited to:* Rhode Island. *G.O. No.:* 326, 18 October 1884. *Citation:* For jumping overboard from the U.S.S. *Trenton,* at Genoa, Italy, 21 September 1880, and rescuing from drowning Hans Paulsen, ordinary seaman.

MORRIS, JOHN

Rank and organization: Corporal, U.S. Marine Corps. *Born:* 25 January 1855, New York, N.Y. *Accredited to:* New York. *G.O. No.:* 326, 18 October 1884. *Citation:* For leaping overboard from the U.S. Flagship *Lancaster,* at Villefranche, France, 25 December 1881, and rescuing from drowning Robert Blizzard, ordinary seaman, a prisoner, who had jumped overboard.

MORSE, WILLIAM

Rank and organization: Seaman, U.S. Navy. *Born:* 1852, Germany. *Accredited to:* New York. *G.O. No.:* 326, 18 October 1884. *Citation:* For jumping overboard from the U.S.S. *Shenandoah* at Rio de Janeiro, Brazil, 19 September 1880, and rescuing from drowning James Grady, first class fireman.

NOIL, JOSEPH B.

Rank and organization: Seaman, U.S. Navy. *Born:* 1841, Nova Scotia. *Accredited to:* New York. *Citation:* Serving on board the U.S.S. *Powhatan* at Norfolk, 26 December 1872, Noil saved Boatswain J. C. Walton from drowning.

NORRIS, J. W.

Rank and organization: Landsman, U.S. Navy. *Born:* 1862, England. *Accredited to:* New York. *G.O. No.:* 326, 18 October 1884. *Citation:* Serving on board the U.S.S. *Jamestown*, New York Navy Yard, 20 December 1883, Norris rescued from drowning A. A. George, who had fallen overboard.

O'CONNER, JAMES F.

Rank and organization: Landsman, Engineer's Force, U.S. Navy. *Born:* 1862, Portsmouth, Va. *Accredited to:* Virginia. *G.O. No.:* 326, 18 October 1884. *Citation:* For jumping overboard from the U.S.S. *Jean Sands*, opposite the Norfolk Navy Yard, on the night of 15 June 1880, and rescuing from drowning a young girl who had fallen overboard.

OHMSEN, AUGUST

Rank and organization: Master-at-Arms, U.S. Navy. *Born:* 1853, Germany. *Accredited to:* New York. *G.O. No.:* 326, 18 October 1884. *Citation:* On board the U.S.S. *Tallapoosa* at the time of the sinking of that vessel, on the night of 21 August 1884. Clearing the berth deck, Ohmsen remained there until the water was waist deep, wading about with outstretched arms, rousing the men out of their hammocks. Then, going on deck, he assisted in lowering the first cutter and then the dinghy, of which he took charge.

O'NEAL, JOHN

Rank and organization: Boatswain's Mate, U.S. Navy. *Born:* 1841, Ireland. *Accredited to:* Pennsylvania. *G.O. No.:* 176, 9 July 1872. *Citation:* Serving on board the U.S.S. *Kansas*, O'Neal displayed great coolness and self-possession at the time Comdr. A. F. Crosman and others were drowned near Greytown, Nicaragua, 12 April 1872, and by personal exertion prevented greater loss of life.

OSBORNE, JOHN

Rank and organization: Seaman, U.S. Navy. *Born:* 1844, New Orleans, La. *Accredited to:* Louisiana. *G.O. No.:* 218, 24 August 1876. *Citation:* Serving on board the U.S.S. *Juniata*, Osborne displayed gallant conduct in rescuing from drowning an enlisted boy of that vessel, at Philadelphia, Pa., 21 August 1876.

OSEPINS, CHRISTIAN

Rank and organization: Seaman, U.S. Navy. *Born:* 1858, Holland. *Accredited to:* New York. *G.O. No.:* 326, 18 October 1884. *Citation:* For jumping overboard from the U.S. Tug *Fortune*, 7 May 1882, at Hampton Roads, Va., and rescuing from drowning James Walters, gunner's mate.

PARKER, ALEXANDER

Rank and organization: Boatswain's Mate, U.S. Navy. *Born:* 1832, Kensington, N.J. *Accredited to:* New Jersey. *G.O. No.:* 215, 9 August 1876. *Citation:* For gallant conduct in attempting to save a shipmate from drowning at the Navy Yard, Mare Island, Calif., on 25 July 1876.

PILE, RICHARD

Rank and organization: Ordinary Seaman, U.S. Navy. *Born:* 1849, West Indies. *Accredited to:* Massachusetts. *G.O. No.:* 176, 9 July 1872. *Citation:* Serving on board the U.S.S. *Kansas*, Pile displayed great coolness and self-possession at the time Comdr. A. F. Crosman and others were drowned, near Greytown, Nicaragua, 12 April 1872, and by his extraordinary heroism and personal exertion prevented greater loss of life.

REGAN, PATRICK

Rank and organization: Ordinary Seaman, U.S. Navy. *Born:* 1852, Ireland. *Accredited to:* New York. *Citation:* Serving on board the U.S.S. *Pensacola*, Regan displayed gallant conduct in the harbor of Coquimbor, Chile, 30 July 1873.

ROUNING, JOHANNES

Rank and organization: Ordinary Seaman, U.S. Navy. Biography not available. *G.O. No.:* 326, 18 October 1884. *Citation:* For jumping overboard from the U.S. Tug *Fortune*, 7 May 1882, at Hampton Roads, Va., and rescuing from drowning James Walters, gunner's mate.

RUSSELL, JOHN

Rank and organization: Seaman, U.S. Navy. *Born:* 1852, New York, N.Y. *Accredited to:* New York. *G.O. No.:* 326, 18 October 1884. *Citation:* For jumping overboard from the U.S.S. *Trenton*, at Genoa, Italy, 21 September 1880, and rescuing from drowning Hans Paulsen, ordinary seaman.

RYAN, RICHARD

Rank and organization: Ordinary Seaman, U.S. Navy. *Born:* 1851, Connecticut. *Accredited to:* Connecticut. *G.O. No.:* 207, 23 March 1876. *Citation:* Serving on board the U.S.S. *Hartford*, Ryan displayed gallant conduct in jumping overboard at Norfolk, Va., and rescuing from drowning one of the crew of that vessel, 4 March 1876.

SADLER, WILLIAM

Rank and organization: Captain of the Top, U.S. Navy. *Born:* 1854, Boston, Mass. *Accredited to:* Massachusetts. *G.O. No.:* 326, 18 October 1884. *Citation:* For jumping overboard from the U.S.S. *Saratoga*, off Coasters Harbor Island, R.I., 25 June 1881, and sustaining until picked up by a boat from the ship, Frank Gallagher, second class boy, who had fallen overboard.

SAPP, ISACC

Rank and organization: Seaman, Engineer's Force, U.S. Navy. *Born:* 1844, Philadelphia, Pa. *Accredited to:* Pennsylvania. *G.O. No.:* 169, 8 February 1872. *Citation:* On board the U.S.S. *Shenandoah* during the rescue of a shipmate at Villefranche, 15 December 1871. Jumping overboard, Sapp gallantly assisted in saving Charles Prince, seaman, from drowning.

SIMPSON, HENRY

Rank and organization: First Class Fireman, U.S. Navy. *Born:* 1859, London, England. *Accredited to:* New York. *G.O. No.:* 326, 18 October 1884. *Citation:* For rescuing from drowning John W. Powers, ordinary seaman on board the U.S.S. *Essex*, at Monrovia, Liberia, 31 October 1877.

SMITH, JAMES

Rank and organization: Seaman, U.S. Navy. *Born:* 1838, Hawaiian Islands. *Accredited to:* New York. *G.O. No.:* 176, 9 July 1872. *Citation:* Serving on board the U.S.S. *Kansas*, Smith displayed great coolness and self-possession at the time Comdr. A. F. Crosman and others were drowned near Greytown, Nicaragua, 12 April 1872, and by extraordinary heroism and personal exertion, prevented greater loss of life.

SMITH, JOHN

Rank and organization: Seaman, U.S. Navy. *Born:* 1854, Bermuda. *Accredited to:* New York. *G.O. No.:* 326, 18 October 1884. *Citation:* For jumping overboard from the U.S.S. *Shenandoah*, at Rio de Janeiro, Brazil, 19 September 1880, and rescuing from drowning James Grady, first class fireman.

SMITH, THOMAS

Rank and organization: Seaman, U.S. Navy. *Born:* 1856, Ireland. *Accredited to:* Virginia. *Citation:* For rescuing from drowning William Kent, coxswain of the U.S.S. *Enterprise*, off Para, Brazil, 1 October 1878.

STEWART, JAMES A.

Rank and organization: Corporal, U.S. Marine Corps. *Born:* 1839, Philadelphia, Pa. *Accredited to:* Pennsylvania. *G.O. No.:* 180, 10 October 1872. *Citation:* Serving on board the U.S.S. *Plymouth*, Stewart jumped overboard in the harbor of Villefranche, France, 1 February 1872 and saved Midshipman Osterhaus from drowning.

SULLIVAN, JAMES F.

Rank and organization: Boatswain's Mate, U.S. Navy. *Born:* 1857, Lowell, Mass. *Accredited to:* Massachusetts. *G.O. No.:* 326, 18 October 1884. *Citation:* For jumping overboard from the U.S. Training Ship *New Hampshire*, at Newport, R.I., 21 April 1882, and rescuing from drowning Francis T. Price, third class boy.

SWEENEY, ROBERT

Rank and organization: Ordinary Seaman, U.S. Navy. *Born:* 1853, Montreal, Canada. *Accredited to:* New Jersey. *G.O. No.:* 326, 18 October 1884. Second award. *Citation:* Serving on board the U.S.S. *Kearsarge*, at Hampton Roads, Va., 26 October 1881, Sweeney jumped overboard and assisted in saving from drowning a shipmate who had fallen overboard into a strongly running tide.

SECOND AWARD

Citation: Serving on board the U.S.S. *Jamestown*, at the Navy Yard, New York, 20 December 1883, Sweeney rescued from drowning A. A. George, who had fallen overboard from that vessel.

SWEENEY, WILLIAM

Rank and organization: Landsman, Engineer's Force, U.S. Navy. *Born:* 1856, Boston, Mass. *Accredited to:* Massachusetts. *G.O. No.:* 326, 18 October 1884. *Citation:* For jumping overboard from the U.S.S. *Jean Sands*, opposite the Navy Yard, Norfolk, Va., on the night of 15 June 1880, and rescuing from drowning a young girl who had fallen overboard.

TAYLOR, RICHARD H.

Rank and organization: Quartermaster, U.S. Navy. *Born:* 1871, Virginia. *Accredited to:* Virginia. *G.O. No.:* 157, 20 April 1904. *Citation:* Serving on board the U.S.S. *Nipsic*, Taylor displayed gallantry during the hurricane at Apia, Samoa, 16 March 1889.

THAYER, JAMES

Rank and organization: Ship's Corporal U.S. Navy. *Born:* 1853, Ireland. *Accredited to:* Pennsylvania. *G.O. No.:* 326, 18 October 1884. *Citation:* For rescuing from drowning a boy serving with him on the U.S.S. *Constitution*, at the Navy Yard, Norfolk, Va., 16 November 1879.

THOMPSON, HENRY

Rank and organization: Seaman, U.S. Navy. Biography not available. *Citation:* For rescuing a man from drowning at Mare Island, Calif., 27 June 1878.

THORNTON, MICHAEL

Rank and organization: Seaman, U.S. Navy. *Born:* 1856, Ireland. *Accredited to:* Pennsylvania. *G.O. No.:* 326, 18 October 1884. *Citation:* For jumping overboard from the U.S. Tug *Leyden*, near Boston, Mass., 26 August 1881, and sustaining until picked up, Michael Drennan, landsman, who had jumped overboard while temporarily insane.

TOBIN, PAUL

Rank and organization: Landsman, U.S. Navy. *Birth:* Plybin, France. *Entered service at:* Brest, France. *G.O. No.:* 180, 10 October 1872. *Citation:* On board the U.S.S. *Plymouth*, Hamburg Harbor, 3 July 1871. Jumping overboard at the imminent risk of his life, Tobin, with a comrade, rescued from drowning one of a party who was thrown from a shore boat into a 4-knot running tide while the boat was coming alongside the ship.

TROUT, JAMES M.

Rank and organization: Second Class Fireman, U.S. Navy. *Born:* 1850, Philadelphia, Pa. *Accredited to:* Pennsylvania. *Citation:* Serving on board the U.S.S. *Frolic*, Trout displayed gallant conduct in endeavoring to save the life of one of the crew of that vessel who had fallen overboard at Montevideo, 20 April 1877.

TROY, JEREMIAH

Rank and organization: Chief Boatswain's Mate, U.S. Navy. *Born:* 1845, New York, N.Y. *Accredited to:* New York. *G.O. No.:* 326, 18 October 1884. *Citation:* For jumping overboard from the U.S. Training Ship *New Hampshire*, at Newport, R.I., 21 April 1882, and rescuing from drowning Francis T. Price, third class boy.

TURVELIN, ALEXANDER HAURE

Rank and organization: Seaman, U.S. Navy. *Born:* 1847, Russia. *G.O. No.:* 326, 18 October 1884. *Citation:* For jumping overboard from the U.S.S. *Trenton*, at Toulon, France, February 1881, and rescuing from drowning Augustus Ohlensen, coxswain.

WEISBOGEL, ALBERT

Rank and organization: Captain of the Mizzen Top, U.S. Navy. *Born:* 1844, New Orleans, La. *Accredited to:* Louisiana. *G.O. No.:* 207, 23 March 1876; 212, 9 June 1876. Second award. *Citation:* For gallant conduct in jumping overboard from the U.S.S. *Benicia*, at sea, and rescuing from drowning one of the crew of that vessel on 11 January 1874.

SECOND AWARD

Citation: For gallant conduct in jumping overboard from the U.S.S. *Plymouth*, at sea, and rescuing from drowning one of the crew of that vessel on 27 April 1876.

WEISSEL, ADAM

Rank and organization: Ship's Cook, U.S. Navy. *Born:* 1854, Germany. *Accredited to:* New York. *G.O. No.:* 326, 18 October 1884. *Citation:* For jumping overboard from the U.S. Training Ship *Minnesota*, at Newport, R.I., 26 August 1881, and sustaining until picked up by a boat from the ship, C. Lorenze, captain of the fore-castle, who had fallen overboard.

WILLIAMS, ANTONIO

Rank and organization: Seaman, U.S. Navy. *Born:* 1825, Malta. *Citation:* For courage and fidelity displayed in the loss of the U.S.S. *Huron*, 24 November 1877.

WILLIAMS, HENRY

Rank and organization: Carpenter's Mate, U.S. Navy. *Born:* 1833, Canada. *Accredited to:* Pennsylvania. *G.O. No.:* 326, 18 October 1884. *Citation:* For going over the stern of the U.S.S. *Constitution*, at sea, 13 February 1879, during a heavy gale, and performing important carpenter's work upon her rudder.

WILLIAMS, LOUIS

Rank and organization: Captain of the Hold, U.S. Navy. *Born:* 1845, Norway. *Accredited to:* California. *G.O. No.:* 326, 18 October 1884. Second award. *Citation:* For jumping overboard from the U.S.S. *Lackawanna*, 16 March 1883, at Honolulu, T.H., and rescuing from drowning Thomas Moran, landsman.

SECOND AWARD

Citation: Serving on board the U.S.S. *Lackawanna*, Williams rescued from drowning William Cruise, who had fallen overboard at Callao, Peru, 13 June 1884.

WILLIS, GEORGE

Rank and organization: Coxswain, U.S. Navy. *Born:* 1839, Boston, Mass. *Accredited to:* Massachusetts. *Citation:* Serving on board the U.S.S. *Tigress*, Willis displayed gallant and meritorious conduct on the night of 22 September 1873 off the coast of Greenland.

WILSON, AUGUST

Rank and organization: Boilermaker, U.S. Navy. *Born:* 1 March 1864, Danzig, Germany. *Accredited to:* New York. *G.O. No.:* 482, 1 November 1897. *Citation:* For gallant conduct while serving on board the U.S.S. *Puritan* and at the time of the collapse of one of the crown sheets of boiler E on that vessel, 1 July 1897. Wrapping wet cloths about his face and arms, Wilson entered the fireroom and opened the safety valve, thus removing the danger of disabling the other boilers.

KOREAN CAMPAIGN
1871

Essentially bent on peaceful missions following the Civil War, the Navy was interrupted in its good-will pursuits in 1871, by trouble in Korea. The Asiatic Squadron under Rear Admiral John Rodgers entered the territorial waters of the Hermit Kingdom to investigate the destruction of the American sailing vessel, *General Sherman*, and the massacre of her crew. At the same time the U.S. Minister to China attempted to negotiate a trade treaty with Korea.

While negotiations were in progress as the ships lay at anchor below the Korean capital, several boat parties, sent out to survey the channel, were treacherously fired upon by fort batteries and 2 Americans wounded.

After waiting 10 days for an apology from the Korean Government, Rear Admiral Rodgers landed several hundred Seamen and Marines. Armed with light artillery and supported by fire from the *Monocacy* and *Palos*, they carried out a land attack against the forts.

The last phase of the operation was the storming of the most important fort, a circular redoubt called the "Citadel." The rushing Sailors and Marines were pounded by showers of stone hurled from the parapet. Hand-to-hand fighting became desperate all along the line and the leader of the assault fell, mortally wounded.

Scaling the ramparts, the men finally drove out the remaining defenders while Private Hugh Purvis and Corporal Charles Brown tore down the enemy flag.

Although the sought-for trade treaty was not forthcoming at the time, the incident had a stabilizing effect and paved the way for a negotiation with Korea a decade later.

ANDREWS, JOHN

Rank and organization: Ordinary Seaman, U.S. Navy. *Born:* 1821, York County, Pennsylvania. *Accredited to:* Maryland. *G.O. No.:* 176, 9 July 1872. *Citation:* On board the U.S.S. *Benicia* in action against Korean forts on 9 and 10 June 1871. Stationed at the lead in passing the forts, Andrews stood on the gunwale on the *Benicia's* launch, lashed to the ridgerope. He remained unflinchingly in this dangerous position and gave his soundings with coolness and accuracy under a heavy fire.

BROWN, CHARLES

Rank and organization: Corporal, U.S. Marine Corps. *Born:* New York, N.Y. *Enlisted at:* Hongkong, China. *G.O. No.:* 169, 8 February 1872. *Citation:* On board the U.S.S. *Colorado* in action against a Korean fort on 11 June 1871. Assisted in capturing the Korean standard in the center of the citadel of the fort.

COLEMAN, JOHN

Rank and organization: Private, U.S. Marine Corps. *Born:* 9 October 1847, Ireland. *Accredited to:* California. *G.O. No.:* 169, 8 February 1872. *Citation:* On board the U.S.S. *Colorado* in action at Korea on 11 June 1871. Fighting hand-to-hand with the enemy, Coleman succeeded in saving the life of Alexander McKenzie.

DOUGHERTY, JAMES

Rank and organization: Private, U.S. Marine Corps. *Born:* 16 November 1839, Langhash, Ireland. *Accredited to:* Pennsylvania. *G.O. No.:* 169, 8 February 1872. *Citation:* On board the U.S.S. *Carondelet* in various actions of that vessel. Wounded several times, Dougherty invariably returned to duty, presenting an example of constancy and devotion to the flag.

FRANKLIN, FREDERICK

Rank and organization: Quartermaster, U.S. Navy. *Born:* 1840, Portsmouth, N.H. *Accredited to:* New Hampshire. G.O. No.: 169, 8 February 1872. *Citation:* On board the U.S.S. *Colorado* during the attack and capture of the Korean forts on 11 June 1871. Assuming command of Company D, after Lt. McKee was wounded, Franklin handled the company with great credit until relieved.

GRACE, PATRICK H.

Rank and organization: Chief Quartermaster, U.S. Navy. *Born:* 1835, Ireland. *Accredited to:* Pennsylvania. *G.O. No.:* 177, 4 December 1915. *Citation:* On board the U.S.S. *Benicia* during the attack on the Korean forts, 10 and 11 June 1871. Carrying out his duties with coolness, Grace set forth gallant and meritorious conduct throughout this action.

HAYDEN, CYRUS

Rank and organization: Carpenter, U.S. Navy. *Born:* 1843, York, Maine. *Accredited to:* Maine. *G.O. No.:* 169, 8 February 1872. *Citation:* On board the U.S.S. *Colorado* during the attack and capture of the Korean forts, 11 June 1871. Serving as color bearer of the battalion, Hayden planted his flag on the ramparts of the citadel and protected it under a heavy fire from the enemy.

LUKES, WILLIAM F.

Rank and organization: Landsman, U.S. Navy. *Born:* 1846, Bohemia. *Enlisted at:* Tientsin, China. *G.O. No.:* 180, 10 October 1872. *Citation:* Served with Company D during the capture of the Korean forts, 9 and 10 June 1871. Fighting the enemy inside the fort, Lukes received a severe cut over the head.

McKENZIE, ALEXANDER

Rank and organization: Boatswain's Mate, U.S. Navy. *Born:* 1837, Scotland. *Accredited to:* New York. *G.O. No.:* 169, 8 February 1872. *Citation:* On board the U.S.S. *Colorado* during the capture of the Korean forts, 11 June 1871. Fighting at the side of Lt. McKee during this action, McKenzie was struck by a sword and received a severe cut in the head from the blow.

McNAMARA, MICHAEL

Rank and organization: Private, U.S. Marine Corps. *Born:* 1841, Clure, Ireland. *Accredited to:* New York. *G.O. No.:* 169, 8 February 1872. *Citation:* On board the U.S.S. *Benicia* during the capture of the Korean forts, 11 June 1871. Advancing to the parapet, McNamara wrenched the match-lock from the hands of an enemy and killed him.

MERTON, JAMES F.

Rank and organization: Landsman, U.S. Navy. *Birth:* England. *G.O. No.:* 180, 10 October 1872. *Citation:* Landsman and member of Company D during the capture of the Korean forts, 9 and 10 June 1871. Merton was severely wounded in the arm while trying to force his way into the fort.

OWENS, MICHAEL

Rank and organization: Private, U.S. Marine Corps. *Born:* 6 February 1853, New York, N.Y. *Accredited to:* New York. *G.O. No.:* 169, 8 February 1872. *Citation:* On board the U.S.S. *Colorado* during the capture of Korean forts, 11 June 1871. Fighting courageously in hand-to-hand combat, Owens was badly wounded by the enemy during this action.

PURVIS, HUGH

Rank and organization: Private, U.S. Marine Corps. *Born:* 5 March 1846, Philadelphia, Pa. *Accredited to:* Pennsylvania. *G.O. No.:* 169, 8 February 1872. *Citation:* On board the U.S.S. *Alaska* during the attack on and capture of the Korean forts, 11 June 1871. Braving the enemy fire, Purvis was the first to scale the walls of the fort and capture the flag of the Korean forces.

ROGERS, SAMUEL F.

Rank and organization: Quartermaster, U.S. Navy. *Born:* 1845, Buffalo, N.Y. *Accredited to:* New York. *G.O. No.:* 169, 8 February 1872. *Citation:* On board the U.S.S. *Colorado* during the attack and capture of the Korean forts, 11 June 1871. Fighting courageously at the side of Lt. McKee during this action, Rogers was wounded by the enemy.

TROY, WILLIAM

Rank and organization: Ordinary Seaman, U.S. Navy. *Born:* 1848, Boston, Mass. *Accredited to:* Massachusetts. *G.O. No.:* 169, 8 February 1872. *Citation:* On board the U.S.S. *Colorado* during the capture of the Korean forts, 11 June 1871. Fighting at the side of Lt. McKee, by whom he was especially commended, Troy was badly wounded by the enemy.

INTERIM 1866 TO 1870

BATES, RICHARD

Rank and organization: Seaman, U.S. Navy. *Born:* 1829, Wales. *Accredited to:* New York. *G.O. No.:* 77, 1 August 1866. *Citation:* For heroic conduct in rescuing from drowning James Rose and John Russell, seamen of the U.S.S. *Winooski*, off Eastport, Maine, 10 May 1866.

BROWN, JOHN

Rank and organization: Captain of the Afterguard, U.S. Navy. *Born:* 1838, Denmark. *Accredited to:* Maryland. *G.O. No.:* 77, 1 August 1866. *Citation:* For heroic conduct with 2 comrades, in rescuing from drowning James Rose and John Russell, seamen, of the U.S.S. *Winooski*, off Eastport, Maine, 10 May 1866.

BURKE, THOMAS

Rank and organization: Seaman, U.S. Navy. *Born:* 1833, Ireland. *Accredited to:* New York. *G.O. No.:* 77, 1 August 1866. *Citation:* For heroic conduct, with 2 comrades, in rescuing from drowning James Rose and John Russell, seamen, of the U.S.S. *Winooski*, off Eastport, Maine, 10 May 1866.

CAREY, JAMES

Rank and organization: Seaman, U.S. Navy. *Born:* 1844, Ireland. *Accredited to:* New York. *Citation:* Seaman on board the U.S.S. *Huron*, saving 3 shipmates from drowning.

Du MOULIN, FRANK

Rank and organization: Apprentice, U.S. Navy. *Born:* 1850, Philadelphia, Pa. *Accredited to:* Pennsylvania. *G.O. No.:* 84, October 1867. *Citation:* On the 5th of September 1867, Du Moulin jumped overboard and saved from drowning Apprentice D'Orsay, who had fallen from the mizzen topmast rigging of the *Sabine*, in New London Harbor, and was rendered helpless by striking the mizzen rigging and boat davit in the fall.

HALFORD, WILLIAM

Rank and organization: Coxswain, U.S. Navy. *Born:* 18 August 1841, Gloucester, England. *Accredited to:* California. *G.O. No.:* 169, 8 February 1872. *Citation:* Halford was sole survivor of the boat's crew sent to the Sandwich Islands for assistance after the wreck of the *Saginaw*, October 1870. Promoted to acting gunner.

ROBINSON, JOHN

Rank and organization: Captain of the Hold, U.S. Navy. *Born:* 1840, Cuba. *Accredited to:* Maine. *G.O. No.:* 82, 23 February 1867. *Citation:* With Acting Ensign James H. Bunting, during the heavy gale which occurred in Pensacola Bay on the night of 19 January 1867, Robinson swam ashore with a line for the purpose of sending off a blowcock, which would facilitate getting up steam and prevent the vessel from stranding, thus voluntarily periling his life to save the vessel and the lives of others.

ROBINSON, THOMAS

Rank and organization: Captain of the Afterguard, U.S. Navy. *Born:* 17 May 1837, Norway. *Accredited to:* New York. *G.O. No.:* 77, 1 August 1866. *Citation:* For heroic efforts to save from drowning Wellington Brocar, landsman, of the *Tallapoosa*, off New Orleans, 15 July 1866.

STACY, WILLIAM B.

Rank and organization: Seaman, U.S. Navy. *Born:* 1838, Massachusetts. *Accredited to:* Massachusetts. *G.O. No.:* 71, 15 January 1866. *Citation:* While coaling ship in the harbor of Cape Haiten, one of the crew of the *Rhode Island* fell overboard, and, after catching a rope, had been forced by exhaustion, to relinquish his hold. Although the sea was running high at the time, Stacy, at the peril of his life, jumped overboard, secured the rope around his shipmate, and thus saved him from drowning.

INDIAN CAMPAIGNS

The first of all Army Medals of Honor was earned by Assistant Surgeon Bernard J. D. Irwin during an Indian campaign in Arizona, 13-14 February 1861. The last Medal of Honor awarded in an Indian campaign was earned by Pvt. Oscar Burkhard on 5 October 1898. With the exception of these two medals, all Indian Campaign Medals of Honor were awarded in operations which took place between 25 March 1865 and 30 December 1891.

ALBEE, GEORGE E.

Rank and organization: First Lieutenant, 41st U.S. Infantry. *Place and date:* At Brazos River, Tex., 28 October 1869. *Entered service at:* Owatonna, Minn. *Birth:* Lisbon, N.H. *Date of issue:* 18 January 1894. *Citation:* Attacked with 2 men a force of 11 Indians, drove them from the hills, and reconnoitered the country beyond.

ALCHESAY

Rank and organization: Sergeant, Indian Scouts. *Place and date:* Winter of 1872–73. *Entered service at:* Camp Verde, Ariz. *Born:* 1853, Arizona Territory. *Date of issue:* 12 April 1875. *Citation:* Gallant conduct during campaigns and engagements with Apaches.

ALLEN, WILLIAM

Rank and organization: First Sergeant, Company I, 23d U.S. Infantry. *Place and date:* At Turret Mountain, Ariz., 27 March 1873. *Entered service at:* Lansingburg, N.Y. *Birth:* Brightstown, N.Y. *Date of issue:* 12 April 1875. *Citation:* Gallantry in action.

ANDERSON, JAMES

Rank and organization: Private, Company M, 6th U.S. Cavalry. *Place and date:* At Wichita River, Tex., 5 October 1870. *Entered service at:* ———. *Birth:* Canada East. *Date of issue:* 19 November 1870. *Citation:* Gallantry during the pursuit and fight with Indians.

ASTON, EDGAR R.

Rank and organization: Private, Company L, 8th U.S. Cavalry. *Place and date:* At San Carlos, Ariz., 30 May 1868. *Entered service at:* ———. *Birth:* Clermont County, Ohio. *Date of issue:* 28 July 1868. *Citation:* With 2 other men he volunteered to search for a wagon passage out of a 4,000-foot valley wherein an infantry column was immobile. This small group passed 6 miles among hostile Apache terrain finding the sought passage. On their return trip down the canyon they were attacked by Apaches who were successfully held at bay.

AUSTIN, WILLIAM G.

Rank and organization: Sergeant, Company E, 7th U.S. Cavalry. *Place and date:* At Wounded Knee Creek, S. Dak., 29 December 1890. *Entered service at:* New York, N.Y. *Birth:* Galveston, Tex. *Date of issue:* 27 June 1891. *Citation:* While the Indians were concealed in a ravine, assisted men on the skirmish line, directing their fire, etc., and using every effort to dislodge the enemy.

AYERS, JAMES F.

Rank and organization: Private, Company H, 6th U.S. Cavalry. *Place and date:* At Sappa Creek, Kans., 23 April 1875. *Entered service at:* ———. *Birth:* Collinstown, Va. *Date of issue:* 16 November 1876. *Citation:* Rapid pursuit, gallantry, energy, and enterprise in an engagement with Indians.

BABCOCK, JOHN B.

Rank and organization: First Lieutenant, 5th U.S. Cavalry. *Place and date:* At Spring Creek, Nebr., 16 May 1869. *Entered service at:* Stonington, Conn. *Birth:* New Orleans, La. *Date of issue:* 18 September 1897. *Citation:* While serving with a scouting column, this officer's troop was attacked by a vastly superior force of Indians. Advancing to high ground, he dismounted his men, remaining mounted himself to encourage them, and there fought the Indians until relieved, his horse being wounded.

BAILEY, JAMES E.

Rank and organization: Sergeant, Company E, 5th U.S. Cavalry. *Place and date:* Winter of 1872–73. *Entered service at:* ———. *Birth:* Dexter, Maine. *Date of issue:* 12 April 1875. *Citation:* Gallant conduct during campaigns and engagements with Apaches.

BAIRD, GEORGE W.

Rank and organization: First Lieutenant and Adjutant, 5th U.S. Infantry. *Place and date:* At Bear Paw Mountain, Mont., 30 September 1877. *Entered service at:* Milford, Conn. *Birth:* Connecticut. *Date of issue:* 27 November 1894. *Citation:* Most distinguished gallantry in action with the Nez Percé Indians.

BAKER, JOHN

Rank and organization: Musician, Company D, 5th U.S. Infantry. *Place and date:* At Cedar Creek, etc., Mont., October 1876 to January 1877. *Entered service at:* Brooklyn, N.Y. *Birth:* Germany. *Date of issue:* 27 April 1877. *Citation:* Gallantry in engagements.

BANCROFT, NEIL

Rank and organization: Private, Company A, 7th U.S. Cavalry. *Place and date:* At Little Big Horn, Mont., 25 June 1876. *Entered service at:* Chicago, Ill. *Birth:* Oswego, N.Y. *Date of issue:* 5 October 1878. *Citation:* Brought water for the wounded under a most galling fire.

BARNES, WILL C.

Rank and organization: Private First Class, Signal Corps, U.S. Army. *Place and date:* At Fort Apache, Ariz., 11 September 1881. *Entered service at:* Washington, D.C. *Birth:* San Francisco, Calif. *Date of issue:* 8 November 1882. *Citation:* Bravery in action.

BARRETT, RICHARD

Rank and organization: First Sergeant, Company A, 1st U.S. Cavalry. *Place and date:* At Sycamore Canyon, Ariz., 23 May 1872. *Entered service at:* ———. *Birth:* Ireland. *Date of issue:* 12 April 1875. *Citation:* Conspicuous gallantry in a charge upon the Tonto Apaches.

BEAUFORD, CLAY

Rank and organization: First Sergeant, Company B, 5th U.S. Cavalry. *Place and date:* Winter of 1872–73. *Entered service at:* ———. *Birth:* Washington County, Md. *Date of issue:* 12 April 1875. *Citation:* Gallant conduct during campaigns and engagements with Apaches.

BELL, JAMES

Rank and organization: Private, Company E, 7th U.S. Infantry. *Place and date:* At Big Horn, Mont., 9 July 1875. *Entered service at:* ———. *Birth:* Ireland. *Date of issue:* 2 December 1876. *Citation:* Carried dispatches to Gen. Crook at the imminent risk of his life.

BERGERNDAHL, FREDERICK

Rank and organization: Private, Band, 4th U.S. Cavalry. *Place and date:* At Staked Plains, Tex., 8 December 1874. *Entered service at:* ———. *Birth:* Sweden. *Date of issue:* 13 October 1875. *Citation:* Gallantry in a long chase after Indians.

BERTRAM, HEINRICH

Rank and organization: Corporal, Company B, 8th U.S. Cavalry. *Place and date:* Arizona, 1868. *Entered service at:* ———. *Birth:* Germany. *Date of issue:* 24 July 1869. *Citation:* Bravery in scouts and actions against Indians.

BESSEY, CHARLES A.

Rank and organization: Corporal, Company A, 3d U.S. Cavalry. *Place and date:* Near Elkhorn Creek, Wyo., 13 January 1877. *Entered service at:* ———. *Birth:* Reading, Mass. *Date of issue:* 15 May 1890. *Citation:* While scouting with 4 men and attacked in ambush by 14 hostile Indians, held his ground, 2 of his men being wounded, and kept up the fight until himself wounded in the side, and then went to the assistance of his wounded comrades.

BISHOP, DANIEL

Rank and organization: Sergeant, Company A, 5th U.S. Cavalry. *Place and date:* At Turret Mountain, Ariz., 25 March 1873. *Entered service at:* ———. *Birth:* Monroe County, Ohio. *Date of issue:* 12 April 1875. *Citation:* Gallantry in engagements.

BLAIR, JAMES

Rank and organization: First Sergeant, Company I, 1st U.S. Cavalry. *Place and date:* Winter of 1872–73. *Entered service at:* ———. *Birth:* Schuyler County, Pa. *Date of issue:* 12 April 1875. *Citation:* Gallant conduct during campaigns and engagements with Apaches.

BLANQUET

Rank and organization: Indian Scouts. *Place and date:* Winter of 1872–73. *Entered service at:* ———. *Birth:* Arizona. *Date of issue:* 12 April 1875. *Citation:* Gallant conduct during campaigns and engagements with Apaches.

BOWDEN, SAMUEL

Rank and organization: Corporal, Company M, 6th U.S. Cavalry. *Place and date:* At Wichita River, Tex., 5 October 1870. *Entered service at:* ———. *Birth:* Salem, Mass. *Date of issue:* 19 November 1870. *Citation:* Gallantry in pursuit of and fight with Indians.

BOWMAN, ALONZO

Rank and organization: Sergeant, Company D, 6th U.S. Cavalry. *Place and date:* At Cibicu Creek, Ariz., 30 August 1881. *Entered service at:* Washington Township, Knox County, Maine. *Born:* 15 June 1848, Washington Township, Knox County, Maine. *Date of issue:* 4 November 1882. *Citation:* Conspicuous and extraordinary bravery in attacking mutinous scouts.

BOYNE, THOMAS

Rank and organization: Sergeant, Company C, 9th U.S. Cavalry. *Place and date:* At Mimbres Mountains, N. Mex., 29 May 1879; at Cuchillo Negro River near Ojo Caliente, N. Mex., 27 September 1879.

Entered service at: ———. *Birth:* Prince Georges County, Md. *Date of issue:* 6 January 1882. *Citation:* Bravery in action.

BRADBURY, SANFORD

Rank and organization: First Sergeant, Company L, 8th U.S. Cavalry. *Place and date:* At Hell Canyon, Ariz., 3 July 1869. *Entered service at:* ———. *Birth:* Sussex County, N.J. *Date of issue:* 3 March 1870. *Citation:* Conspicuous gallantry in action.

BRANAGAN, EDWARD

Rank and organization: Private, Company F, 4th U.S. Cavalry. *Place and date:* At Red River, Tex., 29 September 1872. *Entered service at:* ———. *Birth:* Ireland. *Date of issue:* 19 November 1872. *Citation:* Gallantry in action.

BRANT, ABRAM B.

Rank and organization: Private, Company D, 7th U.S. Cavalry. *Place and date:* At Little Big Horn, Mont., 25 June 1876. *Entered service at:* St. Louis, Mo. *Birth:* New York, N.Y. *Date of issue:* 5 October 1878. *Citation:* Brought water for the wounded under a most galling fire.

BRATLING, FRANK

Rank and organization: Corporal, Company C, 8th U.S. Cavalry. *Place and date:* Near Fort Selden, N. Mex., 8–11 July 1873. *Entered service at:* ———. *Birth:* Germany. *Date of issue:* 12 August 1875. *Citation:* Services against hostile Indians.

BRETT, LLOYD M.

Rank and organization: Second Lieutenant, 2d U.S. Cavalry. *Place and date:* At O'Fallons Creek, Mont., 1 April 1880. *Entered service at:* Malden, Mass. *Born:* 22 February 1856, Dead River, Maine. *Date of issue:* 7 February 1895. *Citation:* Fearless exposure and dashing bravery in cutting off the Indians' pony herd, thereby greatly crippling the hostiles.

BROGAN, JAMES

Rank and organization: Sergeant, Company G, 6th U.S. Cavalry. *Place and date:* At Simon Valley, Ariz., 14 December 1877. *Entered service at:* ———. *Birth:* Ireland. *Date of issue:* 9 January 1880. *Citation:* Engaged singlehanded 2 renegade Indians until his horse was shot under him and then pursued them so long as he was able.

BROPHY, JAMES

Rank and organization: Private, Company B, 8th U.S. Cavalry. *Place and date:* Arizona, 1868. *Entered service at:* Stockton, Calif. *Born:* 20 May 1846, Kilkenny, Ireland. *Date of issue:* 24 July 1869. *Citation:* Bravery in scouts and actions against Indians.

BROWN, BENJAMIN

Rank and organization: Sergeant, Company C, 24th U.S. Infantry. *Place and date:* Arizona, 11 May 1889. *Entered service at:* ———. *Birth:* Spotsylvania County, Va. *Date of issue:* 19 February 1890. *Cita-*

652

tion: Although shot in the abdomen, in a fight between a paymaster's escort and robbers, did not leave the field until again wounded through both arms.

BROWN, JAMES

Rank and organization: Sergeant, Company F, 5th U.S. Cavalry. *Place and date:* At Davidson Canyon near Camp Crittenden, Ariz., 27 August 1872. *Entered service at:* ———. *Birth:* Wexford, Ireland. *Date of issue:* 4 December 1874. *Citation:* In command of a detachment of 4 men defeated a superior force.

BROWN, LORENZO D.

Rank and organization: Private, Company A, 7th U.S. Infantry. *Place and date:* At Big Hole, Mont. 9 August 1877. *Entered service at:* Indianapolis, Ind. *Birth:* Davidson County, N.C. *Date of issue:* 8 May 1878. *Citation:* After having been severely wounded in right shoulder, continued to do duty in a most courageous manner.

BRYAN, WILLIAM C.

Rank and organization: Hospital Steward, U.S. Army. *Place and date:* At Powder River, Wyo., 17 March 1876. *Entered service at:* St. Louis, Mo. *Born:* 9 September 1850, Zanesville, Ohio. *Date of issue:* 15 June 1899. *Citation:* Accompanied a detachment of cavalry in a charge on a village of hostile Indians and fought through the engagements, having his horse killed under him. He continued to fight on foot, and under severe fire and without assistance conveyed 2 wounded comrades to places of safety, saving them from capture.

BURKARD, OSCAR

Rank and organization: Private, Hospital Corps, U.S. Army. *Place and date:* At Leech Lake, Minn., 5 October 1898. *Entered service at:* Hay Creek, Minn. *Born:* 21 December 1877, Achern, Germany. *Date of issue:* 21 August 1899. *Citation:* For distinguished bravery in action against hostile Indians. [Note: This, the last Medal of Honor won in an Indian campaign, was awarded for an action during the uprising of Chippewa Indians, on Lake Leech, northern Minnesota, 5 October 1898.]

BURKE, PATRICK J.

Rank and organization: Farrier, Company B, 8th U.S. Cavalry. *Place and date:* Arizona, 1868. *Entered service at:* ———. *Birth:* Ireland. *Date of issue:* 24 July 1869. *Citation:* Bravery in scouts and actions against Indians.

BURKE, RICHARD

Rank and organization: Private, Company G, 5th U.S. Infantry. *Place and date:* At Cedar Creek, etc., Mont., October 1876 to January 1877. *Entered service at:* ———. *Birth:* Ireland. *Date of issue:* 27 April 1877. *Citation:* Gallantry in engagements.

BURNETT, GEORGE R.

Rank and organization: Second Lieutenant, 9th U.S. Cavalry. *Place and date:* At Cuchillo Negro Mountains, N. Mex., 16 August 1881. *Entered service at:* Spring Mills, Pa. *Birth:* Lower Providence Township, Pa. *Date of issue:* 23 July 1897. *Citation:* Saved the life of a dismounted soldier, who was in imminent danger of being cut off, by alone galloping quickly to his assistance under heavy fire and escorting him to a place of safety, his horse being twice shot in this action.

BUTLER, EDMOND

Rank and organization: Captain, 5th U.S. Infantry. *Place and date:* At Wolf Mountain, Mont., 8 January 1877. *Entered service at:* Brooklyn, N.Y. *Birth:* Ireland. *Date of issue:* 27 November 1894. *Citation:* Most distinguished gallantry in action with hostile Indians.

BYRNE, DENIS

Rank and organization: Sergeant, Company G, 5th U.S. Infantry. *Place and date:* At Cedar Creek, etc., Mont., October 1876 to January 1877. *Entered service at:* ———. *Birth:* Ireland. *Date of issue:* 27 April 1877. *Citation:* Gallantry in engagements.

CABLE, JOSEPH A.

Rank and organization: Private, Company I, 5th U.S. Infantry. *Place and date:* At Cedar Creek, etc., Mont., October 1876 to January 1877. *Entered service at:* Wisconsin. *Birth:* Cape Girardeau, Mo. *Date of issue:* 27 April 1877. *Citation:* Gallantry in action.

CALLEN, THOMAS J.

Rank and organization: Private, Company B, 7th U.S. Cavalry. *Place and date:* At Little Big Horn, Mont., 25–26 June 1876. *Entered service at:* Boston, Mass. *Birth:* Ireland. *Date of issue:* 24 October 1896. *Citation:* Volunteered and succeeded in obtaining water for the wounded of the command; also displayed conspicuously good conduct in assisting to drive away the Indians.

CALVERT, JAMES S.

Rank and organization: Private, Company C, 5th U.S. Infantry. *Place and date:* At Cedar Creek, etc., Mont., October 1876 to January 1877. *Entered service at:* ———. *Birth:* Athens County, Ohio. *Date of issue:* 27 April 1877. *Citation:* Gallantry in action.

CANFIELD, HETH

Rank and organization: Private, Company C, 2d U.S. Cavalry. *Place and date:* At Little Blue, Nebr. 15 May 1870. *Entered service at:* ———. *Birth:* New Meddford, Conn. *Place of issue:* 22 June 1870. *Citation:* Gallantry in action.

CARPENTER, LOUIS H.

Rank and organization: Captain, Company H, 10th U.S. Cavalry. *Place and date:* At Indian campaigns, Kansas and Colorado, September–October 1868. *Entered service at:* Philadelphia, Pa. *Birth:*

Glassboro, N.J. *Date of issue:* 8 April 1898. *Citation:* Was gallant and meritorious throughout the campaigns, especially in the combat of October 15 and in the forced march on September 23, 24 and 25 to the relief of Forsyth's Scouts, who were known to be in danger of annihilation by largely superior forces of Indians.

CARR, JOHN

Rank and organization: Private, Company G, 8th U.S. Cavalry. *Place and date:* At Chiricahua Mountains, Ariz., 29 October 1869. *Entered service at:* ———. *Birth:* Columbus, Ohio. *Date of issue:* 14 February 1870. *Citation:* Gallantry in action.

CARROLL, THOMAS

Rank and organization: Private, Company L, 8th U.S. Cavalry. *Place and date:* Arizona, August to October 1868. *Entered service at:* ———. *Birth:* Ireland. *Date of issue:* 24 July 1869. *Citation:* Bravery in scouts and actions against Indians.

CARTER, GEORGE

Rank and organization: Private, Company B, 8th U.S. Cavalry. *Place and date:* Arizona, August to October 1868. *Entered service at:* ———. *Birth:* Ireland. *Date of issue:* 24 July 1869. *Citation:* Bravery in scouts and actions against Indians.

CARTER, MASON

Rank and organization: First Lieutenant, 5th U.S. Infantry. *Place and date:* At Bear Paw Mountain, Mont., 30 September 1877. *Entered service at:* Augusta, Ga. *Birth:* Augusta, Ga. *Date of issue:* 27 November 1894. *Citation:* Led a charge under a galling fire, in which he inflicted great loss upon the enemy.

CARTER, ROBERT G.

Rank and organization: Second Lieutenant, 4th U.S. Cavalry. *Place and date:* On Brazos, River, Tex., 10 October 1871. *Entered service at:* Bradford, Mass. *Birth:* Bridgeport, Maine. *Date of issue:* 27 February 1900. *Citation:* Held the left of the line with a few men during the charge of a large body of Indians, after the right of the line had retreated, and by delivering a rapid fire succeeded in checking the enemy until other troops came to the rescue.

CARTER, WILLIAM H.

Rank and organization: First Lieutenant, 6th U.S. Cavalry. *Place and date:* At Cibicu, Ariz., 30 August 1881. *Entered service at:* New York, N.Y. *Birth:* Nashville, Tenn. *Date of issue:* 17 September 1891. *Citation:* Rescued, with the voluntary assistance of 2 soldiers, the wounded from under a heavy fire.

CASEY, JAMES S.

Rank and organization: Captain, 5th U.S. Infantry. *Place and date:* At Wolf Mountain, Mont., 8 January 1877. *Entered service at:* New York, N.Y. *Birth:* Philadelphia, Pa. *Date of issue:* 27 November 1894. *Citation:* Led his command in a successful charge against superior numbers of the enemy strongly posted.

CHEEVER, BENJAMIN H., Jr.

Rank and organization: First Lieutenant, 6th U.S. Cavalry. *Place and date:* At White River, S. Dak., 1 January 1891. *Entered service at:* Washington, D.C. *Born:* 7 June 1850, Washington, D.C. *Date of issue:* 25 April 1891. *Citation:* Headed the advance across White River, partly frozen, in a spirited movement to the effective assistance of Troop K, 6th U.S. Cavalry.

CHIQUITO

Rank and organization: Indian Scouts. *Place and date:* Winter of 1871–73. *Entered service at:* ———. *Birth:* Arizona. *Date of issue:* 12 April 1875. *Citation:* Gallant conduct during campaigns and engagements with Apaches.

CLANCY, JOHN E.

Rank and organization: Musician, Company E, 1st U.S. Artillery. *Place and date:* At Wounded Knee Creek, S. Dak., 29 December 1890. *Entered service at:* ———. *Birth:* New York, N.Y. *Date of issue:* 23 January 1892. *Citation:* Twice voluntarily rescued wounded comrades under fire of the enemy.

CLARK, WILFRED

Rank and organization: Private, Company L, 2d U.S. Cavalry. *Place and date:* At Big Hole, Mont., 9 August 1877; at Camas Meadows, Idaho, 20 August 1877. *Entered service at:* ———. *Birth:* Philadelphia, Pa. *Date of issue:* 28 February 1878. *Citation:* Conspicuous gallantry; especial skill as sharpshooter.

CLARKE, POWHATAN H.

Rank and organization: Second Lieutenant, 10th U.S. Cavalry. *Place and date:* At Pinito Mountains, Sonora, Mex., 3 May 1886. *Entered service at:* Baltimore, Md. *Birth:* Alexandria, La. *Date of issue:* 12 March 1891. *Citation:* Rushed forward to the rescue of a soldier who was severely wounded and lay, disabled, exposed to the enemy's fire, and carried him to a place of safety.

COMFORT, JOHN W.

Rank and organization: Corporal, Company A, 4th U.S. Cavalry. *Place and date:* At Staked Plains, Tex., 5 November 1874. *Entered service at:* ———. *Birth:* Philadelphia, Pa. *Date of issue:* 13 October 1875. *Citation:* Ran down and killed an Indian.

CONNOR, JOHN

Rank and organization: Corporal, Company H, 6th U.S. Cavalry. *Place and date:* At Wichita River, Tex., 12 July 1870. *Entered service at:* ———. *Birth:* Ireland. *Date of issue:* 25 August 1870. *Citation:* Gallantry in action.

COONROD, AQUILLA

Rank and organization: Sergeant, Company C, 5th U.S. Infantry. *Place and date:* At Cedar Creek, etc., Mont., October 1876 to January

1877. *Entered service at:* Byran, Ohio. *Birth:* Williams County, Ohio. *Date of issue:* 27 April 1877. *Citation:* Gallantry in action.

CORCORAN, MICHAEL

Rank and organization: Corporal, Company E, 8th U.S. Cavalry. *Place and date:* At Agua Fria River, Ariz., 25 August 1869. *Entered service at:* ———. *Birth:* Philadelphia, Pa. *Date of issue:* 3 March 1870. *Citation:* Gallantry in action.

CO-RUX-TE-CHOD-ISH (Mad Bear)

Rank and organization: Sergeant, Pawnee Scouts, U.S. Army. *Place and date:* At Republican River, Kans., 8 July 1869. *Entered service at:* ———. *Birth:* Nebraska. *Date of issue:* 24 August 1869. *Citation:* Ran out from the command in pursuit of a dismounted Indian; was shot down and badly wounded by a bullet from his own command.

CRAIG, SAMUEL H.

Rank and organization: Sergeant, Company D, 4th U.S. Cavalry. *Place and date:* At Santa Cruz Mountains, Mex., 15 May 1886. *Entered service at:* ———. *Birth:* New Market, N.H. *Date of issue:* 27 April 1887. *Citation:* Conspicuous gallantry during an attack on a hostile Apache Indian Camp; seriously wounded.

CRANDALL, CHARLES

Rank and organization: Private, Company B, 8th U.S. Cavalry. *Place and date:* Arizona, August to October 1868. *Entered service at:* Worcester, Mass. *Birth:* Worcester, Mass. *Date of issue:* 24 July 1869. *Citation:* Bravery in scouts and actions against Indians.

CRIST, JOHN

Rank and organization: Sergeant, Company L, 8th U.S. Cavalry. *Place and date:* Arizona, 26 November 1869. *Entered service at:* ———. *Birth:* Baltimore, Md. *Date of issue:* 3 March 1870. *Citation:* Gallantry in action.

CRISWELL, BANJAMIN C.

Rank and organization: Sergeant, Company B, 7th U.S. Cavalry. *Place and date:* At Little Big Horn River, Mont., 25 June 1876. *Entered service at:* ———. *Birth:* Marshall County, W. Va. *Date of issue:* 5 October 1878. *Citation:* Rescued the body of Lt. Hodgson from within the enemy's lines; brought up ammunition and encouraged the men in the most exposed positions under heavy fire.

CRUSE, THOMAS

Rank and organization: Second Lieutenant, 6th U.S. Cavalry. *Place and date:* At Big Dry Fork, Ariz., 17 July 1882. *Entered service at:* Owensboro, Ky. *Birth:* Owensboro, Ky. *Date of issue:* 12 July 1892. *Citation:* Gallantly charged hostile Indians, and with his carbine compelled a party of them to keep under cover of their breastworks, thus being enabled to recover a severely wounded soldier.

CUBBERLY, WILLIAM G.

Rank and organization: Private, Company L, 8th U.S. Cavalry. *Place and date:* At San Carlos, Ariz., 30 May 1868. *Entered service at:* ———. *Birth:* Butler County, Ohio. *Date of issue:* 28 July 1868. *Citation:* With 2 other men he volunteered to search for a wagon passage out of a 4,000-foot valley wherein an infantry column was immobile. This small group passed 6 miles among hostile Apache terrain finding the sought passage. On their return trip down the canyon they were attacked by Apache who were successfully held at bay.

CUNNINGHAM, CHARLES

Rank and organization: Corporal, Company B, 7th U.S. Cavalry. *Place and date:* At Little Big Horn River, Mont., 25 June 1876. *Entered service at:* New York, N.Y. *Birth:* Hudson, N.Y. *Date of issue:* 5 October 1878. *Citation:* Declined to leave the line when wounded in the neck during heavy fire and fought bravely all next day.

DAILY, CHARLES

Rank and organization: Private, Company B, 8th U.S. Cavalry. *Place and date:* Arizona, August to October 1868. *Entered service at:* ———. *Birth:* Ireland. *Date of issue:* 24 July 1869. *Citation:* Bravery in scouts and actions against Indians.

DANIELS, JAMES T.

Rank and organization: Sergeant, Company L, 4th U.S. Cavalry. *Place and date:* Arizona, 7 March 1890. *Entered service at:* ———. *Birth:* Richland County, Ill. *Date of issue:* 15 May 1890. *Citation:* Untiring energy and cool gallantry under fire in an engagement with Apache Indians.

DAWSON, MICHAEL

Rank and organization: Trumpeter, Company H, 6th U.S. Cavalry. *Place and date:* At Sappa Creek, Kans., 23 April 1875. *Entered service at:* ———. *Birth:* Boston, Mass. *Date of issue:* 16 November 1876. *Citation:* Gallantry in action.

DAY, MATTHIAS W.

Rank and organization: Second Lieutenant, 9th U.S. Cavalry. *Place and date:* At Las Animas Canyon, N. Mex., 18 September 1879. *Entered service at:* Oberlin, Ohio. *Birth:* Mansfield, Ohio. *Date of issue:* 7 May 1890. *Citation:* Advanced alone into the enemy's lines and carried off a wounded soldier of his command under a hot fire and after he had been ordered to retreat.

DAY, WILLIAM L.

Rank and organization: First Sergeant, Company E, 5th U.S. Cavalry. *Place and date:* 1872–73. *Entered service at:* ———. *Birth:* Barron County, Ky. *Date of issue:* 12 April 1875. *Citation:* Gallant conduct during campaigns and engagements with Apaches.

658

DE ARMOND, WILLIAM

Rank and organization: Sergeant, Company I, 5th U.S. Infantry. *Place and date:* At Upper Washita, Tex., 9–11 September 1874. *Entered service at:* ———. *Birth:* Butler County, Ohio. *Date of issue:* 23 April 1875. *Citation:* Gallantry in action.

DEARY, GEORGE

Rank and organization: Sergeant, Company L, 5th U.S. Cavalry. *Place and date:* At Apache Creek, Ariz., 2 April 1874. *Entered service at:* ———. *Birth:* Philadelphia, Pa. *Date of issue:* 12 April 1875. *Citation:* Gallantry in action.

DEETLINE, FREDERICK

Rank and organization: Private, Company D, 7th U.S. Cavalry. *Place and date:* At Little Big Horn, Mont., 25 June 1876. *Entered service at:* Baltimore, Md. *Birth:* Germany. *Date of issue:* 15 October 1878. *Citation:* Voluntarily brought water to the wounded under fire.

DENNY, JOHN

Rank and organization: Sergeant, Company C, 9th U.S. Cavalry. *Place and date:* At Las Animas Canyon, N. Mex., 18 September 1879. *Entered service at:* 1867, Elmira, N.Y. *Birth:* Big Flats, N.Y. *Date of issue:* 27 November 1894. *Citation:* Removed a wounded comrade, under a heavy fire, to a place of safety.

DICKENS, CHARLES H.

Rank and organization: Corporal, Company G, 8th U.S. Cavalry. *Place and date:* At Chiricahua Mountains, Ariz., 20 October 1869. *Entered service at:* ———. *Birth:* Ireland. *Date of issue:* 14 February 1870. *Citation:* Gallantry in action.

DODGE, FRANCIS S.

Rank and organization: Captain, Troop D, 9th U.S. Cavalry. *Place and date:* Near White River Agency, Colo., 29 September 1879. *Entered service at:* Danvers, Mass. *Born:* 11 September 1842, Danvers, Mass. *Date of issue:* 2 April 1898. *Citation:* With a force of 40 men rode all night to the relief of a command that had been defeated and was besieged by an overwhelming force of Indians, reached the field at daylight, joined in the action and fought for 3 days.

DONAHUE, JOHN L.

Rank and organization: Private, Company G, 8th U.S. Cavalry. *Place and date:* At Chiricahua Mountains, Ariz., 20 October 1869. *Entered service at:* ———. *Birth:* Baltimore County, Md. *Date of issue:* 14 February 1870. *Citation:* Gallantry in action.

DONAVAN, CORNELIUS

Rank and organization: Sergeant, Company E, 8th U.S. Cavalry. *Place and date:* At Agua Fria River, Ariz., 25 August 1869. *Entered service at:* ———. *Birth:* Ireland. *Date of issue:* 3 March 1870. *Citation:* Gallantry in action.

DONELLY, JOHN S.

Rank and organization: Private, Company G, 5th U.S. Infantry. *Place and date:* At Cedar Creek, etc., Mont., October 1876 to January 1877. *Entered service at:* Buffalo, N.Y. *Birth:* Ireland. *Date of issue:* 27 April 1877. *Citation:* Gallantry in action.

DOUGHERTY, WILLIAM

Rank and organization: Blacksmith, Company B, 8th U.S. Cavalry. *Place and date:* Arizona, August to October 1868. *Entered service at:* ———. *Birth:* Detroit, Mich. *Date of issue:* 24 July 1869. *Citation:* Bravery in scouts and actions against Indians.

DOWLING, JAMES

Rank and organization: Corporal, Company B, 8th U.S. Cavalry. *Place and date:* Arizona, August to October 1868. *Entered service at:* Cleveland, Ohio. *Birth:* Ireland. *Date of issue:* 24 July 1869. *Citation:* Bravery in scouts and actions against Indians.

EDWARDS, WILLIAM D.

Rank and organization: First Sergeant, Company F, 7th U.S. Infantry. *Place and date:* At Big Hole, Mont., 9 August 1877. *Entered service at:* ———. *Birth:* Brooklyn, N.Y. *Date of issue:* 2 December 1878. *Citation:* Bravery in action.

ELDRIDGE, GEORGE H.

Rank and organization: Sergeant, Company C, 6th U.S. Cavalry. *Place and date:* At Wichita River, Tex., 12 July 1870. *Entered service at:* ———. *Birth:* Sacketts Harbor, N.Y. *Date of issue:* 25 August 1870. *Citation:* Gallantry in action.

ELSATSOOSU

Rank and organization: Corporal, Indian Scouts. *Place and date:* Winter of 1872–73. *Entered service at:* ———. *Birth:* Arizona. *Date of issue:* 12 April 1875. *Citation:* Gallant conduct during campaigns and engagements with Apaches.

ELWOOD, EDWIN L.

Rank and organization: Private, Company G, 8th U.S. Cavalry. *Place and date:* At Chiricahua Mountains, Ariz., 20 October 1869. *Entered service at:* California. *Birth:* St. Louis, Mo. *Date of issue:* 14 February 1870. *Citation:* Gallantry in action.

EMMET, ROBERT TEMPLE

Rank and organization: Second Lieutenant, 9th U.S. Cavalry. *Place and date:* At Las Animas Canyon, N. Mex., 18 September 1879. *Entered service at:* New York, N.Y. *Birth:* New York, N.Y. *Date of issue:* 24 August 1899. *Citation:* Lt. Emmet was in G Troop which was sent to relieve a detachment of soldiers under attack by hostile Apaches. During a flank attack on the Indian camp, made to divert the hostiles, Lt. Emmet and 5 of his men became surrounded when the Indians returned to defend their camp. Finding that the Indians were making for a position from which they could direct their fire on the retreating troop, the Lieutenant held his point with his party until the soldiers reached the safety of a canyon. Lt. Emmet then continued to hold his position while his party recovered their horses. The enemy force consisted of approximately 200.

EVANS, WILLIAM

Rank and organization: Private, Company E, 7th U.S. Infantry. *Place and date:* At Big Horn, Mont., 9 July 1876. *Entered service at:* St. Louis, Mo. *Birth:* Ireland. *Date of issue:* 2 December 1876. *Citation:* Carried dispatches to Brig. Gen. Crook through a country occupied by Sioux.

FACTOR, POMPEY

Rank and organization: Private, Indian Scouts. *Place and date:* At Pecos River, Tex., 25 April 1875. *Entered service at:* ———. *Birth:* Arkansas. *Date of issue:* 28 May 1875. *Citation:* With 3 other men, he participated in a charge against 25 hostiles while on a scouting patrol.

FALCOTT, HENRY

Rank and organization: Sergeant, Company L, 8th U.S. Cavalry. *Place and date:* Arizona, August to October 1868. *Entered service at:* ———. *Birth:* France. *Date of issue:* 24 July 1869. *Citation:* Bravery in scouts and actions against Indians.

FARREN, DANIEL

Rank and organization: Private, Company B, 8th U.S. Cavalry. *Place and date:* Arizona, August to October 1868. *Entered service at:* ———. *Birth:* Ireland. *Date of issue:* 24 July 1869. *Citation:* Bravery in scouts and actions against Indians.

FEASTER, MOSHEIM

Rank and organization: Private, Company E, 7th U.S. Cavalry. *Place and date:* At Wounded Knee Creek, S. Dak., 29 December 1890. *Entered service at:* Schellburg, Pa. *Birth:* Schellburg, Pa. *Date of issue:* 23 June 1891. *Citation:* Extraordinary gallantry.

FEGAN, JAMES

Rank and organization: Sergeant, Company H, 3d U.S. Infantry. *Place and date:* At Plum Creek, Kans., March 1868. *Entered service at:* ———. *Birth:* Ireland. *Date of issue:* 19 October 1878. *Citation:* While in charge of a powder train en route from Fort Harker to Fort Dodge, Kans., was attached by a party of desperadoes, who attempted to rescue a deserter in his charge and to fire the train. Sgt. Fegan, singlehanded, repelled the attacking party, wounding 2 of them, and brought his train through in safety.

FERRARI, GEORGE

Rank and organization: Corporal, Company D, 8th U.S. Cavalry. *Place and date:* At Red Creek, Ariz., 23 September 1869. *Entered service at:* Montgomery County, Ohio. *Birth:* New York, N.Y. *Date of issue:* 23 November 1869. *Citation:* Gallantry in action.

FICHTER, HERMANN

Rank and organization: Private, Company F, 3d U.S. Cavalry. *Place and date:* At Whetstone Mountains, Ariz., 5 May 1871. *Entered service at:* ———. *Birth:* Germany. *Date of issue:* 13 November 1871. *Citation:* Gallantry in action.

FOLEY, JOHN H.

Rank and organization: Sergeant, Company B, 3d U.S. Cavalry. *Place and date:* At Loupe Fork, Platte River, Nebr., 26 April 1872. *Entered service at:* ———. *Birth:* Ireland. *Date of issue:* 22 May 1872. *Citation:* Gallantry in action.

FOLLY, WILLIAM H.

Rank and organization: Private, Company B, 8th U.S. Cavalry. *Place and date:* Arizona, August to October 1868. *Entered service at:* ———. *Birth:* Bergen County, N.J. *Date of issue:* 24 July 1869. *Citation:* Bravery in scouts and actions against Indians.

FORAN, NICHOLAS

Rank and organization: Private, Company L, 8th U.S. Cavalry. *Place and date:* Arizona, August to October 1868. *Entered service at:* ———. *Birth:* Ireland. *Date of issue:* 24 July 1869. *Citation:* Bravery in scouts and actions against Indians.

FORSYTH, THOMAS H.

Rank and organization: First Sergeant, Company M, 4th U.S. Cavalry. *Place and date:* At Powder River, Wyo., 25 November 1876. *Entered service at:* ———. *Birth:* Hartford, Conn. *Date of issue:* 14 July 1891. *Citation:* Though dangerously wounded, he maintained his ground with a small party against a largely superior force after his commanding officer had been shot down during a sudden attack and rescued that officer and a comrade from the enemy.

FOSTER, WILLIAM

Rank and organization: Sergeant, Company F, 4th U.S. Cavalry. *Place and date:* At Red River, Tex., 29 September 1872. *Entered service at:* ———. *Birth:* England, *Date of issue:* 19 November 1872. *Citation:* Gallantry in action.

FREEMEYER, CHRISTOPHER

Rank and organization: Private, Company D, 5th U.S. Infantry. *Place and date:* At Cedar Creek, etc., Mont., 21 October 1876 to 8 January 1877. *Entered service at:* Chicago, Ill. *Birth:* Germany. *Date of issue:* 27 April 1877. *Citation:* Gallantry in action.

GARDINER, PETER W.

Rank and organization: Private, Company H, 6th U.S. Cavalry. *Place and date:* At Sappa Creek, Kans., 23 April 1875. *Entered service at:* ———. *Birth:* Carlisle, N.Y. *Date of issue:* 16 November 1876. *Citation:* With 5 other men he waded in mud and water up the creek to a position directly behind an entrenched Cheyenne position, who were using natural bank pits to good advantage against the main column. This surprise attack from the enemy rear broke their resistance.

GARDNER, CHARLES

Rank and organization: Private, Company B, 8th U.S. Cavalry. *Place and date:* Arizona, August to October 1868. *Entered service at:* ———. *Birth:* Bavaria. *Date of issue:* 24 July 1869. *Citation:* Bravery in scouts and actions against Indians.

GARLAND, HARRY

Rank and organization: Corporal, Company L, 2d U.S. Cavalry. *Place and date:* At Little Muddy Creek, Mont., 7 May 1877; at Camas Meadows, Idaho, 29 August 1877. *Entered service at:* ———. *Birth:* Boston, Mass. *Date of issue:* 28 February 1878. *Citation:* Gallantry in action with hostile Sioux, at Little Muddy Creek, Mont.; having been wounded in the hip so as to be unable to stand, at Camas Meadows, Idaho, he still continued to direct the men under his charge until the enemy withdrew.

GARLINGTON, ERNEST A.

Rank and organization: First Lieutenant, 7th U.S. Cavalry. *Place and date:* At Wounded Knee Creek, S. Dak., 29 December 1890. *Entered service at:* Athens, Ga. *Born:* 20 February 1853, Newberry, S.C. *Date of issue:* 26 September 1893. *Citation:* Distinguished gallantry.

GATES, GEORGE

Rank and organization: Bugler, Company F, 8th U.S. Cavalry. *Place and date:* At Picacho Mountain, Ariz., 4 June 1869. *Entered service at:* ———. *Birth:* Delaware County, Ohio. *Date of issue:* 3 March 1870. *Citation:* Killed an Indian warrior and captured his arms.

GAY, THOMAS H.

Rank and organization: Private, Company B, 8th U.S. Cavalry. *Place and date:* Arizona, August to October 1868. *Entered service at:* ———. *Birth:* Prince Edward Island. *Date of issue:* 24 July 1869. *Citation:* Bravery in scouts and actions against Indians.

GEIGER, GEORGE

Rank and organization: Sergeant, Company H, 7th U.S. Cavalry. *Place and date:* At Little Big Horn River, Mont., 25 June 1876. *Entered service at:* ———. *Birth:* Cincinnati, Ohio. *Date of issue:* 5 October 1878. *Citation:* With 3 comrades during the entire engagement courageously held a position that secured water for the command.

GEORGIAN, JOHN

Rank and organization: Private, Company G, 8th U.S. Cavalry. *Place and date:* At Chiricahua Mountains, Ariz., 20 October 1869. *Entered service at:* ———. *Birth:* Germany. *Date of issue:* 14 February 1870. *Citation:* Bravery in action.

GERBER, FREDERICK W.

Rank and organization: Sergeant Major, U.S. Engineers. *Place and date:* ———, 1839–71. *Entered service at:* ———. *Birth:* Germany. *Date of issue:* 8 November 1871. *Citation:* Distinguished gallantry in many actions and in recognition of long, faithful, and meritorious services covering a period of 32 years.

*GIVEN, JOHN J.

Rank and organization: Corporal, Company K, 6th U.S. Cavalry. *Place and date:* At Wichita River, Tex., 12 July 1870. *Entered service at:* Cincinnati, Ohio. *Birth:* Daviess County, Ky. *Date of issue:* 25 August 1870. *Citation:* Bravery in action.

GLAVINSKI, ALBERT

Rank and organization: Blacksmith, Company M, 3d U.S. Cavalry. *Place and date:* At Powder River, Mont., 17 March 1876. *Entered service at:* ———. *Birth:* Germany. *Date of issue:* 16 October 1877. *Citation:* During a retreat he selected exposed positions, he was part of the rear guard.

GLOVER, T. B.

Rank and organization: Sergeant, Troop B, 2d U.S. Cavalry. *Place and date:* At Mizpah Creek, Mont., 10 April 1879; at Pumpkin Creek, Mont., 10 February 1880. *Entered service at:* ———. *Birth:* New York, N.Y. *Date of issue:* 20 November 1897. *Citation:* While in charge of small scouting parties, fought, charged, surrounded, and captured war parties of Sioux Indians.

GLYNN, MICHAEL

Rank and organization: Private, Company F, 5th U.S. Cavalry. *Place and date:* At Whetstone Mountains, Ariz., 13 July 1872. *Entered service at:* ———. *Birth:* Ireland. *Date of issue:* 4 December 1874. *Citation:* Drove off, singlehanded, 8 hostile Indians, killing and wounding 5.

GODFREY, EDWARD S.

Rank and organization: Captain, 7th U.S. Cavalry. *Place and date:* At Bear Paw Mountain, Mont., 30 September 1877. *Entered service at:* Ottawa, Putnam County, Ohio. *Born:* 9 October 1843, Ottawa, Ohio. *Date of issue:* 27 November 1894. *Citation:* Led his command into action when he was severely wounded.

GOLDEN, PATRICK

Rank and organization: Sergeant, Company B, 8th U.S. Cavalry. *Place and date:* Arizona, August to October 1868. *Entered service at:* ———. *Birth:* Ireland. *Date of issue:* 24 July 1869. *Citation:* Bravery in scouts and actions against Indians.

GOLDIN, THEODORE W.

Rank and organization: Private, Troop G, 7th U.S. Cavalry. *Place and date:* At Little Big Horn, Mont., 26 June 1876. *Entered service at:*

Chicago, Ill. *Born:* 25 July 1855, Avon, Rock County, Wis. *Date of issue:* 21 December 1895. *Citation:* One of a party of volunteers who, under a heavy fire from the Indians, went for and brought water to the wounded.

GOODMAN, DAVID

Rank and organization: Private, Company L, 8th U.S. Cavalry. *Place and date:* At Lyry Creek, Ariz., 14 October 1869. *Entered service at:* ———. *Birth:* Paxton, Mass. *Date of issue:* 3 March 1870. *Citation:* Bravery in action.

GRANT, GEORGE

2. *Rank and organization:* Sergeant, Company E, 18th U.S. Infantry. *Place and date:* At Fort Phil Kearny to Fort C. F. Smith, Dakota Territory, February 1867. *Entered service at:* *IN*. *Birth:* Raleigh, Tenn. *Date of issue:* 6 May 1871. *Citation:* Bravery, energy, and perseverance, involving much suffering and privation through attacks by hostile Indians, deep snows, etc., while voluntarily carrying dispatches.

GREAVES, CLINTON

Rank and organization: Corporal, Company C, 9th U.S. Cavalry. *Place and date:* At Florida Mountains, N. Mex., 24 January 1877. *Entered service at:* Prince Georges County, Md. *Birth:* Madison County, Va. *Date of issue:* 26 June 1879. *Citation:* While part of a small detachment to persuade a band of renegade Apache Indians to surrender, his group was surrounded. Cpl. Greaves in the center of the savage hand-to-hand fighting, managed to shoot and bash a gap through the swarming Apaches, permitting his companions to break free.

GREEN, FRANCIS C.

Rank and organization: Sergeant, Company K, 8th U.S. Cavalry. *Place and date:* Arizona, 1868 and 1869. *Entered service at:* ———. *Birth:* Mount Vernon, Ind. *Date of issue:* 6 September 1869. *Citation:* Bravery in action.

GREEN, JOHN

Rank and organization: Major, 1st U.S. Cavalry. *Place and date:* At the Lava Beds, Calif., 17 January 1873. *Entered service at:* Ohio. *Birth:* Germany. *Date of issue:* 18 November 1897. *Citation:* In order to reassure his command, this officer, in the most fearless manner and exposed to very great danger, walked in front of the line; the command, thus encouraged, advanced over the lava upon the Indians who were concealed among the rocks.

GRESHAM, JOHN C.

Rank and organization: First Lieutenant, 7th U.S. Cavalry. *Place and date:* At Wounded Knee Creek, S. Dak., 29 December 1890. *Entered service at:* Lancaster Courthouse, Va. *Birth:* Virginia. *Date of issue:* 26 March 1895. *Citation:* Voluntarily led a party into a ravine to dislodge Sioux Indians concealed therein. He was wounded during this action.

GRIMES, EDWARD P.

Rank and organization: Sergeant, Company F, 5th U.S. Cavalry. *Place and date:* At Milk River, Colo., 29 September to 5 October 1879. *Entered service at:* ———. *Birth:* Dover, N.H. *Date of issue:* 27 January 1880. *Citation:* The command being almost out of ammunition and surrounded on 3 sides by the enemy, he voluntarily brought up a supply under heavy fire at almost point blank range.

GUNTHER, JACOB

Rank and organization: Corporal, Company E, 8th U.S. Cavalry. *Place and date:* Arizona, 1868 and 1869. *Entered service at:* ———. *Birth:* Schuylkill County, Pa. *Date of issue:* 6 September 1869. *Citation:* Bravery in scouts and actions against Indians.

HADDOO, JOHN

Rank and organization: Corporal, Company B, 5th U.S. Infantry. *Place and date:* At Cedar Creek, etc., Mont., October 1876 to 8 January 1877. *Entered service at:* ———. *Birth:* Boston, Mass. *Date of issue:* 27 April 1877. *Citation:* Gallantry in action.

HALL, JOHN

Rank and organization: Private, Company B, 8th U.S. Cavalry. *Place and date:* Arizona, August to October 1868. *Entered service at:* ———. *Birth:* Logan County, Ill. *Date of issue:* 24 July 1869. *Citation:* Bravery in scouts and actions against Indians.

HALL, WILLIAM P.

Rank and organization: First Lieutenant, 5th U.S. Cavalry. *Place and date:* Near Camp on White River, Colo., 20 October 1879. *Entered service at:* Huntsville, Mo. *Birth:* Randolph County, Mo. *Date of issue:* 18 September 1897. *Citation:* With a reconnoitering party of 3 men, was attacked by 35 Indians and several times exposed himself to draw the fire of the enemy, giving his small party opportunity to reply with much effect.

HAMILTON, FRANK

Rank and organization: Private, Company E, 8th U.S. Cavalry. *Place and date:* At Agua Fria River, Ariz., 25 August 1869. *Entered service at:* ———. *Birth:* Ireland. *Date of issue:* 3 March 1870. *Citation:* Gallantry in action.

HAMILTON, MATHEW H.

Rank and organization: Private, Company G, 7th U.S. Cavalry. *Place and date:* At Wounded Knee Creek, S. Dak., 29 December 1890. *Entered service at:* New York, N.Y. *Birth:* Australia. *Date of issue:* 25 May 1891. *Citation:* Bravery in action.

HANLEY, RICHARD P.

Rank and organization: Sergeant, Company C, 7th U.S. Cavalry. *Place and date:* At Little Big Horn River, Mont., 25 June 1876. *Entered service at:* ———. *Birth:* Boston, Mass. *Date of issue:* 5 October 1878.

Citation: Recaptured, singlehanded, and without orders, within the enemy's lines and under a galling fire lasting some 20 minutes, a stampeded pack mule loaded with ammunition.

HARDING, MOSHER A.

Rank and organization: Blacksmith, Company G, 8th U.S. Cavalry. *Place and date:* At Chiricahua Mountains, Ariz., 20 October 1869. *Entered service at:* ———. *Birth:* Canada West. *Date of issue:* 14 February 1870. *Citation:* Gallantry in action.

HARRINGTON, JOHN

Rank and organization: Private, Company H, 6th U.S. Cavalry. *Place and date:* At Wichita River, Tex., 12 September 1874. *Entered service at:* —MI—. *Birth:* Detroit, Mich. *Date of issue:* 4 November 1874. *Citation:* While carrying dispatches was attacked by 125 hostile Indians, whom he and his comrades fought throughout the day. He was severely wounded in the hip and unable to move. He continued to fight, defending an exposed dying man.

HARRIS, CHARLES D.

Rank and organization: Sergeant, Company D, 8th U.S. Cavalry. *Place and date:* At Red Creek, Ariz., 23 September 1869. *Entered service at:* —NY—. *Birth:* Albion, N.Y. *Date of issue:* 23 November 1869. *Citation:* Gallantry in action.

HARRIS, DAVID W.

Rank and organization: Private, Company A, 7th U.S. Cavalry. *Place and date:* At Little Big Horn River, Mont., 25 June 1876. *Entered service at:* Cincinnati, Ohio. *Birth:* Indianapolis, Ind. *Date of issue:* 5 October 1878. *Citation:* Brought water to the wounded, at great danger to his life, under a most galling fire from the enemy.

HARRIS, WILLIAM M.

Rank and organization: Private, Company D, 7th U.S. Cavalry. *Place and date:* At Little Big Horn River, Mont., 25 June 1876. *Entered service at:* Mt. Vernon, Ky. *Birth:* Madison County, Ky. *Date of issue:* 5 October 1878. *Citation:* Voluntarily brought water to the wounded under fire of the enemy.

HARTZOG, JOSHUA B.

Rank and organization: Private, Company E, 1st U.S. Artillery. *Place and date:* At Wounded Knee Creek, S. Dak., 29 December 1890. *Entered service at:* OHIO. *Birth:* Paulding County, Ohio, *Date of issue:* 24 March 1891. *Citation:* Went to the rescue of the commanding officer who had fallen severely wounded, picked him up, and carried him out of range of the hostile guns.

HAUPT, PAUL

Rank and organization: Corporal, Company L, 8th U.S. Cavalry. *Place and date:* At Hell Canyon, Ariz., 3 July 1869. *Entered service at:* ——→ *Birth:* Prussia. *Date of issue:* 3 March 1870. *Citation:* Gallantry in action.

HAWTHORNE, HARRY L.

Rank and organization: Second Lieutenant, 2d U.S. Artillery. *Place and date:* At Wounded Knee Creek, S. Dak., 29 December 1890. *Entered service at:* Kentucky. *Born:* 1860, Minnesota. *Date of issue:* 11 October 1892. *Citation:* Distinguished conduct in battle with hostile Indians.

HAY, FRED S.

Rank and organization: Sergeant, Company I, 5th U.S. Infantry. *Place and date:* At Upper Wichita, Tex., 9 September 1874. *Entered service at:* **_____** *Birth:* Scotland. *Date of issue:* 23 April 1875. *Citation:* Gallantry in action.

HEARTERY, RICHARD

Rank and organization: Private, Company D, 6th U.S. Cavalry. *Place and date:* At Cibicu, Ariz., 30 August 1881. *Entered service at:* San Francisco, Calif. *Birth:* Ireland. *Date of issue:* 20 July 1888. *Citation:* Bravery in action.

HEISE, CLAMOR

Rank and organization: Private, Company B, 8th U.S. Cavalry. *Place and date:* Arizona, August to October 1868. *Entered service at:* **_____** *Birth:* Germany. *Date of issue:* 24 July 1869. *Citation:* Bravery in scouts and actions against Indians.

HENRY, JOHN

(See p. 313, John H. Shingle, true name.)

HERRON, LEANDER

Rank and organization: Corporal, Company A, 3d U.S. Infantry. *Place and date:* Near Fort Dodge, Kans., 2 September 1868. *Entered service at:* **PA** . *Birth:* Bucks County, Pa. *Date of issue:* Unknown. *Citation:* While detailed as mail courier from the fort, voluntarily went to the assistance of a party of 4 enlisted men, who were attacked by about 50 Indians at some distance from the fort and remained with them until the party was relieved.

HEYL, CHARLES H.

Rank and organization: Second Lieutenant, 23d U.S. Infantry. *Place and date:* Near Fort Hartsuff, Nebr., 28 April 1876. *Entered service at:* Camden, N.J. *Birth:* Philadelphia, Pa. *Date of issue:* 26 October 1897. *Citation:* Voluntarily, and with most conspicuous gallantry, charged with 3 men upon 6 Indians who were entrenched upon a hillside.

HIGGINS, THOMAS P.

Rank and organization: Private, Company B, 8th U.S. Cavalry. *Place and date:* Arizona, August to October 1868. *Entered service at:* **_____** *Birth:* Ireland. *Date of issue:* 24 July 1869. *Citation:* Bravery in scouts and actions against Indians.

HILL, FRANK E.

Rank and organization: Sergeant, Company E, 5th U.S. Cavalry. *Place and date:* At Date Creek, Ariz., 8 September 1872. *Entered service at:* ———. *Birth:* Mayfield, Wis. *Date of issue:* 12 August 1875. *Citation:* Secured the person of a hostile Apache Chief, although while holding the chief he was severely wounded in the back by another Indian.

HILL, JAMES M.

Rank and organization: First Sergeant, Company A, 5th U.S. Cavalry. *Place and date:* At Turret Mountain, Ariz., 25 March 1873. *Entered service at:* ———. *Birth:* Washington County, Pa. *Date of issue:* 12 August 1875. *Citation:* Gallantry in action.

HILLOCK, MARVIN C.

Rank and organization: Private, Company B, 7th U.S. Cavalry. *Place and date:* At Wounded Knee Creek, S. Dak., 29 December 1890. *Entered service at:* Lead City, S. Dak. *Birth:* Michigan. *Date of issue:* 16 April 1891. *Citation:* Distinguished bravery.

HIMMELSBACK, MICHAEL

Rank and organization: Private, Company C, 2d U.S. Cavalry. *Place and date:* At Little Blue, Nebr., 15 May 1870. *Entered service at:* ———. *Birth:* Allegheny County, Pa. *Date of issue:* 22 June 1870. *Citation:* Gallantry in action.

HINEMANN, LEHMANN

Rank and organization: Sergeant, Company L, 1st U.S. Cavalry. *Place and date:* Winter of 1872–73. *Entered service at:* ———. *Birth:* Germany. *Date of issue:* 12 August 1875. *Citation:* Gallant conduct during campaigns and engagements with Apaches.

HOBDAY, GEORGE

Rank and organization: Private, Company A, 7th U.S. Cavalry. *Place and date:* At Wounded Knee Creek, S. Dak., 29 December 1890. *Entered service at:* ———. *Birth:* Pulaski County, Ill. *Date of issue:* 23 June 1891. *Citation:* Conspicuous and gallant conduct in battle.

HOGAN, HENRY

Rank and organization: First Sergeant, Company G, 5th U.S. Infantry. *Place and date:* At Cedar Creek, etc., Mont., October 1876 to 8 January 1877. *Entered service at:* ———. *Birth:* Ireland. *Date of issue:* 26 June 1894. Second award. *Citation:* Gallantry in actions.

SECOND AWARD

Place and date: At Bear Paw Mountain, Mont., 30 September 1877. *Citation:* Carried Lt. Romeyn, who was severely wounded, off the field of battle under heavy fire.

HOLDEN, HENRY

Rank and organization: Private, Company D, 7th U.S. Cavalry. *Place and date:* At Little Big Horn River, Mont., 25 June 1876. *Entered service at:* ———. *Birth:* England. *Date of issue:* 5 October 1878. *Citation:* Brought up ammunition under a galling fire from the enemy.

HOLLAND, DAVID

Rank and organization: Corporal, Company A, 5th U.S. Infantry. *Place and date:* At Cedar Creek, etc., Mont., October 1876 to 8 January 1877. *Entered service at:* ———. *Birth:* Dearborn, Mich. *Date of issue:* 27 April 1877. *Citation:* Gallantry in actions.

*HOOKER, GEORGE

Rank and organization: Private, Company K, 5th U.S. Cavalry. *Place and date:* At Tonto Creek, Ariz., 22 January 1873. *Entered service at:* ———. *Birth:* Frederick, Md. *Date of issue:* 12 August 1875. *Citation:* Gallantry in action in which he was killed.

HOOVER, SAMUEL

Rank and organization: Bugler, Company A, 1st U.S. Cavalry. *Place and date:* At Santa Maria Mountains, Ariz., 6 May 1873. *Entered service at:* ———. *Birth:* Dauphin County, Pa. *Date of issue:* 12 August 1875. *Citation:* Gallantry in action; also services as trailer in May 1872.

HORNADAY, SIMPSON

Rank and organization: Private, Company H, 6th U.S. Cavalry. *Place and date:* At Sappa Creek, Kans., 23 April 1875. *Entered service at:* ———. *Birth:* Hendricks County, Ind. *Date of issue:* 16 November 1876. *Citation:* With 5 other men he waded in mud and water up the creek to a position directly behind an entrenched Cheyenne position, who were using natural bank pits to good advantage against the main column. This surprise attack from the enemy rear broke their resistance.

HOWZE, ROBERT L.

Rank and organization: Second Lieutenant, Company K, 6th U.S. Cavalry. *Place and date:* At White River, S. Dak., 1 January 1891. *Entered service at:* Overton, Rusk County, Tex. *Born:* 22 August 1864, Overton, Rusk County, Tex. *Date of issue:* 25 July 1891. *Citation:* Bravery in action.

HUBBARD, THOMAS

Rank and organization: Private, Company C, 2d U.S. Cavalry. *Place and date:* At Little Blue, Nebr., 15 May 1870. *Entered service at:* ———. *Birth:* Philadelphia, Pa. *Date of issue:* 22 June 1870. *Citation:* Gallantry in action.

HUFF, JAMES W.

Rank and organization: Private, Company L, 1st U.S. Cavalry. *Place and date:* Winter of 1872–73. *Entered service at:* Vanburan, Pa. *Born:*

7 February 1840, Washington, Pa. *Date of issue:* 12 April 1875. *Citation:* Gallant conduct during campaigns and engagements with Apaches.

HUGGINS, ELI L.

Rank and organization: Captain, 2d U.S. Cavalry. *Place and date:* At O'Fallons Creek, Mont., 1 April 1880. *Entered service at:* Minnesota. *Birth:* Illinois. *Date of issue:* 27 November 1894. *Citation:* Surprised the Indians in their strong position and fought them until dark with great boldness.

HUMPHREY, CHARLES F.

Rank and organization: First Lieutenant, 4th U.S. Artillery. *Place and date:* At Clearwater, Idaho, 11 July 1877. *Entered service at:* ———. *Birth:* New York. *Date of issue:* 2 March 1897. *Citation:* Voluntarily and successfully conducted, in the face of a withering fire, a party which recovered possession of an abandoned howitzer and 2 Gatling guns lying between the lines a few yards from the Indians.

HUNT, FRED O.

Rank and organization: Private, Company A, 5th U.S. Infantry. *Place and date:* At Cedar Creek, etc., Mont., October 1876 to 8 January 1877. *Entered service at:* LA. *Birth:* New Orleans, La. *Date of issue:* 27 April 1877. *Citation:* Gallantry in actions.

HUTCHINSON, RUFUS D.

Rank and organization: Sergeant, Company B, 7th U.S. Cavalry. *Place and date:* At Little Big Horn River, Mont., 25 June 1876. *Entered service at:* Cincinnati, Ohio. *Birth:* Butlerville, Ohio. *Date of issue:* 5 October 1878. *Citation:* Guarded and carried the wounded, brought water for the same, and posted and directed the men in his charge under galling fire from the enemy.

HYDE, HENRY J.

Rank and organization: Sergeant, Company M, 1st U.S. Cavalry. *Place and date:* Winter of 1872–73. *Entered service at:* Princeton, Ill. *Birth:* Bangor, Maine. *Date of issue:* 12 August 1875. *Citation:* Gallant conduct during campaigns and engagements with Apaches.

IRWIN, BERNARD J. D.

Rank and organization: Assistant Surgeon, U.S. Army. *Place and date:* Apache Pass, Ariz., 13–14 February 1861. *Entered service at:* New York. *Born:* 24 June 1830, Ireland. *Date of issue:* 24 January 1894. *Citation:* Voluntarily took command of troops and attacked and defeated hostile Indians he met on the way. Surgeon Irwin volunteered to go to the rescue of 2d Lt. George N. Bascom, 7th Infantry, who with 60 men was trapped by Chiricahua Apaches under Cochise. Irwin and 14 men, not having horses began the 100-mile march riding mules. After fighting and capturing Indians, recovering stolen horses and cattle, he reached Bascom's column and help break his siege.

JACKSON, JAMES

Rank and organization: Captain, 1st U.S. Cavalry. *Place and date:* At Camas Meadows, Idaho, 20 August 1877. *Entered service at:* ———. *Birth:* New Jersey. *Date of issue:* 17 April 1896. *Citation:* Dismounted from his horse in the face of a heavy fire from pursuing Indians, and with the assistance of 1 or 2 of the men of his command secured to a place of safety the body of his trumpeter, who had been shot and killed.

JAMES, JOHN

Rank and organization: Corporal, 5th U.S. Infantry. *Place and date:* At Upper Wichita, Tex., 9–11 September 1874. *Entered service at:* ———. *Birth:* England. *Date of issue:* 23 April 1875. *Citation:* Gallantry in action.

JARVIS, FREDERICK

Rank and organization: Sergeant, Company G, 1st U.S. Cavalry. *Place and date:* At Chiricahua Mountains, Ariz., 20 October 1869. *Entered service at:* ———. *Birth:* Essex County, N.Y. *Date of issue:* 14 February 1870. *Citation:* Gallantry in action.

JETTER, BERNHARD

Rank and organization: Sergeant, Company K, 7th U.S. Cavalry. *Place and date:* At Sioux campaign, December 1890. *Entered service at:* ———. *Birth:* Germany. *Date of issue:* 24 April 1891. *Citation:* Distinguished bravery.

JIM

Rank and organization: Sergeant, Indian Scouts. *Place and date:* Winter of 1871–73. *Entered service at:* ———. *Birth:* Arizona Territory. *Date of issue:* 12 April 1875. *Citation:* Gallant conduct during campaigns and engagements with Apaches.

JOHNSON, HENRY

Rank and organization: Sergeant, Company D, 9th U.S. Cavalry. *Place and date:* At Milk River, Colo., 2–5 October 1879. *Entered service at:* ———. *Birth:* Boynton, Va. *Date of issue:* 22 September 1890. *Citation:* Voluntarily left fortified shelter and under heavy fire at close range made the rounds of the pits to instruct the guards; fought his way to the creek and back to bring water to the wounded.

JOHNSTON, EDWARD

Rank and organization: Corporal, Company C, 5th U.S. Infantry. *Place and date:* At Cedar Creek, etc., Mont., October 1876 to 8 January 1877. *Entered service at:* Buffalo, N.Y. *Birth:* Pen Yan, N.Y. *Date of issue:* 27 April 1877. *Citation:* Gallantry in action.

JONES, WILLIAM H.

Rank and organization: Farrier, Company L, 2d U.S. Cavalry. *Place and date:* At Little Muddy Creek, Mont., 7 May 1877; at Camas Meadows, Idaho, 20 August 1877. *Entered service at:* Louisville, Ky.

Birth: Davidson County, N.C. *Date of issue:* 28 February 1878. *Citation:* Gallantry in the attack against hostile Sioux Indians on May 7, 1877 at Muddy Creek, Mont., and in the engagement with Nez Perces Indians at Camas Meadows, Idaho, on 20 August 1877 in which he sustained a painful knee wound.

JORDAN, GEORGE

Rank and organization: Sergeant, Company K, 9th U.S. Cavalry. *Place and date:* At Fort Tularosa, N. Mex., 14 May 1880; at Carrizo Canyon, N. Mex., 12 August 1881. *Entered service at:* Nashville, Tenn. *Birth:* Williamson County, Tenn. *Date of issue:* 7 May 1890. *Citation:* While commanding a detachment of 25 men at Fort Tularosa, N. Mex., repulsed a force of more than 100 Indians. At Carrizo Canyon, N. Mex., while commanding the right of a detachment of 19 men, on 12 August 1881, he stubbornly held his ground in an extremely exposed position and gallantly forced back a much superior number of the enemy, preventing them from surrounding the command.

KAY, JOHN

Rank and organization: Private, Company L, 8th U.S. Cavalry. *Place and date:* Arizona, 21 October 1868. *Entered service at:* ———. *Birth:* England. *Date of issue:* 3 March 1870. *Citation:* Brought a comrade, severely wounded, from under the fire of a large party of the enemy.

KEATING, DANIEL

Rank and organization: Corporal, Company M, 6th U.S. Cavalry. *Place and date:* At Wichita River, Tex., 5 October 1870. *Entered service at:* ———. *Birth:* Ireland. *Date of issue:* 19 November 1870. *Citation:* Gallantry in action and in pursuit of Indians.

KEENAN, BARTHOLOMEW T.

Rank and organization: Trumpeter, Company G, 1st U.S. Cavalry. *Place and date:* At Chiricahua Mountains, Ariz., 20 October 1869. *Entered service at:* ———. *Birth:* Brooklyn, N.Y. *Date of issue:* 14 February 1870. *Citation:* Gallantry in action.

KEENAN, JOHN

Rank and organization: Private, Company B, 8th U.S. Cavalry. *Place and date:* Arizona, August to October 1868. *Entered service at:* ———. *Birth:* Ireland. *Date of issue:* 24 July 1869. *Citation:* Bravery in scouts and actions against Indians.

KELLEY, CHARLES

Rank and organization: Private, Company G, 1st U.S. Cavalry. *Place and date:* At Chiricahua Mountains, Ariz., 20 October 1869. *Entered service at:* ———. *Birth:* Ireland. *Date of issue:* 14 February 1870. *Citation:* Gallantry in action.

KELLY, JOHN J. H.

Rank and organization: Corporal, Company I, 5th U.S. Infantry. *Place and date:* At Upper Wichita, Tex., 9 September 1874. *Entered service at:* ———. *Birth:* Schuyler County, Ill. *Date of issue:* 23 April 1875. *Citation:* Gallantry in action.

KELLY, THOMAS

Rank and organization: Private, Company I, 5th U.S. Infantry. *Place and date:* At Upper Wichita, Tex., 9 September 1874. *Entered service at:* ———. *Birth:* Ireland. *Date of issue:* 23 April 1875. *Citation:* Gallantry in action.

KELSAY

Rank and organization: Indian Scouts. *Place and date:* Winter of 1872–73. *Entered service at:* ———. *Birth:* Arizona. *Date of issue:* 12 April 1875. *Citation:* Gallant conduct during campaigns and engagements with Apaches.

KENNEDY, PHILIP

Rank and organization: Private, Company C, 5th U.S. Infantry. *Place and date:* At Cedar Creek, etc., Mont., 21 October 1876 to 8 January 1877. *Entered service at:* ———. *Birth:* Ireland. *Date of issue:* 27 April 1877. *Citation:* Gallantry in action.

KERR, JOHN B.

Rank and organization: Captain, 6th U.S. Cavalry. *Place and date:* At White River, S. Dak., 1 January 1891. *Entered service at:* Hutchison Station, Ky. *Birth:* Fayette County, Ky. *Date of issue:* 25 April 1891. *Citation:* For distinguished bravery while in command of his troop in action against hostile Sioux Indians on the north bank of the White River, near the mouth of Little Grass Creek, S. Dak., where he defeated a force of 300 Brule Sioux warriors, and turned the Sioux tribe, which was endeavoring to enter the Bad Lands, back into the Pine Ridge Agency.

KERRIGAN, THOMAS

Rank and organization: Sergeant, Company H, 6th U.S. Cavalry. *Place and date:* At Wichita River, Tex., 12 July 1870. *Entered service at:* ———. *Birth:* Ireland. *Date of issue:* 25 August 1870. *Citation:* Gallantry in action.

KILMARTIN, JOHN

Rank and organization: Private, Company F, 3d U.S. Cavalry. *Place and date:* At Whetstone Mountains, Ariz., 5 May 1871. *Entered service at:* ———. *Birth:* Canada. *Date of issue:* 13 November 1871. *Citation:* Gallantry in action.

KIRK, JOHN

Rank and organization: First Sergeant, Company L, 6th U.S. Cavalry. *Place and date:* At Wichita River, Tex., 12 July 1870. *Entered service at:* ———. *Birth:* York, Pa. *Date of issue:* 25 August 1870. *Citation:* Gallantry in action.

KIRKWOOD, JOHN A.

Rank and organization: Sergeant, Company M, 3d U.S. Cavalry. *Place and date:* At Slim Buttes, Dakota Territory, 9 September 1876. *Entered service at:* ———. *Birth:* Allegheny City, Pa. *Date of issue:* 16

October 1877. *Citation:* Bravely endeavored to dislodge some Sioux Indians secreted in a ravine.

KITCHEN, GEORGE K.

Rank and organization: Sergeant, Company H, 6th U.S. Cavalry. *Place and date:* At Upper Wichita, Tex., 9 September 1874. *Entered service at:* ———. *Birth:* Lebanon County, Pa. *Date of issue:* 23 April 1875. *Citation:* Gallantry in action.

KNAAK, ALBERT

Rank and organization: Private, Company B, 8th U.S. Cavalry. *Place and date:* Arizona, August to October 1868. *Entered service at:* ———. *Birth:* Switzerland. *Date of issue:* 24 July 1869. *Citation:* Bravery in scouts and actions against Indians.

KNIGHT, JOSEPH F.

Rank and organization: Sergeant, Troop F, 6th U.S. Cavalry. *Place and date:* At White River, S. Dak., 1 January 1891. *Entered service at:* ———. *Birth:* Danville, Ill. *Date of issue:* 1 May 1891. *Citation:* Led the advance in a spirited movement to the assistance of Troop K, 6th U.S. Cavalry.

KNOX, JOHN W.

Rank and organization: Sergeant, Company I, 5th U.S. Infantry. *Place and date:* At Upper Wichita, Tex., 9 September 1874. *Entered service at:* ———. *Birth:* Burlington, Iowa. *Date of issue:* 23 April 1875. *Citation:* Gallantry in action.

KOELPIN, WILLIAM

Rank and organization: Sergeant, Company I, 5th U.S. Infantry. *Place and date:* At Upper Wichita, Tex., 9 September 1874. *Entered service at:* New York, N.Y. *Birth:* Prussia. *Date of issue:* 23 April 1875. *Citation:* Gallantry in action.

KOSOHA

Rank and organization: Indian Scouts. *Place and date:* Winter of 1872–73. *Entered service at:* ———. *Birth:* Arizona. *Date of issue:* 12 April 1875. *Citation:* Gallant conduct during campaigns and engagements with Apaches.

KREHER, WENDELIN

Rank and organization: First Sergeant, Company C, 5th U.S. Infantry. *Place and date:* At Cedar Creek, etc., Mont., 21 October 1876 to 8 January 1877. *Entered service at:* ———. *Birth:* Prussia. *Date of issue:* 27 April 1877. *Citation:* Gallantry in action.

KYLE, JOHN

Rank and organization: Corporal, Company M, 5th U.S. Cavalry. *Place and date:* Near Republican River, Kans., 8 July 1869. *Entered service at:* ———. *Birth:* Cincinnati, Ohio. *Date of issue:* 24 August 1869. *Citation:* This soldier and 2 others were attacked by 8 Indians, but beat them off and badly wounded 2 of them.

LARKIN, DAVID

Rank and organization: Farrier, Company F, 4th U.S. Cavalry. *Place and date:* At Red River, Tex., 29 September 1872. *Entered service at:* ———. *Birth:* Ireland. *Date of issue:* 19 November 1872. *Citation:* Gallantry in action.

LAWRENCE, JAMES

Rank and organization: Private, Company B, 8th U.S. Cavalry. *Place and date:* Arizona, August to October 1868. *Entered service at:* ———. *Birth:* Scotland. *Date of issue:* 24 July 1869. *Citation:* Bravery in scouts and actions against Indians.

LAWTON, JOHN S.

Rank and organization: Sergeant, Company D, 5th U.S. Cavalry. *Place and date:* At Milk River, Colo., 29 September 1879. *Entered service at:* ———. *Birth:* Bristol, R.I. *Date of issue:* 7 June 1880. *Citation:* Coolness and steadiness under fire; volunteered to accompany a small detachment on a very dangerous mission.

LENIHAN, JAMES

Rank and organization: Private, Company K, 5th U.S. Cavalry. *Place and date:* At Clear Creek, Ariz., 2 January 1873. *Entered service at:* ———. *Birth:* Ireland. *Date of issue:* 12 April 1875. *Citation:* Gallantry in action.

4. LEONARD, PATRICK

Rank and organization: Sergeant, Company C, 2d U.S. Cavalry. *Place and date:* At Little Blue, Nebr., 15 May 1870. *Entered service at:* ———. *Birth:* Ireland. *Date of issue:* 22 June 1870. ~~Second award.~~ *Citation:* Gallantry in action.

5. LEONARD, PATRICK E. ~~SECOND AWARD~~

Rank and organization: Corporal, Company A, 23d U.S. Infantry. *Place and date:* Near Fort Hartsuff, Nebr., 28 April 1876. *Entered service at:* ———. *Birth:* Ireland. *Date of issue:* 26 August 1876. *Citation:* Gallantry in charge on hostile Sioux.

7. LEONARD, WILLIAM

Rank and organization: Private, Company L, 2d U.S. Cavalry. *Place and date:* At Muddy Creek, Mont., 7 May 1877. *Entered service at:* ———. *Birth:* Ypsilanti, Mich. *Date of issue:* 8 August 1877. *Citation:* Bravery in action.

LEWIS, WILLIAM B.

Rank and organization: Sergeant, Company B, 3d U.S. Cavalry. *Place and date:* At Bluff Station, Wyo., 20–22 January 1877. *Entered service at:* ———. *Birth:* Boston, Mass. *Date of issue:* 28 March 1879. *Citation:* Bravery in skirmish.

LITTLE, THOMAS

Rank and organization: Bugler, Company B, 8th U.S. Cavalry. *Place and date:* Arizona, August to October 1868. *Entered service at:* ———. *Birth:* West Indies. *Date of issue:* 24 July 1869. *Citation:* Bravery in scouts and actions against Indians.

LOHNES, FRANCIS W.

Rank and organization: Private, Company H, 1st Nebraska Veteran Cavalry. *Place and date:* At Gilmans Ranch, Nebr., 12 May 1865. *Entered service at:* ———. *Birth:* Oneida County, N.Y. *Date of issue:* 24 July 1865. *Citation:* Gallantry in defending Government property against Indians.

LONG, OSCAR F.

Rank and organization: Second Lieutenant, 5th U.S. Infantry. *Place and date:* At Bear Paw Mountain, Mont., 30 September 1877. *Entered service at:* Utica, N.Y. *Born:* 16 June 1852, Utica, N.Y. *Date of issue:* 22 March 1895. *Citation:* Having been directed to order a troop of cavalry to advance, and finding both its officers killed, he voluntarily assumed command, and under a heavy fire from the Indians advanced the troop to its proper position.

LOWTHERS, JAMES

Rank and organization: Private, Company H, 6th U.S. Cavalry. *Place and date:* At Sappa Creek, Kans., 23 April 1875. *Entered service at:* ———. *Birth:* Boston, Mass. *Date of issue:* 16 November 1876. *Citation:* With 5 other men he waded in mud and water up the creek to a position directly behind an entrenched Cheyenne position, who were using natural bank pits to good advantage against the main column. This surprise attack from the enemy rear broke their resistance.

LOYD, GEORGE

Rank and organization: Sergeant, Company I, 7th U.S. Cavalry. *Place and date:* At Wounded Knee Creek, S. Dak., 29 December 1890. *Entered service at:* ———. *Birth:* Ireland. *Date of issue:* 16 April 1891. *Citation:* Bravery, especially after having been severely wounded through the lung.

LYTLE, LEONIDAS S.

Rank and organization: Sergeant, Company C, 8th U.S. Cavalry. *Place and date:* Near Fort Selden, N. Mex., 8–11 July 1873. *Entered service at:* ———. *Birth:* Warren County, Pa. *Date of issue:* 12 April 1875. *Citation:* Services against hostile Indians.

LYTTON, JEPTHA L.

Rank and organization: Corporal, Company A, 23d U.S. Infantry. *Place and date:* Near Fort Hartsuff, Nebr., 28 April 1876. *Entered service at:* ———. *Birth:* Lawrence County, Ind. *Date of issue:* 26 August 1876. *Citation:* Gallantry in charge on hostile Sioux.

MACHOL

Rank and organization: Private, Indian Scouts. *Place and date:* Arizona, 1872–73. *Entered service at:* ———. *Birth:* Arizona. *Date of issue:* 12 April 1875. *Citation:* Gallant conduct during campaign and engagements with Apaches.

MAHERS, HERBERT

Rank and organization: Private, Company F, 8th U.S. Cavalry. *Place and date:* At Seneca Mountain, Ariz., 25 August 1869. *Entered service at:* ———. *Birth:* Canada. *Date of issue:* 3 March 1870. *Citation:* Gallantry in action.

MAHONEY, GREGORY

Rank and organization: Private, Company E, 4th U.S. Cavalry. *Place and date:* Near Red River, Tex., 26–28 September 1874. *Entered service at:* ———. *Birth:* South Wales. *Date of issue:* 13 October 1875. *Citation:* Gallantry in attack on a large party of Cheyennes.

MARTIN, PATRICK

Rank and organization: Sergeant, Company G, 5th U.S. Cavalry. *Place and date:* At Castle Dome and Santa Maria Mountains, Ariz., June and July 1873. *Entered service at:* ———. *Birth:* Ireland. *Date of issue:* 12 April 1875. *Citation:* Gallant services in operations of Capt. James Burns, 5th U.S. Cavalry.

MATTHEWS, DAVID A.

Rank and organization: Corporal, Company E, 8th U.S. Cavalry. *Place and date:* Arizona, 1868 and 1869. *Entered service at:* ———. *Birth:* Boston, Mass. *Date of issue:* 6 September 1869. *Citation:* Bravery in scouts and actions against Indians.

MAUS, MARION P.

Rank and organization: First Lieutenant, 1st U.S. Infantry. *Place and date:* At Sierra Madre Mountains, Mex., 11 January 1886. *Entered service at:* Tennallytown, Montgomery County, Md. *Birth:* Burnt Mills, Md. *Date of issue:* 27 November 1894. *Citation:* Most distinguished gallantry in action with hostile Apaches led by Geronimo and Natchez.

MAY, JOHN

Rank and organization: Sergeant, Company L, 6th U.S. Cavalry. *Place and date:* At Wichita River, Tex., 12 July 1870. *Entered service at:* ———. *Birth:* Germany. *Date of issue:* 25 August 1870. *Citation:* Gallantry in action.

MAYS, ISAIAH

Rank and organization: Corporal, Company B, 24th U.S. Infantry. *Place and date:* Arizona, 11 May 1889. *Entered service at:* Columbus Barracks, Ohio. *Born:* 16 February 1858, Carters Bridge, Va. *Date of issue:* 19 February 1890. *Citation:* Gallantry in the fight between Paymaster Wham's escort and robbers. Mays walked and crawled 2 miles to a ranch for help.

McBRIDE, BERNARD

Rank and organization: Private, Company B, 8th U.S. Cavalry. *Place and date:* Arizona, August to October 1868. *Entered service at:* ———. *Birth:* Brooklyn, N.Y. *Date of issue:* 24 July 1869. *Citation:* Bravery in scouts and actions against Indians.

McBRYAR, WILLIAM

Rank and organization: Sergeant, Company K, 10th U.S. Cavalry. *Place and date:* Arizona, 7 March 1890. *Entered service at:* New York, N.Y. *Birth:* 14 February 1861, Elizabethtown, N.C. *Date of issue:* 15 May 1890. *Citation:* Distinguished himself for coolness, bravery and marksmanship while his troop was in pursuit of hostile Apache Indians.

McCABE, WILLIAM

Rank and organization: Private, Company E, 4th U.S. Cavalry. *Place and date:* Near Red River, Tex., 26–28 September 1874. *Entered service at:* ———. *Birth:* Ireland. *Date of issue:* 13 October 1875. *Citation:* Gallantry in attack on a large party of Cheyennes.

McCANN, BERNARD

Rank and organization: Private, Company F, 22d U.S. Infantry. *Place and date:* At Cedar Creek, etc., Mont., 21 October 1876 to 8 January 1877. *Entered service at:* ———. *Birth:* Ireland. *Date of issue:* 27 April 1877. *Citation:* Gallantry in action.

McCARTHY, MICHAEL

Rank and organization: First Sergeant, Troop H, 1st U.S. Cavalry. *Place and date:* At White Bird Canyon, Idaho, June 1876 to January 1877. *Entered service at:* ———. *Birth:* St. Johns, Newfoundland. *Date of issue:* 20 November 1897. *Citation:* Was detailed with 6 men to hold a commanding position, and held it with great gallantry until the troops fell back. He then fought his way through the Indians, rejoined a portion of his command, and continued the fight in retreat. He had 2 horses shot from under him, and was captured, but escaped and reported for duty after 3 days' hiding and wandering in the mountains.

McCLERNAND, EDWARD J.

Rank and organization: Second Lieutenant, 2d U.S. Cavalry. *Place and date:* At Bear Paw Mountain, Mont., 30 September 1877. *Entered service at:* Springfield, Ill. *Birth:* Jacksonville, Ill. *Date of issue:* 27 November 1894. *Citation:* Gallantly attacked a band of hostiles and conducted the combat with excellent skill and boldness.

McCORMICK, MICHAEL

Rank and organization: Private, Company G, 5th U.S. Infantry. *Place and date:* At Cedar Creek, etc., Mont., 21 October 1876 to 8 January 1877. *Entered service at:* ———. *Birth:* Rutland, Vt. *Date of issue:* 27 April 1877. *Citation:* Gallantry in action.

McDONALD, FRANKLIN M.

Rank and organization: Private, Company G, 11th U.S. Infantry. *Place and date:* Near Fort Griffin, Tex., 5 August 1872. *Entered service at:* ̶K̶Y̶—. *Birth:* Bowling Green, Ky. *Date of issue:* 31 August 1872. *Citation:* Gallantry in defeating Indians who attacked the mail.

McDONALD, JAMES

Rank and organization: Corporal, Company B, 8th U.S. Cavalry. *Place and date:* Arizona, August to October 1868. *Entered service at:* ———. *Birth:* Scotland. *Date of issue:* 24 July 1869. *Citation:* Bravery in scouts and actions against Indians.

McDONALD, ROBERT

Rank and organization: First Lieutenant, 5th U.S. Infantry. *Place and date:* At Wolf Mountain, Mont., 8 January 1877. *Entered service at:* Fort Sumner, N. Mex. *Birth:* New York. *Date of issue:* 27 November 1894. *Citation:* Led his command in a successful charge against superior numbers of hostile Indians, strongly posted.

McGANN, MICHAEL A.

Rank and organization: First Sergeant, Company F, 3d U.S. Cavalry. *Place and date:* At Rosebud River, Mont., 17 June 1876. *Entered service at:* ———. *Birth:* Ireland. *Date of issue:* 9 August 1880. *Citation:* Gallantry in action.

McGAR, OWEN

Rank and organization: Private, Company C, 5th U.S. Infantry. *Place and date:* At Cedar Creek, etc., Mont., 21 October 1876 to 8 January 1877. *Entered service at:* Pawtucket, R.I. *Birth:* North Attleboro, Mass. *Date of issue:* 27 April 1877. *Citation:* Gallantry in action.

McHUGH, JOHN

Rank and organization: Private, Company A, 5th U.S. Infantry. *Place and date:* At Cedar Creek, etc., Mont., 21 October 1876 to 8 January 1877. *Entered service at:* ———. *Birth:* Syracuse, N.Y. *Date of issue:* 27 April 1877. *Citation:* Gallantry in action.

McKINLEY, DANIEL

Rank and organization: Private, Company B, 8th U.S. Cavalry. *Place and date:* Arizona, August to October 1868. *Entered service at:* ———. *Birth:* Boston, Mass. *Date of issue:* 24 July 1869. *Citation:* Bravery in scouts and actions against Indians.

McLENNON, JOHN

Rank and organization: Musician, Company A, 7th U.S. Infantry. *Place and date:* At Big Hole, Mont., 9 August 1877. *Entered service at:* ———. *Birth:* Fort Belknap, Tex. *Date of issue:* 2 December 1878. *Citation:* Gallantry in action.

McLOUGHLIN, MICHAEL

Rank and organization: Sergeant, Company A, 5th U.S. Infantry. *Place and date:* At Cedar Creek, etc., Mont., 21 October 1876 to 8 January 1877. *Entered service at:* ———. *Birth:* Ireland. *Date of issue:* 27 April 1877. *Citation:* Gallantry in action.

McMASTERS, HENRY A.

Rank and organization: Corporal, Company A, 4th U.S. Cavalry. *Place and date:* At Red River, Tex., 29 September 1872. *Entered service at:* ———. *Birth:* Augusta, Maine. *Date of issue:* 19 November 1872. *Citation:* Gallantry in action.

McMILLAN, ALBERT W.

Rank and organization: Sergeant, Company E, 7th U.S. Cavalry. *Place and date:* At Wounded Knee Creek, S. Dak., 29 December 1890. *Entered service at:* Baltimore, Md. *Birth:* Baltimore, Md. *Date of issue:* 23 June 1891. *Citation:* While engaged with Indians concealed in a ravine, he assisted the men on the skirmish line, directed their fire, encouraged them by example, and used every effort to dislodge the enemy.

McNALLY, JAMES

Rank and organization: First Sergeant, Company E, 8th U.S. Cavalry. *Place and date:* Arizona, 1868 and 1869. *Entered service at:* ———. *Birth:* Ireland. *Date of issue:* 6 September 1869. *Citation:* Bravery in scouts and actions against Indians.

McNAMARA, WILLIAM

Rank and organization: First Sergeant, Company F, 4th U.S. Cavalry. *Place and date:* At Red River, Tex., 29 September 1872. *Entered service at:* ———. *Birth:* Ireland. *Date of issue:* 19 November 1872. *Citation:* Gallantry in action.

McPHELAN, ROBERT

Rank and organization: Sergeant, Company E, 5th U.S. Infantry. *Place and date:* At Cedar Creek, etc., Mont., 21 October 1876 to 8 January 1877. *Entered service at:* ———. *Birth:* Ireland. *Date of issue:* 27 April 1877. *Citation:* Gallantry in action.

McVEAGH, CHARLES H.

Rank and organization: Private, Company B, 8th U.S. Cavalry. *Place and date:* Arizona, August to October 1868. *Entered service at:* ———. *Birth:* New York, N.Y. *Date of issue:* 24 July 1869. *Citation:* Bravery in scouts and actions against Indians.

MEAHER, NICHOLAS

Rank and organization: Corporal, Company G, 1st U.S. Cavalry. *Place and date:* At Chiricahua Mountains, Ariz., 20 October 1869. *Entered service at:* ———. *Birth:* Perry County, Ohio. *Date of issue:* 14 February 1870. *Citation:* Gallantry in action.

MECHLIN, HENRY W. B.

Rank and organization: Blacksmith, Company H, 7th U.S. Cavalry. *Place and date:* At Little Big Horn, Mont., 25 June 1876. *Entered service at:* Pittsburgh, Pa. *Born:* 14 October 1851, Mount Pleasant, Westmoreland County, Pa. *Date of issue:* 29 August 1878. *Citation:* With 3 comrades during the entire engagement courageously held ·a position that secured water for the command.

MERRILL, JOHN

Rank and organization: Sergeant, Company F, 5th U.S. Cavalry. *Place and date:* At Milk River, Colo., 29 September 187ᢒ. *Entered service at:* ———. *Birth:* New York, N.Y. *Date of issue:* 7 June 1880. *Citation:* Though painfully wounded, he remained on duty and rendered gallant and valuable service.

MILLER, DANIEL H.

Rank and organization: Private, Company F, 3d U.S. Cavalry. *Place and date:* At Whetstone Mountains, Ariz., 5 May 1871. *Entered service at:* ———. *Birth:* Fairfield County, Ohio. *Date of issue:* 13 November 1871. *Citation:* Gallantry in action.

MILLER, GEORGE

Rank and organization: Corporal, Company H, 5th U.S. Infantry. *Place and date:* At Cedar Creek, etc., Mont., 21 October 1876 to 8 January 1877. *Entered service at:* ———. *Birth:* Brooklyn, N.Y. *Date of issue:* 27 April 1877. *Citation:* Gallantry in action.

MILLER, GEORGE W.

Rank and organization: Private, Company B, 8th U.S. Cavalry. *Place and date:* Arizona, August to October 1868. *Entered service at:* ———. *Birth:* Philadelphia, Pa. *Date of issue:* 24 July 1869. *Citation:* Bravery in scouts and actions against Indians.

MITCHELL, JOHN

Rank and organization: First Sergeant, Company I, 5th U.S. Infantry. *Place and date:* At Upper Washita, Tex., 9–11 September 1874. *Entered service at:* ———. *Birth:* Ireland. *Date of issue:* 23 April 1875. *Citation:* Gallantry in engagement with Indians.

MITCHELL, JOHN J.

Rank and organization: Corporal, Company L, 8th U.S. Cavalry. *Place and date:* At Hell Canyon, Ariz., 3 July 1869. *Entered service at:* ———. *Birth:* Ireland. *Date of issue:* 3 March 1870. *Citation:* Gallantry in action.

MONTROSE, CHARLES H.

Rank and organization: Private, Company I, 5th U.S. Infantry. *Place and date:* At Cedar Creek, etc., Mont., 21 October 1876 to 8 January 1877. *Entered service at:* St. Louis, Mo. *Birth:* St. Paul, Minn. *Date of issue:* 27 April 1877. *Citation:* Gallantry in action.

MOQUIN, GEORGE

Rank and organization: Corporal, Company F, 5th U.S. Cavalry. *Place and date:* At Milk River, Colo., 29 September to 5 October 1879. *Entered service at:* ———. *Birth:* New York, N.Y. *Date of issue:* 27 January 1880. *Citation:* Gallantry in action.

MORAN, JOHN

Rank and organization: Private, Company F, 8th U.S. Cavalry. *Place and date:* At Seneca Mountain, Ariz., 25 August 1869. *Entered service at:* ———. *Birth:* Ireland. *Date of issue:* 3 March 1870. *Citation:* Gallantry in action.

MORGAN, GEORGE H.

Rank and organization: Second Lieutenant, 3d U.S. Cavalry. *Place and date:* At Big Dry Fork, Ariz., 17 July 1882. *Entered service at:* Minneapolis, Minn. *Birth:* Canada. *Date of issue:* 15 July 1892. *Citation:* Gallantly held his ground at a critical moment and fired upon the advancing enemy (hostile Indians) until he was disabled by a shot.

MORIARITY, JOHN

Rank and organization: Sergeant, Company E, 8th U.S. Cavalry. *Place and date:* Arizona, 1868 and 1869. *Entered service at:* ———. *Birth:* England. *Date of issue:* 6 September 1869. *Citation:* Bravery in scouts and actions against Indians.

MORRIS, JAMES L.

Rank and organization: First Sergeant, Company C, 8th U.S. Cavalry. *Place and date:* Near Fort Selden, N. Mex., 8–11 July 1873. *Entered service at:* ———. *Birth:* Ireland. *Date of issue:* 12 August 1875. *Citation:* Services against hostile Indians.

MORRIS, WILLIAM W.

Rank and organization: Corporal, Company H, 6th U.S. Cavalry. *Place and date:* At Upper Washita, Tex., 9–11 September 1874. *Entered service at:* I N—. *Birth:* Stewart County, Tenn. *Date of issue:* 23 April 1875. *Citation:* Gallantry in engagement with Indians.

MOTT, JOHN

Rank and organization: Sergeant, Company F, 3d U.S. Cavalry. *Place and date:* At Whetstone Mountains, Ariz., 5 May 1871. *Entered service at:* ———. *Birth:* Scotland. *Date of issue:* 13 November 1871. *Citation:* Gallantry in action.

MOYLAN, MYLES

Rank and organization: Captain, 7th U.S. Cavalry. *Place and date:* At Bear Paw Mountain, Mont., 30 September 1877. *Entered service at:* Essex, Mass. *Birth:* Ireland. *Date of issue:* 27 November 1894. *Citation:* Gallantly led his command in action against Nez Percé Indians until he was severely wounded.

MURPHY, EDWARD

Rank and organization: Private, Company G, 1st U.S. Cavalry. *Place and date:* At Chiricahua Mountains, Ariz., 20 October 1869. *Entered service at:* ———. *Birth:* Ireland. *Date of issue:* Unknown. *Citation:* Gallantry in action.

MURPHY, EDWARD F.

Rank and organization: Corporal, Company D, 5th U.S. Cavalry. *Place and date:* At Milk River, Colo., 29 September 1879. *Entered service at:* ———. *Birth:* Wayne County, Pa. *Date of issue:* 23 April 1880. *Citation:* Gallantry in action.

MURPHY, JEREMIAH

Rank and organization: Private, Company M, 3d U.S. Cavalry. *Place and date:* At Powder River, Mont., 17 March 1876. *Entered service at:* ———. *Birth:* Ireland. *Date of issue:* 16 October 1877. *Citation:* Being the only member of his picket not disabled, he attempted to save a wounded comrade.

MURPHY, PHILIP

Rank and organization: Corporal, Company F, 8th U.S. Cavalry. *Place and date:* At Seneca Mountain, Ariz., 25 August 1869. *Entered service at:* ———. *Birth:* Ireland. *Date of issue:* 3 March 1870. *Citation:* Gallantry in action.

MURPHY, THOMAS

Rank and organization: Corporal, Company F, 8th U.S. Cavalry. *Place and date:* At Seneca Mountain, Ariz., 25 August 1869. *Entered service at:* ———. *Birth:* Ireland. *Date of issue:* 3 March 1870. *Citation:* Gallantry in action.

MURRAY, THOMAS

Rank and organization: Sergeant, Company B, 7th U.S. Cavalry. *Place and date:* At Little Big Horn, Mont., 25 June 1876. *Entered service at:* ———. *Birth:* Ireland. *Date of issue:* 5 October 1878. *Citation:* Brought up the pack train, and on the second day the rations, under a heavy fire from the enemy.

MYERS, FRED

Rank and organization: Sergeant, Company K, 6th U.S. Cavalry. *Place and date:* At White River, S. Dak., 1 January 1891. *Entered service at:* Washington, D.C. *Birth:* Germany. *Date of issue:* 4 February 1891. *Citation:* With 5 men repelled a superior force of the enemy and held his position against their repeated efforts to recapture it.

NANNASADDIE

Rank and organization: Indian Scouts. *Place and date:* 1872–73. *Entered service at:* ———. *Birth:* Arizona. *Date of issue:* 12 April 1875. *Citation:* Gallant conduct during campaigns and engagements with Apaches.

NANTAJE (NANTAHE)

Rank and organization: Indian Scouts. *Place and date:* 1872–73. *Entered service at:* ———. *Birth:* Arizona. *Date of issue:* 12 April 1875. *Citation:* Gallant conduct during campaigns and engagements with Apaches.

NEAL, SOLON D.

Rank and organization: Private, Company L, 6th U.S. Cavalry. *Place and date:* At Wichita River, Tex., 12 July 1870. *Entered service at:* ———. *Birth:* Hanover, N.H. *Date of issue:* 25 August 1870. *Citation:* Gallantry in action.

NEDER, ADAM

Rank and organization: Private, Company A, 7th U.S. Cavalry. *Place and date:* Sioux campaign, December 1890. *Entered service at:* ———. *Birth:* Bavaria. *Date of issue:* 25 April 1891. *Citation:* Distinguished bravery.

NEILON, FREDERICK S.

Rank and organization: Sergeant, Company A, 6th U.S. Cavalry. *Place and date:* At Upper Washita, Tex., 9-11 September 1874. *Entered service at:* ———. *Birth:* Boston, Mass. *Date of issue:* 23 April 1875. *Citation:* Gallantry in action.

NEWMAN, HENRY

Rank and organization: First Sergeant, Company F, 5th U.S. Cavalry. *Place and date:* At Whetstone Mountains, Ariz., 13 July 1872. *Entered service at:* ———. *Birth:* Germany. *Date of issue:* 4 December 1874. *Citation:* He and 2 companions covered the withdrawal of wounded comrades from the fire of an Apache band well concealed among rocks.

NIHILL, JOHN

Rank and organization: Private, Company F, 5th U.S. Cavalry. *Place and date:* At Whetstone Mountains, Ariz., 13 July 1872. *Entered service at:* Brooklyn, N.Y. *Born:* 1850, Ireland. *Date of issue:* 4 December 1874. *Citation:* Fought and defeated 4 hostile Apaches located between him and his comrades.

NOLAN, RICHARD J.

Rank and organization: Farrier, Company I, 7th U.S. Cavalry. *Place and date:* At White Clay Creek, S. Dak., 30 December 1890. *Entered service at:* ———. *Birth:* Ireland. *Date of issue:* 1 April 1891. *Citation:* Bravery.

O'CALLAGHAN, JOHN

Rank and organization: Sergeant, Company B, 8th U.S. Cavalry. *Place and date:* Arizona, August to October 1868. *Entered service at:* ———. *Birth:* New York, N.Y. *Date of issue:* 24 July 1869. *Citation:* Bravery in scouts and actions against Indians.

OLIVER, FRANCIS

Rank and organization: First Sergeant, Company G, 1st U.S. Cavalry. *Place and date:* At Chiricahua Mountains, Ariz., 20 October 1869. *Entered service at:* ———. *Birth:* Baltimore, Md. *Date of issue:* 14 February 1870. *Citation:* Bravery in action.

O'NEILL, WILLIAM

Rank and organization: Corporal, Company I, 4th U.S. Cavalry. *Place and date:* At Red River, Tex., 29 September 1872. *Entered service at:* ———. *Birth:* Tariffville, Conn. *Date of issue:* 19 November 1872. *Citation:* Bravery in action.

O'REGAN, MICHAEL

Rank and organization: Private, Company B, 8th U.S. Cavalry. *Place and date:* Arizona, August to October 1868. *Entered service at:* ———. *Birth:* Fall River, Mass. *Date of issue:* 24 July 1869. *Citation:* Bravery in scouts and actions against Indians.

ORR, MOSES

Rank and organization: Private, Company A, 1st U.S. Cavalry. *Place and date:* Winter of 1872–73. *Entered service at:* ———. *Birth:* Ireland. *Date of issue:* 12 April 1875. *Citation:* Gallant conduct during campaigns and engagements with Apaches.

OSBORNE, WILLIAM

Rank and organization: Sergeant, Company M, 1st U.S. Cavalry. *Place and date:* Winter of 1872-73. *Entered service at:* ———. *Birth:* Boston, Mass. *Date of issue:* 12 April 1875. *Citation:* Gallant conduct during campaigns and engagements with Apaches.

O'SULLIVAN, JOHN

Rank and organization: Private, Company I, 4th U.S. Cavalry. *Place and date:* At Staked Plains, Tex., 8 December 1874. *Entered service at:* New York, N.Y. *Birth:* Ireland. *Date of issue:* 13 October 1875. *Citation:* Gallantry in a long chase after Indians.

PAINE, ADAM

Rank and organization: Private, Indian Scouts. *Place and date:* Canyon Blanco tributary of the Red River, Tex., 26–27 September 1874. *Entered service at:* Fort Duncan, Texas. *Birth:* Florida. *Date of issue:* 13 October 1875. *Citation:* Rendered invaluable service to Col. R. S. Mackenzie, 4th U.S. Cavalry, during this engagement.

PARNELL, WILLIAM R.

Rank and organization: First Lieutenant, 1st U.S. Cavalry. *Place and date:* At White Bird Canyon, Idaho, 17 June 1877. *Entered service at:* New York. *Birth:* Ireland. *Date of issue:* 16 September 1897. *Citation:* With a few men, in the face of a heavy fire from pursuing Indians and at imminent peril, returned and rescued a soldier whose horse had been killed and who had been left behind in the retreat.

PAYNE, ISAAC

Rank and organization: Trumpeter, Indian Scouts. *Place and date:* At Pecos River, Tex., 25 April 1875. *Entered service at:* ———. *Birth:* Mexico. *Date of issue:* 28 May 1875. *Citation:* With 3 other men, he participated in a charge against 25 hostiles while on a scouting patrol.

PENGALLY, EDWARD

Rank and organization: Private, Company B, 8th U.S. Cavalry. *Place and date:* At Chiricahua Mountains, Ariz., 20 October 1869. *Entered service at:* ———. *Birth:* England. *Date of issue:* 14 February 1870. *Citation:* Gallantry in action.

PENNSYL, JOSIAH

Rank and organization: Sergeant, Company M, 6th U.S. Cavalry. *Place and date:* At Upper Washita, Tex., 11 September 1874. *Entered service at:* ———. *Birth:* Frederick County, Md. *Date of issue:* 23 April 1875. *Citation:* Gallantry in action.

PHIFE, LEWIS

Rank and organization: Sergeant, Company B, 8th U.S. Cavalry. *Place and date:* Arizona, August to October 1868. *Entered service at:* Marion, Oreg. *Born:* 31 October 1846, Des Moines County, Iowa. *Date of issue:* 24 July 1869. *Citation:* Bravery in scouts and actions against Indians.

PHILIPSEN, WILHELM O.

Rank and organization: Blacksmith, Troop D, 5th U.S. Cavalry. *Place and date:* At Milk River, Colo., 29 September 1879. *Entered service at:* ———. *Birth:* Germany. *Date of issue:* 12 December 1894. *Citation:* With 9 others voluntarily attacked and captured a strong position held by Indians.

PHILLIPS, SAMUEL D.

Rank and organization: Private, Company H, 2d U.S. Cavalry. *Place and date:* At Muddy Creek, Mont., 7 May 1877. *Entered service at:* ———. *Birth:* Butler County, Ohio. *Date of issue:* 8 August 1877. *Citation:* Gallantry in action.

PHOENIX, EDWIN

Rank and organization: Corporal, Company E, 4th U.S. Cavalry. *Place and date:* Near Red River, Tex., 26–28 September 1874. *Entered service at:* Kentucky. *Birth:* St. Louis, Mo. *Date of issue:* 13 October 1875. *Citation:* Gallantry in action.

PLATTEN, FREDERICK

Rank and organization: Sergeant, Company H, 6th U.S. Cavalry. *Place and date:* At Sappa Creek, Kans., 23 April 1875. *Entered service at:* ———. *Birth:* Ireland. *Date of issue:* 16 November 1876. *Citation:* With 5 other men he waded in mud and water up the creek to a position directly behind an entrenched Cheyenne position, who were using natural bank pits to good advantage against the main column. This surprise attack from the enemy rear broke their resistance.

POPPE, JOHN A.

Rank and organization: Sergeant, Company F, 5th U.S. Cavalry. *Place and date:* At Milk River, Colo., 29 September to 5 October 1879. *Entered service at:* ———. *Birth:* Cincinnati, Ohio. *Date of issue:* 27 January 1880. *Citation:* Gallantry in action.

PORTER, SAMUEL

Rank and organization: Farrier, Company L, 6th U.S. Cavalry. *Place and date:* At Wichita River, Tex., 12 July 1870. *Entered service at:* ———. *Birth:* Montgomery County, Md. *Date of issue:* 25 August 1870. *Citation:* Gallantry in action.

POWERS, THOMAS

Rank and organization: Corporal, Company G, 1st U.S. Cavalry. *Place and date:* At Chiricahua Mountains, Ariz., 20 October 1869. *Entered service at:* ———. *Birth:* New York, N.Y. *Date of issue:* 14 February 1870. *Citation:* Gallantry in action.

PRATT, JAMES

Rank and organization: Blacksmith, Company I, 4th U.S. Cavalry. *Place and date:* At Red River, Tex., 29 September 1872. *Entered service at:* Bellefontaine, Ohio. *Birth:* Bellefontaine, Ohio. *Date of issue:* 19 November 1872. *Citation:* Gallantry in action.

PYM, JAMES

Rank and organization: Private, Company B, 7th U.S. Cavalry. *Place and date:* At Little Big Horn River, Mont., 25 June 1876. *Entered service at:* Boston, Mass. *Birth:* Oxfordshire, England. *Date of issue:* 5 October 1878. *Citation:* Voluntarily went for water and secured the same under heavy fire.

RAERICK, JOHN

Rank and organization: Private, Company L, 8th U.S. Cavalry. *Place and date:* At Lyry Creek, Ariz., 14 October 1869. *Entered service at:* ———. *Birth:* Germany. *Date of issue:* 3 March 1870. *Citation:* Gallantry in action with Indians.

RAGNAR, THEODORE

Rank and organization: First Sergeant, Company K, 7th U.S. Cavalry. *Place and date:* At White Clay Creek, S. Dak., 30 December 1890. *Entered service at:* ———. *Birth:* Sweden. *Date of issue:* 13 April 1891. *Citation:* Bravery.

RANKIN, WILLIAM

Rank and organization: Private, Company F, 4th U.S. Cavalry. *Place and date:* At Red River, Tex., 29 September 1872. *Entered service at:* ———. *Birth:* Lewistown, Pa. *Date of issue:* 19 November 1872. *Citation:* Gallantry in action with Indians.

REED, JAMES C.

Rank and organization: Private, Company A, 8th U.S. Cavalry. *Place and date:* Arizona, 29 April 1868. *Entered service at:* ———. *Birth:* Ireland. *Date of issue:* 24 July 1869. *Citation:* Defended his position (with 3 others) against a party of 17 hostile Indians under heavy fire at close quarters, the entire party except himself being severely wounded.

RICHMAN, SAMUEL

Rank and organization: Private, Company E, 8th U.S. Cavalry. *Place and date:* Arizona, 1868 and 1869. *Entered service at:* ———. *Birth:* Cleveland, Ohio. *Date of issue:* 6 September 1869. *Citation:* Bravery in actions with Indians.

ROACH, HAMPTON M.

Rank and organization: Corporal, Company F, 5th U.S. Cavalry. *Place and date:* At Milk River, Colo., 29 September to 5 October 1879. *Entered service at:* —LA—. *Birth:* Concord, La. *Date of issue:* 27 January 1880. *Citation:* Erected breastworks under fire; also kept the command supplied with water 3 consecutive nights while exposed to fire from ambushed Indians at close range.

ROBBINS, MARCUS M.

Rank and organization: Private, Company H, 6th U.S. Cavalry. *Place and date:* At Sappa Creek, Kans., 23 April 1875. *Entered service at:* ———. *Birth:* Elba, Wis. *Date of issue:* 16 November 1876. *Citation:* With 5 other men he waded in mud and water up the creek to a position directly behind an entrenched Cheyenne position, who were using natural bank pits to good advantage against the main column. This surprise attack from the enemy rear broke their resistance.

ROBINSON, JOSEPH

Rank and organization: First Sergeant, Company D, 3d U.S. Cavalry. *Place and date:* At Rosebud River, Mont., 17 June 1876. *Entered service at:* ———. *Birth:* Ireland. *Date of issue:* 23 January 1880. *Citation:* Discharged his duties while in charge of the skirmish line under fire with judgment and great coolness and brought up the lead horses at a critical moment.

ROCHE, DAVID

Rank and organization: First Sergeant, Company A, 5th U.S. Infantry. *Place and date:* At Cedar Creek, etc., Mont., 21 October 1876 to 8 January 1877. *Entered service at:* ———. *Birth:* Ireland. *Date of issue:* 27 April 1877. *Citation:* Gallantry in action.

RODENBURG, HENRY

Rank and organization: Private, Company A, 5th U.S. Infantry. *Place and date:* At Cedar Creek, etc., Mont., 21 October 1876 to 8 January 1877. *Entered service at:* ———. *Birth:* Germany. *Date of issue:* 27 April 1877. *Citation:* Gallantry in action.

ROGAN, PATRICK

Rank and organization: Sergeant, Company A, 7th U.S. Infantry. *Place and date:* At Big Hole, Mont., 9 August 1877. *Entered service at:* ———. *Birth:* Ireland. *Date of issue:* 2 December 1878. *Citation:* Verified and reported the company while subjected to a galling fire from the enemy.

ROMEYN, HENRY

Rank and organization: First Lieutenant, 5th U.S. Infantry. *Place and date:* At Bear Paw Mountain, Mont., 30 September 1877. *Entered service at:* Michigan. *Birth:* Galen, N.Y. *Date of issue:* 27 November 1894. *Citation:* Led his command into close range of the enemy, there maintained his position, and vigorously prosecuted the fight until he was severely wounded.

ROONEY, EDWARD

Rank and organization: Private, Company D, 5th U.S. Infantry. *Place and date:* At Cedar Creek, etc., Mont., 21 October 1876 to 8 January 1877. *Entered service at:* Poughkeepsie, N.Y. *Birth:* Poughkeepsie, N.Y. *Date of issue:* 27 April 1877. *Citation:* Gallantry in action.

ROTH, PETER

Rank and organization: Private, Company A, 6th U.S. Cavalry. *Place and date:* At Wichita River, Tex., 12 September 1874. *Entered service at:* ———. *Birth:* Germany. *Date of issue:* 4 November 1874. *Citation:* While carrying dispatches was attacked by 125 hostile Indians, whom he and his comrades fought throughout the day.

ROWALT, JOHN F.

Rank and organization: Private, Company L, 8th U.S. Cavalry. *Place and date:* At Lyry Creek, Ariz., 14 October 1869. *Entered service at:* Belleville, Ohio. *Birth:* Belleville, Ohio. *Date of issue:* 3 March 1870. *Citation:* Gallantry in action with Indians.

ROWDY

Rank and organization: Sergeant, Company A, Indian Scouts. *Place and date:* Arizona, 7 March 1890. *Entered service at:* ———. *Birth:* Arizona. *Date of issue:* 15 May 1890. *Citation:* Bravery in action with Apache Indians.

ROY, STANISLAUS

Rank and organization: Sergeant, Company A, 7th U.S. Cavalry. *Place and date:* At Little Big Horn, Mont., 25 June 1876. *Entered service at:* ———. *Birth:* France. *Date of issue:* 5 October 1878. *Citation:* Brought water to the wounded at great danger to life and under a most galling fire of the enemy.

RUSSELL, JAMES

Rank and organization: Private, Company G, 1st U.S. Cavalry. *Place and date:* At Chiricahua Mountains, Ariz., 20 October 1869. *Entered service at:* ———. *Birth:* New York, N.Y. *Date of issue:* 14 February 1870. *Citation:* Gallantry in action with Indians.

RYAN, DAVID

Rank and organization: Private, Company G, 5th U.S. Infantry. *Place and date:* At Cedar Creek, etc., Mont., 21 October 1876 to 8 January 1877. *Entered service at:* ———. *Birth:* Ireland. *Date of issue:* 27 April 1877. *Citation:* Gallantry in action.

RYAN, DENNIS

Rank and organization: First Sergeant, Company I, 6th U.S. Cavalry. *Place and date:* At Gageby Creek, Indian Territory, 2 December 1874. *Entered service at:* ———. *Birth:* Ireland. *Date of issue:* 23 April 1875. *Citation:* Courage while in command of a detachment.

SALE, ALBERT

Rank and organization: Private, Company F, 8th U.S. Cavalry. *Place and date:* At Santa Maria River, Ariz., 29 June 1869. *Entered service at:* ———. *Birth:* Broome County, N.Y. *Date of issue:* 3 March 1870. *Citation:* Gallantry in killing an Indian warrior and capturing pony and effects.

SCHNITZER, JOHN

Rank and organization: Wagoner, Troop G, 4th U.S. Cavalry. *Place and date:* At Horseshoe Canyon, N. Mex., 23 April 1882. *Entered service at:* ———. *Birth:* Bavaria. *Date of issue:* 17 August 1896. *Citation:* Assisted, under a heavy fire, to rescue a wounded comrade.

SCHOU, JULIUS

Rank and organization: Corporal, Company I, 22d U.S. Infantry. *Place and date:* Sioux Campaign, 1870. *Entered service at:* ———. *Birth:* Denmark. *Date of issue:* 19 November 1884. *Citation:* Carried dispatches to Fort Buford.

SCHROETER, CHARLES

Rank and organization: Private, Company G, 8th U.S. Cavalry. *Place and date:* At Chiricahua Mountains, Ariz., 20 October 1869. *Entered service at:* ———. *Birth:* Germany. *Date of issue:* 14 February 1870. *Citation:* Gallantry in action.

SCOTT, GEORGE D.

Rank and organization: Private, Company D, 7th U.S. Cavalry. *Place and date:* At Little Big Horn, Mont., 25–26 June 1876. *Entered service at:* Mt. Vernon, Ky. *Birth:* Lancaster County, Ky. *Date of issue:* 5 October 1878. *Citation:* Voluntarily brought water to the wounded under fire.

SCOTT, ROBERT B.

Rank and organization: Private, Company G, 8th U.S. Cavalry. *Place and date:* At Chiricahua Mountains, Ariz., 20 October 1869. *Entered service at:* ———. *Birth:* Washington County, N.Y. *Date of issue:* 14 February 1870. *Citation:* Gallantry in action.

SHAFFER, WILLIAM

Rank and organization: Private, Company B, 8th U.S. Cavalry. *Place and date:* Arizona, August to October 1868. *Entered service at:* ———. *Birth:* Germany. *Date of issue:* 24 July 1869. *Citation:* Bravery in scouts and actions against Indians.

SHARPLESS, EDWARD C.

Rank and organization: Corporal, Company H, 6th U.S. Cavalry. *Place and date:* At Upper Washita, Tex., 9–11 September 1874. *Entered service at:* ———. *Birth:* Marion County, Ohio. *Date of issue:* 23 April 1875. *Citation:* While carrying dispatches was attacked by 125 hostile Indians, whom he (and a comrade) fought throughout the day.

SHAW, THOMAS

Rank and organization: Sergeant, Company K, 9th U.S. Cavalry. *Place and date:* At Carrizo Canyon, N. Mex., 12 August 1881. *Entered service at:* Pike County, Mo. *Birth:* Covington, Ky. *Date of issue:* 7 December 1890. *Citation:* Forced the enemy back after stubbornly holding his ground in an extremely exposed position and prevented the enemy's superior numbers from surrounding his command.

SHEERIN, JOHN

Rank and organization: Blacksmith, Company C, 8th U.S. Cavalry. *Place and date:* Near Fort Selden, N. Mex., 8–11 July 1873. *Entered service at:* ———. *Birth:* Camden County, N.J. *Date of issue:* 12 August 1875. *Citation:* Services against hostile Indians.

SHEPPARD, CHARLES

Rank and organization: Private, Company A, 5th U.S. Infantry. *Place and date:* At Cedar Creek, etc., Mont., 21 October 1876 to 8 January 1877. *Entered service at:* St. Louis, Mo. *Birth:* Rocky Hill, Conn. *Date of issue:* 27 April 1877. *Citation:* Bravery in action with Sioux.

SHINGLE, JOHN H.

Rank and organization: First Sergeant, Troop I, 3d U.S. Cavalry. *Place and date:* At Rosebud River, Mont., 17 June 1876. *Entered service at:* ———. *Birth:* Philadelphia, Pa. *Date of issue:* 1 June 1880. *Citation:* Gallantry in action.

SINGLETON, FRANK

(See p. 306, Frederick S. Neilon, true name.)

SKINNER, JOHN O.

Rank and organization: Contract Surgeon, U.S. Army. *Place and date:* At Lava Beds, Oreg., 17 January 1873. *Entered service at:* Maryland. *Birth:* Maryland. *Date of issue:* Unknown. *Citation:* Rescued a wounded soldier who lay under a close and heavy fire during the assault on the Modoc stronghold after 2 soldiers had unsuccessfully attempted to make the rescue and both had been wounded in doing so.

SMITH, ANDREW J.

Rank and organization: Sergeant, Company G, 8th U.S. Cavalry. *Place and date:* At Chiricahua Mountains, Ariz., 20 October 1869. *Entered service at:* Baltimore, Md. *Birth:* Baltimore, Md. *Date of issue:* 14 February 1870. *Citation:* Gallantry in action.

SMITH, CHARLES E.

Rank and organization: Corporal, Company H, 6th U.S. Cavalry. *Place and date:* At Wichita River, Tex., 12 July 1870. *Entered service at:* ———. *Birth:* Auburn, N.Y. *Date of issue:* 25 August 1870. *Citation:* Gallantry in action.

SMITH, CORNELIUS C.

Rank and organization: Corporal, Company K, 6th U.S. Cavalry. *Place and date:* Near White River, S. Dak., 1 January 1891. *Entered service at:* Helena, Mont. *Birth:* Tucson, Ariz. *Date of issue:* 4 February 1891. *Citation:* With 4 men of his troop drove off a superior force of the enemy and held his position against their repeated efforts to recapture it, and subsequently pursued them a great distance.

*SMITH, GEORGE W.

Rank and organization: Private, Company M, 6th U.S. Cavalry. *Place and date:* At Wichita River, Tex., 12 September 1874. *Entered service at:* ———. *Birth:* Greenfield, N.Y. *Date of issue:* 4 November 1874. *Citation:* While carrying dispatches was attacked by 125 hostile Indians, whom he and his comrades fought throughout the day. Pvt. Smith was mortally wounded during the engagement and died early the next day.

SMITH, OTTO

Rank and organization: Private, Company K, 8th U.S. Cavalry. *Place and date:* Arizona, 1868 and 1869. *Entered service at:* ———. *Birth:* Baltimore, Md. *Date of issue:* 6 September 1869. *Citation:* Bravery in scouts and actions against Indians.

SMITH, ROBERT

Rank and organization: Private, Company M, 3d U.S. Infantry. *Place and date:* At Slim Buttes, Mont., 9 September 1876. *Entered service at:* ———. *Birth:* Philadelphia, Pa. *Date of issue:* 16 October 1877. *Citation:* Special bravery in endeavoring to dislodge Indians secreted in a ravine.

SMITH, THEODORE F.

Rank and organization: Private, Company G, 1st U.S. Cavalry. *Place and date:* At Chiricahua Mountains, Ariz., 20 October 1869. *Entered service at:* ———. *Birth:* Rahway, N.J. *Date of issue:* 14 February 1879. *Citation:* Gallantry in action.

SMITH, THOMAS

Rank and organization: Private, Company G, 1st U.S. Cavalry. *Place and date:* At Chiricahua Mountains, Ariz., 20 October 1869. *Entered service at:* ———. *Birth:* Boston, Mass. *Date of issue:* 14 February 1870. *Citation:* Gallantry in action.

SMITH, THOMAS J.

Rank and organization: Private, Company G, 1st U.S. Cavalry. *Place and date:* At Chiricahua Mountains, Ariz., 20 October 1869. *Entered service at:* ———. *Birth:* England. *Date of issue:* 14 February 1870. *Citation:* Gallantry in action.

SMITH, WILLIAM

Rank and organization: Private, Company G, 8th U.S. Cavalry. *Place and date:* At Chiricahua Mountains, Ariz., 20 October 1869. *Entered service at:* ———. *Birth:* Bath, Maine. *Date of issue:* 14 February 1870. *Citation:* Gallantry in action.

SMITH, WILLIAM H.

Rank and organization: Private, Company G, 1st U.S. Cavalry. *Place and date:* At Chiricahua Mountains, Ariz., 20 October 1869. *Entered service at:* ———. *Birth:* Lapeer County, Mich. *Date of issue:* 14 February 1870. *Citation:* Gallantry in action.

SNOW, ELMER A.

Rank and organization: Trumpeter, Company M, 3d U.S. Cavalry. *Place and date:* At Rosebud Creek, Mont., 17 June 1876. *Entered service at:* ᴹᴬ—. *Birth:* Hardwick, Mass. *Date of issue:* 16 October 1877. *Citation:* Bravery in action; was wounded in both arms.

SPENCE, ORIZOBA

Rank and organization: Private, Company G, 8th U.S. Cavalry. *Place and date:* At Chiricahua Mountains, Ariz., 20 October 1869. *Entered service at:* Tionesta, Pa. *Birth:* Forest County, Pa. *Date of issue:* 14 February 1870. *Citation:* Gallantry in action.

SPRINGER, GEORGE

Rank and organization: Private, Company G, 1st U.S. Cavalry. *Place and date:* At Chiricahua Mountains, Ariz., 20 October 1869. *Entered service at:* ———. *Birth:* York County, Pa. *Date of issue:* 14 February 1870. *Citation:* Gallantry in action.

STANCE, EMANUEL

Rank and organization: Sergeant, Company F, 9th U.S. Cavalry. *Place and date:* At Kickapoo Springs, Tex., 20 May 1870. *Entered service at:* ———. *Birth:* Carroll Parish, La. *Date of issue:* 28 June 1870. *Citation:* Gallantry on scout after Indians.

STANLEY, EBEN

Rank and organization: Private, Company A, 5th U.S. Cavalry. *Place and date:* Near Turret Mountain, Ariz., 25 and 27 March 1873. *Entered service at:* ———. *Birth:* Decatur County, Iowa. *Date of issue:* 12 April 1875. *Citation:* Gallantry in action.

STANLEY, EDWARD

Rank and organization: Corporal, Company F, 8th U.S. Cavalry. *Place and date:* At Seneca Mountain, Ariz., 26 August 1869. *Entered service at:* ———. *Birth:* New York, N.Y. *Date of issue:* 3 March 1870. *Citation:* Gallantry in action.

STAUFFER, RUDOLPH

Rank and organization: First Sergeant, Company K, 5th U.S. Cavalry. *Place and date:* Near Camp Hualpai, Ariz., 1872. *Entered service at:* ———. *Birth:* Switzerland. *Date of issue:* 30 July 1875. *Citation:* Gallantry on scouts after Indians.

STEINER, CHRISTIAN

Rank and organization: Saddler, Company G, 8th U.S. Cavalry. *Place and date:* At Chiricahua Mountains, Ariz., 20 October 1869. *Entered service at:* ———. *Birth:* Germany. *Date of issue:* 14 February 1870. *Citation:* Gallantry in action.

STEWART, BENJAMIN F.

Rank and organization: Private, Company E, 7th U.S. Infantry. *Place and date:* At Big Horn River, Mont., 9 July 1876. *Entered service at:* ———. *Birth:* Norfolk, Va. *Date of issue:* 2 December 1876. *Citation:* Carried dispatches to Gen. Crook at imminent risk of his life.

STICKOFFER, JULIUS H.

Rank and organization: Saddler, Company L, 8th U.S. Cavalry. *Place and date:* At Cienaga Springs, Utah, 11 November 1868. *Entered service at:* ———. *Birth:* Switzerland. *Date of issue:* 3 March 1870. *Citation:* Gallantry in action.

STIVERS, THOMAS W.

Rank and organization: Private, Company D, 7th U.S. Cavalry. *Place and date:* At Little Big Horn, Mont., 25–26 June 1876. *Entered service at:* Mt. Vernon, Ky. *Birth:* Madison County, Ky. *Date of issue:* 5 October 1878. *Citation:* Voluntarily brought water to the wounded under fire.

STOKES, ALONZO

Rank and organization: First Sergeant, Company H, 6th U.S. Cavalry. *Place and date:* At Wichita River, Tex., 12 July 1870. *Entered service at:* ———. *Birth:* Logan County, Ohio. *Date of issue:* 25 August 1870. *Citation:* Gallantry in action.

STRAYER, WILLIAM H.

Rank and organization: Private, Company B, 3d U.S. Cavalry. *Place and date:* At Loupe Forke, Platte River, Nebr., 26 April 1872. *Entered service at:* ———. *Birth:* Maytown, Pa. *Date of issue:* 22 May 1862. *Citation:* Gallantry in action.

STRIVSON, BENONI

Rank and organization: Private, Company B, 8th U.S. Cavalry. *Place and date:* Arizona, August to October 1868. *Entered service at:* ———. *Birth:* Overton, Tenn. *Date of issue:* 24 July 1869. *Citation:* Bravery in scouts and actions against Indians.

SULLIVAN, THOMAS

Rank and organization: Private, Company G, 1st U.S. Cavalry. *Place and date:* At Chiricahua Mountains, Ariz., 20 October 1869. *Entered service at:* ———. *Birth:* Covington, Ky. *Date of issue:* 14 February 1870. *Citation:* Gallantry in action against Indians concealed in a ravine.

SULLIVAN, THOMAS

Rank and organization: Private, Company E, 7th U.S. Cavalry. *Place and date:* At Wounded Knee Creek, S. Dak., 29 December 1890. *Entered service at:* Newark, N.J. *Birth:* Ireland. *Date of issue:* 17 December 1891. *Citation:* Conspicuous bravery in action against Indians concealed in a ravine.

SUMNER, JAMES

Rank and organization: Private, Company G, 1st U.S. Cavalry. *Place and date:* At Chiricahua Mountains, Ariz., 20 October 1869. *Entered service at:* Chicago, Ill., *Birth:* England. *Date of issue:* 14 February 1870. *Citation:* Gallantry in action.

SUTHERLAND, JOHN A.

Rank and organization: Corporal, Company L, 8th U.S. Cavalry. *Place and date:* Arizona, August to October 1868. *Entered service at:* Montgomery County, Ind. *Birth:* Monroe County, Ind. *Date of issue:* 24 July 1869. *Citation:* Bravery in scouts and actions against Indians.

TAYLOR, BERNARD

Rank and organization: Sergeant, Company A, 5th U.S. Cavalry. *Place and date:* Near Sunset Pass, Ariz., 1 November 1874. *Entered service at:* Washington, D.C. *Birth:* St. Louis, Mo. *Date of issue:* 12 April 1875. *Citation:* Bravery in rescuing Lt. King, 5th U.S. Cavalry, from Indians.

TAYLOR, CHARLES

Rank and organization: First Sergeant, Company D, 3d U.S. Cavalry. *Place and date:* At Big Dry Wash, Ariz., 17 July 1862. *Entered service at:* ———. *Birth:* Baltimore, Md. *Date of issue:* 16 December 1882. *Citation:* Gallantry in action.

TAYLOR, WILBUR N.

Rank and organization: Corporal, Company K, 8th U.S. Cavalry. *Place and date:* Arizona, 1868 and 1869. *Entered service at:* ———. *Birth:* Hamden, Maine. *Date of issue:* 6 September 1869. *Citation:* Bravery in actions with Indians.

TEA, RICHARD L.

Rank and organization: Sergeant, Company H, 6th U.S. Cavalry. *Place and date:* At Sappa Creek, Kans., 23 April 1875. *Entered service at:* ———. *Birth:* Philadelphia, Pa. *Date of issue:* 16 November 1876. *Citation:* With 5 other men he waded in mud and water up the creek to a position directly behind an entrenched Cheyenne position, who were using natural bank pits to good advantage against the main column. This surprise attack from the enemy rear broke their resistance.

THOMAS, CHARLES L.

Rank and organization: Sergeant, Company E, 11th Ohio Cavalry. *Place and date:* At Powder River Expedition Dakota Territory, 17 September 1865. *Entered service at:* ———. *Birth:* Philadelphia, Pa. *Date of issue:* 24 August 1894. *Citation:* Carried a message through a country infested with hostile Indians and saved the life of a comrade en route.

THOMPSON, GEORGE W.

Rank and organization: Private, Company C, 2d U.S. Cavalry. *Place and date:* At Little Blue, Nebr., 15 May 1870. *Entered service at:* ———. *Birth:* Victory, N.Y. *Date of issue:* 22 June 1870. *Citation:* Gallantry in action.

THOMPSON, JOHN

Rank and organization: Sergeant, Company G, 1st U.S. Cavalry. *Place and date:* At Chiricahua Mountains, Ariz., 20 October 1869. *Entered service at:* New York, N.Y. *Birth:* Scotland. *Date of issue:* 14 February 1870. *Citation:* Bravery in action with Indians.

THOMPSON, PETER

Rank and organization: Private, Company C, 7th U.S. Cavalry. *Place and date:* At Little Big Horn, Mont., 25 June 1876. *Entered service at:* Pittsburgh, Pa. *Birth:* Scotland. *Date of issue:* 5 October 1878. *Citation:* After having voluntarily brought water to the wounded, in which effort he was shot through the head, he made two successful trips for the same purpose, notwithstanding remonstrances of his sergeant.

TILTON, HENRY R.

Rank and organization: Major and Surgeon, U.S. Army. *Place and date:* At Bear Paw Mountain, Mont., 30 September 1877. *Entered service at:* Jersey City, N.J. *Birth:* Barnegat, N.J. *Date of issue:* 22 March 1895. *Citation:* Fearlessly risked his life and displayed great gallantry in rescuing and protecting the wounded men.

TOLAN, FRANK

Rank and organization: Private, Company D, 7th U.S. Cavalry. *Place and date:* At Little Big Horn, Mont., 25 June 1876. *Entered service at:* Boston, Mass. *Birth:* Malone, N.Y. *Date of issue:* 5 October 1878. *Citation:* Voluntarily brought water to the wounded under fire.

TOY, FREDERICK E.

Rank and organization: First Sergeant, Company G, 7th U.S. Cavalry. *Place and date:* At Wounded Knee Creek, S. Dak., 29 December 1890. *Entered service at:* ———. *Birth:* Buffalo, N.Y. *Date of issue:* 26 May 1891. *Citation:* Bravery.

TRACY, JOHN

Rank and organization: Private, Company G, 8th U.S. Cavalry. *Place and date:* At Chiricahua Mountains, Ariz., 20 October 1869. *Entered service at:* St. Paul, Minn. *Birth:* Ireland. *Date of issue:* 14 February 1870. *Citation:* Bravery in action with Indians.

TRAUTMAN, JACOB

Rank and organization: First Sergeant, Company I, 7th U.S. Cavalry. *Place and date:* At Wounded Knee Creek, S. Dak., 29 December 1890. *Entered service at:* ———. *Birth:* Germany. *Date of issue:* 27 March 1891. *Citation:* Killed a hostile Indian at close quarters, and, although entitled to retirement from service, remained to the close of the campaign.

TURPIN, JAMES H.

Rank and organization: First Sergeant, Company L, 5th U.S. Cavalry. *Place and date:* Arizona, 1872–74. *Entered service at:* ———. *Birth:* Easton, Mass. *Date of issue:* 12 April 1875. *Citation:* Gallantry in actions with Apaches.

VARNUM, CHARLES A.

Rank and organization: Captain, Company B, 7th U.S. Cavalry. *Place and date:* At White Clay Creek, S. Dak., 30 December 1890. *Entered service at:* Pensacola, Fla. *Birth:* Troy, N.Y. *Date of issue:* 22 September 1897. *Citation:* While executing an order to withdraw, seeing that a continuance of the movement would expose another troop of his regiment to being cut off and surrounded, he disregarded orders to retire, placed himself in front of his men, led a charge upon the advancing Indians, regained a commanding position that had just been vacated, and thus insured a safe withdrawal of both detachments without further loss.

VEUVE, ERNEST

Rank and organization: Farrier, Company A, 4th U.S. Cavalry. *Place and date:* At Staked Plains, Tex., 3 November 1874. *Entered service at:* ———. *Birth:* Switzerland. *Date of issue:* 13 October 1875. *Citation:* Gallant manner in which he faced a desperate Indian.

VOIT, OTTO

Rank and organization: Saddler, Company H, 7th U.S. Cavalry. *Place and date:* At Little Big Horn, Mont., 25 June 1876. *Entered service at:* ———. *Birth:* Germany. *Date of issue:* 5 October 1878. *Citation:* Volunteered with George Geiger, Charles Windolph, and Henry Mechlin to hold an exposed position standing erect on the brow of the hill facing the Little Big Horn River. They fired constantly in this manner for more than 20 minutes diverting fire and attention from another group filling canteens of water that were desperately needed.

VOKES, LEROY H.

Rank and organization: First Sergeant, Company B, 3d U.S. Cavalry. *Place and date:* At Loupe Fork, Platte River, Nebr., 26 April 1872. *Entered service at:* ———. *Birth:* Lake County, Ill. *Date of issue:* 22 May 1872. *Citation:* Gallantry in action.

VON MEDEM, RUDOLPH

Rank and organization: Sergeant, Company A, 5th U.S. Cavalry. *Place and date:* 1872–73. *Entered service at:* ———. *Birth:* Germany. *Date of issue:* 12 April 1875. *Citation:* Gallantry in actions and campaigns.

WALKER, ALLEN

Rank and organization: Private, Company C, 3d U.S. Cavalry. *Place and date:* Texas, 30 December 1891. *Entered service at:* ———. *Birth:* Patriot, Ind. *Date of issue:* 25 April 1892. *Citation:* While carrying dispatches, he attacked a party of 3 armed men and secured papers valuable to the United States.

WALKER, JOHN

Rank and organization: Private, Company D, 8th U.S. Cavalry. *Place and date:* At Red Creek, Ariz., 23 September 1869. *Entered service at:* ———. *Birth:* France. *Date of issue:* 23 November 1869. *Citation:* Gallantry in action with Indians.

WALLACE, WILLIAM

Rank and organization: Sergeant, Company C, 5th U.S. Infantry. *Place and date:* At Cedar Creek, etc., Mont., 21 October 1876 to 8 January 1877. *Entered service at:* ———. *Birth:* Ireland. *Date of issue:* 27 April 1877. *Citation:* Gallantry in action.

WALLEY, AUGUSTUS

Rank and organization: Private, Company I, 9th U.S. Cavalry. *Place and date:* At Cuchillo Negro Mountains, N. Mex., 16 August 1881. *Entered service at:* ———. *Birth:* Reistertown, Md. *Date of issue:* 1 October 1890. *Citation:* Bravery in action with hostile Apaches.

WARD, CHARLES H.

Rank and organization: Private, Company G, 1st U.S. Cavalry. *Place and date:* At Chiricahua Mountains, Ariz., 20 October 1869. *Entered service at:* Philadelphia, Pa. *Birth:* England, *Date of issue:* 14 February 1870. *Citation:* Gallantry in action with Indians.

WARD, JAMES

Rank and organization: Sergeant, Company B, 7th U.S. Cavalry. *Place and date:* At Wounded Knee Creek, S. Dak., 29 December 1890. *Entered service at:* Boston, Mass. *Birth:* Quincy, Mass. *Date of issue:* 16 April 1891. *Citation:* Continued to fight after being severely wounded.

WARD, JOHN

Rank and organization: Sergeant, 24th U.S. Infantry Indian Scouts. *Place and date:* At Pecos River, Tex., 25 April 1875. *Entered service at:* Fort Duncan, Tex. *Birth:* Arkansas. *Date of issue:* 28 May 1875. *Citation:* With 3 other men, he participated in a charge against 25 hostiles while on a scouting patrol.

WARRINGTON, LEWIS

Rank and organization: First Lieutenant, 4th U.S. Cavalry. *Place and date:* At Muchague Valley, Tex., 8 December 1874. *Entered service at:* Washington, D.C. *Birth:* Washington, D.C. *Date of issue:* 12 April 1875. *Citation:* Gallantry in a combat with 5 Indians.

WATSON, JAMES C.

Rank and organization: Corporal, Company L, 6th U.S. Cavalry. *Place and date:* At Wichita River, Tex., 12 July 1870. *Entered service at:* ———. *Birth:* Cochecton, N.Y. *Date of issue:* 25 August 1870. *Citation:* Gallantry in action.

WATSON, JOSEPH

Rank and organization: Private, Company F, 8th U.S. Cavalry. *Place and date:* Near Picacho Mountain, Ariz., 4 June 1869. *Entered service at:* St. Joseph, Mich. *Birth:* Union City, Mich. *Date of issue:* 3 March 1870. *Citation:* Killed an Indian warrior and captured his arms.

WEAHER, ANDREW J.

Rank and organization: Private, Company B, 8th U.S. Cavalry. *Place and date:* Arizona, August to October 1868. *Entered service at:* ———. *Birth:* Philadelphia, Pa. *Date of issue:* 24 July 1869. *Citation:* Bravery in scouts and actions against Indians.

WEINERT, PAUL H.

Rank and organization: Corporal, Company E, 1st U.S. Artillery. *Place and date:* At Wounded Knee Creek, S. Dak., 29 December 1890. *Entered service at:* Baltimore, Md. *Birth:* Germany. *Date of issue:* 24 March 1891. *Citation:* Taking the place of his commanding officer, who had fallen severely wounded, he gallantly served his piece, after each fire advancing it to a better position.

WEISS, ENOCH R.

Rank and organization: Private, Company G, 1st U.S. Cavalry. *Place and date:* At Chiricahua Mountains, Ariz., 20 October 1869. *Entered service at:* ———. *Birth:* Kosciusko County, Ind. *Date of issue:* 14 February 1870. *Citation:* Gallantry in action with Indians.

WELCH, CHARLES H.

Rank and organization: Sergeant, Company D, 7th U.S. Cavalry. *Place and date:* At Little Big Horn, Mont., 25–26 June 1876. *Entered service at:* Ft. Snelling, Minn. *Birth:* New York, N.Y. *Date of issue:* 5 October 1878. *Citation:* Voluntarily brought water to the wounded, under fire.

WELCH, MICHAEL

Rank and organization: Sergeant, Company M, 6th U.S. Cavalry. *Place and date:* At Wichita River, Tex., 5 October 1870. *Entered service at:* ———. *Birth:* Poughkeepsie, N.Y. *Date of issue:* 19 November 1870. *Citation:* Gallantry in action.

WEST, FRANK

Rank and organization: First Lieutenant, 6th U.S. Cavalry. *Place and date:* At Big Dry Wash, Ariz., 17 July 1882. *Entered service at:* Mohawk, N.Y. *Birth:* Mohawk, N.Y. *Date of issue:* 12 July 1892. *Citation:* Rallied his command and led it in the advance against the enemy's fortified position.

WHITEHEAD, PATTON G.

Rank and organization: Private, Company C, 5th U.S. Infantry. *Place and date:* At Cedar Creek, etc., Mont., 21 October 1876 to 8 January 1877. *Entered service at:* ———. *Birth:* Russell County, Va. *Date of issue:* 27 April 1877. *Citation:* Gallantry in action.

WIDMER, JACOB

Rank and organization: First Sergeant, Company D, 5th U.S. Cavalry. *Place and date:* At Milk River, Colo., 29 September 1879. *Entered service at:* ———. *Birth:* Germany. *Date of issue:* 4 May 1880. *Citation:* Volunteered to accompany a small detachment on a very dangerous mission.

WILDER, WILBER E.

Rank and organization: First Lieutenant, 4th U.S. Cavalry. *Place and date:* At Horseshoe Canyon, N. Mex., 23 April 1882. *Entered service at:* Detroit, Mich. *Birth:* Atlas, Mich. *Date of issue:* 17 August 1896. *Citation:* Assisted, under a heavy fire, to rescue a wounded comrade.

WILKENS, HENRY

Rank and organization: First Sergeant, Company L, 2d U.S. Cavalry. *Place and date:* At Little Muddy Creek, Mont., 7 May 1877; at Camas Meadows, Idaho, 20 August 1877. *Entered service at:* ———. *Birth:* Germany. *Date of issue:* 28 February 1878. *Citation:* Bravery in actions with Indians.

WILLIAMS, MOSES

Rank and organization: First Sergeant, Company I, 9th U.S. Cavalry. *Place and date:* At foothills of the Cuchillo Negro Mountains, N. Mex., 16 August 1881. *Entered service at:* ———. *Birth:* Carrollton, La. *Date of issue:* 12 November 1896. *Citation:* Rallied a detachment, skillfully conducted a running fight of 3 or 4 hours, and by his coolness, bravery, and unflinching devotion to duty in standing by his commanding officer in an exposed position under a heavy fire from a large party of Indians saved the lives of at least 3 of his comrades.

WILLS, HENRY

Rank and organization: Private, Company C, 8th U.S. Cavalry. *Place and date:* Near Fort Selden, N. Mex., 8–11 July 1873. *Entered service at:* Pennsylvania. *Birth:* Gracon, Pa. *Date of issue:* 12 August 1875. *Citation:* Services against hostile Indians.

WILSON, BENJAMIN

Rank and organization: Private, Company M, 6th U.S. Cavalry. *Place and date:* At Wichita River, Tex., 5 October 1870. *Entered service at:* ———. *Birth:* Pittsburgh, Pa. *Date of issue:* 19 November 1870. *Citation:* Gallantry in action.

WILSON, CHARLES

Rank and organization: Corporal, Company H, 5th U.S. Infantry. *Place and date:* At Cedar Creek, etc., Mont., 21 October 1876 to 8 January 1877. *Entered service at:* Beardstown, Ill. *Birth:* Petersburg, Ill. *Date of issue:* 27 April 1877. *Citation:* Gallantry in action.

WILSON, MILDEN H.

Rank and organization: Sergeant, Company I, 7th U.S. Infantry. *Place and date:* At Big Hole, Mont., 9 August 1877. *Entered service at:* Newark, Ohio. *Birth:* Huron County, Ohio. *Date of issue:* 2 December 1878. *Citation:* Gallantry in forming company from line of skirmishers and deploying again under a galling fire, and in carrying dispatches at the imminent risk of his life.

WILSON, WILLIAM

Rank and organization: Sergeant, Company I, 4th U.S. Cavalry. *Place and date:* At Colorado Valley, Tex., 28 March 1872. *Entered service at:* Philadelphia, Pa. *Birth:* Philadelphia, Pa. *Date of issue:* 27 April 1872. Second award. *Citation:* In pursuit of a band of cattle thieves from New Mexico.

SECOND AWARD

Place and date: At Red River, Tex., 29 September 1872. *Citation:* Distinguished conduct in action with Indians, Red River, Tex.

WILSON, WILLIAM O.

Rank and organization: Corporal, Company I, 9th U.S. Cavalry. *Place and date:* Sioux Campaign, 1890. *Entered service at:* St. Paul, Minn. *Birth:* Hagerstown, Md. *Date of issue:* 17 September 1891. *Citation:* Bravery.

WINDOLPH, CHARLES

Rank and organization: Private, Company H, 7th U.S. Cavalry. *Place and date:* At Little Big Horn, Mont., 25–26 June 1876. *Entered service at:* Brooklyn, N.Y. *Born:* 9 December 1851, Germany. *Date of issue:* 5 October 1878. *Citation:* With 3 comrades, during the entire engagement, courageously held a position that secured water for the command.

702

WINDUS, CLARON A.

Rank and organization: Bugler, Company L, 6th U.S. Cavalry. *Place and date:* At Wichita River, Tex., 12 July 1870. *Entered service at:* ———. *Birth:* Janesville, Wis. *Date of issue:* 25 August 1870. *Citation:* Gallantry in action.

WINTERBOTTOM, WILLIAM

Rank and organization: Sergeant, Company A, 6th U.S. Cavalry. *Place and date:* At Wichita River, Tex., 12 July 1870. *Entered service at:* ———. *Birth:* England. *Date of issue:* 25 August 1870. *Citation:* Gallantry in action.

WITCOME, JOSEPH

Rank and organization: Private, Company B, 8th U.S. Cavalry. *Place and date:* Arizona, August to October 1868. *Entered service at:* ———. *Birth:* Mechanicsburg, Pa. *Date of issue:* 24 July 1869. *Citation:* Bravery in scouts and actions against Indians.

WOOD, LEONARD

Rank and organization: Assistant Surgeon, U.S. Army. *Place and date:* In Apache campaign, summer of 1886. *Entered service at:* Massachusetts. *Birth:* Winchester, N.H. *Date of issue:* 8 April 1898. *Citation:* Voluntarily carried dispatches through a region infested with hostile Indians, making a journey of 70 miles in one night and walking 30 miles the next day. Also for several weeks, while in close pursuit of Geronimo's band and constantly expecting an encounter, commanded a detachment of Infantry, which was then without an officer, and to the command of which he was assigned upon his own request.

WOODALL, ZACHARIAH

Rank and organization: Sergeant, Company I, 6th U.S. Cavalry. *Place and date:* At Wichita River, Tex., 12 September 1874. *Entered service at:* ———. *Birth:* Alexandria, Va. *Date of issue:* 7 November 1874. *Citation:* While in command of 5 men and carrying dispatches, was attacked by 125 Indians, whom he with his command fought throughout the day, he being severely wounded.

WOODS, BRENT

Rank and organization: Sergeant, Company B, 9th U.S. Cavalry. *Place and date:* New Mexico, 19 August 1881. *Entered service at:* Louisville, Ky. *Birth:* Pulaski County, Ky. *Date of issue:* 12 July 1894. *Citation:* Saved the lives of his comrades and citizens of the detachment.

WORTMAN, GEORGE G.

Rank and organization: Sergeant, Company B, 8th U.S. Cavalry. *Place and date:* Arizona, August to October 1868. *Entered service at:* ———. *Birth:* Monckton, New Brunswick. *Date of issue:* 24 July 1869. *Citation:* Bravery in scouts and actions against Indians.

YOUNT, JOHN P.

Rank and organization: Private, Company F, 3d U.S. Cavalry. *Place and date:* At Whetstone Mountains, Ariz., 5 May 1871. *Entered service at:* ~~IND~~. *Birth:* Putnam County, Ind. *Date of issue:* 13 November 1871. *Citation:* Gallantry in action with Indians.

✓ZIEGNER, HERMANN

Rank and organization: Private, Company E, 7th U.S. Cavalry. *Place and date:* At Wounded Knee Creek, and White Clay Creek, S. Dak., 29–30 December 1890. *Entered service at:* ⟨———⟩. *Birth:* Germany. *Date of issue:* 23 June 1891. *Citation:* Conspicuous bravery.

CODY, William Frederick - medal Restored by Act of congress.
(See attached Citation)

CAVALRY GUIDE WILLIAM FREDERICK CODY, UNITED STATES ARMY

BY DIRECTION OF CONGRESS, THE PRESIDENT OF THE UNITED STATE TAKES PLEASURE IN AWARDING THE MEDAL OF HONOR TO CAVALRY GUIDE WILLIAM F. CODY, UNITED STATES ARMY, COMPANY B, 3RD U.S. CAVALRY, FOR ACTION AT LOUPE FORK, PLATTE RIVER, NEBRASKA, 26 APRIL 1872. CITATION: FOR GALLANTRY IN ACTION AT PLATTE RIVER, NEBRASKA, APRIL 26, 1872.

ENTERED SERVICE: LEAVENWORTH, KANSAS
PLACE OF BIRTH: LE CLAIRE, SCOTT COUNTY, IOWA
DATE OF BIRTH: 26 FEBRUARY 1846
DATE OF DEATH: 10 JANUARY 1917
PLACE OF BURIAL: LOOKOUT MOUNTAIN
DENVER, COLORADO

CIVIL WAR

The first Medals of Honor awarded following enactment of the law which established the decoration went to 19 Union Army volunteers of the raiding party sent by General Mitchell in April 1862, to sabotage the vital Confederate rail link between Atlanta and Chattanooga. Disguised as civilians, the raiders captured the locomotive *General* at Big Shanty, Ga., 200 miles deep in enemy territory. Under close pursuit by the Confederates, the party fled north, attempting to burn bridges and destroy track along the way, but after 90 miles, the "Great Locomotive Chase" came to an end. In a few days, all of the raiders were captured and eight were tried and executed. On March 25, 1863, six of the party arrived in Washington after parole from a Confederate prison, and these six men were the first to be presented with Medals of Honor by Secretary of War Stanton. Medals were subsequently awarded to 13 other members of the raiding party, some posthumously.

ADAMS, JAMES F.

Rank and organization: Private, Company D, 1st West Virginia Cavalry. *Place and date:* At Nineveh, Va., 12 November 1864. *Entered service at:* ———. *Birth:* Cabell County, Va. *Date of issue:* 26 November 1864. *Citation:* Capture of State flag of 14th Virginia Cavalry (C.S.A.)

ADAMS, JOHN G. B.

Rank and organization: Second Lieutenant, Company I, 19th Massachusetts Infantry. *Place and date:* At Fredericksburg, Va., 13 December 1862. *Entered service at:* ———. *Birth:* Groveland, Mass. *Date of issue:* 16 December 1896. *Citation:* Seized the 2 colors from the hands of a corporal and a lieutenant as they fell mortally wounded, and with a color in each hand advanced across the field to a point where the regiment was reformed on those colors.

AHEAM, MICHAEL

Rank and organization: Paymaster's Steward, U.S. Navy. *Enlisted in:* France. *G.O. No.:* 45, 31 December 1864. *Citation:* Served on board the U.S.S. *Kearsarge* when she destroyed the *Alabama* off Cherbourg, France, 19 June 1864. Carrying out his duties courageously, PmS. Aheam exhibited marked coolness and good conduct and was highly recommended by his divisional officer for gallantry under enemy fire.

ALBER, FREDERICK

Rank and organization: Private, Company A, 17th Michigan Infantry. *Place and date:* At Spotsylvania, Va., 12 May 1864. *Entered service at:* Manchester, Mich. *Born:* 1838, Germany. *Date of issue:* 30 July 1896. *Citation:* Bravely rescued Lt. Charles H. Todd of his regiment who had been captured by a party of Confederates by shooting down one, knocking over another with the butt of his musket, and taking them both prisoners.

ALBERT, CHRISTIAN

Rank and organization: Private, Company G, 47th Ohio Infantry. *Place and date:* At Vicksburg, Miss., 22 May 1863. *Entered service at:* ———. *Birth:* Cincinnati, Ohio. *Date of issue:* 10 August 1895. *Citation:* Gallantry in the charge of the "volunteer storming party."

ALLEN, ABNER P.

Rank and organization: Corporal, Company K, 39th Illinois Infantry. *Place and date:* At Petersburg, Va., 2 April 1865. *Entered service at:* Bloomington, Ill. *Birth:* Woodford County, Ill. *Date of issue:* 12 May 1865. *Citation:* Gallantry as color bearer in the assault on Fort Gregg.

ALLEN, JAMES

Rank and organization: Private, Company F, 16th New York Infantry. *Place and date:* At South Mountain, Md., 14 September 1862. *Entered service at:* Potsdam, N.Y. *Born:* 6 May 1843, Ireland. *Date of issue:* 11 September 1890. *Citation:* Singlehanded and slightly wounded he accosted a squad of 14 Confederate soldiers bearing the colors of the 16th Georgia Infantry (C.S.A.). By an imaginary ruse he secured their surrender and kept them at bay when the regimental commander discovered him and rode away for assistance.

ALLEN, NATHANIEL M.

Rank and organization: Corporal, Company B, 1st Massachusetts Infantry. *Place and date:* At Gettysburg, Pa., 2 July 1863. *Entered service at:* Boston, Mass. *Birth:* Boston, Mass. *Date of issue:* 29 March 1899. *Citation:* When his regiment was falling back, this soldier, bearing the national color, returned in the face of the enemy's fire, pulled the regimental flag from under the body of its bearer, who had fallen, saved the flag from capture, and brought both colors off the field.

AMES, ADELBERT

Rank and organization: First Lieutenant, 5th U.S. Artillery. *Place and date:* At Bull Run, Va., 21 July 1861. *Entered service at:* Rockland, Maine. *Birth:* East Thomaston, Maine. *Date of issue:* 22 June 1894. *Citation:* Remained upon the field in command of a section of Griffin's Battery, directing its fire after being severely wounded and refusing to leave the field until too weak to sit upon the caisson where he had been placed by men of his command.

AMMERMAN, ROBERT W.

Rank and organization: Private, Company B, 148th Pennsylvania Infantry. *Place and date:* At Spotsylvania, Va., 12 May 1864. *Entered service at:* Center County, Pa. *Birth:* Center County, Pa. *Date of issue:* 31 January 1865. *Citation:* Capture of battle flag of 8th North Carolina (C.S.A.), being one of the foremost in the assault.

ANDERSON, BRUCE

Rank and organization: Private, Company K, 142d New York Infantry. *Place and date:* At Fort Fisher, N.C., 15 January 1865. *Entered service at:* Ephratah, N.Y. *Born:* Mexico, Oswego County, N.Y., 9 June 1845. *Date of issue:* 28 December 1914. *Citation:* Voluntarily advanced with the head of the column and cut down the palisading.

ANDERSON, CHARLES W.

Rank and organization: Private, Company K, 1st New York (Lincoln) Cavalry. *Place and date:* At Waynesboro, Va., 2 March 1865. *Entered service at:* ———. *Birth:* New Orleans, La. *Date of issue:* 26 March 1865. *Citation:* Capture of unknown Confederate flag.

ANDERSON, EVERETT W.

Rank and organization: Sergeant, Company M, 15th Pennsylvania Cavalry. *Place and date:* At Crosbys Creek, Tenn., 14 January 1864. *Entered service at:* Philadelphia, Pa. *Birth:* Louisiana. *Date of issue:* 3 December 1894. *Citation:* Captured, singlehanded, Confederate Brig. Gen. Robert B. Vance during a charge upon the enemy.

ANDERSON, FREDERICK C.

Rank and organization: Private, Company A, 18th Massachusetts Infantry. *Place and date:* At Weldon Railroad, Va., 21 August 1864. *En-*

tered service at: ——— *Birth:* Boston, Mass. *Date of issue:* 6 September 1864. *Citation:* Capture of battle flag of 27th South Carolina (C.S.A.) and the color bearer.

ANDERSON, MARION T.

Rank and organization: Captain, Company D, 51st Indiana Infantry. *Place and date:* At Nashville, Tenn., 16 December 1864. *Entered service at:* Kokomo, Ind. *Birth:* Decatur County, Ind. *Date of issue:* 1 September 1893. *Citation:* Led his regiment over 5 lines of the enemy's works, where he fell, severely wounded.

ANDERSON, PETER

Rank and organization: Private, Company B, 31st Wisconsin Infantry. *Place and date:* At Bentonville, N.C., 19 March 1865. *Entered service at:* ———. *Birth:* Lafayette County, Wis. *Date of issue:* 16 June 1865. *Citation:* Entirely unassisted, brought from the field an abandoned piece of artillery and saved the gun from falling into the hands of the enemy.

ANDERSON, ROBERT

Rank and organization: Quartermaster, U.S. Navy. *Born:* 1841, Ireland. *Accredited to:* New Hampshire. *G.O. No.:* 17, 10 July 1863. *Citation:* Served on board the U.S.S. *Crusader* and the *Keokuk* during various actions of those vessels. Carrying out his duties skillfully while on board the U.S.S. *Crusader*, Q.M. Anderson, on all occasions, set forth the greatest intrepidity and devotion. During the attack on Charleston, while serving on board the U.S.S. *Keokuk*, Q.M. Anderson was stationed at the wheel when shot penetrated the house and, with the scattering of the iron, used his own body as a shield for his commanding officer.

ANDERSON, THOMAS

Rank and organization: Corporal, Company I, 1st West Virginia Cavalry. *Place and date:* At Appomattox Station, Va., 8 April 1865. *Entered service at:* ———. *Birth:* Washington County, Pa. *Date of issue:* 3 May 1865. *Citation:* Capture of Confederate flag.

ANGLING, JOHN

Rank and organization: Cabin Boy, U.S. Navy. *Born:* 1850, Portland, Maine. *Accredited to:* Maine. *G.O. No.:* 59, 22 June 1865. *Citation:* Served on board the U.S.S. *Pontoosuc* during the capture of Fort Fisher and Wilmington, 24 December 1864 to 22 January 1865. Carrying out his duties faithfully during this period, C.B. Angling was recommended for gallantry and skill and for his cool courage while under the fire of the enemy throughout these various actions.

APPLE, ANDREW O.

Rank and organization: Corporal, Company I, 12th West Virginia Infantry. *Place and date:* At Petersburg, Va., 2 April 1865. *Entered service at:* ———. *Birth:* Northampton, Pa. *Date of issue:* 12 May 1865. *Citation:* Conspicuous gallantry as color bearer in the assault on Fort Gregg.

APPLETON, WILLIAM H.

Rank and organization: First Lieutenant, Company H, 4th U.S. Colored Troops. *Place and date:* At Petersburg, Va., 15 June 1864; At New Market Heights, Va., 29 September 1864. *Entered service at:* Portsmouth, N.H. *Born:* 24 March 1843, Chichester, N.H. *Date of issue:* 18 February 1891. *Citation:* The first man of the Eighteenth Corps to enter the enemy's works at Petersburg, Va., 15 June 1864. Valiant service in a desperate assault at New Market Heights, Va., inspiring the Union troops by his example of steady courage.

ARCHER, JAMES W.

Rank and organization: First Lieutenant and Adjutant, 59th Indiana Infantry. *Place and date:* At Corinth, Miss., 4 October 1862. *Entered service at:* Spencer, Ind. *Birth:* Edgar, Ill. *Date of issue:* 2 August 1897. *Citation:* Voluntarily took command of another regiment, with the consent of one or more of his seniors, who were present, rallied the command and led it in the assault.

ARCHER, LESTER

Rank and organization: Sergeant, Company E, 96th New York Infantry. *Place and date:* At Fort Harrison, Va., 29 September 1864. *Entered service at:* ———. *Birth:* Fort Ann, N.Y. *Date of issue:* 6 April 1865. *Citation:* Gallantry in placing the colors of his regiment on the fort.

ARCHINAL, WILLIAM

Rank and organization: Corporal, Company I, 30th Ohio Infantry. *Place and date:* At Vicksburg, Miss., 22 May 1863. *Entered service at:* ———. *Birth:* Germany. *Date of issue:* 10 July 1894. *Citation:* Gallantry in the charge of the "volunteer storming party."

ARMSTRONG, CLINTON L.

Rank and organization: Private, Company D, 83d Indiana Infantry. *Place and date:* At Vicksburg, Miss., 22 May 1863. *Entered service at:* ———. *Birth:* Franklin, Ind. *Date of issue:* 15 August 1894. *Citation:* Gallantry in the charge of the "volunteer storming party."

ARNOLD, ABRAHAM K.

Rank and organization: Captain, 5th U.S. Cavalry, *Place and date:* At Davenport Bridge, Va., 10 May 1864. *Entered service at:* Bedford, Pa. *Born:* 24 March 1837, Bedford, Pa. *Date of issue:* 1 September 1893. *Citation:* By a gallant charge against a superior force of the enemy, extricated his command from a perilous position in which it had been ordered.

ARTHER, MATTHEW

Rank and organization: Signal Quartermaster, U.S. Navy. *Born:* 1835, Scotland. *Entered service at:* Boston, Mass. *G.O. No.:* 17, 10 July 1863. *Citation:* Served on board the U.S.S. *Carondelet* at the reduction of Forts Henry and Donelson, 6 and 14 February 1862 and other actions. Carrying out his duties as signal quartermaster and captain of the rifled bow gun, S/Q.M. Arther was conspicuous for valor and devotion, serving most faithfully, effectively and valiantly.

ASTEN, CHARLES

Rank and organization: Quarter Gunner, U.S. Navy. *Born:* 1834, Halifax, Nova Scotia. *Accredited to:* Illinois. *G.O. No.:* 45, 31 December 1864. *Citation:* Served on board the U.S.S. *Signal*, Red River, 5 May 1864. Proceeding up the Red River, the U.S.S. *Signal* engaged a large force of enemy field batteries and sharpshooters, returning their fire until the Federal ship was totally disabled, at which time the white flag was raised. Although on the sick list, Q.G. Asten courageously carried out his duties during the entire engagement.

ATKINSON, THOMAS E.

Rank and organization: Yeoman, U.S. Navy. *Born:* 1824, Salem, Mass. *Accredited to:* Massachusetts. *G.O. No.:* 45, 31 December 1864. *Citation:* On board the U.S.S. *Richmond*, Mobile Bay, 5 August 1864; commended for coolness and energy in supplying the rifle ammunition, which was under his sole charge, in the action in Mobile Bay on the morning of 5 August 1964. He was a petty officer on board the U.S. Frigate *Congress* in 1842–46; was present and assisted in capturing the whole of the Buenos Ayrean fleet by that vessel off Montevideo; joined the *Richmond* in September 1860; was in the action with Fort McRea, the Head of the Passes of the Mississippi, Forts Jackson and St. Philip, the Chalmettes, the rebel ironclads and gunboats below New Orleans, Vicksburg, Port Hudson, and at the surrender of New Orleans.

AVERY, JAMES

Rank and organization: Seaman, U.S. Navy. *Born:* 1825, Scotland. *Accredited to:* New York. *G.O. No.:* 71, 15 January 1866. *Citation:* Served on board the U.S.S. *Metacomet*. As a member of the boat's crew which went to the rescue of the U.S. monitor *Tecumseh* when that vessel was struck by a torpedo in passing the enemy forts in Mobile Bay, 5 August 1864, S/man Avery braved the enemy fire which was said by the admiral to be "one of the most galling" he had ever seen, and aided in rescuing from death 10 of the crew of the *Tecumseh*, eliciting the admiration of both friend and foe.

AVERY, WILLIAM B.

Rank and organization: Lieutenant, U.S. Army, 1st New York Marine Artillery. *Place and date:* At Tranters Creek, N.C., 5 June 1862. *Entered service at:* Providence, R.I. *Born:* 10 September 1840, Providence, R.I. *Date of issue:* 2 September 1893. *Citation:* Handled his battery with greatest coolness amidst the hottest fire.

AYERS, DAVID

Rank and organization: Sergeant, Company A, 57th Ohio Infantry. *Place and date:* At Vicksburg, Miss., 22 May 1863. *Entered service at:* Upper Sandusky, Ohio. *Birth:* Kalida, Ohio. *Date of issue:* 13 April 1894. *Citation:* Gallantry in the charge of the "volunteer storming party."

AYERS, JOHN G. K.

Rank and organization: Private, Company H, 8th Missouri Infantry. *Place and date:* At Vicksburg, Miss., 22 May 1863. *Entered service at:* Pekin, Tazwell County, Ill. *Birth:* Washlinaw, Mich. *Date of issue:* 31 August 1895. *Citation:* Gallantry in the charge of the "volunteer storming party."

BABCOCK, WILLIAM J.

Rank and organization: Sergeant, Company E, 2d Rhode Island Infantry. *Place and date:* At Petersburg, Va., 2 April 1865. *Entered service at:* South Kingston, R.I. *Birth:* Griswold, Conn. *Date of issue:* 2 March 1895. *Citation:* Planted the flag upon the parapet while the enemy still occupied the line; was the first of his regiment to enter the works.

BACON, ELIJAH W.

Rank and organization: Private, Company F, 14th Connecticut Infantry. *Place and date:* At Gettysburg, Pa., 3 July 1863. *Entered service at:* Berlin, Conn. *Birth:* Burlington, Conn. *Date of issue:* 1 December 1864. *Citation:* Capture of flag of 16th North Carolina regiment (C.S.A.).

BAIRD, ABSALOM

Rank and organization: Brigadier General, U.S. Volunteers. *Place and date:* At Jonesboro, Ga., 1 September 1864. *Entered service at:* Washington, Pa. *Birth:* Washington, Pa. *Date of issue:* 22 April 1896. *Citation:* Voluntarily led a detached brigade in an assault upon the enemy's works.

BAKER, CHARLES

Rank and organization: Quarter Gunner, U.S. Navy. *Born:* 1809, Georgetown, D.C., *Entered service at:* New York, N.Y. *G.O. No.:* 71, 15 January 1866. *Citation:* Served on board the U.S.S. *Metacomet.* As a member of the boat's crew which went to the rescue of the U.S. monitor *Tecumseh* when that vessel was struck by a torpedo in passing the enemy forts in Mobile Bay, 5 August 1864, Q.G. Baker braved the enemy fire which was said by the admiral to be "one of the most galling" he had ever seen, and aided in rescuing from death 10 of the crew of the *Tecumseh*, eliciting the admiration of both friend and foe.

BALDWIN, CHARLES

Rank and organization: Coal Heaver, U.S. Navy. *Born:* 30 June 1839, Delaware. *Accredited to:* Pennsylvania. *G.O. No.:* 45, 31 December 1864. *Citation:* Serving on board the U.S.S. *Wyalusing* and participating in a plan to destroy the rebel ram *Albermarle* in Roanoke River, 25 May 1864. Volunteering for the hazardous mission, C.H. Baldwin participated in the transfer of 2 torpedoes across an island swamp. Weighted by a line which was used to transfer the torpedoes, he swam the river and, when challenged by a sentry, was forced to abandon the plan after erasing its detection and before it could be carried to completion. Escaping the fire of the muskets, C.H. Baldwin spent 2 days and nights of hazardous travel without food, and finally arrived, fatigued, at the mother ship.

BALDWIN, FRANK D.

Rank and organization: Captain, Company D, 19th Michigan Infantry; First Lieutenant, 5th U.S. Infantry. *Place and date:* At Peach Tree Creek, Ga., 12 July 1864. *Entered service at:* Constantine, Mich. *Birth:* Michigan. *Date of issue:* 3 December 1891. Second award. *Citation:* Led his company in a countercharge at Peach Tree Creek, Ga., 12 July 1864, under a galling fire ahead of his own men, and singly entered the enemy's line, capturing and bringing back 2 commissioned officers, fully armed, besides a guidon of a Georgia regiment.

SECOND AWARD

Place and date: At McClellans Creek, Tex., 8 November 1874. *Citation:* Rescued, with 2 companies, 2 white girls by a voluntary attack upon Indians whose superior numbers and strong position would have warranted delay for reinforcements, but which delay would have permitted the Indians to escape and kill their captives.

BALLEN, FREDERICK

Rank and organization: Private, Company B, 47th Ohio Infantry. *Place and date:* At Vicksburg, Miss., 3 May 1863. *Entered service at:* Adrian, Mich. *Born:* 1842, Germany. *Date of issue:* 6 November 1908. *Citation:* Was one of a party that volunteered and attempted to run the enemy's batteries with a steam tug and 2 barges loaded with subsistence stores.

BANKS, GEORGE L.

Rank and organization: Sergeant, Company C, 15th Indiana Infantry. *Place and date:* At Missionary Ridge, Tenn., 25 November 1863. *Entered service at:* Allen County, Ind. *Birth:* ———. *Date of issue:* 28 September 1897. *Citation:* As color bearer, led his regiment in the assault, and, though wounded, carried the flag forward to the enemy's works, where he was again wounded. In a brigade of 8 regiments this flag was the first planted on the parapet.

BARBER, JAMES A.

Rank and organization: Corporal, Company G, 1st Rhode Island Light Artillery. *Place and date:* At Petersburg, Va., 2 April 1865. *Entered service at:* Westerly, R.I. *Birth:* Westerly, R.I. *Date of issue:* 20 June 1866. *Citation:* Was one of a detachment of 20 picked artillerymen who voluntarily accompanied an infantry assaulting party, and who turned upon the enemy the guns captured in the assault.

BARKER, NATHANIEL C.

Rank and organization: Sergeant, Company E, 11th New Hampshire Infantry. *Place and date:* At Spotsylvania, Va., 12 May 1864. *Entered service at:* Manchester, N.H. *Born:* 28 September 1836, Piermont, N.H. *Date of issue:* 23 September 1897. *Citation:* Six color bearers of the regiment having been killed, he voluntarily took both flags of the regiment and carried them through the remainder of the battle.

BARNES, WILLIAM H.

Rank and organization: Private, Company C, 38th U.S. Colored Troops. *Place and date:* At Chapins Farm, Va., 29 September 1864. *Entered service at:* ———. *Birth:* St. Marys County, Md. *Date of issue:* 6 April 1865. *Citation:* Among the first to enter the enemy's works, although wounded.

BARNUM, HENRY A.

Rank and organization: Colonel, 149th New York Infantry. *Place and date:* At Chattanooga, Tenn., 23 November 1863. *Entered service at:* Syracuse, N.Y. *Born:* 24 September 1833, Jamesville, Onondaga County, N.Y. *Date of issue:* July 1889. *Citation:* Although suffering severely from wounds, he led his regiment, inciting the men to greater action by word and example until again severely wounded.

BARNUM, JAMES

Rank and organization: Boatswain's Mate, U.S. Navy. *Born:* 1816, Massachusetts. *Accredited to:* Massachusetts. *G.O. No.:* 59, 22 June 1865. *Citation:* Barnum served on board the U.S.S. *New Ironsides* during action in several attacks on Fort Fisher, 24 and 25 December 1864; and on 13, 14, and 15 January 1865. The ship steamed in and took the lead in the ironclad division close in shore and immediately opened its starboard battery in a barrage of well-directed fire to cause several fires and explosions and dismount several guns during the first 2 days of fighting. Taken under fire as she steamed into position on 13 January, the *New Ironsides* fought all day and took on ammunition at night despite severe weather conditions. When the enemy came out of his bombproofs to defend the fort against the storming party, the ship's battery disabled nearly every gun on the fort facing the shore before the cease-fire orders were given by the flagship. Barnum was commended for highly meritorious conduct during this period.

BARRELL, CHARLES L.

Rank and organization: First Lieutenant, Company C, 102d U.S. Colored Troops. *Place and date:* Near Camden, S.C., April 1865. *Entered service at:* Leighton, Allegan County, Mich. *Birth:* ———. *Date of issue:* 14 May 1891. *Citation:* Hazardous service in marching through the enemy's country to bring relief to his command.

BARRICK, JESSE T.

Rank and organization: Corporal, Company H, 3d Minnesota Infantry. *Place and date:* Near Duck River, Tenn., 26 May–2 June 1863. *Entered service at:* Ft. Snelling, Rice County, Minn. *Born:* 18 January 1841, Columbiana County, Ohio. *Date of issue:* 3 March 1917. *Citation:* While on a scout captured singlehanded 2 desperate Confederate guerrilla officers who were together and well armed at the time.

BARRINGER, WILLIAM H.

Rank and organization: Private, Company F, 4th West Virginia Infantry. *Place and date:* At Vicksburg, Miss., 22 May 1863. *Entered service at:* Jackson County, W. Va. *Birth:* ———. *Date of issue:* 12 July

1894. *Citation:* Gallantry in the charge of the "volunteer storming party."

BARRY, AUGUSTUS

Rank and organization: Sergeant Major, 16th U.S. Infantry. *Place and date:* Unknown, 1863–65. *Entered service at:* ———. *Birth:* Ireland. *Date of issue:* 28 February 1870. *Citation:* Gallantry in various actions during the rebellion.

BARTER, GURDON H.

Rank and organization: Landsman, U.S. Navy. *Born:* 1843, Williamsburgh, N.Y. *Accredited to:* New York. *G.O. No.:* 59, 22 June 1865. *Citation:* On board the U.S.S. *Minnesota* in action during the assault on Fort Fisher, 15 January 1865. Landing on the beach with the assaulting party from his ship, L/man Barter advanced to the top of the sandhill and partly through the breach in the palisades despite enemy fire which killed and wounded many officers and men. When more than two-thirds of the men became seized with panic and retreated on the run, he remained with the party until dark, when it came safely away, bringing its wounded, its arms, and its colors.

BARTON, THOMAS

Rank and organization: Seaman, U.S. Navy. *Born:* 1831, Cleveland, Ohio. *Accredited to:* Ohio. *G.O. No.:* 11, 3 April 1863. *Citation:* On board the U.S.S. *Hunchback* in the attack on Franklin, Va., 3 October 1862. When an ignited shell, with cartridge attached, fell out of the howitzer upon the deck, S/man Barton promptly seized a pail of water and threw it upon the missile, thereby preventing it from exploding.

BASS, DAVID L.

Rank and organization: Seaman, U.S. Navy. *Born:* 1843, Ireland. *Accredited to:* New York. *G.O. No.:* 59, 22 June 1865. *Citation:* On board the U.S.S. *Minnesota* in action during the assault on Fort Fisher, 15 January 1865. Landing on the beach with the assaulting party from his ship, S/man Bass advanced to the top of the sand hill and partly through the breach in the palisades despite enemy fire which killed and wounded many officers and men. When more than two-thirds of the men became seized with panic and retreated on the run, he remained with the party until dark, when it came safely away, bringing its wounded, its arms, and its colors.

BATCHELDER, RICHARD N.

Rank and organization: Lieutenant Colonel and Chief Quartermaster, 2d Corps. *Place and date:* Between Catlett and Fairfax Stations, Va., 13–15 October 1863. *Entered service at:* Manchester, N.H. *Born:* 27 July 1832, Meredith, N.H. *Date of issue:* 20 May 1895. *Citation:* Being ordered to move his trains by a continuous day-and-night march, and without the usual military escort, armed his teamsters and personally commanded them, successfully fighting against heavy odds and bringing his trains through without the loss of a wagon.

BATES, DELAVAN

Rank and organization: Colonel, 30th U.S. Colored Troops. *Place and date:* At Cemetery Hill, Va., 30 July 1864. *Entered service at:* Oswego County, N.Y. *Born:* 1840, Schoharie County, N.Y. *Date of issue:* 22 June 1891. *Citation:* Gallantry in action where he fell, shot through the face, at the head of his regiment.

BATES, NORMAN F.

Rank and organization: Sergeant, Company E, 4th Iowa Cavalry. *Place and date:* At Columbus, Ga., 16 April 1865. *Entered service at:* ———. *Birth:* Vermont. *Date of issue:* 17 June 1865. *Citation:* Capture of flag and bearer.

BAYBUTT, PHILIP

Rank and organization: Private, Company A, 2d Massachusetts Cavalry. *Place and date:* At Luray, Va., 24 September 1864. *Entered service at:* Fall River, Mass. *Birth:* England. *Date of issue:* 19 October 1864. *Citation:* Capture of flag.

BAZAAR, PHILIP

Rank and organization: Ordinary Seaman, U.S. Navy. *Born:* Chile, South America. *Accredited to:* Massachusetts. *G.O. No.:* 59, 22 June 1865. *Citation:* On board the U.S.S. *Santiago de Cuba* during the assault on Fort Fisher on 15 January 1865. As one of a boat crew detailed to one of the generals on shore, O.S. Bazaar bravely entered the fort in the assault and accompanied his party in carrying dispatches at the height of the battle. He was 1 of 6 men who entered the fort in the assault from the fleet.

BEATTY, ALEXANDER M.

Rank and organization: Captain, Company F, 3d Vermont Infantry. *Place and date:* At Cold Harbor, Va., 5 June 1864. *Entered service at:* Vermont. *Born:* 29 July 1828, Ryegate, Vt. *Date of issue:* 25 April 1894. *Citation:* Removed, under a hot fire, a wounded member of his command to a place of safety.

BEATY, POWHATAN

Rank and organization: First Sergeant, Company G, 5th U.S. Colored Troops. *Place and date:* At Chapins Farm, Va., 29 September 1864. *Entered service at:* Delaware County, Ohio. *Birth:* Richmond, Va. *Date of issue:* 6 April 1865. *Citation:* Took command of his company, all the officers having been killed or wounded, and gallantly led it.

BEAUFORT, JEAN J.

Rank and organization: Corporal, Company A, 2d Louisiana Infantry. *Place and date:* At Port Hudson, La., about 20 May 1863. *Entered service:* New Orleans, La. *Birth:* France. *Date of issue:* 20 July 1897. *Citation:* Volunteered to go within the enemy's lines and at the head of a party of 8 destroyed a signal station, thereby greatly aiding in the operations against Port Hudson that immediately followed.

BEAUMONT, EUGENE B.

Rank and organization: Major and Assistant Adjutant General, Cavalry Corps, Army of the Mississippi. *Place and date:* At Harpeth River, Tenn., 17 December 1864; at Selma, Ala., 2 April 1865. *Entered service at:* Wilkes Barre, Pa. *Birth:* Luzerne County, Pa. *Date of issue:* 30 March 1898. *Citation:* Obtained permission from the corps commander to advance upon the enemy's position with the 4th U.S. Cavalry, of which he was a lieutenant; led an attack upon a battery, dispersed the enemy, and captured the guns. At Selma, Ala., charged, at the head of his regiment, into the second and last line of the enemy's works.

BEBB, EDWARD J.

Rank and organization: Private, Company D, 4th Iowa Cavalry. *Place and date:* At Columbus, Ga., 16 April 1865. *Entered service at:* Henry County, Iowa. *Birth:* Butler County, Ohio. *Date of issue:* 17 June 1865. *Citation:* Capture of flag.

BECKWITH, WALLACE A.

Rank and organization: Private, Company F, 21st Connecticut Infantry. *Place and date:* At Fredericksburg, Va., 13 December 1862. *Entered service at:* New London, Conn. *Birth:* New London, Conn. *Date of issue:* 15 February 1897. *Citation:* Gallantly responded to a call for volunteers to man a battery, serving with great heroism until the termination of the engagement.

BEDDOWS, RICHARD

Rank and organization: Private, 34th New York Battery. *Place and date:* At Spotsylvania, Va., 18 May 1864. *Entered service at:* ———. *Birth:* England. *Date of issue:* 10 July 1896. *Citation:* Brought his guidon off in safety under a heavy fire of musketry after he had lost it by his horse becoming furious from the bursting of a shell.

BEEBE, WILLIAM S.

Rank and organization: First Lieutenant, Ordnance Department, U.S. Army. *Place and date:* At Cane River Crossing, La., 23 April 1864. *Entered service at:* Thompson, Conn. *Born:* 14 February 1841, Ithaca, N.Y. *Date of issue:* 30 June 1897. *Citation:* Voluntarily led a successful assault on a fortified position.

BEECH, JOHN P.

Rank and organization: Sergeant, Company B, 4th New Jersey Infantry. *Place and date:* At Spotsylvania Courthouse, Va., 12 May 1864. *Entered service at:* Trenton, N.J. *Born:* 1 May 1844, England. *Date of issue:* 5 June 1894. *Citation:* Voluntarily assisted in working the guns of a battery, all the members of which had been killed or wounded.

BEGLEY, TERRENCE

Rank and organization: Sergeant, Company D, 7th New York Heavy Artillery. *Place and date:* At Cold Harbor, Va., 3 June 1864. *Entered service at:* ———. *Birth:* Ireland. *Date of issue:* 1 December 1864.

Citation: Shot a Confederate color bearer, rushed forward and seized his colors, and although exposed to heavy fire, regained the lines in safety.

BELCHER, THOMAS

Rank and organization: Private, Company I, 9th Maine Infantry. *Place and date:* At Chapins Farm, Va., 29 September 1864. *Entered service at:* Bangor, Maine. *Birth:* Bangor, Maine. *Date of issue:* 6 April 1865. *Citation:* Took a guidon from the hands of the bearer, mortally wounded, and advanced with it nearer to the battery than any other man.

BELL, GEORGE

Rank and organization: Captain of the Afterguard, U.S. Navy. *Born:* 12 March 1839, England. *Accredited to:* New York. *G.O. No.:* 17, 10 July 1863. *Citation:* Served as pilot of the U.S.S. *Santee* when that vessel was engaged in cutting out the rebel armed schooner *Royal Yacht* from Galveston Bay, 7 November 1861, and evinced more coolness, in passing the 4 forts and the rebel steamer *General Rusk*, than was ever before witnessed by his commanding officer. "Although severely wounded in the encounter, he displayed extraordinary courage under the most painful and trying circumstances."

BELL, JAMES B.

Rank and organization: Sergeant, Company H, 11th Ohio Infantry. *Place and date:* At Missionary Ridge, Tenn., 25 November 1863. *Entered service at:* Troy, Ohio. *Birth:* ———. *Date of issue:* Unknown. *Citation:* Though severely wounded, was first of his regiment on the summit of the ridge, planted his colors inside the enemy's works, and did not leave the field until after he had been wounded 5 times.

BENEDICT, GEORGE G.

Rank and organization: Second Lieutenant, Company C, 12th Vermont Infantry. *Place and date:* At Gettysburg, Pa., 3 July 1863. *Entered service at:* Burlington, Vt. *Birth:* Burlington, Vt. *Date of issue:* 27 June 1892. *Citation:* Passed through a murderous fire of grape and canister in delivering orders and re-formed the crowded lines.

BENJAMIN, JOHN F.

Rank and organization: Corporal, Company M, 2d New York Cavalry. *Place and date:* At Sailors Creek, Va., 6 April 1865. *Entered service at:* ———. *Birth:* Orange County, N.Y. *Date of issue:* 3 May 1865. *Citation:* Capture of battle flag of 9th Virginia Infantry (C.S.A.).

BENJAMIN, SAMUEL N.

Rank and organization: First Lieutenant, 2d U.S. Artillery. *Place and date:* From Bull Run to Spotsylvania, Va., from July 1861 to May 1864. *Entered service at:* New York, N.Y. *Birth:* New York, N.Y. *Date of issue:* 11 June 1877. *Citation:* Particularly distinguished services as an artillery officer.

BENNETT, ORREN

Rank and organization: Private, Company D, 141st Pennsylvania Infantry. *Place and date:* At Sailors Creek, Va., 6 April 1865. *Entered service at:* Towanda, Pa. *Birth:* Bradford County, Pa. *Date of issue:* 10 May 1865. *Citation:* Capture of flag.

BENNETT, ORSON W.

Rank and organization: First Lieutenant, Company A, 102d U.S. Colored Troops. *Place and date:* At Honey Hill, S.C., 30 November 1864. *Entered service at:* Michigan. *Born:* 17 November 1841, Union City, Branch County, Mich. *Date of issue:* 9 March 1887. *Citation:* After several unsuccessful efforts to recover 3 pieces of abandoned artillery, this officer gallantly led a small force fully 100 yards in advance of the Union lines and brought in the guns, preventing their capture.

BENSINGER, WILLIAM (2d to receive Medal of Honor)

Rank and organization: Private, Company G, 21st Ohio Infantry. *Place and date:* Georgia, April 1862. *Entered service at:* Hancock County, Ohio. *Born:* 14 January 1840, Wayne County, Ohio. *Date of issue:* 25 March 1863. *Citation:* One of the 19 of 22 men (including 2 civilians) who, by direction of Gen. Mitchell (or Buell), penetrated nearly 200 miles south into enemy territory and captured a railroad train at Big Shanty, Ga., in an attempt to destroy the bridges and track between Chattanooga and Atlanta.

BENYAURD, WILLIAM H. H.

Rank and organization: First Lieutenant, Engineers. *Place and date:* At Five Forks, Va., 1 April 1865. *Entered service at:* Philadelphia, Pa. *Birth:* Philadelphia, Pa. *Date of issue:* 7 September 1897. *Citation:* With one companion, voluntarily advanced in a reconnaissance beyond the skirmishers, where he was exposed to imminent peril; also, in the same battle, rode to the front with the commanding general to encourage wavering troops to resume the advance, which they did successfully.

BETHAM, ASA

Rank and organization: Coxswain, U.S. Navy. *Born:* 1838, New York, N.Y. *Accredited to:* New York. *G.O. No.:* 59, 22 June 1865. *Citation:* Served on board the U.S.S. *Pontoosuc* during the capture of Fort Fisher and Wilmington, 24 December 1864, to 22 January 1865. Carrying out his duties faithfully during this period, Betham was recommended for gallantry and skill and for his cool courage while under the fire of the enemy throughout these various actions.

BETTS, CHARLES M.

Rank and organization: Lieutenant Colonel, 15th Pennsylvania Cavalry. *Place and date:* At Greensboro, N.C., 19 April 1865. *Entered service at:* Philadelphia, Pa. *Birth:* Bucks County, Pa. *Date of issue:* 10 October 1892. *Citation:* With a force of but 75 men, while on a scouting expedition, by a judicious disposition of his men, surprised and captured an entire battalion of the enemy's cavalry.

BEYER, HILLARY

Rank and organization: Second Lieutenant, Company H, 90th Pennsylvania Infantry. *Place and date:* At Antietam, Md., 17 September 1862. *Entered service at:* Philadelphia, Pa. *Birth:* ———. *Date of issue:* 30 October 1896. *Citation:* After his command had been forced to fall back, remained alone on the line of battle, caring for his wounded comrades and carrying one of them to a place of safety.

BIBBER, CHARLES J.

Rank and organization: Gunner's Mate, U.S. Navy. *Born:* 1838, Portland, Maine. *Accredited to:* Maine. *G.O. No.:* 45, 31 December 1864. *Citation:* Bibber served on board the U.S.S. *Agawam*, as one of a volunteer crew of a powder boat which was exploded near Fort Fisher, 23 December 1864. The powder boat, towed in by the *Wilderness* to prevent detection by the enemy, cast off and slowly steamed to within 300 yards of the beach. After fuses and fires had been lit and a second anchor with short scope let go to assure the boat's tailing inshore, the crew again boarded the *Wilderness* and proceeded a distance of 12 miles from shore. Less than 2 hours later the explosion took place, and the following day fires were observed still burning at the forts.

BICKFORD, HENRY H.

Rank and organization: Corporal, Company E, 8th New York Cavalry. *Place and date:* At Waynesboro, Va., 2 March 1865. *Entered service at:* Hartland, Niagara County, N.Y. *Birth:* Michigan. *Date of issue:* 26 March 1865. *Citation:* Recapture of flag.

BICKFORD, JOHN F.

Rank and organization: Captain of the Top, U.S. Navy. *Born:* 1843, Tremont, Maine. *Accredited to:* Maine. *G.O. No.:* 45, 31 December 1864. *Citation:* Served on board the U.S.S. *Kearsarge* when she destroyed the *Alabama* off Cherbourg, France, 19 June 1864. Acting as the first loader of the pivot gun during this bitter engagement, Bickford exhibited marked coolness and good conduct and was highly recommended for his gallantry under fire by his divisional officer.

BICKFORD, MATTHEW

Rank and organization: Corporal, Company G, 8th Missouri Infantry. *Place and date:* At Vicksburg, Miss., 22 May 1863. *Entered service at:* Trivolia, Peoria County, Ill. *Birth:* Peoria County, Ill. *Date of issue:* 31 August 1894. *Citation:* Gallantry in the charge of the "volunteer storming party."

BIEGER, CHARLES

Rank and organization: Private, Company D, 4th Missouri Cavalry. *Place and date:* At Ivy Farm, Miss., 22 February 1864. *Entered service at:* St. Louis, Mo. *Birth:* Germany. *Date of issue:* 8 July 1897. *Citation:* Voluntarily risked his life by taking a horse, under heavy fire, beyond the line of battle for the rescue of his captain, whose horse had been killed in a charge and who was surrounded by the enemy's skirmishers.

BINDER, RICHARD

Rank and organization: Sergeant, U.S. Marine Corps. *Born:* 1840, Philadelphia, Pa. *Accredited to:* Pennsylvania. *Citation:* On board the U.S.S. *Ticonderoga* during the attacks on Fort Fisher, 24 and 25 December 1864, and 13 to 15 January 1865. Despite heavy return fire by the enemy and the explosion of the 100-pounder Parrott rifle which killed 8 men and wounded 12 more, Sgt. Binder, as captain of a gun, performed his duties with skill and courage during the first 2 days of battle. As his ship again took position on the 13th, he remained steadfast as the *Ticonderoga* maintained a well-placed fire upon the batteries on shore, and thereafter, as she materially lessened the power of guns on the mound which had been turned upon our assaulting columns. During this action the flag was planted on one of the strongest fortifications possessed by the rebels.

BINGHAM, HENRY H.

Rank and organization: Captain, Company G, 140th Pennsylvania Infantry. *Place and date:* At Wilderness, Va., 6 May 1864. *Entered service at:* Cannonsburg, Pa. *Born:* 4 December 1841, Philadelphia, Pa. *Date of issue:* 31 August 1893. *Citation:* Rallied and led into action a portion of the troops who had given way under the fierce assaults of the enemy.

BIRDSALL, HORATIO L.

Rank and organization: Sergeant, Company B, 3d Iowa Cavalry. *Place and date:* At Columbus, Ga., 16 April 1865. *Entered service at:* Keokuk, Lee County, Iowa. *Birth:* Monroe County, N.Y. *Date of issue:* 17 June 1865. *Citation:* Capture of flag and bearer.

BISHOP, FRANCIS A.

Rank and organization: Private, Company C, 57th Pennsylvania Infantry. *Place and date:* At Spotsylvania, Va., 12 May 1864. *Entered service at:* ———. *Birth:* Bradford County, Pa. *Date of issue:* 1 December 1864. *Citation:* Capture of flag.

BLACK, JOHN C.

Rank and organization: Lieutenant Colonel, 37th Illinois Infantry. *Place and date:* At Prairie Grove, Ark., 7 December 1862. *Entered service at:* Danville, Ill. *Born:* 27 January 1839, Lexington, Holmes County, Miss. *Date of issue:* 31 October 1893. *Citation:* Gallantly charged the position of the enemy at the head of his regiment, after 2 other regiments had been repulsed and driven down the hill, and captured a battery; was severely wounded.

BLACK, WILLIAM P.

Rank and organization: Captain, Company K, 37th Illinois Infantry. *Place and date:* At Pea Ridge, Ark., 7 March 1862. *Entered service at:* Danville, Ill. *Born:* 11 November 1842, Woodford, Ky. *Date of issue:* 2 October 1893. *Citation:* Singlehandedly confronted the enemy, firing a rifle at them and thus checking their advance within 100 yards of the lines.

BLACKMAR, WILMON W.

Rank and organization: Lieutenant, Company H, 1st West Virginia Cavalry. *Place and date:* At Five Forks, Va., 1 April 1865. *Entered service at:* ———. *Birth:* Bristol, Pa. *Date of issue:* 23 October 1897. *Citation:* At a critical stage of the battle, without orders, led a successful advance upon the enemy.

BLACKWOOD, WILLIAM R. D.

Rank and organization: Surgeon, 48th Pennsylvania Infantry. *Place and date:* At Petersburg, Va., 2 April 1865. *Entered service at:* Philadelphia, Pa. *Born:* 12 May 1838, Ireland. *Date of issue:* 21 July 1897. *Citation:* Removed severely wounded officers and soldiers from the field while under a heavy fire from the enemy, exposing himself beyond the call of duty, thus furnishing an example of most distinguished gallantry.

BLAGHEEN, WILLIAM

Rank and organization: Ship's Cook, U.S. Navy. *Born:* 1832, England. *Accredited to:* New York. *G.O. No.:* 45, 31 December 1864. *Citation:* On board the U.S.S. *Brooklyn* during successful attacks against Fort Morgan, rebel gunboats and the ram *Tennessee* in Mobile Bay, on 5 August 1864. Stationed in the immediate vicinity of the shell whips which were twice cleared of men by bursting shells, Blagheen remained steadfast at his post and performed his duties in the powder division throughout the furious action which resulted in the surrender of the prize rebel ram *Tennessee* and in the damaging and destruction of batteries at Fort Morgan.

BLAIR, ROBERT M.

Rank and organization: Boatswain's Mate, U.S. Navy. *Born:* 1836, Peacham, Vt. *Accredited to:* Vermont. *G.O. No.:* 59, 22 June 1865. *Citation:* Served on board the U.S.S. *Pontoosuc* during the capture of Fort Fisher and Wilmington, 24 December 1864 to 22 January 1865. Carrying out his duties faithfully throughout this period, Blair was recommended for gallantry and skill and for his cool courage while under the fire of the enemy throughout these actions.

BLAKE, ROBERT

Rank and organization: Contraband, U.S. Navy. *Entered service at:* Virginia. *G.O. No.:* 32, 16 April 1864. *Accredited to:* Virginia. *Citation:* On board the U.S. Steam Gunboat *Marblehead* off Legareville, Stono River, 25 December 1863, in an engagement with the enemy on John's Island. Serving the rifle gun, Blake, an escaped slave, carried out his duties bravely throughout the engagement which resulted in the enemy's abandonment of positions, leaving a caisson and one gun behind.

BLASDEL, THOMAS A.

Rank and organization: Private, Company H, 83d Indiana Infantry. *Place and date:* At Vicksburg, Miss., 22 May 1863. *Entered service at:* Guilford, Ind. *Birth:* Dearborn County, Ind. *Date of issue:* 11 August

1894. *Citation:* Gallantry in the charge of the "volunteer storming party."

BLICKENSDERFER, MILTON

Rank and organization: Corporal, Company E, 126th Ohio Infantry. *Place and date:* At Petersburg, Va., 3 April 1865. *Entered service at:* ———. *Birth:* Lancaster, Pa. *Date of issue:* 10 May 1865. *Citation:* Capture of flag.

BLISS, GEORGE N.

Rank and organization: Captain, Company C, 1st Rhode Island Cavalry. *Place and date:* At Waynesboro, Va., 28 September 1864. *Entered service at:* ———. *Birth:* Tiverton, R.I. *Date of issue:* 3 August 1897. *Citation:* While in command of the provost guard in the village, he saw the Union lines returning before the attack of a greatly superior force of the enemy, mustered his guard, and, without orders, joined in the defense and charged the enemy without support. He received three saber wounds, his horse was shot, and he was taken prisoner.

BLISS, ZENAS R.

Rank and organization: Colonel, 7th Rhode Island Infantry. *Place and date:* At Fredericksburg, Va., 13 December 1862. *Entered service at:* Johnston, Maine. *Birth:* Johnston, Maine. *Date of issue:* 30 December 1898. *Citation:* This officer, to encourage his regiment which had never before been in action, and which had been ordered to lie down to protect itself from the enemy's fire, arose to his feet, advanced in front of the line, and himself fired several shots at the enemy at short range, being fully exposed to their fire at the time.

BLODGETT, WELIS H.

Rank and organization: First Lieutenant, Company D, 37th Illinois Infantry. *Place and date:* At Newtonia, Mo., 30 September 1862. *Entered service at:* Chicago, Ill. *Born:* 29 January 1839, Downers Grove, Ill. *Date of issue:* 15 February 1894. *Citation:* With a single orderly, captured an armed picket of 8 men and marched them in prisoners.

BLUCHER, CHARLES

Rank and organization: Corporal, Company H, 188th Pennsylvania Infantry. *Place and date:* At Fort Harrison, Va., 29 September 1864. *Entered service at:* Harrisburgh, Pa. *Birth:* Germany. *Date of issue:* 6 April 1865. *Citation:* Planted first national colors on the fortifications.

BLUNT, JOHN W.

Rank and organization: First Lieutenant, Company K, 6th New York Cavalry. *Place and date:* At Cedar Creek, Va., 19 October 1864. *Entered service at:* Chatham, Four Corners, N.Y. *Birth:* Columbia County, N.Y. *Date of issue:* Unknown. *Citation:* Voluntarily led a charge across a narrow bridge over the creek, against the lines of the enemy.

BOEHM, PETER M.

Rank and organization: Second Lieutenant, Company K, 15th New York Cavalry. *Place and date:* At Dinwiddie Courthouse, Va., 31

March 1865. *Entered service at:* Brooklyn, N.Y. *Birth:* New York. *Date of issue:* 15 December 1898. *Citation:* While acting as aide to General Custer, took a flag from the hands of color bearer, rode in front of a line that was being driven back and, under a heavy fire, rallied the men, re-formed the line, and repulsed the charge.

BOIS, FRANK

Rank and organization: Quartermaster, U.S. Navy. *Entered service at:* Northampton, Mass. *Born:* 1841, Canada. *Date of issue:* 24 November 1916. *G.O. No.:* 17, 10 July 1863. *Citation:* Served as quartermaster on board the U.S.S. *Cincinnati* during the attack on the Vicksburg batteries and at the time of her sinking, 27 May 1863. Engaging the enemy in a fierce battle, the *Cincinnati*, amidst an incessant fire of shot and shell, continued to fire her guns to the last, though so penetrated by enemy shellfire that her fate was sealed. Conspicuously cool in making signals throughout the battle, Bois, after all the *Cincinnati's* staffs had been shot away, succeeded in nailing the flag to the stump of the forestaff to enable this proud ship to go down, "with her colors nailed to the mast."

BOND, WILLIAM

Rank and organization: Boatswain's Mate, U.S. Navy. *Born:* 1839, Boston, Mass. *Accredited to:* Massachusetts. *G.O. No.:* 45, 31 December 1864. *Citation:* Served on board the U.S.S. *Kearsarge* when she destroyed the *Alabama* off Cherbourg, France, 19 June 1864. Carrying out his duties courageously, Bond exhibited marked coolness and good conduct and was highly recommended for his gallantry under fire by his divisional officer.

BONEBRAKE, HENRY G.

Rank and organization: Lieutenant, Company G, 17th Pennsylvania Cavalry. *Place and date:* At Five Forks, Va., 1 April 1865. *Entered service at:* ———. *Birth:* Waynesboro, Pa. *Date of issue:* 3 May 1865. *Citation:* As 1 of the first of Devin's Division to enter the works, he fought in a hand-to-hand struggle with a Confederate to capture his flag by superior physical strength.

BONNAFFON, SYLVESTER, Jr.

Rank and organization: First Lieutenant, Company G, 99th Pennsylvania Infantry. *Place and date:* At Boydton Plank Road, Va., 27 October 1864. *Entered service at:* Philadelphia, Pa. *Birth:* ———. *Date of issue:* 29 September 1893. *Citation:* Checked the rout and rallied the troops of his command in the face of a terrible fire of musketry; was severely wounded.

BOODY, ROBERT

Rank and organization: Sergeant, Company B, 40th New York Infantry. *Place and date:* At Williamsburg, Va., 5 May 1862. At Chancellorsville, Va., 2 May 1863. *Entered service at:* Amesbury, Mass. *Birth:* Lemington, Maine. *Date of issue:* 8 July 1896. *Citation:* This soldier, at Williamsburg, Va., then a corporal, at great personal risk, voluntarily saved the lives of and brought from the battlefield 2 wounded comrades. A year later, at Chancellorsville, voluntarily, and at great personal risk, brought from the field of battle and saved the life of Capt. George B. Carse, Company C, 40th New York Volunteer Infantry.

BOON, HUGH P.

Rank and organization: Captain, Company B, 1st West Virginia Cavalry. *Place and date:* At Sailors Creek, Va., 6 April 1865. *Entered service at:* ———. *Born:* 28 July 1831, Washington, Pa. *Date of issue:* 3 May 1865. *Citation:* Capture of flag.

BOQUET, NICHOLAS

Rank and organization: Private, Company D, 1st Iowa Infantry. *Place and date:* At Wilsons Creek, Mo., 10 August 1861. *Entered service at:* Burlington, Iowa. *Born:* 14 November 1842, Germany. *Date of issue:* 16 February 1897. *Citation:* Voluntarily left the line of battle, and, exposing himself to imminent danger from a heavy fire of the enemy, assisted in capturing a riderless horse at large between the lines and hitching him to a disabled gun, saved the gun from capture.

BOSS, ORLANDO

Rank and organization: Corporal, Company F, 25th Massachusetts Infantry. *Place and date:* At Cold Harbor, Va., 3 June 1864. *Entered service at:* ———. *Birth:* Fitchburg, Mass. *Date of issue:* 10 May 1888. *Citation:* Rescued his lieutenant, who was lying between the lines mortally wounded; this under a heavy fire of the enemy.

BOURKE, JOHN G.

Rank and organization: Private, Company E, 15th Pennsylvania Cavalry. *Place and date:* At Stone River, Tenn., 31 December 1862–1 January 1863. *Entered service at:* Chicago, Ill. *Birth:* Philadelphia, Pa. *Date of issue:* 16 November 1887. *Citation:* Gallantry in action.

BOURNE, THOMAS

Rank and organization: Seaman and Gun Captain, U.S. Navy. *Entered service at:* New York, N.Y. *Birth:* England. *G.O. No.:* 11, 3 April 1863. *Citation:* Served as captain of a gun on board the U.S.S. *Varuna* during an attack on Forts Jackson and St. Philip and while under fire and ramming by the rebel ship *Morgan*, 24 April 1862. During this action at extremely close range while his ship was under furious fire and was twice rammed by the rebel ship *Morgan*, Bourne remained steadfast at his gun and was instrumental in inflicting damage on the enemy until the *Varuna*, badly damaged and forced to beach, was finally sunk.

BOURY, RICHARD

Rank and organization: Sergeant, Company C, 1st West Virginia Cavalry. *Place and date:* At Charlottesville, Va., 5 March 1865. *Entered service at:* Wirt Courthouse, W. Va. *Birth:* Monroe County, Ohio. *Date of issue:* 26 March 1865. *Citation:* Capture of flag.

BOUTWELL, JOHN W.

Rank and organization: Private, Company B, 18th New Hampshire Infantry. *Place and date:* At Petersburg, Va., 2 April 1865. *Entered ser-

vice at: ———. *Birth:* Hanover, N.H. *Date of issue:* Unknown. *Citation:* Brought off from the picket line, under heavy fire, a comrade who had been shot through both legs.

BOWEN, CHESTER B.

Rank and organization: Corporal, Company I, 19th New York Cavalry (1st New York Dragoons). *Place and date:* At Winchester, Va., 19 September 1864. *Entered service at:* ———. *Birth:* Nunda, N.Y. *Date of issue:* 27 September 1864. *Citation:* Capture of flag.

BOWEN, EMMER

Rank and organization: Private, Company C, 127th Illinois Infantry. *Place and date:* At Vicksburg, Miss., 22 May 1863. *Entered service at:* Hampshire, Kane County, Ill. *Birth:* Erie County, N.Y. *Date of issue:* 21 July 1894. *Citation:* Gallantry in the charge of the "volunteer storming party."

BOWMAN, EDWARD R.

Rank and organization: Quartermaster, U.S. Navy. *Born:* 1828, Eastport, Maine. *Accredited to:* Maine. *G.O. No.:* 59, 22 June 1865. *Citation:* On board the U.S.S. *Ticonderoga* during attacks on Fort Fisher, 13 to 15 January 1865. Despite severe wounds sustained during the action Bowman displayed outstanding courage in the performance of duty as his ship maintained its well-placed fire upon the batteries on shore, and thereafter, as she materially lessened the power of guns on the mound which had been turned upon our assaulting columns. During this battle the flag was planted on one of the strongest fortifications possessed by the rebels.

BOX, THOMAS J.

Rank and organization: Captain, Company D, 27th Indiana Infantry. *Place and date:* At Resaca, Ga., 14 May 1864. *Entered service at:* Bedford, Ind. *Birth:* ———. *Date of issue:* 7 April 1865. *Citation:* Capture of flag of the 38th Alabama Infantry (C.S.A.).

BOYNTON, HENRY V.

Rank and organization: Lieutenant Colonel, 35th Ohio Infantry. *Place and date:* At Missionary Ridge, Tenn., 25 November 1863. *Entered service at:* Ohio. *Born:* 22 July 1835, West Stockbridge, Mass. *Date of issue:* 15 November 1893. *Citation:* Led his regiment in the face of a severe fire of the enemy; was severely wounded.

BRADLEY, AMOS

Rank and organization: Landsman, U.S. Navy. *Born:* 1837, Dansville, N.Y. *Accredited to:* New York. *G.O. No.:* 11, 3 April 1863. *Citation:* Served on board the U.S.S. *Varuna* in one of the most responsible positions, during the attacks on Forts Jackson and St. Philip, and while in action against the rebel ship *Morgan*, 24 April 1862. Although guns were raking the decks from behind him, Bradley remained steadfast at the wheel throughout the thickest of the fight, continuing at his station and rendering service with the greatest courage until his ship, repeatedly holed and twice rammed by the rebel ship *Morgan*, was beached and sunk.

BRADLEY, CHARLES

Rank and organization: Boatswain's Mate, U.S. Navy. *Born:* 1838, Ireland. *Accredited to:* New York. *G.O. No.:* 11, 3 April 1863. *Citation:* Served on board the U.S.S. *Louisville.* Carrying out his duties through the thick of battle and acting as captain of a 9-inch gun, Bradley consistently showed, "Attention to duty, bravery, and coolness in action against the enemy."

BRADLEY, THOMAS W.

Rank and organization: Sergeant, Company H, 124th New York Infantry. *Place and date:* At Chancellorsville, Va., 3 May 1863. *Entered service at:* Walden, N.Y. *Born:* 6 April 1844, England. *Date of issue:* 10 June 1896. *Citation:* Volunteered in response to a call and alone, in the face of a heavy fire of musketry and canister, went and procured ammunition for the use of his comrades.

BRADY, JAMES

Rank and organization: Private, Company F, 10th New Hampshire Infantry. *Place and date:* At Chapins Farm, Va., 29 September 1864. *Entered service at:* Kingston, N.H. *Birth:* Boston, Mass. *Date of issue:* 6 April 1865. *Citation:* Capture of flag.

BRANDLE, JOSEPH E.

Rank and organization: Private, Company C, 17th Michigan Infantry. *Place and date:* At Lenoire, Tenn., 16 November 1863. *Entered service at:* Colon, Mich. *Born:* 1839, Seneca County, Ohio. *Date of issue:* 20 July 1897. *Citation:* While color bearer of his regiment, having been twice wounded and the sight of one eye destroyed, still held to the colors until ordered to the rear by his regimental commander.

BRANNIGAN, FELIX

Rank and organization: Private, Company A, 74th New York Infantry. *Place and date:* At Chancellorsville, Va., 2 May 1863. *Entered service at:* Allegheny County, Pa. *Birth:* Ireland. *Date of issue:* 29 June 1866. *Citation:* Volunteered on a dangerous service and brought in valuable information.

BRANT, WILLIAM

Rank and organization: Lieutenant, Company B, 1st New Jersey Veteran Battalion. *Place and date:* At Petersburg, Va., 3 April 1865. *Entered service at:* ———. *Birth:* Elizabeth, N.J. *Date of issue:* 10 May 1865. *Citation:* Capture of battle flag of 46th North Carolina (C.S.A.).

BRAS, EDGAR A.

Rank and organization: Sergeant, Company K, 8th Iowa Infantry. *Place and date:* Spanish Fort, Ala., 8 April 1865. *Entered service at:* Louisa County, Iowa. *Birth:* Jefferson County, Iowa. *Date of issue:* 8 June 1865. *Citation:* Capture of flag.

BRAZELL, JOHN

Rank and organization: Quartermaster, U.S. Navy. *Born:* 1837, Philadelphia, Pa. *Accredited to:* Pennsylvania. *G.O. No.:* 45, 31 December 1864. *Citation:* Served on board the U.S.S. *Richmond* in the action at Mobile Bay, 5 August 1864, where he was recommended for coolness and good conduct as a gun captain during that engagement which resulted in the capture of the rebel ram *Tennessee* and in the destruction of Fort Morgan. Brazell served gallantly throughout the actions with Forts Jackson and St. Philip, the Chalmettes, batteries below Vicksburg, and was present at the surrender of New Orleans while on board the U.S.S. *Brooklyn.*

BREEN, JOHN

Rank and organization: Boatswain's Mate, U.S. Navy. *Born:* 1827, New York. *Accredited to:* New York. *G.O. No.:* 11, 3 April 1863. *Citation:* On board the U.S.S. *Commodore Perry* in the attack upon Franklin, Va., 3 October 1862. With enemy fire raking the deck of his ship and blockades thwarting her progress, Breen remained at his post and performed his duties with skill and courage as the *Commodore Perry* fought a gallant battle to silence many rebel batteries as she steamed down the Blackwater River.

BRENNAN, CHRISTOPHER

Rank and organization: Seaman, U.S. Navy. *Born:* 1832, Ireland. *Accredited to:* Massachusetts. *G.O. No.:* 17, 10 July 1863. *Citation:* On board the U.S.S. *Mississippi* during attacks on Forts Jackson and St. Philip and during the taking of New Orleans, 24–25 April 1862. Taking part in the actions which resulted in the damaging of the *Mississippi* and several casualties on it, Brennan showed skill and courage throughout the entire engagements which resulted in the taking of St. Philip and Jackson and in the surrender of New Orleans.

BREST, LEWIS F.

Rank and organization: Private, Company D, 57th Pennsylvania Infantry. *Place and date:* At Sailors Creek, Va., 6 April 1865. *Entered service at:* ———. *Birth:* Mercer, Pa. *Date of issue:* 10 May 1865. *Citation:* Capture of flag.

BREWER, WILLIAM J.

Rank and organization: Private, Company C, 2d New York Cavalry. *Place and date:* At Appomattox campaign, Va., 4 April 1865. *Entered service at:* ———. *Birth:* Putnam County, N.Y. *Date of issue:* 3 May 1865. *Citation:* Capture of engineer flag, Army of Northern Virginia.

BREYER, CHARLES

Rank and organization: Sergeant, Company I, 90th Pennsylvania Infantry. *Place and date:* At Rappahannock Station, Va., 23 August 1862. *Entered service at:* Philadelphia, Pa. *Birth:* ———. *Date of issue:* 8 July 1896. *Citation:* Voluntarily, and at great personal risk, picked up an unexploded shell and threw it away, thus doubtless saving the life of a comrade whose arm had been taken off by the same shell.

BRIGGS, ELIJAH A.

Rank and organization: Corporal, Company B, 2d Connecticut Heavy Artillery. *Place and date:* At Petersburg, Va., 3 April 1865. *Entered service at:* Salisbury, Conn. *Birth:* Salisbury, Conn. *Date of issue:* 10 May 1865. *Citation:* Capture of battle flag.

BRINGLE, ANDREW

Rank and organization: Corporal, Company F, 10th New York Cavalry. *Place and date:* At Sailors Creek, Va., 6 April 1865. *Entered service at:* ———. *Birth:* Buffalo, N.Y. *Date of issue:* 3 July 1865. *Citation:* Charged the enemy and assisted Sgt. Norton in capturing a field-piece and 2 prisoners.

BRINN, ANDREW

Rank and organization: Seaman, U.S. Navy. *Entered service at:* New York. *Birth:* Scotland. *G.O. No.:* 17, 10 July 1863. *Citation:* Served on board the U.S.S. *Mississippi* during her abandonment and firing in the engagement at Port Hudson, 14 March 1863. Remaining under enemy fire for 2½ hours, Brinn remained on board the grounded vessel until all the abandoning crew had landed. After asking to be assigned some duty, he was finally ordered to save himself and to leave the *Mississippi* which had been deliberately fired to prevent her falling into rebel hands.

BRONNER, AUGUST F.

Rank and organization: Private, Company C, 1st New York Artillery. *Place and date:* At White Oak Swamp, Va., 30 June 1862. At Malvern Hill, Va., 1 July 1862. *Entered service at:* ———. *Birth:* Germany. *Date of issue:* Unknown. *Citation:* Continued to fight after being severely wounded.

BRONSON, JAMES H.

Rank and organization: First Sergeant, Company D, 5th U.S. Colored Troops. *Place and date:* At Chapins Farm, Va., 29 September 1864. *Entered service at:* Delaware County, Ohio. *Birth:* Indiana County, Pa. *Date of issue:* 6 April 1865. *Citation:* Took command of his company, all the officers having been killed or wounded, and gallantly led it.

BROSNAN, JOHN

Rank and organization: Sergeant, Company E, 164th New York Infantry. *Place and date:* At Petersburg, Va., 17 June 1864. *Entered service at:* New York, N.Y. *Birth:* Ireland. *Date of issue:* 18 January 1894. *Citation:* Rescued a wounded comrade who lay exposed to the enemy's fire, receiving a severe wound in the effort.

BROUSE, CHARLES W.

Rank and organization: Captain, Company K, 100th Indiana Infantry. *Place and date:* At Missionary Ridge, Tenn., 25 November 1863. *Entered service at:* Indianapolis, Ind. *Birth:* ———. *Date of issue:* 16 May 1899. *Citation:* To encourage his men whom he had ordered to lie down while under severe fire, and who were partially protected by slight earthworks, himself refused to lie down, but walked along the top of the works until he fell severely wounded.

BROWN, CHARLES

Rank and organization: Sergeant, Company C, 50th Pennsylvania Infantry. *Place and date:* At Weldon Railroad, Va., 19 August 1864. *Entered service at:* ———. *Birth:* Schuylkill County, Pa. *Date of issue:* 1 December 1864. *Citation:* Capture of flag of 47th Virginia Infantry (C.S.A.).

BROWN, EDWARD, JR.

Rank and organization: Corporal, Company G, 62d New York Infantry. *Place and date:* At Fredericksburg and Salem Heights, Va., 3–4 May 1863. *Entered service at:* New York, N.Y. *Born:* 6 July 1841, Ireland. *Date of issue:* 24 November 1880. *Citation:* Severely wounded while carrying the colors, he continued at his post, under fire, until ordered to the rear.

BROWN, HENRI LE FEVRE

Rank and organization: Sergeant, Company B, 72d New York Infantry. *Place and date:* At Wilderness, Va., 6 May 1864. *Entered service at:* Ellicott, N.Y. *Birth:* Jamestown, N.Y. *Date of issue:* 23 June 1896. *Citation:* Voluntarily and under a heavy fire from the enemy, 3 times crossed the field of battle with a load of ammunition in a blanket on his back, thus supplying the Federal forces, whose ammunition had nearly all been expended, and enabling them to hold their position until reinforcement arrived, when the enemy were driven from their position.

BROWN, JAMES

Rank and organization: Quartermaster, U.S. Navy. *Born:* 1826 Rochester, N.Y. *Accredited to:* New York. *G.O. No.:* 32, 16 April 1864. *Citation:* Served on board the U.S.S. *Albatross* during action against Fort De Russy in the Red River Area on 4 May 1863. After the steering wheel and wheel ropes had been shot away by rebel fire, Brown stood on the gun platform of the quarterdeck, exposing himself to a close fire of musketry from the shore, and rendered invaluable assistance by his expert management of the relieving tackles in extricating the vessel from a perilous position, and thereby aided in the capture of Fort De Russy's heavyworks.

BROWN, JEREMIAH Z.

Rank and organization: Captain, Company K, 148th Pennsylvania Infantry. *Place and date:* At Petersburg, Va., 27 October 1864. *Entered service at:* Rimmersburg, Pa. *Birth:* Clarion County, Pa. *Date of issue:* 22 June 1896. *Citation:* With 100 selected volunteers, assaulted and captured the works of the enemy, together with a number of officers and men.

BROWN, JOHN

Rank and organization: Captain of the Forecastle, U.S. Navy. *Born:* 1826, Scotland, *Accredited to:* New York. *G.O. No.:* 45, 31 December

1864. *Citation:* On board the U.S.S. *Brooklyn* during action against rebel forts and gunboats and with the ram *Tennessee* in Mobile Bay, 5 August 1864. Despite severe damage to his ship and the loss of several men on board as enemy fire raked her decks from stem to stern, Brown fought his gun with skill and courage throughout the furious battle which resulted in the surrender of the prize rebel ram *Tennessee* and in the damaging and destruction of batteries at Fort Morgan.

BROWN, JOHN H.

Rank and organization: First Sergeant, Company A, 47th Ohio Infantry. *Place and date:* At Vicksburg, Miss., 19 May 1863. *Entered service at:* Cincinnati, Ohio. *Birth:* Boston, Mass. *Date of issue:* 24 August 1896. *Citation:* Voluntarily carried a verbal message from Col. A. C. Parry to Gen. Hugh Ewing through a terrific fire and in plain view of the enemy.

BROWN, JOHN HARTIES

Rank and organization: Captain, Company D, 12th Kentucky Infantry. *Place and date:* At Franklin, Tenn., 30 November 1864. *Entered service at:* Charlestown, Mass. *Born:* 1834, Canada. *Date of issue:* 13 February 1865. *Citation:* Capture of flag.

*BROWN, MORRIS, JR.

Rank and organization: Captain, Company A, 126th New York Infantry. *Place and date:* At Gettysburg, Pa., 3 July 1863. *Entered service at:* Penn Yan, N.Y. *Born:* August 1842, Hammondsport, N.Y. *Date of issue:* 6 March 1869. *Citation:* Capture of flag.

BROWN, ROBERT

Rank and organization: Captain of the Top, U.S. Navy. *Born:* 1830, Norway. *Accredited to:* New York. *G.O. No.:* 45, 31 December 1864. *Citation:* On board the U.S.S. *Richmond* in action at Mobile Bay on 5 August 1864. Cool and courageous at his station throughout the prolonged action. Brown rendered gallant service as his vessel trained her guns on Fort Morgan and on ships of the Confederacy despite extremely heavy return fire. He participated in the actions at Forts Jackson and St. Philip, with the Chalmette batteries, at the surrender of New Orleans and in the attacks on batteries below Vicksburg.

BROWN, ROBERT B.

Rank and organization: Private, Company A, 15th Ohio Infantry. *Place and date:* At Missionary Ridge, Tenn., 25 November 1863. *Entered service at:* Zanesville. *Born:* 2 October 1844, New Concord, Ohio. *Date of issue:* 27 March 1890. *Citation:* Upon reaching the ridge through concentrated fire, he approached the color bearer of the 9th Mississippi Infantry (C.S.A.), demanded his surrender with threatening gesture and took him prisoner with his regimental flag.

BROWN, URIAH

Rank and organization: Private, Company G, 30th Ohio Infantry. *Place and date:* At Vicksburg, Miss., 22 May 1863. *Entered service at:* ———. *Birth:* Miami County, Ohio. *Date of issue:* 15 August 1894.

Citation: Despite the death of his captain at his side during the assault, he continued carrying his log to the defense ditch. While he was laying his log in place he was shot down and thrown into the water. Unmindful of his own wound he, despite the intense fire, dragged 5 of his comrades from the ditch, wherein they lay wounded, to a place of safety.

BROWN, WILLIAM H.

Rank and organization: Landsman, U.S. Navy. *Born:* 1836, Baltimore, Md. *Accredited to:* Maryland. *G.O. No.:* 45, 31 December 1864. *Citation:* On board the U.S.S. *Brooklyn* during successful attacks against Fort Morgan rebel gunboats and the ram *Tennessee* in Mobile Bay on 5 August 1864. Stationed in the immediate vicinity of the shell whips which were twice cleared of men by bursting shells, Brown remained steadfast at his post and performed his duties in the powder division throughout the furious action which resulted in the surrender of the prize rebel ram *Tennessee* and in the damaging and destruction of batteries at Fort Morgan.

BROWN, WILSON

Rank and organization: Landsman, U.S. Navy. *Born:* 1841, Natchez, Miss. *Accredited to:* Mississippi. *G.O. No.:* 45, 31 December 1864. *Citation:* On board the flagship U.S.S. *Hartford* during successful attacks against Fort Morgan, rebel gunboats and the ram *Tennessee* in Mobile Bay on 5 August 1864. Knocked unconscious into the hold of the ship when an enemy shellburst fatally wounded a man on the ladder above him, Brown, upon regaining consciousness, promptly returned to the shell whip on the berth deck and zealously continued to perform his duties although 4 of the 6 men at this station had been either killed or wounded by the enemy's terrific fire.

BROWN, WILSON W.

Rank and organization: Private, Company F., 21st Ohio Infantry. *Place and date:* Georgia, April 1862. *Entered service at:* Wood County, Ohio. *Birth:* Logan County, Ohio. *Date of issue:* September 1863. *Citation:* One of the 19 of 22 men (including 2 civilians) who, by direction of Gen. Mitchell (or Buell), penetrated nearly 200 miles south into enemy territory and captured a railroad train at Big Shanty, Ga., in an attempt to destroy the bridges and tract between Chattanooga and Atlanta.

BROWNELL, FRANCIS E.

Rank and organization: Private, Company A, 11th New York Infantry. *Place and date:* Alexandria, Va., 24 May 1861. *Entered service at:* Troy, N.Y. *Birth:* New York. *Date of issue:* 26 January 1877. *Citation:* Killed the murderer of Colonel Ellsworth at the Marshall House, Alexandria, Va. First Civil War deed to merit Medal of Honor.

BROWNELL, WILLIAM P.

Rank and organization: Coxswain, U.S. Navy. *Born:* 1838, New York. *Accredited to:* New York. *G.O. No.:* 32, 16 April 1864. *Citation:* Served as coxswain on board the U.S.S. *Benton* during the attack on

Great Gulf Bay, 2 May 1863, and Vicksburg, 22 May 1863. Carrying out his duties with coolness and courage, Brownell served gallantly against the enemy as captain of a 9-inch gun in the attacks on Great Gulf and Vicksburg and as a member of the Battery Benton before Vicksburg.

BRUNER, LOUIS J.

Rank and organization: Private, Company H, 5th Indiana Cavalry. *Place and date:* At Walkers Ford, Tenn., 2 December 1863. *Entered service at:* Clifty Brumer, Ind. *Birth:* Monroe County, Ind. *Date of issue:* 9 March 1896. *Citation:* Voluntarily passed through the enemy's lines under fire and conveyed to a battalion, then in a perilous position and liable to capture, information which enabled it to reach a point of safety.

BRUSH, GEORGE W.

Rank and organization: Lieutenant, Company B, 34th U.S. Colored Troops. *Place and date:* At Ashepoo River, S.C., 24 May 1864. *Entered service at:* New York. *Born:* 4 October 1842, West Kill, N.Y. *Date of issue:* 21 January 1897. *Citation:* Voluntarily commanded a boat crew, which went to the rescue of a large number of Union soldiers on board the stranded steamer *Boston*, and with great gallantry succeeded in conveying them to shore, being exposed during the entire time to heavy fire from a Confederate battery.

BRUTON (BRATON), CHRISTOPHER C.

Rank and organization: Captain, Company C, 22d New York Cavalry. *Place and date:* At Waynesboro, Va., 2 March 1865. *Entered service at:* Riga, Monroe County, N.Y. *Birth:* ———. *Date of issue:* 26 March 1865. *Citation:* Capture of Gen. Early's headquarters flag. Confederate national standard.

BRUTSCHE, HENRY

Rank and organization: Landsman, U.S. Navy. *Born:* 1846, Philadelphia, Pa. *Accredited to:* Pennsylvania. *G.O. No.:* 45, 31 December 1864. *Citation:* Served on board the U.S.S. *Tacony* during the taking of Plymouth, N.C., 31 October 1864. Carrying out his duties faithfully during the capture of Plymouth, Brutsche distinguished himself by a display of coolness when he participated in landing and spiking a 9-inch gun while under a devastating fire from enemy musketry.

BRYANT, ANDREW S.

Rank and organization: Sergeant, Company A, 46th Massachusetts Infantry. *Place and date:* At New Bern, N.C., 23 May 1863. *Entered service at:* Massachusetts. *Born:* 3 March 1841, Springfield, Mass. *Date of issue:* 13 Aguust 1873. *Citation:* By his courage and judicious disposition of his guard of 16 men, stationed in a small earthwork at the head of the bridge, held in check and repulsed for a half hour a fierce attack of a strong force of the enemy, thus probably saving the city New Bern from capture.

*BUCHANAN, GEORGE A.

Rank and organization: Private, Company G, 148th New York Infantry. *Place and date:* At Chapins Farm, Va., 29 September 1864. *Entered service at:* Ontario County, N.Y. *Birth:* New York. *Date of issue:* 6 April 1865. *Citation:* Took position in advance of the skirmish line and drove the enemy's cannoneers from their guns; was mortally wounded.

BUCK, F. CLARENCE

Rank and organization: Corporal, Company A, 21st Connecticut Infantry. *Place and date:* At Chapins Farm, Va., 29 September 1864. *Entered service at:* Windsor, Conn. *Birth:* Hartford, Conn. *Date of issue:* 6 April 1865. *Citation:* Although wounded, refused to leave the field until the fight closed.

BUCK, JAMES

Rank and organization: Quartermaster, U.S. Navy. *Born:* 1808, Baltimore, Md. *G.O. No.:* 11, 3 April 1863. *Citation:* Served on board the U.S.S. *Brooklyn* in the attack upon Forts Jackson and St. Philip and at the taking of New Orleans, 24 and 25 April 1862. Although severely wounded by a heavy splinter, Buck continued to perform his duty until positively ordered below. Later stealing back to his post, he steered the ship for 8 hours despite his critical condition. His bravery was typical of the type which resulted in the taking of the Forts Jackson and St. Philip and in the capture of New Orleans.

BUCKINGHAM, DAVID E.

Rank and organization: First Lieutenant, Company E, 4th Delaware Infantry. *Place and date:* At Rowanty Creek, Va., 5 February 1865. *Entered service at:* ———. *Born:* 3 February 1840, Pleasant Hill, Del. *Date of issue:* 13 February 1895. *Citation:* Swam the partly frozen creek, under fire, in the attempt to capture a crossing.

BUCKLES, ABRAM J.

Rank and organization: Sergeant, Company E, 19th Indiana Infantry. *Place and date:* At Wilderness, Va., 5 May 1864. *Entered service at:* Muncie, Ind. *Birth:* Delaware County, Ind. *Date of issue:* 4 December 1893. *Citation:* Though suffering from an open wound, carried the regimental colors until again wounded.

BUCKLEY, DENIS

Rank and organization: Private, Company G, 136th New York Infantry. *Place and date:* At Peach Tree Creek, Ga., 20 July 1864. *Entered service at:* Avon, N.Y. *Birth:* Canada. *Date of issue:* 7 April 1865. *Citation:* Capture of flag of 31st Mississippi (C.S.A.).

BUCKLEY, JOHN C.

Rank and organization: Sergeant, Company G, 4th West Virginia Infantry. *Place and date:* At Vicksburg, Miss., 22 May 1863. *Entered service at:* ———. *Birth:* Fayette County, W. Va. *Date of issue:* 9 July 1894. *Citation:* Gallantry in the charge of the "volunteer storming party."

BUCKLYN, JOHN K.

Rank and organization: First Lieutenant, Battery E, 1st Rhode Island Light Artillery. *Place and date:* At Chancellorsville, Va., 3 May 1863. *Entered service at:* Rhode Island. *Born:* 15 March 1834, Foster Creek, R.I. *Date of issue:* 13 July 1899. *Citation:* Though himself wounded, gallantly fought his section of the battery under a fierce fire from the enemy until his ammunition was all expended, many of the cannoneers and most of the horses killed or wounded, and the enemy within 25 yards of the guns, when, disabling one piece, he brought off the other in safety.

BUFFINGTON, JOHN E.

Rank and organization: Sergeant, Company C, 6th Maryland Infantry. *Place and date:* At Petersburg, Va., 2 April 1865. *Entered service at:* ———. *Birth:* Carroll County, Md. *Date of issue:* Unknown. *Citation:* Was the first enlisted man of the 3d Division to mount the parapet of the enemy's line.

BUFFUM, ROBERT (3d to receive Medal of Honor)

Rank and organization: Private, Company H, 21st Ohio Infantry. *Place and date:* Georgia, April 1862. *Entered service at:* ———. *Birth:* Salem, Mass. *Date of issue:* 25 March 1863. *Citation:* One of the 19 of 22 men (including 2 civilians) who, by direction of Gen. Mitchell (or Buell), penetrated nearly 200 miles south into enemy territory and captured a railroad train at Big Shanty, Ga., in an attempt to destroy the bridges and track between Chattanooga and Atlanta.

BUHRMAN, HENRY G.

Rank and organization: Private, Company H, 54th Ohio Infantry. *Place and date:* At Vicksburg, Miss., 22 May 1863. *Entered service at:* ———. *Birth:* Cincinnati, Ohio. *Date of issue:* 12 July 1894. *Citation:* Gallantry in the charge of the "volunteer storming party."

BUMGARNER, WILLIAM

Rank and organization: Sergeant, Company A, 4th West Virginia Infantry. *Place and date:* At Petersburg, Va., 2 April 1862. *Entered service at:* Mason City, W. Va. *Birth:* ———. *Date of issue:* 10 July 1894. *Citation:* Gallantry in the charge of the "volunteer storming party."

BURBANK, JAMES H.

Rank and organization: Sergeant, Company K, 4th Rhode Island Infantry. *Place and date:* At Blackwater, near Franklin, Va., 3 October 1862. *Entered service at:* Providence, R.I. *Born:* 5 January 1838, Holland. *Date of issue:* 27 July 1896. *Citation:* Gallantry in action while on detached service on board the gunboat *Barney.*

BURGER, JOSEPH

Rank and organization: Private, Company H, 2d Minnesota Infantry. *Place and date:* At Nolensville, Tenn., 15 February 1863. *Entered service at:* Crystal Lake, Minn. *Birth:* Austria. *Date of issue:* 11 September 1897. *Citation:* Was one of a detachment of 16 men who heroically defended a wagon train against the attack of 125 cavalry, repulsed the attack and saved the train.

BURK, E. MICHAEL

Rank and organization: Private, Company D, 125th New York Infantry. *Place and date:* At Spotsylvania, Va., 12 May 1864. *Entered service at:* Troy, N.Y. *Birth:* Ireland. *Date of issue:* 1 December 1864. *Citation:* Capture of flag, seizing it as his regiment advanced over the enemy's works. He received a bullet wound in the chest while capturing flag.

BURK, THOMAS

Rank and organization: Sergeant, Company H, 97th New York Infantry. *Place and date:* At Wilderness, Va., 6 May 1864. *Entered service at:* Harrisburgh, Lewis County, N.Y. *Born:* 1842, Lewis County, N.Y. *Date of issue:* 24 August 1896. *Citation:* At the risk of his own life, went back while the rebels were still firing and, finding Col. Wheelock unable to move, alone and unaided, carried him off the field of battle.

BURKE, DANIEL W.

Rank and organization: First Sergeant, Company B, 2d U.S. Infantry. *Place and date:* At Shepherdstown Ford, Va., 20 September 1862. *Entered service at:* Connecticut. *Birth:* New Haven, Conn. *Date of issue:* 21 April 1892. *Citation:* Voluntarily attempted to spike a gun in the face of the enemy.

BURKE, THOMAS

Rank and organization: Private, Company A, 5th New York Cavalry. *Place and date:* At Hanover Courthouse, Va., 30 June 1863. *Entered service at:* ———. *Birth:* Ireland. *Date of issue:* 11 February 1878. *Citation:* Capture of battle flag.

BURNS, JAMES M.

Rank and organization: Sergeant, Company B, 1st West Virginia Infantry. *Place and date:* At New Market, Va., 15 May 1864. *Entered service at:* Jefferson County, Ohio. *Birth:* Jefferson County, Ohio. *Date of issue:* 20 November 1896. *Citation:* Under a heavy fire of musketry, rallied a few men to the support of the colors, in danger of capture, and bore them to a place of safety. One of his comrades having been severely wounded in the effort, Sgt. Burns went back a hundred yards in the face of the enemy's fire and carried the wounded man from the field.

BURNS, JOHN M.

Rank and organization: Seaman, U.S. Navy. *Born:* 1835, Hudson, N.Y. *Accredited to:* New York. *G.O. No.:* 45, 31 December 1864. *Citation:* On board the U.S.S. *Lackawanna* during successful attacks against Fort Morgan, rebel gunboats and the ram *Tennessee* in Mobile Bay, on 5 August 1864. Although severely wounded and sent below under the surgeon's charge, Burns promptly returned to his station and assisted the powder division throughout the prolonged action which resulted in the capture of the rebel ram *Tennessee* and in the damaging and destruction of Fort Morgan.

BURRITT, WILLIAM W.

Rank and organization: Private, Company G, 113th Illinois Infantry. *Place and date:* At Vicksburg, Miss., 27 April 1863. *Entered service at:* Chicago, Ill. *Birth:* Campbell, N.Y. *Date of issue:* 8 July 1896. *Citation:* Voluntarily acted as a fireman on a steam tug which ran the blockade and passed the batteries under a heavy fire.

BURTON, ALBERT

Rank and organization: Seaman, U.S. Navy. *Born:* 1838, England. *Accredited to:* New York. *G.O. No.:* 59, 22 June 1865. *Citation:* Served on board the U.S.S. *Wabash* in the assault on Fort Fisher, 15 January 1865. Advancing gallantly through the severe enemy fire while armed only with a revolver and cutlass which made it impossible to return the fire at that range, Burton succeeded in reaching the angle of the fort and going on, to be one of the few who entered the fort. When the rest of the body of men to his rear were forced to retreat under a devastating fire, he was forced to withdraw through lack of support, and to seek the shelter of one of the mounds near the stockade from which point he succeeded in regaining the safety of his ship.

BUTTERFIELD, DANIEL

Rank and organization: Brigadier General, U.S. Volunteers. *Place and date:* At Gaines Mill, Va., 27 June 1862. *Entered service at:* Washington, D.C. *Born:* 31 October 1831, Utica, N.Y. *Date of issue:* 26 September 1892. *Citation:* Seized the colors of the 83d Pennsylvania Volunteers at a critical moment and, under a galling fire of the enemy, encouraged the depleted ranks to renewed exertion.

BUTTERFIELD, FRANK G.

Rank and organization: First Lieutenant, Company C, 6th Vermont Infantry. *Place and date:* At Salem Heights, Va., 4 May 1863. *Entered service at:* Rockingham, Vt. *Birth:* Rockingham, Vt. *Date of issue:* 4 May 1891. *Citation:* Took command of the skirmish line and covered the movement of his regiment out of a precarious position.

BUTTS, GEORGE

Rank and organization: Gunner's Mate, U.S. Navy. *Born:* Rome, N.Y. *Accredited to:* Ohio. *G.O. No.:* 45, 31 December 1864. *Citation:* Served on board the U.S.S. *Signal*, Red River, 5 May 1864. Proceeding up the Red River, the U.S.S. *Signal* engaged a large force of enemy field batteries and sharpshooters, returning their fire until the ship was totally disabled, at which time the white flag was raised. Although entered on the sick list, Butts courageously carried out his duties during the entire engagement.

BYRNES, JAMES

Rank and organization: Boatswain's Mate, U.S. Navy. *Born:* 1838, Ireland. *Accredited to:* New York. *G.O. No.:* 11, 3 April 1863. *Citation:* Served on board the U.S.S. *Louisville*. Carrying out his duties through the thick of battle and acting as captain of a 9-inch gun, Brynes consistently showed "Attention to duty, bravery, and coolness in action against the enemy."

CADWALLADER, ABEL G.

Rank and organization: Corporal, Company H, 1st Maryland Infantry. *Place and date:* At Hatchers Run and Dabneys Mills, Va., 6 February 1865. *Entered service at:* ———. *Birth:* Baltimore, Md. *Date of issue:* 5 January 1897. *Citation:* Gallantly planted the colors on the enemy's works in advance of the arrival of his regiment.

CADWELL, LUMAN L.

Rank and organization: Sergeant, Company B, 2d New York Veteran Cavalry. *Place and date:* At Alabama Bayou, La., 20 September 1864. *Entered service at:* ———. *Birth:* Broome, N.Y. *Date of issue:* 17 August 1894. *Citation:* Swam the bayou under fire of the enemy and captured and brought off a boat by means of which the command crossed and routed the enemy.

CALDWELL, DANIEL

Rank and organization: Sergeant, Company H, 13th Pennsylvania Cavalry. *Place and date:* At Hatchers Run, Va., 6 February 1865. *Entered service at:* ———. *Born:* 1 June 1842, Marble Hill, Montgomery County, Pa. *Date of issue:* 25 February 1865. *Citation:* In a mounted charge, dashed into center of the enemy's line and captured the colors of the 33rd North Carolina Infantry.

CALKIN, IVERS S.

Rank and organization: First Sergeant, Company M., 2d New York Cavalry. *Place and date:* At Sailors Creek, Va., 6 April 1865. *Entered service at:* Willsborough, N.Y. *Birth:* Essex County, N.Y. *Date of issue:* 3 May 1865. *Citation:* Capture of flag of 18th Virginia Infantry (C.S.A.).

CALLAHAN, JOHN H.

Rank and organization: Private, Company B, 122d Illinois Infantry. *Place and date:* At Fort Blakely, Ala., 9 April 1865. *Entered service at:* Macoupin County, Ill. *Birth:* Shelby County, Ky. *Date of issue:* 8 June 1865. *Citation:* Capture of flag.

CAMP, CARLTON N.

Rank and organization: Private, Company B, 18th New Hampshire Infantry. *Place and date:* At Petersburg, Va., 2 April 1865. *Entered service at:* Hanover, N.H. *Birth:* Hanover, N.H. *Date of issue:* Unknown. *Citation:* Brought off from the picket line, under heavy fire, a comrade who had been shot through both legs.

CAMPBELL, JAMES A.

Rank and organization: Private, Company A, 2d New York Cavalry. *Place and date:* At Woodstock, Va., 22 January 1865; At Amelia Courthouse, Va., 5 April 1865. *Entered service at:* ———. *Birth:* New York, N.Y. *Date of issue:* 30 October 1897. *Citation:* While his command was retreating before superior numbers at Woodstock, Va., he voluntarily rushed back with one companion and rescued his commanding officer, who had been unhorsed and left behind. At Amelia Courthouse captured 2 battle flags.

CAMPBELL, WILLIAM

Rank and organization: Boatswain's Mate, U.S. Navy. *Born:* 1838, Indiana. *Accredited to:* Indiana. *G.O. No.:* 59, 22 June 1865. *Citation:* On board the U.S.S. *Ticonderoga* during attacks on Fort Fisher, 24 and 25 December 1864; and 13 to 15 January 1865. Despite heavy return fire by the enemy and the explosion of the 100-pounder Parrott rifle which killed 8 men and wounded 12 more, Campbell, as captain of a gun, performed his duties with skill and courage during the first 2 days of battle. As his ship again took position on the line of the 13th, he remained steadfast as the *Ticonderoga* maintained a well-placed fire upon the batteries on shore, and thereafter, as she materially lessened the power of guns on the mound which had been turned upon our assaulting columns. During this action the flag was planted on one of the strongest fortifications possessed by the rebels.

CAMPBELL, WILLIAM

Rank and organization: Private, Company I, 30th Ohio Infantry. *Place and date:* At Vicksburg, Miss., 22 May 1863. *Entered service at:* ———. *Birth:* Ireland. *Date of issue:* 14 August 1894. *Citation:* Gallantry in the charge of the "volunteer storming party."

CAPEHART, CHARLES E.

Rank and organization: Major, 1st West Virginia Cavalry. *Place and date:* At Monterey Mountain, Pa., 4 July 1863. *Entered service at:* Washington, D.C. *Born:* 1883, Conemaugh Township, Cambria County, Pa. *Date of issue:* 7 April 1898. *Citation:* While commanding the regiment, charged down the mountain side at midnight, in a heavy rain, upon the enemy's fleeing wagon train. Many wagons were captured and destroyed and many prisoners taken.

CAPEHART, HENRY

Rank and organization: Colonel, 1st West Virginia Cavalry. *Place and date:* At Greenbrier River, W. Va., 22 May 1864. *Entered service at:* Bridgeport, Ohio. *Born:* 18 March 1825, Johnstown, Cambria County, Pa. *Date of issue:* 12 February 1895. *Citation:* Saved, under fire, the life of a drowning soldier.

CAPRON, HORACE, JR.

Rank and organization: Sergeant, Company G, 8th Illinois Cavalry. *Place and date:* At Chickahominy and Ashland, Va., June 1862. *Entered service at:* Peoria, Ill. *Birth:* Laurel, Md. *Date of issue:* 27 September 1865. *Citation:* Gallantry in action.

CAREY, HUGH

Rank and organization: Sergeant, Company E, 82d New York Infantry. *Place and date:* At Gettysburg, Pa., 2 July 1863. *Entered service at:* ———. *Birth:* Ireland. *Date of issue:* 6 February 1888. *Citation:* Captured the flag of the 7th Virginia Infantry (C.S.A.), being twice wounded in the effort.

CAREY, JAMES L.

Rank and organization: Sergeant, Company G, 10th New York Cavalry. *Place and date:* At Appomattox Courthouse, Va., 9 April 1865. *Entered service at:* ———. *Birth:* Onondaga County, N.Y. *Date of issue:* Unknown. *Citation:* Daring bravery and urging the men forward in a charge.

CARLISLE, CASPER R.

Rank and organization: Private, Company F, Independent Pennsylvania Light Artillery. *Place and date:* At Gettysburg, Pa., 2 July 1863. *Entered service at:* Allegheny County, Pa. *Birth:* Allegheny County, Pa. *Date of issue:* 21 December 1892. *Citation:* Saved a gun of his battery under heavy musketry fire, most of the horses being killed and the drivers wounded.

CARMAN, WARREN

Rank and organization: Private, Company H, 1st New York (Lincoln) Cavalry. *Place and date:* At Waynesboro, Va., 2 March 1865. *Entered service at:* ———. *Birth:* Seneca County, N.Y. *Date of issue:* 26 March 1865. *Citation:* Capture of flag and several prisoners.

CARMIN, ISAAC H.

Rank and organization: Corporal, Company A, 48th Ohio Infantry. *Place and date:* At Vicksburg, Miss., 22 May 1863. *Entered service at:* ———. *Birth:* Monmouth County, N.J. *Date of issue:* 25 February 1895. *Citation:* Saved his regimental flag; also seized and threw a shell, with burning fuse, from among his comrades.

CARNEY, WILLIAM H.

Rank and organization: Sergeant, Company C, 54th Massachusetts Colored Infantry. *Place and date:* At Fort Wagner, S.C., 18 July 1863. *Entered service at:* New Bedford, Mass. *Birth:* Norfolk, Va. *Date of issue:* 23 May 1900. *Citation:* When the color sergeant was shot down, this soldier grasped the flag, led the way to the parapet, and planted the colors thereon. When the troops fell back he brought off the flag, under a fierce fire in which he was twice severely wounded.

CARR, EUGENE A.

Rank and organization: Colonel, 3d Illinois Cavalry. *Place and date:* At Pea Ridge, Ark., 7 March 1862. *Entered service at:* Hamburg, Erie County, N.Y. *Born:* 10 March 1830, Boston Corner, Erie County, N.Y. *Date of issue:* 16 January 1894. *Citation:* Directed the deployment of his command and held his ground, under a brisk fire of shot and shell in which he was several times wounded.

CARR, FRANKLIN

Rank and organization: Corporal, Company D, 124th Ohio Infantry. *Place and date:* At Nashville, Tenn., 16 December 1864. *Entered service at:* ———. *Birth:* Stark County, Ohio. *Date of issue:* 24 February 1865. *Citation:* Recapture of U.S. guidon from a rebel battery.

740

5. CARR, WILLIAM M.

Rank and organization: Master-at-Arms, U.S. Navy. *Birth:* Baltimore, Md. *G.O. No.:* 45, 31 December 1864. *Citation:* On board the U.S.S. *Richmond* during action against rebel forts and gunboats and with the ram *Tennessee* in Mobile Bay, 5 August 1864. Despite damage to his ship and the loss of several men on board as enemy fire raked her decks, Carr performed his duties with skill and courage throughout the prolonged battle which resulted in the surrender of the rebel ram *Tennessee* and in the successful attacks carried out on Fort Morgan.

CARSON, WILLIAM J.

Rank and organization: Musician, Company E, 1st Battalion, 15th U.S. Infantry. *Place and date:* At Chickamauga, Ga., 19 September 1863. *Entered service at:* North Greenfield, Ohio. *Birth:* Washington County, Pa. *Date of issue:* 27 January 1894. *Citation:* At a critical stage in the battle when the 14th Corps lines were wavering and in disorder he on his own initiative bugled "to the colors" amid the 18th U.S. Infantry who formed by him, and held the enemy. Within a few minutes he repeated his action amid the wavering 2d Ohio Infantry. This bugling deceived the enemy who believed reinforcements had arrived. Thus, they delayed their attack.

CART, JACOB

Rank and organization: Private, Company A, 7th Pennsylvania Reserve Corps. *Place and date:* At Fredericksburg, Va., 13 December, 1862. *Entered service at:* ———. *Birth:* Carlisle, Pa. *Date of issue:* 25 November 1864. *Citation:* Capture of flag of 19th Georgia Infantry (C.S.A.), wresting it from the hands of the color bearer.

3. CARTER, JOHN J.

Rank and organization: Second Lieutenant, Company B, 33d New York Infantry. *Place and date:* At Antietam, Md., 17 September 1862. *Entered service at:* Nunda, N.Y. *Born:* 16 June 1842, Troy, N.Y. *Date of issue:* 10 September 1897. *Citation:* While in command of a detached company, seeing his regiment thrown into confusion by a charge of the enemy, without orders made a countercharge upon the attacking column and checked the assault. Penetrated within the enemy's lines at night and obtained valuable information.

5. CARTER, JOSEPH F.

Rank and organization: Captain, Company D, 3d Maryland Infantry. *Place and date:* At Fort Stedman, Va., 25 March 1865. *Entered service at:* Baltimore, Md. *Birth:* Baltimore, Md. *Date of issue:* 9 July 1891. *Citation:* Captured the colors of the 51st Virginia Infantry (C.S.A.). During the battle he was captured and escaped bringing a number of prisoners with him.

CARUANA, ORLANDO E.

Rank and organization: Private, Company K, 51st New York Infantry. *Place and date:* At New Bern, N.C., 14 March 1862; at South Mountain, Md., 14 September 1862. *Entered service at:* ———. *Birth:*

Ca Valletta, Malta. *Date of issue:* 14 November 1890. *Citation:* At New Bern, N.C., brought off the wounded color sergeant and the colors under a heavy fire of the enemy. Was one of four soldiers who volunteered to determine the position of the enemy at South Mountain, Md. While so engaged was fired upon and his three companions killed, but he escaped and rejoined his command in safety.

CASEY, DAVID

Rank and organization: Private, Company C, 25th Massachusetts Infantry. *Place and date:* At Cold Harbor, Va., 3 June 1864. *Entered service at:* Northbridge, Mass. *Birth:* Ireland. *Date of issue:* 14 September 1888. *Citation:* Two color bearers having been shot dead one after the other, the last one far in advance of his regiment and close to the enemy's line, this soldier rushed forward, and, under a galling fire, after removing the dead body of the bearer therefrom, secured the flag and returned with it to the Union lines.

CASEY, HENRY

Rank and organization: Private, Company C, 20th Ohio Infantry. *Place and date:* At Vicksburg, Miss., 22 April 1863. *Entered service at:* ———. *Birth:* Fayette County, Pa., *Date of issue:* 23 September 1897. *Citation:* Voluntarily served as one of the crew of a transport that passed the forts under a heavy fire.

CASSIDY, MICHAEL

Rank and organization: Landsman, U.S. Navy. *Born:* 1837, Ireland. *Accredited to:* New York. *G.O. No.:* 45, 31 December 1864. *Citation:* Served on board the U.S.S. *Lackawanna* during successful attacks against Fort Morgan, rebel gunboats and the ram *Tennessee*, in Mobile Bay, 5 August 1864. Displaying great coolness and exemplary behavior as first sponger of a gun, Cassidy, by his coolness under fire, received the applause of his officers and the guncrew throughout the action which resulted in the capture of the prize ram *Tennessee* and in the destruction of batteries at Fort Morgan.

CATLIN, ISAAC S.

Rank and organization: Colonel, 109th New York Infantry. *Place and date:* At Petersburg, Va., 30 July 1864. *Entered service at:* Oswego, N.Y. *Birth:* New York. *Date of issue:* 13 January 1899. *Citation:* In a heroic effort to rally the disorganized troops was disabled by a severe wound. While being carried from the field he recovered somewhat and bravely started to return to his command, when he received a second wound, which necessitated amputation of his right leg.

CAYER, OVILA

Rank and organization: Sergeant, Company A, 14th U.S. Volunteers. *Place and date:* At Weldon Railroad, Va., 19 August 1864. *Entered service at:* ———. *Birth:* Canada. *Date of issue:* 15 February 1867. *Citation:* Commanded the regiment, all the officers being disable.

CHAMBERLAIN, JOSHUA L.

Rank and organization: Colonel, 20th Maine Infantry. *Place and date:* At Gettysburg, Pa., 2 July 1863. *Entered service at:* Brunswick, Maine. *Born:* 8 September 1828, Brewer Maine. *Date of issue:* 11 August 1893. *Citation:* Daring heroism and great tenacity in holding his position on the Little Round Top against repeated assaults, and carrying the advance position on the Great Round Top.

CHAMBERLAIN, ORVILLE T.

Rank and organization: Second Lieutenant, Company G, 74th Indiana Infantry. *Place and date:* At Chickamauga, Ga., 20 September 1863. *Entered service at:* Elkhart, Ind. *Birth:* Kosciusko County, Ind. *Date of issue:* 11 March 1896. *Citation:* While exposed to a galling fire, went in search of another regiment, found its location, procured ammunition from the men thereof, and returned with the ammunition to his own company.

CHAMBERS, JOSEPH B.

Rank and organization: Private, Company F, 100th Pennsylvania Infantry. *Place and date:* At Petersburg, Va., 25 March 1865. *Entered service at:* East Brook, Pa. *Birth:* Beaver County, Pa. *Date of issue:* 27 July 1871. *Citation:* Capture of colors of 1st Virginia Infantry (C.S.A.).

CHANDLER, HENRY F.

Rank and organization: Sergeant, Company E, 59th Massachusetts Infantry. *Place and date:* At Petersburg, Va., 17 June 1864. *Entered service at:* ———. *Birth:* Andover, Mass. *Date of issue:* 30 March 1898. *Citation:* Though seriously wounded in a bayonet charge and directed to go to the rear he declined to do so, but remained with his regiment and helped to carry the breastworks.

CHANDLER, JAMES B.

Rank and organization: Coxswain, U.S. Navy. *Born:* 1838, Massachusetts. *Accredited to:* Massachusetts. *G.O. No.:* 45, 31 December 1864. *Citation:* On board the U.S.S. *Richmond* during action against rebel forts and gunboats and with the ram *Tennessee* in Mobile Bay, 5 August 1864. Cool and courageous although he had just come off the sick list, Chandler rendered gallant service throughout the prolonged action as his ship maintained accurate fire against Fort Morgan and ships of the Confederacy despite extremely heavy return fire. He participated in the actions at Forts Jackson and St. Philip, with the Chalmette batteries, at the surrender of New Orleans and in the attacks on batteries below Vicksburg.

CHANDLER, STEPHEN E.

Rank and organization: Quartermaster Sergeant, Company A, 24th New York Cavalry. *Place and date:* At Amelia Springs, Va., 5 April 1865. *Entered service at:* Granby, Oswego County, N.Y. *Birth:* Michigan. *Date of issue:* 4 April 1898. *Citation:* Under severe fire of the enemy and of the troops in retreat, went between the lines to the assistance of a wounded and helpless comrade, and rescued him from death or capture.

CHAPIN, ALARIC B.

Rank and organization: Private, Company G, 142d New York Infantry. *Place and date:* At Fort Fisher, N.C., 15 January 1865. *Entered service at:* Pamelia, N.Y. *Birth:* Ogdensburg, N.Y. *Date of issue:* 28 December 1914. *Citation:* Voluntarily advanced with the head of the column and cut down the palisading.

CHAPMAN, JOHN

Rank and organization: Private, Company B, 1st Maine Heavy Artillery. *Place and date:* At Sailors Creek, Va., 6 April 1865. *Entered service at:* St. John, New Brunswick. *Birth:* St. John, New Brunswick. *Date of issue:* 10 May 1865. *Citation:* Capture of flag.

CHAPUT, LOUIS G.

Rank and organization: Landsman, U.S. Navy. *Born:* 1845, Canada. *Accredited to:* New York. *G.O. No.:* 45, 31 December 1864. *Citation:* On board the U.S.S. *Lackawanna* during successful attacks against Fort Morgan, rebel gunboats and the rebel ram *Tennessee* in Mobile Bay, 5 August 1864. Severely wounded, Chaput remained at his gun until relieved, reported to the surgeon and returned to his gun until the action was over. He was then carried below following the action which resulted in the capture of the prize ram *Tennessee* and in destruction of batteries at Fort Morgan.

CHASE, JOHN F.

Rank and organization: Private, 5th Battery, Maine Light Artillery. *Place and date:* At Chancellorsville, Va., 3 May 1863. *Entered service at:* Augusta, Maine. *Birth:* Chelsea, Maine. *Date of issue:* 7 February 1888. *Citation:* Nearly all the officers and men of the battery having been killed or wounded, this soldier with a comrade continued to fire his gun after the guns had ceased. The piece was then dragged off by the two, the horses having been shot, and its capture by the enemy was prevented.

CHILD, BENJAMIN H.

Rank and organization: Corporal, Battery A, 1st Rhode Island Light Artillery. *Place and date:* At Antietam, Md., 17 September 1862. *Entered service at:* Providence, R.I. *Born:* 8 May 1843, Providence, R.I. *Date of issue:* 20 July 1897. *Citation:* Was wounded and taken to the rear insensible, but when partially recovered insisted on returning to the battery and resumed command of his piece, so remaining until the close of the battle.

CHISMAN, WILLIAM W.

Rank and organization: Private, Company I, 83d Indiana Infantry. *Place and date:* At Vicksburg, Miss., 22 May 1863. *Entered service at:* Wilmington, Ind. *Birth:* Dearborn County, Ind. *Date of issue:* 15 August 1894. *Citation:* Gallantry in the charge of the "volunteer storming party."

CHRISTIANCY, JAMES I.

Rank and organization: First Lieutenant, Company D, 9th Michigan Cavalry. *Place and date:* At Hawes Shops, Va., 28 May 1864. *Entered service at:* Monroe County, Mich. *Birth:* Monroe County, Mich. *Date of issue:* 10 October 1892. *Citation:* While acting as aide, voluntarily led a part of the line into the fight, and was twice wounded.

CHURCHILL, SAMUEL J.

Rank and organization: Corporal, Company G, 2d Illinois Light Artillery. *Place and date:* At Nashville, Tenn., 15 December 1864. *Entered service at:* DeKalb County, Ill. *Birth:* Hubbardton , Vt. *Date of issue:* 20 January 1897. *Citation:* When the fire of the enemy's batteries compelled the men of his detachment for a short time to seek shelter, he stood manfully at his post and for some minutes worked his gun alone.

CILLEY, CLINTON A.

Rank and organization: Captain, Company C, 2d Minnesota Infantry. *Place and date:* At Chickamauga, Ga., 20 September 1863. *Entered service at:* Sasioja, Minn. *Birth:* Rockingham County, N.H. *Date of issue:* 12 June 1895. *Citation:* Seized the colors of a retreating regiment and led it into the thick of the attack.

CLANCY, JAMES T.

Rank and organization: Sergeant, Company C, 1st New Jersey Cavalry. *Place and date:* At Vaughn Road, Va., 1 October 1864. *Entered service at:* ———. *Birth:* Albany, N.Y. *Date of issue:* 3 July 1865. *Citation:* Shot the Confederate Gen. Dunovant dead during a charge, thus confusing the enemy and greatly aiding in his repulse.

CLAPP, ALBERT A.

Rank and organization: First Sergeant, Company G, 2d Ohio Cavalry. *Place and date:* At Sailors Creek, Va., 6 April 1865. *Entered service at:* ———. *Birth:* Pompey, N.Y. *Date of issue:* 24 April 1865. *Citation:* Capture of battle flag of the 8th Florida Infantry (C.S.A.).

CLARK, CHARLES A.

Rank and organization: Lieutenant and Adjutant, 6th Maine Infantry. *Place and date:* At Brooks Ford, Va., 4 May 1863. *Entered service at:* ———. *Birth:* Sangerville, Maine. *Date of issue:* 13 May 1896. *Citation:* Having voluntarily taken command of his regiment in the absence of its commander, at great personal risk and with remarkable presence of mind and fertility of resource led the command down an exceedingly precipitous embankment to the Rappahannock River and by his gallantry, coolness, and good judgment in the face of the enemy saved the command from capture or destruction.

CLARK, HARRISON

Rank and organization: Corporal, Company E, 125th New York Infantry. *Place and date:* At Gettysburg, Pa., 2 July 1863. *Entered service at:* Chatham, N.Y. *Birth:* Chatham, N.Y. *Date of issue:* 11 June 1895.

Citation: Seized the colors and advanced with them after the color bearer had been shot.

CLARK, JAMES G.

Rank and organization: Private, Company F, 88th Pennsylvania Infantry. *Place and date:* At Petersburg, Va., 18 June 1864. *Entered service at:* ———. *Birth:* Germantown, Pa. *Date of issue:* 30 April 1892. *Citation:* Distinguished bravery in action; was severely wounded.

CLARK, JOHN W.

Rank and organization: First Lieutenant and Regimental Quartermaster, 6th Vermont Infantry. *Place and date:* Near Warrenton, Va., 28 July 1863. *Entered service at:* Vermont. *Born:* 21 October 1830, Montpelier, Vt. *Date of issue:* 17 August 1891. *Citation:* Defended the division train against a vastly superior force of the enemy; he was severely wounded, but remained in the saddle for 20 hours afterward, until he had brought his train through in safety.

CLARK, WILLIAM A.

Rank and organization: Corporal, Company H, 2d Minnesota Infantry. *Place and date:* At Nolensville, Tenn., 15 February 1863. *Entered service at:* Shelbyville, Minn. *Birth:* Pennsylvania. *Date of issue:* 11 September 1897. *Citation:* Was one of a detachment of 16 men who heroically defended a wagon train against the attack of 125 cavalry, repulsed the attack and saved the train.

CLARKE, DAYTON P.

Rank and organization: Captain, Company F, 2d Vermont Infantry. *Place and date:* At Spotsylvania, Va., 12 May 1864. *Entered service at:* Hermon, N.Y. *Birth:* Hermon, N.Y. *Date of issue:* 30 June 1892. *Citation:* Distinguished conduct in a desperate hand-to-hand fight while commanding the regiment.

CLAUSEN, CHARLES H.

Rank and organization: First lieutenant, Company H, 61st Pennsylvania Infantry. *Place and date:* At Spotsylvania, Va., 12 May 1864. *Entered service at:* Philadelphia, Pa. *Birth:* Philadelphia, Pa. *Date of issue:* 25 June 1892. *Citation:* Although severely wounded, he led the regiment against the enemy, under a terrific fire, and saved a battery from capture.

CLAY, CECIL

Rank and organization: Captain, Company K, 58th Pennsylvania Infantry. *Place and date:* At Fort Harrison, Va., 29 September 1864. *Entered service at:* ———. *Birth:* Philadelphia, Pa. *Date of issue:* 19 April 1892. *Citation:* Led his regiment in the charge, carrying the colors of another regiment, and when severely wounded in the right arm, incurring loss of same, he shifted the colors to the left hand, which also became disabled by a gunshot wound.

746

CLEVELAND, CHARLES F.

Rank and organization: Private, Company C, 26th New York Infantry. *Place and date:* At Antietam, Md., 17 September 1862. *Entered service at:* ———. *Birth:* Hartford, N.Y. *Date of issue:* 12 June 1895. *Citation:* Voluntarily took and carried the colors into action after the color bearer had been shot.

CLIFFORD, ROBERT T.

Rank and organization: Master-at-Arms, U.S. Navy. *Born:* 1835, Pennsylvania. *Accredited to:* Pennsylvania. *G.O. No.:* 45, 31 December 1864. *Citation:* Served on board the U.S.S. *Shokokon* at New Topsail Inlet off Wilmington, N.C., 22 August 1863. Participating in a strategic plan to destroy an enemy schooner, Clifford aided in the portage of a dinghy across the narrow neck of land separating the sea from the sound. Launching the boat in the sound, the crew approached the enemy from the rear and Clifford gallantly crept into the rebel camp and counted the men who outnumbered his party 3 to 1. Returning to his men, he ordered a charge in which the enemy was routed, leaving behind a schooner and a quantity of supplies.

CLOPP, JOHN E.

Rank and organization: Private, Company F, 71st Pennsylvania Infantry. *Place and date:* At Gettysburg, Pa., 3 July 1863. *Entered service at:* Philadelphia, Pa. *Birth:* Philadelphia, Pa. *Date of issue:* 2 February 1865. *Citation:* Capture of flag of 9th Virginia Infantry (C.S.A.), wresting it from the color bearer.

CLUTE, GEORGE W.

Rank and organization: Corporal, Company I, 14th Michigan Infantry. *Place and date:* At Bentonville, N.C., 19 March 1865. *Entered service at:* ———. *Birth:* Marathon, Mich. *Date of issue:* 26 August 1898. *Citation:* In a charge, captured the flag of the 40th North Carolina (C.S.A.), the flag being taken in a personal encounter with an officer who carried and defended it.

COATES, JEFFERSON

Rank and organization: Sergeant, Company H, 7th Wisconsin Infantry. *Place and date:* At Gettysburg, Pa., 1 July 1863. *Entered service at:* Boscobel, Wis. *Birth:* Grant County, Wis. *Date of issue:* 29 June 1866. *Citation:* Unsurpassed courage in battle, where he had both eyes shot out.

COCKLEY, DAVID L.

Rank and organization: First Lieutenant, Company L, 10th Ohio Cavalry. *Place and date:* At Waynesboro, Ga., 4 December 1864. *Entered service at:* ———. *Born:* 8 June 1843, Lexington, Ohio. *Date of issue:* 2 August 1897. *Citation:* While acting as aide-de-camp to a general officer, he 3 times asked permission to join his regiment in a proposed charge upon the enemy, and in response to the last request, having obtained such permission, joined his regiment and fought bravely at its head throughout the action.

COEY, JAMES

Rank and organization: Major, 147th New York Infantry. *Place and date:* At Hatchers Run, Va., 6 February 1865. *Entered service at:* ———. *Born:* 12 February 1841, New York, N.Y. *Date of issue:* 12 May 1892. *Citation:* Seized the regimental colors at a critical moment and by a prompt advance on the enemy caused the entire brigade to follow him; and, after being himself severely wounded, he caused himself to be lifted into the saddle and a second time rallied the line in an attempt to check the enemy.

COFFEY, ROBERT J.

Rank and organization: Sergeant, Company K, 4th Vermont Infantry. *Place and date:* At Banks Ford, Va., 4 May 1863. *Entered service at:* Montpelier, Vt. *Birth:* Nova Scotia. *Date of issue:* 13 May 1892. *Citation:* Singlehandedly captured 2 officers and 5 privates of the 8th Louisiana Regiment (C.S.A.).

COHN, ABRAHAM

Rank and organization: Sergeant Major, 6th New Hampshire Infantry. *Place and date:* At Wilderness, Va., 6 May 1864; At the mine, Petersburg, Va., 30 July 1864. *Entered service at:* Campton, N.H. *Birth:* Guttentag, Silesia, Prussia. *Date of issue:* 24 August 1865. *Citation:* During Battle of the Wilderness rallied and formed, under heavy fire, disorganized and fleeing troops of different regiments. At Petersburg, Va., 30 July 1864, bravely and coolly carried orders to the advanced line under severe fire.

COLBERT, PATRICK

Rank and organization: Coxswain, U.S. Navy. *Born:* 1840, Ireland. *Accredited to:* New York. *G.O. No.:* 45, 31 December 1864. *Citation:* Served on board the U.S.S. *Commodore Hull* at the capture of Plymouth, 31 October 1864. Painfully wounded by a shell which killed the man at his side, Colbert, as captain of the forward pivot gun, remained at his post until the end of the action, braving the heavy enemy fire and appearing as cool as if at mere target practice.

COLBY, CARLOS W.

Rank and organization: Sergeant, Company G, 97th Illinois Infantry. *Place and date:* At Vicksburg, Miss., 22 May 1863. *Entered service at:* Madison County, Ill. *Birth:* Merrimack, N.H. *Date of issue:* 31 January 1896. *Citation:* Gallantry in the charge of the "volunteer storming party."

COLE, GABRIEL

Rank and organization: Corporal, Company I, 5th Michigan Cavalry. *Place and date:* At Winchester, Va., 19 September 1864. *Entered service at:* New Salem, Mich. *Birth:* Chenango County, N.Y. *Date of issue:* 27 September 1864. *Citation:* Capture of flag, during which he was wounded in the leg.

COLLINS, HARRISON

Rank and organization: Corporal, Company A, 1st Tennessee Cavalry. *Place and date:* At Richland Creek, Tenn., 24 December 1864. *Entered service at:* Cumberland Gap, Tenn. *Born:* 1834, Hawkins County, Tenn. *Date of issue:* 24 February 1865. *Citation:* Capture of flag of Chalmer's Division (C.S.A.).

COLLINS, THOMAS D.

Rank and organization: Sergeant, Company H, 143d New York Infantry. *Place and date:* At Resaca, Ga., 15 May 1864. *Entered service at:* Liberty, Sullivan County, N.Y. *Born:* 14 August 1847, Neversink, N.Y. *Date of issue:* 14 August 1896. *Citation:* Captured a regimental flag of the enemy.

COLLIS, CHARLES H. T.

Rank and organization: Colonel, 114th Pennsylvania Infantry. *Place and date:* At Fredericksburg, Va., 13 December 1862. *Entered service at:* Philadelphia, Pa. *Born:* 4 February 1838, Ireland. *Date of issue:* 10 March 1893. *Citation:* Gallantly led his regiment in battle at a critical moment.

COLWELL, OLIVER

Rank and organization: First Lieutenant, Company G, 95th Ohio Infantry. *Place and date:* At Nashville, Tenn., 16 December 1864. *Entered service at:* ———. *Birth:* Champaign County, Ohio. *Date of issue:* 24 February 1865. *Citation:* Capture of flag.

COMPSON, HARTWELL B.

Rank and organization: Major, 8th New York Cavalry. *Place and date:* At Waynesboro, Va., 2 March 1865. *Entered service at:* Seneca Falls, N.Y. *Birth:* Seneca Falls, N.Y. *Date of issue:* 26 March 1865. *Citation:* Capture of flag belonging to Gen. Early's headquarters.

CONAWAY, JOHN W.

Rank and organization: Private, Company C, 83d Indiana Infantry. *Place and date:* At Vicksburg, Miss., 22 May 1863. *Entered service at:* Hartford, Ind. *Birth:* Dearborn County, Ind. *Date of issue:* 11 August 1894. *Citation:* Gallantry in the charge of the "volunteer storming party."

CONBOY, MARTIN

Rank and organization: Sergeant, Company B, 37th New York Infantry. *Place and date:* At Williamsburg, Va., 5 May 1862. *Entered service at:* New York, N.Y. *Birth:* ———. *Date of issue:* 11 October 1892. *Citation:* Took command of the company in action, the captain having been wounded, the other commissioned officers being absent, and handled it with skill and bravery.

CONGDON, JAMES

Service rendered under name of James Madison.

CONLAN, DENNIS

Rank and organization: Seaman, U.S. Navy. *Born:* 1838, New York, N.Y. *Accredited to:* New York. *G.O. No.:* 45, 31 December 1864. *Citation:* Conlan served on board the U.S.S. *Agawam*, as one of a volunteer crew of a powder boat which was exploded near Fort Fisher, 23 December 1864. The powder boat, towed in by the *Wilderness* to prevent detection by the enemy, cast off and slowly steamed to within 300 yards of the beach. After fuses and fires had been lit and a second anchor with short scope let go to assure the boat's tailing inshore, the crew again boarded the *Wilderness* and proceeded a distance of 12 miles from shore. Less than 2 hours later the explosion took place, and the following day fires were observed still burning at the forts.

CONNELL, TRUSTRIM

Rank and organization: Corporal, Company I, 138th Pennsylvania Infantry. *Place and date:* At Sailors Creek, Va., 6 April 1865. *Entered service at:* Fort Kennedy, Pa. *Birth:* Lancaster, Pa. *Date of issue:* 10 May 1865. *Citation:* Capture of flag.

CONNER, RICHARD

Rank and organization: Private, Company F, 6th New Jersey Infantry. *Place and date:* At Bull Run, Va., 30 August 1862. *Entered service at:* ———. *Birth:* Philadelphia, Pa. *Date of issue:* 17 September 1897. *Citation:* The flag of his regiment having been abandoned during retreat, he voluntarily returned with a single companion under a heavy fire and secured and brought off the flag, his companion being killed.

CONNOR, THOMAS

Rank and organization: Ordinary Seaman, U.S. Navy. *Born:* 1842, Ireland. *Accredited to:* Maryland. *G.O. No.:* 59, 22 June 1865. *Citation:* On board the U.S.S. *Minnesota*, in action during the assault on Fort Fisher, 15 January 1865. Landing on the beach with the assaulting party from his ship, Connor charged up to the palisades and, when more than two-thirds of the men became seized with panic and retreated on the run, risked his life to remain with a wounded officer. With the enemy concentrating his fire on the group, he waited until after dark before assisting in carrying the wounded man from the field.

CONNOR, WILLIAM C.

Rank and organization: Boatswain's Mate, U.S. Navy. *Born:* 1832, Pennsylvania. *Accredited to:* Pennsylvania. *G.O. No.:* 45, 31 December 1864. *Citation:* Served on board the U.S.S. *Howquah* on the occasion of the destruction of the blockade runner *Lynx*, off Wilmington, 25 September 1864. Performing his duty faithfully under the most trying circumstances, Connor stood firmly at his post in the midst of a cross-fire from the rebel shore batteries and our own vessels.

CONNORS, JAMES

Rank and organization: Private, Company E, 43d New York Infantry. *Place and date:* At Fishers Hill, Va., 22 September 1864. *Entered service at:* ———. *Birth:* Ireland. *Date of issue:* 6 October 1864. *Citation:* Capture of flag.

COOK, JOHN

Rank and organization: Bugler, Battery B, 4th U.S. Artillery. *Place and date:* At Antietam Md., 17 September 1862. *Entered service at:* Cincinnati, Ohio. *Birth:* Hamilton County, Ohio. *Date of issue:* 30 June 1894. *Citation:* Volunteered at the age of 15 years to act as a cannoneer, and as such volunteer served a gun under a terrific fire of the enemy.

COOK, JOHN H.

Rank and organization: Sergeant, Company A, 119th Illinois Infantry. *Place and date:* At Pleasant Hill, La., 9 April 1864. *Entered service at:* Quincy, Ill. *Birth:* England. *Date of issue:* 19 September 1890. *Citation:* During an attack by the enemy, voluntarily left the brigade quartermaster, with whom he had been detailed as a clerk, rejoined his command, and, acting as first lieutenant, led the line farther toward the charging enemy.

COOKE, WALTER H.

Rank and organization: Captain, Company K, 4th Pennsylvania Infantry Militia. *Place and date:* At Bull Run, Va., 21 July 1861. *Entered service at:* ———. *Birth:* Norristown, Pa. *Date of issue:* 19 May 1887. *Citation:* Voluntarily served as an aide on the staff of Col. David Hunter and participated in the battle, his term of service having expired on the previous day.

COOPER, JOHN   2 MOH

DOD: 8/22/1891

Rank and organization: Coxswain, U.S. Navy. *Born:* 1832, Ireland. *Accredited to:* New York. *G.O. No.:* 45, 31 December 1864. Second award. *Citation:* On board the U.S.S. *Brooklyn* during action against rebel forts and gunboats and with the ram *Tennessee*, in Mobile Bay, 5 August 1864. Despite severe damage to his ship and the loss of several men on board as enemy fire raked her decks from stem to stern, Cooper fought his gun with skill and courage throughout the furious battle which resulted in the surrender of the prize rebel ram *Tennessee* and in the damaging and destruction of batteries at Fort Morgan.

SECOND AWARD

Citation: Served as quartermaster on Acting Rear Admiral Thatcher's staff. During the terrific fire at Mobile, on 26 April 1865, at the risk of being blown to pieces by exploding shells, Cooper advanced through the burning locality, rescued a wounded man from certain death, and bore him on his back to a place of safety.
G.O. No.: 62, 29 June 1865.

COPP, CHARLES D.

Rank and organization: Second Lieutenant, Company C, 9th New Hampshire Infantry. *Place and date:* At Fredericksburg, Va., 13 December 1862. *Entered service at:* Nashua, N.H. *Born:* 12 April 1840, Warren County, N.H. *Date of issue:* 28 June 1890. *Citation:* Seized the regimental colors, the color bearer having been shot down, and, waving them, rallied the regiment under a heavy fire.

CORCORAN, JOHN

Rank and organization: Private, Company G, 1st Rhode Island Light Artillery. *Place and date:* At Petersburg, Va., 2 April 1865. *Entered service at:* Pawtucket, R.I. *Birth:* Pawtucket, R.I. *Date of issue:* 2 November 1887. *Citation:* Was one of a detachment of 20 picked artillerymen who voluntarily accompanied an infantry assaulting party, and who turned upon the enemy the guns captured in the assault.

CORCORAN, THOMAS E.

Rank and organization: Landsman, U.S. Navy. *Born:* 1838, New York. *Accredited to:* New York. *G.O. No.:* 17, 10 July 1863. *Citation:* Served on board the U.S.S. *Cincinnati* during the attack on the Vicksburg batteries and at the time of her sinking. Engaging the enemy in a fierce battle, the *Cincinnati*, amidst an incessant fire of shot and shell, continued to fire her guns to the last, though so penetrated by shellfire that her fate was sealed. Serving bravely during this action, Corcoran was conspicuously cool under the fire of the enemy, never ceasing to fight until this proud ship went down, "her colors nailed to the mast."

CORLISS, GEORGE W.

Rank and organization: Captain, Company C, 5th Connecticut Infantry. *Place and date:* At Cedar Mountain, Va., 9 August 1862. *Entered service at:* New Haven, Conn. *Birth:* ———. *Date of issue:* 10 September 1897. *Citation:* Seized a fallen flag of the regiment, the color bearer having been killed, carried it forward in the face of a severe fire, and though himself shot down and permanently disabled, planted the staff in the earth and kept the flag flying.

CORLISS, STEPHEN P.

Rank and organization: First Lieutenant, Company F, 4th New York Heavy Artillery. *Place and date:* At South Side Railroad, Va., 2 April 1865. *Entered service at:* ———. *Born:* 26 July 1842, Albany, N.Y. *Date of issue:* 17 January 1895. *Citation:* Raised the fallen colors and, rushing forward in advance of the troops, placed them on the enemy's works.

CORSON, JOSEPH K.

Rank and organization: Assistant Surgeon, 6th Pennsylvania Reserves (35th Pennsylvania Volunteers). *Place and date:* Near Bristoe Station, Va., 14 October 1863. *Entered service at:* Philadelphia, Pa. *Born:* 26 November 1836, Plymouth Meeting, Montgomery County, Pa. *Date of issue:* 13 May 1899. *Citation:* With one companion returned in the face of the enemy's heavy artillery fire and removed to a place of safety a severely wounded soldier who had been left behind as the regiment fell back.

COSGRIFF, RICHARD H.

Rank and organization: Private, Company L, 4th Iowa Cavalry. *Place and date:* At Columbus, Ga., 16 April 1865. *Entered service at:* Wapello, Louisa County, Iowa. *Birth:* Dunkirk County, N.Y. *Date of issue:*

17 June 1865. *Citation:* Capture of flag in a personal encounter with its bearer.

COSGROVE, THOMAS

Rank and organization: Private, Company F, 40th Massachusetts Infantry. *Place and date:* At Drurys Bluff, Va., 15 May 1864. *Entered service at:* East Stoughton, Mass. *Birth:* Ireland. *Date of issue:* 7 November 1896. *Citation:* Individually demanded and received the surrender of 7 armed Confederates concealed in a cellar, disarming and marching them in as prisoners of war.

COTTON, PETER

Rank and organization: Ordinary Seaman, U.S. Navy. *Born:* 1839, New York, N.Y. *Accredited to:* New York. *G.O. No.:* 11, 3 April 1863. *Citation:* Cotton served on board the U.S.S. *Baron De Kalb* in the Yazoo River expedition, 23 to 27 December 1862. Proceeding under orders up the Yazoo River, the *Baron De Kalb*, with the object of capturing or destroying the enemy's transports, came upon the steamers *John Walsh*, *R. J. Locklan*, *Golden Age* and the *Scotland*, sunk on a bar where they were ordered to be burned. Continuing up the river, the *Baron De Kalb* was fired upon but, upon returning the fire, caused the enemy's retreat. Returning down the Yazoo, she destroyed and captured large quantities of enemy equipment and several prisoners. Serving bravely throughout this action, Cotton, as coxswain "distinguished himself in the various actions."

COUGHLIN, JOHN

Rank and organization: Lieutenant Colonel, 10th New Hampshire Infantry. *Place and date:* At Swifts Creek, Va., 9 May 1864. *Entered service at:* Manchester, N.H. *Birth:* Vermont. *Date of issue:* 31 August 1893. *Citation:* During a sudden night attack upon Burnham's Brigade, resulting in much confusion, this officer, without waiting for orders, led his regiment forward and interposed a line of battle between the advancing enemy and Hunt's Battery, repulsing the attack and saving the guns.

COX, ROBERT M.

Rank and organization: Corporal, Company K, 55th Illinois Infantry. *Place and date:* At Vicksburg, Miss., 22 May 1863. *Entered service at:* Prairie City, Ill. *Birth:* Guernsey County, Ohio. *Date of issue:* 31 December 1892. *Citation:* Bravely defended the colors planted on the outward parapet of Fort Hill.

COYNE, JOHN N.

Rank and organization: Sergeant, Company B, 70th New York Infantry. *Place and date:* At Williamsburg, Va., 5 May 1862. *Entered service at:* New York, N.Y. *Born:* 14 November 1839, New York, N.Y. *Date of issue:* 18 April 1888. *Citation:* Capture of a flag after a severe hand-to-hand contest; was mentioned in orders for his gallantry.

CRANSTON, WILLIAM W.

Rank and organization: Private, Company A, 66th Ohio Infantry. *Place and date:* At Chancellorsville, Va., 2 May 1863. *Entered service at:* ———. *Birth:* Champaign County, Ohio. *Date of issue:* 15 December 1892. *Citation:* One of a party of 4 who voluntarily brought in a wounded Confederate officer from within the enemy's line in the face of a constant fire.

CRAWFORD, ALEXANDER

Rank and organization: Fireman, U.S. Navy. *Born:* 1842, Pennsylvania. *Accredited to:* Pennsylvania. *G.O. No.:* 45, 31 December 1864. *Citation:* On board the U.S.S. *Wyalusing*, Crawford volunteered 25 May 1864, in a night attempt to destroy the rebel ram *Albemarle* in the Roanoke River. Taking part in a plan to explode the rebel ram *Albemarle*, Crawford executed his part in the plan with perfection, but upon being discovered, was forced to abandon the plan and retire, leaving no trace of the evidence. After spending two hazardous days and nights without food, he gained the safety of a friendly ship and was then transferred back to the *Wyalusing*. Though the plan failed, his skill and courage in preventing detection were an example of unfailing devotion to duty.

CREED, JOHN

Rank and organization: Private, Company D, 23d Illinois Infantry. *Place and date:* At Fishers Hill, Va., 22 September 1864. *Entered service at:* Chicago, Ill. *Birth:* Ireland. *Date of issue:* 6 October 1864. *Citation:* Capture of flag.

CRIPPS, THOMAS

Rank and organization: Quartermaster, U.S. Navy. *Born:* 1837, Philadelphia, Pa. *Accredited to:* Pennsylvania. *G.O. No.:* 45, 31 December 1864. *Citation:* As captain of a gun on board the U.S.S. *Richmond* during action against rebel forts and gunboats and with the ram *Tennessee* in Mobile Bay, 5 August 1864. Despite damage to his ship and the loss of several men on board as enemy fire raked her decks, Cripps fought his gun with skill and courage throughout a furious 2-hour battle which resulted in the surrender of the rebel ram *Tennessee* and in the damaging and destruction of batteries at Fort Morgan.

CROCKER, HENRY H.

Rank and organization: Captain, Company F, 2d Massachusetts Cavalry. *Place and date:* At Cedar Creek, Va., 19 October 1864. *Entered service at:* California. *Born:* 20 January 1840, Colchester, Conn. *Date of issue:* 10 January 1896. *Citation:* Voluntarily led a charge, which resulted in the capture of 14 prisoners and in which he himself was wounded.

CROCKER, ULRIC L.

Rank and organization: Private, Company M, 6th Michigan Cavalry. *Place and date:* At Cedar Creek, Va., 19 October 1864. *Entered service at:* **OHIO**. *Birth:* Ohio. *Date of issue:* 26 October 1864. *Citation:* Capture of flag of 18th Georgia (C.S.A.).

CROFT, JAMES E.

Rank and organization: Private, 12th Battery, Wisconsin Light Artillery. *Place and date:* At Allatoona, Ga., 5 October 1864. *Entered service at:* Janesville, Wis. *Birth:* England. *Date of issue:* 20 March 1897. *Citation:* Took the place of a gunner who had been shot down and inspired his comrades by his bravery and effective gunnery, which contributed largely to the defeat of the enemy.

CRONIN, CORNELIUS

Rank and organization: Chief Quartermaster, U.S. Navy. *Born:* 1836, Michigan. *Accredited to:* Michigan. *G.O. No.:* 45, 31 December 1864. *Citation:* On board the U.S.S. *Richmond* in action at Mobile Bay on 5 August 1864. Cool and vigilant at his station throughout the prolonged action, Cronin watched for signals and skillfully steered the ship as she trained her guns on Fort Morgan and on ships of the Confederacy despite extremely heavy return fire. He participated in the actions at Forts Jackson and St. Philip, with the Chalmette batteries, at the surrender of New Orleans, and in the attacks on batteries below Vicksburg.

CROSIER, WILLIAM H. H.

Rank and organization: Sergeant, Company G, 149th New York Infantry. *Place and date:* At Peach Tree Creek, Ga., 20 July 1864. *Entered service at:* Skaneateles, N.Y. *Birth:* Skaneateles, N.Y. *Date of issue:* 12 January 1892. *Citation:* Severely wounded and ambushed by the enemy, he stripped the colors from the staff and brought them back into the line.

CROSS, JAMES E.

Rank and organization: Corporal, Company K, 12th New York Infantry. *Place and date:* At Blackburns Ford, Va., 18 July 1861. *Entered service at:* **NY**. *Birth:* Darien, N.Y. *Date of issue:* 5 April 1898. *Citation:* With a companion, refused to retreat when the part of the regiment to which he was attached was driven back in disorder, but remained upon the skirmish line for some time thereafter, firing upon the enemy.

CROWLEY, MICHAEL

Rank and organization: Private, Company A, 22d New York Cavalry. *Place and date:* At Waynesboro, Va., 2 March 1865. *Entered service at:* Rochester, N.Y. *Birth:* Rochester, N.Y. *Date of issue:* 26 March 1865. *Citation:* Capture of flag.

CULLEN, THOMAS

Rank and organization: Corporal, Company I, 82d New York Infantry. *Place and date:* At Bristoe Station, Va., 14 October 1863. *Entered service at:* (——). *Birth:* Ireland. *Date of issue:* 1 December 1864. *Citation:* Capture of flag of 22d or 28th North Carolina (C.S.A.).

CUMMINGS, AMOS J.

Rank and organization: Sergeant Major, 26th New Jersey Infantry. *Place and date:* At Salem Heights, Va., 4 May 1863. *Entered service at:* Irvington, N.J. *Born:* 15 May 1841, Conklin, N.Y. *Date of issue:* 28 March 1894. *Citation:* Rendered great assistance in the heat of the action in rescuing a part of the field batteries from an extremely dangerous and exposed position.

CUMPSTON, JAMES M.

Rank and organization: Private, Company D, 91st Ohio Infantry. *Place and date:* At Shenandoah Valley Campaign, August to November 1864. *Entered service at:* OHIO. *Birth:* Galia County, Ohio. *Date of issue:* Unknown. *Citation:* Capture of flag.

CUNNINGHAM, FRANCIS M.

Rank and organization: First Sergeant, Company H, 1st West Virginia Cavalry. *Place and date:* At Sailors Creek, Va., 6 April 1865. *Entered service at:* Springfield, Pa. *Birth:* Somerset County, Pa. *Date of issue:* 3 May 1865. *Citation:* Capture of battle flag of 12th Virginia Infantry (C.S.A.) in hand-to-hand battle while wounded.

CUNNINGHAM, JAMES S.

Rank and organization: Private, Company D, 8th Missouri Infantry. *Place and date:* At Vicksburg, Miss., 22 May 1863. *Entered service at:* Bloomington, McLean County, Ill. *Birth:* Washington County, Pa. *Date of issue:* 30 July 1894. *Citation:* Gallantry in the charge of the "volunteer storming party."

CURRAN, RICHARD

Rank and organization: Assistant Surgeon, 33d New York Infantry. *Place and date:* At Antietam, Md., 17 September 1862. *Entered service at:* Seneca Falls, N.Y. *Born:* 4 January 1838, Ireland. *Date of issue:* 30 March 1898. *Citation:* Voluntarily exposed himself to great danger by going to the fighting line there succoring the wounded and helpless and conducting them to the field hospital.

CURTIS, JOHN C.

Rank and organization: Sergeant Major, 9th Connecticut Infantry. *Place and date:* At Baton Rouge, La., 5 August 1862. *Entered service at:* Bridgeport, Conn. *Birth:* Bridgeport, Conn. *Date of issue:* 16 December 1896. *Citation:* Voluntarily sought the line of battle and alone and unaided captured 2 prisoners, driving them before him to regimental headquarters at the point of the bayonet.

CURTIS, JOSIAH M.

Rank and organization: Second Lieutenant, Company I, 12th West Virginia Infantry. *Place and date:* At Petersburg, Va., 2 April 1865. *Entered service at:* Ohio County, W. Va. *Birth:* Ohio County, W. Va. *Date of issue:* 12 May 1865. *Citation:* Seized the colors of his regiment after 2 color bearers had fallen, bore them gallantly, and was among the first to gain a foothold, with his flag, inside the enemy's works.

CURTIS, NEWTON MARTIN

Rank and organization: Brigadier General, U.S. Volunteers. *Place and date:* At Fort Fisher, N.C., 15 January 1865. *Entered service at:* De Peyster, N.Y. *Born:* 21 May 1835, De Peyster, N.Y. *Date of issue:* 28 November 1891. *Citation:* The first man to pass through the stockade, he personally led each assault on the traverses and was 4 times wounded.

CUSTER, THOMAS W.

Rank and organization: Second Lieutenant, Company B, 6th Michigan Cavalry. *Place and date:* At Namozine Church, Va., 10 May 1863. *Entered service at:* Monroe, Mich. *Birth:* New Rumley, Ohio. *Date of issue:* 3 May 1865. Second award. *Citation:* Capture of flag on 10 May 1863.

SECOND AWARD

Place and date: At Sailor Creek Va., April 1865. *Date of issue:* 26 May 1865. *Citation:* 2d Lt. Custer leaped his horse over the enemy's works and captured 2 stands of colors, having his horse shot from under him and receiving a severe wound.

CUTCHEON, BYRON M.

Rank and organization: Major, 20th Michigan Infantry. *Place and date:* At Horseshoe Bend, Ky., 10 May 1863. *Entered service at:* Ypsilanti, Mich. *Born:* 11 May 1836, Pembroke, N.H. *Date of issue:* 29 June 1891. *Citation:* Distinguished gallantry in leading his regiment in a charge on a house occupied by the enemy.

CUTTS, JAMES M.

Rank and organization: Captain, 11th U.S. Infantry. *Place and date:* At Wilderness; Spotsylvania; Petersburg, Va., 1864. *Entered service at:* Illinois. *Birth:* Washington, D.C. *Date of issue:* 2 May 1891. *Citation:* Gallantry in actions.

DARROUGH, JOHN S.

Rank and organization: Sergeant, Company F, 113th Illinois Infantry. *Place and date:* At Eastport, Miss., 10 October 1864. *Entered service at:* Concord, Morgan County, Ill. *Birth:* Kentucky. *Date of issue:* 5 February 1895. *Citation:* Saved the life of a captain.

DAVIDSIZER, JOHN A.

Rank and organization: Sergeant, Company A, 1st Pennsylvania Cavalry. *Place and date:* At Paines Crossroads, Va., 5 April 1865. *Entered service at:* Lewiston, Pa. *Birth:* Milford, Pa. *Date of issue:* 3 May 1865. *Citation:* Capture of flag.

DAVIDSON, ANDREW

Rank and organization: Assistant Surgeon, 47th Ohio Infantry. *Place and date:* At Vicksburg, Miss., 3 May 1863. *Entered service at:* Cincinnati, Ohio. *Birth:* Middlebury, Vt. *Date of issue:* 17 October 1892. *Citation:* Voluntarily attempted to run the enemy's batteries.

DAVIDSON, ANDREW

Rank and organization: First Lieutenant, Company H, 30th U.S. Colored Troops. *Place and date:* At the mine, Petersburg, Va., 30 July 1864. *Entered service at:* Otsego County, N.Y. *Born:* 12 February 1840, Scotland. *Date of issue:* 17 October 1892. *Citation:* One of the first to enter the enemy's works, where, after his colonel, major, and one-third the company officers had fallen, he gallantly assisted in rallying and saving the remnant of the command.

DAVIS, CHARLES C.

Rank and organization: Major, 7th Pennsylvania Cavalry. *Place and date:* At Shelbyville, Tenn., 27 June 1863. *Entered service at:* Harrisburg, Pa. *Born:* 15 August 1830, Harrisburg, Pa. *Date of issue:* 14 June 1894. *Citation:* Led one of the most desperate and successful charges of the war.

DAVIS, FREEMAN

Rank and organization: Sergeant, Company B, 80th Ohio Infantry. *Place and date:* At Missionary Ridge, Tenn., 25 November 1863. *Entered service at:* Ohio. *Birth:* Newcomerstown, Ohio. *Date of issue:* 30 March 1898. *Citation:* This soldier, while his regiment was falling back, seeing the 2 color bearers shot down, under a severe fire and at imminent peril recovered both the flags and saved them from capture.

DAVIS, GEORGE E.

Rank and organization: First Lieutenant, Company D, 10th Vermont Infantry. *Place and date:* At Monocacy, Md., 9 July 1864. *Entered service at:* Burlington, Vt. *Birth:* Dunstable, Mass. *Date of issue:* 27 May 1892. *Citation:* While in command of a small force, held the approaches to the 2 bridges against repeated assaults of superior numbers, thereby materially delaying Early's advance on Washington.

DAVIS, HARRY

Rank and organization: Private, Company G, 46th Ohio Infantry. *Place and date:* At Atlanta, Ga., 28 July 1864. *Entered service at:* Ohio. *Birth:* Franklin County, Ohio. *Date of issue:* 2 December 1864. *Citation:* Capture of flag of 30th Louisiana Infantry (C.S.A.).

DAVIS, JOHN

Rank and organization: Quarter Gunner, U.S. Navy. *Born:* Cedarville, N.J. *Accredited to:* New Jersey. *G.O. No.:* 11, 3 April 1863. *Citation:* Served on board the U.S.S. *Valley City* during action against rebel fort batteries and ships off Elizabeth City, N.C., on 10 February 1862. When a shell from the shore penetrated the side and passed through the magazine, exploding outside the screen on the berth deck, several powder division protecting bulkheads were torn to pieces and the forward part of the berth deck set on fire. Showing great presence of mind, Davis courageously covered a barrel of powder with his own body and prevented an explosion, while at the same time passing powder to provide the division on the upper deck while under fierce enemy fire.

DAVIS, JOHN

Rank and organization: Private, Company F, 17th Indiana Mounted Infantry. *Place and date:* At Culloden, Ga., April 1865. *Entered service at:* Indianapolis, Ind. *Birth:* Carroll, Ky. *Date of issue:* 17 June 1865. *Citation:* Capture of flag of Worrill Grays (C.S.A.).

DAVIS, JOSEPH

Rank and organization: Corporal, Company C, 104th Ohio Infantry. *Place and date:* At Franklin, Tenn., 30 November 1864. *Entered service at:* Birth: Wales. *Date of issue:* 4 February 1865. *Citation:* Capture of flag.

DAVIS, MARTIN K.

Rank and organization: Sergeant, Company H, 116th Illinois Infantry. *Place and date:* At Vicksburg, Miss., 22 May 1863. *Entered service at:* Stonington, Christian County, Ill. *Birth:* Marion, Ill. *Date of issue:* 26 July 1894. *Citation:* Gallantry in the charge of the "volunteer storming party."

DAVIS, SAMUEL W.

Rank and organization: Ordinary Seaman, U.S. Navy. *Born:* 1845, Maine. *Accredited to:* Maine. *G.O. No.:* 45, 31 December 1864. *Citation:* On board the U.S.S. *Brooklyn* during successful attacks against Fort Morgan, rebel gunboats and the ram *Tennessee* in Mobile Bay, on 5 August 1864. Despite severe damage to his ship and the loss of several men on board as enemy fire raked her decks from stem to stern, Davis exercised extreme courage and vigilance while acting as a look-out for torpedoes and other obstructions throughout the furious battle which resulted in the surrender of the prize rebel ram *Tennessee* and in the damaging and destruction of batteries at Fort Morgan.

DAVIS, THOMAS

Rank and organization: Private, Company C, 2d New York Heavy Artillery. *Place and date:* At Sailors Creek, Va., 6 April 1865. *Entered service at:* New York. *Birth:* Wales. *Date of issue:* 3 May 1865. *Citation:* Capture of flag.

DAY, CHARLES

Rank and organization: Private, Company K, 210th Pennsylvania Infantry. *Place and date:* At Hatchers Run, Va., 6 February 1865. *Entered service at:* Lycoming County, Pa. *Birth:* Otsego County, N.Y. *Date of issue:* 20 July 1897. *Citation:* Seized the colors of another regiment of the brigade, the regiment having been thrown into confusion and the color bearer killed, and bore said colors throughout the remainder of the engagement.

DAY, DAVID F.

Rank and organization: Private, Company D, 57th Ohio Infantry. *Place and date:* At Vicksburg, Miss., 22 May 1863. *Entered service at:* Ohio. *Birth:* Dallasburg, Ohio. *Date of issue:* 2 January 1895. *Citation:* Gallantry in the charge of the "volunteer storming party."

DEAKIN, CHARLES

Rank and organization: Boatswain's Mate, U.S. Navy. *Born:* 1837, New York, N.Y. *Accredited to:* Pennsylvania. *G.O. No.:* 45, 31 December 1864. *Citation:* As captain of a gun on board the U.S.S. *Richmond* during action against rebel forts and gunboats and with the ram *Tennessee* in Mobile Bay, 5 August 1864. Despite damage to his ship and the loss of several men on board as enemy fire raked her decks, Deakin fought his gun with skill and courage throughout a furious 2-hour battle which resulted in the surrender of the rebel ram *Tennessee* and in the damaging and destruction of batteries at Fort Morgan. He also participated in the actions at Forts Jackson and St. Philip.

DEANE, JOHN M.

Rank and organization: Major, 29th Massachusetts Infantry. *Place and date:* At Fort Stedman, Va., 25 March 1865. *Entered service at:* MA. *Born:* 8 January 1840, Freetown, Mass. *Date of issue:* 8 March 1895. *Citation:* This officer, observing an abandoned gun within Fort Haskell, called for volunteers, and under a heavy fire, worked the gun until the enemy's advancing line was routed.

DE CASTRO, JOSEPH H.

Rank and organization: Corporal, Company I, 19th Massachusetts Infantry. *Place and date:* At Gettysburg, Pa., 3 July 1863. *Entered service at:* ———. *Birth:* Boston, Mass. *Date of issue:* 1 December 1864. *Citation:* Capture of flag of 19th Virginia regiment (C.S.A.).

DE LACEY, PATRICK

Rank and organization: First Sergeant, Company A, 143d Pennsylvania Infantry. *Place and date:* At Wilderness, Va., 6 May 1864. *Entered service at:* Scranton, Pa. *Born:* 25 November 1834, Carbondale, Lackawanna County, Pa. *Date of issue:* 24 April 1894. *Citation:* Running ahead of the line, under a concentrated fire, he shot the color bearer of a Confederate regiment on the works, thus contributing to the success of the attack.

DELAND, FREDERICK N.

Rank and organization: Private, Company B, 40th Massachusetts Infantry. *Place and date:* At Port Hudson, La., 27 May 1863. *Entered service at:* MA. *Born:* 25 December 1843, Sheffield, Mass. *Date of issue:* 22 June 1896. *Citation:* Volunteered in response to a call and, under a heavy fire from the enemy, advanced and assisted in filling with fascines a ditch which presented a serious obstacle to the troops attempting to take the works of the enemy by assault.

DELANEY, JOHN C.

Rank and organization: Sergeant, Company I, 107th Pennsylvania Infantry. *Place and date:* At Danby's mills, Va., 6 February 1860. *Entered service at:* Honesdale, Pa. *Birth:* 22 April 1848, Ireland. *Date of issue:* 29 August 1894. *Citation:* Sprang between the lines and brought out a wounded comrade about to be burned in the brush.

DE LAVIE, HIRAM H.

Rank and organization: Sergeant, Company I, 11th Pennsylvania Infantry. *Place and date:* At Five Forks, Va., 1 April 1865. *Entered service at:* Allegheny County, Pa. *Birth:* Stark County, Ohio. *Date of issue:* 10 May 1865. *Citation:* Capture of flag.

DEMPSTER, JOHN

Rank and organization: Coxswain, U.S. Navy. *Born:* 1839, Scotland. *Accredited to:* Pennsylvania. *G.O. No.:* 59, 22 June 1865. *Citation:* Dempster served on board the U.S.S. *New Ironsides* during action in several attacks on Fort Fisher, 24 and 25 December 1864; and 13, 14, and 15 January 1865. The ship steamed in and took the lead in the ironclad division close inshore and immediately opened its starboard battery in a barrage of well-directed fire to cause several fires and explosions and dismount several guns during the first 2 days of fighting. Taken under fire as she steamed into position on 13 January, the *New Ironsides* fought all day and took on ammunition at night despite severe weather conditions. When the enemy came out of his bomb-proofs to defend the fort against the storming party, the ship's battery disabled nearly every gun on the fort facing the shore before the cease-fire orders were given by the flagship.

DENIG, J. HENRY

Rank and organization: Sergeant, U.S. Marine Corps. *Born:* 1839, York, Pa. *Accredited to:* Pennsylvania. *G.O. No.:* 45, 31 December 1864. *Citation:* On board the U.S.S. *Brooklyn* during action against rebel forts and gunboats and with the ram *Tennessee*, in Mobile Bay, 5 August 1864. Despite severe damage to his ship and the loss of several men on board as enemy fire raked her decks, Sgt. Denig fought his gun with skill and courage throughout the furious 2-hour battle which resulted in the surrender of the rebel ram *Tennessee* and in the damaging and destruction of batteries at Fort Morgan.

DENNING, LORENZO

Rank and organization: Landsman, U.S. Navy. *Born:* 1843, Connecticut. *Entered service at:* New York, N.Y. *G.O. No.:* 45, 31 December 1864. *Citation:* Denning served on board the U.S. Picket Boat No. 1 in action, 27 October 1864, against the Confederate ram *Albemarle* which had resisted repeated attacks by our steamers and had kept a large force of vessels employed in watching her. The picket boat, equipped with a spar torpedo, succeeded in passing the enemy pickets within 20 yards without being discovered and then made for the *Albemarle* under a full head of steam. Immediately taken under fire by the ram, the small boat plunged on, jumped the log boom which encircled the target and exploded its torpedo under the port bow of the ram. The picket boat was destroyed by enemy fire and almost the entire crew taken prisoner or lost.

DENNIS, RICHARD

Rank and organization: Boatswain's Mate, U.S. Navy. *Born:* 1826, Massachusetts. *Accredited to:* Massachusetts. *G.O. No.:* 45, 31

December 1864. *Citation:* On board the U.S.S. *Brooklyn* during successful attacks against Fort Morgan, rebel gunboats and the ram *Tennessee* in Mobile Bay, on 5 August 1864. Despite severe damage to his ship and the loss of several men on board as enemy fire raked her decks from stem to stern, Dennis displayed outstanding skill and courage in operating the torpedo catcher and in assisting in working the bow chasers throughout the furious battle which resulted in the surrender of the prize rebel ram *Tennessee* and in the damaging and destruction of batteries at Fort Morgan.

DENSMORE, WILLIAM

Rank and organization: Chief Boatswain's Mate, U.S. Navy. *Born:* 1834, New York. *Accredited to:* New York. *G.O. No.:* 45, 31 December 1864. *Citation:* As captain of a gun on board the U.S.S. *Richmond* during action against rebel forts and gunboats and with the ram *Tennessee* in Mobile Bay, 5 August 1864. Despite damage to his ship and the loss of several men on board as enemy fire raked her decks, Densmore fought his gun with skill and courage throughout a furious 2-hour battle which resulted in the surrender of the rebel ram *Tennessee* and in the damaging and destruction of batteries at Fort Morgan.

DE PUY, CHARLES H.

Rank and organization: First Sergeant, Company H, 1st Michigan Sharpshooters. *Place and date:* At Petersburg, Va., 30 July 1864. *Entered service at:* St. Louis, Mo. *Birth:* Sherman, Mich. *Date of issue:* 30 July 1896. *Citation:* Being an old artillerist, aided General Bartlett in working the guns of the dismantled fort.

DE WITT, RICHARD W.

Rank and organization: Corporal, Company D, 47th Ohio Infantry. *Place and date:* At Vicksburg, Miss., 22 May 1863. *Entered service at:* Oxford, Ohio. *Birth:* Butler County, Ohio. *Date of issue:* 10 August 1894. *Citation:* Gallantry in the charge of the "volunteer storming party."

DI CESNOLA, LOUIS P.

Rank and organization: Colonel, 4th New York Cavalry. *Place and date:* At Aldie, Va., 17 June 1863. *Entered service at:* New York, N.Y. *Born:* 29 June 1832, Rivarola, Piedmont, Italy. *Date of issue:* Unknown. *Citation:* Was present, in arrest, when, seeing his regiment fall back, he rallied his men, accompanied them, without arms, in a second charge, and in recognition of his gallantry was released from arrest. He continued in the action at the head of his regiment until he was desperately wounded and taken prisoner.

DICKEY, WILLIAM D.

Rank and organization: Captain, Battery M, 15th New York Heavy Artillery. *Place and date:* At Petersburg, Va., 17 June 1864. *Entered service at:* Newburgh, N.Y. *Born:* 11 January 1845, Newburgh, N.Y. *Date of issue:* 10 June 1896. *Citation:* Refused to leave the field, remaining in command after being wounded by a piece of shell, and led his command in the assault on the enemy's works on the following day.

DICKIE, DAVID

Rank and organization: Sergeant, Company A, 97th Illinois Infantry. *Place and date:* At Vicksburg, Miss., 22 May 1863. *Entered service at:* Gillespie, Macoupin County, Ill. *Birth:* Scotland. *Date of issue:* 29 January 1896. *Citation:* Gallantry in the charge of the "volunteer storming party."

DIGGINS, BARTHOLOMEW

Rank and organization: Ordinary Seaman, U.S. Navy. *Born:* 1842, Baltimore, Md. *Accredited to:* Maryland. *G.O. No.:* 391, 12 November 1891. *Citation:* On board the flagship, U.S.S. *Hartford,* during action against rebel forts and gunboats and with the ram *Tennessee* in Mobile Bay, 5 August 1864. Despite damage to his ship and the loss of several men on board as enemy fire raked her decks, Diggins, as loader of a gun, remained steadfast at his post throughout the furious 2-hour battle which resulted in the surrender of the rebel ram *Tennessee* and in the damaging and destruction of batteries at Fort Morgan.

DILGER, HUBERT

Rank and organization: Captain, Battery I, 1st Ohio Light Artillery. *Place and date:* At Chancellorsville, Va., 2 May 1863. *Entered service at:* New York, N.Y. *Born:* 5 March 1836, Germany. *Date of issue:* 17 August 1893. *Citation:* Fought his guns until the enemy were upon him, then with one gun hauled in the road by hand he formed the rear guard and kept the enemy at bay by the rapidity of his fire and was the last man in the retreat.

DILLON, MICHAEL A.

Rank and organization: Private, Company G, 2d New Hampshire Infantry. *Place and date:* At Williamsburg, Va., 5 May 1862. At Oak Grove, Va., 25 June 1862. *Entered service at:* Wilton, N.H. *Birth:* Chelmsford, Mass. *Date of issue:* 10 October 1889. *Citation:* Bravery in repulsing the enemy's charge on a battery, at Williamsburg, Va. At Oak Grove, Va., crawled outside the lines and brought in important information.

DITZENBACK, JOHN

Rank and organization: Quartermaster, U.S. Navy. *Born:* 1828, New York, N.Y. *Accredited to:* Indiana. *G.O. No.:* 59, 22 June 1865. *Citation:* Served on board the U.S. Monitor *Neosho* during the engagement with enemy batteries at Bells Mills, Cumberland River, near Nashville, Tenn., 6 December 1864. Carrying out his duties courageously during the engagement, Ditzenback gallantly left the pilot house after the flag and signal staffs of that vessel had been shot away and, taking the flag which was drooping over the wheelhouse, made it fast to the stump of the highest mast remaining, although the ship was still under a heavy fire from the enemy.

DOCKUM, WARREN C.

Rank and organization: Private, Company H, 121st New York Infantry. *Place and date:* At Sailors Creek, Va., 6 April 1865. *Entered service at:* ———. *Birth:* Clintonville, N.Y. *Date of issue:* 10 May 1865. *Citation:* Capture of flag of Savannah Guards (C.S.A.), after 2 other men had been killed in the effort.

DODD, ROBERT F.

Rank and organization: Private, Company E, 27th Michigan Infantry. *Place and date:* At Petersburg, Va., 30 July 1864. *Entered service at:* Hantramck, Mich. *Born:* 1844, Canada. *Date of issue:* 27 July 1896. *Citation:* While acting as orderly, voluntarily assisted to carry off the wounded from the ground in front of the crater while exposed to a heavy fire.

DODDS, EDWARD E.

Rank and organization: Sergeant, Company C, 21st New York Cavalry. *Place and date:* At Ashbys Gap, Va., 19 July 1864. *Entered service at:* Rochester, N.Y. *Birth:* Canada. *Date of issue:* 11 June 1896. *Citation:* At great personal risk rescued his wounded captain and carried him from the field to a place of safety.

DOLLOFF, CHARLES W.

Rank and organization: Corporal, Company K, 1st Vermont Infantry. *Place and date:* At Petersburg, Va., 2 April 1865. *Entered service at:* St. Johnsbury, Vt. *Birth:* Parishville, N.Y. *Date of issue:* 24 April 1865. *Citation:* Capture of flag.

DONALDSON, JOHN

Rank and organization: Sergeant, Company L, 4th Pennsylvania Cavalry. *Place and date:* At Appomattox Courthouse, Va., 9 April 1865. *Entered service at:* ———. *Birth:* Butler County, Pa. *Date of issue:* 3 May 1865. *Citation:* Capture of flag of 14th Virginia Cavalry (C.S.A.).

DONNELLY, JOHN

Rank and organization: Ordinary Seaman, U.S. Navy. *Born:* 1839, England. *Accredited to:* New York. *G.O. No.:* 71, 15 January 1866. *Citation:* Served on board the U.S.S. *Metacomet*. As a member of the boat's crew which went to the rescue of the U.S. Monitor *Tecumseh* when that vessel was struck by a torpedo in passing the enemy forts in Mobile Bay, 5 August 1864, Donnelly braved the enemy fire which was said by the admiral to be "one of the most galling" he had ever seen and aided in rescuing from death 10 of the crew of the *Tecumseh*, eliciting the admiration of both friend and foe.

DONOGHUE, TIMOTHY

Rank and organization: Private, Company B, 69th New York Infantry. *Place and date:* At Fredericksburg, Va., 13 December 1862. *Entered service at:* ———. *Birth:* Ireland. *Date of issue:* 17 January 1894. *Citation:* Voluntarily carried a wounded officer off the field from between the lines; while doing this he was himself wounded.

DOODY, PATRICK

Rank and organization: Corporal, Company E., 164th New York Infantry. *Place and date:* At Cold Harbor, Va., 7 June 1864. *Entered service at:* New York, N.Y. *Birth:* Ireland. *Date of issue:* 13 December 1893. *Citation:* After making a successful personal reconnaissance, he gallantly led the skirmishers in a night attack, charging the enemy, and thus enabling the pioneers to put up works.

DOOLEN, WILLIAM

Rank and organization: Coal Heaver, U.S. Navy. *Born:* 1841, Ireland. *Accredited to:* Pennsylvania. *G.O. No.:* 45, 31 December 1864. *Citation:* On board the U.S.S. *Richmond* during action against rebel forts and gunboats and with the ram *Tennessee* in Mobile Bay, 5 August 1864. Although knocked down and seriously wounded in the head, Doolen refused to leave his station as shot and shell passed. Calm and courageous, he rendered gallant service throughout the prolonged battle which resulted in the surrender of the rebel ram *Tennessee* and in the successful attacks carried out on Fort Morgan despite the enemy's heavy return fire.

DORE, GEORGE H.

Rank and organization: Sergeant, Company D, 126th New York Infantry. *Place and date:* At Gettysburg, Pa., 3 July 1863. *Entered service at:* ———. *Birth:* England. *Date of issue:* 1 December 1864. *Citation:* The colors being struck down by a shell as the enemy were charging, this soldier rushed out and seized it, exposing himself to the fire of both sides.

DORLEY, AUGUST

Rank and organization: Private, Company B, 1st Louisiana Cavalry. *Place and date:* At Mount Pleasant, Ala., 11 April 1865. *Entered service at:* ———. *Birth:* Germany. *Date of issue:* Unknown. *Citation:* Capture of flag.

DORMAN, JOHN

Rank and organization: Seaman, U.S. Navy. *Born:* 1843, Cincinnati, Ohio. *Accredited to:* Ohio. *G.O. No.:* 32, 18 April 1864. *Citation:* Served on board the U.S.S. *Carondelet* in various actions of that vessel. Carrying out his duties courageously throughout the actions of the *Carondelet*, Dorman, although wounded several times, invariably returned to duty and constantly presented an example of devotion to the flag.

DORSEY, DANIEL A.

Rank and organization: Corporal, Company H, 33d Ohio Infantry. *Place and date:* Georgia, April 1862. *Entered service at:* Fairfield County, Ohio. *Birth:* Waterford, Va. *Date of issue:* 17 September 1863. *Citation:* One of the 19 of 22 men (including 2 civilians) who, by direction of Gen. Mitchell (or Buell), penetrated nearly 200 miles south into enemy territory and captured a railroad train at Big Shanty, Ga., in an attempt to destroy the bridges and track between Chattanooga and Atlanta.

DORSEY, DECATUR

Rank and organization: Sergeant, Company B, 39th U.S. Colored Troops. *Place and date:* At Petersburg, Va., 30 July 1864. *Entered service at:* Baltimore County, Md. *Birth:* Howard County, Md. *Date of issue:* 8 November 1865. *Citation:* Planted his colors on the Confederate works in advance of his regiment, and when the regiment was driven back to the Union works he carried the colors there and bravely rallied the men.

DOUGALL, ALLAN H.

Rank and organization: First Lieutenant and Adjutant, 88th Indiana Infantry. *Place and date:* At Bentonville, N.C., 19 March 1865. *Entered service at:* New Haven, Allen County, Ind. *Birth:* Scotland. *Date of issue:* 16 February 1897. *Citation:* In the face of a galling fire from the enemy he voluntarily returned to where the color bearer had fallen wounded and saved the flag of his regiment from capture.

DOUGHERTY, MICHAEL

Rank and organization: Private, Company B, 13th Pennsylvania Cavalry. *Place and date:* At Jefferson, Va., 12 October 1863. *Entered service at:* Philadelphia, Pa. *Born:* 10 May 1844, Ireland. *Date of issue:* 23 January 1897. *Citation:* At the head of a detachment of his company dashed across an open field, exposed to a deadly fire from the enemy, and succeeded in dislodging them from an unoccupied house, which he and his comrades defended for several hours against repeated attacks, thus preventing the enemy from flanking the position of the Union forces.

DOUGHERTY, PATRICK

Rank and organization: Landsman, U.S. Navy. *Born:* 1844, Ireland. *Accredited to:* New York. *G.O. No.:* 45, 31 December 1864. *Citation:* As a landsman on board the U.S.S. *Lackawanna*, Dougherty acted gallantly without orders when the powder box at his gun was disabled under the heavy enemy fire, and maintained a supply of powder throughout the prolonged action. Dougherty also aided in the attacks on Fort Morgan and in the capture of the prize ram *Tennessee*.

DOW, GEORGE P.

Rank and organization: Sergeant, Company C, 7th New Hampshire Infantry. *Place and date:* Near Richmond, Va., October 1864. *Entered service at:* ———. *Birth:* Atkinson, N.H. *Date of issue:* 10 May 1884. *Citation:* Gallantry while in command of his company during a reconnaissance toward Richmond.

DOW, HENRY

Rank and organization: Boatswain's Mate, U.S. Navy. *Born:* 1840, Scotland. *Accredited to:* Illinois. *G.O. No.:* 17, 10 July 1863. *Citation:* Served on board the U.S.S. *Cincinnati* during the attack on the Vicksburg batteries and at the time of her sinking, 27 May 1863. Engaging the enemy in a fierce battle, the *Cincinnati*, amidst an incessant fire of shot and shell, continued to fire her guns to the last, though so penetrated by enemy shellfire that her fate was sealed. Serving courageously throughout this action, Dow carried out his duties to the end on this proud ship that went down with "her colors nailed to the mast."

DOWNEY, WILLIAM

Rank and organization: Private, Company B, 4th Massachusetts Cavalry. *Place and date:* At Ashepoo River, S.C., 24 May 1864. *Entered service at:* Fall River, Mass. *Birth:* Ireland. *Date of issue:* 21 January 1897. *Citation:* Volunteered as a member of a boatcrew which went to the rescue of a large number of Union soldiers on board the stranded steamer *Boston*, and with great gallantry assisted in conveying them to shore, being exposed during the entire time to a heavy fire from a Confederate battery.

DOWNS, HENRY W.

Rank and organization: Sergeant, Company I, 8th Vermont Infantry. *Place and date:* At Winchester, Va., 19 September 1864. *Entered service at:* Newfane, Vt. *Birth:* Jamaica, Vt. *Date of issue:* 13 December 1893. *Citation:* With one comrade, voluntarily crossed an open field, exposed to a raking fire, and returned with a supply of ammunition, successfully repeating the attempt a short time thereafter.

DRAKE, JAMES M.

Rank and organization: 2d Lieutenant, Company D, 9th New Jersey Infantry. *Place and date:* At Bermuda Hundred, Va., 6 May 1864. *Entered service at:* Elizabeth, N.J. *Birth:* Union County, N.J. *Date of issue:* 3 March 1873. *Citation:* Commanded the skirmish line in the advance and held his position all day and during the night.

DRURY, JAMES

Rank and organization: Sergeant, Company C, 4th Vermont Infantry. *Place and date:* At Weldon Railroad, Va., 23 June 1864. *Entered service at:* Chester, Vt. *Birth:* Ireland. *Date of issue:* 18 January 1893. *Citation:* Saved the colors of his regiment when it was surrounded by a much larger force of the enemy and after the greater part of the regiment had been killed or captured.

DUFFEY, JOHN

Rank and organization: Private, Company B, 4th Massachusetts Cavalry. *Place and date:* At Ashepoo River, S.C., 24 May 1864. *Entered service at:* ———. *Birth:* New Bedford, Mass. *Date of issue:* 21 January 1897. *Citation:* Volunteered as a member of a boatcrew which went to the rescue of a large number of Union soldiers on board the stranded steamer *Boston*, and with great gallantry assisted in conveying them to shore, being exposed during the entire time to a heavy fire from a Confederate battery.

DUNCAN, ADAM

Rank and organization: Boatswain's Mate, U.S. Navy. *Born:* 1833, Maine. *Accredited to:* Maine. *G.O. No.:* 45, 31 December 1864. *Citation:* As captain of a gun on board the U.S.S. *Richmond* during action against rebel forts and gunboats and with the ram *Tennessee* in Mobile Bay, 5 August 1864. Despite damage to his ship and the loss of several men on board as enemy fire raked her decks, Duncan fought his gun with skill and courage throughout the prolonged battle which resulted in the surrender of the rebel ram *Tennessee* and in the successful attacks carried out on Fort Morgan.

DUNCAN, JAMES K. L.

Rank and organization: Ordinary Seaman, U.S. Navy. *Born:* 1845, Frankfort, Pa. *Accredited to:* Pennsylvania. *G.O. No.:* 32, 16 April 1864. *Citation:* Served on board the U.S.S. *Fort Hindman* during the engagement near Harrisonburg, La., 2 March 1864. Following a shell-burst at one of the guns which started a fire at the cartridge tie, Duncan immediately seized the burning cartridge, took it from the gun and threw it overboard, despite the immediate danger to himself. Carrying out his duties through the entire engagement, Duncan served courageously during this action in which the *Fort Hindman* was raked severely with shot and shell from the enemy guns.

DUNLAVY, JAMES

Rank and organization: Private, Company D, 3d Iowa Cavalry. *Place and date:* At Osage, Kans., 25 October 1864. *Entered service at:* Davis County, Iowa. *Birth:* Decatur County, Ind. *Date of issue:* 4 April 1865. *Citation:* Gallantry in capturing Gen. Marmaduke.

DUNN, WILLIAM

Rank and organization: Quartermaster, U.S. Navy. *Born:* Maine. *Accredited to:* Maine. *G.O. No.:* 59, 22 June 1865. *Citation:* On board the U.S.S. *Monadnock* in action during several attacks on Fort Fisher, 24 and 25 December 1864; and 13, 14, and 15 January 1865. With his ship anchored well inshore to insure perfect range against the severe fire of rebel guns, Dunn continued his duties when the vessel was at anchor, as her propellers were kept in motion to make her turrets bear, and the shooting away of her chain might have caused her to ground. Disdainful of shelter despite severe weather conditions, he inspired his shipmates and contributed to the success of his vessel in reducing the enemy guns to silence.

DUNNE, JAMES

Rank and organization: Corporal, Chicago Mercantile Battery, Illinois Light Artillery. *Place and date:* At Vicksburg, Miss., 22 May 1863. *Entered service at:* Chicago, Ill. *Birth:* Detroit, Mich. *Date of issue:* 15 January 1895. *Citation:* Carried with others by hand a cannon up to and fired it through an embrasure of the enemy's works.

DUNPHY, RICHARD D.

Rank and organization: Coal Heaver, U.S. Navy. *Born:* 1840, Ireland. *Accredited to:* New York. *Citation:* On board the flagship U.S.S. *Hartford* during successful attacks against Fort Morgan, rebel gunboats and the rebel ram *Tennessee*, Mobile Bay, 5 August 1864. With his ship under terrific enemy shellfire, Dunphy performed his duties with skill and courage throughout this fierce engagement which resulted in the capture of the rebel ram *Tennessee*.

DU PONT, HENRY A.

Rank and organization: Captain, 5th U.S. Artillery. *Place and date:* At Cedar Creek, Va., 19 October 1864. *Entered service at:* Wilmington, Del. *Birth:* Eleutherean Mills, Del. *Date of issue:* 2 April 1898. *Citation:* By his distinguished gallantry, and voluntary exposure to the enemy's fire at a critical moment, when the Union line had been broken, encouraged his men to stand to their guns, checked the advance of the enemy, and brought off most of his pieces.

DURHAM, JAMES R.

Rank and organization: Second Lieutenant, Company E, 12th West Virginia Infantry. *Place and date:* At Winchester, Va., 14 June 1863. *Entered service at:* Clarksburg, W. Va. *Born:* 7 February 1833, Richmond, W. Va. *Date of issue:* 6 March 1890. *Citation:* Led his command over the stone wall, where he was wounded.

DURHAM, JOHN S.

Rank and organization: Sergeant, Company F, 1st Wisconsin Infantry. *Place and date:* At Perryville, Ky., 8 October 1862. *Entered service at:* Malone, St. Croix County, Wis. *Born:* 1843, New York, N.Y. *Date of issue:* 20 November 1896. *Citation:* Seized the flag of his regiment when the color sergeant was shot and advanced with the flag midway between the lines, amid a shower of shot, shell, and bullets, until stopped by his commanding officer.

ECKES, JOHN N.

Rank and organization: Private, Company E, 47th Ohio Infantry. *Place and date:* At Vicksburg, Miss., 22 May 1863. *Entered service at:* Weston, W. Va. *Birth:* Lewis County, W. Va. *Date of issue:* 21 July 1894. *Citation:* Gallantry in the charge of the "volunteer storming party."

EDDY, SAMUEL E.

Rank and organization: Private, Company D, 37th Massachusetts Infantry. *Place and date:* At Sailors Creek, Va., 6 April 1865. *Entered service at:* Chesterfield, Mass. *Birth:* Vermont. *Date of issue:* 10 September 1897. *Citation:* Saved the life of the adjutant of his regiment by voluntarily going beyond the line and there killing one of the enemy then in the act of firing upon the wounded officer. Was assailed by several of the enemy, run through the body with a bayonet, and pinned to the ground, but while so situated he shot and killed his assailant.

EDGERTON, NATHAN H.

Rank and organization: Lieutenant and Adjutant, 6th U.S. Colored Troops. *Place and date:* At Chapins Farm, Va., 29 September 1864. *Entered service at:* Philadelphia, Pa. *Birth:* ———. *Date of issue:* 30 March 1898. *Citation:* Took up the flag after 3 color bearers had been shot down and bore it forward, though himself wounded.

EDWARDS, DAVID

Rank and organization: Private, Company H, 146th New York Infantry. *Place and date:* At Five Forks, Va., 1 April 1865. *Entered service at:* Sangersfield, N.Y. *Birth:* Wales, England. *Date of issue:* 10 May 1865. *Citation:* Capture of flag.

EDWARDS, JOHN

Rank and organization: Captain of the Top, U.S. Navy. *Born:* 1831, Providence, R.I. *Accredited to:* Rhode Island. *G.O. No.:* 45, 31 December 1864. *Citation:* As second captain of a gun on board the U.S.S. *Lackawanna* during successful attacks against Fort Morgan, rebel gunboats and the ram *Tennessee* in Mobile Bay, on 5 August 1864. Wounded when an enemy shell struck, Edwards refused to go below for aid and, as heavy return fire continued to strike his vessel, took the place of the first captain and carried out his duties during the prolonged action which resulted in the capture of the prize ram *Tennessee* and in the damaging and destruction of batteries at Fort Morgan.

ELLIOTT, ALEXANDER

Rank and organization: Sergeant, Company A, 1st Pennsylvania Cavalry. *Place and date:* At Paines Crossroads, Va., 5 April 1865. *Entered service at:* North Sewickley, Pa. *Birth:* Beaver County, Pa. *Date of issue:* 3 May 1865. *Citation:* Capture of flag.

ELLIOTT, RUSSELL C.

Rank and organization: Sergeant, Company B, 3d Massachusetts Cavalry. *Place and date:* At Natchitoches, La., 19 April 1864. *Entered service at:* Boston, Mass. *Birth:* Concord, N.H. *Date of issue:* 20 November 1896. *Citation:* Seeing a Confederate officer in advance of his command, charged on him alone and unaided and captured him.

ELLIS, HORACE

Rank and organization: Private, Company A, 7th Wisconsin Infantry. *Place and date:* At Weldon Railroad, Va., 21 August 1864. *Entered service at:* Chippewa Falls, Wis. *Birth:* Mercer County, Pa. *Date of issue:* 1 December 1864. *Citation:* Capture of flag of 16th Mississippi (C.S.A.).

ELLIS, WILLIAM

Rank and organization: First Sergeant, Company K, 3d Wisconsin Cavalry. *Place and date:* At Dardanelles, Ark., 14 January 1865. *Entered service at:* Little Rock, Ark. *Birth:* England. *Date of issue:* 8 March 1865. *Citation:* Remained at his post after receiving three wounds, and only retired, by his commanding officer's orders, after being wounded the fourth time.

ELLSWORTH, THOMAS F.

Rank and organization: Captain, Company B, 55th Massachusetts Infantry. *Place and date:* At Honey Hill, S.C., 30 November 1864. *Entered service at:* ———. *Birth:* Ipswich, Mass. *Date of issue:* 18

November 1895. *Citation:* Under a heavy fire carried his wounded commanding officer from the field.

ELSON, JAMES M.

Rank and organization: Sergeant, Company C, 9th Iowa Infantry. *Place and date:* At Vicksburg, Miss., 22 May 1863. *Entered service at:* Shellsburg, Iowa. *Birth:* Coshocton, Ohio. *Date of issue:* 12 September 1891. *Citation:* Carried the colors in advance of his regiment and was shot down while attempting to plant them on the enemy's works.

EMBLER, ANDREW H.

Rank and organization: Captain, Company D, 59th New York Infantry. *Place and date:* At Boydton Plank Road, Va., 27 October 1864. *Entered service at:* New York. *Birth:* New York, N.Y. *Date of issue:* 19 October 1893. *Citation:* Charged at the head of 2 regiments, which drove the enemy's main body, gained the crest of the hill near the Burgess house and forced a barricade on the Boydton road.

ENDERLIN, RICHARD

Rank and organization: Musician, Company B, 73d Ohio Infantry. *Place and date:* At Gettysburg, Pa., 1–3 July 1863. *Entered service at:* Chillicothe, Ohio. *Birth:* Germany. *Date of issue:* 11 September 1897. *Citation:* Voluntarily took a rifle and served as a soldier in the ranks during the first and second days of the battle. Voluntarily and at his own imminent peril went into the enemy's lines at night and, under a sharp fire, rescued a wounded comrade.

ENGLE, JAMES E.

Rank and organization: Sergeant, Company I, 97th Pennsylvania Infantry. *Place and date:* At Bermuda Hundred, Va., 18 May 1864. *Entered service at:* Chester, Pa. *Birth:* Chester, Pa. *Date of issue:* 17 December 1896. *Citation:* Responded to a call for volunteers to carry ammunition to the regiment on the picket line and under a heavy fire from the enemy assisted in carrying a box of ammunition to the front and remained to distribute the same.

ENGLISH, EDMUND

Rank and organization: First Sergeant, Company C, 2d New Jersey Infantry. *Place and date:* At Wilderness, Va., 6 May 1864. *Entered service at:* Newark, N.J. *Born:* 16 November 1841, Ireland. *Date of issue:* 13 February 1891. *Citation:* During a rout and while under orders to retreat seized the colors, rallied the men, and drove the enemy back.

ENGLISH, THOMAS

Rank and organization: Signal Quartermaster, U.S. Navy. *Born:* 1819, New York, N.Y. *Accredited to:* New York. *G.O. No.:* 59, 22 June 1865. *Citation:* English served on board the U.S.S. *New Ironsides* during action in several attacks on Fort Fisher, 24 and 25 December 1864; and 13, 14, and 15 January 1865. The ship steamed in and took the lead in the ironclad division close inshore and immediately opened its starboard battery in a barrage of well-directed fire to cause several fires and explosions and dismount several guns during the first 2 days of fighting. Taken under fire as she steamed into position on 13 January, the *New Ironsides* fought all day and took on ammunition at night despite severe weather conditions. When the enemy came out of his bombproofs to defend the fort against the storming party, the ship's battery disabled nearly every gun on the fort facing the shore before the cease-fire orders were given by the flagship.

ENNIS, CHARLES D.

Rank and organization: Private, Company G, 1st Rhode Island Light Artillery. *Place and date:* At Petersburg, Va., 2 April 1865. *Entered service at:* Charleston, R.I. *Birth:* Stonington, Conn. *Date of issue:* 28 June 1892. *Citation:* Was one of a detachment of 20 picked artillerymen who voluntarily accompanied an infantry assaulting party and who turned upon the enemy the guns captured in the assault.

ERICKSON, JOHN P.

Rank and organization: Captain of the Forecastle, U.S. Navy. *Birth:* London, England. *Accredited to:* New York. *G.O. No.:* 59, 22 June 1865. *Citation:* Served on board the U.S.S. *Pontoosuc* during the capture of Fort Fisher and Wilmington, 24 December 1864, to 22 February 1865. Carrying out his duties faithfully throughout this period, Erickson was so severely wounded in the assault upon Fort Fisher that he was sent to the hospital at Portsmouth, Va. Erickson was recommended for his gallantry, skill, and coolness in action while under the fire of the enemy.

ESTES, LEWELLYN G.

Rank and organization: Captain and Assistant Adjutant General, Volunteers. *Place and date:* At Flint River, Ga., 30 August 1864. *Entered service at:* Penobscot, Maine. *Birth:* Oldtown, Maine. *Date of issue:* 29 August 1894. *Citation:* Voluntarily led troops in a charge over a burning bridge.

EVANS, CORON D.

Rank and organization: Private, Company A, 3d Indiana Cavalry. *Place and date:* At Sailors Creek, Va., 6 April 1865. *Entered service at:* Jefferson County, Ind. *Birth:* Jefferson County, Ind. *Date of issue:* 3 May 1865. *Citation:* Capture of flag of 26th Virginia Infantry (C.S.A.).

EVANS, IRA H.

Rank and organization: Captain, Company B, 116th U.S. Colored Troops, *Place and date:* At Hatchers Run, Va., 2 April 1865. *Entered service at:* Barre, Vt. *Born:* 11 April 1844, Piermont, N.H. *Date of issue:* 24 March 1892. *Citation:* Voluntarily passed between the lines, under a heavy fire from the enemy, and obtained important information.

EVANS, JAMES R.

Rank and organization: Private, Company H, 62d New York Infantry. *Place and date:* At Wilderness, Va., 5 May 1864. *Entered service at:* New York, N.Y. *Birth:* New York, N.Y. *Date of issue:* 25 February 1895. *Citation:* Went out in front of the line under a fierce fire and, in the face of the rapidly advancing enemy, rescued the regimental flag with which the color bearer had fallen.

EVANS, THOMAS

Rank and organization: Private, Company D, 54th Pennsylvania Infantry. *Place and date:* At Piedmont, Va., 5 June 1864. *Entered service at:* Cambria County, Pa. *Birth:* Wales. *Date of issue:* 26 November 1864. *Citation:* Capture of flag of 45th Virginia (C.S.A.).

EVERSON, ADELBERT

Rank and organization: Private, Company D, 185th New York Infantry. *Place and date:* At Five Forks, Va., 1 April 1865. *Entered service at:* Salina, N.Y. *Birth:* Cicero, N.Y. *Date of issue:* 10 May 1865. *Citation:* Capture of flag.

EWING, JOHN C.

Rank and organization: Private, Company E, 211th Pennsylvania Infantry. *Place and date:* At Petersburg, Va., 2 April 1865. *Entered service at:* ———. *Birth:* Westmoreland County, Pa. *Date of issue:* 20 May 1865. *Citation:* Capture of flag.

FALCONER, JOHN A.

Rank and organization: Corporal, Company A, 17th Michigan Infantry. *Place and date:* At Fort Sanders, Knoxville, Tenn., 20 November 1863. *Entered service at:* Manchester, Mich. *Born:* 1844, Wachtenaw, Mich. *Date of issue:* 27 July 1896. *Citation:* Conducted the "burning party" of his regiment at the time a charge was made on the enemy's picket line, and burned the house which had sheltered the enemy's sharpshooters, thus insuring success to a hazardous enterprise.

FALL, CHARLES S.

Rank and organization: Sergeant, Company E, 26th Michigan Infantry. *Place and date:* At Spotsylvania Courthouse, Va., 12 May 1864. *Entered service at:* Hamburg, Mich. *Born:* 1842, Noble County, Ind. *Date of issue:* 13 May 1899. *Citation:* Was one of the first to mount the Confederate works, where he bayoneted two of the enemy and captured a Confederate flag, but threw it away to continue the pursuit of the enemy.

FALLON, THOMAS T.

Rank and organization: Private, Company K, 37th New York Infantry. *Place and date:* At Williamsburg, Va., 5 May 1862. At Fair Oaks, Va., 30–31 May 1862. At Big Shanty, Ga., 14–15 June 1864. *Entered service at:* Freehold, N.J. *Birth:* Ireland. *Date of issue:* 13 February 1891. *Citation:* At Williamsburg, Va., assisted in driving rebel skirmishers to their main line. Participated in action, at Fair Oaks, Va., though excused from duty because of disability. In a charge with his company at Big Shanty, Ga., was the first man on the enemy's works.

*FALLS, BENJAMIN F.

Rank and organization: Color Sergeant, Company A, 19th Massachusetts Infantry. *Place and date:* At Gettysburg, Pa., 3 July 1863.

Entered service at: Lynn, Mass. *Birth:* Portsmouth, N.H. *Date of issue.* 1 December 1864. *Citation:* Capture of flag.

FANNING, NICHOLAS

Rank and organization: Private, Company B, 4th Iowa Cavalry. *Place and date:* At Selma, Ala., 2 April 1865. *Entered service at:* Independence, Buchanan County, Iowa. *Birth:* Carroll County, Ind. *Date of issue:* 17 June 1865. *Citation:* Capture of silk Confederate States flag and 2 staff officers.

FARLEY, WILLIAM

Rank and organization: Boatswain's Mate, U.S. Navy. *Born:* 1835, Whitefield, Maine. *Accredited to:* Maine. *G.O. No.:* 32, 16 April 1864. *Citation:* Served on board the U.S.S. *Marblehead* off Legareville, Stono River, 25 December 1863, during an engagement with the enemy on John's Island. Behaving in a gallant manner, Farley animated his men and kept up a rapid and effective fire on the enemy throughout the engagement which resulted in the enemy's abandonment of his positions, leaving a caisson and 1 gun behind.

FARNSWORTH, HERBERT E.

Rank and organization: Sergeant Major, 10th New York Cavalry. *Place and date:* At Trevilian Station, Va., 11 June 1864. *Entered service at:* ———. *Birth:* Cattaraugus County, N.Y. *Date of issue:* 1 April 1898. *Citation:* Voluntarily carried a message which stopped the firing of a Union battery into his regiment, in which service he crossed a ridge in plain view and swept by the fire of both armies.

FARQUHAR, JOHN M.

Rank and organization: Sergeant Major, 89th Illinois Infantry. *Place and date:* At Stone River, Tenn., 31 December 1862. *Entered service at:* Chicago, Ill. *Birth:* Scotland. *Date of issue:* 6 August 1902. *Citation:* When a break occurred on the extreme right wing of the Army of the Cumberland, this soldier rallied fugitives from other commands, and deployed his own regiment, thereby checking the Confederate advance until a new line was established.

FARRELL, EDWARD

Rank and organization: Quartermaster, U.S. Navy. *Born:* 1833, Saratoga, N.Y. *Accredited to:* New York. *G.O. No.:* 11, 3 April 1863. *Citation:* Served on board the U.S.S. *Owasco* during the attack upon Forts Jackson and St. Philip, 24 April 1862. Stationed at the masthead during these operations, Farrell observed and reported the effect of the fire of our guns in such a manner as to make his intelligence, coolness and capacity conspicuous.

FASNACHT, CHARLES H.

Rank and organization: Sergeant, Company A, 99th Pennsylvania Infantry. *Place and date:* At Spotsylvania, Va., 12 May 1864. *Entered service at:* ———. *Birth:* Lancaster County, Pa. *Date of issue:* 2 April 1878. *Citation:* Capture of flag of 2d Louisiana Tigers (C.S.A.) in a hand-to-hand contest.

FASSETT, JOHN B.

Rank and organization: Captain, Company F, 23d Pennsylvania Infantry. *Place and date:* At Gettysburg, Pa., 2 July 1863. *Entered service at:* Philadelphia, Pa. *Birth:* Philadelphia, Pa. *Date of issue:* 29 December 1894. *Citation:* While acting as an aide, voluntarily led a regiment to the relief of a battery and recaptured its guns from the enemy.

FERNALD, ALBERT E.

Rank and organization: First Lieutenant, Company F, 20th Maine Infantry. *Place and date:* At Five Forks, Va., 1 April 1865. *Entered service at:* Winterport, Maine. *Birth:* Winterport, Maine. *Date of issue:* 10 May 1865. *Citation:* During a rush at the enemy, Lt. Fernald seized, during a scuffle, the flag of the 9th Virginia Infantry (C.S.A.).

FERRELL, JOHN H.

Rank and organization: Pilot, U.S. Navy. *Entered service at:* Illinois. *Born:* 15 April 1823, Tennessee. *G.O. No.:* 59, 22 June 1865. *Citation:* Served on board the U.S. Monitor *Neosho* during the engagement with enemy batteries at Bells Mills, Cumberland River, near Nashville, Tenn., 6 December 1864. Carrying out his duties courageously during the engagement, Ferrell gallantly left the pilothouse after the flag and signal staffs of that vessel had been shot away and, taking the flag which was drooping over the wheelhouse, make it fast to the stump of the highest mast remaining although the ship was still under a heavy fire from the enemy.

FERRIER, DANIEL T.

Rank and organization: Sergeant, Company K, 2d Indiana Cavalry. *Place and date:* At Varnells Station, Ga., 9 May 1864. *Entered service at:* Delphi, Ind. *Birth:* ———. *Date of issue:* 30 March 1898. *Citation:* While his regiment was retreating, voluntarily gave up his horse to his brigade commander who had been unhorsed and was in danger of capture, thereby enabling him to rejoin and rally the disorganized troops. Sgt. Ferrier himself was captured and confined in Confederate prisons, from which he escaped and, after great hardship, rejoined the Union lines.

FERRIS, EUGENE W.

Rank and organization: First Lieutenant and Adjutant, 30th Massachusetts Infantry. *Place and date:* At Berryville, Va., 1 April 1865. *Entered service at:* Lowell, Mass. *Birth:* Springfield, Vt. *Date of issue:* 16 October 1897. *Citation:* Accompanied only by an orderly, outside the lines of the Army, he gallantly resisted an attack of 5 of Mosby's cavalry, mortally wounded the leader of the party, seized his horse and pistols, wounded 3 more, and, though wounded himself, escaped.

FESQ, FRANK

Rank and organization: Private, Company A, 40th New Jersey Infantry. *Place and date:* At Petersburg, Va., 2 April 1865. *Entered service at:* Newark, N.J. *Born:* 4 April 1840, Germany. *Date of issue:* 10

May 1865. *Citation:* Capture of flag of 18th North Carolina (C.S.A.), within the enemy's works.

FINKENBINER, HENRY S.

Rank and organization: Private, Company D, 107th Ohio Infantry. *Place and date:* At Dingles Mill, S.C., 9 April 1865. *Entered service at:* ———. *Birth:* North Industry, Ohio. *Date of issue:* 30 March 1898. *Citation:* While on the advance skirmish line and within direct and close fire of the enemy's artillery, crossed the mill race on a burning bridge and ascertained the enemy's position.

FISHER, JOHN H.

Rank and organization: First Lieutenant, Company B, 55th Illinois Infantry. *Place and date:* At Vicksburg, Miss., 22 May 1863. *Entered service at:* Chicago, Ill. *Birth:* Monmouth, Pa. *Date of issue:* 2 September 1893. *Citation:* Gallantry in the charge of the "volunteer storming party."

FISHER, JOSEPH

Rank and organization: Corporal, Company C, 61st Pennsylvania Infantry. *Place and date:* At Petersburg, Va., 2 April 1865. *Entered service at:* Philadelphia, Pa. *Birth:* Philadelphia, Pa. *Date of issue:* 16 January 1894. *Citation:* Carried the colors 50 yards in advance of his regiment, and after being painfully wounded attempted to crawl into the enemy's works in an endeavor to plant his flag thereon.

FITZPATRICK, THOMAS

Rank and organization: Coxswain, U.S. Navy. *Born:* 1837, Canada. *G.O. No.:* 45, 31 December 1864. *Citation:* As captain of the No. 1 gun on board the flagship U.S.S. *Hartford*, during action against rebel gunboats, the ram *Tennessee* and Fort Morgan in Mobile Bay, 5 August 1864. Although struck several times in the face by splinters, and with his gun disabled when a shell burst between the 2 forward 9-inch guns, killing and wounding 15 men, Fitzpatrick, within a few minutes, had the gun in working order again with new track, breeching and side tackle, had sent the wounded below, cleared the area of other casualties, and was fighting his gun as before. He served as an inspiration to the members of his crew and contributed to the success of the action in which the *Tennessee* was captured.

FLANAGAN, AUGUSTIN

Rank and organization: Sergeant, Company A, 55th Pennsylvania Infantry. *Place and date:* At Chapins Farm, Va., 29 September 1864. *Entered service at:* Chest Springs, Pa. *Birth:* Cambria County, Pa. *Date of issue:* 6 April 1865. *Citation:* Gallantry in the charge on the enemy's works: rushing forward with the colors and calling upon the men to follow him; was severely wounded.

FLANNIGAN, JAMES

Rank and organization: Private, Company H, 2d Minnesota Infantry. *Place and date:* At Nolensville, Tenn., 15 February 1863. *Entered service at:* Louisville, Scott County, Minn. *Birth:* New York. *Date of issue:* 11 September 1897. *Citation:* Was one of a detachment of 16 men who heroically defended a wagon train against the attack of 125 cavalry, repulsed the attack and saved the train.

FLEETWOOD, CHRISTIAN A.

Rank and organization: Sergeant Major, 4th U.S. Colored Troops, *Place and date:* At Chapins Farm, Va., 29 September 1864. *Entered service at:* ———. *Birth:* Baltimore, Md. *Date of issue:* 6 April 1865. *Citation:* Seized the colors, after 2 color bearers had been shot down, and bore them nobly through the fight.

FLOOD, THOMAS

Rank and organization: Boy, U.S. Navy. *Born:* 1840, Ireland. *Accredited to:* New York. *G.O. No.:* 11, 3 April 1863. *Citation:* Served on board the U.S.S. *Pensacola* in the attack on Forts Jackson and St. Philip and at the taking of new Orleans, 24 and 25 April 1862. Swept from the bridge by a shell which wounded the signal quartermaster, Flood returned to the bridge after assisting the wounded man below and taking over his duties, "Performed them with coolness, exactitude and the fidelity of a veteran seaman. His intelligence and character cannot be spoken of too warmly."

FLYNN, CHRISTOPHER

Rank and organization: Corporal, Company K, 14th Connecticut Infantry. *Place and date:* At Gettysburg, Pa., 3 July 1863. *Entered service at:* Sprague, Conn. *Birth:* Ireland. *Date of issue:* 1 December 1864. *Citation:* Capture of flag of 52d North Carolina Infantry (C.S.A.).

FLYNN, JAMES E.

Rank and organization: Sergeant, Company G, 6th Missouri Infantry. *Place and date:* At Vicksburg, Miss., 22 May 1863. *Entered service at:* St. Louis, Mo. *Birth:* Pittsfield, Ill. *Date of issue:* 19 June 1894. *Citation:* Gallantry in the charge of the "volunteer storming party."

FOLLETT, JOSEPH L.

Rank and organization: Sergeant, Company G, 1st Missouri Light Artillery. *Place and date:* At New Madrid, Mo., 3 March 1862; at Stone River, Tenn., 31 December 1862. *Entered service at:* St. Louis, Mo. *Birth:* Newark, N.J. *Date of issue:* 19 September 1890. *Citation:* At New Madrid, Mo., remained on duty though severely wounded. While procuring ammunition from the supply train at Stone River, Tenn., was captured, but made his escape, secured the ammunition, and in less than an hour from the time of his capture had the batteries supplied.

FORCE, MANNING F.

Rank and organization: Brigadier General, U.S. Volunteers. *Place and date:* At Atlanta, Ga., 22 July 1864. *Entered service at:* Cincinnati, Ohio. *Born:* Washington, D.C. 17 December 1824. *Date of issue:* 31 March 1892. *Citation:* Charged upon the enemy's works, and after their capture defended his position against assaults of the enemy until he was severely wounded.

FORD, GEORGE W.

Rank and organization: First Lieutenant, Company E, 88th New York Infantry. *Place and date:* At Sailors Creek, Va., 6 April 1865. *Entered service at:* ———. *Birth:* Ireland. *Date of issue:* 10 May 1865. *Citation:* Capture of flag.

FORMAN, ALEXANDER A.

Rank and organization: Corporal, Company E, 7th Michigan Infantry. *Place and date:* At Fair Oaks, Va., 31 May 1862. *Entered service at:* Jonesville, Mich. *Birth:* Scipio, Mich. *Date of issue:* 17 August 1895. *Citation:* Although wounded, he continued fighting until, fainting from loss of blood, he was carried off the field.

FOUT, FREDERICK W.

Rank and organization: Second Lieutenant, 15th Battery, Indiana Light Artillery. *Place and date:* Near Harpers Ferry, W. Va., 15 September 1862. *Entered service at:* Indianapolis, Ind. *Birth:* Germany. *Date of issue:* 2 November 1896. *Citation:* Voluntarily gathered the men of the battery together, remanned the guns, which had been ordered abandoned by an officer, opened fire, and kept up the same on the enemy until after the surrender.

FOX, HENRY

Rank and organization: Sergeant, Company H, 106th Illinois Infantry. *Place and date:* Near Jackson, Tenn., 23 December 1862. *Entered service at:* Lincoln, Ill. *Birth:* Germany. *Date of issue:* 16 May 1899. *Citation:* When his command was surrounded by a greatly superior force, voluntarily left the shelter of the breastworks, crossed an open railway trestle under a concentrated fire from the enemy, made his way out and secured reinforcements for the relief of his command.

FOX, HENRY M.

Rank and organization: Sergeant, Company M, 5th Michigan Cavalry. *Place and date:* At Winchester, Va., 19 September 1864. *Entered service at:* Coldwater, Mich. *Born:* 1844, Trumbull, Ohio. *Date of issue:* 27 September 1864. *Citation:* Capture of flag.

FOX, NICHOLAS

Rank and organization: Private, Company H, 28th Connecticut Infantry. *Place and date:* At Port Hudson, La., 14 June 1863. *Entered service at:* Greenwich, Conn. *Birth:* ———. *Date of issue:* 1 April 1898. *Citation:* Made 2 trips across an open space, in the face of the enemy's concentrated fire, and secured water for the sick and wounded.

FOX, WILLIAM R.

Rank and organization: Private, Company A, 95th Pennsylvania Infantry. *Place and date:* At Petersburg, Va., 2 April 1865. *Entered service at:* ———. *Birth:* Philadelphia, Pa. *Date of issue:* 28 March 1879. *Citation:* Bravely assisted in the capture of one of the enemy's guns; with the first troops to enter the city, captured the flag of the Confederate customhouse.

FOY, CHARLES H.

Rank and organization: Signal Quartermaster, U.S. Navy. *Birth:* Portsmouth, N.H. *Accredited to:* New Hampshire. *G.O. No.:* 59, 22 June 1865. *Citation:* Served on board the U.S.S. *Rhode Island* during the action with Fort Fisher and the Federal Point batteries, 13 to 15 January 1865. Carrying out his duties courageously during the battle, Foy continued to be outstanding by his good conduct and faithful services throughout this engagement which resulted in a heavy casualty list when an attempt was made to storm Fort Fisher.

FRANKS, WILLIAM J.

Rank and organization: Seaman, U.S. Navy. *Born:* 1830, Chatham County, N.C. *Entered service at:* Duvalls Bluff, Ark. *G.O. No.:* 32, 16 April 1864. *Citation:* Served on board the U.S.S. *Marmora* off Yazoo City, Miss., 5 March 1864. Embarking from the *Marmora* with a 12-pound howitzer mounted on a field carriage, Franks landed with the gun and crew in the midst of heated battle and, bravely standing by his gun despite enemy rifle fire which cut the gun carriage and rammer contributed to the turning back of the enemy during the fierce engagement.

FRANTZ, JOSEPH

Rank and organization: Private, Company E, 83d Indiana Infantry. *Place and date:* At Vicksburg, Miss., 22 May 1863. *Entered service at:* Osgood, Ind. *Birth:* France. *Date of issue:* 13 August 1894. *Citation:* Gallantry in the charge of the "volunteer storming party."

FRASER (FRAZIER), WILLIAM W.

Rank and organization: Private, Company I, 97th Illinois Infantry. *Place and date:* At Vicksburg, Miss., 22 May 1863. *Entered service at:* Alton, Madison County, Ill. *Birth:* Scotland. *Date of issue:* 24 October 1895. *Citation:* Gallantry in the charge of the "volunteer storming party."

FREEMAN, ARCHIBALD

Rank and organization: Private, Company E, 124th New York Infantry. *Place and date:* At Spotsylvania, Va., 12 May 1864. *Entered service at:* Newburgh, N.Y. *Birth:* Goshen, N.Y. *Date of issue:* 1 December 1864. *Citation:* Capture of flag of 17th Louisiana (C.S.A.).

FREEMAN, HENRY B.

Rank and organization: First Lieutenant, 18th U.S. Infantry. *Place and date:* At Stone River, Tenn., 31 December 1862. *Entered service at:* Mount Vernon, Ohio. *Birth:* Mount Vernon, Ohio. *Date of issue:* 17 February 1894. *Citation:* Voluntarily went to the front and picked up and carried to a place of safety, under a heavy fire from the enemy, an acting field officer who had been wounded, and was about to fall into enemy hands.

FREEMAN, MARTIN

Rank and organization: Pilot, U.S. Navy. *Entered service at:* Louisiana. *Born:* 18 May 1814, Germany. *G.O. No.:* 45, 31 December 1864. *Citation:* As pilot of the flagship, U.S.S. *Hartford*, during action against Fort Morgan, rebel gunboats and the ram *Tennessee*, in Mobile Bay, 5 August 1864. With his ship under terrific enemy shellfire, Freeman calmly remained at his station in the maintop and skillfully piloted the ships into the bay. He rendered gallant service throughout the prolonged battle in which the rebel gunboats were captured or driven off, the prize ram *Tennessee* forced to surrender, and the fort successfully attacked.

FREEMAN, WILLIAM H.

Rank and organization: Private, Company B, 169th New York Infantry. *Place and date:* At Fort Fisher, N.C., 15 January 1865. *Entered service at:* Troy, N.Y. *Birth:* Troy, N.Y. *Date of issue:* 27 May 1905. *Citation:* Volunteered to carry the brigade flag after the bearer was wounded.

FRENCH, SAMUEL S.

Rank and organization: Private, Company E, 7th Michigan Infantry. *Place and date:* At Fair Oaks, Va., 31 May 1862. *Entered service at:* Gifford, Mich. *Birth:* Erie County, N.Y. *Date of issue:* 24 October 1895. *Citation:* Continued fighting, although wounded, until he fainted from loss of blood.

FREY, FRANZ

Rank and organization: Corporal, Company H, 37th Ohio Infantry. *Place and date:* At Vicksburg, Miss., 22 May 1863. *Entered service at:* Cleveland, Ohio. *Birth:* Switzerland. *Date of issue:* 14 August 1894. *Citation:* Gallantry in the charge of the "volunteer storming party."

FRICK, JACOB G.

Rank and organization: Colonel, 129th Pennsylvania Infantry. *Place and date:* At Fredericksburg, Va., 13 December 1862. At Chancellorsville, Va., 3 May 1863. *Entered service at:* Pottsville, Pa. *Born:* 23 January 1838, Northumberland, Pa. *Date of issue:* 7 June 1892. *Citation:* At Fredericksburg seized the colors and led the command through a terrible fire of cannon and musketry. In a hand-to-hand fight at Chancellorsville, recaptured the colors of his regiment.

FRISBEE, JOHN B.

Rank and organization: Gunner's Mate, U.S. Navy. *Born:* 1822, Maine, *Accredited to:* Maine. *G.O. No.:* 11, 3 April 1863. *Citation:* Served on board the U.S. Steam Gunboat *Pinola* during action against Forts Jackson and St. Philip, and during the taking of New Orleans, 24 April 1862. While engaged in the bombardment of Fort St. Philip, Frisbee, acting courageously and without personal regard, closed the powder magazine which had been set afire by enemy shelling and shut off his avenue of escape, thereby setting a high example of bravery. He served courageously throughout these engagements which resulted in the taking of the Forts Jackson and St. Philip and in the surrender of New Orleans.

FRIZZELL (FRAZELL), HENRY F.

Rank and organization: Private, Company B, 6th Missouri Infantry. *Place and date:* At Vicksburg, Miss., 22 May 1863. *Entered service at:* Pilot Knob, Iron County, Mo. *Birth:* Madison County, Mo. *Date of issue:* 30 July 1894. *Citation:* Gallantry in the charge of the "volunteer storming party."

FRY, ISAAC N.

Rank and organization: Orderly Sergeant, U.S. Marine Corps. *Accredited to:* Pennsylvania. *G.O. No.:* 59, 22 June 1865. *Citation:* On board the U.S.S. *Ticonderoga* during attacks on Fort Fisher, 13 to 15 January 1865. As orderly sergeant of marine guard, and captain of a gun, Orderly Sgt. Fry performed his duties with skill and courage as the *Ticonderoga* maintained a well-placed fire upon the batteries to the left of the palisades during the initial phases of the 3-day battle, and thereafter, as she considerably lessened the firing power of guns on the mount which had been turned upon our assaulting columns. During this action the flag was planted on one of the strongest fortifications possessed by the rebels.

FUGER, FREDERICK

Rank and organization: Sergeant, Battery A, 4th U.S. Artillery. *Place and date:* At Gettysburg, Pa., 3 July 1863. *Entered service at:* ———. *Birth:* Germany. *Date of issue:* 24 August 1897. *Citation:* All the officers of his battery having been killed or wounded and five of its guns disabled in Pickett's assault, he succeeded to the command and fought the remaining gun with most distinguished gallantry until the battery was ordered withdrawn.

FUNK, WEST

Rank and organization: Major, 121st Pennsylvania Infantry. *Place and date:* At Appomattox Courthouse, Va., 9 April 1865. *Entered service at:* Philadelphia, Pa. *Birth:* Boston, Mass. *Date of issue:* 15 October 1872. *Citation:* Capture of flag of 46th Virginia Infantry (C.S.A.).

FURMAN, CHESTER S.

Rank and organization: Corporal, Company A, 6th Pennsylvania Reserves. *Place and date:* At Gettysburg, Pa., 2 July 1863. *Entered service at:* ———. *Birth:* Columbia, Pa. *Date of issue:* 3 August 1897. *Citation:* Was 1 of 6 volunteers who charged upon a log house near Devil's Den, where a squad of the enemy's sharpshooters were sheltered, and compelled their surrender.

FURNESS, FRANK

Rank and organization: Captain, Company F, 6th Pennsylvania Cavalry. *Place and date:* At Trevilian Station, Va., 12 June 1864. *Entered service at:* Philadelphia, Pa. *Birth:* ———. *Date of issue:* 20 October 1899. *Citation:* Voluntarily carrier a box of ammunition across an open space swept by the enemy's fire to the relief of an outpost whose ammunition had become almost exhausted, but which was thus enabled to hold its important position.

GAGE, RICHARD J.

Rank and organization: Private, Company D, 104th Illinois Infantry. *Place and date:* Elk River, Tenn., 2 July 1863. *Entered service at:* Ottawa, Ill. *Birth:* Grafton County, N.H. *Date of issue:* 30 October 1897. *Citation:* Voluntarily joined a small party that, under a heavy fire, captured a stockade and saved the bridge.

GALLOWAY, GEORGE N.

Rank and organization: Private, Company G, 95th Pennsylvania Infantry. *Place and date:* At Alsops Farm, Va., 8 May 1864. *Entered service at:* ———. *Birth:* Philadelphia, Pa. *Date of issue:* 24 October 1895. *Citation:* Voluntarily held an important position under heavy fire.

GALLOWAY, JOHN

Rank and organization: Commissary Sergeant, 8th Pennsylvania Cavalry. *Place and date:* At Farmville, Va., 7 April 1865. *Entered service at:* ———. *Birth:* Philadelphia, Pa. *Date of issue:* 30 October 1897. *Citation:* His regiment being surprised and nearly overwhelmed, he dashed forward under a heavy fire, reached the right of the regiment, where the danger was greatest, rallied the men and prevented a disaster that was imminent.

GARDINER, JAMES

Rank and organization: Private, Company I, 36th U.S. Colored Troops. *Place and date:* At Chapins Farm, Va., 29 September 1864. *Entered service at:* ———. *Birth:* Gloucester, Va. *Date of issue:* 6 April 1865. *Citation:* Rushed in advance of his brigade, shot a rebel officer who was on the parapet rallying his men, and then ran him through with his bayonet.

GARDNER, CHARLES N.

Rank and organization: Private, Company E, 32d Massachusetts Infantry. *Place and date:* At Five Forks, Va., 1 April 1865. *Entered service at:* ———. *Birth:* South Scituate, Mass. *Date of issue:* 10 May 1865. *Citation:* Capture of flag.

GARDNER, ROBERT J.

Rank and organization: Sergeant, Company K, 34th Massachusetts Infantry. *Place and date:* At Petersburg, Va., 2 April 1865. *Entered service at:* Berkshire County, Mass. *Birth:* Livingston, N.Y. *Date of issue:* 12 May 1865. *Citation:* Was among the first to enter Fort Gregg, clearing his way by using his musket on the heads of the enemy.

GARDNER, WILLIAM

Rank and organization: Seaman, U.S. Navy. *Born:* 1832, Ireland. *Accredited to:* New York. *G.O. No.:* 45, 31 December 1864. *Citation:* As seaman on board the U.S.S. *Galena* in the engagement at Mobile Bay,

5 August 1864. Serving gallantly during this fierce battle which resulted in the capture of the rebel ram *Tennessee* and the damaging of Fort Morgan, Gardner behaved with conspicuous coolness under the fire of the enemy.

GARRETT, WILLIAM

Rank and organization: Sergeant, Company G, 41st Ohio Infantry. *Place and date:* At Nashville, Tenn., 16 December 1864. *Entered service at:* ———. *Birth:* England. *Date of issue:* 24 February 1865. *Citation:* With several companions dashed forward, the first to enter the enemy's works, taking possession of 4 pieces of artillery and captured the flag of the 13th Mississippi Infantry (C.S.A.).

GARRISON, JAMES R.

Rank and organization: Coal Heaver, U.S. Navy. *Born:* 1840, Poughkeepsie, N.Y. *Accredited to:* New York. *G.O. No.:* 45, 31 December 1864. *Citation:* On board the flagship, U.S.S. *Hartford*, during successful engagements against Fort Morgan, rebel gunboats and the ram *Tennessee* in Mobile Bay, on 5 August 1864. When a shell struck his foot and severed one of his toes, Garrison remained at his station at the shell whip and, after crudely bandaging the wound, continued to perform his duties until severely wounded by another shellburst.

GARVIN, WILLIAM

Rank and organization: Captain of the Forecastle, U.S. Navy. *Born:* 1835. *Accredited to:* Virginia. *G.O. No.:* 45, 31 December 1864. *Citation:* Garvin served on board the U.S.S. *Agawam*, as one of a volunteer crew of a powder boat which was exploded near Fort Fisher, 23 December 1864. The powder boat, towed in by the *Wilderness* to prevent detection by the enemy, cast off and slowly steamed to within 300 yards of the beach. After fuses and fires had been lit and a second anchor with short scope let go to assure the boat's tailing inshore, the crew again boarded the *Wilderness* and proceeded a distance of 12 miles from shore. Less than 2 hours later the explosion took place, and the following day fires were observed still burning at the fort.

*GASSON, RICHARD

Rank and organization: Sergeant, Company K, 47th New York Infantry. *Place and date:* At Chapins Farm, Va., 29 September 1864. *Entered service at:* ———. *Birth:* Ireland. *Date of issue:* 6 April 1865. *Citation:* Fell dead while planting the colors of his regiment on the enemy's works.

GAUNT, JOHN C.

Rank and organization: Private, Company G, 104th Ohio Infantry. *Place and date:* At Franklin, Tenn., 30 November 1864. *Entered service at:* Damascoville, Ohio. *Birth:* Columbiana County, Ohio. *Date of issue:* 13 February 1865. *Citation:* Capture of flag.

GAUSE, ISAAC

Rank and organization: Corporal, Company E, 2d Ohio Cavalry. *Place and date:* Near Berryville, Va., 13 September 1864. *Entered service at:* ———. *Birth:* Trumbull County, Ohio. *Date of issue:* 19 September 1864. *Citation:* Capture of the colors of the 8th South Carolina Infantry while engaged in a reconnaissance along the Berryville and Winchester Pike.

GAYLORD, LEVI B.

Rank and organization: Sergeant, Company A, 29th Massachusetts Infantry. *Place and date:* At Fort Stedman, Va., 25 March 1865. *Entered service at:* ———. *Birth:* Boston, Mass. *Date of issue:* 22 June 1896. *Citation:* Voluntarily assisted in working an abandoned gun, while exposed to heavy fire, until the enemy's advancing line was routed by a charge on its left flank.

GEORGE, DANIEL G.

Rank and organization: Ordinary Seaman, U.S. Navy. (Real name is William Smith.) *Born:* 1840, Plaistow, N.H. *Accredited to:* New Hampshire. *G.O. No.:* 45, 31 December 1864. *Citation:* George served on board U.S. Picket Boat No. 1, in action 27 October 1864, against the Confederate ram, *Albemarle*, which had resisted repeated attacks by our steamers and had kept a large force of vessels employed in watching her. The picket boat, equipped with a spar torpedo, succeeded in passing the enemy pickets within 20 yards without being discovered and then made for the *Albemarle* under a full head of steam. Immediately taken under fire by the ram, the small boat plunged on, jumped the log boom which encircled the target and exploded its torpedo under the port bow of the ram. The picket boat was destroyed by enemy fire and almost the entire crew taken prisoner or lost.

GERE, THOMAS P.

Rank and organization: First Lieutenant and Adjutant, 5th Minnesota Infantry. *Place and date:* At Nashville, Tenn., 16 December 1864. *Entered service at:* ———. *Birth:* Chemung County, N.Y. *Date of issue:* 24 February 1865. *Citation:* Capture of flag of 4th Mississippi (C.S.A.).

GESCHWIND, NICHOLAS

Rank and organization: Captain, Company F, 116th Illinois Infantry. *Place and date:* At Vicksburg, Miss., 22 May 1863. *Entered service at:* Pleasant Hill, Ill. *Birth:* France. *Date of issue:* 24 August 1894. *Citation:* Gallantry in the charge of the "volunteer storming party."

GIBBS, WESLEY

Rank and organization: Sergeant, Company B, 2d Connecticut Heavy Artillery. *Place and date:* At Petersburg, Va., 2 April 1865. *Entered service at:* Salisbury, Conn. *Birth:* Sharon, Conn. *Date of issue:* 10 May 1865. *Citation:* Capture of flag.

784

GIFFORD, BENJAMIN

Rank and organization: Private, Company H, 121st New York Infantry. *Place and date:* At Sailors Creek, Va., 6 April 1865. *Entered service at:* German Flats, N.Y. *Birth:* German Flats, N.Y. *Date of issue:* 10 May 1865. *Citation:* Capture of flag.

GIFFORD, DAVID L.

Rank and organization: Private, Company B, 4th Massachusetts Cavalry. *Place and date:* At Ashepoo River, S.C., 24 May 1864. *Entered service at:* ———. *Birth:* Dartmouth, Mass. *Date of issue:* 21 January 1897. *Citation:* Volunteered as a member of a boat crew which went to the rescue of a large number of Union soldiers on board the stranded steamer *Boston* and with great gallantry assisted in conveying them to shore, being exposed during the entire time to a heavy fire from a Confederate battery.

GILE, FRANK S.

Rank and organization: Landsman, U.S. Navy. *Born:* 1845, Massachusetts. *Accredited to:* Massachusetts. *G.O. No.:* 32, 16 April 1864. *Citation:* On board the U.S.S. *Lehigh*, Charleston Harbor, 16 November 1863, during the hazardous task of freeing the *Lehigh*, which had been grounded, and was under heavy enemy fire from Fort Moultrie. After several previous attempts had been made, Gile succeeded in passing in a small boat from the *Lehigh* to the *Nahant* with a line bent on a hawser. This courageous action while under severe enemy fire enabled the *Lehigh* to be freed from her helpless position.

GILLESPIE, GEORGE L.

Rank and organization: First Lieutenant, Corps of Engineers, U.S. Army. *Place and date:* Near Bethesda Church, Va., 31 May 1864. *Entered service at:* Chattanooga, Tenn. *Birth:* Kingston, Tenn. *Date of issue:* 27 October 1897. *Citation:* Exposed himself to great danger by voluntarily making his way through the enemy's lines to communicate with Gen. Sheridan. While rendering this service he was captured, but escaped; again came in contact with the enemy, was again ordered to surrender, but escaped by dashing away under fire.

GILLIGAN, EDWARD L.

Rank and organization: First Sergeant, Company E, 88th Pennsylvania Infantry. *Place and date:* At Gettysburg, Pa., 1 July 1863. *Entered service at:* Philadelphia, Pa. *Birth:* Philadelphia, Pa. *Date of issue:* 30 April 1892. *Citation:* Assisted in the capture of a Confederate flag by knocking down the color sergeant.

GILMORE, JOHN C.

Rank and organization: Major, 16th New York Infantry. *Place and date:* At Salem Heights, Va., 3 May 1863. *Entered service at:* Potsdam, N.Y. *Birth:* Canada. *Date of issue:* 10 October 1892. *Citation:* Seized the colors of his regiment and gallantly rallied his men under a very severe fire.

GINLEY, PATRICK

Rank and organization: Private, Company G, 1st New York Light Artillery. *Place and date:* At Reams Station, Va., 25 August 1864. *Entered service at:* New York, N.Y. *Born:* 22 December 1822, Ireland. *Date of issue:* 31 October 1890. *Citation:* The command having been driven from the works, he, having been left alone between the opposing lines, crept back into the works, put 3 charges of canister in one of the guns, and fired the piece directly into a body of the enemy about to seize the works; he then rejoined his command, took the colors, and ran toward the enemy, followed by the command, which recaptured the works and guns.

GION, JOSEPH

Rank and organization: Private, Company A, 74th New York Infantry. *Place and date:* At Chancellorsville, Va., 2 May 1863. *Entered service at:* Allegheny County, Pa. *Birth:* ———. *Date of issue:* 26 November 1884. *Citation:* Voluntarily and under heavy fire advanced toward the enemy's lines and secured valuable information.

GODLEY, LEONIDAS M.

Rank and organization: First Sergeant, Company E., 22d Iowa Infantry. *Place and date:* At Vicksburg, Miss., 22 May 1863. *Entered service at:* Ashland, Iowa. *Birth:* Mason County, W. Va. *Date of issue:* 3 August 1897. *Citation:* Led his company in the assault on the enemy's works and gained the parapet, there receiving 3 very severe wounds. He lay all day in the sun, was taken prisoner, and had his leg amputated without anesthetics.

GOETTEL, PHILIP

Rank and organization: Private, Company B, 149th New York Infantry. *Place and date:* At Ringgold, Ga., 27 November 1863. *Entered service at:* Syracuse, N.Y. *Birth:* Syracuse, N.Y. *Date of issue:* 28 June 1865. *Citation:* Capture of flag and battery guidon.

GOHEEN, CHARLES A.

Rank and organization: First Sergeant, Company G, 8th New York Cavalry. *Place and date:* At Waynesboro, Va., 2 March 1865. *Entered service at:* ———. *Birth:* Groveland, N.Y. *Date of issue:* 26 March 1865. *Citation:* Capture of flag.

GOLDSBERY, ANDREW E.

Rank and organization: Private, Company E, 127th Illinois Infantry. *Place and date:* At Vicksburg, Miss., 22 May 1863. *Entered service at:* St. Charles, Kane County, Ill. *Birth:* St. Charles, Kane County, Ill. *Date of issue:* 9 August 1894. *Citation:* Gallantry in the charge of the "volunteer storming party."

GOODALL, FRANCIS H.

Rank and organization: First Sergeant, Company G, 11th New Hampshire Infantry. *Place and date:* At Fredericksburg, Va., 13 December 1862. *Entered service at:* Bath, N.H. *Birth:* Bath, N.H. *Date of issue:* 14 December 1894. *Citation:* With the assistance of another soldier brought a wounded comrade into the lines, under heavy fire.

GOODMAN, WILLIAM E.

Rank and organization: First Lieutenant, Company D, 147th Pennsylvania Infantry. *Place and date:* At Chancellorsville, Va., 3 May 1863. *Entered service at:* Philadelphia, Pa. *Born:* 10 December 1838, Philadelphia, Pa. *Date of issue:* 11 January 1894. *Citation:* Rescued the colors of the 107th Ohio Volunteers from the enemy.

GOODRICH, EDWIN

Rank and organization: First Lieutenant, Company D, 9th New York Cavalry. *Place and date:* Near Cedar Creek, Va., November 1864. *Entered service at:* Westfield, N.Y. *Birth:* New York, N.Y. *Date of issue:* 14 May 1894. *Citation:* While the command was falling back, he returned, and in the face of the enemy rescued a sergeant from under his fallen horse.

GOULD, CHARLES G.

Rank and organization: Captain, Company H, 5th Vermont Infantry. *Place and date:* At Petersburg, Va., 2 April 1865. *Entered service at:* Windham, Vt. *Birth:* Windham, Vt. *Date of issue:* 30 July 1890. *Citation:* Among the first to mount the enemy's works in the assault, he received a serious bayonet wound in the face, was struck several times with clubbed muskets, but bravely stood his ground, and with his sword killed the man who bayoneted him.

GOULD, NEWTON T.

Rank and organization: Private, Company G, 113th Illinois Infantry. *Place and date:* At Vicksburg, Miss., 22 May 1863. *Entered service at:* Elk Grove, Ill. *Birth:* Elk Grove, Ill, *Date of issue:* 6 September 1894. *Citation:* Gallantry in the charge of the "volunteer storming party."

GOURAUD, GEORGE E.

Rank and organization: Captain and aide-de-camp, U.S. Volunteers. *Place and date:* At Honey Hill, S.C., 30 November 1864. *Entered service at:* ———. *Birth:* New York, N.Y. *Date of issue:* 21 August 1893. *Citation:* While under severe fire of the enemy, which drove back the command, rendered valuable assistance in rallying the men.

GRACE, PETER

Rank and organization: Sergeant, Company G, 83d Pennsylvania Infantry. *Place and date:* At Wilderness, Va., 5 May 1864. *Entered service at:* Berkshire, Mass. *Birth:* Berkshire, Mass. *Date of issue:* 27 December 1894. *Citation:* Singlehanded, rescued a comrade from 2 Confederate guards, knocking down one and compelling surrender of the other.

GRAHAM, ROBERT

Rank and organization: Landsman, U.S. Navy. *Born:* 1841, England. *Accredited to:* New York. *G.O. No.:* 45, 31 December 1864. *Citation:* Served on board the U.S.S. *Tacony* during the taking of Plymouth,

N.C., 31 October 1864. Carrying out his duties faithfully during the capture of Plymouth, Graham distinguished himself by a display of coolness when he participated in landing and spiking a 9-inch gun while under a devastating fire from enemy musketry.

GRAHAM, THOMAS N.

Rank and organization: Second Lieutenant, Company G, 15th Indiana Infantry. *Place and date:* At Missionary Ridge, Tenn., 25 November 1863. *Entered service at:* Westville, LaPorte County, Ind. *Birth:* ———. *Date of issue:* 15 February 1897. *Citation:* Seized the colors from the color bearer, who had been wounded, and, exposed to a terrible fire, carried them forward, planting them on the enemy's breastworks.

GRANT, GABRIEL

Rank and organization: Surgeon, U.S. Volunteers. *Place and date:* At Fair Oaks, Va., 1 June 1862. *Entered service at:* New York. *Born:* Newark, N.J. *Date of issue:* 21 July 1897. *Citation:* Removed severely wounded officers and soldiers from the field while under a heavy fire from the enemy, exposing himself beyond the call of duty, thus furnishing an example of most distinguished gallantry.

GRANT, LEWIS A.

Rank and organization: Colonel, 5th Vermont Infantry. *Place and date:* At Salem Heights, Va., 3 May 1864. *Entered service at:* Bellow Falls, Vt. *Born:* 17 January 1828, Winhall, Vt. *Date of issue:* 11 May 1893. *Citation:* Personal gallantry and intrepidity displayed in the management of his brigade and in leading it in the assault in which he was wounded.

GRAUL, WILLIAM

Rank and organization: Corporal, Company I, 188th Pennsylvania Infantry. *Place and date:* At Fort Harrison, Va., 29 September 1864. *Entered service at:* Reading, Pa. *Birth:* Reading, Pa. *Date of issue:* 6 April 1865. *Citation:* First to plant the colors of his State on the fortifications.

GRAY, JOHN

Rank and organization: Private, Company B, 5th Ohio Infantry. *Place and date:* At Port Republic, Va., 9 June 1862. *Entered service at:* Hamilton County, Ohio. *Birth:* Scotland. *Date of issue:* 14 March 1864. *Citation:* Mounted an artillery horse of the enemy and captured a brass 6-pound piece in the face of the enemy's fire and brought it to the rear.

GRAY, ROBERT A.

Rank and organization: Sergeant, Company C, 21st Connecticut Infantry. *Place and date:* At Drurys Bluff, Va., 16 May 1864. *Entered service at:* Groton, Conn. *Birth:* Philadelphia, Pa. *Date of issue:* 13 July 1897. *Citation:* While retreating with his regiment, which had been repulsed, he voluntarily returned, in face of the enemy's fire, to a former position and rescued a wounded officer of his company who was unable to walk.

GREBE, M. R. WILLIAM

Rank and organization: Captain, Company F, 4th Missouri Calvary. *Place and date:* At Jonesboro, Ga., 31 August 1864. *Entered service at:* St. Louis, Mo. *Born:* 4 August 1838, Germany. *Date of issue:* 24 February 1899. *Citation:* While acting as aide and carrying orders across a most dangerous part of the battlefield, being hindered by a Confederate advance, seized a rifle, took a place in the ranks and was conspicuous in repulsing the enemy.

GREEN, GEORGE

Rank and organization: Corporal, Company H, 11th Ohio Infantry. *Place and date:* At Missionary Ridge, Tenn., 25 November 1863. *Entered service at:* ———. *Born:* 1840, England. *Date of issue:* 12 January 1892. *Citation:* Scaled the enemy's works and in a hand-to-hand fight helped capture the flag of the 18th Alabama Infantry (C.S.A.).

GREENAWALT, ABRAHAM

Rank and organization: Private, Company G, 104th Ohio Infantry. *Place and date:* At Franklin, Tenn., 30 November 1864. *Entered service at:* Salem, Ohio. *Birth:* Montgomery County, Pa. *Date of issue:* 13 February 1865. *Citation:* Capture of corps headquarters flag (C.S.A.).

GREENE, JOHN

Rank and organization: Captain of the Forecastle, U.S. Navy. *Entered service at:* New York. *Birth:* ———. *G.O. No.* 11, 3 April 1863. *Citation:* Captain of a gun on board the U.S.S. *Varuna* during the attacks on Forts Jackson and St. Philip, and while under fire and ramming by the rebel ship *Morgan*, 24 April 1862. During this action at extremely close range while his ship was under furious fire and twice rammed by the rebel ship *Morgan*, Greene remained steadfast at his gun throughout the thickest of the fight and was instrumental in inflicting damage on the enemy until the *Varuna*, badly damaged and forced to beach, was finally sunk.

GREENE, OLIVER D.

Rank and organization: Major and Assistant Adjutant General, U.S. Army. *Place and date:* At Antietam, Md., 17 September 1862. *Entered service at:* Scott, N.Y. *Born:* 25 January 1833, Scott, N.Y. *Date of issue:* 13 December 1893. *Citation:* Formed the columns under heavy fire and put them into position.

GREGG, JOSEPH O.

Rank and organization: Private, Company F, 133d Ohio Infantry. *Place and date:* Near the Richmond & Petersburg Ry., Va., 16 June 1864. *Entered service at:* ———. *Born:* 5 January 1841, Circleville, Ohio. *Date of issue:* 13 May 1899. *Citation:* Voluntarily returned to the breastworks which his regiment had been forced to abandon to notify 3 missing companies that the regiment was falling back; found the enemy already in the works, refused a demand to surrender, returning to his command under a concentrated fire, several bullets passing through his hat and clothing.

GREIG, THEODORE W.

Rank and organization: Second Lieutenant, Company C, 61st New York Infantry. *Place and date:* At Antietam, Md., 17 September 1862. *Entered service at:* Staten Island, N.Y. *Birth:* New York. *Date of issue:* 10 February 1887. *Citation:* A Confederate regiment, the 4th Alabama Infantry (C.S.A.), having planted its battle flag slightly in advance of the regiment, this officer rushed forward and seized it, and, although shot through the neck, retained the flag and brought it within the Union lines.

GRESSER, IGNATZ

Rank and organization: Corporal, Company D, 128th Pennsylvania Infantry. *Place and date:* At Antietam, Md., 17 September 1862. *Entered service at:* Lehigh County, Pa. *Born:* 15 August 1832, Germany. *Date of issue:* 12 December 1895. *Citation:* While exposed to the fire of the enemy, carried from the field a wounded comrade.

GRIBBEN, JAMES H.

Rank and organization: Lieutenant, Company C, 2d New York Cavalry. *Place and date:* At Sailors Creek, Va., 6 April 1865. *Entered service at:* ———. *Birth:* Ireland. *Date of issue:* 3 May 1865. *Citation:* Capture of flag of 12th Virginia Infantry (C.S.A.).

GRIFFITHS, JOHN

Rank and organization: Captain of the Forecastle, U.S. Navy. *Born:* 1835, Wales. *Accredited to:* Massachusetts. *G.O. No.:* 59, 22 June 1865. *Citation:* On board the U.S.S. *Santiago de Cuba* during the assault on Fort Fisher on 15 January 1865. As one of a boatcrew detailed to one of the generals on shore, Griffiths bravely entered the fort in the assault and accompanied his party in carrying dispatches at the height of the battle. He was one of 6 men who entered the fort in the assault from the fleet.

GRIMSHAW, SAMUEL

Rank and organization: Private, Company B, 52d Ohio Infantry. *Place and date:* At Atlanta, Ga., 6 August 1864. *Entered service at:* ———. *Birth:* Jefferson County, Ohio. *Date of issue:* 5 April 1894. *Citation:* Saved the lives of some of his comrades, and greatly imperiled his own by picking up and throwing away a lighted shell which had fallen in the midst of the company.

GRINDLAY, JAMES G.

Rank and organization: Colonel, 146th New York Infantry. *Place and date:* At Five Forks, Va., 1 April 1865. *Entered service at:* Utica, N.Y. *Birth:* ———. *Date of issue:* 14 August 1891. *Citation:* The first to enter the enemy's works, where he captured 2 flags.

GRISWOLD, LUKE M.

Rank and organization: Ordinary Seaman, U.S. Navy. *Born:* 1837, Massachusetts. *Accredited to:* Massachusetts. *G.O. No.:* 59, 22 June 1865. *Citation:* Served on board the U.S.S. *Rhode Island* which was engaged in saving the lives of the officers and crew of the *Monitor*, 30 December 1862. Participating in the hazardous rescue of the officers and crew of the sinking *Monitor*, Griswold, after rescuing several of the men, became separated in a heavy gale with other members of the cutter that had set out from the *Rhode Island*, and spent many hours in the small boat at the mercy of the weather and high seas until finally picked up by a schooner 50 miles east of Cape Hatteras.

GRUEB, GEORGE

Rank and organization: Private, Company E, 158th New York Infantry. *Place and date:* At Chapins Farm, Va., 29 September 1864. *Entered service at:* New York, N.Y. *Birth:* Germany. *Date of issue:* 6 April 1865. *Citation:* Gallantry in advancing to the ditch of the enemy's works.

GUERIN, FITZ W.

Rank and organization: Private, Battery A, 1st Missouri Light Artillery. *Place and date:* At Grand Gulf, Miss., 28–29 April 1863. *Entered service at:* St. Louis, Mo. *Birth:* New York, N.Y. *Date of issue:* 10 March 1896. *Citation:* With two comrades voluntarily took position on board the steamer *Cheeseman*, in charge of all the guns and ammunition of the battery, and remained in charge of the same for a considerable time while the steamer was unmanageable and subjected to a heavy fire from the enemy.

GUINN, THOMAS

Rank and organization: Private, Company D, 47th Ohio Infantry. *Place and date:* At Vicksburg, Miss., 22 May 1863. *Entered service at:* ———. *Birth:* Clinton County, Ohio. *Date of issue:* 21 August 1894. *Citation:* Gallantry in the charge of the "volunteer storming party."

GWYNNE, NATHANIEL

Rank and organization: Private, Company H, 13th Ohio Cavalry. *Place and date:* At Petersburg, Va., 30 July 1864. *Entered service at:* Fairmount, Mo. *Birth:* Champaign County, Ohio. *Date of issue:* 27 January 1865. *Citation:* When about entering upon the charge, this soldier, then but 15 years old, was cautioned not to go in, as he had not been mustered. He indignantly protected and participated in the charge, his left arm being crushed by a shell and amputated soon afterward.

HACK, JOHN

Rank and organization: Private, Company B, 47th Ohio Infantry. *Place and date:* At Vicksburg, Miss., 3 May 1863. *Entered service at:* Adrian, Mich. *Birth:* 1843, Germany. *Date of issue:* 3 January 1907. *Citation:* Was one of a party which volunteered and attempted to run the enemy's batteries with a steam tug and 2 barges loaded with subsistence stores.

HACK, LESTER G.

Rank and organization: Sergeant, Company F, 5th Vermont Infantry. *Place and date:* At Petersburg, Va., 2 April 1865. *Entered service at:*

Salisbury, Vt. *Born:* 18 January 1841, Bolton, N.Y. *Date of issue:* 10 May 1865. *Citation:* Capture of flag of 23d Tennessee Infantry (C.S.A.) with several of the enemy.

HADLEY, CORNELIUS M.

Rank and organization: Sergeant, Company F, 9th Michigan Cavalry. *Place and date:* At siege of Knoxville, Tenn., 20 November 1863. *Entered service at:* Adrian, Mich. *Born:* 27 April 1838, Sandy Creek, Oswego County, N.Y. *Date of issue:* 5 April 1898. *Citation:* With one companion, voluntarily carried through the enemy's lines important dispatches from Gen. Grant to Gen. Burnside, then besieged within Knoxville, and brought back replies, his comrade's horse being killed and the man taken prisoner.

HADLEY, OSGOOD T.

Rank and organization: Corporal, Company E, 6th New Hampshire Veteran Infantry. *Place and date:* Near Pegram House, Va., 30 September 1864. *Entered service at:* ———. *Birth:* Nashua, N.H. *Date of issue:* 27 July 1896. *Citation:* As color bearer of his regiment he defended his colors with great personal gallantry and brought them safely out of the action.

HAFFEE, EDMUND

Rank and organization: Quarter Gunner, U.S. Navy. *Born:* 1832, Philadelphia, Pa. *Accredited to:* Pennsylvania. *G.O. No.:* 59, 22 June 1865. *Citation:* Haffee served on board the U.S.S. *New Ironsides* during action in several attacks on Fort Fisher, 24 and 25 December 1864; and 13, 14, and 15 January 1865. The ship steamed in and took the lead in the ironclad division close inshore, and immediately opened its starboard battery in a barrage of well-directed fire to cause several fires and explosions and dismount several guns during the first 2 days of fighting. Taken under fire, as she steamed into position on 13 January, the *New Ironsides* fought all day and took on ammunition at night despite severe weather conditions. When the enemy came out of his bombproof to defend the fort against the storming party, the ship's battery disabled nearly every gun on the fort facing the shore before the cease-fire orders were given by the flagship.

HAGERTY, ASEL

Rank and organization: Private, Company A, 61st New York Infantry. *Place and date:* At Sailors Creek, Va., 6 April 1865. *Entered service at:* ———. *Birth:* Canada, *Date of issue:* 10 May 1865. *Citation:* Capture of flag.

HAIGHT, JOHN H.

Rank and organization: Sergeant, Company G, 72d New York Infantry. *Place and date:* At Williamsburg, Va., 5 May 1862. At Bristol Station, Va., 27 August 1862. At Manassas, Va., 29–30 August 1862. *Entered service at:* Westfield, N.Y. *Born:* 1 July 1841, Westfield, N.Y. *Date of issue:* 8 June 1888. *Citation:* At Williamsburg, Va., voluntarily carried a severely wounded comrade off the field in the face of a large force of the enemy; in doing so was himself severely wounded and taken prisoner. Went into the fight at Bristol Station, Va., although severely disabled. At Manassas, volunteered to search the woods for the wounded.

HAIGHT, SIDNEY

Rank and organization: Corporal, Company E, 1st Michigan Sharpshooters. *Place and date:* At Petersburg, Va., 30 July 1864. *Entered service at:* Goodland, Mich. *Born:* 1846, Reading, Mich. *Date of issue:* 31 July 1896. *Citation:* Instead of retreating, remained in the captured works, regardless of his personal safety and exposed to the firing, which he boldly and deliberately returned until the enemy was close upon him.

HALEY, JAMES

Rank and organization: Captain of the Forecastle, U.S. Navy. *Born:* 1824, Ireland. *Accredited to:* Ohio. *G.O. No.:* 45, 31 December 1864. *Citation:* Served as captain of the forecastle on board the U.S.S. *Kearsarge* when she destroyed the *Alabama* off Cherbourg, France, 19 June 1864. Acting as captain of a gun during the bitter engagement, Haley exhibited marked coolness and good conduct and was highly commended by his division officer for his gallantry and meritorious achievement under enemy fire.

HALL, FRANCIS B.

Rank and organization: Chaplain, 16th New York Infantry. *Place and date:* At Salem Heights, Va., 3 May 1863. *Entered service at:* Plattsburgh, N.Y. *Birth:* ———. *Date of issue:* 16 February 1897. *Citation:* Voluntarily exposed himself to a heavy fire during the thickest of the fight and carried wounded men to the rear for treatment and attendance.

HALL, HENRY SEYMOUR

Rank and organization: Second Lieutenant, Company G, 27th New York Infantry; and Captain, Company F, 121st New York Infantry. *Place and date:* At Gaines Mill, Va., 27 June 1862. At Rappahannock Station, Va., 7 November 1863. *Entered service at:* New York. *Birth:* New York. *Date of issue:* 17 August 1891. *Citation:* Although wounded at Gaines Mill, Va., he remained on duty and participated in the battle with his company. At Rappahannock Station, Va., while acting as aide, rendered gallant and prompt assistance in reforming the regiments inside the enemy's works.

HALL, NEWTON H.

Rank and organization: Corporal, Company I, 104th Ohio Infantry. *Place and date:* At Franklin, Tenn., 30 November 1864. *Entered service at:* ———. *Birth:* Portage County, Ohio. *Date of issue:* 13 February 1865. *Citation:* Capture of flag, believed to have belonged to Stewart's Corps (C.S.A.).

HALLOCK, NATHAN M.

Rank and organization: Private, Company K, 124th New York Infantry. *Place and date:* At Bristoe Station, Va., 15 June 1863. *Entered service at:* Middletown, N.Y. *Birth:* Orange County, N.Y. *Date of issue:* 10 September 1897. *Citation:* At imminent peril saved from death or capture a disabled officer of his company by carrying him under a hot musketry fire, to a place of safety.

HALSTEAD, WILLIAM

Rank and organization: Coxswain, U.S. Navy. *Born:* 1837, New York. *Accredited to:* New York. *G.O. No.:* 45, 31 December 1864. *Citation:* On board the U.S.S. *Brooklyn* during action against rebel forts and gunboats and with the ram *Tennessee*, in Mobile Bay, 5 August 1864. Despite severe damage to his ship and the loss of several men on board as enemy fire raked her decks from stem to stern, Halstead fought his gun with skill and courage throughout the furious battle which resulted in the surrender of the prize rebel ram *Tennessee* and in the damaging and destruction of batteries at Fort Morgan.

HAM, MARK G.

Rank and organization: Carpenter's Mate, U.S. Navy. *Born:* 1820, Portsmouth, N.H. *Accredited to:* New Hampshire. *G.O. No.:* 45, 31 December 1864. *Citation:* Served on board the U.S.S. *Kearsarge* when she destroyed the *Alabama* off Cherbourg, France, 19 June 1864. Performing his duties intelligently and faithfully, Ham distinguished himself in the face of the bitter enemy fire and was highly commended by his divisional officer.

HAMILTON, HUGH

Rank and organization: Coxswain, U.S. Navy. *Born:* 1830, New York, N.Y. *Accredited to:* New York. *G.O. No.:* 45, 31 December 1864. *Citation:* On board the U.S.S. *Richmond* during action against rebel forts and gunboats and with the ram *Tennessee* in Mobile Bay, 5 August 1864. Despite damage to his ship and the loss of several men on board as enemy fire raked her decks, Hamilton performed his duties with skill and courage throughout the prolonged battle which resulted in the surrender of the rebel ram *Tennessee* and in the successful attacks carried out on Fort Morgan.

HAMILTON, RICHARD

Rank and organization: Coal Heaver, U.S. Navy. *Born:* 1836, Philadelphia, Pa. *Accredited to:* Pennsylvania *G.O. No.:* 45, 31 December 1864. *Citation:* Hamilton served on board the U.S. Picket Boat No. 1, in action, 27 October 1864, against the Confederate ram *Albemarle* which had resisted repeated attacks by our steamers and had kept a large force of vessels employed in watching her. The picket boat, equipped with a spar torpedo, succeeded in passing the enemy pickets within 20 yards without being discovered and then made for the *Albemarle* under a full head of steam. Immediately taken under fire by the ram, the small boat plunged on, jumped the log boom which encircled the target and exploded its torpedo under the port bow of the ram. The picket boat was destoryed by enemy fire and almost the entire crew taken prisoner or lost.

HAMILTON, THOMAS W.

Rank and organization: Quartermaster, U.S. Navy. *Born:* 1833, Scotland. *Accredited to:* Massachusetts. *G.O. No.:* 17, 10 July 1863. *Citation:* Serving as quartermaster on board the U.S.S. *Cincinnati* during the attack on the Vicksburg batteries and at the time of her sinking, 27 May 1863. Engaging the enemy in a fierce battle, the *Cincinnati*, amidst an incessant fire of shot and shell, continued to fire her guns to the last although so penetrated by enemy shell fire that her fate was sealed. Conspicuously gallant during this action, Hamilton, severely wounded at the wheel, returned to his post and had to be sent below, to hear the incessant roar of guns as the gallant ship went down, "her colors nailed to the mast."

HAMMEL, HENRY A.

Rank and organization: Sergeant, Battery A, 1st Missouri Light Artillery. *Place and date:* At Grand Gulf, Miss., 28–29 April 1863. *Entered service at:* St. Louis, Mo. *Birth:* Germany. *Date of issue:* 10 March 1896. *Citation:* With two comrades voluntarily took position on board the steamer *Cheeseman*, in charge of all the guns and ammunition of the battery, and remained in charge of the same for considerable time while the steamer was unmanageable and subjected to a heavy fire from the enemy.

HAND, ALLEXANDER

Rank and organization: Quartermaster, U.S. Navy. *Born:* 1836, Delaware. *Accredited to:* Delaware. *G.O. No.:* 11, 3 April 1863. *Citation:* Served on board the U.S.S. *Ceres* in the fight near Hamilton, Roanoke River, 9 July 1862. Fired on by the enemy with small arms, Hand courageously returned the raking enemy fire and was spoken of for "good conduct and cool bravery under enemy fire," by the commanding officer.

HANEY, MILTON L.

Rank and organization: Chaplain, 55th Illinois Infantry. *Place and date:* At Atlanta, Ga., 22 July 1864. *Entered service at:* Bushnell, Ill. *Birth:* Ohio. *Date of issue:* 3 November 1896. *Citation:* Voluntarily carried a musket in the ranks of his regiment and rendered heroic service in retaking the Federal works which had been captured by the enemy.

HANFORD, EDWARD R.

Rank and organization: Private, Company H, 2d U.S. Cavalry. *Place and date:* At Woodstock, Va., 9 October 1864. *Entered service at:* ———. *Birth:* Allegany County, N.Y. *Date of issue:* 14 October 1864. *Citation:* Capture of flag of 32d Battalion Virginia Cavalry (C.S.A.).

HANKS, JOSEPH

Rank and organization: Private, Company E, 37th Ohio Infantry. *Place and date:* At Vicksburg, Miss., 22 May 1863. *Entered service at:* Chillicothe, Ohio. *Birth:* Chillicothe, Ohio. *Date of issue:* 19 November 1897. *Citation:* Voluntarily and under fire went to the rescue of a wounded comrade lying between the lines, gave him water, and brought him off the field.

HANNA, MARCUS A.

Rank and organization: Sergeant, Company B, 50th Massachusetts Infantry. *Place and date:* At Port Hudson, La., 4 July 1863. *Entered service at:* Rockport, Mass. *Born:* 3 November 1842, Bristol, Maine. *Date of issue:* 2 November 1895. *Citation:* Voluntarily exposed himself to a heavy fire to get water for comrades in rifle pits.

HANNA, MILTON

Rank and organization: Corporal, Company H, 2d Minnesota Infantry. *Place and date:* At Nolensville, Tenn., 15 February 1863. *Entered service at:* Henderson, Minn. *Birth:* Lickland County, Ohio. *Date of issue:* 11 September 1897. *Citation:* Was one of a detachment of 16 men who heroically defended a wagon train against the attack of 125 cavalry, repulsed the attack and saved the train.

HANSCOM, MOSES C.

Rank and organization: Corporal, Company F, 19th Maine Infantry. *Place and date:* At Bristoe Station, Va., 14 October 1863. *Entered service at:* Bowdoinham, Maine. *Birth:* Danville, Maine. *Date of issue:* 1 December 1864. *Citation:* Capture of the flag of 26th North Carolina (C.S.A.).

HAPEMAN, DOUGLAS

Rank and organization: Lieutenant Colonel, 104th Illinois Infantry. *Place and date:* At Peach Tree Creek, Ga., 20 July 1864. *Entered service at:* Ottawa, Ill. *Born:* 15 January 1839, Ephratah, Fulton County, N.Y. *Date of issue:* 5 April 1898. *Citation:* With conspicuous coolness and bravery rallied his men under a severe attack, re-formed the broken ranks, and repulsed the attack.

HARBOURNE, JOHN H.

Rank and organization: Private, Company K, 29th Massachusetts Infantry. *Place and date:* At Petersburg, Va., 17 June 1864. *Entered service at:* Boston, Mass. *Born:* 9 September 1840, England. *Date of issue:* 24 February 1897. *Citation:* Capture of flag along with 3 enemy men.

HARCOURT, THOMAS

Rank and organization: Ordinary Seaman, U.S. Navy. *Born:* 1841, Boston, Mass. *Accredited to:* Massachusetts. *G.O. No.:* 59, 22 June 1865. *Citation:* On board the U.S.S. *Minnesota* in action during the assault on Fort Fisher, 15 January 1865. Landing on the beach with the assaulting party from his ship, Harcourt advanced to the top of the sandhill and partly through the breach in the palisades despite enemy fire which killed and wounded many officers and men. When more than two-thirds of the men become seized with panic and retreated on the run, he remained with the party until dark when it came safely away, bringing its wounded, its arms and its colors.

*HARDENBERGH, HENRY M.

Rank and organization: Private, Company G, 39th Illinois Infantry. *Place and date:* At Deep Run, Va., 16 August 1864. *Entered service at:*

Bremen, Ill. *Birth:* Noble County, Ind. *Date of issue:* 6 April 1865. *Citation:* Capture of flag. He was wounded in the shoulder during this action. He was killed in action at Petersburg on 28 August 1864.

HARDING, THOMAS

Rank and organization: Captain of the Forecastle, U.S. Navy. *Born:* 1837, Middletown, Conn. *Accredited to:* Connecticut. *G.O. No.:* 45, 31 December 1864. *Citation:* Served as captain of the forecastle on board the U.S.S. *Dacotah* on the occasion of the destruction of the blockade runner *Pevensey*, near Beauford, N.C., 9 June 1864. "Learning that one of the officers in the boat, which was in danger of being, and subsequently was, swamped, could not swim, Harding remarked to him: 'If we are swamped, sir, I shall carry you to the beach or I will never go there myself.' He did not succeed in carrying out his promise, but made desperate efforts to do so, while others thought only of themselves. Such conduct is worthy of appreciation and admiration—a sailor risking his own life to save that of an officer."

HARING, ABRAM P.

Rank and organization: First Lieutenant, Company G, 132d New York Infantry. *Place and date:* At Bachelors Creek, N.C., 1 February 1864. *Entered service at:* New York, N.Y., *Birth:* New York, N.Y. *Date of issue:* 28 June 1890. *Citation:* With a command of 11 men, on picket, resisted the attack of an overwhelming force of the enemy.

HARLEY, BERNARD

Rank and organization: Ordinary Seaman, U.S. Navy. *Born:* 1842, Brooklyn, N.Y. *Accredited to:* New York. *G.O. No.:* 45, 31 December 1864. *Citation:* Harley served on board the U.S. Picket Boat No. 1, in action, 27 October 1864, against the Confederate ram *Albemarle*, which had resisted repeated attacks by our steamers and had kept a large force of vessels employed in watching her. The picket boat, equipped with a spar torpedo, succeeded in passing the enemy pickets within 20 yards without being discovered and then made for the *Albemarle* under a full head of steam. Immediately taken under fire by the ram, the small boat plunged on, jumped the log boom which encircled the target and exploded its torpedo under the port bow of the ram. The picket boat was destroyed by enemy fire and almost the entire crew taken prisoner or lost.

HARMON, AMZI D.

Rank and organization: Corporal, Company K, 211th Pennsylvania Infantry. *Place and date:* At Petersburg, Va., 2 April 1865. *Entered service at:* ———. *Birth:* Westmoreland County, Pa. *Date of issue:* 20 May 1865. *Citation:* Capture of flag.

HARRINGTON, DANIEL

Rank and organization: Landsman, U.S. Navy. *Born:* 1849, Ireland. *Accredited to:* Massachusetts. *G.O. No.:* 11, 3 April 1863. *Citation:* Harrington, a landsman from the U.S.S. *Pocahontas*, participated in a shore mission to procure meat for the ship's crew. While returning to the beach, the party was fired on from ambush and several men killed or wounded. Cool and courageous throughout his action, Harrington rendered gallant service against the enemy and in administering to the casualties.

HARRINGTON, EPHRAIM W.

Rank and organization: Sergeant, Company G, 2d Vermont Infantry. *Place and date:* At Fredericksburg, Va., 3 May 1863. *Entered service at:* Kirby, Vt. *Birth:* Waterford, Maine. *Date of issue:* 13 December 1893. *Citation:* Carried the colors to the top of the heights and almost to the muzzle of the enemy's guns.

HARRIS, GEORGE W.

Rank and organization: Private, Company B, 148th Pennsylvania Infantry. *Place and date:* At Spotsylvania, Va., 12 May 1864. *Entered service at:* Bellefonte, Pa. *Birth:* Schuylkill, Pa. *Date of issue:* 1 December 1864. *Citation:* Capture of flag, wresting it from the color bearer and shooting an officer who attempted to regain it.

HARRIS, JAMES H.

Rank and organization: Sergeant, Company B, 38th U.S. Colored Troops. *Place and date:* At New Market Heights, Va., 29 September 1864. *Entered service at:* ———. *Birth:* St. Marys County, Md. *Date of issue:* 18 February 1874. *Citation:* Gallantry in the assault.

HARRIS, JOHN

Rank and organization: Captain of the Forecastle, U.S. Navy. *Born:* 1839, Scotland. *Accredited to:* New York. *G.O. No.:* 17, 15 January 1866. *Citation:* As captain of the forecastle on board the U.S.S. *Metacomet*, Harris was a member of the boat's crew which went to the rescue of the officers and crew of the U.S. Monitor *Tecumseh*, when that vessel was struck by a torpedo in passing the enemy forts in Mobile Bay, 5 August 1864. Harris braved the enemy fire which was said by the admiral to be "one of the most galling" he had ever seen, and aided in rescuing from death 10 of the crew of the *Tecumseh*, thereby eliciting the admiration of both friend and foe.

HARRIS, MOSES

Rank and organization: First Lieutenant, 1st U.S. Cavalry. *Place and date:* At Smithfield, Va., 28 August 1864. *Entered service at:* New Hampshire. *Birth:* Andover, N.H. *Date of issue:* 23 January 1896. *Citation:* In an attack upon a largely superior force, his personal gallantry was so conspicuous as to inspire the men to extraordinary efforts, resulting in complete rout of the enemy.

HARRIS, SAMPSON

Rank and organization: Private, Company K, 30th Ohio Infantry. *Place and date:* At Vicksburg, Miss., 22 May 1863. *Entered service at:* Olive, Ohio. *Birth:* Noble County, Ohio. *Date of issue:* 10 July 1894. *Citation:* Gallantry in the charge of the "volunteer storming party."

HARRISON, GEORGE H.

Rank and organization: Seaman, U.S. Navy. *Born:* 1842, Massachusetts. *Accredited to:* Massachusetts. *G.O. No. 45,* 31 December 1864. *Citation:* Served on board the U.S.S. *Kearsarge* when she destroyed the *Alabama* off Cherbourg, France, 19 June 1864. Acting as sponger and loader of the 11-inch pivot gun during the bitter engagement, Harrison exhibited marked coolness and good conduct and was highly recommended for his gallantry under fire by the divisional officer.

HART, JOHN W.

Rank and organization: Sergeant, Company D, 6th Pennsylvania Reserves. *Place and date:* At Gettysburg, Pa., 2 July 1863. *Entered service at:* Cumberland, Md. *Birth:* Germany. *Date of issue:* 3 August 1897. *Citation:* Was one of six volunteers who charged upon a log house near the Devil's Den, where a squad of the enemy's sharpshooters were sheltered, and compelled their surrender.

HART, WILLIAM E.

Rank and organization: Private, Company B, 8th New York Cavalry. *Place and date:* At Shenandoah Valley, Va., 1864 and 1865. *Entered service at:* Pittsford, N.Y. *Birth:* Rushville, N.Y. *Date of issue:* 3 July 1872. *Citation:* Gallant conduct and services as scout in connection with capture of the guerrilla Harry Gilmore, and other daring acts.

HARTRANFT, JOHN F.

Rank and organization: Colonel, 4th Pennsylvania Militia. *Place and date:* At Bull Run, Va., 21 July 1861. *Entered service at:* Norristown, Pa. *Born:* 16 December 1830, New Hanover Township, Montgomery County, Pa. *Date of issue:* 26 August 1886. *Citation:* Voluntarily served as an aide and participated in the battle after expiration of his term of service, distinguishing himself in rallying several regiments which had been thrown into confusion.

HARVEY, HARRY

Rank and organization: Corporal, Company A, 22d New York Cavalry. *Place and date:* At Waynesboro, Va., 2 March 1865. *Entered service at:* Rochester, N.Y. *Birth:* England. *Date of issue:* 26 March 1865. *Citation:* Capture of flag and bearer, with two other prisoners.

HASKELL, FRANK W.

Rank and organization: Sergeant Major, 3d Maine Infantry. *Place and date:* At Fair Oaks, Va., 1 June 1862. *Entered service at:* Waterville, Maine. *Born:* 1843, Benton, Maine. *Date of issue:* 8 December 1898. *Citation:* Assumed command of a portion of the left wing of his regiment, all the company officers present having been killed or disabled, led it gallantly across a stream and contributed most effectively to the success of the action.

HASKELL, MARCUS M.

Rank and organization: Sergeant, Company C, 35th Massachusetts Infantry. *Place and date:* At Antietam, Md., 17 September 1862. *Entered service at:* Chelsea, Mass. *Birth:* Chelsea, Mass. *Date of issue:* 18 November 1896. *Citation:* Although wounded and exposed to a heavy fire from the enemy, at the risk of his own life he rescued a badly wounded comrade and succeeded in conveying him to a place of safety.

HASTINGS, SMITH H.

Rank and organization: Captain, Company M, 5th Michigan Cavalry. *Place and date:* At Newbys Crossroads, Va., 24 July 1863. *Entered service at:* ———. *Birth:* Quincy, Mich. *Date of issue:* 2 August 1897. *Citation:* While in command of a squadron in rear guard of a cavalry division, then retiring before the advance of a corps of infantry, was attacked by the enemy and, orders having been given to abandon the guns of a section of field artillery with the rear guard that were in imminent danger of capture, he disregarded the orders received and aided in repelling the attack and saving the guns.

HATCH, JOHN P.

Rank and organization: Brigadier General, U.S. Volunteers. *Place and date:* At South Mountain, Md., 14 September 1862. *Entered service at:* New York, N.Y. *Born:* 9 January 1822, Oswego, N.Y. *Date of issue:* 28 October 1893. *Citation:* Was severely wounded while leading one of his brigades in the attack under a heavy fire from the enemy.

HATHAWAY, EDWARD W.

Rank and organization: Seaman, U.S. Navy. *Entered service at:* Plymouth, Mass. *Born:* 9 July 1838, Plymouth, Mass. *Citation:* On board the U.S.S. *Sciota* prior to the battle Vicksburg, on 28 June 1862. Struck by a bullet which severed his left arm above the elbow, Hathaway displayed exceptional courage as his ship sustained numerous damaging hits from stem to stern while proceeding down the river to fight the battle of Vicksburg.

HAVRON, JOHN H.

Rank and organization: Sergeant, Company G, 1st Rhode Island Light Artillery. *Place and date:* At Petersburg, Va., 2 April 1865. *Entered service at:* Providence, R.I. *Birth:* Ireland. *Date of issue:* 16 June 1866. *Citation:* Was one of a detachment of 20 picket artillerymen who voluntarily accompanied an infantry assaulting party and who turned upon the enemy the guns captured in the assault.

HAWKINS, CHARLES

Rank and organization: Seaman, U.S. Navy. *Born:* 1834, Scotland. *Accredited to:* New Hampshire. *G.O. No.:* 45, 31 December 1864. *Citation:* Hawkins served on board the U.S.S. *Agawam*, as one of a volunteer crew of a powderboat which was exploded near Fort Fisher, 23 December 1864. The powderboat, towed in by the *Wilderness* to prevent detection by the enemy, cast off and slowly steamed to within

300 yards of the beach. After fuses and fires had been lit and a second anchor with short scope let go to assure the boat's tailing inshore, the crew again boarded the *Wilderness* and proceeded a distance of 12 miles from shore. Less than 2 hours later the explosion took place, and the following day fires were observed still burning at the forts.

HAWKINS, GARDNER C.

Rank and organization: First Lieutenant, Company E, 3d Vermont Infantry. *Place and date:* At Petersburg, Va., 2 April 1865. *Entered service at:* Woodstock, Vt. *Birth:* Pomfret, Vt. *Date of issue:* 30 September 1893. *Citation:* When the lines were wavering from the well-directed fire of the enemy, this officer, acting adjutant of the regiment, sprang forward, and with encouraging words cheered the soldiers on and, although dangerously wounded, refused to leave the field until the enemy's works were taken.

HAWKINS, Martin J.

Rank and organization: Corporal, Company A, 33d Ohio Infantry. *Place and date:* Georgia, April 1862. *Entered service at:* Portsmouth, Scioto County, Ohio. *Birth:* Mercer County, Pa. *Date of issue:* September 1863. *Citation:* One of the 19 of 22 men (including 2 civilians) who, by direction of Gen. Mitchell (or Buell), penetrated nearly 200 miles south into enemy territory and captured a railroad train at Big Shanty, Ga., in an attempt to destroy the bridges and track between Chattanooga and Atlanta.

HAWKINS, THOMAS R.

Rank and organization: Sergeant Major, 6th U.S. Colored Troops. *Place and date:* At Chapins Farm, Va., 29 September 1864. *Entered service at:* Philadelphia, Pa. *Birth:* Cincinnati, Ohio. *Date of issue:* 8 February 1870. *Citation:* Rescue of regimental colors.

HAWTHORNE, HARRIS S.

Rank and organization: Corporal, Company F, 121st New York Infantry. *Place and date:* At Sailors Creek, Va., 6 April 1865. *Entered service at:* Otsego, N.Y. *Born:* 1832, Salem, N.Y. *Date of issue:* 29 December 1894. *Citation:* Captured the Confederate Gen. G. W. Custis Lee.

HAYDEN, JOSEPH B.

Rank and organization: Quartermaster, U.S. Navy. *Born:* 1834, Maryland. *Accredited to:* Maryland. *G.O. No.:* 59, 22 June 1865. *Citation:* On board the U.S.S. *Ticonderoga*, as quartermaster in charge of steering the ship into action, during attacks on Fort Fisher, 13 to 15 January 1865. Hayden steered the ship into position in the line of battle where she maintained a well-directed fire upon the batteries to the left of the palisades during the initial phases of the engagement. Although several of the enemy's shots fell over and around the vessel, the *Ticonderoga* fought her guns gallantly throughout 3 consecutive days of battle until the flag was planted on one of the strongest fortifications possessed by the rebels.

HAYES, JOHN

Rank and organization: Coxswain, U.S. Navy. *Born:* 1831, Philadelphia, Pa. *Accredited to:* Pennsylvania. *G.O. No.:* 45, 31 December 1864. *Citation:* Served on board the U.S.S. *Kearsarge* when she destroyed the *Alabama* off Cherbourg, France, 19 June 1864. Acting as second captain of the No. 2 gun during this bitter engagement, Hayes exhibited marked coolness and good conduct and was highly recommended for his gallantry under fire by the divisional officer.

HAYES, THOMAS

Rank and organization: Coxswain, U.S. Navy. *Born:* 1840, Rhode Island. *Accredited to:* Rhode Island. *G.O. No.:* 45, 31 December 1864. *Citation:* As Captain of No. 1 gun on board the U.S.S. *Richmond* during action against rebel forts and gunboats and with the ram *Tennessee* in Mobile Bay, 5 August 1864. Cool and courageous at his station throughout the prolonged action, Hayes maintained fire from his gun on Fort Morgan and on ships of the Confederacy despite extremely heavy return fire.

HAYNES, ASBURY F.

Rank and organization: Corporal, Company F, 17th Maine Infantry. *Place and date:* At Sailors Creek, Va., 6 April 1865. *Entered service at:* Maine. *Birth:* Edinburgh, Maine. *Date of issue:* 10 May 1865. *Citation:* Capture of flag.

HAYS, JOHN H.

Rank and organization: Private, Company F, 4th Iowa Cavalry. *Place and date:* At Columbus, Ga., 16 April 1865. *Entered service at:* Oskaloosa, Mahaska County, Iowa. *Birth:* Jefferson County, Ohio. *Date of issue:* 17 June 1865. *Citation:* Capture of flag and bearer, Austin's Battery (C.S.A.).

HEALEY, GEORGE W.

Rank and organization: Private, Company E, 5th Iowa Cavalry. *Place and date:* At Newnan, Ga., 29 July 1864. *Entered service at:* Dubuque, Iowa. *Birth:* Dubuque, Iowa. *Date of issue:* 13 January 1899. *Citation:* When nearly surrounded by the enemy, captured a Confederate soldier, and with the aid of a comrade who joined him later, captured 4 other Confederate soldiers, disarmed the 5 prisoners, and brought them all into the Union lines.

HEDGES, JOSEPH

Rank and organization: First Lieutenant, 4th U.S. Cavalry. *Place and date:* Near Harpeth River, Tenn., 17 December 1864. *Entered service at:* Ohio. *Birth:* Ohio. *Date of issue:* 5 April 1898. *Citation:* At the head of his regiment charged a field battery with strong infantry supports, broke the enemy's line and, with other mounted troops, captured 3 guns and many prisoners.

HEERMANCE, WILLIAM L.

Rank and organization: Captain, Company C, 6th New York Cavalry. *Place and date:* At Chancellorsville, Va., 30 April 1863. *Entered service at:* Kinderhook, N.Y. *Born:* 28 February 1837, Kinderhook, N.Y. *Date of issue:* 30 March 1898. *Citation:* Took command of the regiment as its senior officer when surrounded by Stuart's Cavalry. The regiment cut its way through the enemy's line and escaped but Capt. Heermance was desperately wounded, left for dead on the field and was taken prisoner.

HELLER, HENRY

Rank and organization: Sergeant, Company A, 66th Ohio Infantry. *Place and date:* At Chancellorsville, Va., 2 May 1863. *Entered service at:* Urbana, Ohio. *Birth:* ———. *Date of issue:* 29 July 1892. *Citation:* One of a party of 4 who, under heavy fire, voluntarily brought into the Union lines a wounded Confederate officer from whom was obtained valuable information concerning the position of the enemy.

HELMS, DAVID H.

Rank and organization: Private, Company B, 83d Indiana Infantry. *Place and date:* At Vicksburg, Miss., 22 May 1863. *Entered service at:* Farmers Retreat, Ind. *Birth:* Dearborn, Ind. *Date of issue:* 26 July 1894. *Citation:* Gallantry in the charge of the "volunteer storming party."

HENRY, GUY V.

Rank and organization: Colonel, 40th Massachusetts Infantry. *Place and date:* At Cold Harbor, Va., 1 June 1864. *Entered service at :* Reading Pa. *Birth:* Fort Smith, Indian Ter. *Date of issue:* 5 December 1893. *Citation:* Led the assaults of his brigade upon the enemy's works, where he had 2 horses shot under him.

HENRY, JAMES

Rank and organization: Sergeant, Company B, 113th Illinois Infantry. *Place and date:* At Vicksburg, Miss., 22 May 1863. *Entered service at:* Kankakee, Ill. *Birth:* Sunfish, Ohio. *Date of issue:* 9 July 1894. *Citation:* Gallantry in the charge of the "volunteer storming party."

HENRY, WILLIAM W.

Rank and organization: Colonel, 10th Vermont Infantry. *Place and date:* At Cedar Creek, Va., 19 October 1864. *Entered service at:* Waterbury, Vt. *Born:* 21 November 1831, Waterbury, Vt. *Date of issue:* 21 December 1892. *Citation:* Though suffering from severe wounds, rejoined his regiment and let it in a brilliant charge, recapturing the guns of an abandoned battery.

HERINGTON, PITT B.

Rank and organization: Private, Company E, 11th Iowa Infantry. *Place and date:* Near Kenesaw Mountain, Ga., 15 June 1864. *Entered service at:* Tipton, Cedar County, Iowa. *Born:* 1840, Michigan. *Date of issue:* 27 November 1899. *Citation:* With one companion and under a fierce fire of the enemy at close range, went to the rescue of a wounded comrade who had fallen between the lines and carried him to a place of safety.

HERRON, FRANCIS J.

Rank and organization: Lieutenant Colonel, 9th Iowa Infantry. *Place and date:* At Pea Ridge, Ark., 7 May 1862. *Entered service at:* Pittsburgh, Pa. *Born:* 17 February 1837, Pittsburgh, Pa. *Date of issue:* 26 September 1893. *Citation:* Was foremost in leading his men, rallying them to repeated acts of daring, until himself disabled and taken prisoner.

HESSELTINE, FRANCIS S.

Rank and organization: Colonel, 13th Maine Infantry. *Place and date:* At Matagorda Bay, Tex., 29-30 December 1863. *Entered service at:* Maine. *Born:* 10 December 1833, Bangor, Maine. *Date of issue:* 2 March 1895. *Citation:* In command of a detachment of 100 men, conducted a reconnaissance for 2 days, baffling and beating back an attacking force of more than a thousand Confederate cavalry, and regained his transport without loss.

HIBSON, JOSEPH C.

Rank and organization: Private, Company C, 48th New York Infantry. *Place and date:* Near Fort Wagner, S.C., 13 July 1863; Near Fort Wagner, S.C., 14 July 1863; Near Fort Wagner, S.C., 18 July 1863. *Entered service at:* New York, N.Y. *Birth:* England. *Date of issue:* 23 October 1897. *Citation:* While voluntarily performing picket duty under fire on 13 July 1863, was attacked and his surrender demanded, but he killed his assailant. The day following responded to a call for a volunteer to reconnoiter the enemy's position, and went within the enemy's lines under fire and was exposed to great danger. On 18 July voluntarily exposed himself with great gallantry during an assault, and received 3 wounds that permanently disabled him for active service.

HICKEY, DENNIS W.

Rank and organization: Sergeant, Company E, 2d New York Cavalry. *Place and date:* At Stony Creek Bridge, Va., 29 June 1864. *Entered service at:* ———. *Birth:* Troy, N.Y. *Date of issue:* 18 April 1891. *Citation:* With a detachment of 3 men, tore up the bridge at Stony Creek, being the last man on the bridge and covering the retreat until he was shot down.

HICKMAN, JOHN

Rank and organization: Second Class Fireman, U.S. Navy. *Born:* 1837, Richmond, Va. *Accredited to:* Virginia. *G.O. No.:* 17, 10 July 1863. *Citation:* Served on board the U.S.S. *Richmond* in the attack on Port Hudson, 14 March 1863. Damaged by a 6-inch solid rifle shot which shattered the starboard safety-valve chamber and also damaged the port safety-valve, the fireroom of the U.S.S. *Richmond* immediately became filled with steam to place it in an extremely critical condition. Acting courageously in this crisis, Hickman persisted in penetrating the steam-filled room in order to haul the hot fires of the furnaces and continued this action until the gravity of the situation had been lessened.

HICKOK, NATHAN E.

Rank and organization: Corporal, Company A, 8th Connecticut Infantry. *Place and date:* At Chapins Farm, Va., 29 September 1864. *Entered service at:* Danbury, Conn. *Birth:* Danbury, Conn. *Date of issue:* 6 April 1865. *Citation:* Capture of flag.

HIGBY, CHARLES

Rank and organization: Private, Company F, 1st Pennsylvania Cavalry. *Place and date:* At Appomattox Campaign, Va., 29 March to 9 April 1865. *Entered service at:* New Brighton, Pa. *Birth:* Pittsburgh, Pa. *Date of issue:* 3 May 1865. *Citation:* Capture of flag.

HIGGINS, THOMAS J.

Rank and organization: Sergeant, Company D, 99th Illinois Infantry. *Place and date:* At Vicksburg, Miss., 22 May 1863. *Entered service at:* Barry, Pike County, Ill. *Birth:* Canada. *Date of issue:* 1 April 1898. *Citation:* When his regiment fell back in the assault, repulsed, this soldier continued to advance and planted the flag on the parapet, where he was captured by the enemy.

HIGHLAND, PATRICK

Rank and organization: Corporal, Company D, 23d Illinois Infantry. *Place and date:* At Petersburg, Va., 2 April 1865. *Entered service at:* Chicago, Ill. *Birth:* Ireland. *Date of issue:* 12 May 1865. *Citation:* Conspicuous gallantry as color bearer in the assault on Fort Gregg.

HILL, EDWARD

Rank and organization: Captain, Company K, 16th Michigan Infantry. *Place and date:* At Cold Harbor, Va., 1 June 1864. *Entered service at:* Detroit, Mich. *Birth:* Liberty, N.Y. *Date of issue:* 4 December 1893. *Citation:* Led the brigade skirmish line in a desperate charge on the enemy's masked batteries to the muzzles of the guns, where he was severely wounded.

HILL, HENRY

Rank and organization: Corporal, Company C, 50th Pennsylvania Infantry. *Place and date:* At Wilderness, Va., 6 May 1864. *Entered service at:* ———. *Birth:* Schuylkill County, Pa. *Date of issue:* 23 September 1897. *Citation:* This soldier, with one companion, would not retire when his regiment fell back in confusion after an unsuccessful charge, but instead advanced and continued firing upon the enemy until the regiment re-formed and regained its position.

HILL, JAMES

Rank and organization: First Lieutenant, Company I, 21st Iowa Infantry. *Place and date:* At Champion Hill, Miss., 16 May 1863. *Entered service at:* Cascade, Iowa. *Birth:* England. *Date of issue:* 15 March 1893. *Citation:* By skillful and brave management captured 3 of the enemy's pickets.

HILL, JAMES

Rank and organization: Sergeant, Company C, 14th New York Heavy Artillery. *Place and date:* At Petersburg, Va., 30 July 1864. *Entered service at:* Lyons, N.Y. *Birth:* Lyons, N.Y. *Date of issue:* 1 December 1864. *Citation:* Capture of flag, shooting a Confederate officer who was rallying his men with the colors in his hand.

HILLIKER, BENJAMIN F.

Rank and organization: Musician, Company A, 8th Wisconsin Infantry. *Place and date:* At Mechanicsburg, Miss., 4 June 1863. *Entered service at:* Waupaca Township, Wis. *Born:* 23 May 1843, Golden, Erie County, N.Y. *Date of issue:* 17 December 1897. *Citation:* When men were needed to oppose a superior Confederate force he laid down his drum for a rifle and proceeded to the front of the skirmish line which was about 120 feet from the enemy. While on this volunteer mission and firing at the enemy he was hit in the head with a minie ball which passed through him. An order was given to "lay him in the shade; he won't last long". He recovered from this wound being left with an ugly scar.

HILLS, WILLIAM G.

Rank and organization: Private, Company E, 9th New York Cavalry. *Place and date:* At North Fork, Va., 26 September 1864. *Entered service at:* ———. *Birth:* 26 June 1841, Conewango, N.Y. *Date of issue:* 26 September 1893. *Citation:* Voluntarily carried a severely wounded comrade out of a heavy fire of the enemy.

HILTON, ALFRED B.

Rank and organization: Sergeant, Company ›H, 4th U.S. Colored Troops. *Place and date:* At Chapins Farm, Va., 29 September 1864. *Entered service at:* ———. *Birth:* Harford County, Md. *Date of issue:* 6 April 1865. *Citation:* When the regimental color bearer fell, this soldier seized the color and carried it forward, together with the national standard, until disabled at the enemy's inner line.

HINCKS, WILLIAM B.

Rank and organization: Sergeant Major, 14th Connecticut Infantry. *Place and date:* At Gettysburg, Pa., 3 July 1863. *Entered service at:* Bridgeport, Conn. *Birth:* Bucksport, Me. *Date of issue:* 1 December 1864. *Citation:* During the highwater mark of Pickett's charge on 3 July 1863 the colors of the 14th Tenn. Inf. C.S.A. were planted 50 yards in front of the center of Sgt. Maj. Hincks' regiment. There were no Confederates standing near it but several were lying down around it. Upon a call for volunteers by Maj. Ellis, commanding, to capture this flag, this soldier and 2 others leaped the wall. One companion was instantly shot. Sgt. Maj. Hincks outran his remaining companion running straight and swift for the colors amid a storm of shot. Swinging his saber over the prostrate Confederates and uttering a terrific yell, he seized the flag and hastily returned to his lines. The 14th Tenn. carried 12 battle honors on its flag. The devotion to duty shown by Sgt. Maj. Hincks gave encouragement to many of his comrades at a crucial moment of the battle.

806

HINNEGAN, WILLIAM

Rank and organization: Second Class Fireman, U.S. Navy. *Born:* 1841, Ireland. *Accredited to:* New York. *G.O. No.:* 45, 31 December 1864. *Citation:* Hinnegan served on board the U.S.S. *Agawam*, as one of a volunteer crew of powder boat which was exploded near Fort Fisher, 23 December 1864. The powder boat, towed in by the *Wilderness* to prevent detection by the enemy, cast off and slowly steamed to within 300 yards of the beach. After fuses and fires had been lit and a second anchor with short scope let go to assure the boat's tailing inshore, the crew again boarded the *Wilderness* and proceeded a distance of 12 miles from shore. Less than 2 hours later the explosion took place, and the following day fires were observed still burning at the forts.

HODGES, ADDISON J.

Rank and organization: Private, Company B, 47th Ohio Infantry. *Place and date:* At Vicksburg, Miss., 3 May 1863. *Entered service at:* Adrian, Mich. *Born:* 1841, Hillsdale, Mich. *Date of issue:* 13 December 1907. *Citation:* Was one of a party that volunteered and attempted to run the enemy's batteries with a steam tug and 2 barges loaded with subsistence stores.

HOFFMAN, HENRY

Rank and organization: Corporal, Company M, 2d Ohio Cavalry. *Place and date:* At Sailors Creek, Va., 6 April 1865. *Entered service at:* ———. *Birth:* Germany. *Date of issue:* 3 May 1865. *Citation:* Capture of flag.

HOFFMAN, THOMAS W.

Rank and organization: Captain, Company A, 208th Pennsylvania Infantry. *Place and date:* At Petersburg, Va., 2 April 1865. *Entered service at:* ———. *Birth:* Perrysburg, Pa. *Date of issue:* 19 July 1895. *Citation:* Prevented a retreat of his regiment during the battle.

HOGAN, FRANKLIN

Rank and organization: Corporal, Company A, 45th Pennsylvania Infantry. *Place and date:* Front of Petersburg, Va., 30 July 1864. *Entered service at:* Howard, Pa. *Birth:* Center County, Pa. *Date of issue:* 1 October 1864. *Citation:* Capture of flag of 6th Virginia Infantry (C.S.A.).

HOGARTY, WILLIAM P.

Rank and organization: Private, Company D, 23d New York Infantry. *Place and date:* At Antietam, Md., 17 September 1862. At Fredericksburg, Va., 13 December 1862. *Entered service at:* ———. *Birth:* New York, N.Y. *Date of issue:* 22 June 1891. *Citation:* Distinguished gallantry in actions while attached to Battery B, 4th U.S. Artillery; lost his left arm at Fredericksburg.

HOLCOMB, DANIEL I.

Rank and organization: Private, Company A, 41st Ohio Infantry. *Place and date:* At Brentwood Hills, Tenn., 16 December 1864. *En-*

tered service at: ———. *Birth:* Hartford, Ohio. *Date of issue:* 22 February 1865. *Citation:* Capture of Confederate guidon.

HOLEHOUSE, JAMES (JOHN)

Rank and organization: Private, Company B, 7th Massachusetts Infantry. *Place and date:* At Marye's Heights, Va., 3 May 1863. *Entered service at:* Fall River, Mass. *Birth:* England. *Date of issue:* 10 September 1897. *Citation:* With one companion voluntarily and with conspicuous daring advanced beyond his regiment, which had been broken in the assault, and halted beneath the crest. Following the example of these 2 men, the colors were brought to the summit, the regiment was advanced and the position held.

HOLLAND, LEMUEL F.

Rank and organization: Corporal, Company D, 104th Illinois Infantry. *Place and date:* At Elk River, Tenn., 2 July 1863. *Entered service at:* La Salle County, Ill. *Birth:* Burlington, Ohio. *Date of issue:* 30 October 1897. *Citation:* Voluntarily joined a small party that, under a heavy fire, captured a stockade and saved the bridge.

HOLLAND, MILTON M.

Rank and organization: Sergeant Major, 5th U.S. Colored Troops. *Place and date:* At Chapins Farm, Va., 29 September 1864. *Entered service at:* Athens, Ohio. *Born:* 1844, Austin, Tex. *Date of issue:* 6 April 1865. *Citation:* Took command of Company C, after all the officers had been killed or wounded, and gallantly led it.

HOLLAT, GEORGE

Rank and organization: Third Class Boy, U.S. Navy. *Entered service at:* New York. *Birth:* ———. *G.O. No.:* 11, 3 April 1863. *Citation:* Hollat served as third class boy on board the U.S.S. *Varuna* during an attack on Forts Jackson and St. Philip, 24 April 1862. He rendered gallant service through the perilous action and remained steadfast and courageous at his battle station despite extremely heavy fire and the ramming of the *Varuna* by the rebel ship *Morgan*, continuing his efforts until his ship, repeatedly holed and fatally damaged, was beached and sunk.

HOLMES, LOVILO N.

Rank and organization: First Sergeant, Company H, 2d Minnesota Infantry. *Place and date:* At Nolensville, Tenn., 15 February 1863. *Entered service at:* Mankato, Minn. *Birth:* Cattaraugus County, N.Y. *Date of issue:* 11 September 1897. *Citation:* Was one of a detachment of 16 men who heroically defended a wagon train against the attack of 125 cavalry, repulsed the attack and saved the train.

HOLMES, WILLIAM T.

Rank and organization: Private, Company A, 3d Indiana Cavalry. *Place and date:* At Sailors Creek, Va., 6 April 1865. *Entered service at:* Indianapolis, Ind. *Birth:* Vermilion County, Ill. *Date of issue:* 3 May 1865. *Citation:* Capture of flag of 27th Virginia Infantry (C.S.A.).

HOLTON, CHARLES M.

Rank and organization: First Sergeant, Company A, 7th Michigan Cavalry. *Place and date:* At Falling Waters, Va., 14 July 1863. *Entered service at:* Battle Creek, Mich. *Born:* 25 May 1838, Potter, N.Y. *Date of issue:* 21 March 1889. *Citation:* Capture of flag of 55th Virginia Infantry (C.S.A.). In the midst of the battle with foot soldiers he dismounted to capture the flag.

HOLTON, EDWARD A.

Rank and organization: First Sergeant, Company I, 6th Vermont Infantry. *Place and date:* At Lees Mills, Va., 16 April 1862. *Entered service at:* Williston, Vt. *Birth:* Westminster, Vt. *Date of issue:* 9 July 1892. *Citation:* Rescued the colors of his regiment under heavy fire, the color bearer having been shot down while the troops were in retreat.

HOMAN, CONRAD

Rank and organization: Color Sergeant, Company A, 29th Massachusetts Infantry. *Place and date:* Near Petersburg, Va., 30 July 1864. *Entered service at:* ———. *Birth:* Roxbury, Mass. *Date of issue:* 3 June 1869. *Citation:* Fought his way through the enemy's lines with the regimental colors, the rest of the color guard being killed or captured.

HOOKER, GEORGE W.

Rank and organization: First Lieutenant, Company E, 4th Vermont Infantry. *Place and date:* At South Mountain, Md., 14 September 1862. *Entered service at:* Boston, Mass. *Birth:* Salem, N.Y. *Date of issue:* 17 September 1891. *Citation:* Rode alone, in advance of his regiment, into the enemy's lines, and before his own men came up received the surrender of the major of a Confederate regiment, together with the colors and 116 men.

HOOPER, WILLIAM B.

Rank and organization: Corporal, Company L, 1st New Jersey Cavalry. *Place and date:* At Chamberlains Creek, Va., 31 March 1865. *Entered service at:* ———. *Birth:* Willimantic, Conn. *Date of issue:* 3 July 1865. *Citation:* With the assistance of a comrade, headed off the advance of the enemy, shooting two of his color bearers; also posted himself between the enemy and the led horses of his own command, thus saving the herd from capture.

HOPKINS, CHARLES F.

Rank and organization: Corporal, Company I, 1st New Jersey Infantry. *Place and date:* At Gaines Mill, Va., 27 June 1862. *Entered service at:* ———. *Birth:* Warren County, N.J. *Date of issue:* 9 July 1892. *Citation:* Voluntarily carried a wounded comrade, under heavy fire, to a place of safety; though twice wounded in the act, he continued in action until again severely wounded.

HORAN, THOMAS

Rank and organization: Sergeant, Company E, 72d New York Infantry. *Place and date:* At Gettysburg, Pa., 2 July 1863. *Entered service at:* Dunkirk, N.Y. *Birth:* ———. *Date of issue:* 5 April 1898. *Citation:* In a charge of his regiment this soldier captured the regimental flag of the 8th Florida Infantry (C.S.A.).

HORNE, SAMUEL B.

Rank and organization: Captain, Company H, 11th Connecticut Infantry. *Place and date:* At Fort Harrison, Va., 29 September 1864. *Entered service at:* Winsted, Conn. *Born:* 3 March 1843, Ireland. *Date of issue:* 19 November 1897. *Citation:* While acting as an aide and carrying an important message, was severely wounded and his horse killed, but delivered the order and rejoined his general.

HORSFALL, WILLIAM H.

Rank and organization: Drummer, Company G, 1st Kentucky Infantry. *Place and date:* At Corinth, Miss., 21 May 1862. *Entered service at :* ———. *Birth:* Campbell County, Ky. *Date of issue:* 17 August 1895. *Citation:* Saved the life of a wounded officer lying between the lines.

HORTON, JAMES

Rank and organization: Gunner's Mate, U.S. Navy. *Born:* 1838, Massachusetts. *Accredited to:* Massachusetts. *G.O. No.:* 59, 22 June 1865. *Citation:* Served as gunner's mate on board the U.S.S. *Montauk*, 21 September 1864. During the night of 21 September, when fire was discovered in the magazine lightroom of the vessel, causing a panic and demoralizing the crew, Horton rushed into the cabin, obtained the magazine keys, sprang into the lightroom and began passing out combustibles, including the box of signals in which the fire originated.

HORTON, LEWIS A.

Rank and organization: Seaman, U.S. Navy. *Born:* 1839, Bristol, Mass. *Accredited to:* Massachusetts. *G.O. No.:* 59, 22 June 1865. *Citation:* Served on board the U.S.S. *Rhode Island*, which was engaged in saving the lives of the officers and crew of the *Monitor*, 30 December 1862. Participating in the hazardous task of rescuing the officers and crew of the sinking *Monitor*, Horton, after rescuing several of the men, became separated in a heavy gale with other members of the cutter that had set out from the *Rhode Island* and spent many hours in the small boat at the mercy of the weather and high seas until finally picked up by a schooner 50 miles east of Cape Hatteras.

HOTTENSTINE, SOLOMON J.

Rank and organization: Private, Company C, 107th Pennsylvania Infantry. *Place and date:* At Petersburg and Norfolk Railroad, Va., 19 August 1864. *Entered service at:* Philadelphia, Pa. *Birth:* Lehigh County, Pa. *Date of issue:* 2 February 1865. *Citation:* Captured flag belonging to a North Carolina regiment, and through a ruse led them into the arms of Federal troops.

HOUGH, IRA

Rank and organization: Private, Company E, 8th Indiana Infantry. *Place and date:* At Cedar Creek, Va., 19 October 1864. *Entered service at:* Henry County, Ind. *Birth:* Henry County, Ind. *Date of issue:* 26 October 1864. *Citation:* Capture of flag.

HOUGHTON, CHARLES H.

Rank and organization: Captain, Company L, 14th New York Artillery. *Place and date:* At Petersburg, Va., 30 July 1864; 25 March 1865. *Entered service at:* Ogdensburg, N.Y. *Born:* 30 April 1842, Macomb, St. Lawrence County, N.Y. *Date of issue:* 5 April 1898. *Citation:* In the Union assault at the Crater (30 July 1864), and in the Confederate assault repelled at Fort Haskell, displayed most conspicuous gallantry and repeatedly exposed himself voluntarily to great danger, was 3 times wounded, and suffered loss of a leg.

HOUGHTON, EDWARD J.

Rank and organization: Ordinary Seaman, U.S. Navy. *Born:* 1843, Mobile, Ala. *Accredited to:* Alabama. *G.O. No.:* 45, 31 December 1864. *Citation:* Houghton served on board the U.S. Picket Boat No. 1 in action, 27 October 1864, against the Confederate ram *Albemarle*, which had resisted repeated attacks by our steamers and had kept a large force of vessels employed in watching her. The picket boat, equipped with a spar torpedo, succeeded in passing the enemy pickets within 20 yards without being discovered and then made for the *Albemarle* under a full head of steam. Immediately taken under fire by the ram, the small boat plunged on, jumped the log boom which encircled the target and exploded its torpedo under the port bow of the ram. The picket boat was destroyed by enemy fire and almost the entire crew taken prisoner or lost.

HOUGHTON, GEORGE L.

Rank and organization: Private, Company D, 104th Illinois Infantry. *Place and date:* At Elk River, Tenn., 2 July 1863. *Entered service at:* Brookfield, Cook County, Ill. *Birth:* Canada. *Date of issue:* 27 March 1900. *Citation:* Voluntarily joined a small party that, under a heavy fire, captured a stockade and saved the bridge.

HOULTON, WILLIAM

Rank and organization: Commissary Sergeant, 1st West Virginia Cavalry. *Place and date:* At Sailors Creek, Va., 6 April 1865. *Entered service at:* ———. *Birth:* Clymer, N.Y. *Date of issue:* 3 May 1865. *Citation:* Capture of flag.

HOWARD, HENDERSON C.

Rank and organization: Corporal, Company B, 11th Pennsylvania Reserves. *Place and date:* At Glendale, Va., 30 June 1862. *Entered service at:* Indiana, Pa. *Birth:* ———. *Date of issue:* 30 March 1898. *Citation:* While pursuing one of the enemy's sharpshooters, encountered 2 others, whom he bayoneted in hand-to-hand encounters; was 3 times wounded in action.

HOWARD, HIRAM R.

Rank and organization: Private, Company H, 11th Ohio Infantry. *Place and date:* At Missionary Ridge, Tenn., 25 November 1863. *Entered service at:* Ohio. *Born:* 17 February 1843, Urbana, Ohio. *Date of issue:* 29 July 1892. *Citation:* Scaled the enemy's works and in a hand-to-hand fight helped capture the flag of the 18th Alabama Infantry (C.S.A.).

HOWARD, JAMES

Rank and organization: Sergeant, Company K, 158th New York Infantry. *Place and date:* At Battery Gregg, near Petersburg, Va., 2 April 1865. *Entered service at:* ———. *Birth:* Newton, N.J. *Date of issue:* 12 May 1865. *Citation:* Carried the colors in advance of the line of battle, the flagstaff being shot off while he was planting it on the parapet of the fort.

HOWARD, MARTIN

Rank and organization: Landsman, U.S. Navy. *Born:* 1843, Ireland. *Accredited to:* New York. *G.O. No.:* 45, 31 December 1864. *Citation:* Served on board the U.S.S. *Tacony* during the taking of Plymouth, N.C., 31 October 1864. Carrying out his duties faithfully during the capture of Plymouth, Howard distinguished himself by a display of coolness when he participated in landing and spiking a 9-inch gun while under a devastating fire from enemy musketry.

HOWARD, OLIVER O.

Rank and organization: Brigadier General, U.S. Volunteers. *Place and date:* At Fair Oaks, Va., 1 June 1862. *Entered service at:* Maine. *Born:* 8 November 1830, Leeds, Maine. *Date of issue:* 29 March 1893. *Citation:* Led the 61st New York Infantry in a charge in which he was twice severely wounded in the right arm, necessitating amputation.

HOWARD, PETER

Rank and organization: Boatswain's Mate, U.S. Navy. *Born:* 1829, France. *Accredited to:* Massachusetts. *G.O. No.:* 17, 10 July 1863. *Citation:* Served on board the U.S.S. *Mississippi* during the action against Port Hudson, 14 March 1863. Running aground during the darkness and in the midst of battle while exposed to a devastating fire from enemy shore batteries, the *Mississippi* was ordered abandoned after a long and desperate attempt to free her. Serving courageously throughout this period in which a steady fire was kept up against the enemy until the ship was enveloped in flames and abandoned. Howard acted gallantly in his duties as boatswain's mate. Soon after the firing of the *Mississippi* and its abandonment, it was seen to slide off the shoal, drift downstream and explode, leaving no possibility of its falling into enemy hands.

HOWARD, SQUIRE E.

Rank and organization: First Sergeant, Company H, 8th Vermont Infantry. *Place and date:* At Bayou Teche, La., 14 January 1863. *Entered service at:* Townshend, Vt. *Birth:* Jamaica, Vt. *Date of issue:* 29 January 1894. *Citation:* Voluntarily carried an important message through the heavy fire of the enemy to bring aid and save the gunboat *Calhoun.*

HOWE, ORION P.

Rank and organization: Musician, Company C, 55th Illinois Infantry. *Place and date:* At Vicksburg, Miss., 19 May 1863. *Entered service at:* Waukegan, Ill. *Birth:* Portage County, Ohio. *Date of issue:* 23 April 1896. *Citation:* A drummer boy, 14 years of age, and severely wounded and exposed to a heavy fire from the enemy, he persistently remained upon the field of battle until he had reported to Gen. W. T. Sherman the necessity of supplying cartridges for the use of troops under command of Colonel Malmborg.

HOWE, WILLIAM H.

Rank and organization: Sergeant, Company K, 29th Massachusetts Infantry. *Place and date:* At Fort Stedman, Va., 25 March 1865. *Entered service at:* MA. *Birth:* Haverhill, Mass. *Date of issue:* 8 March 1895. *Citation:* Served an abandoned gun under heavy fire.

HUBBELL, WILLIAM S.

Rank and organization: Captain, Company A, 21st Connecticut Infantry. *Place and date:* At Fort Harrison, Va., 30 September 1864. *Entered service at:* North Stonington, Conn. *Born:* 19 April 1837, Wolcottville, Conn. *Date of issue:* 13 June 1894. *Citation:* Led out a small flanking party and by a clash and at great risk captured a large number of prisoners.

HUDSON, AARON R.

Rank and organization: Private, Company C, 17th Indiana Mounted Infantry. *Place and date:* At Culloden, Ga., April 1865. *Entered service at:* La Porte County, Ind. *Birth:* Madison County, Ky. *Date of issue:* 17 June 1865. *Citation:* Capture of flag of Worrill Grays (C.S.A.).

HUDSON, MICHAEL

Rank and organization: Sergeant, U.S. Marine Corps. *Born:* 1834, Sligo County, Ireland. *Accredited to:* New York. *G.O. No.:* 45, 31 December 1864. *Citation:* On board the U.S.S. *Brooklyn* during action against rebel forts and gunboats and with the ram *Tennessee* in Mobile Bay, 5 August 1864. Despite severe damage to his ship and the loss of several men on board as enemy fire raked the decks, Sgt. Hudson fought his gun with skill and courage throughout the furious 2-hour battle which resulted in the surrender of the rebel ram *Tennessee.*

HUGHES, OLIVER

Rank and organization: Corporal, Company C, 12th Kentucky Infantry. *Place and date:* At Weldon Railroad, Va., 24 June 1864. *Entered service at:* Albany, Ky. *Born:* 21 January 1841, Fentress County, Tenn. *Date of issue:* 1 August 1865. *Citation:* Capture of flag of 11th South Carolina (C.S.A.).

HUGHEY, JOHN

Rank and organization: Corporal, Company L, 2d Ohio Cavalry. *Place and date:* At Sailors Creek, Va., 6 April 1865. *Entered service at:* ———. *Birth:* Highland, Ohio. *Date of issue:* 3 May 1865. *Citation:* Capture of flag of 38th Virginia Infantry (C.S.A.).

HUIDEKOPER, HENRY S.

Rank and organization: Lieutenant Colonel, 150th Pennsylvania Infantry. *Place and date:* At Gettysburg, Pa., 1 July 1863. *Entered service at:* Philadelphia, Pa. *Born:* 17 July 1839, Meadville, Pa. *Date of issue:* 27 May 1905. *Citation:* While engaged in repelling an attack of the enemy, received a severe wound of the right arm, but instead of retiring remained at the front in command of the regiment.

HUNT, LOUIS T.

Rank and organization: Private, Company H, 6th Missouri Infantry. *Place and date:* At Vicksburg, Miss., 22 May 1863. *Entered service at:* Jefferson County, Mo. *Birth:* Montgomery County, Ind. *Date of issue:* 12 July 1894. *Citation:* Gallantry in the charge of the "volunteer storming party."

HUNTER, CHARLES A.

Rank and organization: Sergeant, Company E, 34th Massachusetts Infantry. *Place and date:* At Petersburg, Va., 2 April 1865. *Entered service at:* Spencer, Mass. *Birth:* Spencer, Mass. *Date of issue:* 12 May 1865. *Citation:* In the assault on Fort Gregg, bore the regimental flag bravely and was among the foremost to enter the work.

HUNTERSON, JOHN C.

Rank and organization: Private, Company B, 3d Pennsylvania Cavalry. *Place and date:* On the Peninsula, Va., 5 June 1862. *Entered service at:* Philadelphia, Pa. *Birth:* Philadelphia, Pa. *Date of issue:* 2 August 1897. *Citation:* While under fire, between the lines of the 2 armies, voluntarily gave up his own horse to an engineer officer whom he was accompanying on a reconnaissance and whose horse had been killed, thus enabling the officer to escape with valuable papers in his possession.

HUSKEY, MICHAEL

Rank and organization: Fireman, U.S. Navy. *Born:* 1841, New York, N.Y. *Accredited to:* New York. *G.O. No.:* 32, 16 April 1864. *Citation:* Fireman on board the U.S.S. *Carondelet*, Deer Creek Expedition, March 1863. Carrying out his duties gallantly, Huskey volunteered to aid in the rescue of the tug *Ivy* under the fire of the enemy, and set forth general meritorious conduct during this hazardous mission.

HYATT, THEODORE

Rank and organization: First Sergeant, Company D, 127th Illinois Infantry. *Place and date:* At Vicksburg, Miss., 22 May 1863. *Entered service at:* Gardner, Ill. *Birth:* Pennsylvania, *Date of issue:* 9 July 1894. *Citation:* Gallantry in the charge of the "volunteer storming party."

HYDE, THOMAS W.

Rank and organization: Major, 7th Maine Infantry. *Place and date:* At Antietam, Md., 17 September 1862. *Entered service at:* Bath, Maine. *Birth:* Italy. *Date of issue:* 8 April 1891. *Citation:* Led his regiment in an assault on a strong body of the enemy's infantry and kept up the fight until the greater part of his men had been killed or wounded, bringing the remainder safely out of the fight.

HYLAND, JOHN

Rank and organization: Seaman, U.S. Navy. *Born:* 1819, Ireland. *Accredited to:* Illinois. *G.O. No.:* 45, 31 December 1864. *Citation:* Served as seaman on board the U.S.S. *Signal* which was attacked by field batteries and sharpshooters and destroyed in Red River, 5 May 1864. Proceeding up the Red River, the U.S.S. *Signal* engaged a large force of enemy field batteries and sharpshooters, returning their fire until the ship was totally disabled, at which time the white flag was raised. Although wounded, Hyland courageously went in full view of several hundred sharpshooters and let go the anchor, and again to slip the cable, when he was again wounded by the raking enemy fire.

HYMER, SAMUEL

Rank and organization: Captain, Company D, 115th Illinois Infantry. *Place and date:* At Buzzard's Roost Gap, Ga., 13 October 1864. *Entered service at:* Rushville, Schuyler County, Ill. *Born:* 17 May 1829, Harrison County, Ind. *Date of issue:* 28 March 1896. *Citation:* With only 41 men under his command, defended and held a blockhouse against the attack of Hood's Division for nearly 10 hours, thus checking the advance of the enemy and insuring the safety of the balance of the regiment, as well as that of the 8th Kentucky Infantry, then stationed at Ringgold, Ga.

ILGENFRITZ, CHARLES H.

Rank and organization: Sergeant, Company E, 207th Pennsylvania Infantry. *Place and date:* At Fort Sedgwick, Va., 2 April 1865. *Entered service at:* Pennsylvania. *Birth:* York County, Pa. *Date of issue:* Unknown. *Citation:* The color bearer falling, pierced by 7 balls, he immediately sprang forward and grasped the colors, planting them upon the enemy's forts amid a murderous fire of grape, canister, and musketry from the enemy.

IMMELL, LORENZO D.

Rank and organization: Corporal, Company F, 2d U.S. Artillery. *Place and date:* At Wilsons Creek, Mo., 10 August 1861. *Entered service at:* ———. *Birth:* Ross, Ohio. *Date of issue:* 19 July 1890. *Citation:* Bravery in action.

INGALLS, LEWIS J.

Rank and organization: Private, Company K, 8th Vermont Infantry. *Place and date:* At Boutte Station, La., 4 September 1862. *Entered service at:* Belvidere, Vt. *Birth:* Boston, Mass. *Date of issue:* 20 October 1899. *Citation:* A railroad train guarded by about 60 men on flat cars having been sidetracked by a misplaced switch into an ambuscade of guerrillas who were rapidly shooting down the unprotected guards, this soldier, under a severe fire in which he was wounded, ran to another switch and, opening it, enabled the train and the surviving guards to escape.

INSCHO, LEONIDAS H.

Rank and organization: Corporal, Company E, 12th Ohio Infantry. *Place and date:* At South Mountain, Md., 14 September 1862. *Entered service at:* Charleston, W. Va. *Birth:* Chatham, Ohio. *Date of issue:* 31 January 1894. *Citation:* Alone and unaided and with his left hand disabled, captured a Confederate captain and 4 men.

IRLAM, JOSEPH

Rank and organization: Seaman, U.S. Navy. *Born:* 1840, England. *Accredited to:* New York. *G.O. No.:* 45, 31 December 1864. *Citation:* Stationed at the wheel on board the U.S.S. *Brooklyn* during action against rebel forts and gunboats and with the ram *Tennessee* in Mobile Bay, 5 August 1864. When heavy enemy fire struck down several men at their guns and replacements were not available, Irlam voluntarily released 2 men who were stationed with him and carried on at the wheel with the assistance of only one of the crew throughout the furious battle.

IRSCH, FRANCIS

Rank and organization: Captain, Company D, 45th New York Infantry. *Place and date:* At Gettysburg, Pa., 1 July 1863. *Entered service at:* New York, N.Y. *Birth:* ———. *Date of issue:* 27 May 1892. *Citation:* Gallantry in flanking the enemy and capturing a number of prisoners and in holding a part of the town against heavy odds while the Army was rallying on Cemetery Hill.

IRVING, JOHN

Rank and organization: Coxswain, U.S. Navy. *Born:* 1839, East Brooklyn, N.Y. *Accredited to:* New York. *G.O. No.:* 45, 31 December 1864. *Citation:* On board the U.S.S. *Brooklyn* during action against rebel forts and gunboats and with the ram *Tennessee*, in Mobile Bay, 5 August 1864. Despite severe damage to his ship and the loss of several men on board as enemy fire raked her decks from stem to stern, Irving fought his gun with skill and courage throughout the furious battle which resulted in the surrender of the prize rebel ram *Tennessee* and in the damaging and destruction of batteries at Fort Morgan.

IRVING, THOMAS

Rank and organization: Coxswain, U.S. Navy. *Born:* 1842, England. *Accredited to:* New York. *G.O. No.:* 32, 16 April 1864. *Citation:* Served on board the U.S.S. *Lehigh*, Charleston Harbor, 16 November 1863, during the harzardous task of freeing the *Lehigh*, which had grounded, and was under heavy enemy fire from Fort Moultrie. Rowing the small boat which was used in the hazardous task of transferring hawsers from the *Lehigh* to the *Nahant*, Irving twice succeeded in making the trip, while under severe fire from the enemy, only to find that each had been in vain when the hawsers were cut by hostile fire and chaffing.

IRWIN, NICHOLAS

Rank and organization: Seaman, U.S. Navy. *Born:* 1833, Denmark. *Accredited to:* New York. *G.O. No.:* 45, 31 December 1864. *Citation:* On board the U.S.S. *Brooklyn* during action against rebel forts and gunboats and with the ram *Tennessee*, in Mobile Bay, 5 August 1864. Despite severe damage to his ship and the loss of several men on board as enemy fire raked her decks from stem to stern, Irwin fought his gun with skill and courage throughout the furious battle which resulted in the surrender of the prize rebel ram *Tennessee* and in the damaging and destruction of batteries at Fort Morgan.

IRWIN, PATRICK

Rank and organization: First Sergeant, Company H, 14th Michigan Infantry. *Place and date:* At Jonesboro, Ga., 1 September 1864. *Entered service at:* Ann Arbor, Mich. *Born:* 1839, Ireland. *Date of issue:* 28 April 1896. *Citation:* In a charge by the 14th Michigan Infantry against the entrenched enemy was the first man over the line of works of the enemy, and demanded and received the surrender of Confederate Gen. Daviel Govan and his command.

JACKSON, FREDERICK R.

Rank and organization: First Sergeant, Company F, 7th Connecticut Infantry. *Place and date:* At James Island, S.C., 16 June 1862. *Entered service at:* New Haven, Conn. *Birth:* New Haven, Conn. *Date of issue:* 1863. *Citation:* Having his left arm shot away in a charge on the enemy, he continued on duty, taking part in a second and a third charge until he fell exhausted from the loss of blood.

JACOBSON, EUGENE P.

Rank and organization: Sergeant Major, 74th New York Infantry. *Place and date:* At Chancellorsville, Va., 2 May 1863. *Entered service at:* New York, N.Y. *Birth:* ———. *Date of issue:* 29 March 1865. *Citation:* Bravery in conducting a scouting party in front of the enemy.

JAMES, ISAAC

Rank and organization: Private, Company H, 110th Ohio Infantry. *Place and date:* At Petersburg, Va., 2 April 1865. *Entered service at:* ———. *Birth:* Montgomery County, Ohio. *Date of issue:* 10 May 1865. *Citation:* Capture of flag.

JAMES, JOHN H.

Rank and organization: Captain of the Top, U.S. Navy. *Born:* 1835, Boston, Mass. *Accredited to:* Massachusetts. *G.O. No.:* 45, 31 December 1864. *Citation:* As captain of a gun on board the U.S.S. *Richmond* during action against rebel forts and gunboats and with the ram *Tennessee* in Mobile Bay, 5 August 1864. Despite damage to his ship and the loss of several men on board as enemy fire raked her decks, James fought his gun with skill and courage throughout a furious 2-hour battle which resulted in the surrender of the rebel ram *Ten-*

nessee and in the damaging and destruction of batteries at Fort Morgan.

JAMES, MILES

Rank and organization: Corporal, Company B, 36th U.S. Colored Troops. *Place and date:* At Chapins Farm, Va., 30 September 1864. *Entered service at:* Norfolk, Va. *Birth:* Princess Anne County, Va. *Date of issue:* 6 April 1865. *Citation:* Having had his arm mutilated, making immediate amputation necessary, he loaded and discharged his piece with one hand and urged his men forward; this within 30 yards of the enemy's works.

JAMIESON, WALTER

Rank and organization: 1st Sergeant, Company B, 139th New York Infantry. *Place and date:* At Petersburg, Va., 30 July 1864; At Fort Harrison, Va., 29 September 1864. *Entered service at:* New York, N.Y. *Birth:* France. *Date of issue:* 5 April 1898. *Citation:* Voluntarily went between the lines under a heavy fire at Petersburg, Va., to the assistance of a wounded and helpless officer, whom he carried within the Union lines. At Fort Harrison, Va., seized the regimental color, the color bearer and guard having been shot down, and, rushing forward, planted it upon the fort in full view of the entire brigade.

JARDINE, JAMES

Rank and organization: Sergeant, Company F, 54th Ohio Infantry. *Place and date:* At Vicksburg, Miss., 22 May 1863. *Entered service at:* Hamilton County, Ohio. *Birth:* Scotland. *Date of issue:* 5 April 1894. *Citation:* Gallantry in the charge of the "volunteer storming party."

JELLISON, BENJAMIN H.

Rank and organization: Sergeant, Company C, 19th Massachusetts Infantry. *Place and date:* At Gettysburg, Pa., 3 July 1863. *Entered service at:* Newburyport, Mass. *Birth:* Newburyport, Mass. *Date of issue:* 1 December 1864. *Citation:* Capture of flag of 57th Virginia Infantry (C.S.A.). He also assisted in taking prisoners.

JENKINS, THOMAS

Rank and organization: Seaman, U.S. Navy. Biography not available. *G.O. No.:* 17, 10 July 1863. *Citation:* Served on board the U.S.S. *Cincinnati* during the attack on the Vicksburg batteries and at the time of her sinking, 27 May 1863. Engaging the enemy in a fierce battle, the *Cincinnati*, amidst an incessant fire of shot and shell, continued to fire her guns to the last, though so penetrated by shell fire that her fate was sealed. Serving bravely during this action, Jenkins was conspicuously cool under the fire of the enemy, never ceasing to fight until this proud ship went down, "her colors nailed to the mast."

JENNINGS, JAMES T.

Rank and organization: Private, Company K, 56th Pennsylvania Infantry. *Place and date:* At Weldon Railroad, Va., 20 August 1864. *Entered service at:* Bucks County, Pa. *Birth:* England. *Date of issue:* 1 December 1864. *Citation:* Capture of flag of 55th North Carolina Infantry (C.S.A.).

JEWETT, ERASTUS W.

Rank and organization: First Lieutenant, Company A, 9th Vermont Infantry. *Place and date:* At Newport Barracks, N.C., 2 February 1864. *Entered service at:* St. Albans, Vt. *Birth:* St. Albans, Vt. *Date of issue:* 8 September 1891. *Citation:* By long and persistent resistance and burning the bridges kept a superior force of the enemy at a distance and thus covered the retreat of the garrison.

JOHN, WILLIAM

Rank and organization: Private, Company E, 37th Ohio Infantry. *Place and date:* At Vicksburg, Miss., 22 May 1863. *Entered service at:* Chillicothe, Ohio. *Birth:* Germany. *Date of issue:* 14 July 1894. *Citation:* Gallantry in the charge of the "volunteer storming party."

JOHNDRO, FRANKLIN

Rank and organization: Private, Company A, 118th New York Infantry. *Place and date:* At Chapins Farm, Va., 30 September 1864. *Entered service at:* ———. *Birth:* Highgate Falls, Vt. *Date of issue:* 6 April 1865. *Citation:* Capture of 40 prisoners.

JOHNS, (JONES) ELISHA

Rank and organization: Corporal, Company B, 113th Illinois Infantry. *Place and date:* At Vicksburg, Miss., 22 May 1863. *Entered service at:* Martintonk, Iroquois County, Ill. *Birth:* Clinton, Ohio. *Date of issue:* 9 August 1894. *Citation:* Gallantry in the charge of the "volunteer storming party."

JOHNS, HENRY T.

Rank and organization: Private, Company C, 49th Massachusetts Infantry. *Place and date:* At Port Hudson, La., 27 May 1863. *Entered service at:* Hinsdale, Mass. *Birth:* ———. *Date of issue:* 25 November 1893. *Citation:* Volunteered in response to a call and took part in the movement that was made upon the enemy's works under a heavy fire therefrom ?of a mile in advance of the general assault.

JOHNSON, ANDREW

Rank and organization: Private, Company G, 116th Illinois Infantry. *Place and date:* At Vicksburg, Miss., 22 May 1863. *Entered service at:* Assumption, Ill. *Birth:* Delaware County, Ohio. *Date of issue:* 9 August 1894. *Citation:* Gallantry in the charge of the "volunteer storming party."

JOHNSON, FOLLETT

Rank and organization: Corporal, Company H, 60th New York Infantry. *Place and date:* At New Hope Church, Ga., 27 May 1864. *Entered service at:* ———. *Birth:* St. Lawrence, N.Y. *Date of issue:* 6 April 1892. *Citation:* Voluntarily exposed himself to the fire of a Confederate sharpshooter, thus drawing fire upon himself and enabling his comrade to shoot the sharpshooter.

JOHNSON, HENRY

Rank and organization: Seaman, U.S. Navy. *Born:* 1824, Norway. *Accredited to:* New York. *G.O. No.:* 82, 23 February 1867. *Citation:* As seaman on board the U.S.S. *Metacomet,* Johnson served as a member of the boat's crew which went to the rescue of the U.S. Monitor *Tecumseh* when that vessel was struck by a torpedo in passing the enemy forts in Mobile Bay, 5 August 1864. He braved the enemy fire which was said by the admiral to be "one of the most galling" he had ever seen, and aided in rescuing from death 10 of the crew of the *Tecumseh,* thereby eliciting the admiration of both friend and foe.

JOHNSON, JOHN

Rank and organization: Private, Company D, 2d Wisconsin Infantry. *Place and date:* At Fredericksburg, Va., 13 December 1862; Antietam. *Entered service at:* Janesville, Rock County, Wis. *Born:* 25 March 1842, Norway. *Date of issue:* 28 August 1893. *Citation:* Conspicuous gallantry in battle in which he was severely wounded. While serving as cannoneer he manned the positions of fallen gunners.

JOHNSON, JOSEPH E.

Rank and organization: First Lieutenant, Company A, 58th Pennsylvania Infantry. *Place and date:* At Fort Harrison, Va., 29 September 1864. *Entered service at:* ———. *Born:* 5 February 1843, Lower Merion, Montgomery County, Pa. *Date of issue:* 1 April 1898. *Citation:* Though twice severely wounded while advancing in the assault, he disregarded his injuries and was among the first to enter the fort, where he was wounded for the third time.

JOHNSON, RUEL M.

Rank and organization: Major, 100th Indiana Infantry. *Place and date:* At Chattanooga, Tenn., 25 November 1863. *Entered service at:* Goshen Ind. *Birth:* ———. *Date of issue:* 24 August 1896. *Citation:* While in command of the regiment bravely exposed himself to the fire of the enemy, encouraging and cheering his men.

JOHNSON, SAMUEL

Rank and organization: Private, Company G, 9th Pennsylvania Reserves. *Place and date:* At Antietam, Md., 17 September 1862. *Entered service at:* Connellsville, Pa. *Born:* 1845, Fayette County, Pa. *G.O. No.:* 160, 30 May 1863. *Citation:* Individual bravery and daring in capturing from the enemy 2 colors of the 1st Texas Rangers (C.S.A.), receiving in the act a severe wound.

JOHNSON, WALLACE W.

Rank and organization: Sergeant, Company G, 6th Pennsylvania Reserves. *Place and date:* At Gettysburg, Pa., 2 July 1863. *Entered service at:* Waverly, N.Y. *Birth:* Newfield, N.Y. *Date of issue:* 8 August 1900. *Citation:* With five other volunteers gallantly charged on a number of the enemy's sharpshooters concealed in a log house, captured them, and brought them into the Union lines.

JOHNSTON, DAVID

Rank and organization: Private, Company K, 8th Missouri Infantry. *Place and date:* At Vicksburg, Miss., 22 May 1863. *Entered service at:* Warsaw County, Ill. *Birth:* Indiana County, Pa. *Date of issue:* 16 August 1884. *Citation:* Gallantry in the charge of the "volunteer storming party."

JOHNSTON, WILLIAM P.

Rank and organization: Landsman, U.S. Navy. *Entered service at:* Chicago, Ill. *Birth:* Chicago, Ill. *G.O. No.:* 32, 16 April 1864. *Citation:* Served on board the U.S.S. *Fort Hindman* during the engagement near Harrisonburg, La., 2 March 1864. Badly wounded in the hand during the action, Johnston, despite his wound, took the place of another man to sponge and lead one of the guns throughout the entire action in which the *Fort Hindman* was raked severely with shot and shell from the enemy guns.

JOHNSTON, WILLIE

Rank and organization: Musician, Company D, 3d Vermont Infantry. *Place and date:* Unknown. *Entered service at:* St. Johnsbury, Vt. *Birth:* Morristown, N.Y. *Date of issue:* 16 September 1863. *Citation:* Date and place of act not on record in War Department.

JONES, ANDREW

Rank and organization: Chief Boatswain's Mate, U.S. Navy. *Born:* 1835, Ireland. *Accredited to:* New York. *G.O. No.:* 45, 31 December 1864. *Citation:* Served as chief boatswain's mate on board the U.S. Ironclad, *Chickasaw*, Mobile Bay, 5 August 1864. Although his enlistment was up, Jones volunteered for the battle of Mobile Bay, going on board the *Chickasaw* from the *Vincennes* where he then carried out his duties gallantly thoughout the engagement with the enemy which resulted in the capture of the rebel ram *Tennessee.*

JONES, DAVID

Rank and organization: Private, Company I, 54th Ohio Infantry. *Place and date:* At Vicksburg, Miss., 22 May 1863. *Entered service at:* ———. *Birth:* Fayette County, Ohio. *Date of issue:* 13 June 1894. *Citation:* Gallantry in the charge of the "volunteer storming party."

JONES, JOHN

Rank and organization: Landsman, U.S. Navy. *Born:* 1837, Bridgeport, Conn. *Accredited to:* New Hampshire, *G.O. No.:* 59, 22 June 1865. *Citation:* Served on board the U.S.S. *Rhode Island,* which was engaged in saving the lives of the officers and crew of the *Monitor,* 30 December 1862. Participating in the hazardous rescue of the officers and crew of the sinking *Monitor,* Jones, after rescuing several of the men, became separated in a heavy gale with other members of the cutter that had set out from the *Rhode Island,* and spent many hours in the small boat at the mercy of the weather and high seas until finally picked up by a schooner 50 miles east of Cape Hatteras.

JONES, JOHN E.

Rank and organization: Quartermaster, U.S. Navy. *Born:* 1834, New York, N.Y. *Accredited to:* New York. *G.O. No.:* 45, 31 December 1864. *Citation:* Served as quartermaster on board the U.S.S. *Oneida* in the engagement at Mobile Bay, 5 August 1864. Stationed at the wheel during the fierce action, Jones, though wounded, carried out his duties gallantly by going to the poop to assist at the signals after the wheel ropes were shot away and remained there until ordered to reeve new wheel ropes.

JONES, THOMAS

Rank and organization: Coxswain, U.S. Navy. *Born:* 1820, Baltimore, Md. *Accredited to:* Maryland. *G.O. No.:* 59, 22 June 1865. *Citation:* On board the U.S.S. *Ticonderoga* during attacks on Fort Fisher, 24 and 25 December 1864; and 13 to 15 January 1865. Despite heavy return fire by the enemy and the explosion of the 100-pounder Parrott rifle which killed 8 men and wounded 12 more, Jones, as captain of a gun, performed his duties with skill and courage during the first 2 days of battle. As his ship again took position on the line on the 13th, he remained steadfast as the *Ticonderoga* maintained a well-placed fire upon the batteries on shore, and thereafter, as she materially lessened the power of guns on the mound which had been turned upon our assaulting columns. During this action the flag was planted on one side of the strongest fortifications possessed by the rebels.

JONES, WILLIAM

Rank and organization: Captain of the Top, U.S. Navy. *Born:* 1831, Philadelphia, Pa. *Accredited to:* Pennsylvania. *G.O. No.:* 45, 31 December 1864. *Citation:* As captain of a gun on board the U.S.S. *Richmond* during action against rebel forts and gunboats and with the ram *Tennessee* in Mobile Bay, 5 August 1864. Despite damage to his ship and the loss of several men on board as enemy fire raked her decks, Jones fought his gun with skill and courage throughout the prolonged battle which resulted in the surrender of the rebel ram *Tennessee* and in the damaging and destruction of batteries at Fort Morgan.

JONES, WILLIAM

Rank and organization: First Sergeant, Company A, 73d New York Infantry. *Place and date:* At Spotsylvania, Va., 12 May 1864. *Entered service at:* New York, N.Y. *Birth:* Ireland. *Date of issue:* 1 December 1864. *Citation:* Capture of flag of 65th Virginia Infantry (C.S.A.).

JORDAN, ABSALOM

Rank and organization: Corporal, Company A, 3d Indiana Cavalry. *Place and date:* At Sailors Creek, Va., 6 April 1865. *Entered service at:* North Madison, Ind. *Birth:* Brown County, Ohio. *Date of issue:* 3 May 1865. *Citation:* Capture of flag.

JORDAN, ROBERT

Rank and organization: Coxswain, U.S. Navy. *Born:* 1826, New York, N.Y. *Accredited to:* New York. *G.O. No.:* 17, 10 July 1863. *Cita-*

tion: Attached to the U.S.S. *Minnesota* and temporarily serving on the U.S.S. *Mount Washington,* during action against the enemy in the Nansemond River, 14 April 1863. When the *Mount Washington* drifted against the bank following several successive hits which struck her boilers and stopped her engines, Jordan boarded the stricken vessel and, for 6 hours as fierce artillery and musketry continued to rake her decks, calmly assisted in manning a 12-pound howitzer which had been mounted on the open hurricane deck.

JORDAN, THOMAS

Rank and organization: Quartermaster, U.S. Navy. *Born:* 1840, Portsmouth, Va. *Accredited to:* Virginia. *G.O. No.:* 59, 22 June 1865. *Citation:* On board the U.S.S. *Galena* during the attack on enemy forts at Mobile Bay, 5 August 1864. Securely lashed to the side of the *Oneida* which had suffered the loss of her steering apparatus and an explosion of her boiler from enemy fire, the *Galena* aided the stricken vessel past the enemy forts to safety. Despite heavy damage to his ship from raking enemy fire, Jordan performed his duties with skill and courage throughout the action.

JOSSELYN, SIMEON T.

Rank and organization: First Lieutenant, Company C, 13th Illinois Infantry. *Place and date:* At Missionary Ridge, Tenn., 25 November 1863. *Entered service at:* Amboy, Ill. *Born:* 14 January 1842, Buffalo, N.Y. *Date of issue:* 4 April 1898. *Citation:* While commanding his company, deployed as skirmishers, came upon a large body of the enemy, taking a number of them prisoner. Lt. Josselyn himself shot their color bearer, seized the colors and brought them back to his regiment.

JUDGE, FRANCIS W.

Rank and organization: First Sergeant, Company K, 79th New York Infantry. *Place and date:* At Fort Sanders, Knoxville, Tenn., 29 November 1863. *Entered service at:* ———. *Birth:* England. *Date of issue:* 2 November 1870. *Citation:* The color bearer of the 51st Georgia Infantry. (C.S.A.), having planted his flag upon the side of the work, Sgt. Judge leaped from his position of safety, sprang upon the parapet, and in the face of a concentrated fire seized the flag and returned with it in safety to the fort.

KAISER, JOHN

Rank and organization: Sergeant, Company E, 2d U.S. Artillery. *Place and date:* At Richmond, Va., 27 June 1862. *Entered service at:* ———. *Birth:* Germany. *Date of issue:* 2 April 1878. *Citation:* Gallant and meritorious service during the 7 days' battles before Richmond, Va.

KALTENBACH, LUTHER

Rank and organization: Corporal, Company F, 12th Iowa Infantry. *Place and date:* At Nashville, Tenn., 16 December 1864. *Entered service at:* Honey Creek, Iowa. *Birth:* Germany. *Date of issue:* 24 February 1865. *Citation:* Capture of flag, of 44th Mississippi Infantry (C.S.A.).

KANE, JOHN

Rank and organization: Corporal, Company K, 100th New York Infantry. *Place and date:* At Petersburg, Va., 2 April 1865. *Entered service at:* ———. *Birth:* Ireland. *Date of issue:* 12 May 1865. *Citation:* Gallantry as color bearer in the assault on Fort Gregg.

KANE, THOMAS

Rank and organization: Captain of the Hold, U.S. Navy. *Born:* 1841, Jersey City, N.J. *Accredited to:* New Jersey. *G.O. No.:* 84, 3 October 1867. *Citation:* On board the U.S.S. *Nereus* during the attack on Fort Fisher, on 15 January 1865. Kane, as captain of the hold, displayed outstanding skill and courage as his ship maintained its well-directed fire against fortifications on shore despite the enemy's return fire. When a rebel steamer was discovered in the river back of the fort, the *Nereus*, with forward rifle guns trained, drove the ship off at the third fire. The gallant ship's participation contributed to the planting of the flag on one of the strongest fortifications possessed by the rebels.

KAPPESSER, PETER   *DOB: 1/8/1839   POB: Bavaria, Germany*

Rank and organization: Private, Company B, 149th New York Infantry. *Place and date:* At Lookout Mountain, Tenn., 24 November 1863. *Entered service at:* Syracuse, N.Y. *Birth:* Germany. *Date of issue:* 28 June 1865. *Citation:* Capture of Confederate flag (Bragg's army).

KARPELES, LEOPOLD

Rank and organization: Sergeant, Company E, 57th Massachusetts Infantry. *Place and date:* At Wilderness, Va., 6 May 1864. *Entered service at:* Springfield, Mass. *Birth:* Hungary. *Date of issue:* 30 April 1870. *Citation:* While color bearer, rallied the retreating troops and induced them to check the enemy's advance.

KAUSS (KAUTZ), AUGUST

Rank and organization: Corporal, Company H, 15th New York Heavy Artillery. *Place and date:* At Five Forks, Va., 1 April 1865. *Entered service at:* New York, N.Y. *Birth:* Germany. *Date of issue:* 10 May 1865. *Citation:* Capture of battle flag.

KEELE, JOSEPH

Rank and organization: Sergeant Major, 182d New York Infantry. *Place and date:* At North Anna River, Va., 23 May 1864. *Entered service at:* Staten Island, N.Y. *Birth:* Ireland. *Date of issue:* 25 October 1867. *Citation:* Voluntarily and at the risk of his life carried orders to the brigade commander, which resulted in saving the works his regiment was defending.

KEEN, JOSEPH S.

Rank and organization: Sergeant, Company D, 13th Michigan Infantry. *Place and date:* Near Chattahoochee River, Ga., 1 October 1864. *Entered service at:* Detroit, Mich. *Born:* 24 July 1843, England. *Date of issue:* 4 August 1899. *Citation:* While an escaped prisoner of war within the enemy's lines witnessed an important movement of the enemy, and at great personal risk made his way through the enemy's lines and brought news of the movement to Sherman's army.

KEENE, JOSEPH

Rank and organization: Private, Company B, 26th New York Infantry. *Place and date:* At Fredericksburg, Va., 13 December 1862. *Entered service at:* ———. *Birth:* England. *Date of issue:* 2 December 1892. *Citation:* Voluntarily seized the colors after several color bearers had been shot down and led the regiment in the charge.

KELLEY, ANDREW J.

Rank and organization: Private, Company E, 17th Michigan Infantry. *Place and date:* At Knoxville, Tenn., 20 November 1863. *Entered service at:* Ypsilanti, Mich. *Born:* 2 September 1845, Lagrange County, Ind. *Date of issue:* 17 April 1900. *Citation:* Having voluntarily accompanied a small party to destroy buildings within the enemy's lines whence sharpshooters had been firing, disregarded an order to retire, remained and completed the firing of the buildings, thus insuring their total destruction; this at the imminent risk of his life from the fire of the advancing enemy.

KELLEY, GEORGE V.

Rank and organization: Captain, Company A, 104th Ohio Infantry. *Place and date:* At Franklin, Tenn., 30 November 1864. *Entered service at:* Massillon, Ohio. *Born:* 23 March 1843, Massillon, Ohio. *Date of issue:* 13 February 1865. *Citation:* Capture of flag supposed to be of Cheatham's Corps (C.S.A.).

KELLEY, JOHN

Rank and organization: Second Class Fireman, U.S. Navy. *Birth:* Ireland. *Accredited to:* Ireland. *G.O. No.:* 11, 3 April 1863. *Citation:* Served as second-class fireman on board the U.S.S. *Ceres* in the fight near Hamilton, Roanoke River, 9 July 1862. When his ship was fired on by the enemy with small arms, Kelley returned the raking fire, courageously carrying out his duties through the engagement and was spoken of for "good conduct and cool bravery under enemy fires," by the commanding officer.

KELLEY, LEVERETT M.

Rank and organization: Sergeant, Company A, 36th Illinois Infantry. *Place and date:* At Missionary Ridge, Tenn., 25 November 1863. *Entered service at:* Rutland, Ill. *Birth:* Schenectady, N.Y. *Date of issue:* 4 April 1900. *Citation:* Sprang over the works just captured from the enemy, and calling upon his comrades to follow, rushed forward in the face of a deadly fire and was among the first over the works on the summit, where he compelled the surrender of a Confederate officer and received his sword.

KELLY, ALEXANDER

Rank and organization: First Sergeant, Company F, 6th U.S. Colored Troops. *Place and date:* At Chapins Farm, Va., 29 September 1864. *Entered service at:* ———. *Birth:* Pennsylvania. *Date of issue:* 6 April

1865. *Citation:* Gallantly seized the colors, which had fallen near the enemy's lines of abatis, raised them and rallied the men at a time of confusion and in a place of the greatest danger.

KELLY, DANIEL

Rank and organization: Sergeant, Company G, 8th New York Cavalry. *Place and date:* At Waynesboro, Va., 2 March 1865. *Entered service at:* ———. *Birth:* Groveland, N.Y. *Date of issue:* 26 March 1865. *Citation:* Capture of flag.

KELLY, THOMAS

Rank and organization: Private, Company A, 6th New York Cavalry. *Place and date:* At Front Royal, Va., 16 August 1864. *Entered service at:* ———. *Birth:* Ireland. *Date of issue:* 26 August 1864. *Citation:* Capture of flag.

KEMP, JOSEPH

Rank and organization: First Sergeant, Company D, 5th Michigan Infantry. *Place and date:* At Wilderness, Va., 6 May 1864. *Entered service at:* Sault Ste. Marie, Mich. *Birth:* Lima, Ohio. *Date of issue:* 1 December 1864. *Citation:* Capture of flag of 31st North Carolina (C.S.A.) in a personal encounter.

KENDALL, WILLIAM W.

Rank and organization: First Sergeant, Company A, 49th Indiana Infantry. *Place and date:* At Black River Bridge, Miss., 17 May 1863. *Entered service at:* Dubois County, Ind. *Birth:* Dubois County, Ind. *Date of issue:* 12 February 1894. *Citation:* Voluntarily led the company in a charge and was the first to enter the enemy's works, taking a number of prisoners.

KENDRICK, THOMAS

Rank and organization: Coxswain, U.S. Navy. *Born:* 1839, Bath, Maine. *Accredited to:* Maine. *G.O. No.:* 45, 31 December 1864. *Citation:* Served as coxswain on board the U.S.S. *Oneida* in the engagement at Mobile Bay, 5 August, 1864. Volunteering for the Mobile Bay action from *Bienville*, Kendrick displayed courageous devotion to duty, and his excellent conduct throughout the battle which resulted in the capture of the rebel ram *Tennessee* and in the damaging of Fort Morgan, attracted the attention of the commanding officer and those serving around him.

KENNA, BARNETT

Rank and organization: Quartermaster, U.S. Navy. *Born:* 1827, England. *Accredited to:* Massachusetts. *G.O. No.:* 45, 31 December 1864. *Citation:* On board the U.S.S. *Brooklyn* during action against rebel forts and gunboats and with the ram *Tennessee*, in Mobile Bay, 5 August 1864. Despite severe damage to his ship and the loss of several men on board as enemy fire raked her decks from stem to stern, Kenna fought his gun with skill and courage throughout the furious action which resulted in the surrender of the rebel ram *Tennessee* and in the damaging and destruction of batteries at Fort Morgan.

KENNEDY, JOHN

Rank and organization: Private, Company M, 2d U.S. Artillery. *Place and date:* At Trevilian Station, Va., 11 June 1864. *Entered service at:* ———. *Birth:* Ireland. *Date of issue:* 19 August 1892. *Citation:* Remained at his gun, resisting with its implements the advancing cavalry, and thus secured the retreat of his detachment.

KENYON, CHARLES

Rank and organization: Fireman, U.S. Navy. *Born:* 1840, New York. *Accredited to:* New York. *G.O. No.:* 11, 3 April 1863. *Citation:* On board the U.S.S. *Galena* in the attack upon Drewry's Bluff, 15 May 1862. Severely burned while extricating a priming wire which had become bent and fixed in the bow gun while his ship underwent terrific shelling from the enemy, Kenyon hastily dressed his hands with cotton waste and oil and courageously returned to his gun while enemy sharpshooters in rifle pits along the banks continued to direct their fire at the men at the guns.

KENYON, JOHN S.

Rank and organization: Sergeant, Company D, 3d New York Cavalry. *Place and date:* At Trenton, N.C., 15 May 1862. *Entered service at:* Schenevus, N.Y. *Born:* 5 May 1843, Grosvenors, Schoharie County, N.Y. *Date of issue:* 28 September 1897. *Citation:* Voluntarily left a retiring column, returned in face of the enemy's fire, helped a wounded man upon a horse, and so enable him to escape capture or death.

KENYON, SAMUEL P.

Rank and organization: Private, Company B, 24th New York Cavalry. *Place and date:* At Sailors Creeks, Va., 6 April 1865. *Entered service at:* Oriskany Falls, N.Y. *Birth:* Ira, N.Y. *Date of issue:* 3 May 1865. *Citation:* Capture of battle flag.

KEOUGH, JOHN

Rank and organization: Corporal, Company E, 67th Pennsylvania Infantry. *Place and date:* At Sailors Creek, Va., 6 April 1865. *Entered service at:* Albany, N.Y. *Birth:* Ireland. *Date of issue:* 3 May 1865. *Citation:* Capture of battle flag of 50th Georgia Infantry (C.S.A.).

KEPHART, JAMES

Rank and organization: Private, Company C, 13th U.S. Infantry. *Place and date:* At Vicksburg, Miss., 19 May 1863. *Entered service at:* ———. *Birth:* Venango County, Pa. *Date of issue:* 13 May 1899. *Citation:* Voluntarily and at the risk of his life, under a severe fire of the enemy, aided and assisted to the rear an officer who had been severely wounded and left on the field.

KERR, THOMAS R.

Rank and organization: Captain, Company C, 14th Pennsylvania Cavalry. *Place and date:* At Moorfield, W. Va., 7 August 1864. *Entered service at:* Pittsburgh, Pa. *Born:* 24 April 1843, Ireland. *Date of issue:*

13 June 1894. *Citation:* After being most desperately wounded, he captured the colors of the 8th Virginia Cavalry (C.S.A.).

KIGGINS, JOHN

Rank and organization: Sergeant, Company D, 149th New York Infantry. *Place and date:* At Lookout Mountain, Tenn., 24 November 1863. *Entered service at:* Syracuse, N.Y. *Birth:* Syracuse, N.Y. *Date of issue:* 12 January 1892. *Citation:* Waved the colors to save the lives of the men who were being fired upon by their own batteries, and thereby drew upon himself a concentrated fire from the enemy.

KIMBALL, JOSEPH

Rank and organization: Private, Company B, 2d West Virginia Cavalry. *Place and date:* At Sailors Creek, Va., 6 April 1865. *Entered service at:* Ironton, Ohio. *Birth:* Littleton, N.H. *Date of issue:* 3 May 1865. *Citation:* Capture of flag of 6th North Carolina Infantry (C.S.A.).

KINDIG, JOHN M.

Rank and organization: Corporal, Company A, 63d Pennsylvania Infantry. *Place and date:* At Spotsylvania, Va., 12 May 1864. *Entered service at:* ———. *Birth:* East Liberty, Pa. *Date of issue:* 1 December 1864. *Citation:* Capture of flag of 28th North Carolina Infantry. (C.S.A.).

KING, HORATIO C.

Rank and organization: Major and Quartermaster, U.S. Volunteers. *Place and date:* Near Dinwiddie Courthouse, Va., 31 March 1865. *Entered service at:* Brooklyn, N.Y. *Born:* 22 December 1837, Portland, Maine. *Date of issue:* 23 September 1897. *Citation:* While serving as a volunteer aide, carried orders to the reserve brigade and participated with it in the charge which repulsed the enemy.

KING, ROBERT H.

Rank and organization: Landsman, U.S. Navy. *Place:* Plymouth, N.C. *Born:* 1845, New York. *Accredited to:* New York. *G.O. No.:* 45, 31 December 1864. *Citation:* King served on board the U.S. Picket Boat No. 1, in action, 27 October 1864, against the Confederate ram, *Albemarle*, which had resisted repeated attacks by our steamers and had kept a large force of vessels employed in watching her. The picket boat, equipped with a spar torpedo, succeeded in passing the enemy pickets within 20 yards without being discovered and then made for the *Albemarle* under a full head of steam. Immediately taken under fire by the ram, the small boat plunged on, jumped the log boom which encircled the target and exploded its torpedo under the port bow of the ram. The picket boat was destroyed by enemy fire and almost the entire crew taken prisoner or lost.

KING, RUFUS, JR.

Rank and organization: First Lieutenant, 4th U.S. Artillery. *Place and date:* At White Oak Swamp Bridge, Va., 30 June 1862. *Entered service at:* New York. *Birth:* New York. *Date of issue:* 2 April 1898. *Citation:* This officer, when his captain was wounded, succeeded to the command of two batteries while engaged against a superior force of the enemy and fought his guns most gallantly until compelled to retire.

KINNAIRD, SAMUEL W.

Rank and organization: Landsman, U.S. Navy. *Born:* 1843, New York, N.Y. *Accredited to:* New York. *G.O. No.:* 45, 31 December 1864. *Citation:* Served as a landsman on board the U.S.S. *Lackawanna* during successful attacks against Fort Morgan, rebel gunboats and the ram *Tennessee* in Mobile Bay, 5 August 1864. Showing a presence of mind and cheerfulness that had much to do with maintaining the crew's morale, Kinnaird served gallantly through the action which resulted in the capture of the prize rebel ram *Tennessee* and in the destruction of batteries at Fort Morgan.

KINSEY, JOHN

Rank and organization: Corporal, Company B, 45th Pennsylvania Infantry. *Place and date:* At Spotsylvania, Va., 18 May 1864. *Entered service at:* ————. *Birth:* Lancaster County, Pa. *Date of issue:* 2 March 1897. *Citation:* Seized the colors, the color bearer having been shot, and with great gallantry succeeded in saving them from capture.

KIRBY, DENNIS T.

Rank and organization: Major, 8th Missouri Infantry. *Place and date:* At Vicksburg, Miss., 22 May 1863. *Entered service at:* St. Louis, Mo. *Born:* 14 September 1838, Niagara, County, N.Y. *Date of issue:* 31 January 1894. *Citation:* Seized the colors when the color bearer was killed and bore them himself in the assault.

KIRK, JONATHAN C.

Rank and organization: Captain, Company F, 20th Indiana Infantry. *Place and date:* At North Anna River, Va., 23 May 1864. *Entered service at:* Wilmington, Ohio. *Birth:* Clinton County, Ohio. *Date of issue:* 13 June 1894. *Citation:* Volunteered for dangerous service and single-handed captured 13 armed Confederate soldiers and marched them to the rear.

KLINE, HARRY

Rank and organization: Private, Company E, 40th New York Infantry. *Place and date:* At Sailors Creek, Va., 6 April 1865. *Entered service at:* Syracuse, N.Y. *Birth:* Germany. *Date of issue:* 10 May 1865. *Citation:* Capture of battle flag.

KLOTH, CHARLES H.

Rank and organization: Private, Chicago Mercantile Battery, Illinois Light Artillery. *Place and date:* At Vicksburg, Miss., 22 May 1863. *Entered service at:* Chicago, Ill. *Birth:* Europe. *Date of issue:* 15 January 1895. *Citation:* Carried with others by hand a cannon up to and fired it through an embrasure of the enemy's works.

KNIGHT, CHARLES H.

Rank and organization: Corporal, Company I, 9th New Hampshire Infantry. *Place and date:* At Petersburg, Va., 30 July 1864. *Entered ser-*

vice at: Keene, N.H. *Birth:* Keene, N.H. *Date of issue:* 27 July 1896. *Citation:* In company with a sergeant, was the first to enter the exploded mine; was wounded but took several prisoners to the Federal lines.

KNIGHT, WILLIAM J.

Rank and organization: Private, Company E, 21st Ohio Infantry. *Place and date:* Georgia, April 1862. *Entered service at:* Farmer Center, Defiance County, Ohio. *Born:* 29 January 1837, Apple Creek, Wayne County, Ohio. *Date of issue:* September 1863. *Citation:* One of the 19 of 22 men (including 2 civilians) who, by direction of Gen. Mitchell (or Buell), penetrated nearly 200 miles south into enemy territory and captured a railroad train at Big Shanty, Ga., in an attempt to destroy the bridges and track between Chattanooga and Atlanta.

KNOWLES, ABIATHER J.

Rank and organization: Private, Company D, 2d Maine Infantry. *Place and date:* At Bull Run, Va., 21 July 1861, *Entered service at:* ———. *Born:* 15 March 1830, LaGrange, Maine. *Date of issue:* 27 December 1894. *Citation:* Removed dead and wounded under heavy fire.

KNOX, EDWARD M.

Rank and organization: Second Lieutenant, 15th New York Battery. *Place and date:* At Gettysburg, Pa., 2 July 1863. *Entered service at:* New York, N.Y. *Birth:* New York, N.Y. *Date of issue:* 18 October 1892. *Citation:* Held his ground with the battery after the other batteries had fallen back until compelled to draw his piece off by hand; he was severely wounded.

KOOGLE, JACOB

Rank and organization: First Lieutenant, Company G, 7th Maryland Infantry. *Place and date:* At Five Forks, Va., 1 April 1865. *Entered service at:* ———. *Birth:* Frederick, Md. *Date of issue:* 10 May 1865. *Citation:* Capture of battle flag.

KOUNTZ, JOHN S.

Rank and organization: Musician, Company G, 37th Ohio Infantry. *Place and date:* At Missionary Ridge, Tenn., 25 November 1863. *Entered service at:* Maumee, Ohio. *Birth:* Maumee, Ohio. *Date of issue:* 13 August 1895. *Citation:* Seized a musket and joined in the charge in which he was severely wounded.

KRAMER, THEODORE L.

Rank and organization: Private, Company G, 188th Pennsylvania Infantry. *Place and date:* At Chapins Farm, Va., 29 September 1864. *Entered service at:* Danville, Pa. *Birth:* Luzerne County, Pa. *Date of issue:* 6 April 1865. *Citation:* Took one of the first prisoners, a captain.

KRETSINGER, GEORGE

Rank and organization: Private, Chicago Mercantile Battery, Illinois Light Artillery. *Place and date:* At Vicksburg, Miss., 22 May 1863. *En-*

tered service at: Chicago, Ill. *Birth:* Herkimer County, N.Y. *Date of issue:* 20 July 1897. *Citation:* Carried with others by hand a cannon up to and fired it through an embrasure of the enemy's works.

KUDER, ANDREW

Rank and organization: Second Lieutenant, Company G, 8th New York Cavalry. *Place and date:* At Waynesboro, Va., 2 March 1865. *Entered service at:* ———. *Birth:* Groveland, N.Y. *Date of issue:* 26 March 1865. *Citation:* Capture of flag.

KUDER, JEREMIAH

Rank and organization: Lieutenant, Company A, 74th Indiana Infantry. *Place and date:* At Jonesboro, Ga., 1 September 1864. *Entered service at:* Warsaw, Ind. *Birth:* Seneca County, Ohio. *Date of issue:* 7 April 1865. *Citation:* Capture of flag of 8th and 19th Arkansas (C.S.A.).

LABILL, JOSEPH S.

Rank and organization: Private, Company C, 6th Missouri Infantry. *Place and date:* At Vicksburg, Miss., 22 May 1863. *Entered service at:* Vandalia, Ill. *Birth:* France. *Date of issue:* 14 August 1894. *Citation:* Gallantry in the charge of the "volunteer storming party."

LADD, GEORGE

Rank and organization: Private, Company H, 22d New York Cavalry. *Place and date:* At Waynesboro, Va., 2 March 1865. *Entered service at:* Carmillus, Onondaga County, N.Y. *Birth:* Carmillus, N.Y. *Date of issue:* 26 March 1865. *Citation:* Captured a standard bearer, his flag, horse and equipment.

LAFFERTY, JOHN

Rank and organization: Fireman, U.S. Navy. *Born:* 1842, New York, N.Y. *Accredited to:* Pennsylvania. *G.O. No.:* 45, 31 December 1864. *Citation:* Served on board the U.S.S. *Wyalusing* and participated in a plan to destroy the rebel ram *Albemarle* in Roanoke River, 25 May 1864. Volunteering for the hazardous mission, Lafferty participated in the transfer of two torpedoes across an island swamp and then served as sentry to keep guard of clothes and arms left by other members of the party. After being rejoined by others of the party who had been discovered before the plan could be completed, Lafferty succeeded in returning to the mother ship after spending 24 hours of discomfort in the rain and swamp.

LAFFEY, BARTLETT

Rank and organization: Seaman, U.S. Navy. *Born:* 1841, Ireland. *Accredited to:* Massachusetts. *G.O. No.:* 32, 16 April 1864. *Citation:* Off Yazoo City, Miss., 5 March 1864, embarking from the *Marmora* with a 12-pound howitzer mounted on a field carriage, Laffey landed with the gun and crew in the midst of heated battle and, bravely standing by his gun despite enemy rifle fire which cut the gun carriage and rammer, contributed to the turning back of the enemy during the fierce engagement.

LAING, WILLIAM

Rank and organization: Sergeant, Company F, 158th New York Infantry. *Place and date:* At Chapins Farm, Va., 29 September 1864. *Entered service at:* New York, N.Y. *Birth:* Hempstead, N.Y. *Date of issue:* 6 April 1865. *Citation:* Was among the first to scale the parapet.

LAKIN, DANIEL

Rank and organization: Seaman, U.S. Navy. *Born:* 1834, Baltimore, Md. *Accredited to:* Maryland. *G.O. No.:* 11, 3 April 1863. *Citation:* On board the U.S.S. *Commodore Perry* in the attack upon Franklin, Va., 3 October 1862. With enemy fire raking the deck of his ship and blockades thwarting her progress, Lakin remained at his post and performed his duties with skill and courage as the *Commodore Perry* fought a gallant battle to silence many rebel batteries as she steamed down the Blackwater River.

LANDIS, JAMES P.

Rank and organization: Chief Bugler, 1st Pennsylvania Cavalry. *Place and date:* At Paines Crossroads, Va., 5 April 1865. *Entered service at:* ―――. *Birth:* Mifflin County, Pa. *Date of issue:* 3 May 1865. *Citation:* Capture of flag.

LANE, MORGAN D.

Rank and organization: Private, Signal Corps, U.S. Army. *Place and date:* Near Jetersville, Va., 6 April 1865. *Entered service at:* Allegany, Mich. *Birth:* Monroe, N.Y. *Date of issue:* 16 March 1866. *Citation:* Capture of flag of gunboat *Nansemond*.

LANFARE, AARON S.

Rank and organization: First Lieutenant, Company B, 1st Connecticut Cavalry. *Place and date:* At Sailors Creek, Va., 6 April 1865. *Entered service at:* Branford, Conn. *Birth:* Branford, Conn. *Date of issue:* 3 May 1865. *Citation:* Capture of flag of 11th Florida Infantry (C.S.A.).

LANGBEIN, J. C. JULIUS

Rank and organization: Musician, Company B, 9th New York Infantry. *Place and date:* At Camden, N.C., 19 April 1862. *Entered service at:* New York, N.Y. *Born:* 29 September 1846, Germany. *Date of issue:* 7 January 1895. *Citation:* A drummer boy, 15 years of age, he voluntarily and under a heavy fire went to the aid of a wounded officer, procured medical assistance for him, and aided in carrying him to a place of safety.

LANN, JOHN S.

Rank and organization: Landsman, U.S. Navy. *Born:* 1842, Rochester, N.Y. *Accredited to:* New York. *G.O. No.:* 59, 22 June 1865. *Citation:* As landsman on board the U.S.S. *Magnolia*, St. Marks, Fla., 5 and 6 March, Lann served with the Army in charge of Navy howitzers during the attack on St. Marks and throughout this fierce engagement made remarkable efforts in assisting transport of the gun. His coolness and determination in standing by his gun while under the fire of the enemy were a credit to the service to which he belonged.

LARIMER, SMITH

Rank and organization: Corporal, Company G, 2d Ohio Cavalry. *Place and date:* At Sailors Creek, Va., 6 April 1865. *Entered service at:* Columbus, Ohio. *Birth:* Richland County, Ohio. *Date of issue:* 3 May 1865. *Citation:* Capture of flag of General Kershaw's headquarters.

LARRABEE, JAMES W.

Rank and organization: Corporal, Company I, 55th Illinois Infantry. *Place and date:* At Vicksburg, Miss., 22 May 1863. *Entered service at:* Mendota, Ill. *Birth:* Rensselaer County, N.Y. *Date of issue:* 2 September 1893. *Citation:* Gallantry in the charge of the "volunteer storming party."

LAWSON, GAINES

Rank and organization: First Sergeant, Company D, 4th East Tennessee Infantry. *Place and date:* At Minville, Tenn., 3 October 1863. *Entered service at:* Tennessee. *Born:* 1841, Hawkins County, Tenn. *Date of issue:* 11 June 1895. *Citation:* Went to the aid of a wounded comrade between the lines and carried him to a place of safety.

LAWSON, JOHN

Rank and organization: Landsman, U.S. Navy. *Born:* 1837, Pennsylvania. *Accredited to:* Pennsylvania. *G.O. No.:* 45, 31 December 1864. *Citation:* On board the flagship U.S.S. *Hartford* during successful attacks against Fort Morgan, rebel gunboats and the ram *Tennessee* in Mobile Bay on 5 August 1864. Wounded in the leg and thrown violently against the side of the ship when an enemy shell killed or wounded the 6-man crew as the shell whipped on the berth deck, Lawson, upon regaining his composure, promptly returned to his station and, although urged to go below for treatment, steadfastly continued his duties throughout the remainder of the action.

LAWTON, HENRY W.

Rank and organization: Captain, Company A, 30th Indiana Infantry. *Place and date:* At Atlanta, Ga., 3 August 1864. *Entered service at:* Ft. Wayne, Allen County, Ind. *Birth:* Ohio. *Date of issue:* 22 May 1893. *Citation:* Led a charge of skirmishers against the enemy's rifle pits and stubbornly and successfully resisted 2 determined attacks of the enemy to retake the works.

LEAR, NICHOLAS

Rank and organization: Quartermaster, U.S. Navy. *Born:* 1826, Rhode Island. *Accredited to:* Pennsylvania. *G.O. No.:* 59, 22 June 1865. *Citation:* Lear served on board the U.S.S. *New Ironsides* during action in several attacks on Fort Fisher, 24 and 25 December 1864; and 13, 14, and 15 January 1865. The ship steamed in and took the lead in the ironclad division close inshore and immediately opened its starboard battery in a barrage of well-directed fire to cause several fires and explosions and dismount several guns during the first 2 days of fighting.

Taken under fire as she steamed into position on 13 January, the *New Ironsides* fought all day and took on ammunition at night despite severe weather conditions. When the enemy came out of his bomb-proofs to defend the fort against the storming party, the ship's battery disabled nearly every gun on the fort facing the shore before the cease-fire order was given by the flagship.

LEE, JAMES H.

Rank and organization: Seaman, U.S. Navy. *Born:* 1840, New York. *Accredited to:* New York. *G.O. No.:* 45, 31 December 1864. *Citation:* Served as seaman on board the U.S.S. *Kearsarge* when she destroyed the *Alabama* off Cherbourg, France, 19 June 1864. Acting as sponger of the No. 1 gun during this bitter engagement, Lee exhibited marked coolness and good conduct and was highly recommended for his gallantry under fire by the divisional officer.

LELAND, GEORGE W.

Rank and organization: Gunner's Mate, U.S. Navy. *Born:* 1834, Savannah, Ga. *Accredited to:* Georgia. *G.O. No.:* 32, 16 April 1864. *Citation:* Serving on board the U.S.S. *Lehigh*, Charleston Harbor, 16 November 1863, during the hazardous task, of freeing the *Lehigh*, which had grounded, and was under heavy enemy fire from Fort Moultrie. Rowing the small boat which was used in the hazardous task of transferring hawsers from the *Lehigh* to the *Nahant*, Leland twice succeeded in making the trip, only to find that each had been in vain when the hawsers were cut by enemy fire and chaffing.

LEON, PIERRE

Rank and organization: Captain of the Forecastle, U.S. Navy. *Born:* 1837, New Orleans, La. *Accredited to:* Pennsylvania. *G.O. No.:* 11, 3 April 1863. *Citation:* Serving on board the U.S.S. *Baron De Kalb*, Yazoo River Expedition, 23 to 27 December 1862. Proceeding under orders up the Yazoo River, the U.S.S. *Baron De Kalb*, with the object of capturing or destroying the enemy's transports, came upon the steamers *John Walsh, R. J. Locklan, Golden Age* and the *Scotland* sunk on a bar where they were ordered fired. Continuing up the river, she was fired on, but upon returning the fire, caused the enemy's retreat. Returning down the Yazoo, she destroyed and captured larger quantities of enemy equipment and several prisoners. Serving bravely throughout this action, Leon, as captain of the forecastle, "distinguished himself in the various actions."

J. LEONARD, EDWIN

Rank and organization: Sergeant, Company I, 37th Massachusetts Infantry. *Place and date:* Near Petersburg, Va., 18 June 1864. *Entered service at:* Agawan, Mass. *Birth:* Agawan, Mass. *Date of issue:* 16 August 1894. *Citation:* Voluntarily exposed himself to the fire of a Union brigade to stop their firing on the Union skirmish line.

3. LEONARD, WILLIAM E.

Rank and organization: Private, Company F, 85th Pennsylvania Infantry. *Place and date:* At Deep Bottom, Va., 16 April 1864. *Entered service at:* Jacksonville, Pa. *Birth:* Greene County, Pa. *Date of issue:* 6 April 1865. *Citation:* Capture of battle flag.

LESLIE, FRANK

Rank and organization: Private, Company B, 4th New York Cavalry. *Place and date:* At Front Royal, Va., 15 August 1864. *Entered service at:* ⟵⟶ *Birth:* England. *Date of issue:* 26 August 1864. *Citation:* Capture of colors of 3d Virginia Infantry (C.S.A.).

LEVY, BENJAMIN

Rank and organization: Private, Company B, 1st New York Infantry. *Place and date:* At Glendale, Va., 30 June 1862. *Entered service at:* —NY—. *Birth:* New York, N.Y. *Date of issue:* 1 March 1865. *Citation:* This soldier, a drummer boy, took the gun of a sick comrade, went into the fight, and when the color bearers were shot down, carried the colors and saved them from capture.

LEWIS, DeWITT CLINTON

Rank and organization: Captain, Company F, 97th Pennsylvania Infantry. *Place and date:* At Secessionville, S.C., 16 June 1862. *Entered service at:* —PA—. *Birth:* West Chester, Pa. *Date of issue:* 23 April 1896. *Citation:* While retiring with his men before a heavy fire of canister shot at short range, returned in the face of the enemy's fire and rescued an exhausted private of his company who but for this timely action would have lost his life by drowning in the morass through which the troops were retiring.

LEWIS, HENRY

Rank and organization: Corporal, Company B, 47th Ohio Infantry. *Place and date:* At Vicksburg, Miss., 3 May 1863. *Entered service at:* Adrian, Mich. *Born:* 14 December 1842, Van Buren Township, Wayne County, Mich. *Date of issue:* 17 April 1917. *Citation:* Was one of a party that volunteered and attempted to run the enemy's batteries with a steam tug and two barges loaded with subsistence stores.

LEWIS, SAMUEL E.

Rank and organization: Corporal, Company G, 1st Rhode Island Light Artillery. *Place and date:* At Petersburg, Va., 2 April 1865. *Entered service at:* Coventry, R.I. *Birth:* Coventry, R.I. *Date of issue:* 16 June 1866. *Citation:* Was one of a detachment of 20 picked artillerymen who voluntarily accompanied an infantry assaulting party and who turned upon the enemy the guns captured in the assault.

LIBAIRE, ADOLPHE

Rank and organization: Captain, Company E, 9th New York Infantry. *Place and date:* At Antietam, Md., 17 September 1862. *Entered service at:* New York, N.Y. *Birth:* —NY—. *Date of issue:* 2 April 1898. *Citation:* In the advance on the enemy and after his color bearer and the entire color guard of 8 men had been shot down, this officer seized the regimental flag and with conspicuous gallantry carried it to the extreme front, urging the line forward.

LILLEY, JOHN

Rank and organization: Private, Company F, 205th Pennsylvania Infantry. *Place and date:* At Petersburg, Va., 2 April 1865. *Entered service at:* —PA—. *Birth:* Mifflin County, Pa. *Date of issue:* 20 May 1865. *Citation:* After his regiment began to waiver he rushed on alone to capture the enemy flag. He reached the works and the Confederate color bearer who, at bayonet point, he caused to surrender with several enemy soldiers. He kept his prisoners in tow when they realized he was alone as his regiment in the meantime withdrew further to the rear.

LITTLE, HENRY F. W.

Rank and organization: Sergeant, Company D, 7th New Hampshire Infantry. *Place and date:* Near Richmond, Va., September 1864. *Entered service at:* New Hampshire. *Birth:* Manchester, N.H. *Date of issue:* 14 January 1870. *Citation:* Gallantry on the skirmish line.

LITTLEFIELD, GEORGE H.

Rank and organization: Corporal, Company G, 1st Maine Veteran Infantry. *Place and date:* At Fort Fisher, Va., 25 March 1865. *Entered service at:* Skowhegan, Maine. *Birth:* Skowhegan, Maine. *Date of issue:* 22 June 1885. *Citation:* The color sergeant having been wounded, this soldier picked up the flag and bore it to the front, to the great encouragement of the charging column.

LIVINGSTON, JOSIAH O.

Rank and organization: First Lieutenant, and Adjutant, 9th Vermont Infantry. *Place and date:* At Newport Barracks, N.C., 2 February 1864. *Entered service at:* Marshfield, Vt. *Birth:* Walden, Vt. *Date of issue:* 8 September 1891. *Citation:* When, after desperate resistance, the small garrison had been driven back to the river by a vastly superior force, this officer, while a small force held back the enemy, personally fired the railroad bridge, and, although wounded himself, asssisted a wounded officer over the burning structure.

LLOYD, BENJAMIN

Rank and organization: Coal Heaver, U.S. Navy. *Born:* 1839. England. *Accredited to:* Pennsylvania. *G.O. No.:* 45, 31 December 1864. *Citation:* Serving on board the U.S.S. *Wyalusing* and participating in a plan to destroy the rebel ram *Albemarle* in Roanoke River, 25 May 1864. Volunteering for the hazardous mission, Lloyd participated in the transfer of two torpedoes across an island swamp. Serving as boatkeeper, he aided in rescuing others of the party who had been detected before the plan could be completed, but who escaped, leaving detection of the plan impossible. By his skill and courage, Lloyd succeeded in returning to the mother ship after spending 24 hours of discomfort in the rain and swamp.

LLOYD, JOHN W.

Rank and organization: Coxswain, U.S. Navy. *Born:* 1831, New York, N.Y. *Accredited to:* New York. *G.O. No.:* 45, 31 December

1864. *Citation:* Serving on board the U.S.S. *Wyalusing* during an attempt to destroy the rebel ram *Albemarle* in Roanoke River, 25 May 1864, Lloyd participated in this daring plan by swimming the Roanoke River heavily weighted with a line which was used for hauling torpedoes across. Thwarted by discovery just before the completion of the plan, Lloyd cut the torpedo guiding line to prevent detection of the plan by the enemy and again swam the river, narrowly escaping enemy musket fire and regaining the ship in safety.

LOCKE, LEWIS

Rank and organization: Private, Company A, 1st New Jersey Cavalry. *Place and date:* At Paines Crossroads, Va., 5 April 1865. *Entered service at:* Jersey City, N.J. *Birth:* Clintonville, N.Y. *Date of issue:* 3 May 1865. *Citation:* Capture of a Confederate flag.

*LOGAN, HUGH

Rank and organization: Captain of the Afterguard, U.S. Navy. *Born:* 1834, Ireland. *Accredited to:* Massachusetts. *G.O. No.:* 59, 22 June 1865. *Citation:* On board the U.S.S. *Rhode Island* which was engaged in rescuing men from the stricken *Monitor* in Mobile Bay, on 30 December 1862. After the *Monitor* sprang a leak and went down, Logan courageously risked his life in a gallant attempt to rescue members of the crew. Although sacrificing his life during the hazardous operation, he had made every effort possible to save the lives of his fellow men.

LONERGAN, JOHN

Rank and organization: Captain, Company A, 13th Vermont Infantry. *Place and date:* At Gettysburg, Pa., 2 July 1863. *Entered service at:* Burlington, Vt. *Birth:* Ireland. *Date of issue:* 28 October 1893. *Citation:* Gallantry in the recapture of 4 guns and the capture of 2 additional guns from the enemy; also the capture of a number of prisoners.

LONGSHORE, WILLIAM H.

Rank and organization: Private, Company D, 30th Ohio Infantry. *Place and date:* At Vicksburg, Miss., 22 May 1863. *Entered service at:* ———. *Birth:* Muskingum County, Ohio. *Date of issue:* 10 August 1894. *Citation:* Gallantry in the charge of the "volunteer storming party."

LONSWAY, JOSEPH

Rank and organization: Private, Company D, 20th New York Cavalry. *Place and date:* At Murfrees Station, Va., 16 October 1864. *Entered service at:* ———. *Birth:* Clayton, N.Y. *Date of issue:* Unknown. *Citation:* Volunteered to swim Blackwater River to get a large flat used as a ferry on other side; succeeded in getting the boat safely across, making it possible for a detachment to cross the river and take possession of the enemy's breastworks.

LORD, WILLIAM

Rank and organization: Musician, Company C, 40th Massachusetts Infantry. *Place and date:* At Drurys Bluff, Va., 16 May 1864. *Entered service at:* Lawrence, Mass. *Birth:* England. *Date of issue:* 4 April 1898. *Citation:* Went to the assistance of a wounded officer lying helpless between the lines, and under fire from both sides removed him to a place of safety.

LORISH, ANDREW J.

Rank and organization: Commissary Sergeant, 19th New York Cavalry (1st New York Dragoons). *Place and date:* At Winchester, Va., 19 September 1864. *Entered service at:* ———. *Born:* 8 November 1832, Dansville, Steuben County, N.Y. *Date of issue:* 27 September 1864. *Citation:* Amid the enemy he grabbed the flag from a color bearer who then called for help. When the bearer's comrades were readying their rifles he dashed directly at them securing their disarming. As he rode away, the Confederates picked up their guns firing at the captor of their flag.

LOVE, GEORGE M.

Rank and organization: Colonel, 116th New York Infantry. *Place and date:* At Cedar Creek, Va., 19 October 1864. *Entered service at:* New York. *Birth:* New York. *Date of issue:* 6 March 1865. *Citation:* Capture of battle flag of 2d South Carolina (C.S.A.).

LOVERING, GEORGE M.

Rank and organization: First Sergeant, Company I, 4th Massachusetts Infantry. *Place and date:* At Port Hudson, La., 14 June 1863. *Entered service at:* East Randolph, Mass. *Born:* 10 January 1832, Springfield, N.H. *Date of issue:* 19 November 1891. *Citation:* During a momentary confusion in the ranks caused by other troops rushing upon the regiment, this soldier, with coolness and determination, rendered efficient aid in preventing a panic among the troops.

LOWER, CYRUS B.

Rank and organization: Private, Company K, 13th Pennsylvania Reserves. *Place and date:* At Wilderness, Va., 7 May 1864. *Entered service at:* ———. *Birth:* Lawrence County, Pa. *Date of issue:* 20 July 1887. *Citation:* Gallant services and soldierly qualities in voluntarily rejoining his command after having been wounded.

LOWER, ROBERT A.

Rank and organization: Private, Company K, 55th Illinois Infantry. *Place and date:* At Vicksburg, Miss., 22 May 1863. *Entered service at:* Elmwood, Ill. *Birth:* Illinois. *Date of issue:* 2 September 1893. *Citation:* Gallantry in the charge of the "volunteer storming party."

LOYD, GEORGE

Rank and organization: Private, Company A, 122d Ohio Infantry. *Place and date:* At Petersburg, Va., 2 April 1865. *Entered service at:* ———. *Birth:* Muskingum County, Ohio. *Date of issue:* 16 April 1891. *Citation:* Capture of division flag of General Heth.

LUCAS, GEORGE W.

Rank and organization: Private, Company C, 3d Missouri Cavalry. *Place and date:* At Benton, Ark., 25 July 1864. *Entered service at:* Mt. Sterling, Brown County, Ill. *Birth:* Adams County, Ill. *Date of issue:* December 1864. *Citation:* Pursued and killed Confederate Brig. Gen. George M. Holt, Arkansas Militia, capturing his arms and horse.

LUCE, MOSES A.

Rank and organization: Sergeant, Company E, 4th Michigan Infantry. *Place and date:* At Laurel Hill, Va., 10 May 1864. *Entered service at:* Hillsdale, Mich. *Born:* 14 May 1842, Payson, Adams County, Ill. *Date of issue:* 7 February 1895. *Citation:* Voluntarily returned in the face of the advancing enemy to the assistance of a wounded and helpless comrade, and carried him, at imminent peril, to a place of safety.

LUDGATE, WILLIAM

Rank and organization: Captain, Company G, 59th New York Veteran Infantry. *Place and date:* At Farmville, Va., 7 April 1865. *Entered service at:* New York, N.Y. *Birth:* England. *Date of issue:* 10 August 1889. *Citation:* Gallantry and promptness in rallying his men and advancing with a small detachment to save a bridge about to be fired by the enemy.

LUDWIG, CARL

Rank and organization: Private, 34th New York Battery. *Place and date:* At Petersburg, Va., 18 June 1864. *Entered service at:* ———. *Birth:* France. *Date of issue:* 30 July 1896. *Citation:* As gunner of his piece, inflicted singly a great loss upon the enemy and distinguished himself in the removal of the piece while under a heavy fire.

LUNT, ALPHONSO M.

Rank and organization: Sergeant, Company F, 38th Massachusetts Infantry. *Place and date:* At Opequan Creek, Va., 19 September 1864. *Entered service at:* Cambridge, Mass. *Birth:* Berwick, Maine. *Date of issue:* 10 May 1894. *Citation:* Carried his flag to the most advanced position where, left almost alone close to the enemy's lines he refused their demand to surrender, withdrew at great personal peril, and saved his flag.

LUTES, FRANKLIN W.

Rank and organization: Corporal, Company D, 111th New York Infantry. *Place and date:* At Petersburg, Va., 31 March 1865. *Entered service at:* ———. *Birth:* Oneida County, N.Y. *Date of issue:* 3 April 1865. *Citation:* Capture of flag of 41st Alabama Infantry (C.S.A.), together with the color bearer and one of the color guard.

LUTHER, JAMES H.

Rank and organization: Private, Company D, 7th Massachusetts Infantry. *Place and date:* At Fredericksburg, Va., 3 May 1863. *Entered service at:* ———. *Birth:* Dighton, Mass. *Date of issue:* 28 June 1890. *Citation:* Among the first to jump into the enemy's rifle pits, he himself captured and brought out three prisoners.

LUTY, GOTLIEB

Rank and organization: Corporal, Company A, 74th New York Infantry. *Place and date:* At Chancellorsville, Va., 3 May 1863. *Entered service at:* West Manchester, Pa. *Birth:* Allegheny County, Pa. *Date of issue:* 5 October 1876. *Citation:* Bravely advanced to the enemy's line under heavy fire and brought back valuable information.

LYMAN, JOEL H.

Rank and organization: Quartermaster Sergeant, Company B, 9th New York Cavalry. *Place and date:* At Winchester, Va., 19 September 1864. *Entered service at:* East Randolph, N.Y. *Birth:* Cattaraugus, N.Y. *Date of issue:* 20 August 1894. *Citation:* In an attempt to capture a Confederate flag he captured one of the enemy's officers and brought him within the lines.

LYON, FREDERICK A.

Rank and organization: Corporal, Company A, 1st Vermont Cavalry. *Place and date:* At Cedar Creek, Va., 19 October 1864. *Entered service at:* Burlington, Vt. *Born:* 25 June 1843, Williamsburg, Mass. *Date of issue:* 26 November 1864. *Citation:* With 1 companion, captured the flag of a Confederate regiment, 3 officers, and an ambulance with its mules and driver.

LYONS, THOMAS

Rank and organization: Seaman, U.S. Navy. *Born:* 1838, Salem, Mass. *Accredited to:* Massachusetts. *G.O. No.:* 169, 8 February, 1872. *Citation:* Served as seaman on board the U.S.S. *Pensacola* in the attack on Forts Jackson and St. Philip, 24 April 1862. Carrying out his duties throughout the din and roar of the battle, Lyons never once erred in his brave performance. Lashed outside of that vessel, on the port-sheet chain, with the lead in hand to lead the ship past the forts, Lyons never flinched, although under a heavy fire from the forts and rebel gunboats.

MacARTHUR, ARTHUR, JR.

Rank and organization: First Lieutenant, and Adjutant, 24th Wisconsin Infantry. *Place and date:* At Missionary Ridge, Tenn., 25 November 1863. *Entered service at:* Milwaukee, Wis. *Birth:* Springfield, Mass. *Date of issue:* 30 June 1890. *Citation:* Seized the colors of his regiment at a critical moment and planted them on the captured works on the crest of Missionary Ridge.

MACHON, JAMES

Rank and organization: Boy, U.S. Navy. *Born:* 1848, England. *Accredited to:* New York. *G.O. No.:* 45, 31 December 1864. *Citation:* On board the U.S.S. *Brooklyn* during successful attacks against Fort Morgan, rebel gunboats and the ram *Tennessee* in Mobile Bay, on 5 August 1864. Stationed in the immediate vicinity of the shell whips which were twice cleared of men by bursting shells, Machon remained steadfast at his post and performed his duties in the powder division throughout the furious action which resulted in the surrender of the prize rebel ram *Tennessee* and in the damaging and destruction of batteries at Fort Morgan.

MACK, ALEXANDER

Rank and organization: Captain of the Top, U.S. Navy. *Born:* 1836, Holland. *Accredited to:* New York. *G.O. No.:* 45, 31 December 1864. *Citation:* On board the U.S.S. *Brooklyn* during successful attacks against Fort Morgan, rebel gunboats and the ram *Tennessee* in Mobile Bay, on 5 August 1864. Although wounded and sent below for treatment, Mack immediately returned to his post and took charge of his gun and, as heavy enemy return fire continued to fall, performed his duties with skill and courage until he was again wounded and totally disabled.

MACK, JOHN

Rank and organization: Seaman, U.S. Navy. *Born:* 1843, Maine. *Accredited to:* Maine. *G.O. No.:* 59, 22 June 1865. *Citation:* As seaman on board the U.S.S. *Hendrick Hudson*, St. Marks, Fla., 5 and 6 March 1865, Mack served with the Army in charge of Navy howitzers during the attack on St. Marks and, throughout this fierce engagement, made remarkable efforts in assisting transport of the gun. His coolness and determination in courageously standing by his gun while under the fire of the enemy were a credit to the service to which he belonged.

MACKIE, JOHN F.

Rank and organization: Corporal, U.S. Marine Corps. *Born:* 1836, New York, N.Y. *Accredited to:* New York. *G.O. No.:* 17, 10 July 1863. *Citation:* On board the U.S.S. *Galena* in the attack on Fort Darling at Drewry's Bluff, James River, on 15 May 1862. As enemy shellfire raked the deck of his ship, Corporal Mackie fearlessly maintained his musket fire against the rifle pits along the shore and, when ordered to fill vacancies at guns caused by men wounded and killed in action, manned the weapon with skill and courage.

MADDEN, MICHAEL

Rank and organization: Private, Company K, 42d New York Infantry. *Place and date:* At Masons Island, Md., 3 September 1861. *Entered service at:* New York, N.Y. *Born:* 28 September 1841, Ireland. *Date of issue:* 22 March 1898. *Citation:* Assisted a wounded comrade to the riverbank and, under heavy fire of the enemy, swam with him across a branch of the Potomac to the Union lines.

MADDEN, WILLIAM

Rank and organization: Coal Heaver, U.S. Navy. *Born:* 1843, England. *Accredited to:* New York. *G.O. No.:* 45, 31 December 1864. *Citation:* On board the U.S.S. *Brooklyn* during the successful attacks against Fort Morgan, rebel gunboats and the ram *Tennessee* in Mobile Bay, on 5 August 1864. Stationed in the immediate vicinity of the shell whips, which were twice cleared of men by bursting shells, Madden remained steadfast at his post and performed his duties in the powder division throughout the furious action which resulted in the surrender of the prize rebel ram *Tennessee* and in the damaging and destruction of batteries at Fort Morgan.

MADISON, JAMES

Rank and organization: Sergeant, Company E, 8th New York Cavalry. *Place and date:* At Waynesboro, Va., 2 March 1865. *Entered service at:* Fairport, N.Y. *Birth:* Niagara, N.Y. *Date of issue:* 26 March 1865. *Citation:* Recapture of Gen. Crook's headquarters flag.

MAGEE, WILLIAM

Rank and organization: Drummer, Company C, 33d New Jersey Infantry. *Place and date:* At Murfreesboro, Tenn., 5 December 1864. *Entered service at:* ———. *Birth:* Newark, N.J. *Date of issue:* 7 February 1866. *Citation:* In a charge, was among the first to reach a battery of the enemy and, with one or two others, mounted the artillery horses and took two guns into the Union lines.

MAHONEY, JEREMIAH

Rank and organization: Sergeant, Company A, 29th Massachusetts Infantry. *Place and date:* At Fort Sanders, Knoxville, Tenn., 29 November 1863. *Entered service at:* Fall River, Mass. *Birth:* ———. *Date of issue:* 1 December 1864. *Citation:* Capture of flag of 17th Mississippi Infantry (C.S.A.).

MANDY, HARRY J.

Rank and organization: First Sergeant, Company B, 4th New York Cavalry. *Place and date:* At Front Royal, Va., 15 August 1864. *Entered service at:* New York, N.Y. *Birth:* England. *Date of issue:* 26 August 1864. *Citation:* Capture of flag of 3d Virginia Infantry (C.S.A.).

MANGAM, RICHARD C.

Rank and organization: Private, Company H, 148th New York Infantry. *Place and date:* At Hatchers Run, Va., 2 April 1865. *Entered service at:* ———. *Birth:* Ireland. *Date of issue:* 21 September 1888. *Citation:* Capture of flag of 8th Mississippi Infantry (C.S.A.).

MANNING, JOSEPH S.

Rank and organization: Private, Company K, 29th Massachusetts Infantry. *Place and date:* At Fort Sanders, Knoxville, Tenn., 29 November 1863. *Entered service at:* ———. *Birth:* Ipswich, Mass. *Date of issue:* 1 December 1864. *Citation:* Capture of flag of 16th Georgia Infantry (C.S.A.).

MARLAND, WILLIAM

Rank and organization: First Lieutenant, 2d Independent Battery, Massachusetts Light Artillery. *Place and date:* At Grand Coteau, La., 3 November 1863. *Entered service at:* ———. *Born:* 11 March 1839, Andover, Mass. *Date of issue:* 16 Feburary 1897. *Citation:* After having been surrounded by the enemy's cavalry, his support having surrendered, he ordered a charge and saved the section of the battery that was under his command.

MARQUETTE, CHARLES

Rank and organization: Sergeant, Company F, 93d Pennsylvania Infantry. *Place and date:* At Petersburg, Va., 2 April 1865. *Entered service at:* Lebanon County, Pa. *Birth:* Lebanon County, Pa. *Date of issue:* 10 May 1865. *Citation:* Sergeant Marquette, although wounded, was one of the first to plant colors on the enemy's breastworks.

MARSH, ALBERT

Rank and organization: Sergeant, Company B, 64th New York Infantry. *Place and date:* At Spotsylvania, Va., 12 May 1864. *Entered service at:* Randolph, N.Y. *Birth* : Cattaraugus County, N.Y. *Date of issue:* 1 December 1864. *Citation:* Capture of flag.

MARSH, CHARLES H.

Rank and organization: Private, Company D, 1st Connecticut Cavalry. *Place and date:* At Back Creek Valley, Va., 31 July 1864. *Entered service at:* New Milford, Conn.. *Birth:* Milford, Conn. *Date of issue:* 23 January 1865. *Citation:* Capture of flag and its bearer.

MARSH, GEORGE

Rank and organization: Sergeant, Company D, 104th Illinois Infantry. *Place and date:* At Elk River, Tenn., 2 July 1863. *Entered service at:* Brookfield, La Salle County, Ill. *Birth:* Brookfield, La Salle County, Ill. *Date of issue:* 17 September 1897. *Citation:* Voluntarily led a small party and, under a heavy fire, captured a stockade and saved the bridge.

MARTIN, EDWARD S.

Rank and organization: Quartermaster, U.S. Navy. *Born:* 1840, Ireland. *Accredited to:* Pennsylvania. *G.O. No.:* 59, 22 June 1865. *Citation:* On board the U.S.S. *Galena* during the attack on enemy forts at Mobile Bay, 5 August 1864. Securely lashed to the side of the *Oneida* which had suffered the loss of her steering apparatus and an explosion of her boiler from enemy fire, the *Galena* aided the stricken vessel past the enemy forts to safety. Despite heavy damage to his ship from raking enemy fire, Martin performed his duties with skill and courage throughout the action.

MARTIN, GEORGE

Service rendered under name of Martin Schwenk.

MARTIN, JAMES

Rank and organization: Sergeant, U.S. Marine Corps. *Born:* 1826, Derry, Ireland. *Accredited to:* Pennsylvania. *G.O. No:* 45, 31 December 1864. *Citation:* As captain of a gun on board the U.S.S. *Richmond* during action against rebel forts and gunboats and with the ram *Tennessee* in Mobile Bay, 5 August 1864. Despite damage to his ship and the loss of several men on board as enemy fire raked her decks, Sgt. Martin fought his gun with skill and courage throughout the furious 2-hour battle which resulted in the surrender of the rebel ram *Tennessee* and in the damaging and destruction of batteries at Fort Morgan.

MARTIN, SYLVESTER H.

Rank and organization: Lieutenant, Company K, 88th Pennsylvania Infantry. *Place and date:* At Weldon Railroad, Va., 19 August 1864. *Entered service at:* ———. *Birth:* Chester County, Pa. *Date of issue:* 5 April 1894. *Citation:* Gallantly made a most dangerous reconnaissance, discovering the position of the enemy and enabling the division to repulse an attack made in strong force.

MARTIN, WILLIAM

Rank and organization: Boatswain's Mate, U.S. Navy. *Born:* 1842, Prussia. *Entered service at:* St. Louis, Mo. *G.O. No.:* 11, 3 April 1863. *Citation:* Serving as boatswain's mate on board the U.S.S. *Benton* during the attack on Haines Bluff, Yazoo River, 27 December 1862. Taking part in the hour-and-a-half engagement with the enemy, who had the dead range of the vessel and was punishing her with heavy fire, Martin served courageously throughout the battle until the *Benton* was ordered to withdraw.

MARTIN, WILLIAM

Rank and organization: Seaman, U.S. Navy. *Born:* 1839, Ireland. *Accredited to:* New York. *G.O. No.:* 11, 3 April 1863. *Citation:* Captain of a gun on board the U.S.S. *Varuna* during an attack on Forts Jackson and St. Philip, 24 April 1862. His ship was taken under furious fire by the rebel *Morgan* and severely damaged by ramming. Steadfast at his station through the thickest of the fight, Martin inflicted damage on the enemy, remaining cool and courageous although the *Varuna*, so badly damaged that she was forced to beach, was finally sunk.

MASON, ELIHU H. (4th to receive Medal of Honor)

Rank and organization: Sergeant, Company K, 21st Ohio Infantry. *Place and date:* Georgia, April 1862. *Entered service at:* Pemberville, Wood County, Ohio. *Birth:* Wayne County, Ind. *Date of issue:* 25 March 1863. *Citation:* One of the 19 of 22 men (including 2 civilians) who, by direction of Gen. Mitchell (or Buell), penetrated nearly 200 miles south into enemy territory and captured a railroad train at Big Shanty, Ga., in an attempt to destroy the bridges and track between Chattanooga and Atlanta.

MATHEWS, WILLIAM H.*

Rank and organization: First Sergeant, Company E, 2d Maryland Veteran Infantry. *Place and date:* At Petersburg, Va., 30 July 1864. *Entered service at:* Baltimore, Md. *Birth:* England. *Date of issue:* 10 July 1892. *Citation:* Finding himself among a squad of Confederates, he fired into them, killing 1, and was himself wounded, but succeeded in bringing in a sergeant and 2 men of the 17th South Carolina Regiment (C.S.A.) as prisoners.

---

*Enlisted in 1861 at Baltimore, Md., under name Henry Sivel, and original Medal of Honor issued under that name. A new medal was issued in 1900 under true name, William H. Mathews.

MATTHEWS, JOHN C.

Rank and organization: Corporal, Company A, 61st Pennsylvania Infantry. *Place and date:* At Petersburg, Va., 2 April 1865. *Entered service at:* ———. *Birth:* Westmoreland County, Pa. *Date of issue:* 13 February 1891. *Citation:* Voluntarily took the colors, whose bearer had been disabled, and, although himself severely wounded, carried the same until the enemy's works were taken.

MATTHEWS, MILTON

Rank and organization: Private, Company C, 61st Pennsylvania Infantry. *Place and date:* At Petersburg, Va., 2 April 1865. *Entered service at:* Pittsburgh, Pa. *Birth:* Pittsburgh, Pa. *Date of issue:* 10 May 1865. *Citation:* Capture of flag of 7th Tennessee Infantry (C.S.A.).

MATTINGLY, HENRY B.

Rank and organization: Private, Company B, 10th Kentucky Infantry. *Place and date:* At Jonesboro, Ga., 1 September 1864. *Entered service at:* ———. *Birth:* Marion County, Ky. *Date of issue:* 7 April 1865. *Citation:* Capture of flag of 6th and 7th Arkansas Infantry (C.S.A.).

MATTOCKS, CHARLES P.

Rank and organization: Major, 17th Maine Infantry. *Place and date:* At Sailors Creek, Va., 6 April 1865. *Entered service at:* Portland, Maine. *Born:* 1840, Danville, Vt. *Date of issue:* 29 March 1899. *Citation:* Displayed extraordinary gallantry in leading a charge of his regiment which resulted in the capture of a large number of prisoners and a stand of colors.

MAXHAM, LOWELL M.

Rank and organization: Corporal, Company F, 7th Massachusetts Infantry. *Place and date:* At Fredericksburg, Va., 3 May 1863. *Entered service at:* ———. *Birth:* Carver, Mass. *Date of issue:* 24 August 1896. *Citation:* Though severely wounded and in face of a deadly fire from the enemy at short range, he rushed bravely forward and was among the first to enter the enemy's works on the crest of Marye's Heights and helped to plant his regimental colors there.

MAY, WILLIAM

Rank and organization: Private, Company H, 32d Iowa Infantry. *Place and date:* At Nashville, Tenn., 16 December 1864. *Entered service at:* Maysville, Franklin County, Iowa. *Birth:* Pennsylvania. *Date of issue:* 24 February 1865. *Citation:* Ran ahead of his regiment over the enemy's works and captured from its bearer the flag of Bonanchad's Confederate battery (C.S.A.).

MAYBERRY, JOHN B.

Rank and organization: Private, Company F, 1st Delaware Infantry. *Place and date:* At Gettysburg, Pa., 3 July 1863. *Entered service at:* Kent County, Del. *Birth:* Smyrna, Del. *Date of issue:* 1 December 1864. *Citation:* Capture of flag.

MAYES, WILLIAM B.

Rank and organization: Private, Company K, 11th Iowa Infantry. *Place and date:* Near Kenesaw Mountain, Ga., 15 June 1864. *Entered service at:* DeWitt, Clinton County, Iowa. *Birth:* Marion County, Ohio. *Date of issue:* 27 November 1899. *Citation:* With one companion and under a fierce fire from the enemy at short range went to the rescue of a wounded comrade who had fallen between the lines and carried him to a place of safety.

MAYNARD, GEORGE H.

Rank and organization: Private, Company D, 13th Massachusetts Infantry. *Place and date:* At Fredericksburg, Va., 13 December 1862. *Entered service at:* ———. *Born:* 2 February 1836, Waltham, Mass. *Date of issue:* 1898. *Citation:* A wounded and helpless comrade, having been left on the skirmish line, this soldier voluntarily returned to the front under a severe fire and carried the wounded man to a place of safety.

McADAMS, PETER

Rank and organization: Corporal, Company A, 98th Pennsylvania Infantry. *Place and date:* At Salem Heights, Va., 3 May 1863. *Entered service at:* Philadelphia, Pa. *Birth:* Ireland. *Date of issue:* 1 April 1898. *Citation:* Went 250 yards in front of his regiment toward the position of the enemy and under fire brought within the lines a wounded and unconscious comrade.

McALWEE, BENJAMIN F.

Rank and organization: Sergeant, Company D, 3d Maryland Infantry. *Place and date:* At Petersburg, Va., 30 July 1864. *Entered service at:* ———. *Birth:* Washington, D.C. *Date of issue:* 4 April 1898. *Citation:* Picked up a shell with burning fuze and threw it over the parapet into the ditch, where it exploded; by this act he probably saved the lives of comrades at the great peril of his own.

McANALLY, CHARLES

Rank and organization: Lieutenant, Company D, 69th Pennsylvania Infantry. *Place and date:* At Spotsylvania, Va., 12 May 1864. *Entered service at:* Philadelphia, Pa. *Birth:* Ireland. *Date of issue:* 2 August 1897. *Citation:* In a hand-to-hand encounter with the enemy captured a flag, was wounded in the act, but continued on duty until he received a second wound.

McCAMMON, WILLIAM W.

Rank and organization: First Lieutenant, Company E, 24th Missouri Infantry. *Place and date:* At Corinth, Miss., 3 October 1862. *Entered service at:* Montgomery County, Mo. *Birth:* Ohio. *Date of issue:* 9 July 1896. *Citation:* While on duty as provost marshal, voluntarily assumed command of his company, then under fire, and so continued in command until the repulse and retreat of the enemy on the following day, the loss to this company during the battle being very great.

McCARREN, BERNARD

Rank and organization: Private, Company C, 1st Delaware Infantry. *Place and date:* At Gettysburg, Pa., 3 July 1863. *Entered service at:* Wilmington, Del. *Birth:* Ireland. *Date of issue:* 1 December 1864. *Citation:* Capture of flag.

McCAUSLIN, JOSEPH

Rank and organization: Private, Company D, 12th West Virginia Infantry. *Place and date:* At Petersburg, Va., 2 April 1865. *Entered service at:* Ohio County, W. Va. *Birth:* Ohio County, W. Va. *Date of issue:* 12 May 1865. *Citation:* Conspicuous gallantry as color bearer in the assault on Fort Gregg.

McCLEARY, CHARLES H.

Rank and organization: First Lieutenant, Company C. 72d Ohio Infantry. *Place and date:* At Nashville, Tenn., 16 December 1864. *Entered service at:* ———. *Birth:* Sandusky County, Ohio. *Date of issue:* 24 February 1865. *Citation:* Capture of flag of 4th Florida Infantry (C.S.A.), while in advance of his lines.

McCLELLAND, JAMES M.

Rank and organization: Private, Company B, 30th Ohio Infantry. *Place and date:* At Vicksburg, Miss., 22 May 1863. *Entered service at:* Ohio. *Birth:* Harrison County, Ohio. *Date of issue:* 13 August 1894. *Citation:* Gallantry in the charge of the "volunteer storming party."

McCLELLAND, MATTHEW

Rank and organization: First Class Fireman, U.S. Navy. *Born:* 1833, Brooklyn, N.Y. *Accredited to:* New York. *G.O. No.:* 17, 10 July 1863. *Citation:* Serving on board the U.S.S. *Richmond* in the attack on Port Hudson, 14 March 1863. Damaged by a 6-inch solid rifle shot which shattered the starboard safety-valve chamber and also damaged the port safety-valve, the fireroom of the *Richmond* immediately became filled with steam to place it in an extremely critical condition. Acting courageously in this crisis, McClelland persisted in penetrating the steam-filled room in order to haul the hot fires of the furnaces and continued this gallant action until the gravity of the situation had lessened.

McCONNELL, SAMUEL

Rank and organization: Captain, Company H, 119th Illinois Infantry. *Place and date:* At Fort Blakely, Ala., 9 April 1865. *Entered service at:* Bushnell, McDonough County, Ill. *Birth:* Belmont County, Ohio. *Date of issue:* 8 June 1865. *Citation:* While leading his company in an assault, Capt. McConnell braved an intense fire that mowed down his unit. Upon reaching the breastworks he found that he had only one member of his company with him, Pvt. Wagner. He was so close to an enemy gun that the blast knocked him down a ditch. Getting up, he entered the gun pit, the guncrew fleeing before him. About 30 paces away he saw a Confederate flag bearer and guard which he captured with the last shot in his pistol.

McCORMICK, MICHAEL

Rank and organization: Boatswain's Mate, U.S. Navy. *Born:* 1833, Ireland. *Accredited to:* Illinois. *G.O. No.:* 45, 31 December 1864. *Citation:* Served as boatswain's mate on board the U.S.S. *Signal*, Red River, 5 May 1864. Proceeding up the Red River, the U.S.S. *Signal* engaged a large force of enemy field batteries and sharpshooters, returning the fire until the ship was totally disabled, at which time the white flag was raised. Serving as gun captain and wounded early in the battle, McCormick bravely stood by his gun in the face of the enemy fire until ordered to withdraw.

McCORNACK, ANDREW

Rank and organization: Private, Company I, 127th Illinois Infantry. *Place and date:* At Vicksburg, Miss., 22 May 1863. *Entered service at:* Rutland, La Salle County, Ill. *Birth:* Kane, Ill. *Date of issue:* 10 January 1895. *Citation:* Gallantry in the charge of the "volunteer storming party."

McCULLOCK, ADAM

Rank and organization: Seaman, U.S. Navy. *Born:* 1830, Maine. *Accredited to:* Maine. *G.O. No.:* 45, 31 December 1864. *Citation:* On board the U.S.S. *Lackawanna* during successful attacks against Fort Morgan, rebel gunboats and the ram *Tennessee* in Mobile Bay, on 5 August 1864. Wounded when an enemy shell struck, and ordered to go below, McCullock refused to leave his station and continued to perform his duties throughout the prolonged action which resulted in the capture of the prize ram *Tennessee* and in the damaging and destruction of Fort Morgan.

McDONALD, GEORGE E.

Rank and organization: Private, Company L, 1st Connecticut Heavy Artillery. *Place and date:* At Fort Stedman, Va., 25 March 1865. *Entered service at:* Warwick, R.I. *Birth:* Warwick, R.I. *Date of issue:* 21 July 1865. *Citation:* Capture of flag.

McDONALD, JOHN

Rank and organization: Boatswain's Mate, U.S. Navy. *Born:* 1817, Scotland. *Accredited to:* Massachusetts. *G.O. No.:* 11, 3 April 1863. *Citation:* Serving on board the U.S.S. *Baron De Kalb*, Yazoo River Expedition, 23 to 27 December 1862. Proceeding under orders up the Yazoo River, the U.S.S. *Baron De Kalb*, with the object of capturing or destroying the enemy's transports, came upon the steamers *John Walsh, R. J. Locklan, Golden Age*, and the *Scotland*, sunk on a bar where they were ordered burned. Continuing up the river, she was fired on but, upon returning the fire, caused the enemy's retreat. Returning down the Yazoo, she destroyed and captured large quantities of enemy equipment and several prisoners. Serving bravely throughout this action, McDonald, as boatswain's mate, "distinguished himself in the various actions."

McDONALD, JOHN WADE

Rank and organization: Private, Company E, 20th Illinois Infantry. *Place and date:* At Pittsburg Landing, Tenn., 6 April 1862. *Entered service at:* Wayneville, DeWitt County, Ill. *Birth:* Lancaster, Ohio. *Date of issue:* 27 August 1900. *Citation:* Was severely wounded while endeavoring, at the risk of his life, to carry to a place of safety a wounded and helpless comrade.

McELHINNY, SAMUEL O.

Rank and organization: Private, Company A, 2d West Virginia Cavalry. *Place and date:* At Sailors Creek, Va., 6 April 1865. *Entered service at:* Point Pleasant, W. Va. *Birth:* Meigs County, Ohio. *Date of issue:* 3 May 1865. *Citation:* Capture of flag.

McENROE, PATRICK H.

Rank and organization: Sergeant, Company D, 6th New York Cavalry. *Place and date:* At Winchester, Va., 19 September 1864. *Entered service at:* New York. *Birth:* Ireland. *Date of issue:* 27 September 1864. *Citation:* Capture of colors of 36th Virginia Infantry (C.S.A.).

McFALL, DANIEL

Rank and organization: Sergeant, Company E, 17th Michigan Infantry. *Place and date:* At Spotsylvania, Va., 12 May 1864. *Entered service at:* Ypsilanti, Mich. *Born:* 1836, Niagara County, N.Y. *Date of issue:* 27 July 1896. *Citation:* Captured Col. Barker, commanding the Confederate brigade that charged the Union batteries; on the same day rescued Lt. George W. Harmon of his regiment from the enemy.

McFARLAND, JOHN

Rank and organization: Captain of the Forecastle, U.S. Navy. *Born:* 1840, Boston, Mass. *Accredited to:* Massachusetts. *G.O. No.:* 45, 31 December 1864. *Citation:* Stationed at the wheel on board the flagship U.S.S. *Hartford* during successful action against Fort Morgan, rebel gunboats and the ram *Tennessee* in Mobile Bay, on 5 August 1864. With his ship under terrific enemy shellfire, McFarland performed his duties with skill and courage and, when the *Lackawanna* ran into his ship and every man at the wheel was in danger of being crushed, remained steadfast at his station and continued to steer the ship.

McGINN, EDWARD

Rank and organization: Private, Company F, 54th Ohio Infantry. *Place and date:* At Vicksburg, Miss., 22 May 1863. *Entered service at:* ———. *Birth:* New York, N.Y. *Date of issue:* 28 June 1894. *Citation:* Gallantry in the charge of the "volunteer storming party."

McGONAGLE, WILSON

Rank and organization: Private, Company B, 30th Ohio Infantry. *Place and date:* At Vicksburg, Miss., 22 May 1863. *Entered service at:* ———. *Birth:* Jefferson County, Ohio. *Date of issue:* 15 August 1894. *Citation:* Gallantry in the charge of the "volunteer storming party."

McGONNIGLE, ANDREW J.

Rank and organization: Captain and Assistant Quartermaster, U.S. Volunteers. *Place and date:* At Cedar Creek, Va., 19 October 1864. *Entered service at:* Cumberland, Md. *Birth:* New York, N.Y. *Date of issue:* 21 July 1897. *Citation:* While acting chief quartermaster of Gen. Sheridan's forces operating in the Shenandoah Valley was severely wounded while voluntarily leading a brigade of infantry and was commended for the greatest gallantry by Gen. Sheridan.

McGOUGH, OWEN

Rank and organization: Corporal, Battery D, 5th U.S. Artillery. *Place and date:* At Bull Run, Va., 21 July 1861. *Entered service at:* —— ——. *Birth:* Ireland. *Date of issue:* 28 August 1897. *Citation:* Through his personal exertions under a heavy fire, one of the guns of his battery was brought off the field; all the other guns were lost.

McGOWAN, JOHN

Rank and organization: Quartermaster, U.S. Navy. *Born:* 1831, Ireland. *Accredited to:* New York. *G.O. No.:* 11, 3 April 1863. *Citation:* McGowan occupied one of the most responsible positions on the U.S.S. *Varuna* during the attacks on Forts Jackson and St. Philip and in action against the rebel ship *Morgan* on 24 April 1862. Although guns were raking the decks from behind him, McGowan remained steadfast at the wheel throughout the thickest of the fight, continuing at his station and rendering service with the greatest courage and skill until his ship, repeatedly holed and twice rammed by the enemy, was beached and sunk.

McGRAW, THOMAS

Rank and organization: Sergeant, Company B, 23d Illinois Infantry. *Place and date:* At Petersburg, Va., 2 April 1865. *Entered service at:* Chicago, Ill. *Birth:* Ireland. *Date of issue:* 12 May 1865. *Citation:* One of the three soldiers most conspicuous for gallantry in the final assault.

McGUIRE, PATRICK

Rank and organization: Private, Chicago Mercantile Battery, Illinois Light Artillery. *Place and date:* At Vicksburg, Miss., 22 May 1863. *Entered service at:* Chicago, Ill. *Birth:* Ireland. *Date of issue:* 15 January 1895. *Citation:* Carried with others by hand a cannon up to and fired it through an embrasure of the enemy's work.

McHALE, ALEXANDER U.

Rank and organization: Corporal, Company H, 26th Michigan Infantry. *Place and date:* At Spotsylvania Courthouse, Va., 12 May 1864. *Entered service at:* Muskegon, Mich. *Born:* 1842, Ireland. *Date of issue:* 11 January 1900. *Citation:* Captured a Confederate color in a charge, threw the flag over in front of the works, and continued in the charge upon the enemy.

McHUGH, MARTIN

Rank and organization: Seaman, U.S. Navy. *Born:* 1837, Cincinnati, Ohio. *Accredited to:* Ohio. *G.O. No.:* 17, 10 July 1863. *Citation:* Serving on board the U.S.S. *Cincinnati* during the attack on the Vicksburg batteries and at the time of her sinking, 27 May 1863. Engaging the enemy in a fierce battle, the *Cincinnati* amidst, an incessant fire of shot and shell, continued to fire her guns to the last, though so penetrated by shellfire that her fate was sealed. Serving bravely during this action, McHugh was conspicuously cool under the fire of the enemy, never ceasing to fire until this proud ship went down, "her colors nailed to the mast."

McINTOSH, JAMES

Rank and organization: Captain of the Top, U.S. Navy. *Born:* 1833, Canada. *Accredited to:* New York. *G.O. No.:* 45, 31 December 1864. *Citation:* On board the U.S.S. *Richmond* during action against rebel forts and gunboats and with the ram *Tennessee* in Mobile Bay, 5 August 1864. Despite damage to his ship and the loss of several men on board as enemy fire raked her decks, McIntosh performed his duties with skill and courage throughout the prolonged battle which resulted in the surrender of the rebel ram *Tennessee* and in the successful attacks carried out on Fort Morgan.

McKAY, CHARLES W.

Rank and organization: Sergeant, Company C, 154th New York Infantry. *Place and date:* At Dug Gap, Ga., 8 May 1864. *Entered service at:* Allegheny, Cattaraugus County, N.Y. *Birth:* Mansfield, N.Y. *Date of issue:* 13 April 1894. *Citation:* Voluntarily risked his life in rescuing under the fire of the enemy a wounded comrade who was lying between the lines.

McKEE, GEORGE

Rank and organization: Color Sergeant, Company D, 89th New York Infantry. *Place and date:* At Petersburg, Va., 2 April 1865. *Entered service at:* ———. *Birth:* Ireland. *Date of issue:* 12 May 1865. *Citation:* Gallantry as color bearer in the assault on Fort Gregg.

McKEEN, NINEVEH S.

Rank and organization: First Lieutenant, Company H, 21st Illinois Infantry. *Place and date:* At Stone River, Tenn., 30 December 1862. At Liberty Gap, Tenn., 25 June 1863. *Entered service at:* Marshall, Clark County, Ill. *Birth:* Marshall, Clark County, Ill. *Date of issue:* 23 June 1890. *Citation:* Conspicuous in the charge at Stone River, Tenn., where he was three times wounded. At Liberty Gap, Tenn., captured colors of 8th Arkansas Infantry (C.S.A.).

McKEEVER, MICHAEL

Rank and organization: Private, Company K, 5th Pennsylvania Cavalry. *Place and date:* At Burnt Ordinary, Va., 19 January 1863. *Entered service at:* Philadelphia, Pa. *Birth:* Ireland. *Date of issue:* 2 August 1897. *Citation:* Was one of a small scouting party that charged and routed a mounted force of the enemy six times their number. He led the charge in a most gallant and distinguished manner, going far beyond the call of duty.

McKNIGHT, WILLIAM

Rank and organization: Coxswain, U.S. Navy. *Born:* 1840, Ulster County, N.Y. *Accredited to:* New York. *G.O. No.:* 11, 3 April 1863. *Citation:* Captain of a gun on board the U.S.S. *Varuna* during the attacks on Forts Jackson and St. Philip and in action against the rebel ship *Morgan*, 24 April 1862. During this action at extremely close range, while his ship was under furious fire and was twice rammed by the rebel ship *Morgan*, McKnight remained steadfast at his gun throughout the thickest of the fight and was instrumental in inflicting damage on the enemy until the *Varuna*, so badly damaged that she was forced to beach, was finally sunk.

McKOWN, NATHANIEL A.

Rank and organization: Sergeant, Company B, 58th Pennsylvania Infantry. *Place and date:* At Chapins Farm, Va., 29 September 1864. *Entered service at:* PA—. *Birth:* Susquehanna County, Pa. *Date of issue:* 6 April 1865. *Citation:* Capture of flag.

McLEOD, JAMES

Rank and organization: Captain of the Foretop, U.S. Navy. *Born:* Scotland. *Accredited to:* Maine. *G.O. No.:* 11, 3 April 1863. *Citation:* Captain of foretop, and a volunteer from the *Colorado*, McLeod served on board the U.S.S. *Pensacola* during the attack upon Forts Jackson and St. Philip and the taking of New Orleans, 24 and 25 April 1862. Acting as gun captain of the rifled howitzer aft which was much exposed, he served this piece with great ability and activity, although no officer superintended it.

McMAHON, MARTIN T.

Rank and organization: Captain, and aide-de-camp, U.S. Volunteers. *Place and date:* At White Oak Swamp, Va., 30 June 1862. *Entered service at:* California. *Born:* 21 March 1838, Canada. *Date of issue:* 10 March 1891. *Citation:* Under fire of the enemy, successfully destroyed a valuable train that had been abandoned and prevented it from falling into the hands of the enemy.

McMILLEN, FRANCIS M.

Rank and organization: Sergeant, Company C, 110th Ohio Infantry. *Place and date:* At Petersburg, Va., 2 April 1865. *Entered service at:* Piqua, Ohio. *Birth:* Bracken County, Ky. *Date of issue:* 10 May 1865. *Citation:* Capture of flag.

*McVEANE, JOHN P.

Rank and organization: Corporal, Company D, 49th New York Infantry. *Place and date:* At Fredericksburg Heights, Va., 4 May 1863. *Entered service at:* Buffalo, N.Y. *Birth:* Canada. *Date of issue:* 21 September 1870. *Citation:* Shot a Confederate color bearer and seized the flag; also approached, alone, a barn between the lines and demanded and received the surrender of a number of the enemy therein.

McWHORTER, WALTER F.

Rank and organization: Commissary Sergeant, Company E, 3d West Virginia Cavalry. *Place and date:* At Sailors Creek, Va., 6 April 1865. *Entered service at:* Harrison County, W. Va. *Birth:* Lewis County, W. Va. *Date of issue:* 3 May 1865. *Citation:* Capture of flag of 6th Tennessee Infantry (C.S.A.).

McWILLIAMS, GEORGE W.

Rank and organization: Landsman, U.S. Navy. *Born:* 1844, Pennsylvania. *Accredited to:* Pennsylvania. *G.O. No.:* 59, 22 June 1865. *Citation:* Served on board the U.S.S. *Pontoosuc* during the capture of Fort Fisher and Wilmington, 24 December 1864, to 22 February 1865. Carrying out his duties faithfully throughout this period, McWilliams was so severely wounded in the assault upon Fort Fisher that he was sent to the hospital at Portsmouth, Va. McWilliams was recommended for his gallantry, skill and coolness in action while under the fire of the enemy.

MEACH, GEORGE E.

Rank and organization: Farrier, Company I, 6th New York Cavalry. *Place and date:* At Winchester, Va., 19 September 1864. *Entered service at:* ———. *Birth:* New York. *Date of issue:* 27 September 1864. *Citation:* Capture of flag.

MEAGHER, THOMAS

Rank and organization: First Sergeant, Company G, 158th New York Infantry. *Place and date:* At Chapins Farm, Va., 29 September 1864. *Entered service at:* Brooklyn N.Y. *Birth:* Scotland. *Date of issue:* 6 April 1865. *Citation:* Led a section of his men on the enemy's works, receiving a wound while scaling a parapet.

MEARS, GEORGE W.

Rank and organization: Sergeant, Company A, 6th Pennsylvania Reserves. *Place and date:* At Gettysburg, Pa., 2 July 1863. *Entered service at:* Bloomsburgh, Pa. *Birth:* Bloomsburgh, Pa. *Date of issue:* 16 February 1897. *Citation:* With five volunteers he gallantly charged on a number of the enemy's sharpshooters concealed in a log house, captured them, and brought them into the Union lines.

MELVILLE, CHARLES

Rank and organization: Ordinary Seaman, U.S. Navy. *Born:* 1828, Dover, N.H. *Accredited to:* New Hampshire. *G.O. No.:* 45, 31 December 1864. *Citation:* On board the flagship U.S.S. *Hartford* during action against rebel gunboats, the ram *Tennessee*, and Fort Morgan in Mobile Bay, 5 August 1864. Wounded and taken below to the surgeon when a shell burst between the two forward 9-inch guns, killing and wounding 15 men, Melville promptly returned to his gun on the deck and, although scarcely able to stand, refused to go below and continued to man his post throughout the remainder of the action resulting in the capture of the rebel ram *Tennessee*.

MENTER, JOHN W.

Rank and organization: Sergeant, Company D, 5th Michigan Infantry. *Place and date:* At Sailors Creek, Va., 6 April 1865. *Entered service at:* Detroit, Mich. *Birth:* Palmer, N.Y. *Date of issue:* 10 May 1865. *Citation:* Capture of flag.

MERRIAM, HENRY C.

Rank and organization: Lieutenant Colonel, 73d U.S. Colored Troops. *Place and date:* At Fort Blakely, Ala., 9 April 1865. *Entered service at:* Houlton, Maine. *Birth:* Houlton, Maine. *Date of issue:* 28 June 1894. *Citation:* Volunteered to attack the enemy's works in advance of orders and, upon permission being given, made a most gallant assault.

MERRIFIELD, JAMES K.

Rank and organization: Corporal, Company C, 88th Illinois Infantry. *Place and date:* At Franklin, Tenn., 30 November 1864. *Entered service at:* Manlius, Bureau County, Ill. *Birth:* Pennsylvania. *Date of issue:* 28 March 1896. *Citation:* Captured 2 battle flags from the enemy and returned with them to his own lines.

MERRILL, AUGUSTUS

Rank and organization: Captain, Company B, 1st Maine Veteran Infantry. *Place and date:* At Petersburg, Va., 2 April 1865. *Entered service at:* Lyndon, Maine. *Birth:* Byron, Maine. *Date of issue:* 23 October 1891. *Citation:* With 6 men, captured 69 Confederate prisoners and recaptured several soldiers who had fallen into the enemy's hands.

MERRILL, GEORGE

Rank and organization: Private, Company I, 142d New York Infantry. *Place and date:* At Fort Fisher, N.C., 15 January 1865. *Entered service at:* ———. *Birth:* Queensberry, N.Y. *Date of issue:* 28 December 1914. *Citation:* Voluntarily advanced with the head of the column and cut down the palisading.

MERRITT, JOHN G.

Rank and organization: Sergeant, Company K, 1st Minnesota Infantry. *Place and date:* At Bull Run, Va., 21 July 1861. *Entered service at:* ———. *Birth:* New York. *Date of issue:* 1 April 1880. *Citation:* Gallantry in action; was wounded while capturing flag in advance of his regiment.

MEYER, HENRY C.

Rank and organization: Captain, Company D, 24th New York Cavalry. *Place and date:* At Petersburg, Va., 17 June 1864. *Entered service at:* Dobbs Ferry, N.Y. *Birth:* Hamburg, N.Y. *Date of issue:* 29 March 1899. *Citation:* During an assault and in the face of a heavy fire rendered heroic assistance to a wounded and helpless officer, thereby saving his life and in the performance of this gallant act sustained a severe wound.

MIFFLIN, JAMES

Rank and organization: Engineer's Cook, U.S. Navy. *Born:* 1839, Richmond, Va. *Accredited to:* Virginia. *G.O. No.:* 45, 31 December 1864. *Citation:* On board the U.S.S. *Brooklyn* during successful attacks against Fort Morgan, rebel gunboats and the ram *Tennessee* in Mobile Bay, on 5 August 1864. Stationed in the immediate vicinity of the shell whips which were twice cleared of men by bursting shells, Mifflin remained steadfast at his post and performed his duties in the powder division throughout the furious action which resulted in the surrender of the prize rebel ram *Tennessee* and in the damaging and destruction of batteries at Fort Morgan.

MILES, NELSON A.

Rank and organization: Colonel, 61st New York Infantry. *Place and date:* At Chancellorsville, Va., 2–3 May 1863. *Entered service at:* Roxbury, Mass. *Birth:* Westminster, Mass. *Date of issue:* 23 July 1892. *Citation:* Distinguished gallantry while holding with his command an advanced position against repeated assaults by a strong force of the enemy; was severely wounded.

MILLER, ANDREW

Rank and organization: Sergeant, U.S. Marine Corps. *Born:* 1836, Germany. *Accredited to:* Washington, D.C. *G.O. No.:* 45, 31 December 1864. *Citation:* As captain of a gun on board the U.S.S. *Richmond* during action against rebel forts and gunboats and with the ram *Tennessee* in Mobile Bay, 5 August 1864. Despite damage to his ship and the loss of several men on board as enemy fire raked her decks, Sgt. Miller fought his gun with skill and courage throughout the furious 2-hour battle which resulted in the surrender of the rebel ram *Tennessee* and in the damaging and destruction of batteries at Fort Morgan.

MILLER, FRANK

Rank and organization: Private, Company M, 2d New York Cavalry. *Place and date:* At Sailors Creek, Va., 6 April 1865. *Entered service at:* Jamaica, N.Y. *Birth:* New York. *Date of issue:* 24 April 1865. *Citation:* Capture of flag of 25th Battalion Virginia Infantry (C.S.A.); was taken prisoner, but successfully retained his trophy until recaptured.

MILLER, HENRY A.

Rank and organization: Captain, Company B, 8th Illinois Infantry. *Place and date:* At Fort Blakely, Ala., 9 April 1865. *Entered service at:* Decatur, Ill. *Birth:* Germany. *Date of issue:* 8 June 1865. *Citation:* Capture of flag.

MILLER, JACOB C.

Rank and organization: Private, Company G, 113th Illinois Infantry. *Place and date:* At Vicksburg, Miss., 22 May 1863. *Entered service at:* Geneva, Kane County, Ill. *Birth:* Bellevue, Ohio. *Date of issue:* 20 August 1894. *Citation:* Gallantry in the charge of the "volunteer storming party."

14.

MILLER, JAMES

Rank and organization: Quartermaster, U.S. Navy. *Born:* 1835, Denmark. *Accredited to:* Massachusetts. *G.O. No.:* 32, 16 April 1864. *Citation:* Served as quartermaster on board the U.S. Steam Gunboat *Marblehead* off Legareville, Stono River, 25 December 1863, during an engagement with the enemy on John's Island. Acting courageously under the fierce hostile fire, Miller behaved gallantly throughout the engagement which resulted in the enemy's withdrawal and abandonment of his arms.

15.

MILLER, JAMES P.

Rank and organization: Private, Company D, 4th Iowa Cavalry. *Place and date:* At Selma, Ala., 2 April 1865. *Entered service at:* Henry County, Iowa. *Birth:* Franklin, Ohio. *Date of issue:* 17 June 1865. *Citation:* Capture of standard of 12th Mississippi Cavalry (C.S.A.).

16.

MILLER, JOHN

Rank and organization: Corporal, Company G, 8th Ohio Infantry. *Place and date:* At Gettysburg, Pa., 3 July 1863. *Entered service at:* Freemont, Sandusky County, Ohio. *Birth:* Germany. *Date of issue:* 1 December 1864. *Citation:* Capture of 2 flags.

17.

MILLER, JOHN

Rank and organization: Private, Company H, 8th New York Cavalry. *Place and date:* At Waynesboro, Va., 2 March 1865. *Entered service at:* Rochester, N.Y. *Birth:* Germany. *Date of issue:* 26 March 1865. *Citation:* Capture of flag.

20.

MILLER, WILLIAM E.

Rank and organization: Captain, Company H, 3d Pennsylvania Cavalry. *Place and date:* At Gettysburg, Pa., 3 July 1863. *Entered service at:* ———. *Born:* 5 February 1836, West Hill, Pa. *Date of issue:* 21 July 1897. *Citation:* Without orders, led a charge of his squadron upon the flank of the enemy, checked his attack, and cut off and dispersed the rear of his column.

MILLIKEN, DANIEL

Rank and organization: Quarter Gunner, U.S. Navy. *Born:* 1838, Maine. *Accredited to:* New York. *G.O. No.:* 59, 22 June 1865. *Citation:* Milliken served on board the U.S.S. *New Ironsides* during action in several attacks on Fort Fisher, 24 and 25 December 1864; and 13, 14, and 15 January 1865. The ship steamed in and took the lead in the ironclad division close inshore and immediately opened its starboard battery in a barrage of well directed fire to cause several fires and explosions and dismount several guns during the first 2 days of fighting. Taken under fire as she steamed into position on 13 January, the *New Ironsides* fought all day and took on ammunition at night despite severe weather conditions. When the enemy came out of his bombproofs to defend the fort against the storming party, the ship's battery disabled nearly every gun on the fort facing the shore before the cease-fire orders were given by the flagship.

MILLS, CHARLES

Rank and organization: Seaman, U.S. Navy. *Born:* 1843, Upster, N.Y. *Accredited to:* New York. *G.O. No.:* 59, 22 June 1865. *Citation:* On board the U.S.S. *Minnesota,* in action during the assault on Fort Fisher, 15 January 1865. Landing on the beach with the assaulting party from his ship, Mills charged up to the palisades and, when more than two-thirds of the men became seized with panic and retreated on the run, risked his life to remain with a wounded officer. With the enemy concentrating his fire on the group, he waited until after dark before assisting the wounded man from the field.

MILLS, FRANK W.

Rank and organization: Sergeant, Company C, 1st New York Mounted Rifles. *Place and date:* At Sandy Cross Roads, N.C., 4 September 1862. *Entered service at:* ———. *Birth:* Middletown, N.Y. *Date of issue:* 2 April 1898. *Citation:* While scouting, this soldier, in command of an advance of but 3 or 4 men, came upon the enemy, and charged them without orders, the rest of the troops following, the whole force of the enemy, 120 men, being captured.

MINDIL, GEORGE W.

Rank and organization: Captain, Company I, 61st Pennsylvania Infantry. *Place and date:* At Williamsburg, Va., 5 May 1862. *Entered service at:* Philadelphia, Pa. *Birth:* Germany. *Date of issue:* 25 October 1893. *Citation:* As aide-de-camp led the charge with a part of a regiment, pierced the enemy's center, silenced some of his artillery, and, getting in his rear, caused him to abandon his position.

MITCHELL, ALEXANDER H.

Rank and organization: First Lieutenant, Company A, 105th Pennsylvania Infantry. *Place and date:* At Spotsylvania, Va., 12 May 1864. *Entered service at:* Hamilton, Pa. *Birth:* Perrysville, Pa. *Date of issue:* 27 March 1890. *Citation:* Capture of flag of 18th North Carolina Infantry (C.S.A.), in a personal encounter with the color bearer.

MITCHELL, THEODORE

Rank and organization: Private, Company C, 61st Pennsylvania Infantry. *Place and date:* At Petersburg, Va., 2 April 1865. *Entered service at:* Pittsburgh, Pa. *Birth:* Tarentum, Pa. *Date of issue:* 10 May 1865. *Citation:* Capture of the flag of the Tennessee Brigade (C.S.A.).

MOFFITT, JOHN H.

Rank and organization: Corporal, Company C, 16th New York Infantry. *Place and date:* At Gaines Mill, Va., 27 June 1862. *Entered service at:* Plattsburg, N.Y. *Born:* 8 January 1843, Chazy, Clinton County, N.Y. *Date of issue:* 3 March 1891. *Citation:* Voluntarily took up the regimental colors after several color bearers had been shot down and carried them until himself wounded.

MOLBONE, ARCHIBALD

Rank and organization: Sergeant, Company G, 1st Rhode Island Light Artillery. *Place and date:* At Petersburg, Va., 2 April 1865. *Entered service at:* West Greenwich, R.I. *Birth:* Coventry, R.I. *Date of issue:* 20 June 1866. *Citation:* Was one of a detachment of 20 picked artillerymen who voluntarily accompanied an infantry assaulting party and who turned upon the enemy the guns captured in the assault.

MOLLOY, HUGH

Rank and organization: Ordinary Seaman, U.S. Navy. *Born:* 1832, Illinois. *Accredited to:* Illinois. *G.O. No.:* 32, 16 April 1864. *Citation:* Served on board the U.S.S. *Fort Hindman* during the engagement near Harrisonburg, La., 2 March 1864. Following a shellburst which mortally wounded the first sponger, who dropped the sponge out of the forecastle port, Molloy jumped out of the port to the forecastle, recovered the sponge and sponged and loaded the gun for the remainder of the action from his exposed position, despite the extreme danger to his person from the raking fire of enemy musketry.

MONAGHAN, PATRICK

Rank and organization: Corporal, Company F, 48th Pennsylvania Infantry. *Place and date:* At Petersburg, Va., 17 June 1864. *Entered service at:* Minersville, Pa. *Birth:* Ireland. *Date of issue:* 1 December 1864. *Citation:* Recapture of colors of 7th New York Heavy Artillery.

MONTGOMERY, ROBERT

Rank and organization: Captain of the Afterguard, U.S. Navy. *Born:* 1838, Ireland. *Accredited to:* Virginia. *G.O. No.:* 45, 21 December 1864. *Citation:* Montgomery served on board the U.S.S. *Agawam,* as one of a volunteer crew of a powder boat which was exploded near Fort Fisher, 23 December 1864. The powder boat, towed in by the *Wilderness* to prevent detection by the enemy, cast off and slowly steamed to within 300 yards of the beach. After fuses and fires had been lit and a second anchor with short scope let go to assure the boat's tailing inshore, the crew again boarded the *Wilderness* and proceeded a distance of 12 miles from shore. Less than 2 hours later the explosion took place, and the following day fires were observed still burning at the forts.

MOORE, CHARLES

Rank and organization: Landsman, U.S. Navy. *Born:* 1839, Ireland. *Accredited to:* New York. *G.O. No.:* 32, 16 April 1864. *Citation:* Serving on board the U.S. Steam Gunboat *Marblehead* off Legareville, Stono River, 25 December 1863, during an engagement with the enemy on John's Island. Wounded in the fierce battle, Moore returned to his quarters until so exhausted by loss of blood that he had to be taken below. This engagement resulted in the enemy's abandonment of his positions, leaving a caisson and one gun behind.

MOORE, CHARLES

Rank and organization: Seaman, U.S. Navy. *Entered service at:* 25 March 1862, Gibraltar, England. *G.O. No.:* 45, 31 December 1864. *Citation:* Served as seaman on board the U.S.S. *Kearsarge* when she destroyed the *Alabama* off Cherbourg, France, 19 June 1864. Acting as sponger and loader of the 11-inch pivot gun of the second division during this bitter engagement, Moore exhibited marked coolness and good conduct and was highly recommended for his gallantry under fire by the divisional officer.

MOORE, DANIEL B.

Rank and organization: Corporal, Company E, 11th Wisconsin Infantry. *Place and date:* At Fort Blakely, Ala., 9 April 1865. *Entered service at:* Mifflin, Wis. *Born:* 12 June 1838, Iowa County, Wis. *Date of issue:* 8 August 1900. *Citation:* At the risk of his own life saved the life of an officer who had been shot down and overpowered by superior numbers.

MOORE, GEORGE

Rank and organization: Seaman, U.S. Navy. *Born:* 1838, Philadelphia, Pa. *Accredited to:* Pennsylvania. *G.O. No.:* 59, 22 June 1865. *Citation:* Served on board the U.S.S. *Rhode Island* which was engaged in saving the lives of the officers and crew of the *Monitor*, 30 December 1862. Participating in the hazardous task of rescuing the officers and crew of the sinking *Monitor*, Moore after rescuing several of the men, became separated in a heavy gale with other members of the cutter that had set out from the *Rhode Island*, and spent many hours in the small boat at the mercy of the weather and high seas until finally picked up by a schooner 50 miles east of Cape Hatteras.

MOORE, GEORGE G.

Rank and organization: Private, Company D, 11th West Virginia Infantry. *Place and date:* At Fishers Hill, Va., 22 September 1864. *Entered service at:* ———. *Birth:* Tyler County W. Va. *Date of issue:* 6 October 1864. *Citation:* Capture of flag.

MOORE, WILBUR F.

Rank and organization: Private, Company C, 117th Illinois Infantry. *Place and date:* At Nashville, Tenn., 16 December 1864. *Entered service at:* Lebanon, St. Clair County, Ill. *Birth:* Lebanon, St. Clair County, Ill. *Date of issue:* 22 February 1865. *Citation:* Captured flag of a Confederate battery while far in advance of the Union lines.

MOORE, WILLIAM

Rank and organization: Boatswain's Mate, U.S. Navy. *Born:* 1834, Boston, Mass. *Accredited to:* Massachusetts. *G.O. No.:* 32, 16 April 1864. *Citation:* Serving as boatswain's mate on board the U.S.S. *Benton* during the attack on Haines Bluff, Yazoo River, 27 December 1862. Wounded during the hour-and-a-half engagement in which the enemy had the dead range of the vessel and was punishing her with heavy fire, Moore served courageously in carrying lines to the shore until the *Benton* was ordered to withdraw.

MOREY, DELANO

Rank and organization: Private, Company B, 82d Ohio Infantry. *Place and date:* At McDowell, Va., 8 May 1862. *Entered service at:* Hardin County, Ohio. *Birth:* Licking County, Ohio. *Date of issue:* 14 August 1893. *Citation:* After the charge of the command had been repulsed, he rushed forward alone with an empty gun and captured two of the enemy's sharpshooters.

MORFORD, JEROME

Rank and organization: Private, Company K, 55th Illinois Infantry. *Place and date:* At Vicksburg, Miss., 22 May 1863. *Entered service at:* Bridgers Corner, Ill. *Birth:* Mercer County, Pa. *Date of issue:* 2 September 1893. *Citation:* Gallantry in the charge of the "volunteer storming party."

MORGAN, JAMES H.

Rank and organization: Captain of the Top, U.S. Navy. *Born:* 1840, New York. *Accredited to:* New York. *G.O. No.:* 45, 31 December 1864. *Citation:* As captain of a gun on board the U.S.S. *Richmond* during action against rebel forts and gunboats and with the *Tennessee* in Mobile Bay, 5 August 1864. Despite damage to his ship and the loss of several men on board as enemy fire raked her decks Morgan fought his gun with skill and courage throughout a furious 2-hour battle which resulted in the surrender of the rebel ram *Tennessee* and in the damaging and destruction of batteries at Fort Morgan.

MORGAN, LEWIS

Rank and organization: Private, Company I, 4th Ohio Infantry. *Place and date:* At Spotsylvania, Va., 12 May 1864. *Entered service at:* Delaware County, Ohio. *Birth:* Delaware County, Ohio. *Date of issue:* 1 December 1864. *Citation:* Capture of flag from the enemy's works.

MORGAN, RICHARD H.

Rank and organization: Corporal, Company A, 4th Iowa Cavalry. *Place and date:* At Columbus, Ga., 16 April 1865. *Entered service at:* Taylor, Freemont County, Iowa. *Birth:* Dubois County, Ind. *Date of issue:* 17 June 1865. *Citation:* Capture of flag inside the enemy's works, contesting for its possession with its bearer.

MORRILL, WALTER G.

Rank and organization: Captain, Company B, 20th Maine Infantry. *Place and date:* At Rappahannock Station, Va., 7 November 1863. *Entered service at:* Brownville, Maine. *Birth:* Brownville, Maine. *Date of issue:* 5 April 1898. *Citation:* Learning that an assault was to be made upon the enemy's works by other troops, this officer voluntarily joined the storming party with about 50 men of his regiment, and by his dash and gallantry rendered effective service in the assault.

MORRIS, WILLIAM

Rank and organization: Sergeant, Company C, 1st New York (Lincoln) Cavalry. *Place and date:* At Sailors Creek, Va., 6 April 1865.

Entered service at: Philadelphia, Pa. *Birth:* Philadelphia, Pa. *Date of issue:* 3 May 1865. *Citation:* Capture of flag of 40th Virginia Infantry (C.S.A.).

MORRISON, FRANCIS

Rank and organization: Private, Company H, 85th Pennsylvania Infantry. *Place and date:* At Bermuda Hundred, Va., 17 June 1864. *Entered service at:* Drakestown, Pa. *Birth:* Fayette County, Pa. *Date of issue:* 2 August 1897. *Citation:* Voluntarily exposed himself to a heavy fire to bring off a wounded comrade.

MORRISON, JOHN G.

Rank and organization: Coxswain, U.S. Navy. *Entered service at:* Lansingburg, N.Y. *Born:* 3 November 1842, Ireland. *G.O. No.:* 59, 22 June 1865. *Citation:* Serving as coxswain on board the U.S.S. *Carondelet*, Morrison was commended for meritorious conduct in general and especially for his heroic conduct and his inspiring example to the crew in the engagement with the rebel ram *Arkansas*, Yazoo River, 15 July 1862. When the *Carondelet* was badly cut up, several of her crew killed, many wounded and others almost suffocated from the effects of escaped steam, Morrison was the leader when boarders were called on deck, and the first to return to the guns and give the ram a broadside as she passed. His presence of mind in time of battle or trial is reported as always conspicuous and encouraging.

MORSE, BENJAMIN

Rank and organization: Private, Company C, 3d Michigan Infantry. *Place and date:* At Spotsylvania, Va., 12 May 1864. *Entered service at:* Grand Rapids, Mich. *Born:* 20 September 1844, Livingston, N.Y. *Date of issue:* 24 February 1891. *Citation:* Capture of colors of 4th Georgia Battery (C.S.A.)

MORSE, CHARLES E.

Rank and organization: Sergeant, Company I, 62d New York Infantry. *Place and date:* At Wilderness, Va., 5 May 1864. *Entered service at:* New York. *Birth:* France. *Date of issue:* 14 January 1890. *Citation:* Voluntarily rushed back into the enemy's lines, took the colors from the color sergeant, who was mortally wounded, and, although himself wounded, carried them through the fight.

MORTON, CHARLES W.

Rank and organization: Boatswain's Mate, U.S. Navy. *Born:* 1836, Ireland. *Accredited to:* Maryland. *G.O. No.:* 11, 3 April 1863. *Citation:* Serving as boatswain's mate on board the U.S.S. *Benton* during the Yazoo River Expedition, 23 to 27 December 1863. Taking part in the hour-and-a-half engagement with the enemy at Drumgould's Bluff, 27 December, Morton served courageously throughout the battle against the hostile forces, who had the dead range of the vessel and were punishing her with heavy fire, until the *Benton* was ordered to withdraw.

MOSTOLLER, JOHN W.

Rank and organization: Private, Company B, 54th Pennsylvania Infantry. *Place and date:* At Lynchburg, Va., 18 June 1864. *Entered service at:* ———. *Birth:* Somerset County, Pa. *Date of issue:* 27 December 1894. *Citation:* Voluntarily led a charge on a Confederate battery (the officers of the company being disabled) and compelled its hasty removal.

MULHOLLAND, ST. CLAIR A.

Rank and organization: Major, 116th Pennsylvania Infantry. *Place and date:* At Chancellorsville, Va., 4–5 May 1863. *Entered service at:* Philadelphia, Pa. *Born:* 1 April 1839, Ireland. *Date of issue:* 26 March 1895. *Citation:* In command of the picket line held the enemy in check all night to cover the retreat of the Army.

MULLEN, PATRICK

Rank and organization: Boatswain's Mate, U.S. Navy. *Entered service at:* Baltimore, Md. *Birth:* Baltimore, Md. *G.O. No.:* 59, 22 June 1865. *Citation:* Served as boatswain's mate on board the U.S.S. *Wyandank* during a boat expedition up Mattox Creek, 17 March 1865. Rendering gallant assistance to his commanding officer, Mullen, lying on his back, loaded the howitzer and then fired so carefully as to kill and wound many rebels, causing their retreat.

SECOND AWARD

G.O. No.: 62, 29 June 1865. Second award. *Citation:* Served as boatswain's mate on board the U.S.S. *Don,* 1 May 1865. Engaged in picking up the crew of picket launch No. 6, which had swamped. Mullen, seeing an officer who was at that time no longer able to keep up and was below the surface of the water, jumped overboard and brought the officer to the boat, thereby rescuing him from drowning, which brave action entitled him to wear a bar on the medal he had already received at Mattox Creek, 17 March 1865.

MUNDELL, WALTER L.

Rank and organization: Corporal, Company E, 5th Michigan Infantry. *Place and date:* At Sailors Creek, Va., 6 April 1865. *Entered service at:* Dallas, Mich. *Born:* 1839, Michigan. *Date of issue:* 10 May 1865. *Citation:* Capture of flag.

MUNSELL, HARVEY M.

Rank and organization: Sergeant, Company A, 99th Pennsylvania Infantry. *Place and date:* At Gettysburg, Pa., 1–3 July 1863. *Entered service at:* Vanango County, Pa. *Birth:* Steuben County, N.Y. *Date of issue:* 5 February 1866. *Citation:* Gallant and courageous conduct as color bearer. (This noncommissioned officer carried the colors of his regiment through 13 engagements.)

MURPHY, CHARLES J.

Rank and organization: First Lieutenant and Quartermaster, 38th New York Infantry. *Place and date:* At Bull Run, Va., 21 July 1861.

Entered service at: ———. *Birth:* England. *Date of issue:* 5 April 1898. *Citation:* Took a rifle and voluntarily fought with his regiment in the ranks; when the regiment was forced back, voluntarily remained on the field caring for the wounded, and was there taken prisoner.

MURPHY, DANIEL J.

Rank and organization: Sergeant, Company F, 19th Massachusetts Infantry. *Place and date:* At Hatchers Run, Va., 27 October 1864. *Entered service at:* Lowell, Mass. *Birth:* Philadelphia, Pa. *Date of issue:* 1 December 1864. *Citation:* Capture of flag of 47th North Carolina Infantry (C.S.A.).

MURPHY, DENNIS J. F.

Rank and organization: Sergeant, Company F, 14th Wisconsin Infantry. *Place and date:* At Corinth, Miss., 3 October 1862. *Entered service at:* ———. *Birth:* Ireland. *Date of issue:* 22 January 1892. *Citation:* Although wounded three times, carried the colors throughout the conflict.

MURPHY, JAMES T.

Rank and organization: Private, Company L, 1st Connecticut Artillery. *Place and date:* At Petersburg, Va., 25 March 1865. *Entered service at:* New Haven, Conn. *Birth:* Canada. *Date of issue:* 29 October 1886. *Citation:* A piece of artillery having been silenced by the enemy, this soldier voluntarily assisted in working the piece, conducting himself throughout the engagement in a gallant and fearless manner.

MURPHY, JOHN P.

Rank and organization: Private, Company K, 5th Ohio Infantry. *Place and date:* At Antietam, Md., 17 September 1862. *Entered service at:* Cincinnati, Ohio. *Birth:* Ireland. *Date of issue:* 11 September 1866. *Citation:* Capture of flag of 13th Alabama Infantry (C.S.A.).

MURPHY, MICHAEL C.

Rank and organization: Lieutenant Colonel, 170th New York Infantry. *Place and date:* At North Anna River, Va., 24 May 1864. *Entered service at:* New York, N.Y. *Birth:* Ireland. *Date of issue:* 15 January 1897. *Citation:* This officer, commanding the regiment, kept it on the field exposed to the fire of the enemy for 3 hours without being able to fire one shot in return because of the ammunition being exhausted.

MURPHY, PATRICK

Rank and organization: Boatswain's Mate, U.S. Navy. *Born:* 1823, Ireland. *Accredited to:* New York. *Citation:* Served as boatswain's mate on board the U.S.S. *Metacomet*, during action against rebel forts and gunboats and with the ram *Tennessee* in Mobile Bay, 5 August 1864. Despite damage to his ship and the loss of several men on board as enemy fire raked her decks, Murphy performed his duties with skill and courage throughout a furious 2-hour battle which resulted in the surrender of the rebel ram *Tennessee* and in the damaging and destruction of batteries at Fort Morgan.

MURPHY, ROBINSON B.

Rank and organization: Musician, Company A, 127th Illinois Infantry. *Place and date:* At Atlanta, Ga., 28 July 1864. *Entered service at:* Oswego, Kendall County, Ill. *Birth:* Oswego, Kendall County, Ill. *Date of issue:* 22 July 1890. *Citation:* Being orderly to the brigade commander, he voluntarily led two regiments as reinforcements into line of battle, where he had his horse shot under him.

MURPHY, THOMAS

Rank and organization: Corporal, Company K, 158th New York Infantry. *Place and date:* At Chapins Farm, Va., 30 September 1864. *Entered service at:* New York, N.Y. *Birth:* New York, N.Y. *Date of issue:* 15 October 1864. *Citation:* Capture of flag.

MURPHY, THOMAS C.

Rank and organization: Corporal, Company I, 31st Illinois Infantry. *Place and date:* At Vicksburg, Miss., 22 May 1863. *Entered service at:* Pekin, Ill. *Birth:* Ireland. *Date of issue:* 14 August 1893. *Citation:* Voluntarily crossed the line of heavy fire of Union and Confederate forces, carrying a message to stop the firing of one Union regiment on another.

MURPHY, THOMAS J.

Rank and organization: First Sergeant, Company G, 146th New York Infantry. *Place and date:* At Five Forks, Va., 1 April 1865. *Entered service at:* New York, N.Y. *Birth:* Ireland. *Date of issue:* 10 May 1865. *Citation:* Capture of flag.

MYERS, GEORGE S.

Rank and organization: Private, Company F, 101st Ohio Infantry. *Place and date:* At Chickamauga, Ga., 19 September 1863. *Entered service at:* ———. *Birth:* Fairfield, Ohio. *Date of issue:* 9 April 1894. *Citation:* Saved the regimental colors by greatest personal devotion and bravery.

MYERS, WILLIAM H.

Rank and organization: Private, Company A, 1st Maryland Cavalry. *Place and date:* At Appomattox Courthouse, Va., 9 April 1865. *Entered service at:* Baltimore, Md. *Birth:* Philadelphia, Pa. *Date of issue:* 14 June 1871. *Citation:* Gallantry in action; was 5 times wounded.

NASH, HENRY H.

Rank and organization: Corporal, Company B, 47th Ohio Infantry. *Place and date:* At Vicksburg, Miss., 3 May 1863. *Entered service at:* Adrian, Mich. *Born:* 4 March 1842, Lanawee, Mich. *Date of issue:* 15 February 1909. *Citation:* Was one of a party that volunteered and attempted to run the enemy's batteries with a steam tug and 2 barges loaded with subsistence stores.

NAYLOR, DAVID

Rank and organization: Landsman, U.S. Navy. *Born:* 1843, Thompsonville, N.Y. *Accredited to:* New York. *G.O. No.:* 45, 31 December 1864. *Citation:* Served on board the U.S.S. *Oneida* in the engagement at Mobile Bay, 5 August 1864. Acting as powder boy at the 30-pounder Parrott rifle, Naylor had his passing box shot from his hands and knocked overboard where it fell in one of the *Galena's* boats which was under the bow. Jumping overboard, Naylor recovered his box, returned to his station and continued to carry out his courageous actions throughout the engagement which resulted in the capture of the rebel ram *Tennessee* and the damaging of Fort Morgan.

NEAHR, ZACHARIAH C.

Rank and organization: Private, Company K, 142d New York Infantry. *Place and date:* At Fort Fisher, N.C., 16 January 1865. *Entered service at:* ———. *Birth:* Canajoharie, N.Y. *Date of issue:* 11 September 1890. *Citation:* Voluntarily advanced with the head of the column and cut down the palisading.

NEIL, JOHN

Rank and organization: Quarter Gunner, U.S. Navy. *Born:* 1837, Newfoundland. *Accredited to:* Virginia. *G.O. No.:* 45, 31 December 1864. *Citation:* Neil served on board the U.S.S. *Agawam,* as one of a volunteer crew of a powder boat which was exploded near Fort Fisher, 23 December 1864. The powder boat, towed in by the *Wilderness* to prevent detection by the enemy, cast off and slowly steamed to within 300 yards of the beach. After fuses and fires had been lit and a second anchor with short scope let go to assure the boat's tailing inshore, the crew again boarded the *Wilderness* and proceeded a distance of 12 miles from shore. Less than 2 hours later the explosion took place, and the following day fires were observed still burning at the forts.

NEVILLE, EDWIN M.

Rank and organization: Captain, Company C, 1st Connecticut Cavalry. *Place and date:* At Sailors Creek, Va., 6 April 1865. *Entered service at:* Waterbury, Conn. *Birth:* ———. *Date of issue:* 3 May 1865. *Citation:* Capture of flag.

NEWLAND, WILLIAM

Rank and organization: Ordinary Seaman, U.S. Navy. *Born:* 1841, Medway, Mass. *Accredited to:* Massachusetts. *G.O. No.:* 45, 31 December 1864. *Citation:* Serving on board the U.S.S. *Oneida* in the engagement at Mobile Bay, 5 August 1864. Carrying out his duties as loader of the after 11-inch gun, Newland distinguished himself on board for his good conduct and faithful discharge of his station, behaving spendidly under the fire of the enemy and throughout the battle which resulted in the capture of the rebel ram *Tennessee* and the damaging of Fort Morgan.

NEWMAN, MARCELLUS J.

Rank and organization: Private, Company B, 111th Illinois Infantry. *Place and date:* At Resaca, Ga., 14 May 1864. *Entered service at:* Richview, Washington County, Ill. *Birth:* Richview, Washington County, Ill. *Date of issue:* 13 May 1899. *Citation:* Voluntarily returned, in the face of a severe fire from the enemy, and rescued a wounded comrade who had been left behind as the regiment fell back.

NEWMAN, WILLIAM H.

Rank and organization: Lieutenant, Company B, 86th New York Infantry. *Place and date:* Near Amelia Springs, Va., 6 April 1865. *Entered service at:* ———. *Birth:* Orange County, N.Y. *Date of issue:* 10 May 1865. *Citation:* Capture of flag.

NIBBE, JOHN H.

Rank and organization: Quartermaster, U.S. Navy. *Born:* 1842, Germany. *Accredited to:* New York. *G.O. No.:* 59, 22 June 1865. *Citation:* Served as quartermaster on board the U.S.S. *Peterel* during its capture in Yazoo River, 22 April 1864. Standing his ground when a shot came through the stern, raking the gundeck and entering and exploding the boilers, when all the others had deserted the flag, Nibbe assisted in getting the wounded off the guard and proceeded to get ready to fire the ship despite the escaping steam from the boilers at which time he was surrounded on all sides by the rebels and forced to surrender.

NICHOLS, HENRY C.

Rank and organization: Captain, Company E, 73d U.S. Colored Troops. *Place and date:* At Fort Blakely, Ala., 9 April 1865. *Entered service at:* ———. *Birth:* Brandon, Vt. *Date of issue:* 3 August 1897. *Citation:* Voluntarily made a reconnaissance in advance of the line held by his regiment and, under a heavy fire, obtained information of great value.

NICHOLS, WILLIAM

Rank and organization: Quartermaster, U.S. Navy. *Born:* 1837, New York, N.Y. *Accredited to:* New York. *G.O. No.:* 45, 31 December 1864. *Citation:* On board the U.S.S. *Brooklyn* during successful attacks against Fort Morgan, rebel gunboats and the ram *Tennessee*, in Mobile Bay, on 5 August 1864. Despite severe damage to his ship and the loss of several men on board as enemy fire raked her decks from stem to stern, Nichols fought his gun with skill and courage throughout the furious battle which resulted in the surrender of the prize rebel ram *Tennessee*, and in the damaging and destruction of batteries at Fort Morgan.

NIVEN, ROBERT

Rank and organization: Second Lieutenant, Company H, 8th New York Cavalry. *Place and date:* At Waynesboro, Va., 2 March 1865. *Entered service at:* Rochester, N.Y. *Born:* 18 December 1833, Harlem, N.Y. *Date of issue:* 26 March 1865. *Citation:* Capture of 2 flags.

NOBLE, DANIEL

Rank and organization: Landsman, U.S. Navy. *Born:* 1840, Bath County, Ky. *G.O. No.:* 71, 15 January 1866. *Citation:* As landsman on board the U.S.S. *Metacomet*, Noble served among the boat's crew which went to the rescue of the U.S. Monitor *Tecumseh* when that vessel was struck by a torpedo in passing enemy forts in Mobile Bay, 5 August 1864. Noble braved the enemy fire which was said by the admiral to be "one of the most galling" he had ever seen and aided in rescuing from death 10 of the crew of the *Tecumseh*, thereby eliciting the admiration of both friend and foe.

NOLAN, JOHN J.

Rank and organization: Sergeant, Company K, 8th New Hampshire Infantry. *Place and date:* At Georgia Landing, La., 27 October 1862. *Entered service at:* Nashua, N.H. *Born:* 24 June 1844, Ireland. *Date of issue:* 3 August 1897. *Citation:* Although prostrated by a cannon shot, refused to give up the flag which he was carrying as color bearer of his regiment and continued to carry it at the head of the regiment throughout the engagement.

NOLL, CONRAD

Rank and organization: Sergeant, Company D, 20th Michigan Infantry. *Place and date:* At Spotsylvania, Va., 12 May 1864. *Entered service at:* Ann Arbor, Mich. *Birth:* Germany. *Date of issue:* 28 July 1896. *Citation:* Seized the colors, the color bearer having been shot down, and gallantly fought his way out with them, though the enemy were on the left flank and rear.

NORTH, JASPER N.

Rank and organization: Private, Company D, 4th West Virginia Infantry. *Place and date:* At Vicksburg, Miss., 22 May 1863. *Entered service at:* Ames, Ohio. *Birth:* ———. *Date of issue:* 27 July 1894. *Citation:* Gallantry in the charge of the "volunteer storming party."

NORTON, ELLIOTT M.

Rank and organization: Second Lieutenant, Company H, 6th Michigan Cavalry. *Place and date:* At Sailors Creek, Va., 6 April 1865. *Entered service at:* Cooper, Mich. *Birth:* Connecticut. *Date of issue:* 3 May 1865. *Citation:* Rushed ahead of his column and captured the flag of the 44th Tennessee Infantry (C.S.A.).

NORTON, JOHN R.

Rank and organization: Lieutenant, Company M, 1st New York (Lincon) Cavalry. *Place and date:* At Sailors Creek, Va., 6 April 1865. *Entered service at:* ———. *Birth:* Ontario County, N.Y. *Date of issue:* 3 May 1865. *Citation:* Capture of flag.

NORTON, LLEWELLYN P.

Rank and organization: Sergeant, Company L, 10th New York Cavalry. *Place and date:* At Sailors Creek, Va., 6 April 1865. *Entered service at:* Cortland County, N.Y. *Birth:* Scott, N.Y. *Date of issue:* 3

July 1865. *Citation:* Charged the enemy and, with the assistance of Corporal Bringle, captured a fieldpiece with 2 prisoners.

NOYES, WILLIAM W.

Rank and organization: Private, Company F, 2d Vermont Infantry. *Place and date:* At Spotsylvania, Va., 12 May 1864. *Entered service at:* Montpelier, Vt. *Birth:* Montpelier, Vt. *Date of issue:* 22 March 1892. *Citation:* Standing upon the top of the breastworks, deliberately took aim and fired no less than 15 shots into the enemy's lines, but a few yards away.

NUGENT, CHRISTOPHER

Rank and organization: Orderly Sergeant, U.S. Marine Corps. *Born:* 1840, County of Caven, Ireland. *Accredited to:* Massachusetts. *G.O. No.:* 32, 16 April 1864. *Citation:* Serving on board the U.S.S. *Fort Henry*, Crystal River, Fla., 15 June 1863. Reconnoitering on the Crystal River on this date and in charge of a boat from the *Fort Henry*, Orderly Sgt. Nugent ordered an assault upon a rebel breastwork fortification. In this assault, the orderly sergeant and his comrades drove a guard of 11 rebels into the swamp, capturing their arms and destroying their camp equipage while gallantly withholding fire to prevent harm to a woman among the fugitives. On 30 July 1863, he further proved his courage by capturing a boat off Depot Key, Fla., containing 2 men and a woman with their baggage.

NUTTING, LEE

Rank and organization: Captain, Company C., 61st New York Infantry. *Place and date:* At Todds Tavern, Va., 8 May 1864. *Entered service at:* ———. *Birth:* Orange County, N.Y. *Date of issue:* 21 August 1893. *Citation:* Led the regiment in charge at a critical moment under a murderous fire until he fell desperately wounded.

O'BEIRNE, JAMES R.

Rank and organization: Captain, Company C, 37th New York Infantry. *Place and date:* At Fair Oaks, Va., 31 May and 1 June 1862. *Entered service at:* New York. *Birth:* Ireland. *Date of issue:* 20 January 1891. *Citation:* Gallantly maintained the line of battle until ordered to fall back.

O'BRIEN, HENRY D.

Rank and organization: Corporal, Company E, 1st Minnesota Infantry. *Place and date:* At Gettysburg, Pa., 3 July 1863. *Entered service at:* St. Anthony Falls, Minn. *Birth:* Maine. *Date of issue:* 9 April 1890. *Citation:* Taking up the colors where they had fallen, he rushed ahead of his regiment, close to the muzzles of the enemy's guns, and engaged in the desperate struggle in which the enemy was defeated, and though severely wounded, he held the colors until wounded a second time.

O'BRIEN, OLIVER

Rank and organization: Coxswain, U.S. Navy. *Born:* 1839, Boston, Mass. *Accredited to:* Massachusetts. *G.O. No.:* 45, 31 December 1864. *Citation:* Served as coxswain on board the U.S. Sloop *John Adams*, Sullivan's Island Channel, 28 November 1864. Taking part in the boarding of the blockade runner *Beatrice* while under heavy enemy fire from Fort Moultrie, O'Brien, who was in charge of one of the boarding launches, carried out his duties with prompt and energetic conduct. This action resulted in the firing of the *Beatrice* and the capture of a quantity of supplies from her.

O'BRIEN, PETER

Rank and organization: Private, Company A, 1st New York (Lincoln) Calvalry. *Place and date:* At Waynesboro, Va., 2 March 1865. *Entered service at:* ———. *Birth:* Ireland. *Date of issue:* 26 March 1865. *Citation:* Capture of flag and of a Confederate officer with his horse and equipment.

O'CONNELL, THOMAS

Rank and organization: Coal Heaver, U.S. Navy. *Born:* 1842, Ireland. *Accredited to:* New York. *G.O. No.:* 45, 31 December 1864. *Citation:* On board the flagship U.S.S. *Hartford*, during successful attacks against Fort Morgan, rebel gunboats and the ram *Tennessee* in Mobile Bay on 5 August 1864. Although a patient in the sick bay, O'Connell voluntarily reported at his station at the shell whip and continued to perform his duties with zeal and courage until his right hand was severed by an enemy shellburst.

O'CONNOR, ALBERT

Rank and organization: Sergeant, Company A, 7th Wisconsin Infantry. *Place and date:* At Gravelly Run, Va., 31 March and 1 April 1865. *Entered service at:* West Point Township, Columbia County, Wis. *Birth:* Canada. *Date of issue:* Unknown. *Citation:* On 31 March 1865, with a comrade, recaptured a Union officer from a detachment of 9 Confederates, capturing 3 of the detachment and dispersing the remainder, and on 1 April 1865, seized a stand of Confederate colors, killing a Confederate officer in a hand-to-hand contest over the colors and retaining the colors until surrounded by Confederates and compelled to relinquish them.

O'CONNOR, TIMOTHY

Rank and organization: Private, Company E, 1st U.S. Cavalry. *Place and date:* Unknown. *Entered service at:* ———. *Birth:* Ireland. *Date of issue:* 5 January 1865. *Citation:* Date and place of act not of record in War Department.

O'DEA, JOHN

Rank and organization: Private, Company D, 8th Missouri Infantry. Place and date: At Vicksburg, Miss., 22 May 1863. *Entered service at:* Clinton, DeWitt County, Ill. *Birth:* Ireland. *Date of issue:* 12 July 1894. *Citation:* Gallantry in the charge of the "volunteer storming party."

O'DONNELL, MENOMEN

Rank and organization: First Lieutenant, Company A, 11th Missouri Infantry. *Place and date:* At Vicksburg, Miss., 22 May 1863. At Fort DeRussey, La., 14 March 1864. *Entered service at:* Illinois. *Born:* 30

April 1830, Ireland. *Date of issue:* 11 September 1897. *Citation:*
Voluntarily joined the color guard in the assault on the enemy's works
when he saw indications of wavering and caused the colors of his regiment to be planted on the parapet. Voluntarily placed himself in the
ranks of an assaulting column (being then on staff duty) and rode with
it into the enemy's works, being the only mounted officer present; was
twice wounded in battle.

O'DONOGHUE, TIMOTHY

Rank and organization: Seaman, U.S. Navy, *Born:* 1841, Rochester,
N.Y. *Accredited to:* New York. *G.O. No.:* 45, 31 December 1864. *Citation:* Served as boatswain's mate on board the U.S.S. *Signal*, Red
River, 5 May 1864. Proceeding up the Red River, the U.S.S. *Signal* engaged a large force of enemy field batteries and sharpshooters, returning the fire until the ship was totally disabled, at which time the white
flag was raised. Serving as gun captain, and wounded early in the battle, O'Donoghue bravely stood by his gun in the face of enemy fire
until ordered to withdraw.

OLIVER, CHARLES

Rank and organization: Sergeant, Company M, 100th Pennsylvania
Infantry. *Place and date:* At Petersburg, Va., 25 March 1865. *Entered
service at:* Allegheny County, Pa. *Birth:* Allegheny County, Pa. *Date of
issue:* 3 July 1865. *Citation:* Capture of flag of 31st Georgia Infantry
(C.S.A.).

OLIVER, PAUL A.

Rank and organization: Captain, Company D. 12th New York Infantry. *Place and date:* At Resaca, Ga., 15 May 1864. *Entered service
at:* New York, N.Y. *Born:* 18 July 1831, at sea in the English Channel
aboard American flagship. *Date of issue:* 12 October 1892. *Citation:*
While acting as aide assisted in preventing a disaster caused by Union
troops firing into each other.

O'NEILL, STEPHEN

Rank and organization: Corporal, Company E, 7th U.S. Infantry.
Place and date: At Chancellorsville, Va., 1 May 1863. *Entered service
at:* ———. *Birth:* St. Johns, New Brunswick. *Date of issue:* 28 September 1891. *Citation:* Took up the colors from the hands of the color
bearer who had been shot down and bore them through the remainder
of the battle.

OPEL, JOHN N.   Born in: BAVARIA

Rank and organization: Private, Company G, 7th Indiana Infantry.
Place and date: At Wilderness, Va., 5 May 1864. *Entered service at:*
Decatur County, Ind. *Birth:* ~~7/29/843~~ *Date of issue:* 1 December 1864.
Citation: Capture of flag of 50th Virginia Infantry (C.S.A.).

ORBANSKY, DAVID

Rank and organization: Private, Company B, 58th Ohio Infantry
Place and date: At Shiloh, Tenn.; Vicksburg, Miss.; etc., 1862 and
1863. *Entered service at:* Columbus, Ohio. *Birth:* Lautenburg, Prussia.
Date of issue: 2 August 1879. *Citation:* Gallantry in actions.

ORR, CHARLES A.

Rank and organization: Private, Company G, 187th New York Infantry. *Place and date:* At Hatchers Run, Va., 27 October 1864. *Entered service at:* Bennington, N.Y. *Birth:* Holland, N.Y. *Date of issue:* 1 April 1898. *Citation:* This soldier and two others, voluntarily and under fire, rescued several wounded and helpless soldiers.

ORR, ROBERT L.

Rank and organization: Major, 61st Pennsylvania Infantry. *Place and date:* At Petersburg, Va., 2 April 1865. *Entered service at:* Philadelphia, Pa. *Born:* 28 March 1836, Philadelphia, Pa. *Date of issue:* 28 November 1892. *Citation:* Carried the colors at the head of the column in the assault after two color bearers had been shot down.

ORTEGA, JOHN

Rank and organization: Seaman, U.S. Navy. *Born:* 1840, Spain. *Accredited to:* Pennsylvania. *G.O. No.:* 45, 31 December 1864. *Citation:* Served as seaman on board the U.S.S. *Saratoga* during actions of that vessel on 2 occasions. Carrying out his duties courageously during these actions, Ortega conducted himself gallantly through both periods. Promoted to acting master's mate.

ORTH, JACOB G.

Rank and organization: Corporal, Company D, 28th Pennsylvania Infantry. *Place and date:* At Antietam, Md., 17 September 1862. *Entered service at:* ———. *Birth:* Philadelphia, Pa. *Date of issue:* 15 January 1867. *Citation:* Capture of flag of 7th South Carolina Infantry (C.S.A.), in hand-to-hand encounter, although he was wounded in the shoulder.

OSBORNE, WILLIAM H.

Rank and organization: Private, Company C, 29th Massachusetts Infantry. *Place and date:* At Malvern Hill, Va., 1 July 1862. *Entered service at:* ———. *Birth:* Scituate, Mass. *Date of issue:* 1 April 1898. *Citation:* Although wounded and carried to the rear, he secured a rifle and voluntarily returned to the front, where, failing to find his own regiment, he joined another and fought with it until again severely wounded and taken prisoner.

OSS, ALBERT

Rank and organization: Private, Company B, 11th New Jersey Infantry. *Place and date:* At Chancellorsville, Va., 3 May 1863. *Entered service at:* Newark, N.J. *Birth:* Belgium. *Date of issue:* 6 May 1892. *Citation:* Remained in the rifle pits after the others had retreated, firing constantly, and contesting the ground step by step.

OVERTURF, JACOB H.

Rank and organization: Private, Company K, 83d Indiana Infantry. *Place and date:* At Vicksburg, Miss., 22 May 1863. *Entered service at:* Holton, Ind. *Birth:* Jefferson County, Ind. *Date of issue:* 13 August 1894. *Citation:* Gallantry in the charge of the "volunteer storming party."

OVIATT, MILES M.

Rank and organization: Corporal, U.S. Marine Corps. *Born:* 1841, Cattaraugus County, N.Y. *Accredited to:* New York. *G.O. No.:* 45, 31 December 1864. *Citation:* On board the U.S.S. *Brooklyn* during action against rebel forts and gunboats and with the ram *Tennessee* in Mobile Bay, 5 August 1864. Despite severe damage to his ship and the loss of several men on board as enemy fire raked the deck, Cpl. Oviatt fought his gun with skill and courage throughout the furious 2-hour battle which resulted in the surrender of the rebel ram *Tennessee*.

PACKARD, LORON F.

Rank and organization: Private, Company E, 5th New York Cavalry. *Place and date:* At Raccoon Ford, Va., 27 November 1863. *Entered service at:* Cuba, N.Y. *Birth:* Cattaraugus County, N.Y. *Date of issue:* 20 August 1894. *Citation:* After his command had retreated, this soldier, voluntarily and alone, returned to the assistance of a comrade and rescued him from the hands of 3 armed Confederates.

PALMER, GEORGE H.

Rank and organization: Musician, 1st Illinois Cavalry. *Place and date:* At Lexington, Mo., 20 September 1861. *Entered service at:* Illinois. *Birth:* New York. *Date of issue:* 10 March 1896. *Citation:* Volunteered to fight in the trenches and also led a charge which resulted in the recapture of a Union hospital, together with Confederate sharpshooters then occupying the same.

PALMER, JOHN G.

Rank and organization: Corporal, Company F, 21st Connecticut Infantry. *Place and date:* At Fredericksburg, Va., 13 December 1862. *Entered service at:* Montville, Conn. *Birth:* Montville, Conn. *Date of issue:* 30 October 1896. *Citation:* First of 6 men who volunteered to assist gunner of a battery upon which the enemy was concentrating its fire, and fought with the battery until the close of the engagement. His commanding officer felt he would never see this man alive again.

PALMER, WILLIAM J.

Rank and organization: Colonel, 15th Pennsylvania Cavalry. *Place and date:* At Red Hill, Ala., 14 January 1865. *Entered service at:* Philadelphia, Pa. *Born:* 16 September 1836, Leipsic, Kent County, Del. *Date of issue:* 24 February 1894. *Citation:* With less than 200 men attacked and defeated a superior force of the enemy, capturing their fieldpiece and about 100 prisoners without losing a man.

PARKER, THOMAS

Rank and organization: Corporal, Company B, 2d Rhode Island Infantry. *Place and date:* At Petersburg, Va., 2 April 1865; at Sailors Creek, Va., 6 April 1865. *Entered service at:* Providence, R.I. *Birth:* England. *Date of issue:* 29 May 1867. *Citation:* Planted the first color on the enemy's works. Carried the regimental colors over the creek after the regiment had broken and been repulsed.

PARKER, WILLIAM

Rank and organization: Captain of the Afterguard, U.S. Navy. *Birth:* Boston, Mass. *Accredited to:* Massachusetts. *G.O. No.:* 11, 3 April 1863. *Citation:* At the wheel on board the U.S.S. *Cayuga* during the capture of Forts St. Philip and Jackson, and New Orleans, 24 and 25 April 1862. As his ship led the advance column toward the barrier and both forts opened fire simultaneously, striking the vessel from stem to stern, Parker conscientiously performed his duties throughout the action in which attempts by 3 rebel steamers to butt and board were thwarted, and the ships driven off. Eleven gunboats were successfully engaged and the enemy garrisons forced to surrender during this battle in which the *Cayuga* sustained 46 hits.

PARKS, GEORGE

Rank and organization: Captain of the Forecastle, U.S. Navy. *Born:* 1823, Schenectady, N.Y. *Accredited to:* New York. *G.O. No.:* 45, 31 December 1864. *Citation:* On board the U.S.S. *Richmond* during action against rebel forts and gunboats and with the ram *Tennessee* in Mobile Bay, 5 August 1864. Despite damage to his ship and the loss of several men on board as enemy fire raked her decks, Parks performed his duties with skill and courage throughout a furious 2-hour battle which resulted in the surrender of the rebel ram *Tennessee* and in the damaging and destruction of batteries at Fort Morgan.

PARKS, HENRY JEREMIAH

Rank and organization: Private, Company A, 9th New York Cavalry. *Place and date:* At Cedar Creek, Va., 19 October 1864. *Entered service at:* Orangeville, N.Y. *Born:* 24 February 1848, Orangeville, N.Y. *Date of issue:* 26 October 1864. *Citation:* While alone and in advance of his unit and attempting to cut off the retreat of a supply wagon, he fought and sent to flight a Confederate color bearer. After capturing the color bearer and leaving him in the rear, he returned to the front and captured 3 more wagons and drivers.

PARKS, JAMES W.

Rank and organization: Corporal, Company F, 11th Missouri Infantry. *Place and date:* At Nashville, Tenn., 16 December 1864. *Entered service at:* Xenia, Clay County, Ill. *Birth:* Lawrence County, Ohio. *Date of issue:* 24 February 1865. *Citation:* Capture of flag.

PARROTT, JACOB (1st to receive Medal of Honor)

Rank and organization: Private, Company K, 33d Ohio Infantry. *Place and date:* Georgia, April 1862. *Entered service at:* Hardin County, Ohio. *Birth:* 17 July 1843, Fairfield County, Ohio. *Date of issue:* 25 March 1863. *Citation:* One of the 19 of 22 men (including 2 civilians) who, by direction of Gen. Mitchell (or Buell) penetrated nearly 200 miles south into enemy territory and captured a railroad train at Big Shanty, Ga., in an attempt to destroy the bridges and tracks between Chattanooga and Atlanta.

PARSONS, JOEL

Rank and organization: Private, Company B, 4th West Virginia Infantry. *Place and date:* At Vicksburg, Miss., 22 May 1863. *Entered service at:* Mason City, W. Va. *Birth:* ———. *Date of issue:* 16 August 1894. *Citation:* Gallantry in the charge of the "volunteer storming party."

PATTERSON, JOHN H.

Rank and organization: First Lieutenant, 11th U.S. Infantry. *Place and date:* At Wilderness, Va., 5 May 1864. *Entered service at:* New York. *Birth:* New York. *Date of issue:* 23 July 1897. *Citation:* Under the heavy fire of the advancing enemy, picked up and carried several hundred yards to a place of safety a wounded officer of his regiment who was helpless and would otherwise have been burned in the forest.

PATTERSON, JOHN T.

Rank and organization: Principal Musician, 122d Ohio Infantry. *Place and date:* At Winchester, Va., 14 June 1863. *Entered service at:* ———. *Birth:* Morgan County, Ohio. *Date of issue:* 13 May 1899. *Citation:* With one companion, voluntarily went in front of the Union line, under a heavy fire from the enemy, and carried back a helpless, wounded comrade, thus saving him from death or capture.

PAUL, WILLIAM H.

Rank and organization: Private, Company E, 90th Pennsylvania Infantry. *Place and date:* At Antietam, Md., 17 September 1862. *Entered service at:* ———. *Birth:* Philadelphia, Pa. *Date of issue:* 3 November 1896. *Citation:* Under a most withering and concentrated fire, voluntarily picked up the colors of his regiment, when the bearer and 2 of the color guard had been killed, and bore them aloft throughout the entire battle.

PAY, BYRON E.

Rank and organization: Private, Company H, 2d Minnesota Infantry. *Place and date:* At Nolensville, Tenn., 15 February 1863. *Entered service at:* Mankato, Minn. *Born:* 21 October 1844, LeRoy Township, Jefferson County, N.Y. *Date of issue:* 11 September 1897. *Citation:* Was one of a detachment of 16 men who heroically defended a wagon train against the attack of 125 cavalry, repulsed the attack and saved the train.

PAYNE, IRVIN C.

Rank and organization: Corporal, Company M, 2d New York Cavalry. *Place and date:* At Sailors Creek, Va., 6 April 1865. *Entered service at:* ———. *Birth:* Wayne County, Pa. *Date of issue:* 3 May 1865. *Citation:* Capture of Virginia State colors.

PAYNE, THOMAS H. L.

Rank and organization: First Lieutenant, Company E, 37th Illinois Infantry. *Place and date:* At Fort Blakely, Ala., 9 April 1865. *Entered service at:* Mendota, La Salle County, Ill. *Born:* 5 October 1840,

Boston, Mass. *Date of issue:* 1 April 1898. *Citation:* While acting regimental quartermaster, learning of an expected assault, requested assignment to a company that had no commissioned officers present; was so assigned, and was one of the first to lead his men into the enemy's works.

PEARSALL, PLATT

Rank and organization: Corporal, Company C, 30th Ohio Infantry. *Place and date:* At Vicksburg, Miss., 22 May 1863. *Entered service at:* ———. *Birth:* Meigs County, Ohio. *Date of issue:* 14 August 1894. *Citation:* Gallantry in the charge of the "volunteer storming party."

PEARSON, ALFRED L.

Rank and organization: Colonel, 155th Pennsylvania Infantry. *Place and date:* At Lewis' Farm, Va., 29 March 1865. *Entered service at:* Pittsburgh, Pa. *Birth:* Pittsburgh, Pa. *Date of issue:* 17 September 1897. *Citation:* Seeing a brigade forced back by the enemy, he seized his regimental color, called on his men to follow him, and advanced upon the enemy under a severe fire. The whole brigade took up the advance, the lost ground was regained, and the enemy was repulsed.

PEASE, JOACHIM

Rank and organization: Seaman, U.S. Navy. *Born:* Long Island, N.Y. *Accredited to:* New York. *G.O. No.:* 45, 31 December 1864. *Citation:* Served as seaman on board the U.S.S. *Kearsarge* when she destroyed the *Alabama* off Cherbourg, France, 19 June 1864. Acting as loader on the No. 2 gun during this bitter engagement, Pease exhibited marked coolness and good conduct and was highly recommended by the divisional officer for gallantry under fire.

PECK, CASSIUS

Rank and organization: Private, Company F, 1st U.S. Sharpshooters. *Place and date:* Near Blackburn's Ford, Va., 19 September 1862. *Entered service at:* ———. *Birth:* Brookfield, Vt. *Date of issue:* 12 October 1892. *Citation:* Took command of such soldiers as he could get and attacked and captured a Confederate battery of 4 guns. Also, while on a reconnaissance, overtook and captured a Confederate soldier.

PECK, OSCAR E.

Rank and organization: Second Class Boy, U.S. Navy. *Born:* 1848, Bridgeport, Conn. *Accredited to:* Connecticut. *G.O. No.:* 11, 3 April 1863. *Citation:* Peck served as second-class boy on board the *Varuna* during an attack on Forts Jackson and St. Philip, 24 April 1862. Acting as powder boy of the after rifle, Peck served gallantly while the *Varuna* was repeatedly attacked and rammed and finally sunk. This was an extremely close-range action and, although badly damaged, the *Varuna* delivered shells abaft the *Morgan's* armor.

PECK, THEODORE S.

Rank and organization: First Lieutenant, Company H, 9th Vermont Infantry. *Place and date:* At Newport Barracks, N.C., 2 February 1864.

Entered service at: Burlington, Vt. *Birth:* Burlington, Vt. *Date of issue:* 8 September 1891. *Citation:* By long and persistent resistance and burning the bridges, kept a superior force of the enemy at bay and covered the retreat of the garrison.

PEIRSOL, JAMES K.

Rank and organization: Sergeant, Company F, 13th Ohio Cavalry. *Place and date:* At Paines Crossroads, Va., 5 April 1865. *Entered service at:* ———. *Birth:* Beaver County, Pa. *Date of issue:* 3 May 1865. *Citation:* Capture of flag.

PELHAM, WILLIAM

Rank and organization: Landsman, U.S. Navy. *Born:* Halifax, Nova Scotia. *Enlisted in:* Nova Scotia. *G.O. No.:* 45, 31 December 1864. *Citation:* On board the flagship U.S.S. *Hartford* during successful actions against Fort Morgan, rebel gunboats and the ram *Tennessee* in Mobile Bay, 5 August 1864. When the other members of his guncrew were killed or wounded under the enemy's terrific shellfire, Pelham calmly assisted the casualties below and voluntarily returned and took his place at an adjoining gun where another man had been struck down. He continued to fight his gun throughout the remainder of the battle which resulted in the capture of the *Tennessee*.

PENNYPACKER, GALUSHA

Rank and organization: Colonel, 97th Pennsylvania Infantry. *Place and date:* At Fort Fisher, N.C., 15 January 1865. *Entered service at:* West Chester, Pa. *Born:* 1 June 1844, Valley Forge, Pa. *Date of issue:* 17 August 1891. *Citation:* Gallantly led the charge over a traverse and planted the colors of one of his regiments thereon; was severely wounded.

PENTZER, PATRICK H.

Rank and organization: Captain, Company C, 97th Illinois Infantry. *Place and date:* At Blakely, Ala., 9 April 1865. *Entered service at:* Gillespie, Macoupin County, Ill. *Birth:* Marion County, Mo. *Date of issue:* 9 October 1879. *Citation:* Among the first to enter the enemy's entrenchments, he received the surrender of a Confederate general officer and his headquarters flag.

PERRY, THOMAS

Rank and organization: Boatswain's Mate, U.S. Navy. *Born:* 1836, New York. *Accredited to:* New York. *G.O. No.:* 45, 31 December 1864. *Citation:* Served as boatswain's mate on board the U.S.S. *Kearsarge* when she destroyed the *Alabama* off Cherbourg, France, 19 June 1864. Acting as captain of the No. 2 gun during this bitter engagement, Perry exhibited marked coolness and good conduct under the enemy fire and was recommended for gallantry by his divisional officer.

PESCH, JOSEPH

Rank and organization: Private, Battery A, 1st Missouri Light Artillery. *Place and date:* At Grand Gulf, Miss., 28–29 April 1863. *Entered service at:* St. Louis, Mo. *Birth:* Prussia. *Date of issue:* 10 March 1896. *Citation:* With 2 comrades voluntarily took position on board the steamer *Cheeseman*, in charge of all the guns and ammunition of the battery, and remained in charge of the same, although the steamer became unmanageable and was exposed for some time to a heavy fire from the enemy.

PETERS, HENRY C.

Rank and organization: Private, Company B, 47th Ohio Infantry. *Place and date:* At Vicksburg, Miss., 3 May 1863. *Entered service at:* Adrian, Mich. *Born:* 29 February 1840, Monroe County, Mich. *Date of issue:* 5 April 1917. *Citation:* Was one of a party that volunteered and attempted to run the enemy's batteries with a steam tug and 2 barges loaded with subsistence stores.

PETERSON, ALFRED

Rank and organization: Seaman, U.S. Navy. *Born:* 1838, Sweden. *Accredited to:* New York. *G.O. No.:* 11, 3 April 1863. *Citation:* On board the U.S.S. *Commodore Perry* in the attack upon Franklin, Va., 3 October 1862. With enemy fire raking the deck of his ship and blockades thwarting her progress, Peterson remained at his post and performed his duties with skill and courage as the *Commodore Perry* fought a gallant battle to silence many rebel batteries as she steamed down the Blackwater River.

PETTY, PHILIP

Rank and organization: Sergeant, Company A, 136th Pennsylvania Infantry. *Place and date:* At Fredericksburg, Va., 13 December 1862. *Entered service at:* Tioga County, Pa. *Born:* 7 May 1840, England. *Date of issue:* 21 August 1893. *Citation:* Took up the colors as they fell out of the hands of the wounded color bearer and carried them forward in the charge.

PHELPS, CHARLES E.

Rank and organization: Colonel, 7th Maryland Infantry. *Place and date:* At Laurel Hill, Va., 8 May 1864. *Entered service at:* Baltimore, Md. *Born:* 1 May 1833, Guilford, Vt. *Date of issue:* 30 March 1898. *Citation:* Rode to the head of the assaulting column, then much broken by severe losses and faltering under the close fire of artillery, placed himself conspicuously in front of the troops, and gallantly rallied and led them to within a few feet of the enemy's works, where he was severely wounded and captured.

PHILLIPS, JOSIAH

Rank and organization: Private, Company E, 148th Pennsylvania Infantry. *Place and date:* At Sutherland Station, Va., 2 April 1865. *Entered service at:* Ulysses, Pa. *Birth:* Wyoming County, N.Y. *Date of issue:* 10 May 1865. *Citation:* Capture of flag.

PHINNEY, WILLIAM

Rank and organization: Boatswain's Mate, U.S. Navy. *Born:* 1824, Norway. *Accredited to:* New York. *G.O. No.:* 45, 31 December 1864.

Citation: On board the U.S.S. *Lackawanna* during successful attacks against Fort Morgan, rebel gunboats and the ram, *Tennessee* in Mobile Bay, 5 August 1864. Serving as a gun captain Phinney showed much presence of mind in managing the gun, and gave much needed encouragement to the crew during the engagement which resulted in the capture of the prize rebel ram *Tennessee* and in the damaging and destruction of Fort Morgan.

PHISTERER, FREDERICK

Rank and organization: First Lieutenant, 18th U.S. Infantry. *Place and date:* At Stone River, Tenn., 31 December 1862. *Entered service at:* Medina County, Ohio. *Birth:* Germany. *Date of issue:* 12 December 1894. *Citation:* Voluntarily conveyed, under a heavy fire, information to the commander of a battalion of regular troops by which the battalion was saved from capture or annihilation.

PICKLE, ALONZO H.

Rank and organization: Sergeant, Company B, 1st Battalion Minnesota Infantry. *Place and date:* At Deep Bottom, Va., 14 August 1864. *Entered service at:* Dover, Minn. *Birth:* Canada. *Date of issue:* 12 June 1895. *Citation:* At the risk of his life, voluntarily went to the assistance of a wounded officer lying close to the enemy's lines and, under fire, carried him to a place of safety.

PIKE, EDWARD M.

Rank and organization: First Sergeant, Company A, 33d Illinois Infantry. *Place and date:* At Cache River, Ark., 7 July 1862. *Entered service at:* Bloomington, Ill. *Birth:* Casce, Maine. *Date of issue:* 29 March 1899. *Citation:* While the troops were falling back before a superior force, this soldier, assisted by one companion, and while under severe fire at close range, saved a cannon from capture by the enemy.

PINGREE, SAMUEL E.

Rank and organization: Captain, Company F, 3d Vermont Infantry. *Place and date:* Lees Mills, Va., 16 April 1862. *Entered service at:* Hartford, Vt. *Birth:* Salisbury, N.H. *Date of issue:* 17 August 1891. *Citation:* Gallantly led his company across a wide, deep creek, drove the enemy from the rifle pits, which were within 2 yards of the farther bank, and remained at the head of his men until a second time severely wounded.

PINKHAM, CHARLES H.

Rank and organization: Sergeant Major, 57th Massachusetts Infantry. *Place and date:* At Fort Stedman, Va., 25 March 1865. *Entered service at:* ———. *Birth:* Grafton, Mass. *Date of issue:* 15 April 1895. *Citation:* Captured the flag of the 57th North Carolina Infantry (C.S.A.), and saved his own colors by tearing them from the staff while the enemy was in the camp.

PINN, ROBERT

Rank and organization: First Sergeant, Company I, 5th U.S. Colored Troops. *Place and date:* At Chapins Farm, Va., 29 September 1864.

Entered service at: Massillon, Ohio. *Born:* 1 March 1843, Stark County, Ohio. *Date of issue:* 6 April 1865. *Citation:* Took command of his company after all the officers had been killed or wounded and gallantly led it in battle.

PIPES, JAMES

Rank and organization: Captain, Company A, 140th Pennsylvania Infantry. *Place and date:* At Gettysburg, Pa., 2 July 1863; At Reams Station, Va., 25 August 1864. *Entered service at:* —'——. *Birth:* Green County, Pa. *Date of issue:* 5 April 1898. *Citation:* While a sergeant and retiring with his company before the rapid advance of the enemy at Gettysburg, he and a companion stopped and carried to a place of safety a wounded and helpless comrade; in this act both he and his companion were severely wounded. A year later, at Reams Station, Va., while commanding a skirmish line, voluntarily assisted in checking a flank movement of the enemy, and while so doing was severely wounded, suffering the loss of an arm.

PITMAN, GEORGE J.

Rank and organization: Sergeant, Company C, 1st New York (Lincoln) Cavalry. *Place and date:* At Sailors Creek, Va., 6 April 1865. *Entered service at:* Philadelphia, Pa. *Birth:* Recklestown N.J. *Date of issue:* 3 May 1865. *Citation:* Capture of flag of the Sumter Heavy Artillery (C.S.A.).

PITTINGER, WILLIAM (5th to receive Medal of Honor)

Rank and organization: Sergeant, Company G, 2d Ohio Infantry. *Place and date:* Georgia, April 1862. *Entered service at:* Jefferson County, Ohio. *Born:* 31 January 1840, Knoxville, Jefferson County, Ohio. *Date of issue:* 25 March 1863. *Citation:* One of the 19 of 22 men (including 2 civilians) who, by direction of Gen. Mitchell (or Buell), penetrated nearly 200 miles south into enemy territory and captured a railroad train at Big Shanty, Ga., in an attempt to destroy the bridges and tract between Chattanooga and Atlanta.

PLANT, HENRY E.

Rank and organization: Corporal, Company F, 14th Michigan Infantry. *Place and date:* At Bentonville, N.C., 19 March 1865. *Entered service at:* Cockery, Mich. *Birth:* Oswego County, N.Y. *Date of issue:* 27 April 1896. *Citation:* Rushed into the midst of the enemy and rescued the colors, the color bearer having fallen mortally wounded.

PLATT, GEORGE C.

Rank and organization: Private, Troop H, 6th U.S. Cavalry. *Place and date:* At Fairfield, Pa., 3 July 1863. *Entered service at:* ———. *Birth:* Ireland. *Date of issue:* 12 July 1895. *Citation:* Seized the regimental flag upon the death of the standard bearer in a hand-to-hand fight and prevented it from falling into the hands of the enemy.

PLIMLEY, WILLIAM

Rank and organization: First Lieutenant, Company F, 120th New York Infantry. *Place and date:* At Hatchers Run, Va., 2 April 1865.

Entered service at: Catskill, N.Y. *Birth:* Catskill, N.Y. *Date of issue:* 4 April 1898. *Citation:* While acting as aide to a general officer, voluntarily accompanied a regiment in an assault on the enemy's works and acted as leader of the movement which resulted in the rout of the enemy and the capture of a large number of prisoners.

PLOWMAN, GEORGE H.

Rank and organization: Sergeant Major, 3d Maryland Infantry. *Place and date:* At Petersburg, Va., 17 June 1864. *Entered service at:* ———. *Birth:* England. *Date of issue:* 1 December 1864. *Citation:* Recaptured the colors of the 2d Pennsylvania Provisional Artillery.

PLUNKETT, THOMAS

Rank and organization: Sergeant, Company E, 21st Massachusetts Infantry. *Place and date:* At Fredericksburg, Va., 11 December 1862. *Entered service at:* West Boylston, Mass. *Birth:* Ireland. *Date of issue:* 30 March 1866. *Citation:* Seized the colors of his regiment, the color bearer having been shot down, and bore them to the front where both his arms were carried off by a shell.

POND, GEORGE F.

Rank and organization: Private, Company C, 3d Wisconsin Cavalry. *Place and date:* At Drywood, Kans., 15 May 1864. *Entered service at:* Fairwater, Fond du Lac County, Wis. *Birth:* Lake County, Ill. *Date of issue:* 16 May 1899. *Citation:* With 2 companions, attacked a greatly superior force of guerrillas, routed them, and rescued several prisoners.

POND, JAMES B.

Rank and organization: First Lieutenant, Company C, 3d Wisconsin Cavalry. *Place and date:* At Baxter Springs, Kans., 6 October 1863. *Entered service at:* Janesville, Rock County, Wis. *Birth:* Allegany, N.Y. *Date of issue:* 30 March 1898. *Citation:* While in command of 2 companies of Cavalry, was surprised and attacked by several times his own number of guerrillas, but gallantly rallied his men, and after a severe struggle drove the enemy outside the fortifications. 1st Lt. Pond then went outside the works and, alone and unaided, fired a howitzer 3 times, throwing the enemy into confusion and causing him to retire.

POOLE, WILLIAM B.

Rank and organization: Quartermaster, U.S. Navy. *Born:* 1833, Maine. *Accredited to:* Maine. *G.O. No.:* 45, 31 December 1864. *Citation:* Service as quartermaster on board the U.S.S. *Kearsarge* when she destroyed the *Alabama* off Cherbourg, France, 19 June 1864. Stationed at the helm, Poole steered the ship during the engagement in a cool and most creditable manner and was highly commended by his divisional officer for his gallantry under fire.

PORTER, AMBROSE

Rank and organization: Commissary Sergeant, Company D, 12th Missouri Cavalry. *Place and date:* At Tallahatchie River, Miss., 7 August 1864. *Entered service at:* Rockport, Atchison County, Mo. *Birth:*

Allegany County, Md. *Date of issue:* 24 August 1905. *Citation:* Was 1 of 4 volunteers who swam the river under a brisk fire of the enemy's sharpshooters and brought over a ferry boat by means of which the troops crossed and dislodged the enemy from a strong position.

PORTER, HORACE

Rank and organization: Captain, Ordnance Department, U.S. Army. *Place and date:* At Chickamauga, Ga., 20 September 1863. *Entered service at:* Harrisburgh, Pa. *Born:* 15 April 1837, Huntington, Pa. *Date of issue:* 8 July 1902. *Citation:* While acting as a volunteer aide, at a critical moment when the lines were broken, rallied enough fugitives to hold the ground under heavy fire long enough to effect the escape of wagon trains and batteries.

PORTER, JOHN R.

Rank and organization: Private, Company G, 21st Ohio Infantry. *Place and date:* Georgia, April 1862. *Entered service at:* Findley, Ohio. *Born:* 14 November 1838, Delaware County, Ohio. *Date of issue:* September 1863. *Citation:* One of the 19 of 22 men (including 2 civilians) who, by direction of Gen. Mitchell (or Buell), penetrated nearly 200 miles south into enemy territory and captured a railroad train at Big Shanty, Ga., in an attempt to destroy the bridges and track between Chattanooga and Atlanta.

PORTER, WILLIAM

Rank and organization: Sergeant, Company H, 1st New Jersey Cavalry. *Place and date:* At Sailors Creek, Va., 6 April 1865. *Entered service at:* ———. *Birth:* New York, N.Y. *Date of issue:* 3 July 1865. *Citation:* Among the first to check the enemy's countercharge.

POST, PHILIP SIDNEY

Rank and organization: Colonel, 59th Illinois Infantry. *Place and date:* At Nashville, Tenn., 15–16 December 1864. *Entered service at:* Galesburg, Ill. *Born:* 19 March 1833, Flordia, Orange County, N.Y. *Date of issue:* 18 March 1893. *Citation:* Led his brigade in an attack upon a strong position under a terrific fire of grape, canister, and musketry; was struck down by a grapeshot after he had reached the enemy's works.

POSTLES, JAMES PARKE

Rank and organization: Captain, Company A, 1st Delaware Infantry. *Place and date:* At Gettysburg, Pa., 2 July 1863. *Entered service at:* Wilmington, Del. *Born:* 28 September 1840, Camden, Del. *Date of issue:* 22 July 1892. *Citation:* Voluntarily delivered an order in the face of heavy fire of the enemy.

POTTER, GEORGE W.

Rank and organization: Private, Company G, 1st Rhode Island Light Artillery. *Place and date:* At Petersburg, Va., 2 April 1865. *Entered service at:* Coventry, R.I. *Birth:* Coventry, R.I. *Date of issue:* 4 March 1886. *Citation:* Was one of a detachment of 20 picked artillerymen who voluntarily accompanied an infantry assaulting party, and who turned upon the enemy the guns captured in the assault.

POTTER, NORMAN F.

Rank and organization: First Sergeant, Company E, 149th New York Infantry. *Place and date:* At Lookout Mountain, Tenn., 24 November 1863. *Entered service at:* Pompey, N.Y. *Birth:* Pompey, N.Y. *Date of issue:* 24 June 1865. *Citation:* Capture of flag (Bragg's army).

POWELL, WILLIAM H.

Rank and organization: Major, 2d West Virginia Cavalry. *Place and date:* At Sinking Creek Valley, Va., 26 November 1862. *Entered service at:* Ironton, Ohio. *Birth:* England. *Date of issue:* 22 July 1890. *Citation:* Distinguished services in raid, where with 20 men, he charged and captured the enemy's camp, 500 strong, without the loss of man or gun.

POWER, ALBERT

Rank and organization: Private, Company A, 3d Iowa Cavalry. *Place and date:* At Pea Ridge, Ark., 7 March 1862. *Entered service at:* Davis County, Iowa. *Birth:* Guernsey County, Ohio. *Date of issue:* 6 March 1899. *Citation:* Under a heavy fire and at great personal risk went to the aid of a dismounted comrade who was surrounded by the enemy, took him up on his own horse, and carried him to a place of safety.

POWERS, WESLEY J.

Rank and organization: Corporal, Company F, 147th Illinois Infantry. *Place and date:* At Oostanaula, Ga., 3 April 1865. *Entered service at:* Virgil, Ill. *Birth:* Canada. *Date of issue:* 24 October 1895. *Citation:* Voluntarily swam the river under heavy fire and secured a ferryboat, by means of which the command crossed.

PRANCE, GEORGE

Rank and organization: Captain of the Main Top, U.S. Navy. *Born:* 1827, France. *Accredited to:* Massachusetts. *G.O. No.:* 59, 22 June 1865. *Citation:* On board the U.S.S. *Ticonderoga* during attacks on Fort Fisher, 24 and 25 December 1864; and 13 to 15 January 1865. Despite heavy return fire by the enemy and the explosion of the 100-pounder Parrott rifle which killed 8 men and wounded 12 more, Prance as captain of a gun, performed his duties with skill and courage during the first 2 days of battle. As his ship again took position on the line on the 13th, he remained steadfast as the *Ticonderoga* maintained a well-placed fire upon the batteries on shore, and thereafter as she materially lessened the power of guns on the mound which had been turned upon our assaulting columns. During this action the flag was planted on one of the strongest fortifications possessed by the rebels.

PRENTICE, JOSEPH R.

Rank and organization: Private, Company E, 19th U.S. Infantry. *Place and date:* At Stone River, Tenn., 31 December 1862. *Entered service at:* ———. *Born:* 6 December 1838, Lancaster, Ohio. *Date of issue:* 3 February 1894. *Citation:* Voluntarily rescued the body of his commanding officer, who had fallen mortally wounded. He brought off the field his mortally wounded leader under direct and constant rifle fire.

PRESTON, JOHN

Rank and organization: Landsman, U.S. Navy. *Born:* 1841, Ireland. *Accredited to:* Massachusetts. *G.O. No.:* 45, 31 December 1864. *Citation:* Served on board the U.S.S. *Oneida* in the engagement at Mobile Bay, 5 August 1864. Severely wounded, Preston remained at his gun throughout the engagement which resulted in the capture of the rebel ram *Tennessee* and the damaging of Fort Morgan, carrying on until obliged to go to the surgeon to whom he reported himself as "only slightly injured." He then assisted in taking care of the wounded below and wanted to be allowed to return to his battle station on deck. Upon close examination it was found that he was wounded quite severely in both eyes.

PRESTON, NOBLE D.

Rank and organization: First Lieutenant and Commissary, 10th New York Cavalry. *Place and date:* At Trevilian Station, Va., 11 June 1864. *Entered service at:* Fulton, N.Y. *Birth:* ———. *Date of issue:* 22 November 1889. *Citation:* Voluntarily led a charge in which he was severely wounded.

PRICE, EDWARD

Rank and organization: Coxswain, U.S. Navy. *Born:* 1840, New York. *Accredited to:* New York. *G.O. No.:* 45, 31 December 1864. *Citation:* On board the U.S.S. *Brooklyn* during successful attacks against Fort Morgan, rebel gunboats and the ram *Tennessee* in Mobile Bay, 5 August 1864. When the sponge broke, leaving the head in the gun and completely disabling the weapon, Price immediately cleared it by pouring powder into the vent and blowing the sponge head out, thereafter continuing to man the weapon until the close of the furious action which resulted in the capture of the prize rebel ram *Tennessee* and in the infliction of damage and destruction on Fort Morgan.

PROVINCE, GEORGE

Rank and organization: Ordinary Seaman, U.S. Navy. *Born:* 1842, New York, N.Y. *Accredited to:* New York. *G.O. No.:* 59, 22 June 1865. *Citation:* On board the U.S.S. *Santiago de Cuba* during the assault on Fort Fisher on 15 January 1865. As one of a boat crew detailed to one of the generals on shore, Province bravely entered the fort in the assault and accompanied his party in carrying dispatches at the height of the battle. He was 1 of 6 men who entered the fort in the assault from the fleet.

PURCELL, HIRAM W.

Rank and organization: Sergeant, Company G, 104th Pennsylvania Infantry. *Place and date:* At Fair Oaks, Va., 31 May 1862. *Entered service at:* ———. *Birth:* Bucks County, Pa. *Date of issue:* 12 May 1894. *Citation:* While carrying the regimental colors on the retreat he returned to face the advancing enemy, flag in hand, and saved the other color, which would otherwise have been captured.

PURMAN, JAMES J.

Rank and organization: Lieutenant, Company A, 140th Pennsylvania Infantry. *Place and date:* At Gettysburg, Pa., 2 July 1863. *Entered service at:* Greene County, Pa. *Birth:* ———. *Date of issue:* 30 October 1896. *Citation:* Voluntarily assisted a wounded comrade to a place of apparent safety while the enemy were in close proximity; he received the fire of the enemy and a wound which resulted in the amputation of his left leg.

PUTNAM, EDGAR P.

Rank and organization: Sergeant, Company D, 9th New York Cavalry. *Place and date:* At Crumps Creek, Va., 27 May 1864. *Entered service at:* Stockton, N.Y. *Birth:* Stockton, N.Y. *Date of issue:* 13 May 1892. *Citation:* With a small force on a reconnaissance drove off a strong body of the enemy, charged into another force of the enemy's cavalry and stampeded them, taking 27 prisoners.

PUTNAM, WINTHROP D.

Rank and organization: Corporal, Company A, 77th Illinois Infantry. *Place and date:* At Vicksburg, Miss., 22 May 1863. *Entered service at:* Peoria, Ill. *Birth:* Southbridge, Mass. *Date of issue:* 4 April 1898. *Citation:* Carried, with others, by hand, a cannon up to and fired it through an embrasure of the enemy's works.

PYNE, GEORGE

Rank and organization: Seaman, U.S. Navy. *Born:* 1841, England. *Accredited to:* New York. *G.O. No.:* 59, 22 June 1865. *Citation:* As seaman on board the U.S.S. *Magnolia*, St. Marks, Fla., 5 and 6 March 1865. Serving with the Army in charge of Navy howitzers during the attack on St. Marks and throughout this fierce engagement, Pyne, although wounded, made remarkable efforts in assisting transport of the gun, and his coolness and determination in courageously standing by his gun while under the fire of the enemy were a credit to the service to which he belonged.

QUAY, MATTHEW S.

Rank and organization: Colonel, 134th Pennsylvania Infantry. *Place and date:* At Fredericksburg, Va., 13 December 1862. *Entered service at: Beaver County, Pa. Born:* 30 September 1833, Dilkburg, Pa. *Date of issue:* 9 July 1888. *Citation:* Although out of service, he voluntarily resumed duty on the eve of battle and took a conspicuous part in the charge on the heights.

QUINLAN, JAMES

Rank and organization: Major, 88th New York Infantry. *Place and date:* At Savage Station, Va., 29 June 1862. *Entered service at:* New York, N.Y. *Born:* 13 September 1833, Ireland. *Date of issue:* 18 February 1891. *Citation:* Led his regiment on the enemy's battery, silenced the guns, held the position against overwhelming numbers, and covered the retreat of the 2d Army Corps.

RAFFERTY, PETER

Rank and organization: Private, Company B, 69th New York Infantry. *Place and date:* At Malvern Hill, Va., 1 July 1862. *Entered service at:* New York, N.Y. *Birth:* Ireland. *Date of issue:* 2 August 1897. *Citation:* Having been wounded and directed to the rear, declined to go, but continued in action, receiving several additional wounds, which resulted in his capture by the enemy and his total disability for military service.

RAMSBOTTOM, ALFRED

Rank and organization: First Sergeant, Company K, 97th Ohio Infantry. *Place and date:* At Franklin, Tenn., 30 November 1864. *Entered service at:* ———. *Birth:* Delaware County, Ohio. *Date of issue:* 24 February 1865. *Citation:* Captured the flag of the 2d Mississippi Infantry (C.S.A.), in a hand-to-hand fight with the color bearer.

RAND, CHARLES F.

Rank and organization: Private, Company K, 12th New York Infantry. *Place and date:* At Blackburns Ford, Va., 18 July 1861. *Entered service at:* Batavia, N.Y. *Birth:* Batavia, N.Y. *Date of issue:* 23 October 1897. *Citation:* Remained in action when a part of his regiment broke in disorder, joined another company, and fought with it through the remainder of the engagement.

RANNAHAN, JOHN

Rank and organization: Corporal, U.S. Marine Corps. *Born:* 1836, County of Monahan, Ireland. *Accredited to:* Pennsylvania. *G.O. No.:* 59, 22 June 1865. *Citation:* On board the U.S.S. *Minnesota* in the assault on Fort Fisher, 15 January 1865. Landing on the beach with the assaulting party from his ship, Cpl. Rannahan advanced to the top of the sandhill and partly through the breach in the palisades despite enemy fire which killed or wounded many officers and men. When more than two-thirds of the men became seized with panic and retreated on the run, he remained with the party until dark when it came safely away, bringing its wounded, its arms and its colors.

RANNEY, GEORGE E.

Rank and organization: Assistant Surgeon, 2d Michigan Cavalry. *Place and date:* At Resaca, Ga., 14 May 1864. *Entered service at:* Detroit, Mich. *Born:* 13 June 1839, Batavia, N.Y. *Date of issue:* 24 April 1901. *Citation:* At great personal risk, went to the aid of a wounded soldier, Pvt. Charles W. Baker, lying under heavy fire between the lines, and with the aid of an orderly carried him to a place of safety.

RANNEY, MYRON H.

Rank and organization: Private, Company G, 13th New York Infantry. *Place and date:* At Bull Run, Va., 30 August 1862. *Entered service at:* ———. *Birth:* Franklinville, N.Y. *Date of issue:* 23 March 1895. *Citation:* Picked up the colors and carried them off the field after the color bearer had been shot down; was himself wounded.

RATCLIFF, EDWARD

Rank and organization: First Sergeant, Company C, 38th U.S. Colored Troops. *Place and date:* At Chapins Farm, Va., 29 September 1864. *Entered service at:* ———. *Birth:* James County, Va. *Date of issue:* 6 April 1865. *Citation:* Commanded and gallantly led his company after the commanding officer had been killed; was the first enlisted man to enter the enemy's works.

RAUB, JACOB F.

Rank and organization: Assistant Surgeon, 210th Pennsylvania Infantry. *Place and date:* At Hatchers Run, Va., 5 February 1865. *Entered servie at:* Weaversville, Pa. *Born:* 13 May 1840, Raubsville, Northhampton County, Pa. *Date of issue:* 20 April 1896. *Citation:* Discovering a flank movement by the enemy, appraised the commanding general at great peril, and though a noncombatant voluntarily participated with the troops in repelling this attack.

RAYMOND, WILLIAM H.

Rank and organization: Corporal, Company A, 108th New York Infantry. *Place and date:* At Gettysburg, Pa., 3 July 1863. *Entered service at:* Penfield, N.Y. *Birth:* Penfield, N.Y. *Date of issue:* 10 March 1896. *Citation:* Voluntarily and under a severe fire brought a box of ammunition to his comrades on the skirmish line.

READ, CHARLES

Rank and organization: Ordinary Seaman, U.S. Navy. *Born:* 1840, Cambridge, N.Y. *Accredited to:* New York. *G.O. No. 59,* 22 June 1865. *Citation:* As seaman on board the U.S.S. *Magnolia,* St. Marks, Fla., 5 and 6 March 1865. Serving with the Army in charge of Navy howitzers during the attack on St. Marks and throughout this fierce engagement, Read made remarkable efforts in assisting transport of the gun, and his coolness and determination in courageously standing by his gun while under the fire of the enemy were a credit to the service to which he belonged.

READ, CHARLES A.

Rank and organization: Coxswain, U.S. Navy. *Born:* 1837, Sweden, *Accredited to:* Ohio. *G.O. No.:* 45, 31 December 1864. *Citation:* Served as coxswain on board the U.S.S. *Kearsarge* when she destroyed the *Alabama* off Cherbourg, France, 19 June 1864. Acting as the first sponger of the pivot gun during this bitter engagement, Read exhibited marked coolness and good conduct and was highly recommended for his gallantry under fire by his divisional officer.

READ, GEORGE E.

Rank and organization: Seaman, U.S. Navy. *Born:* 1838, Rhode Island. *Accredited to:* Rhode Island. *G.O. No.:* 45, 31 December 1864. *Citation:* Served as seaman on board the U.S.S. *Kearsage* when she destroyed the *Alabama* off Cherbourg, France, 19 June 1864. Acting as the first loader of the No. 2 gun during this bitter engagement, Read exhibited marked coolness and good conduct and was highly recommended for his gallantry under fire by his divisional officer.

READ, MORTON A.

Rank and organization: Lieutenant, Company D, 8th New York Cavalry. *Place and date:* At Appomattox Station, Va., 8 April 1865. *Entered service at:* Brockport, N.Y. *Birth:* Brockport, N.Y. *Date of issue:* 3 May 1865. *Citation:* Capture of flag of 1st Texas Infantry (C.S.A.).

REBMANN, GEORGE F.

Rank and organization: Sergeant, Company B, 119th Illinois Infantry. *Place and date:* At Blakely, Ala., 9 April 1865. *Entered service at:* Browning, Schuyler County, Ill. *Birth:* Schuyler County, Ill. *Date of issue:* 8 June 1865. *Citation:* Capture of flag.

REDDICK, WILLIAM H. (6th to receive Medal of Honor)

Rank and organization: Corporal, Company B, 33d Ohio Infantry. *Place and date:* Georgia, April 1862. *Entered service at:* Ohio. *Birth:* Alabama. *Date of issue:* 25 March 1863. *Citation:* One of the 19 of 22 men (including 2 civilians) who, by direction of Gen. Mitchell (or Buell), penetrated nearly 200 miles south into enemy territory and captured a railroad train at Big Shanty, Ga., in an attempt to destroy the bridges and tracks between Chattanooga and Atlanta.

REED, AXEL H.

Rank and organization: Sergeant, Company K, 2d Minnesota Infantry. *Place and date:* At Chickamauga, Ga., 19 September 1863; At Missionary Ridge, Tenn., 25 November 1863. *Entered service at:* Glencoe, Minn. *Birth:* Maine. *Date of issue:* 2 April 1898. *Citation:* While in arrest at Chickamauga, Ga., left his place in the rear and voluntarily went to the line of battle, secured a rifle, and fought gallantly during the 2-day battle; was released from arrest in recognition of his bravery. At Missionary Ridge commanded his company and gallantly led it, being among the first to enter the enemy's works; was severely wounded, losing an arm, but declined a discharge and remained in active service to the end of the war.

REED, CHARLES W.

Rank and organization: Bugler, 9th Independent Battery, Massachusetts Light Artillery. *Place and date:* At Gettysburg, Pa., 2 July 1863. *Entered service at:* ———. *Birth:* Charlestown, Mass. *Date of issue:* 16 August 1895. *Citation:* Rescued his wounded captain from between the lines.

REED, GEORGE W.

Rank and organization: Private, Company E, 11th Pennsylvania Infantry. *Place and date:* At Weldon Railroad, Va., 21 August 1864. *Entered service at:* Johnstown, Pa. *Birth:* Cambria County, Pa. *Date of issue:* 6 September 1864. *Citation:* Capture of flag of 24th North Carolina Volunteers (C.S.A.).

REED, WILLIAM

Rank and organization: Private, Company H, 8th Missouri Infantry. *Place and date:* At Vicksburg, Miss., 22 May 1863. *Entered service at:* Pekin, Tazwell County, Ill. *Birth:* Union County, Pa. *Date of issue:* 12 December 1895. *Citation:* Gallantry in the charge of the "volunteer storming party."

REEDER, CHARLES A.

Rank and organization: Private, Company G, 12th West Virginia Infantry. *Place and date:* At Battery Gregg, near Petersburg, Va., 2 April 1865. *Entered service at:* ———. *Birth:* Harrison, W. Va. *Date of issue:* 3 April 1867. *Citation:* Capture of flag.

REGAN, JEREMIAH

Rank and organization: Quartermaster, U.S. Navy. *Born:* 1832, Boston, Mass. *Accredited to:* Massachusetts. *G.O. No.:* 11, 3 April 1863. *Citation:* As captain of No. 2 gun on board the U.S.S. *Galena* in the attack upon Drewy's Bluff, 15 May 1862. With his ship severely damaged by the enemy's shellfire and several men killed and wounded, Regan, continued to man his gun throughout the engagement despite the concentration of fire directed against men at their guns by enemy sharpshooters in rifle pits along the banks.

REID, ROBERT

Rank and organization: Private, Company G, 48th Pennsylvania Infantry. *Place and date:* At Petersburg, Va., 17 June 1864. *Entered service at:* Pottsville, Pa. *Birth:* Scotland. *Date of issue:* 1 December 1864. *Citation:* Capture of flag of 44th Tennessee Infantry (C.S.A.).

REIGLE, DANIEL P.

Rank and organization: Corporal, Company F, 87th Pennsylvania Infantry. *Place and date:* At Cedar Creek, Va., 19 October 1864. *Entered service at:* Adams County, Pa. *Birth:* Adams County, Pa. *Date of issue:* 26 October 1864. *Citation:* For gallantry while rushing forward to capture a Confederate flag at the stone fence where the enemy's last stand was made.

REISINGER, J. MONROE

Rank and organization: Corporal, Company H, 150th Pennsylvania Infantry. *Place and date:* At Gettysburg, Pa., 1 July 1863. *Entered service at:* Meadville, Pa. *Birth:* Beaver County, Pa. *Date of issue:* Unknown. *Citation:* Specially brave and meritorious conduct in the face of the enemy. *Awarded under Act of Congress, January 25, 1907.*

RENNINGER, LOUIS

Rank and organization: Corporal, Company H, 37th Ohio Infantry. *Place and date:* At Vicksburg, Miss., 22 May 1863. *Entered service at:* ———. *Birth:* Liverpool, Ohio. *Date of issue:* 15 August 1894. *Citation:* Gallantry in the charge of the "volunteer storming party."

REYNOLDS, GEORGE

Rank and organization: Private, Company M, 9th New York Cavalry. *Place and date:* At Winchester, Va., 19 September 1864. *Entered service at:* New York, N.Y. *Birth:* Ireland. *Date of issue:* 27 September 1864. *Citation:* Capture of Virginia State flag.

RHODES, JULIUS D.

Rank and organization: Private, Company F, 5th New York Cavalry. *Place and date:* At Thoroughfare Gap, Va., 28 August 1862. At Bull Run, Va., 30 August 1862. *Entered service at:* Springville, N.Y. *Birth:* Monroe County, Mich. *Date of issue:* 9 March 1887. *Citation:* After having had his horse shot under him in the fight at Thoroughfare Gap, Va., he voluntarily joined the 105th New York Volunteers and was conspicuous in the advance on the enemy's lines. Displayed gallantry in the advance on the skirmish line at Bull Run, Va., where he was wounded.

RHODES, SYLVESTER D.

Rank and organization: Sergeant, Company D, 61st Pennsylvania Infantry. *Place and date:* At Fishers Hill, Va., 22 September 1864. *Entered service at:* Wilkes-Barre, Pa. *Birth:* Plains, Pa. *Date of issue:* 16 February 1897. *Citation:* Was on the skirmish line which drove the enemy from the first entrenchment and was the first man to enter the breastworks, capturing one of the guns and turning it upon the enemy.

RICE, CHARLES

Rank and organization: Coal Heaver, U.S. Navy. *Born:* 1840, Russia. *Accredited to:* Maine. *G.O. No.:* 45, 31 December 1864. *Citation:* On board the U.S.S. *Agawam,* as one of a volunteer crew of a powder boat which was exploded near Fort Fisher, 23 December 1864. The powder boat, towed in by the *Wilderness* to prevent detection by the enemy, cast off and slowly steamed to within 300 yards of the beach. After fuses and fires had been lit and a second anchor with short scope let go to assure the boat's tailing inshore, the crew again boarded the *Wilderness* and proceeded a distance of 12 miles from shore. Less than 2 hours later the explosion took place, and the following day, fires were observed still burning at the fort.

RICE, EDMUND

Rank and organization: Major, 19th Massachusetts Infantry. *Place and date:* At Gettysburg, Pa., 3 July 1863. *Entered service at:* Boston, Mass. *Birth:* Brighton, Mass. *Date of issue:* 6 October 1891. *Citation:* Conspicuous bravery on the third day of the battle on the countercharge against Pickett's division where he fell severely wounded within the enemy's lines.

RICH, CARLOS H.

Rank and organization: First Sergeant, Company K, 4th Vermont Infantry. *Place and date:* At Wilderness, Va., 5 May 1864. *Entered service at:* Northfield, Mass. *Birth:* Canada. *Date of issue:* 4 January 1895. *Citation:* Saved the life of an officer.

RICHARDS, LOUIS

Rank and organization: Quartermaster, U.S. Navy. *Born:* 1835, New York, N.Y. *Accredited to:* New York. *G.O. No.:* 11, 3 April 1863. *Citation:* Richards served as quartermaster on board the U.S.S. *Pensacola* in the attack upon Forts Jackson and St. Philip, and at the taking of New Orleans, 24 and 25 April 1862. Through all the din and roar of battle, he steered the ship through the narrow opening of the barricade, and his attention to orders contributed to the successful passage of the ship without once fouling the shore or the obstacles of the barricade.

RICHARDSON, WILLIAM R.

Rank and organization: Private, Company A, 2d Ohio Cavalry. *Place and date:* At Sailors Creek, Va., 6 April 1865. *Entered service at:* Washington, Ohio. *Birth:* Cleveland, Ohio. *Date of issue:* 7 April 1866. *Citation:* Having been captured and taken to the rear, made his escape, rejoined the Union lines, and furnished information of great importance as to the enemy's position and the approaches thereto.

RICHEY, WILLIAM E.

Rank and organization: Corporal, Company A, 15th Ohio Infantry. *Place and date:* At Chickamauga, Ga., 19 September 1863. *Entered service at:* ———. *Birth:* Athens County, Ohio. *Date of issue:* 9 November 1893. *Citation:* While on the extreme front, between the lines of the combatants single-handed he captured a Confederate major who was armed and mounted.

RICHMOND, JAMES

Rank and organization: Private, Company F, 8th Ohio Infantry. *Place and date:* At Gettysburg, Pa., 3 July 1863. *Entered service at:* Toledo, Ohio. *Birth:* Maine. *Date of issue:* 1 December 1864. *Citation:* Capture of flag.

RICKSECKER, JOHN H.

Rank and organization: Private, Company D, 104th Ohio Infantry. *Place and date:* At Franklin, Tenn., 30 November 1864. *Entered service at:* ———. *Birth:* Springfield, Ohio. *Date of issue:* 3 February 1865. *Citation:* Capture of flag of 16th Alabama Artillery (C.S.A.).

RIDDELL, RUDOLPH

Rank and organization: Lieutenant, Company I, 61st New York Infantry. *Place and date:* At Sailors Creek, Va., 6 April 1865. *Entered service at:* Hamilton, N.Y. *Birth:* Hamilton, N.Y. *Date of issue:* 10 May 1865. *Citation:* Captured the flag of the 6th Alabama Cavalry (C.S.A.).

RILEY, THOMAS

Rank and organization: Private, Company D, 1st Louisiana Cavalry. *Place and date:* At Fort Blakely, Ala., 4 April 1865. *Entered service at:* ———. *Birth:* Ireland. *Date of issue:* 8 June 1865. *Citation:* Captured the flag of the 6th Alabama Cavalry.

RINGOLD, EDWARD

Rank and organization: Coxswain, U.S. Navy. *Born:* 1827, Baltimore, Md. *Accredited to:* Maryland. *G.O. No.:* 17, 10 July 1863. *Citation:* Served as coxswain on board the U.S.S. *Wabash* in the engagement at Pocataligo, 22 October 1862. Soliciting permission to accompany the howitzer corps, and performing his duty with such gallantry and presence of mind as to attract the attention of all around him, Ringold, knowing there was a scarcity of ammunition, went through the whole line of fire with his shirt slung over his shoulder filled with fixed ammunition which he had brought from 2 miles to the rear of the lines.

RIPLEY, WILLIAM Y. W.

Rank and organization: Lieutenant Colonel, 1st U.S. Sharpshooters. *Place and date:* At Malvern Hill, Va., 1 July 1862. *Entered service at:* Rutland, Vt. *Birth:* ———. *Date of issue:* 11 March 1893. *Citation:* At a critical moment brought up two regiments, which he led against the enemy himself, being severely wounded.

ROANTREE, JAMES S.

Rank and organization: Sergeant, U.S. Marine Corps. *Born:* 1835, Dublin, Ireland. *Accredited to:* New York. *G.O. No.:* 45, 31 December 1864. *Citation:* On board the U.S.S. *Oneida* during action against rebel forts and gunboats and with the ram *Tennessee* in Mobile Bay, 5 August 1864. Despite damage to his ship and the loss of several men on board as enemy fire raked her decks and penetrated her boilers, Sgt. Roantree performed his duties with skill and courage throughout the furious battle which resulted in the surrender of the rebel ram *Tennessee* and in the damaging and destruction of batteries at Fort Morgan.

ROBBINS, AUGUSTUS J.

Rank and organization: Second Lieutenant, Company B, 2d Vermont Infantry. *Place and date:* At Spotsylvania, Va., 12 May 1864. *Entered service at:* Grafton, Vt. *Birth:* Grafton, Vt. *Date of issue:* 24 March 1892. *Citation:* While voluntarily serving as a staff officer successfully withdrew a regiment across and around a severely exposed position to the rest of the command; was severely wounded.

ROBERTS, JAMES

Rank and organization: Seaman, U.S. Navy. *Born:* 1837, England. *Accredited to:* Virginia. *G.O. No.:* 45, 31 December 1864. *Citation:* Roberts served on board the U.S.S. *Agawan*, as one of a volunteer crew of a powder boat which was exploded near Fort Fisher, 23 December 1864. The powder boat, towed in by the *Wilderness* to prevent detection by the enemy, cast off and slowly steamed to within 300 yards of the beach. After fuses and fires had been lit and a second anchor with short scope let go to assure the boat's tailing inshore, the crew again boarded the *Wilderness* and proceeded a distance of 12 miles from shore. Less than 2 hours later the explosion took place and the following day fires were observed still burning at the fort.

ROBERTS, OTIS O.

Rank and organization: Sergeant, Company H, 6th Maine Infantry. *Place and date:* At Rappanhannock Station, Va., 7 November 1863. *Entered service at:* Dexter, Maine. *Birth:* Sangerville, Maine. *Date of issue:* 28 December 1863. *Citation:* Capture of flag of 8th Louisiana Infantry (C.S.A.) in a hand-to-hand struggle with the color bearer.

ROBERTSON, ROBERT S.

Rank and organization: First Lieutenant, Company K, 93d New York Infantry. *Place and date:* At Corbins Bridge, Va., 8 May 1864. *Entered service at:* Argyle, N.Y. *Birth:* Argyle, N.Y. *Date of issue:* 2 August 1897. *Citation:* While acting as aide-de-camp to a general officer, seeing a regiment break to the rear, he seized its colors, rode with them to the front in the face of the advancing enemy, and rallied the retreating regiment.

ROBERTSON, SAMUEL

Rank and organization: Private, Company G, 33d Ohio Infantry. *Place and date:* Georgia, April 1862. *Entered service at:* Boarneville, Ross County, Ohio. *Birth:* Muskingum County, Ohio. *Date of issue:* September 1863. *Citation:* One of the 19 of 22 men (including 2 civilians) who by direction of Gen. Mitchell (or Buell) penetrated nearly 200 miles south into enemy territory and captured a railroad train at Big Shanty, Ga., in an attempt to destroy the bridges and tracks between Chattanooga and Atlanta.

ROBIE, GEORGE F.

Rank and organization: Sergeant, Company D, 7th New Hampshire Infantry. *Place and date:* Before Richmond, Va., September 1864. *Entered service at:* ———. *Birth:* Candia, N.H. *Date of issue:* 12 June 1883. *Citation:* Gallantry on the skirmish line.

ROBINSON, ALEXANDER

Rank and organization: Boatswain's Mate, U.S. Navy. *Born:* 1831, England. *Accredited to:* New York. *G.O. No.:* 45, 31 December 1864. *Citation:* Served as boatswain's mate on board the U.S.S. *Howquah* on the occasion of the destruction of the blockade runner, *Lynx*, off Wilmington, 25 September 1864. Performing his duty faithfully under the most trying circumstances, Robinson stood firmly at his post in the midst of a crossfire from the rebel shore batteries and our own vessels.

ROBINSON, CHARLES

Rank and organization: Boatswain's Mate, U.S. Navy. *Born:* 1832, Scotland. *Accredited to:* New York. *G.O. No.:* 11, 3 April 1863. *Citation:* Serving on board the U.S.S. *Baron de Kalb*, Yazoo River Expedition, 23 to 27 December 1862. Proceeding under orders up the Yazoo River, the U.S.S. *Baron de Kalb*, with the object of capturing or destroying the enemy's transports, came upon the steamers *John Walsh, R. J. Locklan, Golden Age*, and the *Scotland* sunk on a bar where they were ordered fired. Continuing up the river, she was fired on by the enemy, but upon returning the fire, caused the rebels to retreat. Returning down the Yazoo, she destroyed and captured large quantities of enemy equipment and several prisoners. Serving bravely throughout this action, Robinson, as boatswain's mate, "distinguished himself in the various actions."

ROBINSON, ELBRIDGE

Rank and organization: Private, Company C, 122d Ohio Infantry. *Place and date:* At Winchester, Va., 14 June 1863. *Entered service at:* — — —. *Birth:* Morgan County, Ohio. *Date of issue:* 5 April 1898. *Citation:* With 1 companion, voluntarily went in front of the Union line, under a heavy fire from the enemy, and carried back a helpless, wounded comrade, thus saving him from death or capture.

ROBINSON, JAMES H.

Rank and organization: Private, Company B, 3d Michigan Cavalry. *Place and date:* At Brownsville, Ark., 27 January 1865. *Entered service at:* Victor, Mich. *Birth.* Oakland County, Mich. *Date of issue:* 4 April 1865. *Citation:* Successfully defended himself, singlehanded against 7 guerrillas, killing the leader (Capt. W. C. Stephenson) and driving off the remainder of the party.

ROBINSON, JOHN C.

Rank and organization: Brigadier General, U.S. Volunteers. *Place and date:* At Laurel Hill, Va., 8 May 1864. *Entered service at:* Binghamton, N.Y. *Birth:* Binghamton, N.Y. *Date of issue:* 28 March 1894. *Citation:* Placed himself at the head of the leading brigade in a charge upon the enemy's breastworks; was severely wounded.

ROBINSON, JOHN H.

Rank and organization: Private, Company I, 19th Massachusetts Infantry. *Place and date:* At Gettysburg, Pa., 3 July 1863. *Entered service at:* Roxbury, Mass. *Birth:* Ireland. *Date of issue:* 1 December 1864. *Citation:* Capture of flag of 57th Virginia Infantry (C.S.A.).

ROBINSON, THOMAS

Rank and organization: Private, Company H, 81st Pennsylvania Infantry. *Place and date:* At Spotsylvania, Va., 12 May 1864. *Entered service at:* Tamaqua, Pa. *Birth:* Ireland. *Date of issue:* 1 December 1864. *Citation:* Capture of flag in a hand-to-hand conflict.

ROCK, FREDERICK

Rank and organization: Private, Company A, 37th Ohio Infantry. *Place and date:* At Vicksburg, Miss., 22 May 1863. *Entered service at:* Cleveland, Ohio. *Birth:* Germany. *Date of issue:* 10 August 1894. *Citation:* Gallantry in the charge of the "volunteer storming party."

ROCKEFELLER, CHARLES M.

Rank and organization: Lieutenant, Company A, 178th New York Infantry. *Place and date:* At Fort Blakely, Ala., 9 April 1865. *Entered service at:* New York. *Birth:* New York. *Date of issue:* 2 August 1897. *Citation:* Voluntarily and alone, under a heavy fire, obtained valuable information which a reconnoitering party of 25 men had previously attempted and failed to obtain, suffering severe loss in the attempt. The information obtained by him was made the basis of the orders for the assault that followed. He also advanced with a few followers, under the fire of both sides, and captured 300 of the enemy who would otherwise have escaped.

RODENBOUGH, THEOPHILUS F.

Rank and organization: Captain, 2d U.S. Cavalry. *Place and date:* At Trevilian Station, Va., 11 June 1864. *Entered service at:* Pennsylvania. *Born:* 5 November 1838, Easton, Pa. *Date of issue:* 21 September 1893. *Citation:* Handled the regiment with great skill and valor; was severely wounded.

ROHM, FERDINAND F.

Rank and organization: Chief Bugler, 16th Pennsylvania Cavalry. *Place and date:* At Reams Station, Va., 25 August 1864. *Entered service at:* Juniata County, Pa. *Birth:* Juniata County, Pa. *Date of issue:* 16 October 1897. *Citation:* While his regiment was retiring under fire voluntarily remained behind to succor a wounded officer who was in great danger, secured assistance, and removed the officer to a place of safety.

ROOD, OLIVER P.

Rank and organization: Private, Company B, 20th Indiana Infantry. *Place and date:* At Gettysburg, Pa., 3 July 1863. *Entered service at:* Terre Haute, Vigo County, Ind. *Birth:* Frankfort County, Ky. *Date of issue:* 1 December 1864. *Citation:* Capture of flag of 21st North Carolina Infantry (C.S.A.).

ROOSEVELT, GEORGE W.

Rank and organization: First Sergeant, Company K. 26th Pennsylvania Infantry. *Place and date:* At Bull Run, Va., 30 August 1862. At Gettysburg, Pa., 2 July 1863. *Entered service at:* Chester, Pa. *Birth:* Chester, Pa. *Date of issue:* 2 July 1887. *Citation:* At Bull Run, Va., recaptured the colors, which had been seized by the enemy. At Gettysburg captured a Confederate color bearer and color, in which effort he was severely wounded.

ROSS, MARION A.

Rank and organization: Sergeant Major, 2d Ohio Infantry. *Place and date:* Georgia, April 1862. *Entered service at:* ———. *Birth:* Champaign County, Ohio. *Date of issue:* September 1863. *Citation:* Nineteen of 22 men (including 2 civilians) who, by direction of Gen. Mitchell (or Buell), penetrated nearly 200 miles south into the enemy's territory and captured a railroad train at Big Shanty, Ga., in an attempt to destroy the bridges and track between Chattanooga and Atlanta.

ROSSBACH, VALENTINE

Rank and organization: Sergeant, 34th New York Battery. *Place and date:* At Spotsylvania, Va., 12 May 1864. *Entered service at:* ———. *Birth:* Germany. *Date of issue:* 10 July 1896. *Citation:* Encouraged his cannoneers to hold a very dangerous position, and when all depended on several good shots it was from his piece that the most effective were delivered, causing the enemy's fire to cease and thereby relieving the critical position of the Federal troops.

ROUGHT, STEPHEN

Rank and organization: Sergeant, Company A, 141st Pennsylvania Infantry. *Place and date:* At Wilderness, Va., 6 May 1864. *Entered service at:* Crampton, Pa. *Birth:* Bradford County, Pa. *Date of issue:* 1 December 1864. *Citation:* Capture of flag of 13th North Carolina Infantry (C.S.A.).

ROUNDS, LEWIS A.

Rank and organization: Private, Company D, 8th Ohio Infantry. *Place and date:* At Spotsylvania, Va., 12 May 1864. *Entered service at:* Huron County, Ohio. *Birth:* Cattaraugus County, N.Y. *Date of issue:* 1 December 1864. *Citation:* Capture of flag.

ROUNTRY, JOHN

Rank and organization: First Class Fireman, U.S. Navy. *Born:* 1840, Massachusetts. *Accredited to:* Massachusetts. *G.O. No.:* 59, 22 June 1865. *Citation:* Served as first class fireman on board the U.S.S. *Montauk*, 21 September 1864. During the night of 21 September when fire was discovered in the magazine lightroom of that vessel, causing a panic and demoralizing the crew, Rountry, notwithstanding the cry of "fire in the magazine," forced his way with hose in hand, through the frightened crowd to the lightroom and put out the flames.

ROUSH, J. LEVI

Rank and organization: Corporal, Company D, 6th Pennsylvania Reserves. *Place and date:* At Gettysburg, Pa., 2 July 1863. *Entered service at:* ———. *Birth:* Bedford County, Pa. *Date of issue:* 3 August 1897. *Citation:* Was 1 of 6 volunteers who charged upon a log house near the Devil's Den, where a squad of the enemy's sharpshooters were sheltered, and compelled their surrender.

ROWAND, ARCHIBALD H., Jr.

Rank and organization: Private, Company K, 1st West Virginia Cavalry. *Place and date:* Winter of 1864–65. *Entered service at:* Pittsburgh, Pa. *Born:* 6 March 1845, Philadelphia, Pa., *Date of issue:* 3 March 1873. *Citation:* Was 1 of 2 men who succeeded in getting through the enemy's lines with dispatches to Gen. Grant.

ROWE, HENRY W.

Rank and organization: Private, Company I, 11th New Hampshire Infantry. *Place and date:* At Petersburg, Va., 17 June 1864. *Entered service at:* Candia, N.H. *Born:* April 1840, Candia, N.H. *Date of issue:* 1 December 1864. *Citation:* With 2 companions, he rushed and disarmed 27 enemy pickets, capturing a stand of flags.

RUNDLE, CHARLES W.

Rank and organization: Private, Company A, 116th Illinois Infantry. *Place and date:* At Vicksburg, Miss., 22 May 1863. *Entered service at:*

Oakley, Macon County, Ill. *Birth:* Cincinnati, Ohio. *Date of issue:* 26 July 1894. *Citation:* Gallantry in the charge of the "volunteer storming party."

RUSH, JOHN

Rank and organization: First Class Fireman, U.S. Navy. *Born:* 1835, Washington, D.C. *Accredited to:* District of Columbia. *G.O. No.:* 17, 10 July 1863. *Citation:* Serving on board the U.S.S. *Richmond* in the attack on Port Hudson, 14 March 1863. Damaged by a 6-inch solid rifle shot which shattered the starboard safety-valve chamber and also damaged the port safety valve, the fireroom of the *Richmond* immediately became filled with steam to place it in an extremely critical condition. Acting courageously in this crisis, Rush persisted in penetrating the steam-filled room in order to haul the hot fires of the furnaces, and continued this action until the gravity of the situation had been lessened.

RUSSELL, CHARLES L.

Rank and organization: Corporal, Company H, 93d New York Infantry. *Place and date:* At Spotsylvania, Va., 12 May 1864. *Entered service at:* Malone, N.Y. *Birth:* Malone, N.Y. *Date of issue:* 1 December 1864. *Citation:* Capture of flag of 42d Virginia Infantry (C.S.A.).

RUSSELL, MILTON

Rank and organization: Captain, Company A, 51st Indiana Infantry. *Place and date:* At Stone River, Tenn., 29 December 1862. *Entered service at:* North Salem, Ind. *Birth:* Hendricks County, Ind. *Date of issue:* 28 September 1897. *Citation:* Was the first man to cross Stone River and, in the face of a galling fire from the concealed skirmishers of the enemy, led his men up the hillside, driving the opposing skirmishers before them.

RUTHERFORD, JOHN T.

Rank and organization: First Lieutenant, Company L, 9th New York Cavalry. *Place and date:* At Yellow Tavern, Va., 11 May 1864; At Hanovertown, Va., 27 May 1864. *Entered service at:* Canton, N.Y. *Birth:* ———. *Date of issue:* 22 March 1892. *Citation:* Made a successful charge at Yellow Tavern, Va., 11 May 1864, by which 90 prisoners were captured. On 27 May 1864, in a gallant dash on a superior force of the enemy and in a personal encounter, captured his opponent.

RUTTER, JAMES M.

Rank and organization: Sergeant, Company C, 143d Pennsylvania Infantry. *Place and date:* At Gettysburg, Pa., 1 July 1863. *Entered service at:* ———. *Birth:* Wilkes-Barre, Pa. *Date of issue:* 30 October 1896. *Citation:* At great risk of his life went to the assistance of a wounded comrade, and while under fire removed him to a place of safety.

RYAN, PETER J.

Rank and organization: Private, Company D, 11th Indiana Infantry. *Place and date:* At Winchester, Va., 19 September 1864. *Entered service at:* Vigo County, Ind. *Birth:* Ireland. *Date of issue:* 4 April 1865.

Citation: With one companion, captured 14 Confederates in the severest part of the battle.

SACRISTE, LOUIS J.

Rank and organization: First Lieutenant, Company D, 116th Pennsylvania Infantry. *Place and date:* At Chancellorsville, Va., 3 May 1863. At Auburn, Va., 14 October 1863. *Entered service at:* Philadelphia, Pa. *Born:* 15 June 1843, New Castle County, Del. *Date of issue:* 31 January 1889. *Citation:* Saved from capture a gun of the 5th Maine Battery. Voluntarily carried orders which resulted in saving from destruction or capture the picket line of the 1st Division, 2d Army Corps.

SAGELHURST, JOHN C.

Rank and organization: Sergeant, Company B, 1st New Jersey Cavalry. *Place and date:* At Hatchers Run, Va., 6 February 1865. *Entered service at:* Buffalo, N.Y. *Birth:* Buffalo, N.Y. *Date of issue:* 3 January 1906. *Citation:* Under a heavy fire from the enemy carried off the field a commissioned officer who was severely wounded and also led a charge on the enemy's rifle pits.

SANCRAINTE, CHARLES F.

Rank and organization: Private, Company B, 15th Michigan Infantry. *Place and date:* At Atlanta, Ga., 22 July 1864. *Entered service at:* Monroe, Mich. *Born:* 1840, Monroe, Mich. *Date of issue:* 25 July 1892. *Citation:* Voluntarily scaled the enemy's breastworks and signaled to his commanding officer in charge; also in single combat captured the colors of the 5th Texas Regiment (C.S.A.).

SANDERSON, AARON

Rank and organization: Landsman, U.S. Navy. *Entered service at:* Philadelphia, Pa. *Birth:* North Carolina. *G.O. No.:* 59, 22 June 1865. *Citation:* Served on board the U.S.S. *Wyandank* during a boat expedition up Mattox Creek, 17 March 1865. Participating with a boat crew in the clearing of Mattox Creek, L/man Anderson carried out his duties courageously in the face of a devastating fire which cut away half the oars, pierced the launch in many places and cut the barrel off a musket being fired at the enemy.

SANDS, WILLIAM

Rank and organization: First Sergeant, Company G, 88th Pennsylvania Infantry. *Place and date:* At Dabney's Mills, Va., 6–7 February 1865. *Entered service at:* Reading, Pa. *Birth:* Reading, Pa. *Date of issue:* 9 November 1893. *Citation:* Grasped the enemy's colors in the face of a deadly fire and brought them inside the lines.

SANFORD, JACOB

Rank and organization: Private, 55th Illinois Infantry. *Place and date:* At Vicksburg, Miss., 22 May 1863. *Entered service at:* Prairie City, Ill. *Birth:* Fulton County, Ill. *Date of issue:* 2 September 1893. *Citation:* Gallantry in the charge of the "volunteer storming party."

SARGENT, JACKSON

Rank and organization: Sergeant, Company D, 5th Vermont Infantry. *Place and date:* At Petersburg, Va., 2 April 1865. *Entered service at:* Stowe, Vt. *Birth:* Stowe, Vt. *Date of issue:* 28 October 1891. *Citation:* First to scale the enemy's works and plant the colors thereon.

SARTWELL, HENRY

Rank and organization: Sergeant, Company D, 123d New York Infantry. *Place and date:* At Chancellorsville, Va., 3 May 1863. *Entered service at:* Ft. Ann, N.Y. *Birth:* Ticonderoga, N.Y. *Date of issue:* 17 November 1896. *Citation:* Was severely wounded by a gunshot in his left arm, went half a mile to the rear but insisted on returning to his company and continue to fight bravely until he became exhausted from the loss of blood and was compelled to retire from the field.

SAUNDERS, JAMES

Rank and organization: Quartermaster, U.S. Navy. *Born:* 1809, Massachusetts. *Accredited to:* Massachusetts. *G.O. No.:* 59, 22 June 1865. *Citation:* Served as quartermaster on board the U.S.S. *Kearsarge* when she destroyed the *Alabama* off Cherbourg, France, 19 June 1864. Carrying out his duties courageously throughout the bitter engagement, Saunders was prompt in reporting damages done to both ships, and it is testified to by Commodore Winslow that he is deserving of all commendation, both for gallantry and for encouragement of others in his division.

*SAVACOOL, EDWIN F.

Rank and organization: Captain, Company K, 1st New York (Lincoln) Cavalry. *Place and date:* At Sailors Creek, Va., 6 April 1865. *Entered service at:* Marshall, Mich. *Born:* 1835, Jackson, Mich. *Date of issue:* 24 April 1865. *Citation:* Capture of flag, during which he was wounded and died several days later in Washington, D.C.

SAVAGE, AUZELLA

Rank and organization: Ordinary Seaman, U.S. Navy. *Born:* 1846, Maine. *Accredited to:* Massachusetts. *G.O. No.:* 59, 22 June 1865. *Citation:* On board the U.S.S. *Santiago de Cuba* in the assault on Fort Fisher, 15 January 1865. When the landing party to which he was attached charged on the fort with a cheer, and the determination to plant the colors on the ramparts, Savage remained steadfast when more than two-thirds of the marines and sailors fell back in panic during the fight. When enemy fire shot away the flagstaff above his hand, he bravely seized the remainder of the staff and brought his colors safely off.

SAXTON, RUFUS

Rank and organization: Brigadier General, U.S. Volunteers. *Place and date:* At Harpers Ferry, W. Va., 26 to 30 May 1862. *Entered service at:* Deerfield, Mass. *Birth:* Greenfield, Mass. *Date of issue:* 25 April 1893. *Citation:* Distinguished gallantry and good conduct in the defense.

898

SCANLAN, PATRICK

Rank and organization: Private, Company A, 4th Massachusetts Cavalry. *Place and date:* At Ashepoo River, S.C., 24 May 1864. *Entered service at:* Spencer, Mass. *Birth:* Ireland. *Date of issue:* 21 January 1897. *Citation:* Volunteered as a member of a boat crew which went to the rescue of a large number of Union soldiers on board the stranded steamer *Boston*, and with great gallantry assisted in conveying them to shore, being exposed during the entire time to a heavy fire from a Confederate battery.

SCHEIBNER, MARTIN E.

Rank and organization: Private, Company G, 90th Pennsylvania Infantry. *Place and date:* At Mine Run, Va., 27 November 1863. *Entered service at:* Berks County, Pa. *Born:* 13 October 1840, Russia. *Date of issue:* 23 June 1896. *Citation:* Voluntarily extinguished the burning fuse of a shell which had been thrown into the lines of the regiment by the enemy.

SCHENCK, BENJAMIN W.

Rank and organization: Private, Company D, 116th Illinois Infantry. *Place and date:* At Vicksburg, Miss., 22 May 1863. *Entered service at:* Maroa, Ill. *Birth:* Butler County, Ohio. *Date of issue:* 14 August 1894. *Citation:* Gallantry in the charge of the "volunteer storming party."

SCHILLER, JOHN

Rank and organization: Private, Company E, 158th New York Infantry. *Place and date:* At Chapins Farm, Va., 29 September 1864. *Entered service at:* New York, N.Y. *Birth:* Germany. *Date of issue:* 6 April 1865. *Citation:* Advanced to the ditch of the enemy's works.

SCHLACHTER, PHILIPP

Rank and organization: Private, Company F, 73d New York Infantry. *Place and date:* At Spotsylvania, Va., 12 May 1864. *Entered service at:* ———. *Birth:* Germany. *Date of issue:* 1 December 1864. *Citation:* Capture of flag of 15th Louisiana Infantry (C.S.A.).

SCHMAL, GEORGE W.

Rank and organization: Blacksmith, Company M, 24th New York Cavalry. *Place and date:* At Paines Crossroads, Va., 5 April 1865. *Entered service at:* Buffalo, N.Y. *Birth:* Germany. *Date of issue:* 3 May 1865. *Citation:* Capture of flag.

SCHMAUCH, ANDREW

Rank and organization: Private, Company A, 30th Ohio Infantry. *Place and date:* At Vicksburg, Miss., 22 May 1863. *Entered service at:* ———. *Birth:* Germany. *Date of issue:* 9 July 1894. *Citation:* Gallantry in the charge of the "volunteer storming party."

SCHMIDT, CONRAD

Rank and organization: First Sergeant, Company K, 2d U.S. Cavalry. *Place and date:* At Winchester, Va., 19 September 1864. *Entered ser-*

DOB: 2 Feb 1830
DoD: 26 Dec 1908

PLACE OF BURIAL: Catholic Cemete
Junction City KANS

CIVIL WAR 899

vice at: Ft. Leavenworth KS. *Birth:* Wortenburg, Germany. *Date of issue:* 16 March 1896. *Citation:* Went to the assistance of his regimental commander, whose horse had been killed under him in a charge, mounted the officer behind him, under a heavy fire from the enemy, and returned him to his command.

SCHMIDT, WILLIAM

Rank and organization: Private, Company G, 37th Ohio Infantry. *Place and date:* At Missionary Ridge, Tenn., 25 November 1863. *Entered service at:* Maumee, Ohio. *Birth:* Tiffin, Ohio. *Date of issue:* 9 November 1895. *Citation:* Rescued a wounded comrade under terrific fire.

SCHNEIDER, GEORGE

Rank and organization: Sergeant, Company A, 3d Maryland Veteran Infantry. *Place and date:* At Petersburg, Va., 30 July 1864. *Entered service at:* ———. *Birth:* Baltimore, Md. *Date of issue:* 27 July 1896. *Citation:* After the color sergeant had been shot down, seized the colors and planted them on the enemy's works during the charge.

SCHNELL, CHRISTIAN

Rank and organization: Corporal, Company C, 37th Ohio Infantry. *Place and date:* At Vicksburg, Miss., 22 May 1863. *Entered service at:* Wapakoneta, Ohio. *Birth:* Virginia. *Date of issue:* 10 July 1894. *Citation:* Gallantry in the charge of the "volunteer storming party."

SCHOFIELD, JOHN M.

Rank and organization: Major, 1st Missouri Infantry. *Place and date:* At Wilsons Creek, Mo., 10 August 1861. *Entered service at:* St. Louis, Mo. *Born:* 29 September 1831, Gerry, N.Y. *Date of issue:* 2 July 1892. *Citation:* Was conspicuously gallant in leading a regiment in a successful charge against the enemy.

SCHOONMAKER, JAMES M.

Rank and organization: Colonel, 14th Pennsylvania Cavalry. *Place and date:* At Winchester, Va., 19 September 1864. *Entered service at:* Maryland. *Born:* 30 June 1842, Pittsburgh, Pa. *Date of issue:* 19 May 1899. *Citation:* At a critical period, gallantly led a cavalry charge against the left of the enemy's line of battle, drove the enemy out of his works, and captured many prisoners.

SCHORN, CHARLES

Rank and organization: Chief Bugler, Company M, 1st West Virginia Cavalry. *Place and date:* At Appomattox, Va., 8 April 1865. *Entered service at:* Mason City, W. Va. *Birth:* Germany. *Date of issue:* 3 May 1865. *Citation:* Capture of flag of the Sumter Flying Artillery (C.S.A.).

SCHUBERT, MARTIN

Rank and organization: Private, Company E, 26th New York Infantry. *Place and date:* At Fredericksburg, Va., 13 December 1862. *Entered service at:* ———. *Birth:* Germany. *Date of issue:* 1 September 1893. *Citation:* Relinquished a furlough granted for wounds, entered the battle, where he picked up the colors after several bearers had been killed or wounded, and carried them until himself again wounded.

SCHUTT, GEORGE

Rank and organization: Coxswain, U.S. Navy. *Born:* 1833, Ireland. *Accredited to:* New York. *G.O. No.:* 59, 22 June 1865. *Citation:* As coxswain on board the U.S.S. *Hendrick Hudson*, St. Marks, Fla., 5 and 6 March 1865. Serving with the army in charge of Navy howitzers during the attack on St. Marks and throughout the fierce engagement, Schutt made remarkable efforts in assisting transport of the gun, and his coolness and determination in courageously remaining by his gun while under the heavy fire of the enemy were a credit to the service to which he belonged.

SCHWAN, THEODORE

Rank and organization: First Lieutenant, 10th U.S. Infantry. *Place and date:* At Peebles Farm, Va., 1 October 1864. *Entered service at:* New York. *Born:* 9 July 1841, Germany. *Date of issue:* 12 December 1898. *Citation:* At the imminent risk of his own life, while his regiment was falling back before a superior force of the enemy, he dragged a wounded and helpless officer to the rear, thus saving him from death or capture.

SCHWENK, MARTIN

Rank and organization: Sergeant, Company B, 6th U.S. Cavalry. *Place and date:* At Millerstown, Pa., July 1863. *Entered service at:* ———. *Birth:* Germany. *Date of issue:* 23 April 1889. *Citation:* Bravery in an attempt to carry a communication through the enemy's lines; also rescued an officer from the hands of the enemy.

SCOFIELD, DAVID H.

Rank and organization: Quartermaster Sergeant, Company K. 5th N.Y., U.S. Cavalry. *Place and date:* At Cedar Creek, Va., 19 October 1864. *Entered service at:* ———. *Birth:* Mamaroneck, N.Y. *Date of issue:* 26 October 1864. *Citation:* Capture of flag of 13th Virginia Infantry (C.S.A.).

SCOTT, ALEXANDER

Rank and organization: Corporal, Company D, 10th Vermont Infantry. *Place and date:* At Monocacy, Md., 9 July 1864. *Entered service at:* Winooski, Vt. *Birth:* Canada. *Date of issue:* 28 September 1897. *Citation:* Under a very heavy fire of the enemy saved the national flag of his regiment from capture.

SCOTT, JOHN M.

Rank and organization: Sergeant, Company F, 21st Ohio Infantry. *Place and date:* Georgia, April 1862. *Entered service at:* Finley, Ohio. *Birth:* Stark County, Ohio. *Date of issue:* 4 August 1866. *Citation:* One of the 19 of 22 men (including 2 civilians) who, by direction of Gen. Mitchell (or Buell), penetrated nearly 200 miles south into enemy territory and captured a railroad train at Big Shanty, Ga., and attempted to destroy the bridges and track between Chattanooga and Atlanta.

SCOTT, JOHN WALLACE

Rank and organization: Captain, Company D, 157th Pennsylvania Infantry. *Place and date:* At Five Forks, Va., 1 April 1865. *Entered service at:* ———. *Born:* 1838, Chester County, Pa. *Date of issue:* 27 April 1865. *Citation:* Capture of the flag of the 16th South Carolina Infantry, in hand-to-hand combat.

SCOTT, JULIAN A.

Rank and organization: Drummer, Company E, 3d Vermont Infantry. *Place and date:* At Lees Mills, Va., 16 April 1862. *Entered service at:* Johnson, Vt. *Birth:* Johnson, Vt. *Date of issue:* February 1865. *Citation:* Crossed the creek under a terrific fire of musketry several times to assist in bringing off the wounded.

SEAMAN, ELISHA B.

Rank and organization: Private, Company A, 66th Ohio Infantry. *Place and date:* At Chancellorsville, Va. 2 May 1863. *Entered service at:* Logan County, Ohio. *Birth:* Logan County, Ohio. *Date of issue:* 24 June 1892. *Citation:* Was 1 of party of 4 who voluntarily brought into the Union lines, under fire, a wounded Confederate officer from whom was obtained valuable information concerning the enemy.

SEANOR, JAMES

Rank and organization: Master-at-Arms, U.S. Navy. *Born:* 1833, Boston, Mass. *Accredited to:* New York. *G.O. No* 45, 31 December 1864. *Citation:* Served as master-at-arms on board the U.S. Ironclad *Chickasaw*, Mobile Bay, 5 August 1864. Although his enlistment was up, Seanor volunteered for the battle of Mobile Bay, going on board the *Chickasaw* from the *Vincennes* where he carried out his duties gallantly throughout the engagement which resulted in the capture of the rebel ram *Tennessee*.

SEARS, CYRUS

Rank and organization: First Lieutenant, 11th Battery, Ohio Light Artillery. *Place and date:* At Iuka, Miss., 19 September 1862. *Entered service at:* Bucyrus, Ohio. *Born:* 10 March 1832, Delaware County, N.Y. *Date of issue:* 31 December 1892. *Citation:* Although severely wounded, fought his battery until the cannoneers and horses were nearly all killed or wounded.

SEAVER, THOMAS O.

Rank and organization: Colonel, 3d Vermont Infantry. *Place and date:* At Spotsylvania Courthouse, Va., 10 May 1864. *Entered service at:* Pomfret, Vt. *Born:* 23 December 1833, Davendish, Vt. *Date of issue:* 8 April 1892. *Citation:* At the head of 3 regiments and under a most galling fire attacked and occupied the enemy's works.

SEITZINGER, JAMES M.

Rank and organization: Private, Company G, 116th Pennsylvania Infantry. *Place and date:* At Cold Harbor, Va., 3 June 1864. *Entered service at:* Worcester, Pa. *Birth:* Germany. *Date of issue:* 1 March 1906.

Citation: When the color bearer was shot down, this soldier seized the colors and bore them gallantly in a charge against the enemy.

SELLERS, ALFRED J.

Rank and organization: Major, 90th Pennsylvania Infantry. *Place and date:* At Gettysburg, Pa., 1 July 1863. *Entered service at:* Pennsylvania. *Born:* 2 March 1836, Plumsteadville, Bucks County, Pa. *Date of issue:* 21 July 1894. *Citation:* Voluntarily led the regiment under a withering fire to a position from which the enemy was repulsed.

*SESTON, CHARLES H.

Rank and organization: Sergeant, Company I, 11th Indiana Infantry. *Place and date:* At Winchester, Va., 19 September 1864. *Entered service at:* New Albany, Ind. *Birth:* New Albany, Ind. *Date of issue:* 6 April 1865. *Citation:* Gallant and meritorious service in carrying the regimental colors.

SEWARD, GRIFFIN

Rank and organization: Wagoner, Company G, 8th U.S. Cavalry. *Place and date:* At Chiricahva Mountains, Ariz., 20 October 1863. *Entered service at:* ———. *Birth:* Dover, Del. *Date of issue:* 14 February 1870. *Citation:* Gallantry in action.

SEWARD, RICHARD E.

Rank and organization: Paymaster's Steward, U.S. Navy. *Place and date:* Ship Island Sound, La., 23 November 1863. *Entered service at:* ———. *Born:* 1840, Kittery, Maine. *Date of issue:* 16 April 1864. *Citation:* Served as paymaster's steward on board the U.S.S. *Commodore*, November 1863. Carrying out his duties courageously, Seward "volunteered to go on the field amidst a heavy fire to recover the bodies of 2 soldiers which he brought off with the aid of others; a second instance of personal valor within a fortnight." Promoted to acting master's mate.

SEWELL, WILLIAM J.

Rank and organization: Colonel, 5th New Jersey Infantry. *Place and date:* At Chancellorsville, Va., 3 May 1863. *Entered service at:* Camden, N.J. *Born:* 6 December 1835, Ireland. *Date of issue:* 25 March 1896. *Citation:* Assuming command of a brigade, he rallied around his colors a mass of men from other regiments and fought these troops with great brilliancy through several hours of desperate conflict, remaining in command though wounded and inspiring them by his presence and the gallantry of his personal example.

SHAFTER, WILLIAM R.

Rank and organization: First Lieutenant, Company I, 7th Michigan Infantry. *Place and date:* At Fair Oaks, Va., 31 May 1862. *Entered service at:* Galesburg, Mich. *Birth:* Kalamazoo, Mich. *Date of issue:* 12 June 1895. *Citation:* Lt. Shafter was engaged in bridge construction and not being needed there returned with his men to engage the enemy participating in a charge across an open field that resulted in casualties to 18 of the 22 men. At the close of the battle his horse was shot from under him and he was severely flesh wounded. He remained on the field that day and stayed to fight the next day only by concealing his wounds. In order not to be sent home with the wounded he kept his wounds concealed for another 3 days until other wounded had left the area.

SHAHAN, EMISIRE

Rank and organization: Corporal, Company A, 1st West Virginia Cavalry. *Place and date:* At Sailors Creek, Va., 6 April 1865. *Entered service at:* ———. *Birth:* Preston County, W. Va. *Date of issue:* 3 May 1865. *Citation:* Capture of flag of 76th Georgia Infantry (C.S.A.).

SHALER, ALEXANDER

Rank and organization: Colonel, 65th New York Infantry. *Place and date:* At Marye's Heights, Va., 3 May 1863. *Entered service at:* New York, N.Y. *Born:* 19 March 1827, Haddam, Conn. *Date of issue:* 25 November 1893. *Citation:* At a most critical moment, the head of the charging column being about to be crushed by the severe fire of the enemy's artillery and infantry, he pushed forward with a supporting column, pierced the enemy's works, and turned their flank.

SHAMBAUGH, CHARLES

Rank and organization: Corporal, Company D, 11th Pennsylvania Reserves. *Place and date:* At Charles City Crossroads, Va., 30 June 1862. *Entered service at:* Indiana County, Pa. *Birth:* Prussia. *Date of issue:* 17 July 1866. *Citation:* Capture of flag.

SHANES, JOHN

Rank and organization: Private, Company K, 14th West Virginia Infantry. *Place and date:* At Carters Farm, Va., 20 July 1864. *Entered service at:* ———. *Birth:* Monomgalis County, W. Va. *Date of issue:* 31 January 1896. *Citation:* Charged upon a Confederate fieldpiece in advance of his comrades and by his individual exertions silenced the piece.

SHAPLAND, JOHN

Rank and organization: Private, Company D, 104th Illinois Infantry. *Place and date:* At Elk River, Tenn., 2 July 1863. *Entered service at:* Ottawa, Ill. *Birth:* England. *Date of issue:* 30 October 1897. *Citation:* Voluntarily joined a small party that, under a heavy fire, captured a stockade and saved the bridge.

SHARP, HENDRICK

Rank and organization: Seaman, U.S. Navy. *Born:* 1815, Spain. *Accredited to:* New York. *G.O. No.:* 45, 31 December 1864. *Citation:* As captain of a 100-pounder rifle gun on topgallant forecastle on board the U.S.S. *Richmond* during action against rebel forts and gunboats and with the ram *Tennessee* in Mobile Bay, 5 August 1864. Despite damage to his ship and the loss of several men on board as enemy fire raked her decks, Sharp fought his gun with skill and courage throughout a furious 2-hour battle which resulted in the surrender of the rebel ram *Tennessee* and in the damaging and destruction of the batteries at Fort Morgan.

904

SHEA, JOSEPH H.

Rank and organization: Private, Company K, 92d New York Infantry. *Place and date:* At Chapins Farm, Va., 29 September 1864. *Entered service at:* ————. *Birth:* Baltimore, Md. *Date of issue:* March 1866. *Citation:* Gallantry in bringing wounded from the field under heavy fire.

SHELLENBERGER, JOHN S.

Rank and organization: Corporal, Company B, 85th Pennsylvania Infantry. *Place and date:* At Deep Run, Va., 16 August 1864. *Entered service at:* Perryopolis, Pa. *Birth:* ————. *Date of issue:* 6 April 1865. *Citation:* Capture of flag.

SHEPARD, IRWIN

Rank and organization: Corporal, Company E, 17th Michigan Infantry. *Place and date:* At Knoxville, Tenn. 20 November 1863. *Entered service at:* Chelsea, Mich. *Birth:* Skaneateles, N.Y. *Date of issue:* 3 August 1897. *Citation:* Having voluntarily accompanied a small party to destroy buildings within the enemy's lines, whence sharpshooters had been firing, disregarded an order to retire, remained and completed the firing of the buildings, thus insuring their total destruction; this at the imminent risk of his life from the fire of the advancing enemy.

SHEPARD, LOUIS C.

Rank and organization: Ordinary Seaman, U.S. Navy. *Born:* 1843, Ohio. *Accredited to:* Ohio. *G.O. No.:* 59, 22 June 1865. *Citation:* Served as seaman on board the U.S.S. *Wabash* in the assault on Fort Fisher, 15 January 1865. Advancing gallantly through severe enemy fire while armed only with a revolver and cutlass which made it impossible to return the fire at that range, Shepard succeeded in reaching the angle of the fort and in going on, to be one of the few who entered the fort. When the rest of the body of men to his rear were forced to retreat under a devastating fire, he was forced to withdraw through lack of support and to seek the shelter of one of the mounds near the stockade from which point he succeeded in regaining the safety of his ship.

SHEPHERD, WILLIAM

Rank and organization: Private, Company A, 3d Indiana Cavalry. *Place and date:* At Sailors Creek, Va., 6 April 1865. *Entered service at:* Dillsboro, Ind. *Birth:* Dearborn County, Ind. *Date of issue:* 3 May 1865. *Citation:* Capture of flag.

SHERIDAN, JAMES

Rank and organization: Quartermaster, U.S. Navy. *Born:* 1831, Newark, N.J. *Accredited to:* New York. *G.O. No.:* 45, 31 December 1864. *Citation:* Served as quartermaster on board the U.S.S. *Oneida* in the engagement at Mobile Bay 5 August 1864. Acting as captain of the after 11-inch gun, and wounded in several places, Sheridan remained at his gun until the firing had ceased and then took the place of the signal quartermaster who had been injured by a fall. Recommended for his gallantry and intelligence, Sheridan served courageously throughout this battle which resulted in the capture of the rebel ram *Tennessee* and the damaging of Fort Morgan.

SHERMAN, MARSHALL

Rank and organization: Private, Company C, 1st Minnesota Infantry. *Place and date:* At Gettysburg, Pa., 3 July 1863. *Entered service at:* St. Paul, Minn. *Birth:* Burlington, Vt. *Date of issue:* 1 December 1864. *Citation:* Capture of flag of 28th Virginia Infantry (C.S.A.).

SHIEL (SHIELDS), JOHN

Rank and organization: Corporal, Company E, 90th Pennsylvania Infantry. *Place and date:* At Fredericksburg, Va., 13 December 1862. *Entered service at:* Cressonville, Pa. *Birth:* ———. *Date of issue:* 21 January 1897. *Citation:* Carried a dangerously wounded comrade into the Union lines, thereby preventing his capture by the enemy.

SHIELDS, BERNARD

Rank and organization: Private, Company E, 2d West Virginia Cavalry. *Place and date:* At Appomattox, Va., 8 April 1865. *Entered service at:* Ironton, Ohio. *Birth:* Ireland. *Date of issue:* 3 May 1865. *Citation:* Capture of flag of the Washington Artillery (C.S.A.).

SHILLING, JOHN

Rank and organization: First Sergeant, Company H, 3d Delaware Infantry. *Place and date:* At Weldon Railroad, Va., 21 August 1864. *Entered service at:* Felton, Del. *Born:* 15 February 1832, England. *Date of issue:* 6 September 1864. *Citation:* Capture of flag.

SHIPLEY, ROBERT F.

Rank and organization: Sergeant, Company A, 140th New York Infantry. *Place and date:* At Five Forks, Va., 1 April 1865. *Entered service at:* ———. *Birth:* Wayne, N.Y. *Date of issue:* 10 May 1865. *Citation:* Captured the flag of the 9th Virginia Infantry (C.S.A.) in hand-to hand combat.

SHIPMAN, WILLIAM

Rank and organization: Coxswain, U.S. Navy. *Born:* 1831, New York, N.Y. *Accredited to:* New York. *G.O. No.:* 59, 22 June 1865. *Citation:* On board the U.S.S. *Ticonderoga* in the attack upon Fort Fisher on 15 January 1865. As captain of No. 2 gun, stationed near the 100-pounder Parrott rifle when it burst into fragments, killing 8 men and wounding 12 more, Shipman promptly recognized the effect produced by the explosion and, despite the carnage surrounding them, and the enemy's fire, encouraged the men at their guns by exclaiming, "Go ahead, boys! This is only the fortunes of war!"

SHIVERS, JOHN

Rank and organization: Private, U.S. Marine Corps. *Born:* 1830, Canada. *Accredited to:* New Jersey. *G.O. No.:* 59, 22 June 1865. *Citation:* On board the U.S.S. *Minnesota*, in the assault on Fort Fisher, 15

January 1865. Landing on the beach with the assaulting party from his ship, Pvt. Shivers advanced to the top of the sandhill and partly through the breach in the palisades despite enemy fire which killed or wounded many officers and men. When more than two-thirds of the men became seized with panic and retreated on the run, he remained with the party until dark when it came safely away, bringing its wounded, its arms and its colors.

SHOEMAKER, LEVI

Rank and organization: Sergeant, Company A, 1st West Virginia Cavalry. *Place and date:* At Nineveh, Va., 12 November 1864. *Entered service at:* ———. *Birth:* Monongalia County, W. Va. *Date of issue:* 26 November 1864. *Citation:* Capture of flag of 22d Virginia Cavalry (C.S.A.).

SHOPP, GEORGE J.

Rank and organization: Private, Company E, 191st Pennsylvania Infantry. *Place and date:* At Five Forks, Va., 1 April 1865. *Entered service at:* Reading, Pa. *Birth:* Equinunk, Pa. *Date of issue:* 27 April 1865. *Citation:* Capture of flag.

SHUBERT, FRANK

Rank and organization: Sergeant, Company E, 43d New York Infantry. *Place and date:* At Petersburg, Va., 2 April 1865. *Entered service at:* ———. *Birth:* Germany. *Date of issue:* 10 May 1865. *Citation:* Capture of two markers.

SHUTES, HENRY

Rank and organization: Captain of the Forecastle, U.S. Navy. *Born:* 1804, Baltimore, Md. *Accredited to:* Maryland. *G.O. No.:* 71, 15 January 1866. *Citation:* Served as captain of the forecastle on board the U.S.S. *Wissahickon* during the battle of New Orleans, 24 and 25 April 1862; and in the engagement at Fort McAllister, 27 February 1863. Going on board the U.S.S. *Wissahickon* from the U.S.S. *Don* where his seamanlike qualities as gunner's mate were outstanding, Shutes performed his duties with skill and courage. Showing a presence of mind and prompt action when a shot from Fort McAllister penetrated the *Wissahickon* below the water line and entered the powder magazine, Shutes contributed materially to the preservation of the powder and safety of the ship.

SICKLES, DANIEL E.

Rank and organization: Major General, U.S. Volunteers. *Place and date:* At Gettysburg, Pa., 2 July 1863. *Entered service at:* New York, N.Y. *Birth:* New York, N.Y. *Date of issue:* 30 October 1897. *Citation:* Displayed most conspicuous gallantry on the field vigorously contesting the advance of the enemy and continuing to encourage his troops after being himself severely wounded.

SICKLES, WILLIAM H.

Rank and organization: Sergeant, Company B, 7th Wisconsin Infantry. *Place and date:* At Gravelly Run, Va., 31 March 1865. *Entered service at:* Columbia County, Wis. *Birth:* Danube, N.Y. *Date of issue:* Unknown. *Citation:* With a comrade, attempted capture of a stand of Confederate colors and detachment of 9 Confederates, actually taking prisoner 3 members of the detachment, dispersing the remainder, and recapturing a Union officer who was a prisoner in hands of the detachment.

SIDMAN, GEORGE E.

Rank and organization: Private, Company C, 16th Michigan Infantry. *Place and date:* At Gaines Mill, Va., 27 June 1862. *Entered service at:* Owosso, Mich. *Born:* 25 November 1844, Rochester, N.Y. *Date of issue:* 6 April 1892. *Citation:* Distinguished bravery in battle. Rallied his comrades to charge vastly superior force until wounded in the hip. He was a 16-year-old drummer.

SIMKINS, LEBBEUS

Rank and organization: Coxswain, U.S. Navy. *Born:* 1836, Utica, N.Y. *Accredited to:* New York. *G.O. No.:* 45, 31 December 1864. *Citation:* On board the U.S.S. *Richmond* during action against rebel forts and gunboats and with the ram *Tennessee* in Mobile Bay, 5 August 1864. Despite damage to his ship and the loss of several men on board as enemy fire raked her decks, Simkins performed his duties with skill and courage throughout a furious 2-hour battle which resulted in the surrender of the rebel ram *Tennessee* and in the damaging and destruction of batteries at Fort Morgan.

SIMMONS, JOHN

Rank and organization: Private, Company D, 2d New York Heavy Artillery. *Place and date:* At Sailors Creek, Va., 6 April 1865. *Entered service at:* Liberty, N.Y. *Birth:* Bethel, N.Y. *Date of issue:* 24 April 1865. *Citation:* Capture of flag.

SIMMONS, WILLIAM T.

Rank and organization: Lieutenant, Company C, 11th Missouri Infantry. *Place and date:* At Nashville, Tenn., 16 December 1864. *Entered service at:* ———. *Born:* 29 January 1843, Green County, Ill. *Date of issue:* 24 February 1865. *Citation:* Capture of flag of 34th Alabama Infantry (C.S.A.). Being the first to enter the works, he shot and wounded the enemy color bearer.

SIMONDS, WILLIAM EDGAR

Rank and organization: Sergeant Major, 25th Connecticut Infantry. *Place and date:* At Irish Bend, La., 14 April 1863. *Entered service at:* Canton, Conn. *Birth:* ———. *Date of issue:* 25 February 1899. *Citation:* Displayed great gallantry, under a heavy fire from the enemy, in calling in the skirmishers and assisting in forming the line of battle.

SIMONS, CHARLES J.

Rank and organization: Sergeant, Company A, 9th New Hampshire Infantry. *Place and date:* At Petersburg, Va., 30 July 1864. *Entered service at:* Exeter, N.H. *Birth:* India. *Date of issue:* 27 July 1896. *Citation:* Was one of the first in the exploded mine, captured a number of prisoners. and was himself captured, but escaped.

SIVEL, HENRY

See William H. Mathews (true name).

SKELLIE, EBENEZER

Rank and organization: Corporal, Company D, 112th New York Infantry. *Place and date:* At Chapins Farm, Va., 29 September 1864. *Entered service at:* Mina, N.Y. *Birth:* Mina, N.Y. *Date of issue:* 6 April 1865. *Citation:* Took the colors of his regiment, the color bearer having fallen, and carried them through the first charge; also, in the second charge, after all the color guards had been killed or wounded he carried the colors up to the enemy's works, where he fell wounded.

SLADEN, JOSEPH A.

Rank and organization: Private, Company A, 33d Massachusetts Infantry. *Place and date:* At Resaca, Ga., 14 May 1864. *Entered service at:* Lowell, Mass. *Birth:* England. *Date of issue:* 19 July 1895. *Citation:* While detailed as clerk at headquarters, voluntarily engaged in action at a critical moment and personal example inspired the troops to repel the enemy.

SLAGLE, OSCAR

Rank and organization: Private, Company D, 104th Illinois Infantry. *Place and date:* At Elk River, Tenn., 2 July 1863. *Entered service at:* Manlius, Ill. *Birth:* Fulton County, Ohio. *Date of issue:* 30 October 1897. *Citation:* Voluntarily joined a small party that, under a heavy fire, captured a stockade and saved the bridge.

SLAVENS, SAMUEL

Rank and organization: Private, Comapny E, 33d Ohio Infantry. *Place and date:* Georgia, April 1862. *Entered service at:* Wakefield, Pike County, Ohio. *Birth:* Pike County, Ohio. *Date of issue:* 28 July 1883. *Citation:* One of the 19 of 22 men (including 2 civilians) who, by direction of Gen. Mitchell (or Buell), penetrated nearly 200 miles south into enemy territory and captured a railroad train at Big Shanty, Ga., in an attempt to destroy the bridges and track between Chattanooga and Atlanta.

SLOAN, ANDREW J.

Rank and organization: Private, Company H, 12th Iowa Infantry. *Place and date:* At Nashville, Tenn., 16 December 1864. *Entered service at:* Colesburg, Delaware County, Iowa. *Birth:* Bedford County, Pa. *Date of issue:* 24 February 1865. *Citation:* Captured flag of 1st Louisiana Battery (C.S.A.).

SLUSHER, HENRY C.

Rank and organization: Private, Company F, 22d Pennsylvania Cavalry. *Place and date:* Near Moorefield, W. Va., 11 September 1863. *Entered service at:* ———. *Birth:* Washington County, Pa. *Date of issue:* 4 April 1898. *Citation:* Voluntarily crossed a branch of the Potomac River under fire to rescue a wounded comrade held prisoner by the enemy. Was wounded and taken prisoner in the attempt.

SMALLEY, REUBEN

Rank and organization: Private, Company F, 83d Indiana Infantry. *Place and date:* At Vicksburg, Miss., 22 May 1863. *Entered service at:* Poston, Ind. *Birth:* Redding, N.Y. *Date of issue:* 9 July 1894. *Citation:* Gallantry in the charge of the "volunteer storming party."

SMALLEY, REUBEN S.

Rank and organization: Private, Company D, 104th Illinois Infantry. *Place and date:* At Elk River, Tenn., 2 July 1863. *Entered service at:* Brookfield, La Salle County, Ill. *Birth:* Washington County, Pa. *Date of issue:* 30 October 1897. *Citation:* Voluntarily joined a small party that, under a heavy fire, captured a stockade and saved the bridge.

SMITH, ALONZO

Rank and organization: Sergeant, Company C, 7th Michigan Infantry. *Place and date:* At Hatchers Run, Va., 27 October 1864. *Entered service at:* Jonesville, Mich. *Born:* 9 August 1842, Niagara County, N.Y. *Date of issue:* 1 December 1864. *Citation:* Capture of flag of 26th North Carolina Infantry (C.S.A.), while outside his lines far from his comrades.

SMITH, CHARLES H.

Rank and organization: Colonel, 1st Maine Cavalry. *Place and date:* At St. Mary's Church, Va., 24 June 1864. *Entered service at:* Maine. *Birth:* Hollis, Maine. *Date of issue:* 11 April 1895. *Citation:* Remained in the fight to the close, although severely wounded.

*SMITH, CHARLES H.

Rank and organization: Coxswain, U.S. Navy. *Born:* 1826, Maine. *Accredited to:* Maine. *G.O. No.:* 59, 22 June 1865. *Citation:* On board the U.S.S. *Rhode Island* which was engaged in rescuing men from the stricken *Monitor* in Mobile Bay, on December 30, 1862. After the *Monitor* sprang a leak and went down, Smith courageously risked his life in a gallant attempt to rescue members of the crew. Although he, too, lost his life during the hazardous operation, he had made every effort possible to save the lives of his fellow men.

SMITH, DAVID L.

Rank and organization: Sergeant, Battery E, 1st New York Light Artillery. *Place and date:* At Warwick Courthouse, Va., 6 April 1862. *Entered service at:* Bath, N.Y. *Birth:* ———. *Date of issue:* 6 August 1906. *Citation:* This soldier, when a shell struck an ammunition chest exploding a number of cartridges and setting fire to the packing tow, procured water and extinguished the fire, thus preventing the explosion of the remaining ammunition.

SMITH, EDWIN

Rank and organization: Ordinary Seaman, U.S. Navy. *Born:* 1841, New York, N.Y. *Accredited to:* New York. *Citation:* On board the U.S.S. *Whitehead* in the attack upon Franklin, Va., 3 October 1862. When his ship became grounded in a narrow passage as she rounded a bend in the Blackwater River, Smith, realizing the hazards of lowering a boat voluntarily swam to shore with a line under the enemy's heavy fire. His fearless action enabled his ship to maintain steady fire and keep the enemy in check during the battle.

SMITH, FRANCIS M.

Rank and organization: First Lieutenant and Adjutant, 1st Maryland Infantry. *Place and date:* At Dabney Mills, Va., 6 February 1865. *Entered service at:* Frederick, Md. *Birth:* Frederick, Md. *Date of issue:* 13 August 1895. *Citation:* Voluntarily remained with the body of his regimental commander under a heavy fire after the brigade had retired and brought the body off the field.

SMITH, HENRY I.

Rank and organization: First Lieutenant, Company B, 7th Iowa Infantry. *Place and date:* At Black River, N.C., 15 March 1865. *Entered service at:* Shell Rock Fall, Cerro Gordo County, Iowa. *Born:* 4 May 1840, England. *Date of issue:* 7 September 1894. *Citation:* Voluntarily and under fire rescued a comrade from death by drowning.

SMITH, JAMES (OVID)

Rank and organization: Private, Company I, 2d Ohio Infantry. *Place and date:* Georgia, April 1862. *Entered service at:* VA *Birth:* Fredericksburg, Va. *Date of issue:* 6 July 1864. *Citation:* One of the 19 of 22 men (including 2 civilians) who, by direction of Gen. Mitchell (or Buell), penetrated nearly 200 miles south into enemy territory and captured a railroad train at Big Shanty, Ga., in an attempt to destroy the bridges and tract between Chattanooga and Atlanta.

SMITH, JAMES

Rank and organization: Captain of the Forecastle, U.S. Navy. *Born:* 1826, Albany, N.Y. *Accredited to:* New York. *G.O. No.:* 45, 31 December 1864. *Citation:* As captain of a gun on board the U.S.S. *Richmond* during action against rebel forts and gunboats and with the ram *Tennessee,* in Mobile Bay, 5 August 1864. Despite damage to his ship and the loss of several men on board as enemy fire raked her decks, Smith fought his gun with skill and courage throughout the prolonged battle which resulted in the surrender of the rebel ram *Tennessee* and in the successful attacks carried out on Fort Morgan.

SMITH, JOHN

Rank and organization: Captain of Forecastle, U.S. Navy. *Born:* 1831, Boston, Mass. *Accredited to:* Massachusetts. *G.O. No.:* 45, 31 December 1864. *Citation:* On board the U.S.S. *Lackawanna* during the successful attacks against Fort Morgan, rebel gunboats and the ram *Tennessee* in Mobile Bay, 5 August 1864. Serving as a gun captain and finding he could not depress his gun when alongside the rebel ironclad *Tennessee,* Smith threw a hand holystone into one of the ports at a rebel using abusive language against the crew of the ship. He continued his daring action throughout the engagement which resulted in the capture of the prize ram *Tennessee* and in the damaging and destruction of Fort Morgan.

SMITH, JOHN

Rank and organization: Second Captain of the Top, U.S. Navy. *Born:* 1826, Albany, N.Y. *Accredited to:* New York. *G.O. No.:* 45, 31 December 1864. *Citation:* As captain of a gun on board the U.S.S. *Richmond* during action against rebel forts and gunboats and with the ram *Tennessee* in Mobile Bay, 5 August 1864. Despite damage to his ship and the loss of several men on board as enemy fire raked her decks, Smith fought his gun with skill and courage throughout a furious 2-hour battle which resulted in the surrender of the rebel ram *Tennessee* and in the damaging and destruction of batteries at Fort Morgan.

SMITH, JOSEPH S.

Rank and organization: Lieutenant Colonel and Commissary of Subsistence, 2d Army Corps. *Place and date:* At Hatchers Run, Va., 27 October 1864. *Entered service at:* Maine. Birth: Wiscasset, Maine. *Date of issue:* 25 May 1892. *Citation:* Led a part of a brigade, saved 2 pieces of artillery, captured a flag, and secured a number of prisoners.

SMITH, OLOFF

Rank and organization: Coxswain, U.S. Navy. *Born:* 1833, Sweden. *Accredited to:* New York. *G.O. No.:* 45, 31 December 1864. *Citation:* On board the U.S.S. *Richmond* during action against rebel forts and gunboats and with the ram *Tennessee* in Mobile Bay, 5 August 1864. Despite damage to his ship and the loss of several men on board as enemy fire raked her decks, Smith performed his duties with skill and courage throughout the furious 2-hour battle which resulted in the surrender of the rebel ram *Tennessee* and in the damaging and destruction of batteries at Fort Morgan.

SMITH, OTIS W.

Rank and organization: Private, Company G, 95th Ohio Infantry. *Place and date:* At Nashville, Tenn., 16 December 1864. *Entered service at:* ———. *Birth:* Logan County, Ohio. *Date of issue:* 24 February 1865. *Citation:* Capture of flag of 6th Florida Infantry (C.S.A.).

SMITH, RICHARD

Rank and organization: Private, Company B, 95th New York Infantry. *Place and date:* At Weldon Railroad, Va., 21 August 1864. *Entered service at:* Harverstraw, Rockland County, N.Y. *Birth:* Harverstraw, Rockland County, N.Y. *Date of issue:* 13 March 1865. *Citation:* Captured 2 officers and 20 men of Hagood's brigade while they were endeavoring to make their way back through the woods.

SMITH, S. RODMOND

Rank and organization: Captain, Company C, 4th Delaware Infantry. *Place and date:* At Rowanty Creek, Va., 5 February 1865. *Entered service at:* Wilmington, Del. *Birth:* Delaware. *Date of issue:* 8 April 1895. *Citation:* Swam the partly frozen creek under fire to establish a crossing.

SMITH, THADDEUS S.

Rank and organization: Corporal, Company E, 6th Pennsylvania Reserve Infantry. *Place and date:* At Gettysburg, Pa., 2 July 1863. *Entered service at:* ———. *Birth:* Franklin County, Pa. *Date of issue:* 5 May 1900. *Citation:* Was 1 of 6 volunteers who charged upon a log house near the Devil's Den, where a squad of the enemy's sharpshooters were sheltered, and compelled their surrender.

SMITH, THOMAS

Rank and organization: Seaman, U.S. Navy. *Born:* 1838, England. *Accredited to:* New York. *G.O. No.:* 59, 22 June 1865. *Citation:* As seaman on board the U.S.S. *Magnolia*, St. Marks, Fla., 5 and 6 March 1865. Serving with the Army in charge of Navy howitzers during the attack on St. Marks and throughout this fierce engagement, Smith made remarkable efforts in assisting transport of the gun, and his coolness and determination in courageously standing by his gun while under the fire of the enemy were a credit to the service to which he belonged.

SMITH, WALTER B.

Rank and organization: Ordinary Seaman, U.S. Navy. *Born:* 1827, New York. *Accredited to:* New York. *G.O. No.:* 45, 31 December 1864. *Citation:* On board the U.S.S. *Richmond* during action against rebel forts and gunboats and with the ram *Tennessee* in Mobile Bay, 5 August 1864. Cool and courageous at his station throughout the prolonged action, Smith rendered outstanding service at the 100-pounder rifle on the topgallant forecastle and while firing his musket into the gun ports of the rebel *Tennessee*.

SMITH, WILLARD M.

Rank and organization: Corporal, U.S. Marine Corps. *Born:* 1840, Alleghany, N.Y. *Accredited to:* New York. *G.O. No.:* 45, 31 December 1864. *Citation:* On board the U.S.S. *Brooklyn* during action against rebel forts and gunboats, and with the ram *Tennessee* in Mobile Bay, 5 August 1864. Despite severe damage to his ship and the loss of several men on board as enemy fire continued to fall, Cpl. Smith fought his gun with skill and courage throughout the furious 2-hour battle which resulted in the surrender of the rebel ram *Tennessee*.

SMITH, WILLIAM

Rank and organization: Quartermaster, U.S. Navy. *Born:* 1838, Ireland. *Accredited to:* New Hampshire. *G.O. No.:* 45, 31 December 1864. *Citation:* Served as second quartermaster on board the U.S.S. *Kearsarge* when she destroyed the *Alabama* off Cherbourg, France, 19 June 1864. Acting as captain of the 11-inch pivot gun of the second division, Smith carried out his duties courageously and deserved special notice for the deliberate and cool manner in which he acted throughout the bitter engagement. It is stated by rebel officers that this gun was more destructive and did more damage than any other gun of *Kearsarge*.

SMITH, WILSON

Rank and organization: Corporal, Battery H, 3d New York Light Artillery. *Place and date:* At Washington, N.C., 6 September 1862. *Entered service at:* Madison, N.Y. *Birth:* Madison, N.Y. *Date of issue:* 24 April 1896. *Citation:* Took command of a gun (the lieutenant in charge having disappeared) and fired the same so rapidly and effectively that the enemy was repulsed, although for a time a hand-to-hand conflict was had over the gun.

SNEDDEN, JAMES

Rank and organization: Musician, Company E, 54th Pennsylvania Infantry. *Place and date:* At Piedmont, Va., 5 June 1864. *Entered service at:* Johntown, Pa. *Birth:* Scotland. *Dates of issue:* 11 September 1897. *Citation:* Left his place in the rear, took the rifle of a disabled soldier, and fought through the remainder of the action.

SOUTHARD, DAVID

Rank and organization: Sergeant, Company C, 1st New Jersey Cavalry. *Place and date.* At Sailors Creek, Va., 6 April 1865. *Entered service at:* ———. *Birth:* Ocean County, N.J. *Date of issue:* 3 July 1865. *Citation:* Capture of flag; and was the first man over the works in the charge.

SOVA, JOSEPH E.

Rank and organization: Saddler, Company H, 8th New York Cavalry. *Place and date:* At Appomattox Campaign, Va., 29 March to 9 April 1865. *Entered service at:* ———. *Birth:* Chili, N.Y. *Date of issue:* 3 May 1865. *Citation:* Capture of flag.

SOWERS, MICHAEL

Rank and organization: Private, Company L, 4th Pennsylvania Cavalry. *Place and date:* At Stony Creek Station, Va., 1 December 1864. *Entered service at:* Allegheny County, Pa. *Born:* 14 September 1844, Pittsburgh, Allegheny County, Pa. *Date of issue:* 16 February 1897. *Citation:* His horse having been shot from under him he voluntarily and on foot participated in the cavalry charge made upon one of the forts, conducting himself throughout with great personal bravery.

SPALDING, EDWARD B.

Rank and organization: Sergeant, Company E, 52d Illinois Infantry. *Place and date:* At Pittsburg Landing, Tenn., 6 April 1862. *Entered service at:* Rockford, Winnebago County, Ill. *Birth:* Ogle County, Ill. *Date of issue:* 15 January 1894. *Citation:* Although twice wounded, and thereby crippled for life, he remained fighting in open ground to the close of the battle.

SPERRY, WILLIAM J.

Rank and organization: Major, 6th Vermont Infantry. *Place and date:* At Petersburg, Va., 2 April 1865. *Entered service at:* Vermont. *Birth:* Cavendish, Vt. *Date of issue:* 12 August 1892. *Citation:* With the assistance of a few men, captured 2 pieces of artillery and turned them upon the enemy.

SPILLANE, TIMOTHY

Rank and organization: Private, Company C, 16th Pennsylvania Cavalry. *Place and date:* At Hatchers Run, Va., 5–7 February 1865. *Entered service at:* Erie, Pa. *Birth:* Ireland. *Date of issue:* 16 September 1880. *Citation:* Gallantry and good conduct in action; bravery in a charge and reluctance to leave the field after being twice wounded.

SPRAGUE, BENONA

Rank and organization: Corporal, Company F, 116th Illinois Infantry. *Place and date:* At Vicksburg, Miss., 22 May 1863. *Entered service at:* Chencys Grove, Ill. *Birth:* Onondaga County, N.Y. *Date of issue:* 10 July 1894. *Citation:* Gallantry in the charge of the "volunteer storming party."

SPRAGUE, JOHN W.

Rank and organization: Colonel, 63d Ohio Infantry. *Place and date:* At Decatur, Ga., 22 July 1862. *Entered service at:* Sandusky, Ohio *Born:* 4 April 1817, White Creek, N.Y. *Date of issue:* 18 January 1894. *Citation:* With a small command defeated an overwhelming force of the enemy and saved the trains of the corps.

SPROWLE, DAVID

Rank and organization: Orderly Sergeant, U.S. Marine Corps. *Born:* 1811, Lisbon, N.Y. *Accredited to:* New York. *G.O. No.:* 45, 31 December 1864. *Citation:* On board the U.S.S. *Richmond* during action against rebel forts and gunboats, and with the ram *Tennessee* in Mobile Bay, 5 August 1864. Despite damage to his ship and the loss of several men on board as enemy fire raked her decks, Orderly Sgt. Sprowle inspired the men of the marine guard and directed a division of great guns throughout the furious battle which resulted in the surrender of the rebel ram *Tennessee* and in the damaging and destruction of batteries at Fort Morgan.

SPURLING, ANDREW B.

Rank and organization: Lieutenant Colonel, 2d Maine Cavalry. *Place and date:* At Evergreen, Ala., 23 March 1865. *Entered service at:* Maine. *Birth:* Cranberry Isles, Maine. *Date of issue:* 10 September 1897. *Citation:* Advanced alone in the darkness beyond the picket line, came upon 3 of the enemy, fired upon them (his fire being returned), wounded 2, and captured the whole party.

STACEY, CHARLES

Rank and organization: Private, Company D, 55th Ohio Infantry. *Place and date:* At Gettysburg, Pa., 2 July 1863. *Entered service at:* –––. *Birth:* England. *Date of issue:* 23 June 1896. *Citation:* Voluntarily took an advanced position on the skirmish line for the purpose of ascertaining the location of Confederate sharpshooters, and under heavy fire held the position thus taken until the company of which he was a member went back to the main line.

STAHEL, JULIUS

Rank and organization: Major General, U.S. Volunteers. *Place and date:* At Piedmont, Va., 5 June 1864. *Entered service at:* New York, N.Y. *Born:* 5 November 1825, Hungary. *Date of issue:* 4 November 1893. *Citation:* Led his division into action until he was severely wounded.

STANLEY, DAVID S.

Rank and organization: Major General, U.S. Volunteers. *Place and date:* At Franklin, Tenn., 30 November 1864. *Entered service at:* Congress, Wayne County, Ohio. *Born:* 1 June 1828, Cedar Valley, Ohio. *Date of issue:* 29 March 1893. *Citation:* At a critical moment rode to the front of one of his brigades, reestablished its lines, and gallantly led it in a successful assault.

STANLEY, WILLIAM A.

Rank and organization: Shell Man, U.S. Navy. *Born:* 1831, Massachusetts. *Accredited to:* Massachusetts. *G.O. No.:* 45, 31 December 1864. *Citation:* Shell man on No. 8 on board the U.S.S. *Hartford* during successful actions against Fort Morgan, rebel gunboats and the ram *Tennessee* in Mobile Bay, on 5 August 1864. Although severely wounded when his ship sustained numerous hits under the enemy's terrific shellfire, Stanley continued to pass shell until forced by the loss of blood to go below.

STARKINS, JOHN H.

Rank and organization: Sergeant, 34th New York Battery. *Place and date:* At Campbell Station, Tenn., 16 November 1863. *Entered service at:* ———. *Birth:* Great Neck, N.Y. *Date of issue:* 30 July 1896. *Citation;* Brought off his piece without losing a man.

STEELE, JOHN W.

Rank and organization: Major and Aide-de-Camp, U.S. Volunteers. *Place and date:* At Spring Hill, Tenn., 29 November 1864. *Entered service at:* Ohio. *Birth:* Vermont. *Date of issue:* 28 September 1897. *Citation:* During a night attack of the enemy upon the wagon and ammunition train of this officer's corps, he gathered up a force of stragglers and others, assumed command of it, though himself a staff officer, and attacked and dispersed the enemy's forces, thus saving the train.

STEINMETZ, WILLIAM

Rank and organization: Private, Company G, 83d Indiana Infantry. *Place and date:* At Vicksburg, Miss., 22 May 1863. *Entered service at:* Sunmans, Ind. *Birth:* Newport, Ky. *Date of issue:* 12 July 1894. *Citation:* Gallantry in the charge of the "volunteer storming party."

STEPHENS, WILLIAM G.

Rank and organization: Private, Chicago Mercantile Battery, Illinois Light Artillery. *Place and date:* At Vicksburg, Miss., 22 May 1863. *Entered service at:* Chicago, Ill. *Birth:* New York, N.Y. *Date of issue:* ? December 1894. *Citation:* Carried with others by hand a cannon uʳ and fired it through an embrasure of the enemy's works.

STERLING, JAMES E.

Rank and organization: Coal Heaver, U.S. Navy. *Born:* 1838, Maine. *Accredited to:* Maine. *G.O. No.:* 45, 31 December 1864. *Citation:* On board the U.S.S. *Brooklyn* during successful attacks against Fort Morgan, rebel gunboats and the ram *Tennessee* in Mobile Bay, on 5 August 1864. Although wounded when heavy enemy return fire raked the decks of his ship, Sterling courageously remained at his post and continued passing shell until struck down a second time and completely disabled.

STERLING, JOHN T.

Rank and organization: Private, Company D, 11th Indiana Infantry. *Place and date:* At Winchester, Va., 19 September 1864. *Entered service at:* Marion County, Ind. *Birth:* Edgar County, Ill. *Date of issue:* 4 April 1865. *Citation:* With one companion captured 14 of the enemy in the severest part of the battle.

STEVENS, DANIEL D.

Rank and organization: Quartermaster, U.S. Navy. *Born:* 1840, Sagnange, Tenn. *Accredited to:* Massachusetts. Letter 15 July 1870, Secretary of the Navy to Hon. S. Hooper. *Citation:* On board the U.S.S. *Canonicus* during attacks on Fort Fisher, on 13 January 1865. As the *Canonicus* moved into position at 700 yards from shore, the enemy troops soon obtained her range and opened with heavy artillery fire, subjecting her to several hits and near misses until late in the afternoon when the heavier ships coming into line drove them into their bombproofs. Twice during the battle, in which his ship sustained 36 hits, the flag was shot away and gallantly replaced by Stevens.

STEVENS, HAZARD

Rank and organization: Captain and Assistant Adjutant General, U.S. Volunteers. *Place and Date:* At Fort Huger, Va., 19 April 1863. *Entered service at:* Olympia, Washington Territory. *Born:* 9 June 1842, Newport, R.I. *Date of issue:* 13 June 1894. *Citation:* Gallanty led a party that assaulted and captured the fort.

STEWART, GEORGE W.

Rank and organization: First Sergeant, Company E, 1st New Jersey Cavalry. *Place and date:* At Paines Crossroads, Va., 5 April 1865. *Entered service at:* ———. *Birth:* Salem, N.J. *Date of issue:* 3 May 1865. *Citation:* Capture of flag.

STEWART, JOSEPH

Rank and organization: Private, Company G, 1st Maryland Infantry. *Place and date:* At Five Forks, Va., 1 April 1865. *Entered service at:* ———. *Birth:* Ireland. *Date of issue:* 27 April 1865. *Citation:* Capture of flag.

STICKELS, JOSEPH

Rank and organization: Sergeant, Company A, 83d Ohio Infantry. *Place and date:* At Fort Blakely, Ala., 9 April 1865. *Entered service at:*

Bethany, Ohio. *Birth:* Butler County, Ohio. *Date of issue:* 8 June 1865. *Citation:* Capture of flag.

STOCKMAN, GEORGE H.

Rank and organization: First Lieutenant, Company C, 6th Missouri Infantry. *Place and date:* At Vicksburg, Miss., 22 May 1863. *Entered service at:* Chicago, Ill. *Birth:* Germany. *Date of issue:* 9 July 1894. *Citation:* Gallantry in the charge of the "volunteer storming party."

STODDARD, JAMES

Rank and organization: Seaman, U.S. Navy. *Born:* 1838, North Carolina. *Accredited to:* North Carolina. *G.O. No.:* 32, 16 April 1864. *Citation:* Off Yazoo City, Miss., 5 March 1864. Embarking from the *Marmora* with a 12-pound howitzer mounted on a field carriage, Stoddard landed with the gun and crew in the midst of heated battle and, bravely standing by his gun despite enemy rifle fire which cut the gun carriage and rammer, contributed to the turning back of the enemy during the fierce engagement.

STOKES, GEORGE

Rank and organization: Private, Company C, 122d Illinois Infantry. *Place and date:* At Nashville, Tenn., 16 December 1864. *Entered service at:* Jerseyville, Ill. *Birth:* England. *Date of issue:* 24 February 1865. *Citation:* Capture of flag.

STOLZ, FRANK

Rank and organization: Private, Company G, 83d Indiana Infantry. *Place and date:* At Vicksburg, Miss., 22 May 1863. *Entered service at:* Sunmans, Ind. *Birth:* Dearborn County, Ind. *Date of issue:* 9 July 1894. *Citation:* Gallantry in the charge of the "volunteer storming party."

STOREY, JOHN H. R.

Rank and organization: Sergeant, Company F, 109th Pennsylvania Infantry. *Place and date:* At Dallas, Ga., 28 May 1864. *Entered service at:* ———. *Birth:* Philadelphia, Pa. *Date of issue:* 29 August 1896. *Citation:* While bringing in a wounded comrade, under a destructive fire, he was himself wounded in the right leg, which was amputated on the same day.

STOUT, RICHARD

Rank and organization: Landsman, U.S. Navy. *Born:* 1836, New York. *Accredited to:* New York. *G.O. No.:* 32, 16 April 1864. *Citation:* Serving on board the U.S.S. *Isaac Smith*, Stono River, 30 January 1863. While reconnoitering on the Stono River on this date the U.S.S. *Isaac Smith* became trapped in a rebel ambush. Fired on from two sides, she fought her guns until disabled. Suffering heavy casualties and at the mercy of the enemy who was delivering a raking fire from every side, she struck her colors out of regard for the wounded aboard, and all aboard were taken prisoners. Carrying out his duties bravely through this action, Stout was severely wounded and lost his right arm while returning the rebel fire.

STRAHAN, ROBERT

Rank and organization: Captain of the Top, U.S. Navy. *Birth:* New Jersey. *G.O. No.:* 45, 31 December 1864. *Accredited to:* New Jersey. *Citation:* Served as captain of the top on board the U.S.S. *Kearsarge* when she destroyed the *Alabama* off Cherbourg, France, 19 June 1864. Acting as captain of the No. 1 gun, Strahan carried out his duties in the face of heavy enemy fire and exhibited marked coolness and good conduct throughout the engagement. Strahan was highly recommended by his division officer for his gallantry and meritorious achievements.

STRAUSBAUGH, BERNARD A.

Rank and organization: First Sergeant, Company A, 3d Maryland Infantry. *Place and date:* At Petersburg, Va., 17 June 1864. *Entered service at:* Warfordsburg, Pa. *Birth:* Adams County, Pa. *Date of issue:* 1 December 1864. *Citation:* Recaptured the colors of 2d Pennsylvania Provisional Artillery.

STREILE, CHRISTIAN

Rank and organization: Private, Company I, 1st New Jersey Cavalry. *Place and date:* At Paines Crossroads, Va., 5 April 1865. *Entered service at:* Jersey City, N.J. *Birth:* Germany. *Date of issue:* 3 May 1865. *Citation:* Capture of flag.

STRONG, JAMES N.

Rank and organization: Sergeant, Company C, 49th Massachusetts Infantry. *Place and date:* At Port Hudson, La., 27 May 1863. *Entered service at:* Pittsfield, Mass. *Birth:* ———. *Date of issue:* 25 November 1893. *Citation:* Volunteered in response to a call and took part in the movement that was made upon the enemy's works under a heavy fire therefrom in advance of the general assault.

STURGEON, JAMES K.

Rank and organization: Private, Company F, 46th Ohio Infantry. *Place and date:* At Kenesaw Mountain, Ga., 15 June 1864. *Entered service at:* ———. *Birth:* Perry County, Ohio. *Date of issue:* 2 January 1895. *Citation:* Advanced beyond the lines, and in an encounter with 3 Confederates shot 2 and took the other prisoner.

SULLIVAN, JAMES

Rank and organization: Ordinary Seaman, U.S. Navy. *Born:* 1833, New York, N.Y. *Accredited to:* New York. *G.O. No.:* 45, 31 December 1864. *Citation:* On board the U.S.S. *Agawam* as one of a volunteer crew of a powder boat which was exploded near Fort Fisher, 2 December 1864. The powder boat, towed in by the *Wilderness* to prevent detection by the enemy, cast off and slowly steamed to within 300 yards of the beach. After fuses and fires had been lit and a second anchor with short scope let go to assure the boat's tailing inshore, the crew boarded the *Wilderness* and proceeded a distance of 12 miles from shore. Less than 2 hours later the explosion took place, and the following day fires were observed still burning at the forts.

SULLIVAN, JOHN

Rank and organization: Seaman, U.S. Navy. *Born:* 1839, New York, N.Y. *Accredited to:* New York. *G.O. No.:* 45, 31 December 1864. *Citation:* Served as seaman on board the U.S.S. *Monticello* during the reconnaissance of the harbor and water defenses of Wilmington, N.C., 23 to 25 June 1864. Taking part in a reconnaissance of enemy defenses which covered a period of 2 days and nights, Sullivan courageously carried out his duties during this action, which resulted in the capture of a mail carrier and mail, the cutting of a telegraph wire, and the capture of a large group of prisoners. Although in immediate danger from the enemy at all times, Sullivan showed gallantry and coolness throughout this action which resulted in the gaining of much vital information of the rebel defenses.

SULLIVAN, TIMOTHY

Rank and organization: Coxswain, U.S. Navy. *Born:* 1835, Ireland. *Accredited to:* New York. *G.O. No.:* 11, 3 April 1863. *Citation:* Served on board the U.S.S. *Louisville* during various actions of that vessel. During the engagements of the *Louisville*, Sullivan served as first captain of a 9-inch gun and throughout his period of service was "especially commended for his attention to duty, bravery, and coolness in action."

SUMMERS, JAMES C.

Rank and organization: Private, Company H, 4th West Virginia Infantry. *Place and date:* At Vicksburg, Miss., 22 May 1863. *Entered service at:* Kanawha County, W. Va. *Born:* 14 February 1838, Kanawha County, W. Va. *Date of issue:* 25 February 1895. *Citation:* Gallantry in charge of the "volunteer storming party."

SUMMERS, ROBERT

Rank and organization: Chief Quartermaster, U.S. Navy. *Born:* 1838, Prussia. *Accredited to:* New York. *G.O. No.:* 59, 22 June 1865. *Citation:* Summers served on board the U.S.S. *Ticonderoga* in the attacks on Fort Fisher, 13 to 15 January 1865. The ship took position in the line of battle and maintained a well-directed fire upon the batteries to the left of the palisades during the initial phase of the engagement. Although several of the enemy's shots fell over and around the vessel, the *Ticonderoga* fought her guns gallantly throughout 3 consecutive days of battle until the flag was planted on one of the strongest fortifications possessed by the rebels.

SURLES, WILLIAM H.

Rank and organization: Private, Company G, 2d Ohio Infantry. *Place and date:* At Perryville, Ky., 8 October 1862. *Entered service at:* Steubenville, Ohio. *Born:* 24 February 1845, Steubenville, Ohio. *Date of issue:* 19 August 1891. *Citation:* In the hottest part of the fire he stepped in front of his colonel to shield him from the enemy's fire.

SWAN, CHARLES A.

Rank and organization: Private, Company K, 4th Iowa Cavalry. *Place and date:* At Selma, Ala., 2 April 1865. *Entered service at:* Mt. Pleasant, Iowa. *Born:* 29 May 1838, Green County, Pa. *Date of issue:* 17 June 1865. *Citation:* Capture of flag (supposed to be 11th Mississippi, C.S.A.) and bearer.

SWANSON, JOHN

Rank and organization: Seaman, U.S. Navy. *Born:* 1842, Sweden. *Accredited to:* Massachusetts. *G.O. No.:* 59, 22 June 1865. *Citation:* On board the U.S.S. *Santiago de Cuba* during the assault on Fort Fisher on 15 January 1865. As one of a boat crew detailed to one of the generals on shore, Swanson bravely entered the fort in the assault and accompanied his party in carrying dispatches at the height of the battle. He was 1 of 6 men who entered the fort in the assault from the fleet.

SWAP, JACOB E.

Rank and organization: Private, Company H, 83d Pennsylvania Infantry. *Place and date:* At Wilderness, Va., 5 May 1864. *Entered service at:* Springs, Pa. *Birth:* Calnehoose, N.Y. *Date of issue:* 19 November 1897. *Citation:* Although assigned to other duty, he voluntarily joined his regiment in a charge and fought with it until severely wounded.

SWATTON, EDWARD

Rank and organization: Seaman, U.S. Navy. *Born:* 1836, New York, N.Y. *Accredited to:* New York. *G.O. No.:* 59, 22 June 1865. *Citation:* On board the U.S.S. *Santiago de Cuba* during the assault on Fort Fisher on 15 January 1865. As one of a boat crew detailed to one of the generals on shore, Swatton bravely entered the fort in the assault and accompanied his party in carrying dispatches at the height of the battle. He was 1 of 6 men who entered the fort in the assault from the fleet.

SWAYNE, WAGER

Rank and organization: Lieutenant Colonel, 43d Ohio Infantry. *Place and date:* At Corinth, Miss., 4 October 1862. *Entered service at:* Columbus, Ohio. *Born:* 10 November 1834, Columbus, Ohio. *Date of issue:* 19 August 1893. *Citation:* Conspicuous gallantry in restoring order at a critical moment and leading his regiment in a charge.

SWEARER, BENJAMIN

Rank and organization: Seaman, U.S. Navy. *Born:* 1825, Baltimore, Md. *Accredited to:* Maryland. *G.O. No.:* 11, 3 April 1863. *Citation:* Embarked in a surfboat from the U.S.S. *Pawnee* during action against Fort Clark, off Baltimore Inlet, 29 August 1861. Taking part in a mission to land troops and to remain inshore and provide protection, Swearer rendered gallant service throughout the action and had the honor of being the first man to raise the flag on the captured fort.

SWEATT, JOSEPH S. G.

Rank and organization: Private, Company C, 6th Massachusetts Infantry. *Place and date:* At Carrsville, Va., 15 May 1863. *Entered service at:* Lowell, Mass. *Born:* 23 October 1843, Boscawen, N.H. *Date of issue:* 22 March 1892. *Citation:* When ordered to retreat this soldier turned and rushed back to the front, in the face of heavy fire of the enemy, in an endeavor to rescue his wounded comrades, remaining by them until overpowered and taken prisoner.

SWEENEY, JAMES

Rank and organization: Private, Company A, 1st Vermont Cavalry. *Place and date:* At Cedar Creek, Va., 19 October 1864. *Entered service at:* Essex, Vt. *Birth:* England. *Date of issue:* 26 October 1864. *Citation:* With one companion captured the State flag of a North Carolina regiment, together with 3 officers and an ambulance with its mules and driver.

SWEGHEIMER, JACOB

Rank and organization: Private, Company I, 54th Ohio Infantry. *Place and date:* At Vicksburg, Miss., 22 May 1863. *Entered service at:* ———. *Birth:* Germany. *Date of issue:* 14 July 1894. *Citation:* Gallantry in the charge of the "volunteer storming party."

SWIFT, FREDERIC W.

Rank and organization: Lieutenant Colonel, 17th Michigan Infantry. *Place and date:* At Lenoire Station, Tenn., 16 November 1863. *Entered service at:* Michigan. *Born:* 30 January 1831, Mansfield Center, Conn. *Date of issue:* 15 February 1897. *Citation:* Gallantly seized the colors and rallied the regiment after 3 color bearers had been shot and the regiment, having become demoralized, was in imminent danger of capture.

SWIFT, HARLAN J.

Rank and organization: Second Lieutenant, Company H, 2d New York Militia Regiment. *Place and date:* At Petersburg, Va., 30 July 1864. *Entered service at:* New York. *Birth:* New Hudson, N.Y. *Date of issue:* 20 July 1897. *Citation:* Having advanced with his regiment and captured the enemy's line, saw 4 of the enemy retiring toward their second line of works. He advanced upon them alone, compelled their surrender and regained his regiment with the 4 prisoners.

SYPE, PETER

Rank and organization: Private, Company B, 47th Ohio Infantry. *Place and date:* At Vicksburg, Miss., 3 May 1863. *Entered service at:* Adrian, Mich. *Born:* 11 October 1841, Monroe County, Mich. *Date of issue:* 12 September 1911. *Citation.* Was one of a party that volunteered and attempted to run the enemy's batteries with a steam tug and 2 barges loaded with subsistence stores.

TABOR, WILLIAM L. S.

Rank and organization: Private, Company K, 15th New Hampshire Infantry. *Place and date:* At the siege of Port Hudson, La., July 1863. *Entered service at:* Concord, N.H. *Born:* 1844, Methenn, Mass. *Date of issue:* 10 March 1896. *Citation:* Voluntarily exposed himself to the enemy only a few feet away to render valuable services for the protection of his comrades.

TAGGART, CHARLES A.

Rank and organization: Private, Company B, 37th Massachusetts Infantry. *Place and date:* At Sailors Creek, Va., 6 April 1865. *Entered service at:* ———. *Birth:* Blandford, Mass. *Date of issue:* 10 May 1865. *Citation:* Capture of flag.

TALBOTT, WILLIAM

Rank and organization: Captain of the Forecastle, U.S. Navy. *Born:* 1812, Maine. *Accredited to:* Massachusetts. *G.O. No.:* 32, 16 April 1865. *Citation:* Served as captain of the forecastle on board the U.S.S. *Louisville* at the capture of the Arkansas post, 10 and 11 January 1863. Carrying out his duties as captain of a 9-inch gun, Talbott was conspicuous for ability and bravery throughout this engagement with the enemy.

*TALLENTINE, JAMES

Rank and organization: Quarter Gunner, U.S. Navy. *Born:* 1840, England. *Accredited to:* Maryland. *G.O. No.:* 45, 31 December 1864. *Citation:* Served as quarter gunner on board the U.S.S. *Tacony* during the taking of Plymouth, N.C., 31 October 1864. Carrying out his duties faithfully during the capture of Plymouth, Tallentine distinguished himself by a display of coolness when he participated in landing and spiking a 9-inch gun while under devastating fire from enemy musketry. Tallentine later gave his life while courageously engaged in storming Fort Fisher, 15 January 1865.

TANNER, CHARLES B.

Rank and organization: Second Lieutenant, Company H, 1st Delaware Infantry. *Place and date:* At Antietam, Md., 17 September 1862. *Entered service at:* Wilmington, Del. *Birth:* Pennsylvania. *Date of issue:* 13 December 1889. *Citation:* Carried off the regimental colors, which had fallen within 20 yards of the enemy's lines, the color guard of 9 men having all been killed or wounded; was himself 3 times wounded.

TAYLOR, ANTHONY

Rank and organization: First Lieutenant, Company A, 15th Pennsylvania Cavalry. *Place and date:* At Chickamauga, Ga., 20 September 1863. *Entered service at:* Philadelphia, Pa. *Born:* 11 October 1837, Burlington, N.J. *Date of issue:* 4 December 1893. *Citation:* Held out to the last with a small force against the advance of superior numbers of the enemy.

TAYLOR, FORRESTER L.

Rank and organization: Captain, Company H, 23d New Jersey Infantry. *Place and date:* At Chancellorsville, Va., 3 May 1863. *Entered service at:* N.J—. *Birth:* Philadelphia, Pa. *Date of issue:* 2 November 1896. *Citation:* At great risk voluntarily saved the lives of and brought from the battlefield 2 wounded comrades.

TAYLOR, GEORGE

Rank and organization: Armorer, U.S. Navy. *Born:* 1830, Watertown, N.Y. *Accredited to:* New York. *G.O. No.:* 45, 31 December 1864. *Citation:* On board the U.S.S. *Lackawanna* during successful attacks against Fort Morgan, rebel gunboats and the ram *Tennessee* in Mobile Bay, on 5 August 1864. When an enemy shell exploded in the shellroom, Taylor although wounded went into the room and, with his hand, extinguished the fire from the explosion. He then carried out his duties during the remainder of the prolonged action which resulted in the capture of the prize rebel ram *Tennessee* and in the damaging and destruction of Fort Morgan.

TAYLOR, HENRY H.

Rank and organization: Sergeant, Company C, 45th Illinois Infantry. *Place and date:* At Vicksburg, Miss., 25 June 1863. *Entered service at:* Galena, Jo Daviess County, Ill. *Birth:* Jo Daviess County, Ill. *Date of issue:* 1 September 1893. *Citation:* Was the first to plant the Union colors upon the enemy's works.

TAYLOR, JOHN

Rank and organization: Seaman, U.S. Navy. Biography not available. *G.O. No.:* 71, 15 January 1866. *Citation:* Seaman in charge of the picket boat attached to the Navy Yard, New York, 9 September 1865. Acting with promptness, coolness and good judgment, Taylor rescued from drowning Commander S. D. Trenchard, of the U.S. Navy, who fell overboard in attempting to get on a ferryboat, which had collided with an English steamer, and needed immediate assistance.

TAYLOR, JOSEPH

Rank and organization: Private, Company E, 7th Rhode Island Infantry. *Place and date:* At Weldon Railroad, Va., 18 August 1864. *Entered service at:* Burrillville, R.I. *Birth:* England. *Date of issue:* 20 July 1897. *Citation:* While acting as an orderly to a general officer on the field and alone, encountered a picket of 3 of the enemy and compelled their surrender.

TAYLOR, RICHARD

Rank and organization: Private, Company E, 18th Indiana Infantry. *Place and date:* At Cedar Creek, Va., 19 October 1864. *Entered service at:* Martin County, Ind. *Birth:* Madison County, Ala. *Date of issue:* 21 November 1864. *Citation:* Capture of flag.

TAYLOR, THOMAS

Rank and organization: Coxswain, U.S. Navy. *Born:* 1834, Bangor, Maine. *Accredited to:* Maine. *G.O. No.:* 59, 22 June 1865. *Citation:* Served on board the U.S.S. *Metacomet* during the action against rebel forts and gunboats and with the rebel ram *Tennessee* in Mobile Bay, 5 August 1864. Despite damage to his ship and the loss of several men on board as enemy fire raked her decks, Taylor encouraged the men of the forward pivot gun when the officer in command displayed cowardice, doing honor to the occasion.

TAYLOR, WILLIAM

Rank and organization: Sergeant, Co. H, and 2d Lt. Co. M, 1st Maryland Inf. *Place and date:* At Front Royal, Va., 23 May 1862. At Weldon Railroad, Va., 19 August 1864. *Entered service at:* ———. *Birth:* Washington, D.C. *Date of issue:* 2 August 1897. *Citation:* When a sergeant, at Front Royal, Va., he was painfully wounded while obeying an order to burn a bridge, but, persevering in the attempt, he burned the bridge and prevented its use by the enemy. Later, at Weldon Railroad, Va., then a lieutenant, he voluntarily took the place of a disabled officer and undertook a hazardous reconnaissance beyond the lines of the army; was taken prisoner in the attempt.

TAYLOR, WILLIAM G.

Rank and organization: Captain of the Forecastle, U.S. Navy. *Born:* 1831, Philadelphia, Pa. *Accredited to:* Pennsylvania. *G.O. No.:* 59, 22 June 1865. *Citation:* On board the U.S.S. *Ticonderoga* during attacks on Fort Fisher, 24 and 25 December 1864. As captain of a gun, Taylor performed his duties with coolness and skill as his ship took position in the line of battle and delivered its fire on the batteries on shore. Despite the depressing effect caused when an explosion of the 100-pounder Parrott rifle killed 8 men and wounded 12 more, and the enemy's heavy return fire, he calmly remained at his station during the 2 days' operations.

TERRY, JOHN D.

Rank and organization: Sergeant, Company E, 23d Massachusetts Infantry. *Place and date:* At New Bern, N.C., 14 March 1862. *Entered service at:* Boston, Mass. *Birth:* Montville, Maine. *Date of issue:* 12 October 1867. *Citation:* In the thickest of the fight, where he lost his leg by a shot, still encouraged the men until carried off the field.

THACKRAH, BENJAMIN

Rank and organization: Private, Company H, 115th New York Infantry. *Place and date:* Near Fort Gates, Fla., 1 April 1864. *Entered service at:* Johnsonville, N.Y. *Birth:* Scotland. *Date of issue:* 2 May 1890. *Citation:* Was a volunteer in the surprise and capture of the enemy's picket.

THATCHER, CHARLES M.

Rank and organization: Private, Company B, 1st Michigan Sharpshooters. *Place and date:* At Petersburg, Va., 30 July 1864. *En-*

tered service at: Eastmanville, Mich. *Born:* 1844, Coldwater, Mich. *Date of issue:* 31 July 1896. *Citation:* Instead of retreating or surrendering when the works were captured, regardless of his personal safety continued to return the enemy's fire until he was captured.

THAXTER, SIDNEY W.

Rank and organization: Major, 1st Maine Cavalry. *Place and date:* At Hatchers Run, Va., 27 October 1864. *Entered service at:* Bangor, Maine. *Birth:* Bangor, Maine. *Date of issue:* 10 September 1897. *Citation:* Voluntarily remained and participated in the battle with conspicuous gallantry, although his term of service had expired and he had been ordered home to be mustered out.

THIELBERG, HENRY

Rank and organization: Seaman, U.S. Navy. *Born:* 1833, Germany. *Accredited to:* Massachusetts. *G.O. No.:* 17, 10 July 1863. *Citation:* Serving temporarily on board the U.S.S. *Mount Washington* during the Nansemond River action, 14 April 1863. After assisting in hauling up and raising the flagstaff, Thielberg volunteered to go up on the pilothouse and observe the movements of the enemy and although 3 shells struck within a few inches of his head, remained at his post until ordered to descend.

THOMAS, HAMPTON S.

Rank and organization: Major, 1st Pennsylvania Veteran Cavalry. *Place and date:* At Amelia Springs, Va., 5 April 1865. *Entered service at:* Pennsylvania. *Born:* 3 November 1837, Quakertown, Bucks County, Pa. *Date of issue:* 15 January 1894. *Citation:* Conspicuous gallantry in the capture of a field battery and a number of battle flags and in the destruction of the enemy's wagon train. Maj. Thomas lost a leg in this action.

THOMAS, STEPHEN

Rank and organization: Colonel, 8th Vermont Infantry. *Place and date:* At Cedar Creek, Va., 19 October 1864. *Entered service at:* Montpelier, Vt. *Birth:* Vermont. *Date of issue:* 25 July 1892. *Citation:* Distinguished conduct in a desperate hand-to-hand encounter, in which the advance of the enemy was checked.

THOMPKINS, GEORGE W.

Rank and organization: Corporal, Company F, 124th New York Infantry. *Place and date:* At Petersburg, Va., 25 March 1865. *Entered service at:* Esport Jervis, N.Y. *Birth:* Orange County, N.Y. *Date of issue:* 6 April 1865. *Citation:* Capture of flag of 49th Alabama Infantry (C.S.A.) from an officer who, with colors in hand, was rallying his men.

THOMPSON, ALLEN

Rank and organization: Private, Company I, 4th New York Heavy Artillery. *Place and date:* At White Oak Road, Va., 1 April 1865. *Entered service at:* Port Jarvis, N.Y. *Birth:* New York, N.Y. *Date of issue:* 22 April 1896. *Citation:* Made a hazardous reconnaissance through timber and slashings preceding the Union line of battle, signaling the troops and leading them through the obstruction.

THOMPSON, CHARLES A.

Rank and organization: Sergeant, Company D, 17th Michigan Infantry. *Place and date:* At Spotsylvania, Va., 12 May 1864. *Entered service at:* Kalamazoo, Mich. *Born:* 1843, Perrysburg, Ohio. *Date of issue:* 27 July 1896. *Citation:* After the regiment was surrounded and all resistance seemed useless, fought singlehanded for the colors and refused to give them up until he had appealed to his superior officers.

THOMPSON, FREEMAN C.

Rank and organization: Corporal, Company F, 116th Ohio Infantry. *Place and date:* At Petersburg, Va., 2 April 1865. *Entered service at:* ———. *Birth:* Monroe County, Ohio. *Date of issue:* 12 May 1865. *Citation:* Was twice knocked from the parapet of Fort Gregg by blows from the enemy muskets but at the third attempt fought his way into the works.

THOMPSON, HENRY A.

Rank and organization: Private, U.S. Marine Corps. *Born:* 1841, England. *Accredited to:* Pennsylvania. *G.O. No.:* 59, 22 June 1865. *Citation:* On board the U.S.S. *Minnesota* in the assault on Fort Fisher, 15 January 1865. Landing on the beach with the assaulting party from his ship, Private Thompson advanced partly through a breach in the palisades and nearer to the fort than any man from his ship despite enemy fire which killed or wounded many officers and men. When more than two-thirds of the men became seized with panic and retreated on the run, he remained with the party until dark, when it came safely away, bringing its wounded, its arms and its colors.

THOMPSON, JAMES

Rank and organization: Private, Company K, 4th New York Heavy Artillery. *Place and date:* At White Oak Road, Va., 1 April 1865. *Entered service at:* Sandy Creek, N.Y. *Birth:* Sandy Creek, N.Y. *Date of issue:* 22 April 1896. *Citation:* Made a hazardous reconnaissance through timber and slashings, preceding the Union line of battle, signaling the troops and leading them through the obstructions.

THOMPSON, JAMES B.

Rank and organization: Sergeant, Company G, 1st Pennsylvania Rifles. *Place and date:* At Gettysburg, Pa., 3 July 1863. *Entered service at:* Perrysville, Pa. *Birth:* Juniata County, Pa. *Date of issue:* 1 December 1864. *Citation:* Capture of flag of 15th Georgia Infantry (C.S.A.).

THOMPSON, J. (JAMES) HARRY

Rank and organization: Surgeon, U.S. Volunteers. *Place and date:* At New Bern, N.C., 14 March 1862. *Entered service at:* New York. *Birth:* England. *Date of issue:* 11 November 1870. *Citation:* Voluntarily reconnoitered the enemy's position and carried orders under the hottest fire.

THOMPSON, JOHN

Rank and organization: Corporal, Company C, 1st Maryland Infantry. *Place and date:* At Hatchers Run, Va., 6 February 1865. *Entered service at:* Baltimore, Md. *Birth:* Denmark. *Date of issue:* 10 September 1897. *Citation:* As color bearer with most conspicuous gallantry preceded his regiment in the assault and planted his flag upon the enemy's works.

THOMPSON, THOMAS

Rank and organization: Sergeant, Company A, 66th Ohio Infantry. *Place and date:* At Chancellorsville, Va., 2 May 1863. *Entered service at:* ———. *Birth:* Champaign County, Ohio. *Date of issue:* 16 July 1892. *Citation:* One of a party of 4 who voluntarily brought into the Union lines, under fire, a wounded Confederate officer from whom was obtained valuable information concerning the enemy.

THOMPSON, WILLIAM

Rank and organization: Signal Quartermaster, U.S. Navy. *Entered service at:* Boston, Mass. *Birth:* Cape May County, N.J. *G.O. No.:* 17, 10 July 1863. *Citation:* During action of the main squadron of ships against heavily defended Forts Beauregard and Walker on Hilton Head, 7 November 1861. Serving as signal quartermaster on board the U.S.S. *Mohican,* Thompson steadfastly steered the ship with a steady and bold heart under the batteries; was wounded by a piece of shell but remained at his station until he fell from loss of blood. Legs since amputated.

THOMPSON, WILLIAM P.

Rank and organization: Sergeant, Company G, 20th Indiana Infantry. *Place and date:* At Wilderness, Va., 6 May 1864. *Entered service at:* Tippecanoe County, Ind. *Birth:* Brooklyn, N.Y. *Date of issue:* 1 December 1864. *Citation:* Capture of flag of 55th Virginia Infantry (C.S.A.).

THOMSON, CLIFFORD

Rank and organization: First Lieutenant, Company A, 1st New York Cavalry. *Place and date:* At Chancellorsville, Va., 2 May 1863. *Entered service at:* New York, N.Y. *Birth:* ———. *Date of issue:* 27 November 1896. *Citation:* Volunteered to ascertain the character of approaching troops; rode up so closely as to distinguish the features of the enemy, and as he wheeled to return they opened fire with musketry, the Union troops returning same. Under a terrific fire from both sides Lieutenant Thomson rode back unhurt to the Federal lines, averting a disaster to the Army by his heroic act.

THORN, WALTER

Rank and organization: Second Lieutenant, Company G, 116th U.S. Colored Troops. *Place and date:* At Dutch Gap Canal, Va., 1 January 1865. *Entered service at:* ———. *Birth:* New York, N.Y. *Date of issue:* 8 December 1898. *Citation:* After the fuze to the mined bulkhead had been lit, this officer, learning that the picket guard had not been withdrawn, mounted the bulkhead and at great personal peril warned the guard of its danger.

TIBBETS, ANDREW W.

Rank and organization: Private, Company I, 3d Iowa Cavalry. *Place and date:* At Columbus, Ga., 16 April 1865. *Entered service at:* Appanoose County, Iowa. *Birth:* Clark County, Ind. *Date of issue:* 17 June 1865. *Citation:* Capture of flag and bearer, Austin's Battery (C.S.A.).

TILTON, WILLIAM

Rank and organization: Sergeant, Company C, 7th New Hampshire Infantry. *Place and date:* At Richmond Campaign, Va., 1864. *Entered service at:* Hanover, N.H. *Birth:* St. Albans, Vt. *Date of issue:* 20 February 1884. *Citation:* Gallant conduct in the field.

TINKHAM, EUGENE M.

Rank and organization: Corporal, Company H, 148th New York Infantry. *Place and date:* At Cold Harbor, Va., 3 June 1864. *Entered service at:* ———. *Birth:* Sprague, Conn. *Date of issue:* 5 April 1898. *Citation:* Though himself wounded, voluntarily left the rifle pits, crept out between the lines and, exposed to the severe fire of the enemy's guns at close range, brought within the lines 2 wounded and helpless comrades.

TITUS, CHARLES

Rank and organization: Sergeant, Company H, 1st New Jersey Cavalry. *Place and date:* At Sailors Creek, Va., 6 April 1865. *Entered service at:* New Brunswick, N.J. *Birth:* Millstone, N.J. *Date of issue:* 3 July 1865. *Citation:* Was among the first to check the enemy's countercharge.

TOBAN, JAMES W.

Rank and organization: Sergeant, Company C, 9th Michigan Cavalry. *Place and date:* At Aiken, S.C., 11 February 1865. *Entered service at:* Northfield, Mich. *Born:* 1844, Northfield, Mich. *Date of issue:* 9 July 1896. *Citation:* Voluntarily and at great personal risk returned, in the face of the advance of the enemy, and rescued from impending death or capture, Maj. William C. Stevens, 9th Michigan Cavalry, who had been thrown from his horse.

TOBIE, EDWARD P.

Rank and organization: Sergeant Major, 1st Maine Cavalry. *Place and date:* At Appomattox Campaign, Va., 29 March to 9 April 1865. *Entered service at:* Lewiston, Maine. *Birth:* Lewiston, Maine. *Date of issue:* 1 April 1898. *Citation:* Though severely wounded at Sailors Creek, 6 April, and at Farmville, 7 April, refused to go to the hospital, but remained with his regiment, performed the full duties of adjutant upon the wounding of that officer, and was present for duty at Appomattox.

TOBIN, JOHN M.

Rank and organization: First Lieutenant and Adjutant, 9th Massachusetts Infantry. *Place and date:* At Malvern Hill, Va., 1 July 1862. *Entered service at:* Boston, Mass. *Birth:* Ireland. *Date of issue:* 11 March 1896. *Citation:* Voluntarily took command of the 9th Massachusetts while adjutant, bravely fighting from 3 p.m. until dusk, rallying and re-forming the regiment under fire; twice picked up the regimental flag, the color bearer having been shot down, and placed it in worthy hands.

TODD, SAMUEL

Rank and organization: Quartermaster, U.S. Navy. *Born:* 1815, Portsmouth, N.H. *Accredited to:* New Hampshire. *G.O. No.:* 45, 31 December 1864. *Citation:* Stationed at the conn on board the U.S.S. *Brooklyn* during action against rebel forts and gunboats and with the ram *Tennessee* in Mobile Bay, 5 August 1864. Despite severe damage to his ship and the loss of several men on board as enemy fire raked her decks from stem to stern, Todd performed his duties with outstanding skill and courage throughout the furious battle which resulted in the surrender of the prize rebel ram *Tennessee* and in the damaging and destruction of batteries at Fort Morgan.

TOFFEY, JOHN J.

Rank and organization: First Lieutenant, Company G, 33d New Jersey Infantry. *Place and date:* At Chattanooga, Tenn., 23 November 1863. *Entered service at:* Hudson, N.J. *Birth:* Duchess, N.Y. *Date of issue:* 10 September 1897. *Citation:* Although excused from duty on account of sickness, went to the front in command of a storming party and with conspicuous gallantry participated in the assault of Missionary Ridge; was here wounded and permanently disabled.

TOMLIN, ANDREW J.

Rank and organization: Corporal, U.S. Marine Corps. *Born:* 1844, Goshen, N.J. *Accredited to:* New Jersey. *G.O. No.:* 59, 22 June 1865. *Citation:* As corporal of the guard on board the U.S.S. *Wabash* during the assault on Fort Fisher, on 15 January 1865. As 1 of 200 marines assembled to hold a line of entrenchments in the rear of the fort which the enemy threatened to attack in force following a retreat in panic by more than two-thirds of the assaulting ground forces, Cpl. Tomlin took position in line and remained until morning when relief troops arrived from the fort. When one of his comrades was struck down by enemy fire, he unhesitatingly advanced under a withering fire of musketry into an open plain close to the fort and assisted the wounded man to a place of safety.

TOMPKINS, AARON B.

Rank and organization: Sergeant, Company G, 1st New Jersey Cavalry. *Place and date:* At Sailors Creek, Va., 5 April 1865. *Entered service at:* ———. *Birth:* Orange, Essex County, N.J. *Date of issue:* 3 July 1865. *Citation:* Charged into the enemy's ranks and captured a battle flag, having a horse shot under him and his cheeks and shoulders cut with a saber.

TOMPKINS, CHARLES H.

Rank and organization: First Lieutenant, 2d U.S. Cavalry. *Place and date:* At Fairfax, Va., 1 June 1861. *Entered service at:* Brooklyn, N.Y. *Birth:* Fort Monroe, Va. *Date of issue:* 13 November 1893. *Citation:* Twice charged through the enemy's lines and, taking a carbine from an enlisted man, shot the enemy's captain.

TOOHEY, THOMAS

Rank and organization: Sergeant, Company F, 24th Wisconsin Infantry. *Place and date:* At Franklin, Tenn., 30 November 1864. *Entered service at:* ———. *Birth:* New York, N.Y. *Date of issue:* Unknown. *Citation:* Gallantry in action; voluntarily assisting in working guns of battery near right of the regiment after nearly every man had left them, the fire of the enemy being hotter at this than at any other point on the line.

TOOMER, WILLIAM

Rank and organization: Sergeant, Company G, 127th Illinois Infantry. *Place and date:* At Vicksburg, Miss., 22 May 1863. *Entered service at:* Chicago, Ill. *Birth:* Ireland. *Date of issue:* 9 July 1894. *Citation:* Gallantry in the charge of the "volunteer storming party."

TORGLER, ERNST

Rank and organization: Sergeant, Company G, 37th Ohio Infantry. *Place and date:* At Ezra Chapel, Ga., 28 July 1864. *Entered service at:* ———. *Birth:* Germany. *Date of issue:* 10 May 1894. *Citation:* At great hazard of his life he saved his commanding officer, then badly wounded, from capture.

TOZIER, ANDREW J.

Rank and organization: Sergeant, Company I, 20th Maine Infantry. *Place and date:* At Gettysburg, Pa., 2 July 1863. *Entered service at:* Plymouth, Maine. *Birth:* Monmouth, Maine. *Date of issue:* 13 August 1898. *Citation:* At the crisis of the engagement this soldier, a color bearer, stood alone in an advanced position, the regiment having been borne back, and defended his colors with musket and ammunition picked up at his feet.

TRACY, AMASA A.

Rank and organization: Lieutenant Colonel, 2d Vermont Infantry. *Place and date:* At Cedar Creek, Va., 19 October 1864. *Entered service at:* Middlebury, Vt. *Birth:* Maine. *Date of issue:* 24 June 1892. *Citation:* Took command of and led the brigade in the assault on the enemy's works.

TRACY, BENJAMIN F.

Rank and organization: Colonel, 109th New York Infantry. *Place and date:* At Wilderness, Va., 6 May 1864. *Entered service at:* Owego, N.Y. *Born:* 26 April 1830, Owego, N.Y. *Date of issue:* 21 June 1895. *Citation:* Seized the colors and led the regiment when other regiments had retired and then reformed his line and held it.

TRACY, CHARLES H.

Rank and organization: Sergeant, Company A, 37th Massachusetts Infantry. *Place and date:* At Spotsylvania, Va., 12 May 1864; At Petersburg, Va., 2 April 1865. *Entered service at:* Springfield, Mass. *Birth:* Jewett City, Conn. *Date of issue:* 19 November 1897. *Citation:* At the risk of his own life, at Spotsylvania, 12 May 1864, assisted in carrying to a place of safety a wounded and helpless officer. On 2 April 1865, advanced with the pioneers, and, under heavy fire, assisted in removing 2 lines of chevaux-de-frise; was twice wounded but advanced to the third line, where he was again severely wounded, losing a leg.

TRACY, WILLIAM G.

Rank and organization: Second Lieutenant, Company I, 122d New York Infantry. *Place and date:* At Chancellorsville, Va., 2 May 1863. *Entered service at:* Onondaga County, N.Y. *Birth:* Onondaga, N.Y. *Date of issue:* 2 May 1895. *Citation:* Having been sent outside the lines to obtain certain information of great importance and having succeeded in his mission, was surprised upon his return by a large force of the enemy, regaining the Union lines only after greatly imperiling his life.

TRAYNOR, ANDREW

Rank and organization: Corporal, Company D, 1st Michigan Cavalry. *Place and date:* At Mason's Hill, Va., 16 March 1864. *Entered service at:* Rome, N.Y. *Birth:* Newark, N.J. *Date of issue:* 28 September 1897. *Citation:* Having been surprised and captured by a detachment of guerrillas, this soldier, with other prisoners, seized the arms of the guard over them, killed 2 of the guerrillas, and enabled all the prisoners to escape.

TREAT, HOWELL B.

Rank and organization: Sergeant, Company I, 52d Ohio Infantry. *Place and date:* At Buzzard's Roost, Ga., 11 May 1864. *Entered service at:* Painesville, Ohio. *Birth:* Painesville, Ohio. *Date of issue:* 14 August 1894. *Citation:* Risked his life in saving a wounded comrade.

TREMAIN, HENRY E.

Rank and organization: Major and Aide-de-Camp, U.S. Volunteers. *Place and date:* At Resaca, Ga., 15 May 1864. *Entered service at:* New York, N.Y. *Birth:* New York, N.Y. *Date of issue:* 30 June 1892. *Citation:* Voluntarily rode between the lines while 2 brigades of Union troops were firing into each other and stopped the firing.

TRIBE, JOHN

Rank and organization: Private, Company G, 5th New York Cavalry. *Place and date:* At Waterloo Bridge, Va., 25 August 1862. *Entered service at:* Oswego, N.Y. *Birth:* Tioga County, N.Y. *Date of issue:* 11 June 1895. *Citation:* Voluntarily assisted in the burning and destruction of the bridge under heavy fire of the enemy.

TRIPP, OTHNIEL

Rank and organization: Chief Boatswain's Mate, U.S. Navy. *Born:* 1826, Maine. *Accredited to:* Maine. *G.O. No.:* 59, 22 June 1865. *Citation:* On board the U.S.S. *Seneca* in the assault on Fort Fisher, 15 January 1865. Despite severe enemy fire which halted an attempt by his assaulting party to enter the stockade, Tripp boldly charged through the gap in the stockade although the center of the line, being totally unprotected, fell back along the open beach and left too few in the ranks to attempt an offensive operation.

TROGDEN, HOWELL G.

Rank and organization: Private, Company B, 8th Missouri Infantry. *Place and date:* At Vicksburg, Miss., 22 May 1863. *Entered service at:* St. Louis, Mo. *Born:* 1840, Cedar Falls, N.C. *Date of issue:* 3 August 1894. *Citation:* Gallantry in the charge of the "volunteer storming party." He carried his regiment's flag and tried to borrow a gun to defend it.

TRUELL, EDWIN M.

Rank and organization: Private, Company E, 12th Wisconsin Infantry. *Place and date:* Near Atlanta, Ga., 21 July 1864. *Entered service at:* Mantson, Wis. *Birth:* Lowell, Mass. *Date of issue:* 11 March 1870. *Citation:* Although severely wounded in a charge, he remained with the regiment until again severely wounded, losing his leg.

TRUETT, ALEXANDER H.

Rank and organization: Coxswain, U.S. Navy. *Born:* 1834, Baltimore, Md. *Accredited to:* Maryland. *G.O. No.:* 45, 31 December 1864. *Citation:* On board the U.S.S. *Richmond* during action against rebel forts and gunboats and with the ram *Tennessee* in Mobile Bay, 5 August 1864. Despite damage to his ship and the loss of several men on board as enemy fire raked her decks, Truett performed his duties with skill and courage throughout a furious 2-hour battle which resulted in the surrender of the rebel ram *Tennessee* and in the damaging and destruction of batteries at Fort Morgan.

TUCKER, ALLEN

Rank and organization: Sergeant, Company F, 10th Connecticut Infantry. *Place and date:* At Petersburg, Va., 2 April 1865. *Entered service at:* Sprague, Conn. *Birth:* Lyme, Conn. *Date of issue:* 12 May 1865. *Citation:* Gallantry as color bearer in the assault on Fort Gregg.

TUCKER, JACOB. R.

Rank and organization: Corporal, Company G, 4th Maryland Infantry. *Place and date:* At Petersburg, Va., 1 April 1865. *Entered service at:* Baltimore, Md. *Birth:* Chester County, Pa. *Date of issue:* 22 April 1871. *Citation:* Was 1 of the 3 soldiers most conspicuous in the final assault.

TWEEDALE, JOHN

Rank and organization: Private, Company B, 15th Pennsylvania Cavalry. *Place and date:* At Stone River, Tenn., 31 December 1862–1 January 1863. *Entered service at:* Philadelphia, Pa. *Born:* 10 June 1841, Frankford, Pa. *Date of issue:* 18 November 1887. *Citation:* Gallantry in action.

TWOMBLY, VOLTAIRE P.

Rank and organization: Corporal, Company F, 2d Iowa Infantry. *Place and date:* At Fort Donelson, Tenn., 15 February 1862. *Entered service at:* Keosauqua, Van Buren County, Iowa. *Birth:* Van Buren County, Iowa. *Date of issue:* 12 March 1897. *Citation:* Took the colors after 3 of the color guard had fallen, and although most instantly knocked down by a spent ball, immediately arose and bore the colors to the end of the engagement.

TYRRELL, GEORGE WILLIAM

Rank and organization: Corporal, Company H, 5th Ohio Infantry. *Place and date:* At Resaca, Ga., 14 May 1864. *Entered service at:* Hamilton County, Ohio. *Birth:* Ireland. *Date of issue:* 7 April 1865. *Citation:* Capture of flag.

UHRL, GEORGE

Rank and organization: Sergeant, Light Battery F, 5th U.S. Artillery. *Place and date:* At White Oak Swamp Bridge, Va., 30 June 1862. *Entered service at:* ———. *Birth:* Germany. *Date of issue:* 4 April 1898. *Citation:* Was 1 of a party of 3 who, under heavy fire of advancing enemy, voluntarily secured and saved from capture a field gun belonging to another battery, and which had been deserted by its officers and men.

URELL, M. EMMET

Rank and organization: Private, Company E, 82d New York Infantry. *Place and date:* At Bristoe Station, Va., 14 October 1863. *Entered service at:* ———. *Birth:* Ireland. *Date of issue:* 6 June 1870. *Citation:* Gallantry in action while detailed as color bearer; was severely wounded.

VALE, JOHN

Rank and organization: Private, Company H, 2d Minnesota Infantry. *Place and date:* At Nolensville, Tenn., 15 February 1863. *Entered service at:* Rochester, Minn. *Birth:* England. *Date of issue:* 11 September 1897. *Citation:* Was one of a detachment of 16 men who heroically defended a wagon train against the attack of 125 cavalry, repulsed the attack and saved the train.

VANCE, WILSON

Rank and organization: Private, Company B, 21st Ohio Infantry. *Place and date:* At Stone River, Tenn., 31 December 1862. *Entered service at:* ———. *Birth:* Hancock County, Ohio. *Date of issue:* 17 September 1897. *Citation:* Voluntarily and under a heavy fire, while his command was falling back, rescued a wounded and helpless comrade from death or capture.

VANDERSLICE, JOHN M.

Rank and organization: Private, Company D, 8th Pennsylvania Cavalry. *Place and date:* At Hatchers Run, Va., 6 February 1865. *Entered service at:* ———. *Birth:* Philadelphia, Pa. *Date of issue:* 1 September 1893. *Citation:* Was the first man to reach the enemy's rifle pits, which were taken in the charge.

VAN MATRE, JOSEPH

Rank and organization: Private, Company G, 116th Ohio Infantry. *Place and date:* At Petersburg, Va., 2 April 1865. *Entered service at:* ———. *Birth:* Mason County, W. Va. *Date of issue:* 12 May 1865. *Citation:* In the assault on Fort Gregg, this soldier climbed upon the parapet and fired down into the fort as fast as the loaded guns could be passed up to him by comrades.

VANTINE, JOSEPH E.

Rank and organization: First Class Fireman, U.S. Navy. *Born:* 1835, Philadelphia, Pa. *Accredited to:* Pennsylvania. *G.O. No.:* 17, 10 July 1863. *Citation:* Serving on board the U.S.S. *Richmond* in the attack on Port Hudson, 14 March 1863. Damaged by a 6-inch solid rifle shot which shattered the starboard safety-valve chamber and also damaged the port safety valve, the fireroom of the *Richmond* immediately filled with steam to place it in an extremely critical condition. Acting courageously in this crisis, Vantine persisted in penetrating the steam-filled room in order to haul the hot fires of the furnaces and continued this action until the gravity of the situation had been lessened.

VAN WINKLE, EDWARD (EDWIN)

Rank and organization: Corporal, Company C, 148th New York Infantry. *Place and date:* At Chapins Farm, Va., 29 September 1864. *Entered service at:* Phelps, N.Y. *Birth:* Phelps, N.Y. *Date of issue:* 6 April 1865. *Citation:* Took position in advance of the skirmish line and drove the enemy's cannoneers from their guns.

VAUGHN, PINKERTON R.

Rank and organization: Sergeant, U.S. Marine Corps. *Born:* 1839, Downingtown, Pa. *Accredited to:* Pennsylvania. *G.O. No.:* 17, 10 July 1863. *Citation:* Serving on board the U.S.S. *Mississippi* during her abandonment and firing in the action with the Port Hudson batteries, 14 March 1863. During the abandonment of the *Mississippi* which had to be grounded, Sgt. Vaughn rendered invaluable assistance to his commanding officer, remaining with the ship until all the crew had landed and the ship had been fired to prevent its falling into enemy hands. Persistent until the last, and conspicuously cool under the heavy shellfire, Sgt. Vaughn was finally ordered to save himself as he saw fit.

VEAL, CHARLES

Rank and organization: Private, Company D, 4th U.S. Colored Troops. *Place and date:* At Chapins Farm, Va., 29 September 1864.

Entered service at: Portsmouth, Va. *Birth:* Portsmouth, Va. *Date of issue:* 6 April 1865. *Citation:* Seized the national colors, after 2 color bearers had been shot down close to the enemy's works, and bore them through the remainder of the battle.

VEALE, MOSES

Rank and organization: Captain, Company F, 109th Pennsylvania Infantry. *Place and date:* At Wauhatchie, Tenn., 28 October 1863. *Entered service at:* Philadelphia, Pa. *Born:* 9 November 1832, Bridgeton, N.J. *Date of issue:* 17 January 1894. *Citation:* Gallantry in action; manifesting throughout the engagement coolness, zeal, judgment, and courage. His horse was shot from under him and he was hit by 4 enemy bullets.

VEAZEY, WHEELOCK G.

Rank and organization: Colonel, 16th Vermont Infantry. *Place and date:* At Gettysburg, Pa., 3 July 1863. *Entered service at:* Springfield, Vt. *Born:* 5 December 1835, Brentwood, N.H. *Date of issue:* 8 September 1891. *Citation:* Rapidly assembled his regiment and charged the enemy's flank; charged front under heavy fire, and charged and destroyed a Confederate brigade, all this with new troops in their first battle.

VERNAY, JAMES D.

Rank and organization: Second Lieutenant, Company B, 11th Illinois Infantry. *Place and date:* At Vicksburg Miss., 22 April 1863. *Entered service at:* Lacon, Marshall County, Ill. *Birth:* Lacon, Ill. *Date of issue:* 1 April 1898. *Citation:* Served gallantly as a volunteer with the crew of the steamer *Horizon* that, under a heavy fire, passed the Confederate batteries.

VERNEY, JAMES W.

Rank and organization: Chief Quartermaster, U.S. Navy. *Born:* 1834, Maine. *Accredited to:* Maine. *G.O. No.:* 59, 22 June 1865. *Citation:* Served as chief quartermaster on board the U.S.S. *Pontoosuc* during the capture of Fort Fisher and Wilmington, 24 December 1864 to 22 February 1865. Carrying out his duties faithfully throughout this period, Verney was recommended for gallantry and skill and for his cool courage while under fire of the enemy throughout these various actions.

VIFQUAIN, VICTOR

Rank and organization: Lieutenant Colonel, 97th Illinois Infantry. *Place and date:* At Fort Blakely, Ala., 9 April 1865. *Entered service at:* Saline County, Nebr. *Birth:* Belgium. *Date of issue:* 8 June 1865. *Citation:* Capture of flag.

VON VEGESACK, ERNEST

Rank and organization: Major and Aide-de-Camp, U.S. Volunteers. *Place and date:* At Gaines Mill, Va., 27 June 1862. *Entered service at:* New York, N.Y. *Birth:* Sweden. *Date of issue:* 23 August 1893. *Citation:* While voluntarily serving as aide-de-camp, successfully and advantageously charged the position of troops under fire.

WAGEMAN, JOHN H.

Rank and organization: Private, Company I, 60th Ohio Infantry. *Place and date:* At Petersburg, Va., 17 June 1864. *Entered service at:* Amelia, Ohio. *Birth:* Clermont County, Ohio. *Date of issue:* 27 July 1896. *Citation:* Remained with the command after being severely wounded until he had fired all the cartridges in his possession, when he had to be carried from the field.

WAGG, MAURICE

Rank and organization: Coxswain, U.S. Navy. *Born:* 1837, England. *Accredited to:* New York. *G.O. No.:* 45, 31 December 1864. *Citation:* Served on board the U.S.S. *Rhode Island*, which was engaged in saving the lives of the officers and crew of the *Monitor* off Hatteras, 31 December 1862. Participating in the hazardous task of rescuing the officers and crew of the sinking *Monitor*, Wagg distinguished himself by meritorious conduct during this operation.

WAGNER, JOHN W.

Rank and organization: Corporal, Company F, 8th Missouri Infantry. *Place and date:* At Vicksburg, Miss., 22 May 1863. *Entered service at:* St. Louis, Mo. *Born:* 1844, Clear Spring, Md. *Date of issue:* 14 December 1894. *Citation:* Gallantry in the charge of the "volunteer storming party."

WAINWRIGHT, JOHN

Rank and organization: First Lieutenant, Company F, 97th Pennsylvania Infantry. *Place and date:* At Fort Fisher, N.C., 15 January 1865. *Entered service at:* West Chester, Pa. *Born:* 13 July 1839, Syracuse, Onondaga County, N.Y. *Date of issue:* 24 June 1890. *Citation:* Gallant and meritorious conduct, where, as first lieutenant, he commanded the regiment.

WALKER, JAMES C.

Rank and organization: Private, Company K, 31st Ohio Infantry. *Place and date:* At Missionary Ridge, Tenn., 25 November 1863. *Entered service at:* Springfield, Ohio. *Birth:* Clark County, Ohio. *Date of issue:* 25 November 1895. *Citation:* After 2 color bearers had fallen, seized the flag and carried it forward, assisting in the capture of a battery. Shortly thereafter he captured the flag of the 41st Alabama and the color bearer.

WALL, JERRY

Rank and organization: Private, Company B, 126th New York Infantry. *Place and date:* At Gettysburg, Pa., 3 July 1863. *Entered service at:* Milo, N.Y. *Birth:* Geneva, N.Y. *Date of issue:* 1 December 1864. *Citation:* Capture of flag.

WALLER, FRANCIS A.

Rank and organization: Corporal, Company I, 6th Wisconsin Infantry. *Place and date:* At Gettysburg, Pa., 1 July 1863. *Entered service at:* DeSoto, Vernon County, Wis. *Birth:* Gurney, Ohio. *Date of issue:* 1

December 1864. *Citation:* Capture of flag of 2d Mississippi Infantry (C.S.A.).

WALLING, WILLIAM H.

Rank and organization: Captain, Company C, 142d New York Infantry. *Place and date:* At Fort Fisher, N.C., 25 December 1864. *Entered service at:* ———. *Birth:* Hartford, N.Y. *Date of issue:* 28 March 1892. *Citation:* During the bombardment of the fort by the fleet, captured and brought the flag of the fort, the flagstaff having been shot down.

WALSH, JOHN

Rank and organization: Corporal, Company D, 5th New York Cavalry. *Place and date:* At Cedar Creek, Va., 19 October 1864. *Entered service at:* ———. *Birth:* Ireland. *Date of issue:* 26 October 1864. *Citation:* Recaptured the flag of the 15th New Jersey Infantry.

WALTON, GEORGE W.

Rank and organization: Private, Company C, 97th Pennsylvania Infantry. *Place and date:* At Fort Hell, Petersburg, Va., 29 August 1864. *Entered service at:* Upper Oxford, Pa. *Birth:* Chester, Pa. *Date of issue:* 6 August 1902. *Citation:* Went outside the trenches, under heavy fire at short range, and rescued a comrade who had been wounded and thrown out of the trench by an exploding shell.

WAMBSGAN, MARTIN

Rank and organization: Private, Company D, 90th New York Infantry. *Place and date:* At Cedar Creek, Va., 19 October 1864. *Entered service at:* Cayuga County, N.Y. *Birth:* Germany. *Date of issue:* 3 November 1896. *Citation:* While the enemy were in close proximity, this soldier sprang forward and bore off in safety the regimental colors, the color bearer having fallen on the field of battle.

WARD, JAMES

Rank and organization: Quarter Gunner, U.S. Navy. *Born:* 1833, New York, N.Y. *Accredited to:* New York. *G.O. No.:* 45, 31 December 1864. *Citation:* Serving as gunner on board the U.S.S. *Lackawanna* during successful attacks against Fort Morgan, rebel gunboats and the ram *Tennessee* in Mobile Bay, 5 August 1864. Although wounded and ordered below, Ward refused to go, but rendered aid at one of the guns when the crew was disabled. He subsequently remained in the chains, heaving the lead, until nearly caught in the collision with the ram *Tennessee*. He continued to serve bravely throughout the action which resulted in the capture of the prize ram *Tennessee* and in the damaging and destruction of Fort Morgan.

WARD, NELSON W.

Rank and organization: Private, Company M, 11th Pennsylvania Cavalry. *Place and date:* At Staunton River Bridge, Va., 25 June 1864. *Entered service at:* ———. *Birth:* Columbiana County, Ohio. *Date of issue:* 10 September 1897. *Citation:* Voluntarily took part in a charge; went alone in front of his regiment under a heavy fire to secure the body of his captain, who had been killed in the action.

WARD, THOMAS J.

Rank and organization: Private, Company C, 116th Illinois Infantry. *Place and date:* At Vicksburg, Miss., 22 May 1863. *Entered service at:* Macon County, Ill. *Birth:* Romney, W. Va. *Date of issue:* 27 July 1894. *Citation:* Gallantry in the charge of the "volunteer storming party."

WARD, WILLIAM H.

Rank and organization: Captain, Company B, 47th Ohio Infantry. *Place and date:* At Vicksburg, Miss., 3 May 1863. *Entered service at:* Adrian, Mich. *Born:* 9 December 1840, Adrian, Mich. *Date of issue:* 2 January 1895. *Citation:* Voluntarily commanded the expedition which, under cover of darkness, attempted to run the enemy's batteries.

WARDEN, JOHN

Rank and organization: Corporal, Company E, 55th Illinois Infantry. *Place and date:* At Vicksburg, Miss., 22 May 1863. *Entered service at:* Lemont, Ill. *Birth:* Cook County, Ill. *Date of issue:* 2 September 1893. *Citation:* Gallantry in the charge of the "volunteer storming party."

WARFEL, HENRY C.

Rank and organization: Private, Company A, 1st Pennsylvania Cavalry. *Place and date:* At Paines Crossroads, Va., 5 April 1865. *Entered service at:* ———. *Birth:* Huntington, Pa. *Date of issue:* 3 May 1865. *Citation:* Capture of Virginia State colors.

WARREN, DAVID

Rank and organization: Coxswain, U.S. Navy. *Born:* 1836, Scotland. *Accredited to:* New York. *G.O. No.:* 45, 31 December 1864. *Citation:* Served as coxswain on board the U.S.S. *Monticello* during the reconnaissance of the harbor and water defenses of Wilmington, N.C., 23 to 25 June 1864. Taking part in a reconnaissance of enemy defenses which lasted 2 days and nights, Warren courageously carried out his duties during this action which resulted in the capture of a mail carrier and mail, the cutting of a telegraph wire, and the capture of a large group of prisoners. Although in immediate danger from the enemy, Warren showed gallantry and coolness throughout this action which resulted in the gaining of much vital information of the rebel defenses.

WARREN, FRANCIS E.

Rank and organization: Corporal, Company C, 49th Massachusetts Infantry. *Place and date:* At Port Hudson, La., 27 May 1863. *Entered service at:* Hinsdale, Mass. *Birth:* Hinsdale, Mass. *Date of issue:* 30 September 1893. *Citation:* Volunteered in response to a call, and took part in the movement that was made upon the enemy's works under a heavy fire therefrom in advance of the general assault.

WEBB, ALEXANDER S.

Rank and organization: Brigadier General, U.S. Volunteers. *Place and date:* At Gettysburg, Pa., 3 July 1863. *Entered service at:* New York, N.Y. *Born:* 15 February 1835, New York, N.Y. *Date of issue:* 28 September 1891. *Citation:* Distinguished personal gallantry in leading his men forward at a critical period in the contest.

WEBB, JAMES

Rank and organization: Private, Company F, 5th New York Infantry. *Place and date:* At Bull Run, Va., 30 August 1862. *Entered service at:* ———. *Birth:* Brooklyn, N.Y. *Date of issue:* 17 September 1897. *Citation:* Under heavy fire voluntarily carried information to a battery commander that enabled him to save his guns from capture. Was severely wounded, but refused to go to the hospital and participated in the remainder of the campaign.

WEBBER, ALASON P.

Rank and organization: Musician, 86th Illinois Infantry. *Place and date:* At Kenesaw Mountain, Ga., 27 June 1864. *Entered service at:* Illinois. *Birth:* Greene County, N.Y. *Date of issue:* 22 June 1896. *Citation:* Voluntarily joined in a charge against the enemy, which was repulsed, and by his rapid firing in the face of the enemy enabled many of the wounded to return to the Federal lines; with others, held the advance of the enemy while temporary works were being constructed.

WEBSTER, HENRY S.

Rank and organization: Landsman, U.S. Navy. *Born:* 1845, Stockholm, N.Y. *Accredited to:* New York. *G.O. No.:* 49, 22 June 1865. *Citation:* On board the U.S.S. *Susquehanna* during the assault on Fort Fisher, 15 January 1865. When enemy fire halted the attempt by his landing party to enter the fort and more than two-thirds of the men fell back along the open beach, Webster voluntarily remained with one of his wounded officers, under fire, until aid could be obtained to bring him to the rear.

WEEKS, CHARLES H.

Rank and organization: Captain of the Foretop, U.S. Navy. *Born:* 1837, New Jersey. *Accredited to:* New Jersey. *G.O. No.:* 84, 3 October 1867. *Citation:* Served as captain of the foretop on board the U.S.S. *Montauk,* 21 September 1864. During the night of 21 September, when fire was discovered in the magazine lightroom of that vessel, causing a panic and demoralizing the crew, Weeks, notwithstanding the cry of "fire in the magazine," displayed great presence of mind and rendered valuable service in extinguishing the flames which were imperiling the ship and the men on board.

WEEKS, JOHN H.

Rank and organization: Private, Company H, 152d New York Infantry. *Place and date:* At Spotsylvania, Va., 12 May 1864. *Entered service at:* Hartwick Seminary, N.Y. *Born:* 15 March 1845, Hampton, Conn. *Date of issue:* 1 December 1864. *Citation:* Capture of flag and color bearer using an empty cocked rifle while outnumbered 5 or 6.

WEIR, HENRY C.

Rank and organization: Captain and Assistant Adjutant General, U.S. Volunteers. *Place and date:* At St. Mary's Church, Va., 24 June 1864. *Entered service at:* ———. *Birth:* West Point, N.Y. *Date of issue:* 18

May 1899. *Citation:* The division being hard pressed and falling back, this officer dismounted, gave his horse to a wounded officer, and thus enabled him to escape. Afterwards, on foot, Captain Weir rallied and took command of some stragglers and helped to repel the last charge of the enemy.

WELCH, GEORGE W.

Rank and organization: Private, Company A, 11th Missouri Infantry. *Place and date:* At Nashville, Tenn., 16 December 1864. *Entered service at:* Keokuk, Lee County, Iowa. *Birth:* Brown County, Iowa. *Date of issue:* 24 February 1965. *Citation:* Captured the flag of the 13th Alabama Infantry (C.S.A.).

WELCH, RICHARD

Rank and organization: Corporal, Company E, 37th Massachusetts Infantry. *Place and date:* At Petersburg, Va., 2 April 1865. *Entered service at:* Williamstown, Mass. *Birth:* Ireland. *Date of issue:* 10 May 1865. *Citation:* Capture of flag.

WELCH, STEPHEN

Rank and organization: Sergeant, Company C, 154th New York Infantry. *Place and date:* At Dug Gap, Ga., 8 May 1864. *Entered service at:* Allegany, Cattaraugus County, N.Y. *Birth:* Groton, N.Y. *Date of issue:* 13 April 1894. *Citation:* Risked his life in rescuing a wounded comrade under fire of the enemy.

*WELLS, HENRY S.

Rank and organization: Private, Company C, 148th New York Infantry. *Place and date:* At Chapins Farm, Va., 29 September 1864. *Entered service at:* Phelps, N.Y. *Birth:* ———. *Date of issue:* 6 April 1865. *Citation:* With 2 comrades, took position in advance of the skirmish line, within short distance of the enemy's gunners, and drove them from their guns.

WELLS, THOMAS M.

Rank and organization: Chief Bugler, 6th New York Cavalry. *Place and date:* At Cedar Creek, Va., 19 October 1864. *Entered service at:* DeKalb, N.Y. *Birth:* Ireland. *Date of issue:* 26 October 1864. *Citation:* Capture of colors of 44th Georgia Infantry (C.S.A.).

WELLS, WILLIAM

Rank and organization: Major, 1st Vermont Cavalry. *Place and date:* At Gettysburg, Pa., 3 July 1863. *Entered service at:* Waterbury, Vt. *Born:* 14 December 1837, Waterbury, Vt. *Date of issue:* 8 September 1891. *Citation:* Led the second battalion of his regiment in a daring charge.

WELLS, WILLIAM

Rank and organization: Quartermaster, U.S. Navy. *Born:* 1832, Germany. *Accredited to:* New York. *G.O. No.:* 45, 31 December 1864. *Citation:* As landsman and lookout on board the U.S.S. *Richmond* during action against rebel forts and gunboats and with the ram *Tennessee* in Mobile Bay, 5 August 1864. Despite damage to his ship the loss of several men on board as enemy fire raked her decks, Wells performed his duties with skill and courage throughout a furious 2-hour battle which resulted in the surrender of the rebel ram *Tennessee* and in the damaging and destruction of batteries at Fort Morgan.

WELSH, EDWARD

Rank and organization: Private, Company D, 54th Ohio Infantry. *Place and date:* At Vicksburg, Miss., 22 May 1863. *Entered service at:* Cincinnati, Ohio. *Birth:* Ireland. *Date of issue:* 11 May 1894. *Citation:* Gallantry in the charge of the "volunteer storming party."

WELSH, JAMES

Rank and organization: Private, Company E, 4th Rhode Island Infantry. *Place and date:* At Petersburg, Va., 30 July 1864. *Entered service at:* Slatersville, R.I. *Birth:* Ireland. *Date of issue:* 3 June 1905. *Citation:* Bore off the regimental colors after the color sergeant had been wounded and the color corporal bearing the colors killed, thereby saving the colors from capture.

WESTERHOLD, WILLIAM

Rank and organization: Sergeant, Company G, 52d New York Infantry. *Place and date:* At Spotsylvania, Va., 12 May 1864. *Entered service at:* ———. *Birth:* Prussia. *Date of issue:* 1 December 1864. *Citation:* Capture of flag of 23d Virginia Infantry (C.S.A.).

WESTON, JOHN F.

Rank and organization: Major, 4th Kentucky Cavalry. *Place and date:* Near Wetumpka, Ala., 13 April 1865. *Entered service at:* Kentucky. *Birth:* Kentucky. *Date of issue:* 9 April 1898. *Citation:* This officer, with a small detachment, while en route to destroy steamboats loaded with supplies for the enemy, was stopped by an unfordable river, but with 5 of his men swam the river, captured 2 leaky canoes, and ferried his men across. He then encountered and defeated the enemy, and on reaching Wetumpka found the steamers anchored in midstream. By a ruse obtained possession of a boat, with which he reached the steamers and demanded and received their surrender.

WHEATON, LOYD

Rank and organization: Lieutenant Colonel, 8th Illinois Infantry. *Place and date:* At Fort Blakely, Ala., 9 April 1865. *Entered service at:* Illinois. *Born:* 15 July 1838, Calhoun County, Mich. *Date of issue:* 16 January 1894. *Citation:* Led the right wing of his regiment, and, springing through an embrasure, was the first to enter the enemy's works, against a strong fire of artillery and infantry.

WHEELER, DANIEL D.

Rank and organization: First Lieutenant, Company G, 4th Vermont Infantry. *Place and date:* At Salem Heights, Va., 3 May 1863. *Entered service at:* Cavendish, Vt. *Birth:* Cavendish, Vt. *Date of issue:* 28 March 1892. *Citation:* Distinguished bravery in action where he was wounded and had a horse shot from under him.

WHEELER, HENRY W.

Rank and organization: Private, Company A, 2d Maine Infantry. *Place and date:* At Bull Run, Va., 21 July 1861. *Entered service at:* Bangor, Maine. *Born:* 1842, Fort Smith, Ark. *Date of issue:* 5 April 1898. *Citation:* Voluntarily accompanied his commanding officer and assisted in removing the dead and wounded from the field under a heavy fire of artillery and musketry.

WHERRY, WILLIAM M.

Rank and organization: First Lieutenant, Company D, 3d U.S. Reserve Missouri Infantry. *Place and date:* At Wilsons Creek, Mo., 10 August 1861. *Entered service at:* St. Louis, Mo. *Born:* 13 September 1836, St. Louis, Mo. *Date of issue:* 30 October 1895. *Citation:* Displayed conspicuous coolness and heroism in rallying troops that were recoiling under heavy fire.

WHITAKER, EDWARD W.

Rank and organization: Captain, Company E, 1st Connecticut Cavalry. *Place and date:* At Reams Station, Va., 29 June 1864. *Entered service at:* Ashford, Conn. *Born:* 15 June 1841, Killingly, Conn. *Date of issue:* 2 April 1898. *Citation:* While acting as an aide voluntarily carried dispatches from the commanding general to Gen. Meade, forcing his way with a single troop of Cavalry, through an Infantry division of the enemy in the most distinguished manner, though he lost half his escort.

WHITE, ADAM

Rank and organization: Corporal, Company G, 11th West Virginia Infantry. *Place and date:* At Hatchers Run, Va., 2 April 1865. *Entered service at:* Parkersburg, W. Va. *Birth:* Switzerland. *Date of issue:* 13 June 1865. *Citation:* Capture of flag.

WHITE, J. HENRY

Rank and organization: Private, Company A, 90th Pennsylvania Infantry. *Place and date:* At Rappanhannock Station, Va., 23 August 1862. *Entered service at:* ———. *Birth:* Philadelphia, Pa. *Date of issue:* 5 May 1900. *Citation:* At the imminent risk of his life, crawled to a nearby spring within the enemy's range and exposed to constant fire filled a large number of canteens, and returned in safety to the relief of his comrades who were suffering from want of water.

WHITE, JOSEPH

Rank and organization: Captain of the Gun, U.S. Navy. *Born:* 1840, Washington, D.C. *Accredited to:* Pennsylvania. *G.O. No.:* 59, 22 June 1865. *Citation:* White served on board the U.S.S. *New Ironsides* during action in several attacks on Fort Fisher, 24 and 25 December 1864; and 13,14, and 15 January 1865. The ship steamed in and took the lead in the ironclad division close inshore and immediately opened its starboard battery in a barrage of well-directed fire to cause several fires and explosions and dismount several guns during the first 2 days of fighting. Taken under fire as she steamed into position on 13 January, the *New Ironsides* fought all day and took on ammunition at night despite severe weather conditions. When the enemy came out of his bombproofs to defend the fort against the storming party, the ships battery disabled nearly every gun on the fort facing the shore before the ceasefire order was given by the flagship.

WHITE, PATRICK H.

Rank and organization: Captain, Chicago Mercantile Battery, Illinois Light Artillery. *Place and date:* At Vicksburg, Miss., 22 May 1863. *Entered service at:* Chicago, Ill. *Born:* 1833, Ireland. *Date of issue:* 15 January 1895. *Citation:* Carried with others by hand a cannon up to and fired it through an embrasure of the enemy's works.

WHITEHEAD, JOHN M.

Rank and organization: Chaplain, 15th Indiana Infantry. *Place and date:* At Stone River, Tenn., 31 December 1862. *Entered service at:* Westville, Ind. *Born:* 6 March 1823, Wayne County, Ind. *Date of issue:* 4 April 1898. *Citation:* Went to the front during a desperate contest and unaided carried to the rear several wounded and helpless soldiers.

WHITFIELD, DANIEL

Rank and organization: Quartermaster, U.S. Navy. *Born:* 1821, Newark, N.J. *Accredited to:* New Jersey. *G.O. No.:* 45, 31 December 1864. *Citation:* Serving as quartermaster on board the U.S.S. *Lackawanna* during successful attacks against Fort Morgan, rebel gunboats and the rebel ram *Tennessee* in Mobile Bay, 5 August 1864. Acting as captain of a gun, Whitfield coolly stood by his gun, holding on to the lock string and waited alongside the rebel ram *Tennessee* until able to fire the shot that entered her port. Whitfield courageously carried out his duties during the prolonged action which resulted in the capture of the prize ram *Tennessee* and in the damaging and destruction of Fort Morgan.

WHITMAN, FRANK M.

Rank and organization: Private, Company G, 35th Massachusetts Infantry. *Place and date:* At Antietam, Md., 17 September 1862. At Spotsylvania, Va., 18 May 1864. *Entered service at:* Ayersville, Mass. *Birth:* Woodstock, Maine. *Date of issue:* 21 February 1874. *Citation:* Was among the last to leave the field at Antietam and was instrumental in saving the lives of several of his comrades at the imminent risk of his own. At Spotsylvania was foremost in line in the assault, where he lost a leg.

WHITMORE, JOHN

Rank and organization: Private, Company F, 119th Illinois Infantry. *Place and date:* At Ft. Blakely, Ala., 9 April 1865. *Entered service at:* Camden, Schuyler County, Ill. *Birth:* Brown County, Ill. *Date of issue:* 8 June 1865. *Citation:* Capture of flag.

WHITNEY, WILLIAM G.

Rank and organization: Sergeant, Company B, 11th Michigan Infantry. *Place and date:* At Chickamauga, Ga., 20 September 1863. *En-*

tered service at: Quincy, Mich. *Born:* 13 December 1840, Allen, Mich. *Date of issue:* 21 October 1895. *Citation:* As the enemy were about to charge, this officer went outside the temporary Union works among the dead and wounded enemy and at great exposure to himself cut off and removed their cartridge boxes, bringing the same within the Union lines, the ammunition being used with good effect in again repulsing the attack.

WHITTIER, EDWARD N.

Rank and organization: First Lieutenant, 5th Battery, Maine Light Artillery. *Place and date:* At Fishers Hill, Va., 22 September 1864. *Entered service at:* Gorham, Maine. *Birth:* Portland, Maine. *Date of issue:* 13 January 1892. *Citation:* While acting as assistant adjutant general, Artillery brigade, 6th Army Corps, went over the enemy's works, mounted, with the assaulting column, to gain quicker possession of the guns and to turn them upon the enemy.

WIDICK, ANDREW J.

Rank and organization: Private, Company B, 116th Illinois Infantry. *Place and date:* At Vicksburg, Miss., 22 May 1863. *Entered service at:* Decatur, Macon County, Ill. *Birth:* Macon County, Ill. *Date of issue:* 11 August 1894. *Citation:* Gallantry in the charge of the "volunteer storming party."

WILCOX, FRANKLIN L.

Rank and organization: Ordinary Seaman, U.S. Navy. *Born:* 1831, Paris, N.Y. *Accredited to:* New York. *G.O. No.:* 59, 22 June 1865. *Citation:* On board the U.S.S. *Minnesota* in action during the assault on Fort Fisher, 15 January 1865. Landing on the beach with the assaulting party from his ship, Wilcox advanced to the top of the sandhill and partly through the breach in the palisades despite enemy fire which killed and wounded many officers and men. When more than two-thirds of the men became seized with panic and retreated on the run, he remained with the party until dark when it came safely away, bringing its wounded, its arms and its colors.

WILCOX, WILLIAM H.

Rank and organization: Sergeant, Company G, 9th New Hampshire Infantry. *Place and date:* At Spotsylvania, Va., 12 May 1864. *Entered service at:* Lempster, N.H. *Birth:* Lempster, N.H. *Date of issue:* 28 July 1896. *Citation:* Took command of his company, deployed as skirmishers, after the officers in command of the skirmish line had both been wounded, conducting himself gallantly; afterwards, becoming separated from command, he asked and obtained permission to fight in another company.

WILEY, JAMES

Rank and organization: Sergeant, Company B, 59th New York Infantry. *Place and date:* At Gettysburg, Pa., 3 July 1863. *Entered service at:* ———. *Birth:* Ohio. *Date of issue:* 1 December 1864. *Citation:* Capture of flag of a Georgia regiment.

WILHELM, GEORGE

Rank and organization: Captain, Company F, 56th Ohio Infantry. *Place and date:* At Champion Hill, or Bakers Creek, Miss., 16 May 1863. *Entered service at:* Lancaster, Ohio. *Born:* 2 April 1830, Scioto County, Ohio. *Date of issue:* 17 November 1887. *Citation:* Having been badly wounded in the breast and captured, he made a prisoner of his captor and brought him into camp.

WILKES, HENRY

Rank and organization: Landsman, U.S. Navy. *Born:* 1845, New York, N.Y. *Accredited to:* New York. *G.O. No.:* 45, 31 December 1864. *Citation:* Wilkes served on board U.S. Picket Boat No. 1 in action, 27 October 1864, against the Confederate Ram, *Albemarle*, which had resisted repeated attacks by our steamers and had kept a large force of vessels employed in watching her. The picket boat, equipped with a spar torpedo, succeeded in passing the enemy pickets within 20 yards without being discovered and them made for the *Albemarle* under a full head of steam. Immediately taken under fire by the ram, the small boat plunged on, jumped the log boom which encircled the target and exploded its torpedo under the port bow of the ram. The picket boat was destroyed by enemy fire and almost the entire crew taken prisoner or lost.

WILKES, PERRY

Rank and organization: Pilot, U.S. Navy. *Entered service at:* Indiana. *Born:* 6 June 1830, Indiana. *G.O. No.:* 45, 31 December 1864. *Citation:* Served as pilot on board the U.S.S. *Signal*, Red River, 5 May 1864. Proceeding up the Red River, the U.S.S. *Signal* engaged a large force of enemy field batteries and sharpshooters, returning their fire until the ship was totally disabled, at which time the white flag was ordered raised. Acting as pilot throughout the battle, Wilkes stood by his wheel until it was disabled in his hands by a bursting enemy shell.

WILKINS, LEANDER A.

Rank and organization: Sergeant, Company H, 9th New Hampshire Infantry. *Place and date:* At Petersburg, Va., 30 July 1864. *Entered service at:* ———. *Birth:* Lancaster, N.H. *Date of issue:* 1 December 1864. *Citation:* Recaptured the colors of 21st Massachusetts Infantry in a hand-to-hand encounter.

WILLCOX, ORLANDO B.

Rank and organization: Colonel, 1st Michigan Infantry. *Place and date:* At Bull Run, Va., 21 July 1861. *Entered service at:* Detroit, Mich. *Birth:* Detroit, Mich. *Date of issue:* 2 March 1895. *Citation:* Led repeated charges until wounded and taken prisoner.

WILLIAMS, ANTHONY

Rank and organization: Sailmaker's Mate, U.S. Navy. *Born:* 1822, Plymouth, Mass. *Accredited to:* Maine. *G.O. No.:* 59, 22 June 1865. *Citation:* Served as sailmaker's mate on board the U.S.S. *Pontoosuc* during the capture of Fort Fisher and Wilmington, 24 December 1864 to 22 February 1865. Carrying out his duties faithfully throughout this period, Williams was recommended for gallantry and skill and for his cool courage while under the fire of the enemy throughout these various actions.

WILLIAMS, AUGUSTUS

Rank and organization: Seaman, U.S. Navy. *Born:* 1842, Norway. *Accredited to:* Massachusetts. *G.O. No:* 59, 22 June 1865. *Citation:* On board the U.S.S. *Santiago de Cuba* during the assault by the fleet on Fort Fisher, on 15 January 1865. When the landing party to which he was attached charged on the fort with a cheer, and with determination to plant their colors on the ramparts, Williams remained steadfast when they reached the foot of the fort and more than two-thirds of the marines and sailors fell back in panic. Taking cover when the enemy concentrated his fire on the remainder of the group, he alone remained with his executive officer, subsequently withdrawing from the field after dark.

WILLIAMS, ELWOOD N.

Rank and organization: Private, Company A, 28th Illinois Infantry. *Place and date:* At Shiloh, Tenn., 6 April 1862. *Entered service at:* Havanna, Ill. *Birth:* Philadelphia, Pa. *Date of issue:* 28 September 1897. *Citation:* A box of ammunition having been abandoned between the lines, this soldier voluntarily went forward with one companion, under a heavy fire from both armies, secured the box, and delivered it within the line of his regiment, his companion being mortally wounded.

WILLIAMS, GEORGE C.

Rank and organization: Quartermaster Sergeant, 1st Battalion, 14th U.S. Infantry. *Place and date:* At Gaines Mill, Va., 27 June 1862. *Entered service at:* ———. *Birth:* England. *Date of issue:* 28 August 1897. *Citation:* While on duty with the wagon train as quartermaster sergeant he voluntarily left his place of safety in the rear, joined a company, and fought with distinguished gallantry through the action.

WILLIAMS, JOHN

Rank and organization: Boatswain's Mate, U.S. Navy. *Entered service at:* New York, N.Y. *Birth:* Elizabethtown, N.J. *G.O. No:* 17, 10 July 1863. *Citation:* Captain of an 11-inch gun aboard the U.S.S. *Mohican* during action of the main squadron of ships against the heavily defended Forts Beauregard and Walker on Hilton Head, and against ships of the Confederate Fleet, 7 November 1861. Cool and courageous at his battle station, Williams maintained steady fire against the enemy while under the fort batteries during a 4-hour engagement which resulted in silencing the batteries of the forts and in the rout of the rebel steamers.

WILLIAMS, JOHN

Rank and organization: Captain of the Maintop, U.S. Navy. *Born:* 1828, New Orleans, La. *Accredited to:* Louisiana. *G.O. No.:* 11, 3 April 1863. *Citation:* Serving as captain of the maintop of the U.S.S. *Pawnee* in the attack upon Mathias Point, 26 June 1861, Williams told his men, while lying off in the boat, that every man must die on his thwart sooner than leave a man behind. Although wounded by a musket ball in the thigh he retained the charge of his boat; and when the staff was shot away, held the stump in his hand, with the flag, until alongside the *Freeborn*.

WILLIAMS, JOHN

Rank and organization: Seaman, U.S. Navy. *Born:* 1832, Pennsylvania. *Accredited to:* Pennsylvania. *G.O. No.:* 11, 3 April 1863. *Citation:* On board the U.S.S. *Commodore Perry* in the attack upon Franklin, Va., 3 October 1862. With enemy fire raking the deck of his ship and blockades thwarting her progress, Williams remained at his post and performed his duties with skill and courage as the *Commodore Perry* fought a gallant battle to silence many rebel batteries as she steamed down the Blackwater River.

WILLIAMS, LE ROY

Rank and organization: Sergeant, Company G, 8th New York Heavy Artillery. *Place and date:* At Cold Harbor, Va., 3 June 1864. *Entered service at:* ———. *Birth:* Oswego, N.Y. *Date of issue:* 1 April 1898. *Citation:* Voluntarily exposed himself to the fire of the enemy's sharpshooters and located the body of his colonel who had been killed close to the enemy's lines. Under cover of darkness, with 4 companions, he recovered the body and brought it within the Union lines, having approached within a few feet of the Confederate pickets while so engaged.

WILLIAMS, PETER

Rank and organization: Seaman, U.S. Navy. *Born:* 1831, Norway, *Accredited to:* Pennsylvania. *G.O. No.:* 11, 3 April 1863. *Citation:* Serving on board the U.S.S. Ironclad Steamer *Monitor*, Hampton Roads, 9 March 1862. During the engagement between the U.S.S. *Monitor* and the C.S.S. *Merrimack*, Williams gallantly served throughout the engagement as quartermaster, piloting the *Monitor* throughout the battle in which the *Merrimack*, after being damaged, retired from the scene of the battle.

WILLIAMS, ROBERT

Rank and organization: Signal Quartermaster, U.S. Navy. *Born:* 1837, New York, N.Y. *Accredited to:* New York. *G.O. No.:* 11, 3 April 1863. *Citation:* Serving as quartermaster on board the U.S.S. *Benton* during the Yazoo River Expedition, 23 to 27 December 1862. Taking part in the hour-and-a-half engagement with the enemy at Drumgould's Bluff, 27 December, Williams served courageously throughout that battle against hostile forces in which the enemy had the dead range of the vessel and were punishing her with heavy fire and, for various other action in which he took part during the Yazoo River Expedition.

WILLIAMS, WILLIAM

Rank and organization: Landsman, U.S. Navy. *Born:* 1840, Ireland. *Accredited to:* Pennsylvania. *G.O. No.:* 32, 16 April 1864. *Citation:* On board the U.S.S. *Lehigh*, Charleston Harbor, 16 November 1863, during the hazardous task of freeing the *Lehigh*, which had been grounded, and was under heavy enemy fire from Fort Moultrie. After several previous attempts had been made, Williams succeeded in passing in a small boat from the *Lehigh* to the *Nahant* with a line bent on a hawser. This courageous action while under severe enemy fire enabled the *Lehigh* to be freed from her helpless position.

WILLIAMS, WILLIAM H.

Rank and organization: Private, Company C, 82d Ohio Infantry. *Place and date:* At Peach Tree Creek, Ga., 20 July 1864. *Entered service at:* Miami County, Ohio. *Birth:* Hancock County, Ohio. *Date of issue:* 19 June 1894. *Citation:* Voluntarily went beyond the lines to observe the enemy; also aided a wounded comrade.

WILLIAMSON, JAMES A.

Rank and organization: Colonel, 4th Iowa Infantry. *Place and date:* At Chickasaw Bayou, Miss., 29 December 1862. *Entered service at:* Des Moines, Iowa. *Born:* 8 February 1829, Columbia, Adair County, Ky. *Date of issue:* 17 January 1895. *Citation:* Led his regiment against a superior force, strongly entrenched, and held his ground when all support had been withdrawn.

WILLIS, RICHARD

Rank and organization: Coxswain, U.S. Navy. *Born:* 1826, England. *Accredited to:* Pennsylvania. *G.O. No.:* 59, 22 June 1865. *Citation:* Willis served on board the U.S.S. *New Ironsides* during action in several attacks on Fort Fisher, 24 and 25 December 1864; and 13, 14 and 15 January 1865. The ship steamed in and took the lead in the ironclad division close inshore and immediately opened its starboard battery in a barrage of well-directed fire to cause several fires and explosions and dismount several guns during the first 2 days of fighting. Taken under fire as she steamed into position on 13 January, the *New Ironsides* fought all day and took on ammunition at night, despite severe weather conditions. When the enemy troops came out of their bomb-proofs to defend the fort against the storming party, the ship's battery disabled nearly every gun on the fort facing the shore before the ceasefire order was given by the flagship.

WILLISTON, EDWARD B.

Rank and organization: First Lieutenant, 2d U.S. Artillery. *Place and date:* At Trevilian Station, Va., 12 June 1864. *Entered service at:* San Francisco, Calif. *Birth:* Norwich, Vt. *Date of issue:* 6 April 1892. *Citation:* Distinguished gallantry.

WILSON, CHARLES E.

Rank and organization: Sergeant, Company A, 1st New Jersey Cavalry. *Place and date:* At Sailors Creek, Va., 6 April 1865. *Entered service at:* ———. *Birth:* Bucks County, Pa. *Date of issue:* 3 July 1865. *Citation:* Charged the enemy's works, colors in hand, and had 2 horses shot from under him.

WILSON, CHRISTOPHER W.

Rank and organization: Private, Company E, 73d New York Infantry. *Place and date:* At Spotsylvania, Va., 12 May 1864. *Entered service at:* West Meriden, Conn. *Birth:* Ireland. *Date of issue:* 30 December 1898. *Citation:* Took the flag from the wounded color bearer and carried it in the charge over the Confederate works, in which charge he also captured the colors of the 56th Virginia (C.S.A.) bringing off both flags in safety.

WILSON, FRANCIS A.

Rank and organization: Corporal, Company B, 95th Pennsylvania Infantry. *Place and date:* At Petersburg, Va., 2 April 1865. *Entered service at:* Philadelphia Pa. *Birth:* Philadelphia, Pa. *Date of issue:* 25 June 1880. *Citation:* Was among the first to penetrate the enemy's lines and himself captured a gun of the 2 batteries captured.

WILSON, JOHN

Rank and organization: Sergeant, Company L, 1st New Jersey Cavalry. *Place and date:* At Chamberlains Creek, Va., 31 March 1865. *Entered service at:* Jersey City, N.J. *Birth:* England. *Date of issue:* 3 July 1865. *Citation:* With the assistance of one comrade, headed off the advance of the enemy, shooting 2 of his color bearers; also posted himself between the enemy and the lead horses of his own command, thus saving the herd from capture.

WILSON, JOHN A.

Rank and organization: Private, Company C, 21st Ohio Infantry. *Place and date:* Georgia, April 1862. *Entered service at:* Wood County, Ohio. *Born:* 25 July 1832, Columbus, Ohio. *Date of issue:* September 1863. *Citation:* One of the 19 of 22 men (including 2 civilians) who, by direction of Gen. Mitchell (or Buell), penetrated nearly 200 miles south into enemy territory and captured a railroad train at Big Shanty, Ga., and attempted to destroy the bridges and track between Chattanooga and Atlanta.

WILSON, JOHN M.

Rank and organization: First Lieutenant, U.S. Engineers. *Place and date:* At Malvern Hill, Va., 6 August 1862. *Entered service at:* Washington Territory. *Birth:* Olympia, Washington Territory. *Date of issue:* 3 July 1897. *Citation:* Remained on duty, while suffering from an acute illness and very weak, and participated in the action of that date. A few days previous he had been transferred to a staff corps, but preferred to remain until the close of the campaign, taking part in several actions.

WINEGAR, WILLIAM W.

Rank and organization: Lieutenant, Company B, 19th New York Cavalry (1st New York Dragoons). *Place and date:* At Five Forks, Va., 1 April 1865. *Entered service at:* ———. *Birth:* Springport, N.Y. *Date of issue:* 3 May 1865. *Citation:* While advancing in front of his company and alone, he found himself surrounded by the enemy. He accosted a nearby enemy flag-bearer demanding the surrender of the group. His effective firing of one shot so demoralized the unit that it surrendered with flag.

WISNER, LEWIS S.

Rank and organization: First Lieutenant, Company K. 124th New York Infantry. *Place and date:* At Spotsylvania, Va., 12 May 1864. *Entered service at:* Wallkill, Orange County, N.Y. *Birth:* Wallkill, Orange County, N.Y. *Date of issue:* 2 January 1895. *Citation:* While serving as an engineer officer voluntarily exposed himself to the enemy's fire.

WITHINGTON, WILLIAM H.

Rank and organization: Captain, Company B, 1st Michigan Infantry. *Place and date:* At Bull Run, Va., 21 July 1861. *Entered service at:* Jackson, Mich. *Born:* 1 February 1835, Dorchester, Mass. *Date of issue:* 7 January 1895. *Citation:* Remained on the field under heavy fire to succor his superior officer.

WOLLAM, JOHN

Rank and organization: Private, Company C, 33d Ohio Infantry. *Place and date:* Georgia, April 1862. *Entered service at:* Jackson, Jackson County, Ohio. *Birth:* Hamilton, Ohio. *Date of issue:* 20 July 1864. *Citation:* One of the 19 of 22 men (including 2 civilians), who, by direction of Gen. Mitchell (or Buell), penetrated nearly 200 miles south into enemy territory and captured a railroad train at Big Shanty, Ga., and attempted to destroy the bridges and track between Chattanooga and Atlanta.

WOOD, H. CLAY

Rank and organization: First Lieutenant, 11th U.S. Infantry. *Place and date:* At Wilsons Creek, Mo., 10 August 1861. *Entered service at:* Winthrop, Maine. *Birth:* Winthrop, Maine. *Date of issue:* 28 October 1893. *Citation:* Distinguished gallantry.

WOOD, MARK

Rank and organization: Private, Company C, 21st Ohio Infantry. *Place and date:* Georgia, April 1862. *Entered service at:* Portage, Ohio. *Birth:* England. *Date of issue:* September 1863. *Citation:* One of the 19 of 22 men (including 2 civilians), who, by direction of Gen. Mitchell (or Buell), penetrated nearly 200 miles south into enemy territory and captured a railroad train at Big Shanty, Ga., and attempted to destroy the bridges and track between Chattanooga and Atlanta.

WOOD, RICHARD H.

Rank and organization: Captain, Company A, 97th Illinois Infantry. *Place and date:* At Vicksburg, Miss., 22 May 1863. *Entered service at:* Woodburn, Macoupin County, Ill. *Birth:* Cumberland, N.J. *Date of issue:* 12 December 1895. *Citation:* Led the "volunteer storming party," which made a most gallant assault upon the enemy's works.

5. WOOD, ROBERT B.

Rank and organization: Coxswain, U.S. Navy. *Born:* New Garden, Ohio. *Accredited to:* Ohio. *G.O. No.:* 17, 10 July 1863. *Citation:* Attached to the U.S.S. *Minnesota* and temporarily serving on the U.S.S. *Mount Washington,* during action against the enemy in the Nansemond River, 14 April 1863. When the U.S.S. *Mount Washington* drifted against the bank and all men were driven from the decks by escaping steam following several successive hits which struck her boilers and stopped her engines, Wood boarded the stricken vessel and, despite a strike on the head by a spent ball, continued at his gun for 6 hours as fierce artillery and musketry continued to rake her decks.

WOODBURY, ERI D.

Rank and organization: Sergeant, Company E, 1st Vermont Calvary. *Place and date:* At Cedar Creek, Va., 19 October 1864. *Entered service at:* St. Johnsbury, Vt. *Birth:* Francistown, N.H. *Date of issue:* 26 October 1864. *Citation:* During the regiment's charge when the enemy was in retreat Sgt. Woodbury encountered 4 Confederate infantrymen retreating. He drew his saber and ordered them to surrender, overcoming by his determined actions their willingness to further resist. They surrendered to him together with their rifles and 12th North Carolina (C.S.A.) regimental flag.

WOODRUFF, ALONZO

Rank and organization: Sergeant, Company I, 1st U.S. Sharpshooters. *Place and date:* At Hatchers Run, Va., 27 October 1864. *Entered service at:* Ionia Mich. *Birth:* Ionia, Mich. *Date of issue:* 29 January 1896. *Citation:* Went to the assistance of a wounded and overpowered comrade, and in a hand-to-hand encounter effected his rescue.

WOODRUFF, CARLE A.

Rank and organization: First Lieutenant, 2d U.S. Artillery. *Place and date:* At Newbys Crossroads, Va., 24 July 1863. *Entered service at:* Washington, D.C. *Born:* Buffalo, N.Y. *Date of issue:* 1 September 1893. *Citation:* While in command of a section of a battery constituting a portion of the rear guard of a division then retiring before the advance of a corps of Infantry was attacked by the enemy and ordered to abandon his guns. Lt. Woodruff disregarded the orders received and aided in repelling the attack and saving the guns.

WOODS, DANIEL A.

Rank and organization: Private, Company K, 1st Virginia Calvary. *Place and date:* At Sailors Creek, Va., 6 April 1865. *Entered service at:* ———. *Birth:* Ohio County, W. Va. *Date of issue:* 3 May 1865. *Citation:* Capture of flag of 18th Florida Infantry (C.S.A.).

WOODS, SAMUEL

Rank and organization: Seaman, U.S. Navy. *Born:* 1835, California. *Accredited to:* California. *G.O. No.:* 17, 10 July 1863. *Citaiton:* As captain of the gun, serving temporarily on board the U.S.S. *Mount Washington,* during the Nansemond River action, 14 April 1863. When one of his comrades was struck by a bullet and knocked overboard, Woods fearlessly jumped into the water and swam after him. Before he reached him, the man sank beneath the surface and Woods promptly swam back to the vessel, went to his gun, and fought it to the close of the action. At the close of the battle, he tirelessly cared for the wounded.

WOODWARD, EVAN M.

Rank and organization: First Lieutenant and Adjutant, 2d Pennsylvania Reserve Infantry. *Place and date:* At Fredericksburg, Va., 13 December 1862. *Entered service at:* ———. *Born:* 11 March 1838, Philadelphia, Pa. *Date of issue:* 14 December 1894. *Citation:* Advanced between the lines, demanded and received the surrender of the 19th Georgia Infantry and captured their battle flag.

WOON, JOHN

Rank and organization: Boatswain's Mate, U.S. Navy. *Born:* 1823, England. *Accredited to:* New York. *G.O. No.:* 17, 10 July 1863. *Citation:* Serving on board the U.S.S. *Pittsburg*, Mississippi River, 29 April 1863. Engaging the enemy batteries at Grand Gulf, the U.S.S. *Pittsburg*, although severely damaged and suffering many personnel casualties, continued to fire her batteries until ordered to withdraw. Taking part in a similar action after nightfall, the U.S.S. *Pittsburg* received further damage, but receiving no personnel casualities in the latter action. Woon showed courage and devotion to duty throughout these bitter engagements.

WORAM, CHARLES B.

Rank and organization: Seaman, U.S. Navy. *Born:* 1845, New York, N.Y. *Accredited to:* New York. *G.O. No.:* 45, 31 December 1864. *Citation:* Served on board the U.S.S. *Oneida* in the engagement at Mobile Bay, 5 August 1864. Acting as an aid to the executive officer, Woram carried orders intelligently and correctly, distinguishing himself by his cool courage throughout the battle which resulted in the capture of the rebel ram *Tennessee* and the damaging of Fort Morgan.

WORTICK (WERTICK), JOSEPH

Rank and organization: Private, Company A, 8th Missouri Infantry. *Place and date:* At Vicksburg, Miss., 22 May 1863. *Entered service at:* Hannibal, Mo. *Birth:* Fayette County, Pa. *Date of issue:* 14 July 1894. *Citation:* Gallantry in the charge of the "volunteer storming party."

WRAY, WILLIAM J.

Rank and organization: Sergeant, Company K, 1st Veteran Reserve Corps. *Place and date:* At Fort Stevens, D.C., 12 July 1864. *Entered service at:* ———. *Birth:* Philadelphia, Pa. *Date of issue:* 15 December 1892. *Citation:* Rallied the company at a critical moment during a change of position under fire.

WRIGHT, ALBERT D.

Rank and organization: Captain, Company G, 43d U.S. Colored Troops. *Place and date:* At Petersburg, Va., 30 July 1864. *Entered ser-*

vice at: ———. *Born:* 10 December 1844, Elkland, Tioga County, Pa. *Date of issue:* 1 May 1893. *Citation:* Advanced beyond the enemy's lines, capturing a stand of colors and its color guard; was severely wounded.

WRIGHT, EDWARD

Rank and organization: Quartermaster, U.S. Navy. *Born:* 1829, New York, N.Y. *Accredited to:* New York. *G.O. No.:* 11, 3 April 1863. *Citation:* On board the U.S.S. *Cayuga* during the capture of Forts St. Philip and Jackson and the taking of New Orleans, 24 and 25 April 1862. As his ship led the advance column toward the barrier and both forts opened fire simultaneously, striking the vessel from stem to stern, Wright conscientiously performed his duties throughout the action in which attempts by 3 rebel steamers to butt and board were repelled, and the ships driven off or forced to surrender. Eleven gunboats were successfully engaged and the enemy garrisons captured during this battle in which the *Cayuga* sustained 46 hits.

WRIGHT, ROBERT

Rank and organization: Private, Company G, 14th U.S. Infantry. *Place and date:* At Chapel House, Farm, Va., 1 October 1864. *Entered service at:* Woodstock, Conn. *Birth:* Ireland. *Date of issue:* 25 November 1869. *Citation:* Gallantry in action.

WRIGHT, SAMUEL

Rank and organization: Corporal, Company H, 2d Minnesota Infantry. *Place and date:* At Nolensville, Tenn., 15 February 1863. *Entered service at:* Swan Lake, Minn. *Birth:* Indiana. *Date of issue:* 11 September 1897. *Citation:* Was one of a detachment of 16 men who heroically defended a wagon train against the attack of 125 cavalry, repulsed the attack and saved the train.

WRIGHT, SAMUEL C.

Rank and organization: Private, Company E, 29th Massachusetts Infantry. *Place and date:* At Antietam, Md., 17 September 1862. *Entered service at:* Plympton, Mass. *Birth:* Plympton, Mass. *Date of issue:* 29 January 1896. *Citation:* Voluntarily advanced under a destructive fire and removed a fence which would have impeded a contemplated charge.

WRIGHT, WILLIAM

Rank and organization: Yeoman, U.S. Navy. *Born:* 1835, London, England. *Accredited to:* Maryland. *G.O. No.:* 45, 31 December 1864. *Citation:* Served as yeoman on board the U.S.S. *Monticello* during the reconnaissance of the harbor and water defenses of Wilmington, N.C., 23 to 25 June 1864. Taking part in a reconnaissance of enemy defenses which covered a period of 2 days and nights, Wright courageously carried out his cutting of a telegraph wire and the capture of a large group of prisoners. Although in immediate danger from the enemy at all times, Wright showed gallantry and coolness throughout this action which resulted in the gaining of much vital information of the rebel defenses.

YEAGER, JACOB F.

Rank and organization: Private, Company H, 101st Ohio Infantry. *Place and date:* At Buzzard's Roost, Ga., 11 May 1864. *Entered service at:* Tiffin, Ohio. *Birth:* Lehigh County, Pa. *Date of issue:* 3 August 1897. *Citation:* Seized a shell with fuze burning that had fallen in the ranks of his company and threw it into a stream, thereby probably saving his comrades from injury.

YOUNG, ANDREW J.

Rank and organization: Sergeant, Company F, 1st Pennsylvania Cavalry. *Place and date:* At Paines Crossroads, Va., 5 April 1865. *Entered service at:* Carmichaelstown, Pa. *Birth:* Greene County, Pa. *Date of issue:* 3 May 1865. *Citation:* Capture of flag.

YOUNG, BENJAMIN F.

Rank and organization: Corporal, Company I, 1st Michigan Sharpshooters. *Place and date:* At Petersburg, Va., 17 June 1864. *Entered service at:* Canada. *Born:* 1844, Canada. *Date of issue:* 1 December 1864. *Citation:* Capture of flag of 35th North Carolina Infantry (C.S.A.).

YOUNG, CALVARY M.

Rank and organization: Sergeant, Company L, 3d Iowa Cavalry. *Place and date:* At Osage, Kans., 25 October 1864. *Entered service at:* Hopeville, Clark County, Iowa. *Birth:* Washington County, Ohio. *Date of issue :* 4 April 1865. *Citation:* Gallantry in capturing Gen. Cabell.

YOUNG, EDWARD B.

Rank and organization: Coxswain, U.S. Navy. *Born:* 1835, Bergan, N.J. *Accredited to:* New Jersey. *G.O. No.:* 59, 22 June 1865. *Citation:* On board the U.S.S. *Galena* during the attack on enemy forts at Mobile Bay, 5 August 1864. Securely lashed to the side of the *Oneida* which had suffered the loss of her steering apparatus and an explosion of her boiler from enemy fire, the *Galena* aided the stricken vessel past the enemy forts to safety. Despite heavy damage to his ship from raking enemy fire, Young performed his duties with skill and courage throughout the action.

YOUNG, HORATIO N.

Rank and organization: Seaman, U.S. Navy. *Born:* 19 July 1845, Calaise, Maine. *G.O. No.:* 32, 16 April 1864. *Citation:* On board the U.S.S. *Lehigh*, Charleston Harbor, 16 November 1863, during the hazardous task of freeing the *Lehigh*, which had grounded, and was under heavy enemy fire from Fort Moultrie. After several previous attempts had been made, Young succeeded in passing in a small boat from the *Lehigh* to the *Nahant* with a line bent on a hawser. This courageous action while under severe enemy fire enabled the *Lehigh* to be freed from her helpless position.

YOUNG, JAMES M.

Rank and organization: Private, Company B, 72d New York Infantry. *Place and date:* At Wilderness, Va., 6 May 1864. *Entered service at:* Chautauqua County, N.Y. *Birth:* Chautauqua County, N.Y. *Date of issue:* 2 April 1898. *Citation:* With 2 companions, voluntarily went forward in the forest to reconnoiter the enemy's position; was fired upon and one of his companions disabled. Pvt. Young took the wounded man upon his back and, under fire, carried him within the Union lines.

YOUNG, WILLIAM

Rank and organization: Boatswain's Mate, U.S. Navy. *Born:* 1835, New York. *Accredited to:* New York. *G.O. No.:* 11, 3 April 1863. *Citation:* On board the U.S.S. *Cayuga* during the capture of Forts St. Philip and Jackson and the taking of New Orleans, 24 and 25 April 1862. As his ship led the advance column toward the barrier and both forts opened fire simultaneously, striking the vessel from stem to stern, Young calmly manned a Parrot gun throughout the action in which attempts by three rebel steamers to butt and board were thwarted and the ships driven off or captured, 11 gunboats were successfully engage and garrisons forced to surrender. During the battle, the *Cayuga* sustained 46 hits.

YOUNKER, JOHN L.

Rank and organization: Private, Company A, 12th U.S. Infantry. *Place and date:* At Cedar Mountain, Va., 9 August 1862. *Entered service at:* — — —. *Birth:* Germany. *Date of issue:* 1 November 1893. *Citation:* Voluntarily carried an order, at great risk of life in the face of a fire of grape and canister; in doing this he was wounded.

RESTORATION OF AWARD

WALKER, DR. MARY E.

Rank and organization: Contract Acting Assistant Surgeon (civilian), U. S. Army. *Places and dates:* Battle of Bull Run, July 21, 1861; Patent Office Hospital, Washington, D.C., October 1861; Chattanooga, Tenn., following Battle of Chickomauga, September 1863; Prisoner of War, April 10, 1864–August 12, 1864, Richmond, Va.; Battle of Atlanta, September 1864. *Entered service at:* Louisville, Ky. *Born:* 26 November 1832, Oswego County, N.Y. In 1917, the Board of Medal Awards (created by the Act of 3 June 1916), after reviewing the merits of the awardees of the Civil War awards, ruled Dr. Walker's Medal, as well as those of 910 other recipients, as unwarranted.

On June 10, 1977, Army Secretary Clifford L. Alexander, Jr., approved the recommendation by the Army Board for Correction of Military Records of May 4, 1977, to restore the Medal of Honor to Dr. Mary E. Walker. The citation by President Andrew Johnson follows:

Whereas it appears from official reports that Dr. Mary E. Walker, a graduate of medicine, "has rendered valuable service to the Government, and her efforts have been earnest and untiring in a variety of ways," and that she was assigned to duty and served as an assistant surgeon in charge of female prisoners at Louisville, Ky., upon the recommendation of Major-Generals Sherman and Thomas, and faithfully served as contract surgeon in the service of the United States, and has devoted herself with much patriotic zeal to the sick and wounded soliders, both in the field and hospitals, to the detriment of her own health, and has also endured hardships as a prisoner of war four months in a Southern prison while acting as contract surgeon; and

Whereas by reason of her not being a commissioned officer in the military service, a brevet or honorary rank cannot, under existing laws, be conferred upon her; and

Whereas in the opinion of the President an honorable recognition of her services and sufferings should be made:

It is ordered, That a testimonial thereof shall be hereby made and given to the said Dr. Mary E. Walker, and that the usual medal of honor for meritorious services be given her.

Given under my hand in the city of Washington, D.C., this 11th day of November, A.D. 1865.

ANDREW JOHNSON,
President.

By the President:
Edwin M. Stanton,
Secretary of War.

PART III

NUMBER OF MEDALS OF HONOR AWARDED BY WARS AND CAMPAIGNS

	Army	Navy	Marine Corps	Air Force*	Coast Guard
Civil War (1861-1865)	1,200	310	17	0	0
Indian Campaigns (1861-1898)	419	0	0	0	0
Korean Campaign (1871)	0	9	6	0	0
Spanish-American War (1898)	30	66	15	0	0
Philippine Insurrection (1899-1913)	70	9	9	0	0
Boxer Rebellion (1900)	4	22	33	0	0
Action Against Philippine Outlaws (1911)	0	5	0	0	0
Mexican Campaign (Vera Cruz) (1911)	1	46	9	0	0
Haitian Campaign (1915)	0	0	6	0	0
Dominican Campaign (1916)	0	0	3	0	0
World War I (1917-1918)	95	21	7	*4	0
Haitian Campaign (1919-1920)	0	0	2	0	0
Second Nicaraguan Campaign (1925)	0	0	2	0	0
Unknowns (1921-1957)	8	0	0	0	0
World War II (1941-1945)	294	57	81	*38	1
Mitchell, William, (Private Law 884)	1	0	0	0	0
Korean Conflict (1950-1953)	78	7	42	4	0
Vietnam Era	155	15	57	12	0
Number of Medals awarded by interim period:					
1866-1870	0	9	0	0	0
1871-1898	0	99	2	0	0
1901-1910	0	46	2	0	0
1915-1916	0	8	0	0	0
1920-1940	2	15	1	*1	0
Total	2,355	744	294	*43 (16)	1

*From 1907 to Sept. 18, 1947, the Air Force was a part of the Army. The awards here tabulated and designated with an asterisk are reported in the Army tabulation.

Note: The grand total number of Medals of Honor awarded by wars is 3,412.

MEDAL OF HONOR AWARDS MADE BY SPECIAL LEGISLATION

BENNETT, Floyd, Machinist, United States Navy.
BYRD, Richard Evelyn, Commander, United States Navy.
CHOLISTER, George Robert, Boatswain's Mate First Class, United States Navy.
DREXLER, Henry Clay, Ensign, United States Navy.
HOBSON, Richmond Pearson, formerly Naval Constructor, United States Navy.
LINDBERGH, Charles A., Captain, United States Army Air Corps Reserve.
GREELY, Adolphus W., Major General, United States Army, Retired.
MITCHELL, William, formerly a Colonel, United States Army (Posthumous).
UNKNOWN SOLDIER of Belgium.
UNKNOWN SOLDIER of Great Britain.
UNKNOWN SOLDIER of France.
UNKNOWN SOLDIER of Italy.
UNKNOWN SOLDIER of Rumania.
UNKNOWN SOLDIER of the United States (1921) – World War I.
UNKNOWN AMERICAN, World War II.
UNKNOWN AMERICAN, Koren Conflict.
UNKNOWN AMERICAN, Vietnam Era.

PART IV
MEDAL OF HONOR RECIPIENTS BY STATE
OF ENTRY INTO SERVICE

[(b) indicates State of birth; *posthumous award; †second award]

ALABAMA

ARMY-AIR FORCE

    BOLDEN, Paul L., S/Sgt., 30th Inf. Div. (Madison) (b. Iowa).
    BOLTON, Cecil H., 1st Lt., 104th Inf. Div. (Huntsville) (b. Fla.).
(b) DAVIS, Charles W., Maj., 25th Inf. Div. (Montgomery).
(b) ERWIN, Henry E., S/Sgt., 20th Air Force (Bessemer).
    *EVANS, Rodney J., Sgt., 1st Cav. Div. (Florala) (b. Mass.).
(b) HOWARD, Robert L., 1st Lt., USA (Montgomery).
    JOHNSTON, Gordon, 1st Lt., U.S. Sig. Cp. (Birmingham) (b. N.C.).
(b) LAWLEY, William R., Jr., 1st Lt., A.C. (Birmingham).
(b) *LEONARD, Matthew, P/Sgt., 1st Inf. Div. (Birmingham).
(b) MANNING, Sidney E., Cpl., 42d Div. (Flomaton).
(b) *MICHAEL, Don Leslie, Sp.4c., 173d Airborne Brig. (Florence).
(b) MIZE, Ola L., M/Sgt., 3d Inf. Div. (Gadsden).
(b) *SEAY, William W., Sgt., 48th Trans. Gp. (Brewton).
    SPRAYBERRY, James M., Capt., 1st Cav. Div. (Montgomery) (b. Ga.).

NAVY-MARINE CORPS

(b) *GRAY, Ross Franklin, Sgt., USMCR (Marvel Valley).
(b) HOUGHTON, Edward J., Ordinary Seamen, USN (Mobile).
(b) *INGRAM, Osmond K., GM1c. USN.
(b) McLAUGHLIN, Alford L., Pfc., 1st Marine Div., Reinf., USMC (Leeds).
(b) *NEW, John Dury, Pfc., USMC.
(b) WILSON, Harold E., T/Sgt., 1st Marine Div., Reinf., USMCR (Birmingham).

ARIZONA

ARMY-AIR FORCE

(b) ALCHESAY, Sgt., Indian Scouts.
    BACON, Nicky Daniel, S/Sgt., 21st Inf., Americal Div. (Phoenix) (b. Ark.).
(b) BLANQUET, Indian Scouts, U.S. Army.
(b) CHIQUITO, Indian Scouts, U.S. Army.
(b) ELSATSOOSU Cpl., Indian Scouts, U.S. Army.
    FERGUSON, Frederick E., CWO, 1st Cav. Div. (Phoenix) (b. Tex.).
    HERRERA, Silvestre S., Pfc., 36th Inf. Div. (Phoenix) (b. Tex.).
(b) JIM, Sgt., Indian Scouts, U.S. Army.
(b) KELSAY, Indian Scouts, U.S. Army.
(b) KOSOHA, Indian Scouts, U.S. Army.
    *LAUFFER, Billy Lane, Pfc., 1st Air Cav. Div. (Phoenix) (b. Ky.).
(b) *LUKE, Frank, Jr., 2d Lt., 1st Pur. Gp., Air Service (Phoenix).
(b) MACHOL, Pvt., Indian Scouts, U.S. Army.
(b) NANNASADDIE, Indian Scouts, U.S. Army.
(b) NANTAJE (NANTAHE), Indian Scouts, U.S. Army.
(b) ROWDY, Sgt., Co. A., Indian Scouts.
    THOMPSON, Max, Sgt., 1st Inf. Div. (Prescott) (b. N.C.).

NAVY-MARINE CORPS

*AUSTIN, Oscar P., Pfc., USMC (Phoenix) (b. Tex.).
*JIMINEZ, Jose Francisco, L/Cpl., USMC (Phoenix) (b. Mexico).
*†PRUITT, John Henry, Cpl., 2d Div., USMC (Phoenix) (b. Ark.). (Awarded both
    Army and Navy Medals of Honor.)
(b)   VARGAS, M. Sando, Jr., Maj. USMC (Winslow).

                Jay R.

ARKANSAS

ARMY-AIR FORCE

(b)   BRITT, Maurice L., Capt., 3d Inf. Div. (Lonoke).
(b)   BURKE, Lloyd L., 1st Lt., 1st Cav. Div. (Stuttgart).
(b) *COLLIER, Gilbert G., Sgt., 40th Inf. Div. (Tichnor).
      DONLON, Roger Hugh C., Capt., USA (Fort Chaffee) (b. N.Y.).
      ELLIS, William, 1st Sgt., 3d Wis. Cav. (Little Rock) (b. England).
(b)   FACTOR, Pompey, Pvt., Indian Scouts.
(b) *GILLILAND, Charles L., Cpl., 3d Inf. Div. (Yellville).
(b)   HENDRIX, James R., S/Sgt., 4th Armd. Div. (Lepanto).
(b) *LLOYD, Edgar H., 1st Lt., 80th Inf. Div. (Blytheville).
(b)   PAYNE, Issac, Trumpeter, 24th U.S. Infantry, Indian Scouts.
(b) *TERRY, Seymour W., Capt., 96th Inf. Div. (Little Rock).

NAVY-MARINE CORPS

      FRANKS, William J., Seaman, USN (b. N.C.).
(b)   GORDON, Nathan Green, Lt., USN (Morrilton).
      WATSON, Wilson Douglas, Pvt., USMCR (b. Ala.).
(b) *WILLIAMS, Jack, PM3c., USNR (Harrison).

CALIFORNIA

ARMY-AIR FORCE

      BACA, John Phillip, Sgt., 1st Cav. Div. (Fort Ord) (b. R.I.).
    *BELLRICHARD, Leslie A., Pfc., 8th Inf. Div. (Oakland) (b. Wis.).
      BROPHY, James, Pvt., 8th U.S. Cav. (Stockton) (b. Ireland).
      CAVAIANI, Jon R., S/Sgt., U.S. Army Vietnam Tr. Adv. Gp. (b. England).
(b)   CRAFT, Clarence B., Pfc., 96th Inf. Div. (Santa Ana).
      CROCKER, Henry H., Capt., 2d Mass. Cav. (b. Conn.).
      DEAN, William F., Maj. Gen., 24th Inf. Div. (b. Ill.).
    *DESIDERIO, Reginald B., Capt., 25th Inf. Div. (San Francisco) (b. Pa.).
(b) *DEVORE, Edward A., Jr., Spec. 4, 9th Inf. Div. (Harbor City).
(b)   DOOLITTLE, James H., Brig. Gen., A.G., USA (Berkeley).
      DUNAGAN, Kern W., Maj., 46th Inf., Americal Div. (Los Angeles) (b. Ariz.).
      ELWOOD, Edwin L., Pvt., 8th U.S. Cav. (b. Mo.).
(b) *EVANS, Donald W., Sp4c., 4th Inf. Div. (Covina).
(b) *GONZALES, David M., Pfc., 32d Inf. Div. (Pacoima).
    *HARMON, Roy W., Sgt., 91st Inf. (Pixley) (b. Okla.).
      HARVEY, Raymond, Capt., 7th Inf. Div. (Pasadena) (b. Pa.).
      HEARTERY, Richard, Pvt., 6th U.S. Cav. (San Francisco) (b. Ireland).
(b)   HERNANDEZ, Rodolfo P., Cpl., Cmbt. Team.
(b)   HIGH, Frank C., Pvt., 2d Oreg. Vol. Inf. (Picard).
      HOLDERMAN, Nelson M., Capt., 77th Inf. Div. (Santa Ana) (b. Nebr.).
      HOOPER, Joe R., S/Sgt., 101st Airborne Div. (Los Angeles) (b. S.C.).
(b) *INGALLS, George Alan, Spec. 4, 1st Cav. Div. (Yorba Linda).
      JENNINGS, Delbert O., S/Sgt., 1st Air Cav. Div. (San Francisco) (b. N. Mex.).
    *KANDLE, Victor L., 1st Lt., 3d Inf. Div. (Redwood City) (b. Wash.).
(b)   KATZ, Phillip C., Sgt., 91st Div. (San Francisco).
      LEAHY, Cornelius J., Pvt., 36th Inf., U.S. Vol. (San Francisco) (b. Ireland).
      LITTRELL, Gary Lee, Sgt., (Los Angeles) (b. Ky.).
      McMAHON, Martin T., Capt., U.S. Vol. (b. Canada).

ARMY-AIR FORCE

*MILLER, Oscar F., Maj., 91st Div. (Los Angeles) (b. Ark.).
*MOLNAR, Frankie Zoly, S/Sgt., 4th Inf. Div. (Fresno) (b. W. Va.).
*MOON, Harold H., Jr., Pvt., 24th Inf. Div. (Gardena) (b. N. Mex.).
(b) *MUNEMORI, Sadao S., Pfc., 442d Combat Team (Los Angeles).
(b) PENRY, Richard Allen, Sgt., 199th Inf. Brig. (Petaluma).
*PIERCE, Larry S., Sgt., 173d Airborne Brig. (Fresno) (b. Okla.).
(b) QUINN, Peter H., Pvt., 4th U.S. Cav. (San Francisco).
REGAN, Patrick, 2d Lt., 20th Div. (Los Angeles) (b. Mass.).
(b) *ROARK, Anund C., Sgt., 4th Inf. Div. (Los Angeles).
(b) *ROBERTS, Harold W., Cpl., 344th Bn., Tank Corps (San Francisco).
ROCCO, Louis R., WO, U.S. Mil. Assist. Com. (Los Angeles) (b. N. Mex.).
(b) RODRIGUEZ, Joseph C., Sgt., 7th Inf. Div. (San Bernardino).
SEIBERT, Lloyd M., Sgt., 91st Div. (Salinas) (b. Mich.).
(b) SHIELS, George F., Surg., U.S. Vol. (San Francisco).
*SHOCKLEY, William R., Pfc., 32d Inf. Div. (Selma) (b. Okla.).
(b) TAYLOR, James Allen, Capt., 1st Cav., Ameri. Div. (San Francisco).
TURNER, George B., Pfc., 14th Armd. Div. (Los Angeles) (b. Tex.).
(b) *VIALE, Robert M., 2d Lt., 37th Inf. Div. (Ukiah).
(b) *VILLEGAS, Ysmael R., S/Sgt., 32 Inf. Div. (Casa Blanca).
*VON SCHLICK, Robert H., Pvt., 9th U.S. Inf. (San Francisco) (b. Germany).
WARE, Keith L., Lt. Col., 3d Inf. Div. (Glendale) (b. Colo.).
(b) WAYBUR, David C., 1st Lt., 3d Inf. Div. (Piedmont).
WEAVER, Amos, Sgt., 36th Inf., U.S. Vol. (San Francisco) (b. Ind.).
WEST, Chester H., 1st Sgt., 91st Div. (Los Banos) (b. Colo.).
WILLISTON, Edward B., 1st Lt., 2d U.S. Arty. (San Francisco) (b. Vt.).
(b) *YOUNG, Robert H., Pfc., 1st Cav. Div. (Vallejo).

NAVY-MARINE CORPS

(b) *ANDERSON, James, Jr., Pfc., 3d Marine Div. (Los Angeles).
BOYDSTON, Erwin Jay, Pvt., USMC (b. Colo.).
BROCK, George F., CM2d., USN (b. Ohio).
BURNES, James, Pvt., USMC (b. Mass.).
(b) *CALLAGHAN, Daniel Judson, Rear Adm., USN.
(b) CLAUSEY, John J., CGM, USN (San Francisco).
COLEMAN, John, Pvt., USMC (b. Ireland).
COVINGTON, Jessie Whitfield, SC3d, USN (b. Tenn.).
*CREEK, Thomas E., L/Cpl., USMC (San Diego) (b. Mo.).
DAHLGREN, John Olof, Cpl., USMC (b. Sweden).
(b) FINN, John William, Lt., USN (Los Angeles).
FISHER, Frederick Thomas, GM1c., USN (b. England).
(b) *FOSTER, Paul Hellstrom, Sgt., USMCR (San Francisco).
(b) *GONSALVES, Harold, Pfc., USMCR (Alameda).
HALFORD, William, Cox., USN (b. England).
HANSEN, Hans A., Seaman, USN (b. Germany).
HEISCH, Henry William, Pvt., USMC (b. Germany).
HENRECHON, George Francis, MM2d, USN (b. Conn.).
HULBERT, Henry Lewis, Pvt., USMC (b. England).
ITRICH, Franz Anton, CCM, USN (b. Germany).
*JOHNSON, Ralph H., Pfc., USMC (Oakland) (b. S.C.).
(b) *JONES, Herbert Charpiot, Ens., USNR (Los Angeles).
(b) *KELSO, Jack W., Pvt., USMC, 1st Marine Div. (Caruthers).
*KOELSCH, John Kelvin, Lt. (jg.), USN (Los Angeles) (b. England).
LAVERTY, John, Flc., USN (b. Ireland).
(b) *MATTHEWS, Daniel P., Sgt., USMC, 1st Marine Div. (Van Nuys).
(b) *MAXAM, Larry Leonard, Cpl., USMC (Burbank).
McALLISTER, Samuel, Ordinary Seaman, USN (b. Ireland).
McGONAGLE, William L., Capt., USN (Thermal) (b. Kans.).
McNALLY, Michael Joseph, Sgt., USMC (b. N.Y.).
(b) MOORE, Albert, Pvt., USMC (Merced).
(b) *OBREGON, Eugene A., Pfc., USMC, 1st Marine Div. (Los Angeles).
ORNDOFF, Harry Westley, Pvt., USMC (b. Ohio).

*PERKINS, William Thomas, Jr., Cpl., USMC (Northridge) (b. N.Y.).
PHARRIS, Jackson Charles, Lt., USN (b. Ga.).
(b)   PHILLIPS, Reuben Jasper, Cpl., USMC (Cambria).
(b) *PHIPPS, Jimmy W., Pfc., USMC (Reseda).
(b)   PITTMAN, R. A., Sgt., USMC (Stockton).
    *POYNTER, James I., Sgt., USMCR, 1st Marine Div. (Donney) (b. Ill.).
(b)   SILVA, France, Pvt., USMC (Haywards).
    SMITH, Eugene P., CWT, USN (b. Ill.).
    STOLTENBERG, Andrew V., GM2c., USN (b. Norway).
    SWETT, James Elms, 1st Lt., USMCR (b. Wash.).
    WESTERMARK, Axel, Seaman, USN (b. Finland).
    †WILLIAMS, Louis, Captain of Hold, USN (b. Norway).
(b)   WOODS, Samuel, Seaman, USN.
    *WORLEY, Kenneth L., L/Cpl., USMCC, 1st Mar. Div. (Fresno) (b. N. Mex.).
    ZION, William, Pvt., USMC (b. Ind.).

COLORADO

*CHILES, Marcellus H., Capt., 89th Div. (Denver) (b. Ark.).
DIX, Drew Dennis, S/Sgt., USA (Denver) (b. N.Y.).
(b)   CRAWFORD, William J., Pvt., 36th Inf. Div. (Pueblo).
(b) *FRYAR, Elmer E., Pvt., 11th Airborne Div. (Denver).
    FUNK, Jesse N., Pfc., 89th Div. (Calhan) (b. Mo.).
    GROVE, William R., Lt. Col., 36th Inf., U.S. Vol. (Denver) (b. Iowa).
    *LINDSTROM, Floyd K., Pfc., 3d Inf. Div. (Colorado Springs) (b. Nebr.).
    *MARTINEZ, Joe P., Pvt., 7th Inf. Div. (Ault) (b. N. Mex.).
    MAXWELL, Robert D., T5g., 3d Inf. Div. (Larimer Co.) (b. Idaho).
(b) *McWETHY, Edgar Lee, Jr., Spec. 5, 1st Cav. Div. (Leadville).
(b) *PUCKET, Donald D., 1st Lt., 98th Bomb. Gp. (Boulder).
    *WALKER, Kenneth N., Brig. Gen., 5th Bomb Comd. (b. N. Mex.).
    WALLACE, George W., 2d Lt., 9th U.S. Inf. (Denver) (b. Ind.).
    *WICKERSHAM, J. Hunter, 2d Lt., 89th Div. (Denver) (b. N.Y.).
    YOUNG, Gerald O., Capt., USAF (Colorado Springs) (b. Ill.).

*COKER, Ronald L., Pfc., USMC (Denver) (b. Nebr.).
McCANDLESS, Bruce, Comdr., USN (b. D.C.).
(b)   MURPHY, Raymond G., 2d Lt., USMC, 1st Marine Div. (Pueblo).
    ROSS, Donald Kirby, Machinist, USN (Denver) (b. Kans.).
    SITTER, Carl L., Capt., USMC, 1st Marine Div. (Pueblo) (b. Mo.).
(b)   UPTON, Frank Monroe, Quartermaster, USN (Loveland).

CONNECTICUT

BABCOCK, John B., 1st Lt., 5th U.S. Cav. (Stonington) (b. La.).
(b)   BACON, Elijah W., Pvt., 14th Conn. Inf. (Berlin).
(b)   BAIRD, George W., 1st Lt. and Adj., 5th U.S. Inf. (Milford).
(b)   BECKWITH, Wallace A., Pvt., 21st Conn. Inf. (New London).
    BEEBE, William S., 1st Lt., Ord. Dept., USA (Thompson) (b. N.Y.).
(b)   BRIGGS, Elijah A., Cpl., 2d Conn. Hvy. Arty. (Salisbury).
(b)   BUCK, F. Clarence, Cpl., 21st Conn. Inf. (Windsor).
(b)   BURKE, Daniel W., 1st Sgt., 2d U.S. Inf.
(b)   CANFIELD, Heth, Pvt., 2d U.S. Cav. (New Medford).
    CORLISS, George W., Capt., 5th Conn. Inf. (New Haven) (b. N.Y.).
(b)   CURTIS, John C., Sgt. Maj., 9th Conn. Inf. (Bridgeport).
    DALY, Michael J., Capt., 3d Inf. Div. (Southport) (b. N.Y.).
    FLYNN, Christopher, Cpl., 14th Conn. Inf. (b. Ireland).
(b)   FORSYTH, Thomas H., 1st Sgt., 4th U.S. Cav. (Hartford).

ARMY-AIR FORCE

FOX, Nicholas, Pvt., 28th Conn. Inf. (Greenwich).
GRAY, Robert A., Sgt., 21st Conn. Inf. (Groton) (b. Pa.).
(b) GIBBS, Wesley, Sgt., 2d Conn. Hvy. Arty. (Salisbury).
*HARTELL, Lee R., 1st Lt., 2d Inf. Div. (Danbury) (b. Pa.).
(b) HICKOK, Nathan E., Cpl., 8th Conn. Inf. (Danbury).
HINCKS, William B., Sgt. Maj., 14th Conn. Inf. (Bridgeport) (b. Maine).
(b) HOOPER, William B., Cpl., 1st N.J. Cav. (Willimantic).
HORNE, Samuel B., Capt., 11th Conn. Inf. (Winsted) (b. Ireland).
(b) HUBBELL, William S., Capt., 21st Conn. Inf. (North Stonington).
(b) JACKSON, Frederick R., 1st Sgt., 7th Conn. Inf. (New Haven).
JOHNSTON, William J., Pfc., 45th Inf. Div. (Colchester) (b. N.Y.).
(b) LANFARE, Aaron S., 1st Lt., 1st Conn. Cav. (Branford).
(b) LEVITOW, John L., Sgt., USAF (New Haven).
*LIBBY, George D., Sgt., 24th Inf. Div. (Waterbury) **(b. Maine)**.
(b) *MAGRATH, John D., Pfc., 10th Mtn. Div. (East Norwalk).
(b) MARSH, Charles H., Pvt., 1st Conn. Cav. (New Milford).
MURPHY, James T., Pvt., 1st Conn. Arty. (b. Canada).
NEVILLE, Edwin M., Capt., 1st Conn. Cav. (Waterbury).
(b) O'NEILL, William, Cpl., 4th U.S. Cav. (Tariffville).
(b) PALMER, John G., Cpl., 21st Conn. Inf. (Montville).
(b) *SHEA, Daniel John, Pfc., 196th Light Inf. Brig., Ameri. Div. (Norwalk).
SIMONDS, William Edgar, Sgt. Maj., 25th Conn. Inf. (Canton).
(b) SODERMAN, William A., Pfc., 2d Inf. Div. (West Haven).
(b) TINKHAM, Eugene M., Cpl., 148th N.Y. Inf. (Sprague).
(b) TUCKER, Allen, Sgt., 10th Conn. Inf. (Sprague).
(b) WHITAKER, Edward W., Capt., 1st Conn. Cav. (Ashford).
WILSON, Christopher W., Pvt., 73d N.Y. Inf. (West Meriden) (b. Ireland).
WRIGHT, Robert, Pvt., 14th U.S. Inf. (Woodstock) (b. Ireland).

NAVY-MARINE CORPS

(b) BARNUM, Harvey C., Jr., Capt., USMC (Cheshire).
CRANDALL, Orson L., CBM, USN (b. Mo.).
(b) HARDING, Thomas, Captain of Forecastle, USN (Middletown).
(b) HILL, Frank, Pvt., USMC (Hartford).
(b) KELLOG, Allan Jay, Jr., Gy/Sgt., 1st Mar. Div. (Bethel).
(b) MANNING, Henry J., Quartermaster, USN (New Haven).
(b) PECK, Oscar E., Second Class Boy, USN (Bridgeport).
(b) *REEVES, Thomas J., CRM, USN (Thomaston).
(b) ROSE, George, Seaman, USN (Stamford).
(b) RYAN, Richard, Ordinary Seaman, USN.
*TALBOT, Ralph, 2d Lt., USMC (b. Mass.).

DELAWARE

ARMY-AIR FORCE

(b) BUCKINGHAM, David E., 1st Lt., 4th Del. Inf. (Pleasant Hill).
(b) CONNOR, James P., Sgt., 3d Inf. Div. (Wilmington).
(b) DU PONT, Henry A., Capt., 5th U.S. Arty. (Wilmington).
(b) MAYBERRY, John B., Pvt., 1st Del. Inf. (Smyrna).
McCARREN, Bernard, Pvt., 1st Del. Inf. (Wilmington) (b. Ireland).
(b) *NELSON, William L., Sgt., 9th Inf. Div. (Wilmington).
PIERCE, Charles H., Pvt., 22d U.S. Inf. (Delaware City) (b. Md.).
(b) POSTLES, James Parke, Capt., 1st Del. Inf. (Wilmington).
(b) SEWARD, Griffin, Wagoner, 8th U.S. Cav. (Dover).
SHILLING, John, 1st Sgt., 3d Del. Inf. (Felton) (b. England).
(b) SMITH, S. Rodmond, Capt., 4th Del. Inf. (Wilmington).
TANNER, Charles B., 2d Lt., 1st Del. Inf. (Wilmington) (b. Pa.).

NAVY-MARINE CORPS

(b) CHADWICK, Leonard, Apprentice First Class, USN (Middletown).

NAVY-MARINE CORPS

(b)   HAND, Allexander, Quartermaster, USN.

DISTRICT OF COLUMBIA

ARMY-AIR FORCE

BARNES, Will C., Pfc., Sig. Cp. (b. Calif.).
(b)   BELL, Dennis, Pvt., 10th U.S. Cav.
BUTTERFIELD, Daniel, Brig. Gen., U.S. Vol. (b. N.Y.).
BYRNE, Bernard A., Capt., 6th U.S. Inf. (b. Va.).
CAPEHART, Charles E., Maj., 1st W. Va. Cav. (b. Pa.).
(b)   CHEEVER, Benjamin H., Jr., 1st Lt., 6th U.S. Cav.
CHURCH, James Robb, Asst. Surg., 1st U.S. Vol. Cav. (b. Ill.).
(b)   McALWEE, Benjamin F., Sgt., 3d Md. Inf.
(b)   *McGOVERN, Robert M., 1st Lt., 1st Cav. Div.
MYERS, Fred, Sgt., 6th U.S. Cav. (b. Germany).
SHAW, George C., 1st Lt., 27th U.S. Inf. (b. Mich.).
(b)   TAYLOR, William, Sgt. and 2d Lt., 1st Md. Inf.
(b)   WARRINGTON, Lewis, 1st Lt., 4th U.S. Cav.
WOODRUFF, Carle A., 1st Lt., 2d U.S. Arty. (b. N.Y.).

NAVY-MARINE CORPS

(b)   BADGER, Oscar Charles, Ens., USN.
*BAUSELL, Lewis Kenneth, Cpl., USMC (b. Va.).
BEHNKE, Heinrich, S1c., USN (b. Germany).
BERKELEY, Randolph Carter, Maj., USMC (b. Va.)
CHAMBERS, Justice M., Col., USMC (b. W. Va.).
(b)   COURTS, George McCall, Lt. (jg), USN.
(b)   HARRINGTON, David, F1c., USN.
(b)   HAYDEN, John, Apprentice, USN.
*JOHNSON, James E., Sgt., USMC, 1st Marine Div. (b. Idaho).
(b)   KEEFER, Philip B., Coppersmith, USN.
(b)   LIPSCOMB, Harry, WT, USN.
McDONALD, James Harper, CM, USN (b. Scotland).
MILLER, Andrew, Sgt., USMC (b. Germany).
MURPHY, John Alphonsus, Drummer, USMC (b. N.Y.).
(b)   PORTER, David Dixon, Col., USMC.
(b)   RUSH, John, F1c., USN.
STEWART, Peter, Gun Sgt., USMC (b. Scotland).
SUTTON, Clarence Edwin, Sgt., USMC (b. Va.).
(b)   WAINWRIGHT, Richard, Jr., Lt., USN.

FLORIDA

ARMY-AIR FORCE

(b)   *BENNETT, Emory L., Pfc., 3d Inf. Div. (Cocoa).
*BOWEN, Hammett L., Jr., S/Sgt., 25th Inf. Div. (Jacksonville) (b. Georgia).
(b)   *CUTINHA, Nicholas J., Spec. 4, 25th Inf. Div. (Fernandina Beach).
*FEMOYER, Robert E., 2d Lt., 711th Heavy Bombing Sq. (Jackson) (b. W. Va.).
McGUIRE, Thomas B., Jr., Maj., AC, 13th Air Force (MacDill Field) (b. N.J.).
(b)   MILLS, James H., Pvt., 3d Inf. Div. (Fort Meade).
*NININGER, Alexander R., Jr., 2d Lt., 57th Inf., Phil. Scouts (Fort Lauderdale) (b. Ga.).
(b)   *SIMS, Clifford Chester, S/Sgt., 101st Airborne Div. (Port St. Joe).
VARNUM, Charles A., Capt. 7th U.S. Cav. (Pensacola) (b. N.Y.).

NAVY-MARINE CORPS

*CARTER, Bruce W., Pfc., 3d Mar. Div. (Jacksonville) (b. N.Y.)
(b)   *CORRY, William Merrill, Jr., Lt. Comdr., USN (Quincy).
(b)   *JENKINS, Robert H., Pfc., USMC (Interlachen).

NAVY-MARINE CORPS

(b) LASSEN, Clyde Everett, Lt., USN (Fort Myers).
(b) *LOPEZ, Baldomero, 1st Lt., USMC, 1st Marine Div. (Tampa).
McCAMPBELL, David, Comdr., USN (b. Ala.).
(b) *McTUREOUS, Robert Miller, Jr., Pvt., USMC (Altoona).
*ORMSBEE, Francis Edward, Jr., CMM, USN (b. R.I.).
*SMEDLEY, Larry Eugene, Cpl., USMC, 1st Mar. Div. (Orlando) (b. Va.).

GEORGIA

ARMY-AIR FORCE

(b) BROWN, Bobbie E., Capt., 1st Inf. Div. (Atlanta).
(b) CARTER, Mason, 1st Lt., 5th U.S. Inf. (Augusta).
*DURHAM, Harold Bascom, Jr., 2d Lt., 1st Inf. Div. (Atlanta) (b. N.C.). *3/16/93*
GARLINGTON, Ernest A., 1st Lt., 7th U.S. Cav. (Athens) (b. S.C.).
(b) JACKSON, Joe M., Lt. Col., USAF (Newnan).
(b) *JOHNSTON, Donald R., Spec. 4, 1st Cav. Div. (Columbus).
(b) LEE, Daniel L., 1st Lt., 117th Cav. Rec. Sq. (Alma).
McCLEERY, Finnis D., Plat. Sgt., 198th Inf. Brig. Ameri. Div. (Fort Benning) (b. Tex.).
(b) *McKIBBEN, Ray, Sgt., 17th Cav. (Felton).
(b) McKINNEY, John R., Sgt., 33d Inf. Div. (Woodcliff).
(b) RAY, Ronald Eric, Capt., 25th Inf. Div. (Cordelle).
(b) *STORY, Luther H., Pfc., 2d Inf. Div. (Buena Vista).
(b) *WILBANKS, Hilliard A., Capt., 21st Tact. Air Support Squadron (Cornelia).
Neth, GA - Highway Dod - June 11, 1992

NAVY-MARINE CORPS

(b) DAVIS, Raymond G., Lt. Col., USMC, 1st Marine Div. (Atlanta).
(b) *DAVIS, Rodney Maxwell, Sgt., USMC, 1st Mar. Div. (Macon).
(b) *DYESS, Aquilla James, Lt. Col., USMCR (Augusta).
(b) *ELROD, Henry Talmage, Capt., USMC (Ashburn).
(b) LELAND, George W., GM, USN (Savannah).
(b) LIVINGSTON, James E., Capt., USMC (McRae).
(b) *PHILLIPS, Lee H., Cpl., USMC, 1st Marine Div. (Ben Hill).
(b) PLESS, Stephen W., Maj., USMC, 1st Mar. Aircraft Wing (Newman).
(b) *THOMASON, Clyde, Sgt., USMCR (Atlanta).

HAWAII

ARMY-AIR FORCE

(b) *KAWAMURA, Terry Teruo, Cpl., 173d Airborne Brig. (Wahiawa).
(b) *MENDONCA, LeRoy A., Sgt., 3d Inf. Div. (Honolulu).
(b) *PILILAAU, Herbert K., Pfc., 2d Inf. Div. (Oahu).
(b) *SMITH, Elmelindo R., P/Sgt., 8th Inf. Div. (Honolulu).
(b) *YANO, Rodney J. T., Sgt., 11th Armd. Cav. Reg. (Kaelakekua, Kona).

IDAHO

ARMY-AIR FORCE

(b) BLEAK, David B., Sgt., 40th Inf. Div. (Shelley).
(b) BROSTROM, Leonard C., Pfc., 7th Inf. Div. (Preston).
FISHER, Bernard Frances, Maj., 1st Air. Com. (Kuna) (b. Calif.).
(b) NEIBAUR, Thomas C., Pvt., 42d Inf. Div. (Sugar City).
(b) *SCHOONOVER, Dan D., Cpl., 7th Inf. Div. (Boise).
(b) *VAN NOY, Junior, Pvt., Engr. Boat and Shore Regt. (Preston).

NAVY-MARINE CORPS

(b) MYERS, Reginald R., Maj. USMC, 1st Marine Div. (Boise).
*REASONER, Frank S., 1st Lt., USMC, 3d Marine Div. (Kellogg) (b. Wash.).

ARMY-AIR FORCE

(b) ALLEN, Abner, P., Cpl., 39th Ill. Inf. (Bloomington).
ALLEX, Jake, Cpl., 33d Div. (Chicago) (b. Serbia, now Yugoslavia).
ANDERSON, Johannes S., 1st Sgt., 33d Div. (Chicago) (b. Finland).
AYERS, John G. K., Pvt., 8th Mo. Inf. (Pekin) (b. Mich.).
BAKER, JOHN F., Jr., Sgt., 25th Inf. Div. (Moline) (b. Iowa).
BANCROFT, Neil, Pvt., 7th U.S. Cav. (Chicago) (b. N.Y.).
(b) BATSON, Matthew A., 1st Lt., 4th U.S. Cav. (Carbondale).
BENDER, Stanley, S/Sgt., 3d Inf. Div. (Chicago) (b. W. Va.).
(b) BERG, George, Pvt., 17th U.S. Inf. (Mt. Erie).
(b) BERTOLDO, Vito R., Sgt., 42d Inf. Div. (Decatur).
(b) BICKFORD, Matthew, Cpl., 8th Mo. Inf. (Trivolia).
BLACK, John C., Lt. Col., 37th Ill. (Danville) (b. Miss.).
BLACK, William P., Capt., 37th Ill. Inf. (Danville) (b. Ky.).
*BLANCHFIELD, Michael R., Spec. 4, 173d Airb. Brig. (Wheeling) (b. Minn.).
(b) BLODGETT, Welis H., 1st Lt., 37th Ill. Inf. (Chicago).
BOURKE, John G., Pvt., 15th Pa. Cav. (Chicago) (b. Pa.).
BOWEN, Emmer, Pvt., 127th Ill. Inf. (Hampshire) (b. N.Y.).
BURRITT, William W., Pvt., 113th Ill. Inf. (Chicago) (b. N.Y.).
CALLAHAN, John H., Pvt., 122d Ill. Inf. (Macoupin County) (b. Ky.).
CAPRON, Horace, Jr., Sgt., 8th Ill. Cav. (b. Md.).
(b) CHOATE, Clyde L., S/Sgt., 601st T. D. Bn. (Anna).
CHURCHILL, Samuel J., Cpl., 2d Ill. Light Arty. (De Kalb County) (b. Vt.).
COLBY, Carlos W., Sgt., 97th Ill. Inf. (Madison County). (b. N.H.).
COOK, John H., Sgt., 119 Ill. Inf. (Quincy) (b. England).
COX, Robert M., Cpl., 55th Ill. Inf. (Prairie City) (b. Ohio).
CREED, John, Pvt., 23rd Ill. Inf. (Chicago) (b. Ireland).
CUNNINGHAM, James S., Pvt., 8th Mo. Inf. (Bloomington) (b. Pa.).
CUTTS, James M., Capt., 11th U.S. Inf. (b. D.C.).
(b) DANIELS, James T., Sgt., 4th U.S. Cav. (Richland County).
DARROUGH, John S., Sgt., 113th Ill. Inf. (Concord) (b. Ky.).
(b) DAVIS, Martin K., Sgt., 116th Ill. Inf. (Stonington).
DICKIE, David, Sgt., 97th Ill. Inf. (Gillespie) (b. Scotland).
(b) DUNHAM, Russell E., T/Sgt., 3d Inf. Div. (Brighton).
DUNNE, James, Cpl., Chicago Mercantile Btry., Ill. Light Arty. (Chicago) (b. Mich.).
ELLIS, Michael B., Sgt., 1st Div. (East St. Louis) (b. Mo.).
FARQUHAR, John M., Sgt. Maj., 89th Ill. Inf. (Chicago) (b. Scotland).
FISHER, John H., 1st Lt., 55th Ill. Inf. (Chicago) (b. Pa.).
FOX, Henry, Sgt. 106th Ill. Inf. (Lincoln) (b. Germany).
FRASER (FRAZIER), William W., Pvt., 97th Ill. Inf. (Alton) (b. Scotland).
FREEMEYER, Christopher, Pvt., 5th U.S. Inf. (Chicago) (b. Germany).
GAGE, Richard J., Pvt., 104th Ill. Inf. (Ottawa) (b. N.H.).
(b) GARMAN, Harold A., Pvt., 5th Inf. Div. (Albion).
(b) GERSTUNG, Robert E., T/Sgt., 79th Inf. Div. (Chicago).
GESCHWIND, Nicholas, Capt., 116th Ill. Inf. (Pleasant Hill) (b. France).
*GIBSON, Eric G., T5, 3d Inf. Div. (Chicago) (b. Sweden).
(b) *GOETTLER, Harold Ernest, 1st. Lt., 50th Aero Sq., Air Serv. (Chicago).
GOLDIN, Theodore, Pvt., 7th U.S. Cav. (Chicago) (b. Wis.).
(b) GOLDSBERY, Andrew E., Pvt., 127th Ill. Inf. (St. Charles).
(b) GOULD, Newton T., Pvt., 113th Ill. Inf. (Elk Grove Village).
GUMPERTZ, Sydney G., 1st Sgt., 33d Div. (Chicago) (b. Calif.).
(b) HALL, John, Pvt., 8th U.S. Cav. (Logan County).
*HAMMOND, Lester, Jr., Cpl., Cmbt. Team (Quincy) (b. Mo.).
HANEY, Milton L., Chaplain, 55th Ill. Inf. (Bushnell) (b. Ohio).
HAPEMAN, Douglas, Lt. Col., 104th Ill. Inf. (Ottawa) (b. N.Y.).
*HARDENBERGH, Henry M., Pvt., 39th Ill. Inf. (Bremen) (b. Ind.).
*HARVEY, Carmel Bernon, Jr., Spec. 4, 5th Cav. Div. (Chicago) (b. W. Va.).
HENRY, James, Sgt., 113th Ill. Inf. (Kankakee) (b. Ohio).
HIGGINS, Thomas J., Sgt., 99th Ill. Inf. (Barry) (b. Canada).
HIGHLAND, Patrick, Cpl., 23d Ill. Inf. (Chicago) (b. Ireland).
(b) HILL, Ralyn M., Cpl., 129th Inf., 33d Div. (Oregon).
(b) HOBDAY, George, Pvt., 7th U.S. Cav. (Pulaski County).

HOLLAND, Lemuel F., Cpl., 104th Ill. Inf. (La Salle County) (b. Ohio).
HOUGHTON, George L., Pvt., 104th Ill. Inf. (Brookfield) (b. Canada).
HOWE, Orion P., Mus., 55th Ill. Inf. (Waukegan) (b. Ohio).
HYATT, Theodore, 1st Sgt., 127th Ill. Inf. (Gardner) (b. Pa.).
HYDE, Henry J., Sgt., 1st U.S. Cav. (Princeton) (b. Maine).
HYMER, Samuel, Capt., 115th Ill. Inf. (Rushville) (b. Ind.).
JOHNS (JONES), Elisha, Cpl., 113th Ill. Inf. (Martintonk) (b. Ohio).
JOHNSON, Andrew, Pvt., 116th Ill. Inf. (Assumption) (b. Ohio).
JOHNSON, Harold I., Pfc., 356th Inf., 89th Div. (Chicago) (b. Kans.).
JOHNSTON, David, Pvt., 8th Mo. Inf. (Warshaw County) (b. Pa.).
JOSSELYN, Simeon T., 1st Lt., 13th Ill. Inf. (Amboy) (b. N.Y.).
(b) KAYS, Kenneth M., Pfc., 101st Airborne Div. (Fairfield).
(b) KELLER, Leonard B., Sgt., 9th Inf. Div. (Rockford).
KELLEY, Leverett M., Sgt., 36th Ill. Inf. (Rutland) (b. N.Y.).
†KELLY, John Joseph, Pvt., 2d Div., USMC (Chicago). (Also awarded Navy Medal of Honor.)
(b) KELLY, John J. H., Cpl., 5th U.S. Inf. (Schuyler County).
KLOTH, Charles H., Pvt., Ill. Light Arty. (Chicago) (b. Europe).
(b) KNIGHT, Joseph F., Sgt., 6th U.S. Cav. (Danville).
KRETSINGER, George, Pvt., Chicago Mercantile Btry., Ill. Light Arty. (Chicago) (b. N.Y.).
(b) *KROTIAK, Anthony L., Pfc., 37th Inf. Div. (Chicago).
(b) *KRYZOWSKI, Edward C., Capt., 2d Inf. Div. (Cicero).
LABILL, Joseph S., Pvt., 6th Mo. Inf. (Vandalia) (b. France).
LARRABEE, James W., Cpl., 55th Ill. Inf. (Mendota) (b. N.Y.).
LOMAN, Berger, Pvt., 33d Div. (Chicago) (b. Norway).
(b) LOWER, Robert A., Pvt., 55th Ill. Inf. (Elmwood).
(b) LUCAS, George W., Pvt., 3d Mo. Cav. (Mt. Sterling).
(b) LYNCH, Allen James, Sgt., 1st Cav. Div. (Airmobile) (Chicago).
(b) MARSH, George, Sgt., 104th Ill. Inf. (Brookfield).
(b) McCLERNAND, Edward J., 2d Lt., 2d U.S. Cav. (Springfield).
McCONNELL, Samuel, Capt., 119th Ill. Inf. (Bushnell) (b. Ohio).
(b) McCORNACK, Andrew, Pvt., 127th Ill. Inf. (Rutland).
McDONALD, John Wade, Pvt., 20th Ill. Inf. (Wayneville) (b. Ohio)
McGRAW, Thomas, Sgt., 23d Ill. Inf. (Chicago) (b. Ireland).
McGUIRE, Patrick, Pvt., Ill. Light Arty. (Chicago) (b. Ireland).
(b) McKEEN, Nineveh S., 1st Lt., 21st Ill. Inf. (Marshall).
MERRIFIELD, James K., Cpl., 88th Ill. Inf. (Manlius) (b. Pa.).
(b) MICHAEL, Edward S., 1st Lt., AC (Chicago).
MILLER, Henry A., Capt., 8th Ill. Inf. (Decatur) (b. Germany).
MILLER, Jacob C., Pvt., 113th Ill. Inf. (Geneva) (b. Ohio).
(b) *MONROE, James H., Pfc., 1st Cav. Div. (Wheaton).
(b) MOORE, Wilburen F., Pvt., 117th Ill. Inf. (Lebanon).
MORELOCK, Sterling, Pvt., 1st Div. (Oquawka) (b. Md.).
MORFORD, Jerome, Pvt., 55th Ill. Inf. (Bridgers Corner) (b. Pa.).
(b) *MOSKALA, Edward J., Pfc., 96th Inf. Div. (Chicago).
(b) MURPHY, Robinson B., Mus., 127th Ill. Inf. (Oswego).
MURPHY, Thomas C., Cpl., 31st Ill. Inf. (Pekin) (b. Ireland).
(b) NEWMAN, Marcellus J., Pvt., 111th Ill. Inf. (Richview).
O'DEA, John, Pvt., 8th Mo. Inf. (Clinton) (b. Ireland).
O'DONNELL, Menomen, 1st Lt., 11th Mo. Inf. (b. Ireland).
(b) OGDEN, Carlos C., 1st Lt., 79th Inf. Div. (Fairmount).
(b) *OLIVE, Milton L., III, Pfc., 173d Airborne Brig. (Chicago).
PALMER, George H., Mus., 1st Ill. Cav. (b. N.Y.).
PARKS. James W., Cpl., 11th Mo. Inf. (Xenia) (b. Ohio).
PAYNE, Thomas H. L., 1st Lt., 37th Ill. Inf. (Mendota) (b. Mass.).
PENTZER, Patrick H., Capt., 97th Ill. Inf. (Gillespie) (b. Mo.).
PEREZ, Manuel, Jr., 11th Airborne Div. (Chicago) (b. Okla.).
PIKE, Edward M., 1st Sgt., 33d Ill. Inf. (Bloomington) (b. Maine).
(b) POPE, Thomas A., Cpl., 33d Div. (Chicago).
POST, Philip Sidney, Col., 59th Ill. Inf. (Galesburg) (b. N.Y.).
POWERS, Wesley J., Cpl., 147th Ill. Inf. (Virgil) (b. Canada).

ARMY-AIR FORCE

PUTNAM, Winthrop D., Cpl., 77th Ill. Inf. (Peoria) (b. Mass.).
(b) REBMANN, George F., Sgt., 119th Ill. Inf. (Browning).
REED, William, Pvt., 8th Mo. Inf. (Pekin) (b. Pa.).
(b) *ROBINSON, James W., Sgt., 1st Inf. Div. (Hinsdale).
RUNDLE, Charles W., Pvt., 116th Ill. Inf. (Oakley) (b. Ohio).
(b) SANFORD, Jacob, Pvt., 55th Ill. Inf. (Prairie City).
SCHENCK, Benjamin W., Pvt., 116th Ill. Inf. (Maroa) (b. Ohio).
SCHOFIELD, John M., Maj., 1st Mo. Inf. (Freeport) (b. N.Y.).
(b) SCHROEDER, Henry F., Sgt., 16th U.S. Inf. (Chicago).
*SEBILLE, Louis J., USAF (Chicago) (b. Mich.).
SHAPLAND, John, Pvt., 104th Ill. Inf. (Ottawa) (b. England).
(b) SIMMONS, William T., Lt., 11th Mo. Inf. (Green County).
SLAGLE, Oscar, Pvt., 104th Ill. Inf. (Manlius) (b. Ohio).
SMALLEY, Reuben S., Pvt., 104th Ill. Inf. (Brookfield) (b. Pa.).
(b) SPALDING, Edward B., Sgt., 52d Ill. Inf. (Rockford).
SPRAGUE, Benona, Cpl., 116th Ill. Inf. (Chencys Grove) (b. N.Y.).
STEPHENS, William G., Pvt., Ill. Light Arty. (Chicago) (b. N.Y.).
STOCKMAN, George H., 1st Lt., 6th Mo. Inf. (Chicago) (b. Germany).
STOKES, George, Pvt., 122d Ill. Inf. (Jerseyville) (b. England).
SUMNER, James, Pvt., 1st U.S. Cav. (Chicago) (b. England).
(b) TAYLOR, Henry H., Sgt., 45th Ill. Inf. (Galena).
TOOMER, William, Sgt., 127th Ill. Inf. (Chicago) (b. Ireland).
(b) *TRUEMPER, Walter E., 2d Lt., 8th AF (Caurora).
(b) VERNAY, James D., 2d Lt., 11th Ill. Inf. (Lacon).
(b) VOKES, Leroy H., 1st Sgt., 3d U.S. Cav. (Lake County).
WARD, Thomas J., Pvt., 116th Ill. Inf. (Macon County) (b. W. Va.).
(b) WARDEN, John, Cpl., 55th Ill. Inf. (Lemont).
WEBBER, Alason P., Mus., 86th Ill. Inf. (b. N.Y.).
WHEATON, Loyd, Lt. Col., 8th Ill. Inf. (b. Mich.).
WHITE, Patrick H., Capt., Chicago Mercantile Btry., Ill. Light Arty. (Chicago) (b. Ireland).
(b) WHITMORE, John, Pvt., 119th Ill. Inf. (Camden).
(b) *WICKAM, Jerry Wayne, Cpl., 11th Arm. Cav. Reg. (Leaf River).
(b) WIDICK, Andrew J., Pvt., 116th Ill. Inf. (Decatur).
WILLIAMS, Ellwood N., Pvt., 28th Ill. Inf. (Havanna) (b. Pa.).
(b) WILSON, Arthur H., 2d Lt., 6th U.S. Cav. (Springfield).
(b) WILSON, Charles, Cpl., 5th U.S. Inf. (Beardstown).
WOOD, Richard H., Capt., 97th Ill. Inf. (Woodburn) (b. N.J.).

NAVY-MARINE CORPS

ASTEN, Charles, Quarter Gunner, USN (b. Nova Scotia).
*BAILEY, Kenneth D., Maj., USMC (Danville) (b. Okla.).
(b) *BIGELOW, Elmer Charles, WT1c., USNR (Hebron).
*BRUCE, Daniel D., Pfc., USMC, 1st Marine Div. (Chicago) (b. Ind.).
(b) *BURKE, Robert C., Pfc., USMC (Monticello).
(b) CATHERWOOD, John, Ordinary Seaman, USN (Springfield).
(b) COURTNEY, Henry C., Seaman, USN (Springfield).
(b) *CROMWELL, John Philip, Capt., USN (Henry).
(b) CRONAN, Willie, BM, USN (Chicago).
*DE LA GARZA, Emilio A., Jr., Cpl., USMC, 1st Marine Div. (Chicago) (b. Ind.).
DOW, Henry, BM, USN (b. Scotland).
(b) DUNLAP, Robert Hugo, Capt., USMCR (Abingdon).
(b) *FARDY, John Peter, Cpl., USMC (Chicago).
FERRELL, John H., Pilot, USN (b. Tenn.).
FLUCKEY, Eugene Bennett, Comdr., USN (b. D.C.).
GRBITCH, Rade, Seaman, USN (b. Austria).
(b) HELMS, John Henry, Sgt., USMC (Chicago).
HOLYOKE, William E., BM1c., USN (b. N.H.).
(b) HULL, James L., F1c., USN (Patoka).
HYLAND, John, Seaman, USN (b. Ireland).
IZAC, Edouard Victor Michel, Lt., USN. (b. Iowa).

NAVY-MARINE CORPS

(b)   JOHNSTON, William P., Landsman, USN (Chicago).
(b)   †KELLY, John Joseph, Pvt., USMC (Chicago). (Also awarded Army Medal of Honor.)
(b)   LEIMS, John Harold, 2d Lt., USMCR (Chicago).
(b)   *LESTER, Fred Faulkner, HA1c., USN (Downers Grove).
(b)   McCARTHY, Joseph Jeremiah, Capt., USMCR·(Chicago).
      McCORMICK, Michael, BM, USN (b. Ireland).
      MEYER, William, CM, USN (b. Germany).
(b)   MOLLOY, Hugh, Ordinary Seaman, USN (b. Ireland).
(b)   MULLIN, Hugh P., Seaman, USN (Richmond).
(b)   *OSBORNE, Weedon E., Lt. (jg.), Dental Corps, USN (Chicago).
(b)   *OZBOURN, Joseph William, Pvt., USMC (Herrin).
      ROBERTS, Charles Church, MM1c., USN (b. Mass.).
      ROBINSON, Robert Guy, Gun. Sgt., USMC (b. N.Y.).
(b)   SCHILT, Christian Frank, 1st Lt., USMC (Richland County).
(b)   STOCKDALE, James B., Rear Adm., USN (Abingdon).
      UPHAM, Oscar J., Pvt., USMC (b. Ohio).
(b)   *WEBER, Lester W., L/Cpl., USMC (Hinsdale).
(b)   WILLIAMS, Ernest Calvin, 1st Lt., USMC (Broadwell).
(b)   *WILSON, Robert Lee, Pfc., USMC (Centralia).
(b)   *WITEK, Frank Peter, Pfc., USMCR (b. Conn.).

INDIANA

ARMY-AIR FORCE

(b)   ANDERSON, Marion T., Capt., 51st Ind. Inf. (Kokomo).
      ARCHER, James W., 1st Lt. and Adj., 59th Ind. Inf. (Spencer) (b. Ill.).
(b)   ARMSTRONG, Clinton L., Pvt., 83d Ind. Inf. (Franklin).
      BANKS, George L., Sgt., 15th Ind. Inf. (Allen County).
(b)   BIDDLE, Melvin E., Pfc., 517th Para. Inf. Rgt. (Anderson).
(b)   BIEGLER, George W., Capt., 28th Inf., U.S. Vol. (Terre Haute).
(b)   BLASDEL, Thomas A., Pvt., 83d Ind. Inf. (Guilford).
      BOX, Thomas J., Capt., 27th Ind. Inf. (Bedford).
      BROUSE, Charles W., Capt., 100th Ind. Inf. (Indianapolis).
      BROWN, Lorenzo D., Pvt., 7th U.S. Inf. (Indianapolis) (b. N.C.).
(b)   BRUNER, Louis J., Pvt., 5th Ind. Cav. (Clifty Brumer).
(b)   BUCKLES, Abram J., Sgt., 18th Ind. Inf. (Muncie).
(b)   CHAMBERLAIN, Orville T., 2d Lt., 74th Ind. Inf. (Elkhart).
(b)   CHISMAN, William W., Pvt., 83d Ind. Inf. (Wilmington).
(b)   CONAWAY, John W., Pvt., 83d Ind. Inf. (Hartford).
(b)   CUMMINS, Andrew J., Sgt., 10th U.S. Inf. (Alexandria).
      DAVIS, John, Pvt., 17th Ind. Mtd. Inf. (Indianapolis) (b. Ky.).
      DAVIS, Sammy L., Sgt., 9th Inf. Div. (Martinsville) (b. Ohio).
      DOUGALL, Allan H., 1st Lt. and Adj., 88th Ind. Inf. (New Haven) (b. Scotland).
(b)   EVANS, Coron D., Pvt., 3d Ind. Cav. (Jefferson County).
(b)   FERRIER, Daniel T., Sgt., 2d Ind. Cav. (Delphi).
      FOUT, Frederick W., 2d Lt., 15th Btry., Ind. Light Arty. (Indianapolis) (b. Germany).
      FRANTZ, Joseph, Pvt., 83d Ind. Inf. (Osgood) (b. France).
      GRAHAM, Thomas N., 2d Lt., 15th Ind. Inf. (Westville).
(b)   GRAVES, Thomas J., Pvt., 17th U.S. Inf. (Millville).
(b)   GREEN, Francis C., Sgt., 8th U.S. Cav. (Mt. Vernon).
(b)   HELMS, David H., Pvt., 83d Ind. Inf. (Farmers Retreat).
      HOLMES, William T., Pvt., 3d Ind. Cav. (Indianapolis) (b. Ill.).
(b)   HORNADAY, Simpson, Pvt., 6th U.S. Cav. (Hendricks County).
(b)   HOUGH, Ira, Pvt., 8th Ind. Inf. (Henry County).
      HUDSON, Aaron R., Pvt., 17th Ind. Mtd. Inf. (La Porte County) (b. Ky.).
      JOHNSON, Ruel M., Maj., 100th Ind. Inf. (Goshen).
      JORDAN, Absalom, Cpl., 3d Ind. Cav. (North Madison) (b. Ohio).
(b)   KENDALL, William W., 1st Sgt., 49th Ind. Inf. (Dubois County).
      KISTERS, Gerry H., 2d Lt., 2d Armd. Div. (Bloomington) (b. Utah).

KUDER, Jeremiah, Lt., 74th Ind. Inf. (Warsaw) (b. Ohio).
LAWTON, Henry W., Capt., 30th Ind. Inf. (Ft. Wayne) (b. Ohio).
(b) LYTTON, Jeptha L., Cpl., 23d U.S. Inf. (Lawrence County).
McCALL, Thomas E., S/Sgt., 36th Inf. Div. (Veedersburg) (b. Kans.).
(b) *McGEE, William D., Pvt., 76th Inf. Div. (Indianapolis).
(b) *MICHAEL, Harry J., 2d Lt., 80th Inf. Div. (Milford).
(b) NOLAN, Joseph A., Artificer, 45th Inf., U.S. Vol. (South Bend).
(b) OPEL, John N., Pvt., 7th Ind. Inf. (Decatur County).
(b) OVERTURF, Jacob H., Pvt., 83d Ind. Inf. (Holton).
ROOD, Oliver P., Pvt., 20th Ind. Inf. (Terre Haute) (b. Ky.).
(b) RUSSELL, Milton, Capt., 51st Ind. Inf. (North Salem).
RYAN, Peter J., Pvt., 11th Ind. Inf. (Terre Haute) (b. Ireland).
(b) *SESTON, Charles H., Sgt., 11th Ind. Inf. (New Albany).
(b) SHEPHERD, William, Pvt., 3d Ind. Cav. (Dillsboro).
SMALLEY, Reuben, Pvt., 83d Ind. Inf. (Poston) (b. N.Y.).
STEINMETZ, William, Pvt., 83d Ind. Inf. (Sunmans) (b. Ky.).
STERLING, John T., Pvt., 11th Ind. Inf. (Marion County) (b. Ill.).
(b) STOLTZ, Frank, Pvt., 83d Ind. Inf. (Sunmans).
(b) SUTHERLAND, John A., Cpl., 8th U.S. Cav. (Montgomery County).
TAYLOR, Richard, Pvt., 18th Ind. Inf. (Martin County) (b. Ala.).
THOMPSON, William P., Sgt., 20th Ind. Inf. (Tippecanoe County) (b. N.Y.).
(b) WALKER, Allen, Pvt., 3d U.S. Cav. (Patriot).
(b) WEISS, Enoch R., Pvt., 1st U.S. Cav. (Kosciusko County).
(b) *WETHERBY, John C., Pvt., 4th U.S. Inf. (Martinsville).
(b) WHITEHEAD, John M., Chaplain, 15th Ind. Inf. (Westville).
(b) WOODFILL, Samuel, 1st Lt., 5th Div. (Bryantsburg).
(b) YOUNT, John P., Pvt., 3d U.S. Cav. (Putnam County).

(b) *ABRELL, Charles G., Cpl., USMC, First Marine Div. (Terre Haute).
(b) ANTRIM, Richard Nott, Comdr., USN (Peru).
BADDERS, William, C.M.M., USN (Indianapolis) (b. Ill.).
(b) BEARSS, Hiram Iddings, Col., USMC (Peru).
(b) BUCHANAN, Allen, Lt. Comdr., USN (Evansville).
(b) CAMPBELL, William, BM, USN.
DITZENBACK, John, Quartermaster, USN (b. N.Y.).
(b) HILL, Frank E., SC1c., USN (La Grange).
(b) INGRAM, Jonas Howard, Lt. (jg.), USN (Jeffersonville).
(b) *SCOTT, Norman, Rear Adm., USN (Indianapolis).
(b) SHOUP, David Monroe, Col., USMC (Tippecanoe).
(b) WILKES, Perry, Pilot, USN.
*WINDRICH, William G., S/Sgt., USMC, 1st Marine Div. (Hammond) (b. Ill.).

IOWA

BEBB, Edward J., Pvt., 4th Iowa Cav. (Henry County) (b. Ohio).
(b) BEYER, Arthur O., Cpl., 603d T.D. Bn. (St. Ansgar).
BIRDSALL, Horatio L., Sgt., 3d Iowa Cav. (Keokuk) (b. N.Y.).
BIRKHIMER, William E., Capt., 3d U.S. Arty. (b. Ohio).
BOQUET, Nicholas, Pvt., 1st Iowa Inf. (Burlington) (b. Germany).
(b) BRAS, Edgar A., Sgt., 8th Iowa Inf. (Louisa County).
(b) BRILES, Herschel F., S/Sgt., 899th Tank Destroyer Battalion (Fort Des Moines).
(b) *CHRISTENSEN, Dale Eldon, 2d Lt., 112th Cav. Regt. (Gray).
COSGRIFF, Richard H., Pvt., 4th Iowa Cav. (Wapello) (b. N.Y.).
(b) DAY, George E., Col., USAF. (Sioux City).
(b) DETHLEFSEN, Merlyn Hans, Maj., U.S. Air Force (Greenville).
DUNLAVY, James, Pvt., 3d Iowa Cav. (Davis County) (b. Ind.).
(b) *EDWARDS, Junior D., Sfc., 2d Inf. Div. (Indianaola).
ELSON, James M., Sgt., 9th Iowa Inf. (Shellsburg) (b. Ohio).
FANNING, Nicholas, Pvt., 4th Iowa Cav. (Independence) (b. Ind.).

ARMY-AIR FORCE

GODLEY, Leonidas M., 1st Sgt., 22d Iowa Inf. (Ashland) (b. W. Va.).
HAYS, John H., Pvt., 4th Iowa Cav. (Oskaloosa) (b. Ohio).
(b) HEALEY, George W., Pvt., 5th Iowa Cav. (Dubuque).
HERINGTON, Pitt B., Pvt., 11th Iowa Inf. (Tipton) (b. Mich.).
*HIBBS, Robert John, 2d Lt., 1st Inf. Div. (Des Moines) (b. Nebr.).
HILL, James, 1st Lt., 21st Iowa Inf. (Cascade) (b. England).
KALTENBACH, Luther, Cpl., 12th Iowa Inf. (Honey Creek). (b. Germany).
(b) KNOX, John W., Sgt., 5th U.S. Inf. (Burlington).
(b) *LINDSEY, Darrell R., Capt., Air Corps (Storm Lake).
MAY, William, Pvt., 32d Iowa Inf. (Maysville) (b. Pa.).
MAYES, William B., Pvt., 11th Iowa Inf. (De Witt) (b. Ohio).
MILLER, James P., Pvt., 4th Iowa Cav. (Henry County) (b. Ohio).
MORGAN, Richard H., Cpl., 4th Iowa Cav. (Taylor) (b. Ind.).
(b) NEPPEL, Ralph G., Sgt., 83d Inf. Div. (Glidden).
(b) *PIKE, Emory J., Lt. Col., 82d Div. (Des Moines).
POWER, Albert, Pvt., 3d Iowa Cav. (Davis County) (b. Ohio).
SLOAN, Andrew J., Pvt., 12th Iowa Inf. (Colesburg) (b. Pa.).
SMITH, Henry I., 1st Lt., 7th Iowa Inf. (Shell Rock Hall) (b. England).
(b) STANLEY, Eben, Pvt., 5th U.S. Cav. (Decatur County).
STRAUB, Paul F., Surg., 36th Inf., U.S. Vol. (b. Germany).
SWAN, Charles A., Pvt., 4th Iowa Cav. (Mt. Pleasant) (b. Pa.).
(b) *THORSON, John F., Pfc., 7th Inf. Div. (Armstrong).
TIBBETS, Andrew W., Pvt., 3d Iowa Cav. (Appanoose County) (b. Ind.).
(b) TITUS, Calvin Pearl, Mus., 14th U.S. Inf. (Vinton).
(b) TWOMBLY, Voltaire P., Cpl., 2d Iowa Inf. (Keosauqua).
(b) WELCH, George W., Pvt., 11th Mo. Inf. (Keokuk).
WILLIAMSON, James A., Col., 4th Iowa Inf. (Des Moines) (b. Ky.).
YOUNG, Calvary M., Sgt., 3d Iowa Cav. (Hopeville) (b. Iowa).

NAVY-MARINE CORPS

(b) DEIGNAN, Osborn, Cox., USN (Sheart).
FITZ, Joseph, Ordinary Seaman, USN (b. Austria).
(b) FLETCHER, Frank Friday, Rear Adm., USN (Oskaloosa).
(b) FLETCHER, Frank Jack, Lt., USN (Marshalltown).
(b) HOWARD, Jimmie E., Gunnery Sgt., 1st Marine Div. (Burlington).
(b) PIERCE, Francis J., PhM1c., USN (Earlville).

KANSAS

ARMY-AIR FORCE

(b) ADAMS, Stanley T., M/Sgt., 24th Inf. Div. (Olathe).
(b) *BLECKLEY, Erwin R., 2d Lt., 130th Field Arty., Obs., 50th Aero Sq., A. S. (Wichita).
*COWAN, Richard Eller, Pfc., 2d Inf. Div. (Wichita) (b. Nebr.).
(b) EHLERS, Walter D., S/Sgt., 1st Inf. Div. (Manhattan).
(b) FERGUSON, Arthur M., 1st Lt., 36th Inf., U.S. Vol. (Burlington).
FUNSTON, Frederick, Col., 20th Kans. Vol. Inf. (Iola) (b. Ohio).
(b) HENDERSON, Joseph, Sgt., 6th U.S. Cav. (Leavenworth).
HUNTSMAN, John A., Sgt., 36th Inf., U.S. Vol. (Lawrence) (b. Iowa).
JOHNSON, Leon W., Col., 9th Air Force (Moline) (b. Mo.).
*PEDEN, Forrest E., T5g., 3d Inf. Div. (Walthena) (b. Mo.).
*PITTS, Riley L., Capt., 25th Inf. Div. (Wichita) (b. Okla.).
(b) ROBB, George S., 1st Lt., 93d Div. (Salina).
(b) TREMBLEY, William B., Pvt., 20th Kans. Vol. Inf. (Kansas City).
(b) WHITE, Edward, Pvt., 20th Kans. Vol. Inf. (Kansas City).

NAVY-MARINE CORPS

(b) *DAVENPORT, Jack A., Cpl., USMC, 1st Marine Div. (Mission).
(b) FOSTER, Paul Frederick, Ens., USN (Wichita).
(b) *TIMMERMAN, Grant Frederick, Sgt., USMC (Americus).

ARMY-AIR FORCE

(b)　BELL, J. Franklin, Col., 36th Inf., U.S. Vol. (Shelbyville).
(b)　*COLLIER, John W., Cpl., 25th Inf. Div. (Worthington).
(b)　*CRAIN, Morris E., T/Sgt., 36th Inf. Div. (Paducah).
(b)　CRUSE, Thomas, 2d Lt., 6th U.S. Cav. (Owensboro).
(b)　DAY, William L., 1st Sgt., 5th U.S. Cav. (Barron County).
(b)　DODD, Carl H., 1st Lt., 24th Inf. Div. (Kenvir).
(b)　HARDAWAY, Benjamin F., 1st Lt., 17th U.S. Inf. (Benleyville).
(b)　HARRIS, William M., Pvt., 7th U.S. Cav. (Madison County).
　　　HAWTHORNE, Harry L., 2d Lt., 2d U.S. Arty. (b. Minn.).
(b)　HORSFALL, William H., Drummer, 1st Ky. Inf. (Campbell County).
　　　HUGHES, Oliver, Cpl., 12th Ky. Inf. (Albany) (b. Tenn.).
　　　JONES, William H., Farrier, 2d U.S. Cav. (Louisville) (b. N.C.).
(b)　KERR, John B., Capt., 6th U.S. Cav. (Hutchison Station).
　　　*LONG, Donald Russell, Sgt., 1st Inf. Div. (Ashland) (b. Ohio).
(b)　MATTINGLY, Henry B., Pvt., 10th Ky. Inf. (Marion County).
(b)　McDONALD, Franklin M., Pvt., 11th U.S. Inf. (Bowling Green).
　　　McGINTY, John J., III, 2d Lt., 3d Mar. Div. (Louisville) (b. Mass.).
(b)　*NASH, David P., Pfc., 9th Inf. Div. (Whitesville).
(b)　NASH, James J., Pvt., 10th U.S. Inf. (Louisville).
　　　PHOENIX, Edwin, Cpl., 4th U.S. Cav. (b. Mo.).
(b)　ROSS, Wilburn, K., Pvt., 3d Inf. Div. (Strunk).
(b)　SANDLIN, Willie, Sgt., 33d Div. (Hyden).
(b)　SCOTT, George D., Pvt., 7th U.S. Cav. (Mt. Vernon).
(b)　SHAW, Thomas, Sgt., 9th U.S. Cav. (Covington).
(b)　*SMITH, David M., Pfc., 2d Inf. Div. (Livingston).
(b)　SPURRIER, Junior J., S/Sgt., 35th Inf. Div. (Riggs).
(b)　*SQUIRES, John C., Sgt., 3d Inf. Div. (Louisville).
　　　*STEWART, Jimmy G., S/Sgt., 1st Cav. Div. (Ashland) (b. W. Va.).
(b)　STIVERS, Thomas W., Pvt., 7th U.S. Cav. (Madison County).
(b)　SULLIVAN, Thomas, Pvt., 1st U.S. Cav. (Covington).
　　　WALKER, Dr. Mary E., Contract Acting Assistant Surgeon, U.S. Army (Louisville) (b. N.Y.).
(b)　WEST, Ernest E., Pfc., 25th Inf. Div. (Wurtland).
(b)　WESTON, John F., Maj., 4th Ky. Cav.
(b)　WOODS, Brent, Sgt., 9th U.S. Cav. (Louisville).

NAVY-MARINE CORPS

(b)　BARBER, William E., Capt., USMC, 1st Marine Div. (West Liberty).
　　　BOERS, Edward William, Seaman USN (b. Ohio).
(b)　BUSH, Richard Earl, Cpl., USMCR (Glasgow).
(b)　CLARY, Edward Alvin, WT, USN (Foxport).
(b)　HOLT, George, Quarter Gunner, USN.
(b)　NOBLE, Daniel, Landsman, USN.
(b)　*PHELPS, Wesley, Pfc., USMCR (Neafus).
(b)　SKAGGS, Luther, Jr., Pfc., USMC (Henderson).

LOUISIANA

ARMY-AIR FORCE

(b)　ANDERSON, Charles W., Pvt., 1st N.Y. (Lincoln) Cav.
　　　BEAUFORT, Jean J., Cpl., 2d La. Inf. (New Orleans) (b. France).
　　　*BENNETT, Steven L., Capt., 20th Tac. Air Sup. Sqr. (Lafayette) (b. Tex.).
(b)　*FOURNET, Douglas B., 1st Lt., 1st Cav. Div. (Airmobile) (Lake Charles).
　　　GREELY, Adolphus W., Maj. Gen., U.S. Army, retired (b. Mass.).
(b)　HUNT, Fred O., Pvt., 5th U.S. Inf. (New Orleans).
(b)　*JOHNSON, Leroy, Sgt., 32d Inf. Div. (Oakdale).
　　　KANE, John R., Col., A.C. (Shreveport) (b. Tex.).
　　　NOVOSEL, Michael J., Chief War. Off., 68th Medical Group, (Kenner) (b. Pa.).
(b)　ROACH, Hampton M., Cpl., 5th U.S. Cav. (Concord).
(b)　SCHOWALTER, Edward R., Jr., 1st Lt., 7th Inf. Div. (Metairie).
(b)　STANCE, Emanuel, Sgt., 9th U.S. Cav. (Carroll Parish).

ARMY-AIR FORCE

(b)   WHITTINGTON, Hulon B., Sgt., 2d Armd. Div. (Bastrop).
(b)   WILLIAMS, Moses, 1st Sgt., 9th U.S. Cav. (Carrollton, La.).
(b)   WISE, Homer L., S/Sgt., 36th Inf. Div. (Baton Rouge).

NAVY-MARINE CORPS

(b)   *CLAUSEN, Raymond M., Pfc., 1st Mar. Aircraft Wing (New Orleans).
(b)   DE BLANC, Jefferson Joseph, 1st Lt., USMCR (Lockport).
       FREEMAN, Martin, Pilot, USN (b. Germany).
       *GILMORE, Howard Walter, Comd., USN (b. Ala.).
(b)   OSBORNE, John, Seaman, USN (New Orleans).
(b)   RYAN, Thomas John, Ensign, USN (New Orleans).
(b)   †WEISBOGEL, Albert, Captain of the Mizzen Top, USN (New Orleans).
       WILKINSON, Theodore Stark, Ens., USN (b. Md.).
(b)   WILLIAMS, John, Captain of Maintop, USN (New Orleans).

MAINE
ARMY-AIR FORCE

(b)   AMES, Adelbert, 1st Lt., 5th U.S. Arty. (Rockland).
(b)   BAILEY, James E., Sgt., 5th U.S. Cav. (Dexter).
(b)   BELCHER, Thomas, Pvt., 9th Maine Inf. (Bangor).
(b)   BLISS, Zenas R., Col., 7th R.I. Inf. (Johnston).
(b)   BOWMAN, Alonzo, Sgt., 6th U.S. Cav. (Washington Township).
(b)   *BUKER, Brian Leroy, Sgt., 1st Spec. Forces (Benton).
(b)   CHAMBERLAIN, Joshua L., Col., 20th Maine Inf. (Brunswick).
(b)   CHASE, John F., Pvt., Maine Light Arty. (Augusta).
(b)   CLARK, Charles A., Lt. and Adj., 6th Maine Inf. (Sangorville).
(b)   CONDON, Clarence M., Sgt., 3d U.S. Arty. (Southbrooksville).
(b)   DAHLGREN, Edward C., 2d Lt., 36th Inf. Div. (Portland).
       DOHERTY, Thomas M., Cpl., 21st U.S. Inf. (Newcastle) (b. Ireland).
(b)   ESTES, Lewellyn G., Capt., and Ass't. Adj. Gen., Vol. (Penobscot).
(b)   FERNALD, Albert E., 1st Lt., 20th Maine Inf. (Winterport).
       *FOURNIER, William G., Sgt., 25th Inf. Div. (Winterport) (b. Conn.).
(b)   *GOODBLOOD, Clair, Cpl., 3d Inf. Div. (Burnham).
(b)   HANSCOM, Moses C., Cpl., 19th Maine Inf. (Bowdoinham).
(b)   HASKELL, Frank W., Sgt. Maj., 3d Maine Inf. (Waterville).
(b)   HAYNES, Asbury F., Cpl., 17th Maine Inf. (Edingburgh).
(b)   HESSELTINE, Francis S., Col., 13th Maine Inf. (Bangor).
(b)   HOWARD, Oliver O., Brig. Gen., U.S. Vol. (Leeds).
       HYDE, Thomas W., Maj., 7th Maine Inf. (Bath) (b. Italy).
(b)   KNOWLES, Abiather J., Pvt., 2d Maine Inf. (La Grange).
(b)   LITTLEFIELD, George H., Cpl., 1st Maine Inf. (Skowhegan).
(b)   *LORING, Charles J., Jr., Maj., USAF (Portland).
       MATTOCKS, Charles P., Maj., 17th Maine Inf. (Portland) (b. Vt.).
       *McMAHON, Thomas J., Spec. 4, 196th Inf. Brig. Amer. Div. (Lewiston) (b. D.C.).
(b)   *McMASTERS, Henry A., Cpl., 4th U.S. Cav. (Augusta).
(b)   MERRIAM, Henry C., Lt. Col., 73d U.S. Colored Troops (Houlton).
(b)   MERRILL, Augustus, Capt., 1st Maine Vet. Inf. (Lyndon).
(b)   MILLETT, Lewis L., Capt., 25th Inf. Div. (Mechanic Falls).
(b)   MORRILL, Walter G., Capt., 20th Maine Inf. (Brownville).
(b)   ROBERTS, Otis O., Sgt., 6th Maine Inf. (Dexter).
(b)   *SKIDGEL, Donald Sidney, Sgt., 1st Cav. Div. (Caribou).
(b)   SMITH, Charles H., Col., 1st Maine Cav. (Hollis).
(b)   SMITH, Joseph S., Lt. Col. and Commissary, 2d Army Corps (Wiscasset).
(b)   SMITH, William, Pvt., 8th U.S. Cav. (Bath).
(b)   SPURLING, Andrew B., Lt. Col., 2d Maine Cav. (Cranberry Isles).
(b)   TAYLOR, Wilbur N., Cpl., 8th U.S. Cav. (Hamden).
(b)   THAXTER, Sidney W., Maj., 1st Maine Cav. (Bangor).
(b)   TOBIE, Edward P., Sgt. Maj., 1st Maine Cav. (Lewiston).
(b)   TOZIER, Andrew J., Sgt., 20th Maine Inf. (Plymouth).
       *WAUGH, Robert T., 1st Lt., 85th Inf, Div. (Augusta) (b. R.I.).

WHEELER, Henry W., Pvt. 2d Maine Inf. (Bangor) (b. Ark.).
(b) WHITTIER, Edward N., 1st Lt., Maine Light Arty. (Gorham).
(b) WOOD, H. Clay., 1st Lt., 11th U.S. Inf. (Winthrop).
ZEAMER, Jay, Jr., Maj., U.S. Army Air Corps (Machias) (b. Pa.)

NAVY-MARINE CORPS

(b) ANGLING, John, Cabin Boy, USN (Portland).
(b) BIBBER, Charles J., GM, USN (Portland).
(b) BICKFORD, John F., Captain of Top, USN (Tremont).
(b) BOWMAN, Edward R., Quartermaster, USN (Eastport).
(b) DAVIS, Samuel W., Ordinary Seaman, USN.
(b) DUNCAN, Adam, BM, USN.
(b) DUNN, William, Quartermaster, USN.
(b) FARLEY, William, BM, USN (Whitehead).
(b) FOSS, Herbert Louis, Seaman, USN (Belfast).
(b) FRISBEE, John B., GM, USN.
(b) GIDDINGS, Charles, Seaman, USN (Bangor).
(b) HAYDEN, Cyrus, Carpenter, USN (York).
(b) KENDRICK, Thomas, Cox., USN (Bath).
(b) MACK, John, Seaman, USN.
(b) McCULLOCK, Adam, Seaman, USN.
McLEOD, James, Captain of Foretop, USN (b. Scotland).
(b) POOLE, William B., Quartermaster, USN.
RICE, Charles, Coal Heaver, USN (b. Russia).
ROBINSON, John, Captain of the Hold, USN (b. Cuba).
(b) SCHONLAND, Herbert Emery, Comdr., USN (Portland).
(b) SEWARD, Richard, Paymaster's Steward, USN (Kittery).
(b) *SMITH, Charles H., Cox., USN.
(b) STERLING, James E., Coal Heaver, USN.
(b) TAYLOR, Thomas, Cox., USN (Bangor).
(b) TRIPP, Othniel, CBM, USN.
(b) VERNEY, James W., CQM, USN.
(b) WILLIAMS, Anthony, Sailmaker's Mate, USN (b. Mass.).
(b) YOUNG, Horatio N., Seaman, USN (Calaise).

MARYLAND

ARMY-AIR FORCE

(b) BARNES, William H., Pvt., 38th U.S. Colored Troops (St. Marys County).
(b) BEAUFORD, Clay, 1st Sgt., 5th U.S. Cav. (Washington County).
(b) BOYNE, Thomas, Sgt., 9th U.S. Cav. (Prince Georges County).
(b) BUFFINGTON, John E., Sgt., 6th Md. Inf. (Carroll County).
(b) CADWALLADER, Abel G., Cpl., 1st Md. Inf. (Baltimore).
(b) CARTER, Joseph F., Capt., 3d Md. Inf. (Baltimore).
CLARKE, Powhatan H., 2d Lt., 10th U.S. Cav. (Baltimore) (b. La.).
(b) *COSTIN, Henry G., Pvt. 29th Div. (Baltimore).
(b) CRIST, John, Sgt., 8th U.S. Cav. (Baltimore).
DEETLINE, Frederick, Pvt., 7th U.S. Cav. (Baltimore) (b. Germany).
(b) DONAHUE, John L., Pvt., 8th U.S. Cav. (Baltimore County).
(b) DORSEY, Decatur, Sgt., 39th U.S. Colored Troops (Baltimore County).
(b) FLEETWOOD, Christian A., Sgt. Maj., 4th U.S. Colored Troops (Baltimore).
(b) GALT, Sterling A., Artificer, 36th Inf., U.S. Vol. (Pawneytown).
*GRAHAM, James A., Capt., 1st Mar. Div. (Prince Georges) (b. Pa.).
GREAVES, Clinton, Cpl., 9th U.S. Cav. (Prince Georges County) (b. Va.).
(b) HARRIS, James H., Sgt., 38th U.S. Colored Troops (St. Marys County).
HART, John W., Sgt., 6th Pa. Res. (Cumberland) (b. Germany).
(b) HILTON, Alfred B., Sgt., 4th U.S. Colored Troops (Harford County).
(b) *HOOKER, George, Pvt., 5th U.S. Cav. (Frederick).
*JACHMAN, Isadore S., S/Sgt., U.S. Army (Baltimore) (b. Germany).
(b) *JECELIN, William R., S/Sgt., 25th Inf. Div. (Baltimore).
(b) KOOGLE, Jacob, 1st Lt., 7th Md. Inf. (Frederick).

MATHEWS, William H., 1st Sgt., 2d Md. Vet. Inf. (b. England).
(b)   MAUS, Marion P., 1st Lt., 1st U.S. Inf. (Tennallytown).
      *McDONALD, Phill G., Pfc., 4th Inf. Div. (Hyattsville) (b. W. Va.).
      McGONNIGLE, Andrew J., Capt. and Asst. Quartermaster, U.S. Vol.
        (Cumberland) (b. N.Y.).
(b)   McMILLAN, Albert W., Sgt., 7th U.S. Cav. (Baltimore).
      MYERS, William H., Pvt., 1st Md. Cav. (Baltimore) (b. Pa.).
(b)   OLIVER, Francis, 1st Sgt., 1st U.S. Cav. (Baltimore).
(b)   PENNSYL, Josiah, Sgt., 6th U.S. Cav. (Frederick County).
      PHELPS, Charles E., Col., 7th Md. Inf. (Baltimore) (b. Vt.).
      *PORTER, Donn F., Sgt., 25th Inf. Div. (Baltimore) (b. Pa.).
(b)   PORTER, Samuel, Farrier, 6th U.S. Cav. (Montgomery County).
(b)   SCHNEIDER, George, Sgt., 3d Md. Vet. Inf. (Baltimore).
(b)   SHEA, Joseph H., Pvt., 92d N.Y. Inf. (Baltimore).
(b)   *SHERIDAN, Carl V., Pfc., 9th Inf. Div. (Baltimore).
(b)   SKINNER, John O., Contract Surg., U.S. Army.
(b)   SMITH, Andrew J., Sgt., 8th U.S. Cav. (Baitimore).
(b)   SMITH, Francis M., 1st Lt. and Adj., 1st Md. Inf. (Frederick).
(b)   SMITH, Otto, Pvt., 8th U.S. Cav. (Baltimore).
(b)   TAYLOR, Charles, 1st Sgt., 3d U.S. Cav. (Baltimore).
      THOMPSON, John, Cpl., 1st Md. Inf. (Baltimore) (b. Denmark).
      TUCKER, Jacob R., Cpl., 4th Md. Inf. (Baltimore) (b. Pa.).
(b)   WALLEY, Augustus, Pvt., 9th U.S. Cav. (Reisterstown).
(b)   *WALMSLEY, John S., Jr., USAF (Baltimore).
      WEINERT, Paul H., Cpl., 1st U.S. Arty. (Baltimore) (b. Germany).
(b)   WIEDORFER, Paul J., Pvt., 80th Inf. Div. (Baltimore).

ANDREWS, John, Ordinary Seaman, USN (b. Pa.).
      BROWN, John, Captain of Afterguard, USN (b. Denmark).
(b)   BROWN, William H., Landsman, USN (Baltimore).
(b)   BUCK, James, Quartermaster, USN (Baltimore).
(b)   CARR, William M., Master at Arms, USN (Baltimore).
(b)   CHATHAM, John Purnell, GM2d, USN (Worchester).
      CONNOR, Thomas, Ordinary Seaman, USN (b. Ireland).
(b)   DIGGINS, Bartholomew, Ordinary Seaman, USN (Baltimore).
(b)   HAMMANN, Charles Hazeltine, Ens., USNRF (Baltimore).
(b)   HAYDEN, Joseph B., Quartermaster, USN.
(b)   JARRETT, Berrie H., Seaman, USN (Baltimore).
      JOHANSON, John P., Seaman, USN (b. Sweden).
(b)   JONES, Thomas, Cox., USN (Baltimore).
(b)   LAKIN, Daniel, Seaman, USN (Baltimore).
(b)   MAGEE, John W., F2d, USN.
(b)   McDONNELL, Edward Orrick, Ens., USN (Baltimore).
(b)   McNAIR, Frederick Vallette, Lt., USN.
      MORTON, Charles W., BM, USN (b. Ireland).
(b)   †MULLEN, Patrick, BM, USN (Baltimore).
      NORRIS, Thomas R., Lt., USN (Silver Spring) (b. Fla.).
      PRESTON, Arthur Murray, Lt., USNR (Silver Spring) (b. D.C.).
(b)   *RICKETTS, Milton Ernest, Lt., USN (Baltimore).
(b)   RINGOLD, Edward, Cox., USN (Baltimore).
(b)   *SHUCK, William E., Jr., S/Sgt., USMC, 1st Marine Div. (Cumberland).
(b)   SHUTES, Henry, Captain of Forecastle, USN (Baltimore).
(b)   SWEARER, Benjamin, Seaman, USN (Baltimore).
      *TALLENTINE, James, Quarter Gunner, USN (b. England).
(b)   *TAYLOR, Karl G., Sr., S/Sgt., 3d Mar. Div. (Laurel).
(b)   TRUETT, Alexander H., Cox., USN (Baltimore).
      WRIGHT, William, Yeoman, USN (b. England).

ARMY-AIR FORCE

(b) ADAMS, John G. B., 2d Lt., 19th Mass. Inf. (Groveland).
(b) ALLEN, Nathaniel M., Cpl., 1st Mass. Inf. (Boston).
(b) ANDERSON, Frederick C., Pvt., 18th Mass. Inf.
(b) *BARNES, John A., III, Pfc., 173d Airborne Brig. (Needham).
BAYBUTT, Philip, Pvt., 2d Mass. Cav. (Fall River) (b. England).
(b) *BEAUDOIN, Raymond O., 1st Lt., 30th Inf. Div. (Holyoke).
(b) BESSEY, Charles A., Cpl., 3d U.S. Cav. (Reading).
BOODY, Robert, Sgt., 40th N.Y. Inf. (Amesbury) (b. Maine).
(b) BOSS, Orlando, Cpl., 25th Mass. Inf. (Fitchburg).
(b) BOWDEN, Samuel, Cpl., 6th U.S. Cav. (Salem).
BRETT, Lloyd M., 2d Lt., 2d U.S. Cav. (Malden) (b. Maine).
BROWN, John H., Capt., 12th Ky. Inf. (Charlestown) (b. Canada).
(b) BRYANT, Andrew S., Sgt., 46th Mass. Inf. (Springfield).
(b) BUFFUM, Robert, Pvt., 21st Ohio Inf. (Salem).
(b) BURT, James M., Capt., 2d Armd. Div. (Lee).
CALLEN, Thomas J., Pvt., 7th U.S. Cav. (Boston) (b. Ireland).
CARNEY, William H., Sgt., 54th Mass. Colored Inf. (New Bedford) (b. Va.).
(b) CARSON, Anthony J., Cpl., 43d Inf., U.S. Vol. (Malden).
CARTER, Robert G., 2d Lt., 4th U.S. Cav. (Bradford) (b. Maine).
CASEY, David, Pvt., 25th Mass. Inf. (Northbridge) (b. Ireland).
(b) CHANDLER, Henry F., Sgt., 59th Mass. Inf. (Andover).
COSGROVE, Thomas, Pvt., 40th Mass. Inf. (E. Stoughton) (b. Ireland).
(b) *CRAIG, Gordon M., Cpl., 1st Cav. Div. (East Bridgewater).
(b) CRANDALL, Charles, Pvt., 8th U.S. Cav. (Worcester).
(b) DAWSON, Michael, Trumpeter, 6th U.S. Cav. (Boston).
(b) DEANE, John M., Maj., 29th Mass. Inf. (Freetown).
(b) DeCASTRO, Joseph H., Cpl., 19th Mass. Inf. (Boston).
(b) *DeFRANZO, Arthur F., S/Sgt., 1st Inf. Div. (Saugus).
(b) DELAND, Frederick N., Pvt., 40th Mass. Inf. (Sheffield).
(b) DODGE, Francis S., Capt., 9th U.S. Cav. (Danvers).
DOWNEY, William, Pvt., 4th Mass. Cav. (Fall River) (b. Ireland).
(b) DUFFEY, John, Pvt., 4th Mass. Cav. (New Bedford).
EDDY, Samuel E., Pvt., 37th Mass. Inf. (Chesterfield) (b. Vt.).
ELLIOTT, Russell C., Sgt., 3d Mass. Cav. (Boston) (b. N.H.).
(b) ELLSWORTH, Thomas F., Capt., 55th Mass. Inf. (Boston).
*FALLS, Benjamin F., Color Sgt., 19th Mass. Inf. (Lynn) (b. N.H.).
FERRIS, Eugene W., 1st Lt. and Adj., 30th Mass. Inf. (Lowell) (b. Vt.).
(b) FOLEY, Robert F., Capt., 25th Inf. Div. (Newton).
(b) GARDNER, Charles N., Pvt., 32d Mass. Inf. (Norwell).
GARDNER, Robert J., Sgt., 34th Mass. Inf. (Berkshire County) (b. N.Y.).
(b) GARLAND, Harry, Cpl., 2d U.S. Cav. (Boston).
(b) GAYLORD, Levi B., Sgt., 29th Mass. Inf. (Boston).
(b) GIBSON, Edward H., Sgt., 27th Inf., U.S. Vol. (Boston).
(b) GIFFORD, David L., Pvt., 4th Mass. Cav. (Dartmouth).
(b) GOODMAN, David, Pvt., 8th U.S. Cav. (Paxton).
(b) GRACE, Peter, Sgt., 83d Pa. Inf. (Berkshire).
(b) *GRANT, Joseph Xavier, Capt., 25th Inf. Div. (Cambridge).
(b) HADDOO, John, Cpl., 5th U.S. Inf. (Boston).
(b) HALL, George J., S/Sgt., 34th Inf. Div. (Stoneham).
(b) HANLEY, Richard P., Sgt., 7th U.S. Cav. (Boston).
HANNA, Marcus A., Sgt., 50th Mass. Inf. (Rockport) (b. Maine).
HARBOURNE, John H., Pvt., 29th Mass. Inf. (Boston) (b. England).
(b) HASKELL, Marcus M., Sgt., 35th Mass. Inf. (Chelsea).
HOLEHOUSE, James (John), Pvt., 7th Mass. Inf. (Fall River) (b. England).
(b) HOMAN, Conrad, Color Sgt., 29th Mass. Inf. (Roxbury).
HOOKER, George W., 1st Lt., 4th Vt. Inf. (Boston) (b. N.Y.).
(b) HOWE, William H., Sgt., 29th Mass. Inf. (Haverhill).
(b) HUNTER, Charles A., Sgt., 34th Mass. Inf. (Spencer).
(b) JELLISON, Benjamin H., Sgt., 19th Mass. Inf. (Newburyport).
JOHNS, Henry T., Pvt., 49th Mass. Inf. (Hinsdale).
*JOHNSON, Elden H., Pvt., 3d Inf. Div. (E. Weymouth) (b. N.J.).
KARPELES, Leopold, Sgt., 57th Mass. Inf. (Springfield) (b. Hungary).

ARMY-AIR FORCE

(b)   LEONARD, Edwin, Sgt., 37th Mass. Inf. (Agawan).
(b)   LEWIS, William B., Sgt., 3d U.S. Cav. (Boston).
      LORD, William, Musician, 40th Mass. Inf. (Lawrence) (b. England).
      LOVERING, George M., 1st Sgt., 4th Mass. Inf. (E. Randolph) (b. N.H.).
(b)   LOWTHERS, James, Pvt., 6th U.S. Cav. (Boston).
      LUNT, Alphonso M., Sgt., 38th Mass. Inf. (Cambridge) (b. Maine).
(b)   LUTHER, James H., Pvt., 7th Mass. Inf. (Dighton).
      MacGILLIVARY, Charles A., Sgt., 44th Inf. Div. (Boston) (b. Canada).
      MAHONEY, Jeremiah, Sgt., 29th Mass. Inf. (Fall River).
(b)   MANNING, Joseph S., Pvt., 29th Mass. Inf.
(b)   MARLAND, William, 1st Lt., Mass. Light Arty. (Andover).
(b)   MATHEWS, George W., Asst. Surg., 36th Inf., U.S. Vol. (Worcester).
(b)   MATTHEWS, David A., Cpl., 8th U.S. Cav. (Boston).
(b)   MAXHAM, Lowell M., Cpl., 7th Mass. Inf. (Taunton).
(b)   MAYNARD, George H., Pvt., 13th Mass. Inf. (Waltham).
(b)   McKINLEY, Daniel, Pvt., 8th U.S. Cav. (Boston).
(b)   MILES, Nelson A., Col., 61st N.Y. Inf. (Roxbury).
(b)   MOSHER, Louis C., 2d Lt., Philippine Scouts (Brockton).
      MOYLAN, Myles, Capt., 7th U.S. Cav. (Essex) (b. Ireland).
      MURPHY, Daniel J., Sgt., 19th Mass. Inf. (Lowell) (b. Pa.).
(b)   *MURPHY, Frederick C., Pfc., 65th Inf. Div. (Weymouth).
(b)   NEE, George H., Pvt., 21st U.S. Inf. (Boston).
(b)   NEILON, Frederick S., Sgt., 6th U.S. Cav.
(b)   O'REGAN, Michael, Pvt., 8th U.S. Cav. (Fall River).
(b)   OSBORNE, William, Sgt., 1st U.S. Cav. (Boston).
(b)   OSBORNE, William H., Pvt., 29th Mass Inf. (Scituate).
(b)   *OUELLETTE, Joseph R., Pfc., 2d Inf. Div. (Lowell).
(b)   *PERKINS, Michael J., Pfc., 101st Inf., 26th Div. (Boston).
(b)   PINKHAM, Charles H., Sgt., Maj., 57th Mass. Inf. (Grafton).
      PLUNKETT, Thomas, Sgt., 21st Mass. Inf. (West Boylston) (b. Ireland).
      *PRUSSMAN, Ernest W., Pfc., 8th Inf. Div. (Brighton) (b. Md.)
      PYM, James, Pvt., 7th U.S. Cav. (Boston) (b. England)
(b)   REED, Charles W., Bug., 9th Independent Btry., Mass. Light Arty. (Charlestown).
(b)   RICE, Edmund, Maj., 19th Mass. Inf. (Boston).
      RICH, Carlos H., 1st Sgt., 4th Vt. Inf. (Northfield) (b. Canada).
      ROBINSON, John H., Pvt., 19th Mass. Inf. (Roxbury) (b. Ireland).
(b)   SAXTON, Rufus, Brig. Gen., U.S. Vol. (Greenfield).
      SCANLAN, Patrick, Pvt., 4th Mass. Cav. (Spencer) (b. Ireland).
(b)   **SINGLETON, Frank, Sgt., 6th U.S. Cav. (See Nielon, Frederick, true name, above).**
      SLADEN, Joseph A., Pvt., 33d Mass. Inf. (Lowell) (b. England)
(b)   SMITH, Thomas, Pvt., 1st U.S. Cav. (Boston).
(b)   SNOW, Elmer T., Trumpeter, 3d U.S. Cav. (Hardwick).
      STRONG, James N., Sgt., 49th Mass. Inf. (Pittsfield).
      SWEATT, Joseph S. G., Pvt., 6th Mass. Inf. (Lowell) (b. N.H.).
(b)   TAGGART, Charles A., Pvt., 37th Mass. Inf. (North Blanford).
      TERRY, John D., Sgt., 23d Mass. Inf. (Boston) (b. Maine).
      TOBIN, John M,. 1st Lt. and Adj., 9th Mass. Inf. (Boston) (b. Ireland).
      TOLAN, Frank, Pvt., 7th U.S. Cav. (Boston) (b. N.Y.).
      TRACY, Charles H., Sgt., 37th Mass. Inf. (Springfield) (b. Conn.).
(b)   *TURNER, Charles W., Sfc., 2d Inf. Div, (Boston).
(b)   TURPIN, James H., 1st Sgt., 5th U.S. Cav. (Boston).
(b)   WALKER, Frank O., Pvt., 46th Inf., U.S. Vol. (Burlington).
(b)   WARD, James, Sgt., 7th U.S. Cav. (Boston).
(b)   WARREN, Francis E., Cpl., 49th Mass. Inf. (Hinsdale).
      WELCH, Richard, Cpl., 37th Mass. Inf. (Williamstown) (b. Ireland).
      WHITMAN, Frank M., Pvt., 35th Mass. Inf. (Ayersville) (b. Maine).
      WHITTLESEY, Charles W., Maj., 308th Inf., 77th Div. (Pittsfield) (b. Wisconsin).
(b)   WILBUR, William H., Col., West. Task Force, N.A. (Palmer).
      *WILKIN, Edward G., Cpl., 45th Inf. Div. (Longmeadow) (b. Vt.).
      WOOD, Leonard, Asst. Surg., U.S. Army (b. N.H.).
(b)   WRIGHT, Samuel C., Pvt., 29th Mass. Inf. (Plympton).

NAVY-MARINE CORPS

(b)   ADAMS, John Mapes, Sgt., USMC (Haverhill).
      ADRIANCE, Harry Chapman, Cpl., USMC (b. N.Y.).
      ARTHER, Matthew, Signal Q.M., USN (Boston) (b. Scotland).
(b)   ATKINSON, Thomas E., Yeoman, USN (Salem).
(b)   BAKER, Benjamin F., Cox., USN (Dennisport).
(b)   BARNUM, James, BM, USN.
      BAZAAR, Philip, Ordinary Seaman, USN (b. Chile, South America).
      BEYER, Albert, Coxs., USN (Boston) (b. Germany).
      BOIS, Frank, Q.M., USN (Northampton) (b. Canada).
(b)   BOND, William, BM, USN (Boston).
(b)   BRADLEY, Alexander, Landsman, USN (Boston).
      BRENNAN, Christopher, Seaman, USN (b. Ireland).
(b)   *CADDY, William Robert, Pfc., USMCR (Quincy).
      CAMPBELL, Daniel, Pvt., USMC (b. Canada).
(b)   *CARON, Wayne Maurice, H.C.M. 3rd c., USN (Middleboro).
(b)   CARR, William Louis, Pvt., USMC (Peabody).
(b)   CHANDLER, James B., Cox., USN.
(b)   CHARETTE, George, G.M. 1c., USN (Lowell).
(b)   CONNOLLY, Michael, Ordinary Seaman, USN (Boston).
      COONEY, James, Pvt., USMC (b. Ireland).
      CRAMEN, Thomas, BM., USN (b. Ireland).
      DEMPSEY, John, Seaman, USN (b. Ireland).
(b)   DENEEF, Michael, Captain of Top, USN.
(b)   DENNIS, Richard, BM., USN.
(b)   *DEWERT, Richard David, Hospital Corpsman, USN (Taunton).
(b)   DORAN, John J., BM2d., USN.
(b)   ENRIGHT, John, Landsman, USN (Lynn).
      FORSTERER, Bruno Albert, Sgt., USMC (b. Germany).
(b)   GILE, Frank S., Landsman, USN.
(b)   GILL, Freeman, GM1c., USN (Boston).
      GISBURNE, Edward A., E3c., USN (b. R.I.)
      GRADY, John, Lt., USN (b. Canada).
      GRIFFITHS, John, Captain of Forecastle, USN (b. Wales).
(b)   GRISWOLD, Luke M., Ordinary Seaman, USN.
      HAMILTON, Thomas W., Quartermaster, USN (b. Scotland).
(b)   HANDRAN, John, Seaman, USN.
      *HANSON, Robert Murray, 1st Lt., USMCR (b. India).
(b)   HARCOURT, Thomas, Ordinary Seaman, USN (Boston).
      HARRINGTON, Daniel, Landsman, USN (b. Ireland).
(b)   HARRISON, George H., Seaman, USN.
(b)   HART, William, M1c., USN.
(b)   HATHAWAY, Edward W., Seaman, USN (Plymouth).
(b)   HILL, Walter Newell, Capt., USMC (Haverhill).
(b)   HORTON, James, GM, USN.
(b)   HORTON, James, Capt. of Top, USN (Boston).
(b)   HORTON, Lewis A., Seaman, USN (Bristol).
      HOWARD, Peter, BM, USN (b. France).
(b)   HUDNER, Thomas Jerome, Jr., Lt. (jg.), USN (Fall River).
      HUNT, Martin, Pvt., USMC (b. Ireland).
(b)   JAMES, John H., Captain of Top, USN (Boston).
(b)   *JULIAN, Joseph Rodolph, Plat. Sgt., USMCR (Sturbridge).
      KEARNEY, Michael, Pvt., USMC (b. Ireland).
(b)   KELLY, Francis, WT., USN (Boston).
(b)   KELLY, Thomas G., Lt., Comdr., USN, River Assault Div. 152 (Boston).
      KENNA, Barnett, Quartermaster, USN (b. England).
      KERSEY, Thomas, Ordinary Seaman, USN (b. Canada).
      KYLE, Patrick J., Landsman, USN (b. Ireland).
      LAFFEY, Bartlett, Seaman, USN (b. Ireland).
      *LOGAN, Hugh, Captain of Afterguard, USN (b. Ireland).
(b)   LYLE, Alexander Gordon, Lt. Comdr., Dental Corps, USN (Gloucester).

NAVY-MARINE CORPS

(b) LYONS, Thomas, Seaman, USN (Salem).
MACKENZIE, John, CBM, USN (b. Conn).
MADDIN, Edward, Ordinary Seaman, USN (b. Canada).
McDONALD, John, BM, USN (b. Scotland).
(b) McFARLAND, John, Captain of Forecastle, USN (Boston).
(b) MIHALOWSKI, John, TM1c., USN (Worcester).
MILLER, Harry Herbert, Seaman, USN (b. Canada).
MILLER, James, Quartermaster, USN (b. Denmark).
MILLER, Willard, Seaman, USN (b. Canada).
(b) MOORE, William, BM, USN (Boston).
MULLER, Frederick, Mate, USN (b. Denmark).
(b) NEWLAND, William, Ordinary Seaman, USN (Medway).
NUGENT, Christopher, Orderly Sgt., USMC (b. Ireland).
(b) O'BRIEN, Oliver, Cox., USN (Boston).
(b) O'CALLAHAN, Joseph Timothy, Comdr., USNR (Boston).
OLSEN, Anton, Ordinary Seaman, USN (b. Norway).
(b) *OUELLET, David G., Seaman, USN (Newton).
(b) PARKER, William, Captain of Afterguard, USN (Boston).
PILE, Richard, Ordinary Seaman, USN (b. West Indies).
(b) POPE, Everett Parker, Capt., USMC (Milton).
(b) *POWER, John Vincent, 1st Lt., USMC (Worcester).
PRANCE, George, Captain of Maintop, USN (b. France).
PRENDERGAST, Thomas Francis, Cpl., USMC (b. Ireland).
PRESTON, John, Landsman, USN (b. Ireland).
PROVINCE, George, Ordinary Seaman, USN (b. N.Y.).
(b) REGAN, Jeremiah, Quartermaster, USN (Boston).
RILLEY, John Phillip, Landsman, USN (b. Pa.).
(b) ROUNTRY, John, F1c., USN.
(b) RYAN, Francis T., Cox., USN.
(b) SADLER, William, Captain of Top, USN (Boston).
(b) SAUNDERS, James, Quartermaster, USN.
SAVAGE, Auzella, Ordinary Seaman, USN (b. Maine).
(b) SCANNELL, David John, Pvt., USMC (Boston).
(b) SCOTT, Joseph Francis, Pvt., USMC (Boston).
SEACH, William, Ordinary Seaman, USN (b. England).
(b) SMITH, John, Captain of Forecastle, USN (Boston).
(b) STACY, William B., Seaman, USN.
(b) STANLEY, William A., Shell Man, USN.
STEVENS, Daniel D., Quartermaster, USN (b. Tenn.).
(b) STICKNEY, Herman Osman, Comdr., USN (Pepperell).
SULLIVAN, Edward, Pvt., USMC (b. Ireland).
(b) SULLIVAN, James F., BM, USN (Lowell).
SWANSON, John, Seaman, USN (b. Sweden).
(b) SWEENEY, William, Landsman Engineers' Force, USN (Boston).
TALBOTT, William, Captain of Forecastle, USN (b. Maine).
THIELBERG, Henry, Seaman, USN (b. Germany).
THOMPSON, William, Sig. Quartermaster, USN (Boston) (b. N.J.).
(b) TROY, William, Ordinary Seaman, USN (Boston).
(b) *VITTORI, Joseph, Cpl., USMCR, 1st Marine Div. (Beverly).
(b) *WALSH, William Gary, Gun. Sgt., USMCR (Roxbury).
(b) WILLEY, Charles H., Machinist, USN (Boston).
WILLIAMS, Augustus, Seaman, USN (b. Norway).
(b) WILLIS, George, Cox., USN (Boston).

MICHIGAN

ARMY-AIR FORCE

ALBER, Frederick, Pvt., 17th Mich. Inf. (Manchester) (b. Germany).
(b) †BALDWIN, Frank D., Capt., 19th Mich. Inf.; 1st Lt., 5th U.S. Inf. (Constantine).
BALLEN, Frederick, Pvt., 47th Ohio Inf. (Adrian) (b. Germany).
BARRELL, Charles L., 1st Lt., 102d U.S. Colored Troops (Leighton).

980 MICHIGAN—Continued

ARMY-AIR FORCE

(b)   BENNETT, Orson W., 1st Lt., l02d U.S. Colored Troops (Union City).
(b)   BONDSTEEL, James Leroy, S/Sgt., 1st Inf. Div. (Jackson).
     BRANDLE, Joseph E., Pvt., 17th Mich. Inf. (Colon) (b. Ohio).
     *BRYANT, William Maud, Sfc., 1st Special Forces (Detroit) (b. Ga.).
(b)   CAWETZKA, Charles, Pvt., 30th Inf., U.S. Vol. (Wayne).
(b)   CHRISTIANCY, James I., 1st Lt., 9th Mich. Cav. (Monroe County).
(b)   CLUTE, George W., Cpl., 14th Mich. Inf. (Marathon).
     COLE, Gabriel, Cpl., 5th Mich. Cav. (New Salem) (b. N.Y.).
(b)   CRAW, Demas T., Col., A.C. (Traverse City).
     †CUSTER, Thomas W., 2d Lt., 6th Mich. Cav. (Monroe) (b. Ohio).
     CUTCHEON, Byron M., Maj., 20th Mich. Inf. (Ypsilanti) (b. N.H.).
     DODD, Robert F., Pvt., 27th Mich. Inf. (Hamtramck) (b. Canada).
(b)   DOUGHERTY, William, Blacksmith, 8th U.S. Cav. (Detroit).
(b)   *ESSEBAGGER, John, Jr., Cpl., 3d Inf. Div. (Holland).
(b)   FALCONER, John A., Cpl., 17th Mich. Inf. (Manchester).
     FALL, Charles S., Sgt., 26th Mich. Inf. (Hamburg) (b. Ind.).
(b)   FORMAN, Alexander A., Cpl., 7th Mich. Inf. (Jonesville).
     FOX, Henry M., Sgt., 5th Mich. Cav. (Coldwater) (b. Ohio).
     FRENCH, Samuel S., Pvt., 7th Mich. Inf. (Gifford) (b. N.Y.).
(b)   FURLONG, Harold A., 1st Lt., 353d Inf., 89th Div. (Detroit).
     HACK, John, Pvt., 47th Ohio Inf. (Adrian) (b. Germany).
     HADLEY, Cornelius M., Sgt., 9th Mich. Cav. (Adrian) (b. N.Y.).
(b)   HAIGHT, Sidney, Cpl., 1st Mich. Sharpshooters (Goodland).
(b)   HARRINGTON, John, Pvt., 6th U.S. Cav. (Detroit).
(b)   HASTINGS, Smith H., Capt., 5th Mich. Cav. (Quincy).
     HILL, EDWARD, Capt., 16th Mich. Inf. (Detroit) (b. N.Y.).
(b)   HODGES, Addison J., Pvt., 47th Ohio Inf. (Adrian).
(b)   HOLLAND, David, Cpl., 5th U.S. Inf. (Dearborn).
     HOLTON, Charles M., 1st Sgt., 7th Mich. Cav. (Battle Creek) (b. N.Y.).
     IRWIN, Patrick, 1st Sgt., 14th Mich. Cav. (Ann Arbor) (b. Ireland).
(b)   JOHNSON, Dwight H., Spec. 5, 4th Inf. Div. (Detroit).
(b)   JOHNSON, Oscar G., Sgt., 91st Inf. Div. (Foster City).
     KEEN, Joseph S., Sgt., 13th Mich. Inf. (Detroit) (b. England).
     KELLEY, Andrew J., Pvt., 17th Mich. Inf. (Ypsilanti) (b. Ind.).
     KEMP, Joseph, 1st Sgt., 5th Mich. Inf. (Sault Ste. Marie) (b. Ohio).
(b)   LAMBERS, Paul Ronald, Sgt., 25th Inf. Div. (Holland).
     LANE, Morgan D., Pvt., Sig. C., U.S. Army (Alleghany) (b. N.Y.).
     LEMON, Peter C., Sgt., 1st Cav. Div. (East Tawas).
(b)   LEONARD, William, Pvt., 2d U.S. Cav. (Ypsilanti).
(b)   LEWIS, Henry, Cpl., 47th Ohio Inf. (Adrian).
     LUCE, Moses A., Sgt., 4th Mich. Inf. (Hillsdale) (b. Ill.).
     McCONNELL, James, Pvt., 33d Inf., U.S. Vol. (Detroit) (b. N.Y.).
     McFALL, Daniel, Sgt., 17th Mich. Inf. (Ypsilanti) (b. N.Y.).
     McHALE. Alexander U., Cpl., 26th Mich. Inf. (Muskegon) (b. Ireland).
     MENTER, John W., Sgt., 5th Mich. Inf. (Detroit) (b. N.Y.).
     MORSE, Benjamin, Pvt., 3d Mich. Inf. (Grand Rapids) (b. N.Y.).
(b)   *MOYER, Donald R., Sfc., 25th Inf. Div. (Oakland).
(b)   MUNDELL, Walter L., Cpl., 5th Mich. Inf. (Dallas) (b. Va.).
(b)   NASH, Henry H., Cpl., 47th Ohio Inf. (Adrian).
     NOLL, Conrad, Sgt., 20th Mich. Inf. (Ann Arbor) (b. Germany).
     NORTON, Elliott M., 2d Lt., 6th Mich. Cav. (Cooper) (b. Conn.).
(b)   PETERS, Henry C., Pvt., 47th Ohio Inf. (Adrian).
     PLANT, Henry E., Cpl., 14th Mich. Inf. (Cockery) (b. N.Y.).
(b)   POLOND, Alfred, Pvt., 10th U.S. Inf. (Lapeer).
(b)   *POXON, Robert Leslie, 1st Lt., 1st Cav. Div. (Detroit).
     RANNEY, George E., Asst. Surg., 2d Mich. Cav. (Detroit) (b. N.Y.).
(b)   ROBINSON, James H., Pvt., 3d Mich. Cav. (Victor).
     ROMEYN, Henry, 1st Lt., 5th U.S. Inf. (b. N.Y.).
(b)   SANCRAINTE, Charles F., Pvt., 15th Mich. Inf. (Monroe).
(b)   *SAVACOOL, Edwin F., Capt., 1st N.Y. Cav. (Marshall).
(b)   SHAFTER, William R., 1st Lt., 7th Mich. Inf. (Galesburg).
     SHEPHARD, Irwin, Cpl., 17th Mich. Inf. (Chelsea) (b. N.Y.).

ARMY-AIR FORCE

SIDMAN, George D., Pvt., 16th Mich. Inf. (Owosso) (b. N.Y.).
(b) SJOGREN, John C., S/Sgt., 40th Inf. Div. (Rockford).
*SKIDGEL, Donald Sidney, Sgt., 1st Cav. Div. (Detroit) (b. Maine).
SMITH, Alonzo, Sgt., 7th Mich. Inf. (Jonesville) (b. N.Y.).
(b) SMITH, Maynard H., Sgt., 423d Bomb. Sq. (Detroit).
(b) SMITH, William H., Pvt., 1st U.S. Cav. (Lapeer).
SWIFT, Frederic W., Lt. Col., 17th Mich. Inf. (b. Conn.).
(b) SYPE, Peter, Pvt., 47th Ohio Inf. (Adrian).
(b) THATCHER, Charles M., Pvt., 1st Mich. Sharpshooters (Eastmanville).
*THOMAS, William H., Pfc., 38th Inf. Div. (Ypsilanti) (b. Ark.).
THOMPSON, Charles A., Sgt., 17th Mich. Inf. (Kalamazoo) (b. Ohio).
(b) TOBAN, James W., Sgt., 9th Mich. Cav. (Northfield).
VLUG, Dirk J., Pfc., 32d Inf. Div. (Grand Rapids) (b. Minn.).
(b) WARD, William H., Capt., 47th Ohio Inf. (Adrian).
(b) WATSON, Joseph, Pvt., 8th U.S. Cav. (St. Joseph).
*WETZEL, Walter C., Pfc., 8th Inf. Div. (Roseville) (b. W. Va.).
(b) WHITNEY, William G., Sgt., 11th Mich. Inf. (Quincy).
*WIGLE, Thomas W., 2d Lt., 34th Inf. Div. (Detroit) (b. Ind.).
(b) WILDER, Wilber E., 1st Lt., 4th U.S. Cav. (Detroit).
(b) WILLCOX, Orlando B., Col., 1st Mich. Inf. (Detroit).
WITHINGTON, William H., Capt., 1st Mich. Inf. (Jackson) (b. Mass.).
(b) WOODRUFF, Alonzo, Sgt., 1st U.S. Sharpshooters (Ionia).
*YNTEMA, Gordon Douglas, Sgt., 5th Special Forces Group (Holland) (b. Md.).
(b) *ZUSSMAN, Raymond, 2d Lt., 756th Tank Bn. (Detroit).

NAVY-MARINE CORPS

*CANNON, George Ham, 1st Lt., USMC (b. Mo.).
(b) CHARETTE, William R., HC3c., USN (Ludington).
(b) CRONIN, Cornelius, CQM, USN (Detroit).
(b) DEWEY, Duane E., Cpl., USMCR, 1st Marine Div. (Muskegon).
(b) *FLAHERTY, Francis C., Ens., USNR (Charlotte).
(b) GLOWIN, Joseph Anthony, Cpl., USMC (Detroit).
(b) *HAMMERBERG, Owen Francis Patrick, BM2c., USN (Daggett).
(b) SIMANEK, Robert E., Pfc., USMC, 1st Marine Div. (Detroit).
*SKINNER, Sherrod E., Jr., 2d Lt., USMCR, 1st Marine Div. (East Lansing) (b. Conn.).
(b) SMITH, Albert Joseph, Pvt., USMC (Calumet).
(b) *WILLIAMS, Dewayne T., Pfc., USMC, 1st Mar. Div. (St. Clair).
(b) ZUIDERVELD, William, HA1c., USN.

MINNESOTA

ARMY-AIR FORCE

ALBEE, George E., 1st Lt., 41st U.S. Inf. (Owatonna) (b. N.H.).
BARRICK, Jesse, Cpl., 3d Minn. Inf. (Rice County) (b. Ohio).
BELL, Harry, Capt., 36 Inf., U.S. Vol. (Minneapolis) (b. Wis.).
(b) *BIANCHI, Willibald C., 1st Lt., 45th Inf., Philippine Scouts (New Ulm).
BURGER, Joseph, Pvt., 2d Minn. Inf. (Crystal Lake) (b. Austria).
BURKARD, Oscar, Pvt., Hosp. Corps, U.S. Army (Hay Creek) (b. Germany).
CILLEY, Clinton A., Capt., 2d Minn. Inf. (Sasioja) (b. N.H.).
CLARK, William A., Cpl., 2d Minn. Inf. (Shelbyville) (b. Pa.).
(b) COLALILLO, Mike, Pfc., 100th Inf. Div. (Duluth).
†CUKELA, Louis, Sgt., 5th Reg., USMC (Minneapolis) (b. Austria). (Also awarded Navy Medal of Honor.)
FLANNIGAN, James, Pvt., 2d Minn. Inf. (Louisville) (b. N.Y.).
HANNA, Milton, Cpl., 2d Minn. Inf. (Henderson) (b. Ohio).
(b) HAWKS, Lloyd C., Pfc., 3d Inf. Div. (Park Rapids).
HOLMES, Lovilo N., 1st Sgt., 2d Minn. Inf. (Mankato) (b. N.Y.).
HUGGINS, Eli L., Capt., 2d U.S. Cav. (b. Ill.).
JOHNSON, John, Pvt., 2d Wis. Inf. (Rochester) (b. Norway).
LINDBERGH, Charles A., Capt., A.C. Res., U.S. Army (Little Falls) (b. Mich.).

ARMY-AIR FORCE

MALLON, George H., Capt., 33d Div. (Minneapolis) (b. Kans.).
MORGAN, George H., 2d Lt., 3d U.S. Cav. (Minneapolis) (b. Canada).
O'BRIEN, Henry D., Cpl., 1st Minn. Inf. (St. Anthony Falls) (b. Maine).
(b) *OLSON, Kenneth L., Spec. 4, 199th Inf. Brig. (Paynesville).
    *PAGE, John U. D., Lt. Col., X Corps Arty. (St. Paul) (b. Malahi Island, Philippine Islands).
    PAY, Byron E., Pvt., 2d Minn. Inf. (Mankato) (b. N.Y.).
    PICKLE, Alonzo H., Sgt., 1st Minn. Inf. (Dover) (b. Canada).
(b) *PRUDEN, Robert J., S/Sgt., 75th Inf. Ameri. Div. (St. Paul).
    *RABEL, Laszlo, S/Sgt., 173d Airborne Brig. (Minneapolis) (b. Hungary).
    REED, Axel H., Sgt., 2d Minn. Inf. (Glencoe) (b. Maine).
(b) RUDOLPH, Donald E., 2d Lt., 6th Inf. Div. (Minneapolis).
    SHERMAN, Marshall, Pvt., 1st Minn. Inf. (St. Paul) (b. Vt.).
(b) THORSNESS, Leo K., Lt. Col., 357th Tactical Fighter Sq. (Walnut Grove).
    TRACY, John, Pvt., 8th U.S. Cav. (St. Paul) (b. Ireland).
    VALE, John, Pvt., 2d Minn. Inf. (Rochester) (b. England).
(b) *WAYRYNEN, Dale Eugene, Spec. 4, 101st Airborne Div. (McGregor).
    WELCH, Charles H., Sgt., 7th U.S. Cav. (Ft. Snelling) (b. N.Y).
    WILSON, William O., Cpl., 9th U.S. Cav. (St. Paul) (b. Md.).
    WRIGHT, Samuel, Cpl., 2d Minn. Inf. (Swan Lake) (b. Ind.).

NAVY-MARINE CORPS

CATLIN, Albertus Wright, Maj., USMC (b. N.Y.).
(b) *COURTNEY, Henry Alexius, Jr., Maj., USMCR (Duluth).
    †CUKELA, Louis, Sgt., USMC (Also awarded Army Medal of Honor) (Minneapolis) (b. Austria).
(b) DYER, Jesse Farley, Capt., USMC (St. Paul).
(b) *FLEMING, Richard E., Capt., USMCR (St. Paul).
(b) *HAUGE, Louis James, Jr., Cpl., USMCR (Ada).
    *KRAUS, Richard Edward, Pfc., USMCR (b. Ill.).
(b) *LA BELLE, James Dennis, Pfc., USMCR (Columbia Heights).
(b) NELSON, Oscar Frederick, MM1c., USN (Minneapolis).
(b) *RUD, George William, CMM, USN (Minneapolis).
(b) SORENSON, Richard Keith, Pvt., USMCR (Anoka).

MISSISSIPPI

ARMY-AIR FORCE

(b) BARFOOT, Van T., 2d Lt., 45th Inf. Div. (Carthage).
    *DIAMOND, James H., Pfc., 24th Inf. Div. (Gulfport) (b. La.).
(b) HEARD, John W., 1st Lt., 3d U.S. Cav. (Woodstock Plantation).
(b) *HENRY, Robert T., Pvt., 1st Inf. Div. (Greenville).
    *JORDAN, Mack A., Pfc., 24th Inf. Div. (Collins).
    LEE, Hubert L., M/Sgt., 2d Inf. Div. (Leland) (b. Mo.).
    LINDSEY, Jake W., T/Sgt., 1st Inf. Div. (Lucedale) (b. Ala.).
(b) PITTMAN, John A., Sgt., 2d Inf. Div. (Tallula).
(b) SLATON, James D., Cpl., 45th Inf. Div. (Gulfport).
(b) WELBORN, Ira C., 2d Lt., 9th U.S. Inf. (Mico).

NAVY-MARINE CORPS

(b) BROWN, Wilson, Landsman, USN (Natchez).
(b) COMMISKEY, Henry A., 1st Lt., USMC, 1st Marine Div. (Hattiesburg).
    MADISON, James Jonas, Lt. Comdr., USNRF (b. N.J.).
(b) *WHEAT, Roy M., L/Cpl., 1st Marine Div. (Moselle).
(b) WILSON, Louis Hugh, Jr., Capt., USMC (Brandon).

ARMY-AIR FORCE

*ADAMS, William E., Maj., 1st Aviation Brig. (b. Wyo.).
(b)   BARGER, Charles D., Pfc., 89th Div. (Stotts City).
(b)   BARKLEY, John L., Pfc., 3d Div. (Blairstown).
BIEGER, Charles, Pvt., 4th Mo. Cav. (St. Louis) (b. Germany).
BRANT, Abram B., Pvt., 7th U.S. Cav. (St. Louis) (b. N.Y.).
BRYAN, William C., Hospital Steward, USA (St. Louis) (b. Ohio).
(b)   BURR, Herbert H., S/Sgt., 11th Armd. Div. (Kansas City).
DE PUY, Charles H., 1st Sgt., 1st Mich. Sharpshooters (St. Louis) (b. Mich.).
(b)   EPPS, Joseph L., Pvt., 33d Inf., U.S. Vol. (Oklahoma, Indian Territory).
EVANS, William, Pvt., 7th U.S. Inf. (St. Louis) (b. Ireland).
FLYNN, James E., Sgt., 6th Mo. Inf. (St. Louis) (b. Ill.).
FOLLETT, Joseph L., Sgt., 1st Mo. Light Arty. (St. Louis) (b. N.J.).
(b)   FORREST, Arthur J., Sgt., 354th Inf., 89th Div. (Hannibal).
(b)   FRIZZELL (FRAZELL), Henry F., Pvt., 6th Mo. Inf. (Pilot Knob).
GREBE, M. R. William, Capt., 4th Mo. Cav. (St. Louis) (b. Germany).
GUERIN, Fitz W., Pvt., 1st Mo. Light Arty. (St. Louis) (b. N.Y.).
GWYNNE, Nathaniel, Pvt., 13th Ohio Cav. (Fairmont) (b. Ohio).
(b)   HALL, William P., 1st Lt., 5th U.S. Cav. (Huntsville).
HAMMEL, Henry A., Sgt., 1st Mo. Light Arty. (St. Louis) (b. Germany).
(b)   HATLER, M. Waldo, Sgt., 356th Inf., 89th Div. (Neosho).
HOWARD, James H., Lt. Col., A.C. (St. Louis) (b. China).
HUNT, Louis T., Pvt., 6th Mo. Inf. (Jefferson County) (b. Ind.).
(b)   *KANELL, Billie G., Pvt., 25th Inf. Div. (Poplar Bluff).
(b)   *KELLEY, Ova A., Pvt., 96th Inf. Div. (Norwood).
KIRBY, Dennis T., Maj., 8th Mo. Inf. (St. Louis) (b. N.Y.).
(b)   *LONG, Charles R., Sgt., 2d Inf. Div. (Kansas City).
McCAMMON, William W., 1st Lt., 24th Mo. Inf. (Montgomery County) (b. Ohio).
MILLER, Archie, 1st Lt., 6th U.S. Cav. (St. Louis) (b. Ill.).
MONTROSE, Charles H., Pvt., 5th U.S. Inf. (St. Louis) (b. Minn.).
PESCH, Joseph, Pvt., 1st Mo. Light Arty. (St. Louis) (b. Germany).
*PETERSEN, Danny J., Sp4c., 25th Inf. Div. (Kansas City) (b. Kans.).
PORTER, Ambrose, Commissary Sgt., 12th Mo. Cav. (Rockport) (b. Md.).
RAY, Charles W., Sgt., 22d U.S. Inf. (St. Louis) (b. N.C.).
*RIORDAN, Paul F., 2d Lt., 34th Inf. Div. (Kansas City) (b. Iowa).
SCHOFIELD, John M., Maj., 1st Mo. Inf. (St. Louis) (b. N.Y.).
SHAW, Thomas, Sgt., 9th U.S. Cav. (Pike County) (b. Ky.)
SHEPPARD, Charles, Pvt., 5th U.S. Inf. (St. Louis) (b. Conn.).
(b)   *SISLER, George K., 1st Lt., 1st Special Forces (Dexter).
(b)   *SKINKER, Alexander R., Capt., 35th Div. (St. Louis).
(b)   *SPECKER, Joe C., Sgt., 48th Engr. Bn. (Odessa).
(b)   TAYLOR, Bernard, Sgt., 5th U.S. Cav. (St. Louis).
TROGDEN, Howell G., Pvt., 8th Mo. Inf. (St. Louis) (b. N.C.).
WAGNER, John W., Cpl., 8th Mo. Inf. (St. Louis) (b. Md.).
(b)   WHERRY, William M., 1st Lt., 3d U.S. Res. Mo. Inf. (St. Louis).
*WILSON, Richard G., Pfc., 11th Abn. Div. (Cape Girardeau) (b. Ill.).
WORTICK, Joseph, Pvt., 8th Mo. Inf. (Hannibal) (b. Pa.).

NAVY-MARINE CORPS

BALCH, John Henry, PhM1c., USN (b. Kans.).
(b)   BALLARD, Donald Everett, H.C.M., 2d c., USN, 3rd Mar. Div. (Kansas City).
(b)   BUTTON, William Robert, Cpl., USMC (St. Louis).
(b)   CARY, Robert Webster, Lt. Comdr., USN (Kansas City).
(b)   *COLE, Darrell Samuel, Sgt., USMCR (Flat River).
(b)   *DAVID, Albert LeRoy, Lt. (jg.), USN (Maryville).
DURNEY, Austin J., Blacksmith, USN (b. Pa.).
(b)   FUQUA, Samuel Glenn, Capt., USN (Laddonia).
(b)   GAIENNIE, Louis Rene, Pvt., USMC (St. Louis).
(b)   HANNEKEN, Herman Henry, 2d Lt., USMC (St. Louis).
(b)   HOLTZ, August, CWT, USN (St. Louis).
MARTIN, William, BM, USN (b. Prussia).

Navy-Marine Corps

(b) McGUIRE, Fred Henry, HA, USN (Gordonville).
(b) O'HARE, Edward Henry, Lt., USN (St. Louis).
(b) *PHILLIPS, George, Pvt., USMCR (Rich Hill).
(b) *SISLER, George K., 1st Lt., 1st Special Forces (Dexter).
(b) TOWNSEND, Julius Curtis, Lt., USN (Athens).

MONTANA

Army-Air Force

(b) *GALT, William Wylie, Capt., 34th Inf. Div. (Stanford).
      MORAN, John E.; Capt., 37th Inf., U.S. Vol. (Cascade County) (b. Vt.).
      *PARRISH, Laverne, T4g., 25th Inf. Div. (Ronan) (b. Mo.).
      POWERS, Leo J., Pfc., 34th Inf. Div. (Alder Gulch) (b. Neb.).
      SCHAUER, Henry, Pfc., 3d Inf. Div. (Scobey) (b. Okla.).
      SMITH, Cornelius C., Cpl., 6th U.S. Cav. (Helena) (b. Ariz.).

Navy-Marine Corps

(b) RUHL, Donald Jack, Pfc., USMCR (Columbus).

NEBRASKA

Army-Air Force

(b) *BOOKER, Robert D., Pvt., 34th Inf. Div. (Callaway).
(b) CO-RUX-TE-CHOD-ISH (Mad Bear), Sgt., Pawnee Scouts, USA.
(b) *FOUS, James W., Pfc., 9th Inf. Div. (Omaha).
(b) HAGEMEISTER, Charles Cris, Spec. 5, 1st Cav. Div. (Lincoln).
(b) KOUMA, Ernest R., M/Sgt., 2d Inf. Div. (Dwight).
      VIFQUAIN, Victor, Lt. Col., 97th Ill. Inf. (Saline County) (b. Belgium).

Navy-Marine Corps

      *BAUER, Harold William, Lt. Col., USMC (b. Kans.).
(b) EHLE, John Walter, F1c., USN (Kearney).
(b) *GOMEZ, Edward, Pfc., USMCR, 1st Marine Div. (Omaha).
      GRAVES, Ora, Seaman, USN (b. Colo.).
(b) *HANSEN, Dale Merlin, Pvt., USMC (Wisner).
      *KEITH, Miguel, L/Cpl., 3rd Mar. Amph. Force (Omaha) (b. Tex.).
(b) KERREY, Joseph Robert, Lt. (jg.), USN, SEAL Force (Lincoln).
(b) *PARLE, John Joseph, Ens., USNR (Omaha).
(b) SCHMIDT, Otto Diller, Seaman, USN (Blair).
(b) VOLZ, Jacob, Carpenter's Mate, USN (Sutton).

NEVADA

Navy-Marine Corps

      *VAN VOORHIS, Bruce Alvery, Lt. Comdr., USN (b. Wash).

NEW HAMPSHIRE

Army-Air Force

(b) APPLETON, William H., 1st Lt., 4th U.S. Colored Troops (Portsmouth).
(b) BARKER, Nathaniel C., Sgt., 11th N.H. Inf. (Manchester).
(b) BATCHELDER, Richard N., Lt. Col. and Chief Qm., 2d Corps (Manchester).
(b) BOUTWELL, John W., Pvt., 18th N.H. Inf. (Hanover).
      BRADY, James, Pvt., 10th N.H. Inf. (Kingston) (b. Mass.).
(b) CAMP, Carlton N., Pvt., 18th N.H. Inf. (Hanover).
(b) CARR, Chris (name changed from Karaberis, Christos H.), Sgt., 337th Inf., 85th
      Inf. Div. (Manchester).
      COHN, Abraham, Sgt. Maj., 6th N.H. Inf. (Campton) (b. Prussia).

ARMY-AIR FORCE

(b) COPP, Charles D., 2d Lt., 9th N.H. Inf. (Nashua).
COUGHLIN, John, Lt. Col., 10th N.H. Inf. (Manchester) (b. Vt.).
(b) CRAIG, Samuel H., Sgt., 4th U.S. Cav. (New Market).
*DILBOY, George, Pfc., 103d Inf., 26th Div. (Keene) (b. Greece).
DILLON, Michael A., Pvt., 2d N.H. Inf. (Wilton) (b. Mass.).
(b) DOW, George P., Sgt., 7th N.H. Inf. (Atkinson).
(b) GOODALL, Francis H., 1st Sgt., 11th N.H. Inf. (Bath).
(b) GRIMES, Edward P., Sgt., 5th U.S. Cav. (Dover).
(b) HADLEY, Osgood T., Cpl., 6th N.H. Vet. Inf. (Nashua).
(b) HARRIS, Moses, 1st Lt., 1st U.S. Cav. (Andover).
KARABERIS, Christos H., Sgt., 85th Inf Div. (Manchester) (Name changed to Chris Carr). (See above.)
(b) KNIGHT, Charles H., Cpl., 9th N.H. Inf. (Keene).
(b) LITTLE, Henry F. W., Sgt., 7th N.H. Inf. (Manchester).
(b) NEAL, Solon D., Pvt., 6th U.S. Cav. (Hanover).
NOLAN, John J., Sgt., 8th N.H. Inf. (Nashua) (b. Ireland).
(b) *PEASE, Harl, Jr., Capt., Bomb. Sq. (H) (Plymouth).
(b) ROBIE, George F., Sgt., 7th N.H. Inf. (Candia).
(b) ROWE, Henry W., Pvt., 11th N.H. Inf. (Candia).
SIMONS, Charles J., Sgt., 9th N.H. Inf. (Exeter) (b. India).
TABOR, William L. S., Pvt., 15th N.H. Inf. (Concord) (b. Mass.).
TILTON, William, Sgt., 7th N.H. Inf. (Hanover) (b. Vt.).
(b) WILCOX, William H., Sgt., 9th N.H. Inf. (Lempster).
(b) WILKINS, Leander A., Sgt., 9th N.H. Inf. (Lancaster).

NAVY-MARINE CORPS

ANDERSON, Robert, Quartermaster, USN (b. Ireland).
(b) FOY, Charles H., Signal Quartermaster, USN (Portsmouth).
(b) FRANKLIN, Frederick, Quartermaster, USN (Portsmouth).
(b) GEORGE, Daniel G., Ordinary Seaman, USN (Plaistow).
(b) HAM, Mark G., CM, USN (Portsmouth).
HAWKINS, Charles, Seaman, USN (b. Scotland).
JONES, John, Landsman, USN (b. Conn.).
(b) MELVILLE, Charles, Ordinary Seaman, USN (Dover).
(b) O'KANE, Richard Hetherington, Cmdr., USN (Dover).
SMITH, William, Quartermaster, USN (b. Ireland).
(b) TODD, Samuel, Quartermaster, USN (Portsmouth).
(b) WEST, Walter Scott, Pvt., USMC (Bradford).

NEW JERSEY

ARMY-AIR FORCE

BART, Frank J., Pvt., 2d Div. (Newark) (b. N.Y.).
BEECH, John P., Sgt., 4th N.J. Inf. (Trenton) (b. England).
*BENJAMIN, George, Jr., Pfc., 77th Inf. Div. (Carney's Point) (b. Pa.).
(b) BRADBURY, Sanford, 1st Sgt., 8th U.S. Cav. (Sussex County).
(b) BRANT, William, Lt., 1st N.J. Vet. Bn. (Elizabeth).
(b) *BRITTIN, Nelson V., Sfc, 24th Inf. Div. (Audubon).
BURKE, Frank (Francis X), 1st Lt., 3d Inf. Div. (Jersey City) (b. N.Y.).
(b) CARMIN, Isaac H., Cpl., 48th Ohio Inf. (Monmouth County).
CASTLE, Frederick W., Brig. Gen., USAAC (Mountain Lake) (b. Philippine Islands).
(b) *COURSEN, Samuel S., 1st Lt., 1st Cav. Div. (Madison).
CUMMINGS, Amos J., Sgt. Maj., 26th N.J. Inf. (Irvington) (b. N.Y.).
(b) DRAKE, James M., 2d Lt., 9th N.J. Inf. (Elizabeth).
*DUTKO, John W., Pfc., 3d Inf. Div. (Riverside) (b. Pa.).
EGGERS, Alan L., Sgt., 27th Div. (Summit). (b. N.Y.).
ENGLISH, Edmund, 1st Sgt., 2d N.J. Inf. (Newark) (b. Ireland).
FALLON, Thomas T., Pvt., 37th N.Y. Inf. (Freehold) (b. Ireland).
FESQ, Frank, Pvt., 40th N.J. Inf. (Newark) (b. Germany).
(b) FOLLY, William H., Pvt., 8th U.S. Cav. (Bergen County).

ARMY-AIR FORCE

GREGG, Stephen R., 2d Lt., 36th Inf. Div. (Bayonne) (b. N.Y.).
HEYL, Charles H., 2d Lt., 23d U.S. Inf. (Camden) (b. Pa.).
(b) HOPKINS, Charles F., Cpl., 1st N.J. Inf. (Warren County).
(b) *HOSKING, Charles Ernest, Jr., M/Sgt., 1st Special Forces (Ramsey).
(b) HOWARD, James, Sgt., 158th N.Y. Inf. (Newton).
(b) JACKSON, James, Capt., 1st U.S. Cav.
JACOBS, Jack H., Capt., U.S. Military Asst. Com. (Trenton) (b. N.Y.).
LATHAM, John C., Sgt., 27th Div. (Rutherford) (b. England).
LOCKE, Lewis, Pvt., 1st N.J. Cav. (Jersey City) (b. N.Y.).
(b) MAGEE, William, Drummer, 33d N.J. Inf. (Newark).
(b) *MAY, Martin O., Pfc., 77th Inf. Div. (Phillipsburg).
*McGRAW, Francis X., Pfc., 1st Inf. Div. (Camden) (b. Pa.).
(b) MEAGHER, John, T/Sgt., 77th Inf. Div. (Jersey City).
MILES, L. Wardlaw, Capt., 77th Div. (Princeton) (b. Md.).
*MINUE, Nicholas, Pvt., 1st Armd. Div. (Carteret) (b. Poland).
(b) ORESKO, Nicholas, M/Sgt., 94th Inf. Div. (Bayonne).
*O'SHEA, Thomas E., Cpl., 27th Div. (Summit) (b. N.Y.).
OSS, Albert, Pvt., 11th N.J. Inf. (Newark) (b. Belgium).
(b) PARKER, James, Lt. Col., 45th Inf., U.S. Vol. (Newark).
(b) *SADOWSKI, Joseph J., Sgt., 4th Armd. Div. (Perth Amboy).
(b) *SAWELSON, William, Sgt., 78th Div. (Harrison).
SEWELL, William J., Col., 5th N.J. Inf. (Camden) (b. Ireland).
(b) SHEERIN, John, Blacksmith, 8th U.S. Cav. (Camden County).
(b) SMITH, Theodore F., Pvt., 1st U.S. Cav. (Rahway).
(b) SOUTHARD, David, Sgt., 1st N.J. Cav. (Ocean County).
(b) STEWART, George W., 1st Sgt., 1st N.J. Cav. (Salem).
STREILE, Christian, Pvt., 1st N.J. Cav. (Jersey City) (b. Germany).
SULLIVAN, Thomas, Pvt., 7th U.S. Cav. (Newark) (b. Ireland).
TAYLOR, Forrester L., Capt., 23d N.J. Inf. (Burlington) (b. Pa.).
(b) THOMPKINS, William H., Pvt., 10th U.S. Cav. (Paterson).
(b) *THORNE, Horace M., Cpl., 9th Armd. Div. (Keyport).
(b) TILTON, Henry R., Maj. and Surg., USA (Jersey City).
(b) TITUS, Charles, Sgt., 1st N.J. Cav. (New Brunswick).
TOFFEY, John J., 1st Lt., 33d New Jersey Inf. (Hudson) (b. N.Y.).
(b) TOMPKINS, Aaron B., Sgt., 1st N.J. Cav. (Orange).
VAN IERSEL, Ludovicus M. M., Sgt., 2d Div. (Glen Rock) (b. Holland).
(b) WANTON, George H., Pvt., 10th U.S. Cav. (Paterson).
(b) *WATTERS, Charles Joseph, Chaplain (Maj.) 173rd Airborne Brig. (Jersey City).
WILSON, John, Sgt., 1st N.J. Cav. (Jersey City) (b. England).
(b) ZABITOSKY, Fred William, Sfc., 5th Spec. Forces Group (Trenton).

NAVY-MARINE CORPS

*BARKER, Jedh C., L/Cpl., 3d Mar. Div., USMC (Park Ridge) (b. N.H.).
BASILONE, John, Sgt., USMC (Rariton) (b. N.Y.).
(b) BEHNE, Frederick, F1c., USN (Lodi).
*BENFOLD, Edward C., HC3c., USN (Camden) (b. N.Y.).
BLUME, Robert, Seaman, USN (b. Pa.).
(b) BREEMAN, George, Seaman, USN (Passaic).
CAFFERATA, Hector A., Jr., Pvt., 1st Marine Div., USMC (Montville) (b. N.Y.).
(b) *CHOLISTER, George Robert, BM1c., USN (Camden).
(b) *CONNOR, Peter S., S/Sgt., 1st Marine Div. (Rein) (Orange).
COONEY, Thomas C., Chief Machinist, USN (b. Canada).
(b) DAVIS, John, Quarter Gunner, USN (Cedarville).
(b) EILERS, Henry A., GM, USN (Newark).
(b) FRYER, Eli Thompson, Capt., USMC (Hightstown).
(b) HAMBERGER, William F., CCM, USN (Newark).
HARVEY, Harry, Sgt., USMC (b. N.Y.).
(b) KANE, Thomas, Captain of the Hold, USN (Jersey City).
(b) MAGER, George Frederick, Apprentice First Class, USN (Phillipsburg).
(b) PARKER, Alexander, BM, USN (Kensington).
PETERSEN, Carl Emil, Chief Machinist, USN (b. Germany).

NAVY-MARINE CORPS

PFEIFER, Louis Fred, Pvt., USMC (b. Pa.).
(b) PRESTON, Herbert Irving, Pvt., USMC (Berkeley).
(b) ROUH, Carlton Robert, 1st Lt., USMCR (Lindenwold).
SHIVERS, John, Pvt., USMC (b. Canada).
SIEGEL, John Otto, BM2d., USN (b. Wisconsin).
(b) SIGLER, Franklin Earl, Pvt., USMCR (Glenridge).
(b) STRAHAN, Robert, Captain of the Top, USN.
†SWEENEY, Robert, Ordinary Seaman, USN (b. Canada).
TEYTAND, August P., QM3d., USN (b. West Indies).
*TOMICH, Peter, CWT, USN (b. Austria).
(b) TOMLIN, Andrew J., Cpl., USMC (Goshin).
(b) VAN ETTEN, Hudson, Seaman, USN (Port Jervis).
(b) WEEKS, Charles H., Captain of Foretop, USN.
(b) WHITFIELD, Daniel, Quartermaster, USN (Newark).
(b) YOUNG, Edward B., Cox., USN (Bergen).

NEW MEXICO

ARMY-AIR FORCE

(b) *FERNANDEZ, Daniel, Spec. 4, 25th Inf. Div. (Albuquerque).
McDONALD, Robert, 1st Lt., 5th U.S. Inf. (Fort Sumner) (b. N.Y.).
*MILLER, Franklin D., S/Sgt., 1st Spec. Forces (Albuquerque) (b. N.C.).
(b) MIYAMURA, Hiroshi H., Cpl., 3d Inf. Div. (Gallup).
(b) RUIZ, Alejandro Renteria, Pfc., 27th Inf. Div. (Carlsbad).
SCOTT, Robert S., Capt., 43d Inf. Div. (Santa Fe) (b. D.C.).

NAVY-MARINE CORPS

*BONNYMAN, Alexander, Jr., 1st Lt., USMCR (b. Ga.).

NEW YORK

ARMY-AIR FORCE

ALLEN, James, Pvt., 16th N.Y. Inf. (Potsdam) (b. Ireland).
(b) ALLEN, William, 1st Sgt., 23d U.S. Inf. (Lansingburg).
(b) ANDERSON, Bruce, Pvt., 142d N.Y. Inf. (Ephratah).
(b) ARCHER, Lester, Sgt., 96th N.Y. Inf. (Fort Ann).
*ASHLEY, Eugene, Jr., Sfc., 1st Spec. Forces (New York) (b. N.C.).
AUSTIN, William G., Sgt., 7th U.S. Cav. (New York) (b. Tex.).
BAKER, John, Musician, 5th U.S. Inf. (Brooklyn) (b. Germany).
(b) *BAKER, Thomas A., Sgt., 27th Inf. Div. (Troy).
(b) BARNUM, Henry A., Col., 149th N.Y. Inf. (Syracuse).
(b) BARRETT, Carlton W., Pvt., 1st Inf. Div. (Luzerne).
(b) BATES, Delavan, Col., 30th U.S. Colored Troops (Oswego County).
(b) BEIKIRCH, Gary B., Sgt., 1st Spec. Forces (Buffalo).
BELL, Bernard P., T/Sgt., 36th Inf. Div. (New York) (b. W.Va.).
(b) BENJAMIN, John F., Cpl., 2d N.Y. Cav. (Orange County).
(b) BENJAMIN, Samuel N., 1st Lt., 2d U.S. Arty. (New York).
BICKFORD, Henry H., Cpl., 8th N.Y. Cav. (Hartland) (b. Mich.).
(b) BLUNT, John W., 1st Lt., 6th N.Y. Cav. (Chatham, Four Corners).
(b) BOEHM, Peter M., 2d Lt., 15th N.Y. Cav. (Brooklyn).
(b) BOWEN, Chester B., Cpl., 19th N.Y. Cav. (1st N.Y. Dragoons) (Nunda).
(b) *BOYCE, George W. G., Jr., 2d Lt., 112th Cav. Regimental Cmbt. Team (New York).
BRADLEY, Thomas W., Sgt., 124th N.Y. Inf. (Walden) (b. England).
(b) BREWER, William J., Pvt., 2d N.Y. Cav. (New York).
(b) BRINGLE, Andrew, Cpl., 10th N.Y. Cav. (Buffalo).
BROSNAN, John, Sgt., 164th N.Y. Inf. (NewYork) (b. Ireland).
BROWN, Edward, Jr., Cpl., 62d N.Y. Inf. (New York) (b. Ireland).
(b) BROWN, Henri Le Fevre, Sgt., 72d N.Y. Inf. (Ellicott).
(b) *BROWN, Morris, Jr., Capt., 126th N.Y. Inf. (Penn Yan).

(b) BROWNELL, Francis E., Pvt., 11th N.Y. Inf. (Troy).
(b) BRUSH, George W., Lt., 34th U.S. Colored Troops (New York).
      BRUTON, Christopher C., Capt., 22d N.Y. Cav. (Riga).
      BUCHA, Paul William, Capt., 101st Airborne Div. (West Point) (b. D.C.).
(b) *BUCHANAN, George A., Pvt., 148th N.Y. Inf. (Ontario County).
      BUCKLEY, Denis, Pvt., 136th N.Y. Inf. (Avon) (b. Canada).
      BURK, E. Michael, Pvt., 125th N.Y. Inf. (Troy) (b. Ireland).
(b) BURK, Thomas, Sgt., 97th N.Y. Inf. (Harrisburg).
      BUTLER, Edmond, Capt., 5th U.S. Inf. (Brooklyn) (b. Ireland).
(b) *BUTTS, John E., 2d Lt., 9th Inf. Div. (Buffalo).
(b) CADWELL, Luman L., Sgt., 2d N.Y. Vet. Cav. (Broome).
(b) CALKIN, Ivers S., 1st Sgt., 2d N.Y. Cav. (Willsborough).
(b) CALL, Donald M., Cpl., 344th Bn., Tank Corps., U.S. Army (Larchmont Manor).
(b) CAMPBELL, James A., Pvt., 2d N.Y. Cav. (New York).
(b) CAREY, James L., Sgt., 10th N.Y. Cav. (Onondaga County).
(b) CARMAN, Warren, Pvt., 1st N.Y. Cav. (Seneca County).
(b) CARR, Eugene A., Col., 3d Ill. Cav. (Hamburg).
(b) CARTER, John J., 2d Lt., 33d N.Y. Inf. (Nunda).
      CARTER, William H., 1st Lt., 6th U.S. Cav. (New York) (b. Tenn.).
      CASEY, James S., Capt., 5th U.S. Inf. (New York) (b. Pa.).
      *CASTLE, Frederick W., Brig. Gen., 8th AF (West Point) (b. P.I.).
(b) CATLIN, Isaac S., Col., 109th N.Y. Inf. (Oswego).
      CHANDLER, Stephen E., Q.M. Sgt., 24th N.Y. Cav. (Granby) (b. Mich.).
(b) CHAPIN, Alaric B., Pvt., 142d N.Y. Inf. (Pamelia).
      *CHARLTON, Cornelius H., Sgt., 25th Inf. Div. (Bronx) (b. W. Va.).
      *CHELI, Ralph, Maj., Air Corps (Brooklyn) (b. Calif.).
(b) CLANCY, James T., Sgt., 1st N.J. Cav. (Albany).
(b) CLANCY, John E., Mus., 1st U.S. Arty. (New York).
(b) CLAPP, Albert A., 1st Sgt., 2d Ohio Cav. (Pompey).
(b) CLARK, Francis J., T/Sgt., 28th Inf. Div. (Salem).
(b) CLARK, Harrison, Cpl., 125th N.Y. Inf. (Chatham).
(b) CLARKE, Dayton P., Capt., 2d Vt. Inf. (Hermon).
(b) CLEVELAND, Charles F., Pvt., 26th N.Y. Inf. (Hartford).
(b) COEY, James, Maj., 147th N.Y. Inf. (New York).
(b) COLLINS, Thomas D., Sgt., 143 N.Y. Inf. (Liberty).
(b) *COLYER, Wilbur E., Sgt., 1st Div. (South Ozone, L.I.).
(b) COMPSON, Hartwell B., Maj., 8th N.Y. Cav. (Seneca Falls).
      CONBOY, Martin, Sgt., 37th N.Y. Inf. (New York).
(b) CONGDON, James. Sgt., 8th N.Y. Cav. (Fairport) (Served as James Madison, see below.)
(b) CORLISS, Stephen P., 1st Lt., 4th N.Y. Hvy. Arty. (Albany).
(b) COYNE, John N., Sgt., 70th N.Y. Inf. (New York).
(b) CROSIER, William H., Sgt., 149th N.Y. Inf. (Skaneateles).
(b) CROSS, James E., Cpl., 12th N.Y. Inf. (Darien).
(b) CROWLEY, Michael, Pvt., 22d N.Y. Cav. (Rochester).
(b) CUNNINGHAM, Charles, Cpl., 7th U.S. Cav. (Hudson).
      CURRAN, Richard, Asst. Surg., 33d N.Y. Inf. (Seneca Falls) (b. Ireland).
(b) CURREY, Francis S., Sgt., 30th Inf. Div. (Hurleyville).
(b) CURTIS, Newton Martin, Brig. Gen., U.S. Vol. (De Peyster).
(b) *DALESSONDRO, Peter J., T/Sgt., 9th Inf. Div. (Watervliet).
      DAVIDSON, Andrew, 1st Lt., 30th U.S. Colored Troops (Oswego County) (b. Scotland).
      DAVIS, John, G.M. 3c, USN (New York) (b. Germany).
      DAVIS, Thomas, Pvt., 2d N.Y. Hvy. Arty. (b. Wales).
(b) *DeGLOPPER, Charles N., Pfc., 82d Airborne Div. (Grand Island).
(b) DENNY, John, Sgt., Company C, 9th U.S. Cav. (Elmira).
      DI CESNOLA, Louis P., Col., 4th N.Y. Cav. (New York) (b. Italy).
(b) DICKEY, William D., Capt., 15th N.Y. Hvy. Arty. (Newburgh).
(b) *DIETZ, Robert H., S/Sgt., 38th Armd. Inf. Bn., 7th Armd. Div. (Kingston).
      DILGER, Hubert, Capt., 1st Ohio Light Arty. (New York) (b. Germany).
      *DOANE, Stephen Holden, 1st Lt., 25th Inf. Div. (Walton) (b. Mass.).
(b) DOCKUM, Warren C., Pvt., 121st N.Y. Inf. (Clintonville).

ARMY-AIR FORCE

DODDS, Edward E., Sgt., 21st N.Y. Cav. (Rochester) (b. Canada).
(b)   DONALDSON, Michael A., Sgt., 165th Inf., 42d Div. (Haverstraw).
      DONELLY, John S., Pvt., 5th U.S. Inf. (Buffalo) (b. Ireland).
(b)   DONAVAN, William Joseph, Lt. Col., 42d Div. (Buffalo).
(b)   DONLON, Roger Hugh C., Capt., U.S. Army (Saugerties).
      DOODY, Patrick, Cpl., 164th N.Y. Inf. (New York) (b. Ireland).
(b)   *DUNN, Parker F., Pfc., 78th Div. (Albany).
      EDWARDS, David, Pvt., 146th N.Y. Inf. (Sangersfield) (b. England).
(b)   EDWARDS, William E., 1st Sgt., 7th U.S. Inf. (Brooklyn).
(b)   ELDRIDGE, George H., Sgt., 6th U.S. Cav. (Sacketts Harbor).
(b)   EMBLER, Andrew H., Capt., 59th N.Y. Inf. (New York).
(b)   EMMET, Robert Temple, 2d Lt., 9th U.S. Cav. (New York).
(b)   EVANS, James R., Pvt., 62d N.Y. Inf. (New York).
(b)   EVERSON, Adelbert, Pvt., 185th N.Y. Inf. (Salina).
(b)   FARNSWORTH, Herbert E., Sgt. Maj., 10th N.Y. Cav. (Cattaraugus County).
(b)   FISHER, Almond E., 2d Lt., 45th Inf. Div. (Brooklyn).
(b)   FOURNIA, Frank O., Pvt., 21st U.S. Inf. (Plattsburg).
      *FRATELLENICO, Frank R., Cpl., 101st Airborne Div. (Chatham) (b. Conn.).
(b)   FREEMAN, Archibald, Pvt., 124th N.Y. Inf. (Newburgh).
(b)   FREEMAN, William H., Pvt., 169th N.Y. Inf. (Troy).
(b)   GAFFNEY, Frank, Pfc., 108th Inf., 27th Div. (Niagara Falls).
(b)   *GARBIARZ, William J., Pfc., 1st Cav. Div. (Buffalo).
(b)   GARDINER, Peter W., Pvt., 6th U.S. Cav. (Carlisle).
(b)   GERE, Thomas P., 1st Lt. and Adj., 5th Minn. Inf. (Chemung County).
      *GERTSCH, John G., S/Sgt., 101st Airborne Div. (Buffalo) (b. N.J.).
(b)   GIFFORD, Benjamin, Pvt., 121st N.Y. Inf. (German Flats).
      GILMORE, John C., Maj., 16th N.Y. Inf. (Potsdam) (b. Canada).
      GINLEY, Patrick, Pvt., 1st N.Y. Light Arty. (New York) (b. Ireland).
(b)   GLOVER, T. B., Sgt., 2d U.S. Cav. (New York).
(b)   GOETTEL, Philip, Pvt., 149th N.Y. Inf. (Syracuse).
(b)   GOHEEN, Charles A., 1st Sgt., 8th N.Y. Cav. (Groveland).
(b)   GOODRICH, Edwin, 1st Lt., 9th N.Y. Cav. (Westfield).
(b)   GOURAUD, George E., Capt. and Aide-de-Camp, U.S. Vol. (New York).
      GRANT, Gabriel, Surg., U.S. Vol. (New York) (b. N.J.).
(b)   GREENE, Oliver D., Maj. and Asst. Adj. Gen., USA (Scott).
(b)   GREIG, Theodore W., 2d Lt., 61st N.Y. Inf. (Staten Island).
      GRINDLAY, James G., Col., 146th N.Y. Inf. (Utica).
      GRUEB, George, Pvt., 158th N.Y. Inf. (New York) (b. Germany).
(b)   *GUENETTE, Peter M., Sp4c., 101st Airborne Div. (Albany).
(b)   HAIGHT, John H., Sgt., 72d N.Y. Inf. (Westfield).
      HALL, Francis B., Chaplain, 16th N.Y. Inf. (Plattsburg).
(b)   HALL, H. Seymour, 2d Lt., 27th N.Y. Inf., and Capt., 121st N.Y. Inf. (New York).
(b)   HALLOCK, Nathan M., Pvt., 124th N.Y. Inf. (Middletown).
      HAMILTON, Mathew H., Pvt., 7th U.S. Cav. (New York) (b. Australia).
(b)   HAMILTON, Pierpont M., Maj., A.C. (New York).
(b)   HANFORD, Edward R., Pvt., 2d U.S. Cav. (Alleghany County).
(b)   HARING, Abram P., 1st Lt., 132d N.Y. Inf. (New York).
(b)   HARRIS, Charles D., Sgt., 8th U.S. Cav. (Albion).
(b)   HART, William E., Pvt., 8th N.Y. Cav. (Pittsford).
      HARVEY, Harry, Cpl., 22d N.Y. Cav. (Rochester) (b. England).
(b)   HATCH, John P., Brig. Gen., U.S. Vol. (Oswego).
(b)   HAWTHORNE, Harris S., Cpl., 121st N.Y. Inf. (Otego).
(b)   HEERMANCE, William L., Capt., 6th N.Y. Cav. (Kinderhook).
      HIBSON, Joseph C., Pvt., 48th N.Y. Inf. (New York) (b. England).
(b)   HICKEY, Dennis W., Sgt., 2d N.Y. Cav. (Troy).
(b)   HILL, James, Sgt., 14th N.Y. Hvy. Arty. (Lyons).
(b)   HILLS, William G., Pvt., 9th N.Y. Cav. (Conewango).
      [1] HOFFMAN, Charles F., Gun. Sgt., 2d Div., USMC (Brooklyn) (Real name: Ernest A. Janson).

---

[1] Note: Later changed name to Janson, Ernest A. Also received Navy Medal of Honor for same act and appears under Janson under Navy and Marine list.

(b) HOGARTY, William P., Pvt., 23d N.Y. Inf. (New York).
     HORAN, Thomas, Sgt., 72d N.Y. Inf. (Dunkirk).
(b) HOUGHTON, Charles H., Capt., 14th N.Y. Arty. (Ogdensburg).
(b) HOULTON, William, Com. Sgt., 1st W. Va. Cav. (Clymer).
(b) HUMPHREY, Charles F., 1st Lt., 4th U.S. Arty. (New York).
     IRSCH, Francis, Capt., 45th N.Y. Inf. (New York).
     IRWIN, Bernard J. D., Asst. Surg., U.S. Army (New York) (b. Ireland).
     JACOBSON, Eugene P., Sgt. Maj., 74th N.Y. Inf. (New York).
     JAMIESON, Walter, 1st Sgt., 139th N.Y. Inf. (New York) (b. France).
(b) JARVIS, Frederick, Sgt., 1st U.S. Cav. (Essex County).
     JOEL, Lawrence, Spec. 6, 173d Airborne Brig. (New York) (b. N.C.).
(b) JOHNSON, Follett, Cpl., 60th N.Y. Inf. (St. Lawrence).
(b) JOHNSON, Wallace W., Sgt., 6th Pa. Res. (Waverly).
(b) JOHNSTON, Edward, Cpl., 5th U.S. Inf. (Buffalo).
     JONES, William, 1st Sgt., 73d N.Y. Inf. (New York) (b. Ireland).
     KAPPESSER, Peter, Pvt., 149th N.Y. Inf. (Syracuse) (b. Germany).
(b) *KAROPCZYC, Stephen Edward, 1st Lt., 25th Inf. Div. (Bethpage).
(b) KAUFMAN, Benjamin, 1st Sgt., 308th Inf., 77th Div. (Brooklyn).
     KAUSS (KAUTZ), August, Cpl., 15th N.Y. Hvy. Arty. (New York) (b. Germany).
(b) *KEDENBURG, John J., Spec. 5, 1st Spec. For. (Massapequa).
     KEELE, Joseph, Sgt. Maj., 182d N.Y. Inf. (Staten Island) (b. Ireland).
(b) KEENAN, Bartholomew T., Trumpeter, 1st U.S. Cav. (Brooklyn).
(b) KELLER, William, Pvt., 10th U.S. Inf. (Buffalo).
(b) KELLY, Daniel, Sgt., 8th N.Y. Cav. (Groveland).
     KELLY, Thomas, Pvt., 6th N.Y. Inf. (b. Ireland).
     KELLY, Thomas, Pvt., 21st U.S. Inf. (New York) (b. Ireland).
(b) KELLY, Thomas J., Cpl., 7th Armd. Div. (Brooklyn).
(b) KENYON, John S., Sgt., 3d N.Y. Cav. (Schenevus).
(b) KENYON, Samuel P., Pvt., 24th N.Y. Cav. (Oriskany Falls).
     KEOUGH, John, Cpl., 67th Pa. Inf. (Albany) (b. Ireland).
(b) KIGGINS, John, Sgt., 149th N.Y. Inf. (Syracuse).
     KING, Horatio C., Maj. and Qm., U.S. Vol. (Brooklyn) (b. Maine).
(b) KING, Rufus, Jr., 1st Lt., 4th U.S. Arty. (New York).
     KLINE, Harry, Pvt., 40th N.Y. Inf. (Syracuse) (b. Germany).
(b) KNOX, Edward M., 2d Lt., 15th N.Y. Btry. (New York).
   †*KOCAK, Matej, Sgt., USMC (New York) (b. Austria) (Also received Navy
        Medal of Honor).
     KOELPIN, William, Sgt., 5th U.S. Inf. (New York) (b. Prussia).
(b) KUDER, Andrew, 2d Lt., 8th N.Y. Cav. (Groveland).
(b) LADD, George, Pvt., 22d N.Y. Cav. (Camillus).
(b) LAING, William, Sgt., 158th N.Y. Inf. (New York).
(b) LANG, George C., Spec. 4, 9th Inf. Div. (Flushing).
     LANGBEIN, J. C. Julius, Musician, 9th N.Y. Inf. (New York) (b. Germany).
    *LANGHORN, Garfield M., Pfc., 1st Aviation Brig. (Riverhead) (b. Va.).
     LAWTON, Louis B., 1st Lt., 9th U.S. Inf. (Auburn) (b. Iowa).
(b) LEVY, Benjamin, Pvt., 1st N.Y. Inf. (New York).
     LIBAIRE, Adolphe, Capt., 9th N.Y. Inf. (New York).
     LITEKY, Angelo J., Chaplain (Capt.) 199th Inf. Brigade (Fort Hamilton) (b.
        D.C.).
(b) LOHNES, Francis W., Pvt., 1st Nebr. Vet. Cav. (Oneida County).
(b) LONG, Oscar F., 2d Lt., 5th U.S. Inf. (Utica).
(b) LONSWAY, Joseph, Pvt., 20th N.Y. Cav. (Clayton).
(b) LORISH, Andrew J., Com. Sgt., 19th N.Y. Cav. (1st N.Y. Dragoons) (Dansville).
(b) LOUE, George M., Col., 116th N.Y. Inf. (New York).
    *LOZADA, Carlos James, Pfc., 173d Airborne Brig. (Bronx) (b. Puerto Rico).
    *LUCAS, Andre C., Lt. Col., 101st Airborne Div. (b. D.C.).
     LUDGATE, William, Capt., 59th N.Y. Vet. Inf. (New York) (b. England).
(b) LUTES, Franklin W., Cpl., 111th N.Y. Inf. (Clyde).
(b) LYMAN, Joel H., Q.M. Sgt., 9th N.Y. Cav. (E. Randolph).
     MADDEN, Michael, Pvt., 42d N.Y. Inf. (New York) (b. Ireland).
(b) MADISON, James, Sgt., 8th N.Y. Cav. (Fairport) (Real name James Congdon (see
        above)).

        MANDY, Harry J., 1st Sgt., 4th N.Y. Cav. (New York) (b. England).
(b) MARSH, Albert, Sgt., 64th N.Y. Inf. (Randolph).
(b) McBRIDE, Bernard, Pvt., 8th U.S. Cav. (Brooklyn).
        McBRYAR, William, Sgt., 10th U.S. Cav. (New York) (b. N.C.).
        McENROE, Patrick H., Sgt., 6th N.Y. Cav. (New York) (b. Ireland).
(b) McGINN, Edward, Pvt., 54th Ohio Inf. (New York).
(b) McHUGH, John, Pvt., 5th U.S. Inf. (Syracuse).
(b) McKAY, Charles W., Sgt., 154th N.Y. Inf. (Allegheny).
        McMURTRY, George G., Capt., 77th Div. (New York) (b. Pennsylvania).
(b) McVEAGH, Charles H., Pvt., 8th U.S. Cav. (New York).
        McVEANE, John P., Cpl., 49th N.Y. Inf. (Buffalo) (b. Canada).
(b) MEACH, George E., Farrier, 6th N.Y. Cav. (New York).
        MEAGHER, Thomas, 1st Sgt., 158th N.Y. Inf. (Brooklyn) (b. Scotland).
(b) *MERRELL, Joseph F., Pvt., 3d Inf. Div. (Staten Island).
(b) MERRILL, George, Pvt., 142d N.Y. Inf. (Queensbury).
(b) MERRILL, John, Sgt., 5th U.S. Cav. (New York).
(b) MERRITT, John G., Sgt., 1st Minn. Inf. (New York).
(b) MEYER, Henry C., Capt., 24th N.Y. Cav. (Dobbs Ferry).
(b) MILLER, Frank, Pvt., 2d N.Y. Cav. (Jamaica).
(b) MILLER, George, Cpl., 5th U.S. Inf. (Brooklyn).
        MILLER, John, Pvt., 8th N.Y. Cav. (Rochester) (b. Germany).
(b) MILLS, Albert L., Capt., U.S. Vol. (New York).
(b) MILLS, Frank W., Sgt., 1st N.Y. Mtd. Rifles (Middletown).
(b) MOFFITT, John H., Cpl., 16th N.Y. Inf. (Plattsburg).
(b) MOQUIN, George, Cpl., 5th U.S. Cav. (New York).
        MORSE, Charles E., Sgt., 62d N.Y. Inf. (New York) (b. France).
    *MULLER, Joseph E., Sgt., 77th Inf. Div. (New York) (b. Mass.).
        MURPHY, Michael C., Lt. Col., 170th N.Y. Inf. (New York) (b. Ireland).
(b) MURPHY, Thomas, Cpl., 158th N.Y. Inf. (New York).
        MURPHY, Thomas J., 1st Sgt., 146th N.Y. Inf. (New York) (b. Ireland).
(b) *MURRAY, Robert C., S/Sgt., 23d Inf. Div. (Bronx).
(b) NEAHR, Zachariah C., Pvt., 142d N.Y. Inf. (Canajoharie).
(b) NEWMAN, William H., Lt., 86th N.Y. Inf. (Orange County).
        NIHILL, John, Pvt., 5th U.S. Cav. (Brooklyn) (b. Ireland).
(b) NIVEN, Robert, 2d Lt., 8th N.Y. Cav. (Rochester).
(b) NORTON, John R., Lt., 1st N.Y. Cav. (Ontario County).
(b) NORTON, Llewellyn P., Sgt., 10th N.Y. Cav. (Cortland County).
(b) NUTTING, Lee, Capt., 61st N.Y. Inf. (Orange County).
        O'BEIRNE, James R., Capt., 37th N.Y. Inf. (New York) (b. Ireland).
(b) *O'BRIEN, William J., Lt. Col., 27th Inf. Div. (Troy).
(b) O'CALLAGHAN, John, Sgt., 8th U.S. Cav. (New York).
        OLIVER, Paul A., Capt., 12th N.Y. Inf. (New York) (b. at Sea).
(b) O'NEIL, Richard W., Sgt., 165th Inf., 42d Div. (New York).
(b) ORR, Charles A., Pvt., 187th N.Y. Inf. (Bennington).
        O'SULLIVAN, John, Pvt., 4th U.S. Cav. (New York) (b. Ireland).
(b) PACKARD, Loron F., Pvt., 5th N.Y. Cav. (Cuba).
(b) PARKS, Henry Jeremiah, Pvt., 9th N.Y. Cav. (Orangeville).
        PARNELL, William R., 1st Lt., 1st U.S. Cav. (New York) (b. Ireland).
(b) PATTERSON, John H., 1st Lt., 11th U.S. Inf. (New York).
(b) PECK, Archie A., Pvt., 307th Inf., 77th Div. (Hornell).
(b) *PETERSON, George, S/Sgt., 1st Inf. Div. (Brooklyn).
(b) PFISTERER, Herman, Mus., 21st U.S. Inf. (New York).
(b) PLIMLEY, William, 1st Lt., 120th N.Y. Inf. (Catskill).
(b) PORTER, William, Sgt., 1st N.J. Cav. (New York).
(b) POTTER, Norman, F., 1st Sgt., 149th N.Y. Inf. (Pompey).
(b) POWERS, Thomas, Cpl., 1st U.S. Cav. (New York).
        PRESTON, Noble D., 1st Lt. and Commissary, 10th N.Y. Cav. (Fulton).
(b) PUTNAM, Edgar P., Sgt., 9th N.Y. Cav. (Stockton).
        QUINLAN, James, Maj., 88th N.Y. Inf. (New York) (b. Ireland).
        RAFFERTY, Peter, Pvt., 69th N.Y. Inf. (New York) (b. Ireland).
(b) RAND, Charles F., Pvt., 12th N.Y. Inf. (Batavia).
(b) RANNEY, Myron H., Pvt., 13th N.Y. Inf. (Franklinville).

(b) *RAY, Bernard J., 1st Lt., 4th Inf. Div. (Baldwin).
(b) RAYMOND, William H., Cpl., 108th N.Y. Inf. (Penfield).
(b) READ, Morton A., Lt., 8th N.Y. Cav. (Brockport).
REYNOLDS, George, Pvt., 9th N.Y. Cav. (New York) (b. Ireland).
RHODES, Julius D., Pvt., 5th N.Y. Cav. (Springville) (b. Mich.).
(b) RIDDELL, Rudolph, Lt., 61st N.Y. Inf. (Hamilton).
(b) ROBERTSON, Robert S., 1st Lt., 93d N.Y. Inf. (Argyle).
(b) ROBINSON, John C., Brig. Gen., U.S. Vol. (Binghamton).
(b) ROCKEFELLER, Charles M., Lt., 178th N.Y. Inf. (New York).
(b) ROONEY, Edward, Pvt., 5th U.S. Inf. (Poughkeepsie).
(b) *ROOSEVELT, Theodore, Jr., Brig. Gen. (Oyster Bay).
(b) RUSSELL, Charles L., Cpl. 93d N.Y. Inf. (Malone).
(b) RUSSELL, James, Pvt., 1st U.S. Cav. (New York).
RUTHERFORD, John T., 1st Lt., 9th N.Y. Cav. (Canton).
(b) SAGE, William H., Capt., 23d U.S. Inf. (Binghamton).
(b) SAGELHURST, John C., Sgt., 1st N.J. Cav. (Buffalo).
(b) SALE, Albert, Pvt., 8th U.S. Cav.
*SANTIAGO-COLON, Hector, Spec. 4, 1st Cav. Div. (New York) (b. Puerto Rico).
(b) SARTWELL, Henry, Sgt., 123d N.Y. Inf. (Fort Ann).
(b) SCHAEFER, Joseph E., S/Sgt., 1st Inf. Div. (Long Island).
SCHILLER, John, Pvt., 158th N.Y. Inf. (New York) (b. Germany).
SCHMAL, George W., Blacksmith, 24th N.Y. Cav. (Buffalo) (b. Germany).
SCHWAN, Theodore, 1st Lt., 10th U.S. Inf. (New York) (b. Germany).
(b) SCOFIELD, David H., Q.M. Sgt., 5th N.Y. Cav. (Mamaroneck).
(b) SCOTT, Robert B., Pvt., 8th U.S. Cav. (Washington County).
SHALER, Alexander, Col., 65th N.Y. Inf. (New York) (b. Conn.).
(b) SHEA, Charles W., 2d Lt., 88th Inf. Div. (New York).
(b) SHIPLEY, Robert F., Sgt., 140th N.Y. Inf. (Wayne).
(b) *SHOUP, Curtis F., S/Sgt., 87th Inf. Div. (Buffalo).
(b) SICKLES, Daniel E., Maj. Gen., U.S. Vol. (New York).
(b) SIMMONS, John, Pvt., 2d N.Y. Hvy. Arty. (Liberty).
(b) SKELLIE, Ebenezer, Cpl., 112th N.Y. Inf. (Mina).
(b) SMITH, Charles E., Cpl., 6th U.S. Cav. (Auburn).
SMITH, David L., Sgt., Btry. E., 1st N.Y. Light Arty. (Bath).
(b) *SMITH, George W., Pvt., 6th U.S. Cav. (Greenfield).
(b) SMITH, Richard, Pvt., 95th N.Y. Inf. (Haverstraw).
(b) SMITH, Wilson, Cpl., 3d N.Y. Light Arty. (Madison).
(b) SOVA, Joseph E., Saddler, 8th N.Y. Cav. (Chili).
STAHEL, Julius, Maj. Gen. U.S. Vol. (New York) (b. Hungary).
(b) STANLEY, Edward, Cpl., 8th U.S. Cav. (New York).
(b) STARKINS, John H., Sgt., 34th N.Y. Btry. (Great Neck).
STEWART, George E., 2d Lt., 19th U.S. Inf. (New York) (b. Australia).
(b) *STONE, Lester R., Jr., Sgt., 23d Inf. Div. (Americal) (Harpursville).
(b) *STRYKER, Robert F., Spec. 4, 26th Inf. Div. (Throop).
(b) SWIFT, Harlan J., 2d Lt., 2d N.Y. Militia Regt. (New York).
THACKRAH, Benjamin, Pvt., 115th N.Y. Inf. (Johnsonville) (b. Scotland).
(b) THOMPKINS, George W., Cpl., 124th N.Y. Inf. (Port Jervis).
(b) THOMPSON, Allen, Pvt., 4th N.Y. Hvy. Arty. (Sandy Creek).
(b) THOMPSON, George W., Pvt., 2d U.S. Cav. (Victory).
(b) THOMPSON, James, Pvt., 4th N.Y. Hvy. Arty. (Sandy Creek).
THOMPSON, J. (James) Harry, Surgeon, U.S. Vol. (New York) (b. England).
THOMPSON, John, Sgt., 1st U.S. Cav. (New York) (b. Scotland).
(b) *THOMPSON, William, Pfc., 25th Inf. Div. (Bronx).
THOMSON, Clifford, 1st Lt., 1st N.Y. Cav. (New York).
(b) THORN, Walter, 2d Lt., 116th U.S. Colored Troops.
TOMPKINS, Charles H., 1st Lt., 2d U.S. Cav. (Brooklyn) (b. Va.).
(b) TOOHEY, Thomas, Sgt., 24th Wis. Inf. (New York).
(b) TOY, Frederick E., 1st Sgt., 7th U.S. Cav. (Buffalo).
(b) TRACY, Benjamin F., Col., 109th N.Y. Inf. (Oswego, N.Y.).
(b) TRACY, William G., 2d Lt., 122d N.Y. Inf. (Onondaga County).
TRAYNOR, Andrew, Cpl., 1st Mich. Cav. (Rome) (b. N.J.).

ARMY-AIR FORCE

(b) TREMAIN, Henry E., Maj. and Aide-de-Camp, U.S. Vol. (New York).
(b) TRIBE, John, Pvt., 5th N.Y. Cav. (Oswego).
   *TURNER, William B., 1st Lt., 27th Div. (Garden City) (b. Mass.).
(b) URBAN, Matt, 2d Bat., 60th Inf. Reg., 9th Inf. Div., (Buffalo).
   VALENTE, Michael, Pvt., 107th Inf. 27th Div. (Ogdensburg) (b. Italy).
   *VANCE, Leon R., Jr., Lt. Col., 8th A.F. (Garden City) (b. Okla.).
(b) VANSCHAICK, Louis J., 1st Lt., 4th U.S. Inf. (Cobleskill).
(b) VAN WINKLE, Edward, Cpl., 148th N.Y. Inf. (Phelps).
   VON VEGESACK, Ernest, Maj., U.S. Vol. (New York) (b. Belgium).
(b) VOSLER, Forrest L., T/Sgt., A.C. (Rochester).
   WAALER, Reidar, Sgt., 105th M.G. Bn., 27th Div. (New York) (b. Norway).
   WAINWRIGHT, Jonathan M., Gen., Commanded USA in Philippines (Skaneateles) (b. Wash.).
(b) WALL, Jerry, Pvt., 126th N.Y. Inf. (Milo).
(b) WALLING, William H., Capt., 142d N.Y. Inf. (Hartford).
   WAMBSGAN, Martin, Pvt., 90th N.Y. Inf. (Cayuga County) (b. Germany).
(b) *WARREN, John E., Jr., 1st Lt., 25th Inf. Div. (Brooklyn).
(b) WATSON, James C., Cpl., 6th U.S. Cav. (Cochecton).
(b) WEBB, Alexander S., Brig. Gen., U.S. Vol. (New York).
(b) WEBB, James, Pvt., 5th N.Y. Inf. (Brooklyn).
   WEEKS, John H., Pvt., 152d N.Y. Inf. (Hartwick Seminary) (b. Conn.).
(b) WEIR, Henry C., Capt., and Asst. Adj. Gen., U.S. Vol. (West Point).
(b) WELCH, Michael, Sgt., 6th U.S. Cav. (Poughkeepsie).
(b) WELCH, Stephen, Sgt., 154th N.Y. Inf. (Cattaraugus County).
   *WELLS, Henry S., Pvt., 148th N.Y. Inf. (Phelps).
   WELLS, Thomas M., Chief Bugler, 6th N.Y. Cav. (DeKalb) (b. Ireland).
(b) WEST, Frank, 1st Lt., 6th U.S. Cav. (Mohawk).
   *WILL, Walter J., 1st Lt., 1st Inf. Div. (W. Winfield) (b. Pa.).
(b) *WILLETT, Louis E., Pfc., 4th Inf. Div. (Brooklyn).
(b) WILLIAMS, Le Roy, Sgt., 8th N.Y. Hvy. Arty. (Oswego).
   WINDOLPH, Charles, Pvt., 7th U.S. Cav. (Brooklyn) (b. Germany).
(b) WINEGAR, William W., Lt., 19th N.Y. Cav. (1st N.Y. Dragoons) (Springport).
(b) WISNER, Lewis S., 1st Lt., 124th N.Y. Inf. (Wallkill).
(b) WRIGHT, Raymond R., Sp 4c, 9th Inf. Div. (Mineville).
(b) YOUNG, James M., Pvt., 72d N.Y. Inf. (Chautauqua County).

NAVY-MARINE CORPS

   AHERN, William, WT, USN (b. Ireland).
   ALLEN, Edward, BM 1c., USN (b. Holland).
   ANDERSON, William, Cox., USN (b. Sweden).
(b) APPLETON, Edwin Nelson, Cpl., USMC (Brooklyn).
(b) AUER, John F., Ordinary Seaman Apprentice, USN (New York).
   AVERY, James, Seaman, USN (b. Scotland).
   BAKER, Charles, Quarter Gunner, USN (New York) (b. D.C.).
(b) BARTER, Gurdon H., Landsman, USN (Williamsburgh).
   BASS, David L., Seaman, USN (b. Ireland).
   BATES, Richard, Seaman, USN (b. Wales).
   BELL, George, Captain of the Afterguard, USN (Brooklyn) (b. England).
(b) BENNETT, Floyd, Machinist, USN (Warrensburg).
(b) BENNETT, James H., CBM, USN (New York).
(b) BETHAM, Asa, Cox., USN (New York).
   BJORKMAN, Ernest H., Ordinary Seaman, USN (b. Sweden).
   BLAGHEEN, William, SC, USN (b. England).
(b) *BOBO, John P., 2d Lt., 3d Marine Div. (Niagara Falls).
   BOURNE, Thomas, Seaman, USN (New York) (b. England).
(b) BRADLEY, Amos, Landsman, USN (Dansville).
   BRADLEY, Charles, BM, USN (b. Ireland).
   BRADY, George F., CGM, USN (b. Ireland).
(b) BREEN, John, BM, USN (New York).
   BRINN, Andrew, Seaman, USN (b. Scotland).
(b) BROWN, Charles, Cpl., USMC (New York) (Enlisted at Hong Kong, China).
(b) BROWN, James, Quartermaster, USN (Rochester).

NAVY-MARINE CORPS

BROWN, John, Captain of Forecastle, USN (b. Scotland).
BROWN, Robert, Captain of Top, USN (b. Norway).
(b) BROWNELL, William P., Cox., USN (New York).
(b) BUCKLEY, Howard Major, Pvt., USMC (Croton Falls).
BURKE, Thomas, Seaman, USN (b. Ireland).
(b) BURNS, John M., Seaman, USN (Hudson).
BURTON, Albert, Seaman, USN (b. England).
BYRNES, James, BM., USN (b. Ireland).
CAHEY, Thomas, Seaman, USN (b. Ireland).
CANN, Tedford H., Seaman, USN (New York) (b. Conn.).
(b) *CAPODANNO, Vincent R., Lt. (Chaplain Corps USNR, 1st Mar. Div. (Staten Island).
CAREY, James, Seaman, USN (Brooklyn) (b. Ireland).
(b) CASAMENTO, Anthony, Corporal, USN (Brooklyn).
CASSIDY, Michael, Landsman, USN (b. Ireland).
CAVANAUGH, Thomas, F1c.,USN (b. Ireland).
CHANDRON, August, SA2d., USN (B. France).
CHAPUT, Louis G., Landsman, USN (b. Canada).
(b) CLANCY, Joseph, Chief, BM, USN (New York).
CLAUSEN, Claus Kristian, Cox., USN (New York) (b. Denmark).
COLBERT, Patrick, Cox., USN (b. Ireland).
(b) CONLAN, Dennis, Seaman, USN (New York).
(b) *COOK, Donald G., Colonel, USN (Brooklyn).
†COOPER, John, Cox., USN (b. Ireland).
CORAHORGI, Demetri, F1c., USN. (b. Austria).
(b) CORCORAN, Thomas E., Landsman, USN.
(b) COREY, William, Landsman, USN (New York).
(b) COSTELLO, John, Ordinary Seaman, USN (Rouses Point).
(b) COTTON, Peter, Ordinary Seaman, USN (New York).
(b) CREELMAN, William J., Landsman, USN (Brooklyn).
(b) CREGAN, George, Cox., USN (New York).
(b) †DALY, Daniel, Gun. Sgt., USMC (Glen Cove).
DAVIS, John, GM3c., USN (New York) (b. Germany).
(b) DECKER, Percy A., BM2d., USN (New York).
DENHAM, Austin, Seaman, USN (b. England).
DENNING, Lorenzo, Landsman, USN (New York) (b. Conn.).
(b) DENSMORE, William, CBM, USN (New York).
DONNELLY, John, Ordinary Seaman, USN (b. England).
DOUGHERTY, Patrick, Landsman, USN (b. Ireland).
DUNPHY, Richard D., Coal Heaver, USN (b. Ireland).
EGLIT, John, Seaman, USN (b. Finland).
(b) ENGLISH, Thomas, SQM, USN (New York).
ERICKSON, John P., Captain of Forecastle, USN (b. England).
ERICKSON, Nick, Cox., USN (b. Finland).
EVERETTS, John, GM1c., USN (b. Canada).
(b) FARRELL, Edward, Quartermaster, USN (Saratoga).
FIELD, Oscar Wadsworth, Pvt., USMC (b. N.J.).
FITZGERALD, John, Pvt., USMC (b. Ireland).
FLANNAGAN, John, BM, USN (b. Ireland).
FLOOD, Thomas, Boy, USN (b. Ireland).
(b) FORBECK, Andrew P., Seaman, USN (New York).
(b) FOWLER, Christopher, Quartermaster, USN.
(b) FRANKLIN, Joseph John, Pvt., USMC (Buffalo).
(b) GALBRAITH, Robert, Apprentice First Class, USN (Brooklyn).
GARDNER, William, Seaman, USN (b. Ireland).
(b) GARRISON, James R., Coal Heaver, USN (Poughkeepsie).
GIBBONS, Michael, Oiler, USN (b. Ireland).
(b) GOWAN, William Henry, BM, USN (Rye).
GRAHAM, Robert, Landsman, USN (b. England).
*GRAVES, Terrence, 2d Lt., USMC (b. Tex.).
GREENE, John, Captain of Forecastle, USN (New York).
HALLING, Luovi, BM1c., USN (b. Sweden).
(b) HALSTEAD, William, Cox., USN.
(b) HAMILTON, Hugh, Cox., USN (New York).

(b) HARLEY, Bernard, Ordinary Seaman, USN (Brooklyn).
      HARRIS, John, Captain of Forecastle, USN (b. Scotland).
(b) HARTIGAN, Charles Conway, Lt., USN (Middletown).
      HILL, George, Chief Quarter Gunner, USN (b. England).
(b) HILL, William L., Captain of Top, USN (Brooklyn).
      HINNEGAN, William, F2c., USN (b. Ireland).
(b) HOBAN, Thomas, Cox., USN (New York).
      HOBSON, Richmond Pearson, Lieutenant, USN (b. Ala.).
      HOLLAT, George, 3c Boy, USN (New York).
      HOWARD, Martin, Landsman, USN (b. Ireland).
      HUDSON, Michael, Sgt., USMC (b. Ireland).
(b) HUGHES, John Arthur, Capt., USMC (New York).
(b) HUSE, Henry McClaren Pinckney, Capt., USN (West Point).
(b) HUSKEY, Michael, Fireman, USN (New York).
(b) *HUTCHINS, Carlton Barmore, Lt., USN (Albany).
      IRLAM, Joseph, Seaman, USN (b. England).
(b) IRVING, John, Cox., USN (Brooklyn).
      IRVING, Thomas, Cox., USN (b. England).
      IRWIN, Nicholas, Seaman, USN (b. Denmark).
(b) JACOBSON, Douglas Thomas, Pfc., USMCR (Rochester).
(b) †JANSON, Ernest August, Gun. Sgt., USMC (Also awarded Army Medal of Honor
      under name of Hoffman, Charles F.) (Brooklyn).
      JOHANSSON, Johan J., Ordinary Seaman, USN (b. Sweden).
      JOHNSON, Henry, Seaman, USN (b. Norway).
      JOHNSON, William, Cooper, USN (b. West Indies).
      JONES, Andrew, CBM, USN (b. Ireland).
(b) JONES, John E., Quartermaster, USN (New York).
(b) JORDAN, Robert, Cox., USN (New York).
(b) KATES, Thomas Wilbur, Pvt., USMC (Shelby Center).
(b) KENYON, Charles, Fireman, USN.
      KING, Hugh, Ordinary Seaman, USN (b. Ireland).
      †KING, John, CWT, USN (b. Ireland).
(b) KING, Robert H., Landsman, USN.
(b) KINNAIRD, Samuel W., Landsman, USN (New York).
      *†KOCAK, Matej, Sgt., 2d Div. USMC (New York) (b. Austria) (Also awarded
      Army Medal of Honor).
      KRAUSE, Ernest, Cox., USN (b. Germany).
      KUCHNEISTER, Hermann William, Pvt., USMC (b. Germany).
(b) LAKIN, Thomas, Seaman, USN.
(b) LANN, John S., Landsman, USN (Rochester).
(b) LEE, James H., Seaman, USN.
      LEJEUNE, Emile, Seaman, USN (b. France).
(b) LEONARD, Joseph, Pvt., USMC (Cohoes).
(b) LLOYD, John W., Cox, USN (New York).
      LOW, George, Seaman, USN (b. Canada).
(b) LUCY, John, Second Class Boy, USN (New York).
      MACHON, James, Boy, USN (b. England).
      MACK, Alexander, Captain of Top, USN (b. Holland).
(b) MACKIE, John F., Cpl., USMC (New York).
      MADDEN, William, Coal Heaver, USN (b. England).
      MARTIN, William, Seaman, USN (b. Ireland).
(b) *McCARD, Robert Howard, Gun. Sgt., USMC (Syracuse).
(b) McCARTON, John, SP, USN (Brooklyn).
(b) McCLELLAND, Matthew, F1c., USN (Brooklyn).
(b) †McCLOY, John, CB, USN (Brewsters).
      McGOWAN, John, Quartermaster, USN (b. Ireland).
      McINTOSH, James, Captain of Top, USN (b. Canada).
      McKENZIE, Alexander, BM, USN (b. Scotland).
(b) McKNIGHT, William, Cox., USN (Ulster County).
      McNAMARA, Michael, Pvt., USMC (b. Ireland).
      MILLIKEN, Daniel S., Quarter Gunner, USN (b. Maine).
(b) MILLMORE, John, Ordinary Seaman, USN (New York).

996   NEW YORK—Continued

NAVY-MARINE CORPS

(b) MILLS, Charles, Seaman, USN (Upster).
(b) MITCHELL, Thomas, Landsman, USN (New York).
     MOORE, Charles, Landsman, USN (b. Ireland).
(b) MOORE, Francis, BM, USN (New York).
(b) MORGAN, James H., Captain of Top, USN (New York).
(b) MORRIS, John, Cpl., USMC (New York).
     MORRISON, John G., Cox., USN (Lansingburg) (b. Ireland).
     MORSE, William, Seaman, USN (b. Germany).
     MURPHY, John Edward, Cox., USN (b. Ireland).
     MURPHY, Patrick, BM, USN (b. Ireland).
(b) MURRAY, William H., Pvt., USMC (Brooklyn).
(b) NAYLOR, David, Landsman, USN (Thompsonville).
     NIBBE, John H., Quartermaster, USN (b. Germany).
(b) NICHOLS, William, Quartermaster, USN (New York).
     NOIL, Joseph B., Seaman, USN (b. Canada).
(b) *NOONAN, Thomas P., L/Cpl., 3rd Mar. Div. USMC (Brooklyn).
(b) NORDSIEK, Charles Luers, Ordinary Seaman, USN (New York).
     NORDSTROM, Isidor, CBM, USN (b. Sweden).
     NORRIS, J. W., Landsman, USN (b. England).
     OAKLEY, William, GM2d, USN (b. England).
     O'CONNELL, Thomas, Coal Heaver, USN (b. Ireland).
(b) O'DONOGHUE, Timothy, Seaman, USN (Rochester).
     OHMSEN, August, Master-at-Arms, USN (b. Germany).
(b) OMALLEY, Robert E., Sgt., 3d Mar. Div. (New York).
     OSEPINS, Christian, Seaman, USN (b. Holland).
(b) OVIATT, Miles M., Cpl., USMC (Cattarangus County).
(b) OWENS, Michael, Pvt., USMC (New York).
(b) PARKS, George, Captain of Forecastle, USN (Schenectady).
(b) PEASE, Joachim, Seaman, USN (Long Island).
(b) PERRY, Thomas, BM, USN.
(b) *PETERS, Lawrence David, Sgt., 1st Mar. Div., USMC (Binghamton).
     PETERSON, Alfred, Seaman, USN (b. Sweden).
     PHILLIPS, George F., M1c., USN (b. Mass).
     PHINNEY, William, BM, USN (b. Norway).
(b) *POWERS, John James, Lt., USN (New York).
(b) PRICE, Edward, Cox., USN.
(b) PROVINCE, George, Ordinary Seaman, USN.
     PYNE, George, Seaman, USN (b. England).
(b) QUICK, Joseph, Cox., USN.
(b) READ, Charles, Ordinary Seaman, USN (Cambridge).
     REGAN, Patrick, Ordinary Seaman, USN (b. Ireland).
     REID, Patrick, CWT, USN (b. Ireland).
(b) RICHARDS, Louis, Quartermaster, USN (New York).
     ROANTREE, James S., Sgt., USMC (b. Ireland).
     ROBINSON, Alexander, BM, USN (b. England).
     ROBINSON, Charles, BM, USN (b. Scotland).
     ROBINSON, Thomas, Captain of Afterguard, USN (b. Norway).
(b) ROGERS, Samuel F., Quartermaster, USN (Buffalo).
     RUSSELL, Henry P., Landsman, USN (b. Canada).
(b) RUSSELL, John, Seaman, USN (New York).
(b) SCHEPKE, Charles S., GM1c., USN (New York).
(b) SCHNEPEL, Fred Jurgen, Ordinary Seaman, USN (New York).
     SCHUTT, George, Cox., USN (b. Ireland).
     SEANOR, James, Master-at-Arms, USN (b. Mass.).
     SHANAHAN, Patrick, CBM, USN (b. Ireland).
     SHARP, Hendrick, Seaman, USN (b. Spain).
     SHERIDAN, James, Quartermaster, USN (b. N.J.).
(b) SHIPMAN, William, Cox., USN (New York).
(b) SIMKINS, Lebbeus, Cox., USN (Utica).
     SIMPSON, Henry, F1c., USN (b. England).
(b) SMITH, Edwin, Ordinary Seaman, USN (New York).
(b) SMITH, James, Captain of Forecastle, USN (Albany).

(b)   SMITH, James, Landsman, USN.
       SMITH, James, Seaman, USN (b. Hawaii).
       SMITH, John, Seaman, USN (b. Bermuda).
(b)   SMITH, John, Second Captain of Top, USN (Albany).
       SMITH, Oloff, Cox., USN (b. Sweden).
       SMITH, Thomas, Seaman, USN (b. England).
(b)   SMITH, Walter B., Ordinary Seaman, USN.
       SMITH, Wilhelm, GM1c., USN (b. Germany).
(b)   SMITH, Willard M., Cpl., USMC (Alleghany).
       SPICER, William, GM1c., USN (b. England).
(b)   SPROWLE, David, Orderly Sgt., USMC (Lisbon).
(b)   STANLEY, Robert Henry, Hospital Apprentice, USN (Brooklyn).
       STANTON, Thomas, CMM, USN (b. Ireland).
       *STOCKHAM, Fred W., Gunnery Sgt., 6th Regt., USMC (New York) (b. Mich.).
(b)   STOKES, John, Chief Master-at-Arms, USN (New York).
(b)   STOUT, Richard, Landsman, USN.
(b)   SULLIVAN, James, Ordinary Seaman, USN (New York).
(b)   SULLIVAN, John, Seaman, USN (New York).
       SULLIVAN, Timothy, Cox., USN (b. Ireland).
       SUMMERS, Robert, Chief Quartermaster, USN (b. Prussia).
       SUNDQUIST, Gustav A., Ordinary Seaman, USN (b. Sweden).
(b)   SWATTON, Edward, Seaman, USN (New York).
(b)   TAYLOR, George, Armorer, USN (Watertown).
       THOMASS, Karl, Cox., USN (b. Germany).
       THORDSEN, William George, Cox., USN (b. Germany).
       TRIPLETT, Samuel, Ordinary Seaman, USN (b. Kans.).
(b)   TROY, Jeremiah, CBM, USN (New York).
       VADAS, Albert, Seaman, USN (b. Austria-Hungary).
       WAGG, Maurice, Cox., USN (b. England).
       WALKER, Edward Alexander, Sgt., USMC (b. Scotland).
(b)   WALSH, James A., Seaman, USN (New York).
(b)   WALSH, Kenneth Ambrose, 1st Lt., USMC (Brooklyn).
(b)   WARD, James, Quarter Gunner, USN (New York).
       WARREN, David, Cox., USN (b. Scotland).
(b)   WEBSTER, Henry S., Landsman, USN (Stockholm).
       WEISSEL, Adam, SC, USN (b. Germany).
       WELLS, William, Quartermaster, USN (b. Germany).
       WESTA, Karl, CMM, USN (b. Norway).
(b)   WILCOX, Franklin L., Ordinary Seaman, USN (Paris).
       WILKE, Julius A. R., BM1c., USN (b. Germany).
(b)   WILKES, Henry, Landsman, USN (New York).
       WILLIAMS, Frank, Seaman, USN (Buffalo) (b. Germany).
       WILLIAMS, John, BM, USN (New York) (b. N.J.).
(b)   WILLIAMS, Robert, Signal Quartermaster, USN (New York).
       WILSON, August, Boilermaker, USN (b. Germany).
       WOON, John, BM, USN (b. England).
(b)   WORAM, Charles B., Seaman, USN (New York).
(b)   WRIGHT, Edward, Quartermaster, USN (New York).
(b)   YOUNG, William, BM, USN.

NORTH CAROLINA

       *BLACKWELL, Robert L., Pvt. 30th Div. (Hurdle Mills) (b. N. Dak.).
(b)   CRUMP, Jerry K., Cpl., 3d Inf. Div. (Forest City).
(b)   *EUBANKS, Ray E., Sgt., 503d Para. Inf. (LaGrange).
(b)   *GEORGE, Charles, Pfc., 45th Inf. Div. (Whittier).
       MURRAY, Charles P., Jr., 1st Lt., 3d Inf. Div. (Wilmington) (b. Md.).
(b)   PARKER, Samuel I., 2d Lt., 1st Div. (Monroe).
(b)   PATTERSON, Robert Martin, Spec. 4, 17th Cav. (Springlake).
       *SIMS, Clifford Chester, S/Sgt., 101st Airborne Div. (Fayetteville) (b. Fla.).

ARMY-AIR FORCE

*STOUT, Mitchell W., Sgt., 44th Arty. (b. Tenn.).
(b)   THOMPSON, Max, Sgt., 1st Inf. Div. (Canton).
(b)   *WARNER, Henry F., Cpl., 1st Inf. Div. (Troy).
(b)   *WOMACK, Bryant H., Pfc., 25th Inf. Div. (Mills Springs).

NAVY-MARINE CORPS

(b)   ANDERSON, Edwin A., Capt., USN (Wilmington).
(b)   *HALYBURTON, William David, Jr., PhM2d., USNR (Canton).
(b)   HERRING, Rufus G., Lt., USNR (Roseboro).
(b)   JOHNSTON, Rufus Zenas, Lt., USN (Lincolnton).
(b)   PARKER, Pomeroy, Pvt., USMC (Gates County).
(b)   STATON, Adolphus, Lt., USN (Tarboro).
(b)   STODDARD, James, Seaman, USN.

NORTH DAKOTA

ARMY-AIR FORCE

(b)   ANDERS, Frank L., Cpl., 1st N. Dak. Vol. Inf. (Fargo).
BLOCH, Orville Emil, 1st Lt., 85th Inf Div. (Streeter) (b. Wis.).
BOEHLER, Otto, Pvt., 1st N. Dak. Vol. Inf. (Wahpeton) (b. Germany).
DAVIS, Charles P., Pvt., 1st N. Dak. Vol. Inf. (Valley City) (b. Minn.).
DOWNS, Willis H., Pvt., 1st N. Dak. Vol. Inf. (Jamestown) (b. Conn.).
(b)   *HAGEN, Loren D., 1st Lt., U.S. Army Tr. Adv. Gp. (Fargo).
JENSEN, Gotfred, Pvt., 1st N. Dak. Vol. Inf. (Devils Lake) (b. Denmark).
KINNE, John B., Pvt., 1st N. Dak. Inf. (Fargo) (b. Wis.).
LONGFELLOW, Richard M., Pvt., 1st N. Dak. Vol. Inf. (Mandan) (b. Ill.).
ROSS, Frank F., Pvt., 1st N. Dak., Vol. Inf. (Langdon) (b. Ill.).
SLETTELAND, Thomas, Pvt., 1st N. Dak. Inf. (Grafton) (b. Norway).
*SMITH, Fred E., Lt. Col., 77th Div. (Bartlett) (b. Ill.).
*WOLD, Nels, Pvt., 138th Inf., 35th Div. (Minnewaukan) (b. Minn.).

NAVY-MARINE CORPS

BRADLEY, Willis Winter, Jr., Comdr., USN (b. N.Y.).
CARTER, Joseph E., Blacksmith, USN (b. England).
(b)   *GURKE, Henry, Pfc., USMC (Neche).

OHIO

ARMY-AIR FORCE

(b)   ALBERT, Christian, Pvt., 47th Ohio Inf. (Cincinnati).
(b)   *ANTOLAK, Sylvester, Sgt., 3d Inf. Div. (St. Clairsville).
(b)   ASTON, Edgar R., Pvt., 8th U.S. Cav. (Clermont County).
(b)   AYERS, David, Sgt., 57th Ohio Inf. (Upper Sandusky).
(b)   *BAESEL, Albert E., 2d Lt., 37th Div. (Berea).
*BAKER, Addison E., Lt. Col., 93d Bomb. Gp. (Akron) (b. Ill.).
BEATY, Powhatan, 1st Sgt., 5th U.S. Colored Troops (Delaware County) (b. Va.).
BELL, James B., Sgt., 11th Ohio Inf. (Troy).
(b)   BENNETT, Edward A., Pfc., 358th Inf., 90th Inf. Div. (Middleport).
(b)   BENSINGER, William, Pvt., 21st Ohio Inf. (Hancock County).
(b)   BICKHAM, Charles G., 1st Lt., 27th U.S. Inf. (Dayton).
(b)   BISHOP, Daniel, Sgt., 5th U.S. Cav. (Monroe County).
BOYNTON, Henry V., Lt. Col., 35th Ohio Inf. (b. Mass.).
BRONSON, James H., 1st Sgt., 5th U.S. Colored Troops (Delaware County) (b. Pa.).
BROOKIN, Oscar, Pvt., 17th U.S. Inf. (Green County) (b. Wis.).
BROWN, John H., 1st Sgt., 47th Ohio Inf. (Cincinnati) (b. Mass.).
(b)   BROWN, Robert B., Pvt., 15th Ohio Inf. (Zanesville).
(b)   BROWN, Uriah, Pvt., 30th Ohio Inf. (Miami County).
(b)   BROWN, Wilson W., Pvt., 21st Ohio Inf. (Wood County).

ARMY-AIR FORCE

(b) BUHRMAN, Henry G., Pvt., 54th Ohio Inf. (Cincinnati).
(b) BURNS, James M., Sgt., 1st W. Va. Inf. (Jefferson County).
(b) CALVERT, James S., Pvt., 5th U.S. Inf. (Athens County).
    CAPEHART, Henry, Col., 1st W. Va. Cav. (Bridgeport) (b. Pa.).
(b) CARR, Franklin, Cpl., 124th Ohio Inf. (Stark County).
(b) CARR, John, Pvt., 8th U.S. Cav. (Columbus).
    CARSON, William J., Mus., 1st Bn., 15th U.S. Inf. (North Greenfield) (b. Pa.).
(b) *CHRISTIAN, Herbert F., Pfc., 3d Inf. Div. (Steubenville).
(b) *CICCHETTI, Joseph J., Pvt., 37th Inf. Div. (Waynesburg).
(b) COCKLEY, David L., 1st Lt., 10th Ohio Cav. (Lexington).
(b) COLWELL, Oliver, 1st Lt., 95th Ohio Inf. (Champaign County).
(b) COOK, John, Bugler, 4th U.S. Arty. (Cincinnati).
(b) COONROD, Aquilla, Sgt., 5th U.S. Inf. (Bryan).
    *CRAIG, Robert, 2d Lt., 3d Inf. Div. (Toledo) (b. Scotland).
(b) CRANSTON, William W., Pvt., 66th Ohio Inf. (Woodstock).
(b) CROCKER, Ulric L., Pvt., 6th Mich. Cav.
(b) CUBBERLY, William G., Pvt., 8th U.S. Cav. (Butler County).
(b) CUMPSTON, James M., Pvt., 91st Ohio Inf. (Gallis County).
    DAVIDSON, Andrew, Asst. Surg., 47th Ohio Inf. (Cincinnati) (b. Vt.).
(b) DAVIS, Freeman, Sgt., 80th Ohio Inf. (Newcomerstown).
(b) DAVIS, Harry, Pvt., 46th Ohio Inf. (Franklin County).
(b) DAY, David F., Pvt., 57th Ohio Inf. (Dallasburg).
(b) DAY, Matthias, W., 2d Lt., 9th U.S. Cav. (Oberlin).
(b) *DE ARMOND, William, Sgt., 5th U.S. Inf. (Butler County).
(b) *DELEAU, Emile, Jr., Sgt., 36th Inf. Div. (Blaine).
(b) DE WITT, Richard W., Cpl., 47th Ohio Inf. (Oxford).
    DORSEY, Daniel, Cpl., 33d Ohio Inf. (Fairfield County) (b. Va.).
    DOWLING, James, Cpl., 8th U.S. Cav. (Cleveland) (b. Ireland).
    ENDERLIN, Richard, Mus., 73d Ohio Inf. (Chillicothe) (b. Germany).
    FERRARI, George, Cpl., 8th U.S. Cav. (Montgomery County) (b. N.Y.).
(b) FINKENBINER, Henry S., Pvt., 107th Ohio Inf. (North Industry).
    *FLEEK, Charles Clinton, Sgt., 25th Inf. Div. (Cincinnati) (b. Ky.).
    FORCE, Manning F., Brig. Gen., U.S. Vol. (Cincinnati) (b. D.C.).
(b) FREEMAN, Henry B., 1st Lt., 18th U.S. Inf. (Mount Vernon).
    FREY, Franz, Cpl., 37th Ohio Inf. (Cleveland) (b. Switzerland).
(b) GATES, George, Bugler, 8th U.S. Cav. (Delaware County).
(b) GAUNT, John C., Pvt., 104th Ohio Inf. (Damascoville).
(b) GAUSE, Isaac, Cpl., 2d Ohio Cav. (Trumbull County).
(b) GEIGER, George, Sgt., 7th U.S. Cav. (Cincinnati).
    *GIVEN, John J., Cpl., 6th U.S. Cav. (Cincinnati) (b. Ky.).
(b) GODFREY, Edward S., Capt., 7th U.S. Cav. (Ottawa).
    GRAY, John, Pvt., 5th Ohio Inf. (Hamilton County) (b. Scotland).
    GREEN, John, Maj., 1st U.S. Cav. (b. Germany).
    GREENAWALT, Abraham, Pvt., 104th Ohio Inf. (Salem) (b. Pa.).
(b) GREGG, Joseph O., Pvt., 133d Ohio Inf. (Circleville).
(b) GRIMSHAW, Samuel, Pvt., 52d Ohio Inf. (Jefferson County).
(b) GUINN, Thomas, Pvt., 47th Ohio Inf. (Clinton County).
(b) *HALL, Lewis, T5g, 25th Inf. Div. (Columbus).
(b) HALL, Newton H., Cpl. 104th Inf. (Portage County).
(b) HANKS, Joseph, Pvt., 37th Ohio Inf. (Chillicothe).
    HARRIS, David W., Pvt., 7th U.S. Cav. (Cincinnati) (b. Ind.).
(b) HARRIS, Sampson, Pvt., 30th Ohio Inf. (Olive).
(b) HARTZOG, Joshua B., Pvt., 1st U.S. Arty. (Paulding County).
(b) *HASTINGS, Joe R., Pfc., 97th Inf. Div. (Magnolia).
    HAWKINS, Martin J., Cpl., 33d Ohio Inf. (Portsmouth) (b. Pa.).
(b) HAYES, Webb·C., Lt. Col., 31st Inf., U.S. Vol. (Freemont).
(b) HEDGES, Joseph, 1st Lt., 4th U.S. Cav.
    HELLER, Henry, Sgt., 66th Ohio Inf. (Urbana) (b. Pa.).
(b) HERDA, Frank A., Sp4c., 101st Airborne Div. (Cleveland).
(b) HOLCOMB, Daniel I., Pvt., 41st Ohio Inf. (Hartford).
    HOLLAND, Milton M., Sgt. Maj., 5th U.S. Colored Troops (Athens) (b. Austin, Tex.).

Army-Air Force

(b)   HOWARD, Hiram R., Pvt., 11th Ohio Inf. (Urbana).
(b)   HUGHEY, John, Cpl., 2d Ohio Cav. (Highland).
(b)   HUTCHINSON, Rufus D., Sgt., 7th U.S. Cav. (Butlerville).
(b)   IMMELL, Lorenzo D., Cpl., 2d U.S. Arty. (Ross).
(b)   JAMES, Isaac, Pvt., 110th Ohio Inf. (Montgomery County).
        JARDINE, James, Sgt., 54th Ohio Inf. (Hamilton County) (b. Scotland).
        JOHN, William, Pvt., 37th Ohio Inf. (Chillicothe) (b. Germany).
(b)   JONES, David, Pvt., 54th Ohio Inf. (Fayette County).
        *KEFURT, Gus, S/Sgt., 3d Inf. Div. (Youngstown) (b. Pa.).
(b)   KELLEY, George V., Capt., 104th Ohio Inf. (Massillon).
(b)   *KESSLER, Patrick L., Pfc., 3d Inf. Div. (Middletown).
        KIMBALL, Joseph, Pvt., 2d W. Va. Cav. (Ironton) (b. N.H.).
(b)   KIRK, Jonathan C., Capt., 20th Ind. Inf. (Wilmington).
(b)   KNIGHT, William J., Pvt., 21st Ohio Inf. (Farmers Center) (Defiance County).
(b)   KOUNTZ, John S., Mus., 37th Ohio Inf. (Maumee).
(b)   KYLE, John, Cpl., 5th U.S. Cav. (Cincinnati).
(b)   *LaPOINTE, Joseph Guy, Jr., Spec. 4, 101st Airb. Div. (Englewood) (Dayton).
(b)   LARIMER, Smith, Cpl., 2d Ohio Cav. (Columbus).
        *LOGAN, John A., Maj., 33d Inf., U.S. Vol. (Youngstown) (b. Ill.).
(b)   LONGSHORE, William H., Pvt., 30th Ohio Inf. (Muskingum County).
(b)   LOYD, George, Pvt., 122d Ohio Inf. (Muskingum County).
        MASON, Elihu H., Sgt., 21st Ohio Inf. (Pemberville) (b. Ind.).
        MAYFIELD, Melvin, Cpl., 6th Inf. Div. (Nashport) (b. W. Va.).
        MAYS, Isaiah, Cpl., 24th U.S. Infantry (Columbus Barracks) (b. Va.).
(b)   McCLEARY, Charles H., 1st Lt., 72d Ohio Inf. (Sandusky County).
(b)   McCLELLAND, James M., Pvt., 30th Ohio Inf. (Harrison County).
(b)   McGONAGLE, Wilson, Pvt., 30th Ohio Inf. (Jefferson County).
        McMILLEN, Francis M., Sgt., 110th Ohio Inf. (Piqua) (b. Ky.).
(b)   MEAHER, Nicholas, Cpl., 1st U.S. Cav. (Perry County).
(b)   *METZGER, William E., Jr., 2d Lt., 8th A.F. (Lima).
(b)   MILLER, Daniel H., Pvt., 3d U.S. Cav. (Fairfield County).
        MILLER, John, Cpl., 8th Ohio Inf. (Freemont) (b. Germany).
(b)   MOREY, Delano, Pvt., 82d Ohio Inf. (Hardin County).
(b)   MORGAN, Lewis, Pvt., 4th Ohio Inf. (Delaware County).
        MURPHY, John P., Pvt., 5th Ohio Inf. (Cincinnati) (b. Ireland).
(b)   MYERS, George S., Pvt., 101st Ohio Inf. (Fairfield).
        NORTH, Jasper N., Pvt., 4th W. Va. Inf. (Ames).
        ORBANSKY, David, Pvt., 58th Ohio Inf. (Columbus) (b. Prussia).
(b)   PARROTT, Jacob, Pvt., 33d Ohio Inf. (Hardin County).
(b)   PATTERSON, John T., Principal Mus., 122d Ohio Inf. (Morgan County).
(b)   PEARSALL, Platt, Cpl., 30th Ohio Inf. (Meigs County).
(b)   *PETRARCA, Frank J., Pfc., 37th Inf. Div. (Cleveland).
(b)   PHILLIPS, Samuel D., Pvt., 2d U.S. Cav. (Butler County).
        PHISTERER, Frederick, 1st Lt., 18th U.S. Inf. (Medina County) (b. Germany).
(b)   PINN, Robert, 1st Sgt., 5th U.S. Colored Troops (Massillon).
(b)   PITTINGER, William, Sgt., 2d Ohio Inf. (Jefferson County).
(b)   POPPE, John A., Sgt., 5th U.S. Cav. (Cincinnati).
(b)   PORTER, John R., Pvt., 21st Ohio Inf. (Findley).
        POWELL, William H., Maj., 2d W. Va. Cav. (Ironton) (b. England).
(b)   PRATT, James, Blacksmith, 4th U.S. Cav. (Bellefontaine).
(b)   PRENTICE, Joseph R., Pvt., 19th U.S. Inf. (Lancaster).
(b)   RAMSBOTTOM, Alfred, 1st Sgt., 97th Ohio Inf. (Delaware County).
        REDDICK, William H., Cpl., 33d Ohio Inf. (b. Ala.).
(b)   RENNINGER, Louis, Cpl., 37th Ohio Inf. (Liverpool).
(b)   RICHARDSON, William R., Pvt., 2d Ohio Cav. (Washington).
(b)   RICHEY, William E., Cpl., 15th Ohio Inf. (Athens County).
(b)   RICHMAN, Samuel, Pvt., 8th U.S. Cav. (Cleveland).
        RICHMOND, James, Pvt., 8th Ohio Inf. (Toledo) (b. Maine).
(b)   RICKENBACKER, Edward V., 1st Lt., 94th Aero Sq., Air Serv. (Columbus).
(b)   RICKSECKER, John H., Pvt., 104th Ohio Inf. (Springfield).
(b)   ROBERTS, Gordon R., Sgt. 101st Airborne Div. (Cincinnati).
(b)   *ROBERTSON, Samuel, Pvt., 33d Ohio Inf. (Barnesville).

(b) ROBINSON, Elbridge, Pvt., 122d Ohio Inf. (Morgan County).
ROCK, Frederick, Pvt., 37th Ohio Inf. (Cleveland) (b. Germany).
(b) *ROSS, Marion A., Sgt. Maj., 2d Ohio Inf. (Champagne County).
(b) ROSSER, Ronald E., Cpl., 2d Inf. Div. (Crooksville).
ROUNDS, Lewis A., Pvt., 8th Ohio Inf. (Huron County) (b. N.Y.).
(b) ROWALT, John F., Pvt., 8th U.S. Cav. (Belleville).
(b) SCHMIDT, William, Pvt., 37th Ohio Inf. (Maumee).
SCHNELL, Christian, Cpl., 37th Ohio Inf. (Wapakoneta) (b. Va.).
(b) *SCOTT, John M., Sgt., 21st Ohio Inf. (Finley).
(b) SEAMAN, Elisha B., Pvt., 66th Ohio Inf. (Logan County).
SEARS, Cyrus, 1st Lt., Ohio Light Arty. (Bucyrus) (b. N.Y.).
(b) SHARPLESS, Edward C., Cpl., 6th U.S. Cav. (Marion County).
SHIELDS, Bernard, Pvt., 2d W. Va. Cav. (Ironton) (b. Ireland).
(b) *SLAVENS, Samuel, Pvt., 33d Ohio Inf. (Wakefield).
(b) SMITH, Otis W., Pvt., 95th Ohio Inf. (Logan County).
SPRAGUE, John W., Col., 63d Ohio Inf. (Sandusky) (b. N.Y.).
(b) STANLEY, David S., Maj. Gen., U.S. Vol. (Congress).
STEELE, John W., Maj. and Aide-de-Camp, U.S. Vol. (b. Vermont).
(b) STICKELS, Joseph, Sgt., 83d Ohio Inf. (Bethany).
(b) STOKES, Alonzo, 1st Sgt., 6th U.S. Cav. (Logan County).
(b) STURGEON, James K., Pvt., 46th Ohio Inf. (Perry County).
(b) SURLES, William H., Pvt., 2d Ohio Inf. (Steubenville).
(b) SWAYNE, Wager, Lt. Col., 43d Ohio Inf. (Columbus).
(b) THOMPSON, Freeman C., Cpl., 116th Ohio Inf. (Monroe County).
(b) THOMPSON, Thomas, Sgt., 66th Ohio Inf. (Champagne County).
(b) *TOWLE, John R., Pvt., 82d Airborne Div. (Cleveland).
(b) TREAT, Howell B., Sgt., 52d Ohio Inf. (Painsville).
TYRRELL, George William, Cpl., 5th Ohio Inf. (Hamilton County) (b. Ireland).
(b) VANCE, Wilson, Pvt., 21st Ohio Inf. (Hancock County).
(b) WAGEMAN, John H., Pvt., 60th Ohio Inf. (Amelia).
(b) WALKER, James C., Pvt., 31st Ohio Inf. (Springfield).
(b) WARD, Nelson W., Pvt., 11th Pa. Cav. (Columbiana County).
WELSH, Edward, Pvt., 54th Ohio Inf. (Cincinnati) (b. Ireland).
WENDE, Bruno, Pvt., 17th U.S. Inf. (Canton) (b. Germany).
(b) WILEY, James, Sgt., 59th N.Y. Inf.
(b) WILHELM, George, Capt., 56th Ohio Inf. (Lancaster).
(b) WILLIAMS, William H., Pvt., 82d Ohio Inf. (Miami County).
(b) WILSON, John A., Pvt., 21st Ohio Inf. (Wood County).
(b) WILSON, Milden H., Sgt., 7th U.S. Inf. (Newark).
*WINDER, David F., Pfc., 11th Inf. Brigade (Mansfield) (b. Pa.).
(b) WOLLAM, John, Pvt., 33d Ohio Inf. (Jackson).
WOOD, Mark, Pvt., 21st Ohio Inf. (Portage) (b. England).
(b) *WOODFORD, Howard E., S/Sgt., 33d Inf. Div. (Barberton).
YEAGER, Jacob F., Pvt., 101st Ohio Inf. (Tiffin) (b. Pa.).
(b) *YOUNG, Rodger W., Pvt., 37th Inf. Div. (Clyde).

(b) BARTON, Thomas C., Seaman, USN (Cleveland).
*BAUGH, William B., Pfc., 1st Marine Div. USMC, (Harrison) (b. Ky.).
(b) BEASLEY, Harry C., Seaman, USN.
(b) *BERRY, Charles Joseph, Cpl., USMC (Lorain).
BUTTS, George, GM., USN (b. N.Y.).
(b) *DICKEY, Douglas E., Pfc., 3d Marine Div. (Greenville).
(b) DORMAN, John, Seaman, USN (Cincinnati).
(b) *EPPERSON, Harold Glenn, Pfc., USMCR (Avon).
*ESTOCIN, Michael J., Captain, USN (Akron) (b. Pa.).
(b) *FOSTER, William Adelbert, Pfc., USMCR (Cleveland).
(b) GARY, Donald Arthur, Lt. (jg.), USN (Findlay).
HALEY, James, Captain of Forecastle, USN (b. Ireland).
(b) HANFORD, Burke, M1c., USN (Toledo).
(b) HARNER, Joseph Gabriel, BM2c., USN (Louisville).

NAVY-MARINE CORPS

    JARDINE, Alexander, F1c., USN (b. Scotland).
(b) *KIDD, Isaac Campbell, Rear Adm., USN (Cleveland).
(b) *MARTIN, Harry Linn, 1st Lt., USMCR (Bucyrus).
    *MASON, Leonard Foster, Pfc., USMC (b. Ky.).
(b) McGUNIGAL, Patrick, SF1c., USN (Hubbard).
(b) McHUGH, Martin, Seaman, USN (Cincinnati).
(b) *NEWLIN, Melvin Earl, Pfc., 1st Mar. Div. (Wellsville).
(b) OSTERMANN, Edward Albert, 1st Lt., USMC (Columbus).
    *PAUL, Joe C., L/Cpl., 3d Marine Div. (Dayton) (b. Ky.).
    READ, Charles A., Cox., USN (b. Sweden).
(b) REID, George Croghan, Maj., USMC (Lorain).
(b) *SCOTT, Robert R., MM1c. USN (Massillon).
(b) SHEPARD, Louis C., Ordinary Seaman, USN.
(b) *STEIN, Tony, Cpl., USMCR (Dayton).
(b) STUPKA, Laddie, F1c., USN (Cleveland).
(b) *WARD, James R., Seaman 1c, USN (Springfield).
    WILLIAMS, Jay, Cox., USN (b. Ind.).
(b) WOOD, Robert B., Cox., USN (New Garden).

OKLAHOMA

ARMY-AIR FORCE

(b) *BURRIS, Tony K., Sfc., 2d Inf. Div. (Blanchard).
(b) CHILDERS, Ernest, 2d Lt., 45th Inf. Div. (Tulsa).
(b) CREWS, John R., S/Sgt., 63d Inf. Div. (Golden).
    EPPS, Joseph L., Pvt., 33d Inf. (Oloagah) (b. Mo.).
(b) *GOTT, Donald J., 1st Lt., 8th A.F. (Arnett) (Okarche).
    HAYS, George Price, 1st Lt., 3d Div. (b. China).
(b) *HENRY, Frederick F., 1st Lt., 2d Inf. Div. (Clinton).
(b) *KINER, Harold G., Pvt., 30th Inf. Div. (Enid).
    *McGILL, Troy A., Sgt., 1st Cav. Div. (Ada) (b. Tenn.).
(b) MONTGOMERY, Jack C., 1st Lt., 45th Inf. Div. (Sallisaw).
(b) *REESE, John N., Jr., Pfc., 37th Inf. Div. (Pryor).
    SAMPLER, Samuel M., Cpl., 36th Div. (Altus) (b. Tex.).
    TREADWELL, Jack L., Capt., 45th Inf. Div. (Snyder) (b. Ala.).
    TURNER, Harold L., Cpl., 36th Div. (Seminole) (b. Mo.).

NAVY-MARINE CORPS

(b) *EVANS, Ernest Edwin, Comdr., USN (Pawnee).
(b) McCOOL, Richard Miles, Jr., Lt., USN:
    *SCHWAB, Albert Earnest, Pfc., USMCR (Tulsa) (b. D.C.).
(b) SMITH, John Lucian, Maj., USMC (Lexington).

OREGON

ARMY-AIR FORCE

    ALLWORTH, Edward C., Capt., 5th Div. (Corvallis) (b. Wash.).
(b) *DAHL, Larry G., Sp4c., 27th Trans. Bat. (Oregon City).
(b) *HOLCOMB, John N., Sgt., 1st Cav. Div. (Corvallis).
(b) *KAUFMAN, Loren R., Sfc., 2d Inf. Div. (The Dalles).
    KILBOURNE, Charles E., 1st Lt., S.C., U.S. Vol. (Portland) (b. Va.).
(b) *KINGSLEY, David R., 2d Lt., A.C. (Portland).
    PHIFE, Lewis, Sgt., 8th U.S. Cav. (Marion) (b. Iowa).
    ROBERTSON, Marcus W., Pvt., 2d Oregon Vol. Inf. (Hood River) (b. Wis.).
(b) *STRYKER, Stuart S., Pfc., 17th Airborne Div. (Portland).
    *YABES, Maximo, 1st Sgt., 25th Inf. Div. (Eugene) (b. Calif).

NAVY-MARINE CORPS

    JACKSON, Arthur J., Pfc., USMC (b. Ohio).

*MARTINI, Gary W., Pfc., 1st Mar. Div. (Portland) (b. Va.).

PENNSYLVANIA

ARMY-AIR FORCE

(b) AMMERMAN, Robert W., Pvt., 148th Pa. Inf. (Center County).
    ANDERSON, Everett W., Sgt., 15th Pa. Cav. (Philadelphia) (b. La.).
(b) ANDERSON, Thomas, Cpl., 1st W. Va. Cav. (Washington County).
(b) APPLE, Andrew O., Cpl., 12th W. Va. Inf.
(b) ARNOLD, Abraham K., Capt., 5th U.S. Cav. (Bedford).
(b) BAIRD, Absalom, Brig. Gen., U.S. Vol. (Washington).
(b) †BEAUMONT, Eugene B., Maj. and Asst. Adj. Gen., Cav. Corps, Army of the Miss.
    (Luzerne County).
(b) BENNETT, Orren, Pvt., 141st Pa. Inf. (Towanda).
(b) BENYAURD, William H. H., 1st Lt., Engr. (Philadelphia).
(b) BETTS, Charles M., Lt. Col., 15th Pa. Cav. (Philadelphia).
    BEYER, Hillary, 2d Lt., 90th Pa. Inf. (Philadelphia).
(b) BINGHAM, Henry H., Capt., 140th Pa. Inf. (Cannonsburg).
(b) BISHOP, Francis A., Pvt., 57th Pa. Inf. (Bradford County).
(b) BLACKMAR, Wilmon W., Lt., 1st W. Va. Cav. (Bristol).
    BLACKWOOD, William R. D., Surgeon, 48th Pa. Inf. (Philadelphia) (b. Ireland).
(b) BLAIR, James, 1st Sgt., 1st U.S. Cav. (Schuylkill County).
(b) BLICKENSDERFER, Milton, Cpl., 126th Ohio Inf. (Lancaster).
    BLUCHER, Charles, Cpl., 188th Pa. Inf. (b. Germany).
(b) BONEBRAKE, Henry G., Lt., 17th Pa. Cav. (Waynesboro).
    BONNAFFON, Sylvester, Jr., 1st Lt., 99th Pa. Inf. (Philadelphia).
(b) BOON, Hugh P., Capt., 1st W. Va. Cav. (Washington).
    BRANNIGAN, Felix, Pvt., 74th N.Y. Inf. (Allegheny County) (b. Ireland).
(b) BREST, Lewis F., Pvt., 57th Pa. Inf. (Mercer).
    BREWSTER, Andre W., Capt., 9th U.S. Inf. (Philadelphia) (b. N.J.).
    BREYER, Charles, Sgt., 90th Pa. Inf. (Philadelphia).
(b) BROWN, Charles, Sgt., 50th Pa. Inf. (Schuylkill County).
(b) BROWN, Jeremiah Z., Capt., 148th Pa. Inf. (Rimmersburg).
(b) *BROWN, Melvin L., Pfc., 1st Cav. Div. (Mahaffey).
(b) BURNETT, George R., 2d Lt., 9th U.S. Cav. (Spring Mills).
(b) BUZZARD, Ulysses G., Pvt., 17th U.S. Inf. (Armstrong).
(b) CALDWELL, Daniel, Sgt., 13th Pa. Cav. (Marble Hill).
(b) *CAREY, Alvin, S/Sgt., 2d Inf. Div. (Laughlinstown).
(b) CARLISLE, Casper R., Pvt., Ind. Pa. Light Arty. (Allegheny County).
    CARPENTER, Louis H., Capt., 10th U.S. Cav. (Philadelphia) (b. N.J.).
(b) CART, Jacob, Pvt., 7th Pa. Res. Corps (Carlisle).
(b) CASEY, Henry, Pvt., 20th Ohio Inf. (Fayette County).
(b) CHAMBERS, Joseph B., Pvt., 100th Pa. Inf. (East Brook).
(b) CLARK, James G., Pvt., 88th Pa. Inf. (Germantown).
(b) CLARK, Wilfred, Pvt., 2d U.S. Cav. (Philadelphia).
(b) CLAUSEN, Charles H., 1st Lt., 61st Pa. Inf. (Philadelphia)
(b) CLAY, Cecil, Capt., 58th Pa. Inf. (Philadelphia).
(b) CLOPP, John E., Pvt., 71st Pa. Inf. (Philadelphia).
    COLLIS, Charles H. T., Col., 114th Pa. Inf. (Philadelphia) (b. Ireland).
(b) COMFORT, John W., Cpl., 4th U.S. Cav. (Philadelphia).
(b) CONNELL, Trustrim, Cpl., 138th Pa. Inf. (Ft. Kennedy).
(b) CONNER, Richard, Pvt., 6th N.J. Inf. (Philadelphia).
(b) COOKE, Walter H., Capt., 4th Pa. Inf. Militia (Norristown).
(b) CORCORAN, Michael, Cpl., 8th U.S. Cav. (Philadelphia).
(b) CORSON, Joseph K., Asst. Surg., 6th Pa. Res. (35th Penn. Vol.) (Philadelphia).
(b) *CRESCENZ, Michael J., Cpl., 196th Inf. Brig., Amer. Div. (Philadelphia).
(b) CUNNINGHAM, Francis M., 1st Sgt., 1st W. Va. Cav. (Springfield).
(b) DAVIDSIZER, John A., Sgt., 1st Pa. Cav. (Lewiston).
(b) DAVIS, Charles C., Maj., 7th Pa. Cav. (Harrisburg).
    DAY, Charles, Pvt., 210th Pa. Inf. (Lycoming County) (b. N.Y.).
(b) DEARY, George, Sgt., 5th U.S. Cav. (Philadelphia).

(b)   DE LACEY, Patrick, 1st Sgt., 143d Pa. Inf. (Scranton).
        DELANEY, John C., Sgt., 107th Pa. Inf. (Honesdale) (b. Ireland).
        DE LAVIE, Hiram H., Sgt., 11th Pa. Inf. (Allegheny) (b. Ohio).
(b)   DE SWAN, John F., Pvt., 21st U.S. Inf. (Philadelphia).
(b)   DOLBY, David Charles, Sgt., 1st Cav. Div. (Norristown).
(b)   DONALDSON, John, Sgt., 4th Pa. Cav. (Butler County).
        DOUGHERTY, Michael, Pvt., 13th Pa. Cav. (Philadelphia) (b. Ireland).
        EDGERTON, Nathan H., Lt. and Adj., 6th U.S. Colored Troops (Philadelphia).
(b)   ELLIOTT, Alexander, Sgt., 1st Pa. Cav. (North Sewickley).
(b)   ENGLE, James E., Sgt., 97th Pa. Inf. (Chester).
(b)   *ENGLISH, Glenn H., Jr., S/Sgt., 173d Airborne Brigade (Altoona).
        EVANS, Thomas, Pvt., 54th Pa. Inf. (Cambria County) (b. Wales).
(b)   EWING, John C., Pvt., 211th Pa. Inf. (Latrobe).
(b)   FASNACHT, Charles H., Sgt., 99th Pa. Inf. (Lancaster County).
(b)   FASSETT, John B., Capt., 23d Pa. Inf. (Philadelphia).
(b)   FEASTER, Mosheim, Pvt., 7th U.S. Cav. (Schellburg).
(b)   FISHER, Joseph, Cpl., 61st Pa. Inf. (Philadelphia).
(b)   FLANAGHAN, Augustine, Sgt., 55th Pa. Inf. (Chest Springs).
(b)   FOX, William R., Pvt., 95th Pa. Inf. (Philadelphia).
(b)   FRICK, Jacob G., Col., 129th Pa. Inf. (Pottsville).
(b)   FUNK, Leonard A., Jr., 1st Sgt., 82d Airborne Div. (Wilkinsburg).
        FUNK, West, Maj. 121st Pa. Inf. (Philadelphia) (b. Mass.).
(b)   FURMAN, Chester S., Cpl., 6th Pa. Res. (Columbia).
        FURNESS, Frank, Capt., 6th Pa. Cav. (Philadelphia).
(b)   GALLOWAY, George N., Pvt., 95th Pa. Inf. (Philadelphia).
(b)   GALLOWAY, John, Com. Sgt., 8th Pa. Cav. (Philadelphia).
(b)   GEDEON, Louis, Pvt., 19th U.S. Inf. (Pittsburgh).
(b)   GILLIGAN, Edward L., 1st Sgt., 88th Pa. Inf. (Philadelphia).
        GION, Joseph, Pvt., 74th N.Y. Inf. (Allegheny County).
(b)   GOODMAN, William E., 1st Lt., 147th Penn. Inf. (Philadelphia).
(b)   GRAUL, William, Cpl., 188th Pa. Inf. (Reading).
        GRESSER, Ignatz, Cpl., 128th Pa. Inf. (Lehigh County) (b. Germany).
(b)   GUNTHER, Jacob, Cpl., 8th U.S. Cav. (Schuylkill County).
(b)   *HALLMAN, Sherwood H., S/Sgt., 29th Inf. Div. (Spring City).
(b)   HARMON, Amzi D., Cpl., 211th Pa. Inf. (Westmoreland County).
(b)   *HARR, Harry R., Cpl., 31st Inf. Div. (East Freedom).
(b)   HARRIS, George W., Pvt., 148th Pa. Inf. (Bellefonte).
(b)   HARTRANFT, John F., Col., 4th Pa. Militia (Norristown).
        HAWKINS, Thomas, Sgt. Maj., 6th U.S. Colored Troops (Philadelphia) (b. Ohio).
        HENRY, Guy V., Col., 40th Mass. Inf. (Reading) (b. Fort Smith,. Indian Ter.).
(b)   HENRY, John., 1st Sgt., 3d U.S. Cav. (Philadelphia) (True name John H. Shingle,
        see below).
(b)   HERRON, Francis J., Lt. Col., 9th Iowa Inf. (Pittsburgh).
(b)   HERRON, Leander, Cpl., 3d U.S. Inf. (Bucks County).
(b)   HIGBY, Charles, Pvt., 1st Pa. Cav. (New Brighton).
(b)   HILL, Henry, Cpl., 50th Pa. Inf. (Schuylkill County).
(b)   HILL, James M., 1st Sgt., 5th U.S. Cav. (Washington County).
(b)   HIMMELSBACK, Michael, Pvt., 2d U.S. Cav. (Allegheny County).
(b)   HOFFMAN, Thomas W., Capt., 208th Pa. Inf. (Perrysburg).
(b)   HOGAN, Franklin, Cpl., 45th Pa. Inf. (Howard).
(b)   HOOVER, Samuel, Bugler, 1st U.S. Cav. (Dauphin County).
(b)   HORNER, Freeman V., S/Sgt., 30th Inf. Div. (Shamokin).
(b)   HOTTENSTINE, Solomon J., Pvt., 107th Pa. Inf. (Philadelphia).
        HOWARD, Henderson C., Cpl., 11th Pa. Res. (Ind.).
(b)   HUBBARD, Thomas, Pvt., 2d U.S. Cav. (Philadelphia).
(b)   HUFF, James W., Pvt., 1st U.S. Cav. (Washington).
(b)   HUIDEKOPER, Henry S., Lt. Col., 150th Pa. Inf. (Meadville).
(b)   HUNTERSON, John C., Pvt., 3d Pa. Cav. (Philadelphia).
(b)   ILGENFRITZ, Charles H., Sgt., 207th Pa. Inf. (York County).
        JENNINGS, James T., Pvt., 56th Pa. Inf. (Bucks County) (b. England).
(b)   JOHNSON, Joseph E., 1st Lt., 58th Pa. Inf. (Lower Merion).
(b)   JOHNSON, Samuel, Pvt., 9th Pa. Res. (Connellsville).

ARMY-AIR FORCE

(b) KELLY, Alexander, 1st Sgt., 6th U.S. Colored Troops (Indiana County).
(b) KELLY, Charles E., Cpl., 36th Inf. Div. (Pittsburgh).
(b) *KELLY, John D., T/Sgt., 79th Inf. Div. (Cambridge Springs).
(b) KEPHART, James, Pvt., 13th U.S. Inf. (Venango County).
     KERR, Thomas R., Capt., 14th Pa. Cav. (Pittsburgh) (b. Ireland).
(b) KINDIG, John M., Cpl., 63rd Pa. Inf. (East Liberty).
(b) KINSEY, John, Cpl., 45th Pa. Inf. (Lancaster County).
(b) KIRK, John, 1st Sgt., 6th U.S. Cav. (York).
(b) KIRKWOOD, John A., Sgt., 3d U.S. Cav. (Allegheny County).
(b) KITCHEN, George K., Sgt., 6th U.S. Cav. (Lebanon County).
(b) KNAPPENBERGER, Alton W., Pfc., 3d Inf. Div. (Spring Mount).
(b) KRAMER, Theodore L., Pvt., 188th Pa. Inf. (Danville).
(b) LANDIS, James P., Chief Bugler, 1st Pa. Cav.
(b) LAWS, Robert E., S/Sgt., 43d Inf. Div. (Altoona).
(b) LEONARD, William E., Pvt., 85th Pa. Inf. (Jacksonville).
(b) LEWIS, DeWitt Clinton, Capt., 97th Pa. Inf. (West Chester).
(b) LILLEY, John, Pvt., 205th Pa. Inf. (Mifflin County).
(b) *LOBAUGH, Donald R., Pvt., 32d Inf. Div. (Freeport).
(b) LOWER, Cyrus B., Pvt., 13th Pa. Res. (Laurence County).
(b) LUTY, Gatlieb, Cpl., 74th N.Y. Inf. (West Manchester).
(b) LYTLE, Leonidas S., Sgt., 8th U.S. Cav. (Warren County).
(b) MacLAY, William P., Pvt., 43d Inf., U.S. Vol. (Altoona).
(b) MARM, Walter Joseph, Jr., 1st Lt., 1st Cav. Div. (Washington).
(b) MARQUETTE, Charles, Sgt., 93d Pa. Inf. (Lebanon County).
(b) MARTIN, Sylvester H., Lt., 88th Pa. Inf. (Chester County).
     *MATHIES, Archibald, Sgt., 8th A.F. (Pittsburgh) (b. Scotland).
(b) MATTHEWS, John C., Cpl., 61st Pa. Inf. (Westmoreland County).
(b) MATTHEWS, Milton, Pvt., 61st Pa. Inf. (Pittsburgh).
     McADAMS, Peter, Cpl., 98th Pa. Inf. (Philadelphia) (b. Ireland).
     McANALLY, Charles, Lt., 69th Pa. Inf. (Philadelphia) (b. Ireland).
     McKEEVER, Michael, Pvt., 5th Pa. Cav. (Philadelphia) (b. Ireland).
(b) McKOWN, Nathaniel A., Sgt., 58th Pa. Inf. (Philadelphia).
(b) *McVEIGH, John J., Sgt., 2d Inf. Div. (Philadelphia)
(b) MEARS, George W., Sgt., 6th Pa. Res. (Bloomsburgh).
(b) MECHLIN, Henry W. B., Blacksmith, 7th U.S. Cav. (Mt. Pleasant).
(b) MERLI, Gino J., Pfc., 1st Inf. Div. (Peckville)
(b) *MESSERSCHMIDT, Harold O., Sgt., 30th Inf. Div. (Chester).
     *MESTROVITCH, James I., Sgt., 111th Inf., 28th Div. (Pittsburgh) (b. Montenegro).
(b) MILLER, George W., Pvt., 8th U.S. Cav. **(Philadelphia).**
(b) MILLER, William E., Capt., 3d Pa. Cav. (West Hill).
     MINDIL, George W., Capt., 61st Pa. Inf. (Philadelphia) (b. Germany).
(b) *MINICK, John W., S/Sgt., 8th Inf. Div. (Carlisle).
(b) MITCHELL, Alexander H., 1st Lt., 105th Pa. Inf. (Hamilton).
(b) MITCHELL, Theodore, Pvt., 61st Pa. Inf. (Pittsburgh).
     MONAGHAN, Patrick, Cpl., 48th Pa. Inf. (Minersville) (b. Ireland).
(b) MORRIS, William, Sgt., 1st N.Y. Cav. (Philadelphia).
(b) MORRISON, Francis, Pvt., 85th Pa. Inf. (Drakestown).
(b) MOSTOLLER, John W., Pvt., 54th Pa. Inf. (Somerset County).
     MULHOLLAND, St. Clair A., Maj., 116th Pa. Inf. (Philadelphia) (b. Ireland).
     MUNSELL, Harvey M., Sgt., 99th Pa. Inf. (Venango County) (b. N.Y.)
(b) MURPHY, Edward F., Cpl., 5th U.S. Cav. (Wayne County).
(b) OLIVER, Charles, Sgt., 100th Pa. Inf. (Allegheny County).
(b) ORR, Robert L., Maj., 61st Pa. Inf. (Philadelphia).
(b) ORTH, Jacob G., Cpl., 28th Pa. Inf. (Philadelphia).
     PALMER, William J., Col., 15th Pa. Cav. (Philadelphia) (b. Del.).
(b) PAUL, William H., Pvt., 90th Pa. Inf. (Philadelphia).
(b) PAYNE, Irvin C., Cpl., 2d N.Y. Cav. (Wayne County).
(b) PEARSON, Alfred L., Col., 155th Pa. Inf. (Pittsburgh).
(b) PEIRSOL, James K., Sgt., 13th Ohio Cav.
(b) PENNYPACKER, Galusha, Col., 97th Pa. Inf. (Valley Forge).
     PETTY, Philip, Sgt., 136th Pa. Inf. (Tioga County) (b. England).

ARMY-AIR FORCE

PHILLIPS, Josiah, Pvt., 148th Pa. Inf. (Ulysses) (b. N.Y.)
(b) *PINDER, John J., T5g., 1st Inf. Div. (Burgettstown).
(b) PIPES, James M., Capt. 140th Pa. Inf. (Green County).
PITMAN, George J., Sgt., 1st N.Y. Cav. (Philadelphia) (b. N.J.)
(b) *PORT, William D., Pfc., 1st Air Cav. Div. (Petersburg).
(b) PORTER, Horace, Capt., Ord. Dept., U.S. Army (Harrisburg).
(b) PURCELL, Hiram W., Sgt. 104th Pa. Inf. (Bucks County).
PURMAN, James J., Lt., 140th Pa. Inf. (Green County).
(b) QUAY, Matthew S., Col., 134th Pa. Inf. (Beaver County).
QUINN, Alexander M., Sgt., 13th U.S. Inf. (Philadelphia) (b. N.J.)
(b) RANKIN, William, Pvt., 4th U.S. Cav. (Lewiston).
(b) RAUB, Jacob F., Asst. Surg., 210th Pa. Inf. (Weaversville).
(b) REED, George W., Pvt., 11th Pa. Inf. (Johnstown).
(b) *REESE, James W., Pvt., 48th Pa. Inf. (Chester).
REID, Robert, Pvt., 48th Pa. Inf. (Pottsville) (b. Scotland).
(b) REIGLE, Daniel P., Cpl., 87th Pa. Inf. (Adams County).
(b) REISINGER, J. Monroe, Cpl., 150th Pa. Inf. (Meadville).
(b) RESSLER, Norman W., Cpl., 7th U.S. Inf. (Dalmatia).
(b) RHODES, Sylvester D., Sgt., 61st Pa. Inf. (Wilkes-Barre).
ROBINSON, Thomas, Pvt., 81st Pa. Inf. (Tamaqua) (b. Ireland).
(b) RODENBOUGH, Theophilus, Capt., 2d U.S. Cav.
(b) *ROEDER, Robert E., Capt., 88th Inf. Div. (Summit Station).
(b) ROHM, Ferdinand F., Chief Bugler, 16th Pa. Cav. (Juniata County).
(b) ROOSEVELT, George W., 1st Sgt., 26th Pa. Inf. (Chester).
(b) ROUGHT, Stephen, Sgt., 141st Pa. Inf. (Crampton).
(b) ROUSH, J. Levi, Cpl., 6th Pa. Res. (Bedford County).
(b) ROWAND, Archibald, H., Jr., Pvt., 1st W. Va. Cav. (Pittsburgh).
(b) RUTTER, James M., Sgt., 143d Pa. Inf. (Wilkes-Barre).
SACRISTE, Louis J., 1st Lt., 116th Pa. Inf. (Philadelphia) (b. Del.).
(b) SANDS, William, 1st Sgt., 88th Pa. Inf. (Reading).
(b) *SARNOSKI, Joseph R., 2d Lt., A. C. (Simpson).
(b) *SAYERS, Foster J., Pfc., 90th Inf. Div. (Howard).
(b) SCHAFFNER, Dwite H., 1st Lt., 77th Div. (Falls Creek).
SCHEIBNER, Martin E., Pvt., 90th Pa. Inf. (Berks County) (b. Russia).
(b) SCHOONMAKER, James M., Col., 14th Pa. Cav. (Pittsburgh).
(b) SCOTT, John Wallace, Capt., 157th Pa. Inf. (Chester County).
SEITZINGER, James M., Pvt., 116th Pa. Inf. (Worcester) (b. Germany).
(b) SELLERS, Alfred J., Maj., 90th Pa. Inf. (Plumstedville).
SHAMBAUGH, Charles, Cpl., 11th Pa. Res. (Indiana County). (b. Prussia).
SHELLENBERGER, John S., Cpl., 85th Pa. Inf. (Perryopolis).
(b) SHEPHERD, Warren J., Cpl., 17th U.S. Inf. (Westover).
SHIEL, (SHIELDS), John, Cpl., 90th Pa. Inf. (Cressonville).
(b) SHINGLE, John H., 1st Sgt., 3d U.S. Cav. (Philadelphia) (Served as John Henry, see above).
(b) SHOMO, William A., Maj., A.C. (Westmoreland County).
(b) SHOPP, George J., Pvt., 191st Pa. Inf. (Reading).
(b) SILK, Edward A., 1st Lt., 100th Inf. Div. (Johnstown).
(b) *SITMAN, William S., Sfc., 2d Inf. Div. (Bellwood).
(b) SLUSHER, Henry C., Pvt., 22d Pa. Cav. (Washington County).
(b) SMITH, Robert, Pvt., 3d U.S. Inf. (Philadelphia).
(b) SMITH, Thaddeus S., Cpl., 6th Pa. Res. Inf. (Franklin County).
SNEDDEN, James, Musician, 54th Pa. Inf. (Johnstown) (b. Scotland).
(b) SOWERS, Michael, Pvt., 4th Pa. Cav. (Allegheny County).
(b) *SPEICHER, Clifton T., Cpl., 40th Inf. Div. (Gray).
(b) SPENCE, Orizoba, Pvt., 8th U.S. Cav. (Tionesta).
SPILLANE, Timothy, Pvt., 16th Pa. Cav. (Erie) (b. Ireland).
(b) SPRINGER, George, Pvt., 1st U.S. Cav. (York County).
(b) STOREY, John H. R., Sgt., 109th Pa. Inf. (Philadelphia).
(b) STRAUSBAUGH, Bernard A., 1st Sgt., 3d Md. Inf. (Warfordsburg).
(b) STRAYER, William H., Pvt., 3d U.S. Cav. (Maytown).
SWAP, Jacob E., Pvt., 83d Pa. Inf. (Springs) (b. N.Y.)
TAYLOR, Anthony, 1st Lt., 15th Pa. Cav. (Philadelphia (b. N.J.).

ARMY-AIR FORCE

(b) TAYLOR, Forrester L., Capt., 23d N.J. Inf.
(b) TEA, Richard L., Sgt., 6th U.S. Cav. (Philadelphia).
(b) THOMAS, Charles L., Sgt., 11th Ohio Cav. (Philadelphia).
(b) THOMAS, Hampton S., Maj., 1st Pa. Vet. Cav. (Quakertown).
(b) THOMPSON, James B., Sgt., 1st Pa. Rifles (Perrysville).
      THOMPSON, Joseph H., Maj., 28th Div. (Beaver Falls) (b. Ireland).
      THOMPSON, Peter, Pvt., 7th U.S. Cav. **(b. Scotland).**
(b) TOMINAC, John J., 1st Lt., 3d Inf. Div. (Conemaugh).
(b) *TURNER, Day G., Sgt., 80th Inf. Div. (Nescopeck).
(b) TWEEDALE, John, Pvt., 15th Pa. Cav. (Philadelphia).
(b) VANDERSLICE, John M., Pvt., 8th Pa. Cav. (Philadelphia).
      VEALE, Moses, Capt., 109th Pa. Inf. (Philadelphia). (b. N.J.)
      WAINWRIGHT, John, 1st Lt., 97th Pa. Inf. (Westchester) (b. N.Y.)
(b) WALTON, George W., Pvt., 97th Pa. Inf. (Upper Oxford).
      WARD, Charles H., Pvt., 1st U.S. Cav. (Philadelphia) (b. England)
(b) WARFEL, Henry C., Pvt., 1st Pa. Cav. (Huntington).
(b) WEAHER, Andrew J., Pvt., 8th U.S. Cav. (Philadelphia).
(b) *WEICHT, Ellis R., Sgt., 36th Inf. Div. (Bedford).
(b) WHITE, J. Henry, Pvt., 90th Pa. Inf. (Philadelphia).
(b) WILLS, Henry, Pvt., 8th U.S. Cav. (Gracon).
(b) *WILSON, Alfred L., T5g., 26th Inf. Div. (Fairchance).
(b) WILSON, Benjamin, Pvt., 6th U.S. Cav. (Pittsburgh).
(b) WILSON, Charles E., Sgt., 1st N.J. Cav. (Bucks County).
(b) WILSON, Francis A., Cpl., 9th Pa. Inf. (Philadelphia).
(b) †WILSON, William, Sgt., 4th U.S. Cav. (Philadelphia)
(b) WITCOME, Joseph, Pvt., 8th U.S. Cav. (Mechanicsburg).
(b) WOODWARD, Evan M., 1st Lt., 2d Pa. Res. Inf. (Philadelphia).
(b) WRAY, William J., Sgt., 1st Vet. Res. Corps. (Philadelphia).
(b) WRIGHT, Albert D., Capt., 43d U.S. Colored Troops.
(b) YOUNG, Andrew J., Sgt., 1st Pa. Cav. (Carmichaelstown).

NAVY-MARINE CORPS

      ANDERSON, Aaron, Landsman, USN (Philadelphia) (b. N.C.) **?**
      BALDWIN, Charles, Coal Heaver, USN (b. Del.).
(b) BARRETT, Edward, F2c., USN.
      *BENFORD, Edward C., HC3c., USN (b. N.Y.).
(b) BINDER, Richard, Sgt., USMC (Philadelphia).
(b) BISHOP, Charles Francis, QM2c., USN (Pittsburgh).
(b) BOONE, Joel Thompson, Lt. (Medical Corps), USN (St. Clair).
(b) BRAZELL, John, Quartermaster, USN (Philadelphia).
(b) BRUTSCHE, Henry, Landsman, USN (Philadelphia).
(b) BUCHANAN, David M., Apprentice, USN (Philadelphia).
(b) †BUTLER, Smedley, Darlington, Maj., USMC (West Chester).
(b) CAMPBELL, Albert Ralph, Pvt., USMC (Williamsport).
(b) CLIFFORD, Robert T., Master-at-Arms, USN.
(b) CONNOR, William C., BM, USN.
(b) CRAWFORD, Alexander, Fireman, USN.
      CRILLEY, Frank William, CGM, USN (b. N.J.).
(b) CRIPPS, Thomas, Quartermaster, USN (Philadelphia).
(b) CROUSE, William Adolphus, WT, USN (Tannetsburg).
(b) CUTTER, George W., Landsman, USN (Philadelphia).
(b) *DAMATO, Anthony Peter, Cpl., USMC (Shenandoah).
(b) DAVIS, Joseph H., Landsman, USN (Philadelphia).
      DEAKIN, Charles, BM, USN (b. N.Y.).
      DEMPSTER, John, Cox., USN (b. Scotland).
(b) DENIG, J. Henry, Sgt., USMC (York).
(b) *DIAS, Ralph E., Pfc., USMC (Shelocta).
      DOOLEN, William, Coal Heaver, USN (b. Ireland).
      DOUGHERTY, James, Pvt., USMC (b. Ireland).

(b) *DREXLER, Henry Clay, Ens., USN (Braddock).
     DRUSTRUP, Neils, Lt., USN (b. Denmark).
(b) DU MOULIN, Frank, Apprentice, USN (Philadelphia).
(b) DUNCAN, James K. L., Ordinary Seaman, USN (Frankfort).
(b) EDWARDS, Walter Atlee, Lt. Comdr., USN (Philadelphia).
(b) *FISHER, Harry, Pvt., USMC (McKeesport).
(b) FOLEY, Alexander Joseph, Sgt., USMC (Heckersville).
(b) FRANCIS, Charles Robert, Pvt., USMC (Doylestown).
     FRY, Isaac N., Orderly Sgt., USMC.
     GAUGHIN, Philip, Sgt., USMC (b. Ireland).
     GIRANDY, Alphonse, Seaman, USN (b. West Indies).
     GRACE, H. Patrick, CQM, USN (b. Ireland).
(b) GROSS, Samuel, Pvt., USMC (Philadelphia).
(b) HAFFEE, Edmund, Quarter Gunner, USN (Philadelphia).
(b) HAMILTON, Richard, Coal Heaver, USN (Philadelphia).
(b) HAYES, John, Cox., USN (Philadelphia).
(b) *HILL, Edwin Joseph, CB, USN (Philadelphia).
     HORTON, William Charlie, Pvt., USMC (b. Ill.).
(b) HUBER, William Russel, MM, USN (Harrisburg).
(b) IAMS, Ross Lindsey, Sgt., USMC (Graysville).
     JOHNSEN, Hans, Chief Machinist, USN (b. Norway).
(b) JOHNSON, John, Seaman, USN (Philadelphia).
     JOHNSON, Peter, F1c., USN (b. England).
(b) JONES, William, Captain of Top, USN (Philadelphia).
     *KELLY, John D., Pfc., USMC, 1st Marine Div. (Homestead) (b. Ohio).
     KILLACKEY, Joseph, Landsman, USN (b. Ireland).
     LAVERTY, John, Fireman, USN (b. N.Y.).
(b) LAWSON, John, Landsman, USN.
     LEAR, Nicholas, Quartermaster, USN (b. R.I.).
     LEON, Pierre, Captain of Forecastle, USN (b. La.).
(b) LEVERY, William, Apprentice First Class, USN.
     LLOYD, Benjamin, Coal Heaver, USN (b. England).
(b) LOWRY, George Maus, Ens., USN (Eve).
(b) MacNEAL, Harry Lewis, Pvt., USMC (Philadelphia).
     MAHONEY, George, F1c., USN (b. Mass.).
(b) MARM, Walter Joseph, Jr., 1st Lt., 1st Cav. Div. (Washington).
     MARTIN, Edward S., Quartermaster, USN (b. Ireland).
     MARTIN, James, Sgt., USMC (b. Iceland).
(b) MATHIAS, Clarence Edward, Pvt., USMC (Royalton).
     MATTHEWS, Joseph, Captain of Top, USN (b. Malta).
     *MAUSERT, Frederick W., III, Sgt., 1st Marine Div. USMC, (Dresher) (b. N.Y.).
(b) McWILLIAMS, George W., Landsman, USN.
(b) MILLER, Hugh, BM, USN (Philadelphia).
(b) MITCHELL, Joseph, GM1c., USN (Philadelphia).
(b) MOORE, George, Seaman, USN (Philadelphia).
(b) *MORGAN, William D., Cpl., USMC, 3rd Mar. Div. (Pittsburgh).
     O'NEAL, John, BM, USN (b. Ireland).
     ORTEGA, John, Seaman, USN (b. Spain).
(b) PAIGE, Mitchell, Platoon Sgt., USMC (Charleroi).
     PETERS, Alexander, BM1c., USN (b. Russia).
     PETTY, Orlando Henderson, Lt., Medical Corps, USNRF (b. Ohio).
(b) *PROM, William R., L/Cpl., USMC, 3rd Mar. Div. (Pittsburgh).
(b) PURVIS, Hugh, Pvt., USMC (Philadelphia).
     QUICK, John Henry, Sgt., USMC (b. W. Va.).
(b) *RAMER, George H., 2d Lt., 1st Marine Div. USMCR (Lewisburg).
     RANNAHAN, John, Cpl., USMC (b. Ireland).
(b) *REEM, Robert D., 2d Lt., 1st Marine Div. USMC (Elizabethtown).
(b) RUSH, William Rees, Capt., USN (Philadelphia).
(b) SAPP, Isaac, Seaman, Engineers' Force, USN (Philadelphia).
(b) SCHMIDT, Oscar, Jr., OGM, USN (Philadelphia).
(b) SEMPLE, Robert, Chief Gunner, USN (Pittsburgh).
     SINNETT, Lawrence C., Seaman, USN (b. W. Va.).

(b) SNYDER, William E., Chief Electrician, USN (South Bethlehem).
(b) STEWART, James A., Cpl., USMC (Philadelphia).
     SUNDQUIST, Axel, CCM, USN (b. Russia).
     *TAYLOR, Karl Gorman, Sr., S/Sgt., 3rd Mar. Div. USMC (Avella) (b. Md.).
(b) TAYLOR, William G., Captain of Forecastle, USN (Philadelphia).
     THAYER, James, Ship's Corporal, USN (b. Ireland).
     THOMPSON, Henry A., Pvt., USMC (b. England).
     THORNTON, Michael, Seaman, USN (b. Ireland).
(b) TROUT, James M., F2d., USN (Philadelphia).
(b) VANTINE, Joseph E., F1c., USN (Philadelphia).
(b) VAUGHN, Pinkerton R., Sgt., USMC (Downingtown).
     WHITE, Joseph, Cox., USN (b. D.C.).
     WILLIAMS, Henry, CM, USN (b. Canada).
(b) WILLIAMS, John, Seaman, USN.
     WILLIAMS, Peter, Seaman, USN (b. Norway).
     WILLIAMS, William, Landsman, USN (b. Ireland).
     WILLIS, Richard, Cox., USN (b. England).

RHODE ISLAND

ARMY-AIR FORCE

(b) AVERY, William B., Lt., 1st N.Y. Marine Arty., U.S. Army (Providence).
     BABCOCK, William J., Sgt., 2d R.I. Inf. (South Kingston) (b. Conn.).
(b) BARBER, James A., Cpl., 1st R.I. Light Arty. (Westerly).
(b) BLISS, George N., Capt., 1st R.I. Cav. (Tiverton).
(b) BUCKLYN, John K., 1st Lt., 1st R.I. Light Arty. (Foster Creek).
     BURBANK, James H., Sgt., 4th R.I. Inf. (Providence) (b. Holland).
(b) CHILD, Benjamin H., Cpl., 1st R.I. Light Arty. (Providence).
(b) CORCORAN, John, Pvt., 1st R.I. Light Arty. (Pawtucket).
     ENNIS, Charles, D., Pvt., 1st R.I. Light Arty. (Charleston) (b. Conn.).
     HAVRON, John H., Sgt., 1st R.I. Light Arty. (Providence) (b. Ireland).
(b) LAWTON, John S., Sgt., 5th U.S. Cav. (Bristol).
(b) LEWIS, Samuel E., Cpl., 1st R.I. Light Arty. (Coventry).
(b) McDONALD, George E., Pvt., 1st Conn. Hvy. Arty. (Warwick).
     McGAR, Owen, Pvt., 5th U.S. Inf. (Pawtucket) (b. Mass.).
(b) MOLBONE, Archibald, Sgt., 1st R.I. Light Arty. (West Greenwich).
     PARKER, Thomas, Cpl., 2d R.I. Inf. (Providence) (b. England).
(b) *PETERS, George J., Pvt., 17th Airborne Div. (Cranston).
(b) POTTER, George W., Pvt., 1st R.I. Arty. (Coventry).
     TAYLOR, Joseph, Pvt., 7th R.I. Inf. (Burrilville) (b. England).
     WELSH, James, Pvt., 4th R.I. Inf. (Slatersville) (b. Ireland).

NAVY-MARINE CORPS

     BRADLEY, George, Chief Gunner, USN (b. N.Y.).
     *CHAMPAGNE, David B., Cpl., USMC, 1st Marine Div. (Wakefield) (b. Md.).
     EADIE, Thomas, CGM, USN (b. Scotland).
(b) EDWARDS, John, Captain of Top, USN (Providence).
(b) GILLICK, Matthew, BM, USN (Providence).
(b) HAYES, Thomas, Cox., USN.
     MOORE, Philip, Seaman, USN (b. Canada).
(b) READ, George E., Seaman, USN.
(b) WALSH, Michael, Chief Machinist, USN (Newport).

SOUTH CAROLINA

ARMY-AIR FORCE

(b) ANDERSON, Webster, Sfc., 101st Airborne Div. (Winnsboro).
(b) ATKINS, Thomas E., Pfc., 32d Inf. Div. (Campobello).
(b) *BARKER, Charles H., Pfc., 7th Inf. Div. (Pickens).
(b) DOZIER, James C., 1st Lt., 30th Div. (Rock Hill).

ARMY-AIR FORCE

(b)   FOSTER, Gary Evans, Sgt., 30th Div. (Inman).
(b)   *HALL, Thomas Lee, Sgt., 30th Div. (Fort Mill).
(b)   *HERIOT, James D., Cpl., 30th Div. (Providence).
(b)   HILTON, Richmond H., Sgt., 30th Div. (Westville).
(b)   KENNEDY, John T., 2d Lt., 6th U.S. Cav. (Orangeburg).
(b)   *KNIGHT, Noah O., Pfc., 3d Inf. Div. (Jefferson).
(b)   MABRY, George L., Jr., Lt. Col., 4th Inf. Div. (Sumter).
(b)   *McWHORTER, William A., Pfc., 32d Inf. Div. (Liberty).
(b)   *SMITH, Furman L., Pvt., 34th Inf. Div. (Central).
(b)   VILLEPIGUE, John C., Cpl., 30th Div. (Camden).
(b)   WILLIAMS, Charles Q., 1st Lt., 5th Special Forces Group (Charleston).

NAVY-MARINE CORPS

(b)   ELLIOTT, Middleton Stuart, Surg., USN (Beaufort).
       FLOYD, Edward, Boilermaker, USN (b. Ireland).
(b)   *HOWE, James D., L/Cpl., 1st Mar. Div. USMC (Fort Jackson, S.C.).
(b)   KENNEMORE, Robert S., S/Sgt., 1st Mar. Div. USMC (Greenville).
       *McGINTY, John J. III, 2d Lt., 3d Mar. Div. (Laurel Bay) (b. Mass.).
(b)   MOFFETT, William A., Comdr., USN.
(b)   *OWENS, Robert Allen, Sgt., USMC (Greenville).
(b)   SULLIVAN, Daniel Augustus Joseph, Ens., USNRF (Charleston).
(b)   THORNTON, Michael Edwin, Petty Officer, Naval Advisory Group (Greenville).
(b)   TRUESDELL, Donald LeRoy, Cpl., USMC (Lugoff).
(b)   *WATKINS, Lewis G., S/Sgt., 1st Mar. Div. USMC (Seneca).
(b)   WHEELER, George Huber, SF1c. USN.
(b)   WILLIAMS, James E., BMFC, USN (Rock Hill).

SOUTH DAKOTA

ARMY-AIR FORCE

       HILLOCK, Marvin C., Pvt., 7th U.S. Cav. (Lead City) (b. Mich.).
       *OLSON, Arlo L., Capt., 3d Inf. Div. (Toronto) (b. Iowa).
       WILSON, William O., Cpl., 9th U.S. Cav. (b. Md.).

NAVY-MARINE CORPS

(b)   FOSS, Joseph Jacob, Capt., USMCR (Sioux Falls).
       *LITTLETON, HERBERT A., Pfc., 1st Mar. Div. USMCR (Black Hawk) (b. Ark.).

TENNESSEE

ARMY-AIR FORCE

(b)   ADKINSON, Joseph B., Sgt., 30th Div. (Atoka).
(b)   CANTRELL, Charles P., Pvt., 10th U.S. Inf. (Nashville).
(b)   CECIL, Josephus S., 1st Lt., 19th U.S. Inf. (New River).
(b)   COLLINS, Harrison, Cpl., 1st Tenn. Cav. (Hawkins County).
(b)   COOLEY, Raymond H., S/Sgt., 25th Inf. Div. (Richard City).
(b)   COOLIDGE, Charles H., T/Sgt., 36th Inf. Div. (Signal Mountain).
(b)   *DUKE, Ray E., Sfc., 24th Inf. Div. (Whitwell).
(b)   *GARDNER, James A., 1st Lt., 101st Airborne Div. (Memphis).
(b)   GILLESPIE, George L., 1st. Lt., Corps of Engrs., U.S. Army (Chattanooga).
(b)   GRANT, George, Sgt., Co. E, 18th U.S. Inf. (Raleigh).
(b)   GREER, Allen J., 2d Lt., 4th U.S. Inf. (Memphis).
(b)   HUFF, Paul B., Cpl., 82d Airborne Div. (Cleveland).
       JENKINS, Don J., S/Sgt., 9th Inf. Div. (Nashville) (b. Ky.).
(b)   JORDAN, George, Sgt., 9th U.S. Cav. (Williamson County).
(b)   KARNES, James E., Sgt., 30th Div. (Knoxville).
(b)   LAWSON, Gaines, 1st Sgt., 4th East Tenn. Inf. (Hawkins County).
       *LEMERT, Milo, 1st Sgt., 30th Div. (Crossville) (b. Iowa).
(b)   *LYELL, William F., Cpl., 7th Inf. Div. (Old Hickory).

ARMY-AIR FORCE

- (b) McGAHA, Charles L., M/Sgt., 25th Inf. Div. (Cosby).
- (b) McGARITY, Vernon, T/Sgt., 99th Inf. Div. (Model).
- (b) MORRIS, William W., Cpl., 6th U.S. Cav. (Stewart County).
- (b) STRIVSON, Benoni, Pvt., 8th U.S. Cav. (Overton).
- (b) TALLEY, Edward R., Sgt., 30th Div. (Russellville).
- (b) WARD, Calvin John, Pvt., 30th Div. (Morristown).
  WELD, Seth L., Cpl., 8th U.S. Inf. (Altamont) (b. Md.).
- (b) YORK, Alvin C., Cpl., 82d Div. (Pall Mall).

NAVY-MARINE CORPS

- (b) BONNEY, Robert Earl, CWT, USN (Nashville).
- (b) HARRISON, Bolden Reush, Seaman, USN (Savannah).
- (b) *KINSER, Elbert Luther, Sgt., USMCR (Greeneville).
- (b) *RAY, David Robert, HC2dc., 1st Mar. Div. USN, (McMinnville).
- (b) *SINGLETON, Walter K., Sgt., 3rd Marine Div. (Memphis).
- (b) *WILLIS, John Harland, PhM1c., USN (Columbia).

TEXAS

ARMY-AIR FORCE

- (b) ADAMS, Lucian, S/Sgt., 3d Inf. Div. (Port Arthur).
- (b) *BARKELEY, David B., Pvt., 89th Div. (San Antonio).
- (b) BENAVIDEZ, Roy P., M/Sgt., Det. B-56, 5th Sp. Fr. Gp. (DeWitt County, Cuero).
- (b) *CARSWELL, Horace S., Jr., Maj., AC, 308th Bomb. Gp. (San Angelo).
- (b) *COLE, Robert G., Lt. Col., 101st Airborne Div. (San Antonio).
- (b) *DAVIS, George Andrew, Jr., Maj., USAF (Lubbock).
- (b) EDWARDS, Daniel R., Pfc., Co. C, 1st Div. (Bruceville).
  EVERHART, Forrest E., T/Sgt., 90th Inf. Div. (Texas City) (b. Ohio).
- (b) FIELDS, James H., 1st Lt., 4th Armd. Div. (Houston).
- (b) *FOWLER, Thomas W., 2d Lt., 1st Armd. Div. (Wichita Falls).
  GARCIA, Marcario, S/Sgt., 4th Inf. Div. (Sugarland) (b. Mexico).
  *HANSON, Jack G., Pfc., 7th Inf. Div. (Galveston) (b. Miss.).
- (b) *HARRIS, James L., 2d Lt., 756th Tank Bn. (Hillsboro).
- (b) HOWZE, Robert L., 2d Lt., 6th U.S. Cav. (Overton).
  *HUGHES, Lloyd H., 2d Lt., A.C. (San Antonio) (b. La.).
- (b) KEARBY, Neel E., Col., A.C. (Dallas).
- (b) *KEATHLEY, George D., S/Sgt., 85th Inf. Div. (Lamesa).
- (b) *KIMBRO, Truman, T4g., 2d Inf. Div. (Houston).
- (b) *KNIGHT, Jack L., 1st Lt., 124th Cav. Reg. (Weatherford).
- (b) *KNIGHT, Raymond L., 1st Lt., A.C. (Houston).
- (b) *LAW, Robert D., Spec. 4, 1st Inf. Div. (Fort Worth).
  *LEE, Milton A., Pfc., 101st Airborne Div. (San Antonio) (b. La.).
- (b) *LEONARD, T. W., 1st Lt., 893d T.D. Bn. (Dallas).
- (b) LOGAN, James M., Sgt., 36th Inf. Div. (Luling).
- (b) LOPEZ, Jose M., Sgt., 2d Inf. Div. (Brownsville).
- (b) *MARTINEZ, Benito, Cpl., 25th Inf. Div. (Fort Hancock).
- (b) *MATHIS, Jack W., 1st Lt., A.C. (San Angelo).
- (b) McCLEERY, Finnis D., P/Sgt., 6th U.S. Inf. (San Angelo).
- (b) McLENNON, John, Musician, 7th U.S. Inf.
  McNERNEY, David H., 1st Sgt., 4th Inf. Div. (Fort Bliss) (b. Mass.).
- (b) MORGAN, John C., 2d Lt., A.C. (Entered service: London, England).
- (b) MURPHY, Audie L., 1st Lt., 3d Inf. Div. (Hunt County, near Kingston).
  PAINE, Adam, Indian Scouts, U.S. Army (Fort Duncan) (b. Fla.).
  *PENDLETON, Charles F., Cpl., 3d Inf. Div. (Forth Worth) (b. Tenn.).
  *ROBINSON, James E., Jr., 1st Lt., 63d Inf. Div. (Waco) (b. Ohio).
- (b) RODRIGUEZ, Cleto, T/Sgt., 37th Inf. Div. (San Antonio).
- (b) SASSER, Clarence Eugene, Spec. 5, 9th Inf. Div. (Rosharon).
- (b) SHELTON, George M., Pvt., 23d U.S. Inf. (Bellington).
- (b) *STEINDAM, Russell A., 1st Lt., 25th Inf. Div. (Austin).
  STONE, James L., 1st Lt., 1st Cav. Div. (Houston) (b. Ark.).
  *WALLACE, Herman C., Pfc., 76th Inf. Div. (Lubbock) (b. Okla.).
  WARD, John, Sgt., 24th U.S. Inf., Indian Scouts (Fort Duncan) (b. Ark.).

ARMY-AIR FORCE

*WATKINS. Travis E., M/Sgt., 2d Inf. Div. (Overton) (b. Ark.).
(b) **WHITELEY, Eli, 1st Lt., 3d Inf. Div. (Georgetown).**
(b) *YOUNG, Marvin R., S/Sgt., 25th Inf. Div. (Odessa).

NAVY-MARINE CORPS

*ANDERSON, Richard Allen, L/Cpl., 1st Mar. Div. (Edinburg) (b. D.C.).
(b) *BORDELON, William James, S/Sgt., USMC (San Antonio).
BULKELEY, John Duncan, Lt. Comdr., USN (b. N.Y.).
*CREEK, Thomas E., L/Cpl., 3rd Mar. Div. USMC, (Amarillo) (b. Mo.).
(b) *DEALEY, Samuel David, Comdr. USN (Dallas).
(b) *GONZALEZ, Alfredo, Sgt., 1st Mar. Div. USMC, (Edinburg).
*GUILLEN, Ambrosio, S/Sgt., 1st Mar. Div. USMC, (b. Colo.).
(b) HARRELL, William George, Sgt., USMC (Rio Grande City).
(b) HARRISON, William Kelly, Comdr., USN (Waco).
*HAWKINS, William Dean, 1st Lt., USMC (El Paso) (b. Kans.).
(b) HAYDEN, David E., HA1c., USN (Florence).
(b) *HUTCHINS, Johnnie David, Sfc., USNR (Weimer).
*KILMER, John E., Hospital Corpsman, USN (b. Ill.).
(b) *LUMMUS, Jack, 1st Lt., USMCR (Ennie).
(b) *MITCHELL, Frank N., 1st Lt., 1st Marine Div. USMC, (Roaring Springs).
(b) *MORELAND, Whitt L., Pfc., 1st Marine Div. USMCR, (Austin).
(b) O'BRIEN, George H., Jr., 2d Lt., 1st Marine Div. USMCR (Big Spring).
(b) *ROAN, Charles Howard, Pfc., USMCR (Claude).
(b) WHEELER, George H., SF1c., USN (San Antonio).
*WILSON, Alfred M., Pfc., 3rd Mar. Div. USMC, (Abilene) (b. Ill.).

UTAH

ARMY-AIR FORCE

THACKER, Brian Miles, 1st Lt., 92d Arty. (Salt Lake City) (b. Ohio).
*VALDEZ, Jose F., Pfc., 3d Inf. Div. (Pleasant Grove) (b. N. Mex.).

NAVY-MARINE CORPS

(b) *BENNION, Mervyn Sharp, Capt., USN (Vernon).
(b) HALL, William E., Lt. (jg.), USNR (Storrs).
(b) WAHLEN, George Edward, PhM2c., USN (Ogden).

VERMONT

ARMY-AIR FORCE

(b) BATES, Norman F., Sgt., 4th Iowa Cav.
(b) BEATTY, Alexander M., Capt., 3d Vt. Inf. (Ryegate).
(b) BENEDICT, George G., 2d Lt., 12th Vt. Inf. (Burlington).
(b) BUTTERFIELD, Frank G., 1st Lt., 6th Vt. Inf. (Rockingham).
(b) CLARK, John W., 1st Lt. and Regimental Qm., 6th Vt. Inf. (Montpelier).
COFFEY, Robert J., Sgt., 4th Vt. Inf. (Montpelier) (b. Canada).
DAVIS, George E., 1st Lt., 10th Vt. Inf. (Burlington) (b. Mass.).
DOLLOFF, Charles W., Cpl., 1st Vt. Inf. (St. Johnsbury) (b. N.Y.).
(b) DOWNS, Henry W., Sgt., 8th Vt. Inf. (Newfane).
DRURY, James, Sgt., 4th Vt. Inf. (Chester) (b. Ireland).
EVANS, Ira H., Capt., 116th U.S. Colored Troops (Barre) (b. N.H.).
(b) GOULD, Charles G., Capt., 5th Vt. Inf. (Windham).
(b) GRANT, Lewis A., Col., 5th Vt. Inf. (Winhall).
HACK, Lester G., Sgt., 5th Vt. Inf. (Salisbury) (b. N.Y.).
HARRINGTON, Ephraim W., Sgt., 2d Vt. Inf. (Kirby) (b. Maine).
(b) HAWKINS, Gardner C., 1st Lt., 3d Vt. Inf. (Woodstock).
(b) HENRY, William W., Col., 10th Vt. Inf. (Waterbury).
(b) HOLTON, Edward A., 1st Sgt., 6th Vt. Inf. (Williston).
(b) HOWARD, Squire E., 1st Sgt., Vt. Inf. (Townshend).

ARMY-AIR FORCE

INGALLS, Lewis J., Pvt., 8th Vt. Inf. (Belvidere) (b. Mass.).
(b) JEWETT, Erastus W., 1st Lt., 9th Vt. Inf. (St. Albans).
(b) JOHNDRO, Franklin, Pvt., 118th N.Y. Inf. (Highgate Falls).
JOHNSTON, Willie, Mus., 3d Vermont Inf. (St. Johnsbury) (b. N.Y.).
(b) LIVINGSTON, Josiah O., 1st Lt. and Adj., 9th Vt. Inf. (Marshfield).
LONERGAN, John, Capt., 13th Vt. Inf. (Burlington) (b. Ireland).
LYON, Frederick A., Cpl., 1st Vt. Cav. (Burlington) (b. Mass.).
(b) McCORMICK, Michael, Pvt., 5th U.S. Inf. (Rutland).
(b) NICHOLS, Henry C., Capt., 73d U.S. Colored Troops (Brandon).
(b) NOYES, William W., Pvt., 2d Vt. Inf. (Montpelier).
(b) PECK, Cassius, Pvt., 1st U.S. Sharpshooters (Brookfield).
(b) PECK, Theodore S., 1st Lt., 9th Vt. Inf. (Burlington).
PINGREE, Samuel E., Capt., 3d Vt. Inf. (Hartford) (b. N.H.).
RIPLEY, William Y. W., Lt. Col., 1st U.S. Sharpshooters (Rutland).
(b) ROBBINS, Augustus J., 2d Lt., 2d Vt. Inf. (Grafton).
(b) SARGENT, Jackson, Sgt., 5th Vt. Inf. (Stowe).
SCOTT, Alexander, Cpl., 10th Vt. Inf. (Winooski) (b. Canada).
(b) SCOTT, Julian A., Drummer, 3d Vt. Inf. (Johnson).
(b) SEAVER, Thomas O., Col., 3d Vt. Inf. (Pomfret).
(b) SPERRY, William J., Maj., 6th Vt. Inf.
SWEENEY, James, Pvt., 1st Vt. Cav. (Essex) (b. England).
(b) THOMAS, Stephen, Col., 8th Vt. Inf. (Montpelier).
TRACY, Amasa A., Lt. Col., 2d Vt. Inf. (Middlebury) (b. Maine).
VEAZEY, Wheelock G., Col., 16th Vt. Inf. (Springfield) (b. N.H.).
(b) WELLS, William, Maj., 1st Vt. Cav. (Waterbury).
(b) WHEELER, Daniel D., 1st Lt., 4th Vt. Inf. (Cavendish).
WOODBURY, Eri D., Sgt., 1st Vt. Cav. (St. Johnsbury) (b. N.H.).

NAVY-MARINE CORPS

(b) BLAIR, Robert M., BM, USN (Peacham).
BREAULT, Henry, Torpedoman Second Class, USN (b. Conn.).
BRESNAHAN, Patrick Francis, WT., USN (b. Mass.).
(b) EDSON, Merritt Austin, Col., USMC (Rutland).
RAMAGE, Lawson Paterson, Comd., USN (b. Mass.).

VIRGINIA

ARMY-AIR FORCE

(b) ADAMS, James F., Pvt., 1st W. Va. Cav. (Cabell County).
(b) AYERS, James F., Pvt., 6th U.S. Cav. (Collinstown).
(b) BROWN, Benjamin, Sgt., 24th U.S. Inf. (Spotsylvania County).
(b) DERVISHIAN, Ernest H., 2d Lt., 34th Inf. Div. (Richmond).
(b) DOSS, Desmond T., Pfc., 77th Inf. Div. (Lynchburg).
*FAITH, Don C., 7th Inf. Div. (Arlington) (b. Ind.).
(b) *FOLLAND, Michael Fleming, Cpl., 199th Inf. Brig. (Richmond).
(b) *GAMMON, Archer T., S/Sgt., 6th Armd. Div. (Roanoke).
(b) GARDINER, James, Pvt., 36th U.S. Colored Troops (Gloucester).
(b) GILLENWATER, James R., Cpl., 36th Inf., U.S. Vol. (Rye Cove).
(b) GREGORY, Earl D., Sgt., 29th Div. (Chase City).
(b) GRESHAM, John C., 1st Lt., 7th U.S. Cav. (Lancaster Courthouse).
(b) JAMES, Miles, Cpl., 36th U.S. Colored Troops (Norfolk).
(b) JOHNSON, Henry, Sgt., 9th U.S. Cav. (Boynton).
(b) *JONES, William A., III, Col., USAF, 602d Spec. Oper. Sq. (Norfolk).
(b) LEE, Fitz, Pvt., 10th U.S. Cav. (Dinwiddie Co.).
(b) *MILLER, Gary L., 1st Lt., 1st Inf. Div. (Covington).
(b) *MONTEITH, Jimmie W., Jr., 1st Lt., 1st Inf. Div. (Richmond).
(b) MORRIS, Charles B., S/Sgt., 173d Airborne Brig. (Roanoke).
NETT, Robert P., Capt., 77th Inf. Div. (Lynchburg) (b. Conn.).
(b) *PEREGORY, Frank D., T/Sgt., 29th Inf. Div. (Charlottesville).
(b) RATCLIFF, Edward, 1st Sgt., 38th U.S. Colored Troops (James County).
(b) *SARGENT, Ruppert L., 1st Lt., 25th Inf. Div. (Hampton).

ARMY-AIR FORCE

(b) *SHEA, Richard T., Jr., 1st Lt., 7th Inf. Div. (Portsmouth).
(b) SMITH, James (Ovid), Pvt., 2d Ohio Inf. (Fredericksburg).
(b) STEWART, Benjamin F., Pvt., 7th U.S. Inf. (Norfolk).
(b) VEAL, Charles, Pvt., 4th U.S. Colored Troops (Portsmouth).
(b) WHITEHEAD, Patton G., Pvt., 5th U.S. Inf. (Russell County).
(b) *WILKINS, Raymond H., Maj., A.C. (Portsmouth).
(b) WOODALL, Zachariah, Sgt., 6th U.S. Cav. (Alexandria).

NAVY-MARINE CORPS

(b) ATKINS, Daniel SC1c., USN (Brunswick).
     BARROW, David D., Seaman, USN (Norfolk) (b. N.C.).
     BLAKE, Robert, Contraband, USN.
(b) BRIGHT, George Washington, Coal Passer, USN (Norfolk).
     BUCK, James, QM, USN (Norfolk) (b. Md.).
(b) BYRD, Richard Evelyn, Comdr., USN (Winchester).
(b) FOX, Wesley L., Capt., USMC, 3d Mar. Div. (Herndon).
(b) GARVIN, William, Captain of Forecastle, USN.
(b) HICKMAN, John, F2c., USN (Richmond).
(b) *HAMMOND, Francis C., Hospital Corpsman, USN (Alexandria).
(b) JORDAN, Thomas, Quartermaster, USN (Portsmouth).
(b) LANGHORNE, Cary DeVall, Surg., USN (Lynchburg).
(b) LANNON, James Patrick, Lt., USN (Alexandria).
     LEE, Howard V., Maj., 3d Mar. Div. (Dumfries) (b. N.Y.).
     LUCAS, Jacklyn Harold, Pfc. USMCR (Norfolk) (b. N.C).
     MEREDITH, James, Pvt., USMC (b. Nebr.).
(b) MIFFLIN, James, Engineer's Cook, USN (Richmond).
     MONTGOMERY, Robert William, Captain of Afterguard, USN (b. Ireland).
     NEIL, John, Quarter Gunner, USN (b. Newfoundland).
(b) NEVILLE, Wendell Cushing, Lt. Col., USMC (Portsmouth).
(b) O'CONNER, James F., Landsman Engineers' Force, USN (Portsmouth).
(b) PENN, Robert, F1c., USN (City Point).
     ROBERTS, James, Seaman, USN (b. England).
(b) SHACKLETTE, William Sidney, Hospital Steward, USN (Delaplane).
     SMITH, Frank Elmer, Oiler, USN (b. Mass.).
     SMITH, Thomas, Seaman, USN (b. Ireland).
(b) STREET, George Levick, III, Comdr., USN (Richmond).
(b) TAYLOR, Richard H., Quartermaster, USN.
     TORGERSON, Martin T., GM3c., USN (b. Norway).
(b) UPSHUR, William Peterkin, Capt., USMC (Richmond).
(b) VANDEGRIFT, Alexander Archer, Maj. Gen., USMC (Charlottesville).
     VOLZ, Robert, Seaman, USN (b. Calif.).

WASHINGTON

ARMY-AIR FORCE

     *ALBANESE, Lewis, Pfc., 1st Cav. Div. (Seattle) (b. Italy).
(b) BJORKLUND, Arnold L., 1st Lt., 36th Inf. Div. (Seattle).
     BRADY, Patrick Henry, Maj., 44th Med. Brig. (Seattle) (b. S. Dak.).
     BRONSON, Deming, 1st Lt., 91st Div. (Seattle) (b. Wis.).
     DROWLEY, Jesse R., S/Sgt., Americal Inf. Div. (Spokane)(b. Mich.).
     FLEMING, James P., Capt., 20th Spec. Oper. Sq. (Pullman) (b. Mo.).
(b) *GRANDSTAFF, Bruce Alan, Plat. Sgt., 4th Inf. Div. (Spokane).
     HAWK, John D., Sgt., 90th Inf. Div. (Bremerton) (b. Calif.).
(b) KERSTETTER, Dexter J., Pfc., 33d Inf. Div. (Centralia).
(b) KINSMAN, Thomas James, Spec. 4, 9th Inf. Div. (Renton).
     *LEISY, Robert Ronald, 2nd Lt., 1st Cav. Div. (Seattle) (b. Calif.).
     LYON, Edward E., Pvt., 2d Oreg. Vol. Inf. (Amboy) (b. Wis.).
(b) *MANN, Joe E., Pfc., 101st Airborne Div. (Seattle).
     McCARTER, Lloyd G., Pvt., 503d Parachute Inf. Regt. (Tacoma) (b. Idaho).
     *PENDLETON, Jack J., S/Sgt., 30th Inf. Div. (Yakima) (b. N. Dak.).
     SCHAUER, Henry, Pfc., 3d Inf. Div. (Palouse) (b. Okla.).

ARMY-AIR FORCE

STEVENS, Hazard, Capt. and Asst. Adj. Gen., U.S. Vol. (Olympia) (b. R.I.).
(b) WILSON, Benjamin F., 1st Lt., 7th Inf. Div. (Vashon).
(b) WILSON, John M., 1st Lt., U.S. Engrs. (Olympia).

NAVY-MARINE CORPS-COAST GUARD

(b) *ANDERSON, Richard Beatty, Pfc., USMC (Tacoma).
      BOYINGTON, Gregory, Maj., USMCR (b. Idaho).
(b) BUSH, Robert Eugene, HA1c., USNR (Tacoma).
      DAVIS, Raymond E., QM3c., USN (Seattle) (b. Minn.).
      FADDEN, Harry D., Cox., USN (b. Oreg.).
(b) GALER, Robert Edward, Maj., USMC (Seattle).
(b) *KEPPLER, Reinhardt John, BM1c., USN (Ralston).
      *MONEGAN, Walter G., Jr., Pfc., 1st Marine Div. USMC (Seattle) (b. Mass.).
      *MUNRO, Douglas Albert, SM1c., USCG (S. Cle Elum) (b. Canada).
(b) *ROOKS, Albert Harold, Capt., USN (Colton).
(b) *SHIELDS, Marvin G., CMTC, Seabee Team 1104 (Port Townsend).
      VAN WINKLE, Archie, S/Sgt., 1st Marine Div. USMCR (Arlington) (b. Alaska).
      WINANS, Roswell, 1st Sgt., USMC (b. Indiana).

WEST VIRGINIA

ARMY-AIR FORCE

APPLE, Andrew O., 12th W. Va. Inf. (New Cumberland) (b. Pa.).
      BARRINGER, William H., Pvt., 4th W. Va. Inf. (Jackson County).
(b) *BELCHER, Ted, Sgt., 25th Inf. Div. (Accoville).
(b) *BENNETT, Thomas W., Cpl., 14th Inf. Div. (Morgantown).
      BOURY, Richard, Sgt., 1st W. Va. Cav. (Wirt Courthouse) (b. Ohio).
(b) BUCKLEY, John C., Sgt., 4th W. Va. Inf. (Fayette County).
      BUMGARNER, William, Sgt., 4th W. Va. Inf. (Mason City).
(b) CRISWELL, Benjamin C., Sgt., 7th U.S. Cav. (Marshall County).
(b) CURTIS, Josiah M., 2d Lt., 12th W. Va. Inf. (Ohio County).
(b) DURHAM, James R., 2d Lt., 12th W. Va. Inf. (Clarksburg).
(b) ECKES, John N., Pvt., 47th Ohio Inf. (Weston).
      GAUJOT, Antoine A., Cpl., 27th Inf., U.S. Vol. (Williamson) (b. Mich.).
      GAUJOT, Julien E., Capt. 1st U.S. Cav. (Williamson) (b. Mich.).
      *HARTSOCK, Robert W., S/Sgt., 25th Inf. Div. (Fairmont) (b. Md.).
(b) *HEDRICK, Clinton M., T/Sgt., 17th Airborne Div. (Riverton).
      INSCHO, Leonidas H., Cpl., 12th Ohio Inf. (Charleston) (b. Ohio).
(b) *KELLEY, Jonah E., S/Sgt., 78th Inf. (Keyser).
      *KYLE, Darwin K., 2d Lt., 3d Inf. Div. (Racine) (b. Ky.).
(b) McCAULSLIN, Joseph, Pvt., 12th W. Va. Inf. (Ohio County).
(b) *McDONALD, Phill G., Pfc., 4th Inf. Div. (Beckley).
      McELHINNY, Samuel O., Pvt., 2d W. Va. Cav. (Point Pleasant) (b. Ohio).
(b) McWHORTER, Walter F., Commissary Sgt., 3d W. Va. Cav. (Harrison County).
(b) MOORE, George G., Pvt., 11th W. Va. Inf. (Tyler County).
      PARSONS, Joel, Pvt., 4th W. Va. Inf. (Mason City).
(b) *POMEROY, Ralph E., Pfc., 7th Inf. Div. (Quinwood).
(b) REEDER, Charles A., Pvt., 12th W. Va. Inf. (Harrison County).
(b) ROGERS, Charles Calvin, Lt. Col., 1st Inf. Div. (Institute).
      SCHORN, Charles, Chief Bugler, 1st W. Va. Cav. (Mason City) (b. Germany).
(b) SHAHAN, Emisire, Cpl., 1st W. Va. Cav. (Preston County).
(b) SHANES, John, Pvt., 14th W. Va. Inf. (Monongalia County).
(b) SHOEMAKER, Levi, Sgt., 1st W. Va. Cav. (Monongalia County).
(b) SUMMERS, James C., Pvt., 4th W. Va. Inf. (Kanawha).
(b) VAN MATRE, Joseph, Pvt., 116th Ohio Inf. (Mason County).
      WHITE, Adam, Cpl., 11th W. Va. Inf. (Parkersburg) (b. Switzerland).
(b) WOODS, Daniel A., Pvt., 1st Va. Cav. (Ohio County).

NAVY-MARINE CORPS

(b) COX, Robert Edward, CGM, USN (St. Albans).

Navy-Marine Corps

(b)   FRAZER, Hugh Carroll, Ens., USN (Martinsburg).
(b)   JONES, Claud Ashton, Comdr., USN (Fire Creek).
     *MARTINI, Gary W., Pfc., 1st Marine Div. (Charleston) (b. Va.).
(b)   NICKERSON, Henry Nehemiah, BM, USN (Edgewood).
     *THOMAS, Herbert Joseph, Sgt., USMCR (b. Ohio).
(b)   WILLIAMS, Hershel Woodrow, Cpl., USMCR (Quiet Dell).

WISCONSIN

Army-Air Force

(b)   ANDERSON, Beauford T., S/Sgt., 96th Inf. Div. (Soldiers Grove).
(b)   ANDERSON, Peter, Pvt., 31st Wis. Inf. (Lafayette County).
(b)   BONG, Richard I., Maj., A.C. (Poplar).
(b)   *BURR, Elmer J., 1st Sgt., 32 Inf. Div. (Menasha).
     CABLE, Joseph A., Pvt., 5th U.S. Inf. (b. Mo.).
(b)   COATES, Jefferson, Sgt., 7th Wis. Inf. (Boscobel).
     CROFT, James E., Pvt., Wis. Light Arty. (Janesville) (b. England).
     DURHAM, John S., Sgt., 1st Wis. Inf. (Malone) (b. N.Y.).
     ELLIS, Horace, Pvt., 7th Wis. Inf. (Chippewa Falls) (b. Pa.).
(b)   *ENDL, Gerald L., S/Sgt., 32d Inf. Div. (Janesville).
     FRITZ, Harold A., Capt., 11th Air Cav. Reg. (Milwaukee) (b. Ill.).
(b)   *GRUENNERT, Kenneth E., Sgt., 32d Inf. Div. (Helenville).
(b)   *HANDRICH, Melvin O., M/Sgt., 25th Inf. Div. (Manawa).
(b)   HILL, Frank E., Sgt., 5th U.S. Cav. (Mayfield).
     HILLIKER, Benjamin F., Mus., 8th Wis. Inf. (Waupaca) (b. N.Y.).
(b)   INGMAN, Einar H., Sgt., 7th Inf. Div. (Tomahawk).
(b)   *JERSTAD, John L., Maj., A.C. (Racine).
     JOHNSON, John, Pvt., 2d Wis. Inf. (Janesville) (b. Norway).
     MacARTHUR, Arthur, Jr., 1st Lt. and Adj., 24th Wis. Inf. (Milwaukee) (b. Mass.).
     MacARTHUR, Douglas, Gen., USA (Ashland) (b. Ark.).
(b)   McGRATH, Hugh J., Capt., 4th U.S. Cav. (Eau Claire).
(b)   *MILLER, Andrew, S/Sgt., 95th Inf. Div. (Two Rivers).
     *MITCHELL, William C., Maj. Gen., A.C. (Milwaukee) (b. Nice, France).
(b)   MOORE, Daniel B., Cpl., 11th Wis. Inf. (Mifflin).
(b)   *MOWER, Charles E., Sgt., 24th Inf. Div. (Chippewa Falls).
(b)   NEWMAN, Beryl R., 1st Lt., 34th Inf. Div. (Baraboo).
(b)   *OLSON, Truman O., Sgt., 3d Inf. Div. (Cambridge).
     O'CONNOR, Albert, Sgt., 7th Wis. Inf. (Columbia County) (b. Canada).
     POND, George F., Pvt., 3d Wis. Cav. (Fairwater) (b. Ill.).
     POND, James B., 1st Lt., 3d Wis. Cav. (Janesville) (b. N.Y.).
(b)   *RED CLOUD, Mitchell, Jr., Cpl., 24th Inf. Div. (Merrillan).
(b)   ROBBINS, Marcus M., Pvt., 6th U.S. Cav. (Elba).
     SICKLES, William H., Sgt., 7th Wis. Inf. (Columbia County) (b. N.Y.).
(b)   *SIJAN, Lance P., Capt., USAF (Milwaukee).
(b)   SLACK, Clayton K., Pvt., 124th M. G. Bn., 33d Div. (Madison).
(b)   STUMPF, Kenneth E., S/Sgt., 25th Inf. Div. (Menasha).
(b)   *SUDUT, Jerome A., 2d Lt., 25th Inf. Div. (Wausau).
     TRUELL, Edwin M., Pvt., 12th Wis. Inf. (Manston) (b. Mass.).
     WALLER, Francis A., Cpl., 6th Wis. Inf. (Desoto) (b. Ohio).
(b)   WETZEL, Gary George, Spec. 4, 173rd Assault Helicopter Comp. (Milwaukee).
(b)   WINDUS, Claron A., Bugler, 6th U.S. Cav. (Janesville).

Navy-Marine Corps

(b)   *AGERHOLM, Harold Christ, Pfc., USMCR (Racine).
     CASTLE, Guy Wilkinson Stuart, Lt., USN.
(b)   *CHRISTIANSON, Stanley R., Pfc., 1st Marine Div. USMC (Mindoro).
(b)   DE SOMER, Abraham, Chief Turret Capt., USN (Milwaukee).
(b)   MODRZEWSKI, Robert J., Maj., 3d Marine Div. (Milwaukee).
(b)   *PETERSON, Oscar Verner, CWT, USN (Prentice).
     *VAN VALKENBURGH, Franklin, Capt., USN (b. Minn.).

NAVY-MARINE CORPS

YOUNG, Cassin, Comdr., USN (b. D.C.).
(b)   YOUNG, Frank Albert, Pvt., USMC (Milwaukee).

WYOMING

ARMY-AIR FORCE

(b)   BAKER, Edward L., Jr., Sgt. Maj., 10th U.S. Cav. (Laramie County).
      *CAREY, Charles F., Jr., T/Sgt., 100th Inf. Div. (Cheyenne) (b. Okla.).
(b)   ROBERTS, Charles D., 2d Lt., 17th U.S. Inf. (Fort Russell).

PUERTO RICO

ARMY-AIR FORCE

(b)   *RUBIO, Euripides, Capt., 1st Inf. Div. RVN (Ponce).

NAVY-MARINE CORPS

(b)   *GARCIA, Fernando L., Pfc., 1st Marine Div. USMC (San Juan).

PART V
FOREIGN BORN MEDAL OF
HONOR RECIPIENTS

AHEAM, Michael, Paymaster's Steward, USN (France).
AHERN, William, WT, USN (Ireland).
ALBANESE, Lewis, Pfc., 1st Cav. Div. (Italy).
ALBER, Frederick, Pvt., 17th Mich. Inf. (Germany).
ALLEN, Edward, BM1c, USN (Holland).
ALLEN, James, Pvt., 16th N.Y. Inf. (Ireland).
ALLEX, Jake, Cpl., 131st Inf. (Serbia, now Yugoslavia).
ANDERSON, Bruce, Pvt., 142d N.Y. Inf. (Mexico).
ANDERSON, James, Pvt., 6th U.S. Cav. (Canada East).
ANDERSON, Johannes S., 1st Sgt., 33d Div. (Finland).
ANDERSON, Robert, QM, USN (Ireland).
ANDERSON, William, Coxs., USN (Sweden).
ARCHINAL, William, Cpl., 30th Ohio Inf. (Germany).
ARTHER, Matthew, Signal QM, USN (Scotland).
ASTEN, Charles, QG, USN (Nova Scotia).
AVERY, James, Seaman, USN (Scotland).
BAKER, John, Musician, 5th U.S. Inf. (Germany).
BALLEN, Frederick, Pvt., 47th Ohio Inf. (Germany).
BARRETT, Richard, 1st Sgt., 1st U.S. Cav. (Ireland).
BARRY, Augustus, Sgt. Maj., 16th U.S. Inf. (Ireland).
BASS, David L., Seaman, USN (Ireland).
BATES, Richard, Seaman, USN (Wales).
BAYBUTT, Philip, Pvt., 2d Mass. Cav. (England).
BAZAAR, Philip, Ordinary Seaman, USN (Chile).
BEAUFORT, Jean J., Cpl., 2d La. Inf. (France).
BEDDOWS, Richard, Pvt., 34th N.Y. Btry. (England).
BEECH, John P., Sgt., 4th N.J. Inf. (England).
BEGLEY, Terrence, Sgt., 7th N.Y. Heavy Arty. (Ireland).
BEHNE, Frederick, FM1c, USN (Germany).
BEHNKE, Heinrich, Seaman 1c, USN (Germany).
BELL, George H., Captain of the Afterguard (England).
BELL, James, Pvt., 7th U.S. Inf. (Ireland).
BELPITT, W. H., Captain of the Afterguard, USN (Australia).
BENSON, James, Seaman, USN (Denmark).
BERGERNDAHL, Frederick, Pvt., 4th U.S. Cav. (Sweden).
BERTRAM, Heinrich, Cpl., 8th U.S. Cav. (Germany).
BEYER, Albert, Coxswain, USN (Germany).
BIEGER, Charles, Pvt., 4th Mo. Cav. (Germany).
BINDER, Richard, Sgt., USMC (Germany).
BJORKMAN, Ernest H., Ordinary Seaman, USN (Sweden).
BLACKWOOD, William R. D., Surg., 48th Pa. Inf. (Ireland).
BLAGHEEN, William, S.C., USN (England).
BLUCHER, Charles, Cpl., 188th Pa. Inf. (Germany).
BOEHLER, Otto, Pvt., 1st Md. Vol. Inf. (Germany).
BOIS, Frank, QM, USN (Canada).
BOQUET, Nicholas, Pvt., 1st Iowa Inf. (Germany).
BOURNE, Thomas, Seaman, USN (England).
BRADLEY, Charles, BM, USN (Ireland).
BRADLEY, Thomas W., Sgt., 124th N.Y. Inf. (England).
BRADY, George F., CGM, USN (Ireland).
BRANAGAN, Edward, Pvt., 4th U.S. Cav. (Ireland).
BRANNIGAN, Felix, Pvt., 74th N.Y. Inf. (Ireland).
BRATLING, Frank, Cpl., 8th U.S. Cav. (Germany).
BRENNAN, Christopher, Seaman, USN (Ireland).
BRINN, Andrew, Seaman, USN (Scotland).
BROGAN, James, Sgt., 6th U.S. Cav. (Ireland).

PART IV.—FOREIGN BORN MEDAL OF HONOR RECIPIENTS—
Continued

BRONNER, August F., Pvt., 1st N.Y. Arty. (Germany).
BROPHY, James, Pvt., 8th U.S. Cav. (Ireland).
BROSNAN, John, Sgt., 164th N.Y. Inf. (Ireland).
BROWN, Edward, Jr., Cpl., 62d N.Y. Inf. (Ireland).
BROWN, James, Sgt., 5th U.S. Cav. (Ireland).
BROWN, John, Captain of Forecastle, USN (Scotland).
BROWN, John, Captain of the Afterguard, USN (Denmark).
BROWN, John H., Captain, 12th Ky. Inf. (Canada).
BROWN, Robert, Captain of Top, USN (Norway).
BUCKLEY, Denis, Pvt., 136th N.Y. Inf. (Canada).
BURBANK, James H., Sgt., 4th R.I. Inf. (Holland).
BURGER, Joseph, Pvt., 2d Minn. Inf. (Austria).
BURK, Michael, Pvt., 125th N.Y. Inf. (Ireland).
BURKARD, Oscar, Pvt., Hosp. Corps, U.S. Army (Germany).
BURKE, Patrick J., Farrier, 8th U.S. Cav. (Ireland).
BURKE, Richard, Pvt., 5th U.S. Inf. (Ireland).
BURKE, Thomas, Pvt., 5th N.Y. Cav. (Ireland).
BURKE, Thomas, Seaman, USN (Ireland).
BURTON, Albert, Seaman USN (England).
BUTLER, Edmond, Capt., 5th U.S. Inf. (Ireland).
BYRNE, Denis, Sgt., 5th U.S. Inf. (Ireland).
BYRNES, James, BM, USN (Ireland).
CAHEY, Thomas, Seaman, USN (Ireland).
CALLEN, Thomas J., Pvt., 7th U.S. Cav. (Ireland).
CALUGAS, Jose, Sgt., 88th F.A., Philippine Scouts (Philippine Islands).
CAMPBELL, Daniel, Pvt., USMC (Canada).
CAMPBELL, William, Pvt., 30th Ohio Inf. (Ireland).
CAREY, Hugh, Sgt., 82d N.Y. Inf. (Ireland).
CAREY, James, Seaman, USN (Ireland).
CARROLL, Thomas, Pvt., 8th U.S. Cav. (Ireland).
CARTER, George, Pvt., 8th U.S. Cav. (Ireland).
CARTER, Joseph E., Blacksmith, USN (England).
CARUANA, Orlando E., Pvt., 51st N.Y. Inf. (Malta).
CASEY, David, Pvt., 25th Mass. Inf. (Ireland).
CASSIDY, Michael, Landsman, USN (Ireland).
CASTLE, Frederick, Brig. Gen., USAAC (Philippines).
CAVANAUGH, Thomas, FM1c, USN (Ireland).
CAVAIANI, Jon R., S/Sgt., U.S. Army Vietnam Tr. Adv. Gp. (England).
CAYER, Ovila, Sgt., 14th U.S. Volunteers (Canada).
CHANDRON, August, Seaman Apprentice 2c, USN (France).
CHAPMAN, John, Pvt., 1st Maine Heavy Arty. (Canada).
CHAPUT, Louis G., Landsman, USN (Canada).
CLAUSEN, Claus Kristian, Coxs., USN (Denmark).
COFFEY, Robert J., Sgt., 4th Vt. Inf. (Canada).
COHN, Abraham, Sgt. Maj., 6th N.H. Inf. (Prussia).
COLBERT, Patrick, Coxs., USN (Ireland).
COLEMAN, John, Pvt., USMC (Ireland).
COLLIS, Charles H.T., Col., 114th Pa. Inf. (Ireland).
CONNOR, John, Cpl., 6th U.S. Cav. (Ireland).
CONNOR, Thomas, Ordinary Seaman, USN (Ireland).
CONNORS, James, Pvt., 43d N.Y. Inf. (Ireland).
COOK, John H., Sgt., 119th Ill. Inf. (England).
COONEY, James, Pvt., USMC (Ireland).
COONEY, Thomas C., Chief Machinist, USN (Canada).
COOPER, John, Coxs., USN (Ireland).
CORAHORGI, Demetri, FM1c, USN (Austria).
CORCORAN, Thomas E., Landsman, USN (Ireland).
COSGROVE, Thomas, Pvt., 40th Mass. Inf. (Ireland).
CRAIG, Robert, 2d Lt., USA (Scotland).
CRAMEN, Thomas, BM, USN (Ireland).
CREED, John, Pvt., 23d Ill. Inf. (Ireland).
CROFT, James E., Pvt., Wis. Light Arty. (England).
CUKELA, Louis, Sgt., USMC (Austria).
CULLEN, Thomas, Cpl., 82d N.Y. Inf. (Ireland).

PART IV.—FOREIGN BORN MEDAL OF HONOR RECIPIENTS— Continued

CURRAN, Richard, Asst. Surg., 33d N.Y. Inf. (Ireland).
DAHLGREN, John Olof, Cpl., USMC (Sweden).
DAILY, Charles, Pvt., 8th U.S. Cav. (Ireland).
DAVIDSON, Andrew, 1st Lt., 30th U.S. Colored Troops (Scotland).
DAVIS, George Fleming, Comdr., USN (Philippine Islands).
DAVIS, John, Ordinary Seaman, USN (Jamaica).
DAVIS, John, GM3c, USN (Germany).
DAVIS, Joseph, Cpl., 104th Ohio Inf. (Wales).
DAVIS, Thomas, Pvt., 2d N.Y. Heavy Arty. (Wales).
DEETLINE, Frederick, Pvt., 7th U.S. Cav. (Germany).
DELANEY, John C., Sgt., 107th Pa. Inf. (Ireland).
DEMPSEY, John, Seaman, USN (Ireland).
DEMPSTER, John, Coxs., USN (Scotland).
DENHAM, Austin, Seaman, USN (England).
DI CESNOLA, Louis P., Col., 4th N.Y. Cav. (Italy).
DICKENS, Charles H., Cpl., 8th U.S. Cav. (Ireland).
DICKIE, David, Sgt., 97th Ill. Inf. (Scotland).
DILBOY, George, Pfc., 103d Infantry (Greece).
DILGER, Hubert, Capt., 1st Ohio Light Arty. (Germany).
DODD, Robert F., Pvt., 27th Mich. Inf. (Canada).
DODDS, Edward E., Sgt., 21st N.Y. Cav. (Canada).
DOHERTY, Thomas M., Cpl., 21st U.S. Inf. (Ireland).
DONAVAN, Cornelius, Sgt., 8th U.S. Cav. (Ireland).
DONELLY, John S., Pvt., 5th U.S. Inf. (Ireland).
DONNELLY, John, Ordinary Seaman, USN (England).
DONOGHUE, Timothy, Pvt., 69th N.Y. Inf. (Ireland).
DOODY, Patrick, Cpl., 164th N.Y. Inf. (Ireland).
DOOLEN, William, Coal Heaver, USN (Ireland).
DORE, George H., Sgt., 126th N.Y. Inf. (England).
DORLEY, August, Pvt., 1st La. Cav. (Germany).
DOUGALL, Allan H., 1st Lt. and Adj., 88th Ind. Inf. (Scotland).
DOUGHERTY, James, Pvt., USMC (Ireland).
DOUGHERTY, Michael, Pvt., 13th Pa. Cav. (Ireland).
DOUGHERTY, Patrick, Landsman, USN (Ireland).
DOW, Henry, BM, USN (Scotland).
DOWLING, James, Cpl., 8th U.S. Cav. (Ireland).
DOWNEY, William, Pvt., 4th Mass. Cav. (Ireland).
DRURY, James, Sgt., 4th Vt. Inf. (Ireland).
DRUSTRUP, Niels, Lt., USN (Denmark).
DUNPHY, Richard D., Coal Heaver, USN (Ireland).
EADIE, Thomas, Chief GM, USN (Scotland).
EDWARDS, David, Pvt., 146th N.Y. Inf. (Wales, England).
EGLIT, John, Seaman, USN (Finland).
ELLIS, William, 1st Sgt., 3d Wis. Cav. (England).
ELMORE, Walter, Landsman, USN (England).
ENDERLIN, Richard, Musician, 73d Ohio Inf. (Germany).
ENGLISH, Edmund, 1st Sgt., 2d N.J. Inf. (Ireland).
ERICKSON, John P., Captain of Forecastle, USN (England).
ERICKSON, Nick, Coxs., USN (Finland).
EVANS, Thomas, Pvt., 54th Pa. Inf. (Wales).
EVANS, William, Pvt., 7th U.S. Inf. (Ireland).
EVERETTS, John, GM1c, USN (Canada).
FALCOTT, Henry, Sgt., 8th U.S. Cav. (France).
FALLON, Thomas T., Pvt., 37th N.Y. Inf. (Ireland).
FARQUHAR, John M., Sgt. Maj., 89th Ill. Inf. (Scotland).
FARREN, Daniel, Pvt., 8th U.S. Cav. (Ireland).
FASSEUR, Isaac L., Ordinary Seaman, USN (Holland).
FEGAN, James, Sgt., 3d U.S. Inf. (Ireland).
FESQ, Frank, Pvt., 40th N.J. Inf. (Germany).
FICHTER, Hermann, Pvt., 3d U.S. Cav. (Germany).
FISHER, Frederick Thomas, GM1c, USN (England).
FITZ, Joseph, Ordinary Seaman, USN (Austria).
FITZGERALD, John, Pvt., USMC (Ireland).
FITZPATRICK, Thomas, Coxs., USN (Canada).

PART IV.—FOREIGN BORN MEDAL OF HONOR RECIPIENTS—
Continued

FLANNAGAN, John, BM, USN (Ireland).
FLOOD, Thomas, Boy, USN (Ireland).
FLOYD, Edward, BM, USN (Ireland).
FLYNN, Christopher, Cpl., 14th Conn. Inf. (Ireland).
FOLEY, John H., Sgt., 3d U.S. Cav. (Ireland).
FORAN, Nicholas, Pvt., 8th U.S. Cav. (Ireland).
FORD, George W., 1st Lt., 88th N.Y. Inf. (Ireland).
FORSTERER, Bruno Albert, Sgt., USMC (Germany).
FOSTER, William, Sgt., 4th U.S. Cav. (England).
FOUT, Frederick W., 2d Lt., Ind. Light Arty. (Germany).
FOX, Henry, Sgt., 106th Ill. Inf. (Germany).
FRANTZ, Joseph, Pvt., 83d Ind. Inf. (France).
FRASER (FRAZIER), William W., Pvt., 97th Ill. Inf. (Scotland).
FREEMAN, Martin, Pilot, USN (Germany).
FREEMEYER, Christopher, Pvt., 5th U.S. Inf. (Germany).
FREY, Franz, Cpl., 37th Ohio Inf. (Switzerland).
FUGER, Frederick, Sgt., 4th U.S. Arty. (Germany).
GARCIA, Marcario, S/Sgt., USA (Mexico).
GARDNER, Charles, Pvt., 8th U.S. Cav. (Germany).
GARDNER, William, Seaman, USN (Ireland).
GARRETT, William, Sgt., 41st Ohio Inf. (England).
GASSON, Richard, Sgt., 47th N.Y. Inf. (Ireland).
GAUGHAN, Philip, Sgt., USMC (Ireland).
GAY, Thomas H., Pvt., 8th U.S. Cav. (Canada).
GEORGIAN, John, Pvt., 8th U.S. Cav. (Germany).
GERBER, Frederick W., Sgt. Maj., U.S. Engr. (Germany).
GESCHWIND, Nicholas, Capt., 116th Ill. Inf. (France).
GIBBONS, Michael, Oiler, USN (Ireland).
GIBSON, Eric G., T/5, USA (Sweden).
GILMORE, John C., Maj., 16th N.Y. Inf. (Canada).
GINLEY, Patrick, Pvt., 1st N.Y. Light Arty. (Ireland).
GIRANDY, Alphonse, Seaman, USN (West Indies).
GLAVINSKI, Albert, Blacksmith, 3d U.S. Cav. (Germany).
GLYNN, Michael, Pvt., 5th U.S. Cav. (Ireland).
GOLDEN, Patrick, Sgt., 8th U.S. Cav. (Ireland).
GRACE, H. Patrick, Chief QM, USN (Ireland).
GRADY, John, Lt., USN (Canada).
GRAHAM, Robert, Landsman, USN (England).
GRAY, John, Pvt., 5th Ohio Inf. (Scotland).
GRBITCH, Rade, Seaman, USN (Austria).
GREBE, M. R. William, Capt., 4th Mo. Cav. (Germany).
GREEN, George, Cpl., 11th Ohio Inf. (England).
GREEN, John, Major, 1st U.S. Cav. (Germany).
GRESSER, Ignatz, Cpl., 128th Pa. Inf. (Germany).
GRIBBEN, James H., Lt., 2d N.Y. Cav. (Ireland).
GRIFFITHS, John, Captain of Forecastle, USN (Wales).
GRUEB, George, Pvt., 158th N.Y. Inf. (Germany).
HACK, John, Pvt., 47th Ohio Inf. (Germany).
HAGERTY, Asel, Pvt., 61st N.Y. Inf. (Canada).
HALEY, James, Captain of Forecastle, USN (Ireland).
HALFORD, William, Coxswain, USN (England).
HALLING, Luovi, BM1c, USN (Sweden).
HAMILTON, Frank, Pvt., 8th U.S. Cav. (Ireland).
HAMILTON, Mathew H., Pvt., 7th U.S. Cav. (Australia).
HAMILTON, Thomas W., QM, USN (Scotland).
HAMMEL, Henry A., Sgt., 1st Mo. Light Arty. (Germany).
HANSEN, Hans A., Seaman, USN (Germany).
HANSON, Robert Murray, 1st Lt., USMCR (India).
HARBOURNE, John H., Pvt., 29th Mass. Inf. (England).
HARDING, Mosher A., Blacksmith, 8th U.S. Cav. (Canada).
HARRINGTON, Daniel, Landsman, USN (Ireland).
HARRIS, John, Captain of Forecastle, USN (Scotland).
HART, John W., Sgt., 6th Pa. Res. (Germany).
HARVEY, Harry, Cpl., 22d N.Y. Cav. (England).

PART IV.—FOREIGN BORN MEDAL OF HONOR RECIPIENTS—
Continued

HAUPT, Paul, Cpl., 8th U.S. Cav. (Prussia).
HAURON, John H., Sgt., 1st R.I. Light Inf. (Ireland).
HAWKINS, Charles, Seaman, USN (Scotland).
HAY, Fred S., Sgt., 5th U.S. Inf. (Scotland).
HAYS, George P., 1st Lt., USA (China).
HEARTERY, Richard, Pvt., 6th U.S. Cav. (Ireland).
HEISCH, Henry William, Pvt., USMC (Germany).
HEISE, Clamor, Pvt., 8th U.S. Cav. (Germany).
HENDRICKSON, Henry, Seaman, USN (Germany).
HIBSON, Joseph C., Pvt., 48th N.Y. Inf. (England).
HIGGINS, Thomas J., Sgt., 99th Ill. Inf. (Canada).
HIGGINS, Thomas P., Pvt., 8th U.S. Cav. (Ireland).
HIGHLAND, Patrick, Cpl., 23d Ill. Inf. (Ireland).
HILL, George, Chief Quarter Gunner, USN (England).
HILL, James, 1st Lt., 21st Iowa Inf. (England).
HINEMANN, Lehmann, Sgt., 1st U.S. Cav. (Germany).
HINNEGAN, William FM2c., USN (Ireland).
HOFFMAN, Henry, Cpl., 2d Ohio Cav. (Germany).
HOGAN, Henry, 1st Sgt., 5th U.S. Inf. (Ireland).
HOLDEN, Henry, Pvt., 7th U.S. Cav. (England).
HOLEHOUSE, James (John), Pvt., 7th Mass. Inf. (England).
HORNE, Samuel B., Capt., 11th Conn. Inf. (Ireland).
HOUGHTON, George L., Pvt., 104th Ill. Inf. (Canada).
HOWARD, James H., Lt. Col., A.C. (China).
HOWARD, Martin, Landsman, USN (Ireland).
HOWARD, Peter, BM, USN (France).
HUDSON, Michael, Sgt., USMC (Ireland).
HULBERT, Henry Lewis, Pvt., USMC (England).
HUNT, Martin, Pvt., USMC (Ireland).
HYDE, Thomas W., Maj., 7th Maine Inf. (Italy).
HYLAND, John, Seaman, USN (Ireland).
IRLAM, Joseph, Seaman, USN (England).
IRVING, Thomas, Coxs., USN (England).
IRWIN, Bernard J., Assist. Surg., U.S. Army (Ireland).
IRWIN, Nicholas, Seaman, USN (Denmark).
IRWIN, Patrick, 1st Sgt., 14th Mich. Inf. (Ireland).
ITRICH, Franz Anton, Chief Carpenter's Mate, USN (Germany).
JACHMAN, Isadore S., S/Sgt., U.S. Army (Germany).
JAMES, John, Cpl., 5th U.S. Inf. (England).
JAMIESON, Walter, 1st Sgt., 139th N.Y. Inf. (France).
JARDINE, Alexander, FM1c, USN (Scotland).
JARDINE, James, Sgt., 54th Ohio Inf. (Scotland).
JENNINGS, James T., Pvt., 56th Pa. Inf. (England).
JENSEN, Gotfred, Pvt., 1st N. Dak. Vol. Inf. (Denmark).
JETTER, Bernhard, Sgt., 7th U.S. Cav. (Germany).
JIMENEZ, Jose Francisco, L/Cpl., USMC (Mexico).
JOHANNESSEN, Johannes J., Chief Watertender, USN (Norway).
JOHANSON, John P., Seaman, USN (Sweden).
JOHANSSON, Johan J., Ordinary Seaman (Sweden).
JOHN, William, Pvt., 37th Ohio Inf. (Germany).
JOHNSEN, Hans, Chief Machinist, USN (Norway).
JOHNSON, Henry, Seaman, USN (Norway).
JOHNSON, John, Pvt., 2d Wis. Inf. (Norway).
JOHNSON, Peter, FM1c, USN (England).
JOHNSON, William, Cooper, USN (West Indies).
JONES, Andrew, Chief BM, USN (Ireland).
JONES, William, 1st Sgt., 73d N.Y. Inf. (Ireland).
JUDGE, Francis W., 1st Sgt., 79th N.Y. Inf. (England).
KAISER, John, Sgt., 2d U.S. Arty. (Germany).
KALTENBACH, Luther, Cpl., 12th Iowa Inf. (Germany).
KANE, John, Cpl., 100th N.Y. Inf. (Ireland).
KAPPESSER, Peter, Pvt., 149th N.Y. Inf. (Germany).
KARPLES, Leopold, Sgt., 57th Mass. Inf. (Hungary).
KAUSS (KAUTZ), August, Cpl., 15th N.Y. Hvy. Arty. (Germany).

**PART IV.—FOREIGN BORN MEDAL OF HONOR RECIPIENTS—
Continued**

KAY, John, Pvt., 8th U.S. Cav. (England).
KEARNEY, Michael, Pvt., USMC (Ireland).
KEATING, Daniel, Cpl., 6th U.S. Cav. (Ireland).
KEELE, Joseph, Sgt. Maj., 182d N.Y. Inf. (Ireland).
KEEN, Joseph S., Sgt., 13th Mich. Inf. (England).
KEENAN, John, Pvt., 8th U.S. Cav. (Ireland).
KEENE, Joseph, Pvt., 26th N.Y. Inf. (England).
KELLEY, Charles, Pvt., 1st U.S. Cav. (Ireland).
KELLEY, John, FM2c., USN (Ireland).
KELLY, Thomas, Pvt., 6th N.Y. Cav. (Ireland).
KELLY, Thomas, Pvt., 5th U.S. Inf. (Ireland).
KELLY, Thomas, Pvt., 21st U.S. Inf. (Ireland).
KENNA, Barnett, QM, USN (England).
KENNEDY, John, Pvt., 2d U.S. Arty. (Ireland).
KENNEDY, Philip, Pvt., 5th U.S. Inf. (Ireland).
KEOUGH, John, Cpl., 67th Pa. Inf. (Ireland).
KERR, Thomas A., Capt., 14th Pa. Cav. (Ireland).
KERRIGAN, Thomas, Sgt., 6th U.S. Cav. (Ireland).
KERSEY, Thomas, Ordinary Seaman, USN (Canada).
KILLACKEY, Joseph, Landsman, USN (Ireland).
KILMARTIN, John, Pvt., 3d U.S. Cav. (Canada).
KING, Hugh, Ordinary Seaman, USN (Ireland).
KING, John, Chief Watertender, USN (Ireland).
KLEIN, Robert, Chief Carpenter's Mate, USN (Germany).
KLINE, Harry, Pvt., 40th N.Y. Inf. (Germany).
KLOTH, Charles H., Pvt., Ill. Light Arty. (Europe).
KNAAK, Albert, Pvt., 8th U.S. Cav. (Switzerland).
KOCAK, Matej, Sgt., USMC (Austria).
KOELPIN, William, Sgt., 5th U.S. Inf. (Prussia).
KOELSCH, John K., Lt. (jg.), USN (England).
KRAMER, Franz, Seaman, USN (Germany).
KRAUSE, Ernest, Coxs., USN (Germany).
KREHER, Wendelin, 1st Sgt., 5th U.S. Inf. (Prussia).
KUCHNEISTER, Hermann William, Pvt., USMC (Germany).
KYLE, Patrick J., Landsman, USN (Ireland).
LABILL, Joseph S., Pvt., 6th Mo. Inf. (France).
LAFFEY, Bartlett, Seaman, USN (Ireland).
LANGBEIN, J. C. Julius, Musician, 9th N.Y. Inf. (Germany).
LARKIN, David, Farrier, 4th U.S. Cav. (Ireland).
LATHAM, John Cridland, Sgt., U.S. Army (England).
LAVERTY, John, FM1c, USN (Ireland).
LAWRENCE, James, Pvt., 8th U.S. Cav. (Scotland).
LEAHY, Cornelius J., Pvt., 36th Inf. U.S., Vol. (Ireland).
LEJEUNE, Emile, Seaman, USN (France).
LEMON, Peter C., Sgt., USMC (Canada).
LENIHAN, James, Pvt., 5th U.S. Cav. (Ireland).
LEONARD, Patrick, Cpl., 23d U.S. Inf. (Ireland).
LEONARD, Patrick, Sgt., 2d U.S. Cav. (Ireland).
LESLIE, Frank, Pvt., 4th N.Y. Cav. (England).
LITTLE, Thomas, Bugler, 8th U.S. Cav. (West Indies).
LLOYD, Benjamin, Coal Heaver, USN (England).
LOGAN, Hugh, Captain of Afterguard, USN (Ireland).
LOMAN, Berger, Pvt., U.S. Army (Norway).
LONERGAN, John, Capt., 13th Vt. Inf. (Ireland).
LORD, William, Musician, 40th Mass. Inf. (England).
LOW, George, Seaman, USN (Canada).
LOYD, George, Sgt., 7th U.S. Cav. (Ireland).
LOZADA, Carlos James, Pfc., U.S. Inf. (Puerto Rico).
LUDGATE, William, Capt., 59th N.Y. Veteran Inf. (England).
LUDWIG, Carl, Pvt., 34th N.Y. Btry. (France).
LUKES, William F., Landsman, USN (Bohemia).
LUTY, Gotlieb, Cpl., 74th N.Y. Inf. (Switzerland).
MacGILLIVARY, Charles A., Sgt., 44th Inf. Div. (Canada).
MACHON, James, Boy, USN (England).

PART IV.—FOREIGN BORN MEDAL OF HONOR RECIPIENTS—
Continued

MACK, Alexander, Captain of Top, USN (Holland).
MADDEN, Michael, Pvt., 42d N.Y. Inf. (Ireland).
MADDEN, William, Coal Heaver, USN (England).
MADDIN, Edward, Ordinary Seaman, USN (Canada).
MAHERS, Herbert, Pvt., 8th U.S. Cav. (Canada).
MAHONEY, Gregory, Pvt., 4th U.S. Cav. (Wales).
MANDY, Harry J., 1st Sgt., 4th N.Y. Cav. (England).
MANGAM, Richard C., Pvt., 148th N.Y. Inf. (Ireland).
MARTIN, Edward S., QM, USN (Ireland).
MARTIN, George, Sgt., 6th U.S. Cav. (Germany).
MARTIN, James, Sgt., USMC (Ireland)
MARTIN, Patrick, Sgt., 5th U.S. Cav. (Ireland).
MARTIN, William, Seaman, USN (Ireland).
MARTIN, William, BM, USN (Prussia).
MATHEWS, William H., 1st Sgt., 2d Md. Vet. Inf. (England).
MATHIES, Archibald, Sgt., USAAC (Scotland).
MATTHEWS, Joseph, Captain of Top, USN (Malta).
MAXWELL, John, FM2c, USN (Ireland).
MAY, John, Sgt., 6th U.S. Cav. (Germany).
McADAMS, Peter, Cpl., 98th Pa. Inf. (Ireland).
McALLISTER, Samuel, Ordinary Seaman, USN (Ireland).
McANALLY, Charles, Lt., 69th Pa. Inf. (Ireland).
McCABE, William, Pvt., 4th U.S. Cav. (Ireland).
McCANN, Bernard, Pvt., 22d U.S. Inf. (Ireland).
McCARREN, Bernard, Pvt., 1st Del. Inf. (Ireland).
McCARTHY, Michael, 1st Sgt., 1st U.S. Cav. (Canada).
McCORMICK, Michael, BM, USN (Ireland).
McDONALD, James, Cpl., 8th U.S. Cav. (Scotland).
McDONALD, James Harper, Chief Metalsmith, USN (Scotland).
McDONALD, John, BM, USN (Scotland).
McENROE, Patrick H., Sgt., 6th N.Y. Cav. (Ireland).
McGANN, Michael A., 1st Sgt., 3d U.S. Cav. (Ireland).
McGOUGH, Owen, Cpl., 5th U.S. Arty. (Ireland).
McGOWAN, John, QM, USN (Ireland).
McGRAW, Thomas, Sgt., 23d Ill. Inf. (Ireland).
McGUIRE, Patrick, Pvt., Ill. Light Arty. (Ireland).
McHALE, Alexander, U., Cpl., 26th Mich. Inf. (Ireland).
McINTOSH, James, Captain of Top, USN (Canada).
McKEE, George, Color Sgt., 89th N.Y. Inf. (Ireland).
McKEEVER, Michael, Pvt., 5th Pa. Cav. (Ireland).
McKENZIE, Alexander, BM, USN (Scotland).
McLEOD, James, Captain of Foretop, USN (Scotland).
McLOUGHLIN, Michael, Sgt., 5th U.S. Inf. (Ireland).
McMAHON, Martin T., Capt., U.S. Vol. (Canada).
McNALLY, James, 1st Sgt., 8th U.S. Cav. (Ireland).
McNAMARA, Michael, Pvt., USMC (Ireland).
McNAMARA, William, 1st Sgt., 4th U.S. Cav. (Ireland).
McPHELAN, Robert, Sgt., 5th U.S. Inf. (Ireland).
McVEANE, John P., Cpl., 49th N.Y. Inf. (Canada).
MEAGHER, Thomas, 1st Sgt., 158th N.Y. Inf. (Scotland).
MERTON, James F., Landsman, USN (England).
MESTROVITCH, James I., Sgt., Company C, 111th Inf. (Montenegro).
MEYER, William, CM, USN (Germany).
MILLER, Andrew, Sgt., USMC (Germany).
MILLER, Harry Herbert, Seaman, USN (Canada).
MILLER, Henry A., Capt., 8th Ill. Inf. (Germany).
MILLER, James, QM, USN (Denmark).
MILLER, John, Cpl., 8th Ohio Inf. (Germany).
MILLER, John, Pvt., 8th N.Y. Cav. (Germany).
MILLER, Willard, Seaman, USN (Canada).
MINDIL, George W., Capt., 61st Pa. Inf. (Germany).
MINUE, Nicholas, Pvt., 1st Armd. Div. (Poland).
MITCHELL, John, 1st Sgt., 5th U.S. Inf. (Ireland).
MITCHELL, John J., Cpl., 8th U.S. Cav. (Ireland).

PART IV.—FOREIGN BORN MEDAL OF HONOR RECIPIENTS— Continued

MOLLOY, Hugh, Ord. Seaman, USN (Ireland).
MONAGHAN, Patrick, Cpl., 48th Pa. Inf. (Ireland).
MONSSEN, Mons, Chief GM, USN (Norway).
MONTAGUE, Daniel, Chief Master-at-Arms, USN (Ireland).
MONTGOMERY, Robert William, Captain of Afterguard, USN (Ireland).
MOORE, Charles, Landsman, USN (Ireland).
MOORE, Charles, Seaman, USN (England).
MOORE, Philip, Seaman, USN (Canada).
MORAN, John, Pvt., 8th U.S. Cav. (Ireland).
MORGAN, George H., 2d Lt., 3d U.S. Cav. (Canada).
MORIARTY, John, Sgt., 8th U.S. Cav. (England).
MORIN, William H., BM2c, USN (England).
MORRIS, James L., 1st Sgt., 8th U.S. Cav. (Ireland).
MORRISON, John G., Coxswain, USN (Ireland).
MORSE, Charles E., Sgt., 62d N.Y. Inf. (France).
MORSE, William, Seaman, USN (Germany).
MORTON, Charles W., BM, USN (Ireland).
MOTT, John, Sgt., 3d U.S. Cav. (Scotland).
MOYLAN, Myles, Capt., 7th U.S. Cav. (Ireland).
MULHOLLAND, St. Clair A., Maj., 116th Pa. Inf. (Ireland).
MULLER, Frederick, Mate, USN (Denmark).
MUNROE, Douglas A., Signalman 1c, USCG (Canada).
MURPHY, Charles J., 1st Lt., 38th N.Y. Inf. (England).
MURPHY, Dennis J. F., Sgt., 14th Wis. Inf. (Ireland).
MURPHY, Edward, Pvt., 1st U.S. Cav. (Ireland).
MURPHY, James T., Pvt., 1st Conn. Arty. (Canada).
MURPHY, Jeremiah, Pvt., 3d U.S. Cav. (Ireland).
MURPHY, John Edward, Coxs., USN (Ireland).
MURPHY, John P., Pvt., 5th Ohio Inf. (Ireland).
MURPHY, Michael C., Lt. Col., 170th N.Y. Inf. (Ireland).
MURPHY, Patrick, BM, USN (Ireland)
MURPHY, Philip, Cpl., 8th U.S. Cav. (Ireland).
MURPHY, Thomas, Cpl., 8th U.S. Cav. (Ireland).
MURPHY, Thomas C., Cpl., 31st Ill. Inf. (Ireland).
MURPHY, Thomas J., 1st Sgt., 146th N.Y. Inf. (Ireland).
MURRAY, Thomas, Sgt., 7th U.S. Cav. (Ireland).
MYERS, Fred, Sgt., 6th U.S. Cav. (Germany).
NEDER, Adam, Pvt., 7th U.S. Cav. (Germany).
NEIL, John, QG, USN (Canada).
NELSON, Lauritz, Sailmaker's Mater, USN (Norway).
NEWMAN, Henry, 1st Sgt., 5th U.S. Cav. (Germany).
NIBBE, John H., QM, USN (Germany).
NIHILL, John, Pvt., 5th U.S. Cav. (Ireland).
NISPEROS, Jose B., Pvt., Philippine Scouts (Philippine Islands).
NOIL, Joseph B., Seaman, USN (Canada).
NOLAN, John J., Sgt., 8th N.H. Inf. (Ireland).
NOLAN, Richard J., Farrier, 7th U.S. Cav. (Ireland).
NOLL, Conrad, Sgt., 20th Mich. Inf. (Germany).
NORDSTROM, Isidor, Chief BM, USN (Sweden).
NORRIS, J. W., Landsman, USN (England).
NUGENT, Christopher, Orderly Sgt., USMC (Ireland).
OAKLEY, William, GM2c, USN (England).
O'BEIRNE, James R., Capt., 37th N.Y. Inf. (Ireland).
O'BRIEN, Peter, Pvt., 1st N.Y. Cav. (Lincoln) (Ireland).
O'CONNELL, Thomas, Coal Heaver, USN (Ireland).
O'CONNOR, Albert, Sgt., 7th Wis. Inf. (Canada).
O'CONNOR, Timothy, Pvt., 1st U.S. Cav. (Ireland).
O'DEA, John, Pvt., 8th Mo. Inf. (Ireland).
O'DONNELL, Menomen, 1st Lt., 11 Mo. Inf. (Ireland).
OHMSEN, August, MA, USN (Germany).
OLSEN, Anton, Ordinary Seaman, USN (Norway).
O'NEAL, John, BM, USN (Ireland).
O'NEILL, Stephen, Cpl., 7th U.S. Inf. (Canada).
ORBANSKY, David, Pvt., 58th Ohio Inf. (Prussia).

PART IV.—FOREIGN BORN MEDAL OF HONOR RECIPIENTS—
Continued

ORR, Moses, Pvt., 1st U.S. Cav. (Ireland).
ORTEGA, John, Seaman, USN (Spain).
OSEPINS, Christian, Seaman, USN (Holland).
OSS, Albert, Pvt., 11th N.J. Inf. (Belgium).
O'SULLIVAN, John, Pvt., 4th U.S. Cav. (Ireland).
PAGE, John U. D., Lt. Col., X Corps Arty. (Philippine Islands).
PARKER, Thomas, Cpl., 2d R.I. Inf. (England).
PARNELL, William R., 1st Lt., 1st U.S. Cav. (Ireland).
PAYNE, Isaac, Trumpeter, Indian Scouts (Mexico).
PELHAM, William, Landsman, USN (Canada).
PENGALLY, Edward, Pvt., 8th U.S. Cav. (England).
PESCH, Joseph, Pvt., 1st Mo. Light Arty. (Germany).
PETERS, Alexander, BM1c, USN (Russia).
PETERSEN, Carl Emil, CMM, USN (Germany).
PETERSON, Alfred, Seaman, USN (Sweden).
PETTY, Philip, Sgt., 136th Pa. Inf. (England).
PHILIPSEN, Wilhelm, O., Blacksmith, 5th U.S. Cav. (Germany).
PHISTERER, Frederick, 1st Lt., 18th U.S. Inf. (Germany).
PHINNEY, William, BM, USN (Norway).
PICKLE, Alonzo H., Sgt., 1st Minn. Inf. (Canada).
PILE, Richard, Ordinary Seaman, USN (West Indies).
PLATT, George C., Pvt., 6th U.S. Cav. (Ireland).
PLATTEN, Frederick, Sgt., 6th U.S. Cav. (Ireland).
PLOWMAN, George H., Sgt. Maj., 3d Md. Inf. (England).
PLUNKETT, Thomas, Sgt., 21st Mass. Inf. (Ireland).
POWELL, William H., Maj., 2d W. Va. Cav. (Wales).
POWERS, Wesley J., Cpl., 147th Ill. Inf. (Canada).
PRANCE, George, Captain of Maintop, USN (France).
PRENDERGAST, Thomas Francis, Cpl., USMC (Ireland).
PRESTON, John, Landsman, USN (Ireland).
PYM, James, Pvt., 7th U.S. Cav. (England).
PYNE, George, Seaman, USN (England).
QUINLAN, James, Maj., 88th N.Y. Inf. (Ireland).
RABEL, Laszlo, S/Sgt., 173 ABN Bgde. (Hungary).
RAERICK, John, Pvt., 8th U.S. Cav. (Germany).
RAFFERTY, Peter, Pvt., 69th N.Y. Inf. (Ireland).
RAGNAR, Theodore, 1st Sgt., 7th U.S. Cav. (Sweden).
RANNAHAN, John, Cpl., USMC (Ireland).
READ, Charles A., Coxs., USN (Sweden).
REED, James C., Pvt., 8th U.S. Cav. (Ireland).
REGAN, Patrick, Ordinary Seaman, USN (Ireland).
REID, Patrick, Chief Watertender, USN (Ireland).
REID, Robert, Pvt., 48th Pa. Inf. (Scotland).
REYNOLDS, George, Pvt., 9th N.Y. Cav. (Ireland).
RICH, Carlos H., 1st Sgt., 4th Vt. Inf. (Canada).
RICE, Charles, Coal Heaver, USN (Russia).
RILEY, Thomas, Pvt., 1st La. Cav. (Ireland).
ROANTREE, James S., Sgt., USMC (Ireland).
ROBERTS, James, Seaman, USN (England).
ROBINSON, Alexander, BM1c, USN (England).
ROBINSON, Charles, BM, USN (Scotland).
ROBINSON, John, Captain of the Hold, USN (Cuba).
ROBINSON, John H., Pvt., 19th Mass. Inf. (Ireland).
ROBINSON, Joseph, 1st Sgt., 3d U.S. Cav. (Ireland).
ROBINSON, Thomas, Captain of Afterguard, USN (Norway).
ROBINSON, Thomas, Pvt., 81st Pa. Inf. (Ireland).
ROCHE, David, 1st Sgt., 5th U.S. Inf. (Ireland).
ROCK, Frederick, Pvt., 37th Ohio Inf. (Germany).
RODENBURG, Henry, Pvt., 5th U.S. Inf. (Germany).
ROGAN, Patrick, Sgt., 7th U.S. Inf. (Ireland).
ROSSBACH, Valentine, Sgt., 34th N.Y. Btry. (Germany).
ROTH, Peter, Pvt., 6th U.S. Cav. (Germany).
ROY, Stanislaus, Sgt., 7th U.S. Cav. (France).
RUBIO, Euripides, Capt., U.S. Inf. (Puerto Rico).

**PART IV.—FOREIGN BORN MEDAL OF HONOR RECIPIENTS—
Continued**

RUSSELL, Henry P., Landsman, USN (Canada).
RYAN, David, Pvt., 5th U.S. Inf. (Ireland).
RYAN, Dennis, 1st Sgt., 6th U.S. Cav. (Ireland).
RYAN, Peter J., Pvt., 11th Ind. Inf. (Ireland).
SANTIAGO-COLON, Hector, Spec. 4, U.S. Cav. (Puerto Rico).
SCANLAN, Patrick, Pvt., 4th Mass. Cav. (Ireland).
SCHEIBNER, Martin E., Pvt., 90th Pa. Inf. (Russia).
SCHILLER, John, Pvt., 158th N.Y. Inf. (Germany).
SCHLACHTER, Philipp, Pvt., 73d N.Y. Inf. (Germany).
SCHMAL, George W., Blacksmith, 24th N.Y. Cav. (Germany).
SCHMAUCH, Andrew, Pvt., 30th Ohio Inf. (Germany).
SCHMIDT, Conrad, 1st Sgt., 2d U.S. Cav. (Germany).
SCHNITZER, John, Wagoner, 4th U.S. Cav. (Germany).
SCHORN, Charles, Chief Bugler, 1st W. VA. Cav. (Germany).
SCHOU, Julius, Cpl., 22d U.S. Inf. (Denmark).
SCHROETER, Charles, Pvt., 8th U.S. Cav. (Germany).
SCHUBERT, Martin, Pvt., 26th N.Y. Inf. (Germany).
SCHUTT, George, Coxs., USN (Ireland).
SCHWAN, Theodore, 1st Lt., 10th U.S. Inf. (Germany).
SCHWENK, Martin, Sgt., 6th U.S. Cav. (Germany).
SCOTT, Alexander, Cpl., 10th Vt. Inf. (Canada).
SEACH, William, Ordinary Seaman, USN (England).
SEITZINGER, James M., Pvt., 116th Pa. Inf. (Germany).
SEWELL, William, J., Col., 5th N.J. Inf. (Ireland).
SHAFFER, William, Pvt., 8th U.S. Cav. (Germany).
SHAMBAUGH, Charles, Cpl., 11th Pa. Res. (Prussia).
SHANAHAN, Patrick, Chief BM, USN (Ireland).
SHAPLAND, John, Pvt., 104th Ill. Inf. (England).
SHARP, Hendrick, Seaman, USN (Spain).
SHIELDS, Bernard, Pvt., 2d W. Va. Cav. (Ireland).
SHILLING, John, 1st Sgt., 3d Del. Inf. (England).
SHIVERS, John, Pvt., USMC (Canada).
SHUBERT, Frank, Sgt. 43d N.Y. Inf. (Germany).
SIMONS, Charles J., Sgt., 9th N.H. Inf. (India).
SIMPSON, Henry, FM1c, USN (England).
SIVEL, Henry, 1st Sgt., 2d Md. Vet. Inf. (England).
SLADEN, Joseph A., Pvt., 33d Mass. Inf. (England).
SLETTELAND, Thomas, Pvt., 1st N. Dak. Inf. (Norway).
SMITH, Henry I., 1st Lt., 7th Iowa Inf. (England).
SMITH, James, Seaman, USN (Sandwich Islands).
SMITH, John, Seaman, USN (Bermuda).
SMITH, Oloff, Coxs., USN (Sweden).
SMITH, Thomas, Seaman, USN (England).
SMITH, Thomas, Seaman USN (Ireland).
SMITH, Thomas J., Pvt., 1st U.S. Cav. (England).
SMITH, Wilhelm, GM1c, USN (Germany).
SMITH, William, QM, USN (Ireland).
SNEDDEN, James, Musician, 54th Pa. Inf. (Scotland).
SPICER, William, GM1c, USN (England).
SPILLANE, Timothy, Pvt., 16th Pa. Cav. (Ireland).
STACEY, Charles, Pvt., 55th Ohio Inf. (England).
STAHEL, Julius, Maj. Gen., U.S. Vol. (Hungary).
STANTON, Thomas, Chief MM, USN (Ireland).
STAUFFER, Rudolph, 1st Sgt., 5th U.S. Cav. (Switzerland).
STEINER, Christian, Saddler, 8th U.S. Cav. (Germany).
STEWART, George E., 2d Lt., 19th U.S. Inf. (New South Wales).
STEWART, Joseph, Pvt., 1st Md. Inf. (Ireland).
STEWART, Peter, Gunnery Sgt., USMC (Scotland).
STICKOFFER, Julius H., Saddler, 8th U.S. Cav. (Switzerland).
STOCKMAN, George H., 1st Lt., 6th Mo. Inf. (Germany).
STOKES, George, Pvt., 122d Ill. Inf. (England).
STOLTENBERG, Andrew V., GM2c, USN (Norway).
STRAUB, Paul F., Surgeon, 36th Inf. (Germany).
STREILE, Christian, Pvt., 1st N.J. Cav. (Germany).

PART IV.—FOREIGN BORN MEDAL OF HONOR RECIPIENTS—
Continued

SULLIVAN, Edward, Pvt., USMC (Ireland).
SULLIVAN, Thomas, Pvt., 7th U.S. Cav. (Ireland).
SULLIVAN, Timothy, Coxs., USN (Ireland).
SUMMERS, Robert, Chief QM, USN (Prussia).
SUMNER, James, Pvt., 1st U.S. Cav. (England).
SUNDQUIST, Axel, Chief CM, USN (Russia).
SUNDQUIST, Gustav A., Ordinary Seaman, USN (Sweden).
SWANSON, John, Seaman, USN (Sweden).
SWEENEY, James, Pvt., 1st Vt. Cav. (England).
SWEENEY, Robert, Ordinary Seaman, USN (Canada).
SWEGHEIMER, Jacob, Pvt., 54th Ohio Inf. (Germany).
TALLENTINE, James, QG, USN (England).
TAYLOR, Joseph, Pvt., 7th R.I. Inf. (England).
TEYTAND, August P., QM3c, USN (West Indies).
THACKRAH, Benjamin, Pvt., 115th N.Y. Inf. (Scotland).
THAYER, James, Ship's Cpl., USN (Ireland)
THIELBERG, Henry, Seaman, USN (Germany).
THOMASS, Karl, Cox., USN (Germany).
THOMPSON, Henry A., Pvt., USMC (England).
THOMPSON, J. (James) Harry, Surg., U.S. Vol. (England).
THOMPSON, John, Cpl., 1st Md. Inf. (Denmark).
THOMPSON, John, Sgt., 1st U.S. Cav. (Scotland).
THOMPSON, Joseph H., Maj., U.S. Army (Ireland).
THOMPSON, Peter, Pvt., 7th U.S. Cav. (Scotland).
THORDSEN, William George, Coxs., USN (Germany).
THORNTON, Michael, Seaman, USN (Ireland).
TOBIN, John M., 1st Lt. and Adj., 9th Mass. Inf. (Ireland).
TOBIN, Paul, Landsman, USN (France).
TOMICH, Peter, Chief Watertender, USN (Austria).
TOOMER, William, Sgt., 127th Ill. Inf. (Ireland).
TORGERSON, Martin T., GM3c, USN (Norway).
TORGLER, Ernst, Sgt., 37th Ohio Inf. (Germany).
TRACY, John, Pvt., 8th U.S. Cav. (Ireland).
TRAUTMAN, Jacob, 1st Sgt., 7th U.S. Cav. (Germany).
TRINIDAD, Telesforo, FM2c, USN (Philippine Islands).
TURVELIN, Alexander, Seaman, USN (Russia).
TYRRELL, George William, Cpl., 5th Ohio Inf. (Ireland).
UHRL, George, Sgt., 5th U.S. Arty. (Germany).
URELL, M. Emmet, Pvt., 82d N.Y. Inf. (Ireland).
VADAS, Albert, Seaman, USN (Austria-Hungary).
VALE, John, Pvt., 2d Minn. Inf. (England).
VALENTE, Michael, Pvt., U.S. Army (Italy).
VAN IERSEL, Ludovicus M.M., Sgt., U.S. Army (Holland).
VEUVE, Ernest, Farrier, 4th U.S. Cav. (Switzerland).
VIFQUAIN, Victor, Lt. Col., 97th Ill. Inf. (Belgium).
VOIT, Otto, Saddler, 7th U.S. Cav. (Germany).
VON MEDEM, Rudolph, Sgt., 5th U.S. Cav. (Germany).
VON SCHLICK, Robert H., Pvt., 9th U.S. Inf. (Germany).
VON VEGESACK, Ernest, Major aide-de-camp, U.S. Vol. (Sweden).
WAALER, Reidar, Sgt., U.S. Army (Norway).
WAGG, Maurice, Cox., USN (England).
WALKER, Edward Alexander, Sgt., USMC (Scotland).
WALKER, John, Pvt., 8th U.S. Cav. (France).
WALLACE, William, Sgt., 5th U.S. Inf. (Ireland).
WALSH, John, Cpl., 5th N.Y. Cav. (Ireland).
WAMBSGAN, Martin, Pvt., 90th N.Y. Inf. (Germany).
WARD, Charles H., Pvt., 1st U.S. Cav. (England).
WARREN, David, Coxs., USN (Scotland).
WEINERT, Paul H., Cpl., 1st U.S. Arty. (Germany).
WEISSEL, Adam, SC, USN (Germany).
WELCH, Richard, Cpl., 37th Mass. Inf. (Ireland).
WELLS, Thomas M., Chief Bugler, 6th N.Y. Cav. (Ireland).
WELLS, William, QM, USN (Germany).
WELSH, Edward, Pvt., 54th Ohio Inf. (Ireland).

PART IV.—FOREIGN BORN MEDAL OF HONOR RECIPIENTS— Continued

WELSH, James, Pvt. 4th R.I. Inf. (Ireland).
WENDE, Bruno, Pvt., 17th U.S. Inf. (Germany).
WESTA, Karl, Chief MM, USN (Norway).
WESTERHOLD, William, Sgt., 52d N.Y. Inf. (Prussia).
WESTERMARK, Axel, Seaman, USN (Finland).
WHITE, Adam, Cpl., 11th W. Va. Inf. (Switzerland).
WHITE, Patrick H., Capt., Chicago Mercantile Btry., Ill. Light Arty. (Ireland).
WIDMER, Jacob, 1st Sgt., 5th U.S. Cav. (Germany).
WILKE, Julius A. R., BM1c, USN (Germany).
WILKENS, Henry, 1st Sgt., 2d U.S. Cav. (Germany).
WILLIAMS, Antonio, Seaman, USN (Malta).
WILLIAMS, Augustus, Seaman, USN (Norway).
WILLIAMS, Frank, Seaman, USN (Germany).
WILLIAMS, George C., Qm. Sgt., 14th U.S. Inf. (England).
WILLIAMS, Henry, CM, USN (Canada).
WILLIAMS, Louis, Captain of Hold, USN (Norway).
WILLIAMS, Peter, Seaman, USN (Norway).
WILLIAMS, William, Landsman, USN (Ireland).
WILLIS, Richard, Coxs., USN (England).
WILSON, August, BM, USN (Germany).
WILSON, Christopher W., Pvt., 73d N.Y. Inf. (Ireland).
WILSON, John, Sgt., 1st N.J. Cav. (England).
WINDOLPH, Charles, Pvt., 7th U.S. Cav. (Germany).
WINTERBOTTOM, William, Sgt., 6th U.S. Cav. (England).
WOOD, Mark, Pvt., 21st Ohio Inf. (England).
WOON, John, BM, USN (England).
WORTMAN, George G., Sgt., 8th U.S. Cav. (Moncton, New Brunswick).
WRIGHT, Robert, Pvt., 14th U.S. Inf. (Ireland).
WRIGHT, William, Yeoman, USN (England).
YOUNG, Benjamin F., Cpl., 1st Mich. Sharpshooters (Canada).
YOUNKER, John L., Pvt., 12th U.S. Inf. (Germany).
ZIEGNER, Hermann, Pvt., 7th U.S. Cav. (Germany).

728

PART VI
DOCUMENTARY BACKGROUND ON
THE MEDAL OF HONOR

Key to the Story of the Medal of Honor

[From the Army Medal of Honor Book, 1948]

The purpose of the Key to the Story of the Medal of Honor is to preserve and make accessible to the public the basic source material for research in the history of the Army Medal of Honor.

When the history of the Medal of Honor was commenced on November 12, 1946, there existed no documentation of the subject in the proper sense of the term, and a major phase of the project has been the search for the basic source-materials concerning the inception and evolution of the decoration.

The documentary material presented in the following pages is divided into two sections: a calendar of letters, other unpublished documents, and the texts of certain Congressional hearings, Statutes, Regulations, General Orders, etc.; and a bibliography of all other printed materials relating to the decoration. The descriptions have been chronologically arranged by the dates of the documents.

CALENDAR OF MEDAL OF HONOR DOCUMENTS

During the Civil War and in the years immediately thereafter, sundry letters, War Department Orders, and related papers concerning the early history of the Army Medal of Honor were laid before Congress and placed on file in the War Department, reference being made to them only occasionally in the records of the Congress or the Department. These papers included letters between the War Department and the United States Mint in Philadelphia, General Orders published by various Army headquarters in the field, credentials submitted to the War Department in support of recommendations made concerning the Medal, lists of Medal winners, and descriptions of medal-presentation cermonies. These letters, orders, and related papers have been found within the War Department proper, in the records contained in the National Archives, in the Library of Congress, and in depositories of information in Philadelphia, New York, and elsewhere. Some were found in widely scattered sources such as contemporary newspapers, "recollections," and "diaries"; others in "War of the Rebellion Records" where they are mixed promiscuously with other materials without any reference to dates or circumstance. After much study and labor, copies of these papers have been brought together in proper order and chronologically arranged as now printed. Although this is called a "Calendar" and is in part a Calendar in the usual sense of a résumé of the contents of documents, nevertheless for a number of hitherto unpublished documents the full test is reproduced.

Inasmuch as the Navy Medal of Honor was the first to be established, the Calendar which follows commences with the correspondence between the United States Mint in Philadelphia and Secretary of the Navy Gideon Welles in Washington, D.C.

Forty-one documents relative to the history of the bestowal of the Medal of Honor during the Civil War are published in 22 of the volumes of the "War of the Rebellion Records." For the purposes of present study "Rebellion Records" has been accepted as a primary source, inasmuch as the documents selected for publication therein were chosen on the basis of an examination of the records of every company, battery, regiment, brigade, division, corps, and army of the Union Army and the records of geographical military departments and divisions, including the files of the War Department and all of its bureaus. "Rebellion Records" were based upon search of these records by experts who were well qualified for the duty by reason of their service in the Army and the War Department. These volumes are available in larger libraries throughout the United States.

1032

Dec. 9, 1861—U.S. Congress. The Congressional Globe, p. 26.

"In Senate . . . Bills introduced . . . Mr. Grimes asked, and by unanimous consent obtained, leave to introduce a bill (S. No. 82) to further promote the efficiency of the Navy; which was read twice by its title, and referred to the Committee on Naval Affairs, and ordered to be printed." This marks the inception of legislation concerning the Medal of Honor. The bill introduced later by Senator Wilson (*see below*, under February 17, 1862) was the first legislation regarding the Army Medal. Concerning the circumstances surrounding the sponsorship of the Navy Medal of Honor, *see* William Salter's *The Life of James W. Grimes.* 1876. pp. 161–163.

Dec. 21, 1861—U.S. Laws, Statutes, etc. An Act to further promote the efficiency of the Navy. 12 Stat. 329–330:

"SEC. 7. *And be it further enacted*, That the Secretary of the Navy be, and is hereby, authorized to cause two hundred 'medals of honor' to be prepared, with suitable emblematic devices, which shall be bestowed upon such petty officers, seamen, landsmen, and marines as shall most distinguish themselves by their gallantry in action and other seamanlike qualities during the present war, and that the sum of one thousand dollars be, and is hereby, appropriated out of any money in the Treasury, for the purpose of carrying this section into effect."

Dec. 30, 1861—Welles, Gideon, Secretary of the Navy. Letter to James Pollock, Superintendent of the U.S. Mint, Philadelphia. *Source: Philadelphia Mint.* Filed: National Archives.

"NAVY DEPARTMENT, *Dec. 30, 1861.*

"SIR. A recent act of Congress—a copy of which is enclosed—Authorizes the Secretary of the Navy to have two hundred medals of honor prepared with suitable emblems and devices to be bestowed on such petty officer, seamen and marines as shall most distinguish themselves by their gallantry in action etc. during the present war, and appropriates $2,000 for the purpose.

"In carrying out the object expressed, the Department would be glad to have your assistance. Your experience in such matters will enable you to give it such data, with regard to the character of the medal that can be gotten up for the sum appropriated, as will enable it to act understandingly. And if you, or any one connected with the establishment under your charge, can suggest an appropriate design for the medals of honor, the Department would be under obligations. It would also be glad if you would suggest a suitable person to engrave the dies after the design for a medal shall have been adopted.

"I am very respecty,
"Yr. obt. svt.

GIDEON WELLES,"

"To The Superintendent of the U.S. Mint, Philadelphia."

Jan. 4, 1862—Pollock, James, Director of Philadelphia Mint. Letter to Gideon Welles, Secretary of the Navy, Washington, D.C. *Source: Philadelphia Mint.* Filed: National Archives.

"MINT OF THE UNITED STATES,
Philada. Jan. 4, 1862.

"SIR: Your letter of the 20th ulto. in relation to the preparation of two hundred 'medals of honor', under an Act of Congress Approved Dec. 21, 1861, entitled 'an Act to further promote the efficiency of the Navy' has been received.

"Designs for the medal in question, are in course of preparation at this institution, and will be finished and enclosed to you in the early part of next week, with my views as to the character of the proposed medal, engraving of dies, etc. The medals can be prepared here at an expense within the appropriation of $2,000.

"Very Respectfully
"Your obedient servant,

"JAS. POLLOCK,
"Director of the Mint."

"HON. GIDEON WELLES,
"Secretary of the Navy,
Washington City."

Jan. 7, 1862—Welles, Gideon. Letter to James Pollock. *Source: Philadelphia Mint.* Filed: National Archives.

Suggests a medal in the shape of a cross, with "three ribbons—the red, white, and blue".

Jan. 11, 1862—Pollack, James. Letter to Gideon Welles. *Source: Philadelphia Mint.* Filed: National Archives.

". . . Designs (including one in the shape of a cross) for the 'medals of honor', will be transmitted to you on Tuesday next, the 14th inst, until which time we must claim your indulgence . . ."

Jan. 14, 1862—Pollock, James. Letter to Gideon Welles. *Source: Philadelphia Mint.* Filed: National Archives.

Encloses three suggested designs.

Jan. 15, 1862—Longacre, James B., Engraver, U.S. Mint, Philadelphia. *Source: Nat. Archives. War Dept. AGO 8847.A (EB)—1882.*

Memorandum describing outline drawings of one of the designs.

Jan. 20, 1862—U.S. War Department. Letter to Wilson and Sons, Silver Smiths, Philadelphia. *Source: Nat. Archives. War Dept. AGO 8847.A (EB)—1882.*

Unsigned note declining an offer by Wilson & Sons to manufacture Medals of Honor as "arrangements have already been made."

Feb. 13, 1862—Welles, Gideon. Letter to James Pollock. *Source: Philadelphia Mint.* Filed: National Archives.

". . . The Department begs leave to remind you of your promise to have other designs of 'medals of honor' prepared; and to ask if I may soon expect them . . ."

Feb. 17, 1862—Pollock, James. Letter to Gideon Welles. *Source: Philadelphia Mint.* Filed: National Archives.

Encloses two additional designs. Also, in this letter, Pollock refers to Welles' statement that $2,000 has been appropriated for manufacture of the medals, and points out that the act appropriates only $1,000. ". . . The . . . amount would not be sufficient to cover the expenses of preparing 200 medals of gold, in a creditable style . . ." In the postscript: "I fear that $2,000 will not be sufficient to get up 200 medals in gold of proper finish. We might prepare 50 in gold and 150 in silver for that amount."

Feb. 17, 1862—U.S. Congress. The Congressional Globe. Feb. 17, 1862. p. 841.

"In Senate . . . Notice of a Bill . . . Mr. Wilson of Massachusetts, gave notice to his intention to ask leave to introduce a bill to authorize the President to distribute medals to privates in the Army of the United States who shall distinguish themselves in battle."

Feb. 20, 1862—Wilson & Sons, Silver Smiths, Philadelphia, Pa. Letter to Mr. Edw. Stanton, Secretary of War, Washington. *Source: Nat. Archives. War Dept. AGO 8847.A (EB)—1882.*

"We notice that silver medals are to be awarded to our Brave Soldiers under a resolution of Congress passed a few days since. We write to say that we are very desirous of submitting a proposition to prepare these medals, and to that end we are now engaged in preparing designs for the same."

Note: The resolution referred to was introduced into the Senate on Feb. 17, 1862 (*see above*), but was not passed until May 13, 1862. There is no source to indicate the foundation for the assumption that the medals were to be made of silver.

March, 1862—The Mitchell Raid. *For documents see National Archives. War Dept. AGO 3313—A (EB)—1879.*

Apr. 17, 1862—Pollock, James. Letter to E. M. Stanton, Secretary of War, Washington, D.C. *Source: Philadelphia Mint.* Filed: National Archives.

Pollock opens correspondence with War Department, noticing that a resolution has been introduced which, if it becomes law, will allow the Army to have a Medal of Honor. He encloses an impression in soft metal and offers the facilities of the Mint for production of a medal.

May 6, 1862—Pollock, James, Director of the Mint, Philadelphia. Letter to Gideon Welles, Secretary of the Navy, Washington, D.C. *Source: Philadelphia Mint.* Filed: National Archives.

Enclosing two additional designs and stating his own preference for the first one.

May 9, 1862—Welles, Gideon. Letter to James Pollock. *Source: Philadelphia Mint.* Filed: National Archives.

"NAVY DEPARTMENT, *May 9, 1862.*

"SIR: Your letter of the 6th instant enclosing designs of medals, No. 1 and No. 2, has been received.

"The Department approves of design No. 1 and desires to know what will be the cost of the medal in bronze, silver and gold respectively.

"I am, respectfully,

"Yr. Obt. servant,

"GIDEON WELLES"

"JAMES POLLOCK, ESQ.

"Director of the Mint, Philadelphia."

May 13, 1862—Longacre, James B., Engraver, Philadelphia Mint. Letter to James Pollock. *Source: Philadelphia Mint.* Filed: National Archives.

Estimates cost of preparing the dies for the medal from $600 to $800.

May 13, 1862. Pollock, James. Letter to Gideon Welles. *Source: Philadelphia Mint.* Filed: National Archives.

Quotes estimates of costs as requested by Welles letter of May 9 (*above*).

". . . In fine gold from $30 to $35 each

". . . In fine silver from $2.00 to $2.50 each

". . . In fine copper (bronzed) about 50 cents ea."

May 13, 1862—U.S. Congress. The Congressional Globe. May 13, 1862.

"In Senate . . . Mr. Wilson, of Massachusetts, from the Committee on Military Affairs and the Militia, to whom the subject was referred, reported a joint resolution (S. No. 82) to provide for the presentation of medals of honor to the enlisted men of the Army and volunteer forces who have or may distinguish themselves in battle during the present rebellion; which was read for the first time and ordered to a second reading."

May 15, 1862—Fox, Gustavus Vasa, Acting Secretary, Navy Department. Letter to James Pollock. *Source: Philadelphia Mint.* Filed: National Archives.

Instructs Pollock to furnish as many medals as possible under the appropriation of $1,000, using the approved design, with inscription on reverse "For personal valor".

May 16, 1862—Fox, Gustavus Vasa. Letter to James Pollock. *Source: Philadelphia Mint.* Filed: National Archives.

Changes the wording on the reverse to "Personal Valor".

May 19, 1862—U.S. Congress. The Congressional Globe, p. 2187.

Senator Wilson's resolution (S. J. R. No. 82) reported to the Senate without amendment, ordered to be engrossed for a third reading, read the third time, and passed.

"Its object is to authorize the President . . . to cause two thousand 'medals of honor' to be prepared with suitable emblematic devices, and to direct that they be presented, in the name of the Congress, to such non-commissioned officers and privates as shall most distinguish themselves by gallantry in action, and other soldier-like qualities; and it appropriates $10,000 for the purpose . . ."

May 20, 1862—Pollock, James. Letter to Gustavus Vasa Fox. *Source: Philadelphia Mint.* Filed: National Archives.

Announcing that preparation of dies is beginning.

June 24, 1862—U.S. Congress. The Congressional Globe, p. 2907.

Reporting referral of Senator Wilson's resolution (S. J. R. 82) to the Committee on Military Affairs.

July 10, 1862—U.S. Congress. The Congressional Globe, p. 3226; 3240.

"House of Representatives . . . Mr. Olin . . . reported back Senate Joint Resolution No. 82 . . . with the recommendation that it do pass . . . The resolution was ordered read a third time; and it was accordingly read a third time, and passed." (*Ibid.*, p. 3226, Message from the House to the Senate announces the House action.)

July 12, 1862—U.S. Laws, Statutes, etc.

"A resolution to provide for the presentation of 'Medals of Honor' to the Enlisted Men of the Army and Volunteer Forces who have distinguished, or may distinguish, themselves in Battle during the present Rebellion. 12 Stat. 623-624.

"*Resolved by the Senate and House of Representatives of the United States of America in Congress assembled,* That the President of the United States be, and he is hereby, authorized to cause two thousand 'medals of honor' to be prepared with suitable emblematic devices, and to direct that the same be presented, in the name of the Congress, to such non-commissioned officers and privates as shall most distinguish themselves by their gallantry in action, and other soldier-like qualities, during the present insurrection. And that the sum of ten thousand dollars be, and the same is hereby, appropriated out of any money in the treasury not otherwise appropriated, for the purpose of carrying this resolution into effect."

"Approved. July 12, 1962."

July 14, 1862—U.S. Congress. The Congressional Globe, p. 3212.

Describes a message from the President to the Senate, announcing that the President has signed the resolution of July 10, 1862.

July 14, 1862—Pollock, James. Letter to E. M. Stanton. *Source: Philadelphia Mint.* Filed: National Archives.

Describes the Medal being made for the Navy and suggests that it might be adopted for the Army.

July 25, 1862—Welles, Gideon. Letter to James Pollock. *Source: Philadelphia Mint.* Filed: National Archives.

Requests date on which the Navy Medals will be ready.

July 28, 1862—Pollock, James. Letter to Gideon Welles. *Source: Philadelphia Mint.* Filed: National Archives.

Reports that the dies for the Navy Medals will be finished in about four weeks.

July 29, 1862—U.S. War Department. General Orders. No. 91, July 29, 1862.

Reprints the resolution which authorizes the Army Medal of Honor.

Sept. 12, 1862—Welles, Gideon. Letter to James Pollock. *Source: Philadelphia Mint.* Filed: National Archives.

Again requests date on which Navy Medals will be finished.

Sept. 15, 1862—Pollock, James. Letter to Gideon Welles. *Source: Philadelphia Mint.* Filed: National Archives.

". . . if no accident occurs in hardening [the dies] we expect to commence striking the medals the last of the present week . . ."

Sept. 30, 1862—Scott, Thomas A., of Pennsylvania Railroad Company, Philadelphia. Letter to Edwin M. Stanton, Secretary of War. *Source: Nat. Archives, War Dept., AGO 8847.A (EB)–1882.*

Introduces R. G. Henkle, member of the firm of William Wilson & Sons, Philadelphia.

Sept. 30, 1862—Pollock, James. Letter to Gideon Welles. *Source: Philadelphia Mint.* Filed: National Archives.

Send three specimen medals by a member of the firm of William Wilson & Sons, Philadelphia and recommends that the firm be allowed to supply attachments for the medals. States that 294 medals may obtained for cost of $999.80.

Oct. 4, 1862—Squier, E. Ego, editor, Frank Leslie's Weekly, 19 City Hall Square, New York City. Letter to James Pollock. *Source: Philadelphia Mint.* Filed: National Archives.

Requests photographs of the medal for publication.

Oct. 7, 1862—Pollock, James. Letter to E. M. Stanton. *Source: Philadelphia Mint.* Filed: National Archives.

Send specimen medal by hands of firm members of William Wilson & Sons; suggests that it would be as appropriate for the Army as the Navy.

Oct. 23, 1862—Welles, Gideon. Letter to James Pollock. *Source: Philadelphia Mint.* Filed: National Archives.

Transmits specimen Medal of Honor with attachment and orders 175 medals struck in copper (bronzed) and turned over to William Wilson & Sons, who will arrange attachments.

Oct. 30, 1862—Wilson & Co., Philadelphia. Letter to E. M. Stanton. *Source: Nat. Archives, War Dept. AGO, 8847.A (EB)–1882.*

Gives rates for work proposed on medal. (Incomplete document.)

Compilation of papers relating to the Medal of Honor, pp. 33-35.

Nov. 17, 1862—Watson, P. H., Assistant Secretary of War, Washington. Letter to James Pollock. *Source: Nat. Archives, War Dept., AGO, *8847.A (EB)–1882.*

Transmits copy of contract of War Department with William Wilson & Son.

Dec. 13, 1862—Pollock, James. Letter to Gideon Welles. *Source: Philadelphia Mint.* Filed: National Archives.

Announces that he is forwarding 175 medals ordered, and bills Navy Department $823.75.

Feb. 14, 1863—U.S. War Department. Memorandum. *Source: Nat. Archives, War Dept., 8847.A (EB)–1882.*

Records receipt of 500 additional medals from William Wilson & Son.

Mar. 3, 1863—U.S. Laws, Statutes, etc.

"SEC. 6. *And be it further enacted,* That the President cause to be struck from the dies recently prepared at the United States Mint for that purpose, 'medals of honor' additional to those authorized by the act (resolution) of July twelfth, eighteen hundred and sixty two, and present the same to such officers, noncommissioned officers, and privates as have most distinguished, or who may hereafter most distinguish, themselves in action; and the sum of twenty thousand dollars is hereby appropriated out of any monies in the treasury not otherwise appropriated, to defray the expenses of the same. "Approved March 3, 1863."

Mar. 3, 1863—U.S. War Department. Memorandum. *Source: Nat. Archives, War Dept., AGO, Consolidated File 92467–S, Slip 489258.*

"There were no medals purchased until subsequent to the passage of the act of Mar. 3, 1863, and of course no presentations were made previous to that date."

Mar. 6, 1863—Washington Chronicle. News story on award of first medals. *Source: Nat. Archives. War Dept., AGO 699273.*

Mar. 12, 1863—U.S. War Department. Memorandum. *Source: Ibid.*

". . . there were 2,000 purchased under contract by the Secretary of War from Wm. Wilson & Sons of Philadelphia, Pa., at a cost of $2 each."

Mar. 24, 1863—U.S. War Department.

No evidence can be found that section 6 of the act approved March 3, 1863, was ever published to the Army in general orders. In General Orders No. 73, 1863, sections 17, 18, 19, and 25 of the act were published, but not section 6.

May 30, 1863—U.S. War Department. AGO. General Orders No. 160. *Source: Library of Congress. Rare Book Room.*

"A medal of honor has been awarded to Pvt. Samuel Johnson, of Company G, 9th Pennsylvania Reserves, for having, by individual bravery and daring, captured from the enemy two colors at the battle of Antietam, September 17, 1862, and received in the act a severe wound. He will be transferred to the Invalid Corps as a commissioned officer.

"By Order of the Secretary of War.

"E. D. TOWNSEND,
"Assistant Adjutant General."

Note: This general order is unique in Civil War history, being the only general orders issued by the War Department in Washington for the award of the Medal of Honor to an individual soldier. The only other instance of a Civil War general order being issued by the War Department relative to the Medal of Honor was the one which follows.

June 3–Aug. 1, 1863—U.S. War Department. Medals of Honor won (21) in the Gettysburg Campaign, Report No. 423. *Source: Reb. Rec., I: XXVII (2): 282.*

June 29, 1863—War Department. Adjutant General's Office. General Orders No. 195. *(See also below:* Mar. 22, 1878).

"The Adjutant General will provide an appropriate Medal of Honor for the troops who, after the expiration of their term, have offered their services to the Government in the present emergency; and also for the volunteer troops from other States that have volunteered their temporary service in the States of Pennsylvania and Maryland.

"By Order of the Secretary of War.

"E. D. TOWNSEND,
"Assistant Adjutant General."

May 4–June 11, 1864—U.S. War Department. Medals of Honor for Campaign from the Rapidan to the James River, Va. Report No. 271. Medals of Honor (31) awarded for distinguished services. *Source: Rebellion Records, I: XXXVI (1): 1020-1021.*

May 1–Sept. 8, 1864—U.S. War Department. The Atlanta (Georgia) Campaign. Report No. 596. Medals of Honor (7) awarded for distinguished services. *Source: Reb. Rec., XXXVIII (3): 612.*

June 11, 1864—Potts, John. Chief Clerk. U.S. War Department. Letter to Wilson & Son, Philadelphia. *Source: Philadelphia Mint.*

Requests terms for an additional 1,000 Medals.

June 13–July 31, 1864—U.S. War Department. The Richmond (Virginia) campaign. Report No. 292, Medals of Honor (16) awarded for distinguished services. *Source: Reb. Rec., I: XL (1): 748.*

Aug. 1–Dec. 31, 1864—U.S. War Department. The Richmond Campaign, August 1-December 31, 1864. Report No. 350. Medals of Honor (61) awarded for distinguished services. *Source: Reb. Rec., I: XLII (1): 848-840.*

Aug. 7–Nov. 28, 1864—U.S. War Department. The Shenandoah Valley Campaign. Report No. 171. Medals of Honor (40) awarded for distinguished services. *Source: Reb. Rec., I: XLIII (1): 550-551.*

Aug. 28, 1864—U.S. War Department. The Atlanta (Georgia) Campaign. Report No. 572 (Addenda). Headquarters, Seventeenth Army Corps. In the Field, Ga., General Orders No. 13. *Source: Reb. Rec., I: XXXVIII (3): 556–558.*

Oct. 11, 1864—U.S. War Department. Headquarters Department of Virginia and North Carolina. Army of the James. Before Richmond. Letter from Ed. W. Smith, Assistant Adjutant General to "Soldiers of the Army of the James". Thirty-eight Medal of Honor Awards mentioned. *Source: Reb. Rec., I: VXLII (3): 161–175.*

Oct. 11, 1864—U.S. War Department. Headquarters Department of Virginia and North Carolina. Army of the James. Before Richmond, Oct. 11, 1864. *Source: Library of Congress. Rare Book Room, Misc. Pamphlets, No. 451.*

Maj. Gen. Benjamin F. Butler, Army Commander, announced, concerning four Negro soldiers: ". . . these gallant colored soldiers were left in command, all their company officers being killed or wounded, and led their unit gallantly and meritoriously through the day. For these services they have most honorable mention, and the Commanding General will cause a special medal to be struck in honor of these gallant colored soldiers."

Oct. 17, 1864—U.S. War Department. Army of the Potomac. Headquarters, Army of the Potomac. *Source: Reb. Rec., III: IV: 814–818.*

List of men to whom Medals of Honor were awarded up to this date.

Oct. 31, 1864—U.S. War Department. Adjutant General's Office. Report to the Secretary of War. *Source: Reb. Rec., III: IV: 810–811: 814.*

Nov. 14, 1864—Jan. 22, 1865—U.S. War Department. The Campaign in North Alabama and Middle Tennessee. Medals of Honor (27) awarded for distinguished services. *Source: Reb. Rec., I: XLV (1): 645–646.*

Dec. 5, 1864—U.S. War Department. Headquarters Army of the Potomac. List of (11) soldiers of the Ninth Army Corps for whom medals of honor have been received by Major General Meade. *Source: Reb. Rec., 1: XLII (3): 815.*

Dec. 5, 1864—U.S. War Department. Headquarters, Second Army Corps. Special Orders, No. 309.
Announces arrangements for ceremonies for presentation of 22 Medals of Honor. *Source: Reb. Rec., I: XLII (3): 812–813.*

Dec. 6, 1864—U.S. War Department. Army of the Potomac. Letter to Major General A. A. Humphreys, Commanding Second Corps. *Source: Reb. Rec., I: XLII (3): 825.*
Adds name of Sgt. Terrence Begley, Co. D., Seventh New York Artillery, to list of Medal winners of the Second Corps.

Dec. 15, 1864—U.S. War Department. Headquarters, Second Army Corps. In Camp, before Petersburg, Va. Special Orders, No. 319, Paragraph 2. *Source: Reb. Rec., I: XLII (3): 1009.*
Announces arrangements for medal presentations.

Dec. 16, 1864—U.S. War Department. Headquarters, Second Division, Ninth Army Corps. Jones House, Va. Letter from Robert B. Potter, Brevet Major General, Commanding, to Lt. Col. P. M. Lydig, Assistant Adjutant General, Ninth Army Corps. *Source: Reb. Rec., I: XLII (3): 1021.*
Reporting arrangements for medal presentations.

Dec. 17, 1864—U.S. War Department. Army of the Potomac. Letter. Headquarters Army of the Potomac. To Commanding Officer Fifth Corps. *Source: Reb. Rec., I: XLII (3): 1028.*
Transmits 3 medals for presentation.

Dec. 22, 1864—U.S. War Department. Army of the Potomac. Special Orders, No. 346. *Source: Reb. Rec., I: XLIII (3): 1857–1858.*
Requests statements be furnished concerning enlisted men entitled to Medals of Honor for conspicuous gallantry.

Dec. 22, 1864—U.S. War Department. Headquarters, 155th Regiment Pennsylvania Volunteers. Letter from Bvt. Col. John Ewing, commanding regiment, to Bvt. Capt. L. C. Bartlett, Acting Assistant Adjutant General. *Source: Reb. Rec., I: LI (1): 1194.*
Two soldiers recommended for Medal of Honor.

Dec. 24, 1864—U.S. War Department. Ninth Army Corps. General Orders. No. 50. Published to the Corps the names of eleven soldiers "to whom were awarded the National Congress medals of honor." *Source: Reb. Rec., I: XLII (3): 1071–1072.*

Dec. 24, 1864—U.S. War Department. 155th Regiment Pennsylvania Volunteers. Letter to L. C. Bartlett, Acting Assistant Adjutant General. *Source: Reb. Rec., I: LI (1): 1194.*
Two soldiers recommended for Medals of Honor in accordance with Special Orders No. 346, Headquarters, Army of the Potomac, December 22, 1864.

Dec. 25, 1864—U.S. War Department. Operations in Maryland, Eastern North Carolina, Pennsylvania, Virginia (except Southwestern), and West Virginia, January 1, 1861–June 30, 1865. Letter from Eli G. Sellers, Lieutenant Colonel, Commanding, 91st Regiment, Pennsylvania Veteran Vols., to Lt. L. C. Bartlett, Acting Assistant Adjutant General. *Source: Reb. Rec., I: LI (1): 1195.*
Three soldiers recommended for Medals of Honor.

Dec. 27, 1864—U.S. War Department. Tenth Vermont Volunteers. Letter to Assistant Adjutant General, Army of the Potomac. *Source: Reb. Rec., I: XLII (3): 1084–1085.*
Four soldiers recommended for Medals of Honor in accordance with Special Orders No. 346, Headquarters, Army of the Potomac, December 22, 1864.

1865—U.S. War Department. Memorandum. *Source: Nat. Archives War Dept. AGO. 92467-S.*
"In 1865, 8,000 additional Medals of Honor were bought from Wilson and Sons."

Feb. 10, 1865—U.S. War Department, Army of the Potomac. Order. *Source: U.S. War Dept. Report of Board of Officers. 1904. p. 15.*
Requested "the names of all such noncommissioned officers and enlisted men as have preeminently distinguished themselves by gallantry in the actions of the 5th, 6th, and 7th of February, 1865."

1865—U.S. War Department. Operations in Arkansas. Report, No. 1—Addenda. Medals of Honor (2) won at Dardanelle, Ark., Jan. 14, 1865 and at Gilman's Ranch, Nebr., May 12, 1865. *Source: Reb. Rec., I: XLVIII: 13.*

1038

Jan. 1–Apr. 3, 1865—U.S. War Department. The Richmond Campaign. Report No. 178. Medals of Honor (11) awarded for distinguished services. *Source: Reb. Rec., I: XLVI (1): 380.*

Jan. 1–June 30, 1865—U.S. War Department. Operations in Louisiana and the Trans-Mississippi States and Territories. Medals of Honor (2) awarded for distinguished services. *Source: Reb. Rec., I: XLVII (1): 13.*

Jan. 1–June 30, 1865—U.S. War Department. The Campaign of the Carolinas. Medals of Honor (3) awarded for distinguished services. *Source: Reb. Rec., I: XLVII (1): 1043.*

Jan. 3–17, 1865—U.S. War Department. Expedition to and capture of Fort Fisher, N.C., and its dependents. Report No. 21. Medals of Honor (4) awarded for distinguished services. *Source: Reb. Rec., I: XLVI (1): 421.*

Feb. 27–Mar. 28, 1865—U.S. War Department. Expedition from Winchester to the Front of Petersburg, Va. Report No. 12. Medals of Honor (16) awarded for distinguished service. *Source: Reb. Rec., I: XLVI (1): 509.*

Mar. 17–May 4, 1865—U.S. War Department. The Mobile (Ala.) Campaign. Report No. 90. Medals of Honor (13) awarded for distinguished services. *Source: Reb. Rec., I: XLIX (1): 313.*

Mar. 22–Apr. 24, 1865—U.S. War Department. Wilson's Raid from Chickasaw to Selma, Ala., and Macon, Ga. Medals of Honor (12) awarded for distinguished services. *Source: Reb. Rec., I: XLIX (1): 504.*

Mar. 28–Apr. 9, 1865—U.S. War Department. Medals of Honor (154) won in the Appomattox (Va.) Campaign, March 28–April 9, 1865. Report No. 266. *Source: Reb. Rec., I: XLVI (1): 1257–1261.*

Apr. 1865—Presentation of 85 Rebel Flags Captured by General Sheridan's Command. Newspaper clipping. (Date and name of newspaper not given.) *Source: Nat. Archives. War Dept., AGO. RPO. 511698.*

Quotes from speech of Secretary of War Stanton: "To each one of you the thanks of the Government. A Medal of Honor will be awarded to each. . . ." Internal evidence indicates the ceremony took place very shortly after the death of President Lincoln (April 14, 1865). *Note.*—This ceremony is not to be confused with the similar one held in Washington in December 1865 and described by Rodenbaugh in *Uncle Sam's Medal of Honor.*

June 8, 1865—U.S. War Department. Letter, from Assistant Adjutant General E. D. Townsend to Maj. Gen. E. R. S. Canby, Commanding Department of the Gulf, New Orleans. *Source: Reb. Rec., I: XLIX (1): 105.*

Transmits nine Medals of Honor for delivery.

June 17, 1865—U.S. War Department. Letter from Assistant Adjutant General E. D. Townsend to Maj. Gen. George H. Thomas, Commanding Department of the Cumberland. *Source: Reb. Rec., I: XLIX (1): 402.*

Transmits 12 Medals of Honor for delivery.

June 17, 1865—U.S. War Department. Wilson's Raid from Chickasaw to Selma, Ala., and Macon, Ga., March 22–April 24, 1865. Letter dated Washington, D.C., to Maj. Gen. George H. Thomas, Commanding Department of the Cumberland. *Source: Reb. Rec., I: XLIX (1): 402.*

Transmits 12 Medals of Honor for delivery.

June 30, 1865—U.S. War Department. Operations in Maryland, Eastern North Carolina, Pennsylvania, Virginia (except Southwestern), and West Virginia. Letter dated June 30, 1865, from Headquarters, 155th Regiment, Pennsylvania Volunteers. *Source: Reb. Rec., I: LI (1): 1194.*

Letter recommended two soldiers for the Medal.

July 6, 1865—U.S. War Department. Correspondence, Orders and Returns from March 16th to June 30, 1865. Headquarters, Sixteenth Army Corps, Montgomery, Ala., General Orders, No. 94. *Source: Reb. Rec., I: XLIX (2): 1070.*

Announced award of 5 Medals of Honor for "gallantry displayed in the capture of rebel flags."

July 10, 1865—U.S. War Department. Headquarters, Seventeenth Army Corps. General Orders, No. 10, Louisville, Ky. *Source: Reb. Rec., I: LII (1): 693.*

Awarded "the silver medal of honor of the corps" to four soldiers.

Sept. 16, 1869—Beaumont, M. H., Editor and Publisher, *The Soldier's Friend.* Letter to General E. D. Townsend, Adjutant General, U.S. Army. *Source: Nat. Archives. War Dept., AGO, Aak-534(EB) 1869.*

Oct. 1869—The Soldier's Friend. *Source: Nat. Archives. War Dept., AGO, Aak-534(EB) 1869.*

List of names of the officers and enlisted men, to whom "Medals of Honor" had been awarded; prepared by the Adjutant General's Office, and transmitted to *The Soldier's Friend* with covering letter dated Sept. 29, 1869.

Nov. 19, 1872—U.S. War Department. General Orders, No. 99.

Announced award of Medals of Honor to nine enlisted men who specially distinguished themselves in an engagement with hostile Indians on the North Fork of the Red River, Texas, September 29, 1872.

Jan. 28, 1875—U.S. War Department. Memorandum. "Special Acts of Gallantry to be stated in each case." *Source: In Nat. Archives no trace of document can be found.* This document is cited in Subject-Index to General Orders, 1860–1880 (p. 164).

Feb. 26, 1878—U.S. War Department. Recommendations of company commanders for conspicuous gallantry at Battle of Little Big Horn. With endorsement by command of Brig. Gen. Terry. *Source: Nat. Archives. War Dept. AGO, 10818-A (EB)-1878.*

Mar. 22, 1878—U.S. War Department. Case of Medal of Honor directed by General Orders 195, of 1863. *Source: Nat. Archives. War Dept., AGO, 771. 1878.* (See above, Jun. 29, 1863.)

Sept. 8, 1878—U.S. War Department. Headquarters of the Army. Adjutant General's Office. Request for Medals of Honor for enlisted men of the 7th Cavalry. *Source: Nat. Archives. War Dept., AGO, 10818-A (EB)-1878.*

Dec. 10, 1884—U.S. War Department. Circular. Circular No. 11.

"The following decisions, rulings etc., have been made during the month of November 1884, and are published to the Army for the information of all concerned:

"MEDALS

"The only decorations allowed to be worn on occasions of ceremony are the 'Army corps badges' authorized by section 1227 of the Revised Statutes; the 'Medal of Honor'; and the several distinctive marks given for excellence in rifle practice, as prescribed by existing orders . . .

"By command of Lieutenant General Sheridan:

"R. C. DRUM,
"*Adjutant General.*"

Dec. 10, 1888—U.S. War Department. Headquarters of the Army. Adjutant General's Office. General Orders No. 109.

"Announcement is made to the Army that it is in contemplation to publish annually, hereafter, at the close of each year, commencing with 1889, an order making mention of gallant or specially meritorious acts or conduct in service, on the part of either commissioned officers or enlisted men of the Army, and containing the names of those who have received Medals of Honor and Certificates of Merit. It is, therefore, directed that whenever an officer or soldier shall have distinguished himself, in any way, by service conspicuous for the skill, fortitude, courage, or gallantry displayed, a full report of the facts be at once made, by any officer cognizant of the same, through the military channel, to The Adjutant General, for the information of the Major General Commanding the Army.

"By command of Major General Schofield:

"R. C. DRUM,
"*Adjutant General.*"

Feb. 11, 1892—U.S. War Department. Circulars. Circular No. 2.

"Headquarters of the Army, Adjutant General's Office.

"The following decisions, rulings, etc., have been made, and are published to the Army for the information of all concerned:

"MEDALS OF HONOR AND CERTIFICATES OF MERIT

"Medals of Honor should be awarded to officers or enlisted men for distinguished bravery in action, while Certificates of Merit should, under the law, be awarded for distinguished service, whether in action or otherwise, of a valuable character to the United States, as, for example, extraordinary exertion in the preservation of human life, or in the preservation of public property, or rescuing public property from destruction by fire or otherwise, or any hazardous service by which the Government is saved loss in men or material. Simple heroism in battle, on the contrary, is fitly rewarded by a Medal of Honor, although such act of heroism may not have resulted in any benefit to the United States. Where the conduct of an enlisted man, noncommissioned officer, or private has been represented to merit both a Medal of Honor and a Certificate of Merit, recommendation may be made for both, either simultaneously or at different times.

"By command of Major General Schofield:

"J. C. KELTON,
"*Adjutant General.*"

1892—U.S. Department of Justice. Opinions of Attorney General of the United States. Vol. 20. 1895. Medal of Honor, pp. 421–423.

A claim for a Medal of Honor for an acting assistant surgeon during the Civil War is rejected.

1895—U.S. War Department. Judge Advocate General. A Digest of Opinions of the Judge Advocate General of the Army. (Winthrop) Washington, GPO. Medal of Honor, pp. 491–492.

May 2, 1896—U.S. Laws, Statutes, etc. 20 Stat. 473. Joint resolution relative to the Medal of Honor authorized by the acts of July twelfth, eighteen hundred and sixty two, and March third, eighteen hundred and sixty three.

Approved, May 2, 1896.

Authorizes . . ."a rosette or knot to be worn in lieu of the medal, and a ribbon to be worn with the medal . . ."

Nov. 10, 1896—U.S. War Department Orders.

"The ribbon to be of silk one inch wide and one inch in length; the center stripe of white one sixteenth of an inch wide, flanked on either side by a stripe of blue seven thirty-seconds of an inch wide, bordered by two stripes of red each one-quarter of an inch wide.

"The knot to be a bowknot of the same combination of colors as the ribbon above described. The ribbon and bowknot are shown in the designs hereto attached."

Feb. 4, 1897—U.S. War Department. Adjutant General's Office. General Orders, No. 4.

Published to the Army the text of the War Department Order quoted above.

Feb. 18, 1897—U.S. War Department. Memorandum.

Contains letter to Tiffany & Co., New York, ordering new ribbons and warning against their unauthorized sale.

June 26, 1897—U.S. War Department. Regulations promulgated respecting the award of the Medal of Honor.

June 30, 1897—U.S. War Department. Adjutant General's Office. General Orders, No. 42.

Published to the Army the Text of the War Department Regulations dated June 26, 1897.

June 30, 1897—U.S. War Department. Award of Medals of Honor, Spanish-American War. *Source: AGO, D & A Branch. Precedent file.*

July 7, 1897—U.S. War Department. Adjutant General's Office. Circular No. 14.

Published to the Army the text of the War Department Memorandum of Feb. 18, 1897.

Sept. 3, 1898—U.S. War Department. General Orders, No. 135.

"II—The following rules will govern the award of Medals of Honor under the resolution of Congress approved July 12, 1862, and under the act approved March 3, 1863, for such officers and enlisted men of the Army, regular and volunteer, as may 'have most distinguished themselves in action.'

"(a) Medals of Honor will not be awarded to officers or enlisted men except for distinguished bravery or conspicuous gallantry, which shall have been manifested in action by conduct that distinguishes a soldier above his comrades, and that involves risk of life, or the performance of more than ordinarily hazardous duty. Recommendations for the award will be governed by this interpretation of extraordinary merit.

"(b) Recommendations should be made only by the officer in command at the time of the 'action,' or by an officer having personal cognizance of the specific act for which the medal was granted. The recommendation must be accompanied by a detailed recital of the circumstances, and by certificates of officers, or affidavits of enlisted men, who were eye-witnesses of the act. The testimony must, when practicable, embrace that of at least two eye-witnesses, and must describe specifically the act or acts by which the person in whose behalf the recommendation is made 'most distinguished' himself, and the facts in the case must be further attested by the official reports of the action, record of events, muster rolls, and returns and descriptive lists.

"By order of the Secretary of War:

"H. C. CORBIN,

"*Adjutant General.*"

1901—U.S. War Department. A Digest of Opinions of the Judge Advocates General of the Army (McClure). Washington, GPO, 876 p. Medals of Honor, pp. 455–456.

Feb. 15, 1901—U.S. War Department. Letter from Secretary of War Elihu Root to Hon. William B. Allison, chairman, Committee on Appropriations, United States Senate. *Source: Nat. Archives. War Dept., AGO, R&P 92467 R–1.*

Encloses proposed legislation on two awards to same person and time limit of three years from date of act.

Mar. 26, 1901—U.S. War Department. Judge Advocate General's Office. Opinion of the Judge Advocate General relative to what constitutes a public record. *Source: War Dept. Cir., May 3, 1901.*

May 3, 1901—U.S. War Department. Unnumbered Circular. 17 p. *Source: Library of the Judge Advocate General. Volume entitled: "Certain Unnumbered Circulars, 1900–1910."*

Opinion and decision of the Judge Advocate General of March 26, 1901, published for the information and guidance of all concerned.

Apr. 19, 1902—U.S. War Department. Special Orders No. 93, Paragraph 14. Appointed the original board of officers appointed by direction of the Secretary of War for the purpose of examining applications and recommendations for Medals of Honor and Certificates of Merit.

June 4, 1902—U.S. War Department. Special Orders, No. 131.

Dissolved board appointed April 19; appointed a new board, and transferred the unfinished business from the old to the new board.

July 17, 1902—U.S. War Department. General Orders, No. 81. Regulations for the uniform of the Army Published in General Orders.

"General Regulations—5. Medals of Honor may be worn by officers and enlisted men entitled to them on all occasions of ceremony; the Medal to be attached to the coat at a point one inch below the opening of the collar."

July 24, 1902—U.S. War Department. Headquarters of the Army. Adjutant General's Office. General Orders, No. 86.

Directs that awards of Medals of Honor and Certificates of Merit will be announced in General Orders, Adjutant General's Office.

Aug. 28, 1902—U.S. War Department. Compilation of papers relating to the Congressional Medal of Honor. 67 p. typescript. *Source: Nat. Archives. War Dept. AGO, RPO 699273.*

1902—U.S. War Department. *Source: Nat. Archives. War Dept., AGO, 461998.* Correspondence relating to the development of the new design of the Medal of Honor.

Sept. 23, 1902—U.S. Department of Justice. Opinion and Decision of the Attorney General. Official Opinions of the Attorneys General of the United States. XXIV: 127–132.

Refers to presentation of Medals of Honor to persons not in service at time of presentation.

Nov. 18, 1902—U.S. Mint. Letter from Director of Mint George E. Roberts to Maj. Gen. H. C. Corbin, Adjutant General, War Department. *Source: Nat. Archives. War Dept., AGO, 461998.*

Suggests inviting a number of well-known artists to compete "for such a sum as you may be pleased to offer."

Nov. 20, 1902—U.S. War Department. Letter from Board of Officers to the Secretary of War. *Source: War Dept. General Orders. 1902. No. 125.*

Remarks of Board of Officers appointed to examine and report on applications and recommendations for Medals of Honor and Certificates of Merit.

Nov. 25, 1902—U.S. Mint. Letter from Charles E. Barber, engraver, Mint Service, U.S. Mint, Philadelphia, to Major General Corbin. *Source: Nat. Archives, War Dept., AGO, 461998.*

Requests from General Corbin fuller details concerning the new medal desired.

Dec. 9, 1902—U.S. War Department. Letter from Adjutant General Corbin to Charles E. Barber, engraver, U.S. Mint. *Source: Nat. Archives. War Dept., AGO, 461998.*

Dec. 11, 1902—U.S. War Department. General Orders, No. 125.

Publishes text of report of Board of Officers (*see above*, Nov. 20, 1902).

Dec. 31, 1902—U.S. War Department. General Orders, No. 132.

Revised regulations for the uniform of the Army.

Feb. 6, 1903—U.S. Department of Justice. Opinion and decision of the Attorney General. Official opinions of the Attorneys General of the United States. XXIV: 580–582.

Discusses time limits. Gives opinion that Medal cannot be awarded if recommendation is made after person involved is discharged.

Mar. 12, 1903—U.S. War Department. General Orders, No. 28.

Paragraph 199½ added to Army Regulations: "Neither a Medal of Honor nor a Certificate of Merit will be awarded in any case when the service of the person recommended, subsequent to the time when he distinguished himself, has not been honorable."

Mar. 16, 1903—U.S. War Department. Circular.

Publishes text of opinions of Department of Justice of September 23, 1902, and February 6, 1903, quoted above.

Nov. 12, 1903—Letter, from Gen. Horatio C. King, Adjutant of the Medal of Honor Legion, New York City, to Elihu Root, Secretary of War, Washington, D.C. *Source: Nat. Archives. War Dept., AGO 92467-R-1.*

Announces that the Legion has adopted a resolution approving change in design of Medal.

Nov. 18, 1903—U.S. War Department. Letter from Elihu Root, Secretary of War, to General King, Brooklyn, N.Y. *Source: Nat. Archives. War Dept., AGO, RPO 62467-R-1.*

Proposes to transmit design of new Medal of Honor to Medal of Honor Legion.

Dec. 10, 1903—U.S. War Department. Letter from Elihu Root, Secretary of War, to the Speaker of the House of Representatives, Washington, D.C. *Source: Nat. Archives. War Dept., AGO, Enc. to 461998.*

Transmits proposed legislation for the new Medal.

Jan. 5, 1904—U.S. War Department. Letter from Elihu Root, Secretary of War, to A. T. Hull, chairman, Committee on Military Affairs, House of Representatives. *Source: Nat. Archives. War Dept., AGO (Encl.)*

Proposes amendments to pending legislation.

Jan. 8, 1904—U.S. War Department. Proceedings of a Board of Officers appointed by Special Orders, No. 131, June 4, 1902. *Published in U.S. War Department. Report of a board of officers,* 1904. (*See below,* Medal of Honor Bibliography—1904.)

Mar. 26, 1904—Estes, L. G. Letter sent to Medal of Honor winners in the city of Washington, D.C. *Source: War Dept., AGO, Decorations & Awards Br., Precedent File.*

Marks inception of a movement in Washington, D.C., to create an organization of Medal of Honor winners.

Apr. 14, 1904—United States Medal of Honor Club. *Source: War Dept., AGO, Dec. & Awards Br., Precedent file.*

Record of first meeting of club noted above.

Apr. 15, 1904—U.S. Laws, Statutes, etc. 33 Stat. 588. Joint Resolution authorizing the issue of duplicate medals where the originals have been lost or destroyed.

Apr. 23, 1904—U.S. Laws, Statutes, etc. 33 Stat. 274. An act making appropriations for the support of the Army for the fiscal year ending June thirtieth, nineteen hundred and five, and for other purposes. * * *

"Ordnance Department . . . Ordnance, Ordnance Stores and Supplies: For three thousand medals of honor to be prepared, with suitable emblematic devices, upon the design of the medal of honor heretofore issued, or upon an improved design, together with appropriate rosettes or other insignia to be worn in lieu of the medal, and to be presented by direction of the President, and in the name of Congress to such officers, noncommissioned officers, and privates as have most distinguished, or may hereafter most distinguish, themselves by their gallantry in action, twelve thousand dollars: *Provided,* That the Secretary of War be, and he is hereby, authorized and directed to use so many of the medals and rosettes or other insignia, provided for by this Act as may be necessary to replace the medals that have been issued under the joint resolution of Congress approved July twelfth, eighteen hundred and sixty-two, and section 6 of the Act of Congress approved March third, eighteen hundred and sixty-three. *And provided further,* That whenever it shall appear from official records in the War Department that any officer or enlisted man of the Army so distinguished himself in action as to entitle him to the award of the congressional medal of honor under the provisions of the sixth section of the Act of Congress approved March third, eighteen hundred and sixty-three, entitled 'An Act making appropriations for the sundry civil expenses of the Government for the year ending June thirtieth, eighteen hundred and sixty-four, and for the year ending thirtieth of June, eighteen hundred and sixty-three, and for other purposes,' the fact that the person who so distinguished himself has since become separated from the military service, or that the award of the medal to him was not specifically recommended or applied for while he was in the said service, shall not be held to prevent the award and presentation of the medal to such person under the provisions of the law hereinbefore cited."

Apr. 28, 1904—U.S. War Department, General Orders, No. 76.

Publishes to the Army text of act of April 23, 1904, relating to the Medal of Honor.

Apr. 29, 1904—U.S. War Department. General Orders, No. 77.

Publishes to the Army text of act of April 15, 1904, relating to the Medal of Honor.

May 11, 1904—U.S. War Department. Orders. Administration of Medal of Honor consolidated under the Military Secretary. *Source: Nat. Archives. War Dept. AGO, R & P 92467-R-2 (Enclosures).*

May 16, 1904—U.S. War Department. Office of the Judge Advocate General. Letter to the Military Secretary, states the basis upon which all awards of the Medal of Honor have been made subsequent to the act approved April 23, 1904.

May 26, 1904—U.S. War Department. Circular.

"Under the act of Congress approved April 23, 1904, the evidence to justify the award of a Medal of Honor must be derived from the official records of the War Department. To entitle a record to be regarded as an official record it must have been made at, or reasonably near, the event of which it purports to be the record, and by an officer whose duty under the law, regulations, or custom of service it was to make it."

Aug. 22, 1904—U.S. War Department. Circular No. 36.

Publishes provisions of act of April 23, 1904.

Sept. 15, 1904—U.S. War Department Orders.

Describes form of inscription on reverse of Medal.

Nov. 22, 1904—U.S. Patent Office. Design Serial No. 37236 and Specification. Application filed Mar. 9, 1904. Term of patent, 14 years.

December 1904—U.S. Patent Office. Transfer of Patent of Medal of Honor Design, under Patent No. 37236. *Source: Nat. Archives. War Dept., AGO, 461998.*

George L. Gillespie, transfers patent design for the new Medal of Honor "to W. H. Taft and his successor or successors as Secretary of War of the United States of America."

Dec. 31, 1904—U.S. War Department. General Orders, No. 197.

Revised regulations for the uniform of the Army published.

". . . the medal shall be worn pendant from the neck; the ribbon passing between the upper and lower hooks of the coat collar so that the medal shall hang about one inch below the opening of the collar."

Apr. 20, 1905—U.S. War Department. Office of The Judge Advocate General. Digest of Opinions of The Judge Advocate General of the Army. 1912. p. 665.

Defines the term "official record" and rules that an oral recommendation is not an official record.

Apr. 29, 1905—U.S. War Department. Circular No. 22.

"4. An oral recommendation for the award of a medal of honor not regarded as an official record . . . "

June 14, 1905—U.S. War Department. Description of the design of the Medal of Honor and correspondence pertaining to its adoption. 16 p.

Part I: Description of the Medal of Honor. Part II: Correspondence on subject of new Medal of Honor Design.

Jan. 25, 1907—U.S. Laws, Statutes, etc. 34 Stat. 1420. Joint Resolution authorizing the Secretary of War to award the Congressional Medal of Honor to Monroe Reisinger for specially brave and meritorious conduct at the Battle of Gettysburg.

Feb. 27, 1907—U.S. Laws, Statutes, etc. 34 Stat. 1422. Joint Resolution relating to the holders of Medals of Honor. 34 Stat. 1422.

" . . . wherever the holders of such Medals of Honor have surrendered them, in order to receive the medals provided by such Act approved April twenty-third, nineteen hundred and four, such medals shall be returned to them: *Provided*, That no recipient of both medals shall wear both medals at the same time."

Mar. 16, 1907—U.S. War Department. General Orders, No. 54.

Publishes text of Joint Resolution of Feb. 27, 1907, relating to the Medal of Honor.

Aug. 14, 1907—U.S. War Department. General Orders, No. 169.

Revised the regulations for the wearing of the Medal of Honor.

Mar. 10, 1908—U.S. War Department. General Orders, No. 33.

Provided for wearing of Medal of Honor ribbon in lieu of the badge under specified conditions.

Dec. 7, 1910—Huidekoper, Frederic L. Letter to General Robert Shaw Oliver, Assistant Secretary of War, War Department, Washington, D.C. *Source: Nat. Archives. War Dept. AGO, RPO 92467 R–1.*

Suggests methods for more publicity being given the Medal.

Dec. 8, 1910—U.S. War Department. Letter from Assistant Secretary of War, Robert Shaw Oliver, to General Frederic L. Huidekoper. *Source: Nat. Archives. War Dept. AGO 92467 R–1.*

Thanks him for the suggestions.

June 23, 1911—Memo from Currier to the Rolls Division regarding George Scott. *Source: National Archives, War Dept. AGO 10818–A(EB)–1878.*

1912—U.S. War Department. A Digest of Opinions of The Judge Advocates General of the Army. Washington, GPO. 1,071 p.

Medals of Honor, pp. 664–666.

May 12, 1913—U.S. War Department Orders. *Source: Nat. Archives. War Dept., AGO, 92467 R-2.*

These Orders distributed business of War Department as between the Secretary of War, the Assistant Secretary of War, and the Assistant and Chief Clerk of the War Department. All business relating to the Medal of Honor and the Certificate of Merit was assigned to the Assistant Secretary of War.

Mar. 4, 1915—U.S. Laws, Statutes, etc. 38 Stat. 1593.

Authorizes the medal for Maj. John O. Skinner, surgeon, United States Army, retired, for gallantry in action while serving as an acting assistant surgeon, United States Army, at the Modoc stronghold during the battle of Jan. 17, 1873, in the Lava Beds, Oreg.

"The medal is made of silver, heavily electroplated in gold, this department from the use of gun metal being necessary as the base metals would not carry the enameling hereinafter mentioned. The chief feature of the old medal, the five-pointed star, has been retained, and in its center appears the head of the heroic Mineva, the highest symbol of wisdom and righteous war. Surrounding this central feature in circular form are the words 'United States of America,' representing nationality. An open laurel wreath, enameled in green, encircles the star, and the oak leaves at the bases of the prongs of the star are likewise enameled in green to give them prominence. 'The medal is suspended by a blue silk ribbon, spangled with thirteen white stars representing the original States, and this ribbon is attached to an eagle supported upon a horizontal bar. Upon the bar, which is attached to two points of the star, appears the word 'valor,' indicative of the distinguished service represented by the medal.

"The reverse side of the medal is engraved with the name of the person honored and the place and date of the distinguished service for which awarded. The medal may be suspended from the neck or attached by pin upon left breast.

"The rosette is hexagonal in form and spangled with thirteen white stars, and is identical in color with the ribbon."

Sept. 20, 1905—U.S. President. Executive Order. Formal presentation of Medals of Honor.

"The presentation of a Medal of Honor to an officer or enlisted man in the military service, awarded under the Joint Resolution of Congress approved July 12, 1862, and the Act of Congress approved March 3, 1863, will always be made with formal and impressive ceremonial.

"The recipient will, when practicable, be ordered to Washington, D.C., and the presentation will be made by the President, as Commander-in-Chief, or by such representative as the President may designate.

"When not practicable to have the presentation at Washington, the details of time, place, and ceremony will be prescribed by the Chief of Staff for each case.

"On campaign, the presentation will be made by the Division or higher commander.

(Signed) THEODORE ROOSEVELT.

THE WHITE HOUSE,
    September 20, 1905."

Sept. 23, 1905—U.S. War Department. General Orders, No. 158. (For all supporting documents see National Archives 956103 M.S.O.)

Publishes text of the Executive Order of the President above.

Nov. 3, 1905—U.S. Department of Justice. Opinion and Decision of the Attorneys General. Official Opinions of the Attorneys General of the United States. XXV: 529–532.

War Department Order requiring surrender of old medals by applicants for the new is upheld.

Apr. 27, 1916—U.S. Laws, Statutes, etc. 39 Stat. 53.

"An Act to establish in the War Department and in the Navy Department, respectively, a roll, designated as 'the Army and Navy medal of honor roll,' and for other purposes.

"*Be it enacted by the Senate and House of Representatives of the United States of America in Congress assembled,* That there is hereby established in the War Department and Navy Department, respectively, a roll designated as 'the Army and Navy medal of honor roll.' Upon written application made to the Secretary of the proper department, and subject to the conditions and requirements hereinafter contained, the name of each surviving person who has served in the military or naval service of the United States in any war, who has attained or shall attain the age of sixty-five years, and who has been awarded a medal of honor for having in action involving actual conflict with an enemy distinguished himself conspicuously by gallantry or intrepidity, at the risk of his life, above, and beyond the call of duty, and who was honorably discharged from service by muster out, resignation, or otherwise, shall be, by the Secretary of the proper department, entered and recorded on said roll. Applications for entry on said roll shall be made in such form and under such regulations as shall be prescribed by the War Department and Navy Department, respectively, and proper blanks and instructions shall be, by the proper Secretary, furnished without charge upon request made by any person claiming the benefits of this Act.

"SEC. 2. That it shall be the duty of the Secretary of War and of the Secretary of the Navy to carry this Act into effect and to decide whether each applicant, under this Act, in his department is entitled to the benefit of this Act. If the official award of the medal of honor to the applicant, or the official notice to him thereof, shall appear to show that the medal of honor was awarded to the applicant for such an act as is required by the provisions of this Act, it shall be deemed sufficient to entitle the applicant to such special pension without further investigation. Otherwise all official correspondence, orders, reports, recommendations, requests, and other evidence now on file in any public office or department shall be considered. A certificate of service and of the act of heroism, gallantry, bravery, or intrepidity for which the medal of honor was awarded, and of enrollment under this Act, and of the right of the special pensioner to be entitled to and to receive the special pension herein granted, shall be furnished each person whose name shall be so entered on said roll. The Secretary of War and the Secretary of the Navy shall deliver to the Commissioner of Pensions a certified copy of each of such of said certificates as he may issue, as aforesaid, and the same shall be full and sufficient authority to the Commissioner of Pensions for the payment by him to the beneficiary named in each such certificate the special pension herein provided for.

"SEC. 3. That each such surviving person whose name shall have been entered on said roll in accordance with this Act shall be entitled to and shall receive and be paid by the Commissioner of Pensions in the Department of the Interior, out of any moneys in the Treasury of the United States not otherwise appropriated, a special pension of $10 per month for life, payable quarter yearly. The Commissioner of Pensions shall make all necessary rules and regulations for making payment of such special pensions to the beneficiaries thereof.

"Such special pension shall begin on the day that such person shall file his application for enrollment on said roll in the office of the Secretary of War or of the Secretary of the Navy after the passage and approval of this Act, and shall continue during the life of the beneficiary.

"Such special pension shall not deprive any such special pensioner of any other pension or of any benefit, right, or privilege to which he is or may hereafter be entitled under any existing or subsequent law, but shall be in addition thereto.

"The special pension allowed under this Act shall not be subject to any attachment, exclusion, levy, tax, lien, or detention under any process whatever.

"SEC. 4. That in case any person has been awarded two or more medals of honor, he shall not be entitled to and shall not receive more than one such special pension.

"Rank in the service shall not be considered in applications filed hereunder.

"Approved April 27, 1916."

June 3, 1916—U.S. Laws, Statutes, etc. 39 Stat. 214.

"SEC. 122: *Investigation concerning Medals of Honor.* A board to consist of five general officers on the retired list of the Army shall be convened . . . for the purpose of investigating and reporting upon past awards or issue of the so-called congressional medal of honor . . . "

June 30, 1916—U.S. Laws, Statutes, etc. 39 Stat. 242. An Act making appropriations for the payment of invalid and other pensions of the United States for the fiscal year ended June thirtieth, nineteen hundred and seventeen, and for other purposes.

Provides that allowances to medal of honor pensioners under the Act of Apr. 27, 1916 "shall be paid from the moneys appropriated for the payment of invalid and other pensions."

Dec. 26, 1916—U.S. War Department. H. P. McCain, The Adjutant General. Letter to Warren G. Harding, United States Senator. *Source: Nat. Archives. War Dept., AGO, 92467 R-2 (Encl.)*

Answers a question of a constituent regarding differences between gratuities connected with Army Medal and Navy Medal.

June 21, 1917—U.S. War Department. Newton D. Baker, Secretary of War. Letter to Hon. George E. Chamberlain, Chairman, Committee on Military Affairs, U.S. Senate. *Source: U.S. Congress. Senate Report No. 73. June 28, 1917.*

" . . . It is the opinion of the War Department that such a bill as the one proposed is very desirable so far as it provides for awards of medals of honor and distinguished

service medals for gallant and distinguished service that may be rendered hereafter."
Continuing, Secretary of War Baker expressed himself as firmly opposed, however, to
awards of the Congressional Medal of Honor or the Distinguished Service Medal for
past deeds: "There are so many angles from which this matter may be approached, if
the past is opened up, and the evidence that would be presented to prove cases is in
such irregular, casual, verbal, and documentary form that it is not believed possible to
do justice to individuals in all cases that would come up for consideration. The War
Department believes that the bill should give us a firm foundation as a course of action for the future, but that it should not involve the War Department in the labor and
annoyance and subject it to the criticism that it is thought would result if the bill provides for the award of distinguished service medals for services performed in the past,
other than the cases for which the certificate of merit has already been granted."
June 28, 1917—P.S. Congress. Senate. Report No. 73. Medals of Honor and Distinguished Service Medals. Report to accompany S. 1720. (*See also*, Sept. 7, 1917,
below.)
"As an important measure of military preparedness, the pending bill (S. 1720)
proposes to make definite and adequate both the mode in which and the basis on
which such recognition of deeds of conspicuous gallantry or other exceptionally meritorious services shall hereafter be extended."
Sept. 7, 1917—U.S. Congress, House. Report No. 140. Medals of Honor and Distinguished Service Medals. Report to accompany S. 1720. (*See also* June 28, 1917,
above.)
Dec. 20, 1917—U.S. War Department. War College Division. Memorandum for the
Chief of Staff. *Source: Memorandum, Mar. 6, 1918 (see above)*.
Recommends that without waiting for legislative action an executive order should be
issued providing for the establishment of a Distinguished Service Cross and a Distinguished Service Medal.
Jan. 11, 1918—U.S. War Department. General Orders, No. 6. Par. 4. Reward for Exceptional Services and Conduct in the Face of the Enemy.
Jan. 12, 1918—U.S. War Department. General Orders, No. 6.
"1. By direction of the President the following decorations and insignia are
authorized:
"(*a*) Distinguished Service Cross . . .
"(*b*) Distinguished Service Medal . . .
"(*c*) War-service chevrons . . .
"(*d*) Wound chevrons . . . "
Feb. 11, 1918—U.S. War Department. General Headquarters. American Expeditionary
Forces. General Orders No. 26. *Source: AGO, Dec. & Awards Br., Precedent File,
"Authorization and Regulations"*.
Contains orders covering award of Medal of Honor to a person apparently fatally
wounded.
Feb. 15, 1918—U.S. War Department. Chief of Staff. Memorandum for The Adjutant
General of the Army. Subject: Posthumous award of the Medal of Honor.
Amends War Department General Orders of Jan. 11, 1918 to read: "The medal so
awarded will be issued to the nearest heir of the deceased person."
Feb. 21, 1918—U.S. War Department. General Orders, No. 20. The last sentence of
paragraph 4, General Orders No. 6, War Department, 1918, is amended to read as fol-
lows:
"The medals so awarded will be issued to the nearest heir of the deceased person."
Mar. 6, 1918—U.S. War Department. Office of The Judge Advocate General. Memoran-
dum for General Crowder. 5 p. typescript. *Source: JAG, Mail & Records Section*.
"A terse history of proceedings in connection with S. 1720, an Act to provide for
the award of Medals of Honor and Distinguished Service Medals."
May 9, 1918—U.S.G.H.Q. American Expeditionary Forces. Bulletin No. 25. France.
Instructions on American awards for gallantry in action and exceptionally meritori-
ous service. Sets standards.
June 9, 1918—U.S. War Department. General Pershing's Order Prescribing Ceremony
for the Presentation of U.S. Army Honors. *Source: The Official Bulletin, Vol. II. June
10, 1918. p. 3*.
July 9, 1918—U.S. Laws, Statutes, etc. 40 Stat. 870. The legislation which clarified all
questions on the Medal of Honor and established the D.S.M., D.S.C., and Silver Star.
"Medals of honor, distinguished service crosses, and distinguished service medals:
That the provisions of existing law relating to the award of medals of honor to officers, noncommissioned officers, and privates of the Army be, and they hereby are,
amended so that the President is authorized to present, in the name of the Congress, a

medal of honor only to each person who, while an officer or enlisted man of the Army, shall hereafter, in action involving actual conflict with an enemy, distinguish himself conspicuously by gallantry and intrepidity at the risk of his life above and beyond the call of duty.

"That the President be, and he is hereby, further authorized to present, but not in the name of Congress, a distinguished service cross of appropriate design and a ribbon, together with a rosette or other device, to be worn in lieu thereof, to any person who, while serving in any capacity with the Army of the United States since the sixth day of April, nineteen hundred and seventeen, has distinguished, or who shall hereafter distinguish, himself or herself by extraordinary heroism in connection with military operations against an armed enemy.

"That the President be, and he is hereby, further authorized to present, but not in the name of Congress, a distinguished service medal of appropriate design and a ribbon, together with a rosette or other device, to be worn in lieu thereof, to any person who, while serving in any capacity with the Army of the United States since the sixth day of April, nineteen hundred and seventeen, has distinguished, or who hereafter shall distinguish, himself or herself by exceptionally meritorious service to the Government in a duty of great responsibility; and said distinguished service medal shall also be issued to all enlisted men of the Army to whom the certificate of merit has been granted up to and including the date of the passage of this act under the provisions of previously existing law, in lieu of such certificates of merit, and after the passage of this act the award of the certificate of merit for distinguished service shall cease; and additional pay heretofore authorized by law for holders of the certificate of merit shall not be paid to them beyond the date of the award of the distinguished service medal in lieu thereof as aforesaid.

"That each enlisted man of the Army to whom there has been or shall be awarded a medal of honor, a distinguished service cross, or a distinguished service medal shall, for each such award, be entitled to additional pay at the rate of $2 per month from the date of the distinguished act or service on which the award is based, and each bar, or other suitable device, in lieu of a medal of honor, a distinguished service cross, or a distinguished service medal, as hereinafter provided for, shall entitle him to further additional pay at the rate of $2 per month from the date of the distinguished act or service for which the bar is awarded, and said additional pay shall continue throughout his active service, whether such service shall or shall not be continuous; but when the award is in lieu of the certificate of merit, as provided for in section three hereof, the additional pay shall begin with the date of the award.

"That no more than one medal of honor or one distinguished service cross or one distinguished service medal shall be issued to any one person; but for each succeeding deed or act sufficient to justify the award of a medal of honor or a distinguished service cross or a distinguished service medal, respectively, the President may award a suitable bar, or other suitable device, to be worn as he shall direct and for each other citation of an officer or enlisted man for gallantry in action published in orders issued from the headquarters of a force commanded by a general officer he shall be entitled to wear, as the President shall direct, a silver star three-sixteenths of an inch in diameter.

"That the Secretary of War be, and he is hereby authorized to extend from the appropriations for contingent expenses of his department from time to time so much as may be necessary to defray the cost of the medals of honor, distinguished services crosses, distinguished service medals, bars, rosettes, and other devices hereinbefore provided for.

"That whenever a medal, cross, bar, ribbon, rosette or other device presented under the provisions of this act shall have been lost, destroyed, or rendered unfit for use, without fault or neglect on the part of the person to whom it was awarded, such medal, cross, bar, ribbon, or device shall be replaced without charge therefor.

"That, except as otherwise prescribed herein, no medals of honor, distinguished service cross, distinguished service medal, or bar, or other suitable device in lieu of either of said medals or of said cross, shall be issued to any person after more than three years from the date of the act justifying the award thereof, nor unless a specific statement or report distinctly setting forth the distinguished service and suggesting or recommending official recognition thereof shall have been made at the time of the distinguished service or within two years thereafter, nor unless it shall appear from official records in the War Department that such person has so distinguished himself as to entitle him thereto; but in case an individual who shall distinguish himself dies before the making of the award to which he may be entitled, the award may, nevertheless, be made and the medal or cross or device presented, within three years from the date of the act justifying the award thereof, to such representative of the deceased as the President may designate; but no medal, cross, bar, or other device, hereinbefore authorized, shall be awarded or presented to any individual whose entire service subsequently to the time he distinguished himself shall not have been honorable; but in cases of officers and enlisted men now in the Army for whom the award of the medal of honor has been recommended in full compliance with then existing regulations but on account of services which, though insufficient fully to justify the award of the medal of honor, appear to have been such as to justify the award of the distinguished service cross or distinguished service medal hereinbefore provided for, such cases may be considered and acted upon under the provisions of this act authorizing the award of the distinguished service cross and distinguished service medal, notwithstanding that said services may have been rendered more than three years before said cases shall have been considered as authorized, by this act, but all consideration of and action upon any of said cases shall be based exclusively upon official records now on file in the War Department; and in the cases of officers and enlisted men now in the Army who have been mentioned in orders, now a part of official records, for extraordinary heroism or especially meritorious services, such as to justify the award of the distinguished service cross or the distinguished service medal hereinbefore provided for, such cases may be considered and acted on under the provisions of this act, notwithstanding that said act or services may have been rendered more than three years before said cases shall have been considered as authorized by this act, but all consideration of and action upon any said cases shall be based exclusively upon official records of the War Department.

"That the President be, and he is hereby, authorized to delegate, under such conditions, regulations, and limitations as he shall prescribe, to the commanding general of a separate army or higher unit in the field, the power conferred upon him by this act to award the medal of honor, the distinguished service cross, and the distinguished service medal; and he is further authorized to make from time to time any and all rules, regulations, and orders which he shall deem necessary to carry into effect the provisions of this act and to execute the full purpose and intention thereof.

"That the President is authorized, under regulations to be prescribed by him, to confer such medals and decorations as may be authorized in the military service of the United States upon officers and enlisted men of the military forces of the countries concurrently engaged with the United States in the present war."

July 22, 1918—U.S. War Department, Bulletin No. 43, 1918. Part I, p. 29; Part II, pp. 42–44. Text of Act of July 9, 1918 published to the Army.

September, 1918—U.S. War Department. The Adjutant General. No more than one Medal of Honor can be issued. *Source: AGO, D & A Sec., Precedent File—Awards for additional acts of gallantry.*

Nov. 22, 1918—U.S. War Department. The Adjutant General. First Medal of Honor Award in World War I. Correspondence. *Source: AGO, D & A Sec., Precedent File—Medal of Honor—First Award.*

Feb. 20, 1919—U.S. War Department. Circular No. 85. Changes in Army Regulations. "No more than one Medal of Honor . . . shall be issued to any one person. . . ."

Aug. 11, 1919—U.S. War Department. War Department General Staff. Staff Memo. Custody of Medals of Honor. *Source: AGO, Dec. & Awards Sec., Equip. 6111, AG 220.52, Misc. Div., Precedent File, "Medal of Honor—Procurement of."*

"1. The request for the transfer of the A. H. G. of all medals of honor, ribbons, etc. now in the War Department Supply Div. as recommended in Par. 7, 3d Ind. is approved. Hereafter the QMC will be responsible for the issue of same . . . FBN/10/20/19."

Aug. 18, 1920—U.S. War Department. Medals of Honor Only to Next of Kin. Memorandum for the Adjutant General of the Army. From Assistant to the Chief of Staff, Director of Operations. *Source: AGO. Dec. & Awards Sec., Precedent File, "Medal of Honor—Heirs Obtaining."*

"The Secretary of War has decided that posthumous awards of medals can be made only to the next of kin of the deceased or to such other person or persons as the next of kin specifically designate."

Oct. 20, 1919—U.S. Fine Arts Commission. Proposed Change in Design of Medal of Honor. Correspondence with Commission on Fine Arts. See letter from Fine Arts Commission submitting new design for Medal of Honor. *Source: AGO Central Files (Pentagon) AGO 210.523, Oct. 20, 1919. (AGO Precedent File, D & A Br.)*

Mar. 4, 1921—U.S. Laws, Statutes, etc. 41 Stat. 1367.

"An Act authorizing bestowal upon the unknown, unidentified British soldier buried in Westminister Abbey and the unknown unidentified French soldier buried in the Arc de Triomphe of the Congressional Medal of Honor."

June 30, 1921—U.S. War Department. Office of the Chief of Staff. Memorandum for The Adjutant General of the Army. Subject: Award of Medals and Decorations. *Source: Nat. Archives. War Dept., AGO, 210.5, June 30, 1921, Decorations Board.*

By this Memorandum the Secretary of War directed that the Adjutant General of the Army "take over from this date all operating functions in connection with the awards of medals and decorations . . ."

July 21, 1921—U.S. War Department. Special Orders. 1921 167-0. Paragraph 47. Created the War Department Decorations Board.

Aug. 24, 1921—U.S. Laws, Statutes, etc. 42 Stat. 191.

"An Act authorizing bestowal upon the unknown, unidentified American to be buried in the memorial Amphitheater of the National Cemetary at Arlington, Virginia, the congressional medal of honor and the distinguished service cross."

Oct. 12, 1921—U.S. Laws, Statutes, etc. 42 Stat. 203.

"Joint Resolution for the bestowal of the Congressional medal of honor upon an unknown, unidentified Italian soldier to be buried in the National Monument to Victor Emmanuel II, in Rome, Italy."

Apr. 7, 1922—U.S. Laws, Statutes, etc. 42 Stat. 493.

"An Act to extend the limitations of time upon the issuance of medals of honor, distinguished service crosses, and distinguished service medals to persons who served in the Army of the United States during the World War."

May 3, 1922—U.S. Laws, Statutes, etc. 42 Stat. 505.

Stipulates monthly (instead of quarterly) pension payment to Medal winners.

Oct. 11, 1922—U.S. War Department. John W. Weeks, Secretary of War. Letter to Chairman, Committee on Military Affairs, United States Senate. Enclosure.

Submitting draft of bill to protect decorations and service medals issued by War Department.

Feb. 24, 1923—U.S. Laws, Statutes, etc. 42 Stat. 1286.

Prohibits unauthorized wearing, manufacture or sale of medals and badges awarded by the War Department.

Oct. 15, 1927—U.S. Army War College. A study of the use of rewards, embodying recommendations for a practical system for regarding organizations and individuals, together with the necessary plan for its operation. Course 1927–1928. G–1 Course No. 12. Report of Committee No. 6. 11 p. mimeographed.

Nov. 11, 1927—U.S. War Department. Office, Chief of Staff. Proposed change in Design of Medal of Honor. Correspondence with Commission on Fine Arts. Letter from Chief of Staff to Mr. Charles Moore, Chairman of Commission. *Source: AGO Central Files, AG 210.523, Oct. 31, 1927.*

Dec. 14, 1927—U.S. Laws, Statutes, etc. Authorized President to present Medal to Lindbergh. (Public Law No. 1, 70th Congress—H.R. 3190.)

Apr. 21, 1928—U.S. Laws, Statutes, etc. 45 Stat. 437. Amends provisions of Act of Feb. 24, 1923 (*above*).

Oct. 27, 1928—U.S. Army War College. Rewards and Commendations. The Army War College, Washington, D.C. Course 1928–29. G–1 Course No. 16. Report of Committee No. 11.

Aug. 27, 1930—U.S. War Department. The Adjutant General. Honors and Annuities for Recipients or Holders of the Congressional Medal of Honor. Letter. *Source: War Dept., AGO, D & A, Precedent File. Honors, annuities, etc.*

Oct. 21, 1930—U.S. Army War College. Personnel Policies and Methods in a Future War. The Army War College, Washington, D.C. Course 1930–31. Report of Committee No. 3.

Feb. 21, 1934—U.S. Department of Justice. Opinions of Attorneys General of the United States, Vol. 37. 1932–34, pp. 544–547.

Persons on the retired list of the Army, holding Medals of Honor, are not eligible under existing legislation to receive the special pension provided by the act of April 27, 1916 (39 Stat. 53).

Mar. 21, 1935—U.S. Laws, Statutes, etc. 49 Stat. part 2, 2048.

Authorizes President to present Medal of Honor to Maj. Gen. Adolphus Washington Greely.

1942—U.S. War Department. A Digest of Opinions of the Judge Advocate General of the Army. 1912–40. Washington, GPO. 1148 p.

Medal of Honor, sections 470, 903, 904, 910, 912, 1434.

Jan. 27, 1945—U.S. War Department. The Adjutant General. Policy Governing Presentation of Duplicate Posthumous Decorations. *Source: War Dept., AGO, D & A, Precedent File—Duplicate Awards—Posthumous.*

May 8, 1945—U.S. War Department. The Adjutant General. Relief of Medal of Honor men from further participation in hazardous Duty. Text of telegram sent to commanding generals, all Service Commands. *Source: War Dept., AGO, D & A, Precedent File.*

June 14, 1945—U.S. War Department. Adjutant General's Office, Decorations and Awards Branch. Letter addressed to commanding generals—all theaters—*Source: AGO, D & A Br., "1945—Outgoing Messages".*

Gives Medal winners choice of White House or overseas presentation.

July 18, 1945—U.S. War Department. General Staff. G–1. Memorandum from the Assistant Chief of Staff, G–1, to The Adjutant General. *Source: War Dept. General Staff File No. WDGAP/200.6*

Centralizes under one authority the control and coordination of all action in connection with presentations of the Medal of Honor.

July 23, 1945—U.S. War Department. Office of Secretary of War. War Department Decorations Board. Medals disapproved for General Pershing and General Eisenhower. Letter of July 23, 1945 from War Department Decorations Board to ASF Military Personnel Divison. *Source: War Dept., AGO, D & A, Precedent File—Eisenhower.*

This letter represents the War Department's first representation to Congress that special gold medals be voted by Congress in such cases of outstanding leadership and that the Medal of Honor be reserved for awarding only gallantry in action.

Oct. 16, 1945—U.S. War Department. Army Ground Forces. Promotion of Medal of Honor awardees. Letter issued by Hq, AGF, Oct. 15, 1945. *Source: War Dept., AGO, D & A, Precedent File. "Promotion of Medal of Honor Men."*

Jan. 10, 1946—U.S. War Department. Decorations Board. Memorandum, Subject: War Department Policy on Decorations and Awards. (Maj. Gen. W. S. Paul.)

July 1, 1946—U.S. War Department. Decorations Board. Memorandum for the Deputy Chief of Staff. Subject: War Department Decorations.

Extracts From the Statutes Authorizing Medals of Honor

[From *The Medal of Honor, 1861–1949—The Navy*]

EXTRACT FROM THE ACT TO PROMOTE THE EFFICIENCY OF THE NAVY

SECTION 7. *And it is further enacted,* That the Secretary of the Navy be, and is hereby, authorized to cause two hundred medals of honor to be prepared with suitable emblematic devices which shall be bestowed upon such petty officers, seamen, landsmen, and marines as shall most distinguish themselves by their gallantry in action and other seamanlike qualities during the present war.

Approved December 21, 1861.

EXTRACT FROM THE ACT TO ESTABLISH AND EQUALIZE THE GRADE OF LINE OFFICERS OF THE UNITED STATES NAVY

SECTION 10. *And be it further enacted,* That . . . seamen distinguishing themselves in battle or by extraordinary heroism in the line of their profession may be promoted to forward warrant officers or acting master's mates, as they may be best qualified, upon the recommendation of their commanding officer, approved by the flag officer and the Department. Upon such promotion they shall receive a gratuity of one hundred dollars and a medal of honor to be prepared by the Navy Department.

Approved May 17, 1864.

EXTRACT FROM THE ACT TO APPOINT CERTAIN OFFICERS OF THE NAVY

SECTION 3. *And be it further enacted,* That . . . seamen distinguishing themselves in battle or by extraordinary heroism in the line of their profession may be promoted to forward warrant officer or acting master's mates, as they may be best qualified, upon the recommendation of their commanding officer, approved by the flag officer and the Department. Upon such promotion they shall receive a gratuity of one hundred dollars and a medal of honor to be prepared by the Navy Department.

Approved May 17, 1864.

AN ACT For the reward of enlisted men of the Navy or Marine Corps.

Be it enacted by the Senate and House of Representatives of the United States of America in Congress assembled, That any enlisted man of the Navy or Marine Corps who shall have distinguished himself in battle or displayed extraordinary heroism in the line of his

profession shall, upon recommendation of his commanding officer, approved by the flag officer and the Secretary of the Navy, receive a gratuity and medal of honor as provided for seamen in section fourteen hundred and seven of the Revised Statutes.
Approved March 3, 1901.

PUBLIC RESOLUTION NO. 23

JOINT RESOLUTION Authorizing the issue of duplicate medals where the originals have been lost or destroyed.

Resolved by the Senate and House of Representatives of the United States of America in Congress assembled, That in any case where the President of the United States has heretofore, under any act or resolution of Congress, caused any medal to be made and presented to any officer or person in the United States on account of distinguished or meritorious services, on a proper showing made by such person to the satisfaction of the President that such medal has been lost or destroyed through no fault of the beneficiary, and that diligent search has been made therefor, the President is hereby authorized to cause to be prepared and delivered to such person a duplicate of such medal, the cost of which shall be paid out of any money in the Treasury not otherwise appropriated.
Approved April 15, 1904.

EXTRACT FROM "AN ACT MAKING APPROPRIATIONS FOR THE NAVAL SERVICE FOR THE FISCAL YEAR ENDING JUNE 30, 1916, AND FOR OTHER PURPOSES."

The President of the United States is hereby empowered to prepare a suitable medal of honor to be awarded to any officer of the Navy, Marine Corps, or Coast Guard who shall have distinguished himself in battle or displayed extraordinary heroism in the line of his profession.
Approved March 3, 1915.

H.R. 12194

AN ACT To provide for the award of medals of honor, distinguished-service medals, and Navy crosses, and for other purposes.

SECTION 1. *Be it enacted by the Senate and House of Representatives of the United States of America in Congress assembled*, That the President of the United States be, and he is hereby, authorized to present, in the name of Congress, a medal of honor to any person who, while in the naval service of the United States, shall, in action involving actual conflict with the enemy, distinguish himself conspicuously by gallantry and intrepidity at the risk of his life above and beyond the call of duty and without detriment to the mission of his command or the command to which attached.
Approved February 4, 1919.

PUBLIC LAW 702—77TH CONGRESS

CHAPTER 551—2D SESSION

S. 2456

AN ACT To amend the Act approved February 4, 1919 (40 Stat. 1056), entitled "An Act to provide for the award of medals of honor, distinguished-service medals, and Navy crosses, and for other purposes", so as to change the conditions for the award of medals, and for other purposes.

Be it enacted by the Senate and House of Representatives of the United States of America in Congress assembled, That the Act approved February 4, 1919 (40 Stat. 1056), entitled "An Act to provide for the award of medals of honor, distinguished-service medals, and Navy crosses, and for other purposes", is hereby amended to read as follows:

"That the President of the United States be, and he is hereby, authorized to present, in the name of Congress, a medal of honor to any person who, while in the naval service of the United States, shall, in action involving actual conflict with the enemy, or in the line of his profession, distinguish himself conspicuously by gallantry and intrepidity at the risk of his life above and beyond the call of duty and without detriment to the mission of his command or to the command to which attached: *Provided*, That the design of this medal shall be the same as that adopted pursuant to the Act approved December 21, 1861 (12 Stat. 330)."

SECTION 2. That section 1407 of the Revised Statutes (Act of May 17, 1864, ch. 89, sec. 3, 13 Stat. 79, 80); the Act of May 4, 1898, numbered 30 (30 Stat. 741), and the Act of March 3, 1901, chapter 850 (31 Stat. 1099), are hereby repealed.

SPECIAL PRIVILEGES WHICH MAY BE CONFERRED UPON RECIPIENTS OF THE MEDAL
OF HONOR UNDER CONDITIONS PRESCRIBED

MEDAL OF HONOR ROLL

AN ACT To establish in the War Department and in the Navy Department, respectively, a roll
designated as "the Army and Navy medal of honor roll," and for other purposes.

Be it enacted by the Senate and House of Representatives of the United States of America in Congress assembled, That there is hereby established in the War Department and Navy Department, respectively, a roll designated as "the Army and Navy medal of honor roll." Upon written application made to the Secretary of the proper department, and subject to the conditions and requirements hereinafter contained, the name of each surviving person who has served in the military or naval service of the United States in any war, who has attained or shall attain the age of sixty-five years, and who has been awarded a medal of honor for having in action involving actual conflict with an enemy distinguished himself conspicuously by gallantry or intrepidity, at the risk of his life, above and beyond the call of duty, and who was honorably discharged from service by muster out, resignation, or otherwise, shall be, by the Secretary of the proper department, entered and recorded on said roll. Applications for entry on said roll shall be made in such form and under such regulations as shall be prescribed by the War Department and Navy Department, respectively, and proper blanks and instructions shall be, by the proper Secretary, furnished without charge upon request made by any person claiming the benefits of this Act.

SECTION 2. That it shall be the duty of the Secretary of War and of the Secretary of the Navy to carry this Act into effect and to decide whether each applicant, under this Act, in his department is entitled to the benefit of this Act. If the official award of the medal of honor to the applicant, or the official notice to him thereof, shall appear to show that the medal of honor was awarded to the applicant for such an act as is required by the provisions of this Act, it shall be deemed sufficient to entitle the applicant to such special pension without further investigation. Otherwise all official correspondence, orders, reports, recommendations, requests, and other evidence now on file in any public office or department shall be considered. A certificate of service and of the act of heroism, gallantry, bravery, or intrepidity for which the medal of honor was awarded, and of enrollment under this Act, and of the right of the special pensioner to be entitled to and to receive the special pension herein granted, shall be furnished each person whose name shall be so entered on said roll. The Secretary of War and the Secretary of the Navy shall deliver to the Veterans' Administration a certified copy of each of such of said certificates as he may issue, as aforesaid, and the same shall be full and sufficient authority to the Veterans' Administration for the payment by him to the beneficiary named in each such certificate the special pension herein provided for.

SECTION 3. That each such surviving person whose name shall have been entered on said roll in accordance with this act shall be entitled to and shall receive and be paid by the Veterans' Administration, out of any money in the Treasury of the United States not otherwise appropriated, a special pension of $10 per month for life, payable quarter yearly. The Veterans' Administration shall make all necessary rules and regulations for making payment of such special pensions to the beneficiaries thereof.

Such special pension shall begin on the day that such person shall file his application for enrollment on said roll in the office of the Secretary of War or of the Secretary of the Navy after the passage and approval of this act, and shall continue during the life of the beneficiary.

Such special pension shall not deprive any such special pensioner of any other pension or of any benefit, right, or privilege to which he is or may hereafter be entitled under any existing or subsequent law, but shall be in addition thereto.

The special pension allowed under this act shall not be subject to any attachment, execution, levy, tax, lien, or detention under any process whatever.

SECTION 4. That in case any person has been awarded two or more medals of honor, he shall not be entitled to and shall not receive more than one such special pension.

Rank in the service shall not be considered in applications filed hereunder.

Approved April 27, 1916.

GOVERNMENT AIR TRANSPORTATION FOR MEDAL OF HONOR RECIPIENTS

The Secretary of Defense has directed that recipients of the Medal of Honor, when properly identified, are authorized to travel as passengers, gratis, in aircraft of the armed service within the continental limits of the United States on a space-available basis, in recognition of their services to the Nation. Cards of authorization are furnished by the chief of Naval Personnel to all present and former members of the naval service who are recipients of the Medal of Honor.

PART VII
MEDAL OF HONOR
ALPHABETICAL INDEX

1060

(P) Photo ......

1070

1074

1076

ALPHABETICAL INDEX

P(3) (3) Photos

1098

STOWERS, Freddie - WWI - Citation on File ✓

Charles A. Windolph
Trumpeter
Medal of Honor
for Reno Hill
procuring water for
besieged command.
7th Cavalry